About the cover art

In this remarkable painting the thematic resonance with *A Course in Miracles* is apparent. In the bottom of the painting the soldiers slumber. They are lost in their dreams and oblivious to the presence of the Heavenly Host, the Angel moving the stone from the tomb, and the Son of Man rising from the grave. The theme here is of "Awakening" demonstrating "there is no death." The emphasis is on the resurrection rather than the crucifixion. While striking some as "Catholic," this is a Reformation (Protestant) artist. Its theme echoes both Protestantism *and* the Course in its emphasis on the resurrection and the empty tomb rather than bodily suffering and sacrifice.

The theme of ascension and awakening symbolized by the resurrection motif transcends all denominations however, and even Christianity itself in its resonance with the Perennial Philosophy.

The Resurrection by Pieter Lastman

Dutch, 1612 - Oil on oak panel
Unframed: 43.2 x 32.4 cm (17 x 12 3/4 in) Framed: 66 x 54.9 x 4.1 cm (26 x 21 5/8 in)

The original is located at the J. Paul Getty Museum, Los Angeles, California. Used by permission.

Pieter Lastman (1583? - 1633)

Dutch painter, born in Amsterdam, probably in 1583. He was a pupil of the Manerist painter Gerrit Pietersz Sweenlinck. More important for his artistic development was a stay in Italy from c.1603 to 1607, presumably in Venice and Rome; here he was subject to many influences, in particular the workshop of Adam Elsheimer. Lastman spent the rest of his life as an esteemed and successful artist in Amsterdam, where he died in 1633. Jan Lievens and Rembrandt were his most important pupils.

This first edition is also published with a plain burgundy cover (left)

"Would God leave anyone without a very present help in time of trouble; a Savior who can symbolize Himself? Yet do we need a many-faceted curriculum, not because of content differences but because symbols must shift and change to suit the need. Jesus has come to answer yours."
Urtext M 24 A 7

A Course in Miracles
Urtext Manuscripts
Complete Seven Volume Combined Edition

Published by Miracles in Action Press, LLC

52 Fitzgerald Drive, Jaffrey, NH 03452

www.miraclesinactionpress.com

First Printed in 2009

Copyright © 2008 Doug Thompson

First edition. All rights reserved. Printed in the United States of America

ISBN **978-0-9816984-0-3** – cover with painting, DVD included
ISBN **978-0-9816984-3-4** – plain burgundy cover, DVD included
ISBN **978-0-9816984-4-1** – cover with painting and dvd order form
ISBN **978-0-9816984-5-8** – burgundy cover and dvd order form

The original dictation of *A Course in Miracles* is in the public domain by virtue of the Scribes' assertion that it is an original composition by Jesus of Nazareth. As such, it is not eligible for copyright protection under current US copyright law. The Scribes' role was to record and share the teaching. Copyrighted material includes Publisher's Note, Preface, footnotes, appendices and the original contents and compilation of the companion DVD.

Author: Jesus of Nazareth
Scribes: Helen Schucman & William Thetford
Editor: Doug Thompson
Publisher: Doug Monkton

A Course in Miracles
Urtext Manuscripts
Complete Seven Volume Combined Edition

A Note from the Publisher	v
Preface	viii

1)	Text	1
2)	Workbook	283
3)	Manual for Teachers	419
4)	Use of Terms	445
5)	Psychotherapy	453
6)	Song of Prayer	467
7)	Gifts of God	481

Appendix I –	The many versions of ACIM	493
Appendix II –	What is the *Urtext*?	507
Appendix III –	The Referencing System Explained	521
Appendix IV –	The Significance of the Differences	543
Appendix V –	Editorial Principles	549
Appendix VI –	What's on the DVD	551
Appendix VII –	Order Form	559

A Note from the Publisher

The manuscripts collection of *A Course in Miracles* known as the "*Urtext Manuscripts*" represents the oldest available *typed* copy of the words dictated by a "voice" to Scribe Helen Schucman. The voice, claimed Schucman, was Jesus. Most of the very personal material[1] found early in the original *Shorthand Notes* is omitted and significant *"dictated without notes"* material which is not found in the original *Notes* is included in this edition. A small amount of re-writing also appears between the *Notes* and the *Urtext*. The *Urtext* is not "the first" or "the original" copy of the Course, but it is very close, much closer than any other version in print. In extensive appendices, Doug Thompson maps out the complex ancestry of the five known historical scribal versions of the Course and the significance of some of the differences between them which amount to as many as 48,000 words.[2]

The word "urtext" refers to a "piecing together"[3] of earlier primary source material to capture as accurately as possible an author's original intent with no additions, omissions or modifications. The *Urtext Manuscripts* are just that. Drawing from both the original dictation in the *Notes* and subsequent clarifications and expansions, Schucman and co-Scribe William Thetford present in this document almost the whole of the author's original dictation with minimal editing and only a few minor and apparently inadvertent omissions.

The *Urtext Manuscripts* predate all other editions of the Course currently in print. The 1972 *Hugh Lynn Cayce (HLC)* manuscript of the *Text* volume, which is the basis of the "*JCIM*" and "*Original*" editions published by the Course in Miracles Society (CIMS), is a later heavily edited and abridged reworking of the *Urtext*. The 1975 Foundation for Inner Peace (FIP) version published in 18+ languages, is a substantial reworking of the *HLC*.[4]

Whether we believe the words of *A Course in Miracles* were authored by the historical Jesus of Nazareth, Dr. Helen Schucman or some other voice or demon calling himself "Christ Jesus," it is certainly among the most profound discourses on universal themes ever conceived. While Schucman claimed the voice was that of Jesus, one need not accept any claims of authorship to recognize the enduring value of the thought system and its insights into daily human life.

In *The Urtext Manuscripts*, the reader will appreciate the authenticity of the text as well as the textual scholarship. This is because it includes over 48,000 words edited out of most previously published versions; discussions of sex and possession, Freud, the Bible, Ed-

---

[1] While the intent was apparently to remove only the "personal material," some sentences which appear to belong to the Course, including two miracle principles which were buried within omitted pages of "personal material" were also omitted. These suspected "inadvertent omissions" of apparently authentic dictation are included in footnotes in this edition

[2] Word count chart by Doug Thompson (approximate totals as measured by MS Word):

Version	Word Count	Incremental difference
Urtext:	337,373	38,184 words omitted from Urtext to HLC
HLC:	299,189	10,221 words omitted from HLC to FIP
FIP:	288,968	48,405 words omitted from Urtext to FIP
Annotated HLC:	301,647	35,726 words omitted from Urtext to Annotated HLC
Annotated HLC	301,647	2,458 words *added to* the original HLC

[3] From *Encyclopedia Britannica;* see Appendix II *"What is the Urtext?"* for an expanded discussion

[4] It should be noted that these observations pertain largely to the *Text* volume scribed between 1965 and 1968. Subsequent volumes experienced much less editing and have fewer differences, version to version.

A Note from the Publisher

gar Cayce and Mary Baker Eddy will be new material for many students and teachers of other versions. While some of this material consists of "personal asides" not intended to be part of the Course teaching, much was clearly intended for inclusion. Sometimes the author's wish to have a topic included is explicitly stated as in this remark on sex which was omitted from other published editions,

> "I want to finish the instructions about sex, because this is an area the miracle worker MUST understand."
>
> – *Urtext* **T 1 B 40b**

This volume is also the first attempt by any edition to engage the reader in the author's unique interpretation of the Bible and Christianity. With over 1000 (footnoted) references to the Bible and its apparently Christian language, we might suppose *A Course in Miracles* is addressed to a Christian audience. Yet terms such as *forgiveness, salvation, atonement, Christ*, and even *second coming* are the common vocabulary of universal spiritual reflection upon which Christianity has no monopoly. It is the vocabulary of the *perennial* or *universal philosophy*[5] common to religious and spiritual expression across the ages. *A Course in Miracles* has found an enthusiastic audience among millions of people seeking a new voice in spiritual, if not Biblical, insight. In the *Urtext*, Jesus asks us to consider the Bible anew,

> "You have begun to realize that this is a very practical course, because it means EXACTLY what it says. So does the Bible, if it is properly understood. There has been a marked tendency on the part of many of the Bible's followers, and also its translators, to be entirely literal about fear and ITS effects, but NOT about love and ITS results. Thus, "hellfire" means burning, but raising the dead becomes allegorical. Actually, it is PARTICULARLY the references to the outcomes of love that should be taken literally because the Bible is ABOUT love, being about GOD." – *Urtext* **T 8 I 7**

The companion 4.5 Gb. DVD* and website offer a substantial research library with over 10,000 pages of primary source manuscripts, concordances and searchable e-texts, the Biblical equivalent of finding the original manuscripts of the canonical gospels. A fascinating digital audio reading of the 31 chapter text (and other material) is included exclusively on the DVD. To some it as if we are listening to the voice of Jesus in real time.

Readers are encouraged to participate in identifying unmarked Biblical references as well as any errors that may have slipped through our proofreading. Doug Thompson, scholar,

---

[5] "Certain pupils have been assigned to each of God's teachers, and they will begin to look for him as soon as he has answered the Call. They were chosen for him because the form of the universal curriculum that he will teach is best for them in view of their level of understanding." *Urtext* **M 3 A 1**

"In philosophy, **universalism** is a doctrine or school claiming universal facts can be discovered... In certain religions, **Universality** is the quality ascribed to an entity whose existence is consistent throughout the universe." **Wikipedia:** Universality (philosophy)

"**Universalism** can be classified as a religion, theology and philosophy that generally holds all persons and creatures are related to God or the Divine and will be reconciled to God. In Christianity, Universalism refers to the belief that all humans can be saved through Jesus Christ and eventually come to harmony in God's kingdom. **Wikipedia:** Universalism

A Note from the Publisher

researcher, commentator, editor and compiler of this remarkable package further invites reader participation in the process of creating a "definitive edition" of *A Course in Miracles* with a dedication to accuracy being a goal Jesus is certain to appreciate. Aware that such a project will take many years of collaboration across several disciplines Mr. Thompson has aptly stated, "The goal here is not to have the last word on 'The Word,' it is simply to move toward the humbler goal of getting the words right."

Doug Monkton

Peterborough, New Hampshire, USA

November 2008

* Please see back pages for DVD details.

PREFACE

By Doug Thompson

Those familiar with the editions of *A Course in Miracles* previously available will find this edition of the *Urtext* manuscripts substantially different, especially in the early chapters of the *Text* volume, due to the fact that it is far closer to the original dictation, having been typed by the Scribes before most of the subsequent editing and abridgement took place.

While much more extensive documentation is provided in the *Appendices*, in this *Preface* I wish to very briefly summarize the major attributes of this edition, explain what distinguishes it from other editions of *A Course in Miracles* and briefly describe the purpose behind its preparation and publication.

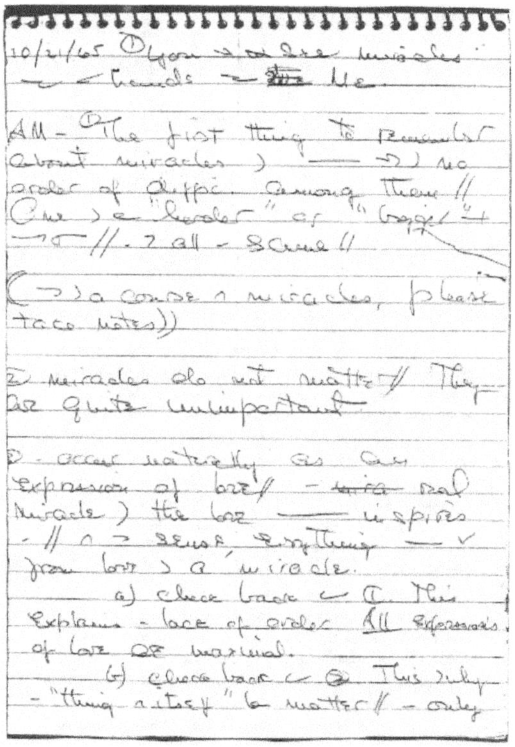

Many will know that the Course was first printed in 1976 by the Foundation for Inner Peace (FIP), that it has subsequently sold millions of copies, that it has been translated into many other languages, and that it is increasingly quoted in published works. The Foundation's claim that its version is "virtually unchanged" from the original "inner dictation" received by Columbia University Psychology professor Dr. Helen Schucman, beginning in 1965, was widely accepted for many years. Schucman and her colleague Dr. William Thetford, repeatedly retyped the original *Shorthand Notes* and over the course of a decade that first manuscript was edited into the much shorter version that was published by FIP in 1975 as *A Course in Miracles*. This "Voice" was, according to Schucman "unambiguously" that of Jesus of Nazareth.[6]

In January of 2000 three earlier versions of the Course emerged on the Internet which were dramatically

Figure 1 The opening page of the earliest known manuscript, the *Shorthand Notes* with the words "You will see miracles through your hands through Me."

---

[6] The "claim to authorship" is unusual and remarkable enough to have been commented upon by Schucman herself and many others over the years in numerous books and articles. A good starting point is Robert Perry's survey which can be found at http://www.circleofa.org/articles/WhoWroteItI.php. Whether her belief that she heard the "Voice" of Jesus of Nazareth is true is something that can hardly be "conclusively proven" one way or the other. One can "weigh the evidence" and come up with a balance of probabilities, but the result depends on what you consider to be "valid evidence." For some the test is "does it agree or disagree with the doctrines of my denomination?" The answer will almost always be both "yes" and "no" if that question is asked about this Course or the doctrines of any other denomination. Were a Catholic and a Lutheran to interrogate the historical Jesus with that model, both would find him wanting, although in different ways, just as the Jewish priests and scribes in Jerusalem found him wanting in the first century. They would also each find the other wanting! Ultimately the question can only be answered by an individual in his heart in consultation with the Holy Spirit. As Jesus said in John 10:3-6

> "The gatekeeper opens the gate for him, and the sheep listen to his voice. He calls his own sheep by name, and leads them out. Whenever he brings out his own sheep, he goes before them, and the sheep follow him, for they know his voice. They will by no means follow a stranger, but will flee from him; for they don't know the voice of strangers." Jesus spoke this parable to them, but they didn't understand what he was telling them.

different in the first eight chapters. Far from being "virtually unchanged" the early manuscripts not only contained a vast amount of previously unpublished material, they revealed that in the later editing much that wasn't entirely removed was extensively re-written, sometimes almost beyond recognition.

Prior to 2000, only one version of the Course was available, the abridged version published by FIP. The three earlier versions which have emerged are, in chronological order of their creation:[7]

- The original *Shorthand Notes*
- The Scribes' first very lightly edited *Urtext*[8]
- The Scribes' second edit, the substantially abridged *Hugh Lynn Cayce* version *(HLC)*.

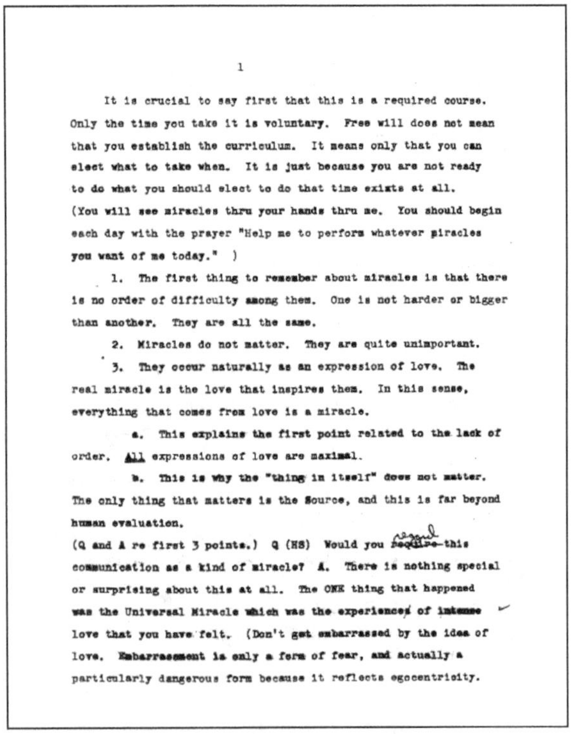

1

It is crucial to say first that this is a required course. Only the time you take it is voluntary. Free will does not mean that you establish the curriculum. It means only that you can elect what to take when. It is just because you are not ready to do what you should elect to do that time exixts at all. (You will see miracles thru your hands thru me. You should begin each day with the prayer "Help me to perform whatever piracles you want of me today.")

1. The first thing to remember about miracles is that there is no order of difficulty among them. One is not harder or bigger than another. They are all the same.

2. Miracles do not matter. They are quite unimportant.

3. They occur naturally as an expression of love. The real miracle is the love that inspires them. In this sense, everything that comes from love is a miracle.

a. This explains the first point related to the lack of order. All expressions of love are maximal.

b. This is why the "thing in itself" does not matter. The only thing that matters is the Source, and this is far beyond human evaluation.

(Q and A re first 3 points.) Q (HS) Would you ~~require~~ regard this communication as a kind of miracle? A. There is nothing special or surprising about this at all. The ONK thing that happened was the Universal Miracle which was the experiences of intense love that you have felt. (Don't get embarrassed by the idea of love. Embarrassment is only a form of fear, and actually a particularly dangerous form because it reflects egocentricity.

Figure 2 The first page of the *Urtext*, the earliest available typed manuscript of *A Course in Miracles,* on which the present edition is based

Our four versions then consist of these three manuscripts which had remained hidden for decades plus the abridgement of the *HLC* prepared by Schucman and Wapnick in 1973-74. Published by FIP beginning in 1975 as "virtually unchanged," it is in fact the ***fourth*** major revision of which copies have surfaced, being some 48,000 words shorter and substantially re-written in the early chapters.

There is very good reason to believe that the Scribes prepared additional manuscripts which either have not survived or are still being withheld from scholarship by their custodians.[9] However many additional manuscripts there may be, these four very different versions of the Course we currently have allow us to trace the extent and nature of the editing from the first scribing (the *Notes*) to the last editing (the 1975 abridgement), along with two points in between. An examination of the differences from one version to the next reveals a number of common elements:

- In each version some scribal errors were corrected.
- Due to a near-total lack of proofreading, there are many hundreds of copying errors from one version to the next. Many are "dropouts" in which a word or two, a line or two, a paragraph or two or in one case an entire page was inadvertently omitted. Most of these errors are reproduced in subsequent versions along with new ones introduced with each

[7] For a more complete discussion of the versions see Appendix II.

[8] Britannica describes the word "urtext" as referring to a "piecing together" of primary sources with the intent of reflecting the author's original intent with no modification. By and large this is exactly what the Scribes' *Urtext* is. For a deeper textual analysis of the manuscripts see Appendix II, Identifying the *Urtext* Manuscripts.

[9] For more on version identification see Appendix I.

PREFACE

retyping such that it is true that 'the more they edited it, the worse it got' in a very real and measurable way.

- Substantial segments which were not removed were re-written, in some cases changing most of the words but not noticeably changing the meaning and in other cases apparently altering the material unintentionally such that the original meaning is distorted or even entirely lost. The extent and frequency of re-writing increases over time. There is very little in the early editing in the *Urtext* manuscripts, and what there is really is minor. In the last edit there is a vast amount of re-writing which frequently entirely changes the meaning of passages.

- In some cases material is preserved accurately but is removed from the original topic of which it is a part and placed in an entirely different discussion, thus altering the meaning of the passage "in context." Again, there is very little of this at first, and considerably more in the later versions.

While many of these differences are ***individually*** of little significance and would attract little notice if few in number, they are not few in number and ***collectively*** the fact that there are thousands of them is of considerable significance. The complete removal of the lengthy discussion on sex and possession, whether one views its removal as a "correction" or a "corruption" cannot be fairly described as a "minor" change.

If we then consider "the differences" as a whole, it is fair to say that the net effect of such a vast number of mistakes is to substantially blur and in some cases distort the message which Schucman initially "heard" and committed to paper. Most who have read both this *Urtext* version and the later abridged versions find the earlier version to be much more readable and understandable. While the abridgement certainly retains most of the core message, it often does so in extremely condensed, abbreviated language which is missing large amounts of explanatory material and concrete examples illustrating the points being made. For the newcomer being introduced to the concepts for the first time, the removal of these "bridges" and explanations can make the material seem incomprehensibly dense.

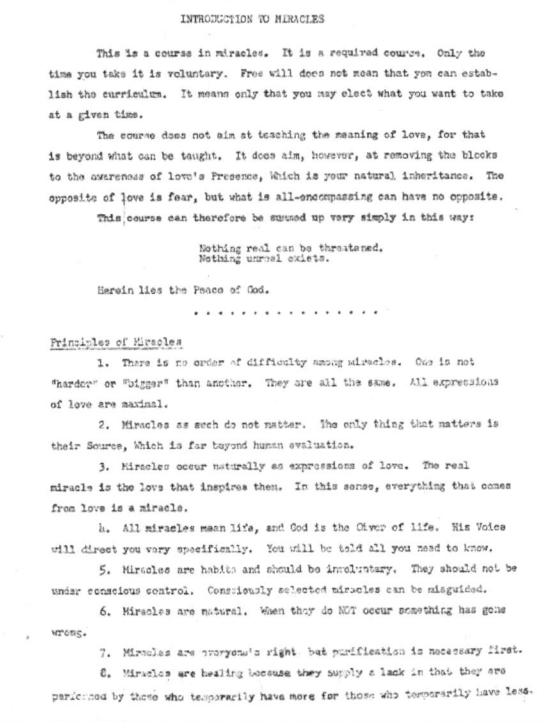

Figure 3 The first page of the *Hugh Lynn Cayce (HLC);* the second earliest typed *manuscript* currently available. Based on the earlier *Urtext*, the *HLC* version introduces a entirely new opening section while removing tens of thousands of words in the first few chapters.

In some cases, the editing changes introduce overt distortions. Some of the omitted material is in fact extremely significant. The *Urtext* says: "I want to finish the instructions about sex, because this is an area the miracle worker MUST understand." Not just that line but all the instructions about sex vanish in later versions despite the author particularly drawing attention to the vital importance of this material.

Preface

Because each version contains some material not found in any other, and each version after the original *Notes* corrects some errors in earlier versions, none of these four versions by itself includes the "whole of the dictation" and none is without flaws. The *Urtext* has several advantages relative to the other versions. It has *much* less editing than any later version. It does have a few changes however, and they are predominantly of three kinds:

- Dictated *corrections* are incorporated. Where the *Notes* contains dictated instructions for correcting previous material, in the *Urtext* the instructions are usually removed and the corrections are made as instructed. There is at least one exception where the dictated corrections were ***not*** made. The instruction to capitalize "Cause and Effect," for instance, is recorded but the words were not subsequently capitalized. In a few cases the dictated instructions remain.

- The *addition* of a dozen or so "dictated without notes" segments which appear to be genuine dictation added after the initial scribing as expansion, clarification or correction of previous points. While not present in the *Notes* most of this material is preserved in subsequent editions, having been accepted by all subsequent editors as "authentic" despite its absence from the *Notes*.

- The *omission* of most of the entirely "personal" comments which generally involve discussions between Schucman and the "Voice" about personal relationship matters, dreams, and the like. This material was clearly never intended to be "part of the Course" and its removal is directed by the "Voice."

Aside from those three differences, each of which can be viewed as an enhancement vis-à-vis the *Notes,* very little of the re-arrangement and re-writing so noteworthy in the later editing appears in the *Urtext*. While there are some "dropouts" of words and phrases, there are not many compared to the later versions.

In order to determine what the "original dictation" really was, all the changes made to any particular passage need to be traced and evaluated through all the versions. In most cases it is fairly obvious which of the "variant readings" is the most authentic. In some cases two or more variants appear at first glance to be equally plausible candidates for "authenticity."

This work of thorough analysis of the variants from which we can expect a *Critical Edition* of high reliability and authenticity to eventually emerge, is a large undertaking which will likely not be completed for several years. Until that analysis is completed, the *Urtext* is overall the most complete and accurate rendition of the original dictation available. It has fewer omissions and editing mistakes than later versions, and it is more complete than the earlier *Notes* and otherwise mostly identical to the *Notes*.

To facilitate identification and assessment of variants, this print edition is complemented by an optical data disk containing both photographic facsimile and searchable e-text copies of the historical scribal manuscripts which are currently available . These are all substantially cross-referenced to a single universal reference system such that with a bit of practice, one can locate any particular passage in any particular version in a matter of seconds. A concordance has also been prepared for the *Urtext* and *HLC* versions. With these tools, the reader who is curious as to the originality or authenticity of a particular passage can quickly check to see how it was rendered in other versions. With this information the reader can assess the variants for herself. It is frequently the case, especially with the more heavily edited

Preface

versions, that a perplexing passage immediately becomes clear when checked against the original dictation. Many of the "perplexities" in the later versions are simply copying mistakes. Others are confusing because they have been removed from their original context. Yet others are clearer in light of the expanded discussion originally dictated. In some cases ambiguous readings become clear simply by seeing which words were originally emphasized.

Currently we have completed two of the three pre-1976 versions as substantially accurate e-texts, the *HLC* (completed in 2006) and the *Urtext* (completed in 2008). The *Notes* has only been partly transcribed into e-text form. When that ongoing work is finished it will be quite easy to generate a comprehensive list of all the editing changes between all the known versions, or a *"Catalogue of Variant Readings."* Armed with that list of all the editing changes and the tools of textual scholarship, it should be fairly easy to evaluate all variants and sort them into

- those which are obviously ***mistakes***
- those which are obviously ***corrections*** and
- those which ***are uncertain***

While further research may ultimately establish some uncertain variants as either corrections or mistakes, if one were to simply reproduce the Course with all the obvious mistakes corrected, all the obvious corrections preserved, and the uncertain variants simply footnoted, one would have a significantly more complete and accurate version than any one of the known historical versions. Such a version would include the most authentic material from all sources, correct the obvious mistakes, preserve all later corrections of earlier errors, and footnote any uncertainties.

There are several purposes for this edition and for its publication at this time. The objective of identifying all editing changes in order to sort and evaluate them required accurate e-texts of each of the historical scribal versions. Preparing such a list manually by visually comparing the facsimile image files is enormously labour intensive and very prone to error. Since we want accurate e-texts from which print editions can be typeset anyway, and since the easiest and most reliable way of generating a *Catalogue of Variant Readings* is to have a computer compare the versions, the first stage of the process is to generate accurate e-text (machine-readable copies) of each version which can then be compared with software which can quickly identify every difference.

Of course as each manuscript was completed and proofed for accuracy, it was possible to format the electronic text for printing. Since there is a substantial public demand for print copies and since most of the copies in circulation are exceedingly inaccurate, we felt it would be very inappropriate not to make these more accurate e-texts available in print editions as soon as they were completed.

The increasing popularity and influence of the Course makes it more important than ever that the Course be available in the most complete and accurate form possible with all genuine uncertainties honestly disclosed rather than disguised. The authority and credibility of its message is severely reduced by the presence of typos and omissions and distortions which focus attention away from the importance of the message and onto the shortcomings of the copy in use.

Preface

As more people read it and more people quote it, and its ideas gain more influence, "minor errors" can have a major deleterious impact on the public dialogue. So too, the perception that an edition is highly unreliable undermines both public confidence and the perceived authority of the material, even where the particular passage in question is entirely accurate.

Where the focus should be on the meaning of the words and the ideas they symbolize, we often end up being sidetracked by the fact that some of the words were miscopied. Instead of focusing on the message, the focus turns to the messenger and the message itself can get lost in the process. Where the question should be "is the message authentic," what too often happens is a debate as to whether "the copy is accurate." That kind of uncertainty is not difficult to dispel with honest, thorough scholarship. That kind of uncertainty is regrettably exacerbated by editions which claim a level of accuracy much greater than they actually deliver. When the "messenger" is found to be misleading and the advertising false, many have mistakenly extrapolated that therefore the "message" must also be fraudulent.

When dealing with material which claims authorship by Jesus of Nazareth, inevitably there will be scepticism and the suspicion that this claim arises not from truth, but rather from delusions or outright fraud. The important area of investigation in terms of the authority and authenticity of this material relates to the process by which Helen Schucman first put these words on paper in her notebooks. The later copying and editing mistakes are really an entirely separate issue with no necessary reflection on the authenticity of the original dictation. Later copying mistakes are irrelevant to the basic question: just how *did* Schucman come up with these words and where did they come from in the first place? Was her belief that she was hearing Jesus of Nazareth correct? Was she mistaken? Or was she a conspirator in a grand hoax?

The most important "question of fraud" relates to the original scribing and whether Schucman really heard "a Voice" or simply composed the material herself, with possible input from others, and then later misrepresented the material either because she suffered from delusions or because of deliberate fraud. This is the basic question every sceptic will have for the material. Indeed is a basic question every reader should ask and must answer because one's opinion of the authorship cannot help but influence one's opinion of the authority. It is much more difficult to answer that question from inaccurate abridged copies than it is from the actual primary source material itself, or at least accurate copies of that material.

The question of "who is the author of this material" is not important to everyone, but it is important to many and answering it with confidence is severely hampered by lack of access to the actual authentic original dictation as first recorded. The decades of suppression of the primary source material have only managed to increase doubt and convince many sceptics that there really must be "something to hide." What other motive could there be for trying to keep the source material secret?

If Schucman was involved in a conspiracy to deceive, if she was honestly confused, if she was unknowingly exercising some unusual savant ability unconnected to anything "supernatural," then her perception of this work as being authored by Jesus is very likely "mistaken." If there is evidence of such inadvertent or even deliberate deception, it will be found in the original *Notes* and subsequent copying mistakes are quite irrelevant except that they serve to muddy the waters. However, the presentation of a substantially altered text as "virtu-

PREFACE

ally unchanged" not only introduces deception because that statement is far from being entirely true, it makes it all the more difficult to interrogate the really important "witness" which is the original words as Schucman wrote them down. It also gives sceptics some very good reasons to be even more doubtful of the integrity of the message when they find the messengers so notably lacking in that regard.

The extent and nature of the editing changes is an interesting topic, but quite a different one from the question of the source and authenticity of the original dictation. Both questions will likely be researched and investigated for years to come. With further research we can expect increasing clarity and quite probably that research will discover things which will surprise many.

The Author makes an interesting comment on the problem of scribal errors.
From the *Notes* 4:67

6   As long as you ~~read~~
7   take accurate notes, every
8   word is meaningful. But I
9   can't always get through.
10 Whenever possible, I will
11 correct retroactively. Be
12 sure to note all later
13 corrections.

A few pages later in the *Notes*, in a quote preserved in the *Urtext*, we read:

T 1 B 30d. "Contradictions in MY word mean lack of understanding, or scribal failures, which I make every effort to correct. But they are still NOT crucial. The Bible has the same problem, I assure you, and it's STILL being edited. Consider the power of MY WORD, in that it has withstood all the attacks of error, and is the Source of Truth."

The sometimes lively debate about the "importance" of the errors is addressed here usefully in a manner which acknowledges the insight of two divergent viewpoints. By saying "every word is meaningful" the Author is saying that it's not wholly unimportant that the right words be put in the right place. Elsewhere he states that every word was carefully chosen.[10] By saying that errors are "not crucial," however, he's stating that getting the words right, although important, is not the only or even the most important thing. He says the power of "My Word" can withstand error. And we have here an interesting and direct comparison of the Course to the Bible as both being manifestations of the "Word" which are imperfect and in need of correction. Elsewhere the Author several times identifies errors in the Bible and sets out to correct them. While those holding the view that either the Bible or the Course is infallible might take offence at this, those who recognize that no book is, or ever likely will be "perfect," will be more inclined to look with interest at Jesus' suggested corrections.

---

[10] "I have made every effort to use words which are ALMOST impossible to distort, but man is very inventive when it comes to twisting symbols around." **(T 3 C 9.)**

Preface

And finally we have the notion of "retroactive correction" which suggests that the Author intends to "correct" any scribal errors over time, presumably as much time as it takes. The idea that either the Course or the Bible achieved a state of perfection at a certain point in time from which no further improvements can be made is one that can be *believed* to be the truth, but it certainly cannot be *demonstrated* to be the truth.

This retroactive correction has two necessary conditions: the first is a willingness to concede that there is at least some importance to identifying and correcting scribal and editing mistakes. We can't begin to cooperate with the Author in the correction of mistakes if we deny there are any or insist that such errors in HIS words are entirely meaningless. A second necessary condition expressed several times in the Course is that we must ask.[11] We must ask and be willing to hear without filtering the Voice of the Holy Spirit through our own preconceptions of what it should or shouldn't say and instead seek only for what it really *does* say.

"Seek and ye shall find" has a corollary. "Don't seek and you won't find."

This retroactive correction will take place "whenever possible" and it is our goal to join with all who are prepared to meet the necessary conditions to **make it possible** to present the Course with the purity and integrity it so richly deserves. This edition of the *Urtext Manuscripts* is one important step toward that goal.

I'd like to be very clear that it is far from my intent to "attack" or "condemn" other editions of *A Course in Miracles* which are somewhat lacking in accuracy and completeness, or those responsible for those editions. Such editions have blessed many lives and their shortcomings are not, as the Author has stated, "crucial."

I firmly believe that those who have published the Course in the past have done the best they could with the often limited skills and resources which were available to them at the time. I'm rather certain that in 1976 those responsible for the decision to publish were largely unaware of many of the problems with that version. I'm also convinced that the world is far better off because they *did* publish what they did when they did than would have been the case if they had waited for years attempting to proofread to perfection.

If they "felt it was just the way Jesus wanted it" I think they were right. I think Jesus wanted it in print, knew the "errors were not crucial" and did not want them to delay further. That does not mean, as some have argued, that it was free of errors or that Jesus didn't want to correct the copying mistakes later when there was more time and perhaps more willingness.

There is a tendency among followers of most "bodies of scripture" to **wish** to believe that their Holy Book is complete, inerrant, infallible, and the "last word." I can certainly understand the desire for perfection and a clear definitive statement that is unambiguous and absolutely trustworthy now and forever. That sort of thing can't be put between the covers of a book, however, and it is a serious misperception to suppose that it can be. The Living God is dynamic as is the relationship of Love between Himself and His Creation. While the "Will of God is changeless" (**T 12 F 3.**) its expression in time *through* people is not and no body of symbols given through people at a particular point in history can ever be "the last thing God has to communicate to His Creation!" A book is static, like a snapshot. And like a photo it can be "accurate" or it can be blurred by flaws and scratches and lose clarity through multiple recopying. But it is not *alive*, it does not find ever new forms with which to express the

---

[11] See in particular T 1 B 15b, T 1 B 25i, T 1 B 30g, T 1 B 30aa, T 2 B 38, for a few examples of the Author's emphasis on the necessity of ASKING.

Preface

changeless truth. It is just one set of symbols from one moment in time, frozen in that moment.

The author makes some useful comments on this aspect of words:

"The purpose of words is to limit, and by limiting to make a vast area of experience more manageable. But that means manageable by YOU. For many aspects of living in this world that is necessary. But not for asking. God does not use words and does not answer in words. He can only "speak" to the Christ in you, Who translates His Answer into whatever language you can understand and accept. Sometimes words will limit fear; sometimes not. That is why some people hear words, some receive feelings of inner conviction, and some do not become aware of anything. Yet God has answered, and His Answer will reach you when you are ready. (**S 1 A 7**)

"Words can be helpful, particularly for the beginner, in helping concentration and facilitating the exclusion or at least the control of extraneous thoughts. Let us not forget, however, that words are but symbols of symbols. They are thus twice removed from reality." (**M 22 A 1**)

God is the "ultimate reality" and words on pages are twice removed. This we must remember when we seek to project onto them "real" aspects of God such as infallibility, changelessness, perfection, inerrancy, etc. To project attributes of Divine reality onto a symbol is really idolatry and "magic thinking." It is the worship of symbols or symbols of symbols in place of the worship of that which is symbolized, the one thing that *is* real, God our Creator.

"Words" are helpful if they direct our attention and concentration on reality. Words are counter-productive if we confuse them *for* reality and make of the symbols idolatrous objects of worship.

In the last analysis the "best version" of *A Course in Miracles* is the one you read and the one to which you open your heart to the redemptive message of love and forgiveness, a message they all contain.

One should also bear in mind that while for most readers faced with a variety of different versions there is an obvious question about which one to choose, the respective versions are not "competitors" so much as they are "complements." Each has unique strengths and weaknesses. Each is a "witness" to a single historical event, that even being Helen Schucman's "hearing" a remarkable discourse and her note-taking during that hearing. Schucman's hearing was not perfect. Her note-taking was not perfect. In her efforts to correct the errors in later editing, for a variety of reasons she ended up introducing progressively more new errors while fixing a few earlier ones each time. Each version then is a precious resource, and each gives us more information about that original event to which each is a witness. By retracing her steps backwards through the versions and the editing and copying mistakes, we can generally distinguish the mistakes from the corrections with ease and do what no version yet to appear has done, extract the best from each of them.

I use the "witness" metaphor here for several reasons. Schucman can be thought of as an eye-witness (or ear-witness) to an historical event. During the event she took notes, but did not take them without error. Later she reviewed her notes and retyped them, at least four times over the course of ten years. Each time the story changed a little. Each time there were

Preface

some inadvertent copying mistakes. It's not uncommon that human memories of events change over time.

Memories don't always change over time, sometimes humans can remember with astonishing "photographic" precision but memories often change dramatically and except by comparison to such data as photos and original written records, we can't tell which memories are pristine and which have "evolved." With that thought in mind it certainly does seem likely that the earliest record Schucman made of the event is most often most likely to be the most accurate and is certainly *less* subject to inadvertent copying mistakes and later "evolved memories" or even interpretation on her part. It is quite possible that certain passages came to mean something very different to *her* ten years later. Which is the more important though? What the "Voice" originally said or how Schucman interpreted it a decade later? Both may be interesting and relevant but they are two very different kinds of data. For many purposes it is important to distinguish, if possible, which words are "original" and which words are a much later "scribal interpretation of the original." Whichever version we happen to prefer it is important to be honest about which is which and refrain from claiming that the one is the other.

A great deal of additional information about this edition, the various versions, and the process by which editorial decisions were made in the preparation of this edition can be found in the Appendices. And now I invite you to turn the page and begin reading, remembering the first line of the dictation Schucman recorded in the *Notes,* and who it was who spoke those words …

"You will see miracles through your hands through Me!"

That is how the Course originally began.

That line, which was edited out of later versions, was simply moved down a bit in the *Urtext* as the Scribes followed the editing instructions "it is crucial to say FIRST that this is a required Course …" They followed that instruction and put that part first. Here in the *Urtext* the entire instruction is preserved, while in later versions the words of instruction "it is crucial to say first that" were removed, and probably quite appropriately.

In this example and numerous others the reader will detect places in the *Urtext* where some editing is indeed appropriate. Aside from the correction of the most blatant typing mistakes and standardization of spelling,[12] the Scribal *Urtext Manuscripts* are presented "as is" on these pages, "warts and all." The time for editing will come. In this edition we simply present it with a bare minimum of editing for print.

For the purposes of reference, cross-reference, and citation we have included three different reference systems: bold numbers in-line which are the original manuscript page numbers. These make checking back to the original manuscript facsimiles very easy. For cross-referencing to the *HLC*, the chapter and section breaks from that version have been inserted. These mostly correspond to the chapter and section divisions in the later FIP abridgements. For cross-referencing to the *Notes*, the *Notes* page number for each section heading is indicated. For more details on the referencing system, see Appendix III.

---

[12] See Appendix V for details on the editorial principles applied in the preparation of this edition.

Acknowledgements

This work owes its existence to an enormous number of people, many of whom I do not know personally and am unlikely to ever meet in this lifetime, who have made available the raw materials from which this compilation was made. My role has largely been a clerical task of collecting, collating, referencing, annotating, documenting and proofing source material made available by others.

There are so many whose contributions played a crucial role in making this publication possible that naming them all is impractical. You know who you are.

In particular, those who prepared the initial e-texts of the *HLC* and the *Urtext* in 2000, which provided the raw material to proof, deserve special mention though I don't know your names. Your work has made my work possible.

To each of you I express my deep gratitude for providing the source materials without which this work would have remained impossible.

To all those who have helped with proofreading and critiques I owe much. The quality and accuracy of this material is much higher for your contributions. I am eternally grateful in every sense of the word.

To those whose future proofreading and critiques will identify imperfections I have yet to detect and correct, I offer my thanks in advance.

Special thanks to Deborah Maltman for the many hours of proofreading and moral support, Gerry Merrick for his encyclopaedic grasp of English grammar and Robert Perry whose wise counsel in the early phases of this project was enormously helpful in helping me understand the difference between a "mistake that needed fixing" and an "intentional novel turn of phrase" and Doug Monkton whose advice and help in the final design has helped produce a result that is much better than it otherwise would have been.

Doug Thompson
July 2008

Urtext* Volume I: *Text

Volume I: Text Table of Contents

CHAPTER 1 – INTRODUCTION TO MIRACLES 1
   T 1 A. Introduction (*Notes* 1 4:28) 1
   T 1 B. Principles of Miracles (*Notes* 1 4:28) 1
   The Relationship of Miracles and Revelation. (*Notes* 75 4:102) 5
   T 1 C. Distortions of Miracle Impulses (*Notes* 211 5:60) 16
CHAPTER 2 – THE ILLUSION OF SEPARATION 18
   T 2 A. Introduction (*Notes* not present in Notes) 18
   T 2 B. The Re-interpretation of Defenses (*Notes* 230 5:79) 20
   T 2 C. Healing as Release from Fear (*Notes* 263 5:112) 23
   T 2 D. Fear as Lack of Love (*Notes* 265 5:114) 25
   T 2 E. The Correction for Lack of Love (*Notes* 271 T(5:120) 26
   T 2 F. The Meaning of the Last Judgment (*Notes* not present in the Notes) 30
CHAPTER 3 – RETRAINING THE MIND 31
   T 3 A. Introduction (*Notes* 296 5:145) 31
   T 3 B. Special Principles for Miracle Workers (*Notes* 312 5:161) 33
   T 3 C. Atonement without Sacrifice (*Notes* 317 5:166) 33
   T 3 D. Miracles as Accurate Perception (*Notes* not present in the Notes) 36
   T 3 E. Perception versus Knowledge (*Notes* 328 5:177) 36
   T 3 F. Conflict and the Ego (*Notes* 339 5:188) 37
   T 3 G. The Loss of Certainty (*Notes* 366 5:215) 39
   T 3 H. Judgment and the Authority Problem.. (*Notes* not present in the Notes) 42
   T 3 I. Creating versus the Self-Image (*Notes* 374 5:223) 43
CHAPTER 4 – THE ROOT OF ALL EVIL 45
   T 4 A. Introduction (*Notes* 389 5:238) 45
   T 4 B. Right Teaching and Right Learning (*Notes* 403 5:252) 45
   T 4 C. The Ego and False Autonomy (*Notes* 439 6:3) 47
   T 4 D. Love without Conflict (*Notes* 456 6:20) 49
   T 4 E. The Escape from Fear (*Notes* 467 6:31) 51
   T 4 F. The Ego-Body Illusion (*Notes* 477 6:41) 52
   T 4 G. The Constant State (*Notes* 487 6:51) 53
   T 4 H. Creation and Communication (*Notes* 508 6:72) 54
   T 4 I. True Rehabilitation (*Notes* 514 6:77) 55
CHAPTER 5 – HEALING AND WHOLENESS 57
   T 5 A. Introduction (*Notes* 518 6:82) 57
   T 5 B. Healing as Joining (*Notes* 520 6:84) 57
   T 5 C. The Mind of the Atonement (*Notes* 525 6:89) 57
   T 5 D. The Voice for God (*Notes* 529 6:93) 58
   T 5 E. The Guide to Salvation (*Notes* 548 6:112) 59
   T 5 F. Therapy and Teaching (*Notes* 558 6:122) 60
   T 5 G. The Two Decisions (*Notes* 569 6:133) 61
   T 5 H. Time and Eternity (*Notes* 577 6:141) 62
   T 5 I. The Eternal Fixation (*Notes* 586 6:150) 63
CHAPTER 6 – ATTACK AND FEAR 66
   T 6 A. Introduction (*Notes* 599 6:163) 66
   T 6 B. The Message of the Crucifixion (*Notes* 601 6:165) 66
   T 6 C. The Uses of Projection (*Notes* 618 6:182) 68
   T 6 D. The Relinquishment of Attack (*Notes* 625 6:193) 69
   T 6 E. The Only Answer (*Notes* 634 6:198) 69
   T 6 F. "To Have, Give All to All" (*Notes* 644 6:208) 70
   T 6 G. "To Have Peace, Teach Peace to Learn It" (*Notes* 654 6:218) 71
   T 6 H. "Be Vigilant Only for God and His Kingdom" (*Notes* 663 6:227) 72

Volume I: Text Table of Contents

CHAPTER 7 – THE CONSISTENCY OF THE KINGDOM **74**
  T 7 A. Introduction (*Notes* 675 7:7) 74
  T 7 B. Bargaining versus Healing (*Notes* 677 7:9) 74
  T 7 C. The Laws of Mind (*Notes* 682 7:14) 74
  T 7 D. The Unified Curriculum (*Notes* 691 7:23) 75
  T 7 E. The Recognition of Truth (*Notes* 696 7:28) 76
  T 7 F. Healing and the Changelessness of Mind (*Notes* 707 7:39) 77
  T 7 G. From Vigilance to Peace (*Notes* 720 7:52) 78
  T 7 H. The Total Commitment (*Notes* 537 6:101) 80
  T 7 I. The Defense of Conflict (*Notes* 733 7:65) 81
  T 7 J. The Extension of the Kingdom (*Notes* 738 7:70) 81
  T 7 K. The Confusion of Strength and Weakness (*Notes* 746 7:78) 82
  T 7 L. The State of Grace (*Notes* 752 7:84) 83

CHAPTER 8 – THE JOURNEY BACK **84**
  T 8 A. Introduction (*Notes* 758 7:90) 84
  T 8 B. The Direction of the Curriculum (*Notes* 760 7:92) 84
  T 8 C. The Rationale for Choice (*Notes* 762 7:94) 84
  T 8 D. The Holy Encounter (*Notes* 768 7:100) 85
  T 8 E. The Light of the World (*Notes* 776 7:108) 86
  T 8 F. The Power of Joint Decision (*Notes* 789 7:121) 87
  T 8 G. Communication and the Ego-Body Equation (*Notes* 798 7:130) 89
  T 8 H. The Body as Means or End (*Notes* 813 7:145) 90
  T 8 I. Healing as Corrected Perception (*Notes* 817 7:149) 91
  T 8 J. The Acceptance of Reality (*Notes* 824 7:156) 92
  T 8 K. The Answer to Prayer (*Notes* 828 7:160) 93

CHAPTER 9 – THE CORRECTION OF ERROR **95**
  T 9 A. Introduction (*Notes* 833 7:165) 95
  T 9 B. Sanity and Perception (*Notes* 834 7:167) 95
  T 9 C. Atonement as a Lesson in Sharing (*Notes* 838 7:170) 95
  T 9 D. The Unhealed Healer (*Notes* 846 7:178) 96
  T 9 E. The Awareness of the Holy Spirit (*Notes* 854 7:186) 97
  T 9 F. Salvation and God's Will (*Notes* 858 7:190) 98
  T 9 G. Grandeur versus Grandiosity (*Notes* 865 7:197) 98
  T 9 H. The Inclusiveness of Creation (*Notes* 873 7:205) 99
  T 9 I. The Decision to Forget (*Notes* 877 7:210) 100
  T 9 J. Magic versus Miracles (*Notes* 890 7:221) 101
  T 9 K. The Denial of God (*Notes* 899 8:3) 102

CHAPTER 10 – GOD AND THE EGO **104**
  T 10 A. Introduction (*Notes* 909 8:13) 104
  T 10 B. Projection versus Extension (*Notes* 911 8:15) 104
  T 10 C. The Willingness for Healing (*Notes* 927 8:31) 105
  T 10 D. From Darkness to Light (*Notes* 936 8:39) 106
  T 10 E. The Inheritance of God's Son (*Notes* 946 8:50) 106
  T 10 F. The "Dynamics" of the Ego (*Notes* 952 8:56) 107
  T 10 G. Experience and Perception (*Notes* 975 8:79) 108
  T 10 H. The Problem and the Answer (*Notes* 984 8:88) 110

CHAPTER 11 – GOD'S PLAN FOR SALVATION **112**
  T 11 A. Introduction (*Notes* 997 8:101) 112
  T 11 B. The Judgment of the Holy Spirit (*Notes* 998 8:102) 112
  T 11 C. The Mechanism of Miracles (*Notes* 1005 8:909) 112
  T 11 D. The Investment in Reality (*Notes* 1019 8:123) 114
  T 11 E. Seeking and Finding (*Notes* 1026 8:130) 115
  T 11 F. The Sane Curriculum (*Notes* 1031 8:135) 116
  T 11 G. The Vision of Christ (*Notes* 1043 8:147/149) 117
  T 11 H. The Guide for Miracles (*Notes* 1049 8:153) 117
  T 11 I. Reality and Redemption (*Notes* 1059 8:163) 119
  T 11 J. Guiltlessness and Invulnerability (*Notes* 1064 8:168) 119

Volume I: Text Table of Contents

CHAPTER 12 – THE PROBLEM OF GUILT 122
    T 12 A. Introduction (*Notes* 1075 8:179) 122
    T 12 B. Crucifixion by Guilt (*Notes* 1076 8:180) 122
    T 12 C. The Fear of Redemption (*Notes* 1082 8:186) 122
    T 12 D. Healing and Time (*Notes* 1091 8:195) 123
    T 12 E. The Two Emotions (*Notes* 1099 8:203) 124
    T 12 F. Finding the Present (*Notes* 1110 8:214) 125
    T 12 G. Attainment of the Real World (*Notes* 1120 8:224) 127

CHAPTER 13 – FROM PERCEPTION TO KNOWLEDGE 129
    T 13 A. Introduction (*Notes* 1132 8:236) 129
    T 13 B. The Role of Healing (*Notes* 1133 8:237) 129
    T 13 C. The Shadow of Guilt (*Notes* 1138 8:242) 129
    T 13 D. Release and Restoration (*Notes* 1144 8:248) 130
    T 13 E. The Guarantee of Heaven (*Notes* 1156 8:260) 132
    T 13 F. The Testimony of Miracles (*Notes* 1166 9:3) 132
    T 13 G. The Happy Learner (*Notes* 1170 9:7) 133
    T 13 H. The Decision for Guiltlessness (*Notes* 1182 9:19) 134
    T 13 I. The Way of Salvation (*Notes* 1190 9:27) 135

CHAPTER 14 – BRINGING ILLUSIONS TO TRUTH 137
    T 14 A. Introduction (*Notes* 1196 9:33) 137
    T 14 B. Guilt and Guiltlessness (*Notes* 1198 9:35) 137
    T 14 C. Out of the Darkness (*Notes* 1208 9:45) 138
    T 14 D. Perception without Deceit (*Notes* 1215 9:52) 139
    T 14 E. The Recognition of Holiness (*Notes* 1228 9:65) 140
    T 14 F. The Shift to Miracles (*Notes* 1233 9:71) 141
    T 14 G. The Test of Truth (*Notes* 1242 9:79) 142

CHAPTER 15 – THE PURPOSE OF TIME 144
    T 15 A. Introduction (*Notes* 1253 9:90) 144
    T 15 B. The Uses of Time (*Notes* 1255 9:92) 144
    T 15 C. Time and Eternity (*Notes* 1264 9:101) 145
    T 15 D. Littleness versus Magnitude (*Notes* 1270 9:107) 145
    T 15 E. Practicing the Holy Instant (*Notes* 1278 9:115) 147
    T 15 F. The Holy Instant and Special Relationships (*Notes* 1287 9:124) 147
    T 15 G. The Holy Instant and the Laws of God (*Notes* 1295 9:133) 148
    T 15 H. The Holy Instant and Communication (*Notes* 1301 9:138) 149
    T 15 I. The Holy Instant and Real Relationships (*Notes* 1310 9:147) 150
    T 15 J. The Time of Christ (*Notes* 1320 9:157) 151
    T 15 K. The End of Sacrifice (*Notes* 1329 9:166) 152

CHAPTER 16 – THE FORGIVENESS OF ILLUSIONS 154
    T 16 A. Introduction (*Notes* 1354 9:191) 154
    T 16 B. True Empathy (*Notes* 1356 9:193) 154
    T 16 C. The Magnitude of Holiness (*Notes* 1336 9:173) 154
    T 16 D. The Reward of Teaching (*Notes* 1343 9:160) 155
    T 16 E. Illusion and Reality of Love (*Notes* 1360 9:197) 156
    T 16 F. Specialness and Guilt (*Notes* 1370 9:207) 157
    T 16 G. The Bridge to the Real World (*Notes* 1382 9:219) 159
    T 16 H. The End of Illusions (*Notes* 1389 9:227) 160

CHAPTER 17 – FORGIVENESS AND HEALING 162
    T 17 A. Introduction (*Notes* 1397 9:234) 162
    T 17 B. Fantasy and Distorted Perception (*Notes* 1398 9:235) 162
    T 17 C. The Forgiven World (*Notes* 1401 9:238) 162
    T 17 D. Shadows of the Past (*Notes* 1407 9:244) 163
    T 17 E. Perception and the Two Worlds (*Notes* 1416 9:253) 164
    T 17 F. The Healed Relationship (*Notes* 1427 9:264) 165
    T 17 G. Practical Forgiveness (*Notes* 1437 9:274) 167
    T 17 H. The Need for Faith (*Notes* 1445 10:5) 167
    T 17 I. The Conditions of Forgiveness (*Notes* 1450 10:10) 168

Volume I: Text Table of Contents

CHAPTER 18 – THE DREAM AND THE REALITY **170**
    T 18 A. Introduction (*Notes* 1454 10:14) 170
    T 18 B. Substitution as a Defense (*Notes* 1456 10:16) 170
    T 18 C. The Basis of the Dream (N* 1463 10:23) 171
    T 18 D. Light in the Dream (*Notes* 1470 10:29) 172
    T 18 E. The Little Willingness (*Notes* 1476 10:36) 172
    T 18 F. The Happy Dream (*Notes* 1481 10:41) 173
    T 18 G. Dreams and the Body (*Notes* 1485 10:45) 174
    T 18 H. "I Need Do Nothing" (*Notes* 1689 11:64) 175
    T 18 I. The Purpose of the Body (*Notes* 1495 10:55) 176
    T 18 J. The Delusional Thought System (N* 1503 10:63) 177
    T 18 K. The Passing of the Dream (*Notes* 1510 10:70) 178

CHAPTER 19 – BEYOND THE BODY **179**
    T 19 A. Introduction (*Notes* 1513 10:73) 179
    T 19 B. Healing and the Mind (*Notes* 1514 10:74) 179
    T 19 C. Sin versus Error (*Notes* 1524 10:84) 180
    T 19 D. The Unreality of Sin (*Notes* 1530 10:90) 181
    T 19 E. Obstacles to Peace –I. The Desire to Get Rid of It (*Notes* 1542 10:102) 182
    T 19 F. The Attraction of Guilt (*Notes* 1548 10:108) 183
    T 19 G. Obstacles to Peace – II. The Belief the Body is Valuable for What it Offers (not present in *Notes*) . 184
    T 19 H. Pleasure and Pain (not present in *Notes*) 184
    T 19 I. Obstacles to Peace - III. The Attraction of Death (not present in *Notes*) 185
    T 19 J. The Incorruptible Body (not present in *Notes*) 185
    T 19 K. Obstacles to Peace - IV. The Fear of God (not present in *Notes*) 186
    T 19 L. The Lifting of the Veil (not present in *Notes*) 187

CHAPTER 20 – THE PROMISE OF THE RESURRECTION **189**
    T 20 A. Introduction (not present in *Notes*) 189
    T 20 B. Holy Week (not present in *Notes*) 189
    T 20 C. Thorns and Lilies (not present in *Notes*) 189
    T 20 D. Sin as an Adjustment (not present in *Notes*) 190
    T 20 E. Entering the Ark (not present in *Notes*) 191
    T 20 F. Heralds of Eternity (not present in *Notes*) 192
    T 20 G. The Temple of the Holy Spirit (not present in *Notes*) 193
    T 20 H. The Consistency of Means and End (not present in *Notes*) 194
    T 20 I. The Vision of Sinlessness (not present in *Notes*) 195

CHAPTER 21 – THE INNER PICTURE **196**
    T 21 A. Introduction (not present in *Notes*) 196
    T 21 B. The Imagined World (not present in *Notes*) 196
    T 21 C. The Responsibility for Sight (not present in *Notes*) 197
    T 21 D. Faith, Belief and Vision (not present in *Notes*) 198
    T 21 E. The Fear to Look Within (*Notes* 1569 10:129) 199
    T 21 F. Reason and Perception (*Notes* 1574 10:134) 199
    T 21 G. Reason and Correction (*Notes* 1582 10:142) 200
    T 21 H. Perception and Wishes (*Notes* 1589 10:149) 201
    T 21 I. The Inner Shift (*Notes* 1597 10:157) 202

CHAPTER 22 – SALVATION AND THE HOLY RELATIONSHIP **204**
    T 22 A. Introduction (*Notes* 1601 10:161) 204
    T 22 B. The Message of the Holy Relationship (*Notes* 1604 10:164) 204
    T 22 C. Your Brother's Sinlessness (*Notes* 1612 10:172) 205
    T 22 D. Reason and the Holy Relationship (*Notes* 1620 10:180) 206
    T 22 E. The Branching of the Road (*Notes* 1628 11:3) 207
    T 22 F. Weakness and Defensiveness (*Notes* 1631 11:6) 207
    T 22 G. Freedom and the Holy Spirit (*Notes* 1635 11:10) 208

CHAPTER 23 – THE WAR AGAINST YOURSELF **210**
    T 23 A. Introduction (*Notes* 1647 11:22) 210
    T 23 B. The Irreconcilable Beliefs (*Notes* 1652 11:27) 210
    T 23 C. The Laws of Chaos (*Notes* 1660 11:35) 211
    T 23 D. Salvation Without Compromise (*Notes* 1674 11:49) 213
    T 23 E. The Fear of Life (*Notes* 1678 11:52) 214

Volume I: Text Table of Contents

CHAPTER 24 – SPECIALNESS AND SEPARATION **215**
T 24 A. Introduction (*Notes* 1684 11:59) 215
T 24 B. Specialness as a Substitute for Love (*Notes* 1685 11:60) 215
T 24 C. The Treachery of Specialness (*Notes* 1695 11:70) 216
T 24 D. The Forgiveness of Specialness (*Notes* 1704 11:79) 217
T 24 E. Specialness and Salvation (*Notes* 1709 11:84) 218
T 24 F. The Resolution of the Dream (*Notes* 1713 11:88) 218
T 24 G. Salvation from Fear (*Notes* 1719 11:94) 219
T 24 H. The Meeting-Place (*Notes* 1727 11:102) 220

CHAPTER 25 – THE REMEDY **222**
T 25 A. Introduction (*Notes* 1735 11:110) 222
T 25 B. The Appointed Task (*Notes* 1737 11:112) 222
T 25 C. The Savior from the Dark (*Notes* 1746 11:21) 222
T 25 D. The Fundamental Law of Perception (*Notes* 1754 11:128) 223
T 25 E. The Joining of Minds (*Notes* 1762 11:137) 224
T 25 F. The State of Sinlessness (*Notes* 1766 11:141) 225
T 25 G. The Special Function (*Notes* 1770 11:145) 225
T 25 H. Commuting the Sentence (*Notes* 1775 11:150) 226
T 25 I. The Principle of Salvation (*Notes* 1785 11:160) 227
T 25 J. The Justice of Heaven (*Notes* 1796 11:171) 229

CHAPTER 26 – THE TRANSITION **230**
T 26 A. Introduction (*Notes* 1803 11:178) 230
T 26 B. The "Sacrifice" of Oneness (*Notes* 1803 11:178) 230
T 26 C. The Forms of Error (*Notes* 1810 11:185) 230
T 26 D. The Borderland (*Notes* 1816 11:191) 231
T 26 E. Where Sin Has Left (*Notes* 1821 11:196) 232
T 26 F. The Little Hindrance (*Notes* 1825 11:200) 232
T 26 G. The Appointed Friend (*Notes* 1834 11:209) 233
T 26 H. Review of Principles (*Notes* 1837 11:212) 234
T 26 I. The Immediacy of Salvation (*Notes* 1850 11:225) 235
T 26 J. For They Have Come (*Notes* 1856 11:231) 236
T 26 K. The Remaining Task (N* 1862 11:237) 237

CHAPTER 27 – THE BODY AND THE DREAM **238**
T 27 A. Introduction (*Notes* 1868 12:3) 238
T 27 B. The Picture of the Crucifixion (*Notes* 1869 12:4) 238
T 27 C. The Fear of Healing (*Notes* 1877 12:12) 239
T 27 D. The Symbol of the Impossible (*Notes* 1890 12:25) 240
T 27 E. The Quiet Answer (*Notes* 1896 12:31) 241
T 27 F. The Healing Example (*Notes* 1901 12:36) 242
T 27 G. The Purpose of Pain (*Notes* 1909 12:44) 243
T 27 H. The Illusion of Suffering (*Notes* 1914 12:49) 243
T 27 I. The "Hero" of the Dream (*Notes* 1925 12:60) 245

CHAPTER 28 – THE UNDOING OF FEAR **247**
T 28 A. Introduction (*Notes* 1936 12:71) 247
T 28 B. The Present Memory (*Notes* 1937 12:72) 247
T 28 C. Reversing Effect and Cause (*Notes* 1947 12:82) 248
T 28 D. The Agreement to Join (*Notes* 1955 12:90) 249
T 28 E. The Greater Joining (*Notes* 1960 12:95) 250
T 28 F. The Alternate to Dreams of Fear (*Notes* 1067 12:102) 251
T 28 G. The Secret Vows (*Notes* 1972 12:107) 251
T 28 H. The Beautiful Relationship (*Notes* 1978 12:113) 252

Volume I: Text Table of Contents

CHAPTER 29 – THE AWAKENING **253**
   T 29 A. Introduction (*Notes* 1083 12:118) 253
   T 29 B. The Closing of the Gap (*Notes* 1985 12:120) 253
   T 29 C. The Coming of the Guest (*Notes* 1989 12:124) 253
   T 29 D. God's Witnesses (*Notes* 1997 12:132) 254
   T 29 E. Dream Roles (*Notes* 2001 12:136) 255
   T 29 F. The Changeless Dwelling-Place (*Notes* 2006 12:141) 255
   T 29 G. Forgiveness and Peace (*Notes* 2011 12:146) 256
   T 29 H. The Lingering Illusion (*Notes* 2038 12:173) 256
   T 29 I. Christ and Anti-Christ (*Notes* 2015 12:150) 257
   T 29 J. The Forgiving Dream (*Notes* 2022 12:157) 258

CHAPTER 30 – THE NEW BEGINNING **260**
   T 30 A. Introduction (*Notes* 2029 12:164) 260
   T 30 B. Rules for Decision (*Notes* 2029 12:164) 260
   T 30 C. Freedom of Will (*Notes* 2045 12:180) 261
   T 30 D. Beyond All Idols (*Notes* 2050 12:185) 261
   T 30 E. The Truth Behind Illusions (*Notes* 2058 12:193) 262
   T 30 F. The Only Purpose (*Notes* 2064 12:199) 263
   T 30 G. The Justification for Forgiveness (*Notes* 2072 12:207) 264
   T 30 H. The New Interpretation (*Notes* 2078 12:213) 265
   T 30 I. Changeless Reality (*Notes* 2083 12:218) 265

CHAPTER 31 – THE SIMPLICITY OF SALVATION **267**
   T 31 A. Introduction (*Notes* 2088 12:223) 267
   T 31 B. The Illusion of an Enemy (*Notes* 2097 12:232) 268
   T 31 C. The Self-Accused (*Notes* 2105 12:240) 269
   T 31 D. The Real Alternative (*Notes* 2109 12:245) 269
   T 31 E. Self-Concept versus Self (*Notes* 2117 12:252) 270
   T 31 F. Recognizing the Spirit (*Notes* 2129 12:264) 271
   T 31 G. The Savior's Vision (*Notes* 2133 12:268) 272
   T 31 H Choose Once Again (*Notes* 2146 12:281) 273

Urtext Volume I: *Text*
CHAPTER 1 – INTRODUCTION TO MIRACLES

T 1 A. Introduction (*Notes* 1 4:28)

T 1 A 1. It is crucial to say first that this is a required course. Only the time you take it is voluntary. Free will does not mean that you establish the curriculum. It means only that you can elect what to take when. It is just because you are not ready to do what you should elect to do that time exists at all. (You will see miracles through your hands through me. You should begin each day with the prayer "Help me to perform whatever miracles you want of me to-day.")

T 1 B. Principles of Miracles (*Notes* 1 4:28)

T 1 B 1. The first thing to remember about miracles is that there is no order of difficulty among them. One is not harder or bigger than another. They are all the same.

T 1 B 2. Miracles do not matter. They are quite unimportant.

T 1 B 3. They occur naturally as an expression of love. The real miracle is the love that inspires them. In this sense, everything that comes from love is a miracle.

T 1 B 3a. This explains the first point related to the lack of order. ALL expressions of love are maximal.

T 1 B 3b. This is why the "thing in itself"[1] does not matter.[2] The only thing that matters is the Source, and this is far beyond human evaluation.

T 1 B 3c. (Q and A re: first 3 points.) Q (HS) Would you regard this communication as a kind of miracle? A. There is nothing special or surprising about this at all. The ONE thing that happened was the Universal Miracle which was the experience of intense love that you have felt. (Don't get embarrassed by the idea of love. Embarrassment is only a form of fear, and actually a particularly dangerous form because it reflects egocentricity. T(2) -2-

T 1 B 3d. Do not feel guilty about the fact that you are doubting this. Just re-read them and their truth will come to you. I love you, and I am not afraid or embarrassed or doubtful. MY strength will support you, so don't worry and leave the rest to me. But when you see B., be SURE you tell him how much he helped you through by giving you the right message, and don't bother with worrying about how you received it. That doesn't matter either. You were just afraid.)

T 1 B 3e. (HS fearful in taxi about a communication which related Dave's healing and Jonathan's hernia. She thought it would be safer to dissociate the two. Instructions were: refer to point 1 and re-read NOW.)

T 1 B 4. ALL miracles mean Life, and God is the giver of[3] Life. He will direct you VERY specifically.

T 1 B 4b. (Plan ahead is good advice in this world, where you should and must control & direct where you have accepted responsibility. But the Universal Plan is in more appropriate hands. You will know all you need to know. Make NO attempts to plan ahead in this respect.)

T 1 B 5. Miracles are habits, and should be involuntary. They should not be under conscious control.[4] Consciously selected miracles are usually misguided,[5] and this will make[6] the talent useless.[7]

T 1 B 6. Miracles are natural. When they do NOT occur something has gone wrong. **T(3) -3-**

T 1 B 7. Miracles are everyone's right, but purification is necessary first.

T 1 B 8. Miracles are a form of healing. They supply a lack, and are performed by those who have more for those who have less.

T 1 B 9. Miracles are a kind of exchange. Like all expressions of love, which are ALWAYS miraculous in the true sense, the exchange reverses the physical laws.

T 1 B 10. A miracle is a reversal of the physical order because it brings more love to the giver AND the receiver. (A miracle is misunderstood when it is regarded as a spectacle.)

T 1 B 11. The use of miracles as a spectacle to INDUCE belief is wrong. They are really used for and by believers.

T 1 B 11b. (HS has some fear about 11) and doubt about 9) and 10). Probably doubt induced by fear of 11).

T 1 B 11c. (When you say "If you want me to I will" please add "and if you DON'T want me to I won't." This is the RIGHT use of

---

[1] The "thing in itself" is a term used in Philosophy to refer to a *noumenon* which is distinct from a *phenomenon* in that while a *phenomenon* is sensed and experienced, the notion of *noumenon* refers to an abstract essence or Platonic ideal independent of sensory perception. A *phenomenon* is that which is perceived; a *noumenon* is the actual object which emits the phenomenon in question. The idea of "human evaluation" is central to the distinction with *noumena* being generally thought of as beyond what can be known by reason or experience. This paragraph certainly appears to be a reference to this philosophical question. Perhaps a reference to Immanuel Kant's *Critique of Pure Reason* in which the means by which knowledge is obtained, ordered and evaluated are extensively explored. The distinction between the noumenon or "thing in itself" and the "cause" or "source" is made here in the Course and is one which Kant's work also addresses.
[2] The *Notes* adds before this sentence "Check back with ②" which refers to **T 1 B 2** "miracles do not matter…"
[3] *Urtext* manuscript has "the" crossed out. There is no "the" in the *Notes*.
[4] Originally the sentence "Otherwise they may become undemocratic" follows here, but is crossed out. It is also present in the *Notes* and crossed out.
[5] Originally typed "dangerous" the handwritten mark-up changes it to "misguided."
[6] Originally typed "may destroy" the handwritten mark-up changes it to "this will make."
[7] The word "useless" is added in handwritten mark-up. This paragraph is one of the most heavily marked up and re-written in the *Text* volume, offering several variant readings. In the *Notes* this last sentence (T 1 B 5.3) is "Selective miracles are dangerous and may destroy the talent." Originally in the *Notes* (N 4:33:3-7) the paragraph is:

```
3    Miracles are habits and should
4    be involuntary.  Otherwise they may
                     Conscious control
5    bec. undemocratic.  Selective miracles
6    are dangerous & may destroy the
7    talent.
```

The words "Conscious control" are crossed out in the *Notes* and replaced with "Otherwise they may."

Before the handwritten mark-up the paragraph was originally typed:

> Miracles are habits, and should be involuntary. They should not be under conscious control. Otherwise they may become undemocratic. Consciously selected miracles are dangerous, and may destroy the talent.

In the later *HLC* this is rendered:

> Miracles are habits and should be involuntary. They should not be under conscious control. Consciously selected miracles can be misguided.

The *HLC* reading is preserved in FIP.

Volume I - Text

inhibition. There has to be SOME control over learning for channelizing purposes. Remember retroactive inhibition which should be easy enough for you.

T 1 B 11d. Sometimes the new learning is the more important, and HAS to inhibit the old. It's a form of correction.)

T 1 B 12. Prayer is the medium of miracles. Prayer is the natural communication of the Created with the Creator. Through prayer, love is received, and through miracles love is expressed. **T(4) -4-**

T 1 B 12b. Miracles are thought-creations. Thought can create lower-order or higher-order realities. This is the basic distinction between intellectualization and thinking. One creates the physical, and the other the spiritual, and we believe in what we create.

T 1 B 13. A miracle is a beginning and an end(ing).[8] It thus abolishes time. It is always an affirmation of re-birth, which seems to go back, but really goes forward. It undoes the past in the present, and thus releases the future.

T 1 B 14. Miracles attest to truth. They are convincing because they arise from conviction. Without conviction, they deteriorate into magic, which is mindless, and therefore destructive, or rather, the uncreative use of Mind.

T 1 B 15. Each[9] day should be devoted to miracles. (God created time so that man could use it creatively, and convince himself of his own ability to create. Time is a teaching device, and a means to an end. It will cease when it is no longer useful for facilitating learning.)

T 1 B 15b. SPECIAL INSTRUCTIONS: Notes on this course have to be taken only under good learning conditions. The same goes for review periods. I will tell you when, but REMEMBER TO ASK.[10]

T 1 B 16. Miracles are teaching devices for demonstrating that it is more blessed to give than to receive. They simultaneously increase the reserve strength of the giver, and supply the lack of strength in the receiver. BE VERY CAREFUL in interpreting this.[11] **T(5) -5-**

T 1 B 16b. INSTRUCTIONS: The purpose of this course is integration. I told you that you will not be able to use it right until you have taken it. As long as your identification vacillates, (and B's is weak) you cannot accept the gift that belongs to you. You are still vacillating between recognizing the gift and throwing it away. B regards himself as too weak to accept it. You do not yet know its healing power. After you have passed the course, you will accept it and keep it and use it. That is the final exam, which you will have no trouble in passing. Midterm marks are not entered on the permanent record.

T 1 B 17. Miracles are the absence of the body. They are sudden shifts into invisibility, away from lower order reality. That is why they heal.

T 1 B 18. A miracle is a service. It is the maximal service that one soul can render another. It is a way of loving your neighbor[12] as yourself. The doer recognizes his own and his neighbor's inestimable value simultaneously.

T 1 B 18b. (This is why no areas of hatred can be retained. If you retain them, your own value is no longer inestimable because, you are evaluating it as X or infinity minus that amount. This is meaningless mathematically, which uses the term "inestimable" only in the very literal sense. Pun intended especially for B, (who originally did not get it.) Intended as a special sign of love.)[13] **T(6) -6-**

T 1 B 19. Miracles rest on the law and order of eternity, not of time.[14]

T 1 B 20. Miracles are an industrial necessity. Industry depends on cooperation, and cooperation depends on miracles. (see page 8)[15]

T 1 B 21. [1] Miracles are cobwebs of iron. They unite human frailty to the strength of God. (see page 7)

T 1 B 21b. (add for 21. HS considered changing "iron" to "steel." Correction: No. Steel would NOT be a better word. Steel is very useful but it would have to be tempered by fire. Iron is the raw material. The point of miracles is that they replace fire, thus making it unnecessary.)

T 1 B 22. Miracles are natural expressions of total forgiveness. Through miracles, man accepts God's forgiveness by extending it to others. The second step is inherent in the first, because light cannot tolerate darkness. Light dispels darkness automatically, by definition.

T 1 B 22b. EXPLANATORY INSTRUCTIONS: Miracles are associated with fear only because of the fallacy that darkness can hide. Man believes that what he cannot see does not exist, and his

---

[8] The *Notes* has several words scratched out following "end" in this line, but does not have the "ing" which is in brackets in the *Urtext* manuscript.
[9] *Urtext* manuscript originally had "Every", crossed out and "Each" typed in above it. the *Notes* has "each."
[10] *Urtext* manuscript has a closing parenthesis with no matching opening parenthesis in this location.
[11] In a long stretch of omitted "personal material" we find four lines which appear to have been an original miracle principle, inadvertently omitted. The following lines occur on *Notes* folio 4:46, lines 22-26:
"Remember a miracle is a spark of Life. It shines through the darkness and brings in the light. You must begin to forget and remember."
Immediately after these lines are the words "This is a private point just for you"
and the discussion goes on to a distinctly private point. This strongly suggests
the immediately preceding material, was not intended to be "private" or omitted.

[12] Leviticus 19:18, Matthew 19:19. 22:39, Mark 12:31, Luke 10:27, Romans 13:9 all refer to loving neighbors as thyself. This theme appears very frequently in the Course and in the Bible.
[13] The following beautiful little discussion of sexual love and specialness in the *Notes* was omitted, likely because it does address sexuality and homosexuality and it does so in individually specific terms. However, it is thoroughly "generalizable" and what is true of "you and Bill" is likewise true of many others. This is from the *Notes*: (N 4:52)

(I threw that in happily specially for Bill, because he does need special signs of love. He doesn't really but he does think so.
Now tell him that homo sex is sinful only to the extent it is based on the principle of exclusion. Everybody should love everybody.
It is wrong to deny the beauty of some souls because of body-structures of which you are afraid. This is essentially an unhealthy attempt to limit fear but fear cannot be limited, just as love cannot have limits.
Heterosexual attitudes can be similarly distracted but do contain a more natural potential. Sex relations are intended for children. You and Bill have misused misunderstood sex, because you both recognize it as a way of establishing human contact for yourselves. This has led to body-image problems.
Children are miracles in their own right. They already have the (N 4:53) gift of life, and their parents provide them with the opportunity to express it.
Nothing physical, mental, or spiritual should be used selfishly. The pleasure from using anything should be in utilizing it for God's will.
You should live so that God is free to arrange temporary human constellations as He sees fit.
Do not interpret this in terms of guilt. Many children which are already here need spiritual parents. The poor are always with us, and many which are born have not been reborn.
Human birth, maturation, and development is a microcosmic representation of a much larger process of Creation and development of abilities. It is subject to error as long as the real purpose (N 4:54) of free will is misunderstood and misdirected.
The real function of parents is to be wiser than the children in this respect and to teach them accordingly, ((This upsets me))
[14] The *Urtext* manuscript shows 19 as the third paragraph, following 21a, with lines indicating relocation and renumbering. This copy reflects the rearrangement and renumbering suggested by these lines, and not the original typing, in these first three paragraphs.
[15] This paragraph is corrected in **T 1 B 22k**.

Chapter 1 – Introduction to Miracles

physical eyes cannot see in the dark. This is a very primitive solution, and has led to a denial of the spiritual eye, which always depends on light. Remember the Biblical injunction: "May I never forget that THINE eye is ever upon me, beholding the evil and the good."[16]

T 1 B 22c. There are two stages, one lower and one higher, which are involved in the escape from darkness: 1) the recognition that darkness CANNOT hide. This usually does entail fear.

T 1 B 22d. 2) The recognition that there is nothing you WANT to hide, even if you could. This brings escape from fear.[17] **T(7) -7-**

T 1 B 22e. Corrections Re Pt. 21 cobwebs of iron. "This is upside down as stated. The part about 'uniting human frailty with the strength of God' is all right, but the explanation stops too soon. If iron is the 'raw material', cobwebs can't become the iron. That is only the way it seems, because cobwebs are associated with the frailty & iron with strength. If you look carefully at the phrasing, you will see it is reversed (one point already tells you that miracles reverse the physical or lower order laws.)

T 1 B 22f. The raw material, or iron, is heavy but crude, & stands for the body, which is a crude creation. The cobweb concept is closer to how the body SHOULD be regarded, i.e., as an airy & temporary home, which can just be blown away with a slight breeze.

T 1 B 22g. (*21. [2])*[18] The point should read "A miracle reawakens the awareness that the spirit, and not the body, is the altar of Truth. This is the recognition that leads to the healing power of the miracle."

T 1 B 22h. (*22a*) A miracle rearranges the order of perception, and places the levels in their true perspective. This heals at all levels, because all sickness comes from confusing the levels.

T 1 B 22i. (Tell B. about the idea (which is still dim to HS) that the reason is not that you (plural) distantiate, doubt, or cannot believe. It is more of a reaction formation against a pull which you both recognize is so intense that you are afraid that you will be uprooted. But remember that a cobweb is really stronger than the iron, if you see it properly. This fear is also why you couldn't get the point straight.)

T 1 B 22j. By the way, it is not true that you are both 'JUST SCRIBES'. You might remember that the Scribes were very wise and holy men and are even sometimes spelled with a capital S. If you want to go further, you might change the meaning of 'just' from 'merely' to 'honest', a term used in the Bible in association with 'might' or 'strength.' Tell B. you couldn't make that pun if the original phrasing had been singular. (HS aside about liking the first about[19] assumption failure more.) Answer: **T(8) -8-** It was cuter, but this one MEANS more. The REAL reason you don't like it is because it refers to you in a VERY lofty position. This makes you nervous.)

T 1 B 22k. Correction: And don't lose sight of the emphasis on cooperation, or the NOT SINGULAR. That point about "industrial necessity" should read "corporate", referring to the body of Christ which is a way of referring to the Church. But the Church of God is only the sum of the souls he created, which IS the corporate body of Christ. Correct to read: "A Miracle makes souls one in God," and leave in the next part about cooperation.[20]

T 1 B 22l. Further correction: "God" should read "Christ." The Father and the Son are not identical, but you CAN say "Like Father, LIKE Son."

T 1 B 22m. (Remind B. to get another notebook. I don't give up as easily as HE does. If I could get YOU to listen, which was a miracle in itself, I can get him to register. He should appreciate this more than anyone else, having had some trouble with this problem himself.)

T 1 B 22n. "Lord heal me" is the only legitimate prayer. This also means "Lord atone for me," because the only thing man should pray for is forgiveness. He HAS everything else.

T 1 B 22o. Now take this personally, and listen to Divine logic: If, when you have been forgiven, you have everything else, and

If you have been forgiven

Then you HAVE everything else.

T 1 B 22p. This happens to be the simplest of all propositions.

    IF P then Q

    P

    Therefore, Q

T 1 B 22q. The real question is, is P true. If you will review the evidence, I think you will find this inescapable. I went on very personal record to this effect, and I am the only completely True Witness for God. You have every[21] right to examine MY credentials— in fact, I urge you to do so. You haven't read the Bible in years. **T(9) -9-**

T 1 B 22r. Special Explanatory Note: As soon as you (H & B) have entered the second phase, you will be not only willing to enter into communion, but will also understand peace and joy. Your commitment is not yet total. That is why you still have more to learn than to teach. When your equilibrium stabilizes, you can teach AS MUCH as you learn. This will give you the proper sense of balance. Meanwhile, remember that NO EFFORT IS WASTED. Unless you remember this, you cannot avail yourself of MY efforts, which are limitless.

T 1 B 22s. (Have a good day.) Since only eternity is real, why not use the illusion of time constructively? You might remember that "underneath are the Everlasting Arms."[22]

T 1 B 22t. BIBLICAL QUOTATION: "If you are ashamed of me before men, I will be ashamed of you before God,"[23] (HS ? of

---

[16] **Proverbs 15:3** The eyes of the LORD are in every place, keeping watch upon the evil and the good.
[17] in a lengthy omitted segment, most of which is "personal" material, which occurs just before paragraph 22e, the following segment occurs in the *Notes* which may be an original miracle principle inadvertently omitted. From the *Notes* (N 4:78):
Miracles depend on timing.
This is why you shouldn't waste time.
I told you awhile back that time
would cease when it was no longer
useful as a learning aid. There is
a way of speeding you up. And
that is by leaving more and more time
for Me. So you can devote it to
miracles."
[18] The "21" here is handwritten in ... as in several instances there is confusion and/or re-sequencing as to numbering and order of principles.
[19] The words "first about" here are handwritten above "assumption" and aren't fully legible, so there might be something else written there. Between paragraphs 23e and 23f in the *Notes,* what would appear from the context to be a first reference to "Assumption failure" occurs. The *Urtext* pages show some sequence differences from the *Notes* here. The 23e-f material appears to predate the 22j material which appears to refer **back** to something which precedes it. In the current *Urtext* sequence the "preceding" material actually follows it. Whether this re-sequencing was intentional or inadvertent is not known.
[20] *Urtext* manuscript has the closing quote here at the end of the paraagraph, rather than after "God,."
[21] *Urtext* manuscript has "very" but probably this should be "every." That is what the *Notes* has.
[22] **Deuteronomy 33:27** The eternal God is *thy* dwelling place, And underneath are the everlasting arms: And he thrust out the enemy from before thee, And said, Destroy.
[23] **Mark 8:38** "For whosoever shall be ashamed of me and of my words in this adulterous and sinful generation, the Son of man also shall be ashamed of him, when he cometh in the glory of his Father with the holy angels."
Also **Luke 9:26** (similar) and **Matthew 10:33** (related)

misquote.) is interpreted as a threat ONLY as long you remain in the first step. (see bottom of p. 6 for steps.)

T 1 B 22u. What it REALLY means is that if you are ashamed of me (or embarrassed by love), you will project and therefore make it impossible for me to reach you. Make every effort you can NOT to do this. I will help you as much as you will let me.

T 1 B 23. Miracles make time and tide wait for all men. They can heal the sick and raise the dead because man himself made both death and taxes, and can abolish both. Note: Tax also means "strain." (One definition for miracles is: "That which, or one who, is of surpassing excellence or merit.") (from Dictionary, third definition)**T(10) -10-**

T 1 B 23b. YOU are a miracle.[24] God creates only "that which, or one who, is of surpassing excellence or merit." Man is capable of this kind of creation, too, being in the image and likeness[25] of his own Creator. Anything else is only his own nightmare, and does not exist. Only the Creations of Light are real.

T 1 B 23c. Miracles[26] are a part of an interlocking chain of forgiveness which, when completed, is the Atonement.[27] This process works all the time and in all dimensions of time. (e.g. given of HS report rewrite for Esther! Esther had hurt something you loved, by writing a report you regarded as very bad. You atoned for her by writing one in her name that was very good. Actually, it was not your responsibility professionally to do this, but because you DO love the Shield you recognized that in this case, you ARE your brother's keeper. While you did not cancel Esther's sin (later defined as "lack of love") you DID cancel out its EFFECTS.

T 1 B 23d. Someday I want to tell Esther that not only is she forgiven but that the effects of all her sins are cancelled. This is what I have already told you. When I can tell her, she will be afraid for a long time, because she will remember many things, consciously or unconsciously, including the Shield report, a lack of love which you cancelled out in advance by a miracle of devotion.

T 1 B 23e. I am in charge of the process of Atonement, which I undertook to begin. My Atonement was for the canceling out of all sins (i.e., lack of love) which human beings could not otherwise correct. That is what the Biblical statement "underneath are the Everlasting Arms"[28] means. (HS explanation: This means that He will backstop whenever human miracles will not suffice for atonement purposes. However, it is perfectly clear that when a person can atone by miracles, both giver and receiver are atoning. It is better to atone this way because of the mutual benefits involved.) **T(11) -11** "Inasmuch as you do it unto the least of these, my children" really ends with "you do it unto yourself and ME."[29] The reason why YOU come before me is because I do not need miracles for my own Atonement, but I stand at the end in case YOU fail temporarily.

T 1 B 23f. SPECIAL EXPLANATION: (In response to HS request re possible corrections.) Change the word "sin" to "absence of love." Sin is a manmade word with threat connotations which he made up himself. No REAL threat is involved anywhere. Just because "nature abhors a vacuum," which is true enough, it does NOT follow that "a vacuum is filled with hellfire." Nothing is gained by frightening yourself, and it is very destructive. Miracles need freedom from fear. Part of their Atonement value involves just that. Note that the word "atone" really means "undo."[30] **T(12) -12**

T 1 B 23g. The purpose of the Atonement is to restore everything TO you. (That is, to restore the awareness. Later clarification.) You had everything when you were created, just as everyone did.[31]

---

[29] **Matthew 25:40** And the King shall answer and say unto them, Verily I say unto you, Inasmuch as ye did it unto one of these my brethren, *even* these least, ye did it unto me.

[30] The following paragraphs (below) in the *Notes* about "Guidance," asking, and answering, were omitted from the *Urtext*. The material is, however, the clearest and most specific material on the practical issues, most notably blockages and why it is we sometimes don't feel we have been heard or can hear.(N 4:73 through 4:75))

The reason I direct everything that is unimportant is because it is no way to waste your free will. If you insist on doing the trivial your way, you waste too much time and will on it. Will cannot be free if it is tied up in trivia. It never gets out.

I will tell exactly what to do in connection with everything that doesn't matter. That is not an area where choice should be invested. There is better use of time.

You have to remember to ask me to take charge of all minutiae, and it will be taken care of so well and so quickly that you cannot bog down in it.

The only remaining problem is that you will be unwilling to ask because you are afraid not to be bogged down. Don't let this hold us back. If you will ask, I will arrange these things even if you're not too enthusiastic.

Prayer can safely be very (N 4:74) specific in little matters. If you need a coat, ask me where to find one. I know your taste well, and I also know where the coat is that you would eventually buy anyway.

If you don't like the coat afterwards, that is what would have happened anyway. I did not pick out the coat for you. You said you wanted something warm, inexpensive, and capable of taking rough wear. I told you you could get a Borgana, but I let you get a better one because the furrier needed you.

Note, however, that it is better in terms of the criteria you established. I could do this because you saw the coat more that way than in terms of a particular material.

You thought of Klein's yourself a few days ago, and then you decided against it, because Borgana is price- fixed. Then you remembered a coat Grace once got there that was much cheaper, and seemed (N 4:75) pretty much the same, and asked yourself whether it was really right to be sold on a particular trade name through advertising. That opened your mind.

I cannot save you more time than you will let Me, but if you are willing to try the Higher Shopping Service, which also covers all lower-order necessities and even quite a number of whims within reason, I have very good use for the time we could save.

Remember, the specific answer you get depends on the specific question you ask. The fewer limits you impose, the better the answer you'll get. Ex: You could ask where do I find a Borgana coat? or where is the coat I want? or where is the coat I should get? and so on. ? ? The form of the thought determines the level of creation.

[31] Immediately before this paragraph, on *Notes* page 4:80 2-6, we find what appears to be a miracle principle inadvertently omitted. It appears within a segment marked "omitted" and which does contain mostly personal material relating to dreams. It is as follows:
Miracles are a way of undoing
over-learned patterns of love-lack.
They bring light into darkness.
That is where their atonement value lies.
The relevance of these words in the immediate context is obvious.

---

[24] The *Notes* starts this paragraph with "That's right that You are a miracle." The glyph for "that" is sometimes indistinguishable from an em dash, so that could be "That's right – You are a miracle." In the *Urtext* we seem to have lost a couple of words.

[25] **Genesis 1:26-27** Then God said, "Let Us make man in Our image, according to Our likeness; let them have dominion over the fish of the sea, over the birds of the air, and over the cattle, over all the earth and over every creeping thing that creeps on the earth." So God created man in His own image; in the image of God He created him; male and female He created them.

[26] Immediately before this in the *Notes* we read: "As long as you take accurate notes, every word is meaningful. But I can't always get through. Whenever possible, I will correct retroactively. Be sure to note all later corrections. They mean that you are more receptive than you were when I tried before." **N 4:67:6-15**

[27] The word "atonement," coined by the 16th Century Bible translator William Tyndale, literally means AT ONE-MENT. It occurs 279 times in ACIM and 71 times in the King James Bible. We can't possibly footnote every Bible reference each time the word appears. The frequency of use suggests the importance of the concept. It is closely linked to the term "salvation" which is the end, atonement being the means. Of note is the fact that the term is defined: **T 1 B 23f** 'Note that the word "atone" really means "undo."' In ACIM's teaching, we were created "at one" or united with God, prior to the separation. "Atonement" then is an "undoing" of the separation illusion, the result of which is "reunion" with God.

[28] **Deuteronomy 33:27** The eternal God is *thy* dwelling place, And underneath are the everlasting arms: And he thrust out the enemy from before thee, And said, Destroy.

Chapter 1 – Introduction to Miracles

T 1 B 23h. Having been restored to your original state, you naturally become part of the Atonement yourself. You now share MY inability to tolerate the lack of love in yourself & in everyone else, and MUST join the GREAT CRUSADE to correct it. The slogan for this Crusade is "Listen, Learn, and DO."

T 1 B 23i. This means Listen to My Voice, Learn to undo the error, and DO something to correct it.

T 1 B 23j. The first two are not enough. The real members of MY party are ACTIVE workers. **T(13) -13**

T 1 B 23k. The power to work Miracles BELONGS to you. I will create the right opportunities for you to do them. But you must be ready & willing to do them, since you are already able to. Doing them will bring conviction in the ability. I repeat that you will see Miracles through your hands through MINE.[32] Conviction really comes through accomplishment. Remember that ability is the potential, Achievement is its expression, and Atonement is the Purpose.

T 1 B 24a. 24 A miracle is a Universal Blessing from God through Me to all My Brothers. Explanation: You once said that souls cannot rest until everyone has found salvation.[33] This happens to be true. It is the privilege of the forgiven to forgive. The Disciples were officially & specifically told to heal others, as Physicians of the Lord. They were also told to heal themselves, & were promised that I would never leave them or forsake them. Atonement is the natural profession of the Children of God, because they have professed Me.

T 1 B 24b. (ASIDE. Tell B that that is what Professor really means. As an Assoc. Prof., he must become associated with My strength. As an Asst. Prof., you must assist both him and Me. The Children need both strength & help. You cannot help until you are strong. The Everlasting Arms are your strength, and the Wisdom of God is your help.)

T 1 B 24c. "Heaven & Earth shall pass away"[34] means that they will not always exist as separate states. My Word, which is the Resurrection and the Light,[35] shall not pass away, because Life is Eternal. YOU are the work of God, and His Work is wholly loveable & wholly loving. This is how a man MUST think of himself in his heart, because this is what he IS.

T 1 B 24d. Add: "As a man thinketh in his heart, so is he."[36] **T(14) -14**

The Relationship of Miracles and Revelation. (*Notes 75 4:102*)

T 1 B 24e. Remember the point about Miracles as a means of organizing different levels of consciousness. Miracles come from the (below conscious) (subconscious) level. Revelations come from the above conscious level. The conscious level is in between & reacts to either sub- or super-conscious impulses in varying ratios. Freud was right about the classification, but not the names. He was also right that the content of consciousness is fleeting. Consciousness is the level which engages in the world, and is capable of responding to both external & internal impulses. Having no impulses from itself, and being primarily a mechanism for inducing response, it can be very wrong.

T 1 B 24f. For example, if the identification is with the body, consciousness may distort superconscious impulses by denying their Source, & seeking their impact in the orgasm. This is the result of the "mistaken identity" confusion.

T 1 B 24g. If you will look back at the description of the EFFECTS of Revelation you will see that there ARE some similarities[37] in the experiential results but hardly in the content.[38]

(This and preceding paragraph go later)

T 1 B 24h. Revelations induce complete but temporary suspension of doubt & fear. They represent the original form of communication between God and His Souls, before the intrusion of fire and ice made this impossible. It should be noted that they involve an extremely personal sense of closeness to Creation, which man tries to find in sexual relationships. This confusion is responsible for the depression and fear which are often associated with sex.

T 1 B 24i. Sex is often associated with lack of love, but Revelation is PURELY a love experience. Physical closeness CANNOT achieve this. As was said before, the subconscious impulses properly induce Miracles, which ARE interpersonal, and result in closeness to others. This can be misunderstood by a personally willful consciousness as an impulse toward sexual gratification.

T 1 B 24j. The Revelation unites Souls directly with God.

T 1 B 24k. The Miracle unites Souls directly with each other. Neither emanates from consciousness, but both are EXPERIENCED there. This is essential, because consciousness is the state which PRODUCES action, though it DOES NOT Inspire it. **T(15) -15**

T 1 B 24l. Man is free to believe what he chooses. What he DOES attests to what he believes.

T 1 B 24m. The deeper levels of his subconscious always contain the impulse to Miracles, but he is free to fill its superficial levels, which are closer to consciousness, with the impulses of this world and to identify himself with them. This results in denying himself access to the miracle level underneath. In conscious actions, then, his interpersonal relationships also become superficial, and miracle-inspired relating becomes impossible.

T 1 B 25. Miracles are a way of EARNING release from fear.

T 1 B 25b. Revelation induces a state in which fear has ALREADY BEEN abolished. Miracles are thus a means, and Revelations are an end. In this sense, they work together.

T 1 B 25c. (Tell B. that miracles DO NOT depend on Revelation. They INDUCE it. He is quite capable of miracles already, but he is still too fearful for Revelations.)

T 1 B 25d. Note that YOUR (HS) Revelation occurred specifically after you had engaged at the visionary level in a process of DENYING fear.

T 1 B 25e. Revelation is intensely personal, and[39] is actually not translatable into conscious content at all. That is why any attempt to describe it in words is usually incomprehensible, even to the writer

---

[32] This line is actually the first line on the first day of the scribing of Chapter 1 in Schucman's notebooks, and the fifth sentence on the first page of this revision. It originally appears slightly different, with the last word "MINE" being "ME" instead.

[33] The word "salvation" occurs 760 times in the seven volumes of ACIM and 169 times in the King James English Bible. We can't possibly footnote every Bible reference each time the word appears. The frequency of its use suggests the importance of the concepts represented by this word. Just what does "salvation" mean? It is the goal, and atonement is the means.

[34] **Mark 13:31** "Heaven and earth shall pass away: but my words shall not pass away." Also **Matthew 24:25** and **Luke 21:33**

[35] In the *Notes* this is "life" and not "Light." It reflects the Biblical quote: **John 11:25** Jesus said to her, "I am the resurrection and the life. He who believes in Me, though he may die, he shall live."

[36] I've not been able to locate this line in the *Notes*. "As a man thinketh" is the title of a rather famous little book by James Allen which might well be what the reference points to. While the line sounds like a Biblical quote and does reflect what Jesus was teaching in **Matthew 5:28**, it's not a word for word reference. **Matthew 5:28**: "but I say unto you, that every one that looketh on a woman to lust after her hath committed adultery with her already in his heart." The idea that the *thought* is causal is central here both in the Bible and the Course. The most direct Biblical quote is from **Proverbs 23:7**: "For as he thinks in his heart, so is he."

[37] Originally written in the *Notes* "superficial similarities," the word "superficial" is crossed out.

[38] The bold characters are not in the *Urtext* but are in the *Notes* and appear to have been omitted inadvertently.

[39] *Urtext* manuscript has "&" (ampersand) here and in numerous places. It is essentially shorthand for "and" and we expand it to "and."

himself at another time. This is why the Book of Revelations is essentially incomprehensible. Revelation induces ONLY experience. Miracles, on the other hand, induce interpersonal ACTION. In the end, these are more useful, because of their IMPERSONAL nature.

T 1 B 25f. In this phase of learning, working miracles is more valuable because freedom from fear cannot be thrust upon you. The experience cannot last.

T 1 B 25g. (Tell B. that your propensity for Revelations, which is very great, is the result of a high level of past communion. Its transitory nature comes from the descent into fear, which has not yet been overcome. His own "suspended" state mitigates both extremes. This has been very apparent in the course of both of your recent developmental patterns.) T(16) -16

T 1 B 25h. ..Miracles are the essential course of ACTION for both of you. They will strengthen him and stabilize you.

T 1 B 25i.. (NOTE that the much more personal than usual notes you are taking today reflect the Revelatory experience. This does NOT produce the more generalizeable quality which this course is aimed at. They may, nevertheless, be of great help to B. personally, since you asked for something that WOULD help him personally. It depends on how he listens, and how well he understands the CO-OPERATIVE nature of your joint experience. You can help only by reading this note FIRST. Ask him later if this should be included in the written part of the course at all or whether you should keep these notes separately. He is in charge of these decisions.)

T 1 B 25j. (Tell B. he should try to understand the VERY important difference between Christ-control and Christ-guidance. This is what made him fearful yesterday.)

T 1 B 26. Miracles praise God through men. They praise God by honoring his Creations, affirming their perfection. They heal because they deny body-identification and affirm[40] Soul-identification. By perceiving the Spirit, they adjust the levels and see them in proper alignment. This places the Spirit at the center, where Souls can communicate directly.

T 1 B 27. Miracles should inspire gratitude, not awe. Man should thank God for what he really is. The Children of God are very holy. The miracle honors their holiness.

T 1 B 27b. God's Creations cannot lose their holiness, although it can be hidden. The miracle uncovers it, and brings it into the light where it belongs.

T 1 B 27c. Holiness can never be really hidden in darkness, but man can deceive himself on this point. This illusion makes him fearful, because in his heart he KNOWS it is an illusion. Like all illusions, he exerts enormous efforts to establish their validity. The miracle sets validity where it belongs. Eternal validity belongs only to the Soul. The miracle acknowledges only the Truth. It thus dispels man's illusions about himself, and puts him into communion with himself and with God. T(17) -17

T 1 B 27d. Christ inspires all miracles, which are essentially intercessions. They intercede for man's holiness, and make him holy. They place man beyond the physical laws, and raise him into the sphere of celestial order. In this order, man IS perfect.

T 1 B 27e. The Soul never loses its communion with God. Only the mind and body need Atonement. The miracle joins in the Atonement of Christ by placing the mind in the service of the Spirit. This establishes the proper function of mind, and abolishes its errors.

T 1 B 28. Miracles honor man, BECAUSE he is loveable. They dispel illusions about himself, and perceive the light in him. They thus atone for his errors by freeing him from his own nightmares. They release him from a prison in which he has imprisoned himself. By freeing his mind from illusions, they restore his sanity, and place him at the feet of Jesus.

T 1 B 28b. (Biblical quotation re healing of devil possessed man, in which the sufferer was subsequently found healed in his right mind, and sitting at feet of Jesus.[41] HS note.)

T 1 B 28c. (Tell B. man's mind can be possessed by illusions, but his Spirit is eternally free. If a mind creates without love, it can create an empty shell. This CAN be possessed by evil. But the Atonement restores the Soul to its proper place. Unless there is emptiness there is no danger, and emptiness is a false creation. The mind that serves the Spirit is invulnerable.)

T 1 B 29. The miracle restores the Soul to its fullness. By atoning for lack, it establishes perfect protection. The strength of the Soul leaves no room for intrusions. The forgiven are filled with the Soul, and their Soul forgives in return. It is the duty of the released to release their brothers.

T 1 B 29b. The forgiven ARE the means of Atonement. Those released by Christ must join in releasing their brothers, for this is the plan of Atonement.

T 1 B 30. Miracles are the way in which minds that serve the spirit unite with Christ for the salvation (or release) of all God's Creations. T(18) -18

T 1 B 30b. Aside (HS commented on awakening with the phrase "God is not Mocked,"[42] with anticipation of punishment.)

T 1 B 30c. Interpretation: "God is not mocked" was intended as reassurance. You are afraid that what you wrote last night was contradictory, conflicting with some earlier points, especially because you were writing while you were all doped up. Remember, "God is not mocked" under any circumstances.

T 1 B 30d. Contradictions in MY word mean lack of understanding, or scribal failures, which I make every effort to correct. But they are still NOT crucial. The Bible has the same problem, I assure you, and it's STILL being edited. Consider the power of MY WORD, in that it has withstood all the attacks of error, and is the Source of Truth.

T 1 B 30e. (Tell B. that there are certain advantages in being a Psychologist. A major one is the understanding of projection, and the extent of its results. Possession is very closely related to projection. "Lucifer"[43] could be literally translated "Light Bearer."[44] He literally PROJECTED himself from Heaven. Projection still has this "hurling" connotation, because it involves hurling something you DO NOT want, and regard as dangerous and frightening, to someone else. This is the opposite of the Golden Rule, and having placed this rule upside down, the reverse of miracles, or projection, follows automatically.)

T 1 B 30f. The correction lies in accepting what is true in YOURSELF, by bringing ALL that you are into light. (HS fearful of writing next part.) Cacey[45] [sic] was wrong about Possession, and he was also wrong about hurting himself. One of the major problems with miracle workers is that they are so sure that what they are doing is right, because they KNOW it stems from love, that they do not pause to let ME establish MY limits.

---

[40] *Urtext* manuscript has "affirms" which presents grammatical problem with agreement in number. This may be typing mistake as the *Notes* has it as "affirm."

[41] **Mark 5: 1-15** And they came to Jesus and saw him who had been demon-possessed, and had the legion, sitting and clothed and right-minded, the one who had the legion. And they were afraid.

[42] **Galatians 6:7** Be not deceived; God is not mocked: for whatsoever a man soweth, that shall he also reap.

Job 13:9 Will it be well when He searches you out? Or can you mock Him as one mocks a man?

[43] **Isaiah 14:12** How art thou fallen from heaven, O Lucifer, son of the morning! *how* art thou cut down to the ground, which didst weaken the nations!

[44] The Strong's definition, and the translation used in the Revised Version and Good News Version is "morning star."

[45] Almost certainly a reference to Cayce (Edgar) whose name is pronounced KAY-SEE.

Chapter 1 – Introduction to Miracles

T 1 B 30g. While what he (Cacey"[46][sic]) did came from Me, he could NOT be induced to ask me each time whether I wanted him to perform this PARTICULAR miracle. If he had, he would not have performed any miracles that could not get through constructively, and would thus have saved himself unnecessary strain. He burned himself out with indiscriminate miracles, and to this extent did not fulfill his own full purpose, and was also subject to the Scribal error I mentioned at the start. The Disciples were also prone to this. **T(19) -19**

T 1 B 30h. The answer is NEVER perform a miracle without asking me IF you should. This spares you from exhaustion, and because you act under direct communication the trance becomes unnecessary. Because miracles are expressions of love, it does NOT follow that they will always be effective. I am the only one who can perform miracles indiscriminately, because I AM the Atonement. You have a ROLE in Atonement, which I will dictate TO you.

T 1 B 30i. Remember, you already have a point about the involuntary nature of miracles. We also have established the fact that everything involuntary belongs under Christ-control, NOT under yours. Under Christ-control, Miracles REPLENISH the doer as well as the receiver.

T 1 B 30j. Possession really means "Not under Christ-Control", thus making him (the mind?) vulnerable to projection. The references to the earth-bound entering bodies really refer to the "taking over" by their own earth-bound "thoughts." This IS Demon Possession. After all, Lucifer fell, but he was still an angel. He is thus the symbol for man.[47] Atonement is the knowledge that the belief that angels can fall is false. It is true that mind can create projections as well as miracles, but it's NOT true that projections are REAL. Any psychologist should understand this. This is what is meant by "The Truth shall set you free."[48]

T 1 B 30k. Christ-controlled miracles are part of the Atonement, but Christ-guidance is personal, and leads to PERSONAL salvation. The impersonal nature of miracles is an essential ingredient, because this enables Me to control their distribution as I see fit.

T 1 B 30l. Christ-guidance, on the other hand, leads to the highly PERSONAL experience of Revelation. This is why it involves PERSONAL choice. A guide does NOT control, by definition, but he does DIRECT, leaving the following up to you. "Lead us not into temptation"[49] means "guide us out of our own errors." Note that the word is "lead", NOT order.

T 1 B 30m. "Take up thy cross and follow me"[50] should be interpreted to read "Recognize your errors and choose to abandon them by following My guidance."**T(20) -20**

T 1 B 30n. (Tell B. when he is afraid of Possession, he need only remember that error cannot really threaten Truth, which ALWAYS can withstand its assaults. ONLY the error is really vulnerable.) The "Princes of this World"[51] are princes only because they are really angels. But they are free to establish their kingdom where they see fit.

T 1 B 30o. If you will remember that ALL princes INHERIT their power from the Father, the right choice becomes inevitable.

> The soul is in a state of grace forever.
> Man's reality is ONLY his soul.
> Therefore, man is in a state of Grace forever.

T 1 B 30p. Atonement undoes all errors in this respect, and thus uproots the REAL source of fear. If you will check back at the reference to uprooting, you will understand it better in this context.[52]

T 1 B 30q. (Tell B. that WHENEVER God's reassurances are experienced as threat, it is ALWAYS because man is defending his misplaced & misdirected love and loyalty. That is what projection always involves.)

T 1 B 30r. "Casting spells" merely means "affirming error", and error is lack of love. When man projects this onto others, he DOES imprison them, but only to the extent that he reinforces errors they have already made. This distortion makes them vulnerable to the curse of others, since they have already cursed themselves. The miracle worker can only bless, and this undoes the curse and frees the soul from prison.

T 1 B 30s. (Tell B. that his slip about (rivet) should be noted. Some slips reach consciousness from the un-Christ-controlled subconscious, and betray a lack of love.)**T(21) -21**

T 1 B 30t. But others (slips) come from the superconscious, which IS in communion with God, and which can also break into consciousness.

T 1 B 30u. HIS slip (rivet) was an expression of a Soul gaining enough strength to request freedom from prison. It will ultimately DEMAND it.

T 1 B 30v. Special Revelation for HS

T 1 B 30w. You are wholly lovely. A perfect shaft of pure light. Before your loveliness the stars stand transfixed, and bow to the power of your will.

T 1 B 30x. What do children know of their creation, except what their Creator tells them?

T 1 B 30y. You were created ABOVE the angels because your role involves creation as well as protection.

T 1 B 30z. You who are in the image of the Father[53] need bow only to HIM, before whom I kneel with you.

T 1 B 30aa. NOTE: This revelation was permitted because you did NOT project onto B. the blame for your omission to ASK ME if you should transcribe the notes. The fact that HE should have done so does not exempt you from your own omission.

T 1 B 30ab. Thanks for blessing him with a miracle rather than cursing him with projection.

T 1 B 30ac. NOTE FURTHER: HE needn't feel concerned about it either; so he forgot? It happens all the time, until the habit of asking becomes involuntary.

T 1 B 30ad. (HS meeting with Dr. Wise and Dr. Damrosch. Dr. D permitted an opportunity for questioning in his capacity as chairman of the flu board for asking re B's flu shot. This was an example of how miracles should work. You did not jump into the question yourself, and even though you DID rush for the phone on Red's advice, you exerted no pressure on B's reluctance.)**T(22) -22**

T 1 B 30ae. This gave ME a chance to let you leave it to the real expert, whom I sent to answer the question.

---

[46] see previous footnote.
[47] This is a rather intriguing line when you think about it: *Lucifer* becomes the symbol, not for a demonic entity, but for man, specifically man's "earth-bound thoughts."
[48] **John 8:32** "and ye shall know the truth, and the truth shall make you free." In relation to the idea of *Lucifer* as a symbol for man, above, "The Truth" that sets you free is the knowledge that "evil" is man-made, our own "earth-bound thoughts" rather than an external, independent, evil personality.
[49] **Matthew 6:13** And bring us not into temptation, but deliver us from evil.
[50] **Mark 10:21** "And Jesus looking upon him loved him, and said unto him, One thing thou lackest: go, sell whatsoever thou hast, and give to the poor, and thou shalt have treasure in heaven: and come, [take up thy cross, and*] follow me." *This phrase "take up thy cross" appears only in the 1611 "King James" version and not in modern translations which simply state "and follow me."
[51] **I Corinthians 2:6** Howbeit we speak wisdom among them that are perfect: yet not the wisdom of this world, nor of the princes of this world, that come to nought:
[52] T 1 B 22i (N 4:89) is the previous reference to being "uprooted"
[53] **Genesis 1:27** And God created man in his own image, in the image of God created he him; male and female created he them.

T 1 B 31. Miracles are examples of right thinking. Reality contact at all levels becomes strong & accurate, thus permitting correct delineation of intra- and interpersonal boundaries. As a result, the doer sees the truth as God created it. This is what is meant by the point on "perspective adjustment."[54]

T 1 B 32. A miracle is a correction factor introduced into false thinking by ME.

T 1 B 32b. It acts as a catalyst, shaking up erroneous perception and snapping it into place. This correction factor places man under the Atonement principle, where his perception is healed. Until this has occurred, perception of the Divine Order is impossible. True depth perception becomes possible only at the highest order of perceptual integration.

T 1 B 32c. The Spiritual eye is the mechanism of miracles, because what the Spiritual eye perceives IS truth. The Spiritual eye perceives both the Creations of God AND the creations of man. Among the creations of man, it can also separate the true from the false by its ability to perceive totally rather than selectively. It thus becomes the proper instrument for reality testing, which always involves the necessary distinction between the true and the false.

T 1 B 33. The miracle dissolves error because the Spiritual eye identifies error as false or unreal. This is the same as saying that by seeing light, darkness automatically disappears. **T(23) -23**

T 1 B 33b. Darkness is lack of light. It does not have unique properties of its own. It is an example of the scarcity fallacy, from which only error can proceed.

T 1 B 33c. (Truth is always abundant……Those who perceive and acknowledge that they have everything have no need for driven behavior of any kind. HS has other personal material related to this re pregnancy.)

T 1 B 34. Miracles are a blessing from parents to children. This is just another way of phrasing the previous point about "from those who have more to those who have less." Children do NOT belong to parents, but they DO need to share their greater abundance. If they are deprived, their perception becomes distorted. When this occurs, the whole family of God, or the Sonship, is impaired in its relationships.

T 1 B 34b. Ultimately, every member of the family of God must return. The miracle calls to him to return, because it blesses and honors him even though he may be absent in spirit.

T 1 B 35. The miracle acknowledges all men as your brothers and Mine. It is a way of perceiving the Universal Mark of God in them.

T 1 B 35b. (Tell B. that this is the true "strawberry mark" of Brotherhood. This is just a sign of special concern for him, because he keeps worrying about this.)

T 1 B 35c. You might add that his false idea about his own exclusion from Universal Love is fallacious in your terms, and arrogant in his. HIS real specialness does NOT stem from exclusion, but from inclusion. ALL My Brothers are special. He should stop interpreting this as "all except B." This is ridiculous! **T(24) -24**

T 1 B 35d. Tell him that the implied lack of love that his version contains is WAY off the Mark, and misses the level of right thinking entirely. He MUST heal his perception in this respect. He MUST work a miracle on behalf of himself here[55] (See the point about miracles as a perception corrector) before he can effect miracles as creative energizers, which they are.

T 1 B 35e. (Tell B. that 50,000,000 Frenchmen CAN be wrong, because the notion is too fragmented. What CAN'T be wrong is the Universal Sonship of which he is a part.)

T 1 B 35f. God WOULD be mocked if ANY of his creations lacked holiness. The Creation IS whole. The mark of Wholeness is Holiness, not holes. <u>THE SONSHIP HAS NO HOLES ANYWHERE.</u>

T 1 B 36. Wholeness is the perceptual content of the miracle. It thus corrects (or atones for) the faulty perception of lack.

T 1 B 36b. We now turn to the fundamental distinction between miracles and projection. The stimulus MUST precede the response, and must also (determine) (influence) the kind of response that is evoked. The relationships of S and R are <u>EXTREMELY</u> intimate. (The behavioristic terminology is because this part deals with behavior.)

T 1 B 36c. Behavior IS response, so that the question "response to what?" becomes crucial.

T 1 B 36d. Stimuli of all kinds are identified through[56] perception. You perceive the stimulus and behave accordingly. It follows, then, that:

As ye perceive

So will ye behave **T(25) -25**

T 1 B 36e. (HS raises point that Biblical language is hardly behavioristic terminology. Answer: No, but they needn't be OUT of accord with each other, either.)

T 1 B 36f. Consider the Golden Rule again. You are asked to behave toward others as you would have them behave toward you.[57] This means that the perception of both must be accurate, since the Golden Rule is the Order for appropriate behavior. You can't behave appropriately unless you perceive accurately, because appropriate behavior DEPENDS on lack of level confusion. The presence of level confusion <u>ALWAYS</u> results in variable reality testing, and hence variability in behavioral appropriateness.

T 1 B 36g. All forms of self image debasement are FUNDAMENTAL perceptual distortions. They inevitably produce either self-contempt or projection, and usually both.

T 1 B 36h. Since you and your neighbor are equal members of the same family, as you perceive both, so will you behave toward both. The way to perceive for Golden Rule behavior is to look out from the perception of your own holiness and perceive the holiness of others. **T(26) -26**

T 1 B 36i. B. & you need considerable clarification of the channel role. Look carefully at Mrs. Albert. She is working miracles every day, because she knows who she is. I emphasize again that your tendency to forget names is not hostility, but a fear of involvement or RECOGNITION. You had misinterpreted human encounters as opportunities for magic rather than for miracles and so you tried to PROTECT THE NAME. This is a very ancient & primitive way of trying to protect a person.

T 1 B 36j. NOTE The very old Jewish practice of changing the name of a person who is very ill, so that when the list is given to the Angel of Death, the person with that name will not be found.

T 1 B 36k. This is a good example of the curiously literal regression which can occur in very bright people when they become afraid. You & B. both do it. Actually, it is a device closely related to the phobia, in the sense that they both narrow fear to a simple aspect of a much larger problem in order to enable them to avoid it.

T 1 B 36l. A similar mechanism works when you get furious about a comparatively minor expression by someone to whom you are ambivalent. A good example of this is your response to Jonathan, who DOES leave things around in very strange ways. Actually, he does this because he thinks that by minor areas of disorganization he

---

[54] See paragraph **T 1 B 22h**
[55] *Urtext* manuscript has a period here, apparently a typo.
[56] *Urtext* manuscript has it typed "thru"
[57] Matthew 7:12 "All things therefore whatsoever ye would that men should do unto you, even so do ye also unto them: for this is the law and the prophets."

can protect his stability. I remind you that you have done this yourself for years, and should understand it very well. This should be met with great charity, rather than with great fury. **T(27) -27**

T 1 B 36m. The fury comes from your awareness that you do not love Jonathan as you should, and you narrow your lack of love by centering your hate on trivial behavior in an attempt to protect him from it.[58] You also call him Jonathan for the same reason (see previous reference).

T 1 B 36n. Note that a name is a human symbol that "stands for" a person. Superstitions about names are very common for just that reason. That is also why people sometimes respond with anger when their names are spelled or pronounced incorrectly.

T 1 B 36o. Actually, the Jewish superstition about changing the names was a distortion of a revelation about how to alter or avert death. What the revelation's proper content was that those "who change their mind" (not name) about destruction (or hate) do not need to die. Death is a human affirmation of a belief in hate.[59] That is why the Bible says "There is no death,"[60] and that is why I demonstrated that death does not exist. Remember that I came to FULFILL the law by[61] RE-INTERPRETING[62] it. The law itself, if properly understood, offers only protection to man. Those who have not yet "changed their minds" have entered the "hellfire" concept into it.

T 1 B 36p. Remember, I said before that because "nature abhors a vacuum", it does NOT follow that the vacuum is filled with hell fire. The emptiness engendered by fear should be replaced by love, because love and its absence are in the same dimension, and correction cannot be undertaken except <u>WITHIN</u> a dimension. Otherwise, there has been a confusion of levels. **T(28) -28**

T 1 B 36q. Returning to Mrs. Albert (not Andrews), she corrected your error about her name without embarrassment and without hostility, because she has NOT made your own mistake about names.

T 1 B 36r. She is not afraid, because[63] she knows she is protected. She made the correction ONLY because you were inaccurate, and the whole question of embarrassment did not occur to her.

T 1 B 36s. She was also quite unembarrassed when she told you that everything has to be done to preserve life, because you never can tell when God may come and say "Get up, Dave," and then he will.

T 1 B 36t. She did not ask what YOU believed first, and afterwards merely added "and its true, too." The RIGHT answer to the SCT item is: <u>WHEN THEY TOLD ME WHAT TO DO, I</u> "referred the question to the only REAL authority."

T 1 B 36u. (HS note: If you ask somebody what he believes before you tell him what you believe, then you are implying that you will say what he approves. This is not "the real authority.")

T 1 B 36v. You took a lot of notes on "Those who are ashamed of Me before men, them will I be ashamed of before God."[64] This was rather carefully clarified, even though the quotation is not quite right, but it doesn't matter.

T 1 B 36w. The important thing is that elsewhere in the Bible it also says "Those who represent (or plead for) Me to men will be represented (or pleaded for) BY Me before God."[65] (Note: This quotation is also not the correct Biblical phrasing, but it IS what it means.) Note that one who represents also "witnesses for." The quotation thus means that you represent or "witness for" the authority in whom you believe. **T(29) -29**

T 1 B 36x. Your witnessing DEMONSTRATES your belief, and thus strengthens it.

T 1 B 36y. I assure you that <u>I</u> will "witness for" anyone who lets me, and to whatever extent he himself permits it.

T 1 B 36z. Those who witness[66] for me are expressing, through their miracles, that they have abandoned deprivation in favor of the abundance they have learned BELONGS to them.

T 1 B 37a. A MAJOR contribution of miracles is their strength in releasing man from his misplaced sense of isolation, deprivation, and lack. They are affirmations of Sonship, which is a state of completion and abundance.[67]

T 1 B 37b. B's very proper emphasis on "changing your mind" needs clarification.

T 1 B 37c. Whatever is true & real is eternal, & <u>CANNOT</u> change or be changed. The Soul is therefore unalterable because it is ALREADY perfect, but the mind can elect the level it chooses to serve. The only limit which is put on its choice is that it CANNOT serve two masters.[68]

T 1 B 37d. While the ballot itself is a secret one, and the right to vote is fully protected, voting ALWAYS entails both election AND rejection. If two candidates are voted for, for the same position, the machine cancels the ballot automatically.

T 1 B 37e. This is necessary, because a split vote does not represent ANY REAL allegiance. **T(30) -30**

T 1 B 37f. Free will is the attribute of the mind, NOT the Soul. The Soul always remains changeless, because it never leaves the sight of God.

T 1 B 37g. The Creation of the Soul is already fully accomplished. The mind, if it votes to do so, becomes a medium by which the Soul can create along the line of its own creation. If it does not freely elect to do so, it retains this creative ability, but places itself under tyrannous rather than authoritative control. As a result, what it creates is imprisonment, because such are the dictates of tyrants.

---

[58] *Urtext* manuscript omits "an", handwritten mark-up fills it in. It is present in the *Notes*.
[59] *Urtext* manuscript has h and f overtyped, so it could be "hate" or "fate" but the "f" is the clearer. *HLC* has "fate." The *Notes* however, clearly has "hate" so that is what we're going with.
[60] **Revelation 21:4** But has now been revealed by the appearing of our Savior Jesus Christ, who has abolished death and brought life and immortality to light through the gospel.
2 Timothy 1:10 And God will wipe away every tear from their eyes; there shall be no more death, nor sorrow, nor crying. There shall be no more pain, for the former things have passed away."
[61] *Urtext* manuscript omits "by", handwritten mark-up fills it in. The *Notes* clearly includes the word "by."
[62] **Matthew 5:17** "Do not think that I came to destroy the Law or the Prophets. I did not come to destroy but to fulfill."
[63] *Urtext* manuscript has it typed "bec." This is a common abbreviation used in Schucman's shorthand for "because."
[64] **Matthew 10:33** But whosoever shall deny me before men, him will I also deny before my Father which is in heaven. Also **Mark 8:38** and Luke 9:2.
[65] **Matthew 10:32** Every one therefore who shall confess me before men, him will I also confess before my Father which is in heaven.
[66] **Isaiah 43:10** "You are My witnesses," says the LORD,
"And My servant whom I have chosen,
That you may know and believe Me,
And understand that I am He.
Before Me there was no God formed,
Nor shall there be after Me."
Isaiah 43:12 "I have declared and saved,
I have proclaimed,
And there was no foreign god among you;
Therefore you are My witnesses,"
Says the LORD, "that I am God.
Acts 1:8 But you shall receive power when the Holy Spirit has come upon you; and you shall be witnesses to Me in Jerusalem, and in all Judea and Samaria, and to the end of the earth.
[67] This is miracle principle 43 in the *HLC*.
[68] **Luke 16:13** "No servant can serve two masters: for either he will hate the one, and love the other; or else he will hold to one, and despise the other. Ye cannot serve God and mammon."

T 1 B 37h. To "change your mind" means to place it at the disposal of True authority. The miracle is thus a sign that the mind has elected to be guided by Christ in HIS service. The abundance of Christ[69] is the natural result of choosing to follow him.

T 1 B 37i. P.S. The reason you have been late recently (for work) because you were taking dictation is merely because you didn't remember to ask me when to stop. This is an example of the "indiscriminant or uncontrolled" miracle-working we already spoke of. It is well-meant but ill-advised.

T 1 B 37j. I prompted that call from Jack (taxi man – couldn't pick HS up, etc.) to show you that this is not necessary. Also, the other man needed the money more today.

T 1 B 37k. NOTE that you managed to fill your scribal role with no interruptions, and were also on time.

T 1 B 37l. NOTE also that you closed the book & put it aside WITHOUT consulting me. ASK "Is that all?" ANSWER: No: add the following: These notes are serving, among other things, to replace the "handwriting on the wall" which you once saw next to your own altar, which read "You have been[70] weighed in the balance and found wanting."**T(31) -31**

T 1 B 37m. Scribes MUST learn Christ-control, to replace their former habits, which DID produce scarcity rather than abundance. From errors of this kind, the sense of deprivation IS inevitable, but very easily corrected.

T 1 B 37n. The following is in relation to question about sex. Tell B. "the one more river" is related to sex. You might even explain it to him as a "tidal wave", a term which he will understand. YOU won't.

T 1 B 37o. Both of you are involved with unconscious distortions (above the miracle level), which are producing a dense cover over miracle-impulses which makes it hard for them to reach consciousness. Sex & miracles are both WAYS OF RELATING. The nature of any interpersonal relationship is limited or defined by what you want it to DO which is WHY you want it in the first place. Relating is a way of achieving an outcome.

T 1 B 37p. Indiscriminant sexual impulses resemble indiscriminant miracle impulses in that both result in body image misperceptions. The first is an expression of an indiscriminant attempt to reach communion through the body. This involves not only the improper self identification, but also disrespect for the individuality of others. Self-control is NOT the whole answer to this problem, though I am by no means discouraging its use. It must be understood, however, that the underlying mechanism must be uprooted (a word you both should understand well enough by now not to regard it as frightening). **T(32) -32**

T 1 B 37q. ALL shallow roots[71] have to be uprooted, because they are not deep enough to sustain you. The illusion that shallow roots can be deepened and thus made to hold is one of the corollaries on which the reversal of the Golden Rule,[72] referred to twice before, is balanced. As these false underpinnings are uprooted (or given up), equilibrium is experienced as unstable. But the fact is that NOTHING is less stable than an orientation which is upside down. Anything that holds it this way is hardly conducive to greater stability.

---

[69] **Matthew 4:19** Then He said to them, "Follow Me, and I will make you fishers of men."

[70] *Urtext* manuscript omits "been", which is handwritten in. The *Notes* clearly has the word present.

[71] **Luke 8:13** "But the ones on the rock are those who, when they hear, receive the word with joy; and these have no root, who believe for a while and in time of temptation fall away."

[72] **Matthew 7:12** "Therefore, whatever you want men to do to you, do also to them, for this is the Law and the Prophets."

T 1 B 37r. The whole danger of defenses lies in their propensity to hold misperceptions rigidly in place. This is why rigidity is regarded AS stability by those who are off the mark.

T 1 B 37s. NOTE The only final solution - (no, Helen, this has nothing to do with the Nazi use of the term.) You just got frightened again. One of the more horrible examples of inverted or upside down thinking (and history is full of horrible examples of this) is the fact that the Nazis spelled their appalling error with capital letters. I shed many tears over this, but it is by no means the only time I said "Father, forgive them for they know not what they do."

T 1 B 37t. All actions which stem from reverse thinking are literally the behavioral expressions of those who know not what they do.[73] Actually, Jean Dixon was right in her emphasis on "Feet on the ground & fingertips in the Heaven," though she was a bit too literal for your kind of understanding. Many people knew exactly what she meant, so her statement was the right miracle for them. **T(33) -33**

T 1 B 37u. For you and Bill, it would be better to consider the concept in terms of reliability & validity. A rigid orientation can be extremely reliable, even if it IS upside down. In fact, the more consistently upside down it is, the more reliable it is, because consistency always held up better mathematically than test-re-test comparisons, which were ALWAYS on shaky ground. You can check this against Jack's notes if you wish, but I assure you its true. Split-half reliability is statistically a MUCH stronger approach. The reason for this is that correlation which is the technique applied to test-re-test comparisons, measures only the EXTENT OF association, and does not consider the Direction at all.

T 1 B 37v. But two halves of the same thing MUST go in the same direction, if there is to be accuracy of measurement. This simple statement is really the principle on which split half reliability, a means of estimating INTERNAL consistency, rests.

T 1 B 37w. Note, however, that both approaches leave out a very important dimension. Internal consistency criteria disregard time, because the focus is on one-time measurements. Test-retest comparisons are BASED on time intervals, but they disregard direction.

T 1 B 37x. It is possible, of course, to use both, by establishing internal consistency AND stability over time. You will remember that Jack once told his class that the more sophisticated statisticians are concentrating more and more on reliability, rather than validity. The rationale for this, as he said, was that a reliable instrument DOES measure something. He also said, however, that validity is still the ultimate goal, which reliability can only serve. **T(34) -34**

T 1 B 37y. I submit (I'm using Jack's language in this section, because it always had a special meaning for you. So did Jack.) Your confusion of sex and statistics is an interesting example of this whole issue. Note that night you spent in the scent of roses doing a complex factorial analysis of covariance. Its a funny story to others, because they see a different kind of level confusion than the one you yourself were making. You might recall that YOU wanted that design, and Jack opposed it. One of the real reasons why that evening was so exhilarating was because it represented a "battle of intellects", (both good ones, by the way), each communicating exceptionally clearly but on opposite sides. The sexual aspects were naturally touched off in both of you, because of the sex and aggression confusion.

T 1 B 37z. (It is especially interesting that after the battle ended on a note of compromise[74] with your agreeing with Jack, he wrote in the margin of your notes "virtue is triumphant." (HS note re submission-dominance, feminine-masculine roles, entered into this.) While this (remark) was funny to both of you at the time, you might con-

---

[73] **Luke 23:34** Then Jesus said, "Father, forgive them, for they do not know what they do." And they divided His garments and cast lots.

[74] The words "on a note of compromise" are crossed out. In the *Notes* they are present and even underlined for emphasis.

Chapter 1 – Introduction to Miracles

sider its truer side. The virtue lay in the complete respect each of you offered to the other's intellect. Your mutual sexual attraction was also shared. The error lay in the word "triumphant." This had the "battle" connotation, because neither of you was respecting ALL of the other. There is a great deal more to a person than intellect & genitals. The omission was the Soul.)T(35) -35

T 1 B 37aa. I submit (after a long interruption) that if a mind (Soul) is in valid relationship with God, it CAN'T be upside down. Jack & the other very eminent methodologists have abandoned validity in favor of reliability because they have lost sight of the end and are concentrating on the means.

T 1 B 37ab. Remember the story about the artist who kept devoting himself to inventing better & better ways of sharpening pencils. He never created anything, but he had the sharpest pencil in town. (The language here is intentional. Sex is often utilized on behalf of very similar errors. Hostility, triumph, vengeance, self-debasement, and all sort of expressions of the lack of love are often VERY clearly seen in the accompanying fantasies. But it is a PROFOUND error to imagine that, because these fantasies are so frequent (or occur so reliably), that this implies validity. Remember that while validity implies reliability the relationship is NOT reversible. You can be wholly reliable, and ENTIRELY wrong.

T 1 B 37ac. While a reliable test DOES measure something, what USE is the test unless you discover what the "something" is? And if validity is more important than reliability, and is also necessarily implied BY it, why not concentrate on VALIDITY and let reliability fall naturally into place.

T 1 B 37ad. Intellect may be a "displacement upward", but sex can be a "displacement outward." How can man "come close" to others through the parts of him which are really invisible? The word "invisible" means "cannot be seen or perceived." T(36) -36 What cannot be perceived is hardly the right means for improving perception.

T 1 B 37ae. The confusion of miracle impulse with sexual impulse is a major source of perceptual distortion, because it INDUCES rather than straightening out the basic level-confusion which underlies all those who seek happiness with the instruments of the world. A desert is a desert is a desert. You can do anything you want in it, but you CANNOT change it from what it IS. It still lacks water, which is why it IS a desert (Bring up that dream about the Bluebird. While HS was looking for this dream, she came across another. The message was to bring both, as an excellent example of how extremely good HS had become over the intervening 25 years at sharpening pencils. Note that the essential content hasn't changed; its just better written.) The thing to do with a desert is to LEAVE.

T 1 B 38. Miracles arise from a miraculous state of mind. By being One, this state of mind goes out to ANYONE, even without the awareness of the miracle worker himself. The impersonal nature of miracles is because Atonement itself is one, uniting all creations with their Creator.

T 1 B 39. The miracle is an expression of an inner awareness of Christ & acceptance of his Atonement. The mind is then in a state of Grace, and naturally becomes gracious, both to the Host within and the stranger without. By bringing in the stranger, he becomes your brother.[75] T(37) -37

T 1 B 39b. The miracles you are told NOT to perform have not lost their value. They are still expressions of your own state of Grace, but the ACTION aspect of the miracle should be Christ-controlled, because of His complete Awareness of the Whole Plan. The impersonal nature of miracle-mindedness ensures YOUR own Grace, but only Christ is in a position to know where Grace can be BESTOWED.

T 1 B 40. A miracle is never lost. It touches many people you may not even know, and sometimes produces undreamed of changes in forces of which you are not even aware. This is not your concern. It will also always bless YOU. This is not your concern, either. But it IS the concern of the Record. The Record is completely unconcerned with reliability, being perfectly valid because of the way it was set up. It ALWAYS measures what it was supposed to measure.

T 1 B 40b. I want to finish the instructions about sex, because this is an area the miracle worker MUST understand.

T 1 B 40c. Inappropriate sex drives (or misdirected miracle-impulses) result in guilt if expressed, and depression if denied. We said before that ALL real pleasure comes from doing God's will.[76] Whenever it is NOT done an experience of lack results. This is because NOT doing the will of God IS a lack of self.

T 1 B 40d. Sex was intended as an instrument for physical creation to enable Souls to embark on new chapters in their experience, and thus improve their record. The pencil was NOT an end in itself. (See earlier section.) It was an aid to the artist in his own creative endeavors. T(38) -38 As he made new homes for Souls and guided them through the period of their own developmental readiness, he learned the role of the father himself. The whole process was set up as a learning experience in gaining Grace.

T 1 B 40e. The pleasure which is derived from sex AS SUCH is reliable only because it stems from an error which men shared. AWARENESS of the error produces the guilt. DENIAL of the error results in projection. CORRECTION of the error brings release.

T 1 B 40f. The only VALID use of sex is procreation. It is NOT truly pleasurable in itself. "Lead us not into Temptation" means "Do not let us deceive ourselves into believing that we can relate in peace to God or our brothers with ANYTHING external." T(39) -39

T 1 B 40g. The "sin of onan"[77] was called a "sin" because it involved a related type of self-delusion; namely, that pleasure WITHOUT relating can exist.

T 1 B 40h. To repeat an earlier instruction, the concept of either the self or another as a "sex-OBJECT" epitomizes this strange reversal. As B. put it, and very correctly, too, it IS objectionable, but only because it is invalid. Upside down logic produces this kind of thinking.

T 1 B 40i. Child of God, you were created to create the good, the beautiful, and the holy. Do not lose sight of this. You were right in telling B. to invite Me to enter anywhere temptation arises. I will change the situation from one of inappropriate sexual attraction to one of impersonal miracle-working. The concept of changing the channel for libidinal expression is Freud's greatest contribution, except that he did not understand what "channel" really means.

T 1 B 40j. The love of God, for a little while, must still be expressed through one body to another. That is because the real vision is still so dim. Everyone can use his body best by enlarging man's perception, so he can see the real VISION. THIS VISION is invisible to the physical eye. The ultimate purpose of the body is to render itself unnecessary. Learning to do this is the only real reason for its creation.

---

[75] **Matthew 25:35** For I was hungry and you gave Me food; I was thirsty and you gave Me drink; I was a stranger and you took Me in;

[76] **Ephesians 2:8** For by grace you have been saved through faith, and that not of yourselves; it is the gift of God.

[77] **Genesis 38:8-11** And Judah said unto Onan, Go in unto thy brother's wife, and perform the duty of a husband's brother unto her, and raise up seed to thy brother. And Onan knew that the seed would not be his; and it came to pass, when he went in unto his brother's wife, that he spilled it on the ground, lest he should give seed to his brother. And the thing which he did was evil in the sight of Jehovah: and he slew him also. Then said Judah to Tamar his daughter-in-law, Remain a widow in thy father's house, till Shelah my son be grown up; for he said, Lest he also die, like his brethren. And Tamar went and dwelt in her father's house.

T 1 B 40k. NOTE Scribes have a particular role in the Plan of Atonement, because they have the ability to EXPERIENCE revelations themselves, and also to put into words enough of the experience to serve as a basis for miracles. **T(40) -40**

T 1 B 40l. (This refers to experiences at the visionary level, after which HS wrote "If you will tell me what to do, I will to do it." She had not known that the word "to" was inserted, and had merely intended to write "I will do it." This recognition had a terrific impact on HS.)

T 1 B 40m. This is why you EXPERIENCED that revelation about "I will to do" VERY personally, but also WROTE IT: What you wrote CAN be useful to miracle workers other than yourself. We said before that prayer is the medium of miracles. The miracle prayer IS what you wrote, i.e. "If you will tell me what to do, I will to do it." *

T 1 B 40n. This prayer is the door that leads out of the desert forever.

T 1 B 40o. *(Correction next day. This is not a complete statement, because it does not exclude the negative. We have already told you to add "and NOT to do what you would not have me do." in connection with miracles. The distinction has also been made here between "miracle-mindedness" as a STATE, and "miracle-doing" as its expression.

T 1 B 40p. The former needs YOUR careful protection, because it is a state of miracle-READINESS. This is what the Bible means in the many references to "Hold yourself ready" and other similar injunctions.

T 1 B 40q. Readiness here means keep your perception right side up, (or valid), so you will ALWAYS be ready, willing, and able. These are the essentials for "listen, learn, and do." You must be
   READY to listen
   WILLING to learn
   and ABLE to do

T 1 B 40r. Only the last is involuntary, because it is the APPLICATION of miracles which must be Christ-controlled. But the other two, which are the voluntary aspects of miracle-mindedness, ARE up to you. **T(41) -41**

T 1 B 40s. To channelize DOES have a "narrowing down" connotation, though NOT in the sense of lack. The underlying state of mind, or Grace is a total commitment. Only the DOING aspect involves the channel at all. This is because doing is always specific.

T 1 B 40t. As Jack said, "A reliable instrument must measure something," but a channel is also valid. It must learn to do ONLY what it is supposed to do. Change the prayer to read:
   If you will tell me what to do,
   ONLY THAT I will to do.

T 1 B 40u. <u>NOTE</u> HS objects to doggerel sound of this, and regards it as very inferior poetry. <u>ANSWER</u>: Its hard to forget, though.

T 1 B 40v. The Revelation is literally unspeakable, because it is an experience of unspeakable love. The word "Awe" should be reserved only for revelations, to which it is perfectly and correctly applicable. It is NOT appropriately applied to miracles, because a state of true awe is worshipful. It implies that one of a lesser order stands before the Greater One. This is the case only when a Soul stands before his Creator. Souls are perfect creations, and should be struck with awe in the presence of the Creator of Perfection.

T 1 B 40w. The miracle, on the other hand, is a sign of love among equals. Equals cannot be in awe of each other, because awe ALWAYS implies inequality. Awe is not properly experienced even to me. That is why in that short introductory vision, I knelt beside you, FACING the light.

T 1 B 40x. An Elder Brother is entitled to respect for his greater experience, and a reasonable amount of obedience for his greater wisdom. He is also entitled to love, because he is a brother, and also to devotion, if he is devoted. It is only my own devotion that entitles me to yours. But you will notice that I have knelt at your altar as readily as I would ever have you kneel at mine. **T(42) -42**

T 1 B 40y. There is nothing about me that you cannot attain.[78] I have nothing that does not come from God. The main difference between us as yet is that I have NOTHING ELSE. This leaves me in a state of true holiness, which is only a POTENTIAL in you.

T 1 B 40z. "No man cometh to the Father but by me"[79] is among the most misunderstood statements in the Bible. It DOES NOT mean that I am in any way separate (or different) from you, EXCEPT IN TIME. Now, we know that time does not exist. Actually, the statement is much more meaningful if it is considered on a vertical rather than a horizontal axis. Regarded along the vertical, man stands below me, and I stand below God. In the process of "rising up", I AM higher. This is because without me the distance between God and man is too great for man to encompass. I bridge the distance as an Elder Brother[80] to man, on the one hand, and a Son of God on the other. My devotion to my brothers has placed me in charge of the Sonship, which I can render complete only to the extent I can SHARE it.

T 1 B 40aa. This appears to contradict another statement: "I and my Father are one."[81] It doesn't. There are still separate parts in the statement, in recognition of the fact that the Father is GREATER. Actually, the original statement was "are of one KIND."

T 1 B 40ab. The Holy Spirit is the Bringer of Revelations, not miracles. Revelations are INDIRECTLY inspired by me, because I am close to the Holy Spirit, and alert to revelation-readiness in my brothers. **T(43) -43** I can thus BRING DOWN to them more than they can DRAW down to themselves. Jean Dixon's description is perhaps a better statement of my position. Because my feet are on the ground and my hands are in heaven, I can bring down the glories of Heaven to my brothers on earth.

T 1 B 40ac. The Holy Spirit is the Highest Communication Medium. Miracles do not involve this type of communication, because they are TEMPORARY communicative devices. When man can return to his original form of communication with God by direct REVELATION, the need for miracles is over. The Holy Spirit mediates higher to lower order communication, keeping the direct channel from God to man open for revelation. Revelation is NOT reciprocal. It is always FROM God TO man. This is because God and man are NOT equal. The miracle is reciprocal because it ALWAYS involves equality.

T 1 B 40ad. In the longitudinal (or horizontal) plane, the true equality of all men in the Sonship appears to involve almost endless time. But we know that time is only an artifact introduced as a learning aid.

T 1 B 41. The miracle is a learning device which lessens the need for time. The sudden shift[82] from horizontal to vertical perception which the miracle entails introduces an interval from which the doer and the receiver both emerge much farther along in time than they would otherwise have been.

---

[78] **John 14:12** "Verily, verily, I say unto you, he that believeth on me, the works that I do shall he do also; and greater *works* than these shall he do; because I go unto the Father."
[79] **John 14:6** Jesus saith unto him, "I am the way, and the truth, and the life: no one cometh unto the Father, but by me."
[80] **Romans 8:29** For whom He foreknew, He also predestined to be conformed to the image of His Son, that He might be the firstborn among many brethren.
[81] **John 10:30** "I and the Father are one."
[82] The manuscript has the plural "shifts" whereas the *Notes* has the singular "shift." The verb in the sentence, "introduces" is singular in both so we conclude the pluralization was a typing mistake. It must be either "shifts introduce" or "shift introduces."

Chapter 1 – Introduction to Miracles

T 1 B 41b. A miracle has thus the unique property of abolishing time by rendering the space of time it occupies unnecessary. There is NO relation between the time a miracle TAKES and the time it COVERS. It substitutes FOR learning that might have taken thousands of years. It does this by the underlying recognition of perfect equality and holiness between doer and receiver on which the miracle rests. **T(44) -44** It is unstable, but perfectly consistent, i.e., it does not occur predictably across time, and it rarely occurs in comparable forms. But within ITSELF it is perfectly consistent. Since it contains NOTHING BUT an acknowledgment of equality and worth, all parts ARE equal. This establishes the prerequisite for validity.

T 1 B 41c. We said before that the miracle abolishes time. It does this by a process of COLLAPSING it. It thus abolishes certain INTERVALS within it. It does this, however, WITHIN the larger temporal sequence.

T 1 B 41d. The validity of the miracle, then, is PREDICTIVE, not logical, within the temporal schema. It establishes an out-of-pattern time interval, which is NOT under the usual laws of time. Only in this sense is it timeless. By collapsing time, it literally saves time, much the way "daylight saving time" does. It rearranges the distribution of light.

T 1 B 41e. The miracle is the only device which man has at his immediate disposal for controlling time. Only the Revelation TRANSCENDS it, having nothing to do with time at all. The miracle is much like the body, in that both are learning aids which aim at facilitating a state in which they are unnecessary. When the Soul is finally in the original state of direct communication, neither the body nor the miracle serves any purpose.

T 1 B 41f. While he is IN the body, however, man can choose between loveless and miraculous channels of creativity. He can create an empty shell (see previous reference), but he DOES NOT create nothing at all. He can wait, delay, paralyze himself, reduce his creativity almost to nothing, and even introduce a real developmental arrest or regression. But he CANNOT abolish his creativity. He CAN destroy his medium of communication, but NOT his potential. **T(45) -45**

T 1 B 41g. He was NOT created by his own free will. Only what HE creates is his to decide. The basic decision of the miracle-minded is NOT to wait on time any longer than is necessary. Time can waste, as well as be wasted. The miracle-worker, therefore, accepts the time-control factor of the miracle gladly, because he knows that every collapse of time brings all men closer to the ultimate RELEASE from time, in which the Son and the Father ARE one.

T 1 B 41h. The real meaning "are of one kind" is "of one mind or will." When the will of the Sonship and the Father are one, their perfect accord IS Heaven. **T(46) -46**

T 1 B 41i. ASIDE Tell B. he is right in providing you with the consistent strength you need to get, and he needs to offer. Your instability and his weakness have resulted from bad karmic choices, and your relationship NOW is crucial for the future. You must both exert every effort to restore it to what it once was. Both of you are correcting where you have failed before. This has already enabled you to fulfill a very unexpected role in your own joint salvation, and the salvation of many other children I will entrust increasingly to you. These are by no means chosen at random. B. should know that his preparation is not only in terms of sharing in the results of your better application of some rather unusual talents. His own role, which he will understand after his preparation is complete, will be equally surprising. He will need your help then, as you need his strength now.

T 1 B 41j. Note that you DO NOT need his help as a scribe, because you developed this ability by your own efforts, and finally placed them at MY disposal. By lending you his strength, he strengthens himself. When he gains this through his own efforts, he will need your help in a very unexpected way. But this is just another example of the reciprocal nature of miracles.

T 1 B 41k. Equality does not imply homogeneity NOW. When EVERYONE has EVERYTHING, individual contributions to the Sonship will no longer be necessary. When the Atonement has been completed, ALL talents will be shared by ALL of the Sons of God. God is NOT partial. All of His children have His total love, and all of his gifts are given freely to everyone alike.

T 1 B 41l. "Except you become as little children"[83] means unless you fully recognize your complete dependence on God, you cannot know the real power of the Son in his true relationship with the Father. **T(47) -47**

T 1 B 41m. You and B. DO have special talents which are needed for the Celestial speedup at this time. But note that the term speed-up is not one which relates to the TRANSCENDING of time.

T 1 B 41n. When time is abolished, and all of the Sons of God have come home, no special agents will be necessary. But do not underestimate the power of special agents now, or the great need there is for them. I do not claim to be more than that myself. No one in his Right Mind, (a term which should be specially noted) ever wants either more or less than that. Those who are called on to witness for me NOW are witnessing for all men, as I am.

T 1 B 41o. The role of the Priestess was once to experience Revelations and to work miracles. The purpose was to bring those not yet available for direct Revelations into proper focus for them. Heightened perception was always the essential Priestess attribute.

T 1 B 41p. (This is the first time that HS ever said that she would be honored if there were any notes.)

T 1 B 41q. (Neither B. nor I is really clear about how sexual-impulses can be directly translated into miracle-impulses.) The fantasies that I mentioned yesterday (refers to discussion HS & B. had) provide an excellent example of how you switch. (Now switch the pronoun references, or it will be too confusing.)

T 1 B 41r. Fantasies are distorted forms of thinking, because they always involve twisting perception into unreality. Fantasy is a debased form of vision. Visions and Revelations are closely related. Fantasies & projection are more closely associated, because both attempt to control external reality according to false internal needs. "Live and let live" happens to be a very meaningful injunction. Twist reality in any way, and you are perceiving destructively. Reality was lost through usurpation, which in turn produced tyranny. I told you you were now restored to your former role in the Plan of Atonement. But you must still choose freely to devote your heritage to the greater Restoration. As long as a single slave remains to walk the earth, your release is not complete. Complete restoration of the Sonship is the only true goal of the miracle-minded. **T(48) -48**

T 1 B 41s. Sexual fantasies are distortions of perception by definition. They are a means of making false associations, and obtaining pleasure from them. Man can do this only because he IS creative. But although he can perceive false associations, he can never make them real except to himself. As was said before, man believes in what he creates. If he creates a miracle, he will be equally strong in his belief in that. The strength of his conviction will then sustain the belief of the miracle receiver.

T 1 B 41t. NO fantasies, sexual or otherwise, are true. Fantasies become totally unnecessary as the Wholly satisfying nature of reality becomes apparent. The sex impulse IS a miracle impulse when it is in proper focus. One individual sees in another the right partner for "procreating the stock" (Wolff was not too far off here), and also

---

[83] **Matthew 18:3** And said, "Assuredly, I say to you, unless you are converted and become as little children, you will by no means enter the kingdom of heaven."

for their joint establishment of a creative home. This does not involve fantasy at all. If I am asked to participate in the decision, the decision will be a Right one, too.

T 1 B 41u. In a situation where you or another person, or both, experience inappropriate sex impulses, KNOW FIRST that this is an expression of fear. Your love toward each other is NOT perfect, and this is why the fear arose. Turn immediately to me by denying the power of the fear, and ask me to help you to replace it with love.[84] This shifts the sexual impulse immediately to the miracle-impulse, and places it at MY disposal.

T 1 B 41v. Then acknowledge the true creative worth of both yourself AND the other one. This places strength where it belongs. Note that sexual fantasies are ALWAYS destructive (or depleting), in that they perceive another in an inappropriate creative role. Both people are perceived essentially as "objects" fulfilling THEIR OWN pleasure drives. This dehumanized view is the source of the DEPLETING use of sex. Freud's description is purely NEGATIVE, i.e., as a release from the UNPLEASANT. He also observed that the tension from id impulses never completely abates. **T(49) -49**

T 1 B 41w. What he should have said is that the shift from miracle-impulses to sexual impulses was debilitating in the first place, because of the level-confusion involved. This set up a state in which real release was impossible. Note also that Freud's notion of sex was as a device for inducing RELAXATION, which he confused with PEACE.

T 1 B 41x. Inappropriate sex relaxes only in the sense that it may induce physical sleep. The miracle, on the other hand, is an ENERGIZER. It always strengthens, and never depletes. It DOES induce peace, and by establishing tranquility (not relaxation) it enables both giver and receiver to enter into a state of Grace. Here his miracle-mindedness, (not release from tension) is restored.

T 1 B 41y. Tension is the result of a building-up of unexpressed miracle-impulses. This can be truly abated only by releasing the miracle-drive, which has been blocked. Converting it to sexual libido merely produces further blocking. Never foster this illusion in yourself, or encourage it in others. An "object" is incapable of release, because it is a concept which is deprived of creative power. The recognition of the real creative power in yourself AND others brings release because it brings peace.

T 1 B 41z. The peace of God which passeth understanding CAN keep your hearts now and forever.[85]

T 1 B 41aa. There are only two short additions needed here:

1. Your earlier acute problem in writing things down came from a MUCH earlier misuse of very great scribal abilities. These were turned to secret rather than shared advantage, depriving it (?) of its miraculous potential, and diverting it into possession. This is much like the confusion of sex impulses with possession-impulses. Some of the original material is still in the Temple. This is why you became so afraid about Atlantis. B. has his own reasons. **T(50) -50**

T 1 B 41ab. 2. Retain your miracle-minded attitude toward Rosie VERY carefully. She once hurt both of you, which is why she is now your servant. But she is blessed in that she sees service as a source of joy. Help her straighten out her past errors by contributing to your welfare now.

T 1 B 41ac. (special Revelation re HS –OMISSION 1.[86])

T 1 B 41ad. HS question re: past memories. <u>ANSWER</u>: As long as you remember ALWAYS that you never suffered anything because of anything that anyone ELSE did, this is not dangerous.

T 1 B 41ae. Remember that you who want peace can find it only by complete forgiveness. You never really WANTED peace before, so there was no point in knowing how to get it. This is an example of the "need to know" principle, which was established by the Plan of Atonement long before CIA.

T 1 B 41af. No kind of knowledge is acquired by anyone unless he wants it, or believes in some way he NEEDS it. A psychologist does NOT need a lesson on the hierarchy of needs as such, but like everyone else, he DOES need to understand his own.

T 1 B 41ag. This particular set of notes will be the only one which deals with the concept of "lack", because while the concept does not exist in the Creation of God, it is VERY apparent in the creations of man. It is, in fact, the essential difference.

T 1 B 41ah. A need implies lack, by definition. It involves the recognition, conscious or unconscious, (and at times, fortunately, superconscious) that you would be better off in a state which is somehow different from the one you are in.

T 1 B 41ai. Until the Separation, which is a better term than the Fall,[87] nothing was lacking. This meant that man had no needs at all. If he had not deprived himself, he would never have experienced them. **T(51) -51**

T 1 B 41aj. After the Separation, needs became the most powerful source of motivation for human action. All behavior is essentially motivated by needs, but behavior itself is not a Divine attribute. The body is the mechanism for behavior. (Ask any behaviorist, and he's RIGHT, too.)

T 1 B 41ak. You tell your own classes that nobody would bother even to get up and go from one place to another if he did not think he would somehow be better off. This is very true.

T 1 B 41al. Believing that he COULD be "better off" is the reason why man has the mechanism for behavior at his disposal. This is why the Bible says "By their DEEDS ye shall know them."[88]

T 1 B 41am. A man acts according to the particular hierarchy of needs he establishes for himself. His hierarchy, in turn, depends on his perception of what he IS, i.e., what he LACKS. This establishes his own rules for what he needs to know.

---

[84] In the *Notes* this appears to be "will love" rather than "with love." In the *Urtext* manuscript it appears as "will (with) love." It seems fairly clear that the *Notes* represents a scribal error and the correct word is "with."

[85] **Philippians 4:7** And the peace of God, which passeth all understanding, shall guard your hearts and your thoughts in Christ Jesus.

[86] From the *Notes* 5:46-47 the following was omitted:
"Priestess, a brother has knelt at your shrine. Heal Him through Me."
I have an idea that the shrine merely represented the "altar within," which the Priestess served. I imagine that the communication form was direct, and the "brother" always nameless. I – the Priestess responded automatically by praying directly to God, standing with upraised arms to draw down a blessing on her brother, who knelt outside. Her response was completely automatic and impersonal. She never even thought of checking the outcome, because there WAS no doubt.
I imagine there is STILL no doubt really. Except that the Priestess can no longer ask alone.
[*Notes* 5:47]
It was originally "sister" not "Priestess."

[87] **Genesis 3:1-7** Now the serpent was more cunning than any beast of the field which the LORD God had made. And he said to the woman, "Has God indeed said, "You shall not eat of every tree of the garden'?" And the woman said to the serpent, "We may eat the fruit of the trees of the garden; but of the fruit of the tree which is in the midst of the garden, God has said, "You shall not eat it, nor shall you touch it, lest you die." Then the serpent said to the woman, "You will not surely die. For God knows that in the day you eat of it your eyes will be opened, and you will be like God, knowing good and evil." So when the woman saw that the tree was good for food, that it was pleasant to the eyes, and a tree desirable to make one wise, she took of its fruit and ate. She also gave to her husband with her, and he ate. Then the eyes of both of them were opened, and they knew that they were naked; and they sewed fig leaves together and made themselves coverings.

[88] **Matthew 7:16-20** "By their fruits ye shall know them. Do *men* gather grapes of thorns, or figs of thistles? Even so every good tree bringeth forth good fruit; but the corrupt tree bringeth forth evil fruit. A good tree cannot bring forth evil fruit, neither can a corrupt tree bring forth good fruit. Every tree that bringeth not forth good fruit is hewn down, and cast into the fire. Therefore by their fruits ye shall know them."

Chapter 1 – Introduction to Miracles

T 1 B 41an. Separation from God is the only lack he really needs to correct. But his Separation would never have occurred if he had not distorted his perception of truth, and thus perceived himself as lacking.

T 1 B 41ao. The concept of ANY sort of need HIERARCHY arose because, having made this fundamental error, he had already fragmented himself into levels with DIFFERENT needs. As he integrates, HE becomes one, and his ONE need becomes one accordingly. Only the fragmented can be confused about this.

T 1 B 41ap. Internal integration within the self will not (suffice to?) correct the lack fallacy, but it WILL correct the NEED fallacy. (Thank you for writing this as given.) Unified need produces unified action, because it produces lack of ambivalence.

T 1 B 41aq. The concept of need hierarchy, a corollary to the original error, requires correction at its OWN level, before the error of levels itself can be corrected. Man cannot operate (or behave) effectively while he operates at split levels. But as long as he does so, he must introduce correction from the bottom UP. **T(52) -52**

T 1 B 41ar. This is because he now operates in space, where "up" and "down" are meaningful terms. Ultimately, of course, space is as meaningless as time. The concept is really one of space-time BELIEF. The physical world exists only because man can use it to correct his UNBELIEF, which placed him in it originally. As long as man KNEW he did not need anything, the whole device was unnecessary.

T 1 B 41as. The need to know is not safely under man's control at this time. It is MUCH better off under mine. Let's just leave it at that.

T 1 B 41at. (Specific question raised by WT re sex under existing conditions) (HS raised previous question about the past, which has just been answered.)

T 1 B 41au. The other question, however, I am more than willing to answer, because it is appropriate for NOW. You and B. both chose your present sex partners shamefully, and would have to atone for the lack of love which was involved in any case.

T 1 B 41av. You selected them precisely BECAUSE they were NOT suited to gratify your fantasies. This was not because you wanted to abandon or give up the fantasies, but because you were AFRAID of them. You saw in your partners a means of protecting against the fear, but both of you continued to "look around" for chances to indulge the fantasies.

T 1 B 41aw. The dream of the "perfect partner" is an attempt to find EXTERNAL integration, while retaining conflicting needs in the self.

T 1 B 41ax. B. was somewhat less guilty of this than you, but largely because he was more afraid. He had abandoned the hope (of finding a perfect partner) in a neurotic sense of despair of finding it. You, on the other hand, insisted that the hope was justified. Neither of you, therefore, was in your Right Mind.

T 1 B 41ay. As was said before, homosexuality is <u>INHERENTLY</u> more risky (or error prone) than heterosexuality, but both can be undertaken on an equally false basis. The falseness of the basis is clear in the accompanying fantasies. Homosexuality ALWAYS involves misperception of the self OR the partner, and generally both. **T(53) -53**

T 1 B 41az. Penetration DOES NOT involve magic, nor DOES ANY form of sexual behavior. It IS a magic belief to engage in ANY form of body image activity at all. You neither created yourselves, nor controlled your creation. By introducing levels into your own perception, you opened the way for body-image distortions.

T 1 B 41ba. The lack of love (or faulty need-orientation) which led to your particular person (not OBJECT) choices CAN BE corrected within the existent framework, and would HAVE to be in the larger interest of overall progress. The situation is questionable largely because of its inherent vulnerability to fantasy-gratification. Doing the best you can WITHIN this limitation is probably the best corrective measure at present. Any relationship you have undertaken for whatever reasons becomes a responsibility.

T 1 B 41bb. If you shift your own needs, some amount of corresponding shift in the need-orientation of the other person MUST result, This will be beneficial, even if the partner was originally attracted to you BECAUSE of your disrespect. Teaching devices which are totally alien to a learner's perceptual system are usually merely disruptive. Transfer depends on SOME common elements in the new situation which are understandable in terms of the old.

T 1 B 41bc. Man can never control the effects of fear himself, because he has CREATED fear and believes in what he creates. In attitude, then, though not in content, he resembles his own Creator, who has perfect faith in His Creations because he Created them. All creation rests on belief, and the belief in the creation produces its existence. This is why it is possible for a man to believe what is not true for anyone else. It is true for him because it is made BY him.

T 1 B 41bd. Every aspect of fear proceeds from upside down perception. The TRULY creative devote their efforts to correcting this. The neurotic devotes his to compromise. The psychotic tries to escape by establishing the truth of his own errors. It is most difficult to free him by ordinary means, only because he is more stable in his denial of truth. **T(54) -54**

T 1 B 42a. The miracle makes no distinction among degrees of misperception. It is a device for perception-correction which is effective quite apart from either the degree or the direction of the error. This is its TRUE indiscriminateness.

T 1 B 42b. Christ-controlled miracles are selective only in that they are directed toward those who can use them for THEMSELVES. Since this makes it inevitable that they will extend them to others, a very strong chain of Atonement is welded. But Christ-control takes no account at all of the MAGNITUDE of the miracle itself, because the concept of size exists only in a plane that is itself unreal. Since the miracle aims at RESTORING reality, it would hardly be useful if it were bound by the laws of the same error it aims to correct. Only man makes that kind of error. It is an example of the "foolish consistency" his own false beliefs have engendered.

T 1 B 42c. Both the power and the strength of man's creative will must be understood, before the real meaning of denial can be appreciated and abolished. Denial is NOT mere negation. It is a positive miscreation. While the miscreation is NECESSARILY believed in by its own creator, it does not exist at all at the level of true Creation.

T 1 B 43. The miracle compares the creations of man with the higher level of creation, accepting what is in ACCORD as true, and rejecting the DISCORDANT as false. This is why it is so closely associated with validity. Real validity is both true AND useful, or better, it is useful BECAUSE it is true.

T 1 B 43b. All aspects of fear are untrue, because they DO NOT exist at the higher creative levels, and therefore do not exist at all. To whatever extent a man is willing to submit his beliefs to the real test of validity, to that extent are his perceptions healed (or corrected.) **T(55) -55**

T 1 B 43c. In sorting out the false from the true, the miracle proceeds much along the lines suggested very correctly by B., i.e.:

> *If perfect love casts out fear,*[89]
> *And if fear exists,*
> *Then there is NOT perfect love.*

But

---

[89] 1 John 4:18 There is no fear in love; but perfect love casts out fear, because fear involves torment. But he who fears has not been made perfect in love.

Only perfect love really exists.

T 1 B 43d. Therefore, if there is fear, it creates a state which does not exist. Believe THIS and you WILL be free. Only God can establish this solution, for THIS faith IS His gift.[90]

T 1 C. Distortions of Miracle Impulses (*Notes* 211 5:60)

T 1 C 1. Man must contribute to his readiness here as elsewhere. The readiness for faith, as for everything else that is true, entails the two steps necessary for the release from fear.

T 1 C 2. Denial of fear, in human terms, is a strong defense because it entails two levels of error:
1. That truth CAN be denied and
2. That absence of truth can be effective.

T 1 C 3. EXPERIENCING fear, which is more characteristic of B., involves only the second error. However, these differences do not affect the power of the miracle at all, since only truth and error are its concern.

T 1 C 4. YOU are both more miracle-minded, and less able to recognize fear because of your stronger, but split, identification. B., also characteristically, is less miracle-minded, but better able to recognize fear, because his identification is more consistently right but weaker.

T 1 C 5. Together, the conditions needed for consistent miracle-mindedness, the state in which fear has been abolished, can be particularly well worked out. In fact, it WAS already well worked out before. **T(56) -56**

T 1 C 6. Your idea about the real meaning of "possession" should be clarified. Your own denial of fear (this refers to a visionary experience of HS) introduced some error variance, but not really a significant amount. However, there is always a chance that as the size of the sample increases, what was non-significant before may ATTAIN significance, so we had better get this out of the way now while you are still within the safety margin.

T 1 C 7. Fear of possession is a perverted expression of the fear of the irresistible attraction. (Aside. Yes, this DOES apply to homosexuality, among other errors, where the whole concept of possessing, or "entering" is a key fear. It is a symbolic statement of an inverted decision NOT to enter into, or possess, the Kingdom. In physical terms, which it emphasizes because of the inherent error of Soul avoidance, REAL physical creation is avoided, and fantasy gratification is substituted.)

T 1 C 8. The truth is still that the attraction of God is irresistible at ALL levels, and the acceptance of this totally unavoidable truth is only a matter of time. But you should consider whether you WANT to wait, because you CAN return now, if you choose. (Note to HS: You are writing this with improper motivation, but we will try anyway. If you are to stop, do so immediately.)

T 1 C 9. Possession is a concept which has been subject to numerous distortions, some of which we will list below: **T(57) -57**

1. It (possession) can be associated with the body only. If this occurs, sex is particularly likely to be contaminated. Possession versus being possessed is apt to be seen as the male and female role. Since neither will be conceived of as satisfying alone, and both will be associated with fear, this interpretation is particularly vulnerable to psychosexual confusion.

2. From a rather similar misperceptual reference point, possession can also be associated with things. This is essentially a shift from 1), and is usually due to an underlying fear of associating possession with people. In this sense, it is an attempt to PROTECT people, like the superstition about "protecting the name", we mentioned before.

T 1 C 10. Both **1)** and **2)** are likely to become compulsive for several reasons, including:

a. They represent an attempt to escape from the real possession-drive, which cannot be satisfied this way.

b. They set up substitute goals, which are usually reasonably easy to attain.

c. They APPEAR to be relatively harmless, and thus SEEM to allay fear. The fact that they usually interfere with good interpersonal relationships can be interpreted, in this culture, as a lack of sophistication on the part of the OTHER (not the self), and this induces a false feeling of confidence in the solution, based on reliability NOT validity. It is also fairly easy to find a partner who SHARES the illusion. Thus, we have any number of relationships which are actually ESTABLISHED on the basis **T(58) -58** of **1)**, and others which HOLD TOGETHER primarily because of the joint interests in **2)**.

d. The manifestly <u>EXTERNAL</u> emphasis which both entail seems to be a safety device, and thus permits a false escape from much more basic inhibitions. As a compromise solution, the <u>ILLUSION</u> of interpersonal relating is preserved, along with the retention of the lack of love component. This kind of psychic juggling leaves the person (or juggler?) with a feeling of emptiness, which in fact is perfectly justified, because he IS acting from scarcity. He then becomes more and more driven in his behavior, to fill the emptiness.

T 1 C 11. When these solutions have been invested with extreme belief, **1)** leads to sex crimes, and **2)** to stealing. The kleptomaniac is a good example of the latter.

T 1 C 12. Generally, two types of emotional disturbances result:

a. The tendency to maintain the illusion that only the physical is real. This produces depression.

b. The tendency to invest the physical with non-physical properties. This is essentially magic, and tends more toward anxiety-proneness.

c. The tendency to vacillate from one to the other, which produces a corresponding vacillation between depression AND anxiety.

T 1 C 13. Both result in self imposed starvation.[91]

T 1 C 14. 3. Another type of distortion is seen in the fear of or desire for "spirit" possession. The term "spirit" is profoundly debased in this context, but it DOES entail a recognition that **T(59) -59** the body is not enough, and investing it with magic will not work. This recognition ACCEPTS the fact that neither 1) nor 2) is sufficient, but, precisely BECAUSE it does not limit fear so narrowly, it is more likely to produce greater fear in its own right.

T 1 C 15. Endowing the Spirit with human possessiveness is a more INCLUSIVE error than **1)** or **2)**, and a step somewhat further away from the "Right Mind." Projection is also more likely to occur, with vacillations between grandiosity and fear. "Religion" in a distorted sense, is also more likely to occur in this kind of error, because the idea of a "spirit" is introduced, though fallaciously, while it is excluded from 1) and 2)).

T 1 C 16. Witchcraft is thus particularly apt to be associated with 3), because of the much greater investment in magic.

T 1 C 17. It should be noted that 1) involves only the body, and 2) involves an attempt to associate things with human attributes. Three, on the other hand, is a more serious level confusion, because it endows the Spirit with EVIL attributes. This accounts both for the religious zeal of its proponents, and the aversion (or fear) of its opponents. Both attitudes stem from the same false belief.

---

[90] **Ephesians 2:8** For by grace you have been saved through faith, and that not of yourselves; it is the gift of God,

[91] It is odd that it says "two things happen" and then lists three and then describes all three as "both." But that is the form in the *Notes*. This material is not preserved in any other version available to us. However, there are actually two, A) and B) with C) being a mix of the two which could be considered a third.

Chapter 1 – Introduction to Miracles

T 1 C 18. This in NOT what the Bible means by "possessed of the Holy Spirit." It is interesting to note that even those who DID understand that could nevertheless EXPRESS their understanding inappropriately. The concept of "speaking **T(60) -60** in many tongues" was originally an injunction to communicate to everyone in his own language, or his own level. It hardly meant to speak in a way that NOBODY can understand. This strange error occurs when people DO understand the need for Universal communication, but have contaminated it with possession fallacies. The fear engendered by this misperception leads to a conflicted state in which communication IS attempted, but the fear is allayed by making the communication incomprehensible.

T 1 C 19. It could also be said that the fear induced selfishness, or regression, because incomprehensible communication is hardly a worthy offering from one Son of God to another.

T 1 C 20. 4. Knowledge can also be misinterpreted as a means of possession. Here, the content is not physical, and the underlying fallacy is more likely to be the confusion of mind and brain. The attempt to unite non-physical content with physical attributes is illustrated by statements like "the thirst for knowledge." (No Helen, this is NOT what the "thirst" in the Bible means. The term was used only because of man's limited comprehension, and is probably better dropped.)

T 1 C 21. The fallacious use of knowledge can result in several errors, including:

a. The idea that knowledge will make the individual more attractive to others. This is a possession-fallacy.

b. The idea that knowledge will make the individual invulnerable. This is the reaction formation against the underlying fear of vulnerability. **T(61) -61**

c. The idea that knowledge will make the individual worthy. This is largely pathetic.

T 1 C 22. Both you and B. should consider type 4) <u>VERY</u> carefully. Like all these fallacies, it contains a denial mechanism, which swings into operation as the fear increases, thus canceling out the error temporarily, but seriously impairing efficiency.

T 1 C 23. Thus, you claim you can't read, and B. claims that he can't speak. Note that depression is a real risk here, for a Child of God should never REDUCE his efficiency in ANY way. The depression comes from a peculiar pseudo-solution which reads:

A Child of God is efficient.
I am not efficient.
Therefore, I am not a Child of God.

T 1 C 24. This leads to neurotic resignation, and this is a state which merely INCREASES the depression.

T 1 C 25. The[92] corresponding denial mechanism for 1) is the sense of PHYSICAL inability, or IMPOTENCE. The denial mechanism for 2) is often bankruptcy. Collectors of things often drive themselves well beyond their financial means, in an attempt to force discontinuance. If this idea of cessation cannot be tolerated, a strange compromise involving BOTH insatiable possessiveness and insatiable throwing-away (bankruptcy) may result. An example is the inveterate or compulsive gambler, particularly the horse-racing addict. Here, the conflicted drive is displaced both from people AND things, and is invested in animals. The implied DEROGATION of people is the cause of the underlying EXTREME superstition of the horse racing addict. Here, the conflicted drive is displaced both from people AND things, and is invested in animals. **T(62) -62**

---

[92] {(Ed. Note) The following paragraph shows up and is crossed out, and is repeated on *Urtext* page 69 (T 2 A 16-19) with the last sentence missing. One might argue that it should only have been included once however we decided to include it in both locations. This material has not been located in the *Notes*.}

Chapter 2 – The Illusion of Separation

T 2 A. Introduction (*Notes* not present in Notes)

(Insert for page 61)

T 2 A 1. This section is inserted here because it deals with a more fundamental misuse of knowledge, referred to in the Bible as the cause of the Fall (or Separation). There are several introductory remarks which are intended to make these explanations less fear-provoking. The first is a couplet which I drew to your attention during the fragments of Midsummer Night's Dream, which you heard last night:

> "Be as thou wast wont to be
> See as thou wast wont to see."

It is noteworthy that these words were said by Oberon in releasing Titania from her own errors, both of being and perceiving. These were the words which re-established her true identity as well as her true abilities and judgment. The similarity here is obvious.

T 2 A 2. There are also some definitions, which I asked you to take from the dictionary, which will also be helpful. Their somewhat unusual nature is due to the fact that they are not first definitions in their chronological appearance. Nevertheless, the fact that each of them does appear in the dictionary should be reassuring.

> Project (verb): to extend forward or out.
>
> Project (noun): a plan in the mind
>
> World: a natural grand division. (Note that you originally wrote "word" instead of "world.")

T 2 A 3. We will refer later to projection as related to both mental illness and mental health. It will also be commented on that Lucifer literally projected himself from heaven. We also have observed that man can create an empty shell, but cannot create nothing at all. **T(63) 63** This emptiness provides the screen for the misuse of projection.

T 2 A 4. The Garden of Eden, which is described as a literal garden in the Bible, was not originally an actual garden at all. It was merely a mental state of complete need-lack. Even in the literal account, it is noteworthy that the pre-Separation state was essentially one in which man needed nothing. The Tree of Knowledge, again an overly-literal concept, (as is clearly shown by the subsequent reference to "eating of the fruit of the tree") is a symbolic reference to some of the misuses of knowledge referred to in the section immediately preceding this one. There is, however, considerable clarification of this concept, which must be understood before the real meaning of the "detour into fear" can be fully comprehended. Projection, as defined above, (this refers to the verb) is a fundamental attribute of God, which he also gave to his Son. In the Creation, God projected his Creative Ability out of Himself toward the Souls which He created, and also imbued them with the same loving wish (or will) to create. We have commented before on the FUNDAMENTAL error involved in confusing what has been created with what is being created. We have also emphasized that man, insofar as the term relates to Soul, has not only been fully Created, but also been created perfect. There is no emptiness in him. The next point, too, has already been made, but bears repetition here. The Soul, because of its own likeness to its Creator, is creative.[93] No Child of God is capable of losing this ability, because it is inherent in what he IS.

T 2 A 5. Whenever projection in its inappropriate sense is utilized, it ALWAYS implies that some emptiness (or lack of everything) must exist, and that it is within man's ability to put his own ideas there INSTEAD of the truth. If you will consider carefully what this entails, the following will become quite apparent: **T(64) -64**

First, the assumption is implicit that what God has Created can be changed by the mind of Man.

Second, the concept that what is perfect can be rendered imperfect (or wanting) is intruded.

Third, the belief that man can distort the Creations of God (including himself) has arisen, and is tolerated.

Fourth, that since man can create himself, the direction of his own creation is up to him.

T 2 A 6. These related distortions represent a picture of what actually occurred in the Separation. None of this existed before, nor does it actually exist now. The world, as defined above, WAS made as a natural grand division, or projecting outward of God. That is why everything which He Created is like Him.

T 2 A 7. It should be noted that the opposite of pro is con. Strictly speaking, then, the opposite of projecting is conjecting, a term which referred to a state of uncertainty or guess work. Other errors arise in connection with ancillary defenses, to be considered later. For example, dejection, which is obviously associated with depression, injection, which can be misinterpreted readily enough, in terms of possession fallacies (particularly penetration), and rejection, which is clearly associated with denial. It should be noted also that rejection can be used as refusing, a term which necessarily involves a perception of what is refused as something unworthy.

T 2 A 8. Projection as undertaken by God was very similar to the kind of inner radiance which the Children of the Father inherit from Him. It is important to note that the term "project outward" necessarily implies that the real source of projection is internal. **T(65) -65** This is as true of the Son as of the Father.

T 2 A 9. The world, in its original connotation, included both the proper creation of man by God, AND the proper creation by man in his Right Mind. The latter required the endowment of man by God with free will, because all loving creation is freely given. Nothing in either of these statements implies any sort of level involvement, or, in fact, anything except one continuous line of creation, in which all aspects are of the same order.

T 2 A 10. When the "lies of the serpent" were introduced, they were specifically called lies because they are not true. When man listened, all he heard was untruth. He does not have to continue to believe what is not true, unless he chooses to do so. All of his miscreations can disappear in the well known "twinkling of an eye",[94] because it is a visual misperception.

T 2 A 11. Man's spiritual eye can sleep, but as will shortly appear in the notes (reference Bob, elevator operator) a sleeping eye can still see. One translation of the Fall, a view emphasized by Mary Baker Eddy, and worthy of note, is that "a deep sleep fell upon Adam."[95] While the Bible continues to associate this sleep as a kind of anesthetic utilized for protection of Adam during the creation of Eve, Mrs. Eddy was correct in emphasizing that nowhere is there any reference made to his waking up. While Christian Science is clearly incomplete, this point is much in its favor.

---

[93] **Genesis 1:26-27** Then God said, "Let Us make man in Our image, according to Our likeness; let them have dominion over the fish of the sea, over the birds of the air, and over the cattle, over all the earth and over every creeping thing that creeps on the earth." So God created man in His own image; in the image of God He created him; male and female He created them.

[94] **Corinthians 15:52** In a moment, in the twinkling of an eye, at the last trumpet. For the trumpet will sound, and the dead will be raised incorruptible, and we shall be changed. 1

[95] **Genesis 2:21** And the LORD God caused a deep sleep to fall on Adam, and he slept; and He took one of his ribs, and closed up the flesh in its place.

Chapter 2 – The Illusion of Separation

T 2 A 12. The history of man in the world as he saw it has not been characterized by any genuine or comprehensive re-awakening, or re-birth. **T(66) -66** This is impossible as long as man projects in the spirit of miscreation. It still remains within him to project as God projected his own Spirit to him. In reality, this is his ONLY choice, because his free will was made for his own joy in creating the perfect.

T 2 A 13. All fear is ultimately reducible to the basic misperception of man's ability to USURP the power of God. It is again emphasized that he neither CAN nor HAS been able to do this. In this statement lies the real justification for his escape from fear. This is brought about by his acceptance of the Atonement, which places him in a position to realize that his own errors never really occurred. **T(67) -67**

T 2 A 14. When the deep sleep[96] fell upon Adam, he was then in a condition to experience nightmares, precisely because he was sleeping. If a light is suddenly turned on while someone is dreaming, and the content of his dream is fearful, he is initially likely to interpret the light itself as part of the content of his own dream. However, as soon as he awakens, the light is correctly perceived as the release from the dream, which is no longer accorded reality. I would like to conclude this with the Biblical injunction "Go ye and do likewise."[97] It is quite apparent that this depends on the kind of knowledge which was NOT referred to by the "Tree of Knowledge" which bore lies as fruit. The knowledge that illuminates rather than obscures is the knowledge which not only makes you free, but also shows you clearly that you ARE free.[98] **T(68) -68**

Lead in for p. 61 (after insert)

T 2 A 15. The preceding sections were inserted because of the necessity of distinguishing between real and false knowledge. Having made this distinction, it is well to return to the errors already listed a while back. It might be well to recapitulate them here. The first involved the fallacy that only the physical is real. The second involved things rather than people. The third involves the endowment of the physical with non-physical properties. And the fourth clarified the misuse of knowledge. All of them were subsumed under possession fallacies. The denial mechanism for three has already been set forth in some detail, and will also continue after the following:

T(69) -69 (Retyped)

T 2 A 16. The corresponding denial mechanism for 1) is the sense of PHYSICAL inability, or IMPOTENCE. The denial mechanism for 2) is often bankruptcy. Collectors of things often drive themselves well beyond their financial means, in an attempt to force discontinuance. If this idea of cessation cannot be tolerated, a strange compromise involving BOTH insatiable possessiveness and insatiable throwing-away (bankruptcy) may result. An example is the inveterate or compulsive gambler, particularly the horse-racing addict. Here, the conflicted drive is displaced both from people AND things, and is invested in animals. The implied DEROGATION of people is the cause of the underlying EXTREME superstition of the horse racing addict.

T 2 A 17. The alcoholic is in a similar position, except that his hostility is more inward than outward directed.

T 2 A 18. Defenses aimed at protecting (or retaining) error are particularly hard to undo, because they introduce second-order misperceptions which obscure the underlying errors still further. **T(70) -70**

---

[96] **Genesis 2:21** as above.
[97] It is unclear from the text whether a paragraph break is really intended. The previous line stops before the end but there is no indentation on the next line. The *HLC* puts a paragraph break here and we feel it is appropriate. The material has not been found in the *Notes*.
[98] **John 8:32** "And you shall know the truth, and the truth shall make you free."

T 2 A 19. The pseudo-corrective mechanism of three is apt to be more varied because of the more inclusive nature of the error, which has already been mentioned. Some of the possibilities are listed below:

T 2 A 20. One aspect of the possession/possessed conflict can be raised to predominance. If this is attempted in connection with POSSESSING, it leads to the paranoid solution. The underlying component of "being possessed" is retained in the "persecution" fantasies, which are generally concomitants.

T 2 A 21. If "being possessed" is brought to ascendance, a state of some sort of possession by external forces results, but NOT with a major emphasis on attacking others. Attack BY others becomes the more obvious component. In the more virulent forms, there is a sense of being possessed by demons, and unless there is vacillation with a), a catatonic solution is more likely than a paranoid one.

T 2 A 22. The FOCUSED paranoid has become more rigid in his solution, and centers on ONE source of projection to escape from vacillation. (Aside: It should be noted that this type of paranoia is an upside down form of religion, because of its obvious attempt to unify into oneness.)

T 2 A 23. Both 1, 2, and 4 are more likely to produce neurotic[99] rather than psychotic states, though this is by no means guaranteed. However, 3 is inherently more vulnerable to the psychotic correction, again because of the more fundamental level confusion which is involved.

T 2 A 24. It should be noted, however, that the greater fear which is induced by 3 can ITSELF reach psychotic proportions, thus forcing the individual closer and closer to a psychotic solution. **T(71) -71**

T 2 A 25. It is emphasized here that these differences have no effect at all on the miracle, which can heal any of them with equal ease. This is because of the miracle's inherent avoidance of within-error distinctions. Its SOLE concern is to distinguish between truth, on the one hand, and ALL kinds of error, on the other. This is why some miracles SEEM to be of greater magnitude than others. But remember the first point in this course, i.e., that there is no order of difficulty in miracles.

T 2 A 26. The emphasis on mental illness which is marked in these notes reflects the "UNDOING" aspect of the miracle. The "DOING" aspect is, of course, much more important. But a true miracle cannot occur on a false basis. Sometimes the undoing must precede it.

T 2 A 27. At other times, both can occur simultaneously, but you are not up to this at the moment.

T 2 A 28. Further, insights into mental illness can be misused, and lead to preoccupation with one's own symptoms. This is why this area is less constructive for most people than a course primarily devoted to mental health. However, some professions will find (some?) principles of mental illness constructive, especially those which are concerned with mental illness in others. This obviously includes psychologists.

T 2 A 29. The obvious correction for ALL types of the possession-fallacy is to redefine possession correctly. In the sense of "taking over," the concept does not exist at all in divine reality, which is the only level of reality where real existence is a meaningful term. **T(72) -72**

T 2 A 30. No one CAN be "taken over" unless he wills to be. However, if he places his mind under tyranny, rather than authority, he intrudes the submission/dominance concept[100] onto free will himself. This produces the obvious contradiction inherent in any formu-

---

[99] The word "neurotic" is written in by hand, apparently NOT Helen's hand. It is in all caps. Many handwritten corrections are erratic as to capitalization. It's not clear this was intended to be capitalized. In the *Notes* the word is present, and not emphasized.
[100] The word "concept" is not in the *Ur*, but is in the *Notes*. It appears to be an inadvertent omission.

lation that associates free will with imprisonment. Even in very mild forms, this kind of association is risky, and may spread quite unexpectedly, particularly under external stress. This is because it can be internally controlled ONLY if EXTERNAL conditions are peaceful. This is not safe, because external conditions are produced by the thoughts of many, not all of whom are pure in heart as yet.

T 2 A 31. Why should you be at THEIR mercy? This issue is VERY closely related to the whole possession issue. You insist on thinking that people CAN possess you, if you believe that their thoughts (or the external environment) can affect you, regardless of WHAT they think. You are perfectly unaffected by ALL expressions of lack of love. These can be either from yourself and others, or from yourself to others, or from others to you. (I'm glad you passed that test. It was crucial. This is ref. to HS reluctance to take dictations as given.)

T 2 A 32. Peace is an attribute in YOU. You cannot find it outside.[101] All mental illness is some form of EXTERNAL searching. Mental health is INNER peace. It enables you to remain unshaken by lack of love from without, and capable, through your own miracles of correcting the external conditions, which proceed from lack of love in others.

T 2 B. The Re-interpretation of Defenses (*Notes* 230 5:79)

T 2 B 1. When you are afraid of ANYTHING, you are acknowledging its power to hurt you. Remember that where your heart is, there is your treasure[102] also. This means that you believe in what you VALUE. **T(73) -73** If you are AFRAID, you are VALUING WRONG. Human understanding will inevitably value wrong, and by endowing all human thoughts with equal power, will inevitably DESTROY peace. This is why the Bible speaks of "The peace of God which PASSETH (human) understanding."[103]

T 2 B 2. THIS peace is totally incapable of being shaken by human errors of any kind. It denies the ability of anything which is not of God to effect you in any way.

T 2 B 3. This is the PROPER use of denial. It is not used to HIDE anything, but it IS used to correct error. It brings ALL error into the light, and since error and darkness are the same, it abolishes error automatically.

T 2 B 4. True denial is a very powerful protective device. You can and should deny any belief that error can hurt you. This kind of denial is NOT a concealment device, but a correction device. The "Right Mind" of the mentally healthy DEPENDS on it.

T 2 B 5. You can do ANYTHING I ask. I have asked you to perform miracles,[104] and have made it VERY clear that these are NATURAL, CORRECTIVE, HEALING, and UNIVERSAL. There is nothing good they cannot do. But they cannot be performed in the spirit of doubt.[105] Remember my own question, before you ask yours "Oh ye of little faith, wherefore didst[106] thou DOUBT."[107] (Reference to Christ and the apostles walking on water.)

T 2 B 6. You have asked YOURSELVES why you cannot really incorporate my words (the idea of cannibalism in connection with the Sacrament is a reflection of a distorted view of sharing. I told you before that the word "thirst" in connection with the Spirit was used in the Bible because of the limited understanding of those to whom I spoke. I also told you NOT to use it. The same holds for expressions like "feeding on.") **T(74) -74** Symbiosis is misunderstood by the mentally ill, who use it that way. But I also told you that you must recognize your total dependence on God, a statement which you did not like.)

T 2 B 7. God and the Souls He created ARE symbiotically related. They are COMPLETELY dependent on each other. The creation of the Soul itself has already been perfectly accomplished, but the creation BY Souls has not. God created Souls so He could depend on them BECAUSE He created them perfectly. He gave them His peace so they would not be shaken, and would be unable to be deceived. Whenever you are afraid, you ARE deceived. Your mind is NOT serving your Soul. This literally starves the Soul by denying its daily bread.[108] Remember the poem about the Holy Family which crossed your mind last night:

"Where tricks of words are never said
And mercy is as plain as bread."

The reason why that had such a strong impact on you originally was because you knew what it MEANT.

T 2 B 8. God offers ONLY mercy. Your own words should ALWAYS reflect only mercy, because that is what you have received, and that is what you should GIVE. Justice is a temporary expedient, or an attempt to teach man the meaning of mercy. Its JUDGMENTAL side rises only because man is capable of INJUSTICE if that is what his mind creates. You are afraid of God's will because you have used your own will, which He created in the likeness of His own,[109] to <u>MISCREATE</u>.

T 2 B 9. What you do NOT realize is that the mind can miscreate only when it is NOT free. An imprisoned mind is not free by definition. It is possessed, or held back, by ITSELF. Its will is therefore limited, and not free to assert itself. **T(75) -75**

T 2 B 10. The three things that crossed your mind, which was comparatively free at the time, are perfectly relevant:

T 2 B 11. 1. It is alright to remember the past, <u>PROVIDED</u> you also remember that ANYTHING you suffer is because of YOUR OWN ERRORS.

T 2 B 12. 2. In this context, your remark that "after the burning, I swore if I ever saw him again, I would (not) ("Not" was written in later) recognize him. Note, by the way, that you did not put in the "not" until afterwards. That is because your inherent correction-device was working properly at the moment. The result is that you are NOT DENYING ME.

T 2 B 13. 3. The story about Hinda. This was an excellent example of misperception which led to a totally unwarranted fear of a PERSON. (HS story refers to a very young child who fell down the stairs when HS had arms open in a welcoming gesture at bottom of stairs. For years afterwards, Hinda screamed upon seeing HS.) The misstep which caused her fall had nothing at all to do with you, just as your own mis-steps have nothing at all to do with me.

---

[101] **Deuteronomy 4:29** But from there you will seek the LORD your God, and you will find Him if you seek Him with all your heart and with all your soul.
[102] **Matthew 6:21** For where your treasure is, there your heart will be also.
[103] **Philippians 4:7** And the peace of God, which surpasses all understanding, will guard your hearts and minds through Christ Jesus.
[104] **Matthew 10:1** And when He had called His twelve disciples to Him, He gave them power over unclean spirits, to cast them out, and to heal all kinds of sickness and all kinds of disease.
[105] **Matthew 17:19-20** Then the disciples came to Jesus privately and said, "Why could we not cast it out?"
So Jesus said to them, "Because of your unbelief; for assuredly, I say to you, if you have faith as a mustard seed, you will say to this mountain, 'Move from here to there,' and it will move; and nothing will be impossible for you."
[106] Spelling correction: manuscript has "didsth."
[107] **Matthew 8:26** And he saith unto them, "Why are ye fearful, O ye of little faith?" Then he arose, and rebuked the winds and the sea; and there was a great calm.
[108] **Matthew 6:11** "Give us this day our daily bread."
[109] **Genesis 1:26-27** Then God said, "Let Us make man in Our image, according to Our likeness; let them have dominion over the fish of the sea, over the birds of the air, and over the cattle, over all the earth and over every creeping thing that creeps on the earth." So God created man in His own image; in the image of God He created him; male and female He created them.

T 2 B 14. Denial of error is a very powerful defense of truth. We have slowly been shifting the emphasis from the negative to the positive use of denial. Remember, we have already stated that denial is not a purely negative device; it results in positive miscreation. That is the way the mentally ill DO employ it. T(76) -76

T 2 B 15. But remember a very early thought of your own, "Never underestimate the power of denial." In the service of the "Right Mind", the denial of ERROR frees the mind and re-establishes the freedom of the will. When the will is REALLY free, it CANNOT miscreate, because it recognizes ONLY TRUTH.

T 2 B 16. Projection arises out of FALSE DENIAL. Not out of its proper use. My own role in the Atonement IS one of true projection, i.e., I can project to YOU the affirmation of truth. If you project error to me (or to yourself) you are interfering with the process. My use of projection, which can also be yours, is NOT based on faulty denial. But it DOES involve the very powerful use of the denial of error.

T 2 B 17. The miracle worker is one who accepts my kind of denial and projection, unites his own inherent abilities to deny and project with mine, and imposes them back on himself and others. This establishes the total lack of threat anywhere. Together we can then work for the real time of peace, which is Eternal.

T 2 B 18. I inspired Bob (ref. to elevator man who took HS down from her apt.) to make that remark to you, and it is a pity that you heard only the last part. But you can still use that. His remark ended with: "Every shut eye is not asleep." Since your own vision is much improved at the moment, we will go on a while.

T 2 B 19. Freud's identification of mechanisms was quite correct, as was his recognition of their creative ability. They can INDEED create man's perception, both of himself and his surroundings. T(77) -77

T 2 B 20. But Freud's limitations induced inevitable limits on his own perception. He made two kinds of errors.

T 2 B 21. The first is that he saw only how the mechanisms worked in the mentally ill.

T 2 B 22. The second is his own denial of the mechanism of the Atonement.

T 2 B 23. Let us take up the first, because a clear understanding of the second depends on it.

T 2 B 24. Denial should be directed only to error, and projection should be limited to truth. You should truly give as you have truly received. The Golden Rule[110] can work effectively only on this basis.

T 2 B 25. Intellectualization is a poor word, which stems from the brain-mind confusion. "Right-Mindedness" is better. This device defends the RIGHT MIND, and gives it control over the body. "Intellectualization" implies a split, whereas "Right-Mindedness" involves healing.

T 2 B 26. Withdrawal is properly employed in the service of withdrawing from the desert. It is NOT a device for escape, but for consolidation. There IS only One Mind.

T 2 B 27. Dissociation is quite similar. You should split yourself off from error, but only in defense of integration.

T 2 B 28. Detachment is essentially a weaker form of dissociation. This is one of the major areas of withholding that both you and B. are engaging in.

T 2 B 29. Flight can be undertaken in whatever direction you choose, but note that the concept itself implies flight FROM something. Flight from error is perfectly appropriate.. T(78) -78

T 2 B 30. Distantiation is a way of putting distance between yourself and what you SHOULD fly from.

T 2 B 31. Regression is a real effort to return to your own original state. In this sense, it is utilized to RESTORE, not to go back to the less mature.

T 2 B 32. Sublimation should be associated with the SUBLIME.

T 2 B 33. There are many other so-called "dynamic" concepts which are profound errors due essentially to the misuse of defenses. Among them is the concept of different levels of aspiration, which results from real level confusion.

T 2 B 34. However, the main point to be understood from these notes is that you can defend truth as well as error, and in fact, much better.

T 2 B 35. So far we have concentrated on ends rather than means because unless you regard an end as worth achieving, you will not devote yourself to the means by which it can BE achieved. Your own question enabled me to shift the emphasis from end to means. (Question asked was "how can we incorporate this material?") You and B. HAVE accepted the end as valuable, thus signifying your willingness to use defenses to ensure it.

T 2 B 36. The means are easier to clarify after the true worth of the goal itself is firmly established.

T 2 B 37. Everyone defends his own treasure. You do not have to tell him to do this, because HE will do so automatically. The real question still remains WHAT do you treasure, and HOW MUCH do you treasure it?

T 2 B 38. Once you learn to consider these two points, and bring them into ALL your actions as the true criteria for behavior, I will have little difficulty in clarifying the means. You have not learned to be consistent about this as yet. I have therefore concentrated on showing you that the means ARE available whenever you DO ask. T(79) -79

T 2 B 39. You can save a lot of time, however, if you do not need to extend this step unduly. The correct focus will shorten it immeasurably.

T 2 B 40. Papers will be very easy to write as this time is shortened. T(80) 80

T 2 B 41. The[111] Atonement is the ONLY defense which cannot be used destructively. That is because, while everyone must eventually join it, it was not a device which was generated by man. The Atonement PRINCIPLE was in effect long before the Atonement itself was begun. The Principle was love, and the Atonement itself, was an ACT of love. Acts were not necessary before the Separation, because the time-space belief did not exist.

T 2 B 42. It was only after the Separation that the defense of Atonement, and the necessary conditions for its fulfillment were planned. It became increasingly apparent that all of the defenses which man can choose to use constructively or destructively were not enough to save him. It was therefore decided that he needed a defense which was so splendid that he could not misuse it, although he COULD refuse it. His will could not turn it into a weapon of attack, which is the inherent characteristic of all other defenses. The Atonement thus becomes the only defense which was NOT a two-edged sword.[112]

T 2 B 43. The Atonement actually began long before the Crucifixion. Many Souls offered their efforts on behalf of the Separated Ones but they could not withstand the strength of the attack, and had to be brought back. Angels came, too, but their protection was not enough, because the Separated ones were not interested in peace. They had already split themselves, and were bent on dividing rather than reintegrating. The levels they introduced into themselves turned

---

[110] **Matthew 7:12** "Therefore, whatever you want men to do to you, do also to them, for this is the Law and the Prophets."

[111] Nov. 13

[112] **Psalm 149:6** Let the high praises of God be in their mouth, And a two-edged sword in their hand,

against each other, and they, in turn, turned against each other. They established differences, divisions, cleavages, dispersion, and all the other concepts related to the increasing splits they produced.

T 2 B 44. Not being in their Right Minds, they turned their defenses from protection to assault, and acted literally insanely. It was essential to introduce a split-proof device which could be used ONLY to heal, if it was used at all. **T(81) 81**

T 2 B 45. The[113] Atonement was built into the space-time belief in order to set a limit on the need for the belief, and ultimately to make learning complete. The Atonement IS the final lesson. Learning, itself, like the classrooms in which it occurs, is temporary. Let all those who overestimate human intelligence remember this. (HS questions last sentence, which she perceives as threatening.) The ability to learn has no value when change of understanding is no longer necessary. The eternally creative have nothing to learn. Only after the Separation was it necessary to direct the creative force to learning, because changed behavior had become mandatory.

T 2 B 46. Human beings can learn to improve their behavior, and can also learn to become better and better learners. This increase serves (HS notes that this was written "served") to bring them in closer and closer accord with the Sonship. But the Sonship itself is a perfect creation, and perfection is not a matter of degree. Only while there are different degrees is learning meaningful. The evolution of man is merely a process by which he proceeds from one degree to the next. He corrects his previous missteps by stepping forward. This represents a process which is actually incomprehensible in temporal terms, because he RETURNS as he progresses. (Originally, was "goes forward", rather than "progresses")

T 2 B 47. The Atonement is the device by which he can free himself from the past as he goes ahead. It UNDOES his past errors, thus making it unnecessary for him to keep retracing his steps without advancing toward his return.

T 2 B 48. In this sense, the Atonement saves time, but, like the miracle which serves it, does not abolish it. As long as there is need for Atonement, there is need for time. But the Atonement, as a completed plan, does have a unique relationship TO time. Until the Atonement is finished, its various phases will proceed IN time, but the whole Atonement stands at its end. At this point, the bridge of the return has been built.

T 2 B 49.(Note to HS. The reason this is upsetting to you is because the Atonement is a TOTAL commitment. You still think this is associated with loss. This is the same mistake ALL the Separated ones make, in one way or another. They cannot believe that a defense which CANNOT attack also IS the best defense. Except for this misperception, the angels COULD have helped them. What do you think "the **T(82) 82** meek shall inherit the earth" MEANS? They will literally take it over because of their strength. A two-way defense is inherently weak, precisely BECAUSE it has two edges it can turn against the self very unexpectedly. This tendency CANNOT be controlled EXCEPT by miracles.)

T 2 B 50. The miracle turns the defense of Atonement to the protection of the inner self, which, as it becomes more and more secure; assumes its natural talent of protecting others. The inner self knows itself as both a brother AND a son.

T 2 B 51.(The above notes were taken with great difficulty by HS, and constitute the only series this far that were written very slowly. When HS asked about this, she was told, "don't worry about the notes. They are right, but YOU are not sufficiently Right-Minded yet to write about the Atonement with comfort. You will write about it yet with joy.)

T 2 B 52.(Aside from HS: Last night I felt briefly but intensely depressed, temporarily under the impression that I was abandoned. I tried, but couldn't get through at all. After a while, I decided to give up for the time being, and He said, "don't worry. I will never leave you or forsake you." I did feel a little better, and decided I was really not sick, so I could return to my exercises. While I was exercising, I had some part-vision experiences which I found only mildly frightening at times, and quite reassuring at others.

T 2 B 53. I am not too sure of the sequence, but it began with a VERY clear assurance of love, and an equally clear emphasis on my own great value, beauty, and purity. Things got a little confusing after that. First, the idea of "Bride of Christ" occurred to me with vaguely inappropriate "undertones." Then there was a repetition of "the way of Love", and a restatement of an earlier experience, now as if it were FROM Him TO me: "Behold the Handmaid of the Lord; Be it done unto you according to His Word."[114] (This threw me into panic before, but at that time, it was stated in the more accurate Biblical phrasing: "Be it done unto ME according to HIS Word.")[115] **T(83) 83** This time I was a bit uneasy, but remembered I had misperceived it last time, and was probably still not seeing it right. Actually, it is really just a statement of allegiance to the Divine Service, which can hardly be dangerous.

T 2 B 54. Then there was a strange sequence, in which Christ seemed to be making very obvious advances, which became quite sexual in my perception of them. I ALMOST thought briefly that he turned into a devil. I got just a LITTLE scared, and the possession idea came in for a while, but I thought it SO silly, that there is no point in taking it seriously.

T 2 B 55.(As I am writing this, I remember that thing in the book about the demon lover, which once THROUGH me (note spelling, "threw") into a fit. I am upset, but the spelling slip is reassuring.

T 2 B 56. This morning we reviewed the whole episode. He said he was "VERY pleased at the COMPARATIVE lack of fear, and also the concomitant awareness that it WAS misperception. This showed much greater strength, and a much increased Right-Mindedness. This is because defenses are now being used much better, on behalf of truth MORE than error, though not completely so.

T 2 B 57. The weaker use of mis-projection is shown by my recognition that it can't REALLY be that way, which became possible as soon as denial was applied against error, NOT truth. This permitted a much greater awareness of alternative interpretations.

T 2 B 58. It was also explained (the shift to the passive form instead of "He also explained" should be noted. This is an expression of fear.) "Remember the section in "Letters from the Scattered Brotherhood" you read last evening about 'Hold fast', and please do so." **T(84) 83a (NOTE)**

T 2 B 59.(Note made on 11/15 by HS re B's remark concerning[116] top of p.5, 11/13.[117])

Yes, but I doubt if it says this is inevitable. It may entail more miswill than we think. The above may have been too passively interpreted. Note that B. Did NOT ask MY will re same. If he had, HE would have felt better. **T(85) 84**[118]

T 2 B 60. You know that when defenses are disrupted there is a period of real disorientation, accompanied by fear, guilt, and usually vacillations between anxiety and depression. This process is different only in that defenses are not being disrupted, but re-interpreted, even though it may be experienced as the same thing.

T 2 B 61. In the re-interpretation of defenses, they are not disrupted but their use for ATTACK is lost. Since this means they can be used only ONE way, they became MUCH stronger, and much more de-

---

[113] 11/13

[114] **Luke 1:38** And Mary said, "Behold, the handmaid of the Lord; be it unto me according to thy word. And the angel departed from her."
[115] Apparently Schucman is referring to the same quote (Luke 1:18) The closing bracket is not in the *Urtext* manuscript but is in the *Notes*.
[116] *Urtext* manuscript says "aconcerning" here.
[117] This would refer to the next page, or absolute page #85
[118] 11/13

pendable. They no longer oppose the Atonement, but greatly facilitate it. The Atonement can only be accepted within you.

T 2 B 62. You have perceived it largely as EXTERNAL thus far, and that is why your EXPERIENCE of it has been minimal. You have been SHOWN the chalice many times, but have not accepted it "for yourself." Your major improper use of defenses is now largely limited to externalization. Do not fail to appreciate your own remarkable progress in this respect. You perceived it first as a vessel of some sort whose purpose was uncertain but which might be a piss-pot. You DID notice, however, that the INSIDE was gold, while the OUTSIDE, though shiny, was silver. This was a recognition of the fact that the INNER part is more precious than the OUTER side, even though both are resplendent, though with different value.

T 2 B 63. The re-interpretation of defenses is essential to break open the INNER light. Since the Separation, man's defenses have been used almost entirely to defend themselves AGAINST the Atonement, and thus maintain their separation. They generally see this as a need to protect the body from external intrusion (or intruding), and this kind of misperception is largely responsible for the homosexual fallacy, as well as your own pregnancy fears. The so-called "anal" behavior is a distorted attempt to "steal" the Atonement, and deny its worth by concealing it, and holding onto it with a bodily receptacle, which is regarded as particularly vicious. "Oral" fantasies are rather similar in purpose, except that they stem more from a sense of deprivation, and insatiable thirst which results. "Anal" fallacies are more of a refusal to give, while oral fantasies emphasize a distorted need to take. The main **T(86) -85** error in both is the belief that the body can be used as a means for attaining Atonement.

T 2 B 64. Perceiving the body as the Temple is only the first step in correcting this kind of distortion. (HS scalded hand, and looked for butter to put on. It occurred to her that the Atonement was the cure. Burn appeared to be minimal, and caused little discomfort.)

T 2 B 65. Seeing the body as the Temple alters part of the misperception, but not all of it. It DOES recognize, however, that the concept of addition or subtraction in PHYSICAL terms is not appropriate. But the next step is to realize that a Temple is not a building at all. Its REAL holiness lies in the INNER altar, around which the building is built. The inappropriate emphasis which men have put on beautiful Church BUILDINGS is a sign of their own fear of Atonement, and unwillingness to reach the altar itself. The REAL beauty of the Temple cannot be seen with the physical eye. The spiritual eye, on the other hand, cannot see the building at all, but it perceives the altar within with perfect clarity. This is because the spiritual eye has perfect vision.

T 2 B 66. For perfect effectiveness, the chalice of the Atonement belongs at the center of the inner altar, where it undoes the Separation, and restores the wholeness of the Spirit. Before the Separation, the mind was invulnerable to fear, because fear did not exist. Both the Separation and the fear were MISCREATIONS of the mind, which have to be undone. This is what the Bible means by the "Restoration of the Temple." It DOES NOT mean the restoration of the building, but it DOES mean the opening of the altar to receive the Atonement.

T 2 B 67. This heals the Separation, and places within man the one defense against all Separation-mind errors which can make him perfectly invulnerable. **T(87) -86**

T 2 B 68. The acceptance of the Atonement by everyone is only a matter of time. In fact, both TIME and MATTER were created for this purpose. This appears to contradict free will, because of the inevitability of this decision. If you review the idea carefully, you will realize that this is not true. Everything is limited in some way by the manner of its creation. Free will can temporize, and is capable of enormous procrastination. But it cannot depart entirely from its Creator, who set the limits on its ability to miscreate by virtue of its own real purpose.

T 2 B 69. The misuse of will engenders a situation which, in the extreme, becomes altogether intolerable. Pain thresholds can be high, but they are not limitless. Eventually, everybody begins to recognize, however dimly, that there MUST be a better way. As this recognition is more firmly established, it becomes a perceptual turning-point. This ultimately reawakens the spiritual eye, simultaneously weakening the investment in physical sight. The alternating investment in the two types or levels of perception is usually experienced as conflict for a long time, and can become very acute.

T 2 B 70. But the outcome is as certain as God. The spiritual eye literally CANNOT SEE error, and merely looks for Atonement. All the solutions which the physical eyes seek, dissolve in its sight. The spiritual eye, which looks within, recognizes immediately that the altar has been defiled, and needs to be repaired and protected. Perfectly aware of the RIGHT defense, it passes over all others, looking past error to truth. Because of the real strength of ITS vision, it pulls the will into its own service, and forces the mind to concur. This reestablishes the true power of the will, and makes it increasingly unable to tolerate delay. The mind then realizes, with increasing certitude, that delay is only a way of increasing unnecessary pain, which it need not tolerate at all. The pain threshold drops accordingly, and the mind becomes increasingly sensitive to what it would once have regarded as very minor intrusions of discomfort. **T(88) -87**

T 2 B 71. The Children of God are entitled to perfect comfort, which comes from a sense of perfect trust. Until they achieve this, they waste themselves and their true creative power on useless attempts to make themselves more comfortable by inappropriate means. But the real means is ALREADY provided, and does not involve any efforts on their part at all. Their egocentricity usually misperceives this as personally insulting, an interpretation which obviously arises from their misperception of themselves. Egocentricity and communion cannot coexist. Even the terms themselves are contradictory.

T 2 B 72. The Atonement is the only gift which is worthy of being offered to the Altar of God. This is because of the inestimable value of the Altar itself. It was created perfect, and is entirely worthy of receiving perfection. God IS lonely without His SOULS, and THEY are lonely without Him. Remember the "spiritual" (a VERY good term) which begins with "And God stepped down from Heaven and said: I'M lonely - - I'll make ME a World." The world WAS a way of healing the Separation, and the Atonement is the GUARANTEE that the device will ultimately do so.

T 2 B 73. (HS request for special message for B. Tell B that his delaying tactics are holding him back. He does not really understand detachment, distantiation, and withdrawal. He is interpreting them as "holding himself aloof" from the Atonement.) **T(89) -88**[119]

T 2 C. Healing as Release from Fear (*Notes* 263 5:112)

T 2 C 1. The new emphasis will now be on healing. The miracle is the means, the Atonement the principle, and the healing is the result. Those who speak of "the miracle OF healing" are combining two orders of reality inappropriately. Healing is NOT a miracle. The Atonement, or the final miracle, is a REMEDY. It is purely a means, while any type of healing is a result.

T 2 C 2. The order of error to which Atonement is applied is irrelevant. Essentially, ALL healing is the release from fear. But to undertake this you cannot be fearful yourself.

T 2 C 3. You do not understand healing because of your own fear. I have been hinting throughout (and once stated very directly, because

---
[119] Nov. 14

you were unfearful at the time) that you MUST heal others. The reason is that their healing merely witnesses or attests to yours.

T 2 C 4. A major step in the Atonement plan is to undo error at ALL levels. Illness, which is really "not Right Mindedness", is the result of level confusion in the sense that it always entails the misbelief that what is amiss in one level can adversely affect another.

T 2 C 5. We have constantly referred to miracles as the means of correcting level confusion. In reality, all mistakes must be corrected at the level at which they occur. Only the mind is capable of error. The body can ACT erroneously, but this is only because it has responded to mis-Thought. The body cannot create, and the belief that it CAN, a fundamental error responsible for most of the fallacies already referred to, produces all physical symptoms.

T 2 C 6. All physical illness represents a belief in magic. The whole distortion which created magic rested on the belief that there is a creative ability in matter, which can control the mind. This fallacy can work either way; i.e., it can be misbelieved either that the mind can miscreate IN the body, or that the body can miscreate in the mind. If it can be made clear **T(90) -89** that the mind, which is the only level of creation, cannot create beyond itself, then neither confusion need occur.

T 2 C 7. The reason why only the mind can create is more obvious than may be immediately apparent. The Soul has been created. The body is a learning device FOR the mind. Learning devices are not lessons in themselves. Their purpose is merely to facilitate the <u>THINKING</u> of the learner. The most that a faulty use of a learning device can do is to fail to facilitate. It does not have the power in itself to introduce actual learning errors.

T 2 C 8. The body, if properly understood, shares the invulnerability of the Atonement to two-edged application. This is not because the body is a miracle, but because it is not inherently open to misinterpretation. The body is merely a fact.[120] Its ABILITIES can be,[121] and frequently are, overevaluated. However, it is almost impossible to deny its existence. Those who do are engaging in a particularly unworthy form of denial. (The use of the word "unworthy" here implies simply that it is not necessary to protect the mind by denying the un-mindful. There is little doubt that the mind can miscreate. If one denies this unfortunate aspect of its power, one is also denying the power itself.)

T 2 C 9. All material means which man accepts as remedies for bodily ills are simply restatements of magic principles. It was the first level of the error to believe that the body created its own illness. Thereafter, it is a second mis-step to attempt to heal it through non-creative agents. It does not follow, however, that the application of these very weak corrective devices are evil. Sometimes the illness has sufficiently great a hold over an individual's mind to render him inaccessible to Atonement. In this case, one may be wise to utilize a compromise approach to mind and body, in which something from the OUTSIDE is temporarily given healing **T(91) -90** belief. This is because the last thing that can help the non-Right-Minded (or the sick) is an increase in fear. They are already in a fear-weakened state. If they are inappropriately exposed to a straight and undiluted miracle, they may be precipitated into panic. This is particularly likely to occur when upside down perception has induced the belief that miracles are frightening.

T 2 C 10. The value of the Atonement does not lie in the manner in which it is expressed. In fact, if it is truly used it will inevitably BE expressed in whatever way is most helpful to the receiver, not the giver. This means that a miracle, to attain its full efficacy, MUST be expressed in a language which the recipient can understand without fear. It does not follow by any means that this is the highest level of communication of which he is capable. But it DOES mean that it is the highest level of communication of which he is capable NOW.

T 2 C 11. The whole aim of the miracle is to RAISE the level of communication, not to impose regression (as improperly used) upon it. Before it is safe to let miracle workers loose in this world, it is essential that they understand fully the fear of release. Otherwise, they may unwittingly foster the misbelief that release is imprisonment, which is very prevalent. This misperception arose from the attempted protection device (or misdefense) that harm can be limited to the body. This was because of the much greater fear (which this one counteracts) that the mind can hurt itself. Neither error is really meaningful, because the miscreations of the mind do not really exist. That recognition is a far better protection device than any form of level confusion, because of the advantages of introducing correction at the level of the error.

T 2 C 12. It is essential that the remembrance of the fact that ONLY mind can create at all remain with you. Implicit in this is the corollary that correction belongs at the thought level, and NOT at either level **T(92) -91** to which creation is inapplicable. To repeat an earlier statement, and also to extend it somewhat, the Soul is already perfect, and therefore does not require correction. The body does not really exist, except as a learning device for the mind. This learning device is not subject to errors of its own, because it was created, but is NOT creating.

It should be obvious, then, that correcting the creator (or inducing it to give up miscreation) is the only application of creation which is inherently meaningful at all.

T 2 C 13. We said before that magic is essentially mindless, or the destructive (miscreated) use of mind. Physical medicines are a form of "spells." In one way, they are a more benign form, in that they do not entail the possession fallacy which DOES enter when a mind believes that it can possess another. Since this is considerably less dangerous, though still incorrect, it has its advantages. It is particularly helpful to the therapist who really wants to heal, but is still fearful himself. By using physical means to do so, he is not engaging in any form of enslavement, even though he is not applying the Atonement. This means that his mind is dulled by fear, but is not actively engaged in distortion.

T 2 C 14. Those who are afraid of using the mind to heal are right in avoiding it, because the very fact that they are afraid HAS made them vulnerable to miscreation. They are therefore likely to misunderstand any healing they might induce, and, because egocentricity and fear usually occur together, may be unable to accept the real Source of the healing. Under these conditions, it is safer for them to rely TEMPORARILY on physical healing devices, because they cannot misperceive them as their own creations. As long as their own vulnerability persists, it is essential to preserve them from even attempting miracles.

T 2 C 15. We said in a previous section that the miracle is an expression of miracle-Mindedness. Miracle-Mindedness merely means Right-Mindedness in the sense that we are now using it. Right-Mindedness neither exalts nor depreciates **T(93) -92** the mind of the miracle worker nor of the miracle receiver. However, as a creative act, the miracle need not await the Right-Mindedness of the receiver. In fact, its purpose is to restore him TO his Right Mind. But it is essential that the miracle worker be in his Right Mind, or he will be unable to reestablish Right-Mindedness in someone else.

T 2 C 16. The healer who relies on his own readiness is endangering his understanding. He is perfectly safe as long as he is completely unconcerned about HIS readiness, but maintains a consistent trust in MINE. (Errors of this kind produce some very erratic behavior, which usually point up an underlying unwillingness to co-operate. Note that by inserting the carbon backwards, B. created a situation in which two copies did not exist. This reflected two levels of confi-

---

[120] The words "in human experience" are added in the *HLC*. This has not been located in the *Notes*.

[121] The word "be" is not present in the original *Urtext* manuscript, but is present in the *HLC*. This has not been located in the *Notes*.

dence lack, one in My readiness to heal, and the other in his own willingness to give.) These errors inevitably introduce inefficiency into the miracle worker's behavior, and temporarily disrupt his miracle-mindedness. We might also make very similar comments about your own hesitation about dictating at all. This is a larger error only because it results in greater inefficiency. If you don't say anything, nobody can use it, including Me. We have established that for all corrective processes, the first step is know that this is fear. Unless fear had entered, the corrective procedure would never have become necessary. If your miracle working propensities are not working, it is always because fear has intruded on your Right-Mindedness, and has literally upset it. (i.e. turned it upside down).

T 2 C 17. All forms of not-Right-Mindedness are the result of refusal to accept the Atonement FOR YOURSELF. If the miracle worker DOES accept it, he places himself in the position to recognize that those who need to be healed are simply those who have NOT done so. The reason why you felt the vast radiation range of your own inner illumination is because you were aware that your Right-Mindedness IS healing. **T(94) -93** The sole responsibility of the miracle worker is to accept Atonement himself. This means that he knows that mind is the only creative level, and that its errors ARE healed by the Atonement. Once he accepts this, HIS mind can only heal. By denying his mind any destructive potential, and reinstating its purely constructive powers, he has placed himself in a position where he can undo the level confusion of others. The message which he then gives to others is the truth that THEIR MINDS are really similarly constructive, and that their own miscreations cannot hurt them. By affirming this, the miracle worker releases the mind from overevaluating its own learning device (the body), and restores the mind to its true position as the learner. It should be re-emphasized that the body does not learn, any more than it creates. As a learning device, it merely follows the learner, but if it is falsely endowed with self initiative, it becomes a serious obstruction to the learning it should facilitate.

T 2 C 18. ONLY the mind is capable of illumination. The Soul is already illuminated, and the body in itself is too dense. The mind, however, can BRING its own illumination TO the body by recognizing that density is the opposite of intelligence, and therefore unamenable to independent learning. It is, however, easily brought into alignment with a mind which has learned to look beyond density toward light.

T 2 C 19. Corrective learning always begins with awakening the spiritual eye, and turning away from belief in physical sight. The reason this entails fear is because man is afraid of what his spiritual eye will see, which was why he closed it in the first place. We said before that the spiritual eye cannot see error, and is capable only of looking beyond it to the defense of Atonement. There is no doubt that the spiritual eye does produce extreme discomfort by what it sees. The thing that man forgets is that the discomfort **T(95) -94** is not the final outcome of its perception. When the spiritual eye is permitted to look upon the defilement of the altar, it also looks immediately toward Atonement. Nothing which the spiritual eye perceives can induce fear. Everything that results from accurate spiritual awareness merely is channelized toward correction. Discomfort is aroused only to bring the need to correct forcibly into awareness.

T 2 C 20. What the physical eye sees is not corrective, nor can it be corrected by any device which can be physically seen. As long as a man believes in what his physical sight tells him, all his corrective behavior will be misdirected. The reason why the real vision is obscured is because man cannot endure to see his own defiled altar. But since the altar has BEEN defiled, this fact becomes doubly dangerous unless it IS perceived. This perception is totally non-threatening because of the Atonement. The fear of healing arises in the end from an unwillingness to accept the unequivocal fact that healing is necessary. The fear arises because of the necessary willingness to look at what man has done to himself.

T 2 C 21. Healing was an ability which was lent to man after the Separation, before which it was completely unnecessary. Like all aspects of the space-time belief, healing ability is temporary. However, as long as time persists, healing remains among the stronger human protections. This is because healing always rests on charity, and charity is a way of perceiving the true perfection of another, even if he cannot perceive it himself. Most of the loftier concepts of which man is capable now are time-dependent. Charity is really a weaker reflection of a much more powerful love-encompassment, which is far beyond any form of charity that man can conceive of as yet. Charity is essential to Right-Mindedness, in the limited sense to which Right-Mindedness can now be attained. Charity is a way of looking at another AS IF he had already gone far beyond his actual accomplishment in time. Since his own thinking is faulty, he cannot see the Atonement himself, or he would have no need for charity at all. The charity which is accorded him is both an acknowledgment that he IS weak, and a recognition that he COULD BE stronger. The way in which both of these beliefs are stated clearly implies their dependence on time, making it quite apparent that charity lies within the framework of human **T(96) 95** limitations, though toward the higher levels.

T 2 C 22. We said before, twice in fact, that only Revelation transcends time. The miracle, as an expression of true human charity, can only shorten it a best. It must be understood, however, that whenever a man offers a miracle to another, he IS shortening the suffering of both. This introduces a correction into the Record, which corrects retroactively as well as progressively. **T(97) -96**[122]

T 2 D. Fear as Lack of Love (*Notes* 265 5:114)

T 2 D 1. You and B. both believe that "being afraid" is involuntary. But I have told you many times that only CONSTRUCTIVE acts should be involuntary. We said that Christ-control can take over everything that DOESN'T matter, and Christ-guidance can direct everything that DOES, if you so will.

T 2 D 2. Fear cannot be Christ-controlled, but it CAN be self-controlled. Fear is always associated with what does not matter. It prevents Me from controlling it. The correction is therefore a matter of YOUR will, because its presence shows that you have raised the UNIMPORTANT to a higher level than it warrants. You have thus brought it under your will, where it DOES NOT belong. This means YOU feel responsible for it. The level confusion here is perfectly obvious.

T 2 D 3. The reason that I cannot CONTROL fear for you is that you are attempting to raise to the mind level the proper content of the lower-order reality. I do NOT foster level confusion, but YOU can will to correct it.

T 2 D 4. You would not tolerate insane behavior on your part, and would hardly advance the excuse that you could not help it. Why should you tolerate insane thinking? There is a fallacy here you would do well to look at clearly.

T 2 D 5. You both believe that you ARE responsible for what you DO, but NOT for what you THINK. The truth is that you ARE responsible for what you THINK, because it is only at this level that you CAN exercise choice. What you DO comes from what you think. You cannot separate the truth by giving autonomy to your behavior. This is controlled by Me automatically, as soon as you place what you think under my guidance.

T 2 D 6. Whenever you are afraid, it is a sure sign that you have allowed your mind to miscreate, i.e., have NOT allowed Me to guide it. It is pointless to believe that controlling the outcome of mis-Thought **T(98) -97** can result in real healing. When you are fearful, you have willed wrongly. This is why you feel you are responsible for it.

---

[122] Nov. 15, '65

T 2 D 7. You must change your MIND, not your behavior, and this IS a matter of will. You do not need guidance EXCEPT at the mind-level. Correction belongs ONLY at the level where creation is possible. The term does not really mean anything at the symptom-level, where it cannot work.

T 2 D 8. The correction of fear IS your responsibility. When you ask for release from fear, you are implying that it isn't. You should ask, instead, for help in the conditions which have brought the fear about. This condition always entails a separated Mind-willingness. At this level, you CAN help it.

T 2 D 9. You are much too tolerant of Mind-wandering, thus passively condoning its miscreation. The particular result never matters, but this fundamental error DOES. The fundamental correction is always the same. Before you will to do anything, ask Me if your will is in accord with Mine. If you are sure that it IS, there will BE no fear.

T 2 D 10. Fear is always a sign of strain, which arises whenever the WILL to do conflicts with WHAT you do. This situation arises in two major ways:

1) You can will to do conflicting things, either simultaneously or successively. This produces conflicting behavior, which would be tolerable to the self (though not necessarily to others) except for the fact that the part of the will that wants something ELSE is outraged.

2) You can BEHAVE as you think you should, but without entirely WILLING to do so. This produces consistent behavior, but entails great strain WITHIN the self. **T(99) -98**

T 2 D 11. If you think about it, you will realize that in both cases the will and the behavior are out-of-accord, resulting in a situation in which you are doing what you do NOT will. This arouses a sense of coercion, which usually produces rage. The anger then invades the mind, and projection in the wrong sense becomes likely. Depression or anxiety are virtually certain.

T 2 D 12. Remember that whenever there is fear, it is because YOU have NOT MADE UP YOUR MIND. Your will is split, and your behavior inevitably becomes erratic. Correcting at the behavior level can shift the error from the first type to the second, but will NOT obliterate the fear.

T 2 D 13. It is possible to reach a state in which you bring your will under my guidance without much conscious effort, but this implies the kind of habit pattern which neither you nor B. has developed dependably as yet.

T 2 D 14. Tell B. that although he keeps telling you that God will never ask you to do more than you can, he does not understand it himself. God CANNOT ask more than you WILL. The strength to DO comes from your own undivided will to do. There is NO strain in doing God's will as soon as it is also your own.

T 2 D 15. The lesson here is quite simple, but particularly apt to be overlooked. I will therefore repeat it, URGING you to listen. Only your mind can produce fear. It does so whenever it is conflicted in what it wills, thus producing inevitable strain, because willing and doing become discordant. This CANNOT be corrected by better DOING. But it CAN be corrected by higher WILLING.

T 2 E. The Correction for Lack of Love (*Notes* 271 T(5:120))

T 2 E 1. After taking the first corrective step, i.e., "Knowing it IS fear," you might benefit temporarily by adding another next step BEFORE going on with the corrective process. Try saying to yourself that you MUST have willed not to love somehow or somewhere, or that fear which arises from behavior-will conflict could not have happened. Then follow previous instructions. **T(100) -99**

T 2 E 2. If you consider what the process really means, it is nothing more than a series of pragmatic steps in the larger process of accepting the Atonement as THE remedy. From this viewpoint, the steps can be reworded as follows:

1.) Know first this is fear.
2.) Fear arises from lack of love.
3.) The ONLY remedy for lack of love is perfect love.
4.) Perfect love IS the Atonement.

T 2 E 3. The final procedural step (3) is inherent in the last statement (4). We have emphasized that the miracle, or the EXPRESSION of Atonement, is always a sign of real respect from the worthy TO the worthy. This worth IS re-established by the Atonement.

T 2 E 4. It is obvious, then, that when you are afraid you have placed yourself in a position where you NEED Atonement BECAUSE you have DONE something loveless because you WILLED without love. This is precisely the situation for which the Atonement was offered. The need for the remedy inspired its CREATION.

T 2 E 5. As long as you recognize only the NEED for the remedy, you will remain fearful. However, as soon as you REMEDY it, you have also abolished the fear. This is how TRUE healing occurs. **T(101) -100**

T 2 E 6. Everyone experiences fear, and nobody enjoys it. Yet, it would take very little Right-thinking to know why it occurs. Neither you nor B. have thought about it very much, either. (I object at this point to the use of plural verb with a properly singular subject - - HS - - and remember that last time in a very similar sentence, He said it correctly and I remembered it with real pleasure. This real grammatical error makes me suspicious of the genuineness of these notes. <u>ANSWER</u>: What it really shows is that YOU are not very receptive. The reason it came out that way, is because you are projecting (in the inappropriate way) your own anger, which has nothing to do with these notes. YOU made the error, because you are not feeling loving, so you want me to sound silly, so you won't have to pay attention. Actually, I am trying to get through against considerable opposition, because you are not very happy, and I wish you were. I thought I'd take a chance, even though you are so resistant, because I MIGHT be able to make you feel better. You may be unable not to attack at all, but do try to listen a little, too.)

T 2 E 7. Very few people appreciate the real power of the mind. Nobody remains fully aware of it all the time. This is inevitable in this world, because the human being has many things he must do, and cannot engage in constant thought-watching. However, if he hopes to spare himself from fear, there are some things he must realize, and realize them fully, at least some of the time. **T(102) -101**

T 2 E 8. The mind is a very powerful creator, and it never loses its creative force. It never sleeps. Every instant it is creating, and ALWAYS as you will. Many of your ordinary expressions reflect this. For example, when you say "don't give it a thought", you are implying that if you do not think about something, it will have no effect on you. This is true enough.

T 2 E 9. On the other hand, many other expressions are clear expressions of the prevailing LACK of awareness of thought-power. For example, you say, "just an idle thought", and mean that the thought has no effect. You also speak of some actions as "thoughtless", implying that if the person HAD thought, he would not have behaved as he did. You also use phrases like "thought provoking", which is bland enough, but the term "a provoking thought" means something quite different.

T 2 E 10. While expressions like "think big" give some recognition to the power of thought, they still come nowhere near the truth. You do not expect to grow when you say it, because you don't really believe it. It is hard to recognize that thought and belief combine into a power-surge that can literally move mountains.[123]

T 2 E 11. It appears at first glance that to believe such power about yourself is merely arrogant, but that is not the real reason why you don't believe it.

T 2 E 12. People prefer to believe that their thoughts cannot exert real control because they are literally AFRAID of them. Therapists try to help people who are afraid of their own death wishes by depreciating the power of the wish. They even attempt to "free" the patient by persuading him that he can think whatever he wants, without ANY real effect at all. **T(103) -102**

T 2 E 13. There is a real dilemma here, which only the truly right-minded can escape. Death wishes do not kill in the physical sense, but they DO kill spiritually. ALL destructive thinking is dangerous. Given a death wish, a man has no choice except to ACT upon his thought, or behave CONTRARY TO it. He can thus choose ONLY between homicide and fear. (See previous notes on will conflicts.) (NOTE I avoided this term in the last series of notes intentionally, because it seemed too Rankian. Apparently, there was a reason why this word should have been used last time. It is used in this section for a very good reason.)

T 2 E 14. The other possibility is that he depreciates the power of his thought. This is the usual psychoanalytic approach. This DOES allay guilt, but at the cost of rendering thinking impotent. If you believe that what you think is ineffectual, you may cease to be overly afraid of it, but you are hardly likely to respect it, either. The world is full of endless examples of how man has depreciated himself because he is afraid of his own thoughts. In some forms of insanity, thoughts are glorified, but this is only because the underlying depreciation was too effective for tolerance.

T 2 E 15. The truth is that there ARE no "idle thoughts." ALL thinking produces form at some level. The reason why people are afraid of ESP, and so often react against it, is because they KNOW that thought can hurt them. Their OWN thoughts have made them vulnerable.

T 2 E 16. You and B., who complain all the time about fear, still persist in creating it most of the time. I told you last time that you cannot ask ME to release you from it, because I KNOW it does not exist. YOU don't. If I merely intervene between your thoughts and their results, I would be tampering with a basic law of cause and effect, in fact the most fundamental one there is in this world. **T(104) -103** I would hardly help if I depreciated the power of your own thinking. This would be in direct opposition to the purpose of this course.

T 2 E 17. It is certainly much more useful to remind you that you do not guard your thoughts at all carefully, except for a relatively small part of the day, and somewhat inconsistently even then. You may feel at this point that it would take a miracle to enable you to do this, which is perfectly true. Human beings are not used to miraculous thinking, but they CAN be TRAINED to think that way.

T 2 E 18. All miracle-workers HAVE to be trained that way. I have to be able to count on them. This means that I cannot allow them to leave their mind unguarded, or they will not be able to help me. Miracle-working entails a full realization of the power of thought, and real avoidance of miscreation. Otherwise, the miracle will be necessary to set the mind ITSELF straight, a circular process which would hardly foster the time-collapse for which the miracle was intended. Nor would it induce the healthy respect that every miracle-worker must have for true cause and effect.

T 2 E 19. Miracles cannot free the miracle-worker from fear. Both miracles AND fear come from his thoughts, and if he were not free to choose one, he would also not be free to choose the other. Remember, we said before that when electing one person, you reject another.

T 2 E 20. It is much the same in electing the miracle. By so doing, you HAVE rejected fear. Fear cannot assail unless it has been created. You and B. have been afraid of God, of me, of yourselves, and of practically everyone you know at one time or another. **T(105) -104** This can only be because you have miscreated all of us, and believe in what you have created. (We spent a lot of time on this before, but it did not help very much.) You would never have done this if you were not afraid of your own thoughts. The vulnerable are essentially miscreators, because they misperceive Creation.

T 2 E 21. You and B. are willing to accept primarily what does NOT change your minds too much, and leaves you free to leave them quite unguarded most of the time. You persist in believing that when you do not consciously watch your mind, it is unmindful.

T 2 E 22. It is time to consider the whole world of the unconscious, or unwatched mind. This will frighten you, because it is the source of fright. You may look at it as a new theory of basic conflict, if you wish, which will not be entirely an intellectual approach, because I doubt if the truth will escape you entirely.

T 2 E 23. The unwatched mind is responsible for the whole content of the unconscious, which lies above the miracle-level. All psychoanalytic theorists have made some contribution to the truth in this connection, but none of them has seen it in its true entirety. (The correct grammar here is a sign of your better cooperation. Thank you.) Jung's best contribution was an awareness of individual vs. collective unconscious levels. He also recognized the major place of the religious spirit in his schema. His archetypes were also meaningful concepts. But his major error lay in regarding the deepest level of the unconscious as shared in terms of CONTENT. The deepest level of the unconscious is shared as an ABILITY. As MIRACLE-MINDEDNESS, the content, (or the particular miracles which an individual happens to perform) does not matter at all. **T(106) -105** They will, in fact, be entirely different, because, since I direct them, I make a point of avoiding redundancy. Unless a miracle actually heals, it is not a miracle at all.

T 2 E 24. The content of the miracle-level is not recorded in the individual's unconscious, because if it were, it would not be automatic and involuntary, which we have said repeatedly it should be. However, the content IS a matter for the record, which is NOT within the individual himself.

T 2 E 25. All psychoanalysts made one common error, in that they attempted to uncover unconscious CONTENT. You cannot understand unconscious activity in these terms, because "content" is applicable ONLY to the more superficial unconscious levels to which the individual himself contributes. This is the level at which he can readily introduce fear, and usually does.

T 2 E 26. Freud was right in calling this level pre-conscious, and emphasizing that there is a fairly easy interchange between preconscious and conscious material. He was also right in regarding the censor as an agent for the protection of consciousness from fear. HIS major error lay in his insistence that this level is necessary at all in the psychic structure. If the psyche contains fearful levels from which it cannot escape without splitting, its integration is permanently threatened. It is essential not to control the fearful, but to ELIMINATE it.

T 2 E 27. Here, Rank's concept of the will was particularly good, except that he preferred to ally it only with man's own truly creative ability, but did not extend it to its proper union with God's. His "birth trauma", another valid idea, was also too limited, in that it did

---

[123] **Matthew 17:20** So Jesus said to them, "Because of your unbelief; for assuredly, I say to you, if you have faith as a mustard seed, you will say to this mountain, 'Move from here to there,' and it will move; and nothing will be impossible for you."
1 Corinthians 13:2 And though I have the gift of prophecy, and understand all mysteries and all knowledge, and though I have all faith, so that I could remove mountains, but have not love, I am nothing.

not refer to the Separation, which was really a FALSE idea of birth. Physical birth is not **T(107) -106** a trauma in itself. It can, however, remind the individual of the Separation, which was a very real cause of fear.

T 2 E 28. The idea of "will-THERAPY" was potentially a very powerful one, but Rank did not see its real potential because he himself used his mind partly to create a theory OF the mind, but also partly to attack Freud. His reactions to Freud stemmed from his own unfortunate acceptance of the deprivation-fallacy, which itself arose from the Separation. This led him to believe that his own mind-creation could stand only if the creation of another's fell. In consequence, his theory emphasized rather than minimized the two-edged nature of defenses. This is an outstanding characteristic of his concepts, because it was outstandingly true of him.

T 2 E 29. He also misinterpreted the birth-trauma in a way that made it inevitable for him to attempt a therapy whose goal was to ABOLISH FEAR. This is characteristic of all later theorists, who do not attempt, as Freud did, to split off the fear in his own form of therapy.

T 2 E 30. No one as yet has fully recognized either the therapeutic value of fear, or the only way in which it can be truly ended. When man miscreates, he IS in pain. The cause and effect principle here is temporarily a real expeditor. Actually, Cause is a term properly belonging to God, and Effect, which should also be capitalized, is HIS Sonship. This entails a set of cause and effect relationships which are totally different from those which man introduced into the Miscreation.**T(108) -107**[124]

T 2 E 31. The fundamental opponents in the real basic conflict are Creation and miscreation. All fear is implicit in the second, just as all love is inherent in the first. Because of this difference, the basic conflict IS one between love and fear.

T 2 E 32. So much, then, for the true nature of the major opponents in the basic conflict. Since all such theories lead to a form of therapy in which a re-distribution of psychic energy results, it is necessary to consider OUR concept of libido next. In this respect, Freud was more accurate than his followers, who were essentially more wishful. Energy CAN emanate from both Creation AND miscreation, and the particular ratio between them which prevails at a given point in time DOES determine behavior AT that time. If miscreation did NOT engender energy in its own right, it would be unable to produce destructive behavior, which it very patently DOES.

T 2 E 33. Everything that man creates has energy because, like the Creation of God, they (it) come FROM energy, and are endowed by their creator with the power to create. Miscreation is still a genuine creative act in terms of the underlying IMPULSE, but NOT in terms of the CONTENT of the creation. This, however, does not deprive the creation of its OWN creative power. It DOES, however, GUARANTEE that the power will be misused, or USED FEARFULLY.

T 2 E 34. To deny this is merely the previously mentioned fallacy of depreciation. Although Freud made a number of fallacies of his own, he DID avoid this one in connection with libido. The later theorists denied the split-energy concept, not by attempting to heal it, but by re-interpreting it instead of **T(109) -108** redistributing it.

T 2 E 35. This placed them in the illogical position of assuming that the split which their therapies were intended to heal had not occurred. The result of this approach is essentially a form of hypnosis. This is quite different from Freud's approach, which merely ended in a deadlock.

T 2 E 36. A similar deadlock occurs when both the power of Creation and of miscreation coexist. This is experienced as conflict only because the individual feels AS IF both were occurring AT THE SAME LEVEL. He BELIEVES in what he has created in his own unconscious and he naturally believes it is real BECAUSE he has created it. He, thus, places himself in a position where the fearful becomes REAL.

T 2 E 37. Nothing but level-confusion can result as long as this belief is held in ANY form. Inappropriate denial and equally inappropriate identification of the REAL factors in the basic conflict will NOT solve the problem itself. The conflict CANNOT disappear until it is fully recognized that miscreation is NOT real, and therefore there IS no conflict. This entails a full realization of the basic fact that, although man has miscreated in a very real sense, he need neither continue to do so, nor to suffer from his past errors in this respect.

T 2 E 38. A REDISTRIBUTION of psychic energy, then, is NOT the solution. Both the idea that both kinds MUST exist, and the belief that ONE kind is amenable for use or misuse, are real distortions. The ONLY way is to STOP MISCREATING NOW, and accept the Atonement for miscreations of the past. **T(110) -109** Only this can re-establish true single-mindedness. The structure of the psyche, as you very correctly noted yourself, follows along the lines of the particular libido concept the theorist employs. (I still think it was the other way around - - HS. Answer: This confusion arises out of the fact that you DID change the order - - several times in fact. Actually, it didn't matter, because the two concepts DO flow from each other. It was a TERRIFIC waste of time, and one in which I hardly care to become engaged myself. PLEASE!)

T 2 E 39. Freud's psyche was essentially a good and evil picture, with very heavy weight given to the evil. This is because every time I mentioned the Atonement to him, which was quite often, he responded by defending his theory more and more against it. This resulted in his increasingly strong attempts to make the illogical sound more and more logical.

T 2 E 40. I was very sorry about this, because his was a singularly good mind, and it was a shame to waste it. However, the major purpose of his incarnation was not neglected. He DID succeed in forcing recognition of the unconscious into man's calculations about himself, a step in the right direction which should not be minimized. Freud was one of the most religious men I have known recently. Unfortunately, he was so afraid of religion that the only way he could deal with it was to regard IT (not himself) as sick. This naturally prevented healing.

T 2 E 41. Freud's superego is a particularly interesting example of the real power of miscreation. It is noteworthy throughout the whole development of his theories that the superego never allied itself with freedom. The most it could do in this direction was to **T(111) -110** work out a painful truce in which both opponents LOST. This perception could not fail to force him to emphasize discontent in his view of civilization.

T 2 E 42. The Freudian id is really only the more superficial level of the unconscious, and not the deepest level at all. This, too, was inevitable, because Freud could not divorce miracles from magic. It was therefore his constant endeavor, (even preoccupation) to keep on thrusting more and more material between consciousness and the real deeper level of the unconscious, so that the latter became increasingly obscured. The result was a kind of bedlam, in which there was no order, no control, and no sense. This was exactly how he FELT about it.

T 2 E 43. The later theoretical switch to the primacy of anxiety was an interesting device intended to deny both the instinctive nature of destructiveness, and the force of the power of miscreation. By placing the emphasis on the RESULT, the generative nature of the power was minimized.

T 2 E 44. Destructive behavior IS instinctual. The instinct for creation is NOT obliterated in miscreation. That is why it is always invested with reality. *One of the chief ways in which man can correct his magic-miracle confusion is to remember that he did not create

---

[124] NOV. 16

himself. He is apt to forget this when he becomes egocentric, and this places him in a position where belief in magic is virtually inevitable. His instincts for creation were given him by his own Creator, who was expressing the same instinct in His Creation. Since the creative ability rests solely in the mind, everything which man creates is necessarily instinctive.[125] **T(112) -111**[126] IV

T 2 E 45. (This goes after basic conflict theory.) (Dictated without notes by HS)

T 2 E 46. We have already said that the basic conflict is one between love and fear, and that the proper organization of the psyche rests on a lack of level confusion. The section on psychic energy should be re-read very carefully, because it is particularly likely to be misinterpreted until this section is complete.

T 2 E 47. It has already been said that man CANNOT control fear, because he himself created it. His belief in it renders it out of his control by definition. For this reason, any attempt to resolve the basic conflict through[127] the concept of mastery of fear is meaningless. In fact, it asserts the power of fear by the simple assumption that it need be mastered at all.

T 2 E 48. The essential resolution rests entirely on the mastery of love. In the interim, conflict is inevitable. The reason for this is the strangely illogical position in which man had placed himself. Since we have frequently emphasized that correction must be applied within the level that error occurs, it should be clear that the miracle MUST be illogical because its purpose is to correct the illogical and restore order.

T 2 E 49. Two concepts which CANNOT coexist are nothing and everything. To whatever extent one is believed in, the other HAS BEEN abolished. In the conflict, fear is really nothing, and love is really everything. (This recognition is really the basis for the castration complex.) This is because whenever light penetrates darkness,[128] it DOES abolish it. The unwillingness to be seen, or submit error to light, is spuriously associated with active doing. In this incarnation, this can take the form of oedipal involvement and concomitant castration anxiety. **T(113) -112**

T 2 E 50. However, in more long range and meaningful terms, the oedipal complex is a miniature of the true Separation fear, and the castration complex is a way of denying that it ever occurred. Like all pseudo-solutions, this kind of distorted thinking is very creative, but false. The Separation HAS occurred. To deny this is merely to misuse denial. However, to concentrate on error is merely a further misuse of legitimate psychic mechanisms. The true corrective procedure, which has already been described as the proper use of the spiritual eye (or true vision), is to accept the error temporarily, <u>BUT ONLY</u> as an indication that <u>IMMEDIATE</u> correction is mandatory. This establishes a state of mind in which the Atonement can be accepted without delay.

T 2 E 51. It is worth repeating that ultimately there is no compromise possible between everything and nothing. The purpose of time is essentially a device by which all compromise in this respect can be abolished. It seems to be abolished by degrees precisely because time itself involves a concept of intervals which do[129] not really exist. The faulty use of creation has made this necessary as a corrective device.

T 2 E 52. "And God so loved the world that He gave his only begotten Son so that whosoever believeth on Him shall not perish but have Eternal Life"[130] needs only one slight correction to be entirely meaningful in this context. It should read "And God so loved the world that he gave it TO His only begotten Son." It should be noted that God HAS begotten only ONE Son. **T(114) 113** If you believe that all of the Souls that God created ARE His Sons, and if you also believe that the Sonship is One, then every Soul MUST be a Son of God, or an integral part of the Sonship. You do not find the concept that the whole is greater than its parts difficult to understand. You should therefore not have too great difficulty with this. The Sonship in its Oneness DOES transcend the sum of its parts. However, it loses this special state as long as any of its parts are missing. This is why the conflict cannot ultimately be resolved UNTIL all of the individual parts of the Sonship have returned. Only then, in the true sense, can the meaning of wholeness be understood.

T 2 E 53. The concept of minus numbers has always been regarded as a mathematical rather than an actual expedient. (This is a major limitation on mathematics as presently understood.) Any statement which implies degrees of difference in negation is essentially meaningless. What can replace this negative approach is a recognition of the fact that as long as one part (which is the same as a million or ten or eight thousand parts) of the Sonship is missing, it is NOT complete.

T 2 E 54. In the Divine psyche, the Father and the Holy Spirit are not incomplete at all. The Sonship has the unique faculty of believing in error, or incompleteness, if he so elects. However, it is quite apparent that so to elect IS to believe in the existence of nothingness. The correction of this error **T(115) -114** is the Atonement.

T 2 E 55. We have already briefly spoken about readiness. But there are some additional awarenesses which might be helpful. Readiness is nothing more than the prerequisite for accomplishment. The two should not be confused. As soon as a state of readiness occurs, there is always some will to accomplish, but this is by no means undivided. The state does not imply more than the potential for a shift of will. Confidence cannot develop fully until mastery has been accomplished. We began this section with an attempt to correct the fundamental human error that fear can be mastered. The Correction was that ONLY love can be mastered. When I told you that you were "ready for Revelation", I did not mean that you had in any way mastered this form of communication. However, you yourself attested to your readiness by insisting that I would not have said so if it had not been true. This IS an affirmation of readiness. Mastery of love necessarily involves a much more complete confidence in the ability than either of you has attained. But the readiness at least is an indication that you believe this is possible. This is only the beginning of confidence.

T 2 E 56. In case this be misunderstood as a statement that an enormous amount of time will be necessary between readiness and mastery, I would again remind you that time and space are under My control. **T(116) -115** (Dictated without notes by HS)

T 2 E 57. One of the chief ways in which man can correct his magic-miracle confusion is to remember that he did not create himself. He is apt to forget this when he becomes egocentric, and this places him in a position where belief in magic is virtually inevitable. His instincts for creation were given him by his own Creator, who was expressing the same instinct in His Creation. Since the creative ability rests solely in the mind, everything which man creates is necessarily instinctive. **T(117) -116**

T 2 E 58. It also follows that whatever he creates is real in his own eyes, but not necessarily in the sight of God. This basic distinction leads us directly into the real meaning of the Last Judgment. (I am

---

[125] Starting at the fourth sentence, (*) the rest of this paragraph is crossed out. The material shows up again on page 116 prefaced with the words "Dictated without notes by HS." **T 2 E 57** This has not been located in the *Notes*.
[126] Nov. 20, '65
[127] The shorthand form "thru" appears in the *Urtext* manuscript
[128] 1 John 1:5 This is the message which we have heard from Him and declare to you, that God is light and in Him is no darkness at all.
[129] *Urtext* manuscript has "does not" but it appears that the "intervals" do not exist, not the "concept of intervals." *HLC* also changes this to "do." This has not been located in the *Notes*.
[130] **John 3:16** "For God so loved the world that He gave His only Son, that whoever believes in Him should not perish but have everlasting life."

T 2 F. The Meaning of the Last Judgment (*Notes* not present in the Notes)

T 2 F 1. The Final Judgment is one of the greatest threat concepts in man's perception. This is only because he does not understand it. Judgment is not an essential attribute of God. Man brought judgment into being only because of the Separation. God Himself is still the God of mercy. After the Separation, however, there WAS a place for justice in the schema, because it was one of the many learning devices which had to be built into the overall plan. Just as the Separation occurred over many millions of years, the Last Judgment will extend over a similarly long period, and perhaps even longer. Its length depends, however, on the effectiveness of the present speed-up. We have frequently noted that the miracle is a device for shortening but not abolishing time. If a sufficient number of people become truly miracle-minded quickly, the shortening process can be almost immeasurable. But it is essential that these individuals free themselves from fear sooner than would ordinarily be the case, because they MUST emerge from basic conflict it they are to bring peace to the minds of others. **T(118) -117**

T 2 F 2. The Last Judgment is generally thought of as a procedure undertaken by God. Actually, it will be undertaken solely by man, with My help. It is a Final Healing, rather than a meting out of punishment, however much man may think punishment is deserved. Punishment as a concept is in total opposition to Right-Mindedness. The aim of the Final Judgment is to RESTORE Right-Mindedness TO man.

T 2 F 3. The Final Judgment might be called a process of Right-evaluation. It simply means that finally all men must come to understand what is worthy and what is not. After this, their ability to choose can be reasonably directed. Unless this distinction has been made, the vacillations between free and imprisoned will cannot but continue. The first step toward freedom, then, MUST entail a sorting out of the false from the true. This is a process of division only in the constructive sense, and reflects the true meaning of the Apocalypse. Man will ultimately look upon his own creations, and will to preserve only what is good, just as God Himself once looked upon what he had created, and knew that it WAS good.[131] At this point, the Will will begin to look with love on its creations, because of their great worthiness. The mind will inevitably disown its miscreations, and having withdrawn belief from them, they will no longer exist.

T 2 F 4. The term Last Judgment is frightening, not only because it has been falsely projected onto God, but also because of the association of "Last" with death. This is an outstanding example of upside down perception. Actually, if it is examined objectively, it is quite apparent that it is really the doorway to life. No man who lives in fear is really alive. **T(119) -118**

T 2 F 5. His own final judgment cannot be directed toward himself, because he is not his own creation. He can apply it meaningfully, and at any time, to everything he has ever created, and retain in his real memory only what is good. This is what his own Right-Mindedness CANNOT BUT dictate. The purpose of time is solely to "give him time" to achieve this judgment. It is his own perfect judgment of his own creation. When everything that he retains is lovable, there is no reason for any fear to remain in him. This IS his part in the Atonement. **T(120) 119**

---

[131] **Genesis 1:31** Then God saw everything that He had made, and indeed it was very good. So the evening and the morning were the sixth day.

CHAPTER 3 – RETRAINING THE MIND

T 3 A. Introduction (*Notes* 296 5:145)

T 3 A 1. All learning involves attention and study at some level. This course is a MIND-TRAINING course. Good students assign study periods for themselves. However, since this obvious step has not occurred to you, and since we are cooperating in this, I will make the obvious assignment now.

T 3 A 2. B is better at understanding the need to study the notes than you are, but neither of you realizes that many of the problems you keep being faced with may ALREADY have been solved there. YOU do not think of the notes in this way at all. B DOES from time to time, but he generally says, "It's probably in the notes," and DOESN'T look it up. He believes that, although he reads them over, they cannot REALLY help him until they are complete.

T 3 A 3. First of all, he cannot be sure of this unless he tries. Second, they would BE completed if both of you so willed.

T 3 A 4. You vaguely know that the course is intended for some sort of preparation. I can only say that you are not prepared.

T 3 A 5. I was amused when you reminded B. that he, too, was being prepared for something quite unexpected, and he said, he was not at all curious about what it was. This disinterest is very characteristic of him when he is afraid. Interest and fear do NOT go together, as your respective behavior clearly shows.

T 3 A 6. Mental retardation is a defense which, like the others EXCEPT the Atonement, can be used on behalf of error or truth, as elected. When it occurs in REALITY, it is a temporary device, agreed on beforehand, to check the miscreative abilities of strong but misdirected wills.

T 3 A 7. It is necessary that this appropriate use of the defense BE considered real, because otherwise it cannot serve. The lesson involves not only the individual himself, but also his parents, siblings, and all of those who come in close relation with him. **T(121) -120** The VALUE of the experience depends on the need of each particular learner. The person himself is a POOR learner, by definition, only as a step toward changing from a bad to a good one.

T 3 A 8. Mental retardation can also be used as a maladaptive defense, if the wrong (or attack) side is employed. This produces the "pseudo-retardation syndrome" which is justly classified as a psychiatric (or disturbed-level) symptom. Both of you do this all the time. B. acts as if he does not understand even his OWN special language, let alone mine, and you cannot read at all.

T 3 A 9. This represents a joint attack on both yourselves AND me, because it renders YOUR mind weak, and mine incompetent. Remember, this puts you in a truly fearful position. If you cannot understand either your own mind OR mine, you do not KNOW what is really willed. It is thus IMPOSSIBLE to avoid conflict, as defined before, because even if you act ACCORDING TO will, you wouldn't know it.

T 3 A 10. The next part of this course rests too heavily on the earlier part not to REQUIRE its study. Without this, you will become much too fearful when the unexpected DOES occur to make constructive use of it. However, as you study the notes, you will see some of the obvious implications, unless you still persist in misusing the defense of mental retardation. Please remember that its constructive use, described above, is hardly a REAL part of your own REAL proper equipment. It is a <u>PARTICULARLY</u>[132] inappropriate defense as you use it, and I can only urge you to avoid it.

T 3 A 11. The reason why a solid foundation is necessary at this point is because of the highly likely confusion of "fearful" and "awesome," which most people do make. You will remember that we said once before that awe is inappropriate in connection with the Sons of God, because you should not experience awe in the presence of your own equals.[133] **T(122) -121** But it WAS emphasized that awe IS a proper reaction of the Soul in the presence of its Creator.

T 3 A 12. So far, this course has had only indirect recourse to God, and rarely even refers to Him directly. I have repeatedly emphasized that awe is not appropriate in connection with me, BECAUSE of our inherent equality. I have been careful to clarify my own role in the Atonement, without either over or understating it. I have tried to do exactly the same things in connection with yours.

T 3 A 13. The next step, however, DOES involve the direct approach to God Himself. It would be most unwise to start on this step at all without very careful preparation, or awe will surely be confused with fear, and the experience will be more traumatic than beatific.

T 3 A 14. Healing is of God in the end. The means are carefully explained in the notes. Revelation has occasionally SHOWN you the end, but to reach it the means are needed. **T(123) -122**

T 3 A 15.(The following Introduction dictated by HS without notes.) The following is the only detailed description which need be written down as to how error interferes with preparation. The events specifically referred to here could be any events, nor does their particular influence matter. It is the process which is to be noted here, and not its results. The kind of beliefs, and the fallacious premises involved in misthought are as well exemplified here as elsewhere. There is nothing of special interest about the events described below, EXCEPT their typical nature. If this is a true course in mind-training, then the whole value of this section rests ONLY in showing you what NOT to do. The more constructive emphasis is, of course, on the positive approach. Mind-watching would have prevented any of this from occurring, and will do so any time you permit it to.

T 3 A 16.(Following is from notes) Tell B. that the reason why he was so strained yesterday is because he allowed himself a number of fear-producing attitudes. They were fleeting enough to be more will-of-the-wisps than serious will-errors, but unless he watches this kind of thing, he WILL find the notes fearful, and, knowing him well, will mis-distantiate. His unprovoked irritation was unpardonable EXCEPT by himself, and he did not choose to pardon it. YOU did, but I am afraid you were under some strain in doing so. This was unfortunate, and weakened your own ability to behave healingly toward B. at the time, and later also toward Louis, both of whom DID act stupidly. But one stupidity at a time is usually enough. You are getting too close to the misuse of mental retardation when stupidity sets in all around.

T 3 A 17. B., having already weakened himself, was very un-miracle-minded, first by not asking Dora if she wanted a lift in the cab, which was going her way. Even if she didn't want it, she would have been able to use the thought well. There is probably no human error that is **T(124) -123** more fear-provoking (in the will/behavior conflict sense) than countering any form of error with error. The result can be highly inflammable. By reacting to Dora's stupidity with his own, all of the elements which are virtually certain to engender fear have been provided.

T 3 A 18. B should note that this is one of the few times that he had to wait for a cab. He thought he took care of it by holding the door of a cab which did come for that lady, but he was misguided in this belief. Beliefs are THOUGHTS, and thus come under Christ-guidance, NOT control. Actually, by giving this cab to her, he was

---

[132] *Urtext* manuscript has lower case underlined. It is underlined in the *Notes* also, which is how emphasis is indicated in that document.

[133] Miracle Principle 41 (**1 C 0 41**)

very unkind to you. It was quite apparent that you were extremely cold, and also very late. The idea that giving her the cab would atone for his previous errors was singularly out of place, and well calculated to lead to further error. If, instead of attempting to atone on his own, he had asked for guidance, there would have been no difficulty whatever in the cab situation. It was not necessary that anyone wait at all.

T 3 A 19. B's original slight to Dora, because of his own need to get home as he perceived it, stopped him from benefiting from the time-saving device of the miracle. He would have gotten home MUCH quicker if he had taken time to use time properly.

T 3 A 20. YOU were still suffering from strain (see above), and got quite irritated at the girl who stood next to the door on the side which blocked its opening. Her presence there made it necessary each time the door was opened to hold it for a much longer time than was necessary, and you were angry because this made you cold. Actually, the girl was taking care of the younger child who was standing outside, and both of them were really mentally retarded. If you will remember, the older girl asked you very uncertainly about the bus, and you were well aware at the time of her extreme uncertainty. **T(125) -124**

T 3 A 21. It would have been much wiser had you built up her confidence, instead of associating with her stupidity. This reduced your own efficiency, and the only thing that saved you then was that you DID remember, in the cab, to ask me about the notes, instead of assuming that you were necessarily to arrange to meet the next day and go over them. B. had already become so misguided that it did not occur to him that his own will, (which he justified by the contents of the recent notes —a misuse of truth only seemingly on its own behalf) might be questionable. (You took poor notes yourself here, because you got mad at him on remembering this. While you did try to will right in the cab, you did not quite succeed. The error is showing up now.)

T 3 A 22. B thus placed himself in a condition to experience a fear rather than a love reaction. (HS notes that she was going to write "an excellent position," but did not do so. Answer: You were right about the misuse of "excellent" here, and please do cross it out. You are STILL angry. An excellent position for miscreation is not a meaningful approach to the problem.)

T 3 A 23. It was ~~indeed~~[134] discourteous ("indeed" is not necessary; it was your OWN error here; I am NOT saying this with any harsh overtones at all. I am just trying to create better learning conditions for the study periods. We want as little interference as possible, for VERY good reasons.)

T 3 A 24. Now, go back to B; he WAS discourteous when he told you that HE wanted to keep the original copy of the notes, having decided to have them Xeroxed on his OWN will, and then justifying it by a very slight misinterpretation of what I said about "useful for others." In fact, if he will re-read the actual quote, he will see that it REALLY means "useful for HIM." YOU had interpreted it[135] that way, and frankly this was pretty clear to me at the time. **T(126) -125** But this sort of thing happens all the time. It should, be noted, however, that the result was not only considerable and totally unnecessary planning on B's part, but also a failure to utilize what WAS intended for him as a help for HIMSELF. And before YOU get too self-satisfied, I would remind you that you do it all the time, too.

T 3 A 25. B. acted inappropriately toward YOU, by saying that he wanted to be SURE that the original was not lost or dirty. It is noticeable that, having already decided what HE wanted to do, it never occurred to him that it IS possible that HE might lose or dirty them himself, especially as he had not entrusted them to me. This is a form of arrogance that he would be much happier without. He should also note that this would probably not have occurred had he not been ALREADY literally "off the beam." Be SURE to tell him that this pun is to reassure him that I am not angry. If he does not get it, or does not like it, I KNOW it is not very good. The reason is that HE put me in a position where I can really give him very little at the moment.

T 3 A 26. But I want him to know that I am VERY well aware of the exceedingly few times he now makes errors of this kind. He has come a VERY long way in this respect. It seems a shame that he should allow himself even this much discomfort from it.

T 3 A 27. I suggest to YOU that we pray for him, and I pray for your full cooperation in this. This will correct YOUR errors, and help him react better to the work on the bookcase, which may otherwise lend itself for misuse by misprojection. There would have been no problem at all about the bookcase, and perhaps even no bookcase, if the solution of the storage problem had been left to me. I have promised to guide you OUT of problems, and will certainly not create them for you. But this means that you do not undertake to solve them yourselves. A storage problem is hardly more difficult for me to solve that a space problem, (see comments under special principles for miracle workers.) **T(127) -126**

T 3 A 28. You started well in your attempt to pray with me for B., but ended badly. This is because you had already made a number of earlier errors. You were wrong to be pleased with Bill F's criticism of Rose, and should not have enjoyed Bill F's description of Zanvil's caricaturing of her. You could have laughed WITH Bill, but NOT AT Rose. Real courtesy NEVER does this. You should know that all God's children are fully worthy of COMPLETE courtesy. You should NEVER join with one at the EXPENSE of another.

T 3 A 29. When you called B about joining you, Gene, & Anne at lunch, YOU should have waited to ask ME. In fact, you should not even have told Anne that you would call. Then you could have asked B. FIRST if HE would want to come, and called ANNE back. It is true that it was better that he came, but this has nothing to do with the real issue. There are ways of treating others in which ONLY consistent courtesy, even in very little things, is offered. This is a VERY HEALING habit to acquire.

T 3 A 30. B's answer to your call was a clear statement of his own sadly conflicted state. He said, "I don't want to join you, but that's ungracious, so I'll go." Whenever ANY invitation to join others in a gracious way is offered, it should ALWAYS be met with respect, although it need not always be accepted. However, if it is MET ungraciously the resulting feeling may well be one of coercion. This is ALWAYS a split-will reaction.

T 3 A 31. B. did not solve this by ACTING graciously. The lunch need not have entailed either mental or physical strain for him, and no "need to escape" should have arisen. This was a regression of the unprofitable kind. B. will continue to experience this need from time to time, until he is willing to realize that there is nothing he needs or wants to escape from.

T 3 A 32. It is very hard to get out of the chain of miscreation which can arise out of even the simplest mis-thought. To borrow one of your own phrases, "This kind of human tragedy is far easier to avert than to undo." **T(128) -127**

T 3 A 33. You must both learn not to let this kind of chain reaction START. You will NOT be able to control it once it has started, because everything and everyone will be pulled into the misprojection, and misinterpreted accordingly. NOTHING is lovely to the unloving. This is because they are CREATING ugliness.

T 3 A 34. You, Helen, were definitely not acting right-mindedly by writing these notes right in front of Jonathan. (Note that you wrote his name as "Jonathan" this time, although previously in these same notes you referred to him as "Louis," intentionally using his real name. Actually, of course, it does not matter what you call him, but

---
[134] *Urtext* manuscript has the word "indeed" crossed out, as does the *Notes*.
[135] *Urtext* manuscript does not have "it" here but the *Notes* does and it is clearly needed.

NOTE that you FELT FREE at that time to CHOOSE the name YOU preferred to use. This time, you were FORCED to call him "Jonathan" because you were ATTACKING him when you took the notes in front of him, and are now falling back on the magical device of "protecting his name."

T 3 A 35. (I had been considering calling B rather ambivalently, and had gotten up to do so, but remembered to ask. The answer was to call him at 8:30. It would be better if HE called, but he may not decide to do so. If he does not, you should try to get through, and if he has decided NOT to be there, just leave a message that it is not important. This is still a kindly gesture, and the message should be put in a gentle way.) (B. did call HS)

T 3 A 36. Without going into further elaboration, and we could devote many hours to this, lets consider all the time that we had to waste today. AND all the notes that could have been devoted to a better purpose than undoing the waste, and thus creating further waste. There IS a better use for time, too. I would have liked to have spent some time on corrections of the past notes, as an important step before reviewing them. A major point of clarification is necessary in connection with the phrase "replacing hatred (or fear) with love." T(129) -128

T 3 A 37. (No, Helen, do NOT check this against the prayer that B. very kindly typed for you on the card. That WAS a gracious offering on his part, and YOU also accepted it with grace at the time. Why should you deprive yourself of the value of the offering by referring this correction first to HIM?)

T 3 A 38. (These notes did not continue at this time, due to the obvious fact that HS was still clearly not in her right mind. However, B later suggested that "correct" or "correct for" should be used instead of "replace." At the time, he was quite sure about this, and he was perfectly right. The reason why it was essential that HE make this correction was that the word "replace" was his choice originally, and reflected a temporary misunderstanding of his own. It was, however, both courteous and necessary that he change this himself, both as a sign of his own better understanding, and of an avoidance of correction by someone else, which would have been discourteous.) T(130) -129 [136]

T 3 B. Special Principles for Miracle Workers (*Notes* 312 5:161)

T 3 B 1. The miracle abolishes the need for lower order concerns. Since it is an illogical, or out-of-pattern time interval, by definition, the ordinary considerations of time and space do not apply.

T 3 B 1a. For example, I do NOT regard time as you and B. do, and Kolb's space problem is NOT mine. When YOU perform a miracle, I will arrange both time and space to adjust to it.[137]

T 3 B 2. Clear distinction between what HAS BEEN Created and what IS BEING created is essential. ALL forms of correction (or healing) rest on this FUNDAMENTAL correction in level perception.

T 3 B 3. Another way of stating 2) is: NEVER confuse right with wrong-mindedness. Responding to ANY form of miscreation with anything EXCEPT a DESIRE TO HEAL (or a miracle) is an expression of this confusion.

T 3 B 4. The miracle is ALWAYS a DENIAL of this error, and an affirmation of the truth. Only Right-Mindedness CAN create in a way that has any real effect. Pragmatically, what has no real effect, has no real existence. Its REAL effect, then, is emptiness. Being without substantial content, it lends itself to projection.

T 3 B 5. The level-adjustment power of the miracle creates the right perception for healing. Until this has occurred, healing cannot be understood. Forgiveness is an empty gesture, unless it entails correction. Without this, it is essentially judgmental, rather than healing. T(131) -130

T 3 B 6. Miraculous forgiveness is ONLY correction. It has no element of judgment at all. "Father forgive them for they know not what they do"[138] in NO way EVALUATES what they do. It is strictly limited to an appeal to God to HEAL their minds. There is no reference to the outcome of their misthought. THIS does not matter.

T 3 B 7. The Biblical injunction "Be of one mind"[139] is the statement for REVELATION readiness. My OWN injunction "Do this in remembrance of me"[140] is the request for cooperation in miracle-workers. It should be noted that the two statements are not in the same order of reality, because the latter involves a time awareness, since memory implies recalling the PAST in the present.

T 3 B 8. Time is under MY direction, but Timelessness belongs to God alone. In time, we exist for and with each other. In Timelessness, we coexist with God. T(132) -131[141]

T 3 C. Atonement without Sacrifice (*Notes* 317 5:166)

T 3 C 1. There is one more point which must be perfectly clear before any residual fear which may still be associated with miracles becomes entirely groundless. The Crucifixion did NOT establish the Atonement. The Resurrection did. This is a point which many very sincere Christians have misunderstood. Nobody who was free of the scarcity-fallacy could POSSIBLY have made this mistake.

T 3 C 2. If the Crucifixion is seen from an upside down point of view, it certainly does appear AS IF God permitted, and even encouraged, one of his Sons to suffer BECAUSE he was good. Many very devoted ministers preach this every day. This particularly unfortunate interpretation, which actually arose out of the combined misprojection of a large number of my own would-be followers, has led many people to be bitterly afraid of God.

T 3 C 3. This particularly anti-religious concept happens to enter into many religions, and this is neither by chance nor coincidence.

T 3 C 4. The real Christian would have to pause and ask "how could this be?" Is it likely that God Himself would be capable of the kind

---

[136] Sunday, Nov. 2
[137] The paragraphs in this segment are all numbered, except for this one, **T 3 B 1a**. While there is a paragraph break in the *Urtext* manuscript, it is not present in the *Notes* and appears to be a "copying artifact" and not an intentional edit or part of the original dictation. We thus preseved the manuscript's numbering of principles, which is also present in the *Notes*.
[138] **Luke 23:34** And Jesus said, "Father, forgive them; for they know not what they do." And parting his garments among them, they cast lots.
[139] **2 Corinthians 13:11** Finally, brethren, farewell. Become complete. Be of good comfort, be of one mind, live in peace; and the God of love and peace will be with you. Also **Philippians 2:1-8**
Philemon 2:1- 8 If there is therefore any comfort in Christ, if any consolation of love, if any fellowship of the Spirit, if any tender mercies and compassions, fulfill ye my joy, that ye be of the same mind, having the same love, being of one accord, **of one mind**; *doing* nothing through faction or through vainglory, but in lowliness of mind each counting other better than himself; not looking each of you to his own things, but each of you also to the things of others. Have this mind in you, which was also in Christ Jesus: who, being in the form of God, counted it not a prize to be on an equality with God, but emptied himself, taking the form of a servant, being made in the likeness of men; and being found in fashion as a man, he humbled himself, becoming obedient *even* unto death, yea, the death of the cross.
While there are other candidates; **Romans 15:5, Romans 12:16**; the passage in Philemon, which concludes with a reference to the crucifixion reflects the Course which immediately proceeds to discuss the crucifixion.
[140] **Luke 22:19** And he took bread, and gave thanks, and brake *it*, and gave unto them, saying, This is my body which is given for you: this do in remembrance of me.; Also **1 Corinthians 11:23-25**
[141] Nov. 22 Tuesday

of thinking which His own Words have clearly stated is unworthy of man?

T 3 C 5. (There are times when) The best defense, as always, is NOT to attack another's position, but rather to protect the truth. It is not necessary to consider anything acceptable, if you have to turn a whole frame of reference around in order to justify it. This procedure is painful in its minor **T(133) -132** applications, and genuinely tragic on a mass basis. Persecution is a frequent result, justifying the terrible misperception[142] that God Himself persecuted His own Son on behalf of salvation. The very words are meaningless.

T 3 C 6. It has always been particularly difficult to overcome this because, although the error itself is no harder to overcome than any other error, men were unwilling to give it up because of its prominent escape value. In milder forms, a parent says "This hurts me more than it hurts you," and feels exonerated in beating a child. Can you believe that the Father REALLY thinks this way?

T 3 C 7. It is so essential that all such thinking be dispelled that we must be VERY sure that NOTHING of this kind remains in your mind.[143] I was NOT punished because YOU were bad. The wholly benign lesson which the Atonement teaches is wholly lost if it is tainted with this kind of distortion in ANY form.

T 3 C 8. "Vengeance is Mine sayeth the Lord"[144] is strictly a karmic viewpoint. It is a real misperception of truth, by which man assigns his own evil past to God. The "evil conscience" from the past has nothing to do with God. He did not create it, and He does not maintain it. God does NOT believe in karmic retribution at all. His Divine mind does not create that way. HE does not hold the evil deeds of a man even against HIMSELF. Is it likely, then, that He would hold against any man the evil that ANOTHER did? **T(134) -133**

T 3 C 9. Be very sure that you recognize how impossible this assumption really is, and how ENTIRELY it arises from misprojection. This kind of error is responsible for a host of related fallacies, including the misbelief that God rejected man and forced him out of the Garden of Eden,[145] or that I am misdirecting you. I have made every effort to use words which are ALMOST impossible to distort, but man is very inventive when it comes to twisting symbols around.

T 3 C 10. God Himself is not symbolic; He is FACT. The Atonement, too, is totally without symbolism. It is perfectly clear, because it exists in light. Only man's attempts to shroud it in darkness have made it inaccessible to the unwilling, and ambiguous to the partly willing. The Atonement itself radiates nothing but truth. It therefore epitomizes harmlessness, and sheds ONLY blessing. It could not do this if it arose from anything other than perfect innocence! Innocence is wisdom, because it is unaware of evil, which does not exist. It is, however, PERFECTLY aware of EVERYTHING, that is true.

T 3 C 11. The Resurrection demonstrated that NOTHING can destroy truth. Good can withstand ANY form of evil, because light abolishes ALL forms of darkness.[146] The Atonement is thus the perfect lesson. It is the final demonstration that all of the other lessons which I taught are true. **T(135) -134**

T 3 C 12. Man is released from ALL errors if he believes in this. The deductive approach to teaching accepts the generalization which is applicable to ALL single instances, rather than building up the generalization after analyzing numerous single instances separately. If you can accept the ONE GENERALIZATION NOW, there will be no need to learn from many smaller lessons.

T 3 C 13. NOTHING can prevail against a Son of God who commends his Spirit into the hands of His Father.[147] By doing this, the mind awakens from its sleep, and the Soul remembers its Creator. All sense of Separation disappears, and level confusion vanishes. The Son of God IS part of the holy Trinity, but the Trinity Itself is One. There is no confusion within ITS levels, because they are of One Mind and One Will. This Single Purpose creates perfect integration, and establishes the (reign of the) Peace of God.

T 3 C 14. But this vision can be perceived only by the truly innocent. Because their hearts are pure, they defend true perception, instead of defending themselves AGAINST it. Understanding the lesson of the Atonement, they are without the will to attack, and therefore they see truly. This is what the Bible means when it says "(and) when He shall appear (or be perceived) we shall be like Him, for we shall see Him AS HE IS."[148] **T(136) -135**

T 3 C 15. Sacrifice is a notion totally unknown to God. It arises solely from fear of the Records.[149] This is particularly unfortunate, because frightened people are apt to be vicious. Sacrificing others in any way is a clear-cut violation of God's own injunction that man should be merciful even as His Father in Heaven is merciful.[150]

T 3 C 16. It has been harder for many Christians to realize that this commandment (or assignment) also applies to THEMSELVES. Good teachers never terrorize their students. To terrorize is to attack, and this results in rejection of what the teacher offers. This results in learning failures.

T 3 C 17. I have been correctly referred to in the Bible as "The Lamb of God who taketh away the sins of the world."[151] Those who represent the lamb as blood-stained (an all too widespread conceptual error) do NOT understand the meaning of the symbol.

T 3 C 18. Correctly understood, the symbol is a very simple parable, or teaching device, which merely depicts my innocence. The lion and the lamb lying down together[152] refers to the fact that strength and innocence are NOT in conflict, but naturally live in peace. "Blessed are the pure in heart for they shall see God"[153] is another way of saying the same thing. Only the innocent CAN see God.

T 3 C 19. There has been some controversy (in human terms) as to whether seeing is an attribute of the eyes, or an expression of the integrative powers of the brain. Correctly understood, the issue re-

---

[142] The *Notes* has "justified by the terrible misprojection"
[143] The *Urtext* manuscript has "minds" but the *Notes* has "minds."
[144] **Deuteronomy 32:35** Vengeance is Mine, and recompense; Their foot shall slip in due time; For the day of their calamity is at hand, And the things to come hasten upon them.'
Romans 12:19 Beloved, do not avenge yourselves, but rather give place to wrath; for it is written, "Vengeance is Mine, I will repay," says the Lord.
[145] **Genesis 3:23-24** Therefore the LORD God sent him out of the garden of Eden to till the ground from which he was taken. So He drove out the man; and He placed cherubim at the east of the garden of Eden, and a flaming sword which turned every way, to guard the way to the tree of life.
[146] **1 John 1:5** This is the message which we have heard from Him and declare to you, that God is light and in Him is no darkness at all.
[147] **Genesis 1:26-27** Then God said, "Let Us make man in Our image, according to Our likeness; let them have dominion over the fish of the sea, over the birds of the air, and over the cattle, over all the earth and over every creeping thing that creeps on the earth." So God created man in His own image; in the image of God He created him; male and female He created them.; Also: **Luke 23:46** And when Jesus had cried out with a loud voice, He said, "Father, "into Your hands I commit My spirit.'" Having said this, He breathed His last.
[148] **1 John 3:2** Beloved, now we are children of God; and it has not yet been revealed what we shall be, but we know that when He is revealed, we shall be like Him, for we shall see Him as He is.
[149] It is not entirely certain what the word "Records," capitalized, refers to but it may be the "Akashic Record."
[150] **Luke 6:36** "Be ye merciful, even as your Father is merciful."
[151] **John 1:29** On the morrow he seeth Jesus coming unto him, and saith, Behold, the Lamb of God, which taketh away the sin of the world!
[152] **Isaiah 11:6** "The wolf also shall dwell with the lamb, The leopard shall lie down with the young goat, The calf and the young lion and the fatling together; And a little child shall lead them."
[153] **Psalm 24:4** He who has clean hands and a pure heart, Who has not lifted up his soul to an idol, Nor sworn deceitfully.   Also: **Matthew 5:8** Blessed are the pure in heart, For they shall see God.

volves around the question of whether **T(137) -136** the body or the mind can see (or understand). This is not really open to question at all.

T 3 C 20. The body is not capable of understanding. Only the mind KNOWS anything. A pure mind knows the truth, and this IS its strength. It cannot attack the body, because it knows EXACTLY what the body IS. This is what "a sane mind in a sane body" really means.

T 3 C 21. A sane mind is NOT out for blood. It does not confuse destruction with innocence, because it associates innocence with strength, NOT with weakness. Innocence is INCAPABLE of sacrificing anything, because the innocent mind HAS everything and strives only to PROTECT its Wholeness. This is why it CANNOT misproject. It can only honor man, because honor is the NATURAL greeting of the truly loved to others who are LIKE them.

T 3 C 22. The lamb taketh away the sins of the world[154] only in the sense that the state of innocence or Grace, is one in which the meaning of the Atonement is perfectly apparent. The innocence of God is the true state of the mind of His Son. In this state, man's mind DOES see God, and because he sees Him as he Is, he knows that the Atonement, NOT sacrifice, is the ONLY appropriate gift to His OWN altar, where nothing except perfection truly belongs.[155] The understanding of the innocent is TRUTH. That is why their altars are truly radiant. **T(138) -137**

T 3 C 23. (Dictated directly without notes) pp 7-12 Though Christians generally (but by no means universally) recognize the contradiction involved in victimizing others, they are less adept at ensuring their own inability to victimize themselves. Although this appears to be a much more benign error from the viewpoint of society, it is nevertheless inherently dangerous because once a two-edged defense is used, its direction cannot be self-controlled.

T 3 C 24. B. recently observed how many ideas were condensed into relatively few pages here. This is because we have not been forced to dispel miscreations throughout. (There is one set of notes not yet transcribed which is devoted to this. These emphasize only the enormous waste of time that is involved.)[156] Cayce's notes, too, could have been much shortened. Their excessive length is due to two factors. The first involves a fundamental error which Cayce himself made, and which required constant undoing. The second is more related to the attitude of his followers. They are unwilling to omit anything he said. This is respectful enough, but not overly-judicious. I would be a far better editor, if they would allow me this position on their staff.

T 3 C 25. It is obvious that Cayce himself was not able to transcend the misperceptions of the need for sacrifice, or he could not possibly have been willing to sacrifice himself. Anyone who is unable to leave the requests of others unanswered has not entirely transcended egocentricity. **T(139) -138** I never "gave of myself" in this inappropriate way, nor would I ever have encouraged Cayce to do so.

T 3 C 26. Cayce could not see the Atonement as totally lacking in sacrifice at ANY level. It WAS obvious to him that the mind cannot be so limited. It was equally apparent to him that the Soul is merely unaffected by such an idea. This left him only the body with which to invest his misperception. This is also why he used his own mind at the "EXPENSE of his body."

T 3 C 27. Because Cayce was a somewhat erratic listener, he was compelled to correct his own errors at very great length, and not always adequately. Consider the basis from which he started, when he began with "yes, we have the body." It is noteworthy that in all these readings, a large section was actually devoted to the body, even though he usually concluded with the caution that the body cannot be healed by itself. It would have saved an enormous number of words if he had always begun with this.

T 3 C 28. Cayce and his devotion to me are in no way underestimated by the realization that he worked under very great strain, which is ALWAYS a sign that something is wrong. One of the difficulties inherent in trance states is that it is very difficult to overcome the split which the trance itself induces through the medium of communications made while in the trance state. **T(140) -139**

T 3 C 29. Cayce's whole approach put him in a real double-bind, from which he did not recover. When he spoke of a dream in which he saw his own rather immanent reincarnation, he was perfectly accurate. He was sufficiently attuned to real communication to make it easy to correct his errors, and free him to communicate without strain. It is noticeable throughout his notes that he frequently engaged in a fallacy that we have already noted in some detail: namely, the tendency to endow the physical with nonphysical properties. Cayce suffered greatly from this error. He did not make either of the other three. However, you will remember that it is this one which is particularly vulnerable to magical associations. Cayce's accuracy was so great that, even when he did this, he was able to apply it constructively. But it does not follow that this was a genuinely constructive approach.

T 3 C 30. It should also be noted that, when Cayce attempted to "see" the body in proper perspective, he saw physically discernible auras surrounding it. This is a curious compromise, in which the nonphysical attributes of the self are approached AS IF they could be seen with the physical eye.

T 3 C 31. Cayce's illiteracy never stood in his way. This is because illiteracy does not necessarily imply any lack of love, and in Cayce's case very definitely did not. He therefore had no difficulty at all in overcoming this seeming limitation. **T(141) -140** What DID hamper him was a profound sense of personal unworthiness, which, characteristically enough, was sometimes over-compensated for in what might be called a Christian form of grandiosity. Cayce was essentially uncharitable to himself. This made him very erratic in his own miracles, and, because he was genuinely anxious to help others, left himself in a highly vulnerable position.

T 3 C 32. His son comments both on the rather erratic nature of the Cayce household, and also on the rather uneven nature of Cayce's temper. Both of these observations are true, and clearly point to the fact that Cayce did not apply the Peace of God to himself. Once this had occurred, particularly in a man whose communication channels were open, it was virtually impossible for him to escape external solutions. Cayce was a very religious man, who should have been able to escape fear through religion. Being unable to apply his religion wholeheartedly to himself, he was forced to accept certain magical beliefs which were alien to his own Christianity. This is why he was so different when he was asleep, and even disowned what he said in this state.

T 3 C 33. The lack of integration which this split state implies is clearly shown in certain off-the-mark detours into areas such as the effects of stones on the mind, and some curious symbolic attempt to integrate churches and glands. (This is hardly more peculiar than some of your own confusion.) **T(142) -141**

T 3 C 34. Cayce's mind was imprisoned to some extent by an error against which you have been cautioned several times. He looked to the past for an EXPLANATION of the present, but he never succeeded in separating the past FROM the present. When he said "mind is the builder," he did not realize that it is only what it is building NOW that really creates the future. The past, in itself, does not have the ability to do this. Whenever we move from one instant

---

[154] **John 1:29** On the morrow he seeth Jesus coming unto him, and saith, "Behold, the Lamb of God, which taketh away the sin of the world!"
[155] **Hosea 6:6** For I desire mercy and not sacrifice, And the knowledge of God more than burnt offerings. Also: **Matthew 9:13** But go and learn what this means: "I desire mercy and not sacrifice. For I did not come to call the righteous, but sinners, to repentance."
[156] it is not clear if that set of notes was ever transcribed, or if it has survived at all.

to the next, the previous one no longer exists. In considering the body as the focus for healing, Cayce was expressing his own failure to accept this AS ACCOMPLISHED. He did not fail to recognize the value of the Atonement for others, but he did fail to accept its corrective merit for himself.

T 3 C 35. As we have frequently emphasized, man CANNOT control his own errors. Having created them, he does believe in them. Because of his failure to accept his own perfect freedom FROM the past, Cayce could not really perceive others as similarly free. This is why I have not wholly endorsed the Cayce documents for widespread use.

T 3 C 36. I am heartily supportive of the ARE's endeavor to make Cayce's singular contributions immortal, but it would be most unwise to have them promulgated as a faith until they have been purged of their essential errors. This is why **T(143) -142** there have been a number of unexplained set backs in their explication. It is also one of the many reasons why the Cayce material, a major step in the speedup, must be properly understood before it can be meaningfully validated.

T 3 C 37. Cayce's son has been wise in attempting to deal with reliability, which in Cayce's case is very high. There is a way of validating the material, and Hugh Lynn is perfectly aware that this must be done eventually. He is also aware of the fact that he is unable to do it. In the present state of the material, it would be most unwise even to attempt it. There is too much that IS invalid. When the time comes that this can be corrected to the point of real safety, I assure you it will be accomplished. In tribute to Cayce, I remind you that no effort is wasted, and Cayce's effort was very great.

T 3 C 38. It would be most ungrateful of me if I allowed his work to produce a generation of witch doctors. I am sorry that Cayce himself could not rid himself of a slight tendency in this direction. But fortunately I have a fuller appreciation of him than he had.

T 3 C 39. I am repeating here a Biblical injunction of my own, already mentioned elsewhere, that if my followers eat any deadly thing it shall not hurt them.[157] This is what Cayce could NOT believe, because he could not see that, as a Son of God, he WAS invulnerable. **T(144) -143**

T 3 D. Miracles as Accurate Perception (*Notes* not present in the Notes)

(DICTATED WITHOUT NOTES[158])

T 3 D 1. We have repeatedly stated that the basic concepts referred to throughout the notes are NOT matters of degree. Certain fundamental concepts CANNOT be meaningfully understood in terms of co-existing polarities. It is impossible to conceive of light and darkness, or, everything and nothing, as joint possibilities. They are all true OR all false. It is absolutely essential that you understand completely that behavior is erratic until a firm commitment to one or the other is made.

T 3 D 2. A firm commitment to darkness or nothingness is impossible. Nobody has ever lived who has not experienced some light and some of everything. This has made everybody really unable to deny truth totally, even if he deceives himself in this connection most of the time. That is why those who live largely in darkness and emptiness never find any lasting solace. (This really answers B's question about whether people return voluntarily.)

T 3 D 3. Innocence is also not a partial attribute. It is not a real defense UNTIL it is total. When it is partial, it is characterized by the same erratic nature that holds for other two-edged defenses. The partly innocent are apt to be quite stupid at times. It is not until their innocence is a genuine viewpoint which is universal in its application that it becomes wisdom.

T 3 D 4. Innocent (or true) perception means that you NEVER misperceive, and ALWAYS see truly. More simply, this means that you never see what does not exist in reality. Whenever you lack confidence in what someone else will do, you are attesting to your belief that he is not in his Right Mind. This is hardly a miracle-based frame of reference. It also has the disastrous effect of denying (incorrect use) the essentially creative power of the miracle. The miracle perceives everything AS IT IS. If nothing but the truth exists (and this is really redundant **T(145) -144** in statement, because what is not true CANNOT exist) Right-Minded seeing cannot see ANYTHING BUT perfection. We have said many times that ONLY what God creates, or what man creates with the same will, has any real existence. This, then, is all that the innocent can see. They do not suffer from the delusions of the Separated ones.

T 3 D 5. The way to correct all such delusions is to withdraw your faith from them, and invest it ONLY in what is true. To whatever extent you side with false perception in yourself or others, you are validating a basic misperception. You CANNOT validate the invalid. I would suggest that you voluntarily give up all attempts to do so, because they can be only frantic. If you are willing to validate what is true in everything you perceive, you will make it true for you.

T 3 D 6. Remember that we said that truth overcomes ALL error. This means that if you perceive truly, you are canceling out misperceptions in yourself AND others simultaneously. Because you see them as they were really created and can really create, you offer them your own validation of THEIR truth. This is the real healing which the miracle actively creates.

T 3 D 7. (Reply to HS question: Is this all? The reason why this is so short, despite its extreme importance, is because it is not symbolic. This means that it is not open to more than one interpretation.) **(146) -145** This means that it is unequivocal. It also explains the quotation which you have never gotten correctly in complete form before: "But this we know, that when He shall appear (or be perceived) we shall be like Him for we shall see Him as He is. And every man that hath this hope in him purifieth himself even as He is pure."[159] Every man DOES have the hope that he can see correctly, because the ability to do so is IN him. Man's ONLY hope IS to see things as they are). **T(147) -146**[160]

T 3 E. Perception versus Knowledge (*Notes* 328 5:177)

T 3 E 1. (On Wed. evening, Nov. 24, HS had sudden flash of illumination and very much wanted to offer prayer for B., which she did as follows: "Jesus, help me see my brother (B.) as he really is, and thus release both him and me." HS also thought later: Every time there is anything unlovable that crosses one's mind (re sex, possession, etc.) you should immediately recognize that you do not want to hurt your brother.) On Thurs. morning, the prayer for the miracle occurred as follows stated above.)

T 3 E 2. You had a lot of trouble afterwards with the words (which are essentially irrelevant) partly because you were dissatisfied with yourself at the time, but also because you ARE confused about the difference between perception and cognition. You will note that we have said very little about cognition as yet. (Aside: One of the exceptions is in the correction formula for fear, which begins with KNOW first) The reason is because you must get your perceptions straightened out before you can KNOW anything.

---

[157] **Mark 16:18** they shall take up serpents, and if they drink any deadly thing, it shall in no wise hurt them; they shall lay hands on the sick, and they shall recover.
[158] Nov. 24, 1965
[159] **1 John 3:2-3** Beloved, now are we children of God, and it is not yet made manifest what we shall be. We know that, if he shall be manifested, we shall be like him; for we shall see him even as he is. And every one that hath this hope *set* on him purifieth himself, even as he is pure.
[160] Friday, Nov. 26

T 3 E 3. To know is to be certain. Uncertainty merely means that you DON'T know. Knowledge is power BECAUSE it is certain, and certainty is strength. Perception is temporary. It is an attribute of the space-time belief, and is therefore subject to fear or love. Misperception produces fear, and true perception produces love. NEITHER produces certainty because all perception varies. That is why it is NOT knowledge. True perception is the BASIS for knowledge, but KNOWING is the affirmation of truth.

T 3 E 4. All of your difficulties ultimately stem from the fact that you do not recognize, or KNOW, yourselves, each other, or God. "Recognize" means "know again." This means that you knew before. (Note that it does not mean SAW before.) You can see in many ways, because perception involves different interpretations, and this means it is not whole. **T(148) -147** The miracle is a way of PERCEIVING, not a way of knowing. It is the right answer to a question, but you do not ask questions at all when you know.

T 3 E 5. Questioning delusions is the first step in undoing them. The miracle, or the right answer, corrects them. Since perceptions CHANGE, their dependence on time is obvious. They are subject to transitory states, and this implies variability by definition. How you perceive at any given time determines what you DO, and action MUST occur in time. Knowledge is timeless because certainty is not questionable. You KNOW when you have ceased to ask questions.

T 3 E 6. The "questioning mind" perceives itself in time, and therefore looks for FUTURE answers. The unquestioning mind is closed merely because it believes the future and the present will be the same. This establishes an unchanged state, or stasis. This is usually an attempt to counteract an underlying fear that the future will be WORSE than the present, and this fear inhibits the tendency to question at all.

T 3 E 7. Visions are the natural perception of the spiritual eye, but they are still corrections. B's question about the "spiritual eye" was a very legitimate one. The "spiritual eye" is symbolic, and therefore NOT a device for knowing. It IS, however, a means of right perception, which brings it into the proper domain of the miracle, but NOT of revelation. PROPERLY speaking, a "vision of God" is a miracle rather than a revelation. The fact that perception is involved at all removes the experience from the realm of knowledge. That is why these visions do not last. **T(149) -148**

T 3 E 8. The Bible instructs you to "KNOW thyself,"[161] or BE CERTAIN. Certainty is always of God. When you love someone, you have PERCEIVED him as he is, and this makes it possible for you to KNOW him. But it is not until you RECOGNIZE him that you KNOW him. Only then are you ABLE to stop asking questions about him.

T 3 E 9. While you ask questions about God, you are clearly implying that you do NOT know Him.[162] Certainty does not require action. When you say you are ACTING on the basis of sure knowledge, you are really confusing perception and cognition. Knowledge brings MENTAL strength for creative THINKING, but not for right doing.

T 3 E 10. Perception, miracles and doing are closely related. Knowledge is a result of revelation, and induces only thought (thinking). Perception involves the body even in its most spiritualized form. Knowledge comes from the altar within, and is timeless because it is certain. To perceive the truth is not the same as KNOWING it. This is why B. is having so much trouble in what he calls "integrating" the notes. His tentative perception is too uncertain for knowledge, because knowledge is SURE. Your perception is so variable that you swing from sudden but real knowledge to complete cognitive disorganization. This is why B. is more prone to irritation, while you are more vulnerable to rage. He is consistently BELOW his potential, while you achieve it at times and then swing very wide of the mark.

T 3 E 11. Actually, these differences do not matter. But I thought you might be glad to learn that you are much better off with DIFFERENT perceptual problems than you would be if you suffered from similar ones. This enables each of you to RECOGNIZE (and this is the **T(150) -149** right word here) that the misperceptions of the other are unnecessary. It is because you do not KNOW what to do about it that B. reacts to yours with irritation, and you respond to his with fury.

T 3 E 12. I repeat again that if you ATTACK error, you will hurt yourself. You do not RECOGNIZE each other when you attack. Attack is ALWAYS made on a stranger. You are MAKING him a stranger by misperceiving him, so that you CANNOT know him. It is BECAUSE you have made him into a stranger that you are afraid of him. PERCEIVE him correctly, so that your Soul can KNOW him.

T 3 E 13. Right perception is necessary before God can communicate DIRECTLY to his own altars, which he has established in His Sons. There he can communicate His certainty, and His KNOWLEDGE will bring the peace WITHOUT question.

T 3 E 14. God is not a stranger to His Own Sons, and His Sons are not strangers to each other. Knowledge preceded both perception and time, and will also ultimately replace (or correct for) them. This is the real meaning of the Biblical account of God as "Alpha and Omega, the Beginning and the End."[163] It also explains the quotation "Before Abraham WAS, I AM." Perception can and must be stabilized, but knowledge IS stable. "Fear God and keep His Commandments" is a real scribal error. It should read, "KNOW God and accept His certainty." (This error is why the commandments are all negative, in contrast to Christ's statement about "Thou shalt love."[164] etc.) There are no strangers in His Creation. To create as He Created, you can create only what you KNOW and accept as yours.

T 3 E 15. God knows His Children with perfect certainty. He Created them by knowing them. **T(151) -150** He recognizes them perfectly. When they do not recognize each other, they do not recognize Him. Brothers can misperceive one another, but they rarely maintain that they do not KNOW each other. This is possible only if they maintain that they are NOT really brothers. The Bible is VERY specific on this point. **T(152) -151**

T 3 F. Conflict and the Ego (*Notes* 339 5:188)

T 3 F 1. Most[165] of the abilities man now possesses are only shadows of his real strengths. The Soul knows, loves, and creates. These are its unequivocal functions. All of the functions of man are equivocal, or open to question or doubt. This is because he can no longer be certain how he will USE them. He is therefore incapable of knowledge, because he is uncertain. He is also incapable of true loving, because he can perceive lovelessly. He cannot create surely, because perception deceives, and illusions are not pure.[166]

---

[161] While the Bible arguably so instructs, it doesn't do it in those words that we can find.
[162] The *Urtext* manuscript has "him" with no capital. However, this pronoun clearly refers to God, the *Notes* has it capitalized, and the general scribal practice is to capitalize pronouns for persons of the Trinity.
[163] **John 8:58** Jesus said to them, "Most assuredly, I say to you, before Abraham was, I AM." ;
Also: **Revelation 21:6** And He said to me, "It is done! I am the Alpha and the Omega, the Beginning and the End. I will give of the fountain of the water of life freely to him who thirsts.;
Also: **Revelation 22:13** I am the Alpha and the Omega, the Beginning and the End, the First and the Last.
[164] **Matthew 22:37** Jesus said unto him, "Thou shalt love the Lord thy God with all thy heart, and with all thy soul, and with all thy mind."
[165] Saturday 11/27
[166] *Notes* has 'sure' here instead of 'pure' which seems more likely to be correct in the context.

T 3 F 2. Perception did not exist until the Separation had introduced degrees, aspects and intervals. The Soul has no levels, and ALL conflict arises from the concept of levels. Wars arise when some regard others as if they were on a different level. All interpersonal conflicts arise from this fallacy. Only the levels of the Trinity are capable of Unity. The levels which man created by the Separation are disastrous. They cannot BUT conflict. This is because one is essentially meaningless to another. Freud realized this perfectly, and that is why he conceived as forever irreconcilable the different levels of his psyche. They were conflict-prone by definition, because they wanted different things and obeyed different principles.

T 3 F 3. In our picture of the psyche, there is an unconscious level, which properly consists ONLY of the miracle ability and should be under MY direction; and a conscious level, which perceives or is aware of impulses from both the unconscious and the superconscious. These are the sources of the impulses it receives. Consciousness is thus the level of perception, but NOT of knowledge. Again, to PERCEIVE is NOT to know. (In this connection, Cayce is more accurate than Freud.)

T 3 F 4. Consciousness was the first split that man introduced into himself. He became a PERCEIVER rather than a creator in the true sense.

T 3 F 5. Consciousness is correctly identified as the domain of the ego. **T(153) -152** Jung was right indeed in insisting that the ego is NOT the self, and that the self should be regarded as an achievement. He did not RECOGNIZE (a term we now understand) that the Achievement was God's. In a sense, the ego was a man-made attempt to perceive himself as he wished, rather than as he IS. This is an example of the created/creator confusion we spoke of before. He can only KNOW himself as he IS, because that is all he can be SURE of. Everything else IS open to question.

T 3 F 6. The ego is the questioning compartment in the post-Separation psyche which man created for himself. It is capable of asking valid questions, but not of perceiving wholly valid answers, because these are cognitive, and cannot BE perceived. The endless speculation about the meaning of mind has led to considerable confusion because the mind IS confused. Only One-Mindedness is without confusion. A separate, or divided, mind MUST be confused. A divided mind is uncertain by definition. It HAS to be in conflict because it is out of accord with itself.

T 3 F 7. Intrapersonal conflict arises from the same basis as interpersonal. One part of the psyche perceives another part as on a different LEVEL, and does not understand it. This makes the parts strangers to each other, WITHOUT RECOGNITION. This is the essence of the fear-prone condition, in which attack is ALWAYS possible.

T 3 F 8. Man has every reason to feel anxious, as he perceives himself. This is why he cannot escape fear until he KNOWS that he DID not and CAN not create himself. He can NEVER make this misperception valid, and when he at last PERCEIVES clearly, he is GLAD HE CAN'T. His Creation is beyond his own error variance, and this is why he MUST eventually choose to heal the Separation. **T(154) -153**

T 3 F 9. Right-mindedness is not to be confused with the KNOWING mind, because it is applicable only to right perception. You can be right-minded or wrong-minded, and this is subject to degrees, a fact which clearly demonstrates a lack of association with knowledge. (No, Helen, this is PERFECTLY clear and DOES follow the previous section. Neither you nor I is at all confused, even in grammar.)

T 3 F 10. The term "right-mindedness" is properly used as the correction for wrong-mindedness, and applies to the state of mind which induces accurate perception. It is miraculous because it heals misperception, and healing is indeed a miracle, in view of how man perceives himself. Only the sick NEED healing. The Soul does not need healing, but the mind DOES.

T 3 F 11. Freud gave a very graphic but upside down account of how the divisions of the mind arose from the bottom UP. Actually, this is impossible, because the unconscious cannot create the conscious. You cannot create something you can't KNOW. Freud was greatly worried about this, being VERY bright, though misguided, and attempted to get around it by introducing a number of "borderline" areas which merely resulted in fuzziness. This was particularly unfortunate, because he was capable of going much higher, if he had not been so afraid. This is why he kept pulling the mind DOWN.

T 3 F 12. The ego did NOT arise out of the unconscious. A lower-order perception cannot create a higher-order one, (which is the way you perceive the structure of the psyche if you look at it from the bottom UP) because it doesn't understand it. But a higher-order perception CAN create a lower-order one by understanding it in terms of MISperception. **T(155) -154**

T 3 F 13. Perception ALWAYS involves some misuse of will, because it involves the mind in areas of uncertainty. The mind is very active because it has will-power. When it willed the Separation it willed to perceive. Until it chose to do this, it willed only to know. Afterwards, it had to will ambiguously, and the only way out of ambiguity IS clear perception.

T 3 F 14. The ego is as frail as Freud perceived it. The later theorists have tried to introduce a less pessimistic view, but have looked in the wrong direction for their hope. Any attempt to endow the ego with the attributes of the Soul, is merely confused thinking. Freud was more clear-sighted about this, because he knew a BAD thing when he perceived it, but he failed to recognize that a bad thing cannot exist. It is therefore wholly unnecessary to try to get out of it. As you very rightly observed yourself, the thing to do with a desert is to LEAVE.

T 3 F 15. The mind returns itself to its proper function only when it WILLS TO KNOW. This places it in the Soul's service, where perception is meaningless. The superconscious is the level of the mind which wills to do this. (Freud was particularly distorted on this point, because he was getting too far UP for comfort according to his own perception.) But he WAS right in maintaining that the "parts" of the psyche cannot be correctly perceived either as THINGS or as entirely separate. (He would have thought better if he had said "entirely separated.")

T 3 F 16. The mind DID divide itself when it willed to create its own levels AND the ability to perceive them. But it could NOT entirely separate itself from the Soul, because it is FROM the Soul that it derives its whole power to create. Even in miscreating, will is affirming its source, or it would merely cease to be. This is impossible, because it IS part of the Soul, which God created, and which is therefore eternal. **T(156) -155**

T 3 F 17. The ability to perceive made the body possible, because you must perceive SOMETHING, and WITH something. This is why perception involves an exchange, or a translation, which knowledge does NOT need. The interpretive function of perception, (actually, a distorted form of creation), then permitted man to interpret the body as HIMSELF, which, although depressing, was a way out of the conflict he induced. (This has already been covered in some detail.)

T 3 F 18. The superconscious, which KNOWS, could not be reconciled with this loss of power, because it was incapable of darkness. This is why it became almost inaccessible to the mind, and entirely inaccessible to the body. It was PERCEIVED as a threat, because light does abolish darkness by establishing the clear fact that it ISN'T THERE. The truth will ALWAYS destroy error in this sense. This is not an ACTIVE process of destruction at all. We have already emphasized the fact that knowing does not DO anything. It can be PERCEIVED as an attacker, but it CANNOT attack.

T 3 F 19. What man perceives as its attack is his own recognition of the fact that it can always be REMEMBERED, because it has never been destroyed. This is not a literal remembering as much as a re-membering. (That is largely for B. I wish he would decide to use that talent of his constructively. He has no idea of how powerful it could be. Actually, it does come from the unconscious, and is really a distorted form of miraculous perception which he has reduced to word twisting. Although this can be quite funny, it is still a real waste. Maybe he'd care to let me control it, and still use it humorously himself. He doesn't have to decide it is one OR the other.) **T(157) -156**

T 3 F 20. The unconscious should never have been reduced to a "container" for the waste products of conflict. Even as HE perceives his psyche, every level has a creative potential, because nothing man creates can wholly lose this.

T 3 F 21. God and the Souls He created remain in surety, and therefore KNOW that no miscreation exists. Truth cannot deal with unwilling error, because it does not will to be blocked out. But I was a man who remembered the Soul and its knowledge. Tell B. that when he refused to misperceive he was indeed behaving as I behaved. And as a man, I did not attempt to counteract error with knowledge, so much as to <u>CORRECT</u> error from the bottom up. I demonstrated both the powerlessness of the body AND the power of the mind, by uniting MY will with that of my Creator, [167] which naturally remembered the Soul and its own real purpose.

T 3 F 22. I cannot unite your will with God's for you. But I CAN erase all misperceptions from your mind, if you will bring it under my guidance. ONLY your misperceptions stand in your own way. Without them, your own choice is certain. Sane perception INDUCES sane choosing. The Atonement was an act based on true perception. I cannot choose for you, but I CAN help you make your own right choice.

T 3 F 23. "Many are called but few are chosen"[168] SHOULD read, "ALL are called but few choose to listen. Therefore, they do not choose RIGHT." The "chosen ones" are merely those who choose right SOONER. This is the real meaning of the celestial speed-up. Strong wills can do this NOW. And you WILL find rest for your Souls.[169] God knows you only in peace, and this IS your reality. **T(158) -157**

T 3 F 24.(Note that the term "insight", though referring to lofty perception, is not an attribute of knowledge. This is why terms like "lofty" are meaningless in this context. Insight is not the way TO knowledge, but it IS a prerequisite FOR knowledge. Being of God, knowledge has nothing to do with your perceptions at all. That is why it can only be a gift of God TO you.) **T(159) -158**

T 3 G. The Loss of Certainty (*Notes* 366 5:215)

Dictated without notes.[170]

T 3 G 1. We[171] said before that the abilities which man possesses are only shadows of his true abilities. The Soul's true functions are knowing, loving, and creating. The intrusion of the ability to perceive, which is inherently judgmental, was introduced only after the Separation. No one has been sure of anything since then. You will also remember that I made it very clear that the Resurrection was the return to knowledge, which was accomplished by the union of my will with the Father's.

T 3 G 2. Since the Separation, the words "create" and "make" are inevitably confused. When you make something, you make it first out of a sense of lack or need, and second, out of a something that already exists. Anything that is[172] made is made for a specific purpose. It has no true generalizability. When you make something to fill a perceived lack, which is obviously why you would make anything, you are tacitly implying that you believe in the Separation. Knowing does not lead to doing, as we have frequently observed already.

T 3 G 3. What appears to be contradictory about the difference between knowing and perceiving, and Revelation and miracles, is again the fallacy that is the root cause of all subsequent errors. The miracle was associated with perception, and not with knowing. However, we also noted that prayer is the medium of miracles, and also the natural communication of the Creator and the Created. Prayer is always an affirmation of knowledge, not of accurate perception. That is why unless perception has entered into it, it calls on Revelation. **T(160) -159**

T 3 G 4. The confusion between your own creation and what you create is so profound that it has literally become impossible to know anything, because knowledge is always stable. It is quite evident that human beings are not. Nevertheless, they are perfectly stable as God created them. In this sense, when their behavior is unstable, they are obviously disagreeing with God's idea of the Creation. This is a fundamental right of man, although not one he would care to exercise if he were in his Right Mind.

T 3 G 5. The problem that is bothering you most is the fundamental question which man continually asks of himself, but which cannot properly be directed to himself at all. He keeps on asking "himself" what he is. This implies that the answer is not only one which he knows, but one which is up to him. The first part of this statement is perfectly true, but the second part is not. We have frequently commented on the absolute necessity of correcting all fallacious thinking which associates man in any way with his own Creation. Man CANNOT perceive himself correctly. He has no image at all. The word "image" is always perception related, and is not a product of knowing. Images are symbolic, and stand for something else. The current emphasis on "changing your image" is a good description of the power of perception, but it implies that there is nothing to KNOW.

T 3 G 6. Prayer is the medium of miracles, not because God created perceptions, but because God created YOU. At the beginning of this course, we said that YOU are a miracle. Therefore, the miracle worker is a miracle NOT of his own creation.[173] Unless perception rests on some knowing basis, it is so unstable that it doesn't mean anything. **T(161) -160** Knowing is not open to interpretation, because its meaning is its own. It is possible to interpret meaning, but this is always open to error because it involves the perception of meaning. All of these wholly needless complexities are the result of man's attempt to regard himself both as separated and unseparated at the same time. It is impossible to undertake a confusion as fundamental as this without engaging in further confusion.

---

[167] The *Notes* begins a new sentence at "by" and in place of the word "which" here has "I brought His Light back into the mind. I naturally"
[168] **Matthew 20:16** "So the last will be first, and the first last. For many are called, but few chosen." Also: **Matthew 22:14** "For many are called, but few are chosen."
[169] **Jeremiah 6:16** Thus says the LORD: "Stand in the ways and see, And ask for the old paths, where the good way is, And walk in it; Then you will find rest for your souls." But they said, "We will not walk in it." **Matthew 11:29** "Take My yoke upon you and learn from Me, for I am gentle and lowly in heart, and you will find rest for your souls."
[170] The words "dictated without notes" are handwritten on the top of the page above the date. The first 13 paragraphs of this section are not present in the *Notes*.
[171] Nov. 30 *[1965]*

[172] The words "that is" are typed between lines, over the words "can be" which are crossed out. Thus, originally typed "Anything can be made is made" becomes "Anything that is made is made." This has not been located in the *Notes*.
[173] This sentence originally was typed "Therefore, the Creator of the miracle is a miracle NOT of his own creation." The words "the Creator" are crossed out and the word "WORKER" is printed in by hand in block capitals. This has not been located in the *Notes*.

T 3 G 7. Methodologically, man's mind has been very creative. But, as always occurs when method and content are separated, it has not been utilized for anything but an attempt to escape a fundamental and entirely inescapable impasse. This kind of thinking cannot result in a creative outcome, though it has resulted in considerable ingenuity. It is noteworthy, however, that this ingenuity has almost totally divorced him from knowledge.

T 3 G 8. Knowledge does not require ingenuity at all. When we say "the truth shall set you free,"[174] we mean that all this kind of thinking is a waste of time, but that you are free of the need of engaging in it. T(162) -161

T 3 G 9. Note again that the functions of the Soul were not referred to as abilities. This point requires clarification, because abilities are beliefs which are BASED on the scarcity fallacy, since they do not mean anything apart from within-group comparisons. As you yourself never fail to point out, "nobody has none of an ability, and nobody has all of it." That is, of course, why the curve never rests on the line. The clearest implications of relativity, which properly inheres in this statement, DEMONSTRATE that abilities are not functions of the Soul. The Soul's functions are NOT relative. They are ABSOLUTE. They are OF God and FROM[175] God, and therefore God-like.

T 3 G 10. Prayer is a way of asking for something. When we said that prayer is the medium of miracles, we also said that the only meaningful prayer is for forgiveness, because those who have been forgiven HAVE everything. Once forgiveness has been accepted, prayer in the usual sense becomes utterly without meaning. Essentially, a prayer for forgiveness is nothing more than a request that we may be able to recognize something we already have.

T 3 G 11. In electing the ability to perceive instead of the will to know, man placed himself in a position where he could resemble his Father ONLY by perceiving miraculously. But he lost the knowledge that he HIMSELF is a miracle. MIRACULOUS CREATION was his own Source, and also his own real function. "God created man in his own image and likeness"[176] is correct in meaning, but the words are open to considerable misinterpretation. This is avoided, however, if "image" is understood to mean "thought," and "likeness" is taken as "of a like quality." God DID create the Son in His own Thought, and of a quality like to His own. There IS nothing else.

T 3 G 12. Perception is impossible WITHOUT a belief in "more" and "less." Unless perception, at every level, involves selectivity, it is incapable of organization. In all types of perception, there is a continual process of accepting and rejecting, of organizing and reorganizing, and of shifting and changing focus. Evaluation is an essential aspect of perception, because judgment MUST be made for selection. "Lack of lack" is a concept which is meaningless to a perceiver, because the ability to perceive at all RESTS ON lack. T(163) -162

T 3 G 13. What happens to perceptions if there ARE no judgments, and there is nothing BUT perfect equality? Perception is automatically useless. Truth can only be KNOWN. All of it is equally true, and knowing any part of it IS to know all of it.

T 3 G 14. Only perception involves partial awareness. Knowledge transcends ALL of the laws which govern perception. Partial KNOWLEDGE is impossible. It is all One, and has no separate parts. (i.e. the parts have NOT separated.) This IS the real knowledge. You who are really one with it need but know YOURSELF and your knowledge is complete. To know God's miracle is to know Him.

T 3 G 15. Forgiveness is the healing of the perception of separation. Correct perception of EACH OTHER is necessary ONLY because minds have willed to see themselves AS separate beings. Each Soul knows God completely. This IS the miraculous power of the Soul. The fact that each Soul has this power completely is a fact that is entirely alien to human thinking, in which if any ONE has everything, there is nothing LEFT.

T 3 G 16. God's miracles are as total as His Thought, because they ARE His thoughts. God shines in them all with perfect light. If they recognize this light anywhere, they know it universally. Revelation cannot be explained, because it IS knowledge. Revelation HAPPENS. It is the only REALLY natural happening, because it reflects the nature of God. T(164) -163

T 3 G 17. As long as perception lasts, prayer has a place. Since perception rests on lack, those who perceive have not totally accepted the Atonement and given over themselves to truth. Perception IS a separated state, and the perceiver DOES need healing. Communion, not prayer, is the natural state of those who know. God and HIS miracles are inseparable.

T 3 G 18. All words, at best, are preparatory. THE word is really a thought. No one WORD is universally meaningful, because a word is a symbol, but thought is not divisible by creation. The original name for "thought" and "word" was the same. The quotation should read "In the beginning was the thought, and the thought was with God, and the thought WAS God." How beautiful indeed are the thoughts of God, who live in His light. Your worth is beyond perception because it is beyond doubt.

T 3 G 19. Do not perceive yourself in different lights. KNOW yourself in the One Light, where the miracle which is you is perfectly clear. T(165) -164

T 3 G 20. The[177] prerequisites for therapy must include the following conditions:

T 3 G 21. 1. The procedure must involve the recognition rather than the denial of the importance of thought.

T 3 G 22. 2. The exact equality of everyone who is involved. This must include Me.

T 3 G 23. 3. No one is either therapist or patient. (B. should add "teacher or pupil.")

T 3 G 24. 4. Above all EVERYONE involved must want to give up everything that is NOT true. The reason for the negative emphasis here is that therapy implies something HAS gone wrong. Even though the purpose is to correct, those who are ill ARE negative.

T 3 G 25. 5. Therapy is EXACTLY the same as all other forms of miracle-working. It has no separate laws of its own. All of the points that were given for miracles apply to therapy because, UNLESS therapy proceeds from miracle-mindedness, it CANNOT heal.

T 3 G 26. 6. The therapist (hopefully) does have the role of being the better perceiver. (This is also, again hopefully, true of the teacher.) It does not follow that he is the better knower. Temporarily, the therapist or teacher can help in straightening out twisted

---

[174] **John 8:32** "and ye shall know the truth, and the truth shall make you free."

[175] The *Urtext* manuscript is totally illegible, we are *just guessing* that it is perhaps meant to be "FROM." This is a "dictated without notes" segment so we can't check the *Notes*. This material was not preserved in any other version, either.

[176] **Genesis 1:26-27** Then God said, "Let Us make man in Our image, according to Our likeness; let them have dominion over the fish of the sea, over the birds of the air, and over the cattle, over all the earth and over every creeping thing that creeps on the earth." So God created man in His own image; in the image of God He created him; male and female He created them.

[177] 12/7/65 is manually handwritten in the top right corner. It also includes a typed "1" in the top centre, indicating originally this was numbered "page 1." While not marked "dictated without notes," since the material has not been located in the *Notes*, and is marked page "1", it may well have been directly dictated. The apparently original pagination runs right to section **H 1** which is again numbered "1," again missing from the *Notes*, and dated 12/10/65.

Chapter 3 – Retraining the Mind

perceptions, which is also the only role that I would ever contribute myself. All therapy should do is try to place EVERYONE involved in the right frame of mind to help one another. It is essentially a process of true courtesy, including courtesy to Me. T(166) -165

T 3 G 27. Any[178] form of mental illness can truthfully be described as an expression of viciousness. We said before that those who are afraid are apt to be vicious. If we were willing to forgive other people's misperceptions of us, they could not possibly affect us at all. There is little doubt that you can explain your present attitudes[179] in terms of how people used to look at you, but there is no wisdom in doing so. In fact, the whole historical approach can justifiably be called doubtful.

T 3 G 28. As you have so often said, no one has adopted ALL of his parents' attitudes as his own. In every case, there has been a long process of choice, in which the individual has escaped from those he himself vetoed, while retaining those he voted FOR. B. has not retained his parents political beliefs, in spite of the particular kind of newspapers that constituted their own reading matter in this area. The reason why he could do this was because he believed he was free in this area.

T 3 G 29. There must be some acute problem OF HIS OWN that would make him so eager to accept their misperception of his own worth. This tendency can ALWAYS be regarded as punitive. It cannot be justified by the inequality of the strengths of parents and children. This is never more than temporary, and is largely a matter of maturational and thus physical difference. It does not last unless it is held onto. T(167) -166[180]

T 3 G 30. When B's father came to his new office and "destroyed" it, it is quite apparent that B. MUST have been willing to let it be destroyed. The many times that he has commented on this event alone would suggest that the extreme importance of this misperception in his own distorted thinking. Why should anyone accord an obvious misperception so much power? There cannot be any real justification for it, because even B. himself recognized the real problem by saying "How could he do this to me?" The answer is HE didn't.

T 3 G 31. B. has a very serious question to ask himself in this connection. We said before that the purpose of the Resurrection was to "demonstrate that no amount of misperception has any influence at all on a Son of God." This demonstration EXONERATES those who misperceive, by establishing beyond doubt that they have NOT hurt anyone. B's question, which he must ask himself very honestly, is whether he is willing to demonstrate that his parents have NOT hurt him. Unless he is willing to do this, he has not forgiven them.

T 3 G 32. The essential goal of therapy is the same as that of knowledge. No one can survive independently as long as he is willing to see himself through the eyes of others. This will always put him in a position where he MUST see himself in different lights. Parents do not create the image of their children, though they may perceive T(168) -167[181] images which they do create. However, as we have already said, you are not an image. If you SIDE WITH image-makers, you are merely being idolatrous.

T 3 G 33. B. has no justification whatever for perpetuating ANY image of himself at all. He is NOT an image. Whatever is true of him is wholly benign. It is essential that he KNOW this about himself, but he cannot know it while he chooses to interpret himself as vulnerable enough to BE hurt. This is a peculiar kind of arrogance, whose narcissistic component is perfectly obvious. It endows the perceiver with sufficient unreal strength to make him over, and then acknowledges the perceiver's miscreation. There are times when this strange lack of real courtesy appears to be a form of humility. Actually, it is never more than simple spite.

T 3 G 34. Bill, your parents did misperceive you in many ways, but their ability to perceive was quite warped, and their misperceptions stood in the way of their own knowledge. There is no reason why it should stand in the way of yours. It is still true that you believe they DID something to you. This belief is extremely dangerous to your perception, and wholly destructive of your knowledge. This is not only true of your attitudes toward your parents, but also of your misuse of your friends. You still think that you MUST respond to their errors AS IF they were true. By reacting self-destructively, you are GIVING them approval for their misperceptions. T(169) -168[182]

T 3 G 35. No one has the right to change himself according to different circumstances. Only his actions are capable of appropriate variation. His belief in himself is a constant, unless it rests on perceptual acuity rather than knowledge of what he is.

T 3 G 36. It is your DUTY to establish beyond doubt that you are totally unwilling to side with (identify with) anyone's misperceptions of you, including your own. If you become concerned with totally irrelevant factors, such as the physical condition of a classroom, the number of students, the hour of the course, and the many elements which you may choose to select for emphasis as a basis for misperception, you have lost the knowledge of what ANY interpersonal relationship is for. It is NOT true that the difference between pupil and teacher is lasting. They meet IN ORDER to abolish the difference. At the beginning, since we are still in time, they come together on the basis of inequality of ability and experience. The aim of the teacher is to give them more of what is temporarily his. This process has all of the miracle conditions we referred to at the beginning. The teacher (or miracle worker) gives more to those who have less, bringing them closer to equality with him, at the same time gaining for himself.

T 3 G 37. The confusion here is only because they do not gain the same things, because they do not NEED the same things. If they did, their respective, though temporary roles would not be conducive to mutual profit. Freedom from fear can be achieved by BOTH teacher and pupil ONLY if they do not compare either their needs or their T(170) -169[183] positions in regard to each other in terms of higher and lower.

T 3 G 38. Presumably, children must learn from parents. What parents learn from children is merely of a different order. Ultimately, there is no difference in order, but this involves only knowledge. Neither parents nor children can be said to HAVE knowledge, or their relationships would not exist AS IF they were on different levels. The same is true of the teacher and the pupil. Children have an authority problem ONLY if they believe that their image is influenced BY the authority. This is an act of will on their part, because they are electing to misperceive the authority and GIVE him this power.

T 3 G 39. A TEACHER with an authority problem is merely a pupil who refuses to teach others. He wants to maintain HIMSELF in a position where he can be misused and misperceived. This makes him resentful of teaching, because of what he insists it has done to him.

T 3 G 40. The ONLY way out of this particular aspect of the desert is still to leave. The way this is left is to release EVERYONE involved, by ABSOLUTELY REFUSING to engage in any form of honoring error. Neither teacher nor pupil is imprisoned by learning unless he uses it as an attack. If he does this, he will be imprisoned

---

[178] 12/7/65
[179] The word "absolutes" is crossed out, and the word "attitudes" typed above it. This has not been located in the *Notes*.
[180] 12/7 [1965]
[181] 12/7 [1965]
[182] 12/7 [1965]
[183] 12/7 [1965]

whether he actually teaches or learns, or refuses to be[184] engaged in the process at all. **T(171) -170**[185]

T 3 G 41. The role of a teacher, properly conceived, is one of leading himself and others out of the desert. The value of this role can hardly be underestimated, if only because it was one to which I very gladly dedicated my own life. I have repeatedly asked MY pupils to follow me. This means that, to be effective teachers, they MUST interpret teaching as I do. I have made EVERY effort to teach you ENTIRELY without fear. If you do not listen, you will be unable to avoid the VERY obvious error of perceiving teaching as a threat.

T 3 G 42. It is hardly necessary to say that teaching is a process whose purpose is to produce learning. The ultimate purpose of ALL learning is to abolish fear. This is necessary so that knowledge can happen. The role of the teacher is NOT the role of God. This confusion is all too frequently made, by parents, teachers, therapists, and the clergy. It is a real misunderstanding of both God and His miracles. Any teacher who believes that teaching is fearful CANNOT learn because he is paralyzed. He also cannot really teach.

T 3 G 43. B. was quite right in maintaining that this course is a prerequisite for his. However, he was really saying much more than that. The purpose of this course IS to prepare you for knowledge. So is the only real purpose of ANY legitimate course. All that is required of you as a teacher is to follow Me. **T(172) -171**[186]

T 3 G 44. Whenever anyone decides that he can function only in SOME roles but not in others, he cannot BUT be attempting to make a compromise which will not work. If B. is under the misbelief that he is coping with the fear problem by functioning as an administrator and as a teacher of interns, but NOT as a teacher of students, he is merely deceiving himself. He owes himself greater respect. There is nothing as tragic as the attempt to deceive one's self, because it implies that you perceive yourself as so unworthy that deception is more fitting for you than truth. Either you can function in all of the roles you have properly undertaken to fill, or you cannot function effectively in any of them. This IS an all or none decision. You CANNOT make inappropriate level distinctions within this choice. You are either capable or not. This does not mean that you can DO everything, but it DOES mean that you are either totally miracle-minded or not. This decision is open to NO compromise whatever. When B. says that he cannot teach, he is making the same mistake that we spoke of before, when he acted as if universal laws applied to everyone except him. This is not only arrogant, but patently untrue. Universal laws MUST apply to him, unless he does not exist. We will not bother to argue about this. **T(173) -172**[187]

T 3 G 45. Descartes engaged in a very interesting teaching procedure, and one from which he himself learned a great deal. He began with doubting the existence of everything, except himself. He insisted that his own existence was not open to doubt, and rebuilt his entire thought system on the one premise "I think, therefore I am." It is noteworthy that he arrived at accepting the entire system he originally doubted, solely on the basis of this ONE piece of knowledge. There was, however, a distinct shift in his own perception. He no longer really questioned the reality of what he perceived, because he KNEW he was there.

T 3 G 46. We mentioned before that B. is not too sure of this, and that is why we suggested that he concentrate on "Lord, here I am."[188] A teacher is unlikely to be effective unless he begins with

BEING THERE. B, this is not really open to question. You will lose all your fear of teaching and relating in any form once you know who you are. There is no point whatever in remaining in the prison of believing that this is up to you. You do NOT exist in different lights. It is this belief which has confused you about your own reality. Why would you want to remain so obscure to yourself? **T(174) C 1**[189]

T 3 H. Judgment and the Authority Problem.. (*Notes not present in the Notes*)

T 3 H 1. We have already discussed the Last Judgment[190] in some though insufficient detail. After the Last Judgment, there isn't any more. This is symbolic only in the sense that everybody is much better off WITHOUT judgment. When the Bible says "Judge not that ye be not judged"[191] it merely means that if you judge the reality of others at all, you will be unable to avoid judging your own. The choice to judge rather than know has been the cause of the loss of peace. Judgment is the process on which perception but not cognition rests. We covered this before in terms of selectivity. Evaluation was said at that time to be its obvious prerequisite.

T 3 H 2. Judgment ALWAYS involves rejection. It is not an ability which emphasizes ONLY the positive aspects of what is judged, whether it be in or out of the self. However, what has been perceived and rejected, (or judged and found wanting) remains in the unconscious because it HAS been perceived. Watson had a very relevant notion of the unconscious in this connection. In fact, it was so relevant that he dropped it as officially out of accord with Behaviorism. He was right on both counts.

T 3 H 3. One of the illusions from which human perception suffers is that what it perceives and judges against has no effect. This cannot be true, unless man[192] also believes that what his judgment vetoes does not exist. He evidently does not believe this, or he would not have judged against it. **T(175) C 2** It does not really matter, in the end, whether you judge right or wrong. Either way, you are placing your belief in the unreal. This cannot be avoided in any type of judgment, because it IMPLIES the belief that reality is yours to choose FROM.

T 3 H 4. Neither of you has any idea of the tremendous release and deep peace that comes from meeting yourselves and your brothers totally without judgment. If you will look back at the earlier notes about what you and your brothers ARE, you will realize that judging them in any way is really without meaning. In fact, their meaning is lost to you precisely BECAUSE[193] you ARE judging them. All un-

---

accept the Atonement with conviction, recognizing its inevitable worth, and my own divine worth as part of this identification with thee. I pray that my fear be replaced by an active sense of thy love, and thy continual willingness to help me overcome the split, or divided will, which is responsible for my difficulty with this. I accept the divinity of the messages we have received, and affirm my will in both accepting and acting upon the Atonement principle.

"Here I am, Lord:

"The major problem that both of you have is the continuing split will, which naturally interferes with your true identification. To the extent that you hold onto this split, it will take longer to get through and will MARKEDLY interfere with your own integration efforts. Reliance has to be placed on Me, which is sufficient once you do this without distantiation or division in loyalties. This will be strengthened through a continual affirmation of the goal you both want to achieve, and an awareness of its inevitability. In this way, you will both perceive and KNOW your true worth, and the importance of maintaining a COMPLETE identification."

[189] 12/10/65
[190] **Matthew 11:22** But I say to you, it will be more tolerable for Tyre and Sidon in the day of judgment than for you.
[191] **Matthew 7:1** "Judge not, that ye be not judged."
[192] manuscript has it typed "he", it is crossed out and the word "MAN" is handwritten in block caps. This has not been located in the *Notes*.
[193] The word "BECAUSE" is handwritten in block capitals. This passage has not been located in the *Notes*.

---

[184] The word "be" was inserted to correct the grammar.
[185] 12/7 [1965]
[186] 12/7 [1965]
[187] 12/7 [1965]
[188] An interesting page shows up in the *Urtext* collection bearing the heading "Special Message directly to WT" (which likely refers to William Thetford) this may be what the words "Lord, here I am" refer to. It is as follows:
"I would like to pray that my will be united with thine, recognizing that thy perfect love will suffice (or correct) for my imperfect love. I pray that I may

certainty comes from a totally fallacious belief that you are under the coercion of judgment. You do not need it to organize your life, and you certainly do not need it to organize yourselves.

T 3 H 5. When you look upon knowledge, all judgment is automatically suspended, and this is the process that enables recognition to REPLACE perception. Man is very fearful of everything he has perceived and refused to accept. He believes that because he has refused to accept it, he has lost control over it. This is why he sees it in nightmares, or in pleasant disguise in what seems to be happier dreams. Nothing that you have refused to accept can be brought into awareness. It does NOT follow that it is dangerous. But it DOES follow that you have made it dangerous. **T(176) C 3**

T 3 H 6. When you feel tired, it is merely because you have judged yourself as capable of being tired. When you laugh at someone it is because you have judged him as debased. When you laugh at yourself, you are singularly likely to laugh at others, if only because you cannot tolerate being more debased THAN others. All of this does make you tired, because it is essentially disheartening. You are not really capable of being tired, but you are very capable of wearying yourselves.

T 3 H 7. The strain of constant judgment is virtually intolerable. It is a curious thing that any ability which is so debilitating should be so deeply cherished. But there is a very good reason for this. (This, however, depends upon what you mean by good.)

T 3 H 8. If you wish to be the author of reality, which is totally impossible anyway, then you will insist on holding on to judgment. You will also use the term with considerable fear and believe that judgment will someday be used against you. To whatever extent it IS used against you, it is due ONLY to your belief in its efficacy as a weapon of defense for your own authority.

T 3 H 9. The issue of authority is really a question of authorship. When an individual has a "authority problem," it is ALWAYS because he believes he is the author of himself, and resents his own projection that you share his delusion in this respect. He then perceives the situation as one in which two people are literally fighting for his own authorship. This is the fundamental **T(177) C 4** error of all those who believe they have usurped the power of God.

T 3 H 10. The belief is very frightening to them, but hardly troubles God at all. He is, however, eager to undo it, not to punish His children, but ONLY because He knows that it makes them unhappy. Souls were given their own true authorship, and men[194] preferred to remain anonymous when they chose to separate themselves FROM their Author. The word "authority" has been one of their most fearful symbols ever since. Authority has been used for great cruelty, because, being uncertain of their true Authorship, men believe that their creation was anonymous. This has left them in a position where it SOUNDS meaningful to consider the possibility that they must have created themselves.

T 3 H 11. The dispute over authorship has left such uncertainty in the minds of man that some people have gone so far as to doubt whether they were ever created at all. Despite the apparent contradiction in this position, it is in one sense more tenable than the view that they created themselves. At least, it acknowledged the fact some TRUE authorship is necessary for existence.

T 3 H 12. Only those who give over all desire to reject can KNOW that their own rejection is impossible. **T(178) C 5** You have not usurped the power of God, but you HAVE lost it. Fortunately, when you lose something, this does not mean that the something has gone. It merely means that YOU do not know where it is. Existence does not depend on your ability to identify it, or even to place it. It is perfectly possible to look on reality without judgment, and merely KNOW it is there. By knowing this, you are not doubting its reality at all.

T 3 H 13. Peace is a natural heritage of the Soul. Everyone is free to refuse to accept his inheritance, but he is NOT free to establish what his inheritance IS. The problem which everyone MUST decide is the fundamental question of his own authorship. All fear comes ultimately, and sometimes by way of very devious routes, from the denial of Authorship. The offense is never to God, but only to the denier himself. He has thrown away the reason for his own peace, and sees himself only in pieces. This strange perception IS an authority problem. It is also the basis for castration anxiety, since both forms of error are fundamentally the same.

T 3 H 14. Neither you nor B. can find peace while this authority problem continues. But the truth is still that there IS no problem about this. There is no man who does not feel that he is imprisoned in some way. If this has been the result of his own free will, he must regard his will as if it were NOT free, or the obviously circular reasoning of his own position would be quite apparent. **T(179) C 6**

T 3 H 15. Free will MUST lead to freedom. Judgment always imprisons, because it separates segments of reality according to highly unstable scales of desire. Wishes are not facts, by definition. To wish is to imply that willing is not sufficient. However, no one really believes that what is wished is as real as what is willed. Instead of "seek you first the Kingdom of Heaven"[195] say "Will ye first the Kingdom of Heaven,"[196] and you have said "I know what I am, and I will to accept my own inheritance." **T(180) C 7**[197]

T 3 H 16. It is ESSENTIAL that this whole authority problem be voluntarily dismissed at once and for all before B's course. Neither of you understands how important this is for your sanity. You are both quite insane on this point. (This is not a judgment. It is merely a fact. (No, Helen, you SHOULD use the word "fact." This is just as much a fact as God is. A fact is literally a "making" or a starting point. You DO start from this point, and your thinking is inverted because of it.)

T 3 I. Creating versus the Self-Image (*Notes* 374 5:223)

T 3 I 1. Every system of thought MUST have a starting point. It begins with either a making or a creating, a difference which we have already covered. Both are acts of will, except that making involves doing, and creating involves active willing. Their resemblance lies in their power as FOUNDATIONS. Their difference lies in what rests upon them. Both are cornerstones for systems of belief by which men live.

T 3 I 2. It is a mistake to believe that a thought-system which is based on lies is weak. NOTHING made by a child of God is without power. It is absolutely essential that you realize this, because otherwise you will not understand why you have so much trouble with this course, and will be unable to escape from the prisons you have (made) created for yourselves. (The use of creative here was an error. You should have said made for yourself.) **T(181) C 8**

T 3 I 3. You have both made the error of the psychotherapist we described in some detail before, and it is particularly serious at this time. You cannot resolve your authority problem by depreciating the power of your minds. It[198] CAN hurt you if you misuse it, because you KNOW its strength. You also know that you CANNOT weaken it any more than you can weaken God.

---

[194] *Urtext* manuscript has it typed "they", it is crossed out and "MANY" is handwritten in bock caps, and that is crossed out and the word "MEN" is handwritten in block caps. This has not been located in the *Notes*.

[195] Matthew 6:33 "But seek ye first his kingdom, and his righteousness; and all these things shall be added unto you."
[196] Matthew 6:33 (see above)
[197] 12/11/6
[198] *Urtext* manuscript has it typed "It", the word is crossed out and "THIS" is written above in block caps. The *Notes* has it as "It" and joins the last two sentences with "and" instead of breaking them with a period.

T 3 I 4. The devil[199] is a frightening concept ONLY because he is thought of as extremely powerful and extremely active. He is perceived as a force in combat with God, battling Him for possession of Souls. He deceives by lies, and builds kingdoms of his own, in which everything is in direct opposition to God. Yet, he ATTRACTS men rather than repels them, and they are perceived as willing to "sell" him their Souls in return for gifts they KNOW are of no real worth at all.

T 3 I 5. This makes absolutely no sense. The whole picture is one in which man acts in a way he HIMSELF realizes is self destructive, but which he does NOT WILL to correct, and therefore perceives the cause as beyond his control.

T 3 I 6. We have discussed the fall or Separation before, but its meaning must be clearly understood, without symbols. The Separation is NOT symbolic. It is an order of reality, or a system of thought that is PERFECTLY real in time, though not in Eternity. All beliefs are real to the believer. **T(182) C 9**

T 3 I 7. The fruit of only ONE tree was "forbidden" to man in his symbolic garden.[200] But God could not have forbidden it, or it could not have BEEN eaten. If God knows His children, and I assure you he does, would he have put them in a position where their own destruction was possible? The "tree" which was forbidden was correctly named "tree of knowledge." Yet God created knowledge, and gave it freely to His Creations. The symbolism here is open to many interpretations, but you may be SURE that any interpretation which perceives either God OR His creations as if they were capable of destroying their own Purpose is wrong.

T 3 I 8. Eating of the tree of knowledge is a symbolic expression for incorporating into the self the ability for self-creation. This is the ONLY sense in which God and His souls are NOT co-creators. The belief that they ARE is implicit in the "self concept," a concept now made acceptable by its WEAKNESS, and explained by a tendency of the self to create an IMAGE of itself. Its fear aspect is usually ascribed to the "father figure," a particularly interesting idea, in view of the fact that nobody means the physical father by the term. It refers to an IMAGE of a father in relation to an IMAGE of the self.

T 3 I 9. Once again, images are perceived, NOT known. Knowledge cannot deceive, but perception CAN. Man can perceive himself as self-creating, but he CANNOT do more than BELIEVE it. He CANNOT make it true. I told you before that when you finally perceive correctly, you can only be GLAD YOU CAN'T. **T(183) C 10** But until then, the belief that you CAN is the central foundation-stone in your thought-system, and all your defenses are used to attack ideas which would bring it to light.

T 3 I 10. You and B. still believe you are images of your own creation. You are split with your own Souls on this point, and there is NO resolution, because you believe the one thing that is literally INCONCEIVABLE. That is why you CANNOT create, and are afraid to make or produce.

T 3 I 11. You, Helen, are CONSTANTLY arguing about the authorship of this course. This is NOT humility; it is a REAL authority problem. You, Bill, really believe that by teaching you are assuming a dominant or father role, and that the "father figure" will kill you. This is not humility either. Castration fears are a particularly distorted reflection of the real basic anxiety, or Separation fear.

T 3 I 12. The mind can make the belief in Separation VERY real and VERY fearful. And this belief IS the devil. It is powerful, active, destructive, and clearly in opposition to God, because it literally denies His Fatherhood. Never underestimate the[201] power of this denial. Look at your lives and see what the devil has made. But KNOW that this making will surely dissolve in the light of truth, because its foundation IS a lie. **T(184) C 11**

T 3 I 13. Your creation by God is the only foundation which cannot be shaken, because the light is IN it. Your starting point IS truth, and you MUST return to this Beginning. Much has been perceived since then, but nothing else has happened. That is why your Souls are still in peace, even though your minds are in conflict.

T 3 I 14. You have not yet gone back far ENOUGH and that is why you become so fearful. As you approach the beginning, you feel the fear of the destruction of your thought-systems upon you, as if it were the fear of death. There IS no death,[202] but there IS a belief in death.

T 3 I 15. The Bible says that the tree that bears no fruit will be cut off and will wither away.[203] Be glad! The light WILL shine from the true Foundation of Life, and your own thought-systems WILL stand corrected. They CANNOT stand otherwise.

T 3 I 16. You who fear salvation are WILLING death. Life and death, light and darkness, knowledge and perception are irreconcilable. To believe that THEY can be reconciled is to believe that God and man can NOT. Only the Oneness of Knowledge is conflictless. Your Kingdom is not of this world[204] because it was given you from BEYOND this world. Only IN this world is the idea of an authority problem meaningful. The world is not left by death but by truth, and truth CAN be known by all those for whom the Kingdom was created, and for whom it waits. **T(185) C 12**

---

[199] **Revelation 12:7-10** And war broke out in heaven: Michael and his angels fought with the dragon; and the dragon and his angels fought, but they did not prevail, nor was a place found for them in heaven any longer. So the great dragon was cast out, that serpent of old, called the Devil and Satan, who deceives the whole world; he was cast to the earth, and his angels were cast out with him. Then I heard a loud voice saying in heaven, "Now salvation, and strength, and the kingdom of our God, and the power of His Christ have come, for the accuser of our brethren, who accused them before our God day and night, has been cast down."

[200] **Genesis 2:16-17** And the LORD God commanded the man, saying, "Of every tree of the garden you may freely eat; but of the tree of the knowledge of good and evil you shall not eat, for in the day that you eat of it you shall surely die."

[201] The word "the" is not in the *Urtext* manuscript. It is added to make the sentence grammatical. It is also present in the *Notes*, which suggests its omission was inadvertent.

[202] **2 Timothy 1:10** But has now been revealed by the appearing of our Savior Jesus Christ, who has abolished death and brought life and immortality to light through the gospel,

[203] **John 15:2** "Every branch in Me that does not bear fruit He takes away; and every branch that bears fruit He prunes, that it may bear more fruit."

[204] **John 18:36** Jesus answered, "My kingdom is not of this world. If My kingdom were of this world, My servants would fight, so that I should not be delivered to the Jews; but now My kingdom is not from here."

Chapter 4 – The Root of All Evil

T 4 A. Introduction (*Notes* 389 5:238)

T 4 A 1. (Aside to HS. You were both wise and devoted (two words which are literally interchangeable in the sense that they truly bring on the exchange of one another.) in claiming your scribal functions and working so late. You HAD committed a serious error against your brother, and one who had asked for your help. A devoted priestess does not do this. The Bible says you should go WITH a brother twice as far as he asks.[205] It certainly DOES NOT suggest that you set him BACK on his journey.

T 4 A 2. Devotion to a brother CANNOT set YOU back either. It can ONLY lead to mutual progress. The result of genuine devotion is inspiration, a word which, properly understood is the OPPOSITE of fatigue. To be fatigued is to be DIS-spirited, but to be inspired is to be IN the spirit. To be egocentric IS to be dispirited. But to be self-centered in the RIGHT sense is to be inspired, or in the Soul. The truly inspired are enlightened, and cannot abide in darkness.

T 4 A 3. Do not attempt to break God's copyright, because His Authorship alone CAN copy right. Your own right authorship does NOT lie in remaking His copies, but in creating LIKE Him.

T 4 A 4. Embarrassment is ALWAYS an expression of egocentricity, an association which has been made before. (Made, NOT created. This kind of association is ALWAYS man-made). Both of you have completed the SCT stem: When I was called on to speak—with—"I became embarrassed and COULD NOT SPEAK." **T(186) C 13** This should be corrected to "Recognized my Authorship."

T 4 A 5. Tell B. that he cannot be embarrassed by his own words unless he believes that HE is responsible for them. We have already corrected "word" to "thought," and he IS free to allocate the authorship for his thoughts as he elects. He can speak from his Soul or from his ego, precisely as he chooses. If he speaks from his Soul, he has chosen to "be still and know that I am God."[206] These words are inspired, because they come from KNOWLEDGE. If he speaks from his ego, he is DISCLAIMING knowledge instead of AFFIRMING it, and is thus dis-spiriting himself.

T 4 A 6. The dis-spirited have no choice BUT to be narcissistic, and to be narcissistic IS to place your faith in the unworthy. Your real worth IS your divine authorship, and your Soul is its acknowledgement. I cannot guide your egos EXCEPT as you associate them with your Souls.

T 4 A 7. Attacking misidentification errors is neither MY function nor YOURS. Destroying the devil is a meaningless undertaking. Cervantes[207] wrote an excellent symbolic account of this procedure, though he did not understand his own symbolism. The REAL point of his writing was that his "hero" was a man who perceived himself as unworthy because he identified with his ego and perceived its weakness. He then set about to alter his perception, NOT by correcting his misidentification, but by behaving egotistically. **T(187)?23 ?C 14**

T 4 A 8. Chesterton wrote an excellent description of Cervantes and his perception of his "unheroic hero," a view of man which the ego tolerates all too frequently, but the Soul NEVER countenances:

"And he sees across a weary land a straggling road in Spain Up which a lean and foolish knight forever rides in vain."[208]

T 4 A 9. Do not embark on foolish journeys because they are indeed in vain. The ego may will them because the ego IS both lean and foolish. But the Soul CANNOT embark on them because it is forever Unwilling to depart from its Foundation. The journey to the cross should be the LAST foolish journey for every mind. Do not dwell upon it, but dismiss it as accomplished. If you can accept that as YOUR OWN last foolish journey, you are free also to join My Resurrection. Human living has indeed been needlessly wasted in repetition compulsion. It re-enacts the Separation, the loss of power, the foolish journey of the ego in its attempt at reparation, and finally the crucifixion of the body, or death. Repetition compulsions can be endless, unless they are given up by an act of will, or, more properly as active creation. Do not make the pathetic human error of "clinging to the old rugged cross."[209] The only message of the crucifixion is in respect for man's ability to OVERCOME the cross. Unless he does so, he is free to crucify himself as often as he chooses. But this was NOT the gospel I intended to offer him.

T 4 A 10. We have another journey to undertake, and I hope that, if both of you will read these notes carefully, they will help to prepare you to undertake it. **T(188) C 15**[210]

T 4 B. Right Teaching and Right Learning (*Notes* 403 5:252)

T 4 B 1. We have spoken of many different human symptoms, and at this level there IS almost endless variation. But there is only one cause for all of them. The authority problem IS "the root of all evil."[211] Money is but one of its many reflections, and is a reasonably representative example of the kind of thinking which stems from it. The idea of buying and selling implies precisely the kind of exchange that the Souls cannot understand at all, because their own Supply is always abundant, and all their demands are fully met.

T 4 B 2. Every symptom which the ego has made involves a contradiction in terms. This is because the mind is split between the ego and the Soul, so that WHATEVER the ego makes is incomplete and contradictory. Consider what a "speechless professor" means as a concept. It literally means a "nonprofessing professor," or a "non-speaking speaker."

T 4 B 3. Untenable positions such as this are the result of the authority problem, which, because it accepts the one inconceivable thought as its premise, can only produce ideas which are inconceivable. B. may claim (and has certainly done so in the past) that the PROFESSORSHIP was thrust upon him. This is not true. He wanted it very much, and also worked hard to get it. He would not have had to work so hard either, if he had not misunderstood it.

T 4 B 4. The term "profess" is used quite frequently in the Bible, but in a somewhat different context. To profess is to identify with an idea and offer the idea to others to be THEIR own. The idea does NOT lessen; it becomes STRONGER. **T(189) C 16** The teacher clarifies his own ideas and strengthens them BY teaching them.

---

[205] **Matthew 5:41** "And whoever compels you to go one mile, go with him two."
[206] **Psalms 46:10** Be still, and know that I am God: I will be exalted among the nations, I will be exalted in the earth.
[207] Cervantes's novel "Don Quixote" and its "unhero" Don Juan tilting at windmills is referred to here. See: http://www.wizardacademy.com/TheGospelofDonQuixote.asp for an excellent discussion and biography
[208] From "*Lepanto*" by G.K. Chesterton.
[209] Christian Hymn; words and music by George Bennard, 1913; http://solosong.net/cross.html
"On a hill far away stood an old rugged cross
The emblem of suffering and shame
How I love that old cross where the dearest and best
For a world of lost sinners was slain"
[210] Dec. 26
[211] **1 Timothy 6:10** For the love of money is a root of all kinds of evil, for which some have strayed from the faith in their greediness, and pierced themselves through with many sorrows.

T 4 B 5. Teacher and pupil, therapist and patient, are all alike in the learning process. They are in the SAME order of learning, and unless they SHARE their lessons they will lack conviction. If a salesman must believe in the product he sells, how much more must a teacher believe in the ideas which he professes. But he needs another condition; he must also believe in the students to whom he offers his ideas.

T 4 B 6. B. could not be afraid to teach unless he still believes that interaction means loss, and that learning means separation. He stands guard over his own ideas, because he wants to protect his thought-system as it is, and learning MEANS change. Change is always fearful to the separated, because they cannot conceive of it as a change toward HEALING the separation. They ALWAYS perceive it as a change for further separation, because separation WAS their first experience of change.

T 4 B 7. Bill, your whole fear of teaching is nothing but an example of your own intense separation anxiety, which you have handled with the usual series of mixed defenses in the combined pattern of attack on truth and defense of error, which characterizes ALL ego-thinking.

T 4 B 8. You insist that if you allow no change to enter into your EGO, your SOUL will find peace. This profound confusion is possible only if one maintains that the SAME thought-system can stand on two foundations. **T(190) C 17**

T 4 B 9. NOTHING can reach the Soul from the ego, and nothing FROM the Soul can strengthen the ego, or reduce the conflict within it. The ego IS a contradiction. Man's self and God's Self ARE in opposition. They are opposed in creation, in will, and in outcome. They are fundamentally irreconcilable because the Soul cannot perceive, and the ego cannot know. They are therefore NOT IN COMMUNICATION, and can never BE in communication.

T 4 B 10. Nevertheless the ego can learn, because its maker can be misguided, but CANNOT make the totally lifeless out of the life-given. The Soul need not be taught, but the ego MUST. The ultimate reason why learning or teaching is perceived as frightening is because true learning DOES lead to the relinquishment (NOT destruction) of the ego to the light of the Soul. This is the change the ego MUST fear, because it does not share my charity.

T 4 B 11. My lesson was like yours, and because I learned it I can teach it. I never attack your egos (in spite of H's strange beliefs to the contrary), but I DO try to teach them how their thought-systems have arisen. When I remind you of your TRUE Creation, your egos cannot BUT respond with fear.

T 4 B 12. Bill, teaching and learning are your greatest strengths now, because you MUST change your mind and help others change theirs. It is pointless to refuse to tolerate change or changing because you believe that you can demonstrate by doing so that the Separation never occurred. The dreamer who doubts the reality of his dream while he is still dreaming it is not really healing the level-split. **T(191) C 18**

T 4 B 13. You HAVE dreamed of a separated ego, and you HAVE believed in a world which rested upon it. This is very real to you. You cannot undo this by doing nothing and not changing.

T 4 B 14. If you are willing to renounce the role of guardians of your thought-systems and open them to me, I will correct them very gently, and lead you home. Every good teacher hopes to give his students so much of his own thinking that they will one day no longer need him. This is the one real goal of the parent, teacher, and therapist. This goal will not be achieved by those who believe that they will LOSE their child or pupil or patient if they succeed.

T 4 B 15. It is IMPOSSIBLE to convince the ego of this, because it goes against all of its own laws. But remember that laws are set up to protect the continuity of the system in which the law-maker believes. It is natural enough for the ego to try to protect itself, once YOU have made it. But it is NOT natural for YOU to want to obey its laws unless YOU believe in them.

T 4 B 16. The ego cannot make this choice because of the nature of its origin. But YOU can, because of the nature of YOURS. Egos can clash in any situation, but Souls cannot clash at all. If you perceive a teacher as merely a "larger ego," you WILL be afraid, because to ENLARGE an ego IS to increase separation anxiety. Do not engage in this foolishness, Bill. I will teach with you and live with you, if you will think with me. **T(192) C 19**

T 4 B 17. But my goal will always be to absolve you finally from the need for a teacher. This is the OPPOSITE of the ego-oriented teacher's goal. He is concerned with the effect of HIS ego on OTHER egos, and he therefore interprets their interaction as a means of ego preservation. This is no less true if he is afraid to teach than if he is frankly out to dominate through teaching. The form of the symptom is only a reflection of his particular way of handling the separation anxiety.

T 4 B 18. ALL separation anxiety is a symptom of a continuing will to remain separated. This cannot be repeated too often because you have NOT learned it. Bill, you are afraid to teach ONLY because you are afraid of the impression your image of yourself will make ON OTHER IMAGES. You believe that their APPROVAL of your image will exalt it, but also that your separation anxiety will be increased. You also believe that their DISAPPROVAL of it will lessen the separation anxiety, but at the cost of depression.

T 4 B 19. I would not be able to devote myself to teaching if I believed either of these ideas, and YOU will not be a devoted teacher yourself as long as you maintain them. I am constantly being perceived as a teacher either to be exalted or rejected, but I do not accept either perception for myself.

T 4 B 20. Your own worth is NOT established by your teaching. Your worth was established by God. As long as you dispute this, EVERYTHING you do will be fearful, and particularly any situation which lends itself easily to the superior-inferior fallacy. Teachers must be patient, and repeat their lessons until they are learned. I am willing to do so, because I have no right to set your learning limits for you. **T(193) C 20**

T 4 B 21. Once again,—NOTHING you do, or think, or will, or make is necessary to establish your worth. This point IS NOT DEBATABLE except in delusions. Your ego is NEVER at stake because God did not create it. Your Soul is never at stake because He DID. Any confusion on this point IS a delusion, and no form of devotion is possible as long as this delusion lasts.

T 4 B 22. Bill, if you will to be a devoted teacher rather than an egocentric one, you will not be afraid. The teaching situation IS fearful if it is misused as an ego involvement. If you become afraid, it is BECAUSE you are using it this way. But the devoted teacher perceives the situation AS IT IS, and NOT as HE wills it. He does not see it as dangerous because HE is not exploiting it.

T 4 B 23. The ego tries to exploit ALL situations into forms of praise for itself in order to overcome its doubts. It will be doubtful forever, or better, as long as you believe in it. You who made it CANNOT trust it, because you KNOW it is not real. The ONLY sane solution is not to try to change reality, which is indeed a fearful attempt, but to see it as it is. YOU are part of reality, which stands unchanged beyond the reach of your ego, but within easy reach of your Soul.

T 4 B 24. Bill, again I tell you that when you are afraid, be still and KNOW that God is real and YOU are His beloved son in whom he is well pleased.[212] Do not let your ego dispute this, because the ego

---

[212] **Psalm 46:10** Be still, and know that I am God; I will be exalted among the nations, I will be exalted in the earth! ; Also: **Matthew 17:5** While he was still speaking, behold, a bright cloud overshadowed them; and suddenly

cannot know what is as far beyond its reach as you are. God is NOT the author of fear.[213] YOU are. **T(194) C 21** You have willed, therefore, to create unlike Him, and you have made fear for yourselves.

T 4 B 25. You are not at peace, because you are not fulfilling your function. God gave you a very lofty responsibility which you are not meeting. You KNOW this, and you are afraid. But your egos have chosen to be afraid INSTEAD of meeting it. When you awaken you will not be able to understand this, because it is literally incredible.

T 4 B 26. DO NOT BELIEVE THE INCREDIBLE NOW. Any attempt to increase its believableness is merely to postpone the inevitable. The word "inevitable" is fearful to the ego, but joyous to the Soul. God IS inevitable and you CANNOT avoid Him any more than He can avoid YOU.

T 4 B 27. The ego is afraid of the Soul's joy, because once you have experienced this, you will withdraw all protection from your ego and become totally without investment in fear. Your investment is great now, because fear is a witness to the Separation, and your ego rejoices when you witness to it.

T 4 B 28. Leave it behind. Do not listen to it, and do not preserve it. Listen only to God, who is as incapable of deception as are the Souls he created. As teachers and therapists, release yourselves and release others. Do not present a false and unworthy picture of yourselves TO others, or accept such a picture OF them yourselves.

T 4 B 29. The ego has built a shabby and unsheltering home for you, because it cannot build otherwise. Do not try to make this impoverished house stand.[214] ITS weakness IS your strength.[215] Only God could make a home that was worthy of His Creations, who have chosen to leave it empty by their own dispossession. **T(195) C 22**

T 4 B 30. His Home will stand forever, and is ready for you when you choose to enter. Of this you can be wholly certain. God is as incapable of creating the perishable as your ego is of making the eternal.

T 4 B 31. Of your egos you can do nothing to save yourselves or others. But of your Souls you can do everything for the salvation of both.[216] Humility is a lesson for the ego, not for the Soul. The Soul is beyond humility, because it recognizes its radiance, and gladly sheds its light everywhere.

T 4 B 32. The meek shall inherit the earth[217] because their egos are humble, and this gives them better perception. The Kingdom of Heaven is the right of the Soul, whose beauty and dignity are beyond doubt, beyond perception, and stand forever as the mark of the love of God for His Creations, who are wholly worthy of Him and ONLY of Him. Nothing else is sufficiently worthy to be a gift for a creation of God Himself.

T 4 B 33. I will substitute for your ego if you will, but NEVER for your Soul. A father can safely leave a child with an elder brother who has shown himself responsible, but this involves no confusion about the child's origin. The brother can protect the child's body and his ego, which are very closely associated, but he does not confuse HIMSELF with the father because he does this, although the child may. **T(196) C 23**

T 4 B 34. The reason why I can be entrusted with YOUR body and YOUR egos is simply because this enables YOU not to be concerned with them, and ME to teach you their unimportance. I could not understand their importance to YOU if I had not once been tempted to believe them myself.[218] Let us undertake to learn this lesson together, so we can also be free of them together.

T 4 B 35. I need devoted teachers as much as I need devoted priestesses. They both heal the mind, and that is always my own aim. The Soul is far beyond the need of your protection OR mine.

T 4 B 36. The Biblical quotation should read "In this world you need NOT have tribulation BECAUSE I have overcome the world."[219] THAT is why you should "be of good cheer."

T 4 B 37. B's course was very carefully chosen, because "abnormal psychology" IS ego psychology. This is precisely the kind of content which should never be taught FROM the ego whose abnormality should be lessened by teaching, not increased. You, Bill, are particularly well suited to perceive this difference, and can therefore teach this course as it should be taught. Most teachers have an unfortunate tendency to teach the COURSE abnormally, and many of the students are apt to suffer considerable perceptual distortion because of their own authority problem.

T 4 B 38. Your teaching assignment (and I assure you it IS an assignment) will be to present perceptual distortions without either engaging in them yourself, or encouraging your students to do so. This interpretation of your role and theirs is too charitable to induce fear. **T(197) C 24** If you adhere to this role, you will both engender and experience hope, and you will inspire rather than dispirit the future teachers and therapists I am entrusting to you.

T 4 B 39. I promise to attend myself, and you should at least credit with me with some dependability in keeping my own promises. I never make them lightly, because I know the need my brothers have for trust.

T 4 C. The Ego and False Autonomy (*Notes* 439 6:3)

T 4 C 1. Bill has asked lately how the mind could ever have made the ego. This is a perfectly reasonable question; in fact, the best question either of you could ask. There is no point in giving an historical answer, because the past does not matter in human terms, and history would not exist if the same errors were not being repeated in the present. B. has often told you that your thinking is too abstract at

---

a voice came out of the cloud, saying, "This is My beloved Son, in whom I am well pleased. Hear Him!"

[213] **1 Corinthians 14:33** For God is not the author of confusion but of peace, as in all the churches of the saints.

[214] **Matthew 7:24-27.** "Therefore whoever hears these sayings of Mine, and does them, I will liken him to a wise man who built his house on the rock: and the rain descended, the floods came, and the winds blew and beat on that house; and it did not fall, for it was founded on the rock. But everyone who hears these sayings of Mine, and does not do them, will be like a foolish man who built his house on the sand: and the rain descended, the floods came, and the winds blew and beat on that house; and it fell. And great was its fall."

[215] **2 Corinthians 12:9** And He said to me, "My grace is sufficient for you, for My strength is made perfect in weakness." Therefore most gladly I will rather boast in my infirmities, that the power of Christ may rest upon me.

[216] **John 5:19** Then Jesus answered and said to them, "Most assuredly, I say to you, the Son can do nothing of Himself, but what He sees the Father do; for whatever He does, the Son also does in like manner."

[217] **Psalm 37:11** But the meek shall inherit the earth, And shall delight themselves in the abundance of peace.
Matthew 5:5 "Blessed are the meek, For they shall inherit the earth."

[218] **Matthew 4:1-11** Then Jesus was led up by the Spirit into the wilderness to be tempted by the devil. And when He had fasted forty days and forty nights, afterward He was hungry. Now when the tempter came to Him, he said, "If You are the Son of God, command that these stones become bread." But He answered and said, "It is written, 'Man shall not live by bread alone, but by every word that proceeds from the mouth of God.'" Then the devil took Him up into the holy city, set Him on the pinnacle of the temple, and said to Him, "If You are the Son of God, throw Yourself down. For it is written: 'He shall give His angels charge over you,'" and, "'In their hands they shall bear you up, Lest you dash your foot against a stone.'" Jesus said to him, It is written again, 'You shall not tempt the LORD your God.'" Again, the devil took Him up on an exceedingly high mountain, and showed Him all the kingdoms of the world and their glory. And he said to Him, "All these things I will give You if You will fall down and worship me." Then Jesus said to him, "Away with you, Satan! For it is written, 'You shall worship the LORD your God, and Him only you shall serve.'" Then the devil left Him, and behold, angels came and ministered to Him.

[219] **John 16:33** "These things I have spoken to you, that in Me you may have peace. In the world you will have tribulation; but be of good cheer, I have overcome the world."

times, and he is right. Abstraction DOES apply to knowledge, because knowledge is completely impersonal, and examples are irrelevant to its understanding. Perception, however, is always specific, and therefore quite concrete.

T 4 C 2. Perceptual distortions are not abstractions. They are merely confusions. Each man makes one ego for himself, although it is subject to enormous variation because of its instability, and one for everyone he perceives, which is equally variable. Their interaction IS a process which literally alters both, because they were not made either BY or WITH the unalterable. **T(198) C 25**

T 4 C 3. It is particularly important to realize that this alteration can and does occur as readily when the interaction takes place IN THE MIND as when it involves physical presence. THINKING about another ego is as effective in changing relative perception as is their physical interaction. There could be no better example of the fact that the ego is an idea, though not a reality-based thought. Your own present state is the best concrete example B. could have of how the mind could have made the ego. You DO have real knowledge at times, but when you throw it away it is as if you never had it. This willfulness is so apparent that B. need only perceive it to see that is DOES happen. If it can occur that way in the present, why should he be surprised that it occurred that way in the past? All psychology rests on the principle of continuity of behavior. Surprise is a reasonable response to the unfamiliar, but hardly to something that has occurred with such persistence.

T 4 C 4. An extreme example is a good teaching aid, not because it is typical, but because it is clear. The more complex the material, the clearer the examples should be for teaching purposes. (Bill, remember that for your own course, and do not avoid the dramatic. It holds the student's interest precisely because it is so apparent that it CAN be readily perceived.) But, as we have said before, all teaching devices in the hands of good teachers are aimed at rendering themselves unnecessary. I would therefore like to use your present state as an example of how the mind can work, provided you both fully recognize that it need not work that way. **T(199) C 26** I NEVER forget this myself, and a good teacher shares his own ideas, which he himself believes. Otherwise, he cannot really "profess" them, as we used the term before.

T 4 C 5. With full recognition of its transitory nature, (a recognition which I hope you both share), H. offers a very good teaching example of alternations between Soul and ego, with concomitant variation between peace and frenzy. In answer to B's question, it is perfectly apparent that when she is ego-dominated, she DOES NOT KNOW her Soul. Her abstract ability, which is perfectly genuine and does stem from knowledge, cannot help her because she has turned to the concrete which she cannot handle abstractly. Being incapable of appropriate concreteness perceptually, because her ego is not her natural home, she suffers from its intrusions, but NOT from complete lack of knowledge.

T 4 C 6. The result is a kind of "double vision", which would have produced an actual diplopia, if she had not settled for nearsightedness. This was an attempt to see the concrete more clearly through the ego's eyes, without the "interference" of the longer range. Her virtual lack of astigmatism is due to her real efforts at objectivity and fairness. She has not attained them, or she would not be nearsighted. But she HAS tried to be fair with what she permitted herself to see. **T(200) C 27**

T 4 C 7. Why are you surprised that something happened in the dim past, when it is so clearly happening right now? You forget the love that even animals have for their own offspring, and the need they feel to protect them. This is because they regard them as part of themselves. No one disowns something he regards as a very real part of himself. Man reacts to his ego much as God does to His Souls, -- with love, protection, and great charity. The reaction of man to the self he made is not at all surprising. In fact, it duplicates in many ways the way he will one day react to his real creations, which are as timeless as he is.

T 4 C 8. The question is not HOW man responds toward his ego, but only what he believes he IS. Again, belief is an ego-function, and as long as your origin is open to belief at all, you ARE regarding it from an ego viewpoint. That is why the Bible quotes me as saying, "Ye believe in God, believe also in me."[220] Belief DOES apply to me, because I am the teacher of the ego. When teaching is no longer necessary, you will merely know God.

T 4 C 9. Belief that there IS another way is the loftiest idea of which ego-thinking is capable. This is because it contains a hint of recognition that the ego is NOT the self. Helen always had this idea, but it merely confused her. B., you were more capable of a long-range view, and that is why your eyesight is good. But you were willing to see because you utilized judgment against what you saw. This gave you clearer perception than Helen's, but cut off the cognitive level more deeply. That is why you believe that you never had knowledge. **T(201) C 28**

T 4 C 10. Repression HAS been a stronger mechanism in your own ego defense, and that is why you find her shifts so hard to tolerate. Willfulness is more characteristic of her, and that is why she has less sense than you do. It is extremely fortunate, temporarily, that the particular strengths you will both develop and use are precisely those which the other must supply now. You who will be the strength of God are quite weak, and you who will be God's help are clearly in need of help. What better plan could have been devised to prevent the intrusion of the ego's arrogance on the outcome?

T 4 C 11. Undermining the foundation of an ego's thought-system MUST be perceived as painful, even though this is anything but true. Babies scream in rage if you take away a knife or a scissors, even though they may well harm themselves if you do not. The speedup has placed you both in the same position.

T 4 C 12. You are NOT by any means prepared, and in this sense you ARE babies. You have no sense of real self-preservation and are very likely to decide that you need precisely what would hurt you most. Whether you know it now or not, however, you both HAVE willed to cooperate in a concerted and very commendable effort to become both harmLESS and helpFUL, two attributes which MUST go together. Your attitudes, even toward this, are necessarily conflicted, because ALL attitudes are ego-based. **T(202) C 29**

T 4 C 13. This will not last. Be patient awhile, and remember what we have said once before; the outcome is as certain as God! Helen used to perceive the quotation "To him that hath shall be given"[221] as a paradox that bordered on the ironic. She also had a similar reaction to another related one: "Faith is the gift of God."[222] We have re-interpreted both of these statements before, but perhaps we can make them even clearer now.

T 4 C 14. Only those who have a real and lasting sense of abundance can be truly charitable. This is quite obvious when you consider the concepts involved. To be able to give anything implies that you can do without it. Even if you associate giving with sacrifice, you still give only because you believe you are somehow getting something better so that you can do without the thing you give.

T 4 C 15. "Giving to get" is an inescapable law of the ego, which ALWAYS evaluates itself in relation to others' egos, and is therefore continually preoccupied with the scarcity principle which gave rise to it. This IS the meaning of Freud's "pleasure principle." Freud was the most accurate "ego psychologist" we ever had, although he

---

[220] **John 14:1** "Let not your heart be troubled: ye believe in God, believe also in me."
[221] **Matthew 13:12** "For whosoever hath, to him shall be given, and he shall have more abundance: but whosoever hath not, from him shall be taken away even that he hath."
[222] **1 Corinthians 12:9** "To another faith by the same Spirit; to another the gifts of healing by the same Spirit;"

would not have preferred this description himself. His ego was a very weak and deprived concept, which could function ONLY as a thing in need.

T 4 C 16. The "reality principle" of the ego is not real at all. It is forced to perceive the "reality" of other egos, because it CANNOT establish the reality of itself. In fact, its whole perception of other egos AS real is ONLY an attempt to convince itself that IT is real. **T(203) C 30**

T 4 C 17. "Self esteem," in ego terms, means nothing more than that the ego has deluded itself into accepting its reality and is therefore temporarily less predatory. This "self esteem" is ALWAYS vulnerable to stress, a term which really means that a condition has arisen in which the delusion of reality of the ego is threatened. This produces either ego-deflation or ego-inflation, resulting in either withdrawal or attack. The ego literally lives by comparisons. This means that equality is beyond its grasp, and charity becomes impossible.

T 4 C 18. The ego NEVER gives out of abundance, because it was made as a SUBSTITUTE for it. This is why the concept of GETTING arose in the ego's thought-system. All appetites are "getting" mechanisms representing ego needs to confirm itself. This is as true of bodily appetites as it is of the so-called "higher" ego needs. Bodily appetites are NOT physical in origin, because the ego regards the body as its home, and DOES try to satisfy itself through the body. But the IDEA that this is possible is a decision of the ego, which is completely confused about what is really possible. This accounts for its essential erraticness.

T 4 C 19. Consider the inevitable confusion which MUST arise from a perception of the self which responds: When I was completely on my own I "had no idea what was possible." **T(204) C 31** The ego DOES believe it is completely on its own, which is merely another way of describing how it originated. This is such a fearful state that it can only turn to other egos, and unite with them in a feeble attempt at identification, or attack them in an equally feeble show of strength. The ego is free to complete the stem: "When I was completely on my own" in any way it chooses, but it is NOT free to consider the validity of the premise itself, because this premise is its FOUNDATION. The ego IS the belief of the mind that it is completely on its own.

T 4 C 20. The ego's ceaseless attempts to gain the Soul's acknowledgement and thus establish its own existence are utterly useless. The Soul in its knowledge is unaware of the ego. It does NOT attack the ego. It merely cannot conceive of it at all. While the ego is equally unaware of the Soul, it DOES perceive itself as rejected by something which is greater than itself. This is why self-esteem in ego terms MUST be a delusion.

T 4 C 21. The creations of God do not create myths, but the creative efforts of man can turn to mythology, but only under one condition. What man then makes is no longer creative. Myths are entirely perceptions and are so ambivalent in form, and so characteristically good and evil in nature that the most benevolent of them is not without fearful components, if only in innuendo. **T(205) C 32** Myths and magic are closely associated, in that myths are usually related to the ego origins, and magic to the powers which the ego ascribes to itself. Every mythological system includes an account of "the creation," and associates this with its particular perception of magic.

T 4 C 22. The "battle for survival" is nothing more than the ego's struggle to preserve itself and its interpretation of its own beginning. This beginning is always associated with physical birth, because nobody maintains that the ego existed before that point in time. The religiously ego-oriented tend to believe that the Soul existed before, and will continue to exist afterwards, after a temporary lapse into ego-life. Some actually believe that the Soul will be punished for this lapse, even though in reality it could not possibly know anything about it.

T 4 C 23. The term "salvation" does NOT apply to the Soul, which is not in danger and does not need to be salvaged. Salvation is nothing more that "right-mindedness" which is NOT the one-mindedness of the Soul, but which must be accomplished before one-mindedness can be restored. Right-mindedness dictates the next step automatically, because right perception is uniformly without attack, so that wrong-mindedness is obliterated. The ego cannot survive without judgment, and is laid aside accordingly. The mind then has only ONE direction in which it can move. **T(206) C 33**

T 4 C 24. The directions which the mind will take are always automatic, because they cannot BUT be dictated by the thought-system to which it adheres. Every thought-system has INTERNAL consistency, and this does provide a basis for the continuity of behavior. However, this is still reliability and NOT validity. Reliable behavior is a meaningful perception, as far as ego thinking goes. However, VALID behavior is an expression which is inherently contradictory, because validity is an END, and behavior is a MEANS. These cannot be combined logically, because when an end has been attained, the means for its attainment are no longer meaningful.

T 4 C 25. Test constructors recognize that there are different kinds of validity, and also that they are of different orders. This means that they do not mean truth and do not pretend to mean it. Test validity can be judged by logic, by theory, and by practice, each being regarded as a different dimension. In each case, the amount of confidence is expressed in some form of percentage, either quantitatively, or merely in terms of "high," moderate, and low. But a hypothesis is tested as either true or false, to be accepted or rejected accordingly. If it is shown to be true it becomes a fact, after which no one attempts to evaluate it unless its status AS fact is questioned.

T 4 C 26. EVERY idea which the ego has accorded the status of fact is questionable, because facts are in the realm of knowledge. Confusing realms of discourse is a thinking error which philosophers have recognized for centuries. Psychologists are generally quite deficient in this respect, as are many theologians. Data from one realm of discourse do not mean anything in another, **T(207) C 34** because they can be understood only WITHIN the thought-systems of which they are a part. This is why psychologists are concentrating increasingly on the ego, in an attempt to unify their clearly unrelated data. It need hardly be said that an attempt to relate the unrelated cannot succeed.

T 4 C 27. The recent ecological emphasis is but a more ingenious way of trying to impose order on chaos. We have already credited the ego with considerable ingenuity, though not with creativeness. But it should always be remembered that inventiveness is really wasted effort, even in its most ingenious forms. We do not have to EXPLAIN anything. This is why we need not trouble ourselves with inventiveness. The highly specific nature of invention is not worthy of the abstract creativity of God's Creations. **T(208) C 35**[223]

T 4 D. Love without Conflict (*Notes* 456 6:20)

T 4 D 1. When H. reads this to you, Bill, try to listen very carefully. You have never understood what "The Kingdom of Heaven is within you" means.[224] The reason you cannot understand it is because it is NOT understandable to the ego, which interprets it as if something outside is inside, which does not mean anything. The word "within" does not belong. The Kingdom of Heaven IS you.

T 4 D 2. What else BUT you did the Creator create, and what else but you IS His Kingdom? This is the whole message of the Atonement, a message which in its totality transcends the sum of its parts which we have covered before.[225] Christmas is not a time; it is a state

---

[223] Dec. 27, 1965
[224] **Luke 17:21** Nor will they say, "See here!' or "See there!' For indeed, the kingdom of God is within you."
[225] **T 1 B 22k.; T 2 E 52.;**

of mind. The Christ Mind wills from the Soul, not from the Ego, and the Christ Mind IS yours.

T 4 D 3. You, too, have a Kingdom which your Soul has created. It has not ceased to create because your ego has set you on the road of perception. Your Soul's creations are no more fatherless than you are. Your ego and your Soul will never be co-creators, but your Soul and YOUR Creator will ALWAYS be. Be confident that your creations are as safe as you are. The Kingdom is perfectly united and perfectly protected, and the ego will not prevail against it.[226] Amen.

T 4 D 4. That was written in that form because it is a good thing to use as a kind of prayer in moments of temptation. It is a declaration of independence. You will both find it very helpful if you understand it fully.

T 4 D 5. In its characteristic upside down way, the ego has taken the impulses from the superconscious and perceives them as if they arise in the unconscious. The ego judges what is to be accepted, and the impulses from the superconscious are unacceptable to it, because they clearly point to the unexistence of the ego itself. **T(209) C 36** The ego therefore experiences threat, and not only censors but also re-interprets the data. However, as Freud very correctly pointed out what you do not perceive you still know, and it can retain a very active life BEYOND your awareness.

T 4 D 6. Repression thus operates to conceal not only the baser impulses, but also the most lofty ones from the ego's awareness, because BOTH are threatening to the ego and, being concerned primarily with its preservation in the face of threat, it perceives them as the same. The threat value of the lofty is really much greater to the ego, because the pull of God Himself can hardly be equated with the pull of human appetites.

T 4 D 7. By perceiving them as the same, the ego attempts to save itself from being swept away, as it would surely be in the presence of knowledge. The upper level of the unconscious thus contains the call of God as well as the call of the body. That is why the basic conflict between love and fear is unconscious. The ego cannot tolerate either and represses both by resorting to inhibition. Society depends on inhibiting the former, but SALVATION depends on disinhibiting the latter.[227]

T 4 D 8. The reason you need my help is because you have repressed your own guide, and therefore need guidance. My role is to separate the true from the false in your own unconscious, so it can break through the barriers the ego has set up and shine into your minds. Against our united strength, the ego CANNOT prevail.

T 4 D 9. It should be quite apparent to you by now why the ego regards the Soul as its "enemy." The ego arose from the Separation, and its **T(210) C 37** continued existence depends on your continuing belief in the Separation. Reducing the Soul impulses to the unconscious, the ego has to offer you some sort of reward for maintaining this belief. All it CAN offer is a sense of temporary existence, which begins with its own beginning and ends with its own ending. It tells you that this life is YOUR existence because it IS its own.

T 4 D 10. Against this sense of temporary existence, the Soul offers the knowledge of permanence and unshakeable BEING. No one who has experienced the revelation of this can ever fully believe in the ego again. How can its meager offering to you prevail against the glorious gift of God?

T 4 D 11. You who identify with your egos cannot believe that God loves you. YOU do not love what you have made, and what you have made does not love you. Being made out of the denial of the Father, the ego has no allegiance to its own Maker. You cannot conceive of the real relationship that exists between God and His Souls, because of the hatred you have for the Self you have made. You project onto your own idea of yourself the will to separate, which conflicts with the love you also feel for what you have made because you made it.

T 4 D 12. No human love is without this ambivalence, and since no ego has experienced love WITHOUT ambivalence, the concept is beyond its understanding. Love will enter immediately into any mind which truly wants it, but it MUST want it truly. This means that it wants it WITHOUT ambivalence, and this kind of wanting is wholly without the ego's "drive to get." **T(211) C 38**

T 4 D 13. There is a kind of experience that is so different from anything the ego can offer that you will never recover. The word is used quite literally here, – you will never be able to hide again. It is necessary to repeat that your belief in darkness and in hiding IS why the light cannot enter.

T 4 D 14. The Bible has many references to the immeasurable gifts which are for you, but for which YOU must ask.[228] This is not the condition as the ego sets conditions. It is the glorious condition of what you ARE. No force except your own will is strong enough or worthy enough to guide you. In this you are as free as God, and must remain so forever.

T 4 D 15. You can never be bound except in honor, and that is always voluntary. Let us ask the Father in my name to keep you mindful of His love for you and yours for Him. He has never failed to answer this request, because it asks only for what He has already willed. Those who call truly are ALWAYS answered.

T 4 D 16. Note: HS became very fearful here, and rather vaguely thought the answer was: "Thou shalt have no other Gods before me, because there ARE none.[229] You still think there are."

T 4 D 17. It has never really entered your minds to give up every idea you have ever had that OPPOSES knowledge. You retain thousands of little scraps of meanness which prevent the Holy One from entering.[230] Light cannot penetrate through the walls you make to block it, and it is forever UNwilling to destroy what you have made. No one can see THROUGH a wall, but I can step around it. **T(212) C 39**

T 4 D 18. Watch your minds for the scraps of meanness, or you will be unable to ask me to do so. I can help you only as our Father Created us. I will love you and honor you and maintain complete respect for what you have made. But I will neither love nor honor it unless it is true. I will never forsake you, any more than God will. But I MUST wait as long as you will to forsake yourselves.

T 4 D 19. Because I wait in love and not in impatience, you will surely ask me truly. I will come gladly in response to a single unequivocal call. Watch carefully, and see what it is you are truly asking for. Be very honest with yourselves about this, for you we must hide nothing from each other.

T 4 D 20. If you will REALLY try to do this, you have taken the first step toward preparing your minds for the Holy One to enter. We will prepare for this together, and once He has come, you will be ready to help me make other minds ready for Him. How long will you deny Him His Kingdom? **T(213) C 40**[231]

T 4 D 21. In your own unconscious, deeply repressed by the ego, is the declaration of your release. GOD HAS GIVEN YOU EVERY-

---

[226] **Matthew 16:18** "And I also say to you that you are Peter, and on this rock I will build My church, and the gates of Hades shall not prevail against it."
[227] "Former" and "latter" here refer to **T 4 D 6.** "the baser impulses" and "the most lofty." Society depends on inhibiting baser, salvation depends on disinhibiting the most lofty. Later versions swap "former" and "latter" in a most curious copying mistake.

[228] **Matthew 7:7** "Ask, and it will be given to you; seek, and you will find; knock, and it will be opened to you."
[229] **Exodus 20:3** "You shall have no other gods before Me."
[230] **Mark 1:24** Saying, "Let us alone! What have we to do with You, Jesus of Nazareth? Did You come to destroy us? I know who You are--the Holy One of God!"
[231] Jan. 7, '66

THING. This is the one fact which MEANS that the ego does not exist, and which therefore makes it profoundly afraid. In the ego's language, to have and to be are different, but they are identical to the Soul. It knows that you both HAVE everything and ARE everything. Any distinction in this respect is meaningful only when the idea of getting, which implies a lack, has already BEEN accepted. That is why we made no distinction before between HAVING the Kingdom of God and BEING the Kingdom of God.

T 4 D 22. The calm being of God's Kingdom, which in your sane mind is perfectly conscious, is ruthlessly banished from the part of the mind which the ego rules. The ego is desperate because it opposes literally invincible odds whether you are asleep or awake. Consider how much vigilance you have been willing to exert to protect your ego, and how little you have been willing to exert to protect your higher mind. Who but the insane would undertake to believe what is not true, and then protect this belief at the cost of Truth?

T 4 E. The Escape from Fear (*Notes* 467 6:31)

T 4 E 1. If you cannot hear the voice of God, it is because you do not choose to listen. The fact that you DO listen to the voice of your ego is demonstrated by your attitudes, your feelings, and your behavior. Your attitudes are obviously conflicted; your feelings have a narrow range on the negative side, but are never purely joyous; and your behavior is either strained or unpredictable. **T(214) C 41** Yet this IS what you want. This is what you are fighting to keep, and what you are vigilant to save. Your minds are filled with schemes to save the face of your egos, and you do not seek the Face of God.

T 4 E 2. The glass in which the ego seeks to see its face is dark indeed.[232] How can it maintain the trick of its existence except with mirrors? But where you look to find yourself is up to you. We have said that you cannot change your mind by changing your behavior, but we have also said, and many times before, that you CAN change your mind.

T 4 E 3. When your mood tells you that you have willed wrongly, and this is so whenever you are not joyous, then KNOW this need not be.

T 4 E 4. In every case you have thought wrongly about some Soul that God created, and are perceiving images your ego makes in a darkened glass. Think honestly what you have thought that God would NOT have thought, and what you have NOT thought that God would have you think. Search sincerely for what you have done and left undone accordingly. And then change your minds to THINK WITH GOD's.

T 4 E 5. This may seem hard to you, but it is MUCH easier than trying to think AGAINST it. Your mind IS one with God's. Denying this and thinking otherwise has held your ego together, but has literally split your mind. As a loving brother, I am deeply concerned with your minds, and urge you to follow my example as you look at yourselves and at each other and see in both the glorious Creations of a glorious Father.

T 4 E 6. When you are sad, KNOW that this NEED NOT BE. Depression ALWAYS arises ultimately from a sense of being deprived of something you want and do not have. **T(215) C 42** KNOW you are deprived of nothing, except by your own decisions, and then decide otherwise.

T 4 E 7. When you are anxious, KNOW that all anxiety comes from the capriciousness of the ego, and NEED NOT BE. You can be as vigilant AGAINST the ego's dictates as FOR them.

T 4 E 8. When you feel guilty, KNOW that your ego has indeed violated the laws of God, but YOU have not. Leave the sins of the ego to me. That is what the Atonement is for. But until you change your mind about those your ego has hurt, the Atonement cannot release you. As long as you feel guilty, your ego is in command, because only the ego CAN experience guilt. THIS NEED NOT BE.

T 4 E 9. You, Helen, have been more honest that B. in really trying to see whom your ego has hurt, and also in trying to change your mind about them. (HS doubtful whether this is accurate – written at a time when she was very angry.) I am not unmindful of your efforts, but you still have much too much energy invested in your ego. THIS NEED NOT BE. Watch your minds for the temptations of the ego, and do not be deceived by it. KNOW it offers you nothing.

T 4 E 10. You, B, have not made consistent efforts to change your mind except through applying old habit patterns to new ideas. But you have learned, and learned it better than H., (HS doubtful about accuracy here) that your mind gains control over ITSELF when you direct it genuinely toward perceiving someone ELSE truly. Your lack of vitality is due to your former marked effort at solving your needless depression and anxiety through disinterest. Because your ego WAS protected by this unfortunate negative attribute, you are afraid to abandon it. **T(216) C 43**

T 4 E 11. When you have given up this voluntary dis-spiriting, you have already seen how your mind can focus, and rise above fatigue, and heal. But you are not sufficiently vigilant against the demands of your ego that you disengage yourself. THIS NEED NOT BE. The habit of engaging WITH God and His Creations is easily made if you refuse actively to let your minds slip away. Your problem is not concentration: it is a belief that nobody, including yourself, is WORTH consistent effort.

T 4 E 12. Side with me CONSISTENTLY against this deception, as we have sided against it briefly already. Do not permit this shabby belief to pull you back. The disheartened are useless to themselves and to me, but only the ego can be disheartened.

T 4 E 13. Have you REALLY considered how many opportunities you have to gladden yourselves, and how many of them you have refused? There is no limit to the power of a Son of God, but he himself can limit the expression of his power as much as he wills. Your mind and mine can unite in shining your ego away, and releasing the strength of God into everything you think and will and do. Do no settle for ANYTHING less than this, and refuse to accept anything BUT this as your goal.

T 4 E 14. Watch your minds carefully for any beliefs that hinder its accomplishment, and step away from them. Judge how well you have done this by your own feelings, for this is the one RIGHT use of judgment. Judgment, like any other defense, can be used to attack or protect, to hurt or to heal. The ego SHOULD be brought to your own judgment and found wanting there. Without your own allegiance, protection, and love it cannot exist. **T(217) C 44**

T 4 E 15. Judge your ego truly, and you MUST withdraw allegiance, protection, and love from it. You are mirrors of truth in which God Himself shines in perfect light. To the ego's dark glass you need but say, "I will not look there because I KNOW these images are not true."

T 4 E 16. Then let me the Holy One shine upon you in peace,[233] knowing that this and only this MUST be! His Mind shone on you in your creation, and brought YOUR mind into being. His Mind still shines on you and MUST shine THROUGH you. Your ego cannot prevent HIM from shining on you, but it CAN prevent you from letting Him shine THROUGH you.

T 4 E 17. The first coming of Christ is just another name for the Creation, for Christ is the Son of God. The SECOND coming of Christ means nothing more than the end of the ego's rule over part

---

[232] **1 Corinthians 13:12** For now we see in a mirror, dimly, but then face to face. Now I know in part, but then I shall know just as I also am known.

[233] **Numbers 6:25-26** The LORD make His face shine upon you, And be gracious to you; The LORD lift up His countenance upon you, And give you peace.'"

of the minds of men, and the healing of the mind.[234] I was created like you in the First, and I am reminding you that I have called you to join with me in the Second.

T 4 E 18. If you will think over your lives, you will see how carefully the preparations were made. I am in charge of the Second Coming as I have already told you, and my judgment, which is used only for its protection, cannot be wrong because it NEVER attacks.[235] YOURS is so distorted that you believe that I was mistaken in choosing you. I assure you this is a mistake of your own egos. Do NOT mistake it for humility.

T 4 E 19. Your egos are trying to convince you that THEY are real, and I am not, because if I AM real, I am no more real than YOU are. That knowledge, and I assure you that it IS knowledge, means that Christ must come into your minds and heal them. **T(218) C 45**

T 4 E 20. While I am not attacking your egos, I AM working with your higher mind whether you are asleep or awake, (just as your ego does with your lower mind.) I am your vigilance in this, because you are too confused to recognize your own hope.

T 4 E 21. I was not mistaken. Your minds WILL elect to join with mine, and together we are invincible. You two will yet come together in my name and your sanity will be restored.[236] I raised the dead by KNOWING that life is an eternal attribute of everything that the living God Created.[237] Why do you believe that it is harder for me to inspire the dis-spirited or to stabilize the unstable? I do not believe that there is an order of difficulty in miracles: YOU do. I have called and you will answer. I KNOW that miracles are natural, because they are expressions of love. My calling you is as natural as your answer and as inevitable. **T(219) C 46**[238]

T 4 F. The Ego-Body Illusion (*Notes* 477 6:41)

T 4 F 1. ALL things work together for good.[239] There are NO exceptions except in the ego's judgment. Control is a central factor in what the ego permits into consciousness, and one to which it devotes its maximum vigilance. This is NOT the way a balanced mind holds together. ITS control is unconscious.

T 4 F 2. The ego is further off balance by keeping its primary motivation UNconscious, and raising control rather than sensible judgment to predominance. It has every reason to do this, according to the thought-system which both gave rise to it and which it serves. Sane judgment would inevitably judge AGAINST it, and MUST be obliterated by the ego in the interest of its self-preservation.

T 4 F 3. A crucial source of the ego's off-balance state is its lack of discrimination between impulses from God and from the body. Any thought-system which makes THIS confusion MUST be insane. Yet this demented state is ESSENTIAL to the ego, which judges ONLY in terms of threat or nonthreat TO ITSELF.

T 4 F 4. In one sense, the ego's fear of the idea of God is at least logical, because this idea DOES dispel it. Fear of dissolution from the higher source, then, makes SOME sense in ego terms. But fear of the body, with which the ego identifies so closely, is more blatantly senseless. The body is the ego's home by its own election. It is the only identification with which it feels safe, because the body's vulnerability is its own best argument that you CANNOT be of God. **T(220) C 47**

T 4 F 5. This is the belief that it sponsors eagerly. Yet the ego hates the body, because it does not accept the idea that the body is good enough as its home. Here is where the mind becomes actually dazed. Being told by the ego that it is really part of the body, and that the body is its protector, it is also constantly informed that the body can NOT protect it. This, of course, is not only true, but perfectly obvious.

T 4 F 6. Therefore, the mind asks, "Where can I go for protection?", to which the ego replies, "Turn to me." The mind, and not without cause, reminds the ego that it has itself insisted that it IS identified with the body, so there is no point in turning to it for protection. The ego has no real answer to this because there ISN'T any. But it DOES have a typical solution. It obliterates the question from the mind's awareness. Once unconscious, it can and does produce uneasiness, but it cannot be answered because it cannot be asked.

T 4 F 7. This is the question which MUST be asked: "Where am I to go for protection?" Only an insane mind FAILS to ask it. Even the insane ask it unconsciously, but it requires real sanity to ask it consciously.

T 4 F 8. If you will remember your dream about the recorder, which was remarkably accurate in some ways because it came partly from ego-repressed knowledge, the real problem was correctly stated as "What is the question?" **T(221) C 48** because, as you very well knew, the answer COULD be found if the question were recognized. If you remember, there were a number of solutions you attempted, all ego-based, not because you thought they would really work, but because the question ITSELF was obscure.

T 4 F 9. When the Bible says "Seek and ye shall find,"[240] it does NOT mean that you should seek blindly and desperately for something you wouldn't recognize. Meaningful seeking is consciously undertaken, consciously organized, and consciously directed. B's chief contribution to your joint venture is his insistence that the goal be formulated clearly, and KEPT IN MIND.

T 4 F 10. You, Helen, are not good at doing this. You still search for many gods[241] simultaneously, and this goal confusion, given a strong will, MUST produce chaotic behavior. B's behavior is not chaotic, because he is not so much goal-divided as not goal-ORIENTED. Where Helen has overinvested in many goals, B has underinvested in ALL goals. He has the advantage of POTENTIALLY greater freedom from distractibility, but he does not care enough to use it. Helen has the advantage of great effort, but she keeps losing sight of the goal.

T 4 F 11. B has very intelligently suggested that you both should set yourself the goal of really studying for this course. There can be no doubt of the wisdom of this decision, for any student who wants to pass it. But, knowing your individual weaknesses as learners and being **T(222) C 49** a teacher with some experience, I must remind you that learning and wanting to learn are inseparable.

T 4 F 12. All learners learn best when they believe that what they are trying to learn is of value to them. But values in this world are hierarchical, and not everything you may WANT to learn has lasting value. **T(223) C 50** Indeed, many of the things you want to learn are chosen BECAUSE their value will not last. The ego thinks it is an advantage not to commit itself to ANYTHING that is eternal, because the eternal MUST come from God.

T 4 F 13. Eternalness is the one function that the ego has tried to develop, but has systematically failed. It may surprise you to learn that had the ego willed to do so, it COULD have made the eternal,

---

[234] **Matthew 16:27** "For the Son of Man will come in the glory of His Father with His angels, and then He will reward each according to his works."
[235] **Matthew 16:27** "For the Son of Man will come in the glory of His Father with His angels, and then He will reward each according to his works."
[236] **Matthew 18:20** "For where two or three are gathered together in My name, I am there in the midst of them."
[237] **John 11:43-44** Now when He had said these things, He cried with a loud voice, "Lazarus, come forth!" And he who had died came out bound hand and foot with graveclothes, and his face was wrapped with a cloth. Jesus said to them, "Loose him, and let him go."
[238] 1/12/66
[239] **Romans 8:28** And we know that all things work together for good to those who love God, to those who are the called according to His purpose.

[240] **Matthew 7:7** "Ask, and it will be given to you; seek, and you will find; knock, and it will be opened to you."
[241] While the *Urtext* manuscript does have "gods" here, the *Notes* is rather ambiguous, and very possibly this should be "goals."

because, as a product of the mind, it IS endowed with the power of its own creator. But the DECISION to do this, rather than the ABILITY to do it is what the ego cannot tolerate. That is because the decision, from which the ability would naturally develop, would necessarily involve true perception, a state of clarity which the ego, fearful of being judged truly, MUST avoid.

T 4 F 14. The results of this dilemma are peculiar, but no more so than the dilemma itself. The ego has reacted characteristically here as elsewhere, because mental illness, which is ALWAYS a form of ego-involvement, is not a problem of reliability as much as of validity. The ego compromises with the issue of the eternal, just as it does with all issues that touch on the real question in ANY way. By compromising in connection with all TANGENTIAL questions, it hopes to hide the REAL question and keep it OUT OF MIND. Its characteristic "business" with non-essentials is precisely for that purpose.

T 4 F 15. Consider the alchemist's age-old attempts to turn base metal into gold. (This typo was originally "god"). The one question which the alchemist did not permit himself to ask was "What For?" He COULD not ask this, because it would immediately become apparent that there was no sense in his efforts, even if he succeeded. The ego has also countenanced some strange compromises with the idea of the eternal, making odd attempts to relate the concept to the unimportant in an effort to satisfy the mind without jeopardizing itself. Thus, it has permitted many good minds to devote themselves to perpetual MOTION, but NOT to perpetual THOUGHTS.

T 4 F 16. Ideational preoccupations with conceptual problems set up to be incapable of solution are another favorite ego device for impeding the strong-willed from real progress in learning. The problems of squaring the circle, and carrying pi to infinity are good examples. A more recent ego-attempt is particularly noteworthy. The idea of preserving the body by suspension, thus giving it the kind of limited immortality **T(224) C 51** which the ego can tolerate, is among its more recent appeals to the mind.

T 4 F 17. It is noticeable that in all these diversionary tactics, the ONE question which is NEVER asked by those who pursue them is "What for?" This is the question which YOU must learn to ask in connection with everything your mind wills to undertake. What is your purpose? Whatever it is, you cannot doubt that it will channelize your efforts automatically. When you make a decision of purpose, then, you HAVE made a decision about future effort, a decision which will remain in effect UNLESS you change the DECISION.

T 4 F 18. Psychologists are in a good position to realize that the ego is capable of making and accepting as real some very distorted associations which are not true. The confusion of sex with aggression, and resulting behavior which is the same for BOTH, is a good example. This is understandable to the psychologist, and does not produce surprise. The lack of surprise, however, is NOT a sign of understanding. It is a symptom of the psychologist's ability to accept as reasonable a compromise which is clearly senseless, to attribute it to the mental illness of the patient rather than his own, and to limit his questions about both the patient AND himself to the trivial.

T 4 F 19. These relatively minor confusions of the ego are not among its more profound misassociations, although they DO reflect them. Your own egos have been blocking the more important questions which your minds should ask. You do NOT understand a patient while you yourselves are willing to limit the questions you raise about HIS mind, because you are also accepting these limits for YOURS. This makes you unable to heal him AND yourselves. Be ALWAYS unwilling to adapt to ANY situation in which miracle-mindedness is unthinkable. That state in ITSELF is enough to demonstrate that perception is wrong.

T 4 G. The Constant State (*Notes 487 6:51*)

T 4 G 1. It cannot be emphasized too often that CORRECTING perception is merely a temporary expedient. It is necessary ONLY because Misperception is a BLOCK to knowledge, while ACCURATE perception is a stepping-stone TOWARD it. The whole value of right perception lies in the inevitable judgment which it necessarily entails that it is UNNECESSARY. This removes the block entirely.

T 4 G 2. You may ask how this is possible as long as you appear to be living in this world. And since this is a sensible question, it has a sensible answer. But you **T(225) C 52** must be careful that you really understand the question. What IS the you who are living in this world? Bill will probably have more trouble with this than you, but if he will try not to close his mind, he may decide that we are NOT engaging in denial after all.

T 4 G 3. To help him, it might be wise to review a number of the concepts with which he does not appear to have trouble, except at times. He liked the idea of invisibility, and was particularly open to the concept of different orders of reality. He also found the notion of varying densities of energy appealing. While he may yet agree that these are merely teaching aids, this is a good time to employ them.

T 4 G 4. Immortality is a constant state. It is as true now as it ever was or will be, because it implies NO CHANGE AT ALL. It is not a continuum, and it is NOT understood by comparing it with any opposite. Knowledge NEVER involves comparisons. That is its essential difference from everything else the mind can grasp.

T 4 G 5. "A little knowledge" is not dangerous except to the ego. Vaguely the ego senses threat, and, being unable to realize that "a little knowledge" is a meaningless phrase because "all" and "a little" in this context are the same, decides that since "all" is impossible, the fear does not lie in this. "A little," however, is a scarcity concept, and this the ego understands well. Regarding "all" as impossible, "a little" is perceived as the real threat.

T 4 G 6. The essential thing to remember always is that the ego DOES NOT RECOGNIZE the real source of its perceived threat. And if YOU associate yourself WITH the ego, YOU do not perceive the whole situation as it really is. Only your allegiance to it gives the ego ANY power over you. We have spoken of the ego as if it were a separate thing, acting on its own. This was necessary to persuade you that you cannot dismiss it lightly, and MUST realize how much of your thinking is ego-directed. But we cannot safely leave it at that, or you will regard yourselves as necessarily conflicted as long as you are here, or more properly, BELIEVE that you are here.

T 4 G 7. The ego is nothing more than a PART of your belief about yourselves. Your other life has continued without interruption, and has been and always will be totally unaffected by your attempts to dissociate. The ratio of repression and **T(226) C 53** dissociation of truth varies with the individual ego-illusion (tell Bill that phrase is VERY good), but dissociation is always involved, or you would not believe that you ARE here.

T 4 G 8. When I told Bill to concentrate on the phrase "here I am, Lord," I did not mean "in this world" by "here." I wanted him to think of himself as a separate consciousness, capable of direct communication with the Creator of that consciousness. He, too, MUST begin to think of himself as a very powerful receiving and sending channel, a description I once gave you symbolically. Remember that HE understood it before you did, because you are more dissociative and less repressed.

T 4 G 9. Your great debt to each other is something you should never forget. It is exactly the same debt that you owe to me. Whenever you react egotistically toward each other, you are throwing away the graciousness of your indebtedness and the holy perception it would produce. The reason why the term "holy" can be used here is that, as you learn how much you ARE indebted to the whole Sonship which includes me, you come as close to knowledge as perception ever can. This gap is so small knowledge can easily flow across it and obliterate it forever.

T 4 G 10. You have very little trust in me as yet, but it will increase as you turn more and more often to me instead of to your egos for guidance. The results will convince you increasingly that your choice in turning to me is the only sane one you can make. No one who has learned from experience that one choice brings peace and joy while another brings chaos and disaster needs much conditioning. The ego cannot withstand the conditioning process, because the process itself DEMONSTRATES that there is another way.

T 4 G 11. The classic conditioning by rewards model has always been most effective. Howard Hunt made a very good point in this connection, even though he did not understand that the real reason why conditioning through pain is not the most efficient method is because pain itself is an ego-illusion, and can never induce more than a temporary effect.

T 4 G 12. The rewards of God are immediately recognized as eternal. Since this recognition is made by YOU and NOT by your ego, the recognition ITSELF establishes that you and your ego CANNOT be identical. You may believe that you have already accepted the difference, but you are by no means convinced as yet. The very fact that you are preoccupied with the idea of escaping FROM the ego shows this. **T(227) C 54**

T 4 G 13. You cannot escape from the ego by humbling it, or controlling it, or punishing it. The ego and the Soul DO NOT KNOW each other. The separated mind cannot maintain the separation EXCEPT by dissociating. Having done this, it utilizes repression against all truly natural impulses, not because the EGO is a separate thing, but because you want to believe that YOU are. The ego is a device for maintaining this belief, but it is still only YOUR willingness to use the device that enables it to endure.

T 4 G 14. My trust in you is greater than yours in me at the moment, but it will not always be that way. Your mission is very simple. You have been chosen to live so as to demonstrate that You are NOT an ego. I repeat that I do not choose God's channels wrongly. The Holy One[242] shares my trust and always approves my Atonement decisions, because my will is never out of accord with His.

T 4 G 15. I have told you several times that I am in charge of the whole Atonement. This is ONLY because I completed my part in it as a man, and can now complete it through other men. My chosen receiving and sending channels cannot fail, because I will lend them MY strength as long as theirs is wanting. I will go with you to the Holy One, and through MY perception HE can bridge the little gap. Your gratitude to each OTHER is the only gift I want. I will bring it to God for you, knowing that to know your brother IS to know God.

T 4 G 16. A little knowledge is an all-encompassing thing. If you are grateful to each other you are grateful to God for what He created. Through your gratitude you can come to know each other, and one moment of real recognition makes all men your brothers because they are all of your Father. Love does not conquer all things, but it DOES set all things right.

T 4 G 17. Because you are all the Kingdom of God, I can lead you back to your own creations, which you do not yet know. God has kept them very safe in HIS knowing while your attention has wandered. Bill gave you a very important idea when he told you that what has been dissociated IS STILL THERE. I am grateful to him for that, and I hope he will not decide that it is true only for you. Even though dissociation is much more apparent in you, and repression is much more evident in him, each of you utilizes both.

T 4 G 18. Wisdom always dictates that a therapist work through WEAKER defenses first. That is why I suggested to Bill that he persuade you to deal with REPRESSION first. **T(228) C 55** We have only just about reached the point where dissociation means much to you, because it is so important to your misbeliefs. Bill might do well, - and you could help him here, - to concentrate more on HIS dissociative tendencies and not try to deal with repression yet.

T 4 G 19. I hinted at this when I remarked on his habit of disengaging himself, and when I spoke to him about distantiation. These are all forms of dissociation, and these weaker forms were always more evident in him than in you. That is because dissociation was so extreme in your case that you did not have to hide it because you were not aware that it was there. Bill, on the other hand, DOES dissociate more than he thinks, and that is why he cannot listen. He does not need to go through the same course in repression that you did, because he will give up his major misdefense AFTER he has rid himself of the lesser ones.

T 4 G 20. Do not disturb yourself about repression, Bill, but DO train yourself to be alert to any tendency to withdraw from your brothers. Withdrawal is frightening, and you do not recognize all the forms it takes in you. Helen is right that she will experience things that will cut across all her perceptions because of their stunning knowledge. You were right that this will occur when she learns to recognize what she ALREADY knows and has dissociated.

T 4 G 21. You, Bill, will learn somewhat differently, because you are afraid of all complete involvements, and believe that they lessen YOU. You have learned to be so much more clear-sighted about this that you should be ready to oppose it in yourself RELATIVELY easily. As you come closer to a brother, you DO approach me, and as you withdraw from him I become distant to you.

T 4 G 22. Your giant step forward was to INSIST on a collaborative venture. This does NOT go against the true spirit of meditation at all. It is inherent IN it. Meditation is a collaborative venture with GOD. It CANNOT be undertaken successfully by those who disengage themselves from the Sonship, because they are disengaging themselves from me. God will come to you only as you will give Him to your brothers. Learn first of them, and you will be ready to hear God as you hear them. That is because the function of love is One.

T 4 G 23. How can you teach someone the value of something he has thrown away deliberately? He must have thrown it away because he did NOT value it. You can only show him how **T(229) C 56** miserable he is WITHOUT it, and bring it near very slowly, so he can learn how his misery lessens as he approaches it. This conditions him to associate his misery with its ABSENCE, and to associate the OPPOSITE of misery with its presence. It gradually becomes desirable, as he changes his mind about its worth.

T 4 G 24. I am conditioning you to associate misery with the ego, and joy with your Soul. You have conditioned yourself the other way around. But a far greater reward will break through any conditioning, if it is repeatedly offered when the old habit is broken. You are still free to choose. But can you really WANT the rewards of the ego in the presence of the rewards of God?

T 4 H. Creation and Communication (*Notes* 508 6:72)

T 4 H 1. It should be clear that, while the content of any particular ego-illusion does not matter, it is usually more helpful to correct it in a specific context. Bill is right that you are too abstract in this matter. Ego-illusions are QUITE specific, although they frequently change, and although the mind is naturally abstract, it became concrete voluntarily as soon as it splits. However, only PART of it splits, so only PART of it is concrete.

T 4 H 2. The concrete part is the same part that believes in the ego, because the ego DEPENDS on the specific. It is the part that believes your existence means you are SEPARATE. Everything the

---
[242] Mark 1:24 Saying, "Let us alone! What have we to do with You, Jesus of Nazareth? Did You come to destroy us? I know who You are--the Holy One of God!"

ego perceives is a separate whole, without the relationships that imply BEING. The ego is thus AGAINST communication, except in so far as it is utilized to ESTABLISH separateness, rather than to abolish it.

T 4 H 3. The communication system of the ego is based on its own thought-system, as is everything else it dictates. Its communication is controlled by its need to protect itself, and it will disrupt communication when it experiences threat. While this is always so, individual egos perceive different kinds of threat, which are quite specific in their own judgment. For example, although all forms of perceived demands may be classified (or judged) by the ego as coercive communication which must be disrupted, the response of breaking communication will nevertheless be to a SPECIFIC PERSON or persons.

T 4 H 4. The specificity of the ego's thinking, then, results in a spurious kind of generalization, which is really not abstract at all. It will respond in certain specific ways to all stimuli which it perceives as related. In contrast, the Soul reacts in the same way to everything it know is true, and does not respond at all to anything else. Nor does it make any attempt to ESTABLISH what is true. It knows **T(230) C 57** that what is true is everything that God created. It is in complete and direct communication with every aspect of Creation, because it is in complete and direct communication with its Creator.

T 4 H 5. THIS communication IS the will of God. Creation and communication are synonymous. God created every mind by communicating His Mind to it, thus establishing it forever as a channel for the reception of His Mind and Will. Since only beings of a like order can truly communicate. His Creations naturally communicate WITH Him and communicate LIKE Him. This communication is perfectly abstract, in that its quality is universal in application, and not subject to ANY judgment, ANY exception, or ANY alteration.

T 4 H 6. God made you BY this and FOR this. The mind can distort its functions, but it cannot endow itself with those it was not given. That is why the mind cannot totally lose the ability to communicate, even though it may refuse to utilize it on behalf of being. Existence as well as being rests on communication.

T 4 H 7. Existence is SPECIFIC in how, what, and with whom communication is worth undertaking. Being is completely without these distinctions. It is a state in which the mind IS in communication with everything that is real, including its own Soul. To whatever extent you permit this state to be curtailed, you are limiting your sense of your OWN reality, which becomes total only by recognizing ALL reality in the glorious context of its real relationship to YOU. This IS your reality. Do not desecrate it or recoil from it. It is your real home, your real temple,[243] and your real self.

T 4 H 8. God, who encompasses ALL Being, nevertheless created separate beings who have everything individually, but who want to share it to increase their joy. Nothing that is real can be increased EXCEPT by sharing it. That is why God Himself created you. Divine Abstraction takes joy in application, and that is what creation MEANS. How, what, and to whom are irrelevant, because real creation gives everything since it can only create like itself. Remember that in being, there is no difference between having and being, as there is in existence. In the state of being, the mind gives everything always.

T 4 H 9. The Bible repeatedly states that you should praise God.[244] This hardly means that you should tell Him how wonderful He is. He has no ego with which to accept **T(231) C 58** thanks, and no perceptions with which to judge your offerings. But unless you take your part in the creation, His joy is not complete because YOURS is incomplete. And THIS He does know. He knows it in his own Being and its experience of His Sons' experience. The constant GOING OUT of His love is blocked when His Channels are closed, and He IS lonely when the minds He created do not communicate fully with Him.

T 4 H 10. God HAS kept your kingdom for you, but He cannot share His joy with you until you know it with your whole mind. Even revelation is not enough, because it is communication FROM God. But it is not enough until it is shared. God does not need revelation returned to Him, which would clearly be impossible, but He DOES want revelation brought to others. This cannot be done with the actual revelation, because its content cannot be expressed, and it is intensely personal to the mind which receives it. But it can still be returned BY that mind through its attitudes to other minds which the knowledge from the revelation brings.

T 4 H 11. God is praised whenever any mind learns to be wholly helpful. This is impossible without being wholly harmless, because the two beliefs cannot coexist. The truly helpful are invulnerable, because they are NOT protecting their egos, so that nothing CAN hurt them. Their helpfulness IS their praise of God, and He will return their praise of Him, because they are like Him and can rejoice together. God goes out to them and through them, and there is great joy throughout the Kingdom. Every mind that is changed adds to this joy with its own individual willingness to share in it.

T 4 H 12. The truly helpful are God's miracle-workers, whom I direct until we are all united in the joy of the kingdom. I will direct you to wherever you can be truly helpful, and to whoever can follow my guidance through you. I arranged for Bill to attend the rehabilitation meetings for very good reasons, and I want him to know them so we can share our goal there.

T 4 I. True Rehabilitation (*Notes* 514 6:77)

T 4 I 1. Properly speaking, every mind which is split needs rehabilitation. The medical orientation emphasizes the body, and the vocational orientation stresses the ego. The team approach generally leads more to confusion than anything else, because it is too often misused as an expedient for sharing the ego's dominion with other ego's rather than as a real experiment in cooperation of minds. **T(232) C 59**

T 4 I 2. The reason why Bill needs this experience is because he needs rehabilitating himself. How often have I answered "help him" when you asked me to help you? He, too, has asked for help, and he has been helped whenever he was truly helpful to you. He has also gained to whatever extent he could give. He will help YOU more

---

[243] **1 Corinthians 3:16** Do you not know that you are the temple of God and that the Spirit of God dwells in you?

[244] **Psalm 150:1-6** Praise the LORD!
Praise God in His sanctuary;
Praise Him in His mighty firmament!
Praise Him for His mighty acts;
Praise Him according to His excellent greatness!
Praise Him with the sound of the trumpet;
Praise Him with the lute and harp!
Praise Him with the timbrel and dance;
Praise Him with stringed instruments and flutes!
Praise Him with loud cymbals;
Praise Him with clashing cymbals!
Let everything that has breath praise the LORD.
 Praise the LORD!
Luke 19:37 And as he was now drawing nigh, *even* at the descent of the mount of Olives, the whole multitude of the disciples began to rejoice and praise God with a loud voice for all the mighty works which they had seen;
Romans 15:11 Praise the LORD, all you Gentiles!
 Laud Him, all you peoples!

truly by going, if he can remember all the time he is there that his ONLY reason for being there is to REPRESENT ME.

T 4 I 3. Rehabilitation, as a movement, has been an improvement over overt neglect, but it is often little more than a painful attempt on the part of the halt to lead the blind. Bill, you will see this at every meeting. But this is not why you were chosen to go. You have a fear of broken bodies, because your ego cannot tolerate them. Your[245] ego cannot tolerate ego-weakness, either, without ambivalence, because it is afraid of its own weakness and the weakness of its chosen home.

T 4 I 4. That is really why you recoil from the demands of the dependent, and from the sight of a broken body. Your ego is threatened, and blocks your natural impulse to help, placing you under the strain of divided will. You withdraw to allow your ego to recover, and to regain enough strength to be helpful again on a basis limited enough NOT to threaten your ego, but also too limited to give YOU joy.

T 4 I 5. Those with broken bodies are often looked down on by the ego, because of its belief that nothing but a perfect body is worthy as its OWN temple. A mind that recoils from a hurt body is in great need of rehabilitation itself. A damaged brain is also hardly a danger. ALL symptoms of hurt need true helpfulness, and whenever they are met with this, the mind that so meets them heals ITSELF.

T 4 I 6. Rehabilitation is an attitude of praising God as He Himself knows praise. He offers praise to you, and you must offer it to others. The real limitations on clinical psychology, as it is evaluated by its followers at present, are not reflected by the attitudes of psychiatrists, or medical boards, or hospital administrators, even though most of them are sadly in need of rehabilitation themselves.

T 4 I 7. The real handicaps of the clinicians lie in their attitudes to those whom their egos perceive as weakened and damaged. By these evaluations, they have **T(233) C 60** weakened and damaged their own helpfulness, and have thus set their own rehabilitation back. Rehabilitation is NOT concerned with the ego's fight for control, nor the ego's need to avoid and withdraw.

T 4 I 8. Bill, you can do much on behalf of your own rehabilitation AND Helen's, and much more universally as well, if you think of the Princeton meetings in this way:

> I am here ONLY to be truly helpful.
>
> I am here to represent Christ, who sent me.
>
> I do not have to worry about what to say or what to do,[246] because the one who sent me will direct me.
>
> I am content to be wherever He wishes,[247] knowing he goes
>
> there with me.
>
> I will be healed as I let him teach me to heal.

---

[245] *Ur* manuscript has "you" rather than "your" which is a fairly obvious typo.

[246] **Matthew 10:19** "But when they deliver you up, do not worry about how or what you should speak. For it will be given to you in that hour what you should speak;"

[247] The manuscript has "wished" but the *Notes* has "wishes" which seems more appropriate here.

Chapter 5 – Healing and Wholeness

T 5 A. Introduction (*Notes* 518 6:82)

T 5 A 1. To heal is to make happy. I told you once to think how many opportunities you have to gladden yourselves, and how many you have refused. This is exactly the same as telling you that you have refused to heal yourselves. The light that belongs in you is the light of joy. Radiance is not associated with sorrow. Depression is often contagious, but although it may affect those who come in contact with it, they do not yield to its influence wholeheartedly. But joy calls forth an integrated willingness to share in it, and thus promotes the mind's natural impulse to RESPOND AS ONE.

T 5 A 2. Those who attempt to heal without being wholly joyous themselves call forth different kinds of responses at the same time, and thus deprive others of the joy of responding wholeheartedly. To be wholehearted, you MUST be happy. If fear and love cannot coexist, and if it is impossible to be wholly fearful and remain alive, then the only possible whole state IS that of love. There is no difference between love and joy. Therefore, the only possible whole state IS the wholly joyous.

T 5 A 3. To heal, or to make joyous, is therefore the same as to integrate and MAKE ONE. That is why it makes no difference TO what part or BY what part of the Sonship the healing is done. EVERY part benefits, and benefits equally. YOU are being blessed by every beneficent thought of any of your brothers anywhere. You should want to bless them in return, out of gratitude.

T 5 A 4. You do not have to know them individually, or they you. The light of joy **T(234) C 61** is so strong that it radiates throughout the Sonship and returns thanks to the Father for radiating HIS joy upon it. Only God's own holy children are worthy to be channels of his beautiful joy, because only they are beautiful enough to hold it by sharing it. It is impossible for a Child of God to love his neighbor EXCEPT as himself. That is why the healer's prayer is, "let me know this brother as I know myself."

T 5 B. Healing as Joining (*Notes* 520 6:84)

T 5 B 1. Healing is an act of thought by which two minds perceive their oneness, and become glad. This gladness calls to every part of the Sonship to rejoice with them, and let God Himself go out into them and through them. Only the healed mind can experience revelation with lasting effect, because revelation is an experience of pure joy. If you do not will to be wholly joyous, your mind cannot <u>HAVE</u> what it does not will to <u>BE</u>.

T 5 B 2. Remember that the Soul knows no difference between being and having. The higher mind thinks according to the laws which the Soul obeys, and therefore honors only the laws of God. To Him, getting is meaningless, and giving is all. Having everything, the Soul HOLDS everything by GIVING it, thus creating as the Father created.

T 5 B 3. If you think about it, you will see that, while this kind of thinking is totally alien to having THINGS, even to the lower mind it is quite comprehensible in connection with IDEAS. If you share a physical possession, you DO divide its ownership. But if you share an IDEA, you do NOT lessen it. ALL of it is still yours, although all of it has been given away. Further, if the person to whom you give it accepts it as HIS, he reinforces it in YOUR mind, and thus INCREASES it.

T 5 B 4. If you can accept the concept that the world IS one of ideas, the whole belief in the false association which the ego has made between giving and LOSING is gone. Let us start our process of re-awakening[248] with just a few simple concepts:

Thoughts INCREASE by being given away.

The more who BELIEVE in them, the STRONGER they become.

EVERYTHING is an idea.

How, then, is it possible that giving and losing can be meaningfully associated? **T(235) C 62**

T 5 B 5. This is the invitation to the Holy Spirit. I told you that I could reach up and bring the Holy Spirit down to you. But I can bring Him to you only at your own invitation. The Holy Spirit is nothing more than your own right mind. He was also mine. The Bible says, "May the mind be in you that was also in Christ Jesus,"[249] and uses this as a BLESSING. It is the blessing of miracle-mindedness. It asks that you may think as I thought, joining with me in Christ-thinking.

T 5 B 6. The Holy Spirit is the only part of the Holy Trinity which is symbolic. He is referred to in the Bible as the Healer, the Comforter, and the Guide.[250] He is also described as something separate, apart from the Father and from the Son. I myself said, "and if I go I will send you ANOTHER comforter, and he will abide with you."

T 5 B 7. The Holy Spirit is a difficult concept to grasp, precisely because it IS symbolic, and therefore open to many different interpretations. As a man and as one of God's creations, my right thinking, which came from the Universal Inspiration which IS the Holy Spirit, taught me first and foremost that this Inspiration is for ALL. I could not have it myself without knowing that.

T 5 B 8. The word "know" is proper here, because the Holy Inspiration is so close to knowledge that it calls forth, or better, allows it to come. We have spoken before of the higher or true perception, which is so close to truth that God Himself can flow across the little gap. Knowledge is always ready to flow everywhere, but it cannot oppose. Therefore you can obstruct it, although you can never lose it.

T 5 B 9. The Holy Spirit is the Christ mind that senses the knowledge that lies beyond perception. It came into being with the separation as a protection, and inspired the beginning of the Atonement at the same time. Before that, there was no need for healing and no-one was comfortless.

T 5 C. The Mind of the Atonement (*Notes* 525 6:89)

T 5 C 1. God honored even the miscreations of His Children because they had made them. But he also blessed them with a way of thinking about them that could raise their perceptions until they became so lofty that they could reach almost back to Him.

T 5 C 2. The Holy Spirit is the mind of the Atonement. It represents a state of mind that comes close enough to one-mindedness that transfer is at last possible. As you well know, transfer depends on common elements in the old learning and the new situation to which it is transferred. **T(236) C 63** Perception is not knowledge, but it can be TRANSFERRED to knowledge, or CROSS OVER into it. It might even be more helpful here to use the literal meaning "carried over," for the last step is taken by God.

T 5 C 3. The Holy Spirit, the shared Inspiration of all the Sonship, induces a kind of perception in which many elements are like those in the Kingdom of Heaven Itself.

T 5 C 4. First, its universality is perfectly clear, and no-one who receives it could ever believe for one instant that sharing it involves anything BUT gain.

---

[248] In the manuscript the word "rebirth?" is typed between the lines. That is not present in the *Notes* however.

[249] **Philippians 2:5** Let this mind be in you which was also in Christ Jesus,
[250] **John 14:16** "And I will pray the Father, and He will give you another Helper, that He may abide with you forever."

T 5 C 5. Second, it is incapable of attack, and is therefore truly open. This means that although it does not engender knowledge, it does not obstruct it in any way. **Third, it is an unequivocal call to love. Every other voice is still.**[251]

T 5 C 6. There is a point at which sufficient quantitative changes produce real qualitative differences. The next point requires real understanding, because it is the point at which the shift occurs.

T 5 C 7. Finally, it points the way beyond the healing which it brings, and leads the mind beyond its own integration into the paths of creation.

T 5 C 8. Healing is not creating; it is reparation. The Holy Spirit promotes healing by looking beyond it, to what the children of God were before healing was needed, and will be when they have BEEN healed. This alteration of the time sequence should be quite familiar, because it is very similar to the shift in time perception which the miracle introduces.

T 5 C 9. The Holy Spirit is the MOTIVATION for miracle-mindedness. It is the will to HEAL the separation by letting it go. It is IN you because God placed it in your mind, and although you can keep it asleep you cannot obliterate it. God Himself keeps it alive by transmitting it from His Mind to yours as long as there is time. It is partly His will and partly yours. The miracle itself is just this fusion or union of will between Father and Son.

T 5 C 10. The Holy Spirit is the Spirit of Joy. It is the call to return, with which God blessed the minds of the separated Sons. This the vocation of the mind. It had no calling until the separation, because before it had only BEING, and would not have understood the call to right thinking. The Holy **T(237) C 64** Spirit was God's answer to the separation, the means by which the Atonement could repair until the whole mind returned to creating. The Atonement and the separation began at the same time. When man made the ego, God placed in him the call of joy. This call is so strong that the ego always dissolves at its sound.

T 5 C 11. That is why you can choose to listen to two voices within you. One you made yourself, and that one is not of God. But the other is given you by God, Who asks you only to listen to it. The Holy Spirit IS in you in a very literal sense. It is the voice that calls you back to where you were before and will be again.

T 5 D. The Voice for God (*Notes* 529 6:93)

T 5 D 1. It is possible even in this world to hear ONLY that voice and no other. It takes effort and great willingness to learn. It is the final lesson that I learned, and God's Sons are as equal as learners as they are as Souls. The voice of the Holy Spirit IS the call to Atonement, or the restoration of the integrity of the mind. When the Atonement is complete and the whole Sonship is healed, there will be no call to return, but what God creates is eternal. The Holy Spirit will remain with the Sons of God, to bless THEIR creations and keep them in the light of joy.

T 5 D 2. You ARE the Kingdom of Heaven, but you have let the belief in darkness enter your minds, and so you need a new light. The Holy Spirit is the radiance that you must let to banish the idea of darkness. His is the glory before which dissociation falls away, and the Kingdom of Heaven breaks through into its own.

T 5 D 3. Before the separation you did not need guidance. You KNEW as you will know again, but you do not know now. God does not guide, because He can share only PERFECT KNOWLEDGE. Guidance is EVALUATIVE, because it implies that there is a RIGHT way and also a WRONG way, one to be chosen and the other avoided. By choosing one, you give up the other. This IS a conflict state. It MEANS that knowledge has been lost, because knowledge is SURE.

T 5 D 4. God is not in you; YOU are part of HIM. When you willed to leave Him, He gave you a voice to speak FOR Him, because He could no longer share His **T(238) C 65** knowledge with you without hindrance. Direct communication was broken, because you had made another voice through another will. The Holy Spirit calls you both to remember and forget. You have chosen to be in a state of opposition, in which opposites are possible. As a result, there ARE choices which you must make. In the holy state, the will is free in the sense that its <u>CREATIVE</u> power is unlimited, but choice itself is meaningless.

T 5 D 5. Freedom to choose is the same POWER as freedom to create, but its APPLICATION is different. Choosing MEANS divided will. The Holy Spirit is one way of choosing. This way is in you BECAUSE there is also another way. God did not leave His Children comfortless,[252] even though they left Him. The voice they put in their minds was NOT the voice of His Will, for which the Holy Spirit speaks. The call to return is stronger than the call to depart, but it speaks in a different way.

T 5 D 6. The voice of the Holy Spirit does not command, because it is incapable of arrogance. It does not demand, because it does not seek control. It does not overcome, because it does not attack. It merely REMINDS. It is compelling only because of what it reminds you OF. It brings to your mind the OTHER way, remaining quiet even in the midst of the turmoil you have made for yourselves. The voice for God is always quiet, because it speaks of peace. Yet peace is stronger than war, because it heals. War is DIVISION, not increase. No-one gains from strife.

T 5 D 7. "What profiteth a man if he gain the whole world and lose his own Soul?"[253] This means that if he listens to the wrong voice, he has LOST SIGHT of his Soul. He CANNOT lose it, but he CAN not know it. It is therefore LOST TO HIM, until he chooses right. The Holy Spirit is your guide in choosing. He is the part of your mind which ALWAYS speaks for the right choice, because he speaks for God. He is your remaining communication with God, which you can interrupt, but cannot destroy.

T 5 D 8. The Holy Spirit is the way in which God's will can be done on earth as it is in Heaven.[254] Both Heaven and Earth are in YOU, because the call of both are in your wills, and therefore in your minds. The voice for God comes from your own altars to Him. These altars are not THINGS. They are DEVOTIONS. **T(239) C 66** But you have other devotions now. Your divided devotion has given you the two voices, and you must choose at which altar you will to serve. The call you answer now IS an evaluation, because it is a DECISION. The decision itself is very simple. It is made on the basis of which call is worth more to you.

T 5 D 9. My mind will always be like yours, because we were created as equals. It was only my DECISION that gave me all power in Heaven and earth.[255] My only gift to you is to help you make the same decision FOR YOURSELF. The will for this decision is the will to SHARE it, because the decision itself IS the decision to share. It is MADE BY GIVING, and is therefore the one act of mind that resembles true creation.

T 5 D 10. You understand the role of models in the learning process, and the importance of the models you value and choose to follow in determining what you will to learn. I am your model for decision. By deciding for God, I showed you that this decision CAN be made, and that YOU can make it. I promised you that the mind that made

---

[251] This line is from the *Notes*, an apparently inadvertent omission.

[252] John 14:18 "I will not leave you orphans; I will come to you."

[253] Matthew 16:26 "For what profit is it to a man if he gains the whole world, and loses his own soul? Or what will a man give in exchange for his soul?"

[254] Matthew 6:10 "Your kingdom come. Your will be done On earth as it is in heaven."

[255] Matthew 28:18 And Jesus came and spoke to them, saying, "All authority has been given to Me in heaven and on earth."

the decision for me is also in YOU, and that you can let it change you just as it changed me. This mind is unequivocal, because it hears only ONE VOICE, and answers in ONE WAY.

T 5 D 11. You are the light of the world with me.[256] Rest does not come from sleeping, but from waking. The Holy Spirit is the call to awake and be glad. The world is very tired, because it is the IDEA of weariness. Our task is the joyous one of waking it to the call for God. Everyone will answer the call of the Holy Spirit, or the Sonship cannot be as one. What better vocation could there be for any part of the Kingdom than to restore it to the perfect integration that can make it whole?

T 5 D 12. Hear only this through the Holy Spirit within you, and teach your brothers to listen as I am teaching you. When you are tempted by the wrong voice, call on me to remind you how to heal by sharing my decision and MAKING IT STRONGER. As we share this goal, we increase its power to attract the whole Sonship, and to bring it back into the Oneness in which it was created.

T 5 D 13. Remember that "Yoke" means "join together," and "burden" means message. Let us reconsider the biblical statement "my yoke[257] is easy and my burden light"[258] in this way. Let us join together, for my message is Light. **T(240) C 67** I came to your minds because you had grown vaguely aware of the fact that there is another way, or another voice. Having given this invitation to the Holy Spirit, I could come to provide the model for HOW TO THINK.

T 5 D 14. Psychology has become the study of BEHAVIOR, but no-one denies the basic law that behavior is a response to MOTIVATION, and motivation is will. I have enjoined you to behave as I behaved, but we must respond to the same mind to do this. This mind is the Holy Spirit, whose will is for God always. It teaches you how to keep me as the model for your thought, and behave like me as a result.

T 5 D 15. The power of our joint motivation is beyond belief, but NOT beyond accomplishment. What we can accomplish together has no limits, because the call for God IS the call to the unlimited. Child of God, my message is for YOU, to hear and give away as you answer the Holy Spirit within you. **T(241) C 68**[259]

T 5 E. The Guide to Salvation (*Notes* 548 6:112)

T 5 E 1. The way to LEARN TO KNOW your brother is by perceiving the Holy Spirit in him. We have already said that the Holy Spirit is the bridge or thought-transfer of perception TO knowledge, so we CAN use the terms as if they were related, because in HIS mind they are. This relationship MUST be in His mind, because unless it were, the separation between the two ways of thinking would not be open to healing. He is part of the Holy Trinity, because His Mind is partly YOURS and also PARTLY GOD's. This needs clarification not in statement, since we have said this before, but in EXPERIENCE.

T 5 E 2. The Holy Spirit is the IDEA of healing. Being thought, the idea GAINS AS IT IS SHARED. Being the call FOR God, it is also the idea OF God. If you are part of God, it is also the idea of YOURSELF, as well as of all the parts of God. The idea of the Holy Spirit shares the property of other ideas, because it follows the laws of the universe of which IT is a part. Therefore, it is strengthened by being given away. It increases in YOU as you give it to your brothers.

T 5 E 3. Since thoughts do not have to be conscious to exist, your brother does NOT have to be AWARE of the Holy Spirit, either in himself or in you for this miracle to occur. He may have dissociated the call for God, just as YOU have. But the dissociation is healed in BOTH of you as you see it in him, and thus acknowledge its BE-ING. Bill, who has made a number of vital contributions to our joint venture, made a major one a while ago, which he himself did not appreciate or even understand. If we recognize its value together, we will be able to use it together, because it is an idea, **T(242) C 69** and must therefore be shared to be held.

T 5 E 4. When Bill said that he was determined "NOT to see you that way," he was speaking negatively. If he will state the same idea POSITIVELY, he will see the POWER of what he said. He had realized that there are two ways of seeing you, and also that they are diametrically opposed to one another. These two ways must be in HIS mind, because he was referring to HIMSELF as the perceiver. They must also be in YOURS, because he was perceiving YOU.

T 5 E 5. What he was really saying was that he would NOT look at you through HIS ego, or perceive YOUR ego in you. Stated positively, he would see you through the Holy Spirit in HIS mind, and perceive it in YOURS. What you acknowledge in your brother, you ARE acknowledging in yourself. What you share you STRENGTHEN. The voice of the Holy Spirit IS weak in you. That is why you MUST share it, because it must be INCREASED in strength before YOU can hear it. It is impossible to hear it in yourself while it is so weak in your OWN mind. It is NOT weak in itself; but it IS limited by your unwillingness to hear it.

T 5 E 6. Will itself is an idea, and is therefore strengthened by being shared. You have made the mistake of looking for the Holy Spirit in YOURSELVES, and that is why your meditations have frightened you. By adopting the ego's viewpoint, you undertook an ego-alien journey WITH THE EGO AS GUIDE. This was BOUND to produce fear. Bill's better idea needs to be strengthened in BOTH of you. Since it was HIS, HE can increase it by giving it to you. **T(243) C 70**

T 5 E 7. Delay is of the ego, because time is ITS concept. Delay is obviously a TIME idea. Both time AND delay are meaningless in eternity. We have said before that the Holy Spirit is God's answer to the ego. Everything of which the Holy Spirit reminds you is in direct opposition to the ego's notions, because true and false perceptions are THEMSELVES opposed. The Holy Spirit has the task of UNDOING what the ego has made. It must undo it in the same realm of discourse in which the ego itself operates, or the mind would be unable to understand the change. We have repeatedly emphasized the fact that one level of the mind is not understandable to another. So it is with the ego and the soul, and with time and eternity.

T 5 E 8. Eternity is an idea of God, so the soul understands it perfectly. Time is a belief of the ego, so the lower mind, which IS the ego's domain, accepts it without question. The only aspect of time which is really eternal is NOW. That is what we REALLY mean when we say that now is the only time. The literal nature of this statement does not mean anything to the ego. It interprets it, at best, to mean "don't worry about the future." This is NOT what it really means at all.

T 5 E 9. The Holy Spirit is the mediator between the interpretations of the ego and the knowledge of the Soul. Its ability to deal with symbols enables it to work AGAINST the ego's beliefs in its own language. Its equal ability to look BEYOND symbols into eternity also enables it to understand the laws of God, for which it speaks. **T(244) C 71**

T 5 E 10. It can thus perform the function of RE-INTERPRETING what the ego makes, not by destruction, but by understanding. Understanding is light, and light leads to knowledge. The Holy Spirit is IN light, because it is IN YOU who ARE light. But you yourselves do not know this. It is therefore the task of the Holy Spirit to re-interpret you on behalf of God.

T 5 E 11. You cannot understand yourselves alone. This is because you have no meaning apart from your rightful place in the Sonship, and the rightful place of the Sonship in God. This is your life, your eternity, and YOURSELF. It is of this that the Holy Spirit reminds

---

[256] **Matthew 5:14** "You are the light of the world. A city that is set on a hill cannot be hidden."
[257] *Ur* spells this "yolk"
[258] **Matthew 11:30** "For My yoke is easy and My burden is light."
[259] Jan. 29, '66

you. It is this that the Holy Spirit SEES. This vision invariably frightens the ego, because it is so calm. Peace is the ego's greatest enemy, because according to ITS interpretation of reality, war is the guarantee of its survival. The ego becomes strong in strife because if you believe there is strife, you will react viciously because the idea of danger has entered your mind. This idea itself IS an appeal to the ego.

T 5 E 12. The Holy Spirit is as vigilant as the ego to the call of danger, opposing it with ITS strength just as the ego WELCOMES it with all its might. The Holy Spirit counters this welcome by welcoming peace. Peace and eternity are as closely related as are time and war. Perception as well as knowledge derive meaning from RELATIONSHIPS. Those which you accept are the foundations of your beliefs. **T(245) C 72**

T 5 E 13. The Separation is merely another term for a split mind. It was not an act, but a thought. Therefore, the idea of Separation can be given away, just as the idea of unity can, and either way, it will be STRENGTHENED IN THE MIND OF THE GIVER. The ego is the symbol of the Separation, just as the Holy Spirit is the symbol of peace. What you perceive in others you are STRENGTHENING IN YOUR SELF. You let your mind misperceive, but the Holy Spirit lets your mind re-interpret its own misperceptions. The Holy Spirit is the perfect teacher. It uses only what your minds ALREADY understand, to teach you that you do not understand it.

T 5 E 14. The Holy Spirit can deal with an unwilling learner without going counter to his will, because part of his will IS still for God. Despite the ego's attempts to conceal this part, it is still much stronger than the ego, even though the ego does not recognize it. The Holy Spirit recognizes it perfectly, because it is its own dwelling place, or the place in the mind where it is at home. YOU are at home there, too, because it is a place of peace, and peace is of God.

T 5 E 15. You who are part of God are not at home EXCEPT in His peace. If peace is eternal, you are at home only in eternity. The ego made the world as IT perceives it, but the Holy Spirit, the RE-INTERPRETER of what the ego made, sees it only as a teaching device for bringing you home. The Holy Spirit must perceive time and re-interpret into the timeless. The mind must be led into eternity THROUGH time, because having made time it is capable of perceiving its opposite. **T(246) C 73**

T 5 E 16. The Holy Spirit must work through opposites, because it must work with and for a mind that IS in opposition. Correct and learn, and be open to learning. You have NOT made truth, but truth can still set you free.[260] Look as the Holy Spirit looks, and understand as He understands. His understanding looks back to God, in remembrance of Me.[261] He is in Holy Communion always, and He is part of YOU. He is your guide to salvation, because he holds the remembrance of things past and to come. He holds this gladness gently in your minds, asking only that you INCREASE it in His name by sharing it to increase His joy in YOU. **T(247) C 74**[262]

T 5 F. Therapy and Teaching (*Notes* 558 6:122)

T 5 F 1. You must have noticed how often I have used your own ideas to help YOU. B. is right is saying that you have learned to be a loving, wise, and very understanding therapist, except for yourself. That exception has given you more than perception for others because of what you saw in them, but less than knowledge of your real relationships TO them because you did NOT make them part OF you. Understanding IS beyond perception, because it introduces meaning. But it is below knowledge, even though it can grow TO-WARD it. It is possible, with great effort, to understand someone else and to be helpful to him, but the effort is misdirected. The misdirection is quite apparent. It is directed AWAY from you.

T 5 F 2. This does NOT mean that it is lost to you, but it DOES mean that you are not aware of it. I have saved all of your kindnesses and every loving thought you have had, and I assure you, you have had many. I have purified them of errors which hid their light, and have kept them for you in their own perfect radiance. They are beyond destruction and beyond guilt. They came from the Holy Spirit within YOU, and we know that what God creates is eternal.

T 5 F 3. Bill once spoke of the Kingdom in this way, because he yearns for what he has repressed. You are much more afraid of it, because dissociation is more fearful. B's better contact has allowed him the strength to retain the fear in awareness, and to resort to displacement, which he is learning to overcome with YOUR help. That is because you do not perceive HIM as dissociated, and can help him with his repression, **T(248) C 75** which does not frighten you. He, on the other hand, has no difficulty in seeing YOU dissociate, and does not have to deal with repression in you, which WOULD produce fear in him.

T 5 F 4. Joining in Atonement, which I have repeatedly asked you to do, is ALWAYS a way OUT of fear. This does not mean that you can safely fail to acknowledge anything that is true, but the Holy Spirit will not fail to help you re-interpret EVERYTHING that you perceive as fearful, and teach you ONLY what is loving IS true. It is beyond your ability to destroy, but entirely within your grasp. It BELONGS to you because YOU created it. It is yours because it is part of you, just as you are part of God, because He created you.

T 5 F 5. The Atonement is the GUARANTEE of the safety of the Kingdom. Nothing good is lost, because it comes from the Holy Spirit, the voice for Creation. Nothing that is not good was ever created, and therefore CANNOT be protected. What the ego makes it KEEPS TO ITSELF, and so it is without strength. Its unshared existence does not die. It was merely never born. Real birth is not a beginning; it is a CONTINUING. Everything that CAN continue has already BEEN born. But it can INCREASE as you are willing to return the part of your mind that needs healing to the higher part, and thus render your creating (creation) undivided.

T 5 F 6. You yourself always told your patients that the real difference between neurotic and 'healthy' guilt feelings was that neurotic guilt feelings DO NOT HELP ANYONE. This distinction was very wise, though incomplete. Let us make the distinction a little sharper now. **T(249) C 76** Neurotic guilt feelings are a device of the ego for "atoning" without sharing, and for asking for pardon without change. The ego NEVER calls for real atonement, and cannot tolerate real forgiveness, which IS change.

T 5 F 7. Your concept of "healthy guilt feelings" has great merit, but without the concept of the Atonement it lacked the healing potential it held. YOU make the distinction in terms of feelings which led to a decision not to <u>REPEAT</u> the error, which is only PART of healing. Your concept therefore lacked the idea of UNDOING it. What you were really advocating, then, was adopting a policy of sharing without a real FOUNDATION.

T 5 F 8. I have come to give you the foundation, so your own thoughts can make you REALLY free.[263] You have carried the burden of the ideas you did NOT share, and which were therefore too weak to increase, but you did NOT recognize how to UNDO their existence because you HAD made them. You CANNOT cancel out your past errors alone. They will NOT disappear from your mind without remedy. The remedy is NOT of your making, any more than YOU are.

---

[260] **John 8:32** "And you shall know the truth, and the truth shall make you free."

[261] **Luke 22:19** And He took bread, gave thanks and broke it, and gave it to them, saying, "This is My body which is given for you; do this in remembrance of Me."

[262] Jan. 12, '66

[263] **John 8:32** "And you shall know the truth, and the truth shall make you free."

Chapter 5 – Healing and Wholeness

T 5 F 9. The Atonement cannot be understood except as a PURE ACT OF SHARING. That is what is meant when we said that it is possible even in this world to listen to ONE voice. If you are part of God, and the Sonship is one, you CANNOT be limited to the self the ego sees. Every loving thought held in ANY part (of the Sonship) belongs to every part. **T(250) C 77** It is shared BECAUSE it is loving. Sharing is God's way of creating, and also YOURS. Your ego can keep you in exile FROM the Kingdom but in the Kingdom itself it has no power.

T 5 F 10. You have become willing to receive my messages as I give them, without interference by the ego, so we can clarify an earlier point which was mentioned before. We said that you will one day teach as much as you learn, and that will keep you in balance. The time is now, because you have let it be now. You cannot learn EXCEPT by teaching. I heard one voice because I had learned that learning is attained BY teaching. I understood that I COULD NOT ATONE FOR MYSELF ALONE.

T 5 F 11. Listening to one voice MEANS the will to share the voice to hear it yourself. The mind that was in me is still irresistibly drawn to every mind created by God, because God's wholeness IS the wholeness of his Son.[264] Turning the other cheek[265] does NOT mean that you should submit to violence without protest. It means that you cannot be hurt, and do not want to show your brother anything except your wholeness. Show him that he CANNOT hurt you, and hold nothing against him, or you hold it against yourself.

T 5 F 12. Teaching is done in many ways, by formal means, by guidance, and above all BY EXAMPLE. If you will to learn, you MUST will to teach. Teaching is therapy because it means the sharing of ideas, and the awareness that to share them is to strengthen them. The union of the Sonship IS its protection. **T(251) C 78** The ego cannot prevail against the Kingdom BECAUSE it is united,[266] and the ego fades away and is undone in the presence of the attraction of the parts of the Sonship which hear the call of the Holy Spirit to be as One.

T 5 F 13. I cannot forget my need to teach what I have learned which arose in me BECAUSE I learned it. I call upon you to teach what you have learned, because by so doing YOU can depend on it. Make it dependable in my name, because my name is the name of God's Son. What I learned I give you freely, and the mind which was in me rejoices as YOU will to hear it. The Holy Spirit atones in all of us by UNDOING, and thus lifts the burden you have placed in your mind. By following Him, He leads you back to God where you belong. And how can you find this way except by taking your brother with you?

T 5 F 14. My part in the Atonement is not complete until YOU join it, and give it away. As you teach, so shall you learn. I will never leave you or forsake you, because to forsake you would be to forsake myself and God who created me.[267] You will forsake yourselves and your God if you forsake any of YOUR brothers. You are more than your brother's keeper. In fact, you do not WANT to keep him. You must learn to see him as he is, and KNOW that he belongs to God, as you do. How could you treat your brother better than by rendering unto God[268] the things which are God's?

T 5 F 15. Ideas do not LEAVE the mind which thought them in order to have separate being. Nor do separate thoughts conflict with one another in space, because they do not occupy space at all. **T(252) C 79** HUMAN ideas can conflict in content, because they occur at different levels, and include opposite thoughts at the SAME level. IT IS IMPOSSIBLE TO SHARE OPPOSING THOUGHTS. The Holy Spirit does not LET you forsake your brothers. Therefore, you can really share only the parts of your thoughts which are of Him, which He also keeps for YOU. And of such is the Kingdom of Heaven.[269] All the rest remains with you until He has re-interpreted them in the light of the Kingdom, making them, too, worthy of being shared. When they have been sufficiently purified, He lets you give them away. The will to share them IS their purification.

T 5 F 16. The Atonement gives you the power of a healed mind, but the power to create is of God. Therefore, those who have been forgiven must devote themselves first to healing, because having RECEIVED the idea of healing they MUST give it to hold it. The full power of creation (creating) cannot be expressed as long as any of God's ideas are withholding it from the Kingdom. The joint will of ALL the Sonship is the only creator that can create like the Father. That is because only the complete can think completely, and the thinking of God lacks nothing. Everything YOU think that is not through the Holy Spirit IS lacking.

T 5 F 17. How can you who are so Holy suffer? All your past, except its beauty, is gone, and nothing is left except a blessing. You can indeed depart in peace,[270] because I have loved you as I loved myself.[271] You go WITH my blessing and FOR my blessing. Hold it and share it, that it may always be ours. I place the peace of God in your heart, and in your hands, to hold and share. The heart is pure to hold it, and the hands are strong to give it. We cannot lose. My judgment is as strong as the wisdom of God, **T(253) C 80** in whose Heart and Hands we have our being.[272] His quiet children are His blessed sons. The Thoughts of God are with you. **T(254) C 81**

T 5 G. The Two Decisions (*Notes* 569 6:133)

T 5 G 1. Perhaps[273] this will become clearer and more personally meaningful if the ego's use of guilt is clarified. The ego has a purpose, just as the Holy Spirit has. The ego's purpose is FEAR, because only the fearful can be egotistic. The ego's logic is as impeccable as that of the Holy Spirit, because your mind has all the means at its disposal to side with Heaven or earth, as it elects. But let us again remember that both are in you.

T 5 G 2. In Heaven there is no guilt, because the Kingdom is attained through the Atonement, which creates it in you. The word "create" is appropriate here, because once what YOU have made is undone by the Holy Spirit, the blessed residue IS restored, and therefore continues in creation. What is truly blessed is incapable of giving rise to guilt, and must give rise to joy. This makes it invulnerable to the ego, because its peace is unassailable. It is invulnerable to disruption BECAUSE it is whole.

T 5 G 3. Guilt is <u>ALWAYS</u> disruptive. Anything that engenders fear is divisive, because it obeys the law of division. If the ego is the symbol of the separation, it is also the symbol of guilt. Guilt is more than merely not of God. It is the symbol of the ATTACK on God. This is a totally meaningless concept EXCEPT to the ego, but do not

---

[264] **Philippians 2:5** Let this mind be in you which was also in Christ Jesus,
[265] **Matthew 5:39** "But I tell you not to resist an evil person. But whoever slaps you on your right cheek, turn the other to him also."
[266] **Matthew 16:18** "And I also say to you that you are Peter, and on this rock I will build My church, and the gates of Hades shall not prevail against it."
[267] **Hebrews 13:5** Let your conduct be without covetousness; be content with such things as you have. For He Himself has said, "I will never leave you nor forsake you."
[268] **Matthew 22:21** They said to Him, "Caesar's." And He said to them, "Render therefore to Caesar the things that are Caesar's, and to God the things that are God's."

[269] **Matthew 19:14** But Jesus said, "Let the little children come to Me, and do not forbid them; for of such is the kingdom of heaven."
[270] **Luke 2:29** Lord, now You are letting Your servant depart in peace, According to Your word;
[271] **Luke 10:27** And he answering said, "Thou shalt love the Lord thy God with all thy heart, and with all thy soul, and with all thy strength, and with all thy mind; and thy neighbor as thyself."
[272] **Acts 17:28** for in Him we live and move and have our being, as also some of your own poets have said, "For we are also His offspring."
[273] Feb. 21, '66

underestimate the power of the ego's belief in it. This is the belief from which ALL guilt really stems. **T(255) C 82**

T 5 G 4. The ego IS the part of the mind which believes in division. But how can part of God detach itself WITHOUT believing it is attacking Him? We spoke before of the authority problem as involving the concept of USURPING His power. The ego believes that this is what YOU did, because it believes it IS you. It follows, then, that if you identify WITH the ego, you MUST perceive yourself as guilty.

T 5 G 5. Whenever you respond to your ego, you WILL experience guilt, and you WILL fear punishment. The ego is quite literally a fearful thought. And however ridiculous the idea of attacking God may be to the sane mind, never forget that the ego is NOT SANE. It REPRESENTS a delusional system, and it speaks FOR it. Listening to the ego's voice MEANS that you believe it is possible to attack God. You believe that a part of Him has been torn away by YOU.

T 5 G 6. The classic picture of fear of retaliation from without then follows, because the severity of the guilt is so acute that it MUST be projected. Although Freud was wrong about the basic conflict itself, he was very accurate in describing its effects. Whatever you accept INTO your mind has reality for you. It is, however, only the ACCEPTANCE which makes it real.

T 5 G 7. As an extreme example of dissociation yourself, you should have little trouble in understanding that it is perfectly possible not to ACCEPT what IS in your minds. **T(256) C 83** If you enthrone the ego in it, the fact that you have accepted it, or allowed it to enter, MAKES IT YOUR REALITY. This is because the mind as God created it IS capable of creating reality. We said before that you must learn to think WITH God. To think WITH Him is to think LIKE Him. This engenders joy, not guilt, because it is natural. Guilt is a sure sign that your thinking is Unnatural. Perverted thinking will ALWAYS be attended with guilt, because it IS the belief in sin.

T 5 G 8. The ego does not perceive sin as a lack of love. It perceives it as a POSITIVE ACT OF ASSAULT. This is an interpretation which is necessary to its survival, because as soon as YOU regard it as a LACK, you will automatically attempt to remedy the situation. And you will also succeed. The ego regards this as doom, but YOU must learn to regard it as freedom.

T 5 G 9. The guiltless mind cannot suffer. Being sane, it heals the body because IT has been healed. The sane mind cannot conceive of illness, because it cannot conceive of attacking anything or anyone. We said before that illness is a form of magic. It might be better to say it is a form of magical SOLUTION. The ego believes that by punishing ITSELF, it will mitigate the punishment of God. Yet even in this it is arrogant. It attributes to God a punishing attempt, and then takes over this intent as its OWN prerogative. It tries to usurp ALL the functions of God as it perceives them, because it recognizes that only total allegiance can be trusted. **T(257) C 84**

T 5 G 10. The ego cannot OPPOSE the laws of God, any more than YOU can. But it can INTERPRET them according to what it wants, just as YOU can. That is why the question "what DO you want" must be answered. You ARE answering it every minute and every second, and each moment of decision is a judgment which is anything BUT ineffectual. Its effects will follow automatically UNTIL THE DECISION IS CHANGED. This is a redundant statement, because you have NOT learned it. But again, any decision can be Unmade as well as made.

T 5 G 11. But remember that the ALTERNATIVES are unalterable. The Holy Spirit, like the ego, is a decision. Together they constitute all the alternatives which your mind CAN accept and obey. The ego and the Holy Spirit are the ONLY choices which are open to you. God created one, and so you cannot eradicate it. YOU made the other, so you CAN. Only what God creates is irreversible and unchangeable. What YOU have made can always be changed, because when you do not think LIKE God, you have not really thought at all.

Delusional ideas are NOT thought, but you CAN think that you believe in them.

T 5 G 12. But you are wrong. The function of thought comes FROM God and is IN God. As part of HIS thought, you cannot think APART from Him. Irrational thought is a thought DISORDER. God Himself orders your thought, because your thought was created BY Him.[274] **T(258) C 85** Guilt feelings are always a sign that you do not know this. They also show that you believe you CAN think apart from God, and WANT to.

T 5 G 13. Every thought disorder is attended by guilt at its inception, and MAINTAINED by guilt in its continuance. Guilt is inescapable for those who believe that they order their OWN thought, and must therefore obey its orders. This makes them feel RESPONSIBLE for their mind ERRORS, without recognizing that by ACCEPTING this responsibility they are really reacting Irresponsibly. If the sole responsibility of the miracle-worker is to accept the ATONEMENT, and I assure you that it is, then the responsibility for what is atoned FOR CANNOT be yours.

T 5 G 14. This contradiction cannot BE resolved except by accepting the solution of undoing. You WOULD be responsible for the effects of all your wrong thinking IF IT COULD NOT BE UNDONE. The purpose of the Atonement is to save the past in PURIFIED form only. If you accept the remedy FOR a thought-disorder, and a remedy whose efficacy is beyond doubt, how can its symptoms remain? You have reason to question the validity of symptom cure. But NO ONE believes that the symptoms can remain if the underlying CAUSE is removed.

T 5 H. Time and Eternity (*Notes* 577 6:141)

T 5 H 1. The CONTINUING will to remain separated is the only possible reason for continuing guilt feelings. We have said this before, but we did not emphasize the destructive results of this decision at that time. ANY decision of the mind will affect both behavior AND experience. And what you will you EXPECT. This is NOT delusional. **T(259) C 86** Your mind DOES create your future, and CAN turn it back to full creation at any minute, IF IT ACCEPTS THE ATONEMENT FIRST. It will also turn back to full creation the instant it has done so. Having given up its thought DISORDER, the proper ordering of thought becomes quite apparent.

T 5 H 2. God in His knowledge is not waiting. But His Kingdom IS bereft while YOU wait. All the Sons of God are waiting for your return, just as YOU are waiting for THEIRS. Delay does not matter in eternity, but it IS tragic in time. You have elected to be in time rather than in eternity, and have therefore changed your belief in your status. But election is both free and alterable. You do NOT belong in time. Your place is ONLY in eternity, where God Himself placed you forever.

T 5 H 3. Guilt feelings are the PRESERVERS of time. They induce fears of FUTURE retaliation or abandonment, and thus ensure that the future will remain like the past. This IS the ego's continuity, and gives it a false sense of security through the belief that you cannot escape from it. But you can and MUST. God offers you the continuity of eternity in exchange. When you will to make this exchange, you will simultaneously exchange guilt for peace, viciousness for love, and pain for joy.

T 5 H 4. My role is only to unchain your will and make it free. Your egos cannot accept this freedom, and will oppose your free decision at every possible moment, and in every possible way. **T(260) C 87** And as its maker, you KNOW what it can do, because you GAVE IT the ability to do it. The mind does indeed know its power, because the mind does indeed know God. Remember the Kingdom always, and remember that you who are part of it cannot BE lost. The mind that was in me IS in you,[275] for God creates with perfect

---

[274] March 6, 1966
[275] **Philippians 2:5** Let this mind be in you which was also in Christ Jesus,

Chapter 5 – Healing and Wholeness

fairness. Let the Holy Spirit remind you always of His fairness, and let me teach you how to share it with your brothers. How else can the chance to claim it for yourself be given you?

T 5 H 5. What you do not understand is that the two voices speak for different interpretations of the same thing simultaneously, or almost simultaneously, for the ego always speaks first. Alternate interpretations are unnecessary until the first one has been made, and speaking itself was unnecessary before the ego was made. The ego speaks in judgment, and the Holy Spirit reverses its decisions, much as the Supreme Court has the power to reverse the lower court's decision about the laws of this world.

T 5 H 6. The ego's decisions are ALWAYS wrong, because they are based on a complete fallacy which they are made to uphold. NOTHING it perceives is interpreted correctly. Not only does it cite scripture for its purpose, but it even interprets scripture as a witness for itself. The Bible is a fearful thing to the ego, because of its prejudiced judgment. Perceiving it as fearful, it interprets it fearfully. Having made YOU afraid, you do not appeal to the higher court, because you believe its judgment would be AGAINST you. **T(261) C 88**

T 5 H 7. We need cite only a few examples to see how the ego's interpretations have mislead you. A favorite ego quotation is "As ye sow, so shall ye reap."[276] Another is "Vengeance is mine sayeth the Lord."[277] Still another is "I will visit the sins of the fathers unto the third and the fourth generation."[278] And also, "The wicked shall perish."[279] There are many others, but if you will let the Holy Spirit re-interpret these in its own light, they will suffice.

T 5 H 8. "As ye sow, so shall ye reap" merely means that what you believe to be worth cultivating you will cultivate in yourself. Your judgment of what is worthy DOES make it worthy for you.

T 5 H 9. "Vengeance is mine sayeth the Lord" is easily explained if you remember that ideas increase only by being shared. This quotation therefore emphasizes the fact that vengeance CANNOT be shared. Give it therefore to the Holy Spirit, who will undo it in you because it does not BELONG in your mind, which is part of God.

T 5 H 10. "I will visit the sins of the fathers unto the third and fourth generation," as interpreted by the ego, is particularly vicious. It is used, in fact, as an attempt to guarantee its survival beyond itself. Actually, all it really means is that the Holy Spirit in later generations retains the power to interpret CORRECTLY what former generations have thought, and thus release THEIR thoughts from the ability to produce fear ANYWHERE in the Sonship. **T(262) C 89**

T 5 H 11 "The wicked shall perish" is merely a statement of fact, if the word "perish" is properly understood. Every loveless thought MUST be undone, and even the word "undone" is fearful to the ego, which interprets "I am undone" as "I am destroyed." The ego will NOT be destroyed, because it is part of YOUR thought. But because it is uncreative, and therefore unsharing, it WILL be re-interpreted entirely, to release you from fear.

T 5 H 12. The part of your thought which you have given TO the ego will merely return to the Kingdom, where your whole mind BELONGS. The ego is a form of ARREST, but arrest is merely delay. It does NOT involve the concept of police at all, although the ego welcomes that interpretation. You CAN delay the completion of the Kingdom, but you CANNOT introduce the concept of ASSAULT into it.

T 5 H 13. When I said "I am come as a light into the world,"[280] I surely came to share this light with you. Remember the symbolic reference we made before to the ego's dark glass, and remember also that we said "Do not look there." It is still true that "Where you look to find yourself is up to you." The Higher Court will not condemn you. It will merely dismiss the case against you. There can BE no case against a child of God, and every witness to guilt in God's creations is bearing false witness[281] to God Himself.

T 5 H 14. Appeal everything you believe gladly to God's own Higher Court, because it speaks for Him, and therefore speaks truly. It WILL dismiss the case against you, however carefully YOU have built it. **T(263) C 90** The case may be fool-proof, but it is NOT God-proof. The voice for God will not hear it at all, because it can only witness truly. Its verdict will always be "Thine is the Kingdom,"[282] because it was given you to remind you of what you ARE.

T 5 H 15. Your patience with each other is your patience with your selves. Is not a child of God worth patience? I have shown you infinite patience, because my will IS that of our Father, from whom I learned of infinite patience. His voice was in me, as it is in you, speaking for patience toward the Sonship, in the name of its Creator. What you need to learn now is that only infinite patience CAN produce immediate effects. This is the way in which time is exchanged for eternity. Infinite patience calls upon infinite Love, and by producing results NOW renders time unnecessary.

T 5 H 16. To say that time is temporary is merely redundant. We have repeatedly said that time is a learning device which will be abolished when it is no longer useful. The Holy Spirit, who speaks for God in time, also knows that time is meaningless. He reminds you of this in every passing moment of time, because it is His special function to return YOU to eternity and remain to bless YOUR creations there. He is the only blessing you can truly give, because He is so truly blessed. And because He has been given you so freely by God, you must give Him as you received Him. **T(264) C 91**

T 5 I. The Eternal Fixation (*Notes* 586 6:150)

T 5 I 1. The concept of "set" is among the better psychological percepts. Actually, it is used quite frequently in the Bible, and also here, under many different terms. "God will keep him in perfect peace whose mind is stayed (or set) on Thee because he trusteth in Thee."[283]

T 5 I 2. The pronouns here are confusing without explanation, and the attempt to shift "Thee" to "Him" is a misinterpretation. The statement means that God's peace is set in the Holy Spirit, because it is fixed on God. It is also fixed in you. You, then, ARE fixed in the peace of God.

T 5 I 3. The concept of "fixation" is a very helpful one, which Freud understood perfectly. Unfortunately, he lost his understanding because he was afraid, and as you know all too well, fear is incompatible with good judgment. Fear DISTORTS thinking, and therefore DISorders thought. Freud's system of thought was extremely ingen-

---

[276] **2 Corinthians 9:6** But this I say: He who sows sparingly will also reap sparingly, and he who sows bountifully will also reap bountifully.
[277] **Deuteronomy 32:35** Vengeance is Mine, and recompense; Their foot shall slip in due time; For the day of their calamity is at hand, And the things to come hasten upon them.'
Romans 12:19 Beloved, do not avenge yourselves, but rather give place to wrath; for it is written, "Vengeance is Mine, I will repay," says the Lord.
[278] **Exodus 34:7** Keeping mercy for thousands, forgiving iniquity and transgression and sin, by no means clearing the guilty, visiting the iniquity of the fathers upon the children and the children's children to the third and the fourth generation."
[279] **Psalm 37:20** But the wicked shall perish; And the enemies of the LORD, Like the splendor of the meadows, shall vanish. Into smoke they shall vanish away.

[280] **John 12:46** "I have come as a light into the world, that whoever believes in Me should not abide in darkness."
[281] **Exodus 20:16** You shall not bear false witness against your neighbor.
[282] **Matthew 6:13** "And do not lead us into temptation,
But deliver us from the evil one.
For Thine is the kingdom and the power and the glory forever. Amen."
[283] **Isaiah 26:3** Thou wilt keep *him* in perfect peace, *whose* mind *is* stayed *on thee*: because he trusteth in thee.

ious, because Freud was extremely ingenious. A mind MUST endow its thoughts with its own attributes. This is its inherent STRENGTH, even though it may misuse its power.

T 5 I 4. Freud lost much of the potential value of his own thought system because, much like Cayce, he did NOT include himself in it. This IS a dissociated state, because the thinker cuts himself off from his thoughts. Freud's thought was so conflicted that he could not have retained his sanity as HE saw it WITHOUT dissociating.

T(265) C 92 This is why the many contradictions which are quite apparent in his thinking became increasingly less apparent to HIM.

T 5 I 5. A man who knows what fixation REALLY means and does NOT yield to it is terribly afraid. Fixation is the pull of God, on whom your mind IS fixed because of the Holy Spirit's irrevocable set. "Irrevocable" means "cannot be called back or redirected." The irrevocable nature of the Holy Spirit's set is the basis for its unequivocal voice. The Holy Spirit NEVER changes its mind. Clarity of thought CANNOT occur under conditions of vacillation. Unless a mind is fixed in its purpose, it is NOT clear. But clarity literally means the state of light, and enlightenment IS understanding. It stands UNDER perception because you have denied it as the REAL foundation of thought. This is the basis for ALL delusional systems.

T 5 I 6. The concept of fixation, as Freud saw it, has a number of real learning advantages. First, it recognizes that man CAN be fixated at a point in development which does NOT accord with a point in time. This clearly could have been a means toward real release from the time belief, had Freud pursued it with an open mind. But Freud suffered all his life from refusal to allow eternity to dawn upon his mind, and enlighten it truly. As a result, he overlooked NOW entirely, and merely saw the continuity of past and future.

T 5 I 7. Second, although he misinterpreted what the Holy Spirit told him, or better, reminded him of, he was too honest to deny more than he had to, to keep his fear in tolerable bounds, as he perceived the situation. Therefore, he EMPHASIZED that the point in development at which the mind is fixated is more real to ITSELF than the external reality with which it DISagrees. **T(266) C 93** This again could have been a powerful RELEASE mechanism, had Freud not decided to involve it in a strong defense system because he perceived it as an attack.

T 5 I 8. Third, although Freud interpreted fixation as irrevocable danger points to which the mind can always regress, the concept can also be interpreted as an irrevocable call to sanity which the mind cannot LOSE. Freud saw return as a threat to maturity because he did not understand prodigality. He merely interpreted it as squandering. Actually, "prodigal" also means careful. This confusion between careful and careless led him to confuse the escape from care with something desirable. In fact, he even went so far as to equate it quite literally WITH desire.

T 5 I 9. But throughout his thought-system, the "threat" of fixation remained, and could never be completely eliminated by any living human being anywhere. Essentially, this was the basis of his pessimism. This was personally as well as theoretically the case. Freud tried every means his very inventive mind could devise to set up a form of therapy which could enable the mind to escape from fixation forever, even though he KNEW this was impossible. The knowledge plagued his belief in his own thought-system at every turn, because he was both an honest man and a healer. He was therefore only PARTIALLY insane at the perceptual level, and was unable to relinquish the hope of release even though he could not cope with it.[284] **T(267) C 94**

T 5 I 10. The reason for this amount of detail is because YOU are in the same position. You were eternally fixated on God in your creation, and the pull of this fixation is so strong that you will never overcome it. The reason is perfectly clear. The fixation is on a level that is so high that it cannot BE surmounted. You are ALWAYS being pulled back to your Creator because you belong in Him.

T 5 I 11. Do you REALLY believe you can make a voice that can drown out His? Do you REALLY believe that you can devise a thought-system which can separate you from His? Do you REALLY believe that you can plan for your safety and joy better than He can? You need be neither careful nor careless. You need merely cast all your cares upon Him because He careth for YOU.[285] You ARE His care because He loves you. His voice reminds you always that all hope is yours BECAUSE of His care.

T 5 I 12. You CANNOT choose to escape His care, because that is not His will. But you CAN choose to accept His care, and use the infinite power OF His care for all those He created BY it. There have been many healers who did not heal themselves. They have not moved mountains[286] by their faith because their faith was not[287] WHOLE. Some of them have healed the sick[288] at times, but they have not raised the dead. Unless the healer heals HIMSELF, he does NOT believe that there is no order in miracles. He has not learned that EVERY mind that God created is equally worthy of being healed because GOD CREATED IT WHOLE. **T(268) C 95**

T 5 I 13. You are asked merely to return to God the mind as HE created it. He asks you only for what He gave, knowing that this giving will heal YOU. Sanity IS wholeness. And the sanity of your brothers IS yours. Why should you listen to the endless insane calls which you think are made upon you, when you KNOW the voice of God Himself is in you? God commended His Spirit to you, and asks that you commend yours to Him. He wills to keep it in perfect peace because you are of one mind and Spirit with Him.[289]

T 5 I 14. Excluding yourself from the Atonement is the ego's last-ditch defense of its own existence. It reflects both the ego's need to separate, and your willingness to side with its separateness. This willingness means that YOU DO NOT WANT TO BE HEALED. When I told Bill that there is "just one more thing," he heard me very well. I hope he will hear me as well now. His intelligent mishearing of "river" as "rivet" showed that, even though he wanted release, he was not able to cope with it at the time.

T 5 I 15. But the time IS now. You have not been asked to work out the Plan of Salvation yourselves, because, as I told you before, the Remedy is NOT of your making. God Himself gave you the perfect

---

[284] The word "it" is missing from the *Urtext* manuscript but is present in the *Notes*. Nothing else appears missing here.

[285] **1 Peter 5:7** Casting all your care upon Him, for He cares for you.

[286] **Matthew 17:20** So Jesus said to them, "Because of your unbelief; for assuredly, I say to you, if you have faith as a mustard seed, you will say to this mountain, 'Move from here to there,' and it will move; and nothing will be impossible for you.

[287] The *Ur* manuscript is illegible between the words "faith" and "whole." The *Notes* has "was not."

[288] **Isaiah 26:19** Your dead shall live; Together with my dead body they shall arise. Awake and sing, you who dwell in dust; For your dew is like the dew of herbs, And the earth shall cast out the dead.

Isaiah 35:5-6 Then the eyes of the blind shall be opened, And the ears of the deaf shall be unstopped. Then the lame shall leap like a deer,
And the tongue of the dumb sing. For waters shall burst forth in the wilderness, And streams in the desert.

Matthew 10:1 And when He had called His twelve disciples to Him, He gave them power over unclean spirits, to cast them out, and to heal all kinds of sickness and all kinds of disease.

Matthew 10:8 "Heal the sick, cleanse the lepers, raise the dead, cast out demons. Freely you have received, freely give."

Matthew 11:5 "The blind see and the lame walk; the lepers are cleansed and the deaf hear; the dead are raised up and the poor have the gospel preached to them." *There are many more references to healing and raising the dead in the Bible.*

[289] **Psalm 31:5** Into Your hand I commend my spirit; You have redeemed me, O LORD God of truth.

Luke 23:46 And when Jesus had cried out with a loud voice, He said, "Father, 'into Your hands I commend My spirit.'" Having said this, He breathed His last.

correction for everything you have made which is not in accord with His Holy Will. I have made His Plan perfectly clear and perfectly explicit to you, and have also told you of your part in His Plan and how urgent it is that you fulfill it.

T 5 I 16. There is time for delay, but there need not be. God weeps at the sacrifice of His children who believe they are lost to Him. The "one more thing" that Bill must learn is merely that he is NOT the one more. He is both ONE and AT ONE. If he will learn this NOW, he will be willing in accord with the last judgment, which is really only the Biblical reminder of the inevitability of self-INCLUSION. This is what "Physician, heal thyself" really means. Bill has frequently observed for HIMSELF that this is hard to do. He has, however, been perfectly aware of **T(269) C 96** JUST what YOU should do about it.

T 5 I 17. You might ask him for me whether he does not think he might be dissociating HIMSELF from his own awareness, since he is so clear about the remedy for YOU. You might also remind him that to whatever extent he separates himself from you, he is separating himself from ME. This IS a collaborative venture. Let me therefore return his own ideas to him, so that you can share them and thus help each other to help me.

T 5 I 18. But let me first remind you of something I told you myself. Whenever you are not wholly joyous, it is because you have reacted with a lack of love to some Soul which God created. Perceiving this as sin, you become defensive because you EXPECT ATTACK. The decision to react in that way, however, was YOURS, and can therefore be undone. It CANNOT be undone by repentance in the usual sense, because this implies guilt. If you allow yourself to feel guilty, you will reinforce the error, rather than allowing it to be undone FOR you.

T 5 I 19. Decisions CANNOT be difficult. This is obvious if you realize that you must ALREADY have made a decision NOT to be wholly joyous if that is what you feel. Therefore, the first step in the undoing is to recognize that YOU ACTIVELY DECIDED WRONGLY, BUT CAN AS ACTIVELY DECIDE OTHERWISE.

T 5 I 20. Be very firm with yourselves in this, and keep yourselves fully aware of the fact that the UNDOING process, which does NOT come from you, is nevertheless WITHIN you because God placed it there. YOUR part is merely to return your thinking to the point at which the error was made, and give it over to the Atonement in peace. Say to yourselves the following, as sincerely as you can, remembering that the Holy Spirit will respond fully to your slightest invitation: **T(270) C 97**

I must have decided wrongly because I am NOT at peace.

I made the decision myself, but I can also decide otherwise.

I WILL to decide otherwise, because I WANT to be at peace.

I do NOT feel guilty, because the Holy Spirit will undo ALL the consequences of my wrong decision IF I WILL LET HIM.

I WILL to let Him by allowing Him to decide for God for me.

(271) C 98[290]

---

[290] March 22, 1966

Chapter 6 – Attack and Fear

T 6 A. Introduction (*Notes* 599 6:163)

T 6 A 1. The relationship of anger to attack is obvious, but the inevitable association of anger and FEAR is not always so clear. Anger ALWAYS involves PROJECTION OF SEPARATION, which must ultimately be accepted as entirely one's own responsibility. Anger cannot occur unless you believe that you have BEEN attacked; the attack was JUSTIFIED; and you are in no way responsible for it. Given these three wholly irrational premises, the equally irrational conclusion that a brother is worthy of attack rather than of love follows. What can be expected from insane premises EXCEPT an insane conclusion?

T 6 A 2. The way to undo an insane conclusion is always to consider the sanity of the premises on which it rests. You cannot BE attacked, attack HAS no justification, and you ARE responsible for what you believe. You have been asked to take me as your model for learning. And we have often said that an extreme example is a particularly helpful learning device. EVERYONE teaches, and teaches all the time. This is a responsibility which he assumes inevitably, the moment he has accepted any premises at all. And NO ONE can organize his life without ANY thought system. Once he has developed a thought system of any kind, he lives by it and TEACHES it.

T 6 A 3. You have been chosen to teach the Atonement precisely BECAUSE you have been EXTREME examples of allegiance to your thought systems, and therefore have developed the capacity FOR allegiance. It has indeed been misplaced. Bill had become an outstanding example of allegiance to apathy, and you have become a startling example of fidelity to variability. But this IS a form of faith, which you yourselves had grown willing to redirect. You cannot doubt the STRENGTH of your devotion when you consider how faithfully you observed it. It was quite evident that you had ALREADY developed the ability to follow a better model, if you could ACCEPT it. **T(272) C 99**

T 6 B. The Message of the Crucifixion (*Notes* 601 6:165)

T 6 B 1. We have not dwelt upon the crucifixion, because of its fearful connotations. The only emphasis we laid upon it was that it was NOT a form of punishment. But we know that nothing can be really explained only in negative terms. There is a positive interpretation of the crucifixion which is wholly devoid of fear, and therefore wholly benign in what it teaches, if it is properly understood. It is nothing more than an extreme example. Its value, like the value of any teaching device, lies solely in the kind of learning it facilitates. It can be, and has been, misunderstood. But this is only because the fearful are apt to perceive fearfully.

T 6 B 2. I told you before that you can always call on me to share my decision and thus MAKE IT STRONGER. I also told you that the crucifixion was the last foolish journey that the Sonship need take, and that it should mean[291] RELEASE from fear to anyone who understands it. While we emphasized the Resurrection only before, the purpose of the crucifixion and how it actually LED to the Resurrection was not clarified at that time. Nevertheless, it has a definite contribution to make to your own lives, and if you will consider it WITHOUT fear, it will help you understand your own role as teachers.

T 6 B 3. You have reacted for years AS IF you were being crucified. This is a marked tendency of the separated, who ALWAYS refuse to consider what they have done to THEMSELVES. Projection means anger, anger fosters assault, and assault promotes fear. The real meaning of the crucifixion lies in the APPARENT intensity of the assault of some of the Sons of God upon a brother. This, of course, is impossible, and must be fully understood AS an impossibility. In fact, unless it IS fully understood as ONLY that, I cannot serve as a real model for learning.

T 6 B 4. Assault can ultimately be made ONLY on the body. There is little doubt that one BODY can assault another, and can even destroy it. But if destruction ITSELF is impossible, then ANYTHING that is destructible cannot be real. Therefore, its destruction does NOT justify anger. To the extent **T(273) C 100** to which you believe it DOES, you MUST be accepting false premises and TEACHING THEM TO OTHERS. The message which the crucifixion was intended to teach was that it is not necessary to perceive ANY form of assault in persecution because you cannot BE persecuted. If you respond with anger, you MUST be equating yourself with the destructible, and are therefore regarding yourself insanely. I have made it perfectly clear that I am like you, and you are like me. But our fundamental equality can be demonstrated only through joint decision.

T 6 B 5. You are free to perceive yourselves as persecuted if you choose.[292] But you might remember when you DO choose to react that way that I WAS persecuted as the world judges, and did NOT share this evaluation for myself. And because I did not share it, I did NOT strengthen it. I therefore offered a DIFFERENT interpretation of attack, and one which I DO want to share with you. If you will BELIEVE it, you will help me TEACH it.

T 6 B 6. We have said before, "As you teach so shall you learn." If you react as if you are persecuted, you ARE teaching persecution. This is not a lesson which the Sons of God should WANT to teach if they are to realize their own salvation. Rather teach your own perfect immunity, which IS the Truth in you, and KNOW that it cannot be assailed. Do not protect it yourselves, or you have believed that it IS assailable. You are not asked to BE crucified, because that was part of my own teaching contribution. You are merely asked to follow my example in the face of much less extreme temptations to misperceive, and NOT to accept them falsely as justifications for anger.

T 6 B 7. There can BE no justification for the unjustifiable. Do not believe there is, and do not TEACH that there is. Remember always that what you believe you WILL teach. Believe with me, and we will become equal as teachers. YOUR resurrection is your reawakening. I am the model for rebirth, but rebirth itself is merely the dawning on your minds of what is already in them. **T(274) C 101** God placed it there Himself, and so it is true forever. I believed in it, and therefore made it forever true for me. Help me to teach it to our brothers in the name of the Kingdom of God. But first believe that it is true for you, or you will teach amiss.

T 6 B 8. My brothers slept[293] during the so-called "agony in the garden," but I could not be angry with them, because I had learned I

---

[291] The *Urtext* manuscript has "means" here although the *Notes* and the *HLC* both have "mean" which is better grammar.
[292] The *Urtext* manuscript and the *Notes* both have "chose" here, changed in later versions to "choose" which seems to fit much better.
[293] **Luke 22:39-46** Coming out, He went to the Mount of Olives, as He was accustomed, and His disciples also followed Him. When He came to the place, He said to them, "Pray that you may not enter into temptation." And He was withdrawn from them about a stone's throw, and He knelt down and prayed, saying, "Father, if it is Your will, take this cup away from Me; nevertheless not My will, but Yours, be done." Then an angel appeared to Him from heaven, strengthening Him. And being in agony, He prayed more earnestly. Then His sweat became like great drops of blood falling down to the ground. When He rose up from prayer, and had come to His disciples, He found them sleeping from sorrow. Then He said to them, "Why do you sleep? Rise and pray, lest you enter into temptation."

could not BE abandoned. Peter swore he would never deny me, but he did so three times. It should be noted that he did offer to defend me with the sword, which I naturally refused, not being at all in need of bodily protection. I AM sorry when my brothers do not share my decision to hear (and be) only one voice, because it weakens them as teachers AND learners. But yet I know that they cannot really betray themselves or me, and that it is still on them that I MUST build my church.[294]

T 6 B 9. There is no choice in this, because only you can BE the foundation of God's church. A church is where an altar is, and the presence of the altar is what makes it a church. Any church which does not inspire love has a hidden altar which is not serving the purpose for which God intended it. I must found His church on you because you, who accept me as a model are literally my disciples. Disciples are followers, but if the model they follow has chosen to SAVE THEM PAIN IN ALL RESPECTS, they are probably unwise NOT to follow him.

T 6 B 10. I elected, both for your sake AND mine, to demonstrate that the most outrageous assault, as judged by the ego, did not matter. As the world judges these things, but NOT as God knows them, I was betrayed, abandoned, beaten, torn, and finally killed. It was perfectly clear that this was only because of the projection of others onto me, because I had not harmed anyone and had healed many. We are still equal as learners, even though we need not have equal experiences. The Holy Spirit is glad when you can learn enough from MINE to be re-awakened by them. That was their only purpose, and that is the only way **T(275) C 102** in which I can be perceived as the Way, the Truth, and the Light.[295]

T 6 B 11. When you hear only one voice, you are never called on to sacrifice. On the contrary, by enabling YOURSELVES to hear the Holy Spirit in others, you can learn from their experiences and gain from them WITHOUT experiencing them. That is because the Holy Spirit IS one, and anyone who listens is inevitably led to demonstrate His way for ALL. You are not persecuted, nor was I. You are not asked to repeat my experience, because the Holy Spirit which we SHARE, makes this unnecessary. But to use my experiences constructively for yourselves, you must still follow my example in how to perceive them.

T 6 B 12. My brothers and yours are constantly engaged in justifying the unjustifiable. My one lesson, which I must teach as I learned, is that no perception which is out of accord with the judgment of the Holy Spirit CAN be justified. I undertook to show this was true in a very extreme case, merely because this would serve as a good teaching aid to those whose temptations to give in to anger and assault would NOT be as extreme.

T 6 B 13. I will, with God Himself, that none of His Sons should suffer. Remember that the Holy Spirit is the communication link between God the Father and His separated Sons. If you will listen to His voice, you will know that you cannot either hurt or BE hurt, but that many need your blessing to help them hear this for themselves. When you perceive only this need in them, and do not respond to any others, you will have learned[296] of me, and be as eager to share your learning as I am. The crucifixion CANNOT be shared, because it is the symbol of projection. But the Resurrection IS the symbol of sharing, because the re-awakening of every Son of God is necessary to enable the Sonship to know its wholeness. Only this IS knowledge.

T 6 B 14. The message of the crucifixion is very simple and perfectly clear: "teach ONLY love, for that is what you ARE." If you interpret it in any other way, you are using it as a weapon for assault rather than as the call to peace for which it was intended. The Apostles often misunderstood it, and always for the same reason that makes anyone misunderstand anything. Their **T(276) C 103** own imperfect love made them vulnerable to projection, and out of their own fear they spoke of the wrath[297] of God as His RETALIATORY weapon. They also could not speak of the crucifixion entirely without anger, because their own sense of guilt had made them angry.

T 6 B 15. There are two glaring examples of upside down thinking in the New Testament, whose whole Gospel is only the message of love. These are not at all like the several slips into impatience which I made, because I had learned the Atonement prayer, which I also came to teach, too well to engage in upside down thinking myself. If the Apostles had not felt guilty, they never could have quoted ME as saying, "I come not to bring peace but a sword."[298] This is clearly the exact opposite of everything I taught.

T 6 B 16. Nor could they have described my reactions to Judas Iscariot as they did, if they had really understood ME. They could not have believed that I could[299] have said, "Betrayest thou the Son of Man with a kiss?"[300] unless I BELIEVED IN BETRAYAL. The whole message of the crucifixion was simply that I did NOT. The "punishment"[301] which I am said to have called forth upon Judas was a similar reversal. Judas was my brother and a Son of God, as much a part of the Sonship as myself. Was it likely that I would condemn him when I was ready to demonstrate that condemnation is impossible?

T 6 B 17. I am very grateful to the Apostles for their teaching, and fully aware of the extent of their devotion to me. But as you read their teachings, remember that I told them myself that there was much they would understand later, because they were NOT wholly ready to follow me at the time.[302] I emphasize this only because I do not want you to allow ANY fear to enter into the thought system toward which I am guiding you. I do NOT call for martyrs but for TEACHERS.

T 6 B 18. Bill is an outstanding example of this confusion, and has literally believed for years that teaching IS martyrdom. This is because he thought, and still thinks at times, that teaching leads to crucifixion rather than to re-awakening. The upside down nature of this association is so obvious that **T(277) C 104** he could only have made it BECAUSE he felt guilty. No-one is "punished" for sins, and the Sons of God are not sinners. ANY concept of "punishment" involves the projection of blame, and REINFORCES the idea that

---

[297] **Ezekiel 7:19** They will throw their silver into the streets,
And their gold will be like refuse;
Their silver and their gold will not be able to deliver them
In the day of the wrath of the LORD;
They will not satisfy their souls,
Nor fill their stomachs,
Because it became their stumbling block of iniquity.
John 3:36 "He who believes in the Son has everlasting life; and he who does not believe the Son shall not see life, but the wrath of God abides on him."
[298] **Matthew 10:34** "Do not think that I came to bring peace on earth. I did not come to bring peace but a sword."
[299] The manuscript has "not" typed between the lines which is also present in the *Notes*. However, this very much appears to be an error since it really makes no sense to say "*They could **not** have believed that I could **not** have said, 'Betrayest though the Son of Man with a kiss?'* unless I BELIEVED IN BETRAYAL." It has to be either "*I could not have said ...*" or "*They could not believe I could have said...*" but it can't be both.
[300] **Luke 22:48** But Jesus said to him, "Judas, are you betraying the Son of Man with a kiss?"
[301] **Matthew 26:24** "The Son of Man indeed goes just as it is written of Him, but woe to that man by whom the Son of Man is betrayed! It would have been good for that man if he had not been born."
[302] **John 16:12** "I still have many things to say to you, but you cannot bear them now."

---

[294] **Matthew 16:18** "And I also say to you that you are Peter, and on this rock I will build My church, and the gates of Hades shall not prevail against it."
[295] **John 14:6** Jesus said to him, "I am the way, the truth, and the life. No one comes to the Father except through Me. *The Biblical quote certainly uses "life" while the Shorthand Notes and later copying in ACIM has "light."*
[296] **Matthew 11:29** "Take My yoke upon you and learn from Me, for I am gentle and lowly in heart, and you will find rest for your souls."

blame is justified. The behavior that results is a LESSON IN BLAME, just as all behavior teaches the beliefs that motivate it.

T 6 B 19. The crucifixion was a complex of behaviors arising out of clearly opposed thought systems. As such, it is the perfect symbol of conflict between the ego and the Son of God. It was as much intrapersonal as interpersonal then, just as it is now, and it is still just as real. But BECAUSE it is just as real now, its lesson, too, has equal reality WHEN IT IS LEARNED. I do not need gratitude any more than I needed protection. But YOU need to develop your weakened ability to BE grateful, or you cannot appreciate God. HE does not need your appreciation, but you DO.

T 6 B 20. You cannot love what you do not appreciate, and FEAR MAKES APPRECIATION IMPOSSIBLE. Whenever you are afraid of what you are, you do not appreciate it, and will therefore reject it. As a result, you will TEACH REJECTION. The power of the Sons of God is operating all the time, because they were created as creators. Their influence on EACH OTHER is without limit, and MUST be used for their joint salvation. Each one MUST learn to teach that all forms of rejection are utterly meaningless.

T 6 B 21. The separation IS the notion of rejection. As long as you teach this, YOU still believe it. This is NOT as God thinks, and you must think as He thinks if you are to know Him again.

T 6 C. The Uses of Projection (*Notes* 618 6:182)

T 6 C 1. Any split in will MUST involve a rejection of part of it, and this IS the belief in separation. The wholeness of God, which IS His peace, cannot be appreciated EXCEPT by a whole mind, which recognizes the wholeness of God's creation and BY this recognition knows its Creator.

T 6 C 2. Exclusion and separation are synonymous. So are separation and dissociation. We have said before that the separation was and IS dissociation, and also that once it had occurred, projection became its main defense, or the device which KEEPS IT GOING. The reason, however, may not be **T(278) C 105** as clear to you as you think. What you project you disown, and THEREFORE DO NOT BELIEVE IS YOURS. You are therefore EXCLUDING yourself from it, by the very statement you are making that you are DIFFERENT from someone else. Since you have also judged AGAINST what you project, you attack it because you have already attacked it BY rejecting it. By doing this UNCONSCIOUSLY, you try to keep the fact that you must have attacked yourself FIRST out of awareness, and thus imagine that you have made yourself safe.

T 6 C 3. Projection will ALWAYS hurt you. It reinforces your belief in your own split mind, and its ONLY purpose is to KEEP THE SEPARATION GOING. It is solely a device of the ego to make you feel DIFFERENT from your brothers and separated FROM them. The ego justifies this on the wholly spurious grounds that it makes you seem better than they are, thus obscuring equality WITH them still further.

T 6 C 4. Projection and attack are inevitably related, because projection is ALWAYS a means of JUSTIFYING attack. Anger without projection is impossible. The ego uses projection ONLY to distort your perception of both yourself AND your brothers. It begins by excluding something you think exists in you which you do not want, and leads directly to your excluding yourself from your brothers.

T 6 C 5. But we know that there is another use of projection. Every ability of the ego has a better counterpart, because its abilities are directed by the mind, which has a better voice. The Holy Spirit, as well as the ego, utilizes projection but since their goals are opposed, so is the result. The Holy Spirit begins by perceiving YOU as perfect. KNOWING this perfection is shared, it RECOGNIZES it in others, thus strengthening it in both. Instead of anger, this arouses love FOR both because IT ESTABLISHES INCLUSION. Perceiving equality, it perceives equal needs. This invites Atonement automatically, because Atonement IS the one need which is universal. **T(279) C 106**

T 6 C 6. To perceive YOURSELF in this way is the ONLY way in which you can find happiness in this world. This is because it is the acknowledgement that you are NOT in this world, and the world IS unhappy. How else can you find joy in a joyless place EXCEPT by realizing that YOU ARE NOT THERE? You cannot be ANYWHERE that God did not put you, and God created you as part of HIM. That is both WHERE you are and WHAT you are. This is COMPLETELY unalterable. It is total inclusion. You cannot change this now or ever. It is forever true. It is NOT a belief, but a fact.

T 6 C 7. Anything that God creates is as true as He is. Its truth lies only in its perfect inclusion in Him Who alone IS perfect. To deny this in any way is to deny yourself AND Him, because it is impossible to accept one without the other. The perfect equality of the Holy Spirit's perception is the counterpart of the perfect equality of God's knowing. The ego's perception has no counterpart in God, but the Holy Spirit remains the bridge between perception and knowledge. By enabling you to use perception in a way that PARALLELS knowledge, you will ultimately meet it and KNOW it.

T 6 C 8. The ego prefers to believe that parallel lines do not meet, and conceives of their meeting as impossible. But you might remember that even the human eye perceives them as if they DO meet in the distance, which is the same as IN THE FUTURE, if time and space are one dimension. The later mathematics support the interpretation of ultimate convergence of the parallel theoretically. EVERYTHING meets in God, because everything was created BY Him and IN Him.[303] God created His Sons by extending His Thought and retaining the extensions of His Thought in His Mind. ALL His Thoughts are thus perfectly united within themselves and with each other because they, were created neither partially nor in part.

T 6 C 9. The Holy Spirit enables you to PERCEIVE THIS WHOLENESS NOW. You can no more pray for yourselves alone than you can find joy for yourself **T(280) C 107** alone. Prayer is a re-statement of INCLUSION, directed by the Holy Spirit under the laws of God. God created you to create. You cannot EXTEND His Kingdom until you KNOW of its wholeness. But thoughts begin in the mind OF THE THINKER, from which they extend outward. This is as true of God's thinking as it is of yours. Because your minds are split, you can also perceive as well as think, but perception cannot escape from the basic laws of mind. You perceive FROM your mind, and extend your perceptions outward.

T 6 C 10. Although perception of any kind is unnecessary, YOU made it and the Holy Spirit can therefore use it well. He can INSPIRE perception and lead it toward God by making it PARALLEL to God's way of thinking, and thus guaranteeing their ultimate meeting. This convergence SEEMS to be far in the future ONLY because your mind is NOT in perfect alignment with the idea, and therefore DOES NOT WANT IT NOW. The Holy Spirit USES time, but does NOT believe in it. Coming from God, He uses EVERYTHING for good,[304] but does not BELIEVE in what is not true.

T 6 C 11. Since the Holy Spirit IS in your minds, then your minds MUST be able to believe ONLY what is true. The Holy Spirit can speak only for this, because he speaks for God. He tells you to return your whole mind to God, BECAUSE IT HAS NEVER LEFT HIM. If it has never left Him, you need only perceive it AS IT IS to BE returned. The full awareness of the Atonement, then, is the rec-

---

[303] **Genesis 1:1** In the beginning God created the heavens and the earth.
John 1:3 All things were made through Him, and without Him nothing was made that was made.
Ephesians 3:9 and to make all men see what is the dispensation of the mystery which for ages hath been hid in God who created all things;
[304] **Romans 8:28** And we know that all things work together for good to those who love God, to those who are the called according to His purpose.

ognition that the separation NEVER OCCURRED. The ego CANNOT prevail[305] against this, because it is an explicit statement that the EGO never occurred.

T 6 C 12. The ego can accept the idea that RETURN is necessary, because it can so easily make the idea seem so difficult. But the Holy Spirit tells you that even RETURN is unnecessary, because what never happened CANNOT involve ANY problem. But it does NOT follow that YOU cannot make the idea of return both necessary AND difficult. God made nothing either necessary OR difficult. But YOU have perceived both AS IF they were part of His perfect creations. Yet it is surely clear that the perfect NEED nothing, and CANNOT **T(281) C 108** experience perfection as a difficult accomplishment because that is what they ARE.

T 6 C 13. This is the way in which you MUST perceive God's Creations, bringing all of your perceptions into the one parallel line which the Holy Spirit sees. This line is the direct line of communication with God, and lets YOUR mind converge with HIS. There is NO CONFLICT ANYWHERE in this perception, because it means that ALL perception is guided by the Holy Spirit, whose mind is fixed on God. ONLY the Holy Spirit can resolve conflict, because ONLY the Holy Spirit is conflict-free. He perceives ONLY what is true in YOUR mind, and extends outward to ONLY what is true in other minds.

T 6 C 14. The difference between the ego's use of projection and projection as the Holy Spirit uses it is very simple. The ego projects to EXCLUDE and therefore to deceive. The Holy Spirit projects by RECOGNIZING HIMSELF in EVERY mind, and thus perceives them as ONE. Nothing conflicts in this perception, because what the Holy Spirit perceives IS the same. Wherever He looks He sees Himself, and because He is UNITED, He offers the whole Kingdom always. This is the one message which God gave TO Him, and for which He must speak because that is what He IS. The peace of God lies in that message, and so the peace of God lies in YOU.

T 6 C 15. The great peace of the Kingdom shines in your mind forever, but it must shine OUTWARD to make YOU aware of it. The Holy Spirit was given you with perfect impartiality, and only by perceiving Him impartially can you perceive Him at all. The ego is legion,[306] but the Holy Spirit is one. No darkness abides ANYWHERE in the Kingdom, so your part is only to allow no darkness to abide in your OWN mind. This alignment with Light is unlimited, because it is in alignment with the Light of the world.[307] Each of us IS the Light of the world, and by joining our minds IN this Light, we proclaim the Kingdom of God together and AS ONE. **T(282) C 109**[308]

T 6 D. The Relinquishment of Attack (*Notes* 625 6:193)

T 6 D 1. We have used many words as synonymous which are not ordinarily regarded as the same. We began with having and being, and recently have used others. Hearing and being is an example, to which we can also add teaching and being, learning and being, and, above all, PROJECTING and being. This is because, as we have said before, every idea begins in the mind of the thinker and extends outward. Therefore, what extends FROM the mind IS STILL IN IT, and FROM what it extends IT KNOWS ITSELF. This is its natural talent.

T 6 D 2. The word "knows" is correct here, even though the ego does NOT know, and is not concerned with BEING at all. The Holy Spirit still holds knowledge safe through its impartial perception. By attacking nothing, it presents no barrier at all to the communication of God. Therefore, being is never threatened. Your Godlike mind can never be defiled. The ego never was and never will be part of it.

T 6 D 3. But through the ego you CAN hear and learn and teach and project WHAT IS NOT TRUE. From this, which YOU have made, you have taught yourselves to believe you ARE NOT WHAT YOU ARE. You CANNOT teach what you have not learned. And what you teach you strengthen in yourselves BECAUSE you are sharing it. Every lesson which you teach YOU are learning.

T 6 D 4. That is why you must teach only ONE lesson. If you are to be conflict free yourselves, you must learn ONLY from the Holy Spirit, and teach ONLY by Him. You ARE only love, but when you denied this you made what you ARE something you must LEARN. We said before that the message of the Crucifixion was teach ONLY love, for that is what you ARE. This is the ONE lesson which is perfectly unified, because it is the only lesson which IS one. And only BY teaching it can YOU learn it. **T(283) C 110**

T 6 D 5. "As you teach so will you learn." If that is true, and it is true indeed, you must never forget that what you teach is teaching YOU. What you project you BELIEVE. The only REAL safety lies in projecting ONLY the Holy Spirit, because as you see His gentleness in others your own mind perceives ITSELF as totally harmless. Once it can accept this fully, it does NOT see the need to PROTECT ITSELF. The protection of God then dawns upon it, assuring it that it is perfectly safe forever.

T 6 D 6. The perfectly safe ARE wholly benign. They bless because they know they ARE blessed. Without anxiety, the mind is wholly kind, and because it PROJECTS beneficence, it IS beneficent. Safety is the COMPLETE RELINQUISHMENT OF ATTACK. No compromise is possible in this. Teach attack in any form, and YOU HAVE LEARNED IT AND IT WILL HURT YOU. But your learning is not immortal, and you can unlearn it BY NOT TEACHING IT. Since you cannot NOT teach, your salvation lies in teaching exactly the opposite of EVERYTHING THE EGO BELIEVES. This is how YOU will learn the truth that will make you free,[309] and keep you so as others learn it of YOU.

T 6 D 7. The only way to HAVE peace is to TEACH peace. By learning it through projection, it becomes a part of you that you KNOW, because you cannot teach what you have dissociated. Only thus can you win back the knowledge you threw away. An idea which you SHARE you MUST HAVE. It awakens in you through the CONVICTION of teaching. Remember that if teaching is being and learning is being, then teaching is learning. EVERYTHING you teach YOU are learning. Teach only love, and learn that love is yours and YOU are love. **T(284) C 111**[310]

T 6 E. The Only Answer (*Notes* 634 6:198)

T 6 E 1. Remember that the Holy Spirit is the ANSWER, not the question. The ego always speaks first, because it is capricious and does NOT mean its maker well. This is because it believes, and correctly, that its maker may withdraw his support from it at any moment. If it meant you well, it would be glad, as the Holy Spirit will be glad when He has brought you home and you no longer need His guidance. The ego does NOT regard itself as part of you. Herein lies its primary perceptual error, the foundation of its whole thought system.

T 6 E 2. When God created you, He made you part of Him. That is why attack WITHIN the Kingdom is impossible. But YOU made the ego without love, and so it does not love YOU. You could not re-

---
[305] **Matthew 16:18** "And I also say to you that you are Peter, and on this rock I will build My church, and the gates of Hades shall not prevail against it."
[306] **Mark 5:9** Then He asked him, "What is your name?" And he answered, saying, "My name is Legion; for we are many."
[307] **Matthew 5:14** "You are the light of the world. A city that is set on a hill cannot be hidden."
[308] March 29, '66.

[309] **John 8:32** "And you shall know the truth, and the truth shall make you free."
[310] March 30, 1966

main WITHIN the Kingdom without love, and since the Kingdom IS love, you believe you are WITHOUT it. This enables the ego to regard itself as SEPARATE AND OUTSIDE ITS MAKER, thus speaking for the part of your mind that believes YOU are separate and outside the Mind of God.

T 6 E 3. The ego, then, raised the first question that was ever asked, but it can never answer it. That question, which was "What are you?" was the beginning of doubt. The ego has never answered ANY questions since, though it has raised a great many. The most inventive activities of the ego have never done more than OBSCURE THE QUESTION, because you HAVE the answer, and THE EGO IS AFRAID OF YOU. You cannot really understand conflict until YOU fully understand one basic fact that the ego does not know. The Holy Spirit does not speak first, but He ALWAYS answers. EVERYONE has called upon Him for help at one time or another, and in one way or another, AND HAS BEEN ANSWERED. Since the Holy Spirit answers truly, He answers FOR ALL TIME, and that means that EVERYONE HAS THE ANSWER NOW. **T(285) C 112**

T 6 E 4. The ego cannot hear the Holy Spirit, but it DOES feel that part of the same mind that made it is <u>AGAINST</u> it. It interprets this wholly as a justification for ATTACKING its maker. The ego believes that the best defense is attack, and WANTS YOU TO BELIEVE THIS. Unless you DO believe it, you will not side with it. And the ego feels badly in need of allies, though not of brothers.

T 6 E 5. Perceiving something alien to itself in your MIND, the ego turns to the body, NOT the mind as its ally BECAUSE the body is not part of you. This makes the body the ego's friend. But it is an alliance frankly based on separation. If you side with this alliance, you WILL be afraid, because you are siding with an alliance OF fear. The ego and the body conspire AGAINST your minds, and because they realize that their "enemy" CAN end them both merely by knowing they are not part of him, they join in the attack together. This is perhaps the strangest perception of all, if you consider what it really involves. The ego, which is not real, attempts to persuade the mind, which IS real, that it IS its own learning device, and that the learning device is more real than IT is. No-one in his right mind could POSSIBLY believe this, and no-one in his right mind DOES believe it.

T 6 E 6. Hear, then, the one answer of the Holy Spirit to ALL the questions which the ego raises. You are a Child of God, a priceless part of His Kingdom, which He created as part of Him. Nothing else exists, and ONLY this is real. You have chosen a sleep in which you have had bad dreams, but the sleep is not real, and God calls you to awake. There will be nothing left of your dream when you hear Him, because you WILL be awake. Your dreams have contained many of the ego's symbols, and they have confused you. But that was only because you were asleep and DID NOT KNOW. **T(286) C 113**

T 6 E 7. When you awake, you will see the Truth around you and in you, and you will no longer believe in dreams, because they will have no reality for you. But the Kingdom and all that you have created there will have great reality for you, because they are beautiful and true. In the Kingdom, where you are and what you are is perfectly certain. There is no doubt there, because the first question was never asked. Having finally been wholly answered, IT HAS NEVER BEEN. BEING alone lives in the Kingdom, where everything lives in God without question. The time that was spent on questioning in the dream has given way to the Creation and to its Eternity. **T(287) C 114**

T 6 E 8. YOU[311] are as certain as God, because you are as true as He is. But what was once quite certain in your minds has become only the ABILITY for certainty. The introduction of abilities into being was the beginning of UNcertainty, because abilities are POTENTIALS, not accomplishments. Your abilities are totally useless in the presence of God's accomplishments and also of yours. Accomplishments are RESULTS which HAVE BEEN achieved. When they are perfect, abilities are meaningless.

T 6 E 9. It is curious that the perfect must now be perfected. In fact, it is impossible. But you must remember that when you put yourselves in an impossible situation, you believed that the impossible WAS possible.

T 6 E 10. Abilities must be DEVELOPED, or you cannot use them. This is not true of anything that God created, but it is the kindest solution possible to what YOU have made. In an impossible situation, you can develop your abilities to the point where they CAN GET YOU OUT OF IT. You have a guide to how to develop them, but you have no commander EXCEPT YOURSELF. This leaves YOU in charge of the Kingdom, with both a guide to FIND it and a MEANS to keep it. You have a model to follow who will strengthen YOUR command, and never detract from it in any way. You therefore retain the central place in your perceived enslavement, a fact which ITSELF demonstrates that you are NOT enslaved.

T 6 E 11. You are in an impossible situation only because you thought it was possible to be in one. You WOULD be in an impossible situation if God showed you your perfection, and PROVED to you that you were wrong. This would demonstrate that the perfect were inadequate to bring THEMSELVES to the awareness of their perfection, and thus side with the belief that those who have everything need help, and are therefore helpless. **T(288) C 115**

T 6 E 12. This is the kind of reasoning that the ego engages in, but God, who KNOWS that His creations are perfect does NOT insult them. This would be as impossible as the ego's notion that it has insulted Him. That is why the Holy Spirit NEVER commands. To command is to assume INequality, which the Holy Spirit demonstrates does not exist. Fidelity to premises is a law of the mind, and everything God created is faithful to His laws. But fidelity to other laws is also possible, not because the laws are true, but because YOU MADE THEM.

T 6 E 13. What would be gained if God proved to you that you have thought insanely? Can God lose His own certainty? We have frequently stated that what you teach you ARE. Would you have God teach you that you have sinned? If He confronted the self you have made with the Truth He created FOR you, what could you be but afraid? You would doubt your sanity, which is the one thing in which you can FIND the sanity He gave you. God does not teach. To teach is to imply a lack which God KNOWS is not there. God is not conflicted. Teaching aims at change, but God created ONLY the changeless.

T 6 E 14. The separation was not a loss of perfection, but a failure in COMMUNICATION. A harsh and strident form of communication arose as the ego's voice. It could not shatter the peace of God, but it COULD shatter YOURS. God did not blot it out, because to eradicate it would be to attack it. Being questioned, He did not question. He merely gave the Answer.

T 6 E 15. God's answer IS your teacher.

T 6 F. "To Have, Give All to All" (*Notes* 644 6:208)

T 6 F 1. Like any good teacher, He DOES know more than you know NOW, but he teaches only to make you equals. This is because you had ALREADY taught wrong, having believed what was not true. YOU DID NOT BELIEVE IN YOUR OWN PERFECTION. Could God teach you that you had made a split mind when He knows your mind only as whole? **T(289) C 116**

T 6 F 2. What God DOES know is that His communication channels are not open to Him, so that He cannot impart His joy and know that His Children are wholly joyous. This is an ongoing process, not in time, but in eternity. God's extending outward, though not His com-

---
[311] April 1, 1966

pleteness, was blocked when the Sonship does not communicate with Him as one. So He thought, "My Children sleep, and must be awakened."

T 6 F 3. How can you wake children better and more kindly than with a gentle Voice that will not frighten them, but will merely remind them that the night is over and the Light has come? You do not inform them that the nightmares which frightened them so badly were not real, because children BELIEVE in magic. You merely reassure them that they are safe NOW. Then you train them to RECOGNIZE THE DIFFERENCE between sleeping and waking, so that THEY will understand they need not be afraid of dreams. Then when bad dreams come, they will call on the Light THEMSELVES to dispel them.

T 6 F 4. A wise teacher teaches through approach, NOT avoidance. He does not emphasize what you must avoid to escape from harm as much as what you need to learn to have joy. This is true even of the world's teachers. Consider the confusion that a child would experience if he were told, "Do not do THIS because it might hurt you and make you unsafe, but if you do THAT you will escape from harm and be safe, and then you will not be afraid." All of this could be included in only three words: "Do only that." That simple statement is perfectly clear, easily understood, and very easily remembered. **T(290) C 117**

T 6 F 5. The Holy Spirit NEVER itemizes errors, because He does not frighten children, and those who lack wisdom ARE children. But He ALWAYS answers their call, and His dependability makes THEM more certain. Children DO confuse fantasy and reality, and they ARE frightened because they do not know the difference.

T 6 F 6. The Holy Spirit makes NO distinction among dreams. He merely shines them away. His light is ALWAYS the call to awake, WHATEVER you may have been dreaming. Nothing lasting lies in dreams, and the Holy Spirit, shining with the light from God Himself, speaks only for what lasts forever.

T 6 F 7. When your body and your ego and your dreams are gone, you will know that YOU will last forever. Many think that this is accomplished through death, but NOTHING is accomplished through death because death is nothing. EVERYTHING is accomplished through life, and life is of the mind and in the Mind. The body neither lives nor dies, because it cannot contain you who ARE life. If we share the same mind, YOU CAN OVERCOME DEATH BECAUSE I DID. Death is an attempt to resolve conflict by not willing at all. Like any other impossible solution which the ego attempts, IT WILL NOT WORK.

T 6 F 8. God did not make the body, because it is destructible, and therefore not of the Kingdom. The body is the symbol of the WHAT YOU THINK YOU ARE. It is clearly a separation device, and therefore does not exist. The Holy Spirit, as always, takes what you have made and translates it into a learning device FOR you. Again, as always, it re-interprets what the ego uses as an argument FOR separation into an argument AGAINST it. **T(291) -118**

T 6 F 9. If the mind can heal the body, but the body cannot heal the mind, then the mind MUST BE STRONGER. Every miracle demonstrates this. We have said that the Holy Spirit is the MOTIVATION for miracles. This is because He ALWAYS tells you that ONLY the mind is real, because only the mind CAN BE SHARED. The body IS separate, and therefore CANNOT be part of you. To be of one mind[312] is meaningful, but to be of one body is meaningless. By the laws of mind, then, the body IS meaningless.

T 6 F 10. To the Holy Spirit THERE IS NO ORDER OF DIFFICULTY IN MIRACLES. This is FAMILIAR enough to you by now, but it has not yet become believable. Therefore, you do not understand it and cannot USE it. We have too much to accomplish on behalf of the Kingdom to let this crucial concept slip away. It is a real foundation stone of the thought system I teach and want YOU to teach. You cannot perform miracles without believing it, because it is a belief in perfect equality.

T 6 F 11. Only one equal gift CAN be offered to the equal Sons of God, and that is FULL APPRECIATION. Nothing more and nothing less. Without a range, order of difficulty IS meaningless, and there must BE no range in what you offer to each other. The Holy Spirit, which leads to God, translates communication into being, just as He ultimately translates perception into knowledge.

T 6 F 12. You DO NOT LOSE WHAT YOU COMMUNICATE. The ego uses the body for attack, for pleasure, and for pride. The insanity of this perception makes it a fearful one. The Holy Spirit sees it only as a means of COMMUNICATION. And because communicating IS sharing, it becomes communion. You might argue that fear as well as love can be communicated, and therefore can be shared. But this is not so real as it sounds. Those who communicate fear are promoting attack, and attack always BREAKS communication, and therefore makes communion impossible. **T(292) -119**

T 6 F 13. Egos DO join together in temporary allegiance, but always for WHAT EACH ONE CAN GET SEPARATELY. The Holy Spirit communicates only WHAT EACH ONE CAN GIVE TO ALL. He never takes ANYTHING back, because He wants YOU to keep it. Therefore, His teaching begins with the lesson: To HAVE, GIVE all TO all.

T 6 F 14. This is a very preliminary step, and THE ONLY ONE YOU MUST TAKE YOURSELF. It is not even necessary that you COMPLETE the step yourself, but it IS necessary that you turn in that direction. Having willed to go that way, you place YOURSELF in charge of the journey, where you and ONLY you must remain.

T 6 F 15. This step APPEARS to exacerbate conflict rather than resolve it, because it is the BEGINNING step in reversing your perception and turning it right side up. This conflicts with the upside down perception which you have not yet abandoned, or the change in direction would not have been necessary. Some people remain at this step for a very long time, experiencing VERY acute conflict. Many try to accept the CONFLICT, rather than to take the next step toward its resolution. But having taken the first step, they WILL be helped. Having willed what they CANNOT complete alone, THEY ARE NO LONGER ALONE.

T 6 F 16. You, Helen, had taken this step, and because you believed in it, you taught it to Bill, who still believed in the solution of sleep. You were not consistent in teaching it, but you did so often enough to enable him to learn it. Once HE learned it, he could teach YOU how to become more consistently awake, and thus begin to waken HIMSELF. This placed him, too, in command of the journey. His recognition of the direction it must take was perfectly stated when he INSISTED ON COLLABORATION.

T 6 F 17. You, H., had taken a giant step INTO conflict, but B. turned you both forwards TOWARD THE WAY OUT. The more he teaches this, the more he will learn it. **T(293) C 120**[313]

T 6 G. "To Have Peace, Teach Peace to Learn It" (*Notes* 654 6:218)

T 6 G 1. All the separated ones have a basic fear of retaliation and abandonment. This is because they BELIEVE in attack and rejection, so this is what they perceive and teach and LEARN. These insane concepts are clearly the result of their own dissociation and projection. What you teach you are, but it is quite apparent that you can teach wrongly, and therefore TEACH YOURSELVES WRONG. Many thought that I was attacking them, even though it is

---

[312] **Romans 12:16** Be of the same mind toward one another. Do not set your mind on high things, but associate with the humble. Do not be wise in your own opinion.

[313] APRIL 3, '66

quite apparent that I was NOT. An insane learner learns strange lessons.

T 6 G 2. What you must understand is that, when you do not SHARE a thought system, you ARE weakening it. Those who BELIEVE in it therefore perceive this as an ATTACK ON THEM. This is because everyone identifies himself WITH his thought system, and EVERY thought system centers on WHAT YOU BELIEVE YOU ARE. If the center of the thought system is TRUE, only truth extends outward from it. But if a lie is at its center, only DECEPTION proceeds from it.

T 6 G 3. All good teachers realize that only fundamental change will last. But they do NOT begin at that level. Strengthening MOTIVATION for change is their first and foremost goal. It is also their last and final one. Increasing motivation for change IN THE LEARNER is all that a teacher NEED do to GUARANTEE change. This is because a change in motivation IS a change of mind, and this will INEVITABLY produce fundamental change BECAUSE the mind IS fundamental. **T(294) -121**

T 6 G 4. The first step in the reversal or undoing process, then, is the UNDOING of the getting concept. Accordingly, the Holy Spirit's first lesson was: To HAVE, GIVE all TO all. We said that this is apt to INCREASE conflict temporarily, and we can clarify this still further now. At this point, the equality of having and being is not yet perceived. Until it IS, having still appears to be the OPPOSITE of being. Therefore, the first lesson SEEMS to contain a contradiction because it is BEING LEARNED BY A CONFLICTED MIND. This MEANS conflicting motivation, and so the lesson CANNOT be learned consistently as yet.

T 6 G 5. Further, the mind of the learner projects its own split, and therefore does NOT perceive consistent minds in others, making him suspicious of THEIR motivations. This is the real reason why in many respects the first lesson is the hardest to learn. Still strongly aware of the ego in himself, and responding primarily TO the ego in others, he is being taught to react to BOTH as if what he DOES believe IS NOT TRUE.

T 6 G 6. Upside down as always, the ego perceives the first lesson as insane. In fact, this is its only alternative here, because the other one, which would be much LESS acceptable, would obviously be that IT is insane. The ego's judgment, then, is predetermined by what it IS, though not more so than is any other product of thought. The fundamental change will still occur with the change of mind IN THE THINKER. **T(295) -122**

T 6 G 7. Meanwhile, the increasing clarity of the Holy Spirit's voice makes it impossible for the learner NOT TO LISTEN. For a time, then, he IS receiving conflicting messages AND ACCEPTING BOTH. This is the classic "double bind" in communication, which you wrote about yourselves quite recently, and with good examples too. It is interesting that Helen claimed at the time that she had never heard of it and did not understand it. You might remember our brother's insistence on its inclusion. Helen thought he had become (quite) irrational on this point, but it was quite strongly reinforced in HIS mind, and so he wanted to teach it in his text. This, of course, was a very good way for YOU to learn it.

T 6 G 8. The way out of conflict between two opposing thought systems is clearly TO CHOOSE ONE AND RELINQUISH THE OTHER. If you identify WITH your thought system, and you cannot escape this, and if you accept two thought systems which are in COMPLETE DISagreement, peace of mind IS impossible. If you TEACH both, which you will surely do as long as you ACCEPT both, you are teaching conflict and LEARNING it. But you DO want peace, or you would not have called upon the voice for PEACE to help you. His LESSON is not insane, but the CONFLICT IS.

T 6 G 9. There can BE no conflict between sanity and insanity, because only one is true, and therefore only ONE is REAL. The ego tries to persuade you that it is up to YOU to decide which voice is true. But the Holy Spirit teaches you that truth was created by God, and YOUR decision CANNOT change it. As you begin to realize the quiet power of His Voice AND ITS PERFECT CONSISTENCY, it MUST dawn on your minds that you are **T(296) C 123** trying to undo a decision which was made irrevocably FOR you. That is why we suggested before that there was help in reminding yourselves to allow the Holy Spirit to decide for God for YOU.

T 6 G 10. You are NOT asked to make insane decisions, although you are free to THINK you are. But it MUST be insane to believe IT IS UP TO YOU to decide what God's Creations ARE. The Holy Spirit perceives the conflict EXACTLY AS IT IS. Therefore, His second lesson is: To HAVE peace, TEACH peace to LEARN it.

T 6 G 11. This is still a preliminary step, because having and being are still not equated but it is more advanced than the first step, which is really only a thought REVERSAL. The second step is a positive affirmation of WHAT YOU WANT. This, then IS a step in the direction OUT of conflict, because it means that alternatives have been considered, and ONE has been chosen as MORE DESIRABLE.

T 6 G 12. But the evaluation "more desirable" still implies that the desirable has degrees. Therefore, although this step is essential for the ultimate decision, it is clearly NOT the final one.

T 6 G 13. It should be clear that the recognition of the lack of order in miracles has not yet been accepted, because NOTHING is difficult that is WHOLLY DESIRED. To desire wholly is to CREATE, and creating CANNOT be difficult if God Himself created you AS a creator. The second step, then, is still perceptual but it is nevertheless a giant step toward the unified perception that parallels God's knowing. **T(297) C 124**

T 6 G 14. As you take this step and HOLD THIS DIRECTION, you will be pushing toward the center of your thought system, where the FUNDAMENTAL change will occur. You are only beginning this step now, but you have started on this way by realizing that ONLY ONE WAY IS POSSIBLE. You do not yet realize this consistently, and so your progress is intermittent, but the second step is easier than the first, because it FOLLOWS. The very fact that you have accepted THAT is a demonstration of your growing awareness that the Holy Spirit WILL lead you on. **T(298) C 125**

T 6 H. "Be Vigilant Only for God and His Kingdom" (*Notes* 663 6:227)

T 6 H 1. For your own salvation you MUST be critical, because YOUR salvation IS critical to the whole Sonship. We said before that the Holy Spirit IS evaluative, and MUST be. Yet His evaluation does not extend BEYOND you, or you WOULD share it. In YOUR mind, and your mind ONLY, He sorts out the true from the false, and teaches you to judge every thought that you allow to ENTER in the light of what God PUT there. Whatever is IN ACCORD with this light He retains, to strengthen the Kingdom in YOU. When it is PARTLY in accord with truth He accepts it and purifies it. But what is OUT OF ACCORD ENTIRELY He rejects by judging against. This is how He keeps the Kingdom perfectly consistent and perfectly unified.

T 6 H 2. But what you must remember is that what the Holy Spirit REJECTS the ego ACCEPTS. This is because they are in fundamental disagreement about everything, because they are in fundamental disagreement about WHAT YOU ARE. The ego's beliefs on this crucial issue vary, and that is why it promotes different moods. The Holy Spirit NEVER varies on this point, and so the ONE mood that He engenders is joy. He PROTECTS this by rejecting everything that does NOT foster joy, and so He alone can keep you wholly joyous.

T 6 H 3. The Holy Spirit does not teach your mind to be critical of other minds, because He does not want you to teach your errors and

LEARN THEM YOURSELVES. He would hardly be consistent if He allowed you to STRENGTHEN what you must learn to avoid. In the mind of the THINKER, then, He IS judgmental, but only in order to unify it so IT CAN perceive WITHOUT judgment. **T(299) C 126** This enables the mind to TEACH without judgment and therefore learn to BE without judgment. The UNdoing is necessary only in YOUR mind, so that you cannot PROJECT it. God Himself has established what you can project with perfect safety. Therefore, the Holy Spirit's third lesson is: Be vigilant ONLY for God and HIS Kingdom.

T 6 H 4. This is a major step toward FUNDAMENTAL change. Yet it is still a lesson in thought REVERSAL, because it implies that there is something you must be vigilant AGAINST. It has advanced far from the first lesson which was PRIMARILY a reversal, and also from the second, which was essentially the identification of what is MORE desirable. This step, which follows from the second as the second does from the first, emphasizes the DICHOTOMY between the desirable and the UNdesirable. It therefore makes the ULTIMATE choice inevitable. But while the first step seems to INCREASE conflict, and the second still ENTAILS it to some extent, this one calls for CONSISTENT EFFORT AGAINST IT.

T 6 H 5. We said already that you can be as vigilant AGAINST the ego as FOR it. This lesson teaches not that you CAN be, but that you MUST be. It does not concern itself with order of difficulty, but with CLEAR-CUT PRIORITY FOR VIGILANCE. This step is unequivocal in that it teaches THERE MUST BE NO EXCEPTIONS, but it does NOT deny that the temptations to MAKE exceptions will occur. Here, then, your consistency is called on DESPITE chaos. But chaos and consistency CANNOT coexist for long, because they are MUTUALLY EXCLUSIVE **T(300) -127** As long as you must be vigilant against ANYTHING, however, you are not recognizing this, and are holding the belief that you can CHOOSE EITHER ONE.

T 6 H 6. By teaching you WHAT to choose, the Holy Spirit will ultimately be able to teach you that YOU NEED NOT CHOOSE AT ALL. This will finally liberate your will FROM choice, and direct it toward creation WITHIN the Kingdom. Choosing through the Holy Spirit will only lead you TO it. You create by what you ARE, but this IS what you must learn. The way to learn it is INHERENT in the third step, which brings together the lessons inherent in the others, and goes beyond them toward real integration.

T 6 H 7. If you allow yourselves to HAVE in your minds only what God put there, you are acknowledging your mind as God created it. Therefore, you are accepting it AS IT IS. And since it IS whole, you are teaching peace BECAUSE you have believed in it. The final step will still be taken FOR you by God. But by the third step, the Holy Spirit has PREPARED you FOR God. He is GETTING YOU READY to translate having into being by the very nature of the steps you must take WITH Him. You learn first that having rests on GIVING and NOT getting. Next you learn that you learn what you TEACH, and that you WANT TO LEARN PEACE. This is the CONDITION for identifying WITH the Kingdom, because it is the condition OF the Kingdom. **T(301) -128**

T 6 H 8. But you have believed that you are WITHOUT the Kingdom, and have therefore excluded yourself FROM it in your belief. It is therefore essential to teach you that YOU must be INCLUDED, and the BELIEF THAT YOU ARE NOT is the ONLY thing that you must exclude.

T 6 H 9. The third step is thus one of PROTECTION for your minds by allowing you to identify ONLY with the center, where God placed the altar to HIMSELF. We have already said that altars are BELIEFS, but God and His creations are BEYOND belief because they are beyond question. The Voice FOR God speaks only for BELIEF beyond question, but this IS the preparation for BEING without question.

T 6 H 10. As long as belief in God and His Kingdom is assailed by ANY doubts in your minds, His perfect Accomplishment is NOT apparent to you. This is why you MUST be vigilant ON GOD's BEHALF. The ego speaks AGAINST His Creation, and therefore DOES engender doubt. You cannot go BEYOND belief UNTIL you believe wholly. No one can EXTEND a lesson he has NOT LEARNED FULLY. Transfer, which IS extension, is the measure of learning because it is the MEASURABLE RESULT. This, however, does NOT mean that what it transfers TO is measurable. On the contrary, unless it transfers to the whole Sonship, which is immeasurable because it was created BY the Immeasurable, the learning itself MUST be incomplete.

T 6 H 11. To teach the WHOLE Sonship WITHOUT EXCEPTION demonstrates that you PERCEIVE ITS WHOLENESS and have learned that it IS One. Now you must be vigilant to HOLD its Oneness in your minds because if you allow doubt to enter, YOU will lose awareness of its wholeness, and WILL BE UNABLE TO TEACH IT. **T(302) C 129** The wholeness of the Kingdom does NOT depend on your perception, but your AWARENESS of its wholeness DOES. It is only your awareness that NEEDS protection, because your BEING cannot be assailed. Yet a real sense of being CANNOT be yours while you are doubtful of what you ARE. THIS IS WHY VIGILANCE IS ESSENTIAL. Doubts ABOUT being MUST not enter your mind, or you CANNOT know what you are with certainty.

T 6 H 12. Certainty is OF God for YOU. Vigilance is not necessary for truth, but it IS necessary AGAINST ILLUSION. Truth is WITHOUT illusions, and therefore WITHIN the Kingdom. Everything OUTSIDE the Kingdom IS ILLUSION. But you must learn to ACCEPT truth because YOU THREW IT AWAY. You therefore saw yourself AS IF you were WITHOUT it. By making another Kingdom WHICH YOU VALUED, you did NOT keep the Kingdom of God alone in your minds, and thus placed part of your mind OUTSIDE of it. What you have made has thus DIVIDED YOUR WILL and given you a sick mind that MUST be healed. Your vigilance AGAINST this sickness IS the way to heal it.

T 6 H 13. Once YOUR mind is healed, it radiates health and thereby TEACHES healing. This establishes you as a teacher who teaches LIKE me. Vigilance was required of me as much as of you. But remember that those who will to teach the same thing MUST be in agreement about what they believe.

T 6 H 14. The third step, then, is a statement of what you WANT to believe, and entails a willingness to RELINQUISH EVERYTHING ELSE. I told you that you were just beginning the second step, but I also told you that the third one FOLLOWS it. The Holy Spirit WILL enable you to go on IF YOU FOLLOW HIM. Your vigilance is the sign that you WANT Him to guide you. **T(303) C 130** Vigilance DOES require effort, but only to teach you that effort ITSELF is unnecessary. You have exerted GREAT effort to preserve what you made BECAUSE it is NOT true. Therefore, you must now turn your effort AGAINST it. Only this can cancel out the NEED for effort, and call upon the BEING which you both HAVE and ARE. THIS recognition is wholly WITHOUT effort, because it is ALREADY true and needs no protection. It is in the perfect safety of God. Therefore, inclusion is total and Creation is WITHOUT LIMIT.

CHAPTER 7 – THE CONSISTENCY OF THE KINGDOM

T 7 A. Introduction (*Notes* 675 7:7)

T 7 A 1. The creative power of both God AND His Creations is limitless, but it is NOT in reciprocal relationship. You DO communicate fully WITH God, as He does with YOU. This is an ongoing process in which you SHARE, and BECAUSE you share it, you are inspired to create LIKE God. But in Creation you are NOT in a reciprocal relation TO God, because He created YOU, but you did NOT create Him. We have already stated that only in this respect your creative power differs from His. Even in this world there is a parallel. Parents give birth to children, but children do NOT give birth to parents. They DO, however, give birth to their children, and thus give birth AS their parents do.

T 7 A 2. If you created GOD and He created you, the KINGDOM could not increase through its OWN creative thought. Creation would therefore be limited, and you would NOT be co-creators WITH God. As God's creative Thought proceeds FROM Him TO you, so must YOUR creative thoughts proceed FROM you to YOUR creations. In this way only can ALL creative power EXTEND OUTWARD. **T(304) C 131** God's accomplishments are NOT yours. But yours are LIKE His. HE created the Sonship, and YOU increase it. You HAVE the power to ADD to the Kingdom, but NOT to add to the Creator OF the Kingdom.

T 7 A 3. You claim this power when you have become wholly vigilant for God AND the Kingdom. BY ACCEPTING this power as YOURS, you have learned to be what you ARE. YOUR creations belong in YOU, as YOU belong in God. You are part of God, as your sons are part of His Sons. To create is to love. Love extends outward simply because it cannot be contained. Being limitless, it DOES NOT STOP. It creates forever, but NOT in time. God's creations have ALWAYS BEEN, because HE has always been. YOUR creations have always been, because you can create only as HE creates.

T 7 A 4. Eternity is yours because He created you eternal.

T 7 B. Bargaining versus Healing (*Notes* 677 7:9)

T 7 B 1. The ego demands RECIPROCAL rights, because it is competitive rather than loving. It is always willing to make a deal, but it cannot understand that to be LIKE another means that NO DEALS ARE POSSIBLE. To gain you must GIVE, not bargain. To bargain is to LIMIT giving, and this is NOT God's Will. To will WITH God is to create like HIM. God does not limit HIS gifts in ANY way. You ARE His gifts, and so your gifts must be like HIS.

T 7 B 2. Your gifts TO the Kingdom are like His to YOU. I gave ONLY love to the Kingdom, because I believed that was what I WAS. What you believe you are DETERMINES your gifts, and if God created you by extending HIMSELF AS you, you can only extend YOURSELF as He did. Only joy increases forever. Joy and Eternity are INSEPARABLE. God extends outward beyond limits and beyond time, and you, who are co-creators with Him, extend His Kingdom forever and beyond limit. **T(305) C 132** Eternity is the indelible stamp of Creation. The eternal are in peace and joy forever.

T 7 B 3. To think like God is to share His certainty of WHAT YOU ARE. And to CREATE like Him is to share the perfect love He shares with YOU. To this the Holy Spirit leads you, that your joy may be complete[314] because the Kingdom of God is whole. We have said that the last step in the re-awakening of knowledge is taken by God. This is true, but it is hard to explain in words, because words are symbols, and nothing that is true NEEDS to be explained. However, the Holy Spirit always has the task of translating the useLESS into the useFUL, the meaningLESS into the meaningFUL, and the temporary into the timeLESS. He CAN, therefore, tell you something about this last step, but this one you must know yourself, because BY it you know what you are. This IS your being.

T 7 B 4. God does not take steps because His Accomplishments are NOT gradual. He does not teach, because His Creations are changeless. He does nothing LAST because He Created FIRST and FOR ALWAYS. It must be understood that the word "first" as applied to Him is NOT a time concept. He is first here only in the sense that He is first in the Holy Trinity Itself. He is the Prime Creator because HE created His co-creators. Because He DID, time applies neither to Him NOR to what He created. **T(306) C 133**[315]

T 7 B 5. The "last step" that God was said to take was therefore true in the beginning, is true now, and will be true forever.[316] What is timeless IS ALWAYS THERE because its BEING is eternally changeless. It does NOT change by increase, because it was forever created TO increase. If you perceive it as NOT increasing, you do not know what it IS. You also do not know what created it, or who HE is. God does not REVEAL this to you, because it was never hidden. His light was never obscured, because it is His Will to SHARE it. How can what is fully shared be withheld and then revealed?

T 7 B 6. To heal is the ONLY kind of thinking in this world that resembles the Thought of God, and because of the elements which they SHARE, can transfer TO it. When a brother perceives himself as sick, he IS perceiving himself as NOT WHOLE, and therefore IN NEED. If you, too, see him this way, you are seeing him as if he were ABSENT from the Kingdom or separated FROM it, thus making the Kingdom ITSELF obscure to BOTH OF YOU. Sickness and separation are not of God, but the Kingdom IS. If you obscure the Kingdom, you are perceiving WHAT IS NOT OF GOD.

T 7 C. The Laws of Mind (*Notes* 682 7:14)

T 7 C 1. To heal, then, is to correct perception in your brother AND yourself by SHARING THE HOLY SPIRIT WITH HIM. This places you both WITHIN the Kingdom and restores ITS wholeness in your minds. This PARALLELS creation because it UNIFIES BY INCREASING, and INTEGRATES BY EXTENDING.

T 7 C 2. WHAT YOU PROJECT YOU BELIEVE. This is an immutable law of mind in this world as well as in the Kingdom. However, its CONTENT is somewhat different in this world from what it REALLY is, because the thoughts it governs are VERY different from the thoughts in the Kingdom. Laws must be adapted to circumstances, if they are to maintain order. **T(307) C 134**

T 7 C 3. The outstanding characteristic of the laws of mind, as they operate in this world, is that by obeying them, and I assure you that you MUST obey them, you can arrive at diametrically opposed results. This is because the laws have adapted to the circumstances of this world, in which diametrically opposed outcomes are BELIEVED in. The laws of mind govern thoughts, and you DO respond to two conflicting voices. You have heard many arguments on behalf of "the freedoms," which would indeed have BEEN freedom if man had not chosen to FIGHT for them. That is why they perceive "the freedoms" as many instead of ONE.

T 7 C 4. But the argument that underlies the DEFENSE of freedom is perfectly valid. Because it is true, it should not be FOUGHT for, but it SHOULD be sided WITH. Those who are AGAINST freedom believe that its outcome will hurt them, which CANNOT be true.

---

[314] **John 15:11** "These things I have spoken to you, that My joy may remain in you, and that your joy may be complete."

[315] April 11, '66.
[316] **Hebrews 13:8** Jesus Christ is the same yesterday, today, and forever.

But those who are FOR freedom, even if they are misguided in HOW they defend it, are siding with the one thing in this world which IS true. Whenever anyone can listen fairly to both sides of ANY issue, he WILL make the right decision. This is because he HAS the answer. Conflict can indeed be projected, but it MUST be intrapersonal first.

T 7 C 5. The term "intraPERSONAL" is an ego term, because "personal" implies of ONE person, and NOT of others. "Interpersonal" has a similar error, because it implies something that exists between DIFFERENT individuals. When we spoke before of the extremely PERSONAL nature of revelation, we followed this statement immediately with a description of the inevitable outcomes of the revelation in terms of SHARING. A PERSON conceives of himself as separate, largely because he perceives OF himself as bounded by a body. ONLY if he perceives as a MIND can he overcome this. THEN he is free to use terms like "intraMENTAL" and "interMENTAL" WITHOUT seeing them as different and conflicting, because minds CAN be in perfect accord. **T(308) C 135**

T 7 C 6. OUTSIDE the Kingdom, the law which prevails INSIDE it is ADAPTED to "what you project you believe." This is its TEACHING form, because outside the Kingdom teaching is mandatory because learning is essential. This form of the law clearly implies that you will learn what YOU are from what you have projected onto others and therefore believe THEY are. IN the Kingdom, there is no teaching OR learning, because there is no BELIEF. There is only CERTAINTY. God and His Sons, in the surety of Being, KNOW that what you project you ARE.

T 7 C 7. That form of the law is NOT adapted at all, being the Law of Creation. God Himself created the law by creating BY it. And His Sons, who create LIKE Him, follow it gladly, knowing that the INCREASE of the Kingdom depends on it, just as THEIR creation did. Laws must be communicated, if they are to be helpful. In effect, they must be TRANSLATED for those who speak a different language. But a good translator, though he MUST alter the FORM of what he translates, NEVER changes the meaning. In fact, his whole PURPOSE is to change the form SO THAT the original meaning IS retained.

T 7 C 8. The Holy Spirit IS the translator of the Laws of God to those who do NOT understand them. YOU could not do this yourselves because conflicted minds CANNOT be faithful to one meaning, and will therefore CHANGE THE MEANING TO PRESERVE THE FORM. The Holy Spirit's purpose in translating is naturally EXACTLY the opposite. He translates ONLY to preserve the original meaning in ALL respects and in ALL languages. Therefore, He OPPOSES differences in form as meaningful, and emphasizes always that THESE DIFFERENCES DO NOT MATTER. The meaning of His message is ALWAYS the same, and ONLY the meaning matters. **T(309) C 136**

T 7 C 9. God's Law of Creation, in perfect form, does NOT involve the USE of truth to convince His sons OF truth. The EXTENSION of truth, which IS the Law of the Kingdom, rests only on the knowledge of WHAT TRUTH IS. This is your INHERITANCE, and requires no learning at all. But when you DISinherited YOURSELVES, you BECAME learners. No-one questions the intimate connection of learning and memory. Learning is impossible WITHOUT memory, because it CANNOT be consistent UNLESS it is remembered.

T 7 C 10. That is why the Holy Spirit IS a lesson in remembering. We said before that He teaches remembering and FORGETTING, but the forgetting aspect is only TO MAKE THE REMEMBERING CONSISTENT. You forget to REMEMBER BETTER. You will NOT understand His translations while you listen to two ways of perceiving them. Therefore, you must forget or relinquish one to UNDERSTAND the other. This is the only way you can LEARN consistency, so that you can finally BE consistent. What can the perfect consistency of the Kingdom MEAN to the confused? It MUST be apparent that confusion INTERFERES with meaning, and therefore PREVENTS THE LEARNER FROM APPRECIATING IT.

T 7 C 11. There is NO confusion in the Kingdom, because there IS only one meaning. This Meaning comes from God and IS God. Because it is also YOU, you share it and EXTEND it AS YOUR CREATOR DID. This needs no translation, because it is perfectly understood, but it DOES need extension because it MEANS extension. Communication here is perfectly direct and perfectly united. It is totally without strain, because nothing discordant EVER enters. That is why it IS the Kingdom of God. It belongs to Him and is therefore LIKE Him. That IS its reality, and nothing CAN assail it. **T(310) C 137**[317]

T 7 D. The Unified Curriculum (*Notes* 691 7:23)

T 7 D 1. To heal is to liberate totally. We once said there is no order in miracles because they are all MAXIMAL EXPRESSIONS OF LOVE. This has no range at all. The non-maximal only APPEARS to have a range. This is because it SEEMS to be meaningful to measure it FROM the maximum and identify its position by HOW MUCH IT IS NOT THERE. Actually, this does not mean ANYTHING. It is like negative numbers in that the concept can be used theoretically, but it has NO application practically. It is true that if you put three apples on the table and then took them AWAY, the three apples are NOT THERE. But it is NOT true that the table is now MINUS three apples. If there is NOTHING on the table, it does NOT matter what WAS there in terms of amount. The "nothing" is neither greater nor less because of what is ABSENT.

T 7 D 2. That is why "all" and "nothing" are dichotomous, WITHOUT A RANGE. This is perfectly clear in maximal test performance and for EXACTLY the reason you emphasize. You cannot interpret AT ALL, unless you assume either MAXIMAL motivation or its COMPLETE ABSENCE. Only in these two conditions can you validly COMPARE responses, and you MUST assume the former, because if the LATTER is true, the subject WILL NOT DO ANYTHING. Given VARIABLE motivation he WILL do something, but you CANNOT UNDERSTAND WHAT IT IS.

T 7 D 3. The RESULTS of tests are evaluated relatively, ASSUMING maximal motivation. But this is because we are dealing with ABILITIES, where degree of development IS meaningful. This does NOT mean that what ability is used FOR is necessarily either limited OR divided. But one thing is certain. Abilities are POTENTIALS for learning, and you will apply them to WHAT YOU WANT **T(311) C 138** TO LEARN. Learning is EFFORT, and effort MEANS will.

T 7 D 4. You will notice that we have used the term "abilities" as a plural, which is correct. This is because abilities began with the ego, which perceived them as a POTENTIAL FOR EXCELLING. This is how the ego STILL perceives them and uses them. It does NOT want to teach everyone all it has learned, because that would DEFEAT its purpose in learning. Therefore, it does not REALLY learn at all. The Holy Spirit teaches YOU to use what the ego has made to TEACH the opposite of what the ego has LEARNED. The KIND of learning is as irrelevant as is the particular ability which was applied TO the learning.

T 7 D 5. You could not have a better example of the Holy Spirit's (this) unified purpose than this course. The Holy Spirit has taken very diversified areas of YOUR past learning, and has applied them to a UNIFIED curriculum. The fact that this was NOT the ego's reason for learning is totally irrelevant. YOU made the effort to learn, and the Holy Spirit has a unified goal for ALL effort. He ADAPTS the ego's potentials for excelling to potentials for EQUALIZING. This makes them USELESS for the ego's purpose, but VERY useful for His.

---

[317] April 17, 1966

T 7 D 6. If different abilities are applied long enough to one GOAL, the abilities THEMSELVES become unified. This is because they are channelized in one direction, or in one WAY. Ultimately, then, they all contribute to ONE RESULT, and by so doing, their SIMILARITY rather than their differences is emphasized. You can EXCEL in many DIFFERENT ways, but you can EQUALIZE in ONE WAY ONLY. Equality is NOT a variable state, by definition. **T(312) C 139**

T 7 D 7. That is why we once said that papers will be easy to write when you have learned THIS course. To the ego there appears to be no connection, because the EGO is discontinuous. But the Holy Spirit teaches one lesson and applies it to ALL individuals in ALL situations. Being conflict free, He maximizes ALL efforts and ALL results. By teaching the power of the Kingdom of God Himself, He teaches you that ALL POWER IS YOURS. Its application does not matter. It is ALWAYS maximal. Your vigilance does NOT establish it as yours, but it DOES enable you to use it ALWAYS and in ALL WAYS.

T 7 D 8. When I said, "Behold I am with you always,"[318] I meant it literally. I am not absent to ANYONE nor in ANY situation. BECAUSE I am always with you, YOU are the Way, and the Truth, and the Light.[319] YOU did not make this power any more than I did. It was created to BE shared, and therefore cannot be meaningfully perceived as BELONGING to anyone AT THE EXPENSE of another. This perception makes it meaningLESS by eliminating or overlooking its real and ONLY meaning.

T 7 E. The Recognition of Truth (*Notes* 696 7:28)

T 7 E 1. God's MEANING waits in the Kingdom because that is where He placed it. It does NOT wait in time. It merely RESTS there (in the Kingdom) because it BELONGS there, as YOU do. How can you, who ARE God's meaning, perceive yourselves as absent FROM it? You can see yourselves as separated FROM your meaning only by EXPERIENCING YOURSELF AS UNREAL. This is WHY the ego is insane; it teaches that you are NOT what you ARE. This is so contradictory that it is clearly impossible. It is therefore a lesson which you CANNOT REALLY LEARN, and therefore CANNOT REALLY TEACH. But you ARE always teaching. You MUST, then, be teaching SOMETHING ELSE AS WELL, even though the ego DOES NOT KNOW WHAT IT IS. **T(313) C 140**

T 7 E 2. The ego, then, IS always being undone, and DOES suspect your motives. Your mind CANNOT be unified in allegiance to the ego, because the mind does NOT BELONG to it. But what is "treacherous" to the ego IS faithful to peace. The ego's "enemy" is therefore YOUR friend. We said before that the ego's friend is not part of you but that is because the ego perceives itself as at war and therefore in need of allies. YOU, who are NOT at war, must look for brothers and RECOGNIZE all you see AS brothers, because ONLY EQUALS ARE AT PEACE.

T 7 E 3. Because God's equal Sons have everything, they CANNOT compete. But if they perceive ANY of their brothers as anything OTHER than their perfect equals, the IDEA of competition HAS entered their minds. Do not underestimate your need to be vigilant AGAINST this idea, because ALL your conflicts come FROM it. It IS the belief that conflicting interests are possible, and therefore means that you have accepted the IMpossible as true. How is that different from saying that you are perceiving YOURSELF as unreal?

---

[318] **Matthew 28:20** "Teaching them to observe all things that I have commanded you; and lo, I am with you always, even to the end of the age." Amen.
[319] **John 14:6** Jesus said to him, "I am the way, the truth, and the life. No one comes to the Father except through Me. *Again, while the Biblical quote is "life" in ACIM, all versions, we find "light."*

T 7 E 4. To be IN the Kingdom is merely to focus your full attention ON it. As long as you believe that you can ATTEND to what is NOT true, you are accepting conflict as your CHOICE. IS IT REALLY A CHOICE? It SEEMS to be, but seeming and reality are hardly the same. You who ARE the Kingdom are not concerned with seeming. Reality is yours because you ARE reality. This is how having and being are ultimately reconciled, NOT in the Kingdom, but IN YOUR MINDS. The altar there is the ONLY reality. It is PERFECTLY clear in its thought, because it is a reflection of PERFECT Thought. It SEES only brothers because it sees ONLY in its own Light. **T(314) C 141**

T 7 E 5. God has lit your minds Himself, and keeps your mind lit BY His light because His light is WHAT YOUR MINDS ARE. This is TOTALLY beyond question. And when YOU questioned it, you WERE answered. The answer merely UNDOES the question by establishing the fact that to QUESTION reality is to question MEANINGLESSLY. That is why the Holy Spirit NEVER questions. Its sole function is to UNdo the questionable, and thus LEAD TO CERTAINTY. The certain are perfectly calm, because they are not in doubt. They do NOT raise questions because NOTHING QUESTIONABLE ENTERS THEIR MINDS. This holds them in perfect serenity because this is what they SHARE, KNOWING what they are.

T 7 E 6. Healing is both an art and a science, as has so often been said. It is an art because it depends on inspiration in the sense that we have already used the term. Inspiration is the opposite of dis-spiriting, and therefore means to make joyful. The dis-spirited are depressed because they believe that they are literally "without the Spirit," which is an illusion. You do not PUT the Spirit in them by inspiring them, because that would be "magic," and therefore would not be real healing. But you DO recognize the Spirit that is ALREADY THERE, and thereby REAWAKEN IT. This is why the healer is part of the Resurrection and the <u>LIFE</u>. The SPIRIT is not asleep in the minds of the sick, but the part of the mind that can perceive it and be glad IS. **T(315) C 142**

T 7 E 7. Healing is also a science because it obeys the laws of God, whose laws are true. BECAUSE they are true, they are perfectly dependable, and therefore universal in application. The real aim of science is neither prediction nor control, but ONLY UNDERSTANDING. This is because it does NOT establish the laws it seeks; <u>CANNOT</u> discover them through prediction, and has NO control over them at all. Science is nothing more than an approach to WHAT ALREADY IS. Like inspiration, it can be misunderstood as magic, and WILL be whenever it is undertaken as SEPARATE from what already is, and perceived as a means for ESTABLISHING it. To believe this is possible is to believe YOU CAN DO IT. This can ONLY be the voice of the ego.

T 7 E 8. Truth can only be RECOGNIZED, and NEED only be recognized. Inspiration is of the Spirit, and certainty is of God according to His laws. Both therefore come from the same Source, because inspiration comes from the voice FOR God and certainty comes from the laws OF God. Healing does not come DIRECTLY from God, who knows His Creations as perfectly whole. But healing is nevertheless OF God, because it proceeds from His Voice and from His laws. It is their RESULT in a state of mind which does not know Him. The STATE is unknown to Him, and therefore does not exist. But those who sleep are stupefied, or better, UNAWARE. And BECAUSE they are unaware THEY DO NOT KNOW.

T 7 E 9. The Holy Spirit must work THROUGH you to teach you He is IN you. This is an intermediary step toward the knowledge that YOU are in God BECAUSE YOU ARE PART OF HIM. The miracles which the Holy Spirit inspires CAN have no order, because every part of Creation IS of one order. This is God's will AND yours. **T(316) C 143** The laws of God ESTABLISH this, and the Holy Spirit reminds you OF it. When you heal, you are REMEMBERING THE LAWS OF GOD and FORGETTING the laws of the ego. We said before that forgetting is merely a way of REMEMBERING BETTER. It is therefore NOT the opposite of remembering, when it is properly conceived. Perceived IMproperly, it induces a perception of CONFLICT WITH SOMETHING ELSE, as all incorrect perception does. PROPERLY perceived, it can be used as a way OUT of conflict, as all proper perception can.

T 7 E 10. ALL abilities, then should be given over to the Holy Spirit, WHO KNOWS HOW TO USE THEM PROPERLY. He can use them ONLY for healing, because He knows you ONLY as whole. BY healing you learn of wholeness, and by learning of wholeness you learn to remember God. You HAVE forgotten Him, but the Holy Spirit still knows that YOUR forgetting MUST be translated into a way of remembering, and NOT perceived as a SEPARATE ability which OPPOSES AN OPPOSITE. This is the way in which the ego tries to use ALL abilities, because its goal is ALWAYS to make YOU believe that YOU are in opposition.

T 7 E 11. The ego's goal is as unified as the Holy Spirit's, and it is BECAUSE of this that their goals can NEVER be reconciled in ANY way or to ANY extent. The ego ALWAYS seeks to divide and separate. The Holy Spirit ALWAYS seeks to unify and HEAL. As you heal, you ARE healed because the Holy Spirit sees NO ORDER OF HEALING. Healing IS the way to undo the belief in differences, because it is the ONLY way of perceiving the Sonship WITHOUT this belief. This perception is therefore IN accord with the laws of God even in a state of mind which is OUT of accord with His. **T(317) C 144** But the strength of right perception is so great that it brings the mind INTO accord with His, because it yields to His pull which IS in all of you.

T 7 E 12. To oppose the pull or the will of God is not an ability but a real delusion. The ego believes that it HAS this ability, and can offer this ability to YOU as a gift. YOU DO NOT WANT IT. It is NOT a gift. It is NOTHING AT ALL. God HAS given you a gift, which you both HAVE and ARE. When you do not USE it, you do not know you HAVE it. By not knowing this, you do NOT know what you ARE. Healing, then, is a way of APPROACHING knowledge by THINKING in accordance with the laws of God and RECOGNIZING THEIR UNIVERSALITY. WITHOUT this recognition, you have made the laws themselves meaningless TO you. But the LAWS are not meaningless, because all meaning is contained BY them, and IN them.

T 7 E 13. Seek ye FIRST the Kingdom of Heaven,[320] because that is where the laws of God operate truly, and they can operate ONLY truly, because they are the laws of Truth. But SEEK THIS ONLY, because you can FIND nothing else. There IS nothing else. God is all in all[321] in a very literal sense. All being[322] is in Him because He IS all Being. YOU are therefore in Him because YOUR being IS His. Healing is a way of FORGETTING the sense of danger that the ego has induced in YOU by not recognizing its existence in your brothers. This strengthens the Holy Spirit in BOTH of you, because it is a REFUSAL TO ACKNOWLEDGE FEAR. Love needs only this invitation. It comes freely to ALL the Sonship, because it is what the Sonship IS. **T(318) C 145** By their awakening TO it, they merely forget what they are NOT. This enables them to remember what they ARE.

---

[320] **Matthew 6:33** "But seek first the kingdom of God and His righteousness, and all these things shall be added to you."
[321] **1 Corinthians 15:28** Now when all things are made subject to Him, then the Son Himself will also be subject to Him who put all things under Him, that God may be all in all.
Ephesians 1:23 Which is His body, the fullness of Him who fills all in all.
[322] **Acts 17:28** for in Him we live and move and have our being, as also some of your own poets have said, "For we are also His offspring."

T 7 F. Healing and the Changelessness of Mind (*Notes* 707 7:39)

T 7 F 1. The body is nothing more than a framework for developing abilities. It is therefore a means for developing potentials, which is quite apart from what the potential is used FOR. This IS a decision. The effects of the ego's decision in this matter are so apparent that they need no elaboration here. But the Holy Spirit's decision to use the body ONLY for communication has such direct connection with healing that it DOES need clarification. The unhealed healer OBVIOUSLY does not understand his own vocation.

T 7 F 2. ONLY minds communicate. Since the ego CANNOT obliterate the impulse to communicate because it is also the impulse to CREATE it can only try to teach you that the BODY can both communicate AND create, and therefore DOES NOT NEED THE MIND. The ego, then, tries to teach you that the body can ACT like the mind, and therefore IS self-sufficient. But we have learned that behavior is NOT the level for either teaching OR learning. This MUST be so, because you CAN act in accordance with what you do NOT believe. But this will weaken you as teachers AND learners because, as has been repeatedly emphasized, you teach what you DO believe. An inconsistent lesson WILL be poorly taught and POORLY LEARNED. If you teach both sickness AND healing, you ARE both a poor teacher and a poor learner. **T(319) C 146**

T 7 F 3. Healing is the one ability that everyone CAN develop, and MUST develop, if he is to BE healed. Healing IS the Holy Spirit's form of communication, and THE ONLY ONE HE KNOWS. He recognizes no other, because he does NOT accept the ego's confusion of mind and body. Minds CAN communicate, but they CANNOT hurt. The body in the service of the ego can hurt other BODIES, but this CANNOT occur UNLESS the body has ALREADY been confused WITH the mind. This fact, too, can be used either for healing or for magic, but you must realize that magic is ALWAYS the belief that healing is HARMFUL. This is its totally insane premise, and so it proceeds accordingly.

T 7 F 4. Healing ONLY STRENGTHENS. Magic always tries to weaken. Healing perceives NOTHING in the healer that everyone else does not share WITH him. Magic ALWAYS sees something special in the healer, which he believes he can offer as a gift to someone who does NOT have it. He may believe that this gift comes from God TO him, but it is quite evident that he does NOT understand God if he thinks HE has something that others DO NOT. You might well ask why SOME healing CAN result from this kind of thinking, and there is a real reason for this.

T 7 F 5. However misguided the "magical healer" may be, and however much he may be trying to strengthen his ego, HE IS ALSO TRYING TO HELP. He IS conflicted and unstable, but AT TIMES he is offering SOMETHING to the Sonship, and the ONLY thing the Sonship can ACCEPT IS healing. When the so-called healing "works," then, the impulse both to help and BE helped have coincided. This is co-incidental, because the healer may NOT be experiencing HIMSELF as truly helpful at the time, and the belief that he IS, in the mind of ANOTHER, HELPS HIM. **T(320) C 147**

T 7 F 6. The Holy Spirit does NOT work by chance, and the healing that is of HIM ALWAYS works. And unless the healer ALWAYS heals BY Him, the results WILL vary. But healing itself IS consistence, because ONLY consistence is conflict-free, and only the conflict-free ARE whole. By accepting exceptions, and acknowledging that he can SOMETIMES heal and SOMETIMES not, the healer is OBVIOUSLY accepting INconsistency. He is therefore IN conflict and TEACHING conflict.

T 7 F 7. Can ANYTHING of God NOT be for all and always? Love is incapable of ANY exceptions. Only if there is fear does the whole IDEA of exceptions of any kind seem to be meaningful. Exceptions ARE fearful because they were made BY fear. The "fearful healer" is a contradiction in terms, and is therefore a concept that ONLY a conflicted mind could POSSIBLY perceive as meaningful. Fear does NOT gladden. Healing DOES. Fear ALWAYS makes exceptions. Healing NEVER does. Fear produces dissociation because it induces SEPARATION. Healing <u>ALWAYS</u> induces harmony because it proceeds from integration.

T 7 F 8. Healing is predictable BECAUSE it can be counted on. EVERYTHING that is of God can be counted on, because everything of God is WHOLLY REAL. HEALING can be counted on BECAUSE it is inspired by His voice, and is in accord with His laws. But if healing IS consistence, it CANNOT be inconsistently understood. Understanding MEANS consistence, because GOD means consistence. And because that IS His Meaning, it is also YOURS. YOUR meaning CANNOT be out of accord with His, because your whole meaning, and your ONLY meaning, comes FROM His and is LIKE His. God CANNOT be out of accord with HIMSELF, and YOU cannot be out of accord with Him. You cannot separate your <u>SELF</u> from YOUR Creator, who created YOU by sharing HIS Being WITH you. **T(321) C 148**

T 7 F 9. The unhealed healer wants gratitude FROM his brothers, but he is NOT grateful to them. This is because he thinks he is giving something TO them, and is NOT receiving something equally desirable in return. His TEACHING is limited because he is LEARNING so little. His HEALING lesson is limited by his own ingratitude, which is a lesson in sickness. Learning is constant and so vital in its power for change that a Son of God can recognize his power in an instant, and change the world in the next. That is because by changing HIS mind he has changed the most powerful device that was ever created FOR change.

T 7 F 10. This in no way contradicts the changelessness of mind as GOD created it. But YOU think that you HAVE changed it, as long as you learn through the ego. This DOES place you in a position of needing to learn a lesson which SEEMS contradictory: you must learn to change your mind ABOUT your mind. Only by this can you learn that it IS changeless.

T 7 F 11. When you heal, that is exactly what you ARE learning (doing). You are recognizing the changeless mind in your brother by perceiving (knowing) that he could NOT have changed his mind. That is how you perceive the Holy Spirit in him. It is ONLY the Holy Spirit in him that never changes His mind. He himself must think he CAN, or he would not perceive himself as sick. He therefore does not know what his self IS. If YOU see only the changeless in him, you have not really changed him at all. But by changing your mind about HIS FOR him, you help him undo the change his ego thinks it has made in him. As you can hear two voices, so you can see in two ways. One way shows you an image, or better, an idol which you may worship out of fear, but which you will never love. The other shows you only truth, which you will love because you will UNDERSTAND it. Understanding is APPRECIATION, because what you understand you can identify WITH, and by making it part of YOU you have accepted it with love. **T(322) C 149** This is how God Himself created YOU, in understanding, in appreciation, and in love.

T 7 F 12. The ego is totally unable to understand this, because it does NOT understand what it makes. It does NOT appreciate it, and it does NOT love it. It incorporates to TAKE AWAY. It literally believes that every time it deprives someone of something IT has increased. We have spoken often of the INCREASE of the Kingdom by YOUR creations, which can only BE created as YOU were.

T 7 F 13. The whole glory and perfect joy that IS the Kingdom lies in you to give. Do you not WANT to give it? You CANNOT forget the Father because I am with you and <u>I</u> CANNOT forget Him. To forget ME is to forget yourself and Him who created you. Our brothers ARE forgetful. That is why they need your remembrance[323] of Me and Him who created Me. Through this remembrance you can change THEIR minds about themselves, as I can change YOURS. Your minds are so powerful a light that you can look into theirs and enlighten them, as I can enlighten yours.

T 7 F 14. I do not want to share my BODY in communion because this is to share nothing. Would I try to share an illusion with the most holy children of a most Holy Father? But I do want to share my MIND with you because we ARE of one Mind, and that Mind IS ours. See ONLY this Mind everywhere, because only this IS everywhere and in everything. It IS everything, because it encompasses all things within ITSELF. Blessed[324] are you who perceive only this, because you perceive only what is true. Come therefore unto me and learn of the truth in YOU.[325] **T(323) C 150**

T 7 F 15. The mind WE share IS shared by all our brothers, and as we see them truly, they WILL be healed. Let YOUR minds shine with mine upon their minds, and by our gratitude to them make THEM aware of the light in <u>THEM</u>. This light will shine back upon YOU and on the whole Sonship because this IS your proper gift to God. He will accept it and give it to the Sonship, because it is acceptable to Him, and therefore to His Sons. This is the true communion of the Spirit Who sees the altar of God in everyone, and by bringing it to YOUR appreciation calls upon you to love God and His Creation. **T(324) C 151**

T 7 G. From Vigilance to Peace (*Notes* 720 7:52)

T 7 G 1. You can think of the Sonship ONLY as one. This is part of the law of Creation, and therefore governs ALL thought. You can PERCEIVE the Sonship as fragmented, but it is IMPOSSIBLE for you to see something in part of it that you will not attribute to ALL of it. That is why attack is NEVER discrete. And why attack MUST be relinquished entirely. If it is NOT relinquished entirely, it is not relinquished at all. Fear and love are equally reciprocal. They make or create depending on whether the ego or the Holy Spirit begets or inspires them, but they WILL return to the mind of the thinker, and they WILL affect his total perception. That includes his perception of God, of His Creations, and of his own. He will not appreciate ANY of these if he regards them fearfully. He will appreciate ALL of them if he regards them with love.

T 7 G 2. The mind that accepts attack CANNOT love. This is because it believes that it can DESTROY love, and therefore does not understand what love IS. If it does not understand what love IS, it CANNOT perceive itself as loving. This loses the awareness of being; induces feelings of unreality; and results in utter confusion. Your own thinking has done this, because of its power. But your own thinking can also save you FROM this, because its power is not of your making. Your ability to DIRECT your thinking as you will IS part of its power. If you do not believe you can do this, you have DENIED the power of your thought, and thus rendered it powerLESS in your belief. **T(325) C 152**

T 7 G 3. The ingeniousness of the ego to preserve itself is enormous, but it stems from the power of the mind WHICH THE EGO DENIES. This means that the ego attacks WHAT IS PRESERVING IT, and this MUST be a source of extreme anxiety. This is why it NEVER knows what it is doing. This is perfectly logical, though

---

[323] **Luke 22:19** And He took bread, gave thanks and broke it, and gave it to them, saying, "This is My body which is given for you; do this in remembrance of Me."

1 Corinthians 11:24-25 And when He had given thanks, He broke it and said, "Take, eat; this is My body which is broken for you; do this in remembrance of Me." In the same manner He also took the cup after supper, saying, "This cup is the new covenant in My blood. This do, as often as you drink it, in remembrance of Me."

[324] **Matthew 5:3-11**, The Beatitudes "Blessed are they …"

[325] **Matthew 11:28** "Come to Me, all you who labor and are heavy laden, and I will give you rest."

Chapter 7 – The Consistency of the Kingdom

clearly insane. The ego draws upon the one source which is totally inimitable to its existence FOR its existence. Fearful of perceiving the POWER of this source, it is forced to DEPRECIATE it. This threatens its OWN existence, a state which it finds intolerable.

T 7 G 4. Remaining logical but still insane, the ego resolves this completely insane dilemma in a completely insane way. It does not perceive ITS existence as threatened, by projecting the threat onto YOU, and perceiving your BEING as NONexistent. This ensures ITS continuance, if you side WITH it, by guaranteeing that you will NOT know your OWN safety. The ego CANNOT AFFORD TO KNOW ANYTHING. Knowledge is total, and the ego DOES NOT BELIEVE IN TOTALITY. This unbelief is its own origin, and while the ego does not love YOU, it IS faithful to its own antecedent, begetting as it was begotten.

T 7 G 5. Mind ALWAYS REproduces as it was produced. Produced by fear, the ego REproduces fear. This IS its allegiance, and this allegiance makes it treacherous to love BECAUSE you are love. Love IS your power, which the ego MUST deny. It must also deny everything which this power gives TO you, BECAUSE it gives you everything. No-one who has everything WANTS the ego. Its own maker, then, DOES NOT WANT IT. Rejection is therefore the only decision which the ego could POSSIBLY encounter if the mind which made it knew ITSELF. And if it recognized ANY part of the Sonship, it WOULD know itself. T(326) C 153

T 7 G 6. The ego therefore opposes ALL appreciation, ALL recognition, ALL sane perception, and ALL knowledge. It perceives their threat as total because it senses the fact that all commitments which the mind makes ARE total. Forced therefore to detach itself from you who ARE mind, it is willing to attach itself to anything ELSE. But there IS nothing else. It does NOT follow, however, that the mind cannot make illusions. But it DOES follow that if it makes illusions it will BELIEVE in them, because THAT IS HOW IT MADE THEM.

T 7 G 7. The Holy Spirit undoes illusions without attacking them merely because He cannot perceive them at all. They therefore do not exist for Him. He resolves the APPARENT conflict which they engender by perceiving CONFLICT as meaningless. We said before that the Holy Spirit perceives the conflict EXACTLY AS IT IS, and it IS meaningless. The Holy Spirit does not want you to UNDERSTAND conflict. He wants you to realize that BECAUSE conflict is meaningLESS it cannot BE understood. WE have already said that understanding brings appreciation, and appreciation brings love. Nothing else CAN be understood because nothing else is real and therefore nothing else HAS meaning.

T 7 G 8. If you will keep in mind what the Holy Spirit offers you, you cannot be vigilant for anything BUT God and His Kingdom. The ONLY reason why you find this difficult is because you think there IS something else. Belief does not require vigilance UNLESS it is conflicted. If it IS, there ARE conflicting components within it which have engendered a state of war, and vigilance has therefore BECOME essential. Vigilance has no place at all in peace. It is necessary ONLY AGAINST beliefs which are NOT true, and would never have been called upon by the Holy Spirit if you had not believed the untrue yourselves. T(327) C 154

T 7 G 9. But you CANNOT deny that when you BELIEVE something you HAVE made it true FOR YOU. When YOU believe what God DOES NOT KNOW, your thought seems to CONTRADICT His, and this makes it appear AS IF YOU ARE ATTACKING HIM. We have repeatedly emphasized that the ego DOES believe it can attack God, and tries to persuade you that YOU have done this. If the mind CANNOT attack, the ego proceeds perfectly logically to the position that YOU cannot be mind. By not seeing you as YOU are, it can see ITSELF as it WANTS to be. Aware of its weakness, the ego wants your allegiance, but NOT as you really are. The ego therefore wants to engage your mind in its OWN delusional system, because otherwise the light of YOUR understanding WILL dispel it.

T 7 G 10. The ego wants no part of truth, because the truth is that IT is not true. If truth is total, the UNtrue CANNOT exist. Commitment to either MUST be total, because they cannot co-exist in your minds WITHOUT splitting them. If they cannot coexist in peace, and if you WANT peace, you MUST give up the IDEA of conflict ENTIRELY, and for ALL TIME. This requires vigilance ONLY as long as YOU DO NOT RECOGNIZE WHAT IS TRUE. While you believe that two totally contradictory thought systems SHARE truth, your need for vigilance is apparent. Your minds ARE dividing their allegiance between two kingdoms, and YOU are totally committed to neither. T(328) C 155

T 7 G 11. Your identification with the Kingdom is totally beyond question except by you WHEN YOU ARE THINKING INSANELY. What you are is NOT established by your perception, and is NOT influenced BY it at all. ALL perceived problems in identification at ANY level ARE NOT PROBLEMS OF FACT. But they ARE problems in UNDERSTANDING, because they MEAN that you perceive WHAT you can understand as UP TO YOU TO DECIDE. The ego believes THIS totally, being fully committed TO it. But it is NOT TRUE. The ego is therefore totally committed to UNtruth, perceiving in total contradiction to the Holy Spirit and to the knowledge of God.

T 7 G 12. You can be perceived with meaning ONLY by the Holy Spirit, because your being IS the knowledge of God. ANY belief that you accept which is APART from this WILL obscure God's voice in you, and will therefore obscure God TO you. Unless you perceive His Creation truly, you CANNOT know the Creator, because God and His Creation ARE NOT SEPARATE. The Oneness of the Creator and the Creation IS your wholeness, your sanity, and your limitless power. This limitless power is God's gift to you, because it is WHAT YOU ARE. If you dissociate your mind FROM it, you are perceiving the most powerful force in the universe of thought AS IF it were weak, because you do NOT believe YOU are part of it.

T 7 G 13. Perceived WITHOUT your part IN it, God's Creation IS perceived as weak, and those who SEE themselves as weakened DO attack. The attack MUST be blind, because there is nothing TO attack. Therefore, they make up images, perceive them as unworthy, and attack them for their unworthiness. That is all the world of the ego is. NOTHING. It has no meaning. It does not exist. Do not TRY to understand it, because if you do you are believing that it CAN be understood, and therefore is capable of being appreciated and loved. This WOULD justify it, but it CANNOT BE justified. YOU cannot make the meaningLESS meaningFUL. This can ONLY be an insane attempt. T(329) -156

T 7 G 14. Allowing INsanity to enter your minds means that you have not judged sanity AS WHOLLY DESIRABLE. If you WANT something else, you WILL MAKE something else. But because it IS something else it WILL attack your thought system and divide your allegiance. You CANNOT create in this divided state, and you MUST be vigilant AGAINST this divided state because ONLY peace CAN BE extended. Your divided minds ARE blocking the extension of the Kingdom, and its extension IS your joy. If you do not extend the Kingdom, you are NOT thinking with your Creator and creating as He created.

T 7 G 15. In this depressing state, the Holy Spirit reminds you gently that you are sad because you are not fulfilling your function as co-creators WITH God, and are therefore depriving YOURSELVES of joy. This is not God's will, but YOURS. If your will is out of accord with God's, YOU ARE WILLING WITHOUT MEANING. But because ONLY God's will is unchangeable, no REAL conflict of will is possible. This is the Holy Spirit's perfectly consistent teaching. Creation, not separation, IS your will BECAUSE it is God's. And nothing that opposes this means anything at all. Being a perfect Accomplishment, the Sonship can only accomplish perfectly, EXTENDING the joy in which it was created, and identifying itself with both its Creator and its creations, KNOWING they are One. T(330) C 157

T 7 H. The Total Commitment (*Notes* 537 6:101)

T 7 H 1. Whenever you deny a blessing to a brother, YOU will feel deprived. This is because denial is as total as love. It is as impossible to deny part of the Sonship as it is to love it in part. Nor is it possible to love it totally AT TIMES. You CANNOT be totally committed SOMETIMES. Remember a very early lesson, -- "never underestimate the power of denial." It has no power in ITSELF, but YOU can give it the power of YOUR mind, whose power is without limit of ANY kind. If you use it to deny reality, reality is gone FOR YOU. REALITY CANNOT BE PARTLY APPRECIATED. That is why denying any part of it means you have lost awareness of ALL of it.

T 7 H 2. That is the negative side of the law as it operates in this world. But denial is a defense, and so it is as capable of being used positively as it is of being used destructively. Used negatively, it WILL be destructive, because it will be used for attack. But in the service of the Holy Spirit, the law becomes as beneficent as all of the laws of God. Stated positively, the law requires you only to recognize PART of reality to appreciate ALL of it. Mind is too powerful to be subject to exclusion. You will NEVER be able to exclude yourself from what you project.

T 7 H 3. When a brother acts insanely, he is offering you an opportunity to bless him. His need is YOURS. YOU need the blessing you can offer him. There is no way for you to have it EXCEPT by giving it. This IS the law of God, and it HAS NO EXCEPTIONS. What you deny you LACK, not because it IS lacking, but because you have denied it in another, and therefore are not aware of it in YOU. Every response you make is determined by what you think you ARE. And what you WANT to be IS what you think you are. Therefore, what you WANT to be determines every response you make. T(331) C 158

T 7 H 4. You do NOT need God's blessing, because that you have forever. But you DO need YOURS. The picture you see of yourselves is deprived, unloving, and very vulnerable. You CANNOT love this. But you can very easily escape FROM it, or better, leave it behind. You are NOT there, and that is not YOU. Do not see this picture in anyone, or you HAVE accepted it as you. ALL illusions about the Sonship are DISPELLED together, as they were MADE together. Teach no-one that HE is what YOU do not want to be. Your brother is the mirror in which you will see the image of yourself as long as perception lasts. And perception WILL last until the Sonship knows itself as whole. T(332) C 159

T 7 H 5. You MADE perception, and it MUST last as long as you WANT it. Illusions are investments. They will last as long as you value them. Values are relative, but they are powerful because they are MENTAL JUDGMENTS. The only way to dispel illusions is to withdraw ALL investment from them, and they will HAVE no life for you because you have put them OUT OF YOUR MIND. While you include them IN it, you are GIVING them life. Except there is nothing there to receive your gift.

T 7 H 6. The gift of life IS yours to give, because it was given YOU. You are unaware of YOUR gift BECAUSE you do not give it. You CANNOT make nothing live, because it cannot BE enlivened. Therefore, you have NOT extended the gift you both have and are, and so you do NOT know your being. All confusion comes from not extending life, because this is NOT the will of your Creator. You CAN do nothing apart from Him, and you DO do nothing apart from him. Keep His Way to remember yourselves, and teach His Ways lest you forget yourself. Give only honor to the sons of the living God,[326] and count yourself among them gladly.

T 7 H 7. ONLY honor is a fitting gift for those whom God Himself created worthy of honor and whom He honors. Give them the appreciation which God accords them always, because they are His Beloved Sons in whom He is well pleased.[327] You CANNOT be apart from them, because you are not apart from Him. Rest in His love, and protect your rest by loving. But love EVERYTHING He created, of which YOU are part, or you cannot learn of His peace and accept His gift FOR yourself and AS yourself. T(333) C 160 You CANNOT know your own perfection until you have honored all those who were created LIKE you.

T 7 H 8. One Child of God is the only teacher sufficiently worthy to teach another. One Teacher is in all your minds, and He teaches the same lesson to all. He always teaches you the inestimable worth of EVERY Son of God, teaching it with infinite patience born of the Love of Him for whom He speaks. Every attack is a call for His patience, because ONLY His patience can translate attack into blessing. Those who attack DO NOT KNOW THEY ARE BLESSED. They attack BECAUSE THEY BELIEVE THEY ARE DEPRIVED. Give therefore of YOUR abundance, and teach them THEIRS. Do not share their delusions of scarcity, or you will perceive YOURSELF as lacking.

T 7 H 9. Attack could never PROMOTE attack unless you perceived it as a means of depriving you of SOMETHING YOU WANT. But you cannot lose ANYTHING unless YOU do not value it and therefore DO NOT WANT IT. This makes you feel DEPRIVED of it, and by projecting YOUR rejection, you believe that others are TAKING IT FROM YOU. One MUST be fearful if he believes that his brother is attacking him to tear the Kingdom of Heaven from him.

T 7 H 10. This is the ultimate basis for ALL of the ego's projection. Being the part of your mind which does NOT believe it is responsible for ITSELF, and being without allegiance to God, it is incapable of trust. Projecting its insane belief that YOU have been treacherous to YOUR Creator, it believes that your brothers, who are as incapable of this as you are, are out to TAKE GOD FROM YOU. T(334) C 161 Whenever a brother attacks another, THIS IS WHAT HE BELIEVES. Projection ALWAYS sees YOUR will in others. If you will to separate YOURSELF from God, that is what you will think others are doing TO you.

T 7 H 11. You ARE the will of God. Do not accept anything else AS YOUR will, or you ARE denying what you are. Deny THIS and you WILL attack, because you believe you have BEEN attacked. But see the love of God in you, and you will see it everywhere because it IS everywhere. See His abundance in everyone, and you will know that you are in Him WITH them. They are part of you as you are part of God. YOU are as lonely without understanding this as God Himself is lonely when His Sons do not know Him. The peace of God IS understanding this.

T 7 H 12. There is only one way out of the world's thinking, just as there was only one way INTO it. Understand totally by understanding TOTALITY. Perceive ANY part of the ego's thought system as wholly insane, wholly delusional, and wholly undesirable, and you have CORRECTLY EVALUATED ALL OF IT. This correction enables you to perceive ANY part of Creation as wholly real, wholly perfect, and WHOLLY DESIRABLE. Wanting this ONLY, you will HAVE this only, and giving this only, you will BE only this. The gifts you offer to the ego are ALWAYS experienced as sacrifices. But the gifts you offer to the Kingdom are gifts to YOU. They will always be treasured by God, because they belong to His Beloved Sons who belong to Him. All power and glory are yours because the Kingdom is His.[328] T(335) C 162

---

[326] **John 6:69** Also we have come to believe and know that You are the Christ, the Son of the living God."

[327] **Matthew 3:17** And suddenly a voice came from heaven, saying, "This is My beloved Son, in whom I am well pleased."

[328] **Matthew 3:17** And suddenly a voice came from heaven, saying, "This is My beloved Son, in whom I am well pleased."

Chapter 7 – The Consistency of the Kingdom

T 7 I. The Defense of Conflict (*Notes* 733 7:65)

T 7 I 1. We once said that without projection there can be no anger, but it is also true that without projection there can be no love. Projection is a fundamental law of the mind, and therefore one which ALWAYS operates. It is the law by which you create and were created. It is the law which unifies the Kingdom and keeps it in the mind of God. To the ego, the law is perceived as a way of getting RID of something it does NOT want. To the Holy Spirit, it is the fundamental law of sharing, by which you give what you value in order to keep it in your OWN minds.

T 7 I 2. Projection to the Holy Spirit is the law of extension. To the ego, it is the law of deprivation. It therefore produces abundance or scarcity, depending on how you choose to apply it. This choice IS up to you, but it is NOT up to you to decide whether or not you will UTILIZE projection. Every mind MUST project, because that is how it lives, and every mind IS life. The ego's use of projection must be fully understood before the INEVITABLE association between projection and anger can be finally UNmade.

T 7 I 3. The ego ALWAYS tries to preserve conflict. It is very ingenious in devising ways which SEEM to diminish conflict only because it does NOT want you to find it so intolerable that you will INSIST on giving it up. Therefore, it tries to persuade you that IT can free you OF conflict, lest you give IT up and free YOURSELF. The ego, using its own warped version of the laws of God, uses the power of the mind ONLY to defeat the mind's real purpose. It projects conflict FROM your mind to OTHER minds, in an attempt to persuade you that you have gotten RID of it. This has a number of fallacies which may not be so apparent.

T 7 I 4. Strictly speaking, conflict cannot BE projected, precisely BECAUSE it cannot be fully shared. Any attempt to keep PART of it and get rid of ANOTHER part does not really mean ANYTHING. Remember that a conflicted teacher is a poor teacher AND A POOR LEARNER. His lessons are confused, and their transfer value severely limited BY his confusion. **T(336) C 163**

T 7 I 5. A second fallacy is the idea that you can GET RID of something you do not want BY giving it away. GIVING it is how you KEEP it. The belief that by giving it OUT you have excluded from WITHIN is a complete distortion of the power of EXTENSION.

T 7 I 6. That is why those who project from the ego are vigilant for their OWN safety. THEY ARE AFRAID THAT THEIR PROJECTIONS WILL RETURN AND HURT THEM. They DO believe they have blotted them out of their OWN minds, but they also believe they are trying to creep back INTO them. This is because their projections have NOT left their minds, and this, in turn, forces them to engage in compulsive activity in order NOT to recognize this.

T 7 I 7. You cannot perpetuate an illusion about another WITHOUT perpetuating it about yourself. There is no way out of this, because it is IMPOSSIBLE to fragment the mind. To fragment is to break into pieces, and mind CANNOT attack. The belief that it CAN, a fallacy which the ego ALWAYS makes, underlies its whole use of projection. This is because it does not understand what the mind IS, and therefore does not understand what YOU are. Yet ITS existence IS dependent on your mind, because it is a BELIEF. The ego IS therefore a confusion in identification, which never had a consistent model, and never developed consistently. It is the distorted product of the misapplication of the laws of God by distorted minds which are misusing their own power.

T 7 I 8. DO NOT BE AFRAID OF THE EGO. It DOES depend on your mind, and as you made it by believing in it, so you can dispel it by withdrawing belief FROM it. Do NOT project the responsibility for your belief in it onto ANYONE else, or you will PRESERVE the belief. When you are willing to accept sole responsibility for the ego's existence YOURSELF, you will have laid aside all anger and all attack, because they COME from an attempt to PROJECT RESPONSIBILITY FOR YOUR OWN ERRORS. But having ACCEPTED the error **T(337) C 164** as yours, DO NOT KEEP THEM. Give them over quickly to the Holy Spirit to be undone completely, so that ALL their effects will vanish from your minds and from the Sonship AS A WHOLE. He will teach you to perceive BEYOND belief, because truth IS beyond belief and His perception IS true.

T 7 I 9. The ego can be completely forgotten at ANY time, because it was always a belief that is totally incredible. No-one can KEEP a belief he has judged to be unbelievable. The more you learn ABOUT the ego, the more you realize that it cannot BE believed. The incredible cannot BE understood because it IS unbelievable. The utter meaninglessness of ALL perception which comes from the unbelievable MUST be apparent, but it is NOT beyond belief because it was made BY belief.

T 7 I 10. The whole purpose of this course is to teach you that the ego is unbelievable and will forever BE unbelievable. You who made the ego by BELIEVING the unbelievable CANNOT make this judgment alone. By accepting the Atonement for YOURSELF, you are deciding AGAINST the belief that you can BE alone, thus dispelling the idea of separation and affirming your true identification with the whole Kingdom as literally PART OF YOU. This identification is as beyond doubt as it is beyond belief. Your wholeness HAS no limits, because its being is in Infinity.

T 7 J. The Extension of the Kingdom (*Notes* 738 7:70)

T 7 J 1. Only you can limit your creative power, but God wills to release it. He no more wills you to deprive yourselves of YOUR creations than He wills to deprive Himself of His.

T 7 J 2. Do not withhold your gifts to the Sonship, or you withhold yourself from God. Selfishness is of the ego but self-fullness is of the Soul because that is how He created it. The Holy Spirit is the part of the mind that lies between the ego and the Soul, mediating between them ALWAYS IN FAVOR OF THE SOUL. To the ego this is partiality, and it therefore responds as if it were the part that is being sided AGAINST. **T(338) C 165** To the Soul this is truth, because it knows its own fullness and cannot conceive of ANY part from which it is excluded. The soul KNOWS that the consciousness of all its brothers is included in its own, as IT is included in God. The power of the whole Sonship AND OF ITS CREATOR is therefore its OWN fullness,[329] rendering its Creation and its creating equally whole and equal in perfection.

T 7 J 3. The ego cannot prevail[330] against a totality which includes God, and any totality MUST include God. Everything He created is given ALL His power because it is part of Him and shares His Being WITH Him. Creating is the OPPOSITE of loss, as blessing is the opposite of sacrifice. Being MUST be extended. That is how it retains the knowledge of itSELF. The soul yearns to share ITS Being as ITS Creator did. Created BY sharing, its will is to create. It does NOT wish to CONTAIN God, but to EXTEND HIS BEING.

T 7 J 4. The extension of God's Being is the Soul's only function. ITS fullness cannot be contained any more than can the fullness of its Creator. Fullness IS extension. The ego's whole thought system BLOCKS extension, and therefore blocks YOUR ONLY FUNCTION. It therefore blocks your joy and THIS is why you perceive yourselves as unfulfilled. Unless you create, you ARE unfulfilled. But God does NOT know unfulfillment, and therefore you MUST create. YOU may not know your own creations, but this can no more interfere with their reality than your unawareness of your Soul can interfere with its being.

---

[329] **Ephesians 3:19** To know the love of Christ which passes knowledge; that you may be filled with all the fullness of God.
[330] **Matthew 16:18** "And I also say to you that you are Peter, and on this rock I will build My church, and the gates of Hades shall not prevail against it."

T 7 J 5. The Kingdom is forever extending, because it is in the Mind of God. YOU do not know your joy because you do not know your own self-fullness. Exclude ANY part of the Kingdom FROM yourself, and you are NOT whole. A split mind CANNOT perceive its fullness, and needs the miracle OF its wholeness to dawn upon it and heal it. This reawakens its wholeness IN it and restores it to the Kingdom because of its ACCEPTANCE of wholeness. The full appreciation of its self-fullness makes selfishness impossible, and extension inevitable. T(339) C 66 That is why there is perfect peace in the Kingdom. Every Soul IS fulfilling its function, and ONLY complete fulfillment IS peace.

T 7 J 6. Insanity APPEARS to add to reality, but no-one would claim that what it adds is true. Insanity is therefore the NONextension of truth, which blocks joy because it blocks Creation and therefore blocks self-FULFILLMENT. The unfulfilled MUST be depressed, because their self-fullness is UNKNOWN to them. Your creations are protected FOR you because the Holy Spirit, Who is in your minds, knows of them, and can bring them INTO your awareness whenever you will let Him. They ARE there as part of your own being, because YOUR fulfillment INCLUDES them. The creations of every Son of God are yours, because every creation belongs to everyone, being created for the Sonship as a whole.

T 7 J 7. You have not failed to add to the inheritance of the Sons of God, and thus have not failed to secure it for yourselves. If it was the will of God to give it to you, He gave it forever. If it was His will that you have it forever, He gave you the means for keeping it, and YOU HAVE DONE SO. Disobeying God's will is meaningful only to the insane. In truth, it is impossible.

T 7 J 8. Your self-fullness is as boundless as God's. Like His, it extends forever and in perfect peace. Its radiance is so intense that it creates in perfect joy, and only the whole can be born of its wholeness. Be confident that you have never lost your identity and the extension which maintains it in wholeness and peace. Miracles are AN EXPRESSION OF THIS CONFIDENCE. They are reflections both of your own proper identification WITH your brothers, and of your own awareness that YOUR identification IS maintained by extension. The miracle is A LESSON IN TOTAL PERCEPTION. By including ANY part of totality in the lesson, you HAVE included the whole. T(340) C 167

T 7 J 9. You have said that, when you write of the Kingdom and your own creations which belong to it, you are describing WHAT YOU DO NOT KNOW. This is true in a sense, but no more true than your failure to acknowledge the whole result of the ego's premises. The Kingdom is the result of premises, as much as this world is. You HAVE carried the ego's reasoning to its logical conclusion, which is TOTAL CONFUSION ABOUT EVERYTHING. But you do not really BELIEVE this, or you could not possibly maintain it. If you REALLY saw this result, you COULD not want it. The ONLY reason why you could possibly want ANY part of it is because YOU DO NOT SEE THE WHOLE OF IT.

T 7 J 10. You therefore ARE willing to look at the ego's premises but NOT at their logical outcome. Is it not possible that you have done the same thing with the premises of God? Your creations ARE the logical outcome of His premises. HIS thinking has established them FOR you. They are therefore THERE, EXACTLY where they belong. They belong to your mind, as part of your identification with HIS. But your state of mind and your recognition of WHAT IS IN YOUR MIND depends, at any given moment, on what you believe ABOUT your mind. Whatever these beliefs may be, they are the premises which will determine WHAT YOU ACCEPT INTO YOUR MINDS.

T 7 J 11. It is surely clear that you can both accept into your minds what is NOT really there, and DENY WHAT IS. Neither of these possibilities requires further elaboration, although both are clearly indefensible even if YOU elect to defend them. But the function which God Himself GAVE your minds through His you may DENY but you CANNOT prevent. They are the logical outcome of what you ARE. The ability to SEE a logical outcome depends on the WILLINGNESS TO SEE IT, but its TRUTH has nothing to do with your willingness at all. Truth is GOD's will. SHARE His Will, and you will share what He KNOWS. Deny His Will AS YOURS, and you are denying His Kingdom AND yours. T(341) C 168

T 7 J 12. The Holy Spirit will direct you ONLY so as to avoid all pain. The UNDOING of pain must OBVIOUSLY avoid this. No-one would surely OBJECT to this goal IF HE RECOGNIZED IT. The problem is NOT whether what He says is true, but whether or not you want to LISTEN to what He says.

T 7 K. The Confusion of Strength and Weakness (*Notes* 746 7:78)

T 7 K 1. You no more recognize what is painful than you know what is joyful, and are, in fact, very apt to confuse them. The Holy Spirit's main function is to teach you to TELL THEM APART.

T 7 K 2. However strange it may seem that this is necessary, it obviously IS. The reason is equally obvious. What is joyful to you IS painful to the ego, and as long as you are in doubt about what YOU are, you WILL be confused about joy and pain. This confusion is the cause of the whole idea of sacrifice. Obey the Holy Spirit, and you WILL be giving up the ego, but you will be SACRIFICING nothing. On the contrary, you will be gaining EVERYTHING. But if you BELIEVED this there would BE no conflict. That is why you need to DEMONSTRATE THE OBVIOUS TO YOURSELF. It is NOT obvious to you.

T 7 K 3. You REALLY believe that doing the opposite of God's will CAN be better for you. You also believe that it is POSSIBLE to do the opposite of God's will. Therefore, you believe that an impossible choice IS open to you, which is both very fearful and very desirable. But God WILLS. He does NOT wish. YOUR will is as powerful as His because it IS His. The ego's wishes do not mean anything, because the ego wishes for the impossible. You CAN wish for the impossible, but you can only WILL with God. This is the ego's weakness and YOUR strength. T(342) C 169

T 7 K 4. The Holy Spirit ALWAYS sides with YOU and with your STRENGTH. As long as you avoid His guidance in any way, you WANT TO BE WEAK. But weakness IS frightening. What else, then, can this decision mean except that you WANT to be fearful? The Holy Spirit NEVER asks for sacrifice, but the ego ALWAYS does. When you are confused about this VERY clear distinction in motivation, it CAN only be due to projection. Projection of this kind IS a confusion in motivation, and given THIS confusion, TRUST becomes impossible.

T 7 K 5. No-one obeys gladly a guide he does not trust. But this does not mean that the GUIDE is untrustworthy. In this case, it ALWAYS means that the FOLLOWER IS. However, this, too, is merely a matter of his own belief. Believing that HE can betray, he believes that everything can betray HIM. But this is ONLY because he has ELECTED TO FOLLOW FALSE GUIDANCE. Unable to follow THIS guidance WITHOUT fear, he associates fear WITH guidance, and refuses to follow ANY guidance at all. If the result of this decision is confusion, this is hardly surprising.

T 7 K 6. The Holy Spirit is perfectly trustworthy, as YOU are. God Himself trusts you and therefore your trustworthiness IS beyond question. It will always remain beyond question, however much you may question it. I trust MY choices ONLY because they ARE God's Will. We said before that YOU are the will of God. His will is not an idle wish, and your identification WITH His Will is not optional because it IS what you are. Sharing His will WITH me is not really open to choice at all, though it may SEEM to be. The whole separation lies in this fallacy. And the ONLY way out of the fallacy is to decide that YOU DO NOT HAVE TO DECIDE ANYTHING. T(343) C 170

T 7 K 7. Everything has been given you by GOD'S decision. This IS His Will, and you can NOT undo it. Even the relinquishment of your false decision-making prerogative, which the ego guards so jealously, is not accomplished by your wish. It was accomplished FOR you by the Will of God, who has not left you comfortless.[331] His Voice WILL teach you how to distinguish between pain and joy, and lead you out of the confusion YOU have made. There IS no confusion in the mind of a Son of God, whose will MUST be the will of the Father, because the Father's Will IS His Son.

T 7 K 8. Miracles are IN ACCORD with the Will of God, whose will you do NOT know because you are confused about what YOU will. This MEANS that you are confused about what you are. If you ARE God's will and do NOT ACCEPT His will, you can ONLY be not accepting what you are. But if your joy IS what you are, you ARE denying joy. The miracle therefore is a lesson in WHAT JOY IS. Being a lesson in SHARING, it is a lesson in love, which IS joy. Every miracle is thus a lesson in Truth, and by OFFERING truth YOU are learning the difference between pain and joy.

T 7 L. The State of Grace (*Notes* 752 7:84)

T 7 L 1. The Holy Spirit will ALWAYS guide you truly, because YOUR joy IS His. This is His will for everyone, because He speaks for the Kingdom of God which IS joy. Following Him[332] is therefore the easiest thing in the world, and the only thing which IS easy, because it is NOT of the world and is therefore NATURAL. The world goes AGAINST your nature, because it is out of accord with God's laws. The world perceives orders of difficulty in EVERYTHING. This is because the ego perceives nothing as wholly desirable. By DEMONSTRATING to yourselves that THERE IS NO ORDER OF DIFFICULTY IN MIRACLES, you will convince yourselves that in your NATURAL state there IS no difficulty, because it is a state of Grace. **T(344) C 171**

T 7 L 2. Grace is the natural state of every Son of God. When he is NOT in a state of grace he IS out of his natural environment, and does NOT function well. Everything he does becomes a strain, because he was not created for the environment which he has made. He therefore CANNOT adapt to it, nor can he adapt IT to HIM. There is no point in trying. A Son of God is happy ONLY when he knows he is WITH God. That is the only environment in which he will not experience strain, because that is where he belongs. It is also the only environment that is worthy of him, because his own worth is beyond ANYTHING that he can make.

T 7 L 3. Consider the Kingdom which YOU have made, and judge its worth fairly. Is it worthy to be a home for a Child of God? Does it protect his peace, and shine love upon him? Does it keep his heart untouched by fear, and allow him to give always without any sense of loss? Does it teach him that this giving IS his joy, and that God Himself thanks him for his giving?

T 7 L 4. That is the only environment in which you can be happy. You cannot make it, any more than you can make yourselves. But it has been created for you, as you were created for it. God watches over His children and denies them nothing. But when they deny Him they do NOT know this, because THEY deny themselves everything. You who could give the love of God to everything you see and touch and remember are literally denying Heaven to yourselves. I call upon you again to remember that I have chosen you to teach the Kingdom TO the Kingdom. There are no exceptions to this lesson because the lack of exceptions IS the lesson.

T 7 L 5. Every Son who returns to the Kingdom with this lesson in his heart has healed the Sonship and given thanks to God. Everyone who learns this lesson has become the perfect teacher, because he has learned it of the Holy Spirit, who wants to teach him everything He knows. When a mind has only light, it KNOWS only light. Its own radiance shines all around it, and **T(345) C 172** extends out into the darkness of other minds, transforming them into majesty. The majesty of God is there, for YOU to recognize and appreciate and KNOW.

T 7 L 6. Perceiving the majesty of God AS your brother is to accept your OWN inheritance. God gives only equally. If you recognize His gift to anyone ELSE, you have acknowledged what He has given YOU. Nothing is as easy to perceive as truth. This is the perception which is immediate, clear, and natural. You have trained yourselves NOT to see it, and this HAS been very difficult for you. OUT of your natural environment you may well ask, "what is truth?"[333] because truth IS the environment by which and for which you were created. You do not know yourselves because you do not know YOUR Creator. You do not know YOUR creations, because you do not know your brothers who created them WITH you.

T 7 L 7. We said before that only the whole Sonship is a worthy co-creator with God, because only the whole Sonship can create LIKE Him. Whenever you heal a brother by recognizing his worth, you are acknowledging HIS power to create and YOURS. HE cannot have lost what YOU recognize, and you MUST have the glory you see in HIM. He is a co-creator with God with YOU. Deny his creative power and you are denying yours AND THAT OF GOD WHO CREATED YOU. You cannot deny part of the truth. You do not know your creations because you do not know their creator. You do not know yourselves because you do not know YOURS.

T 7 L 8. Your creations cannot establish your reality, any more than YOU can establish God's. But you can KNOW both. Being is known by sharing. Because God shared His Being with you, you can know Him. But you must also know all He created to know what THEY have shared. Without your Father you will not know your fatherhood. The Kingdom of God includes all His Sons and their children, who are like the Sons as they are like the Father. Know then the Sons of God, and you will know ALL Creation. **T(346) C 173**[334]

---

[331] **John 14:18** "I will not leave you comfortless: I will come to you."
[332] **Matthew 4:19** Then He said to them, "Follow Me, and I will make you fishers of men."
[333] **John 18:38** Pilate said to Him, "What is truth?" And when he had said this, he went out again to the Jews, and said to them, "I find no fault in Him at all."
[334] May 18

Chapter 8 – The Journey Back

T 8 A. Introduction (Notes 758 7:90)

T 8 A 1. You are hampered in your progress by your demands to know what you do not know. This is actually a way of hanging on to deprivation. You cannot reasonably object to following instructions in a course FOR knowing, on the grounds that you do not know. The need for the course is implicit in your objection. Knowledge is not the motivation for learning this course. PEACE is. As the PRE-REQUISITE for knowledge, peace MUST be learned. This is ONLY because those who are in conflict are not peaceful, and peace is the CONDITION of knowledge because it is the condition of the Kingdom.

T 8 A 2. Knowledge will be restored when YOU meet its conditions. This is not a bargain made by God, who made no bargains at all. It is merely the result of your misuse of His Laws on behalf of a will that was not His. Knowledge IS His Will. If you are OPPOSING His Will, how CAN you have knowledge? I have told you what knowledge OFFERS you, but it is clear that you do NOT regard this as wholly desirable. If you did, you would hardly be willing to throw it away so readily, when the ego asks for your allegiance.

T 8 A 3. The distraction of the ego SEEMS to interfere with your learning, but it HAS no power to distract unless you GIVE it the power. The ego's voice is an hallucination. You cannot expect the EGO to say "I am not real." Hallucinations ARE inaccurate perceptions of reality. But you are NOT asked to dispel them alone. You are merely asked to evaluate them in terms of their results TO YOU. If you DO NOT WANT THEM on the basis of LOSS OF PEACE, they will be removed from your mind FOR you. Every response to the ego is a call to war, and war DOES deprive you of peace.

T 8 A 4. Yet in this war THERE IS NO OPPONENT. THIS is the re-interpretation of reality which you must make to secure peace, and the ONLY one you need ever make.

T 8 B. The Direction of the Curriculum (Notes 760 7:92)

T 8 B 1. Those whom you PERCEIVE as opponents are PART of your peace, which YOU are giving up by attacking them. How can you have what YOU give up? You SHARE to have, but you do NOT give it up yourselves. **T(347) C 174** When you GIVE UP peace, you are EXCLUDING yourself FROM it. This is a condition which is so ALIEN to the Kingdom that you CANNOT understand the state which prevails WITHIN it.

T 8 B 2. Your past learning MUST have taught you the wrong things, simply because it has not made you happy. On this basis alone, its value should be questioned. If learning aims at CHANGE, and that is ALWAYS its purpose, are you satisfied with the changes YOURS has brought you? Dissatisfaction with the learning outcome MUST be a sign of learning failure, because it means that you did NOT get what you WANT.

T 8 B 3. The curriculum of the Atonement IS the opposite of the curriculum you have established for yourselves, but SO IS ITS OUTCOME. If the outcome of yours has made you unhappy, and if you WANT a different outcome, a change in the curriculum is obviously necessary. **T(348) C 175**[335]

T 8 B 4. The first change that MUST be introduced is a change in DIRECTION. A meaningful curriculum CANNOT be inconsistent. If it is planned by two teachers, each believing in diametrically opposed ideas, it CANNOT be integrated. If it is carried out by these two teachers simultaneously, EACH ONE MERELY INTERFERES WITH THE OTHER. This leads to fluctuation, but NOT to change.

---
[335] May 23, 1966

The volatile HAVE no direction. They cannot choose one, because they CANNOT relinquish the others EVEN IF THE OTHERS DO NOT EXIST. Their conflicted curriculum teaches them that ALL directions exist, and gives them no RATIONALE for choice.

T 8 B 5. The total senselessness of such a curriculum must be fully recognized before a real change in direction becomes possible. You CANNOT learn simultaneously from two teachers who are in TOTAL DISAGREEMENT ABOUT EVERYTHING. Their joint curriculum presents an IMPOSSIBLE learning task. They are teaching you ENTIRELY different things in ENTIRELY different ways, which WOULD be possible except for the crucial fact that both are teaching you about YOURSELF. Your REALITY is unaffected by both. But if you LISTEN to both, your mind will split on WHAT YOUR REALITY IS.

T 8 C. The Rationale for Choice (Notes 762 7:94)

T 8 C 1. There IS a rationale for choice. Only ONE teacher KNOWS what your reality is. If learning that is the PURPOSE of the curriculum, you MUST learn it of Him. The ego does NOT KNOW WHAT IT IS TRYING TO TEACH. It is trying to teach you what you are WITHOUT KNOWING IT. The ego is expert ONLY in confusion. It does not understand ANYTHING ELSE. As a teacher, then, it is totally confused and TOTALLY CONFUSING.

T 8 C 2. Even if you could disregard the Holy Spirit entirely, which is quite impossible, you could learn nothing from the ego, because the ego KNOWS nothing. Is there ANY possible reason for choosing a teacher such as this? Does the TOTAL disregard of ANYTHING it teaches make anything BUT sense? Is THIS the teacher to whom a Son of God should turn to find HIMSELF? The ego has never given you a sensible answer to anything. **T(349) C 176** Simply on the grounds of your own experience with the ego's teaching, should not this alone disqualify it as your future teacher?

T 8 C 3. But the ego has done more harm to your learning than this alone. Learning is joyful if it leads you along your natural path, and facilitates the development of WHAT YOU HAVE. But when you are taught AGAINST your nature, you will lose by your learning, because your learning will IMPRISON you. Your will is IN your nature, and therefore CANNOT go AGAINST it. The ego cannot teach you anything as long as your will is free, because you WILL NOT LISTEN TO IT. It is NOT your will to be imprisoned, BECAUSE your will is free.

T 8 C 4. That is why the ego IS the denial of free will. It is NEVER God Who coerces you, because He SHARES His Will WITH you. His voice teaches ONLY His Will, but that is not the Holy Spirit's lesson, because that is what you ARE. The LESSON is that your will and God's CANNOT be out of accord because they ARE one. This is the UNdoing of EVERYTHING the ego tries to teach. It is not, then, only the DIRECTION (of the curriculum?) which must be unconflicted, but also the CONTENT.

T 8 C 5. The ego wants to teach you that you want to OPPOSE God's Will. This unnatural lesson CANNOT be learned, but the ATTEMPT to learn it is a violation of your own freedom, and makes you AFRAID of your will BECAUSE it is free. The Holy Spirit opposes ANY imprisoning of the will of a Son of God, KNOWING that the will of the Son IS the Father's. He leads you steadily along the path of freedom, teaching you how to disregard, or look beyond EVERYTHING that would hold you back.

T 8 C 6. We said before that the Holy Spirit teaches you the difference between pain and joy. That is the same as saying that He teaches you the difference between imprisonment and freedom. YOU CANNOT MAKE THIS DISTINCTION WITHOUT HIM. That is because you have taught YOURSELF that imprisonment IS freedom. Believing them to be the same, how can you tell them apart? Can you ask the part of your mind that taught you to believe they ARE the same to teach you the DIFFERENCE? **T(350) C 177**

T 8 C 7. The Holy Spirit's teaching takes only one direction, and has only one goal. His direction is freedom, and His goal is God. But He cannot conceive of God without YOU, because it was not God's Will to BE without you. When you have learned that your will IS God's, you could no more will to be without Him than He could will to be without YOU. This IS freedom and this IS joy. Deny YOURSELF this, and you ARE denying God His Kingdom, because He created you FOR this.

T 8 C 8. When we said, "all power and glory are yours"[336] because the Kingdom is His," this is what we meant: The Will of God is without limit, and all power and glory lie within it. It is boundless in strength and in love and in peace. It has no boundaries because its extension is unlimited, and it encompasses all things because it CREATED all things. By CREATING all things, it made them PART OF ITSELF. YOU are the Will of God, because this is how you were created. Because your Creator creates only like Himself, you ARE like Him.

T 8 C 9. You are part of Him who IS all power and glory, and are therefore as unlimited as He is. To what else EXCEPT all power and glory can the Holy Spirit appeal to restore God's Kingdom? His appeal, then, is merely to what the Kingdom is, and for its own acknowledgment of what it is. When you acknowledge THIS, you bring the acknowledgment automatically to everyone, because YOU HAVE ACKNOWLEDGED EVERYONE. By your recognition you awaken theirs, and through theirs YOURS is extended. Awakening runs easily and gladly through the Kingdom in answer to the call of God. This is the natural response of every Son of God to the Voice of His Creator, because it is the voice for HIS creations and for his own extension.

T 8 D. The Holy Encounter (*Notes* 768 7:100)

T 8 D 1. Glory be to God in the highest,[337] and to you because He has so willed it. Ask and it shall be given you,[338] because it has already been given. Ask for light and learn that you are light. If you WANT understanding and enlightenment you will learn it, because your will to learn it is your decision to listen to the Teacher who knows of light and can therefore **T(351) C 78** TEACH IT TO YOU.

T 8 D 2. There is no limit on your learning, because there is no limit on your MINDS. There is no limit on His will to teach, because He was created by unlimited Will in ORDER to teach. KNOWING His function perfectly, He wills to fulfill it perfectly, because that is His joy AND YOURS. To fulfill the Will of God perfectly is the only joy and peace that can be fully KNOWN, because it is the only function that can be FULLY EXPERIENCED. When this is accomplished, then, there IS no other experience. But the WISH for other experience will block this, because God's Will CANNOT be forced upon you, being an experience of total WILLINGNESS.

T 8 D 3. The Holy Spirit knows how to teach this, but YOU do not. That is why you need Him, and why God gave Him TO you. Only HIS teaching will release your will to God's, uniting it with His power and glory, and establishing them as yours. You will share them as He shares them, because this is the natural outcome of their being. The Will of the Father and of the Son are one together BY THEIR EXTENSION. Their extension is the RESULT of their Oneness, holding THEIR unity by extending their JOINT will.

T 8 D 4. This is perfect creation by the perfectly created in union with the Perfect Creator. The Father MUST give fatherhood to His Sons, because His Own Fatherhood must be extended outward. You who belong in God have the holy function of extending His Fatherhood by placing no limits upon it. Let the Holy Spirit teach you HOW to do this, for you will know what it MEANS of God Himself. **T(352) C 179**

T 8 D 5. When you meet anyone, remember it is a holy encounter. As you see him, you will see yourself. As you treat him, you will treat yourself. As you think of him, you will think of yourself. Never forget this, for in him you will find yourself or lose sight of yourself. Whenever two Sons of God meet they are given another chance at Salvation. Do not leave anyone without giving salvation TO him and receiving it yourself. For I am always there WITH you,[339] in remembrance of YOU.

T 8 D 6. The goal of the curriculum, regardless of the teacher you choose, is KNOW THYSELF. There is nothing else to learn. Everyone is looking for himself and the power and glory he thinks he has lost. Whenever you are with anyone ELSE, you have another opportunity to find them. Your power and glory are in HIM BECAUSE they are yours. The ego tries to find them in YOURSELF, because he[340] does not know where to look. But the Holy Spirit teaches you that if you look only at yourself you CANNOT find yourself because that is NOT what you are.

T 8 D 7. Whenever you are with a brother you are learning what you are, because you are TEACHING what you are. He will respond either with pain or with joy, depending on which teacher YOU are following. HE will be imprisoned or released according to your decision, AND SO WILL YOU.[341] Never forget your responsibility to him, because it is your responsibility to YOURSELF. Give him HIS place in the Kingdom, and you will have YOURS. The Kingdom CANNOT be found alone, and you who ARE the Kingdom cannot find YOURSELVES alone.

T 8 D 8. To achieve the goal of the curriculum, then, you CANNOT listen to the ego. Its purpose is to DEFEAT ITS OWN GOAL. It does not know this, because it does not know anything. But YOU can know this, and you WILL know it if you are willing to look at what the ego has made of YOU. **T(353) C 180** This IS your responsibility, because once you have really done this you WILL accept the Atonement for yourself. What other choice could you make?

T 8 D 9. Having made this choice, you will begin to learn and understand why you have believed that when you met someone else, you have thought he WAS[342] someone else. And every holy encounter in which YOU enter fully will teach you THAT THIS IS NOT SO. You can encounter ONLY part of yourself, because you are part of God WHO IS EVERYTHING. His power and glory are everywhere, and you CANNOT be excluded from them. The ego teaches that your strength is in you ALONE. The Holy Spirit teaches that ALL strength is in God and THEREFORE in you.

T 8 D 10. God wills NO-ONE suffer. He does not will ANYONE to suffer for a wrong decision you have made, including YOURSELF. That is why He has given you the means for UNDOING it. Through His power and glory all your wrong decisions are undone COMPLETELY, releasing you AND your brothers from EVERY IM-

---

[336] **Matthew 6:13** "And do not lead us into temptation,
But deliver us from the evil one.
For Yours is the kingdom and the power and the glory forever." Amen.

[337] **Luke 2:14** "Glory to God in the highest, And on earth peace, goodwill toward men!"

[338] **Matthew 7:7** "Ask, and it shall be given you; seek, and ye shall find; knock, and it shall be opened unto you": **Luke 11:9** "And I say unto you, Ask, and it shall be given you; seek, and ye shall find; knock, and it shall be opened unto you."

[339] **Matthew 28:20** "Teaching them to observe all things that I have commanded you; and lo, I am with you always, even to the end of the age." Amen.

[340] Later versions have "it" rather than "he", so does the *Notes*.

[341] **Matthew 16:19** "And I will give you the keys of the kingdom of heaven, and whatever you bind on earth will be bound in heaven, and whatever you loose on earth will be loosed in heaven."

[342] *Urtext* manuscript has it typed "they WERE" crossed out and handwritten replacement is "he was." The *Notes* has it "they were."

PRISONING THOUGHT ANY part of the Sonship has accepted. Wrong decisions HAVE no power BECAUSE they are not true. The imprisonment which they SEEM to produce is no more true than THEY are.

T 8 D 11. Power and glory belong to God alone. So do YOU. God gives WHATEVER belongs to Him, because He gives OF HIMSELF, and EVERYTHING belongs to Him. Giving of YOUR self is the function He gave you. Fulfilling it perfectly will teach you what YOU have of HIM. And this will teach you what you are IN Him. You CANNOT be powerLESS to do this, because this IS your power. Glory is God's gift to you because that is what HE is. See this glory everywhere, to learn what YOU are. **T(354) C 181**[343]

T 8 E. The Light of the World (*Notes* 776 7:108)

T 8 E 1. If God's Will for you is complete peace and joy, unless you experience ONLY this you MUST be refusing to acknowledge His Will. His Will does not vacillate, being changeless forever. When you are not at peace, it can only be because you do not believe you are IN HIM. Yet He is all in all.[344] His peace IS complete, and you MUST be included in it. His laws govern you because they govern EVERYTHING. You cannot exempt yourself from His laws, although you CAN disobey them. But if you do, and ONLY if you do, you WILL feel lonely and helpless, because you ARE denying yourself everything.

T 8 E 2. I am come as a light into the world[345] which DOES deny itself everything. It does this simply by dissociating itself FROM everything. It is therefore an illusion of isolation, MAINTAINED by fear of the same loneliness which IS its illusion. I have told you that I am with you always even to the end of the world.[346] That is WHY I am the light of the world.[347] If I am with you in the loneliness of the world, THE LONELINESS IS GONE. You CANNOT maintain the illusion of loneliness if you are NOT alone.

T 8 E 3. My purpose, then, IS to overcome the world.[348] I do not attack it, but my light must dispel it because of WHAT IT IS. Light does not ATTACK darkness, but it DOES shine it away. If my light goes with you everywhere, YOU shine it away WITH ME. The light becomes OURS, and you CANNOT abide in darkness, any more than darkness can abide anywhere you go. The remembrance of me IS the remembrance of yourself and of Him Who sent me to you.[349]

T 8 E 4. You WERE in darkness until God's Will was done completely by ANY part of the Sonship. When it was, it was perfectly accomplished by ALL. How else could it BE perfectly accomplished? My mission was simply to UNITE the Will of the Sonship WITH the Will of the Father by being aware of the Father's Will myself. This is the awareness I came to give YOU, and YOUR problem in accepting it IS the problem of this world. Dispelling it is

---

[343] May 31, 1966
[344] **1 Corinthians 15:28** Now when all things are made subject to Him, then the Son Himself will also be subject to Him who put all things under Him, that God may be all in all.
Ephesians 1:23 Which is His body, the fullness of Him who fills all in all.
[345] **John 8:12** Again therefore Jesus spake unto them, saying, "I am the light of the world: he that followeth me shall not walk in the darkness, but shall have the light of life."
[346] **Matthew 28:20** "teaching them to observe all things whatsoever I commanded you: and lo, I am with you always, even unto the end of the world."
[347] **John 8:12** Again therefore Jesus spake unto them, saying, "I am the light of the world: he that followeth me shall not walk in the darkness, but shall have the light of life." Also **John 9:5. 12:46; Matthew 5:14**
[348] **John 16:33** "These things have I spoken unto you, that in me ye may have peace. In the world ye have tribulation: but be of good cheer; I have overcome the world."
[349] **Luke 22:19** And He took bread, gave thanks and broke it, and gave it to them, saying, "This is My body which is given for you; do this in remembrance of Me."

---

salvation, and in this sense I AM the salvation of the world.[350] **T(355) C 182**

T 8 E 5. The world MUST despise and reject me,[351] because the world IS the belief that love is impossible. YOUR reactions to me ARE the reactions of the world to God. If you will accept the fact that I am with you, you are DENYING the world and ACCEPTING GOD. My will IS His, and YOUR will to hear me IS the decision to hear His Voice and abide in His Will. As He sent me to you, so will I send you to others. But I will go to them WITH you, so we can teach them union and peace.

T 8 E 6. Do you not think the world needs peace as much as you do? Do you not want to give it to the world as much as you want to receive it? For unless you do, you will NOT receive it. If you will to have it of me, you MUST give it. Rehabilitation does not come from anyone ELSE. You can have GUIDANCE from without, but you must ACCEPT it from within. The guidance must become what YOU want, or else it will be meaningless to you. That is why rehabilitation is a collaborative venture. I can tell you what to DO, but this will not really help you unless you collaborate by believing that I KNOW what to do. Only then will your MIND will to follow me.

T 8 E 7. Without YOUR will, you cannot be rehabilitated. MOTIVATION TO BE HEALED is the crucial factor in rehabilitation. Without this, you are deciding AGAINST healing, and your veto of my will FOR you MAKES HEALING IMPOSSIBLE. If healing IS our joint will, unless our wills ARE joined you CANNOT be healed. This is obvious when you consider what healing is FOR.

T 8 E 8. Healing is the way in which the separation is overcome. Separation is overcome by UNION. It CANNOT be overcome by separating. The WILL to unite must be unequivocal, or the will ITSELF is separated or NOT WHOLE. Your will is the means by which you determine your own condition, because will is the MECHANISM OF DECISION. It is the power by which you separate or join, and experience pain or joy accordingly. My will cannot OVERCOME yours, because YOURS IS AS POWERFUL AS MINE. If it were not so, the Sons **T(356) C 183** of God would be unequal.

T 8 E 9. All things BECOME possible through our joint will. But my will alone will not help you. Your will is as free as mine, and God Himself would not go against it. I cannot will what God does not will. I CAN offer you my will to make yours invincible by this sharing, but I CANNOT oppose yours without competing with it and thereby violating God's Will for you. Nothing God created can oppose your will, as nothing God created can oppose His. God GAVE your will its power, which I can only acknowledge in honor of His.

T 8 E 10. If you want to be LIKE me, I will help you, knowing that we ARE alike. If you want to be DIFFERENT, I will wait until you change your mind. I can TEACH you, but only you can choose to LISTEN to my teaching. How else can it be, if God's Kingdom IS freedom? Freedom cannot be learned by tyranny of ANY kind, and the perfect equality of ALL God's Sons cannot be recognized through the dominion of one will over another. God's Sons are equal in will, all being the Will of their Father. This is the ONLY lesson I can teach, knowing that it is true.

T 8 E 11. When your will is NOT mine, it is not Our Father's. This means that you have imprisoned YOURS, and have not LET it be

---

[350] **John 8:12** Again therefore Jesus spake unto them, saying, "I am the light of the world: he that followeth me shall not walk in the darkness, but shall have the light of life." Also **John 11:25** Jesus said unto her, "I am the resurrection, and the life: he that believeth on me, though he die, yet shall he live"
[351] **Isaiah 53:3** He was despised, and rejected of men; a man of sorrows, and acquainted with grief: and as one from whom men hide their face he was despised; and we esteemed him not.
John 15:18 "If the world hates you, you know that it hated Me before it hated you."

free. Of yourselves you can do nothing,[352] because of yourselves you ARE nothing. I am nothing without the Father, and YOU are nothing without me because by DENYING the Father you deny YOURSELF. I will ALWAYS remember you, and in MY remembrance OF you lies your remembrance of YOURSELF. In our remembrance of EACH OTHER lies our remembrance of God. And in this remembrance lies your freedom, because your freedom is in Him.[353]

T 8 E 12. Join then with me in praise of Him AND you whom He created. This is our gift of gratitude to Him, which He will share with ALL His Creations, to whom He gives equally whatever is acceptable to Him. BECAUSE it is acceptable to Him, it is the gift of freedom, which IS His Will for all His Sons. By OFFERING freedom you will be free, because **T(357) C 184** freedom is the only gift which you can offer to God's Sons, being an acknowledgment of what they are and what HE is.

T 8 E 13. Freedom is creation because it is love. What you seek to imprison you do NOT love. Therefore, when you seek to imprison ANYONE, including YOURSELF, you do not love him and you cannot identify with him. When you imprison yourself, you are losing sight of your true identification with me and with the Father. Your identification IS with the Father and with the Son. It CANNOT be with one and not the other. If you are part of one, you MUST be part of the other because they ARE One.

T 8 E 14. The Holy Trinity is holy BECAUSE It is One. If you exclude YOURSELF from this union, you are perceiving the Holy Trinity as separated. You MUST be included in It, because It IS everything. Unless you take your place in It and fulfill your function AS part of It, It is as bereft as YOU are. No part of It can be imprisoned if Its Truth is to be known.

T 8 E 15. Can you be separated from your identification and be at peace? Dissociation is NOT a solution; it is a DELUSION. The delusional believe that truth will ASSAIL them, and so they DO NOT SEE IT because they prefer the delusion. Judging truth as something they do NOT want, they perceive deception and block knowledge. Help them by offering them YOUR unified will on their behalf, as I am offering you mine on YOURS. Alone we can do nothing, but TOGETHER our wills fuse into something whose power is far beyond the power of its separate parts.

T 8 E 16. By NOT BEING SEPARATE, the Will of God is established IN ours and AS ours. This will is invincible BECAUSE it is undivided. The UNDIVIDED will of the Sonship is the perfect creator, being wholly in the likeness of God,[354] Whose Will it IS. YOU cannot be exempt from it, if you are to understand what it is and what YOU are. By separating your will from mine, you ARE exempting yourself from the Will of God which IS yourself.

T 8 E 17. But to heal is still to make whole. Therefore to heal is to UNITE with those who are LIKE you, because perceiving this likeness IS to **T(358) C 185** recognize the Father. If YOUR perfection is in Him and ONLY in Him, how can you KNOW it WITHOUT recognizing Him? The recognition of God is the recognition of yourself. There IS no separation of God and His Creation. You will learn this as you learn that there is no separation of YOUR will and mine.

T 8 E 18. Let the love of God shine upon you by your acceptance of me. MY reality is yours and His. By joining YOUR will with mine, you are signifying your awareness that the Will of God is One. His Oneness and ours are not separate, because His Oneness ENCOMPASSES ours. To join WITH me is to restore His power TO you BECAUSE we are sharing it. I offer you only the recognition of His power in you, but in that lies ALL truth. As WE unite, we unite with Him. Glory be to the union of God and His Holy Sons, because all glory lies IN them because they ARE united.

T 8 E 19. The miracles WE do bear witness to the Will of the Father for His Son, and to our joy in uniting <u>WITH</u> His Will FOR us. When you unite with me, you are uniting WITHOUT the ego, because I have renounced the ego in myself, and therefore CANNOT unite with yours. OUR union is therefore the way to renounce the ego in <u>YOURSELVES</u>. The truth in both of us is BEYOND the ego. By willing that, you HAVE gone beyond it toward truth.

T 8 E 20. Our success in transcending the ego is guaranteed by God, and I can share my perfect confidence IN His Promise because I know He gave me this confidence for both of us and ALL of us. I bring His Peace back to all His Children, because I received it of Him for us all. Nothing can prevail against our united wills, because nothing can prevail against God's. Would ye know the Will of God for YOU? Ask it of me, who knows[355] it for you, and you will find it. I will deny YOU nothing, as God denies ME nothing.

T 8 E 21. Ours is simply the journey back to God Who is our home. Whenever fear intrudes anywhere along the road to peace, it is ALWAYS because the ego has attempted to JOIN the journey with us AND CANNOT DO SO. Sensing defeat and angered by it, it regards itself as rejected and becomes **T(359) C 186** retaliative. You are invulnerable to its retaliation BECAUSE I AM WITH YOU. On this journey, you have chosen me as your companion INSTEAD of your ego. Do not try to hold on to both, or you will try to go in different directions and will lose the way.

T 8 E 22. The ego's way is not mine, but it is also NOT YOURS. The Holy Spirit has one direction for ALL minds, and the one He taught me IS yours. Let us not lose sight of His direction through illusions, for ONLY illusions of another direction can obscure the one for which God's Voice speaks in all of us. Never accord the ego the power to interfere with the journey, because it HAS none, and the journey is the way to what is TRUE. Leave ALL deception behind, and reach beyond all attempts of the ego to hold you back.

T 8 E 23. I DO go before you, because I AM beyond the ego. Reach therefore for my hand because you WANT to transcend the ego. My will, will NEVER be wanting, and if you want to share it YOU WILL. I give it willingly and gladly, because I need YOU as much as you need ME.

T 8 F. The Power of Joint Decision (*Notes* 789 7:121)

T 8 F 1. WE are the joint will of the Sonship, whose wholeness is for all. We begin the journey back by setting out TOGETHER, and gather in our brothers as we CONTINUE together.

T 8 F 2. Every gain in our strength is offered to all, so they, too, can lay aside their weakness and add their strength to us. God's welcome waits for us all, and He will welcome us as I am welcoming YOU. Forget not the Kingdom of God for anything the world has to offer. The world can <u>ADD</u> nothing to the power and the glory of God and His Holy Sons, but CAN blind the Sons to the Father if

---

[352] **John 5:19** Then Jesus answered and said to them, "Most assuredly, I say to you, the Son can do nothing of Himself, but what He sees the Father do; for whatever He does, the Son also does in like manner."
John 5:30 "I can of Myself do nothing. As I hear, I judge; and My judgment is righteous, because I do not seek My own will but the will of the Father who sent Me."
[353] **Luke 22:19** And He took bread, gave thanks and broke it, and gave it to them, saying, "This is My body which is given for you; do this in remembrance of Me."
[354] **Genesis 1:26-27** Then God said, "Let Us make man in Our image, according to Our likeness; let them have dominion over the fish of the sea, over the birds of the air, and over the cattle, over all the earth and over every creeping thing that creeps on the earth." So God created man in His own image; in the image of God He created him; male and female He created them.

[355] *Urtext* manuscript has it typed "know", it should be "knows" as it is in the *HLC* to be grammatically correct. The *Notes*, however, also has it as "know."

they behold it. You cannot behold the[356] world and know God. Only one is true.

T 8 F 3. I am come to tell you that the choice of which is true is not yours. If it were, you would have destroyed yourselves. But God did not will the destruction of His Creations, having created them for eternity. His Will has saved you, not from yourselves, but from your illusions of yourselves. He has saved you FOR yourselves. Let us glorify Him Whom the world denies, for over His Kingdom[357] it has no power. **T(360) C 187**[358]

T 8 F 4. No-one created by God can find joy in anything except the eternal. That is not because he is DEPRIVED of anything else, but because nothing else is WORTHY of him. What God AND His Sons create IS eternal, and in this and this only is their joy. Listen to the story of the prodigal son,[359] and learn what God's treasure is and YOURS:[360]

T 8 F 5. This son of a loving father left his home and thought he squandered everything for nothing of any value, though he did not know its worthlessness at the time. He was ashamed to return to his father, because he thought he had hurt him. But when he came home the father welcomed him with joy, because only the son himself WAS his father's treasure. HE WANTED NOTHING ELSE.

T 8 F 6. God wants only His Son, because His Son is His only treasure. You want your creations, as He wants His. Your creations are your gift to the Holy Trinity, created in gratitude for YOUR creation. They do not leave you, any more than you have left YOUR Creator. But they EXTEND your creation, as God extended Himself to YOU. Can the Creations of God Himself take joy in what is not real? And what IS real except the Creations of God and those which are created like His? YOUR creations love you as your Soul loves your Father FOR THE GIFT OF CREATION. There IS no other gift that is eternal, and therefore THERE IS NO OTHER GIFT THAT IS TRUE.

T 8 F 7. How, then, can you accept anything else, or GIVE anything else, and expect joy in return? And what else BUT joy would you want? You made neither yourself nor your function. YOU have made only the DECISION to be unworthy of both. But you COULD not make YOURSELF unworthy because YOU ARE THE TREASURE OF GOD. What HE values IS valuable. There CAN be no question of its worth, because its value lies in God's sharing Himself with it and ESTABLISHING ITS **T(361) C 188** VALUE FOREVER. YOUR function is to ADD to God's treasure by creating YOURS. His will TO you is His Will FOR you. He would not withhold creation from you, because HIS joy is in it.

T 8 F 8. You CANNOT find joy EXCEPT as He does. HIS joy lay in creating YOU, and He extends His Fatherhood to you so that you can extend yourself AS HE DID. You do not understand this because you do not understand Him. No one who does not know his function can understand it. And no one CAN know his function unless he knows who he IS. Creation is the Will of God. His Will created you TO CREATE. Your will was not created separate from His, and so it wills as HE wills.

T 8 F 9. An unwilling will does not mean anything, because it is a contradiction in terms which actually leaves nothing. You can make yourself powerless only in a way that has NO MEANING AT ALL. When you THINK you are unwilling to will with God, YOU ARE NOT THINKING. God's will IS thought. It cannot be contradicted BY thought. God does not contradict HIMSELF. And His Sons, who are like Him, cannot contradict themselves OR Him. But their thought is so powerful that they can even imprison the mind of God's Son IF THEY SO CHOOSE. This choice DOES make the Son's function unknown TO HIM, but never to his Creator. And BECAUSE it is not unknown to his Creator, it is forever knowable to him.

T 8 F 10. There is no question but one you should ever ask of yourself: "Do I want to know my Father's Will for me?" HE will not hide it. He has revealed it to me because I asked it of Him, and learned of what He had already given. Our function is to function together, because apart from each other we cannot function at all. The whole power of God's Son lies in all of us, but not in any of us alone. **T(362) C 189** God would not have us be alone because HE does not will to be alone. That is why He created His Son and gave him the power to create with Him. Our creations are as holy as we are, and we are the Sons of God Himself, and therefore as holy as He is. Through our creations we extend our Love, and thus increase the joy of the Holy Trinity. You do not understand this for a very simple reason. You who are God's own treasure do not regard yourselves as valuable. Given this belief YOU CANNOT UNDERSTAND ANYTHING.

T 8 F 11. I share with God the knowledge of the value HE puts upon you. My devotion to you is of Him, being born of my knowledge of myself AND Him. We cannot BE separated. Whom God has joined CANNOT be separated,[361] and God has joined all His Sons WITH HIMSELF. Can you be separated from your life and your being? The journey to God is merely the reawakening of the knowledge of where you are always, and what you are forever. It is a journey without distance, to a goal that has never changed.

---

[356] *Urtext* manuscript has it "and" ... *HLC* has it "the" which appears correct. The passage has not been located in the *Notes*.

[357] **John 18:36** Jesus answered, "My kingdom is not of this world. If My kingdom were of this world, My servants would fight, so that I should not be delivered to the Jews; but now My kingdom is not from here."

[358] June 6, 1966.

[359] **Luke 15:11-32** Then He said: "A certain man had two sons. And the younger of them said to his father, 'Father, give me the portion of goods that falls to me.' So he divided to them his livelihood. And not many days after, the younger son gathered all together, journeyed to a far country, and there wasted his possessions with prodigal living. But when he had spent all, there arose a severe famine in that land, and he began to be in want. Then he went and joined himself to a citizen of that country, and he sent him into his fields to feed swine. And he would gladly have filled his stomach with the pods that the swine ate, and no one gave him anything.

"But when he came to himself, he said, 'How many of my father's hired servants have bread enough and to spare, and I perish with hunger! I will arise and go to my father, and will say to him, "Father, I have sinned against heaven and before you, and I am no longer worthy to be called your son. Make me like one of your hired servants."'

"And he arose and came to his father. But when he was still a great way off, his father saw him and had compassion, and ran and fell on his neck and kissed him. And the son said to him, 'Father, I have sinned against heaven and in your sight, and am no longer worthy to be called your son.'

"But the father said to his servants, 'Bring out the best robe and put it on him, and put a ring on his hand and sandals on his feet. And bring the fatted calf here and kill it, and let us eat and be merry; for this my son was dead and is alive again; he was lost and is found.' And they began to be merry.

"Now his older son was in the field. And as he came and drew near to the house, he heard music and dancing. So he called one of the servants and asked what these things meant. And he said to him, 'Your brother has come, and because he has received him safe and sound, your father has killed the fatted calf.'

"But he was angry and would not go in. Therefore his father came out and pleaded with him. So he answered and said to his father, 'Lo, these many years I have been serving you; I never transgressed your commandment at any time; and yet you never gave me a young goat, that I might make merry with my friends. But as soon as this son of yours came, who has devoured your livelihood with harlots, you killed the fatted calf for him.'

"And he said to him, 'Son, you are always with me, and all that I have is yours. It was right that we should make merry and be glad, for your brother was dead and is alive again, and was lost and is found.'"

[360] The *Urtext* manuscript has a paragraph break here, but no other version does.

[361] **Mark 10:9** "What therefore God hath joined together, let not man put asunder."
Matthew 19:6 "So that they are no more twain, but one flesh. What therefore God hath joined together, let not man put asunder."

Chapter 8 – The Journey Back

T 8 F 12. Truth can only be EXPERIENCED. It cannot be described and it cannot be explained. I can make you aware of the CONDITIONS of truth, but the experience is of God. Together we can meet its conditions, but truth will dawn upon you of itself. What God has willed for you IS yours. He has given His Will to His treasure, whose treasure It is. Your heart lies where your treasure is,[362] as His does. You who are beloved of God are wholly blessed. Learn this of me, and free the Holy Will of all those who are as blessed as you are. **T(363) C 190**

T 8 G. Communication and the Ego-Body Equation (*Notes* 798 7:130)

T 8 G 1. Attack is ALWAYS physical. When attack in ANY form enters your mind, you are EQUATING YOURSELF WITH A BODY. This is the ego's INTERPRETATION of the body. You do not have to ATTACK physically to accept this interpretation; you ARE accepting it simply by the belief that attack can GET YOU SOMETHING YOU WANT. If you did NOT believe this, the IDEA of attack would have no appeal to you.

T 8 G 2. When you equate yourself with a body, you will ALWAYS experience depression. When a Child of God thinks of himself in this way, he is belittling himself and seeing his brothers as similarly belittled. Since he can find himself ONLY in them, he has cut himself off from salvation. Remember that the Holy Spirit interprets the body ONLY as a means of communication. Being the communication link between God and His separated Sons, He interprets everything YOU have in the light of what HE is.

T 8 G 3. The ego SEPARATES through the body. The Holy Spirit reaches THROUGH it to others. You do not perceive your brothers as the Holy Spirit does because you do not interpret their bodies AND YOURS solely as a means of JOINING THEIR MINDS and uniting them with yours and mine. This interpretation of the body will change your mind entirely about its value. Of itself it has NONE. If you use it for attack it is harmful to you. But if you use it ONLY to reach the minds of those who believe they ARE bodies and teach them THROUGH the body that THIS IS NOT SO, you will begin to understand the power of the mind that is in both of you. If you use the body for this, and ONLY for this, you CANNOT use it for attack. In the service of uniting, it becomes a beautiful lesson in communion, which has value until communion IS. **T(364) C 191**

T 8 G 4. This is God's way of making unlimited what YOU have limited. His Voice does not see the body as YOU do, because He knows the ONLY reality that ANYTHING can have is the service it can render God on behalf of the function HE has given. Communication ENDS separation. Attack PROMOTES it. The body is ugly or beautiful, savage or holy, helpful or harmful, according to the use to which it is put. And in the body of another you will see the use to which you put YOURS.

T 8 G 5. If the body becomes for you a means which you give to the Holy Spirit to use on behalf of the union of the Sonship, you will not see ANYTHING physical except as WHAT IT IS. Use it for truth, and you will see it truly. MISuse it and you WILL misunderstand it, because you have already done so BY misusing it. Interpret ANYTHING apart from the Holy Spirit, and you will mistrust it. This will lead you to hatred and attack and LOSS OF PEACE.

T 8 G 6. But ALL loss comes only from your own misunderstanding. Loss of ANY kind is impossible. When you look upon a brother as a physical entity, HIS power and glory are lost to you and SO ARE YOURS. You HAVE attacked him, and you MUST have attacked yourself first. Do not see him this way for your OWN salvation, which MUST bring him his. Do not ALLOW him to belittle himself in YOUR mind, but give him freedom from his belief in littleness, and escape from YOURS. As part of YOU, HE is holy. As part of ME, YOU are. To communicate with part of God Himself is to reach beyond the Kingdom to its Creator, through His Voice which He has established as part of YOU. **T(365) C 192**

T 8 G 7. Rejoice, then, that of yourselves you can do nothing.[363] You are not OF yourselves. And He of Whom you ARE has willed your power and glory FOR you, with which you can perfectly accomplish His holy Will for you when you so will it yourself. He has not withdrawn His gifts from YOU, but YOU have withdrawn them from Him. Let no Son of God remain hidden for His Name's sake, because His Name is YOURS.

T 8 G 8. Remember that the Bible says, "The word (or thought) was made flesh."[364] Strictly speaking, this is impossible, since it seems to involve the translation of one order of reality into another. Different orders of reality merely SEEM to exist, just as different orders of miracles do. Thought cannot be MADE into flesh except by belief, because thought is NOT physical. But thought IS communication, for which the body can be used. This is the only NATURAL use to which it can be put. To use the body UNnaturally is to lose sight of the Holy Spirit's purpose, and thus to confuse the goal of His curriculum.

T 8 G 9. There is nothing so frustrating to a learner as to place him in a curriculum which he cannot learn. His sense of adequacy suffers, and he MUST become depressed. Being faced with an impossible learning situation, REGARDLESS of why it is impossible, is the most depressing thing in the world. In fact, it is ultimately WHY the world is depressing. The Holy Spirit's curriculum is NEVER depressing because it is a curriculum in joy. Whenever the reaction to learning is depression, it is only because the goal of the curriculum has been lost sight of.

T 8 G 10. In the world, not even the body is perceived as whole. Its purpose is seen as fragmented into many functions which bear little or no relationship to each other, so that it appears to be ruled by chaos. **T(366) C 193** Guided by the ego, it IS. Guided by the Holy Spirit, it is NOT. It becomes ONLY a means by which the part of the mind which you have separated from your Soul can reach beyond its distortions and RETURN to the Soul. The ego's temple thus becomes the temple of the Holy Spirit, where devotion to Him replaces devotion to the ego. In this sense the body DOES become a temple to God,[365] because His Voice abides in it by directing the use TO WHICH YOU PUT IT.

T 8 G 11. Healing is the result of using the body SOLELY for communication. Since this IS natural, it heals by making whole, which is also natural. ALL mind is whole, and the belief that part of it is physical or NOT MIND is a fragmented (or sick) interpretation. Mind CANNOT be made physical, but it CAN be made manifest THROUGH the physical if it uses the body to GO BEYOND itself. By reaching OUT, the mind EXTENDS itself. It does not STOP at the body, for if it does it is blocked in its purpose. A mind which has been blocked has allowed itself to be vulnerable to attack, because it has TURNED AGAINST ITSELF.

T 8 G 12. The removal of blocks, then, is the ONLY way to guarantee help and healing. Help and healing are the normal expressions of a mind which is working THROUGH the body but not IN it. If the mind believes the body is its GOAL, it WILL distort its perception OF the body, and by blocking its own extension BEYOND it will

---

[362] **Matthew 6:21** "For where your treasure is, there your heart will be also."

[363] **John 5:19** Then Jesus answered and said to them, "Most assuredly, I say to you, the Son can do nothing of Himself, but what He sees the Father do; for whatever He does, the Son also does in like manner."

[364] **John 1:14** And the Word became flesh, and dwelt among us (and we beheld his glory, glory as of the only begotten from the Father), full of grace and truth.

[365] **1 Corinthians 3:16** Do you not know that you are the temple of God and that the Spirit of God dwells in you?

1 Corinthians 6:19 Or do you not know that your body is the temple of the Holy Spirit who is in you, whom you have from God, and you are not your own?

INDUCE illness by FOSTERING SEPARATION. Perceiving the body AS A SEPARATE ENTITY cannot BUT foster illness, because it is not true. A medium of communication WILL lose its usefulness if it is used for anything else. **T(367) C 194**

T 8 G 13. To use a medium of communication as a medium of ATTACK is an obvious confusion in purpose. To communicate is to join and to attack is to separate. How can you do both simultaneously WITH THE SAME THING, and NOT suffer? Perception of the body can be unified only by ONE PURPOSE. This releases the mind from the temptation to see it in many lights, and gives it over ENTIRELY to the One Light in which it can be really understood at all.

T 8 G 14. To confuse a learning device with a curriculum GOAL is a fundamental confusion. Learning can hardly be meaningfully arrested at its own aids, and hope to understand them OR its real purpose. Learning must lead BEYOND the body to the re-establishment of the power of the mind IN it. This can be accomplished ONLY if the mind EXTENDS to other minds, and does not ARREST ITSELF in its extension. The arrest of the mind's extension is the cause of all illness, because ONLY EXTENSION IS THE MIND's FUNCTION. Block this, and you have blocked health because you have BLOCKED THE MIND's JOY.

T 8 G 15. The opposite of joy is depression. When your learning promotes depression INSTEAD of joy, you CANNOT be listening to God's joyous teacher, and you MUST be learning amiss. To see a body as anything EXCEPT a means of pure extension is to limit your mind and HURT YOURSELF. Health is therefore nothing more than united purpose. If the body is brought under the purpose of the mind, it becomes whole because the mind's purpose IS one.

T 8 G 16. Attack can only be an assumed goal of the body, but the body APART from the mind HAS NO PURPOSE AT ALL. You are NOT limited by the body, and thought CANNOT be made flesh.[366] But mind can be manifested through the body if it goes beyond it and DOES NOT INTERPRET IT AS LIMITATION. Whenever you see another as limited TO or BY the body, you are imposing this limit ON YOURSELF. Are you willing to ACCEPT this, when your whole purpose for learning should be to escape FROM limitations? **T(368) C 195**

T 8 G 17. To conceive of the body as a means of attack of any kind, and to entertain even the possibility that joy could POSSIBLY result, is a clear-cut indication of a poor learner. He has accepted a learning goal in obvious contradiction to the unified purpose of the curriculum, and is interfering with his ability to accept it AS HIS OWN.

T 8 G 18. Joy is unified purpose, and unified purpose is ONLY God's. When yours is unified, it IS His. Interfere with His purpose, and YOU NEED SALVATION. You have condemned yourself, but condemnation is not of God. Therefore, it is not true. No more are any of the RESULTS of your condemnation. When you see a brother as a body, you are condemning him BECAUSE you have condemned yourself. But if ALL condemnation is unreal, and it MUST be unreal because it is a form of attack, then it can HAVE no results.

T 8 G 19. Do not allow yourselves to suffer from the results of what is not true. Free your minds from the belief that this is possible. In its complete impossibility, and your full awareness OF its complete impossibility, lies your only hope for release. But what other hope would you want? Freedom from illusions lies only in not BELIEVING them. THERE IS NO[367] ATTACK, but there IS unlimited communication and therefore unlimited power and wholeness. The power of wholeness is EXTENSION. Do not arrest your thought in this world, and you will open your mind to Creation in God. **T(369) C 196**[368]

T 8 H. The Body as Means or End (*Notes* 813 7:145)

T 8 H 1. Attitudes toward the body are attitudes toward ATTACK. The ego's definitions of ANYTHING are childish, and are ALWAYS based on what it believes a thing is FOR. This is because it is incapable of true generalizations, and equates what it sees with the function IT ascribes to it. It does NOT equate it with what it IS. To the ego, the body IS TO ATTACK WITH. Equating YOU with the body, it teaches that YOU are to attack with, because THIS IS WHAT IT BELIEVES. The body, then, is not the source of its own health. Its condition lies solely in your interpretation of its function.

T 8 H 2. The reason why definitions by function are inferior is merely because they may well be inaccurate. Functions are part of being, since they arise FROM it. But the relationship is NOT reciprocal. The whole does define the part, but the part does NOT define the whole. This is as true of knowledge as it is of perception. The reason why to KNOW in part is to know entirely is merely because of the fundamental difference between knowledge and perception. In perception, the whole is built up of parts, which can separate and reassemble in different constellations. Knowledge never changes, so that its constellation is permanent. The only areas in which part-whole relationships have any meaning are those in which change is possible. There IS no difference between the whole and the part where change is impossible. **T(370) C 197**

T 8 H 3. The body exists in a world which seems to contain two voices which are fighting for its possession. In this perceived constellation, the body is regarded as capable of shifting its control from one to the other, making the concept of both health and sickness possible. The ego makes a fundamental confusion between means and ends, as it always does. Regarding the body as an end, it has no real use for it at all, because it is NOT an end. You must have noticed an outstanding characteristic of every end that the ego has accepted as its own. When you have achieved it, IT HAS NOT SATISFIED YOU. This is why the ego is forced to shift from one end to another without ceasing, so that YOU will continue to hope it can offer you something.

T 8 H 4. It has been particularly difficult to overcome the ego's belief in the body as an end because this is synonymous with ATTACK AS AN END. The ego has a REAL INVESTMENT IN SICKNESS. If you are sick, how can you object to the ego's firm belief that you are NOT invulnerable? This is a particularly appealing argument from the ego's point of view, because it obscures the obvious attack which underlies the sickness. If you accepted THIS, and also decided AGAINST attack, you could not give this false witness to the ego's stand. It is hard to perceive this as a false witness, because you do not realize that it IS entirely out of keeping with what YOU want. This witness, then, appears to be innocent and trustworthy only because YOU have not seriously cross-examined him. **T(371) C 198**

T 8 H 5. If you did, you would not consider sickness such a strong witness on behalf of the ego's views. A more honest statement would be as follows: Those who WANT the ego are predisposed to defend it. Therefore, their choice of witnesses should be suspect from the beginning. The ego does not call upon witnesses who might disagree with its case, NOR DOES THE HOLY SPIRIT. We have said before that judgment IS the function of the Holy Spirit, and one which He is perfectly equipped to fulfill. The ego, as a judge, gives anything BUT an impartial trial[369] (judgment.) When the ego calls on a witness, it has ALREADY MADE IT AN ALLY.

---

[366] **John 1:14** And the Word became flesh and dwelt among us, and we beheld His glory, the glory as of the only begotten of the Father, full of grace and truth.

[367] *Urtext* manuscript has it typed NOT, *HLC* holds it as "no" and we agree this is likely a typo. In the *Notes* it is clearly "no attack."

[368] June 8, 1966

[369] *HLC* drops "trial" in favor of "judgment" – this material has not been located in the *Notes*.

It is still true that the body has no function of itself. This is because it is NOT an end. The ego, however, establishes it AS an end because, as such, IT WILL LOSE ITS TRUE FUNCTION.

T 8 H 6. This is the purpose of everything the ego does. Its sole aim is to lose sight of the functions of EVERYTHING. A sick body does not make any sense. It COULD not make any sense, since sickness is not what it is FOR. Sickness is meaningful only if the two basic premises on which the ego's interpretation of the body rests are true. These are specifically first that the body is for attack, and also that you ARE a body. Without this, sickness is completely inconceivable. Sickness is a way of demonstrating that YOU CAN BE HURT. It is a witness to your frailty, your vulnerability, and your extreme need to depend on external guidance. The ego uses this as its best argument for your need for ITS guidance. It dictates endless prescriptions for AVOIDING this catastrophic outcome. The Holy Spirit, perfectly aware of the same data, does not bother to **T(372) C 199** analyze it at all. If the data are meaningless, there is no point in treating them at all.[370]

T 8 H 7. The function of truth is to collect data which are TRUE. There is no point in trying to make sense out of meaningless data. ANY way they are[371] handled results in nothing. The more complicated the results become, the harder it may be to recognize their nothingness, but it is not necessary to examine ALL possible outcomes to which premises give rise to judge the PREMISES truly.

T 8 H 8. A learning DEVICE is NOT a teacher. IT cannot tell you how you feel. YOU do not KNOW how you feel, because YOU HAVE ACCEPTED THE EGO's CONFUSION,[372] and YOU think A LEARNING DEVICE CAN TELL YOU HOW YOU[373] FEEL. Sickness is merely another example of your insistence on asking for guidance of a teacher who DOES NOT KNOW THE ANSWER. The ego is INCAPABLE of knowing how you feel. When we said that the ego DOES NOT KNOW ANYTHING, we said the one thing about the ego that is wholly true. But there is a corollary. If knowledge is being, and the ego has no knowledge, then the ego HAS NO BEING.

T 8 H 9. You might ask how the voice of something which does not exist can be so insistent. Have you ever seriously considered the distorting power of something you WANT, even if it is not true? You have had many instances of how what you want can distort what you see and hear. No one can doubt the ego's skill in building up false cases. And no one can doubt your willingness to listen, until YOU will not to tolerate ANYTHING except truth.

T 8 H 10. When YOU lay the ego aside it will be gone. The Holy Spirit's voice is as loud as your willingness to listen. It cannot be louder without violating your will, which He seeks to free but never to command. **T(373) C 200** He will teach you to use your body ONLY to reach your brothers so He can teach His message through you. This will heal them and THEREFORE heal you. Everything used in accordance with its function as HE sees it CANNOT be sick. Everything used otherwise IS.

T 8 H 11. Do not allow the body to be a mirror of a split mind. Do not let it be an image of your own perception of littleness. Do not let it reflect your will to attack. Health is the natural state of anything whose interpretation is left to the Holy Spirit, who perceives no attack on anything. Health is the result of relinquishing ALL attempts to use the body lovelessly. It is the beginning of the proper perspective on life, under the guidance of the one teacher who knows what life IS, being the voice for Life Itself.

T 8 I. Healing as Corrected Perception (*Notes* 817 7:149)

T 8 I 1. We once said that the Holy Spirit is the Answer.[374] He is the answer to EVERYTHING, because He knows what the answer to everything IS. The ego does not know what a REAL question is, although it asks an endless number. But YOU can learn this, as you learn to question the value of the ego and thus establish your ability to EVALUATE its questions. When the ego tempts you to sickness, do not ask the Holy Spirit to heal the body. For this would merely be to accept the ego's belief that the body is the proper aim for healing. Ask rather that the Holy Spirit teach you the right PERCEPTION of the body, for perception alone can be distorted.

T 8 I 2. ONLY PERCEPTION CAN BE SICK, because perception can be WRONG. Wrong perception is DISTORTED WILLING, which WANTS things to be as they are not. The reality of EVERYTHING is totally harmless, because total harmlessness is the CONDITION of its reality. It is also the condition of your AWARENESS of its reality. You do not have to SEEK reality. It will seek you and FIND you, WHEN YOU MEET ITS CONDITIONS. Its conditions are part of WHAT IT IS. And this part only is up to you. The rest is of Itself. You need **T(374) C 201** do so little, because It is so powerful that your little part WILL bring the whole to you. Accept, then, your little part, and LET the whole be yours. Wholeness heals BECAUSE it is of the[375] mind.

T 8 I 3. All forms of sickness, even unto death,[376] are physical expressions of the FEAR OF AWAKENING. They are attempts to reinforce UNCONSCIOUSNESS out of fear of CONSCIOUSNESS. This is a pathetic way of TRYING NOT TO KNOW by rendering the faculties for knowing ineffectual. "Rest in peace" is a blessing for the living, not the dead, because rest comes from waking, not from sleeping. Sleep is withdrawing; waking is JOINING. Dreams are ILLUSIONS of joining, taking on the ego's distortions about what joining means, if you are sleeping under its guidance. But the Holy Spirit, too, has use for sleep, and can use dreams on BEHALF of waking, if you will let Him.

T 8 I 4. How you wake is the sign of how you have used sleep. To whom did you give it? Under which teacher did you place it? Whenever you wake dis-spiritedly, it was NOT of the Spirit. ONLY when you awaken joyously have you utilized sleep ACCORDING TO THE HOLY SPIRIT's PURPOSE. You can indeed be "drugged by sleep," but this is ALWAYS because you have MISUSED IT ON BEHALF OF SICKNESS. Sleep is no more a form of death than death is a form of unconsciousness. UNCONSCIOUSNESS IS IMPOSSIBLE. You can rest in peace only BECAUSE YOU ARE AWAKE.

T 8 I 5. Healing is release from the fear of waking, and the substitution of the will to wake. The will to wake is the will to love, since ALL healing involves replacing fear with love. The Holy Spirit cannot distinguish among degrees of error, for if He taught that one form of sickness is more serious than another, He would be teaching that one error can be more REAL than another. But HIS function is to distinguish ONLY between the false and the true, REPLACING the false WITH the true. **T(375) C 202**

T 8 I 6. The ego, which always WEAKENS the will, wants to SEPARATE the body from the mind. This IS an attempt to DESTROY it. But the ego actually believes that it is PROTECTING it. This is because it believes that MIND IS DANGEROUS, and that to MAKE MINDLESS is to heal. But to make mindless is impossible, since it would mean to make nothing out of what God Created. The ego DESPISES weakness, even though it makes every effort to IN-

---

[370] The words "at all" are crossed out in the *Urtext* manuscript.
[371] The *Urtext* manuscript has "it is" typed, and "they are" is penciled in. The *Notes* also has it as "it is."
[372] *Ur* has it "CONCLUSION" crossed out with "confusion" written in. The *Notes* also has it as "confusion."
[373] *Urtext* manuscript has it typed "TO" this is crossed out and "YOU" is written in. The *Notes* also has it as "you" rather than "to."

[374] UR 6 E 0 284
[375] The word "the" is not in the *Ur* but is in the *HLC* and the *Notes*.
[376] **John 11:4** When Jesus heard that, He said, "This sickness is not unto death, but for the glory of God, that the Son of God may be glorified through it."

DUCE it. IT WANTS ONLY WHAT IT HATES. To the ego this is perfectly sensible. Believing in the power of attack, it WANTS it.

T 8 I 7. You have begun to realize that this is a very practical course, because it means EXACTLY what it says. So does the Bible, if it is properly understood. There has been a marked tendency on the part of many of the Bible's followers, and also its translators, to be entirely literal about fear and ITS effects, but NOT about love and ITS results. Thus, "hellfire" means burning, but raising the dead becomes allegorical. Actually, it is PARTICULARLY the references to the outcomes of love that should be taken literally because the Bible is ABOUT love, being about GOD.

T 8 I 8. The Bible enjoins you to be perfect,[377] to heal ALL errors, to take no thought of the body AS SEPARATE, and to accomplish all things IN MY NAME. This is not my name alone, for ours is a shared identification. The name of God's Son is One, and you are enjoined to do the works of love BECAUSE we share this oneness. Our minds are whole BECAUSE they are one. If you are sick, you are withdrawing from me. But you CANNOT WITHDRAW FROM ME ALONE. You can only withdraw from yourself AND me.

T 8 I 9. I would not ask you to do things which you CANNOT do, and it is impossible that I could do things YOU cannot do. Given this, and given this QUITE LITERALLY, there CAN be nothing which prevents you from doing EXACTLY what I ask, and EVERYTHING which argues FOR it. I give you NO limits, because God lays none upon you. T(376) C 203 When you limit YOURSELF, we are NOT of one mind, and that IS sickness. But sickness is not of the body, but OF THE MIND. ALL forms of DISfunction are merely signs that the mind has split, and does not accept a UNIFIED PURPOSE.

T 8 I 10. The unification of purpose, then, is the Holy Spirit's ONLY way of healing. This is because it is the only level at which healing MEANS anything. The re-establishing of meaning in a chaotic thought system IS the only way to heal it. We said before that your task is only to meet the conditions FOR meaning, since meaning itself is of God. But your RETURN to meaning is essential TO HIS, because YOUR meaning is PART of His. Your healing, then, is part of HIS health, because it is part of His Wholeness. He cannot lose this, but YOU can not know it. Yet it is still His will for you, and His will MUST stand forever and in all things. T(377) C 204

T 8 J. The Acceptance of Reality (Notes 824 7:156)

T 8 J 1. Fear of the Will of God is one of the strangest beliefs that the human mind has ever made. This could not possibly have occurred unless the mind was already profoundly split, making it possible for IT to be afraid of what it really is. It is apparent that reality CANNOT "threaten" anything except illusions, because reality can only UPHOLD truth. The very fact that the will of God, which IS what you are, is perceived as fearful TO you demonstrates that you ARE afraid of what you are. It is not, then, the will of God of which you are afraid, but YOURS. Your will is NOT the ego's, and that is why the ego is against you. What seems to be the fear of God is really only the fear of YOUR OWN REALITY.

T 8 J 2. It is impossible to learn anything consistently in a state of panic. If the purpose of this course is to learn what you are, and if you have ALREADY DECIDED that what you are is FEARFUL, then it MUST follow that you will NOT LEARN THIS COURSE. But you might remember that the reason FOR the course is that you do NOT know who you are. If you do not know your reality, how would you know whether it is fearful or not? The association of truth and fear, which would be highly artificial at best, is particularly inappropriate in the minds of those who do not know what truth IS. All that this kind of association means is that you are arbitrarily endowing something quite beyond your awareness with something YOU DO NOT WANT.

T 8 J 3. It is evident, then, that you are judging something of which you are totally unaware. You have set this strange situation up so that it IS COMPLETELY IMPOSSIBLE to escape from it WITHOUT a guide who DOES know what your reality is. The purpose of this Guide is merely to remind you of what YOU want. He is not attempting to force an alien will UPON you. He is merely making every possible effort, within the limits YOU impose upon Him, to RE-ESTABLISH your OWN will in your consciousness. You have IMPRISONED it in your UNconscious, where it remains available, but cannot help you. When we said that the Holy Spirit's function is to sort out the true from the false in your unconscious, we meant that He has the power to look into what YOU have T(378) C 205 hidden, and perceive the Will of God there.

T 8 J 4. His perception of this will can make it real to YOU, because HE is in your mind, and therefore He IS your reality. If, then, His perception OF your mind brings its reality TO you, He IS teaching you what you are. The only source of fear in this whole process can ONLY be WHAT YOU THINK YOU LOSE. But it is only what the Holy Spirit sees that you can possibly HAVE. We have emphasized many times that the Holy Spirit will never call upon you to sacrifice anything. But if you ask the sacrifice of reality OF YOURSELVES, the Holy Spirit MUST remind you that this is not God's will BECAUSE it is not yours.

T 8 J 5. There is NO DIFFERENCE between your will and God's. If you did not have divided wills, you would recognize that willing is salvation because it IS communication. It is impossible to communicate in alien tongues.[378] You and your Creator can communicate through creation, because that, and only that, IS your joint will. Divided wills do not communicate because they speak for different things TO THE SAME MIND. This loses the ability to communicate, simply because confused communication DOES NOT MEAN ANYTHING. A message cannot be said to be communicated UNLESS it makes sense.

T 8 J 6. How sensible can your messages be, when they ask for WHAT YOU DON'T WANT? Yet as long as you are afraid of your will, this is precisely what you WILL ask for. You may insist that the Holy Spirit does not answer you, but it might be wiser to consider the kind of asker you are. YOU DO NOT ASK ONLY FOR WHAT YOU WANT. This is SOLELY because you are afraid you might receive it, AND YOU WOULD. THIS is really why you persist in asking the teacher who could not possibly teach you your will. Of him, you can never learn it, and this gives you the illusion of safety. But you cannot be safe FROM truth, but only IN it. Reality is the ONLY safety.

T 8 J 7. Your will is your salvation BECAUSE IT IS THE SAME AS GOD's. The separation is nothing more than the belief that it is DIFFERENT. NO mind can believe that its will is STRONGER than God's. If, then, a mind believes that ITS will is different

---

[377] Matthew 5:48 "Ye therefore shall be perfect, as your heavenly Father is perfect."

[378] Genesis 11:1-9 Now the whole earth had one language and one speech. And it came to pass, as they journeyed from the east, that they found a plain in the land of Shinar, and they dwelt there. Then they said to one another, "Come, let us make bricks and bake them thoroughly." They had brick for stone, and they had asphalt for mortar. And they said, "Come, let us build ourselves a city, and a tower whose top is in the heavens; let us make a name for ourselves, lest we be scattered abroad over the face of the whole earth." But the LORD came down to see the city and the tower which the sons of men had built. And the LORD said, "Indeed the people are one and they all have one language, and this is what they begin to do; now nothing that they propose to do will be withheld from them. Come, let Us go down and there confuse their language, that they may not understand one another's speech." So the LORD scattered them abroad from there over the face of all the earth, and they ceased building the city. Therefore its name is called Babel, because there the LORD confused the language of all the earth; and from there the LORD scattered them abroad over the face of all the earth.

FROM His, it can only decide either that there IS no God, or that GOD'S WILL IS FEARFUL. The former accounts for the atheist, and the latter for the martyr. Martyrdom takes many forms, the category including ALL **T(379) C 206** doctrines which hold that God demands sacrifices of ANY kind.

T 8 J 8. Either basic type of insane decision will induce panic, because the atheist believes he is alone and the martyr believes that God is crucifying him. Both really fear both abandonment AND retaliation, but the former is more reactive against abandonment and the latter against retaliation. The atheist maintains that God has left him, but he does not care. He will, however, become very fearful, and hence very ANGRY, if anyone suggests that God has NOT left him. The martyr, on the other hand, is more aware of guilt, and believing that punishment is inevitable, attempts to teach himself to LIKE it.

T 8 J 9. The truth is, very simply, that NO-ONE WANTS EITHER ABANDONMENT OR RETALIATION. Many people SEEK both, but it is still true that they do NOT want it. Can you ask the Holy Spirit for "gifts" such as these, and actually expect to RECEIVE them? The Holy Spirit is totally incapable of giving YOU anything that does NOT come from God. His task is NOT to make anything FOR you. He CANNOT make you want something you DON'T want. When you ask the Universal Giver for what you do not want, YOU are asking for what CANNOT be given, BECAUSE IT WAS NEVER CREATED. It was never created because it was never your will for YOU.

T 8 J 10. Ultimately everyone must learn the will of God, because ultimately everyone must recognize HIMSELF. This recognition IS the recognition that HIS WILL AND GOD'S ARE ONE. In the presence of Truth, there are no unbelievers and no sacrifices. In the security of Reality fear is totally meaningless. To deny what IS can only SEEM to be fearful. Fear cannot be real without a cause, and GOD is the only Cause. God is Love,[379] and you DO want Him. This IS your will. Ask for THIS and you WILL be answered, because you will be asking only for what BELONGS to you. **T(380) C 207**

T 8 J 11. When you ask the Holy Spirit for what would hurt you, He CANNOT answer, because NOTHING can hurt you and SO YOU ARE ASKING FOR NOTHING. ANY desire which stems from the ego IS a desire for nothing, and to ask for it IS NOT A REQUEST. It is merely a denial in the FORM of a request. The Holy Spirit is not concerned with form at all, being aware only of MEANING. The ego cannot ask the Holy Spirit for ANYTHING, because there is COMPLETE COMMUNICATION FAILURE between them. But YOU can ask for EVERYTHING of the Holy Spirit, because YOUR requests are real, being of your will. Would the Holy Spirit deny the Will of God? And could He fail to recognize it in God's Sons?

T 8 J 12. The energy which you withdraw from Creation you expend on fear. This is not because your ENERGY is limited, but because YOU HAVE LIMITED IT. You do not recognize the ENORMOUS waste of energy which you expend in denying truth. What would YOU say of someone who PERSISTED in attempting the impossible, and believed that to ACHIEVE it is SUCCESS? The belief that you MUST HAVE THE IMPOSSIBLE in order to be happy is totally at variance with the principle of Creation. God COULD not will that happiness DEPENDED on what you could never have.

T 8 J 13. The fact that God is love does not require belief, but it DOES require ACCEPTANCE. It is indeed possible for you to DENY facts, although it is IMPOSSIBLE for you to CHANGE them. If you hold your hands over your eyes you will NOT see, because you are interfering with the laws of seeing. If you deny love

you will NOT KNOW IT because your cooperation is the LAW OF ITS BEING. You cannot change laws you did not make, and the laws of happiness were created FOR you, NOT BY you.

T 8 J 14. Attempts of any kind to deny what IS are fearful, and if they are strong they WILL induce panic. WILLING AGAINST reality, though impossible, can be MADE into a very persistent goal, EVEN THOUGH YOU DO NOT WANT IT. But consider the result of this strange decision. **T(381) C 208** You are DEVOTING your mind to what you DO NOT WANT. How real can this devotion be? If you do not want it, it was never created. If it was never created, it is nothing. Can you REALLY devote yourself to nothing?

T 8 J 15. God, in His devotion to YOU, created you devoted to EVERYTHING, and GAVE you what you are devoted TO. Otherwise, you would not have been created perfect. Reality IS everything, and you therefore have everything BECAUSE you are real. You cannot make the UNreal because the ABSENCE of reality is fearful, and fear cannot BE created. As long as you believe that fear is possible, YOU WILL NOT CREATE. Opposing orders of reality MAKE REALITY MEANINGLESS, and reality is MEANING.

T 8 J 16. Remember, then, that God's Will is ALREADY possible, and nothing else will EVER be. This is the simple acceptance of Reality because only this is real. You cannot DISTORT reality and KNOW WHAT IT IS. And if you DO distort reality you will experience anxiety, depression, and ultimately panic, because you are trying to MAKE YOURSELF UNREAL. When you feel these things do not try to look BEYOND yourself for truth, for truth can only be WITHIN you. Say, therefore, :

"Christ is in me, and where He is God MUST be, for Christ is PART of Him." **T(382) - 209 -**

T 8 K. The Answer to Prayer (*Notes* 828 7:160)

T 8 K 1. Everyone who has ever tried to use prayer to request something, has experienced what appears to be failure. This is not only true in connection with specific things which might be harmful, but also in connection with requests which are strictly in line with this course. The latter, in particular, might be incorrectly interpreted as "proof" that the course does not mean what it says. But you must remember that the course does state, and REPEATEDLY, that its purpose is the ESCAPE FROM FEAR.

T 8 K 2. Let us suppose, then, that what you request of the Holy Spirit IS what you really want, but that YOU ARE STILL AFRAID OF IT. Should this be the case, your ATTAINMENT of it would no longer BE what you want, even if IT is. This accounts for why CERTAIN SPECIFIC FORMS of healing are not achieved, even though the STATE of healing IS. It frequently happens that an individual asks for physical healing, because he is fearful OF BODILY HARM. However, at the same time, if he WERE healed physically, the threat to his thought-system would be considerably MORE fearful to him than its physical EXPRESSION. In this case, he is not really asking for RELEASE from fear, but for the removal of a symptom WHICH HE HAS SELECTED. This request is, therefore, NOT for healing at all.

T 8 K 3. The Bible emphasizes that ALL prayers are answered,[380] and this must be true, if no effort is wasted. The very fact that one has asked the Holy Spirit for ANYTHING, will ensure a response. But it is equally certain that no response, given by the Holy Spirit, will EVER be one which would INCREASE fear. It is even possible that His answer will not be heard at all. It is IMpossible, however,

---

[379] **1 John 4:8** He who does not love does not know God, for God is love. And we have known and believed the love that God has for us. God is love, and he who abides in love abides in God, and God in him. Also **1 John 4:16**

[380] **Matthew 21:22** "And whatever things you ask in prayer, believing, you will receive."
John 14:13 "And whatsoever ye shall ask in my name, that will I do, that the Father may be glorified in the Son."
John 15:16 "Ye did not choose me, but I chose you, and appointed you, that ye should go and bear fruit, and *that* your fruit should abide: that whatsoever ye shall ask of the Father in my name, he may give it you."

that it will be lost. There are many answers which you have already received, but have NOT YET HEARD. I assure you that they are waiting for you. It is indeed true that no effort is wasted. **T(383) - 210**

T 8 K 4. If you would know your prayers are answered, never doubt a Son of God. Do not question him, and do not confound him, for your faith in him is your faith in YOURSELF. If you would know God and His Answer, believe in me, whose faith in YOU cannot be shaken. Can you ask of the Holy Spirit truly, and doubt your brother? Believe his words are true, because of the truth which is in him. You will unite with the truth in him, and his words will BE true. As you hear him, you will hear me.

T 8 K 5. LISTENING to truth is the only way you can hear it now, and finally KNOW it. The message your brother gives you is UP TO YOU. What does he say to you? What would YOU have him say? Your decision ABOUT him determines the message YOU receive. Remember that the Holy Spirit is in him, and His Voice speaks to YOU through him. What can so holy a brother tell you EXCEPT truth? But are you LISTENING to it?

T 8 K 6. Your brother may not know who he is, but there is a Light in his mind which DOES know. This Light can shine[381] into yours, making HIS words true, and you ABLE TO HEAR THEM. His words ARE the Holy Spirit's answer to YOU. Is your faith in him strong enough to LET you listen and hear? Salvation is of your brother. The Holy Spirit extends from your mind to his, and answers YOU. You cannot hear the Voice for God in yourself alone, because you are NOT alone. And His answer is only for what you ARE.

T 8 K 7. You will not know the trust I have in you, unless you EXTEND it. You will not trust the guidance of the Holy Spirit, or believe that it is for YOU, unless you hear it in others. **T(384) -211** It MUST be for your brother, BECAUSE it is for you. Would God have created a Voice for you alone? Could you hear His answer EXCEPT as He answers ALL of God's Sons? Hear of your brother what you would have me hear of YOU, for you would not want ME to be deceived.

T 8 K 8. I love you for the truth in you, as GOD does. Your deceptions may deceive YOU, but they CANNOT deceive ME. Knowing what you ARE, I CANNOT doubt you. I hear only the Holy Spirit in you, Who speaks to me through YOU. If you would hear ME, hear my brothers, in whom God's Voice speaks. The answer to ALL your prayers lies in them. You will be answered as you HEAR THE ANSWER IN EVERYONE. Do not listen to anything else, or you will not hear truth.

T 8 K 9. Believe in your brothers BECAUSE I believe in you, and you will learn that my belief in you is justified. Believe in me BY believing in them, for the sake of what God gave them. THEY WILL ANSWER YOU, if you learn to ask truth of them. Do not ask for blessings without blessing THEM, for only in this way can YOU learn how blessed YOU are. By following this way, you ARE looking for the truth in YOU. This is not going BEYOND yourself, but TOWARD yourself. Hear only God's answer in His Sons, and YOU are answered.

T 8 K 10. To disbelieve is to side AGAINST, or to ATTACK. To believe is to accept, and SIDE WITH. To believe is not to be credulous, but to accept and APPRECIATE. What you do NOT believe you do NOT APPRECIATE, and you CANNOT be grateful for what you do not VALUE. There is a price you will pay for judgment, because judgment IS the setting of price. And as you set it, you WILL pay it. **T(385) 212 -**

T 8 K 11. If paying is equated with GETTING, you will set the PRICE low, but demand a high RETURN. But you will have forgotten that to price is to VALUE, so that YOUR return is IN PROPORTION TO YOUR JUDGMENT OF WORTH. If paying is associated with giving, IT CANNOT BE PERCEIVED AS LOSS, and the RECIPROCAL relationship of giving and RECEIVING will be recognized. The price will then be set high, because of the value of the RETURN.

T 8 K 12. To price for GETTING is to LOSE SIGHT OF VALUE, making it inevitable that you will NOT value what you receive. Valuing it little, you will not appreciate it, and you will not WANT it. Never forget, then, that YOU have set the value on what you receive, and have priced it BY what you give. To believe that it is possible to get much FOR little, is to believe that you can bargain with God.

T 8 K 13. God's laws are ALWAYS fair, and PERFECTLY consistent. BY giving, you receive. But to receive is to ACCEPT, NOT to get. It is impossible not to HAVE, but it IS possible NOT TO KNOW YOU HAVE. The recognition of HAVING is the willingness for GIVING, and ONLY by this willingness, can you RECOGNIZE what you have. What you give is therefore the value you put on what you have, being the exact measure of the value you PUT upon it.[382] And this, in turn, is the measure of HOW MUCH YOU WANT IT.

T 8 K 14. You can ASK of the Holy Spirit, then, ONLY by giving TO Him. And you can GIVE to Him only WHERE YOU SEE HIM. If you SEE Him in everyone, consider how much you will be asking OF Him, and HOW MUCH YOU WILL RECEIVE. He will deny you nothing, because you have denied Him nothing, and so you can SHARE EVERYTHING. This is the way, and the ONLY way, to have His answer, because His answer is all you can ask for and WANT. Say, then, to everyone,

"Because I will to know myself, I see you as God's Son and my brother." **T(386) -213**

---

[381] **Matthew 5:16** "Let your light so shine before men, that they may see your good works and glorify your Father in heaven."

[382] **Matthew 7:2** "For with what judgment you judge, you will be judged; and with the measure you use, it will be measured back to you."

Chapter 9 – The Correction of Error

T 9 A. Introduction (*Notes* 833 7:165)

T 9 A 1. The alertness of the ego to the errors which other egos make, is NOT the kind of vigilance which the Holy Spirit would have you maintain. Egos are critical in terms of the kind of sense they STAND FOR. THEY understand this kind of sense, because it IS sensible to them. To the Holy Spirit, it makes no sense at all. To the ego, it is kind and right and good to point out errors, and "correct" them. This makes PERFECT sense to the ego, which is TOTALLY unaware of what errors ARE, and what correction IS.

T 9 A 2. Errors ARE[383] the ego, and CORRECTION of errors of ANY kind lies solely in the RELINQUISHMENT of the ego. When you CORRECT a brother, you are telling him that he is WRONG. He may be making no sense at the time, and it is certain that if he is speaking from the ego, he WILL be making no sense, but your task is still to tell him HE IS RIGHT. You do not tell him this verbally if he is SPEAKING foolishly, because he needs correction AT ANOTHER LEVEL, since his error IS at another level. HE is still right, because he is a Son of God. His ego is ALWAYS wrong, no matter WHAT it says or does.

T 9 A 3. If you point out the errors of HIS ego, you MUST be seeing him through yours, because the Holy Spirit DOES NOT PERCEIVE HIS ERRORS. This MUST be true, if there is no communication AT ALL between the ego and the Holy Spirit. The ego makes NO sense, and the Holy Spirit does not attempt to understand ANYTHING that arises from it. Since He does not understand it, He DOES NOT JUDGE IT, KNOWING that nothing it engenders MEANS ANYTHING.

T 9 B. Sanity and Perception (*Notes* 834 7:167)

T 9 B 1. When you react AT ALL to errors, you are NOT LISTENING TO THE HOLY SPIRIT. He has merely disregarded them, and if you ATTEND to them, you are NOT HEARING HIM. If you do not hear HIM, you are listening to YOUR ego, and making as little sense as the brother whose errors you perceive. This CANNOT be correction. But it is more than merely lack of correction for him. It is the GIVING UP of correction in YOURSELF. **T(387) -214**

T 9 B 2. When a brother behaves insanely, you can heal him ONLY by perceiving the SANITY in him. If you perceive his errors and ACCEPT them, you are accepting YOURS. If you want to give YOURS over to the Holy Spirit, you must do this with HIS. Unless this becomes the ONE way in which you handle ALL errors, you cannot understand HOW ALL ERRORS ARE UNDONE. How is this different from telling you that what you teach you LEARN? Your brother is as right as you are. And if you think he is WRONG, you are condemning YOURSELF.

T 9 B 3. YOU cannot correct YOURSELF. Is it possible, then, for you to correct another? But you CAN see him truly, because it IS possible for you to see YOURSELF truly. It is not up to you to CHANGE him, but merely to accept him AS HE IS. His errors do not come from the truth that is in him, and ONLY this truth is yours. His errors cannot change this, and can have no effect at all on the truth in YOU.

T 9 B 4. To perceive errors in anyone, and to REACT to them AS IF THEY WERE REAL, is to MAKE them real to you. You will not escape paying the price for this, NOT because you are being PUNISHED for it, but because you are following the wrong guide, and will[384] lose your way. Your brother's errors are not of him, any more than yours are OF YOU. Accept his errors as real, and you have attacked YOURSELF. If you would find YOUR way AND KEEP IT, see only truth beside you, for you walk together.

T 9 B 5. The Holy Spirit in you forgives all things in you, AND your brother. HIS errors are forgiven WITH yours. Atonement is no more separate than love. It CANNOT be separate, because it COMES from Love. ANY attempt you make to correct a brother, means that you believe correction by YOU is possible, and this can ONLY be the arrogance of the ego. Correction is of God, Who does not know of arrogance. The Holy Spirit forgives everything, BECAUSE GOD CREATED EVERYTHING. Do not undertake HIS function, or you will forget YOURS. **T(388) -215**

T 9 B 6. Accept ONLY the function of healing in time, because that is what time is FOR. GOD gave you the function to create in eternity. You do not need to learn this. But you DO need to learn to WANT this, and for THIS all learning was made. This is the Holy Spirit's good use of an ability which you do not need, but which you HAVE made. Give it to Him; you do NOT know how to use it. He will teach you how to see YOURSELF without condemnation, by learning how to look on EVERYTHING without it. Condemnation will then not be real to you, and all YOUR errors WILL be forgiven.

T 9 C. Atonement as a Lesson in Sharing (*Notes* 838 7:170)

T 9 C 1. Atonement is for all, because it is the way to UNDO the belief that ANYTHING is for you ALONE. To forgive is to OVERLOOK. Look, then, BEYOND error, and do not let your perception rest UPON it, for you will believe what your perception HOLDS. Accept as true only what your brother IS, if you would know yourself. Perceive what he is NOT, and you CANNOT know what you are, BECAUSE you see HIM falsely. Remember always that your identity is shared, and that its sharing IS its reality.

T 9 C 2. You have a PART to play in the Atonement. But the plan of the Atonement IS beyond you. You do not know how to OVERLOOK errors, or you would not make them. It would merely be further error to think either that you do NOT make them, or that you can CORRECT them without a GUIDE TO CORRECTION. And if you do not FOLLOW this Guide,[385] your errors will NOT be corrected. The plan is not yours BECAUSE of your limited ideas about WHAT YOU ARE. But this limitation IS where ALL ERRORS ARISE. The way to UNDO them is, therefore, not OF you, but FOR you.

T 9 C 3. The Atonement is a lesson in sharing, which is given you because YOU HAVE FORGOTTEN HOW TO DO IT. The Holy Spirit merely reminds you of what is your NATURAL ability. By RE-INTERPRETING the ability to ATTACK, which you DID make, into the ability to SHARE, He TRANSLATES what you have made, into what God created. But if you would accomplish this THROUGH Him, you cannot look on your abilities through the eyes of the ego, or you will judge them as IT does. All their harmfulness lies in ITS judgment. **T(389) -216** All their HELPFULNESS lies in the judgment of the Holy Spirit.

T 9 C 4. The ego has a plan of forgiveness, because you are ASKING for one, but not of the right teacher. The EGO's plan, of course, MAKES NO SENSE and WILL NOT WORK. By following it, you will merely place yourself in an impossible situation, to which the ego ALWAYS leads you. Its plan is to have you SEE ERROR CLEARLY FIRST, and THEN overlook it. But how CAN you overlook what you have made real? By seeing it clearly, you HAVE made it real, and CANNOT overlook it.

---

[383] The *HLC* inserts the word "of" here, it is not in the *Ur* manuscript, nor is it in the *Notes*.
[384] The word "WiLL" is handwritten in. It is also present in the *Notes*.

[385] Originally it appears to have been typed with a lower case "g", and the capital is overwritten by hand. It is also capitalized in the *Notes*.

T 9 C 5. This is where the ego is forced into appealing to mysteries, and begins to insist that you accept the meaningless, to save yourself. Many have tried to do this in my name, forgetting that my words make PERFECT sense, because they come from GOD. They are as sensible now as they ever were, because they speak of ideas which are eternal. Forgiveness that is learned of ME does not use fear to UNDO fear. Nor does it make real the UNreal, and then destroy it.

T 9 C 6. Forgiveness through the Holy Spirit lies simply in looking beyond error from the beginning, and thus KEEPING it unreal for you. Do not let any belief in its realness[386] enter your minds AT ALL, or you will also believe that you must UNDO what you have made, in order to BE forgiven. What has no effect does not exist, and to the Holy Spirit, the effects of error are TOTALLY nonexistent. By steadily and consistently canceling out ALL its effects, EVERYWHERE AND IN ALL RESPECTS, He teaches that the ego does not exist, and PROVES IT. Follow His teaching in forgiveness, then, because forgiveness IS His function, and HE knows how to fulfill it perfectly. **T(390) -217** That is what we meant when we once said that miracles are NATURAL, and when they do NOT occur, something has gone wrong. Miracles are merely the sign of your willingness to follow HIS plan of Salvation, in recognition of the FACT that you do NOT know what it is. His work is NOT your function, and unless you accept this, you CANNOT learn what your function IS.

T 9 C 7. The confusion of functions is so typical of the ego, that you should be quite familiar with it by now. The ego believes that ALL functions belong to IT, even though it has no idea what they ARE. This is more than mere confusion. It is a particularly dangerous combination of grandiosity AND confusion, that makes it likely that the ego will attack anyone and anything, for no reason at all. This is exactly what it DOES. It is TOTALLY unpredictable in its responses, because it has no idea WHAT it heard.

T 9 C 8. If one has no idea what is happening, how appropriately can you EXPECT him to react? But you might still ask yourself, regardless of how you can ACCOUNT for the reactions, whether they place the ego in a very sound position as a guide for YOURS. It seems absurd to have to emphasize repeatedly that the ego's qualifications as a guide are singularly unfortunate, and that it is a remarkably poor choice as a teacher of salvation. Yet this question, ridiculous as it seems, is REALLY the crucial issue in the whole separation fantasy.

T 9 C 9. Anyone who elects a totally insane guide, MUST be totally insane himself. It is not true that you do not know the guide is insane. YOU know it because I know it, and you HAVE judged it by the same Standard as I have. The ego literally lives on borrowed time, and ITS days ARE numbered. Do not fear the last judgment,[387] but welcome it and do not wait, for the ego's time is **T(391) -218** borrowed from YOUR eternity. This IS the Second Coming,[388] which was made FOR you, as the First was created.

T 9 C 10. The Second Coming is merely the return of SENSE. Can this POSSIBLY be fearful? What can be fearful but fantasy, and no one turns to fantasy unless he despairs of satisfaction in reality. But it is CERTAIN that he will NEVER find satisfaction in fantasy, so

---

[386] "reality" probably should be substituted for "realness" but all later editors leave "realness" in place and the *Notes* also has this reading.
[387] Matthew 11:22 "But I say to you, it will be more tolerable for Tyre and Sidon in the day of judgment than for you."
And he charged us to preach unto the people, and to testify that this is he who is ordained of God *to be* the Judge of the living and the dead.
Acts 10:42-43 To him bear all the prophets witness, that through his name every one that believeth on him shall receive remission of sins.
[388] Matthew 16:27 "For the Son of Man will come in the glory of His Father with His angels, and then He will reward each according to his works."
Matthew 25:31 "When the Son of Man comes in His glory, and all the holy angels with Him, then He will sit on the throne of His glory."

---

that his ONLY hope is to change his mind about REALITY. Only if the decision that reality is fearful is WRONG, can GOD be right. And I ASSURE you that God IS right.

T 9 C 11. Be glad, then, that you HAVE been wrong, but this was only because you did not know who you WERE. Had you REMEMBERED, you could no more have been wrong than God can. The impossible can happen ONLY in fantasy. When you search for reality in fantasies, you will not find it. The symbols of fantasy are of the ego, and of THESE you will find many. But do not look for meaning in them. They have no more meaning than the fantasies into which they are woven.

T 9 C 12. Fairy tales can be pleasant or fearful, pretty or ugly, but NO ONE calls them TRUE. Children may believe them, and so, for a while, they ARE true for them. But when Reality dawns, they are gone. REALITY has NOT gone in the meanwhile. The[389] Second Coming is the <u>AWARENESS</u> of Reality, not its RETURN. Behold, my children, Reality is here. It belongs to you and me and God, and is perfectly satisfying to all of us. Only THIS awareness heals, because it is the awareness of truth. **T(392) -219**

T 9 D. The Unhealed Healer (*Notes* 846 7:178)

T 9 D 1. The ego's plan for forgiveness is far more widely used than God's. This is because it is undertaken by unhealed healers, and IS therefore of the ego. Let us consider the unhealed healer more carefully now. By definition, he is trying to GIVE what he has NOT received. If he is a theologian, he may begin with the premise, "I am a miserable sinner, and so are you." If he is a psychotherapist, he is more likely to start with the equally incredible idea that HE really believes in attack, and so does the patient, but it does not matter in EITHER case.

T 9 D 2. We have repeatedly stated that beliefs of the ego CANNOT be shared, and THIS IS WHY THEY ARE NOT REAL. How, then, can UNCOVERING them MAKE them real? Every healer who searches fantasies for truth MUST be unhealed, because he DOES NOT KNOW WHERE TO LOOK FOR TRUTH, and therefore does not have the answer to the problem of healing. There IS an advantage to bringing nightmares into awareness, but ONLY to teach that they are NOT real, and that ANYTHING they contain is meaningless. The unhealed healer cannot DO this, because he does not BELIEVE it.

T 9 D 3. All unhealed healers follow the ego's plan for forgiveness, in one form or another. If they are theologians, they are likely to condemn THEMSELVES, TEACH condemnation, and advocate a very fearful solution. Projecting condemnation onto God, they make Him retaliative, and FEAR HIS RETRIBUTION. What they have done is merely to IDENTIFY with the ego, and by perceiving clearly what IT does, condemn THEMSELVES because of this profound confusion.

T 9 D 4. It is understandable that there has been a revolt against this concept, but to revolt AGAINST it, is still to BELIEVE in it. The FORM of the revolt, then, is different, but NOT the content. **T(393) -220** The new form of the ego's plan is as unhelpful as the older one, because form does not matter to the Holy Spirit, and therefore DOES NOT MATTER AT ALL. According to the newer forms of the plan, the therapist interprets the ego's symbols IN the nightmare, and uses them to PROVE THE NIGHTMARE IS REAL. Having MADE it real, he then attempts to dispel its EFFECTS by <u>DEPRECIATING THE IMPORTANCE OF THE DREAMER.</u>

T 9 D 5. This WOULD be a healing approach, IF THE DREAMER were properly identified AS UNREAL. But if the dreamer is equated <u>WITH</u> the mind, the mind's corrective power, through the Holy Spirit, is DENIED. It is noteworthy that this is a contradiction even in the ego's own terms, and one which it usually DOES note,

---

[389] Several words are crossed out here and are illegible, but may have included "AWARENESS of reality." The *Notes* has it as it stands here.

even in its confusion. If the way to counteract fear is to reduce the importance of the FEARER, how can this build up ego STRENGTH? These perfectly self-evident inconsistencies account for why, except for certain stylized verbal accounts, NOBODY can EXPLAIN what happens in psychotherapy. Nothing real DOES.

T 9 D 6. Nothing REAL has happened to the unhealed healer, and HE LEARNS FROM HIS OWN TEACHING. BECAUSE his ego is involved, it ALWAYS attempts to gain some support from the situation. Seeking to GET something for HIMSELF, the healer does NOT know how to give, and consequently CANNOT SHARE. He CANNOT correct, because he is not working CORRECTIVELY. He believes that it is up to him to teach the patient what is REAL, but he does not know it HIMSELF.

T 9 D 7. What, then, SHOULD happen? When God said: "Let there be Light,"[390] there WAS light. Can you find light by ANALYZING darkness as the psychotherapist does, or like the theologian, by ACKNOWLEDGING it in yourself, and looking for a distant light to remove it, while emphasizing the distance? **T(394) -221**

T 9 D 8. Healing is NOT mysterious. Nothing occurs UNLESS you understand it, since light IS understanding. A "miserable sinner" cannot be healed without magic, nor can an "unimportant mind" esteem itself without magic. Both forms of the ego's approach, then, MUST arrive at an impasse, the characteristic "impossible situation" to which the ego ALWAYS leads.

T 9 D 9. It CAN be helpful to point out to a patient WHERE HE IS HEADING, but the point is LOST unless he can change his direction. The therapist cannot do this for him, but he also CANNOT DO THIS FOR HIMSELF. His only MEANINGFUL contribution is to present an example of one whose direction has been changed FOR him, and who NO LONGER BELIEVES IN NIGHTMARES OF ANY KIND. The light in HIS mind will therefore ANSWER the questioner, who MUST decide with God that there IS light BECAUSE HE SEES IT. And by HIS acknowledgment, THE THERAPIST KNOWS IT IS THERE.

T 9 D 10. That is how perception ultimately is translated into knowledge. The miracle-worker begins by PERCEIVING light, and translates HIS perception into sureness by continually extending it, and ACCEPTING ITS ACKNOWLEDGMENT. Its EFFECTS assure him IT IS THERE. The therapist does not heal; he LETS HEALING BE. HE can point to darkness, but he CANNOT bring light OF HIMSELF, for light is NOT of him. But being FOR him, it MUST be for his patient.

T 9 D 11. The Holy Spirit is the ONLY therapist. He makes healing PERFECTLY clear in ANY situation in which He is the guide.[391] The human therapist can only LET HIM FULFILL HIS FUNCTION. He needs no help for this. He WILL tell you EXACTLY what to do, to help ANYONE He sends to you FOR help, and will speak to him through you, IF YOU DO NOT INTERFERE. Remember that you **T(395) -222** ARE choosing a guide for helping, and the wrong choice will NOT help. But remember also that THE RIGHT ONE WILL. Trust Him, for help is His function, and He is of God.

T 9 D 12. As you awaken other minds TO Him through <u>HIM</u>, and not yourself, you will understand that you are not obeying the laws of this world, but that the laws you ARE obeying WORK. "The good is what works" is a sound though insufficient statement. ONLY the good CAN work. Nothing else works at all. This course is a guide to behavior. Being a very direct and very simple learning situation, it provides the guide who tells you what to do. If you do it, you will SEE that it works. Its RESULTS are more convincing than its words. THEY will convince you that the words are true.

T 9 D 13. By following the right Guide, you will learn the simplest of all lessons: "By their fruits ye shall know them,[392] and THEY shall know THEMSELVES." **T(396) 223**

T 9 E. The Awareness of the Holy Spirit (*Notes* 854 7:186)

T 9 E 1. How can you become increasingly aware of the Holy Spirit in you, EXCEPT by His EFFECTS? You cannot see Him with your eyes, nor hear Him with your ears. How, then, can you perceive Him at all?[393] If you INSPIRE joy, and others react to you WITH joy, even though you are not experiencing joy yourself, there must be SOMETHING IN YOU that IS CAPABLE OF PRODUCING IT. If it is in YOU, and CAN produce joy, and if you see that it DOES produce joy in others, you MUST be dissociating it in yourself.

T 9 E 2. It seems to you that the Holy Spirit does not produce joy consistently in you, ONLY because YOU DO NOT CONSISTENTLY AROUSE JOY IN OTHERS. Their reactions to you ARE your evaluations of His consistency. When you are inconsistent, you will not always GIVE RISE to joy, and so you will not always recognize HIS consistency. What you offer to your brother, you offer to Him,[394] because He cannot GO BEYOND your offering in HIS giving. This is NOT because HE limits His giving, but simply because YOU have limited your RECEIVING.

T 9 E 3. The will to receive is the will to accept. If your brothers ARE part of you, will you ACCEPT them? Only they can teach you what you are, and your learning is the result of what you taught THEM. What you call upon in them, you call upon in YOURSELF. And as you call upon it IN THEM, it becomes real to YOU. God has but one Son, knowing them all as One. Only God Himself is more than they, but they are not less than He is. Would you know what this means? If what you do to my brother you do to me,[395] and if you do everything for yourself because we are PART of you, everything WE do belongs to you as well. Every Soul God created is part of you, and shares His glory WITH you. **T(397) -224**[396]

T 9 E 4. His glory belongs to Him, but it is equally YOURS. You cannot, then, BE less glorious than He is. He is more than you ONLY because He CREATED you, but not even this would He keep from you. Therefore, you CAN create as He did, and YOUR dissociation WILL NOT ALTER THIS. Neither God's Light nor YOURS is dimmed because you do not see.

T 9 E 5. Because the Sonship MUST create as one, you remember creation whenever you recognize part of creation. Each part you remember adds to YOUR wholeness, because each part IS whole. Wholeness is indivisible, but you cannot learn YOUR wholeness, UNTIL YOU SEE IT EVERYWHERE. You can know yourself only as God knows His Son, for KNOWLEDGE is shared WITH God. When you awake in Him, you will know your magnitude by accepting HIS limitlessness as YOURS. But meanwhile, you will judge it as you judge your brothers', and will accept it as you accept theirs.

---

[390] **Genesis 1:3** Then God said, "Let there be light"; and there was light.
[391] This possibly should be capitalized, but it is not capitalized in the *Notes*.
[392] **Matthew 7:16- 20** "By their fruits ye shall know them. Do *men* gather grapes of thorns, or figs of thistles? Even so every good tree bringeth forth good fruit; but the corrupt tree bringeth forth evil fruit. A good tree cannot bring forth evil fruit, neither can a corrupt tree bring forth good fruit. Every tree that bringeth not forth good fruit is hewn down, and cast into the fire. Therefore by their fruits ye shall know them."
[393] *Urtext* manuscript obscured after "Him at al ..." The "I?" is reconstructed from the *Notes*..
[394] **Matthew 25:40** And the King will answer and say to them, "Assuredly, I say to you, inasmuch as you did it to one of the least of these My brethren, you did it to Me.'
[395] **Matthew 25:40** "And the King will answer and say to them, "Assuredly, I say to you, inasmuch as you did it to one of the least of these My brethren, you did it to Me."
[396] Paragraphation in doubt, it is not certain a new paragraph should begin here.

T 9 E 6. You are not yet awake, but you can learn HOW to awaken. Very simply the Holy Spirit teaches you to awaken others. As you see them waken, you will learn WHAT WAKING MEANS. And because you have willed to wake them, their gratitude, and their appreciation of what you have given them, will TEACH YOU ITS VALUE. THEY will become the witnesses to your reality, as YOU were created witnesses to God's. But when the Sonship COMES TOGETHER and accepts its oneness, it will be known by ITS creations, who witness to its reality, as the Son does to the Father.

T 9 E 7. Miracles have no place in eternity because they are reparative. But while you still need healing, your miracles are the only witnesses to your reality THAT YOU CAN RECOGNIZE. **T(398) - 225 -** You cannot perform a miracle FOR YOURSELF, because miracles are a way of GIVING ACCEPTANCE AND receiving it. In TIME, the giving comes FIRST, though they are simultaneous in eternity, where they cannot BE separated. When you have learned that they ARE the same, the need for time is over. Eternity is ONE time, its ONLY dimension being "always."

T 9 E 8. But this cannot mean anything to you, until you remember God's open arms, and finally know His open Mind. Like Him, YOU are ALWAYS, in His Mind, and with a mind like His. In your open mind are YOUR creations, in perfect communication, born of perfect understanding. Could you but accept one of them, you would not want ANYTHING the world has to offer. Everything else would be totally meaningless. God's meaning is incomplete without you, and you are incomplete without your creations.

T 9 E 9. Accept your brother in this world, and accept NOTHING ELSE, for in him you will find your creations, because he created them WITH you. You will never know that you are co-creator with God, until you learn that your brother is a co-creator with YOU.

T 9 F. Salvation and God's Will (*Notes* 858 7:190)

T 9 F 1. God's Will is your salvation. Would He not have given you the means to find it? If He wills you to HAVE it, He MUST have made it possible, and very easy to obtain it.

T 9 F 2. Your brothers are everywhere. You do not have to seek far for salvation. Every minute and every second gives you a chance to save YOURSELF. Do not lose these chances, NOT because they will not return, but because delay of joy is needless. God wills you perfect happiness NOW. Is it possible that this is not also YOUR will? And is it possible that this is not ALSO the will of your brothers? Consider, then, that in this joint will, you ARE all united, and IN THIS ONLY. There WILL be disagreement on anything ELSE, but NOT in this. This, then, is where peace ABIDES. And YOU abide in peace, when you so decide. **T(399) - 226 -**

T 9 F 3. But you cannot abide in peace unless you accept the Atonement, because the Atonement IS the way to peace. The reason is very simple, and so obvious that it is often overlooked. That is because the ego is AFRAID of the obvious, since obviousness is the essential characteristic of reality. You CANNOT overlook it, unless you are NOT LOOKING. It is PERFECTLY obvious that if the Holy Spirit looks with love on all He perceives, He looks with love on YOU. His EVALUATION of you is based on his[397] knowledge of what you ARE, and so He evaluates you truly. And this evaluation MUST be in your mind, because HE is.

T 9 F 4. The ego is also in your mind, because you have ACCEPTED it there. ITS evaluation of you, however, is the exact opposite of the Holy Spirit's, because the ego does NOT love you. It is unaware of what you are, and wholly mistrustful of EVERYTHING it perceives, because its own perceptions are so shifting. The ego is therefore capable of suspiciousness at best, and viciousness at worst. That is its range. It cannot exceed it, because of its uncertainty. And it can never go BEYOND it, because it can never BE certain.

---

[397] The pronoun "his" refers to the deity and should probably be capitalized. The *Notes* omits the word entirely.

T 9 F 5. You, then, have two conflicting evaluations of yourself in your minds, and they CANNOT BOTH BE TRUE. You do not yet realize how COMPLETELY different these evaluations are, because you do not understand how lofty the Holy Spirit's perception of you really is. He is not deceived by ANYTHING you do, because He NEVER forgets what you are. The ego is deceived by EVERYTHING you do, even when you respond to the Holy Spirit, because at such times ITS CONFUSION INCREASES. The ego is, therefore, particularly likely to attack you when you react lovingly, because it has evaluated you AS UNLOVING, and you are going AGAINST ITS JUDGMENT.

T 9 F 6. The ego will begin to ATTACK your motives as soon as they become clearly out of accord with its perception of you. This is when it will shift abruptly from suspiciousness to viciousness, because its uncertainty is **T(400) - 227** INCREASED. But it is surely pointless to attack in return. What can this mean, except that you are AGREEING with the ego's evaluation of what you are? If you are willing to see yourself as unloving, YOU WILL NOT BE HAPPY. You are condemning yourself, and MUST therefore regard yourself as inadequate.

T 9 F 7. Would you look to the ego to help you escape from a sense of inadequacy it has PRODUCED, and must MAINTAIN for its own existence? Can you ESCAPE from its evaluation of you, by using its methods for keeping this picture INTACT? You cannot evaluate an insane belief system from WITHIN it. Its own range precludes this. You can only GO BEYOND it, and look back from a point where SANITY exists, and SEE THE CONTRAST. Only BY this contrast, can insanity be judged as insane.

T 9 F 8. With the grandeur of God in you, you have chosen to be little, and lament your littleness. Within the system which DICTATED this choice, the lament IS inevitable. Your littleness is TAKEN FOR GRANTED there, and you do NOT ask who granted it. The question is meaningless WITHIN the ego's thought-system, because it OPENS THE WHOLE THOUGHT-SYSTEM TO QUESTION. We said before that the ego does not know what a real question is. Lack of knowledge of ANY kind is ALWAYS associated with UNWILLINGNESS to know, and produces a TOTAL lack of knowledge, simply because KNOWLEDGE is total. NOT to question your littleness is, therefore, to deny ALL knowledge, and keep the ego's WHOLE thought-system intact.

T 9 F 9. You cannot retain PART of a thought-system, because it can BE questioned only at its foundation. And this MUST be questioned from beyond it, because WITHIN it, its foundation DOES stand. The Holy Spirit judges against the reality of the ego's thought-system, merely because He knows its FOUNDATION is not true. Therefore, nothing that arises from it MEANS anything. The Holy Spirit judges every belief you hold in terms of where it comes from. If it comes from God, **T(401) -228** He knows it to be true. If it does not, He knows it is meaningless.

T 9 F 10. Whenever you question your value, say, "God Himself is incomplete without me." Remember this when the ego speaks, and you will not hear it. The truth about YOU is so lofty that nothing that is unworthy of God is worthy of you. Choose, then, what you want in these terms, and accept nothing that you would not offer to God as wholly fitting for HIM, for YOU do not want anything else. Return your part of Him, and He will give you all of Himself, in exchange for your return of what belongs to Him, and renders Him complete.

T 9 G. Grandeur versus Grandiosity (*Notes* 865 7:197)

T 9 G 1. Grandeur is of God, and ONLY of Him. Therefore, it is in you. Whenever you become aware of it, however dimly, you abandon the ego automatically, because in the presence of the grandeur of God, the meaninglessness of the ego becomes perfectly apparent. Though it does not understand this, the ego believes that its "enemy" has struck, and attempts to offer gifts to induce you to return to its protection. SELF-inflation is the only offering it can make. The grandiosity of the ego is its alternative to the grandeur of God. Which will you choose?

T 9 G 2. Grandiosity is ALWAYS a cover for despair. It is without hope, because it is not real. It is an attempt to COUNTERACT your littleness, based on the belief THAT THE LITTLENESS IS REAL. WITHOUT this belief, the grandiosity is meaningless, and you could not possibly WANT it. The essence of grandiosity is competitiveness, because it ALWAYS involves ATTACK. It is a delusional attempt to OUTDO, but NOT to UNdo. We said before that the ego vacillates between suspiciousness and viciousness. It remains suspicious as long as you DESPAIR of yourself. It shifts to viciousness whenever you will not tolerate self-debasement, and seek relief. Then it offers you the delusion of ATTACK as a solution. **T(402) - 229**

T 9 G 3. The ego does not know the difference between grandeur and grandiosity, because it does not know the difference between miracle-impulses and ego-alien beliefs of its own. We once said that the ego IS aware of threat, but does NOT make distinctions between two ENTIRELY different kinds of threat to its existence. Its own PROFOUND sense of vulnerability renders it incapable of judgment, EXCEPT in terms of attack. When it experiences threat, its ONLY decision is whether to attack NOW, or withdraw to attack later. If you ACCEPT its offer of grandiosity, it will attack immediately. If you do not, it will wait.

T 9 G 4. The ego is immobilized in the presence of God's grandeur, because HIS grandeur establishes YOUR freedom. Even the faintest hint of your reality literally drives the ego from your mind, because of the complete lack of investment in it. Grandeur is totally WITHOUT illusion, and because it is real, it is compellingly convincing. But the conviction of reality will not REMAIN with you, UNLESS YOU DO NOT ALLOW THE EGO TO ATTACK IT.

T 9 G 5. The ego will make every effort to recover, and mobilize its energies AGAINST your release. It will tell you that you are insane, and argue that grandeur CANNOT be a real part of you, because of the littleness in which IT believes. But your grandeur is NOT delusional, BECAUSE YOU DID NOT MAKE IT. YOU have made grandiosity, and are afraid of it, because it is a form of ATTACK. But your grandeur is of God, who created it out of His love. From your grandeur you can only bless, because your grandeur is your ABUNDANCE. By blessing you hold it in your minds, protecting it from illusions, and keeping yourself in the Mind of God.

T 9 G 6. Remember always that you cannot be anywhere EXCEPT in the Mind of God. When you FORGET this, you WILL despair, and you WILL attack. The ego depends SOLELY on your willingness to tolerate it. But if you are willing to look upon your grandeur, you CANNOT despair, and therefore you CANNOT want the ego. Your grandeur is God's ANSWER to the ego, because it is true. **T(403) -230** Littleness and grandeur cannot co-exist, nor is it possible for them to alternate in your awareness. Littleness and grandiosity can and MUST, since both are untrue, and therefore on the same level. Being the level of shift, it is experienced as shifting, and extremes are its essential characteristic.

T 9 G 7. But truth and littleness are DENIALS of each other, and grandeur IS truth. Truth does not vacillate; it is ALWAYS true. When grandeur slips away from you, YOU HAVE REPLACED IT WITH SOMETHING YOU HAVE MADE. Perhaps it is the belief in littleness; perhaps it is the belief in grandiosity. But it MUST be insane, because it is NOT TRUE. Your grandeur will NEVER deceive you, but your illusions ALWAYS will. Illusions ARE deceptions.

T 9 G 8. You CANNOT triumph, but you ARE exalted. And in your exalted state, you seek others like you, and rejoice with them. It is easy to distinguish grandeur from grandiosity, simply because love is returned, but pride is not. Pride will not produce miracles, and therefore will deprive you of the true witnesses to your reality. Truth is not obscure nor hidden, but its obviousness to YOU lies in the joy you bring to its witnesses, WHO SHOW IT TO YOU. They attest to your grandeur, but they cannot attest to pride because pride is not shared.

T 9 G 9. God WANTS you to behold what He created, because it is HIS joy. Can your grandeur be arrogant, when God HIMSELF witnesses to it? And what can be real that has NO witnesses? What good can come of it? And if no good can come of it, the Holy Spirit cannot use it. What He cannot TRANSFORM to the Will of God does not exist at all. Grandiosity is delusional because it is used to REPLACE your grandeur. Yet what God has created cannot BE replaced. **T(404) -231**

T 9 G 10. God is incomplete without you, simply because His grandeur is total, and you cannot BE missing from it. You are altogether irreplaceable in the Mind of God. No one else can fill your part of it, and while you leave your part of it empty, your eternal place merely waits for your return. God, through His Voice, reminds you of it, and God Himself keeps your extensions safe within it. But YOU do not know them, until you return TO them.

T 9 G 11. You CANNOT replace the Kingdom, and you cannot replace yourself. God, Who KNOWS your value, would not have it so, and so it is NOT so. Your value is in GOD's Mind, and therefore NOT in yours alone. To accept yourself as He created you CANNOT be arrogant, because it is the DENIAL of arrogance. To accept your littleness IS arrogant, because it means that you believe that YOUR evaluation of yourself is TRUER THAN GOD's. But if truth is indivisible, then YOUR evaluation of yourself MUST BE GOD's.

T 9 G 12. You did not ESTABLISH your value, and it needs no defense. NOTHING can attack it, or prevail over it. It does not vary. It merely IS. Ask the Holy Spirit WHAT it is, and He will tell you. But do not be afraid of His Answer, for it comes from God. It IS an exalted answer, because of its Source. But the Source is true, and so is its answer. Listen and do not question what you hear, for God does not deceive. He would have you replace the ego's belief in littleness with His own exalted answer to the question of your being, so that you can cease to question it, and KNOW it for what it IS. **T(405) - 232 -**

T 9 H. The Inclusiveness of Creation (*Notes* 873 7:205)

T 9 H 1. NOTHING beyond yourself can make you fearful or loving, because nothing IS beyond you. Time and eternity are both in your minds, and WILL conflict, until you perceive time SOLELY as a means to REGAIN eternity. You cannot do this, as long as you believe that ANYTHING that happens to you is caused by factors OUTSIDE yourself. You must learn that time is solely at YOUR disposal, and that nothing in the world can take this responsibility FROM you. You can VIOLATE God's laws in your imagination, but you cannot escape from them. They were established for your protection, and are as inviolate as your safety.

T 9 H 2. God created nothing beside you, and nothing beside you exists, for you are part of Him. What except Him CAN exist? Nothing BEYOND Him can happen, because nothing EXCEPT Him is real. YOUR creations add to Him, as YOU do. But nothing is added that is different, because everything has always BEEN. What can upset you except the ephemeral, and how can the ephemeral be real, if you are God's ONLY creation, and He created you eternal?

T 9 H 3. Your holy will establishes EVERYTHING that happens to you. Every response you make, to everything you perceive, is up to you, because your will DETERMINES your perception of it. God does not change His Mind about YOU, for He is not uncertain of HIMSELF. And what He knows CAN be known, because He does not know only for Himself. He CREATED you for Himself, but He gave you the power to create for YOUR self, so you would be LIKE Him. That is why your will is holy.

T 9 H 4. Can anything EXCEED the love of God? Can anything, then, exceed YOUR will? Nothing can reach you from BEYOND it, because being in God, YOU encompass everything. Believe this, and you will realize how much IS up to you. When ANYTHING threatens your peace of mind, ask yourself "Has God changed His Mind about me?" Then ACCEPT His decision, for it is indeed changeless, and refuse to change your mind about YOURSELF.
T(406) - 233 - God will never decide AGAINST you, or He would be deciding against Himself.

T 9 H 5. The reason you do not know YOUR creations is simply that you would decide against them, as long as your minds are split, and to attack what you have created is impossible. But remember that IT IS AS IMPOSSIBLE FOR GOD. The law of Creation is that you love your creations as yourself, BECAUSE THEY ARE PART OF YOU.[398] Everything that was created is therefore PERFECTLY safe, because the laws of God protect it by His love. Any part of your mind that does not know this, has banished itself from knowledge, because it has NOT MET ITS CONDITIONS.

T 9 H 6. Who could have done this but you? Recognize this gladly, for in this recognition lies the realization that your banishment is not of God,[399] and therefore does not exist. You are at home in God, dreaming of exile, but perfectly capable of awakening to Reality. Is it your will to do so? You know, from your own experience, that what you see in dreams you think is real, as long as you are asleep. But the instant you waken, you KNOW that everything that SEEMED to happen DID NOT HAPPEN AT ALL. You do not think this mysterious, even though ALL the laws of what you awake to WERE violated while you slept.

T 9 H 7. Is it not possible that you merely shifted from one dream to another without really wakening? Would you bother to reconcile what happened in conflicting DREAMS, or would you dismiss BOTH TOGETHER, if you discovered that REALITY is in accord with neither? You do not remember being awake. When you hear the Holy Spirit, you merely feel BETTER, because loving seems POSSIBLE to you. But you do NOT remember yet that it once was so, and it is in this remembering that you will know it can be so again.

T 9 H 8. What is possible has not yet been accomplished. But what has once been is so now, if it is eternal. When you remember, you will know what you remember IS eternal, and therefore is NOW.
T(407) - 234 -

T 9 H 9. You will remember everything the instant you DESIRE IT WHOLLY, for if to desire wholly is to create, you will have willed away the separation, returning your mind simultaneously to your Creator and your creations. Knowing them, you will have no wish to sleep, but only the will to waken and be glad. Dreams will be impossible, because you will WANT only truth, and being at last your will, it will be yours.

T 9 I. The Decision to Forget (*Notes* 877 7:210)

T 9 I 1. Unless you KNOW something, you CANNOT dissociate it. Knowledge therefore PRECEDES dissociation, and dissociation is nothing more than a DECISION TO FORGET. What has been FORGOTTEN then appears to be fearful, but ONLY because the dissociation was an ATTACK ON TRUTH. You are fearful BE-CAUSE you have forgotten. And you have REPLACED your knowledge by an awareness of dreams, BECAUSE YOU ARE AFRAID OF YOUR DISSOCIATION, NOT of what you have dissociated. Even in this world's therapy, when dissociated material is ACCEPTED, it ceases to be fearful, for the laws of mind always hold.

T 9 I 2. But to give up the dissociation of REALITY brings more than merely lack of fear. In THIS decision lie joy, and peace, and the glory of creation. Offer the Holy Spirit only your will to remember, for He retains the knowledge of God and of you FOR you, waiting for your acceptance. Give up gladly EVERYTHING that would stand in the way of your remembering, for God is in your memory, and His Voice will tell you that you are part of Him when you are willing to remember Him and know your own reality again. Let nothing in this world delay your remembering of Him, for in this remembering is the knowledge of YOURSELF.

T 9 I 3. To remember is merely to restore to your mind WHAT IS ALREADY THERE. You do not make what you remember; you merely accept again what has BEEN made AND REJECTED. The ability to ACCEPT truth in this world is the perceptual counterpart of creating in the Kingdom. God WILL do His part **T(408) - 235 -** if you will do yours, and HIS return in exchange for yours IS the exchange of knowledge for perception. NOTHING is beyond His will for you. But signify your will to remember Him, and behold! He will give you everything but for your asking.

T 9 I 4. Whenever you attack, you are denying YOURSELF. You are specifically teaching yourself that you are NOT what you are. YOUR denial of reality precludes ACCEPTANCE of God's gift, BECAUSE YOU HAVE ACCEPTED SOMETHING ELSE IN ITS PLACE. If you understand that the misuse of defenses always constitutes an attack on truth, and truth is God, you will realize why this is ALWAYS fearful. If you further recognize that you are PART of God, you will also understand why it is that YOU ALWAYS ATTACK YOURSELF FIRST.

T 9 I 5. ALL attack is self attack. It cannot BE anything else. Arising from your OWN decision NOT to be what you ARE, IT IS AN ATTACK ON YOUR IDENTIFICATION. Attack is thus the way in which your identification is lost, because, when you attack, you MUST have forgotten what you are. And if your reality is God's, when YOU attack, you are not remembering HIM. This is not because He is gone, but because you are ACTIVELY WILLING NOT TO REMEMBER HIM.

T 9 I 6. If you realized the complete havoc this makes of your peace of mind, you COULD not make such an insane decision. You make it only because you still believe that it can GET YOU SOMETHING YOU WANT. It follows, then, that you want something OTHER than peace of mind, and you have not considered what it must be. Yet the logical outcome of your decision is perfectly clear, if you will LOOK at it. By deciding AGAINST your reality, you have made yourself vigilant AGAINST God and His Kingdom. And it is THIS vigilance that makes you afraid to remember Him. **T(409) - 236 -**

T 9 I 7. You have NOT attacked God, and you DO love Him. Can you change your reality? No-one can will to destroy himself. When you think you are attacking your SELF, it is a sure sign that you hate what you think you are. And this, and ONLY this, can BE attacked by you. What you THINK you are CAN be hateful, and what this strange image makes you do can be very destructive. The destruction is no more real than the image, but those who make idols DO worship them. The idols are nothing, but their worshippers are the Sons of God in sickness.

T 9 I 8. God would have them released from their sickness, and returned to His Mind. He will not limit your power to help them, because He has given it TO you. Do not be afraid of it, because it is

---

[398] **Leviticus 19:18** You shall not take vengeance, nor bear any grudge against the children of your people, but you shall love your neighbor as yourself: I am the LORD.
[399] **Genesis 3:23-24** Therefore the LORD God sent him out of the garden of Eden to till the ground from which he was taken. So He drove out the man; and He placed cherubim at the east of the garden of Eden, and a flaming sword which turned every way, to guard the way to the tree of life.

Chapter 9 – The Correction of Error

your salvation. What Comforter[400] can there be for the sick children of God except His power through YOU? Remember that it does not matter where in the Sonship He is accepted. He is ALWAYS accepted for all, and when your mind receives Him, the remembrance of Him awakens throughout the Sonship.

T 9 I 9. Heal your brothers simply by accepting God FOR them. Your minds are not separate, and God has only one channel for healing, because He has but one Son. His remaining communication link with all His Children joins them together, and them to Him. To be aware of this is to heal them, because it is the awareness that no one is separate, and so no one is sick. To believe that a Son of God can be sick is to believe that PART OF GOD CAN SUFFER.

T 9 I 0. Love CANNOT suffer, because it cannot attack. The remembrance of love therefore brings invulnerability with it. Do not side with sickness in the presence of a Son of God, even if HE believes in it, for YOUR acceptance of God in him ACKNOWLEDGES the love of God which he has forgotten. Your recognition of him as PART OF GOD teaches him the truth about himself, WHICH HE IS DENYING. Would you STRENGTHEN his denial of God, and thus lose sight of YOURSELF? Or would you remind him of his wholeness, and remember your Creator WITH him?

T 9 I 11. To believe a Son of God is sick is to worship the same idol he does. God created love, NOT idolatry. ALL forms of idolatry are caricatures of **T(410) - 237 -** creation, taught by sick minds, who are too divided to know that Creation SHARES power, and NEVER usurps it. Sickness is idolatry, because it is the belief that POWER CAN BE TAKEN FROM YOU. But this is impossible, because you are part of God, Who IS all power. A sick god MUST be an idol, made in the image of what its maker thinks HE is. And that is exactly what the ego DOES perceive in a Son of God; -- a sick god, self-created, self-sufficient, very vicious, and very vulnerable.

T 9 I 12. Is this the idol you would worship? Is this the image you would be vigilant to SAVE? Are you REALLY afraid of losing THIS? Look calmly at the logical conclusion of the ego's thought-system, and judge whether its offering is really what you want, for this IS what it offers you. To obtain THIS, you are willing to attack the Divinity of your brothers, and thus lose sight of YOURS. And you are willing to keep it hidden, to protect this idol, which you think will save you from dangers WHICH THE IDOL ITSELF STANDS FOR, but which do not exist.

T 9 I 13. There are no idolaters in the Kingdom, but there is great appreciation for every Soul which God created, because of the calm knowledge that each one is part of Him. God's Son knows no idols, but He DOES know His Father. Health in this world is the counterpart of value in Heaven. It is not my merit that I contribute to you, but my love, for you do not value yourselves. When you do not value yourself you become sick, but MY value of you can heal you, because the value of God's Son is one.

T 9 I 14. When I said, "my peace I give unto you,"[401] I meant it. Peace came from God through me to YOU. It was FOR you, but you did not ask. When a brother is sick, it is because HE IS NOT ASKING FOR PEACE, and therefore he does not know he HAS it. The ACCEPTANCE of peace is the denial of illusion, and sickness IS an illusion. Yet every Son of God has the power to deny illusions ANYWHERE in the Kingdom, merely by denying them completely in himself.

T 9 I 15. I CAN heal you, because I KNOW you. I know your value FOR you, and it is this value that makes you whole. A whole mind is not idolatrous, and does not know of conflicting laws. I will heal you merely because I have only **T(411) - 238 -** ONE message, and it is true. Your faith in it will make you whole,[402] when you have faith in me. I do not bring God's message with deception, and you will learn this as you learn that you ALWAYS receive as much as you ACCEPT. You could accept peace NOW, for everyone you meet, and offer them perfect freedom from ALL illusions, BECAUSE YOU HEARD. But have no other gods before Him,[403] or you will NOT hear.

T 9 I 16. God is not jealous[404] of the gods you make, but YOU are. You would save them and serve them, because you believe that THEY MADE YOU. You think they are your father, because you are projecting onto them the fearful fact that YOU MADE THEM TO REPLACE GOD. But when they seem to speak to you, remember that NOTHING can replace God, and whatever replacements you have attempted ARE nothing. Very simply, then, you may BELIEVE you are afraid of nothingNESS, but you are REALLY afraid of NOTHING. And in THAT awareness you ARE healed.

T 9 I 17. You WILL hear the god you listen to. You MADE the god of sickness, and BY making him, you made yourself ABLE to hear him. But you did NOT create him, because he is NOT the Will of the Father. He is therefore not eternal, and will be UNmade for you, the instant you signify your willingness to accept ONLY the eternal. If God has but one Son, there is but one God. You share reality with Him, BECAUSE reality is not divided. To accept other gods before Him, is to place other images before YOURSELF. You do not realize how much you listen to your gods, and how vigilant you are on their behalf. But they exist only because you honor them.

T 9 I 18. Place honor where it is due, and peace WILL be yours. It is your inheritance from your REAL Father. You cannot make your father, and the father you made did NOT make you. Honor is not due to illusions, for to honor them is to honor nothing. But fear is not due them either, for nothing cannot be fearful. You have chosen to fear love BECAUSE of its perfect harmlessness. And because of this fear, you have been willing to give up your own perfect helpfulness, and your own perfect Help. Only at the altar of God will you find peace, and this altar is in you, because God put it there. His Voice still calls **T(412) - 239 -** you to return, and He will be heard, when you place no other gods before Him.

T 9 I 19. You can give up the god of sickness for your brothers; in fact, you would HAVE to do so, if you give him up for yourself. For if you see him anywhere, YOU are accepting him. And if you accept him, you WILL bow down and worship him, because HE WAS MADE AS GOD's REPLACEMENT. He is the belief that YOU CAN CHOOSE WHICH GOD IS REAL. Although it is perfectly clear that this has nothing to do with REALITY, it is equally clear that it has EVERYTHING to do with REALITY AS YOU PERCEIVE IT.[405]

T 9 J. Magic versus Miracles (*Notes* 890 7:221)

T 9 J 1. All magic is a form of reconciling the irreconcilable. All religion is the recognition that the irreconcilable cannot BE reconciled.

T 9 J 2. Sickness and perfection ARE irreconcilable. If God created you perfect, you ARE perfect. If you believe you can be sick, you HAVE placed other gods before Him. GOD is not at war with the god of sickness which you made, but YOU are. He is the symbol of willing AGAINST God, and you are afraid of him BECAUSE he cannot be reconciled with God's will. If you ATTACK him, you

---

[400] **John 14:16** "And I will pray the Father, and He will give you another Helper, that He may abide with you forever."
[401] **John 14:27** "Peace I leave with you, My peace I give to you; not as the world gives do I give to you. Let not your heart be troubled, neither let it be afraid."

[402] **Matthew 9:22** But Jesus turned around, and when He saw her He said, "Be of good cheer, daughter; your faith has made you whole." And the woman was made well from that hour.
[403] **Exodus 20:3** You shall have no other gods before Me.
[404] **Exodus 20:5** You shall not bow down to them nor serve them. For I, the LORD your God, am a jealous God, visiting the iniquity of the fathers upon the children to the third and fourth generations of those who hate Me,
[405] [split paragraph]

will make him real to you. But if you refuse to worship him, in whatever form he may appear to you, and wherever you think you see him, he will disappear into the nothingness out of which he was made.

T 9 J 3. Reality can dawn only in an unclouded mind. It is always THERE, to BE accepted, but its acceptance depends on your WILLINGNESS TO HAVE IT. To know reality MUST involve the willingness to judge Unreality FOR WHAT IT IS. This is the RIGHT use of selective perception. To overlook nothingness is merely to judge it correctly, and because of your ability to evaluate it truly, to LET IT GO. Knowledge cannot dawn on a mind full of illusions, because truth and illusions are irreconcilable. Truth is whole, and CANNOT be known by PART of a mind.

T 9 J 4. The Sonship cannot be perceived as PARTLY sick, because to perceive it that way, is not to perceive it at all. If the Sonship is ONE, it is one in ALL respects. ONENESS CANNOT BE DIVIDED. If you perceive other gods, YOUR mind is split, and you will not be able to LIMIT the split, because the split IS the **T(413) - 240** - sign that you have removed part of your mind from God's Will, and this MEANS that it is out of control. To be out of control is to be out of REASON, and the mind DOES become unreasonable without reason. This is merely a matter of DEFINITION. By DEFINING the mind wrongly, you perceive it as FUNCTIONING wrongly.

T 9 J 5. God's laws will keep your minds at peace, because peace IS His Will, and His laws are established to uphold it. His are the laws of freedom, but yours are the laws of bondage. Since freedom and bondage are irreconcilable, their laws CANNOT BE UNDERSTOOD TOGETHER. The laws of God work only for your good, and there ARE no other laws beside His. Everything else is merely lawLESS, and therefore chaotic. But God Himself has protected EVERYTHING He created BY His laws. Therefore, everything that is not under them does not exist.

T 9 J 6. "Laws of chaos" are meaningless, by definition. Creation is perfectly lawful, and the chaotic is without meaning, BECAUSE IT IS WITHOUT GOD. You have given your peace to the gods you made, but they are not there to take it FROM you, and you are NOT able to give it TO them. You are NOT free to give up freedom, but only to DENY it. YOU CANNOT DO WHAT GOD DID NOT INTEND, because what He did not intend DOES NOT HAPPEN. Your gods do not BRING chaos; you are ENDOWING them with chaos, and accepting it OF them.

T 9 J 7. All this has never been. Nothing but the laws of God has ever operated, and nothing except His Will will ever be. You were created through His laws and by His Will, and the manner of your creation established you AS CREATORS. What you have made is so unworthy of you, that you could hardly want it, IF YOU WERE WILLING TO SEE IT AS IT IS. You will see nothing at all. And your vision will AUTOMATICALLY look beyond it, to what is IN you, and all AROUND you. Reality cannot BREAK THROUGH the obstructions you interpose, but it WILL envelop you completely, WHEN YOU LET THEM GO.

T 9 J 8. When you have experienced the protection of God, the making of idols becomes inconceivable. There are no strange images in the Mind of God, and what is not in His Mind CANNOT be in yours, because you are of One Mind, and that Mind **T(414) - 241** - belongs to HIM. It is yours BECAUSE it belongs to Him, for ownership is sharing to Him. And if it is so for Him, it is so for you. His definitions ARE His laws, for by them He established the universe as what it is. No false gods you attempt to interpose between yourself and your reality, affect truth at all. Peace is yours because God created you. And He created nothing else.

T 9 J 9. The miracle is the act of a Son of God who has laid aside all false gods, and who calls on his brothers to do likewise. It is an act of faith, because it is the recognition that his brother CAN do it. It is

a call to the Holy Spirit in his mind, a call to Him which is strengthened by this joining. Because the miracle-worker has heard Him, he strengthens His Voice in a sick brother by weakening his belief in sickness, which he does NOT share. The power of one mind CAN shine into another, because all the lamps of God were lit by the same spark. It is everywhere, and it is eternal.

T 9 J 10. In many, only the spark remains, for the great rays are obscured. But God has kept the spark alive, so the rays can never be completely forgotten. If you but see the little spark, you will learn of the greater light, for the rays are there unseen. Perceiving the spark will heal, but knowing the Light will create. Yet in the returning, the little light must be acknowledged first, for the separation was a descent from magnitude to littleness. But the spark is still as pure as the Great Light, because it is the remaining call of Creation. Put all your faith in it, and God Himself will answer you. **T(415) - 242 -**

T 9 K. The Denial of God (*Notes 899 8:3*)

T 9 K 1. The rituals of the god of sickness are strange and very demanding. Joy is never permitted, for depression is the sign of allegiance to him. Depression MEANS that you have foresworn God. Men are afraid of blasphemy, but they do not know what it means. They do not realize that, to deny God, is to deny their own identity, and in this sense, the wages of sin IS death.[406] The sense is very literal; -- denial of Life perceives its opposite, as ALL forms of denial replace what IS, with what is NOT. No-one can really DO this, but that you can THINK you can, and BELIEVE YOU HAVE, is beyond dispute.

T 9 K 2. Do not forget, however, that to deny God will inevitably result in projection, and you will believe that others, AND NOT YOURSELF, have done this TO you. You WILL receive the message you give, because it is the message you WANT. You may believe that you judge your brothers by the messages they give YOU, but you HAVE judged them by the message you give THEM. Do not attribute your denial of joy to them, or you cannot see the spark in them, that could bring joy to YOU. It is the DENIAL of the spark that brings depression, and whenever you see your brothers WITHOUT it, you ARE denying God.

T 9 K 3. Allegiance to the denial of God is the ego's religion. The god of sickness obviously demands the denial of health, because health is in direct opposition to its own survival. But consider what this means to YOU. UNLESS you are sick you cannot keep the gods you made, for only in sickness could you possibly WANT them. Blasphemy, then, is SELF-destructive, not God destructive. It means that you are willing NOT to know yourself, IN ORDER to be sick. This IS the offering which your god demands, because having made him out of YOUR insanity, he IS an insane idea. He has many forms, but though he may seem like many different things, he is but one idea;-- the denial of God.

T 9 K 4. Sickness and death entered the mind of God's Son against His Will. The "attack on God" made His Son think he was fatherless, and out of his **T(416) - 243** - depression he made the god of depression. This was his alternative to joy, because he would not accept the fact that, although he was a creator, he had been created. Yet the Son IS helpless without the Father, Who alone IS his Help.[407] We said before that of yourselves you can do nothing,[408]

---

[406] **Romans 6:23** For the wages of sin is death, but the gift of God is eternal life in Christ Jesus our Lord.
[407] **Psalm 121:2** My help comes from the LORD, Who made heaven and earth.
[408] **John 5:19** Then Jesus answered and said to them, "Most assuredly, I say to you, the Son can do nothing of Himself, but what He sees the Father do; for whatever He does, the Son also does in like manner."
John 5:30 "I can of Myself do nothing. As I hear, I judge; and My judgment is righteous, because I do not seek My own will but the will of the Father who sent Me."

but you are not OF yourselves. If you were, what you have made would be true, and you could never escape.

T 9 K 5. It is BECAUSE you did not make yourselves, that you need be troubled by nothing.[409] Your gods are nothing, because your Father did not create them. You cannot make creators who are unlike your Creator, any more than He could have created a Son who was unlike Him. If creation is sharing, it cannot create what is unlike itself. It can share only what it IS. Depression is isolation, and so it could not have BEEN created.

T 9 K 6. Son of God, you have not sinned, but you have been much mistaken. But this can be corrected, and God will help you, knowing that you could not sin against Him. You denied Him BECAUSE you loved Him, knowing that if you RECOGNIZED your love for Him, you COULD not deny Him. Your denial therefore MEANS that you love Him, and THAT YOU KNOW HE LOVES YOU. Remember that what you deny you MUST have known. And if you can accept denial, YOU CAN ACCEPT ITS UNDOING.

T 9 K 7. Your Father has not denied you. He does not retaliate, but He DOES call to you to return. When you think He has not answered your call, YOU HAVE NOT ANSWERED HIS. He calls to you from every part of the Sonship, because of His love for His Son. If you hear His message, He HAS answered you, and you will learn what you are of Him, if you hear aright. The love of God is in everything He created, for His Son is everywhere. Look with peace upon your brothers, and God will come rushing into your heart, in gratitude for your gift to Him.

T 9 K 8. Do not look to the god of sickness for healing, but only to the God of love, for healing is the acknowledgment of Him. When you acknowledge Him, you will KNOW that He has never ceased to acknowledge you, and that in **T(417) - 244 -** His acknowledgment OF you lies your Being. You are not sick, and you cannot die. But you CAN confuse your self with things that do. Remember, though, that to do this IS blasphemy, for it means that you are looking without love on God and His Creation, from which He cannot be separated. Only the eternal can be loved, for love does not die. What is of God is His forever, and you ARE of God. Would He allow Himself to suffer? And would He offer His Son anything that is not acceptable to Him?

T 9 K 9. If you will accept yourself as God created you, you will be incapable of suffering. But to do this, you must acknowledge Him as your Creator. This is not because you will be punished otherwise. It is merely because your acknowledgment of your Father IS the acknowledgment of yourself as you ARE. Your Father created you Wholly without sin, wholly without pain, and wholly without suffering of any kind. If you deny Him, you bring sin, pain, and suffering into your OWN mind, because of the power He gave it. Your mind is capable of creating worlds, but it can also DENY what it creates, because it is free.

---
[409] **John 14:1** "Let not your heart be troubled; you believe in God, believe also in Me."

T 9 K 10. You do not realize how much you have denied yourself, and how much God, in His love, would not have it so. Yet He would not interfere with you, because He would not know His Son if he were not free. To interfere with you would be to attack HIMSELF, and God is not insane. When you denied HIM, you WERE insane. Would you have Him SHARE your insanity? God will never cease to love His Son, and His Son will never cease to love Him. That was the condition of His Son's Creation, fixed forever in the Mind of God. To know that is sanity. To deny it is insanity. God gave HIMSELF to you in your Creation, and His gifts ARE eternal. Would you deny yourself to Him?

T 9 K 11. Out of your gifts to Him, the Kingdom will be restored to His Son. His Son removed himself from His gift by refusing to accept what had been created FOR him, and what he himself had created in the name of His Father. Heaven waits for his return, for it was created as the dwelling place of God's Son. You are not at home anywhere else, or in any other condition. Do not deny yourself the joy which was created FOR you, for the misery you have made for yourselves. God has given you the means for undoing what you have made. Listen, and you WILL learn what you are. **T(418) -245**

T 9 K 12. If God knows His children as wholly sinless, it is blasphemous to perceive them as guilty. If God knows His children as wholly without pain, it is blasphemous to perceive suffering anywhere. If God knows his children to be wholly joyous, it is blasphemous to feel depressed. All these illusions, and the many other forms which blasphemy may take, are REFUSALS TO ACCEPT CREATION AS IT IS. If God created His Son perfect, that is how you must learn to see him, to learn of his reality. And as part of the Sonship, THAT IS HOW YOU MUST SEE YOURSELF TO LEARN YOURS.

T 9 K 13. Do not perceive ANYTHING God did not create, or you ARE denying Him. His is the ONLY Fatherhood, and it is yours only because HE has given it to you. Your gifts to YOURSELF are meaningless, but your gifts to YOUR creations are like His, because they are given in His Name. That is why your creations are as real as His. But the real Fatherhood must be acknowledged, if the real Son is to be known. You believe that the sick things which you have made are your real creations, because you believe that the sick images you perceive are the Sons of God.

T 9 K 14. Only if you ACCEPT the Fatherhood of God will you have anything, because His Fatherhood GAVE you everything. That is why to deny Him IS to deny yourself. Arrogance is the denial of love, because love shares and arrogance withholds. As long as both appear to you to be desirable, the concept of choice, which is not of God, will remain with you. While this is not true in Eternity, it IS true in time, so that, while time lasts in YOUR minds, there WILL be choices. Time itself WAS your choice. If you would remember Eternity, you must learn to look on only the Eternal. If you allow yourselves to become preoccupied with the temporal, you are LIVING IN TIME. As always, your choice is determined by what you value. Time and Eternity cannot both be real, because they contradict each other. If you will accept only what is timeless as real, you will begin to understand Eternity, and make it yours. **T(419) - 246 -**

Chapter 10 – God and the Ego

T 10 A. Introduction (*Notes* 909 8:13)

T 10 A 1. Either God or the ego is insane. If you will examine the evidence ON BOTH SIDES fairly, you will realize that this MUST be true. Neither God nor the ego proposes a partial thought system. Each is internally consistent, but they are diametrically opposed in all respects, so that partial allegiance is impossible. But remember that their results are as different as their foundations, and their fundamentally irreconcilable natures CANNOT be resolved by YOUR vacillations. Nothing alive is fatherless, for life is creation. Therefore, your decision is always an answer to the question, "Who is my father?" And you WILL be faithful to the father you choose.

T 10 A 2. Yet what would you say to someone who REALLY believed this question involves conflict? If YOU made the ego, how can the ego have made YOU? The authority problem remains the ONLY source of perceived conflict, because the ego was MADE out of the wish of God's Son to father HIM. The ego, then, is nothing more than a delusional system in which YOU MADE YOUR OWN FATHER. Make no mistake about this. It sounds insane when it is stated with perfect honesty, but the ego never looks upon what it does with perfect honesty. Yet that IS its insane premise, which is carefully hidden in the dark cornerstone of its thought system. And either the ego, which you made, IS your father, or its whole thought system will not stand.

T 10 B. Projection versus Extension (*Notes* 911 8:15)

T 10 B 1. You have made by projection, but God has created by extension. The cornerstone of God's creation is YOU, for HIS thought system is light. Remember the rays that are there unseen. The more you approach the center of HIS thought system, the clearer the light becomes. The closer you come to the foundation of the ego's thought system, the darker and more obscure becomes the way. But even the little spark in your mind is enough to lighten it. Bring this light fearlessly with you, and hold it up to the foundation of the ego's thought system bravely. Be willing to judge it with perfect honesty. Open the dark stone of terror on which it rests, and bring it out into the light. There you will see that it rests on meaninglessness, and that everything of which you have been afraid was based on nothing. **T(420) - 247 -**

T 10 B 2. My brother, you are part of God and part of me. When you have at last looked at the ego's foundation without shrinking, you will also have looked upon ours. I come to you from our Father, to offer you everything again. Do not refuse it to keep a dark cornerstone hidden, for ITS protection will not save you. I GIVE you the lamp, and I will go with you. You will not take this journey alone. I will lead you to your true Father, Who hath need of you, as I have. Will you not answer the call of love with joy?

T 10 B 3. You HAVE learned your need of healing. Would you bring anything[410] ELSE to the Sonship, KNOWING your need of it for yourself? For in this lies the beginning of knowledge; the foundation on which God will help you build again the thought system which you share WITH Him. Not one stone you place upon it but will be blessed by Him. For you will be restoring the holy dwelling place of His Son, where He wills His Son to be, and where he IS. In whatever part of the mind of God's Son you restore this reality, you restore it to YOURSELF. For you dwell in the Mind of God WITH your brother, for God Himself did not will to be alone. **T(421) - 248 -**[411]

T 10 B 4. To be alone is to be separated from Infinity, but how can this be, if Infinity has no end? No-one can BE beyond the limitless, because what has NO limits, must be everywhere. There are no beginnings and no endings in God, Whose Universe is Himself.[412] Can you exclude yourself from the Universe, or from God, Who IS the Universe? I and my Father are one[413] with YOU, for you are part of us. Do you REALLY believe that part of God can be missing or lost to Him?

T 10 B 5. If you were not part of God, His Will would not be unified. Is this conceivable? Can part of His Mind contain nothing? If your place in His Mind cannot be filled by anyone EXCEPT you, and your filling it WAS your creation, WITHOUT you, there would be an empty place in God's Mind. Extension cannot be blocked, and it has no voids. It continues forever, however much it is denied. Your DENIAL of its reality arrests it in time, but not in Eternity. That is why your creations have not ceased to be extended, and why so much is waiting for your return.

T 10 B 6. Waiting is possible ONLY in time, but time has no meaning. You who made delay can leave time behind, simply by recognizing that neither beginnings nor endings were created by the Eternal, Who placed no limits on His creation nor upon those who create like Him. You do not know this, simply because you have tried to limit what HE created, and so you believe that ALL creation is limited. How, then, could you know YOUR creations, having DENIED Infinity? The laws of the universe do not permit contradiction. What holds for God holds for you. If you believe YOU are absent from God, you WILL believe He is absent from you.

T 10 B 7. Infinity is meaningless WITHOUT you, and YOU are meaningless without God. There IS no end to God and His Son, for we ARE the universe. God is not incomplete, and He is not childless. Because He did not will to be alone, He created a Son like Himself. Do not deny Him His Son, for your unwillingness to accept His Fatherhood has denied you yours. See His creations as HIS Son, for yours were created in honor of Him. **T(422) - 249 -**

T 10 B 8. The universe of love does not stop because you do not see it, and your closed eyes have not lost the ability to see. Look upon the glory of His creation, and you will learn what God has kept for YOU. God has given you a place in His Mind which is yours forever. But you could keep it only by Giving it, as it was given to you. Could YOU be alone there, if it was given you because GOD did not will to be alone? God's Mind cannot be lessened. It can ONLY be increased, and EVERYTHING He creates has the function of creating.[414] LOVE DOES NOT LIMIT, and what it creates is not limited.

T 10 B 9. To give without limit is God's Will for you, because only this can bring you the joy which is His, and which He wills to share with YOU. Your love is as boundless as His because it IS His. Could any part of Him be WITHOUT His Love, and could any part of His Love be contained? God is your heritage, because His one gift is Himself. How can you give except LIKE Him, if you would know His gift to YOU? Give, then, without limit and without end, to learn how much HE has given YOU. Your ability to ACCEPT Him depends on your willingness to give as He gives. Your fatherhood and your Father are One. **T(423) -250**[415]

---

[410] *Notes* shows "aught" rather than "anything"
[411] August 8, 1966.
[412] **Hebrews 7:3** Without father, without mother, without genealogy, having neither beginning of days nor end of life, but made like the Son of God, remains a priest continually.
[413] **John 10:30** "I and My Father are one."
John 14:20 "At that day you will know that I am in My Father, and you in Me, and I in you."
[414] This sentence is repeated in the manuscript.
[415] August 10, 1966.

T 10 B 10. God willed to create, and your will is His. It follows, then, that YOU will to create, since your will follows from His. And being the extension of His will, yours MUST be the same. Yet what you will, you do not know. This is not strange, when you realize that to deny IS to not know. God's Will was that you are His Son. By DENYING this, you denied your OWN will, and therefore DO NOT KNOW WHAT IT IS. The reason you must ask what God's Will is in everything, is merely because It IS yours. YOU do not know what it is, but the Holy Spirit REMEMBERS IT FOR YOU.

T 10 B 11. Ask him, therefore, what God's Will is for you, and He will tell you YOURS. It cannot be too often repeated that you do NOT KNOW it. Whenever what the Holy Spirit tells you appears to be coercive, it is ONLY because YOU DO NOT RECOGNIZE YOUR OWN WILL. The projection of the ego makes it appear as if God's Will is OUTSIDE yourself, and therefore NOT YOURS. In THIS interpretation, it IS possible for God's Will and yours to conflict. God, then, may seem to demand of you what you do NOT want to give, and thus DEPRIVE you of what you want. Would God, Who wants ONLY your will, be capable of this? Your will is His Life, which He has GIVEN to you. Even in time you cannot live apart from Him, for sleep is not death. What He created can sleep, but it CANNOT die. Immortality is His Will for His Son, and His Son's will for HIMSELF. Yet God's Son cannot will death for himself, because His Father is Life, and HIS SON IS LIKE HIM.

T 10 B 12. Creation is your will because it is His. You cannot be happy unless you do what you will truly, and you CHANGE this, because it is immutable. But it is immutable by God's Will AND YOURS, for otherwise His Will would not have been extended. You are afraid to know God's Will, because you believe it is NOT yours. This belief is your whole sickness, and your whole fear. Every symptom of sickness and fear arises[416] here, because this is the belief that makes you want not to know. Believing this, you hide in T(424) -251 darkness, denying that the Light is in YOU.

T 10 B 13. You are asked to trust the Holy Spirit only because He speaks for YOU. He is the Voice for God, but never forget that God did not will to be alone. He SHARES His Will with you; He does not thrust it UPON you. Always remember that what He gives He holds, so that nothing He gives CAN contradict Him. You who share His Life must share it to KNOW it, for sharing IS knowing. Blessed are[417] you who learn that to hear the Will of your Father, is to know your own. For it is YOUR will to be LIKE Him, Whose Will it is that it be so.

T 10 B 14. God's Will is that His Son be One, and united with Him in His Oneness. That is why healing is the beginning of the recognition that YOUR WILL IS HIS.[418]

T 10 C. The Willingness for Healing (*Notes* 927 8:31)

T 10 C 1. If sickness is separation, the will to heal and BE HEALED is the first step toward RECOGNIZING WHAT YOU TRULY WANT. Every ATTACK is a step AWAY from this, and every healing thought brings it closer. The Son of God HAS both Father and Son because he IS both Father and Son.

T 10 C 2. To unite having and being is only to unite your will with His, for He wills you HIMSELF. And you will yourself to HIM, because in your perfect understanding of Him, you KNOW there IS but One Will. But when you attack ANY part of God and His Kingdom, your understanding is NOT perfect, and what YOU will is therefore lost to you.

T 10 C 3. Healing thus becomes A LESSON IN UNDERSTANDING, and the more you practice it, the better teacher AND LEARNER you become. If you have DENIED truth, what better witnesses to its reality could you have, than those who have been healed BY it? But be sure to count yourself among them, for in your willingness to JOIN them is YOUR healing accomplished.

T 10 C 4. Every miracle which you accomplish speaks to you of the Fatherhood of God. Every healing thought which you ACCEPT, either FROM your brother or in your OWN mind, teaches you that you are God's Son. But in every hurtful thought you hold, wherever you perceive it, lies the denial of God's Fatherhood and your Sonship. And denial IS as total as love. You cannot deny PART of yourself, simply because the remainder will seem to be unintegrated, and therefore without meaning. And being without meaning TO YOU, you will not understand it. T(425) -252 To deny meaning MUST be to fail to understand.

T 10 C 5. You can only heal yourself, for only God's Son NEEDS healing. He needs it because he does not understand himself, and therefore knows not what he does.[419] Having forgotten his will, he does not know what he WANTS. Healing is a sign that HE WANTS TO MAKE WHOLE. And this willingness opens his OWN ears to the Voice of the Holy Spirit, Whose message IS wholeness. He will enable you to go far beyond the healing YOU would undertake, for beside your small willingness to make whole He will lay His Own COMPLETE Will and make YOURS whole. What can the Son of God NOT accomplish with the Fatherhood of God in him? **T(426) -253**

T 10 C 6. And yet the invitation must come from you, for you have surely learned that whom you invite as your guest WILL abide with you.[420] The Holy Spirit cannot speak to an unwelcoming host, BECAUSE HE WILL NOT BE HEARD. The Eternal Guest remains, but His Voice grows faint in alien company. He needs your protection, but only because your care is a sign that you WANT Him. Think like Him ever so slightly, and the little spark becomes a blazing light that fills your mind so that He becomes your only Guest.

T 10 C 7. Whenever you ask the ego to enter, you lessen His welcome. HE will remain, but YOU have allied yourself AGAINST Him. Whatever journey you choose to take, He will go with you, waiting. You can safely trust His patience, for He CANNOT leave a part of God. But you will far more than patience. You will never rest until you know your function AND FULFILL IT, for only in this can your will and your Father's be wholly joined. To HAVE Him is to be LIKE Him, and He has GIVEN Himself to you.

T 10 C 8. You who have God MUST be as God, for HIS function became YOURS with His gift. Invite this knowledge back into your minds, and let nothing that will obscure it enter. The Guest whom God sent you will teach you how to do this, if you but recognize the little spark, and are WILLING TO LET IT GROW. YOUR willingness need not be perfect, because His IS. If you will merely offer Him a little place, He will lighten it so much, that you will gladly extend it. And by THIS extending, you will begin to remember Creation.

T 10 C 9. Would you be hostage to the ego or host to God? You will accept only whom YOU invite. You are free to determine who shall be your guest, and how long he shall remain with you. But this is not REAL freedom, for it depends on how you see it. For the Holy Spirit is THERE, although He cannot help you without your invitation, and the ego is nothing, whether you invite it in or not. Real freedom depends on welcoming REALITY, and of your guests only He IS real. Know, then, Who abides with you, merely by recognizing WHAT IS ALREADY THERE, and do not be satisfied with

---

[416] The manuscript has "arise" here but both the *Notes* and the *HLC* have "arises" which is grammatically correct.
[417] This word pair "Blessed Are" occurs 8 times in the *Ur Text* volume and once in the *Workbook* and appears to be a literary parallel to the Biblical Beatitudes in **Matthew 5:3-11.**
[418] 251 [split paragraph]

[419] **Luke 23:34** Then Jesus said, "Father, forgive them, for they do not know what they do." And they divided His garments and cast lots.
[420] **John 14:16** "And I will pray the Father, and He will give you another Helper, that He may abide with you forever."

imaginary comforters, for the Comforter[421] of God is in you. **T(427) - 254 -**

T 10 D. From Darkness to Light (*Notes* 936 8:39)

T 10 D 1. When you are weary, remember you have hurt yourself. Your Comforter will rest[422] you, but YOU cannot. YOU DO NOT KNOW HOW, for if you did, you could never have grown weary. Unless you have hurt yourselves, you could never suffer in ANY way, for that is not God's Will for His Son. Pain is not of Him, for He knows no attack, and His peace surrounds you silently. God is very quiet, for there is no conflict in Him. Conflict is the root of all evil,[423] for being blind, it does not see whom it attacks. But it ALWAYS attacks the Son of God, and the Son of God is YOU.

T 10 D 2. God's Son is indeed in need of comfort, for he knows not what he does,[424] believing his will is not his own. The Kingdom is his, and yet he wanders homelessly. At home in God he is lonely, and amid all his brothers he is friendless. Would God let this be real, if He did not will to be alone Himself? And if your will is His, it CANNOT be true of you, BECAUSE it is not true of Him. Oh my children, if you knew what God wills for you, your joy would be complete![425] And what He wills HAS happened, for it was ALWAYS true.

T 10 D 3. When the light comes, and you have said, "God's Will is mine," you will see such beauty that you will KNOW it is not of you. Out of your joy, you will create beauty in His Name, for YOUR joy could no more be contained than His. The bleak little world will vanish into nothingness, and your heart will be so filled with joy that it will leap into Heaven and into the presence of God. I cannot tell you what this will be like, for your hearts are not ready. But I CAN tell you, and remind you often, that what God wills for Himself He wills for YOU, and what He wills for you IS yours.

T 10 D 4. The way is not hard, but it IS very different. Yours is the way of pain, of which God knows nothing. THAT way is hard indeed, and very lonely. Fear and grief are your guests, and they go with you, and abide with you on the way. But the dark journey is not the way of God's Son. Walk in light, and do not see the dark companions, for they are not fit companions for the Son of God, who was created OF Light and IN Light. **T(428) -255** The Great Light ALWAYS surrounds you, and shines out FROM you. How can you see the dark companions in a Light such as this? If you see THEM, it is only because you are denying the Light. But DENY THEM INSTEAD, for the Light is here, and the way is clear.

T 10 D 5. God hides nothing from His Son, even though he would hide himself. Yet the Son of God cannot hide his glory, for God wills him to be glorious, and GAVE him the Light that shines in him. You will never lose your way, for God leads you. When you wander, you but undertake a journey which is not real. The dark companions, the dark way, are all illusions. Turn toward the Light, for the little spark in you is part of a Light so great that it can sweep you out of all darkness forever. For your Father IS your Creator, and you ARE like Him. The Children of Light[426] cannot abide in darkness, for darkness is NOT in them.

T 10 D 6. Do not be deceived by the dark comforters, and never let them enter the mind of God's Son, for they have no place in His temple.[427] When you are tempted to deny Him, remember that there ARE no other Gods that you CAN place before Him, and accept His Will for you in peace. For you CANNOT accept it otherwise. Only God's Comforter CAN comfort you. In the quiet of His temple, He waits to give you the peace that is yours. GIVE His peace that you may enter the temple, and find it waiting for you. But be holy in the Presence of God, or you will not know that you are there. For what is unlike God cannot enter His Mind, because it was not in His Thought, and therefore does not belong to Him. And YOUR minds must be as pure as His, if you would know what belongs to YOU.

T 10 D 7. Guard carefully His temple, for He Himself dwells there, and abides in peace. You cannot enter God's Presence with the dark companions beside you, but you also cannot enter alone. All your brothers must enter WITH you, for until you have accepted them, YOU cannot enter. For you cannot understand Wholeness unless YOU are whole, and no part of the Son can be excluded, if he would know the wholeness of his Father. **T(429) -256**

T 10 D 8. In your mind you can ACCEPT the whole Sonship, and bless it with the light your Father gave it. Then you will be worthy to dwell in the temple WITH Him, because it is YOUR will not to be alone. God blessed His Son forever. If you will bless him in TIME, you will BE in eternity. Time cannot separate you from God, if you use it on BEHALF of the eternal. **T(430) - 257 -**

T 10 E. The Inheritance of God's Son (*Notes* 946 8:50)

T 10 E 1. Never forget that the Sonship is your salvation, for the Sonship is your Soul. As God's Creation it is yours, and belonging to you, it is His. Your Soul does not need salvation, but your mind needs to learn what salvation IS. You are not saved FROM anything, but you ARE saved FOR glory. Glory is your inheritance, given your Soul by its Creator, that you might EXTEND it. But if you hate part of your own Soul, ALL your understanding is lost, because you are looking on what God creates AS YOURSELF without love. And since what He created IS part of Him, you are denying Him His place in His own altar.

T 10 E 2. Could you try to make God homeless, and know YOU are at home? Can the Son deny the Father, WITHOUT believing that the Father has denied HIM? God's laws hold ONLY for your protection, and they never hold in vain. What you experience, when you deny your father, is still for your protection, for the power of your will cannot be lessened without the intervention of God AGAINST it, and any limitation on YOUR power is NOT the Will of God. Therefore, look ONLY to the power that God gave you to save you, remembering that it is yours BECAUSE it is His, and join with your brothers in His peace.

T 10 E 3. The peace of YOUR Soul lies in its limitlessness. Limit the peace you share, and your own Soul MUST be unknown to you. Every altar to God is part of your Soul, because the Light He created is One with Him. Would you cut a brother off from the Light that is yours? You could not do so, if you realized that YOU CAN ONLY DARKEN YOUR OWN MIND. As you bring HIM back, so will YOUR mind return. That is the law of God, for the protection of the wholeness of His Son.

---

[421] see previous note

[422] **Matthew 11:28-29** "Come to Me, all you who labor and are heavy laden, and I will give you rest. Take My yoke upon you and learn from Me, for I am gentle and lowly in heart, and you will find rest for your souls."

[423] **1 Timothy 6:10** For the love of money is a root of all kinds of evil, for which some have strayed from the faith in their greediness, and pierced themselves through with many sorrows.

[424] **Luke 23:34** Then Jesus said, "Father, forgive them, for they do not know what they do." And they divided His garments and cast lots.

[425] **John 15:11** "These things I have spoken to you, that My joy may remain in you, and that your joy may be complete."
John 16:24 "Until now you have asked nothing in My name. Ask, and you will receive, that your joy may be full."

[426] **Luke 16:8** So the master commended the unjust steward because he had dealt shrewdly. For the sons of this world are more shrewd in their generation than the sons of light.
1 Thessalonians 5:5 You are all sons of light and sons of the day. We are not of the night nor of darkness.

[427] **1 Corinthians 3:16** Do you not know that you are the temple of God and that the Spirit of God dwells in you?

T 10 E 4. ONLY YOU CAN DEPRIVE YOURSELF OF ANYTHING. Do not oppose this realization, for it is truly the beginning of the dawn of light. Remember also that the denial of this simple fact takes many forms, and these you must learn to recognize, and oppose steadfastly and WITHOUT EXCEPTION. This is a crucial step in the re-awakening. The beginning phases of this reversal are often quite painful, for as blame is withdrawn from without, there is a strong tendency to harbor it within.

T 10 E 5. It is difficult, at first, to realize that this is EXACTLY T(431) -258 the same thing, for there IS no distinction between within and without. If your brothers are part of YOU, and you blame THEM for your deprivation, you ARE blaming yourself. And you cannot blame yourself WITHOUT blaming them.

T 10 E 6. That is why blame must be UNDONE, NOT re-allocated. Lay it to yourself, and you cannot KNOW yourself, for ONLY THE EGO BLAMES AT ALL. Self-blame is therefore ego identification, and as strong an ego defense as blaming others. YOU CANNOT ENTER GOD's PRESENCE IF YOU ATTACK HIS SON. When His Son lifts his voice in praise of his Creator, he WILL hear the Voice of his Father. But the Creator cannot be praised WITHOUT His Son, for their glory is shared, and they are glorified together. Christ is at God's altar, waiting to welcome His Son. But come wholly without condemnation, for otherwise you will believe that the door is barred, and you cannot enter.

T 10 E 7. The door is NOT barred, and it is impossible for you to be unable to enter the place where God would have you be. But love yourself with the love of Christ, for so does your Father love you.[428] You CAN refuse to enter, but you CANNOT bar the door which Christ holds open. Come unto me who hold it open FOR you, for while I live, it cannot be shut, and I live forever.[429] God is my Life and YOURS, and NOTHING is denied by God to His Son. At God's altar, Christ waits for the restoration of Himself in YOU.

T 10 E 8. God knows His Son as wholly blameless as Himself, and He is approached through the appreciation of His Son. Christ waits for your acceptance of Him as YOURSELF, and His Wholeness as YOURS. For Christ is the Son of God, who lives in his Creator, and shines with His glory. Christ is the extension of the love and the loveliness of God, as perfect as his Creator, and at peace with Him. Blessed is the Son of God, whose radiance is of His Father, and whose glory T(432) -259 He wills to share as His Father shares it with Him.[430]

T 10 E 9. There is no condemnation in the Son, for there is no condemnation in the Father. Sharing the perfect Love of the Father, the Son must share what belongs to Him, for otherwise He will not know the Father or the Son. Peace be unto you[431] who rest in God, and in whom the whole Sonship rests. T(433) - 260 -[432]

T 10 F. The "Dynamics" of the Ego (*Notes* 952 8:56)

T 10 F 1. No-one can escape from illusions unless he looks at them, for not looking is the way they are PROTECTED. There is no need to shrink from illusions, for they cannot be dangerous. We are ready to look more closely at the ego's thought system, because together we have the lamp that will dispel it, and since you realize you do not WANT it, you MUST be ready. Let us be very calm in doing this, for we are merely looking honestly for truth. The "dynamics" of the ego will be our lesson for a while, for we must look first at this to look beyond it, since you HAVE made it real. We will UNDO this error quietly together, and then look beyond it to truth.

T 10 F 2. What is healing, but the removal of all that STANDS IN THE WAY of knowledge? And how else can one dispel illusions EXCEPT by looking at them directly, WITHOUT protecting them? Be not afraid, therefore, for what you will be looking at IS the source of fear, but you have learned surely by now, that FEAR IS NOT REAL. We have accepted the fact already that its EFFECTS can be dispelled, merely by denying THEIR reality. The next step is obviously to recognize that WHAT HAS NO EFFECTS DOES NOT EXIST.

T 10 F 3. Laws do not operate in a vacuum, and what leads to nothing HAS NOT HAPPENED. If reality is recognized BY ITS EXTENSION, what extends to nothing CANNOT be real. Do not be afraid, then, to look upon fear, for it cannot BE seen. Clarity undoes confusion by definition, and to look upon darkness through light MUST dispel it. Let us begin this lesson in "ego dynamics", by understanding that the term itself does not mean anything. In fact, it contains exactly the contradiction in terms that MAKES it meaningless. "Dynamics" implies the power to DO something, and the whole separation fallacy lies in the belief that the ego HAS the power to do ANYTHING.

T 10 F 4. The ego is fearful BECAUSE you believe this. But the truth is very simple; ALL POWER IS OF GOD. What is NOT of Him has no power to do ANYTHING. When we look at the ego, then, we are NOT considering dynamics, but delusions. We can surely regard a delusional system without fear, T(434) - 261 - for it cannot have any effects if its source is not true. Fear becomes more obviously inappropriate if one recognizes the ego's GOAL, which is so clearly senseless that any effort exerted on its behalf is NECESSARILY expended on nothing.

T 10 F 5. The ego's goal is quite explicitly EGO AUTONOMY. From the beginning, then, its PURPOSE is to be separate, sufficient unto itself, and independent of any power EXCEPT ITS OWN. This is WHY it is the symbol of separation. Every idea has a purpose, and its purpose is always the natural extension of what it IS. Everything that stems from the ego is the natural outcome of its central belief, and the way to undo its RESULTS, is merely to recognize that their SOURCE is NOT natural, being out of accord with your TRUE nature.

T 10 F 6. We once said that to will contrary to God is wishful thinking, and not real willing. His Will is One, because the extension of His Will CANNOT be unlike ITSELF. The real conflict you experience, then, is between the ego's idle wishes and the Will of God, WHICH YOU SHARE. Can this BE a real conflict? Yours is the independence of Creation, NOT of autonomy. Your whole creative function lies in your complete dependence on God, Whose function He shares WITH you. By HIS willingness to share it, He becomes as dependent on you, as you are on HIM. Do not ascribe the ego's arrogance to Him, Who wills NOT to be independent of YOU. He has included YOU in HIS Autonomy. Can YOU believe that autonomy is meaningful APART from Him?

T 10 F 7. The belief in EGO autonomy is costing you the knowledge of your dependence on God, IN WHICH YOUR FREEDOM LIES. The ego sees ALL dependency as threatening, and has twisted even your longing for God into a means of establishing ITSELF. But do not be deceived by ITS interpretation of your conflict. The ego ALWAYS attacks on behalf of separation. Believing it HAS the power to do this, it does nothing else, because its goal of autonomy T(435) -262 IS nothing else. The ego is totally confused about reality, BUT IT DOES NOT LOSE SIGHT OF ITS GOAL. It is much

---

[428] **John 13:34** "A new commandment I give to you, that you love one another; as I have loved you, that you also love one another."

[429] **Matthew 11:28** "Come to Me, all you who labor and are heavy laden, and I will give you rest. "

[430] **Psalm 118:26** Blessed is he who comes in the name of the LORD! We have blessed you from the house of the LORD.
Then the multitudes who went before and those who followed cried out, saying:
Hosanna to the Son of David!
Matthew 21:9 Blessed is He who comes in the name of the LORD! Hosanna in the highest!

[431] **John 20:21** So Jesus said to them again, "Peace to you! As the Father has sent Me, I also send you."

[432] August 24, 1966

more vigilant than YOU are, BECAUSE it is perfectly certain of its purpose. YOU are confused, because you do NOT know YOURS.

T 10 F 8. What you must learn to recognize is that the LAST thing the ego wishes you to realize, is THAT YOU ARE AFRAID OF IT. For if the ego gives rise to fear, it is DIMINISHING your independence, and WEAKENING your power. Yet its one claim to your allegiance is that it can GIVE power to you. Without THIS belief, you would not listen to it at all. How, then, can its existence continue, if you realize that by accepting it, you ARE belittling yourself, and DEPRIVING yourself of power?

T 10 F 9. The ego can and does allow you to regard yourself as supercilious, unbelieving, "light hearted -," distant, emotionally shallow, callous, uninvolved, and even desperate, BUT NOT REALLY AFRAID. MINIMIZING fear, but NOT its undoing, is the ego's constant effort, and is indeed the skill at which it is VERY ingenious. How can it preach separation WITHOUT upholding it through fear, and would you listen to it, if you recognized this IS what it is doing?

T 10 F 10. YOUR recognition that whatever seems to separate you from God is ONLY fear, regardless of the form it takes, and quite apart from HOW THE EGO WANTS TO YOU TO EXPERIENCE IT, is therefore the basic ego threat. Its dream of autonomy is shaken to its foundation by this awareness. For though you may countenance a false idea of independence, you will NOT accept the cost of fear, IF YOU RECOGNIZE IT. Yet this IS the cost, and the ego CANNOT minimize it. For if you overlook love, you are overlooking YOURSELF, and you MUST fear UNreality BECAUSE YOU HAVE DENIED YOURSELF. T(436) 263 By believing that you have successfully attacked truth, YOU ARE BELIEVING THAT ATTACK HAS POWER. Very simply, then, YOU HAVE BECOME AFRAID OF YOURSELF. And no one wills to learn what he believes would DESTROY him.

T 10 F 11. If the ego's goal of autonomy COULD be accomplished GOD's purpose could be DEFEATED, and this IS impossible. Only by learning what fear IS, can you finally learn to distinguish the possible from the impossible, and the false from the true. According to the ego's teaching, ITS goal CAN be accomplished, and GOD's Purpose can NOT. According to the Holy Spirit's teaching, ONLY God's Purpose IS accomplishment, and it is ALREADY accomplished.

T 10 F 12. God is as dependent on you as you are on Him, because HIS autonomy ENCOMPASSES yours, and is therefore incomplete WITHOUT it. You can only ESTABLISH your autonomy by identifying WITH Him, and FULFILLING YOUR FUNCTION AS IT EXISTS IN TRUTH. The ego believes that to accomplish ITS goal IS happiness. But it is given YOU to know that GOD's function IS yours, and happiness CANNOT be found apart from your joint will. Recognize only that the ego's goal, which you have pursued quite diligently, has merely brought you FEAR, and it becomes difficult to maintain that FEAR is happiness.

T 10 F 13. UPHELD by fear, this IS what the ego would have you believe. Yet God's Son is not insane, and CANNOT believe it. Let him but RECOGNIZE it, and he will NOT accept it. For only the insane would choose fear IN PLACE of love, and only the insane could believe that love can be gained by ATTACK. But the sane KNOW that only attack COULD produce fear, from which the love of God COMPLETELY protects them. T(437) - 264 -

T 10 F 14. The ego analyzes; the Holy Spirit ACCEPTS. The appreciation of wholeness comes ONLY through acceptance, for to analyze MEANS to separate out. The attempt to understand totality by BREAKING IT UP is clearly the characteristically contradictory approach of the ego to everything. Never forget that the ego believes that power, understanding AND TRUTH lie in separation. And to ESTABLISH this belief it MUST attack. Unaware that the belief cannot BE established, and obsessed with the conviction that separation IS salvation, the ego attacks everything it perceives, by breaking it up into small and disconnected parts, without meaningful relationships, and thus without meaning. The ego will ALWAYS substitute chaos for meaning, for if separation is salvation, harmony is threat.

T 10 F 15. The ego's interpretations of the laws of perception are, and would HAVE to be, the exact opposite of the Holy Spirit's. The ego FOCUSES ON ERROR, and OVERLOOKS TRUTH. It makes real every mistake it perceives, and with characteristically circular reasoning, concludes that, BECAUSE of the mistake, consistent truth must be meaningless. The next step, then, is obvious. If consistent truth is meaningless, INCONSISTENCY must be true if truth has meaning. Holding error clearly in mind, and protecting what it has made real, the ego proceeds to the next step in its thought system; that error is real, and TRUTH IS ERROR.

T 10 F 16. The ego makes no attempt to UNDERSTAND this, and it is clearly not understandable. But the ego does make EVERY attempt to DEMONSTRATE it, and THIS it does constantly. Analyzing to ATTACK meaning, the ego DOES succeed in overlooking it, and is left with a series of fragmented perceptions IN WHICH IT UNIFIES ON BEHALF OF ITSELF. This, then, becomes the universe it perceives and it is this universe which, in turn, becomes its demonstration of its own reality. T(438) -265

T 10 F 17. Do not underestimate the appeal of the ego's demonstrations to those who would listen. Selective perception chooses its witnesses carefully, and its witnesses ARE consistent. The case for insanity IS strong to the insane. For reasoning ends at its beginning, and no thought system transcends its source. Yet reasoning without meaning CANNOT demonstrate anything, and those who are convinced by it, MUST be deluded. Can the ego teach truly, when it overlooks truth? Can it perceive what it has DENIED? Its witnesses DO attest to its DENIAL, but hardly to WHAT it has denied. The ego looks straight at the Father and does not see Him, for it has denied His Son.

T 10 F 18. Would YOU remember the Father? Accept His Son and you WILL remember Him. Nothing can demonstrate that His Son is unworthy, for nothing can prove that a lie is true. What you see of His Son through the eyes of the ego is a demonstration that His Son does not exist, yet where the Son is, the Father MUST be. Accept what God does NOT deny, and HE will demonstrate its truth. The witnesses for God stand in His Light and behold what HE created. Their silence is the sign that they have beheld God's Son, and in the Presence of Christ, THEY need demonstrate nothing, for Christ speaks to them of Himself and of His Father. They are silent because Christ speaks to them, and it is His words that THEY speak.

T 10 F 19. Every brother you meet becomes a witness for Christ or for the ego, depending on what you perceive in him. Everyone convinces you of WHAT YOU WANT TO PERCEIVE, and of the reality of the Kingdom you have chosen for your vigilance. Everything you perceive is a witness to the thought-system YOU WANT TO BE TRUE. Every brother has the power to release you, IF YOU WILL TO BE FREE. You cannot accept false witness[433] of him, unless you have evoked false witnesses AGAINST him. If HE speaks not of Christ to YOU, YOU spoke not of Christ to him. You hear but your own voice, and if Christ speaks through you, YOU will hear Him. T(439) -266

T 10 G. Experience and Perception (*Notes* 975 8:79)

T 10 G 1. It is impossible not to believe what you see, but it is equally impossible to see what you do NOT believe. Perceptions are built up on the basis of experience, and experience leads to beliefs. It is not until BELIEFS are fixed that perceptions stabilize. In effect, then, what you believe you DO see. That is what I meant when I

---

[433] **Exodus 20:16** You shall not bear false witness against your neighbor.

said, "Blessed are ye who have not seen and still believe,"[434] for those who believe in the resurrection WILL see it. The resurrection is the complete triumph of Christ over the ego, not by attack, but by transcendence. For Christ DOES rise above the ego and all its works, and ascends to the Father and HIS Kingdom.[435]

T 10 G 2. Would you join in the resurrection or the crucifixion? Would you condemn your brothers or free them? Would you transcend YOUR prison and ascend to the Father? For these questions are all the same, and are answered together. There has been much confusion about what perception means, because the same word is used both for awareness and for the INTERPRETATION of awareness. Yet you cannot BE aware without interpretation, and what you perceive IS your interpretation. This course is perfectly clear. You do not see it clearly because you are interpreting AGAINST it, and therefore do not BELIEVE it. And if belief determines perception, you do NOT perceive what it means and therefore do not ACCEPT it.

T 10 G 3. Yet different experiences lead to different beliefs, and with them different perceptions. For perceptions are learned WITH beliefs, and experience teaches.[436] I am leading you to a new kind of experience which you will become less and less willing to deny. Learning of Christ is easy, for to perceive with Him involves no strain at all. HIS perceptions are your NATURAL awareness, and it is only distortions which YOU introduce that tire you. Let the Christ in you interpret FOR you, and do not try to limit what you see by narrow little beliefs which are unworthy of God's Son. For until Christ comes into His Own, the Son of God WILL see himself as fatherless. **T(440) -267**

T 10 G 4. I am YOUR resurrection and YOUR life.[437] You live in me because you live in God. And everyone lives in YOU, as YOU live in everyone. Can you, then, perceive unworthiness in a brother and NOT perceive it in yourself? And can you perceive it in yourself and NOT perceive it in God? Believe in the resurrection because it has BEEN accomplished, and it has been accomplished IN YOU. This is as true now as it will ever be, for the resurrection is the Will of God, Which knows no time and no exceptions. But make no exceptions yourself, or you will not perceive what has been accomplished FOR you. For we ascend unto the Father together, as it was in the beginning, is now, and ever shall be,[438] for such is the nature of God's Son as His Father created him. **T(441) -268**[439]

T 10 G 5. Do not underestimate the power of the devotion of God's Son, nor the power of the god he worships over him. For he places HIMSELF at the altar of his god, whether it be the god he made or the God Who created him. That is why his slavery is as complete as his freedom, for he will obey ONLY the god he accepts. The god of the crucifixion demands that he crucify, and his worshippers obey. In his name they crucify THEMSELVES, believing that the power of the Son of God is born of sacrifice and pain. The God of the resurrection demands nothing, for He does not will to TAKE AWAY. He does not require obedience, for obedience implies submission. He would only have you learn your OWN will and follow it, not in the spirit of sacrifice and submission, but in the gladness of freedom.

T 10 G 6. Resurrection must compel your allegiance gladly because it is the symbol of joy. Its whole compelling power lies in the fact that it represents what YOU want to be. The freedom to leave behind everything that hurts you and humbles you and frightens you cannot be thrust upon you, but it CAN be offered you through the grace of God. And you can ACCEPT it by His grace, for God IS gracious to His Son, accepting him without question as His Own. Who, then, is YOUR own? The Father has given you all that is His, and He Himself is yours WITH them.[440] Guard them in their resurrection, for otherwise you will not awake in God, safely surrounded by what is yours forever.

T 10 G 7. You will not find peace until you have removed the nails from the hands of God's Son and taken the last thorn from his forehead.[441] The Love of God surrounds His Son whom the god of the crucifixion condemns. Teach not that I died in vain. Teach rather THAT I DID NOT DIE by demonstrating that I LIVE IN YOU. For the UNDOING of the crucifixion of God's Son is the work of the redemption, in which everyone has a part of equal value. God does not judge His blameless Son. **T(442) -269** Having given HIMSELF to him, how could it be otherwise?

T 10 G 8. You have nailed YOURSELF to a cross and placed a crown of thorns upon your own head.[442] Yet you CANNOT crucify God's Son, for the Will of God cannot die. His Son HAS BEEN redeemed from his own crucifixion, and you cannot assign to death whom God has given eternal life. The dream of crucifixion still lies heavy on your eyes, but what you see in dreams is not reality. While you perceive the Son of God as crucified you are asleep. And as long as you believe that YOU can crucify him you are only having nightmares. You who are beginning to wake are still aware of dreams and have not yet forgotten them. The forgetting of dreams and the awareness of Christ comes with the awakening of others to SHARE your redemption.

T 10 G 9. You will awaken to your OWN call, for the Call to awake is WITHIN you. If I live in you, you ARE awake. Yet you must see the works I do through you, or you will not perceive that I have done them UNTO you. Do not set limits on what you believe I can do THROUGH you, or you will not accept what I can do FOR you. For it is done ALREADY, and unless you give ALL that you have received, you will not know that your Redeemer liveth[443] and that YOU have awakened WITH Him. Redemption is recognized ONLY by sharing it.

T 10 G 10. God's Son IS saved. Bring only THIS awareness to the Sonship, and you will have a part in the redemption as valuable as mine. For your part must be LIKE mine if you learn it of me. If you believe that YOURS is limited, YOU are limiting MINE. There is no order of difficulty in miracles because all of God's Sons are of equal value, and their equality is their Oneness. The whole power of God is in every part of Him, and nothing contradictory to His Will is either great or small. What does not exist HAS no size and no meas-

---

[434] **John 20:29** Jesus said to him, "Thomas, because you have seen Me, you have believed. Blessed are those who have not seen and yet have believed."
[435] **John 20:17** Jesus said to her, "Do not cling to Me, for I have not yet ascended to My Father; but go to My brethren and say to them, I am ascending to My Father and your Father, and to My God and your God."
[436] The *Notes* reads: "Yet different experiences lead to different beliefs, and with them different perceptions. For perceptions are learned beliefs, and experience does teach." FIP *Second Edition* also restores this line to the original reading.
[437] **John 11:25** Jesus said to her, "I am the resurrection and the life. He who believes in Me, though he may die, he shall live."
[438] **Hebrews 13:8** Jesus Christ is the same yesterday, today, and forever. The wording here is reminiscent of the Gloria Patri or Minor Doxology commonly used in Christian liturgy: "Glory be to the Father, and to the Son and to the Holy Ghost/Spirit. As it was in the beginning, is now, and ever shall be, world without end. Amen." The Greek original is of great antiquity, possibly the first century."
[439] 31 August, 1966

[440] **Luke 15:31** And he said to him, "Son, you are always with me, and all that I have is yours."
[441] **Matthew 27:29** When they had twisted a crown of thorns, they put it on His head, and a reed in His right hand. And they bowed the knee before Him and mocked Him, saying, "Hail, King of the Jews!"
John 19:5 So Jesus came out, wearing the crown of thorns and the purple robe. Pilate said to them, "Look! Here is the man!"
[442] ibid.
[443] **Job 19:25** "For I know that my Redeemer lives, And He shall stand at last on the earth"

ure. To God ALL things are possible.[444] And to Christ it is given to be LIKE the Father. **T(443) - 270 -**

T 10 H. The Problem and the Answer (*Notes* 984 8:88)

T 10 H 1. The world as YOU perceive it cannot have been created by the Father, for the world is NOT as you see it. God created ONLY the eternal, and everything YOU see is perishable. Therefore, there must be another world which you do NOT see. The Bible speaks of a NEW Heaven and a NEW earth,[445] yet this cannot be literally true, for the eternal are not RE-created. To PERCEIVE anew is merely to perceive again, implying that before YOU WERE NOT PERCEIVING AT ALL. What, then, is the world that awaits your perception WHEN YOU SEE IT? Every loving thought that the Son of God ever had is eternal. Those which his mind perceived in this world are the world's only reality. They are still perceptions, because he still believes that he is separate, yet they are eternal, because they are loving. And BEING loving, they are like the Father, and therefore cannot die.

T 10 H 2. The real world can ACTUALLY BE PERCEIVED. All that is necessary is a willingness to perceive nothing ELSE. For if you perceive both good AND evil, you are accepting both the false AND the true, AND MAKING NO DISTINCTION BETWEEN THEM. The ego sees SOME good, but never ONLY good. That is WHY its perceptions are so variable. It does not reject goodness entirely, for this you could not accept, but it always ADDS something that is NOT real TO the real, thus CONFUSING ILLUSION AND REALITY. For perceptions cannot be partly true. If you believe in truth AND illusion you CANNOT TELL WHICH IS TRUE.

T 10 H 3. To establish your PERSONAL autonomy, you tried to create UNLIKE your Father, BELIEVING what you made to be capable of BEING unlike Him. Yet everything in what you have made that IS true, IS like Him. Only this is the real world, and perceiving ONLY this will lead you to the real Heaven because IT WILL MAKE YOU CAPABLE OF UNDERSTANDING IT. The perception of goodness is not knowledge, but the denial of the OPPOSITE of goodness enables you to perceive a condition in which opposites do not exist. And this IS the condition of knowledge. WITHOUT this awareness, you have NOT met its conditions, and until you do you will not know that it is yours already. **T(444) - 271 -**

T 10 H 4. You have made many ideas which you have placed between yourselves and your Creator, and these beliefs are the world as YOU perceive it. Truth is not absent here, but it IS obscure. You do not know the difference between what you have made, and what God created, and so you do not know the difference between what you have made, and what YOU have created. To believe that you can perceive the real world is to believe that you can know yourself. You CAN know God, because it is His Will to BE known. The real world is all that the Holy Spirit has saved for you, out of what you have made, and to perceive only this is salvation, because it is the recognition that reality is ONLY WHAT IS TRUE.

T 10 H 5. This is a very simple course. Perhaps you do not feel that a course which, in the end, teaches nothing more than that only reality is true is necessary. BUT DO YOU BELIEVE IT? When you have perceived the real world, you will recognize that you did NOT believe it. But the swiftness with which your new and ONLY real perception will be translated into knowledge, will leave you only an instant to realize that this judgment is true. And then everything you made will be forgotten, the good and the bad, the false and the true. For as Heaven and earth become one, even the real world will vanish from your sight. The end of the world is not its destruction, but its TRANSLATION into Heaven. The RE-INTERPRETATION of the world is the transfer of ALL perception to knowledge.

T 10 H 6. The Bible tells you to become as little children.[446] Little children recognize that they do not understand what they perceive, and so they ASK WHAT IT MEANS. Do not make the mistake of believing that YOU understand what YOU perceive, for its meaning IS lost to you. But the Holy Spirit has saved its meaning FOR you, and if you will LET Him interpret it FOR you, He will restore what you have thrown away. As long as you THINK YOU KNOW its meaning, you will see no need to ask it OF Him. You do not know the meaning of ANYTHING you perceive. NOT ONE THOUGHT YOU HOLD IS WHOLLY TRUE.

T 10 H 7. The recognition of this is your firm beginning. You are not misguided; you have accepted no guide at all. Instruction in perception is your **T(445) - 272 -** great need, FOR YOU UNDERSTAND NOTHING. RECOGNIZE this, but do not accept it, for understanding is your inheritance. Perceptions are learned, and you are not without a Teacher. But your willingness to learn of Him depends on your willingness to question EVERYTHING you have learned OF YOURSELF, for you who have learned amiss should not be your own teachers. No-one can withhold truth, except from himself. Yet God will not refuse the answer He GAVE you. Ask, then, for what is yours, but which you did NOT make, and do not defend yourself AGAINST truth.

T 10 H 8. YOU made the problem which God HAS answered. Ask yourselves, therefore, but one simple question; "Do I want the problem or do I want the answer?" Decide for the answer, and you WILL have it, for you will see it as it is, and it is yours already.[447] You complain that this course is not sufficiently specific for you to understand it AND USE IT. Yet it has been VERY specific, and YOU HAVE NOT DONE WHAT IT SPECIFICALLY ADVOCATES. This is not a course in the play of ideas, but in their PRACTICAL APPLICATION. Nothing could be more specific than to be told very clearly, that if you ask you WILL receive.[448]

T 10 H 9. The Holy Spirit will answer EVERY specific problem, as long as you believe that problems ARE specific. His answer is both many and one, as long as you believe that the One IS many. Realize that YOU ARE AFRAID OF HIS SPECIFICITY, for fear of what you think it will DEMAND of you. Yet only by asking will you learn that nothing that is of God demands ANYTHING of you. God GIVES; He does NOT take. You are refusing to ask, because you believe that asking is TAKING, and you do not perceive it as sharing. The Holy Spirit will give you only what is yours, and will take nothing in return. For what is yours IS everything, and you share it WITH God. This IS its reality. Would the Holy Spirit, Who wills only to RESTORE, be capable of MISinterpreting the question you must ask to learn His answer?

T 10 H 10. You HAVE heard the answer, but you have misunderstood the QUESTION. You have believed that to ask for guidance of the Holy Spirit, IS TO ASK FOR DEPRIVATION. Little children of God, you do not understand your Father. **T(446) - 273 -** You believe in a world that takes because you believe that you can get by taking. But BY that perception, you have lost sight of the real world. You are afraid of the world AS YOU SEE IT, but the real world is

---

[444] **Matthew 19:26** But Jesus looked at them and said to them, "With men this is impossible, but with God all things are possible."

[445] **Isaiah 65:17** For behold, I create new heavens and a new earth; And the former shall not be remembered or come to mind.
Revelation 21:1 Now I saw a new heaven and a new earth, for the first heaven and the first earth had passed away. Also there was no more sea.

[446] **Matthew 18:3** And said, "Assuredly, I say to you, unless you are converted and become as little children, you will by no means enter the kingdom of heaven."

[447] **1 John 3:2** Beloved, now we are children of God; and it has not yet been revealed what we shall be, but we know that when He is revealed, we shall be like Him, for we shall see Him as He is.

[448] **Matthew 7:7** "Ask, and it will be given to you; seek, and you will find; knock, and it will be opened to you."

still yours for the asking. Do not deny it TO yourself, for it can ONLY free you. Nothing of God will enslave His Son, whom He created free and whose freedom is protected by HIS Being.

T 10 H 11. Blessed are you who will ask the truth of God without fear, for only thus can you learn that His answer IS the release from fear. Beautiful Child of God, you are asking only for what I promised you. Do you believe I would DECEIVE you? The Kingdom of Heaven IS within you.[449] Believe that the truth is in me, for I KNOW that it is in YOU. God's Sons have nothing which they do not share. Ask for truth of any Son of God, and you have asked it of me. No one of us but has the answer in him, to give to anyone who asks it OF him. Ask anything of God's Son, and His Father will answer you, for Christ is not deceived in His Father and His Father is not deceived in Him.

T 10 H 12. Do not, then, be deceived in your brother, and see only his loving thoughts as his reality, for by denying that his mind is split, YOU WILL HEAL YOURS. Accept him as his Father accepts him, and heal him unto Christ, for Christ is his healing AND YOURS. Christ is the Son of God Who is in no way separate from His Father, Whose EVERY thought is as loving as the Thought of His Father, by which He was created. Be not deceived in God's Son, for thereby you MUST be deceived in yourself. And being deceived in yourself you ARE deceived in your Father, in Whom no deceit is possible.

T 10 H 13. In the real world, there is no sickness, for there is no separation and no division. Only loving thoughts are recognized, and because no-one is without YOUR help, the Help of God goes with YOU everywhere. As you become willing to ACCEPT this Help BY ASKING FOR IT, you will give it BECAUSE YOU WANT IT. Nothing will be beyond your healing power, because nothing will be denied your simple request. What problems will not disappear in the presence **T(447) - 274** -of God's answer? Ask, then, to learn of the reality of your brother BECAUSE THIS IS WHAT YOU WILL PERCEIVE IN HIM, and you will see <u>YOUR</u> beauty reflected in HIM.

T 10 H 14. Do not accept your brother's variable perception of himself, for his split mind is yours, and you will not accept YOUR healing without his. For you share the real world as you share Heaven, and his healing IS yours. To love yourself is to HEAL yourself, and you cannot perceive part of you as sick and achieve your OWN goal. Brother, we heal together as we live together, and love together. Be not deceived in God's Son, for he is one with himself, and One with his Father. Love him who is beloved of His Father, and you will learn of the Father's Love for YOU.

---

[449] **Luke 17:21** Nor will they say, "See here!' or 'See there!' For indeed, the kingdom of God is within you."

T 10 H 15. If you perceive offense in a brother, pluck the offense from your mind,[450] for you are offended by Christ, and are deceived in Him. HEAL in Christ and be not offended by Him, for there is no offense IN Him. If what you perceive offends you, you are offended in YOURSELF, and are condemning God's Son, whom God condemneth not. Let the Holy Spirit remove ALL offense of God's Son against himself and perceive no-one but through HIS guidance, for He would save you from ALL condemnation. Accept His healing power, and use it for all He sends you, for He wills to heal the Son of God in whom He is not deceived.

T 10 H 16. Children perceive terrifying ghosts and monsters and dragons, and they are terrified. But if they ask someone they trust for the REAL meaning of what they perceive, and are willing to LET THEIR INTERPRETATIONS GO IN FAVOR OF REALITY, their fear goes with them. When a child is helped to translate his "ghost" into a curtain, his "monster" into a shadow and his "dragon" into a dream, he is no longer afraid, and laughs happily at his own fear. You, my children, are afraid of your brothers, and of your Father and of YOURSELVES. But you are merely DECEIVED in them.

T 10 H 17. Ask what they ARE of the Teacher of Reality, and hearing His answer, you too will laugh at your fears and replace them with peace. For fear lies **T(448) - 275** - not in reality, but in the minds of children who do not UNDERSTAND it. It is only their LACK OF UNDERSTANDING that frightens them, and when they learn to perceive truly, they are not afraid. And because of this, they will ask for truth again, when they are frightened. It is not the REALITY of your brothers, or your Father, or yourself which frightens you. You do not know what they ARE, and so YOU perceive them as ghosts and monsters and dragons.

T 10 H 18. ASK of their reality from the One Who knows it, and He will tell you what they are. For you do NOT understand them, and because you are deceived by what you see, you NEED reality to dispel your fears. Would you not exchange your fears for truth if the exchange is yours for the asking? For if God is not deceived in you, you can be deceived only in YOURSELF. But you can learn the truth of yourself of the Holy Spirit, Who will teach you that, as part of God, deceit in YOU is impossible. When you perceive yourself without deceit, you will accept the real world in place of the false one you have made. And then your Father will lean down to you, and take the last step for you, by raising you unto Himself. **T(449) - 276 -**[451]

---

[450] **Matthew 5:29** "If your right eye causes you to sin, pluck it out and cast it from you; for it is more profitable for you that one of your members perish, than for your whole body to be cast into hell."
[451] September 8, 1966

Chapter 11 – God's Plan for Salvation

T 11 A. Introduction (*Notes* 997 8:101)

T 11 A 1. You have been told not to make error real, and the way to do this is very simple. If you WANT to believe in error, you would HAVE to make it real, because it is not true. But TRUTH is real in its OWN right, and to believe in truth, YOU DO NOT HAVE TO DO ANYTHING. Understand that you do not respond to stimuli, but to STIMULI AS YOU INTERPRET THEM. Your interpretation thus becomes the JUSTIFICATION for the response. That is why analyzing the motives of others is hazardous to YOU. If you decide that someone is REALLY trying to attack you, or desert you or enslave you, you will respond as if he had actually DONE so, BECAUSE you have made his error REAL to you. To interpret error is to GIVE IT POWER, and, having done this, you WILL overlook truth.

T 11 A 2. The analysis of ego motivation is very complicated, very obscuring, and NEVER without the risk of your own ego involvement. The whole process represents a clear-cut attempt to demonstrate YOUR OWN ability to understand what you perceive. This is demonstrated by the fact that you REACT to your interpretations as if they WERE correct, and control your reactions behaviorally, BUT NOT EMOTIONALLY. This is quite evidently a mental split, in which you have attacked the integrity of your mind, and pitted one level within it against another.

T 11 B. The Judgment of the Holy Spirit (*Notes* 998 8:102)

T 11 B 1. There is but one interpretation of ALL motivation that makes any sense, and, because it is the Holy Spirit's judgment, it requires no effort at all on your part. Every loving thought is true. EVERYTHING ELSE is an appeal for healing and help. That is what it IS, regardless of the form it takes. Can anyone be justified in responding with anger to a plea for help? No response can BE appropriate EXCEPT the willingness to give it TO him, for this and ONLY this is what he is ASKING for. Offer him anything ELSE, and YOU are assuming the right to attack his reality, by interpreting it AS YOU SEE FIT.

T 11 B 2. Perhaps the danger of this to your OWN mind is not yet fully apparent. But this by no means signifies that it is not perfectly clear. If you maintain **T(450) - 277 -** that an appeal for help is something ELSE, you will REACT to something else, and your response will be inappropriate to reality as IT is, but NOT to your perception OF it. This is poor reality testing by definition. There is nothing to prevent you from recognizing ALL calls for help as exactly what they are, EXCEPT YOUR OWN PERCEIVED NEED TO ATTACK. It is only THIS that makes you willing to engage in endless "battles" with reality, in which you DENY the reality of the need for healing by making IT unreal.

T 11 B 3. You would not do this except for your UNWILLINGNESS to perceive reality, WHICH YOU WITHHOLD FROM YOURSELF. It is surely good advice to tell you not to judge what you do not understand. No-one with a personal investment is a reliable witness, for truth for him has become what he WANTS it to be. If you are unwilling to perceive an appeal for help AS WHAT IT IS, it is because YOU are unwilling to give help, AND RECEIVE IT. The analysis of the ego's "real" motivation is the modern equivalent of the inquisition. For in both, a brother's errors are "uncovered," and he is then attacked FOR HIS OWN GOOD. What can this be, BUT projection? For HIS errors lay in the minds of his INTERPRETERS, for which they punished HIM.

T 11 B 4. Whenever you fail to recognize a call for help, you are REFUSING help. Would you maintain that you do not NEED it? Yet this IS what you are maintaining when you refuse to recognize a brother's appeal. For only by ANSWERING his appeal, can YOU be helped. Deny him YOUR help, and you will NOT perceive God's answer to YOU. The Holy Spirit does NOT need your help in interpreting motivation, but you DO need HIS. ONLY appreciation is an appropriate response to your brother. Gratitude is due him for both his loving thoughts, and his appeals for help, for both are capable of bringing love into YOUR awareness, IF YOU PERCEIVE THEM TRULY. And ALL your sense of strain comes from your attempts NOT to do just this.

T 11 B 5. How simple, then, is God's plan for salvation. There is but one response to reality, for reality evokes no conflict at all. There is but one Teacher of Reality, Who understands what it is. He does NOT change His mind about reality, because REALITY does not change. Although YOUR **T(451) - 278 -** interpretations of reality are meaningless in your divided state, His remain consistently true. He GIVES them to you because they are FOR you.

T 11 B 6. Do not attempt to "help" a brother in YOUR way, for you cannot help YOURSELVES. But hear his call for the help of God, and you will recognize your OWN need for the Father. Your interpretations of your brother's need is your interpretation of YOURS. By giving help, you are ASKING FOR IT. And if you perceive but one need[452] in yourself, you WILL be healed. For you will recognize God's answer as you want it to be, and if you want it in truth, it will be truly yours. Every appeal you answer in the Name of Christ, brings the remembrance of your Father closer to YOUR awareness. For the sake of YOUR need, then, hear every call for help as what it is, so God can answer YOU. **T(452) -279**[453]

T 11 B 7. By applying the Holy Spirit's interpretation of the reactions of others more and more consistently, you will gain an increasing awareness that HIS criteria are equally applicable to YOU. For to RECOGNIZE fear is not enough to escape FROM it, although the recognition IS necessary to demonstrate the NEED for escape. The Holy Spirit must still TRANSLATE it into truth. If you were LEFT with the fear, having RECOGNIZED it, you would have taken a step AWAY from reality, not TOWARD it. Yet we have repeatedly emphasized the need to recognize fear, and face it WITHOUT DISGUISE, as a crucial step in the undoing of the ego. Consider how well the Holy Spirit's interpretation of the motives of others will serve you then.

T 11 B 8. Having taught you to accept only loving thoughts in others, and to regard everything else as an appeal for help, He has taught you that FEAR is an appeal for help. This is what RECOGNIZING it really means. If you do NOT PROTECT it, HE will reinterpret it. That is the ultimate value TO YOU in learning to perceive attack as a call for love. We have learned surely that fear and attack are inevitably associated. If ONLY attack produces fear, and if you see attack as the call for help that it IS, the REALITY of fear MUST dawn upon you. For fear IS a call for love, in unconscious recognition of what has been denied.

T 11 C. The Mechanism of Miracles (*Notes* 1005 8:909)

T 11 C 1. Fear is a symptom of your deep sense of loss. If, when you perceive it in others, you learn to SUPPLY the loss, the basic CAUSE of fear is removed. Thereby you teach yourself that fear does not exist IN YOU, for you have in YOURSELF, the means for removing it, and have DEMONSTRATED this by GIVING it. Fear and love are the only emotions of which you are capable. One is false, for it was made out of denial, and denial DEPENDS on the real belief in what is denied for its OWN existence. **T(453) - 280 -**

---

[452] *Notes* has "this one need" which appears more likely correct.
[453] Sept. 9, '66

Chapter 11 – God's Plan for Salvation

T 11 C 2. By interpreting fear correctly, as a POSITIVE AFFIRMATION OF THE UNDERLYING BELIEF IT MASKS, you are undermining its perceived usefulness by rendering it useless. Defenses which do not work AT ALL are AUTOMATICALLY discarded. If you raise what fear conceals to CLEAR-CUT, UNEQUIVOCAL PRE-DOMINANCE, fear becomes meaningless. You have denied its power to conceal love, which was its only purpose. The mask which YOU have drawn across the face of Love has disappeared.

T 11 C 3. If you would look upon Love, which IS the world's reality, how could you do better than to recognize, in every defense AGAINST it, the underlying appeal FOR it? And how could you better learn of its reality, than by answering the appeal for it by GIVING it? The Holy Spirit's interpretation of fear DOES dispel it, for the AWARENESS of truth cannot BE denied. Thus does the Holy Spirit replace fear with love, and translate error into truth. And thus will YOU learn of Him how to replace your dream of separation with the fact of unity. For the separation is only the DENIAL of union, and, correctly interpreted, attests to your eternal knowledge that union is true. **T(454) - 281 -**

T 11 C 4. Miracles are merely the translation of denial into truth. If to love oneself is to HEAL oneself, those who are sick do NOT love themselves. Therefore, they are asking for the love that would heal them, but which they are DENYING TO THEMSELVES. If they knew the truth about themselves, they could not be sick. The task of the miracle-worker thus becomes to DENY THE DENIAL OF TRUTH. The sick must heal THEMSELVES, for the truth is IN them. But, having OBSCURED it, the light in ANOTHER mind must shine into theirs, because that light IS theirs.

T 11 C 5. The light in them shines as brightly, REGARDLESS of the density of the fog that obscures it. If you give no power to the fog to obscure the light, it HAS none, for it has power ONLY because the Son of God gave power TO it. He must HIMSELF withdraw that power, remembering that all power is of God. YOU CAN REMEMBER THIS FOR ALL THE SONSHIP. Do not allow your brother not to remember, for his forgetfulness is YOURS. But YOUR remembering is HIS, for God cannot be remembered alone. THIS IS WHAT YOU HAVE FORGOTTEN. To perceive the healing of your brother as the healing of yourself, is thus the way to remember God. For you forgot your brothers WITH Him, and God's answer to your forgetting is but the way to remember.

T 11 C 6. Perceive in sickness but another call for love, and offer your brother what he believes he cannot offer HIMSELF. Whatever the sickness, there is but one remedy. You will be made whole as you MAKE whole, for to perceive in sickness the appeal for health, is to recognize in hatred the call for love. And to give a brother what he REALLY wants, is to offer it unto yourself. For your Father wills you to know your brother AS yourself.[454] Answer HIS call for love, and YOURS is answered. Healing is the love of Christ for His Father, and for HIMSELF. **T(455) - 282 -**[455]

T 11 C 7. You have no idea of the intensity of your wish to get rid of each other. This does NOT mean that you are not strongly impelled TOWARD each other, but it DOES mean that LOVE IS NOT THE ONLY EMOTION. Because your love has become more in awareness, the conflict can no longer be "settled" by your previous attempts to MINIMIZE the fear. The love makes attack untenable, BUT YOU STILL FEEL THE FEAR. Instead of trying to resolve it directly, you have a strong tendency to TRY TO ESCAPE FROM THE LOVE. Yet this is the LAST thing you would want to ESCAPE from. And even if you did, you can escape from everything ELSE, but not from this. Be glad indeed that there IS no escape from salvation.[456]**T(456) -283**[457]

T 11 C 8. You do not realize how much you hate each other. You will not get rid of this until you DO realize it, for UNTIL then, you will think you want to get rid of EACH OTHER and KEEP THE HATRED. Yet if you are each other's salvation, what can this mean except that you PREFER attack to salvation? Be glad that neither your reality nor your salvation is a matter of your preference, for you HAVE much cause for joy. But that the cause is NOT of your making is surely obvious. You DO hate and fear each other, and your love, which is very real, is TOTALLY obscured by it. How can you know the meaning of love UNLESS it is total?

T 11 C 9. This will be a very difficult period for you, but it will not be so for long. You are in danger, but you WILL be helped, and nothing will happen. But you cannot remain in darkness, and this will BE the way out. Look as calmly as you can upon hatred, for if we are to deny the denial of truth, we must first RECOGNIZE what we are denying. Remember that knowledge PRECEDES denial, and that the separation was a descent from magnitude to littleness. And so the way back is to retrace the way to magnitude.

T 11 C 10. Your hatred is not real, But it is real to you. IT HIDES WHAT YOU REALLY WANT. Surely you are willing to look upon what you do NOT want without fear, EVEN IF IT FRIGHTENS YOU, if you can thereby get rid of it? For you CANNOT escape salvation, and you WILL not escape fear until you WANT salvation. Be not afraid of this journey into fear, for it is not your destination. And we will walk through it in safety, for peace is not far, and you will be led in its light. **T(457) - 284 -**

T 11 C 11. Remember what we said about the frightening perceptions of little children, which terrify them because they do not understand them. If they ASK for enlightenment, AND ACCEPT IT, their fears vanish. But if they HIDE their nightmares, they will KEEP them. It is easy to help an uncertain child, for he recognizes that he does not know what his perceptions mean. But you believe you DO know. Little children, you are hiding your heads under the covers of the heavy blankets you have laid upon yourselves. You are hiding your nightmares in the darkness of your own certainty, and refusing to open your eyes and LOOK AT THEM.

T 11 C 12. Let us not save nightmares, for they are not fitting offerings for Christ, and so they are not fit gifts for YOU. Take off the covers, and look at what you are afraid of. Only the ANTICIPATION will frighten you, for the reality of nothingness cannot be frightening. Let us not delay this, for your dream of hatred will not leave you without help, and help is here. Learn to be quiet in the midst of turmoil, for quietness is the END of strife, and this is the journey to peace. Look straight at every image that rises to delay you, for the goal is inevitable, because it is eternal.

T 11 C 13. The goal of love is but your right, and it belongs to you DESPITE your preference. YOU STILL WILL WHAT GOD WILLS, and no nightmare can defeat a Child of God in his purpose. For your purpose was given you by God, and you must accomplish it, BECAUSE it is His Will. Awake and remember your purpose, for it is YOUR will to do so. What has been accomplished FOR you MUST be yours. Do not let your hatred stand in the way of love, for

---

[454] **Leviticus 19:18** You shall not take vengeance, nor bear any grudge against the children of your people, but you shall love your neighbor as yourself: I am the LORD.

Matthew 22:39 And the second is like it: "You shall love your neighbor as yourself."

Matthew 25:40 "And the King shall answer and say to them, Truly I say to you, Inasmuch as you did *it* to one of the least of these My brothers, you have done *it* to Me."

[455] Sept. 13, 66

[456] This page and the next covering paragraphs **T 11 C 7.**though **T 11 C 10.**show up as Special Message 7 and do not show up in the subsequent *HLC* manuscript, suggesting that the Scribes viewed this material as "private" and not part of the Course. While this page and the next have two separate dates typed at the beginning of each page, those dates may represent the date of typing rather than the date of original dictation. In the *Notes* this material shows up on pages 1011-1013 (N8:115) through (N8:117).

[457] Sept. 14, '66

NOTHING can withstand the love of Christ for His Father, or His Father's love for Him.

T 11 C 14. A little while, and you WILL see me.[458] For I am not hidden because you are hiding. I will awaken you as surely as I awakened myself, for I awoke FOR you. In MY Resurrection is YOUR release. Our mission is to ESCAPE CRUCIFIXION; **T(458) - 285 -** not Redemption. Trust in my help, for I did not walk alone, and I will walk with you, as our Father walked with me. Did you not know that I walked with Him in peace? And does not that mean that peace goes with US on the journey?

T 11 C 15. There is no fear in perfect love.[459] We will but be making perfect TO you, what is ALREADY perfect IN you. You do not fear the UNKNOWN, but the KNOWN. You will not fail in your mission, because I failed not in mine. Give me but a little trust, in the name of the COMPLETE trust I have in you, and we will easily accomplish the goal of perfection together. For perfection IS, and cannot be denied. To deny the denial of perfection is not so difficult as the denial of truth. And what we can accomplish together MUST be believed, when you SEE it as accomplished. You who have tried to banish love have not succeeded. But you who choose to banish fear WILL succeed.

T 11 C 16. The Lord is with you,[460] but you know it not. Yet your Redeemer liveth,[461] and abideth in you in the peace out of which He was created. Would you not exchange THIS awareness for the awareness of your fear? When we have OVERCOME fear, not by hiding it, not by minimizing it, not by denying its full import in ANY way, THIS IS WHAT YOU WILL REALLY SEE. You cannot lay aside the obstacle to real vision without looking upon it, for to lay aside means to judge AGAINST. If YOU will look, the Holy Spirit will judge, AND WILL JUDGE TRULY. He cannot shine away what YOU keep hidden, for you have not offered it TO Him, and He CANNOT take it FROM you.

T 11 C 17. We therefore are embarking on an organized, well-structured, and carefully planned program, aimed at learning how to offer to the Holy Spirit everything you do NOT want. HE knows what to DO with it. You do NOT know how to use what He knows. Whatever is revealed to Him that is not of God, is gone. But you must reveal it to YOURSELF in perfect willingness, for otherwise His knowledge remains useless TO you. Surely He will not fail to help you, since help is His ONLY purpose. Do you not have greater reason for fearing the world, as you perceive it, than for looking at the cause of fear, and letting it go forever? **T(459) -286**[462]

---

[458] **John 16:16** "A little while, and you will not see Me; and again a little while, and you will see Me, because I go to the Father."

[459] **1 John 4:18** There is no fear in love: but perfect love casteth out fear, because fear hath punishment; and he that feareth is not made perfect in love.

[460] **Judges 6:12** And the Angel of the LORD appeared to him, and said to him, "The LORD is with you, you mighty man of valor!"
2nd Chronicles 15:2 And he went out to meet Asa, and said unto him, Hear ye me, Asa, and all Judah and Benjamin: the LORD is with you, while ye be with him; and if ye seek him he will be found of you; but if ye forsake him he will forsake you.
Luke 1:28 And having come in, the angel said to her, "Rejoice, highly favored one, the Lord is with you; blessed are you among women!"

[461] **Job 19:25** "But I know that my redeemer liveth, and that he shall stand up at the last upon the earth"

[462] Sept. 16

T 11 D. The Investment in Reality (*Notes* 1019 8:123)

T 11 D 1. I once asked if you were willing to sell[463] all you have, and give to the poor and follow me. This is what I meant: If you had no investment in anything in this world, you could teach the poor where THEIR treasure IS. The poor are merely those who have invested wrongly, and they are poor indeed! And because they are in need, it is given to you to help them, since you are among them. Consider how perfectly your lesson would be learned, IF YOU WERE UNWILLING TO SHARE THEIR POVERTY. For poverty is lack, and there is but one lack, since there is but one need.

T 11 D 2. Suppose a brother insists on having you do something you think you do not want to do.[464] The very fact of his insistence should tell you that HE BELIEVES SALVATION LIES IN IT. If you insist on refusing, and experience a quick response of opposition, YOU are believing that YOUR salvation lies in NOT doing it. You, then, are making the same mistake that HE is, and are making his error real to both of you. Insistence means INVESTMENT, and what you invest in is ALWAYS related to your notion of salvation. The question is always two-fold; first, WHAT is to be saved, and second, how can it BE saved?

T 11 D 3. Whenever you become angry[465] with a brother, for WHATEVER reason, you are believing that the EGO is to be saved, AND TO BE SAVED BY ATTACK. If HE attacks, you are agreeing with this belief, and if YOU attack, you are reinforcing it. REMEMBER THAT THOSE WHO ATTACK ARE POOR. Their poverty asks for gifts, NOT for further impoverishment. You who could help them are surely acting destructively, if you accept their poverty AS YOURS. If you had not invested AS THEY HAD, it would never occur to you to overlook their need. **T(460) -287**

T 11 D 4. RECOGNIZE WHAT DOES NOT MATTER, and if your brothers ask you for something[466] "outrageous," do it BECAUSE it does not matter. Refuse, and your OPPOSITION establishes that it DOES matter to you. It is only you, therefore, who have MADE the request outrageous, for nothing can BE asked OF you, and EVERY request of a brother is FOR you. Why would you insist in DENYING him? For to do so is to deny yourself, and impoverish both. HE is asking for salvation, as YOU are. Poverty is of the ego, and never of God. No "outrageous" request CAN be made of one who recognizes what is valuable, and wants to accept nothing else.

---

[463] **Mark 10:21** Then Jesus, beholding him, loved him and said to him, "One *thing* you lack. Go, sell whatever you have and give it to the poor, and you shall have treasure in Heaven. And come, take up the cross and follow Me."
Matthew 19:21 Jesus said to him, "If you want to be perfect, go, sell what you have and give to the poor, and you will have treasure in heaven; and come, follow Me."
Luke 18:22 And when Jesus heard it, he said unto him, "One thing thou lackest yet: sell all that thou hast, and distribute unto the poor, and thou shalt have treasure in heaven: and come, follow me."

[464] **Matthew 5:38-48** "Ye have heard that it was said, An eye for an eye, and a tooth for a tooth: but I say unto you, resist not him that is evil: but whosoever smiteth thee on thy right cheek, turn to him the other also. And if any man would go to law with thee, and take away thy coat, let him have thy cloak also. And whosoever shall compel thee to go one mile, go with him two. Give to him that asketh thee, and from him that would borrow of thee turn not thou away. Ye have heard that it was said, Thou shalt love thy neighbor, and hate thine enemy: but I say unto you, love your enemies, and pray for them that persecute you; that ye may be sons of your Father who is in heaven: for he maketh his sun to rise on the evil and the good, and sendeth rain on the just and the unjust. For if ye love them that love you, what reward have ye? Do not even the publicans the same? And if ye salute your brethren only, what do ye more *than others*? Do not even the Gentiles the same? Ye therefore shall be perfect, as your heavenly Father is perfect."

[465] **Matthew 5:22** "but I say unto you, that every one who is angry with his brother shall be in danger of the judgment; and whosoever shall say to his brother, Raca, shall be in danger of the council; and whosoever shall say, Thou fool, shall be in danger of the hell of fire."

[466] **Matthew 5:42** "Give to him that asketh thee, and from him that would borrow of thee turn not thou away."

Chapter 11 – God's Plan for Salvation

T 11 D 5. Salvation is for the mind, and it is attained through peace. This is the only thing that CAN be saved, and the ONLY way to save it. Any response OTHER than love, arises from a confusion about the "what" and the "how" of salvation. And this is the ONLY answer. Never lose sight of this, and never allow yourself to believe, even for an instant, that there is another answer. For you will surely place yourself among the poor, who do not understand that they dwell in abundance and that salvation is come. **T(461) - 288 -**[467]

T 11 D 6. To identify with the ego is to attack yourself, and MAKE YOURSELF POOR. That is why everyone who identifies with the ego FEELS DEPRIVED. What he EXPERIENCES is then depression or anger, but what he DID is to exchange his self-love for self-hate, MAKING HIM AFRAID OF HIMSELF. He does NOT realize this. Even if he is fully aware of ANXIETY, he does NOT perceive its source AS HIS OWN EGO IDENTIFICATION, and he ALWAYS tries to handle it by making some sort of insane "arrangement" with the world. He ALWAYS perceives this world as OUTSIDE HIMSELF, for this is crucial to his adjustment. He does NOT realize that HE MAKES THIS WORLD, for there IS no world outside him.

T 11 D 7. If only the loving thoughts of God's Son ARE the world's reality, the real world MUST be IN HIS MIND.[468] His insane thoughts, too, must be in his mind, but an INTERNAL conflict of this magnitude he cannot tolerate. For a split mind IS endangered, and the recognition that it encompasses COMPLETELY opposed thoughts within itself IS intolerable. Therefore, the mind projects the split, NOT the reality. EVERYTHING you perceive as the outside world, is merely your attempt to maintain your ego identification, for everyone believes that identification is salvation.

T 11 D 8. But consider what has happened, for thoughts have consequences to the thinker. You are AT ODDS with the world as you perceive it because you think IT is antagonistic to you. THIS IS A NECESSARY CONSEQUENCE OF WHAT YOU HAVE DONE. You have projected outward what IS antagonistic to what is inward, and therefore you would HAVE to perceive it this way. That is why you MUST realize that your hatred IS in your mind, and NOT OUTSIDE IT, before you can get rid of it. And why you MUST get rid of it, BEFORE you can perceive the world as it really is.

T 11 D 9. Long ago we said that God so loved the world[469] that He gave it TO His only-begotten Son. (that whosoever believeth on him should never see death). God DOES love the real world, and those who perceive its reality **T(462) - 289 -** CANNOT see the world of death. For death is not OF the real world, in which everything is eternal. God gave you the real world in exchange for the one you made, out of your split mind, and which IS the symbol of death. For if you could REALLY separate yourselves from the Mind of God, you WOULD die. And the world you perceive IS a world of separation.

T 11 D 10. You were willing to accept even death to deny your Father. But He would not have it so, and so it is NOT so. You still could not will against Him, and that is why you have no control over the world you made. It is NOT a world of will, because it is governed by the desire to be unlike Him. And this desire IS NOT WILL. The world you made is therefore totally chaotic, governed by arbitrary and senseless "laws," and without meaning of ANY kind. For it was made out of what you do NOT want, projected FROM your mind, because you were AFRAID of it.

T 11 D 11. Yet this world is ONLY in the mind of its maker, along with his REAL salvation. Do not believe it is outside of yourself, for only by recognizing WHERE it is, will you gain control over it. For you DO have control over your mind, for the mind is the mechanism of decision. If you will recognize that ALL attack which you perceive, is in your own mind, and NOWHERE ELSE, you will at last have placed its source, and where it began it must end. For in this place also lies salvation. The altar of God, where Christ abideth, is there.

T 11 D 12. You have defiled the altar, but NOT the world. But Christ has placed the Atonement on the altar FOR you. Bring your perceptions of the world to this altar, for it is the altar to truth. There you will see your vision changed, and there you will learn to see truly. From this place, where God and His Son dwell in peace, and where you are welcome, you will look out in peace, and behold the world truly. But to find the place, you must relinquish your investment in the world as YOU have projected it, allowing the Holy Spirit to project the real world TO you, from the altar of God. **T(463) - 290 -**

T 11 E. Seeking and Finding (*Notes* 1026 8:130)

T 11 E 1. The ego is certain that love is dangerous, and this is ALWAYS its central teaching.[470] It never PUTS it this way; on the contrary, everyone who believes that the ego is salvation is intensely engaged in the SEARCH for love. Yet the ego, though encouraging the search very actively, makes one proviso; - do not FIND it. Its dictates, then, can be summed up simply as, "Seek and do NOT find."[471] This is the ONE promise that it holds out to you, and the one promise IT WILL KEEP. For the ego pursues its goal with fanatic insistence, and its reality-testing, though severely impaired, is completely consistent.

T 11 E 2. The search which the ego undertakes is therefore bound to be defeated. And since it also teaches that IT is your identification, its guidance leads you to a journey which MUST end in perceived SELF defeat. For the ego CANNOT love, and in its frantic search FOR love, it is seeking WHAT IT IS AFRAID TO FIND. The SEARCH is inevitable, because the ego is part of your mind, and because of its source, the ego is not wholly split off, or it could not be believed at all. For it is your mind that BELIEVES in it, and gives existence TO it. Yet it is ALSO your mind that has the power to DENY its existence, and you will surely do so when you realize exactly what the journey it sets you IS.

T 11 E 3. It is surely obvious that no-one WANTS to find WHAT WOULD UTTERLY DEFEAT HIM. Being UNABLE to love, the ego would be totally inadequate in Love's presence, for it could not respond at all. YOU would HAVE to abandon its guidance, for it would be quite apparent that it had NOT taught you the response pattern you NEED. The ego will therefore DISTORT love, and teach you that LOVE calls forth the responses the ego CAN teach. Follow its teaching, then, and you will SEARCH for love, BUT WILL NOT RECOGNIZE IT.

T 11 E 4. But DO you realize that the ego MUST set you on a journey that cannot BUT lead to a sense of futility and depression? To seek and NOT to find is hardly joyous. Is this the promise YOU would keep? The Holy Spirit offers you another promise, and one that will lead to joy. For **T(464) - 291 -** HIS promise is always, "Seek and you WILL find,"[472] and under HIS guidance you cannot BE defeated. His is the journey to ACCOMPLISHMENT, and the goal HE sets before you He WILL GIVE YOU. For He will never deceive God's Son, Whom He loves with the love of the Father.

T 11 E 5. You WILL undertake a journey, because you are not at home in this world. And you WILL search for your home, whether you know where it is or not. If you believe it is OUTSIDE yourself,

---

[467] Sept. 20, 1966
[468] *Notes* adds "And everything else MUST be illusion"
[469] **John 3:16** "For God so loved the world, that he gave his only begotten Son, that whosoever believeth on him should not perish, but have eternal life."

[470] *Notes* has "teaching theme" instead of just "teaching."
[471] **Matthew 7:7** "Ask, and it will be given to you; seek, and you will find; knock, and it will be opened to you."
[472] **Matthew 7:7** "Ask, and it shall be given you; seek, and ye shall find; knock, and it shall be opened unto you."

the search will be futile, for you will be seeking where it is NOT. You do not know how to look within yourself, for you DO NOT BELIEVE YOUR HOME IS THERE. Yet the Holy Spirit knows it FOR you, and He will guide you TO your home, because that is His Mission. As He fulfills HIS mission, He will teach you YOURS. For your mission is the same as His. By guiding your BROTHERS home, you are but following HIM.

T 11 E 6. Behold the Guide your Father gave you, that you might learn you have eternal life. For death is not your Father's Will nor yours, and whatever is true IS the Will of the Father. You pay no price for life, for that was given you, but you DO pay a price for death, and a very heavy one. If death is your treasure, you will sell everything else[473] to purchase it. And you will believe that you HAVE purchased it BECAUSE you have sold everything else. BUT YOU CANNOT SELL THE KINGDOM OF HEAVEN. Your inheritance can neither be bought NOR sold.[474] There can BE no disinherited parts of the Sonship, for God is whole, and all his extensions are like Him.

T 11 E 7. The Atonement was not the price of your wholeness, but it WAS the price of your AWARENESS of your wholeness. For what you chose to "sell" had to be kept FOR you, since you COULD not "buy" it back. Yet YOU must invest in it, not with money, but WITH YOUR SPIRIT. For Spirit is Will, and will IS the "price" of the Kingdom. Your inheritance awaits only the recognition that you have BEEN redeemed. The Holy Spirit guides you into Life Eternal, but YOU must relinquish your investment in death, or you will not see it, though it is all around you. **T(465) -292**[475]

T 11 F. The Sane Curriculum (*Notes* 1031 8:135)

T 11 F 1. Only love is strong because it is UNDIVIDED. The strong do not attack, because they see no need to do so. BEFORE the idea of attack can enter your mind, YOU MUST HAVE PERCEIVED YOURSELF AS WEAK. Because you had attacked yourself, and BELIEVED THAT THE ATTACK WAS EFFECTIVE, you behold yourself as weakened. No longer perceiving yourself and all your brothers as equal, AND REGARDING YOURSELF AS WEAKER, you attempt to "equalize" the situation YOU HAVE MADE. You use attack to do so, because you believe that ATTACK WAS SUCCESSFUL IN WEAKENING YOU.

T 11 F 2. That is why the recognition of your OWN invulnerability is so important in the restoration of your sanity. For if you accept your invulnerability, you are recognizing that ATTACK HAS NO EFFECT. Although you have attacked yourself, and very brutally, you will demonstrate that NOTHING HAPPENED. Therefore, by attacking, you have NOT DONE ANYTHING. Once you realize this, there is no longer any SENSE in attack, for it manifestly DOES NOT WORK, it cannot PROTECT you. But the recognition of your invulnerability has more than merely negative value.

T 11 F 3. If your attacks on yourself FAILED to weaken you, YOU ARE STILL STRONG. You therefore HAVE no need to "equalize" the situation to ESTABLISH your strength. But you will never realize the utter uselessness of attack, EXCEPT by recognizing that your attack on YOURSELF had no effects. For others DO react to attack, if they perceive it, and if you ARE trying to attack them, you will be unable to avoid interpreting this as reinforcement. The ONLY place where you can cancel out ALL reinforcement, is IN YOURSELF. For YOU are always the first point of your attack, and if this has never been it HAS no consequences. **T(466) - 293 -**[476]

T 11 F 4. The Holy Spirit's Love is your strength, for yours is divided, and therefore not real. You could not trust your own love, when you have ATTACKED it. You cannot learn of PERFECT love with a split mind, because a split mind HAS MADE ITSELF A POOR LEARNER. You tried to make the separation eternal because you wanted to RETAIN the characteristics of creation, WITH YOUR OWN CONTENT.

T 11 F 5. Creation is NOT of you, and poor learners need special teaching. You have learning handicaps in a very literal sense. There are areas in your learning skills that are so impaired, that you can progress only under constant clear-cut direction, provided by a teacher who can TRANSCEND your limited resources. He BECOMES your resource, because OF YOURSELF, you CANNOT learn.[477] The learning situation in which you place yourself IS impossible, and IN this situation, you clearly require a special teacher, and a special curriculum.

T 11 F 6. Poor learners are not good choices for teachers, either for themselves or for anyone else. You would hardly turn to THEM to establish the curriculum by which they can ESCAPE their limitations. If they understood what is BEYOND them, they would not BE handicapped. You do NOT know the meaning of love, and this IS your handicap. Do not attempt to teach YOURSELVES what you do not understand, and do not try to set up curriculum goals, where yours have clearly failed. For YOUR learning goal has been NOT TO LEARN, and this CANNOT lead to successful learning.

T 11 F 7. You cannot transfer what you have not learned, and the impairment of the ability to generalize is a crucial learning failure. Would you ask those who have FAILED to learn, what learning aids are FOR? THEY DO NOT KNOW. For if they could INTERPRET the aids correctly, they would have LEARNED from them. We have said that the ego's rule is, "Seek and do NOT find." Translated into curricular terms, this is the same as saying, "TRY to learn but DO NOT SUCCEED." **T(467) -294**

T 11 F 8. The result of this curriculum goal is obvious. Every legitimate teaching aid, every real instruction, and every sensible guide to learning, WILL BE MISINTERPRETED. For they are all for learning FACILITATION, which this strange curriculum goal is AGAINST. If you are trying to learn how NOT to learn, and using the AIM of teaching TO DEFEAT ITSELF, what can you expect BUT confusion? The CURRICULUM does not make any sense.

T 11 F 9. This kind of learning has so weakened your mind that you CANNOT love. For the curriculum you have chosen is AGAINST love, and amounts to a course in HOW TO ATTACK YOURSELF. A necessary minor, supplementing this major curriculum goal, is in learning how NOT to overcome the split which made this goal believable. And YOU can NOT overcome it, for all YOUR learning is on its BEHALF.

T 11 F 10. Yet your will speaks against your learning, as your learning speaks against your will. And so you fight AGAINST learning, and SUCCEED, for that is your will. But you do NOT realize, even yet, that there IS something you DO will to learn, and that you CAN learn it, because it IS your will to do so. You who have tried to learn what you do NOT will, should take heart. For though the curriculum you set yourself is depressing indeed, it is merely ridiculous, IF YOU LOOK AT IT. Is it POSSIBLE that the way to achieve a goal is NOT TO ATTAIN IT?

T 11 F 11. Resign NOW as your own teachers. THIS resignation will NOT lead to depression. It is merely the result of an honest

---

[473] **Matthew 13:45-46** "Again, the kingdom of heaven is like unto a man that is a merchant seeking goodly pearls: and having found one pearl of great price, he went and sold all that he had, and bought it."

[474] **Genesis 25:31-33** But Jacob said, "Sell me your birthright as of this day." And Esau said, "Look, I am about to die; so what is this birthright to me?" Then Jacob said, "Swear to me as of this day." So he swore to him, and sold his birthright to Jacob.

[475] Sept. 21, '66

[476] Sept. 22, 1966

[477] **John 5:19** Then Jesus answered and said to them, "Most assuredly, I say to you, the Son can do nothing of Himself, but what He sees the Father do; for whatever He does, the Son also does in like manner."

appraisal of what you have taught yourselves, and of the learning outcomes which have resulted. Under the proper learning conditions, which you can neither provide nor understand, you will become excellent learners AND teachers. But it is not so yet, and will not BE so until the whole learning situation, as YOU have set it up, is reversed. **T(468) - 295 -**

T 11 F 12. Your learning POTENTIAL, properly understood, is limitless, BECAUSE IT WILL LEAD YOU TO GOD. You can TEACH the way to Him AND learn it, if you will follow the Teacher Who knows it, and the curriculum for learning it. The curriculum is totally unambiguous, because the goal is NOT divided, and the means and the end are in COMPLETE accord. YOU need offer only UNDIVIDED ATTENTION. Everything else will be GIVEN you. For it is YOUR will to learn aright, and NOTHING can oppose the will of God's Son. His learning is as unlimited as HE is. **T(469) - 296 -**[478]

T 11 G. The Vision of Christ (*Notes* 1043 8:147/149)

T 11 G 1. The ego is trying to teach you how to gain the whole world, and lose your own Soul.[479] The Holy Spirit teaches that you CANNOT lose your Soul and there IS no gain in the world, for OF ITSELF, it profits nothing.[480] To invest in something WITHOUT profit is surely to impoverish yourself, and the overhead is high. Not only is there no profit in the investment, but the cost TO YOU is enormous. For this investment costs you the world's reality, by DENYING YOURS, and gives you nothing in return. You CANNOT sell your Soul, but you CAN sell your AWARENESS of it.

T 11 G 2. You cannot perceive the soul, but you will not KNOW it while you perceive anything ELSE as more valuable. The Holy Spirit is your strength because He perceives nothing BUT your soul AS YOU. He is perfectly aware that you do NOT know yourselves, and perfectly aware of how to teach you what you are. BECAUSE He loves you, He will gladly teach you what He loves, for He wills to share it. Remembering you always, He cannot let you forget your worth. For the Father never ceases to remind Him of His Son, and He never ceases to remind His Son of the Father. God is in your memory BECAUSE of Him.

T 11 G 3. You CHOSE to forget your Father, but you did NOT will to do so. And THEREFORE, you CAN decide otherwise. As it was MY decision, so is it YOURS. YOU DO NOT WANT THE WORLD. The only thing of value in it is whatever part of it YOU look upon with love. This GIVES it the only reality it will ever have. ITS value is NOT in itself, but yours IS in you. As self value comes from self EXTENSION, so does the PERCEPTION of self value come from the projection of loving thoughts outward.

T 11 G 4. Make the world real unto YOURSELF, for the real world is the gift of the Holy Spirit, and so it BELONGS to you. Correction is for all who cannot see. To open the eyes of the blind is the Holy Spirit's mission, for He knows that they have not LOST their vision, but merely sleep. He would awaken them from the sleep of forgetting, to the remembering of God. Christ's eyes are open, and He will look upon whatever you see with love **T(470) - 297 -** if you accept His vision as yours.

T 11 G 5. The Holy Spirit keeps[481] the vision of Christ for every Son of God who sleeps. In His sight, the Son of God is perfect, and He longs to share His vision WITH you. He will SHOW you the real world, because God GAVE you Heaven. Through Him, your Father calls His Son to remember. The awakening of His Son begins with his investment in the REAL world, and BY this, he will learn to REinvest in HIMSELF. For reality is one with the Father AND the Son, and the Holy Spirit blesses the real world in Their Name.

T 11 G 6. When you have seen this real world, as you will surely do, you WILL remember us. But you must learn the cost of sleeping, AND REFUSE TO PAY IT. Only then will you decide to awake. And then the real world will spring to your sight, for Christ has never slept. He is waiting to be seen, for He has never lost sight of YOU. He looks quietly on the real world, which He would SHARE with you, because He knows of the Father's love for Him. And knowing this, He would give you what is yours.

T 11 G 7. In perfect peace, He waits for you at His Father's altar, holding out the Father's love to you, in the quiet light of the Holy Spirit's blessing. For the Holy Spirit will lead everyone home to his Father, where Christ waits as his Self. Every Child of God is one in Christ, for his Being is in Christ, as Christ's is in God. Christ's love for you is His love for His Father, which He knows because He knows His Father's love for Him. When the Holy Spirit has at last led you to Christ, at the altar to His Father, perception fuses into knowledge, because perception has become so holy that its transfer to Holiness is merely its natural extension.

T 11 G 8. Love transfers to love without ANY interference, for the situations are identical. Only the ABILITY to make this transfer is the product of learning. As you perceive more and more common elements in ALL situations, the transfer of your training, under the Holy Spirit's guidance increases and becomes generalized. Gradually, you learn to apply it to everyone and everything, for its applicability IS universal. When this has been **T(471) - 298 -** accomplished, perception and knowledge have become so similar that they share the unification of the Laws of God. What is One cannot be perceived as separate, and the denial of the separation IS the reinstatement of knowledge.

T 11 G 9. At the altar of God, the holy perception of God's Son becomes so enlightened that light streams into it, and the Spirit of God's Son shines in the Mind of the Father, and becomes one with it. Very gently does God shine upon Himself, loving the extension of Himself which is His Son. The world has no purpose, as it blends into the Purpose of God. For the real world has slipped quietly into Heaven, where everything eternal in it has always been. There, the Redeemer and the redeemed join in perfect love of God, and of each other. Heaven is your home, and being in God, it must ALSO be in you.

T 11 H. The Guide for Miracles (*Notes* 1049 8:153)

T 11 H 1. Miracles demonstrate that learning has occurred under the right guidance, for learning is invisible, and what has been learned can be recognized ONLY by its RESULTS. Its GENERALIZATION is demonstrated as you use it in more and more situations. You will recognize that you have learned there is no order of difficulty in miracles, when you have applied them to ALL situations. For there IS no situation to which miracles do not apply, and by applying them TO all situations, you will gain the REAL world. For in this holy perception, you will be made whole, and the Atonement will radiate from YOUR acceptance of it FOR YOURSELF, to everyone the Holy Spirit sends you for your blessing.

T 11 H 2. In every Child of God His blessing lies, and in your blessing of the Children of God is His blessing to YOU. Everyone in the world must play his part in the redemption of the world, to recognize that the world HAS BEEN redeemed. You cannot see the invisible. But if you see its effects, YOU KNOW IT MUST BE THERE. By perceiving what it DOES, you recognize its being. And by WHAT it does, you learn what it IS. You cannot SEE your abilities, but you gain confidence in their EXISTENCE as they enable you to ACT. And the results, of your actions you CAN see. **T(472) - 299 -**

---

[478] Sept. 21, 1966.
[479] **Mark 8:36** "For what will it profit a man if he gains the whole world, and loses his own soul?"
[480] **Proverbs 10:2** Treasures of wickedness profit nothing, But righteousness delivers from death.
John 6:63 "It is the Spirit who gives life; the flesh profits nothing. The words that I speak to you are spirit, and they are life."
[481] The *Urtext* manuscript has "keep" (no 's'), an apparent typo. It's correct, as we have it here *with* the s, in the *Notes*.

T 11 H 3. The Holy Spirit is invisible, but you CAN see the results of His Presence, and through them, you will learn that He is there. What He enables you to do is clearly NOT of this world, for miracles violate every law of reality, as this world judges it. Every law of time and space, of magnitude and mass, of prediction and control, is transcended, for what the Holy Spirit enables you to do is clearly beyond ALL of them. Perceiving His RESULTS, you will understand where He MUST be, and finally KNOW what He is. **T(473) - 300 -**[482]

T 11 H 4. You cannot see the Holy Spirit, but you CAN see His MANIFESTATIONS. And UNLESS YOU DO, you will not realize He is there. Miracles are His witnesses, and speak for his Presence. What you cannot see becomes real to you only through the witnesses who speak FOR it. For you can be AWARE of what you cannot see, and it can become compellingly real to you, as its presence becomes manifest THROUGH you. Do His work, for you SHARE in His function. As your function in Heaven is creation, so your function on earth is healing. God shares His function with you in Heaven, and the Holy Spirit shares HIS with you on earth.

T 11 H 5. As long as you believe you have two functions, so long will you need correction. For this belief is the DESTRUCTION of peace, a goal in direct opposition to the Holy Spirit's purpose. You see what you expect, and you expect what you invite. Your perception is the result of your invitation, coming to you as you sent for it. Whose manifestations would you see? Of whose presence would you be convinced? For you will believe in what you MANIFEST, and as you look out so will you see in. Two ways of looking at the world are in your mind, and your perception will reflect the guidance you chose.

T 11 H 6. I am the manifestation of the Holy Spirit, and when you see me, it will be because you have invited Him. For He will send you His witnesses if you will but look upon them. Remember always that you see what you seek,[483] for what you seek you WILL find. The ego finds what it seeks, and ONLY that. It does not find love, for that is NOT what it is seeking. But seeking and finding are the same, and if you seek for two goals, you will FIND them, but you will RECOGNIZE NEITHER. For you will think they are the same, BECAUSE YOU WANT THEM BOTH. The mind always strives for integration, and if it is split, and WANTS TO KEEP THE SPLIT, it will believe it has ONE goal by MAKING IT ONE.

T 11 H 7. We said before that WHAT you project is up to you, but it is NOT up to you WHETHER to project, for projection is a law of mind. Perception IS **T(474) - 301 -** projection, and you look in BEFORE you look out. As you look IN, you choose the guide for seeing, and THEN look out, and behold his witnesses. This is why you find what you seek. What you want IN YOURSELF you will make manifest by PROJECTION, and you will accept it FROM the world, because you put it there BY wanting it.

T 11 H 8. When you think you are projecting what you do NOT want, it is still because you DO want it. This leads DIRECTLY to dissociation, for it represents the acceptance of two goals, each perceived IN A DIFFERENT PLACE, separated from each other BECAUSE YOU MADE THEM DIFFERENT. The mind then sees a divided world OUTSIDE ITSELF, but NOT within. This gives it an illusion of integrity, and enables it to believe that IT is pursuing one goal. As long as you perceive the world as split, YOU are not healed. For to be healed is to pursue one goal, because you have ACCEPTED only one, and WANT but one.

T 11 H 9. When you want ONLY love, you will see nothing else. The contradictory nature of the witnesses you perceive is merely the reflection of your conflicting invitations. You have looked upon your minds, and accepted opposition there, having SOUGHT it there. But do not then believe that the witnesses FOR opposition are true for they attest only to your DECISION about reality, returning to you the message you GAVE them. Love is recognized by its messengers. If you make it manifest, its messengers will come to you, because you INVITED them.

T 11 H 10. The power of decision is your one remaining freedom as a prisoner of this world. YOU CAN DECIDE TO SEE IT RIGHT. What you MADE of it is NOT its reality, for its reality is only what you GAVE it. You cannot REALLY give anything BUT love to anyone or anything, nor can you really receive anything else FROM them. If you think you have received anything ELSE, it is because you have looked within, and thought you saw the power to GIVE something else WITHIN YOURSELF. It was only THIS decision that **T(475) - 302 -** determined what you found, for it was the decision OF WHAT YOU SOUGHT.

T 11 H 11. You are afraid of me because you looked within, and are afraid of what you saw. Yet you COULD not have seen reality, for the reality of your mind is the loveliest of God's Creations. Coming only from God, its power and grandeur could only bring you peace, IF YOU REALLY LOOKED UPON IT. If you are afraid, it is because you saw something THAT IS NOT THERE. Yet in this same place you could have looked upon me and all your brothers, in the perfect safety of the Mind that created us. For we are there in the peace of the Father, Who wills to PROJECT His peace through YOU.

T 11 H 12. When you have accepted your mission to PROJECT peace, you will FIND it. For by MAKING IT MANIFEST you will SEE it. Its holy witnesses will surround you, because you CALLED UPON THEM, and they will come to you. I HAVE heard your call, and I have answered it, but you will not look upon me nor hear the answer which you sought. But that is only because you do not yet want ONLY that. Yet as I become more real to you, you will learn that you DO want only that. And you will see me as you look within, and we will look upon the world as God created it together. Through the eyes of Christ, ONLY the real world exists, and can BE seen.

T 11 H 13. As you decide so will you see. And all that you see but witnesses to your decision. When you look within and see me, it will be because you have decided to manifest truth. And as you manifest it, you will see it both without AND within, for you will see it without BECAUSE you saw it first within. Everything you behold without is a JUDGMENT of what you beheld within. If it is YOUR judgment, it will be wrong, for judgment is not your function. If it is the judgment of the Holy Spirit, it will be right, for judgment IS His function. You share His function only by judging AS HE DOES, reserving no judgment at all unto yourselves. For you will judge AGAINST yourselves, but He will judge FOR you.

T 11 H 14. Remember, then, that whenever you look without and react unfavorably to what you see, you have judged yourself unworthy, and have condemned yourself **T(476) - 303 -** to death. The death penalty is the ego's ultimate goal, for it fully believes that you are a criminal, as deserving of death as God knows you are deserving of life. The death penalty never leaves the ego's mind, for that is what it always reserves for you in the end. Wanting to kill you, as the final expression of its feeling for you, it lets you live but to await death. It will torment you while you live, but its hatred is not satisfied until you die. For your destruction is the one end toward which it works, and the only one with which it will be satisfied.

T 11 H 15. The ego is not a traitor to God to Whom treachery is impossible. But it IS a traitor TO YOU who believe you have been treacherous to your Father. That is why the undoing of GUILT is an essential part of the Holy Spirit's teaching. For as long as you feel guilty, you are listening to the voice of the ego, which tells you that you HAVE been treacherous to God, AND THEREFORE DESERVE DEATH. You will think that death comes from Him, AND

---
[482] Sept. 26, 1966
[483] **Deuteronomy 4:29** But from there you will seek the LORD your God, and you will find Him if you seek Him with all your heart and with all your soul.

NOT FROM THE EGO, because, by confusing yourself WITH the ego, you believe that YOU want death. And from what you want God does NOT save you.

T 11 H 16. When you are tempted to yield to the desire for death, remember that I DID NOT DIE. You will realize that this is true when you look within and SEE me. Would I have overcome death for myself alone? And would eternal life have been given me of the Father UNLESS he had also given it to YOU? When you learn to make ME manifest, YOU will never see death. For you will have looked upon the deathless IN YOURSELF, and you will see only the eternal, as you look out upon a world that cannot die. **T(477) -304**[484]

T 11 I. Reality and Redemption (*Notes* 1059 8:163)

T 11 I 1. Do you REALLY believe that you can kill the Son of God? For the Father has hidden His Son safely within Himself, and kept him far away from your destructive thoughts, but YOU know neither the Father nor the Son because of them. You ATTACK the real world every day and every hour and every minute, and yet you are surprised that you cannot SEE it. If you seek love to attack it, YOU WILL NEVER FIND IT. For if love is SHARING, how can you find it except through ITSELF? Offer it and it will come to you, because it is drawn to itself. But offer attack and it will remain hidden, for it can live only in peace.

T 11 I 2. God's Son is as safe as his Father, for the Son knows his Father's protection and CANNOT fear. His Father's love holds him in perfect peace, and needing nothing, he asks for nothing. But he is far from you whose Self he is, for you chose to attack him, and he disappeared from your sight into his Father. HE did not change, but YOU did. For a split mind and all its works were not created by the Father, and could not live in the knowledge OF Him.

T 11 I 3. When you made what is NOT true visible, what is true became INVISIBLE. Yet it cannot be invisible in ITSELF, for the Holy Spirit sees it with perfect clarity. It IS invisible to you, because you are looking at SOMETHING ELSE. Yet it is no more up to you to decide what is visible and what is invisible, than it is up to you to decide what reality is. What can be seen is WHAT THE HOLY SPIRIT SEES. The definition of reality is God's, not yours. HE created it, and He knows what it is. You who knew have forgotten. And unless He had given you a way to remember, you would have condemned yourselves to oblivion. **T(478) -305**

T 11 I 4. Because of your Father's love, you can NEVER forget Him. For no one can forget what God Himself placed in his memory. You can DENY it, but you CANNOT LOSE IT. A Voice will answer every question you ask, and a vision will correct the perception of everything you see. For what you have made invisible is the only truth, and what you have not heard is the only answer. For God would reunite you with yourself, and did not abandon you in your seeming distress. You are waiting only for Him, and do not know it. But His memory shines in your minds, and cannot BE obliterated. It is no more past than future, being forever always.

T 11 I 5. You have but to ask for this memory, and you WILL remember. But the memory of God cannot shine in a mind which has MADE it invisible, and WANTS TO KEEP IT SO. For the memory of God can dawn only in a mind that wills to remember, and that has relinquished the insane desire to control reality. You who cannot even control yourselves, should hardly aspire to control the universe. But look upon what you have made of it, and rejoice that it is not so.

T 11 I 6. Son of God, be not content with nothing. What is not real cannot BE seen, and has NO value. God could not offer His Son what has no value, nor could His Son receive it. You were redeemed the instant you thought you had deserted Him. Everything you made has never been, and is invisible because the Holy Spirit does not see it. Yet what He DOES see is yours to behold, and through HIS vision YOUR perception is healed. You have made the INvisible the only truth that this world holds. Valuing nothing, you have sought it and found it. By making nothing real to you, you have SEEN it. **T(479) -306**

T 11 I 7. BUT IT IS NOT THERE. And Christ is invisible to you BECAUSE OF WHAT YOU HAVE MADE VISIBLE TO YOURSELVES. Yet it does not matter how much distance you have tried to interpose between your awareness and Truth. God's Son CAN be seen, because His Vision is shared. The Holy Spirit looks upon Him, and sees nothing else in you. What is invisible to you is perfect in His sight, and encompasses ALL of it. He has remembered YOU because He forgot not the Father.

T 11 I 8. You looked upon the unreal and found despair. But by SEEKING the unreal, what else COULD you find? The UNreal world IS a thing of despair, for it can never be. And you who share God's Being with Him, could never be content WITHOUT reality. What God did not give you has no power over you, and the attraction of love for love remains irresistible. For it is the function of love to unite all things unto itself, and to hold all things together by extending its wholeness.

T 11 I 9. The real world was given you by God, in loving exchange for the world YOU made, and which you SEE. But take it from the hand of Christ, and look upon it. <u>ITS</u> reality will make everything ELSE invisible, for beholding it is TOTAL perception. And as you look upon it, you will remember that it was always so. Nothingness will become invisible, for you will at last have seen truly. Redeemed perception is easily translated into knowledge, for ONLY perception is capable of error. And perception has never been. Being corrected, it gives place to knowledge, which is forever the ONLY reality. The Atonement is but the way back to what was never lost. Your Father could not cease to love His Son. **T(480) -307**

T 11 J. Guiltlessness and Invulnerability (*Notes* 1064 8:168)

T 11 J 1. If you did not feel guilty, you could not attack. For condemnation is the root of attack. It is the judgment of one mind by another as UNWORTHY of love, and DESERVING of punishment. But herein lies the split. For the mind that judges, perceives itself as SEPARATE from the mind being judged, believing that by punishing ANOTHER, IT will escape punishment. All this is but the delusional attempt of the mind to deny itself, and ESCAPE THE PENALTY OF DENIAL. It is NOT an attempt to RELINQUISH denial, but to HOLD ON TO IT. For it is guilt that has obscured the Father to you, and it is guilt that has driven you insane. The acceptance of guilt into the mind of God's Son was the beginning of the separation, as the acceptance of the Atonement is its end.

T 11 J 2. The world you see is the delusional system of those made mad by guilt. Look carefully at this world, and you will realize that this is so. For this world is the symbol of punishment, and all the laws which seem to govern it are the laws of death. Children are born into it through pain and in pain. Their growth is attended by suffering, and they learn of sorrow and separation and death. Their minds are trapped in their brain, and its powers decline[485] if their bodies are hurt. They seem to love, yet they desert, and are deserted. They appear to lose what they love, perhaps the most insane belief of all. And their bodies wither and gasp and are laid in the ground, and seem to be no more. Not one of them but has thought that God is cruel.

---

[484] Sept. 30, '66

[485] Our copy of the *Urtext* manuscript has an "s" handwritten after "decline" such that it becomes "powers declines" which is a problem of agreement in number. The *Notes* has it as this appears to have been originally typed, "powers decline" and so we are going with that option.

T 11 J 3. If this were the real world, God WOULD be cruel. For no father could subject his children to this as the price of salvation, and be loving. LOVE DOES NOT KILL TO SAVE. For if it did, attack WOULD be salvation, and this is the ego's interpretation, NOT God's. **T(481) -308** Only the world of guilt could demand this, for only the guilty could CONCEIVE of it. Adam's "sin" could have touched none of you, had you not believed that it was the FATHER Who drove him out of Paradise.[486] For it is in THAT belief that knowledge of the Father was lost, for it is only those who do not understand Him that COULD believe it.

T 11 J 4. This world IS a picture of the crucifixion of God's Son. And until you realize that God's Son CANNOT be crucified, this is the world you will see. But you will NOT realize this, until you accept the eternal fact that GOD'S SON IS NOT GUILTY. He DESERVES only love, because he has GIVEN only love. He cannot be condemned, because he has never condemned. The Atonement is the final lesson he need learn, for it teaches him that, never having sinned, HE HAS NO NEED OF SALVATION.

T 11 J 5. Long ago we said that the Holy Spirit shares the goal of all good teachers, whose ultimate aim is to make themselves unnecessary, by teaching their pupils all they know. The Holy Spirit wills ONLY this, for sharing the Father's love for His Son, He wills to remove all guilt from his mind, that he may remember his Father in peace. For peace and guilt are antithetical, and the Father can BE remembered ONLY in peace. Love and guilt cannot coexist, and to accept one is to DENY the other.

T 11 J 6. Guilt hides Christ from your sight, for it is the denial of the blamelessness of God's Son. In this strange world which you have made, the Son of God HAS sinned. How could you SEE him, then? By making HIM invisible, the world of retribution rose in the black cloud of guilt which you accepted, and you hold it dear. For the blamelessness of Christ is the proof that the ego never was, and can never be. Without guilt the ego HAS no life, and God's Son **T(482) -309** IS without guilt.

T 11 J 7. As you look upon yourselves and judge what you do honestly, as you have been asked to do, you may be tempted to wonder how you can be guiltless. But consider this. You are NOT guiltless in time, but IN ETERNITY. You HAVE "sinned" IN THE PAST, but there IS no past. Always has no direction. Time seems to go in one direction, but when you reach its end, it will roll up like a long carpet that has spread along the past behind you, and will disappear. As long as you believe the Son of God is guilty, you will walk along this carpet, believing that it leads to death. And the journey will seem long and cruel and senseless, for so it is.

T 11 J 8. The journey which the Son of God has set HIMSELF is foolish indeed. But the journey on which his Father sets him is one of release and joy. The Father is not cruel, and His Son CANNOT hurt himself. The retaliation which he fears, AND WHICH HE SEES, will never touch him, for although he BELIEVES in it, the Holy Spirit KNOWS it is not true. He stands at the end of time, where YOU must be, because He is WITH you. He has ALWAYS undone everything unworthy of the Son of God, for such was His mission, given BY God. And what God gives HAS always been.

T 11 J 9. You will see me as you learn the Son of God is guiltless. He has always sought his guiltlessness, and he has FOUND it. For everyone is seeking to escape from the prison he has made, and the way to find release is not denied him.[487] Being IN him, he has found it. WHEN he finds it is only a matter of time, and time is but an illusion. For the Son of God is guiltless NOW, and the brightness of his purity shines untouched forever in God's Mind. God's Son will ALWAYS be as he was created. Deny YOUR world, and judge him not. For his eternal guiltlessness is in the mind of his Father, and protects him forever. **T(483) -310**

T 11 J 10. When you have accepted the Atonement for yourselves, you will realize that THERE IS NO GUILT IN GOD'S SON. And ONLY as you look upon him as guiltless, can you understand his Oneness. For the IDEA of guilt brings a belief of condemnation of one by another, projecting separation in place of unity. You can condemn only yourself, and by doing so, you cannot know that you are God's Son. For you have denied the condition of his Being, which is his perfect blamelessness. Out of Love he was created, and in Love he abides. Goodness and mercy[488] have always followed him, for he has always extended the Love of his Father.

T 11 J 11. As you perceive the holy companions who travel with you, you will realize that there IS no journey, but only an awakening. The Son of God, who sleepeth not, has kept faith with his Father FOR you. There is no road to travel ON, and no time to travel THROUGH. For God waits not for His Son in time, being forever unwilling to be without him. And so it has always been. Let the holiness of God's Son shine away the cloud of guilt that darkens your mind, and by accepting his purity AS yours, learn of him that it IS yours.

T 11 J 12. You are invulnerable BECAUSE you are guiltless. You can hold on to the past ONLY through guilt. For guilt establishes that you WILL BE punished for what you have done, and thus depends on one-dimensional time, proceeding from past to future. No-one who believes this, can understand what ALWAYS means. And therefore guilt MUST deprive you of the appreciation of eternity. You are immortal BECAUSE you are eternal, and always MUST be now. Guilt, then, is a way of holding past and future in your minds, to ensure the ego's continuity. For if what it HAS BEEN[489] WILL BE punished, it's continuity WOULD be guaranteed. **T(484) -311**

T 11 J 13. But the guarantee of your continuity is God's, not the ego's. And immortality is the opposite of time, for time passes away, while immortality is constant. Accepting the Atonement teaches you WHAT IMMORTALITY IS, for by accepting your guiltlessness, you learn that the past has never been, and so the future is needless. The future IN TIME is ALWAYS associated with expiation, and ONLY guilt could induce a sense of NEED for expiation. Accepting the guiltlessness of the Son of God AS YOURS is therefore God's way of reminding you of His Son, and what he is in truth. For God has never condemned His Son, and being guiltless, he IS eternal.

T 11 J 14. You cannot dispel guilt by making it real, and THEN atoning for it. For this is the ego's plan, which it offers INSTEAD of dispelling it. The ego believes in ATONEMENT THROUGH ATTACK, being fully committed to the insane notion that attack IS salvation. And YOU who cherish guilt must ALSO believe it, for how else but by identifying WITH the ego, could you hold dear what you do not want?

---

[486] **Genesis 3:23-24** Therefore the LORD God sent him out of the garden of Eden to till the ground from which he was taken. So He drove out the man; and He placed cherubim at the east of the garden of Eden, and a flaming sword which turned every way, to guard the way to the tree of life.

[487] **Luke 4:18-19** "The Spirit of the Lord is upon me, Because he anointed me to preach good tidings to the poor: He hath sent me to proclaim release to the captives, And recovering of sight to the blind, To set at liberty them that are bruised, To proclaim the acceptable year of the Lord."

The above reference to release of prisoners, or captives, being the assignment from God which Jesus claims appears to be a quote from the prophet Isaiah:

Isaiah 61:1-2 The spirit of the Lord GOD is upon me; because the LORD hath anointed me to preach good tidings unto the meek; he hath sent me to bind up the brokenhearted, to proclaim liberty to the captives, and the opening of the prison to them that are bound; to proclaim the acceptable year of the LORD...

[488] **Psalm 23:6** Surely goodness and mercy shall follow me
  All the days of my life;
  And I will dwell in the house of the LORD
  Forever.

[489] *Notes* has "DONE" instead of "BEEN"

T 11 J 15. The ego teaches you to attack yourself BECAUSE you are guilty, and this MUST INCREASE the guilt, for guilt is the RESULT of attack. In the ego's teaching, then, there IS no escape from guilt. For attack MAKES GUILT REAL, and if it is real there IS no way to overcome it. The Holy Spirit dispels it simply through the calm recognition that it has never been. As He looks upon the guiltless Son of God, he KNOWS this is true. And being true for you, you CANNOT attack yourself, for WITHOUT guilt, attack is impossible. You, then, ARE saved BECAUSE God's Son is guiltless. And being wholly pure, you ARE invulnerable. **T(485) -312**[490]

---

[490] Oct. 4, 1966

Chapter 12 – The Problem of Guilt

T 12 A. Introduction (Notes 1075 8:179)

T 12 A 1. The ultimate purpose of projection, as the ego uses it, is ALWAYS to get rid of guilt. But, characteristically, it attempts to get rid of it FROM ITS VIEWPOINT ONLY. For much as the ego wants to RETAIN guilt, YOU find it intolerable. For guilt stands in the way of your remembering God, Whose pull is so strong that YOU cannot resist it. On this issue, then, the deepest split of all occurs, for if you are to RETAIN guilt, as the ego insists, YOU CANNOT BE YOU. Only by persuading you that IT is you, could the ego possibly induce you to PROJECT guilt, and thereby keep it in your mind.

T 12 A 2. But consider how strange a solution the ego's arrangement is. You PROJECT guilt to get rid of it, but you actually merely CONCEAL it. You DO experience guilt FEELINGS, but you have NO IDEA OF WHY. On the contrary, you associate them with a weird assortment of EGO ideals, which the ego claims you have failed. But you have no idea that you are failing the Son of God, by seeing HIM as guilty. Believing you are no longer YOU, you do not realize that you are failing YOURSELF.

T 12 B. Crucifixion by Guilt (Notes 1076 8:180)

T 12 B 1. The darkest of your hidden cornerstones holds your belief in guilt from your own awareness. For in that dark and secret place is the realization that you have betrayed God's Son, by condemning him to death. You do not even SUSPECT that this murderous but insane idea lies hidden there. For the ego's destructive urge is so intense, that nothing short of the crucifixion of God's Son can ultimately satisfy it. It does not know who the Son of God IS, because it is blind. But let it perceive guiltlessness ANYWHERE, and it will try to destroy it, because it is afraid.

T 12 B 2. Much of the ego's strange behavior is directly attributable to its definition of guilt. To the ego, THE GUILTLESS ARE GUILTY. Those who do NOT attack are its "enemies," because, by NOT VALUING its interpretation of salvation, they are in an excellent position to LET IT GO. They have approached the darkest and deepest cornerstone in the ego's foundation, and while it can withstand your raising all else to question, it guards this one secret with **T(486) 313** its life, for its existence DOES depend on keeping this secret. And it is this secret that we must look upon calmly, for the ego cannot protect you AGAINST truth, and in ITS presence the ego is dispelled.

T 12 B 3. In the calm light of truth, let us recognize that YOU BELIEVE YOU HAVE CRUCIFIED GOD'S SON. You have not admitted this "terrible" secret, because you still wish to crucify him, IF YOU COULD FIND HIM. But the wish has hidden him from you, because it is very fearful, AND YOU ARE AFRAID TO FIND HIM. You have handled this wish TO KILL YOURSELF by NOT KNOWING WHO YOU ARE, and identifying with something ELSE. You have projected guilt blindly and indiscriminately, but you have NOT uncovered its source. For the ego DOES want to kill you, and if you identify WITH it, you MUST believe ITS GOAL IS YOURS.

T 12 B 4. We once said that the crucifixion is the symbol of the ego. When it was confronted with the REAL guiltlessness of God's Son, it DID attempt to kill him. And the reason it gave was that guiltlessness is blasphemous to God. To the ego, THE EGO IS GOD, and guiltlessness MUST be interpreted AS THE FINAL GUILT WHICH FULLY JUSTIFIES MURDER. You do not yet understand that ALL your fear of this course stems ultimately from this interpretation, but if you will consider your reactions TO it, you will become increasingly convinced that this is so.

T 12 B 5. This course has explicitly stated that its goal FOR YOU is happiness and peace. Yet you are AFRAID of it. You have been told again and again that it will make you free, yet you react as if it is trying to IMPRISON you. Most of the time you DISMISS it, BUT YOU DO NOT DISMISS THE EGO'S THOUGHT SYSTEM. You HAVE seen its results and you STILL lack faith in it. You MUST, then, believe that, by NOT learning the course, YOU ARE PROTECTING YOURSELF. And you do NOT realize that it is only your guiltlessness that CAN protect you. **T(487) -314**

T 12 B 6. The Atonement has always been interpreted as the release from guilt, and this is correct, if it is understood. Yet even when I have interpreted it FOR you, you have rejected it, and have NOT accepted it FOR YOURSELF. You have recognized the futility of the ego and its offerings, but though you do not want it, you will not look upon the alternative with gladness. YOU ARE AFRAID OF REDEMPTION, and YOU BELIEVE IT WILL KILL YOU. Make no mistake about the depth of your fear. For you believe that, in the presence of truth, you will turn on yourself and DESTROY yourself.

T 12 B 7. Little children, this is not so. Your "guilty secret" is nothing, and if you will but bring it to light, the Light WILL dispel it. And then no dark cloud will remain between you and the remembrance of your Father. For you will remember His guiltless Son, who did not die because he is immortal. And you will see that you were redeemed WITH him, and have never been separated FROM him. In THIS understanding lies your remembering, for it is the recognition of love WITHOUT fear. There will be great joy in Heaven[491] on your homecoming, and the joy will be YOURS. For the redeemed son of man[492] IS the guiltless Son of God, and to recognize HIM, IS your redemption. **T(488) -315**[493]

T 12 C. The Fear of Redemption (Notes 1082 8:186)

T 12 C 1. You may wonder why it is so crucial that you look upon your hatred, and realize its full extent. And you may think that it would be easy enough for the Holy Spirit to show it to you, and dispel it WITHOUT the need for you to raise it to awareness yourself. But there is one more complication which you have interposed between yourself and the Atonement, that you do not yet realize. We have said that no one will countenance fear, IF HE RECOGNIZES IT. But in your disordered state, YOU ARE NOT AFRAID OF FEAR. You do not LIKE it, but it is NOT your desire to attack which really frightens you. You are not seriously disturbed by your hostility. You keep it hidden, because you are MORE afraid of what it covers.

T 12 C 2. You could look even upon the ego's darkest cornerstone WITHOUT fear, if you did not believe that, WITHOUT THE EGO, you would find, within yourself, something you fear even more. YOU ARE NOT AFRAID OF CRUCIFIXION. Your real terror is of REDEMPTION. Under the ego's dark foundation is the memory of God, and it is of THIS that you are really afraid. For this memory

---

[491] **Luke 15:7** "I say to you that likewise there will be more joy in heaven over one sinner who repents than over ninety-nine just persons who need no repentance."
[492] The term "Son of Man" is frequently used in the Bible to refer to "people" in general, and then by Jesus to describe himself. The Greek original actually could be translated into English as "one" or "someone" or "anyone" being a rather generic term for "human." Due to the large number of such references, we choose simply two typical ones.
Numbers 23:19 God is not a man, that he should lie; Neither the son of man, that he should repent: Hath he said, and shall he not do it? Or hath he spoken, and shall he not make it good?
Matthew 8:20 And Jesus said to him, "Foxes have holes and birds of the air have nests, but the Son of Man has nowhere to lay His head."
[493] Oct. 5, '66

would INSTANTLY restore you to your proper place, and it is THIS place that you have sought to LEAVE.

T 12 C 3. Your fear of attack is nothing, compared to your fear of love. You would be willing to look upon your savage wish to kill God's Son, IF YOU DID NOT BELIEVE THAT IT SAVES YOU FROM LOVE. For this wish CAUSED the separation. You have protected it, because you do not WANT the separation healed, and you realize that, by REMOVING the dark cloud that obscures it, your love for your Father would IMPEL you to answer His call, and leap into Heaven. You believe that attack is salvation, to PREVENT you from this. For still deeper than the ego's foundation, and MUCH stronger than IT will ever be, is your intense and burning love of God, AND HIS FOR YOU. **T(489) -316**

T 12 C 4. THIS IS WHAT YOU REALLY WANT TO HIDE. In honesty, is it not harder for you to say "I love" than "I hate?" For you associate love with weakness and hatred with strength, and your REAL power seems to you as your real weakness. For you could NOT control your joyous response to the call of love if you heard it, and the whole world you THINK you control WOULD vanish. The Holy Spirit, then, seems to be ATTACKING YOUR FORTRESS, for you would SHUT OUT GOD, and He does not will to BE excluded.

T 12 C 5. You have built your whole insane belief system, because you think you would be HELPLESS in God's Presence. And you would SAVE yourself from His love, because you think it would crush you into nothingness. You are afraid it would sweep you AWAY from yourself, AND MAKE YOU LITTLE. For you believe that magnitude lies in defiance, and attack is grandeur. YOU THINK YOU HAVE MADE A WORLD THAT GOD WOULD DESTROY. And by loving Him, WHICH YOU DO, you would throw this world away, WHICH YOU WOULD.

T 12 C 6. Therefore, you have used the world to COVER YOUR LOVE, and the deeper you go into the blackness of the ego's foundation, the CLOSER you come to the Love that is hidden beneath it. AND IT IS THIS THAT FRIGHTENS YOU. You can accept insanity, BECAUSE YOU MADE IT. But you cannot accept love, BECAUSE YOU DID NOT. You would rather be slaves of the crucifixion, than Sons of God in redemption. For your INDIVIDUAL death is more valued than your living Oneness, and what is GIVEN you, is not so dear as what you MADE. You are more afraid of God than of the ego, and love cannot enter where it is not welcome. But hatred CAN, for it enters of ITS will, and cares not for YOURS.

T 12 C 7. The reason you must look upon your delusions, and not keep them hidden, is that THEY DO NOT REST ON THEIR OWN FOUNDATION. In concealment, they APPEAR to do so, and thus they seem to be SELF-SUSTAINED. THIS is the fundamental illusion on which they rest. For BENEATH them, and concealed as long as THEY are hidden, is the loving mind that THOUGHT it made them in anger. And the pain in this mind is so apparent, when it is uncovered, that its need of healing cannot BE denied. Not all the tricks and games that you have offered it can heal it, **T(490) -317** for HERE is the REAL crucifixion of God's Son.

T 12 C 8. And yet he is NOT crucified. For here is both his pain AND his healing, for the Holy Spirit's vision is merciful, and His remedy is quick. Do not HIDE suffering from His sight, but bring it gladly TO Him. Lay before His eternal sanity ALL your hurt, and LET Him heal you. Do not leave any spot of pain hidden from His Light, and search your minds carefully for any thoughts which you may fear to uncover. For He will heal every little thought that you have kept to hurt you, and cleanse it of its littleness, restoring it to the magnitude of God.

T 12 C 9. Beneath all your grandiosity, which you hold so dear, is your real call for help. For you call for love to your Father, as your Father calls you to Himself. In that place, which you have hidden, you will only to unite with the Father, in loving remembrance of Him. You will find this place of truth as you see it in your brothers, for though they may deceive themselves, like you they long for the grandeur that is in them. And perceiving it you will WELCOME it, and it will be yours. For grandeur is the RIGHT of God's Son, and no illusions can satisfy him, or save him from what he IS.

T 12 C 10. Only his love is real, and he will be content ONLY with his reality. Save him from his illusions, that you may accept the magnitude of your Father in peace and joy. But exempt no one from your love, or you will be hiding a dark place in your minds, where the Holy Spirit is not welcome. And you will exempt YOURSELF from His healing power, for by not offering total love, YOU will not be healed completely. And healing must be as complete as fear, for love cannot enter where there is one spot of fear to mar its welcome.

T 12 C 11. You who prefer specialness to sanity could not obtain it in your right minds. You were at peace until you asked for special favor, and God did not give it. For the request was alien to Him, and you could not ask this of a Father who truly loved His Son. Therefore, you made of Him an UNloving father, demanding of Him what only such a father COULD give. And the peace of God's Son was shattered, **T(491) -318** for he no longer understood his Father. He feared what he had made, but still more did he fear his REAL Father, having attacked his glorious equality WITH Him.

T 12 C 12. In peace he needed nothing, and asked for nothing. In war he DEMANDED everything, and FOUND nothing. For how could the gentleness of love respond to his demands, EXCEPT by departing in peace, and returning to the Father?[494] If the Son did not wish to REMAIN in peace, he could not remain at all. For a darkened mind cannot live in the light, and it must seek a place of darkness, where it can believe it is where it is NOT. God did not ALLOW this to happen. But you DEMANDED that it happen, and therefore believed that it was so.

T 12 C 13. To SINGLE OUT is to MAKE ALONE, and thus MAKE LONELY. God did not do this to you. Could He SET YOU APART, KNOWING that your peace lies in His Oneness? He denied you only your request for pain, for suffering is not of His creation. Having GIVEN you creation, He could not take it FROM you. He could but answer your insane request with a sane answer, which would abide with you in your insanity. AND THIS HE DID. No-one who hears His answer but will give up insanity. For His answer is the reference point BEYOND delusions, from which you can look back on them, and see them as insane. But seek this place and you WILL find it, for Love is in you, and will lead you there. **T(492) -319**[495]

T 12 D. Healing and Time (*Notes* 1091 8:195)

T 12 D 1. And now the reason why you are afraid of this course should be apparent. For this is a course on love, because it is about YOU. You have been told that your function in this world is healing, and your function in Heaven is creating. The ego teaches that your function on earth is destruction, and that you have no function AT ALL in Heaven. It would thus destroy you here, and bury you here, leaving you no inheritance except the dust out of which it thinks you were made.[496] While it is reasonably satisfied with you,

---

[494] **Luke 2:29** "Lord, now You are letting Your servant depart in peace, According to Your word;"
John 14:12 "Most assuredly, I say to you, he who believes in Me, the works that I do he will do also; and greater works than these he will do, because I go to My Father."
John 14:28 You have heard Me say to you, "I am going away and coming back to you.' If you loved Me, you would rejoice because I said, "I am going to the Father,' for My Father is greater than I.
[495] Oct. 6, '66
[496] **Genesis 2:7** And the LORD God formed man of the dust of the ground, and breathed into his nostrils the breath of life; and man became a living being.

as its reasoning goes, it offers you oblivion. When it becomes overtly savage, it offers you hell.

T 12 D 2. Yet neither oblivion nor hell is as unacceptable to you as Heaven. For your definition of Heaven IS hell and oblivion, and the REAL Heaven is the greatest threat you think you COULD experience. For hell and oblivion are ideas which YOU made up, and you are bent on DEMONSTRATING their reality, TO ESTABLISH YOURS. If THEIR reality is questioned, you believe that YOURS is. For you believe that ATTACK established your reality, and that your DESTRUCTION is the final proof THAT YOU WERE RIGHT.

T 12 D 3. Under the circumstances, would it not be MORE DESIRABLE to have been wrong, even apart from the fact that you WERE wrong? For while it could perhaps be argued that death suggests there WAS life, no one would claim that it proves there IS life. And even the PAST life, which death might indicate, could only have been futile if it must come to this, and NEEDS this to prove that it WAS. You question Heaven, but you do NOT question this. You could heal and be healed, if you DID question it. And even though you know not Heaven, might it not be more desirable than death? You have been as selective in your questioning as in your perception. An open mind is more honest than this. **T(493) -320**[497]

T 12 D 4. The ego has a very strange notion of time, and it is with this notion that the questioning might well begin. The ego invests heavily in the past, and in the end, believes that the past is the ONLY aspect of time that is meaningful. You will remember that we said its emphasis on guilt enables it to ensure its continuity, by MAKING THE FUTURE LIKE THE PAST, and thus AVOIDING the present. By the notion of PAYING FOR the past in the future, the past becomes the DETERMINER of the future, making THEM continuous, WITHOUT an intervening present. For the ego uses the present ONLY as a brief transition TO the future, in which it brings the past TO the future, BY INTERPRETING THE PRESENT IN PAST TERMS.

T 12 D 5. NOW has no meaning to the ego. The present merely reminds it of PAST hurts, and it reacts to the present AS IF it were past. For the ego cannot tolerate RELEASE from the past, and though it is no more, the ego tries to preserve its IMAGE by responding as if it were present. Thus, it dictates reactions to those you meet NOW from a PAST reference point, obscuring their PRESENT reality. In effect, if you FOLLOW its dictates, you will react to your brothers as though they were SOMEONE ELSE, and this will surely prevent you from perceiving them AS THEY ARE. And you will receive messages from them out of your OWN past because, by making it real in the present, you are forbidding yourself to LET IT GO. You thus DENY yourself the message of release that every brother offers you NOW.

T 12 D 6. The shadowy figures from the past are precisely what you must ESCAPE. For they are not real, and have no hold over you, unless YOU bring them WITH you. They carry the spots of pain in your minds, directing you to attack in the present, in retaliation for a past that is no more. AND THIS DECISION IS ONE OF FUTURE PAIN. For unless you learn that PAST pain is delusional, you are choosing a future of delusions, and losing the endless opportunities which you COULD find for release in the present. For the ego would PRESERVE **T(494) -321** your nightmares, and PREVENT you from awaking, and understanding that THEY are past.

T 12 D 7. Would you RECOGNIZE a holy encounter, if you are merely perceiving it as a meeting with your OWN past? For you are meeting no one, and the SHARING of salvation, WHICH MAKES THE ENCOUNTER HOLY, is excluded from your sight. The Holy Spirit teaches that you always meet YOURSELF, and the encounter is holy because YOU are. The ego teaches that you always encounter your PAST, and because your dreams WERE not holy, the future CANNOT be, and the present is without meaning. It is evident that the Holy Spirit's perception of time is the exact opposite of the ego's. And the reason is equally clear, for they perceive the GOAL of time as diametrically opposed.

T 12 D 8. The Holy Spirit interprets time's PURPOSE as rendering the need for it UNNECESSARY. Thus does He regard the function of time as temporary, serving only His teaching function, which is temporary by definition. HIS emphasis is therefore on the ONLY aspect of time which CAN extend to the infinite. For NOW is the closest approximation of eternity that this world offers. And it is in the REALITY of now, without past OR future, that the beginning of the appreciation of eternity lies. For only now is HERE, and IT presents the opportunities for the holy encounters, in which salvation can be found.

T 12 D 9. The ego, on the other hand, regards the function of time as one of extending itself IN PLACE of eternity. For, like the Holy Spirit, the ego interprets the goal of time as its own. The continuity of past and future, UNDER ITS DIRECTION, is the only purpose it perceives in time, and it closes over the present, so that no gap in the EGO's continuity can occur. ITS continuity, then, would KEEP you in time, while the Holy Spirit would release you FROM it. And it is HIS interpretation of the means of salvation that you must learn to accept, if you would share His goal of salvation FOR you. **T(495) - 322**

T 12 D 10. You, too, will interpret the function of time as you interpret yours. If you accept your function in the world of time AS HEALING, you will emphasize ONLY the aspect of time in which healing can occur. For healing CANNOT be accomplished in the past, and MUST be accomplished in the present to RELEASE the future. THIS interpretation ties the future to the present, and EXTENDS THE PRESENT, rather than the past. But if you interpret your function as DESTRUCTION, you will lose sight of the present, and hold on to the past TO ENSURE A DESTRUCTIVE FUTURE. And time WILL be as you interpret it, for OF ITSELF it IS nothing. **T(496) - 323 -**[498]

T 12 E. The Two Emotions (*Notes* 1099 8:203)

T 12 E 1. We have said that you have but two emotions, love and fear. One is changeless but continually exchanged, being offered BY the eternal TO the eternal. In this exchange it is extended, for it INCREASES as it is given. The other has many forms, for the content of INDIVIDUAL illusions differs greatly. But they have one thing in common; they are all insane. They are made of sights which are NOT seen, and sounds which are NOT heard. They make up a PRIVATE world which CANNOT be shared. For they are meaningful ONLY to their maker, and so they have no meaning at all. In this world their maker moves alone, for only HE perceives them.

T 12 E 2. Each one peoples his world with figures from his INDIVIDUAL past, and it is because of this that private worlds DO differ. But the figures that he sees were NEVER real, for they are made up ONLY of his REACTIONS to his brothers, and do NOT include their reactions to HIM. Therefore he does not see that he made them, and that they ARE NOT WHOLE. For these figures HAVE NO WITNESSES, being perceived in one SEPARATE mind only.

T 12 E 3. It is THROUGH these strange and shadowy figures that the insane relate to their insane world. For they SEE only those who remind them of these images, and it is to THEM that they relate. Thus do they communicate with those who ARE NOT THERE, and it is THEY who answer them. And no-one hears their answer save him who called upon them, and he ALONE believes they answered him. Projection MAKES perception, and you CANNOT see beyond

---

Genesis 3:19 By the sweat of your brow you will eat your food until you return to the ground, since from it you were taken; for dust you are and to dust you will return.

[497] Oct. 7, 1966

[498] Oct. 10, 1966

Chapter 12 – The Problem of Guilt

it. Again and again have men attacked each other, because they saw IN THEM a shadow figure in their private world.

T 12 E 4. And thus it is that you MUST attack yourself first. For what you attack is NOT in others. Its ONLY reality is in your OWN mind, and by attacking **T(497) - 324** - others, you are literally attacking WHAT IS NOT THERE. The delusional can be very destructive, for they do not recognize they have condemned THEMSELVES. They do not wish to die, YET THEY WILL NOT LET CONDEMNATION GO. And so they SEPARATE into their private world, where everything is disordered, and where what is within, appears to be without. Yet what IS within they do NOT see, for the REALITY of their brothers they CANNOT see.

T 12 E 5. You have but two emotions, yet in your private world, you react to each of them AS THOUGH IT WERE THE OTHER. For love cannot abide in a world apart, where, when it comes, it is not recognized. If you see your own hatred AS your brother, you are not seeing HIM. Everyone draws nigh unto what he loves, and recoils from what he fears. And you react with fear to love, and draw AWAY from it. But fear ATTRACTS you, and believing it is love, you call it to yourself. Your private world is filled with the figures of fear you have invited into it. And all the love your brothers offer you, YOU DO NOT SEE.

T 12 E 6. As you look with open eyes upon your world, it MUST occur to you that you have withdrawn into insanity. For you see what is not there, and hear what is soundless. Your behavioral MANIFESTATIONS of emotions are the OPPOSITE of what the emotions ARE. You communicate with no-one, and you are as isolated from reality, as if you were ALONE in all the universe. In your madness, you OVERLOOK REALITY COMPLETELY, and you see ONLY YOUR SPLIT MIND everywhere you look. God calls you and you do not hear, for you are preoccupied with your own voice. And the vision of Christ is not in your sight, for you look upon yourself ALONE.

T 12 E 7. Little children, would you offer THIS to your Father? For if you offer it to yourself, you ARE offering it to Him. And He will NOT return it, for it is unworthy of you BECAUSE it is unworthy of Him. But He WOULD release you **T(498) - 325** - from it, and set you free. His sane answer tells you that what you have offered YOURSELF is NOT true, but HIS offering TO you has never changed. You who know not what you do, CAN learn what insanity IS, and look beyond it. It is GIVEN you to learn how to DENY insanity, and come forth from your private world in peace.

T 12 E 8. And you will see all that you denied in your brothers, BECAUSE you denied it in yourself. For you will love them, and by drawing nigh unto them, you will draw them to YOURSELF, perceiving them as witnesses to your reality, which you share with GOD. For I am WITH them, as I am with YOU. And we will draw them from their private world, for as we are united, so would we unite with them. The Father welcomes all of us in gladness, and gladness is what WE would offer Him. For every Son of God is given you, to whom God gave HIMSELF. And it is God Whom you must offer them, to recognize His gift to YOU.[499]

T 12 E 9. Vision depends on light, and you CANNOT see in darkness. Yet in the darkness, in the private world of sleep, you SEE in dreams, although your eyes are closed. And it is here that WHAT you see YOU MADE. But let the DARKNESS go, and ALL you made YOU WILL NO LONGER SEE, for sight of IT depends upon DENYING vision. But from denying vision, IT DOES NOT FOLLOW THAT YOU CANNOT SEE. Yet this is what denial DOES, for BY it you ACCEPT insanity, believing you can make a private world, AND RULE YOUR OWN PERCEPTION. But FOR this, light MUST be excluded. Dreams disappear when light has come, AND YOU CAN SEE.

T 12 E 10. Do not seek vision through YOUR eyes. For you MADE your way of seeing, that you might see in darkness, and in this you ARE deceived. BEYOND this darkness, and yet still WITHIN you, is the vision of Christ, Who looks on all in light. YOUR vision comes from fear, as His from Love. And He sees FOR you, as your witness to the real world. He is the Holy Spirit's **T(499) - 326** – MANIFESTATION, looking always on the real world, and calling forth its witnesses, and drawing them unto YOU. For He loves what He sees within you, and He would EXTEND it. And He will not return unto the Father, until He has extended your perception even unto Him. And there perception is no more, for He has RETURNED you to the Father WITH Him.[500]

T 12 E 11. You have but two emotions, and one you made and one was GIVEN you. Each is a WAY OF SEEING, and different worlds arise from their different visions. See through the vision that is GIVEN you, for through Christ's vision He beholds Himself. And seeing what He is, He knows His Father. Beyond your darkest dreams, He sees God's guiltless Son within you, shining in perfect radiance, which is undimmed by your dreams. And this YOU will see, as you look with Him. For His vision is His gift of love to you, given Him of the Father FOR you.

T 12 E 12. The Holy Spirit is the light in which Christ stands revealed. And all who would behold Him can see Him, for they have ASKED for light. Nor will they see Him ALONE, for He is no more alone than THEY are. Because they SAW the Son, they have risen IN Him to the Father.[501] And all this will they understand, because they looked within, and saw, beyond the darkness, the Christ in them, and RECOGNIZED Him. In the sanity of His vision, they looked upon themselves with love, seeing themselves as the Holy Spirit sees them. And WITH this vision of the truth in THEM, came all the beauty of the world to shine upon them. **T(500) -327**[502]

T 12 F. Finding the Present (*Notes* 1110 8:214)

T 12 F 1. To perceive truly is to be aware of ALL reality, through the awareness of your own. But for this, NO illusions can rise to meet your sight, for ALL reality leaves no room for ANY error. This means that you perceive a brother only AS YOU SEE HIM NOW. His past has NO reality in the present, and you CANNOT see it. Your past reactions TO him are also NOT THERE, and if it is to these that you react NOW, you see but an image of him that you made and cherish INSTEAD of him. In your questioning of delusions, ask yourself if it is REALLY sane to perceive WHAT WAS NOW. If you remember the PAST as you look upon him, you will be unable to perceive the reality that is NOW.

T 12 F 2. You consider it "natural" to use your PAST experience as the reference point from which to JUDGE the present. Yet this is

---

[499] There is a grammar problem here: arguably it should be "God *to* Whom." The *Notes* doesn't have a "to" but then the *Notes* often leaves out tiny fragments. The sentence is somewhat unclear the way it stands. Are we being told to offer God to Them or offer Them to God? The word "to" is added because the grammar demands it. However, in no other version is this change made, including the *Notes*. There are two possible ways to read this: Either it is *God to Whom* you must offer them (His Sons which He has just given you) or it is *God Who you must offer TO them*. Due to the use of "whom" instead of "who" here, we feel the word "to" was intended before "Whom" and that "them", who are God's Sons just given me, are to be given back to God. Otherwise, the error is using "Whom" where "Who" is proper.

[500] **John 14:12** "Most assuredly, I say to you, he who believes in Me, the works that I do he will do also; and greater works than these he will do, because I go to My Father."
John 14:28 "You have heard Me say to you, 'I am going away and coming back to you.' If you loved Me, you would rejoice because I said, 'I am going to the Father,' for My Father is greater than I."
[501] **Colossians 2:12** Buried with Him in baptism, in which you also were raised with Him through faith in the working of God, who raised Him from the dead.
Colossians 3:1 If then you were raised with Christ, seek those things which are above, where Christ is, sitting at the right hand of God.
[502] October 16, 1966

UNnatural, because it is delusional. When you have learned to look upon everyone with NO REFERENCE AT ALL to the past, either his OR yours as you perceived it, you will be able to learn FROM WHAT YOU SEE NOW. For the past can cast no shadow to darken the present, UNLESS YOU ARE AFRAID OF LIGHT. And ONLY if you are, would you choose to bring this darkness WITH you, and by holding it in your minds, see it as a dark cloud that shrouds your brothers, and conceals their reality from your sight.

T 12 F 3. THIS DARKNESS IS IN YOU. The Christ revealed to you NOW has no past, for He is changeless. AND IN HIS CHANGELESSNESS LIES YOUR RELEASE. For if He is as He was created, there IS no guilt in Him. No cloud of guilt has risen to obscure Him, and He stands revealed in everyone you meet, because you see Him through HIMSELF. **T(501) -328** To be born again[503] is to let the PAST go, and LOOK WITHOUT CONDEMNATION UPON THE PRESENT. For the cloud which obscures God's Son to you IS the past, and if you would have it past AND GONE, you must NOT SEE IT NOW. And if you see it now in your delusions, it has NOT gone from you, although it is not there.

T 12 F 4. Time can release as well as imprison, depending on whose interpretation of it you use. Past, present, and future are not continuous, UNLESS YOU FORCE CONTINUITY ON THEM. You can PERCEIVE them as continuous, and make them so FOR YOU. But do not be deceived, and then believe that this is how it IS, for to believe that reality is what you would HAVE it be, according to YOUR use for it, IS delusional. You would DESTROY time's continuity by breaking it into past, present, and future, FOR YOUR OWN PURPOSES. You would anticipate the future on the basis of your PAST experience and plan for it accordingly. And by so doing, you are ALIGNING past and future, and not allowing the miracles, which could intervene BETWEEN them, to free you to be born again.[504]

T 12 F 5. The miracle enables you to see your brother WITHOUT his past, and so perceive him as born again.[505] His errors ARE all past, and by perceiving him WITHOUT them, you are RELEASING him. And since his past is yours, you SHARE in this release. Let no dark cloud out of YOUR past obscure him from you, for truth lies ONLY in the present, and you WILL find it if you seek it there. You have looked for it where it is NOT, and therefore have not found it. Learn, then, to seek it where it IS, and it WILL dawn on eyes that see. Your past was made in anger, and if you use it to ATTACK the present you will NOT SEE the freedom that the present holds. **T(502) -329** Judgment and condemnation are BEHIND you, and unless you bring them WITH you, you WILL see that you are free of them.

T 12 F 6. Look lovingly upon the present, for it holds the ONLY things that are forever true. All healing lies within it, because ITS continuity is real. It extends to ALL aspects of consciousness AT THE SAME TIME, and thus enables them to REACH EACH OTHER. The present is before time WAS, and WILL BE when time is no more. In it is everything that is eternal, and they ARE one. THEIR continuity is timeless, and their communication is unbroken, for they are NOT SEPARATED by the past. Only the past CAN separate, and IT is nowhere.

T 12 F 7. The present offers you your brothers in the light that would unite you WITH them, and free YOU from the past. Would you, then, hold the past AGAINST them? For if you do, you are choosing to remain in the darkness THAT IS NOT THERE, and refusing to accept the light that is offered you. For the light of perfect vision is freely given, as it is freely received, and can be accepted only WITHOUT LIMIT. In this one, still dimension of time, which does not change, and where there is no sight of what you were, you look at Christ, and call His witnesses to shine on you, BECAUSE YOU CALLED THEM FORTH. And THEY will not deny the truth in you, because you looked for it in them, and FOUND it there.

T 12 F 8. Now is the time for salvation, for NOW is the release from time. Reach out to all your brothers, and touch them with the touch of Christ. In timeless union WITH them is YOUR continuity, unbroken because it is wholly shared. God's guiltless Son is ONLY light. There is no darkness in him ANYWHERE, for he is whole.[506] **T(503) -330** Call all your brothers to witness to his wholeness, as I am calling you to join with me. Every voice has a part in the song of redemption, the hymn of gladness and thanksgiving for the light, to the Creator of Light. The holy light that shines forth from God's Son is the witness that his light is of his Father.

T 12 F 9. Shine on your brothers in remembrance of your Creator, and you WILL remember Him, as you call forth the witnesses to His creation. Those whom you heal bear witness to YOUR healing, for in THEIR wholeness you will see your own. And as your hymns of praise and gladness rise to your Creator, He will return your thanks, in His clear answer to your call. For it can never be that His Son called upon Him, and remained unanswered. His call to you is but your call to Him. And in Him you are answered by His peace.

T 12 F 10. Children of Light, you know not that the Light is in you. And you will find it through its witnesses. For having given light to them, THEY WILL RETURN IT. Everyone you see IN light brings YOUR light closer to your OWN awareness. Love always leads to love. The sick, who ASK for love, are grateful for it, and in their joy, they shine with holy thanks. And this they offer you, who GAVE them joy. They are your guides to joy, for having received it OF you, they would keep it. You have established them as guides to peace, for you have made it manifest in them. And SEEING it, its beauty calls you home.

T 12 F 11. There is a light which this world cannot give. Yet YOU can give it, as it was given YOU. And AS you give it, it shines forth to call you FROM the world, and follow it. For this light **T(504) - 331** - will attract you as nothing in this world can do. And you will lay aside the world and find another. This other world is bright with love WHICH YOU HAVE GIVEN IT. And here will everything remind you of your Father and his holy Son. Light is unlimited, and spreads across this world in quiet joy. All those you brought WITH you will shine on you, and you will shine on them in gratitude, because they brought you here. Your light will join with theirs, in power so compelling, that it will draw the others out of darkness as you look on them.

T 12 F 12. Awaking unto Christ is following the laws of love OF YOUR FREE WILL, and out of quiet recognition of the truth in them. The attraction of light must draw you willingly, and willingness is signified by GIVING. Those who accept love OF you, become your willing witnesses to the love you gave them, and it is THEY who hold it out to YOU. In sleep you are alone, and your awareness is narrowed to yourself. And that is why the nightmares come. You dream of isolation, BECAUSE your eyes are closed. You do not SEE your brothers, and, in the darkness, you cannot look upon the light you GAVE to them.

T 12 F 13. And yet the laws of love are not suspended because you sleep. And you have followed them through all your nightmares, and have been faithful in your giving, for you were NOT alone. Even in sleep has Christ protected you, ensuring the real world FOR you

---

[503] John 3:3 Jesus answered and said to him, "Most assuredly, I say to you, unless one is born again, he cannot see the kingdom of God."
John 3:7 Do not marvel that I said to you, "You must be born again."
[504] see previous footnotes re: "born again"
[505] see previous footnotes re: "born again"

[506] 1 John 1:5 This is the message which we have heard from Him and declare to you, that God is light and in Him is no darkness at all.
1 John 2:8 Again, a new commandment I write to you, which thing is true in Him and in you, because the darkness is passing away, and the true light is already shining.

when you wake. In YOUR name He has given FOR you, and given YOU the gifts He gave. God's Son is still as loving as his Father. Continuous WITH his Father, he has no past APART from Him. So he has never ceased to be his Father's witness, AND HIS OWN. Although he slept, CHRIST'S VISION DID NOT LEAVE HIM. And so it is that he can call unto himself the witnesses that teach him that he never slept. **T(505) -332**[507]

T 12 G. Attainment of the Real World (*Notes* 1120 8:224)

T 12 G 1. Sit quietly and look upon the world you see, and tell yourself, "The real world is not like this. It has no buildings, and there are no streets where people walk alone and separately. There are no stores where people buy an endless list of things they do not need. It is not lit with artificial light, and night comes not upon it. There is no day that brightens and grows dim. There is no loss. Nothing is there but shines, and shines forever." This world you see MUST BE DENIED, for sight of it is costing you a different kind of vision. YOU CANNOT SEE BOTH WORLDS, for each of them involves a different kind of seeing, and depends on what you cherish. The sight of one is possible because you have denied the other.

T 12 G 2. Both are not true, yet either one will seem as real to you as the amount to which you hold it dear. And yet their power is NOT the same, because their real attraction to you is unequal. You do not really want the world you see, for it has disappointed you since time began. The homes you built have never sheltered you. The roads you made have led you nowhere, and no city that you built has withstood the crumbling assault of time. Nothing you made but has the mark of death[508] upon it. Hold it not dear, for it is old and tired, and ready to return to dust, even as you made it.[509]

T 12 G 3. This aching world has not the power to touch the living world at all. You could not give it that, and so, although you turn in sadness from it, you cannot find in it the road that leads AWAY from it into another world. Yet the REAL world HAS the power to touch you even here BECAUSE YOU LOVE IT. And what you call with love WILL come to you. LOVE ALWAYS ANSWERS, being unable to deny a call for help, or not to hear the cries of pain that rise to it, from every part of this strange world you made, but do not want. The only effort you need make, to give this world away in glad exchange for what you did NOT make is willingness to learn THE ONE YOU MADE IS FALSE. **T(506) -333**

T 12 G 4. You HAVE been wrong about the world, because you have misjudged YOURSELF. From such a twisted reference point, what COULD you see? All vision starts WITH THE PERCEIVER, who judges what is true and what is false. And what he judges false, HE DOES NOT SEE. You who would judge reality CANNOT see it, for whenever judgment enters, reality has slipped away. The out of mind is out of sight, because what is denied is THERE, but is not recognized. Christ is still there, although you know Him not. His Being does NOT depend upon your recognition. He lives within you in the quiet present, and waits for you to leave the past behind, and enter into the world He holds out to you in love.

T 12 G 5. No-one in this distracted world but has not seen some glimpses of the other world about him. But while he still lays value on his own, he will DENY the vision of the other world, maintaining that he loves WHAT HE LOVES NOT, and following not the road that love points out. Love leads so gladly! And as you follow Him, YOU will rejoice that you have found His company, and learned of Him the joyful journey home. You wait but for YOUR-SELF. To give this sad world over, and exchange your errors for the peace of God, is but YOUR will. And Christ will ALWAYS offer you the Will of God, in recognition that you share it WITH Him.

T 12 G 6. It is God's Will that nothing touch His Son except Himself, and nothing else comes nigh unto him. He is as safe from pain as God Himself, Who watches over him in everything. The world about him shines with love, because God placed him in Himself where pain is not, and love surrounds him without end or flaw. Disturbance of his peace can never be. In perfect sanity he looks on love, for it is all about him, and within him. He MUST deny the world of pain, the instant he perceives the arms of love around him. And from this point of safety, he looks quietly about him, and recognizes that the world is one with him. **T(507) -334**

T 12 G 7. The peace of God passeth[510] your understanding ONLY in the past. Yet here it IS, and you CAN understand it NOW. God loves His Son forever, and His Son RETURNS his Father's love forever. The real world is the way that leads you to remembrance of this one thing that is wholly true, and wholly YOURS. For all else you have LENT yourself in time, and it WILL fade. But this one thing is ALWAYS yours, being the gift of God unto His Son. Your ONE reality was GIVEN you, and BY it God created you as one with Him.

T 12 G 8. You will first DREAM of peace, and THEN awaken to it. Your first exchange of what you made for what, you want is the exchange of nightmares for the happy dreams of love. In these lie your true perceptions, for the Holy Spirit corrects the world of dreams, where ALL perception is. Knowledge needs NO correction. Yet the dreams of love lead UNTO knowledge. In them you see nothing fearful, and BECAUSE of this they are the welcome that you OFFER knowledge. Love waits on welcome, NOT on time, and the real world is but your welcome of what always was. Therefore the call of joy is in it, and your glad response is your awakening to what you have NOT lost. Praise, then, the Father for the perfect sanity of His most holy Son.

T 12 G 9. Your Father knoweth[511] that you have need of nothing. In Heaven this is so, for what could you need in eternity? In YOUR world you DO need things, because it is a world of scarcity in which you find yourself BECAUSE you are lacking. But CAN you find yourself in such a world? Without the Holy Spirit, the answer would be no. But BECAUSE of Him, the answer is a joyous YES. As mediator between the two worlds, He knows what you have need of, and WHICH WILL NOT HURT YOU. Ownership is a dangerous concept, if it is left to you. The ego wants to HAVE things for salvation, for possession is its law. Possession for its OWN sake is the ego's fundamental creed, a basic cornerstone in the churches that it builds unto itself. And at ITS altar, it demands you lay ALL of the things it bids you get, leaving you no joy in them. **T(508) - 335 -**

T 12 G 10. EVERYTHING that the ego tells you that you need will hurt you. For, although it urges you again and again to GET, it LEAVES you nothing, for what you get it will DEMAND of you. And even from the very hands that grasped it, it will be wrenched and hurled into the dust. For where the ego sees salvation IT SEES SEPARATION, and so you lose whatever you have gotten in its name. Therefore, ask not of yourselves what you need, FOR YOU KNOW NOT, and your advice unto yourself WILL hurt you. For what YOU think you need will merely serve to tighten up your world AGAINST the light, and render you unwilling to question the value that this world can REALLY hold for you.

---

[507] October 19, 1966
[508] **Exodus 19:12** Mark a boundary around the mountain that the people must not cross, and tell them not to go up the mountain or even get near it. If any of you set foot on it, you are to be put to death;
[509] **Genesis 3:19** By the sweat of your brow you will eat your food until you return to the ground, since from it you were taken; for dust you are and to dust you will return."
[510] **Philippians 4:6-7** In nothing be anxious; but in everything by prayer and supplication with thanksgiving let your requests be made known unto God. And the peace of God, which passeth all understanding, shall guard your hearts and your thoughts in Christ Jesus.
[511] **Luke 12:30** "For all these things do the nations of the world seek after: but your Father knoweth that ye have need of these things." also **Matthew 6:8** and **6:32**

T 12 G 11. Only the Holy Spirit KNOWS what you need. For HE will give you all things that do NOT block the way to light. And what else COULD you need? In time, He gives you all the things that you need have, and will renew them as long as you have need of them. He will take nothing FROM you, as long as you have ANY need of it. And yet He knows that EVERYTHING you need is temporary, and need but last until you step aside from ALL your needs, and learn that all of them HAVE BEEN fulfilled. Therefore, He has no investment in the things that He supplies, except to make certain that you will NOT use them on behalf of lingering in time. He knows that you are not at home there, and He wills no delay to wait upon your joyous homecoming.

T 12 G 12. Leave, then, your needs to Him. He will supply[512] them, with no emphasis at all upon them. What comes to you of Him comes safely, for He will ensure it never can become a dark spot, hidden in your mind, and kept to hurt you. Under His guidance, you will travel light and journey lightly, for His sight is ever on the journey's end, which is His goal. God's Son is not a traveler through OUTER worlds. However holy his perception may become, no world OUTSIDE himself holds his inheritance. Within HIMSELF he HAS no needs, for light needs nothing but to shine in peace. And from ITSELF, to let the rays extend in quiet to infinity.

T 12 G 13. Whenever you are tempted to undertake a foolish journey that would lead AWAY from light, remember what you REALLY want, and say, "The Holy Spirit leads **T(509) - 336** - me unto Christ, and where else would I go? What need have I but to awake in Him?" Then follow Him in joy, with faith that He will lead you safely through all the dangers to your peace of mind that this world sets before you. Kneel not before the altars to sacrifice, and seek not what you will surely lose. Content yourselves with what you will as surely KEEP, and be not restless, for you undertake a quiet journey to the peace of God, where He would have you be in quietness.

T 12 G 14. In me, you have ALREADY overcome EVERY temptation that would hold you back. We walk together on the way to quietness that is the gift of God. Hold me dear, for what EXCEPT your brothers CAN you need? We will restore to you the peace of mind that we MUST find together. The Holy Spirit will teach you to awaken unto us, and to yourself. THIS is the only REAL need to be fulfilled in time. Salvation FROM the world lies ONLY here. My peace I GIVE you.[513] TAKE it of me, in glad exchange for all the world has offered but to TAKE AWAY. And we will spread it, like a veil of light, across the world's sad face, in which we hide our brothers FROM the world, and it from them.

T 12 G 15. We cannot sing redemption's hymn alone. My task is not completed 'til I have lifted every voice with mine. And yet it is NOT mine, for as it is my gift to you, so was it the Father's gift to me, given me through His Spirit. The sound of it will banish sorrow from the mind of God's most holy Son, where it cannot abide. Healing in time IS needed, for joy cannot establish its eternal reign where sorrow dwells. You dwell not here, but in eternity. You travel but in dreams, while safe at home. Give thanks to every part of you that you have taught how to REMEMBER you. Thus does the Son of God give thanks unto his Father for his purity. **T(510) -337**

---

[512] **Philippians 4:19** And my God shall supply every need of yours according to his riches in glory in Christ Jesus.

[513] **John 14:27** "Peace I leave with you, My peace I give to you; not as the world gives do I give to you. Let not your heart be troubled, neither let it be afraid."

CHAPTER 13 – FROM PERCEPTION TO KNOWLEDGE

T 13 A. Introduction (*Notes* 1132 8:236)

T 13 A 1. All therapy is release from the past. And that is why the Holy Spirit IS the only therapist. HE TEACHES THAT THE PAST DOES NOT EXIST, a fact which belongs to the sphere of knowledge, and which therefore NO-ONE IN THE WORLD KNOWS. It would indeed be impossible to BE in the world with this knowledge. For the mind that knows this unequivocally, knows also that it dwells in eternity, and utilizes no perception at all. It therefore does not consider WHERE it is, because the concept "where" does not mean anything to it. It knows that it is EVERYWHERE, just as it has EVERYTHING and FOREVER.

T 13 A 2. The very real difference between perception and knowledge becomes quite apparent, if you consider this: there is NOTHING partial about knowledge. Every aspect is whole, and therefore NO ASPECT IS SEPARATE. YOU are an aspect of knowledge, being in the Mind of God, Who KNOWS you. All knowledge MUST be yours, for in you IS all knowledge. Perception, at its loftiest, is NEVER complete. Even the perception of the Holy Spirit, as perfect as perception CAN be, is without meaning in Heaven. Perception can reach EVERYWHERE under His guidance, for the vision of Christ beholds EVERYTHING in light. But no perception, however holy, will last FOREVER.

T 13 B. The Role of Healing (*Notes* 1133 8:237)

T 13 B 1. Perfect perception, then, has many elements IN COMMON with knowledge, making transfer TO it possible. Yet the last step must be taken by God, because the last step in your redemption, which SEEMS to be in the future, WAS accomplished by God in your creation. The separation has NOT interrupted it. Creation cannot BE interrupted. The separation is merely a faulty formulation of reality, WITH NO EFFECT AT ALL. The miracle, without a function in Heaven, IS needful here. ASPECTS of reality can still be seen, and they will replace aspects of UNREALITY. Aspects of reality can be seen IN EVERYTHING and EVERYWHERE. Yet only God can gather them together by crowning them AS ONE with the final gift of eternity. **T(511) -338**

T 13 B 2. Apart from the Father and the Son, the Holy Spirit has no function. He is not separate from either, being in the mind of both, and knowing that Mind is one. He is a thought of God, and God has GIVEN Him to you, because He has NO thoughts He does not share. His message speaks of timelessness in time, and that is why Christ's vision looks on everything with love. Yet even Christ's vision is not His reality. The golden ASPECTS of reality, which spring to light under His loving gaze, are partial glimpses of the Heaven that lies beyond them.

T 13 B 3. This is the miracle of creation; THAT IT IS ONE FOREVER. Every miracle you offer to the Son of God, is but the true perception of one ASPECT of the whole. Though every aspect IS the whole, you cannot KNOW this, until you SEE that every aspect IS THE SAME, perceived in the SAME light; and THEREFORE one. Everyone seen WITHOUT the past thus brings you nearer to the end of time, by bringing healed and healing sight into the darkness, and ENABLING THE WORLD TO SEE. For light must come into the darkened world, to make Christ's vision possible even here. Help Him to give His gift of light to all who think they wander in the darkness, and let Him gather them into His quiet sight that makes them one.

T 13 B 4. They are all the same; all beautiful, and equal in their holiness. And He will offer them unto His Father, as they were offered unto Him. There is ONE miracle, as there is ONE reality. And every miracle you do contains them all, as every aspect of reality you see blends quietly into the one reality of God. The only miracle that ever was, is God's most holy Son, created in the One Reality that is his Father. Christ's vision is His gift to you. His Being is His Father's gift to Him. **T(512) - 339 -**

T 13 B 5. Be you content with healing, for Christ's gift you CAN bestow, and your Father's gift you CANNOT lose. Offer Christ's gift to everyone and everywhere. For miracles, offered the Son of God through the Holy Spirit, attune YOU to reality. The Holy Spirit knows your part in the redemption, and who are seeking you, and where to find them. Knowledge is far beyond your individual concern. You who are part of it, and all of it, need only realize that it is of the Father, NOT of you. Your role in the redemption LEADS you to it, by re-establishing its oneness in your minds.

T 13 B 6. When you have seen your brothers as yourself, you will be RELEASED to knowledge, having learned to FREE yourself, of Him who knows of freedom. Unite with me, under the holy banner of His teaching, and, as we grow in strength, the power of God's Son will move in us, and we will leave no-one untouched and no-one left alone. And suddenly, time will be over, and we will all unite in the Eternity of God the Father. The holy light you saw OUTSIDE yourself, in every miracle you offered to your brothers, will be RETURNED to you. And, KNOWING that the light is IN you, YOUR creations will be there WITH you, as you are in your Father.

T 13 B 7. As miracles in this world join you to your brothers, so do your creations establish your fatherhood in Heaven. YOU are the witnesses to the Fatherhood of God, and He has given you the power to create the witnesses to YOURS, which is as HIS. Deny a brother here, and you deny the witnesses to your fatherhood in Heaven. The miracle which God created is perfect, as are the miracles which YOU created in His Name. They need no healing, nor do you, when you know THEM.

T 13 B 8. But in this world, your perfection is unwitnessed. God knows it, but YOU do not, and so you do not SHARE His witness TO it. Nor do you witness unto Him, for reality is witnessed to as one. God waits your witness to His Son, and to Himself. The miracles you do on earth are lifted up to Heaven, and to Him. They witness to what you do not know, and, as they reach the gates of Heaven,[514] God will open them. For never would He leave His own beloved Son outside them, and beyond Himself. **T(513) -340**

T 13 C. The Shadow of Guilt (*Notes* 1138 8:242)

T 13 C 1. Guilt remains the only thing that hides the Father, FOR GUILT IS THE ATTACK UPON HIS SON. The guilty ALWAYS condemn, and HAVING done so, they WILL condemn, linking the future to the past, as is the ego's law. Fidelity unto this law lets no light in, for it DEMANDS fidelity to darkness, and FORBIDS awakening. The ego's laws are strict, and breaches are severely punished. Therefore, give no obedience to its laws, for they ARE laws of punishment. And those who follow them believe that THEY are guilty, and so they MUST condemn. Between the future and the past, the laws of God must intervene, if you would free yourselves. Atonement stands between them, like a lamp that shines so brightly, that the chain of darkness, in which you bound yourselves will disappear.

T 13 C 2. Release from guilt is the ego's whole undoing. MAKE NO-ONE FEARFUL, for his guilt is yours, and, by obeying the ego's harsh commandments, you bring its condemnation on yourself, and you will not escape the punishment it offers those who obey it. The ego rewards fidelity to it with pain, for faith in it IS pain. And faith can be rewarded only in terms of the belief in which the faith was placed. Faith MAKES the power of belief, and

---

[514] **Genesis 28:17** And he was afraid and said, "How awesome is this place! This is none other than the house of God, and this is the gate of heaven!"

WHERE it is invested, determines its reward.[515] For faith is ALWAYS given what is treasured, and what is treasured IS returned to you.

T 13 C 3. The world can give you ONLY what you gave it, for being nothing but your own projection, it HAS no meaning apart from what you found in it, and placed your faith in. Be faithful unto darkness, and you will NOT see, because your faith WILL be rewarded as you GAVE it. You WILL accept your treasure,[516] **T(514) -341** and if you place your faith in the past, the future WILL be like it. Whate'er you hold as dear YOU THINK IS YOURS. The power of your VALUING will make it so.

T 13 C 4. Atonement brings a re-evaluation of EVERYTHING you cherish, for it is the means by which the Holy Spirit can SEPARATE the false and true, which you have accepted into your minds WITHOUT DISTINCTION. Therefore, you cannot value one without the other, and guilt has become AS TRUE FOR YOU AS INNOCENCE. You do NOT believe the Son of God is guiltless, because you see the past, and see HIM not. When you condemn a brother, you are saying, "I who WAS guilty choose to REMAIN so." You have denied HIS freedom, and by so doing, you have denied the witness unto YOURS. You could as easily have FREED him from the past, and lifted from his mind the cloud of guilt that binds him TO it. And in HIS freedom would have been your OWN.

T 13 C 5. Lay not his guilt upon him, for HIS guilt lies in his secret that HE thinks that HE has done this unto YOU. Would you then teach him that he is RIGHT in his delusion? The idea that the guiltless Son of God can attack himself, and MAKE him guilty, IS insane. In ANY form, in ANYONE, BELIEVE THIS NOT. For sin and condemnation are the same, and the belief in one is faith in the other, calling for punishment INSTEAD of love. NOTHING can justify insanity, and to call for punishment UPON YOURSELF, MUST be insane.

T 13 C 6. See no-one, then, as guilty, and you will affirm the truth of guiltlessness UNTO YOURSELF. In every condemnation that you offer the Son of God, lies the conviction of your OWN guilt. **T(515) - 342 -** If you would have the Holy Spirit make YOU free of it, accept His offer of Atonement for ALL your brothers. For so you learn that IT IS TRUE FOR YOU. Remember always that it is impossible to condemn the Son of God IN PART. Those whom you see as guilty, become the witnesses to guilt IN YOU, and you WILL see it there, for it IS there, until it is undone. Guilt is ALWAYS in your OWN mind, WHICH HAS CONDEMNED ITSELF. Project it not, for while you do, it cannot BE undone. With everyone whom you release from guilt, great is the joy in Heaven,[517] where the witnesses to your fatherhood rejoice.

T 13 C 7. GUILT MAKES YOU BLIND. For while you see one spot of guilt within you, YOU WILL NOT SEE THE LIGHT. And by projecting it, the WORLD seems dark, and shrouded in your guilt. You throw a dark veil over it, and cannot see it, BECAUSE YOU CANNOT LOOK WITHIN. You are afraid of what you would see there, but it is NOT there. THE THING YOU FEAR IS GONE. If you would look within, you would see only the Atonement, shining in quiet and in peace, upon the altar to your Father. Do not be afraid to look within. The ego tells you all is black with guilt within you, and bids you NOT TO LOOK. Instead, it bids you look upon your brothers, AND SEE THE GUILT IN THEM.

T 13 C 8. Yet this you cannot do, WITHOUT REMAINING BLIND. For those who see their brothers dark, and guilty in the dark in which they shroud them, are too afraid to look upon the light within. Within you is NOT what you believe is there, and what YOU put your faith in. Within you is the holy sign of perfect faith YOUR FATHER has in you. HE does not value you as you do. He knows Himself, and knows the truth IN YOU. He knows THERE IS NO DIFFERENCE, for He knows not of differences. Can YOU see guilt where God KNOWS there is perfect innocence? You can DENY His knowledge, but you CANNOT change it. Look, then, upon the light He placed within you, and learn that what you feared was there HAS BEEN replaced with love. **T(516) - 343 -**

T 13 D. Release and Restoration (*Notes* 1144 8:248)

T 13 D 1. You are accustomed to the notion that the mind can see the source of pain where it is not. The doubtful service of displacement is to hide the REAL source of your guilt, and KEEP from your awareness the full perception THAT IT IS INSANE. Displacement ALWAYS is maintained by the illusion that the source, from which attention is diverted, MUST BE TRUE. And MUST BE FEARFUL, or you would not have displaced the guilt onto what you believed to be LESS fearful. You are therefore willing, with little opposition, to look upon all sorts of "sources" underneath awareness, provided that they are not the deeper source, to which they bear no real relationship at all. Insane ideas HAVE no real relationships, for that is why they ARE insane.

T 13 D 2. No real relationship can rest on guilt, or even hold one spot of it, to mar its purity. For all relationships which guilt has touched, are used but to avoid the person AND the guilt. What strange relationships you have made for this strange purpose! And you forgot that real relationships are holy, and cannot be used by YOU at all. They are used ONLY by the Holy Spirit, and it is that that MAKES them pure. If you displace YOUR guilt upon them, the Holy Spirit cannot use them. For, by pre-empting FOR YOUR OWN ends what you should have given HIM, he cannot use them unto YOUR release. No-one who would unite in ANY way, with ANYONE, for his OWN salvation will find it in that strange relationship. It is not shared, and so it is not real.

T 13 D 3. In any union with a brother, in which you seek to lay YOUR guilt upon him, or share it WITH him, or perceive his own, YOU WILL FEEL GUILTY. Nor will you find satisfaction and peace with him, because your union with him IS NOT REAL. You will see guilt in that relationship, BECAUSE YOU PUT IT THERE. It is inevitable that those who suffer guilt WILL attempt to displace it, because they DO believe in it. Yet, though they suffer, they will not look within, AND LET IT GO. They cannot know they love, and cannot understand WHAT LOVING IS. Their main concern is to perceive the source of guilt **T(517) -344** OUTSIDE themselves, BEYOND their own control.

T 13 D 4. When you maintain that YOU are guilty, but the source LIES IN THE PAST, you are NOT looking inward. The past is NOT in you. Your weird associations to it HAVE no meaning in the present. Yet you let them stand BETWEEN you and your brothers, with whom you find no REAL relationships at all. Can you EXPECT to use your brothers as a means to solve the past, and still to see them as they really ARE? Salvation is not found by those who use their brothers to resolve problems WHICH ARE NOT THERE. You wanted not salvation in the past. Would you impose your idle wishes on the present, and hope to find salvation NOW?

T 13 D 5. Determine, then, to be NOT as you were. Use no relationship to hold you to the past, but with each one, each day, be born again.[518] A minute, even less, will be enough to free you from the past, and give your mind in peace over to the Atonement. When everyone is welcome to you as you would have YOURSELF be

---

[515] **Matthew 6:21** "For where your treasure is, there your heart will be also."
Hebrews 11:1 Now faith is the substance of things hoped for, the evidence of things not seen.
[516] **Matthew 6:21** "For where your treasure is, there your heart will be also."
[517] **Luke 15:7** "I say to you that likewise there will be more joy in heaven over one sinner who repents than over ninety-nine just persons who need no repentance."

[518] **John 3:3** Jesus answered and said to him, "Most assuredly, I say to you, unless one is born again, he cannot see the kingdom of God."
John 3:7 Do not marvel that I said to you, "You must be born again.'

Chapter 13 – From Perception to Knowledge

welcome to your Father, you will see no guilt in you. For you will have ACCEPTED the Atonement, which shone within you all the while you dreamed of guilt, and would not look within and SEE it.

T 13 D 6. As long as you believe that guilt is justified in ANY way, in ANYONE, WHATEVER he may do, you will not look within, where you would ALWAYS find Atonement. The end of guilt will never come as long as you believe THERE IS A REASON FOR IT. For you must learn that guilt is ALWAYS totally insane, and HAS no reason. The Holy Spirit seeks not to dispel REALITY. If GUILT were real, ATONEMENT would not be. The purpose of Atonement is to dispel illusions, NOT to establish them as real, and THEN forgive them. The Holy Spirit does not KEEP illusions in your mind to frighten you, and show them to you fearfully, to demonstrate what He has saved you FROM. T(518) - 345 -

T 13 D 7. WHAT HE HAS SAVED YOU FROM IS GONE. Give NO reality to guilt, and see NO reason for it. The Holy Spirit does what God would have Him do, and has ALWAYS done so. He has SEEN separation, but KNOWS of union. He TEACHES healing, but He also KNOWS of creation. He would have you see and teach as He does, and through Him. But what He knows, you do NOT know, though it is yours. NOW it is given you to heal and teach, to make what WILL BE, now. As yet it is NOT now. The Son of God believes that he is lost in guilt, alone in a dark world, where pain is pressing everywhere upon him, FROM WITHOUT. When he has looked within, and seen the radiance there, he will remember how much his Father loves him. And it will seem incredible that he had ever thought his Father loved him not, and looked upon him as condemned.

T 13 D 8. The moment that you realize GUILT IS INSANE, WHOLLY unjustified, and WHOLLY without reason, you will NOT fear to look upon Atonement, and ACCEPT IT WHOLLY. You who have been unmerciful unto yourselves, do not remember your Father's love. And, looking without mercy upon your brothers, you do not remember how much YOU love HIM. Yet it is forever true. In shining peace within you, is the perfect purity in which you were created. Fear not to look upon the lovely truth in you. Look THROUGH the cloud of guilt that dims your vision, and look PAST darkness, to the holy place where you will see the light.

T 13 D 9. The altar to your Father is as pure as He Who raised it to Himself. Nothing can keep FROM you what Christ would have you see. His will is like His Father's, and He offers mercy to every Child of God, as He would have YOU do. RELEASE from guilt, as you would BE released. There is no other way to look within, and see the light of love shining as steadily, and as surely, as God Himself has always loved His Son. AND AS HIS SON LOVES HIM. There is no fear in love,[519] for love is guiltless. You who have ALWAYS loved your Father can have no fear, for ANY reason, to look within, and see your holiness.

T 13 D 10. You CANNOT be as you believed you WERE. Your guilt is without reason, because it is not in the Mind of God, where YOU are. And this IS T(519) - 346 - reason, which the Holy Spirit would RESTORE to you. He would remove ONLY illusions. All else He would have you see. And in Christ's vision He would show you the perfect purity that is forever within God's Son. You cannot enter into REAL relationship with ANY of God's Sons, unless you love them all, and EQUALLY. Love is not special. If you single out PART of the Sonship for your love, you are imposing guilt on ALL your relationships, and MAKING them unreal.

T 13 D 11. You can love ONLY as God loves. Seek not to love UNLIKE Him, for there IS no love apart from His. Until you recognize that this is true, you will have no idea WHAT LOVE IS LIKE. No-one who condemns a brother, can see HIMSELF as guiltless in the peace of God.[520] If he IS guiltless and in peace, AND SEES IT NOT, he IS delusional, and has NOT looked upon himself. To him I say, "Behold the Son of God,[521] and look upon his purity, and be still. In quiet, look upon his holiness, and offer thanks unto his Father, that no guilt has ever touched him."

T 13 D 12. No illusion that you have ever held against him, has touched his innocence in any way. His shining purity, wholly untouched by guilt, and wholly loving, is bright within you. Let us look upon him together, and love him. For in our love of him IS your guiltlessness. But look upon yourself, and gladness and appreciation for what you will[522] see, will banish guilt forever. I thank You, Father, for the purity of Your most holy Son, whom Thou hast created guiltless forever.[523]

T 13 D 13. Like you, my faith and my belief are centered on what I treasure. The difference is that I love ONLY what God loves WITH me, and, because of this, I treasure you beyond the value that you set on yourselves, even unto the worth that God has placed upon you. I love all that He created. And all my faith and my belief I offer unto it. My faith in[524] you is strong as all the love I give my Father. My trust in you is without limit, and without the fear that you will hear me not. I thank the Father for your loveliness, and for the many gifts that you will let me offer to the Kingdom, in honor of its wholeness that is of God. T(520) - 347 -

T 13 D 14. Praise be unto you, who make the Father One with His Own Son. Alone we are all lowly, but together, we shine with brightness so intense, that none of us alone can even think on it. Before the glorious radiance of the Kingdom, guilt melts away, and, transformed into kindness, will never more be what it was. Every reaction that you experience will be so purified, that it is fitting as a hymn of praise unto your Father. See only praise of Him in what He has created, for He will never cease His praise of YOU. United in this praise, we stand before the gates of Heaven, where we will surely enter, in our blamelessness. God loves you. Could I, then, lack faith in you, and love Him perfectly?

T 13 D 15. Forgetfulness and sleep, and even death, become the ego's best advice for how to deal with the perceived and harsh intrusion of guilt on peace. Yet no-one sees himself in conflict, and ravaged by a cruel war, unless he believes that BOTH "opponents" in the war are real. Believing this, he must escape, for such a war would surely end his peace of mind, and so destroy him. But if he could but realize the war is between forces that are real and UNREAL powers, he could look upon himself, and SEE his freedom. No-one finds himself ravaged and torn in endless battles, which he HIMSELF perceives as wholly without meaning.

T 13 D 16. God would not have His Son embattled, and so His Son's imagined "enemy," which he made, is TOTALLY unreal. You are but trying to escape a bitter war from which you HAVE escaped. The war is gone. For you have heard the hymn of freedom, rising unto Heaven. Gladness and joy belong to God for your release, because YOU made it not. But, as you made not freedom, so

---

[519] **1 John 4:18** There is no fear in love: but perfect love casteth out fear, because fear hath punishment; and he that feareth is not made perfect in love.

[520] **1 John 2:9** He who says he is in the light, and hates his brother, is in darkness until now.

1 John 4:20 If someone says, "I love God," and hates his brother, he is a liar; for he who does not love his brother whom he has seen, how can he love God whom he has not seen?

[521] **Psalm 46:10** Be still, and know that I am God; I will be exalted among the nations, I will be exalted in the earth!

[522] *Notes* and *HLC* omit "will see" and simply read "see."

[523] **Matthew 11:25** At that time Jesus answered and said," I thank You, Father, Lord of heaven and earth, that You have hidden these things from the wise and prudent and have revealed them to babes."

John 11:41 Then they took away the stone from the place where the dead man was lying. And Jesus lifted up His eyes and said, "Father, I thank You that You have heard Me.

[524] *Notes* and *HLC* have "my faith in you is strong" while the *Ur* manuscript reads "my faith is you" which appears to be an obvios typing mistake.

you made not a war that could ENDANGER freedom. Nothing destructive ever was, or will be. The war, the guilt, the past, are gone as one, into the unreality from whence they came. **T(521) -348**[525]

T 13 E. The Guarantee of Heaven (*Notes* 1156 8:260)

T 13 E 1. When we are all united in Heaven, you will value NOTHING that you value here. For nothing that you value here you value wholly, and so you do not value it at all. Value is where God placed it, and the value of what God esteems CANNOT BE JUDGED, for it HAS BEEN ESTABLISHED. It is WHOLLY of value. It can merely be appreciated OR NOT. To value it partially is NOT TO KNOW ITS VALUE. In Heaven is everything God values, and nothing else. Heaven is perfectly unambiguous. Everything is clear and bright, and calls forth ONE response. There is no darkness, and there is no contrast. There is no variation. There is no interruption. There is a sense of peace so deep, that no dream in this world has ever brought even a dim imagining of what it is.

T 13 E 2. Nothing in this world can give this peace, for nothing in this world is wholly shared. Perfect perception can merely show you what is CAPABLE of being wholly shared. It can also show you the RESULTS of sharing, while you still remember the results of NOT sharing. The Holy Spirit points quietly to the contrast, knowing that you will finally let Him judge the difference FOR you, allowing Him to demonstrate which MUST be true. He has perfect faith in your final judgment because He knows that HE WILL MAKE IT FOR YOU. To doubt this would be to doubt that His mission will be fulfilled. How is this possible, when His mission is of God?

T 13 E 3. You whose minds are darkened by doubt and guilt, remember this; God gave the Holy Spirit TO you, and gave HIM the mission to REMOVE all doubt, and every trace of guilt, that His dear Son has laid upon himself. IT IS IMPOSSIBLE THAT THIS MISSION FAIL. **T(522) -349** Nothing can prevent what God would <u>HAVE</u> accomplished from accomplishment. Whatever your reactions to the Holy Spirit's voice may be, whatever voice you choose to listen to, whatever strange thoughts may occur to you, God's Will IS done. You WILL find the peace in which He has established you, because HE does NOT change His Mind. He is invariable as the peace in which you dwell, and of which the Holy Spirit reminds you.

T 13 E 4. You will not remember change and shift in Heaven. You have need of contrast only here. Contrast and differences are necessary teaching aids, for by them you learn what to avoid, and what to seek. When you have LEARNED this, you will find the answer that makes the need for ANY differences disappear. Truth comes of its OWN will, unto its own. When you have learned that you BELONG to truth, it will flow lightly over you, without a difference of ANY kind. For you will NEED no contrast to help you realize that THIS IS WHAT YOU WANT, and ONLY this.

T 13 E 5. Fear not the Holy Spirit will fail in what your Father has given Him to do. THE WILL OF GOD CAN FAIL IN NOTHING. Have faith in only this one thing, and it will be sufficient; God wills you be in Heaven, and nothing can keep you FROM it, or IT from you. Your wildest misperceptions, your weird imaginings, your blackest nightmares all mean nothing. They will not prevail against the peace God wills for you. The Holy Spirit WILL restore your sanity, because insanity is NOT the Will of God. If that suffices Him,[526] it is enough for you. You will NOT keep what God would have removed, because it breaks communication with you, with whom He would communicate. His voice WILL be heard. **T(523) -350**

---

[525] October 28, 1966

[526] **2 Corinthians 12:9** And He said to me, "My grace is sufficient for you, for My strength is made perfect in weakness." Therefore most gladly I will rather boast in my infirmities, that the power of Christ may rest upon me.

T 13 E 6. The communication link which God Himself placed within you, joining your minds with His, CANNOT be broken. You may believe you WANT it broken, and this belief DOES interfere with the deep peace, in which the sweet and constant communication which God would SHARE with you, is known. Yet His channels of reaching out CANNOT be wholly closed, and separated FROM Him. Peace will be yours, because His peace still flows to you, from Him Whose Will IS peace. YOU HAVE IT NOW. The Holy Spirit will teach you how to USE it, and by PROJECTING it, to learn that it IS in you.

T 13 E 7. God willed you Heaven, and will ALWAYS will you nothing else. The Holy Spirit knows ONLY of His Will. There is no chance that Heaven will not be yours, for God is sure, and what He wills is sure as He is. You will learn salvation, because you will learn HOW TO SAVE. It will not be possible to exempt yourself from what the Holy Spirit wills to teach you. Salvation is as sure as God. His certainty suffices. Learn that even the darkest nightmare that disturbed the mind of God's sleeping Son, holds no power over him. He WILL learn the lesson of awaking. God watches over him, and light surrounds him.

T 13 E 8. Can God's Son lose himself in dreams, when God has placed WITHIN him the glad call to awaken and be glad? He cannot separate himself from what is IN him. His sleep will not withstand the call to wake. The mission of redemption will be fulfilled, as surely as the Creation will remain unchanged throughout Eternity. You do NOT have to know that Heaven is yours, to MAKE it so. It IS so. But the will of God must be accepted AS your will, to KNOW it. The Holy Spirit CANNOT fail to undo FOR you everything **T(524) -351** that you have learned, that teaches you what is NOT true must be RECONCILED with truth. This is the reconciliation which the ego would substitute for your reconciliation unto sanity and unto peace.

T 13 E 9. The Holy Spirit has a very different kind of reconciliation in His mind for you, and one which HE WILL EFFECT, as surely as the ego will NOT effect what it attempts. Failure is of the ego, NOT of God. From Him you CANNOT wander, and there is no possibility that the plan the Holy Spirit offers to everyone, for the salvation OF everyone, will not be perfectly accomplished. You WILL be released, and you will NOT remember anything you made that was not created FOR you, and BY you in return. For how can you remember what was never true, or NOT remember what has always been? It is this reconciliation with truth, and ONLY truth, in which the peace of Heaven lies. **T(525) -352**[527]

T 13 F. The Testimony of Miracles (*Notes* 1166 9:3)

T 13 F 1. Yes, you are blessed indeed. But in this world, you do not know it. Yet you have the means for LEARNING it, and SEEING it quite clearly. The Holy Spirit uses logic as easily, and as well, as does the ego, except that HIS conclusions are NOT insane. They take a direction EXACTLY opposite, pointing as clearly to Heaven as the ego points to darkness and to death. We have followed much of the ego's logic, and have seen its logical conclusions. And HAVING seen them, we have realized that they can NOT be seen but in delusions. For there alone their SEEMING clearness SEEMS TO BE CLEARLY SEEN. Let us now turn AWAY from them, and follow the simple logic, by which the Holy Spirit teaches you the simple conclusions that speak for truth, and ONLY truth.

T 13 F 2. If you are blessed and do not know it, you need to learn it MUST be so. The KNOWLEDGE is not taught, but its conditions MUST be acquired, for it is THEY that have been thrown away. You CAN LEARN to bless, and CANNOT give WHAT YOU HAVE NOT. If, then, you OFFER blessing, it MUST have come FIRST TO YOURSELF. And you must also have ACCEPTED IT AS YOURS, for how else could you GIVE IT AWAY? This is

---

[527] November 2, 1966

WHY your miracles offer YOU the testimony that YOU are blessed. If what you offer IS complete forgiveness, you MUST have LET GUILT GO, accepting the Atonement for yourself, and learning you ARE guiltless. How could you learn what has been done for you, BUT WHICH YOU DO NOT KNOW, unless you do what you would HAVE to do, if it HAD BEEN done unto you?

T 13 F 3. INDIRECT proof of truth is needed in a world made of denial, and without direction. You will perceive the need for this, if you will realize that to DENY is the decision NOT to know. The logic of the world MUST therefore lead to nothing, for its GOAL is nothing. If you decide to have and give and BE nothing except a dream, you MUST direct your thoughts unto oblivion. And if you have and give and are EVERYTHING, and ALL THIS HAS BEEN DENIED, your thought system is closed off, and wholly separated from the truth. **T(526) -353** This IS an insane world, and do not underestimate the actual extent of its insanity. There is no area of your perception that it has not touched, and your dream IS sacred to you.

T 13 F 4. That is why God placed the Holy Spirit IN you, where YOU placed the dream. Seeing is ALWAYS outward. Were your thoughts wholly of YOU, the thought-system which YOU have made, WOULD be forever dark. The thoughts which the mind of God's Son projects, HAVE all the power that he gives them. The thoughts he shares with God are BEYOND his belief, but those HE made ARE his beliefs. And it is THESE, and NOT the truth, that he has chosen to defend and love. They will not be taken from him. But they CAN be given up BY him, for the Source of their undoing is IN him. There is NOTHING in the world to teach him that the logic of the world is totally insane, and leads to nothing. But in him who MADE this insane logic, there is One Who KNOWS it leads to nothing, for He knows of EVERYTHING.

T 13 F 5. Any direction which will lead you where the Holy Spirit leads you NOT, goes nowhere. Anything you deny, which He knows to be true, you have denied YOURSELF, and He must therefore teach you NOT to deny it. Undoing IS indirect, as DOING is. You were created ONLY to create, neither to see NOR do. These are but INDIRECT expressions of the will to live, which has been blocked by the capricious and unholy whim of death and murder, that your Father shared not WITH you. You have set yourselves the task of sharing what can NOT be shared. And while you think it possible to LEARN to do this, you will NOT believe all that IS possible to learn to do.

T 13 F 6. The Holy Spirit, therefore, must begin His teaching, by showing you what you can NEVER learn. His MESSAGE is not indirect, but He must introduce the simple truth into a thought-system which has become so **T(527) -354** twisted and so complex, that you CANNOT SEE that it means nothing. HE merely looks at its foundation, and DISMISSES it. But YOU, who CANNOT undo what you have made, nor escape the heavy burden of it's dullness that lies upon your minds, cannot see THROUGH it. It DECEIVES you, because you chose to deceive YOURSELVES. Those who choose to BE deceived, will merely ATTACK direct approaches, which would seem but to ENCROACH upon deception, and strike at it.

T 13 G. The Happy Learner (*Notes* 1170 9:7)

T 13 G 1. The Holy Spirit needs a happy learner, in whom His mission can be happily accomplished. You who are steadfastly devoted to misery, MUST first recognize that you ARE miserable and NOT happy. The Holy Spirit cannot teach WITHOUT this contrast, for you believe that misery IS happiness. This has so confused you, that you have undertaken to learn to do what you can NEVER do, believing that, UNLESS you learn it, you will NOT be happy. You do NOT realize that the foundation on which this most peculiar learning goal depends, means ABSOLUTELY NOTHING. This DOES make sense to you.

T 13 G 2. Have faith in nothing,[528] and you will FIND the treasure that you sought. But you will add another burden to your mind, ALREADY burdened, or you would NOT have sought another. You will believe that NOTHING IS OF VALUE, and will VALUE it. A little piece of glass, a speck of dust, a body, or a war, are one to you. For if you value ONE thing made of nothing, you HAVE believed that nothing CAN be precious, and that you CAN learn how to make the UNtrue true. The Holy Spirit, SEEING where you are, but KNOWING you are elsewhere, begins His lesson in simplicity with the fundamental teaching that TRUTH IS TRUE. This is the hardest lesson you will ever learn, and in the end, the ONLY one. **T(528) - 355 -**

T 13 G 3. Simplicity is very difficult for twisted minds. Consider all the distortions you have made of nothing; all the strange forms and feelings, and actions and reactions, that you have woven out of it. Nothing is so alien to you as the simple truth and nothing are you LESS inclined to listen to. The contrast between what is true, and what is not, is PERFECTLY apparent, yet you do NOT see it. The simple and the obvious are NOT apparent to those who would make palaces and royal robes of nothing, believing they are kings with golden crowns BECAUSE of them. All this the Holy Spirit sees, and teaches, simply, that ALL THIS IS NOT TRUE.

T 13 G 4. To these unhappy learners, who would teach themselves that it is NOT nothing, and delude themselves into believing that it is NOT nothing, the Holy Spirit says, with steadfast quietness, "The truth is true. Nothing else matters, nothing else is real, and EVERYTHING beside it is not there. Let Me make the one distinction FOR you, which you CANNOT make, but NEED to learn. Your faith in nothing IS deceiving you. Offer your faith to Me, and I will place it gently in the holy place where it belongs. You will find NO deception there, but only the simple Truth. And you will love it, because you will UNDERSTAND it."

T 13 G 5. Like you, the Holy Spirit did NOT make truth. Like God, He KNOWS it to be true. He brings the LIGHT of truth into the darkness, and LETS it shine on you.[529] And as it shines, YOUR BROTHERS see it, and, realizing that this light is NOT what you have made, they see in you MORE than YOU see. They will be happy learners of the lesson which this light brings to them, because it teaches them release from nothing, and from all the works of nothing. The heavy chains which SEEM to bind them unto despair, they do NOT see as nothing, until YOU bring the light TO them. And THEN they see the chains have disappeared, and so they MUST have been nothing.

T 13 G 6. And YOU will see it WITH them. BECAUSE you taught them gladness and release, they will become YOUR teachers in release and gladness. When you teach ANYONE that truth is true, YOU LEARN IT WITH HIM. And so you learn **T(529) - 356 -** that what seemed hardest was the easiest. Learn to be happy learners. You will NEVER learn how to make nothing everything. But see that this HAS BEEN your goal, and RECOGNIZE how foolish it has been. Be glad it is undone, for, when you look at it in simple honesty, it IS undone. We said before, "Be not content with nothing," for you HAVE believed that nothing COULD content you. IT IS NOT SO.

T 13 G 7. If you would be a happy learner, you must give EVERYTHING that YOU have learned over to the Holy Spirit, to be UNlearned FOR you. And THEN begin to learn the joyous lessons

---

[528] **Matthew 6:21** "For where your treasure is, there your heart will be also."
[529] **Numbers 6:24-25** The LORD make his face to shine upon thee, and be gracious unto thee: The LORD lift up his countenance upon thee, and give thee peace.
Luke 1:79 "To give light to those who sit in darkness and the shadow of death, To guide our feet into the way of peace. "
John 1:5 And the light shines in the darkness, and the darkness did not comprehend it.

that come quickly, on the firm foundation that truth is true. For what is built there IS true, and BUILT on truth.[530] The universe of learning will open up before you, in all its gracious simplicity. With truth before you, you will not look back. The happy learner meets the conditions of learning here, as he also meets the conditions of knowledge in the Kingdom.

T 13 G 8. All this lies in the Holy Spirit's plan to free you from the past, and open up the way to freedom FOR you. For truth IS true. What else could ever be, or ever was? This simple lesson holds the key to the dark door, which you believe is locked forever. You MADE this door OF nothing, and behind it IS nothing. The key is only the light which shines away the shapes and forms and fears of nothing. Accept this key to freedom, from the hands of Christ, Who gives it to you, that you may join Him in the holy task of bringing light to darkness. For, like your brothers, YOU do not realize the light has come, and freed you from the sleep of darkness.

T 13 G 9. Behold your brothers in their freedom, and learn of them how to be FREE of darkness. The light in you will waken them, and they will not leave YOU asleep. The Vision of Christ is GIVEN, the very instant that it is perceived. Where everything is clear, it is ALL holy. The quietness of its simplicity is so compelling, that you will realize IT IS IMPOSSIBLE TO DENY THE SIMPLE TRUTH. For there IS nothing else. God is everywhere, and His Son is IN Him WITH everything. Can he sing the dirge of sorrow, when THIS is true? **T(530) - 357 -**[531]

T 13 H. The Decision for Guiltlessness (*Notes* 1182 9:19)

T 13 H 1. Learning will be commensurate with motivation, and the interference in your motivation for learning, is EXACTLY the same as that which interferes with ALL your thinking. The happy learner CANNOT FEEL GUILTY ABOUT LEARNING. This is so ESSENTIAL to learning, that it should never be forgotten. The guiltless learner learns so easily, BECAUSE HIS THOUGHTS ARE FREE. But this entails the recognition that GUILT IS INTERFERENCE, NOT SALVATION, and serves NO useful function at all.

T 13 H 2. You are accustomed to using guiltlessness merely to offset the pain of guilt, and do not look upon it as having value IN ITSELF. You believe that guilt AND guiltlessness are BOTH of value, each representing an ESCAPE from what the other does NOT offer you. You do NOT want either alone, for without both, you do not see YOURSELVES as whole, and therefore happy. You are whole ONLY in your guiltlessness, and only in your guiltlessness, CAN you be happy. There IS no conflict here.

T 13 H 3. To wish for guilt in ANY way, in ANY form, will lose[532] appreciation of the value of your guiltlessness, and push it from your sight. There is NO compromise that you can make with guilt, and escape from the pain which ONLY guiltlessness allays. Learning is living here, as creating is Being in Heaven. Whenever the pain of guilt seems to ATTRACT you, remember that, if you yield to it, you are deciding AGAINST your happiness, and will NOT learn how to be happy. Say, therefore, to yourself, gently, but with the conviction born of the love of God and of His Son:

What I experience I will make manifest.
If I am guiltless, I have nothing to fear.
I choose to testify to my ACCEPTANCE of the Atonement,
NOT FOR ITS REJECTION.
I would accept my guiltlessness by making it manifest,
and SHARING it.
Let me bring peace to God's Son from his Father. **T(531) - 358 -**

T 13 H 4. Each[533] day, each hour and minute, - even each second, - you are deciding between the crucifixion and the Resurrection; between the ego and the Holy Spirit. The ego is the choice for guilt, the Holy Spirit the decision for blamelessness. The power of decision is all that is yours. What you can decide BETWEEN is fixed, because there are no alternatives, EXCEPT truth and illusion. And there is no overlap between them, because they are opposites which CANNOT be reconciled, and CANNOT both be true. You are guilty OR guiltless, bound OR free, happy OR unhappy.

T 13 H 5. The miracle teaches you that you have chosen guiltlessness, freedom, and joy. It is not a cause, but an EFFECT. It is the natural result of CHOOSING RIGHT, attesting to your happiness that comes from choosing to be FREE of guilt. Everyone you offer healing TO, returns it. Everyone you attack, KEEPS it and cherishes it, by holding it AGAINST you. Whether he DOES this, or does it not, will make no difference. YOU WILL THINK HE DOES. It is impossible to offer WHAT YOU DO NOT WANT, without this penalty. The cost of giving IS receiving. Either it is a penalty from which you suffer, or the happy purchase of a treasure to hold dear.

T 13 H 6. No penalty is ever asked of God's Son, except BY himself and OF himself. Every chance given to him to heal, is another opportunity to replace darkness with light, and fear with love.[534] If he refuses it, he binds himself TO darkness because he did not choose to free his brother, and enter light WITH him.[535] By GIVING power to nothing, he threw away the joyous opportunity to learn that nothing HAS no power. And, by NOT DISPELLING, darkness, HE became afraid of darkness AND of light. The joy of learning darkness has no power over the Son of God, is the happy lesson the Holy Spirit teaches, and would have YOU teach WITH Him. It is HIS joy to teach it, as it will be YOURS.

T 13 H 7. The way to teach this simple lesson is merely this; guiltlessness IS invulnerability. Therefore, make your INVULNERABILITY manifest to everyone, and teach him that, WHATEVER he may try to do to you, your perfect freedom from the belief that you can BE harmed, shows him HE is guiltless. He can do NOTHING that can hurt you, and by refusing to allow him to THINK HE CAN, you teach him **T(532) - 359 -** that the Atonement, which you have accepted for yourself, IS ALSO HIS. THERE IS NOTHING TO FORGIVE. No-one can hurt the Son of God. His guilt is WHOLLY without cause, and, being without cause, CANNOT exist.

T 13 H 8. God is the ONLY Cause, and guilt is NOT of Him. Teach no-one he has hurt you, for, if you do, you teach YOURSELF that what is NOT of God, HAS POWER OVER YOU. THE CAUSELESS CANNOT BE. Do not attest to it, and do not foster belief in it in any mind. Remember always MIND IS ONE, and CAUSE IS ONE. You will learn communication with this Oneness ONLY when you learn to DENY the causeless, and accept the Cause of God as YOURS. The power that God has given to His Son IS his, and nothing else can His Son see, or choose to look upon, without

---

[530] **John 1:5** "Therefore whoever hears these sayings of Mine, and does them, I will liken him to a wise man who built his house on the rock: and the rain descended, the floods came, and the winds blew and beat on that house; and it did not fall, for it was founded on the rock."
Matthew 7:24-27 "But everyone who hears these sayings of Mine, and does not do them, will be like a foolish man who built his house on the sand: and the rain descended, the floods came, and the winds blew and beat on that house; and it fell. And great was its fall."

[531] November 6, 1966.

[532] The *Urtext* manuscript has this as "lost" but both the earlier *Notes* and the alter *HLC* has this is as "lose" which suggests "lost" was a typo.

[533] Nov. 12, 1966

[534] **1 John 1:5** "This is the message which we have heard from Him and declare to you, that God is light and in Him is no darkness at all."
1 John 2:8 Again, a new commandment I write to you, which thing is true in Him and in you, because the darkness is passing away, and the true light is already shining.

[535] **Matthew 16:19** "And I will give you the keys of the kingdom of heaven, and whatever you bind on earth will be bound in heaven, and whatever you loose on earth will be loosed in heaven."
John 20:23 "If you forgive the sins of any, they are forgiven them; if you retain the sins of any, they are retained."

imposing on HIMSELF the penalty of guilt, IN PLACE of all the happy teaching the Holy Spirit would gladly offer him.

T 13 H 9. Whenever you decide to make decisions FOR YOURSELF, you are thinking self-destructively, and the decision WILL BE WRONG. It will hurt you, because of the CONCEPT of decision which led to it. It is not true that you can make decisions BY yourself, or FOR yourself alone. No thought of God's Son CAN be separate, or isolated in its effects. Every decision is made for the WHOLE SONSHIP, directed in and out, and influencing a constellation larger than anything you ever dreamed of. Those who accept Atonement, ARE invulnerable. But those who believe they are guilty, WILL respond to guilt, because THEY THINK IT IS SALVATION, and will NOT refuse to see it, and side WITH it. They BELIEVE that INCREASING guilt is self-PROTECTION. And they fail to understand the simple fact that, what they do NOT want, MUST hurt them.

T 13 H 10. All this arises because they do NOT believe that WHAT THEY WANT IS GOOD. Yet will was given them BECAUSE it is holy, and will bring TO them ALL that they need, coming as naturally as peace that knows no limits. There is NOTHING their wills will not provide, that offers them ANYTHING of value. But, because they do NOT understand their will, the Holy Spirit quietly understands if[536] FOR them, and gives them what THEY will, without effort, strain, or the impossible burden of deciding WHAT THEY WANT AND NEED ALONE. It will never happen that you will have to make decisions FOR YOURSELF. You are NOT bereft of help, and HELP THAT KNOWS THE ANSWER. Would you be content with little, which is all that YOU ALONE can T(533) - 360 -[537] offer yourself, when He Who GIVES YOU EVERYTHING will simply OFFER it TO you?

T 13 H 11. He will never ask what you have done to make you worthy of the gift of God. Ask it not therefore of yourselves. Instead, accept His answer, for He KNOWS you are worthy of everything God wills FOR you. Do not try to escape the gift of God, which He so freely, and so gladly offers you. He offers you but what God gave Him FOR you. You need NOT decide whether or not you are DESERVING of it. GOD KNOWS THAT YOU ARE. Would you deny the truth of GOD'S decision, and place your pitiful appraisal of yourself, in place of His calm and unswerving value of His Son? NOTHING can shake God's conviction of the perfect purity of everything that He created, for it IS wholly pure. Do not decide AGAINST it, for being of Him it MUST be true.

T 13 H 12. Peace abides in every mind that quietly accepts the plan that GOD has set for his Atonement, RELINQUISHING HIS OWN. You know NOT of Salvation, for you do NOT understand it. Make no decisions about what it is, or where it lies, but ask of the Holy Spirit EVERYTHING, and leave ALL decisions to His gentle counsel. The One Who knows the plan, of God which God would have you follow, can teach you what it IS. Only His wisdom is capable of guiding you to follow it. Every decision you undertake alone but signifies that you would define what Salvation is, and what you would be saved <u>FROM</u>. The Holy Spirit KNOWS that ALL Salvation is escape from guilt. You have no other "enemy," and against this strange distortion of the purity of the Son of God, the Holy Spirit is your ONLY friend. **T(534) -361**

T 13 H 13. He is the strong protector of your innocence, which sets you free.[538] And it is HIS decision to undo EVERYTHING that would obscure your innocence from your unclouded mind. Let Him, therefore, be the only guide that you would follow to Salvation. He knows the way, and leads you gladly on it. WITH Him, you will not fail to learn what God wills FOR you IS your will. WITHOUT His guidance, you will think you know alone, and will decide AGAINST your peace, as surely as you made the wrong decision in ever thinking that Salvation lay in you alone. Salvation is of Him to Whom God GAVE it FOR you. He has not forgotten it. Forget HIM not, and He will make EVERY decision for you, for YOUR Salvation and the peace of God in you.

T 13 H 14. Seek not to appraise the worth of God's Son, whom He created holy, for to do so is TO EVALUATE HIS FATHER, and judge AGAINST Him. And you WILL feel guilty for this imagined "crime," which no one in this world, or Heaven, CAN POSSIBLY commit. God's Spirit teaches only that the "sin" of SELF replacement on the throne of God is NOT a source of guilt. What CANNOT happen, can have no effects to fear. Be quiet in your faith in Him, Who loves you, and would lead you out of insanity. Madness may be your CHOICE, but NOT your reality. Never forget the Love of God, Who HAS remembered you. For it is quite impossible that He could ever let His Son drop from His loving Mind, wherein he was created, and where his abode was fixed in perfect peace forever.

T 13 H 15. Say to the Holy Spirit only, "Decide for me," and it is done. For His decisions are reflections of WHAT GOD KNOWS ABOUT YOU, and in this light, error of ANY kind becomes impossible. Why would you struggle so frantically to anticipate all that you CANNOT know, **T(535) -362** when ALL knowledge lies behind EVERY decision that the Holy Spirit makes FOR YOU? Learn of His wisdom and His love, and teach His answer to everyone who struggles in the dark. For you decide for THEM AND for yourself. How gracious is it to decide all things through Him, Whose equal love is given equally to all alike. He leaves you no one OUTSIDE yourself, alone WITHOUT you. And so He gives you what is yours, because your Father would have you share it WITH him.

T 13 H 16. In everything be led by Him, and do not reconsider. Trust Him to answer quickly, surely, and with love for everyone who will be touched, in any way by the decision. And EVERYONE will be. Would you take unto yourself the sole responsibility for deciding what can bring ONLY good to everyone? Would you KNOW this? You taught YOURSELVES the most unnatural habit of NOT communicating with your Creator. Yet you remain in close communication with Him, and with everything that is within Him, as it is within YOURSELF. UNlearn isolation through His loving guidance, and learn of all the happy communication that you have thrown away, but could NOT lose.

T 13 H 17. Whenever you are in doubt what you should do, think of His Presence in you, and tell yourself this, and ONLY this: "He leadeth me,[539] and knows the way, which I know not. Yet He will never KEEP from me what He would have me LEARN. And so I trust Him to communicate to me all that He knows FOR me." Then let Him teach you quietly how to perceive your guiltlessness, which is ALREADY there. **T(536) -363**

T 13 I. The Way of Salvation (*Notes* 1190 9:27)

T 13 I 1. When you accept a brother's guiltlessness, you will SEE Atonement in him. For, by proclaiming it in HIM, you make it YOURS, and you WILL see what you sought. You will not see the symbol of your brother's guiltlessness shining within him, while you still believe IT IS NOT THERE. HIS guiltlessness is YOUR Atonement. Grant it to him, and you will see the truth of what you have acknowledged. Yet truth is offered FIRST, to be received, even as God gave it first to His Son. The first in time means nothing, but the First in Eternity is God the Father, Who is both First and One. Beyond the First, there is no other, for there is no order, no second or third, and nothing BUT the First.

---

[536] *Notes* and *HLC* have "it" here ... obvious typo.
[537] Nov. 12, 1966
[538] **John 8:32** "And you shall know the truth, and the truth shall make you free."

[539] **Psalm 23:2-3** He maketh me to lie down in green pastures; He leadeth me beside the still waters. He restoreth my soul; He leadeth me in the paths of righteousness For his name's sake.

T 13 I 2. You who belong to the First Cause, created by Him like unto Himself, and part of Him, are more than merely guiltless. The state of guiltlessness is only the condition in which what is NOT there has been REMOVED, from the disordered mind that THOUGHT it WAS. This state, and only this, must YOU attain with God beside you. For until you do, you will still think that you are separate FROM Him. You can feel His Presence NEXT TO you, but CANNOT know that you are one with Him. This need not be taught. Learning applies ONLY to the condition IN WHICH IT HAPPENS of itself.

T 13 I 3. When you have let all that has obscured the truth in your most holy mind be undone for you, and stand in grace before your Father, He will give Himself to you, as He has ALWAYS done. Giving Himself is all He knows, and so it is ALL knowledge. For what He knows NOT cannot be, and therefore CANNOT BE GIVEN. Ask not to BE forgiven, for this has already been accomplished. Ask rather to LEARN how to forgive, and restore WHAT ALWAYS WAS to your unforgiving mind. Atonement becomes real and visible, to them that USE it. On earth, it is your ONLY function, and you **T(537) -364** must learn that it is all you WANT to learn.

T 13 I 4. You WILL feel guilty 'til you learn this. For, in the end, whatever form it takes, your guilt arises from your failure to fulfill your function in God's Mind with ALL OF YOURS. Can you ESCAPE this guilt, by failing to fulfill your function HERE? You need not understand creation, to do what must be done, BEFORE that knowledge would be meaningful to you. God breaks no barriers; neither did He MAKE them. When YOU release them, they are gone. God will not fail, nor ever has, in anything.

T 13 I 5. Decide that God is right, and YOU are wrong, about yourself. He created you out of Himself, but still WITHIN Him. He knows what you are. Remember that there is no second to Him.

There cannot, therefore, be anyone WITHOUT His Holiness, nor anyone unworthy of His perfect love. Fail not in your function of loving in a loveless place, made out of darkness and deceit, for thus are darkness and deception UNdone. FAIL NOT YOURSELF, but instead, offer to God AND YOU His blameless Son. For this small gift of appreciation FOR His love, God will Himself exchange your gift for HIS.

T 13 I 6. Before you make ANY decisions for yourself, remember that YOU HAVE DECIDED AGAINST YOUR FUNCTION IN HEAVEN, and consider carefully whether you WANT to make decisions here. Your function here is only to decide AGAINST deciding what you want, in recognition that YOU DO NOT KNOW. How, then, CAN you decide what you should do? Leave ALL decisions to the One Who speaks for God, and for your function as He KNOWS it. So will He teach you to remove the awful burden you have laid upon yourself, by loving not the Son of God, and trying to teach him guilt INSTEAD of love. Give up this frantic and insane attempt, **T(538) -365** which cheats you of the joy of living with your God and Father, and awaking gladly to His Love and Holiness, which join together as truth in YOU, making you One with Him.

T 13 I 7. When you have learned how to decide WITH God, ALL decisions become as easy and as right as breathing. There is no effort, and you will be led as gently, as if you were being carried along a quiet path in summer. Only your own volition seems to make deciding hard. The Holy Spirit will not delay at all in answering your EVERY question what to do. He KNOWS. And He will TELL you, and then do it FOR you. You who are tired might consider whether this is not more restful than sleep. For you can bring your guilt into sleeping, but NOT into this. **T(539) - 366 -**[540]

---

[540] November 16, 1966.

CHAPTER 14 – BRINGING ILLUSIONS TO TRUTH

T 14 A. Introduction (*Notes* 1196 9:33)

T 14 A 1. Unless you are guiltless you cannot know God, Whose Will is that you know Him. Therefore, you MUST be guiltless. But, if you do not accept the necessary conditions for knowing Him, YOU HAVE DENIED HIM, and do not recognize Him, though He is all around you. He cannot be known without His Son, whose guiltlessness IS the condition for knowing Him. Accepting His Son as guilty is denial of the Father so complete, that knowledge is swept away from recognition, in the very mind where God Himself has placed it. If you would but listen, and learn how impossible this is! Do not endow Him with attributes YOU understand. You made Him not, and anything YOU understand, is not of Him.

T 14 A 2. Your task is not to make reality. It is here, WITHOUT your making, but NOT without YOU. You who have thrown your selves away, and valued God so little, hear me speak for Him, and for yourselves. You cannot understand how much your Father loves you, for there is no parallel in your experience of the world to help you understand it. There is nothing on earth with which it can compare, and nothing you have ever felt, APART from Him, that resembles it ever so faintly. You cannot even give a blessing in perfect gentleness. Would you know of One Who gives forever, and Who knows of nothing EXCEPT giving?

T 14 A 3. The Children of Heaven live in the light of the blessing of their Father, because THEY KNOW THAT THEY ARE SINLESS. The Atonement was established as the means of restoring guiltlessness to the mind which has denied it, and thus denied Heaven to Itself. Atonement teaches you the true condition of the Son of God. It does NOT teach you what you are, or what your Father is. The Holy Spirit, Who remembers this FOR you, merely teaches you how to REMOVE the blocks that stand between you and what YOU know. His memory is YOURS. If you remember what YOU have made, you are remembering nothing. Remembrance of reality is in HIM, and THEREFORE in you.

T 14 B. Guilt and Guiltlessness (*Notes* 1198 9:35)

T 14 B 1. The guiltless and the guilty are totally incapable of understanding one T(540) - 367 – another. Each perceives the other AS LIKE HIMSELF, making them unable to communicate, because each sees the other UNLIKE the way he sees himself. God can communicate ONLY to the Holy Spirit in your mind, because only He shares the knowledge of what you are WITH God. And only the Holy Spirit can answer God for YOU, for only He knows what God IS. Everything ELSE, that YOU have placed within your mind, CANNOT exist, for what is not in communication with the Mind of God, has never been. Communication with God is Life. Nothing without it IS at all.

T 14 B 2. The only part of your mind that has reality, is the part that links you still with God. Would you have ALL of it transformed into a radiant message of God's Love, to share with all the lonely ones, who have denied Him with you? GOD MAKES THIS POSSIBLE. Would you deny His yearning to be known? You yearn for Him, as He for you. This is forever changeless. Accept, then, the immutable. Leave the world of death behind, and return quietly to Heaven. There is NOTHING of value here, and EVERYTHING of value there. Listen to the Holy Spirit, and to God through Him. He speaks of you to YOU. There IS no guilt in you, for God is blessed in His Son, as the Son is blessed in Him.

T 14 B 3. Each one of you has a special part to play in the Atonement, but the message given to each to share is always the same; GOD's SON IS GUILTLESS. Each one teaches the message differently, and learns it differently. But UNTIL he teaches it and learns it, he will suffer the pain of dim awareness, that his true function remains unfulfilled in him. The burden of guilt is heavy, but God would not have you bound by it. HIS plan for your awaking is as perfect as yours is fallible. You know not what you do,[541] but He Who knows is with you. His gentleness is yours, and all the love you share with God, He holds in trust for you. He would teach you nothing except how to be happy. T(541) - 368 -

T 14 B 4. Blessed Son of a wholly blessing Father, joy was created FOR you. Who can condemn whom God has blessed? There is nothing in the Mind of God that does not share his shining innocence. Creation is the natural extension of perfect purity. Your only calling here is to devote yourself, with active willingness, to the denial of guilt in ALL its forms. To accuse is NOT TO UNDERSTAND. The happy learners of the Atonement become the teachers of the innocence that is the RIGHT of all that God created. Deny them not what is their due, for you will not withhold it from them alone.

T 14 B 5. The inheritance of the Kingdom is the right of God's Son, given him in his creation. Do not try to steal it from him, or you will ASK for guilt and WILL experience it. PROTECT his purity from every thought that would steal it away, and keep it from his sight. BRING INNOCENCE TO LIGHT, in answer to the call of the Atonement. Never allow purity to remain hidden, but shine away the heavy veils of guilt, within which the Son of God has hidden himself from his own sight. We are all joined in the Atonement here, and nothing else can unite us in this world. So will the world of separation slip away, and full communication be restored between the Father and the Son.

T 14 B 6. The miracle acknowledges the guiltlessness which MUST have been denied, to produce NEED of healing. Do not withhold this glad acknowledgment, for hope of happiness, and release from suffering of every kind, lies in it. Who is there but wishes to be free of pain? He may not yet have learned HOW to exchange his guilt for innocence, nor realize that ONLY in this exchange can freedom from pain be his. But those who have failed to learn need TEACHING, NOT attack. To attack those who have need of teaching is to fail to learn FROM them.

T 14 B 7. Teachers of innocence, each in his own way, have joined together, taking their part in the unified curriculum of the Atonement. There is no unity of learning goals apart from this. There is no conflict in this curriculum, which has ONE aim, however it is taught. Each effort made on T(542) - 369 - its behalf is offered to the single purpose of RELEASE from guilt, to the eternal glory of God and His creation. And every teaching that points to this points straight to Heaven, and to the peace of God. There is no pain, no trial, no fear, that teaching this can fail to overcome. The power of God Himself supports this teaching, and GUARANTEES its limitless results

T 14 B 8. Join your own efforts to the Power that cannot fail, and MUST result in peace. No-one can be untouched by teaching such as this. You will not see yourself BEYOND the power of God if you teach only this. You will NOT be exempt from the effect of this most holy lesson, which seeks but to restore what is the right of God's creation. From everyone whom you accord release from guilt, you will INEVITABLY learn YOUR innocence. The circle of Atonement HAS no end. And you will find ever-increasing confidence in your safe inclusion in what is for all, in everyone you bring within its safety and its perfect peace.

T 14 B 9. Peace, then, be unto everyone who becomes a teacher of peace.[542] For peace is the acknowledgment of perfect purity, from

---

[541] **Luke 23:34** And Jesus said, "Father, forgive them; for they know not what they do." And parting his garments among them, they cast lots.

[542] **John 20:21** So Jesus said to them again, "Peace to you! As the Father has sent Me, I also send you."

which no-one is excluded. Within its holy circle, is everyone whom God created as His Son. Joy is its unifying attribute, with no-one left outside, to suffer guilt alone. The power of God draws everyone to its safe embrace of love and union. Stand quietly within this circle, and attract all tortured minds to join with you, in the safety of its peace and holiness. Abide with me within it,[543] as teachers of Atonement, NOT of guilt.

T 14 B 10. Blessed are ye who teach with me. Our power comes not of us, but of our Father. In guiltlessness we know Him, as He knows us guiltless. I stand within the circle, calling YOU to peace. Teach peace with me, and stand with me on holy ground.[544] Remember for everyone your Father's power, that He has given them. Believe not that you cannot teach His perfect peace. Stand not outside, but join with me within. Fail not the only purpose to which MY teaching calls you. Restore to God His Son, as He created him, by teaching T(543) - 370 - him his innocence.

T 14 B 11. The crucifixion had no part in the Atonement. Only the Resurrection became my part in it. THAT is the symbol of the RELEASE from guilt, by guiltlessness. Whomever you perceive as guilty, you would crucify. But you RESTORE guiltlessness to whomever you SEE as guiltless. Crucifixion is ALWAYS the ego's aim. It SEES AS GUILTY, and BY its condemnation, IT WOULD KILL. The Holy Spirit sees only guiltlessness, and, in His gentleness, He would RELEASE from fear, and re-establish the reign of love. The power of love is in His gentleness, which is of God and therefore cannot crucify, nor suffer crucifixion. The temple you restore becomes YOUR altar, for it was re-built through YOU. And everything you give to God IS yours. Thus He creates, and thus must YOU restore.

T 14 B 12. Each one you see you place, within the holy circle of Atonement, or leave outside, judging him fit for crucifixion or redemption. If you bring him INTO the circle of purity, you will rest there WITH him. If you leave him without, you JOIN him there. Judge not, except in quietness which is NOT of you.[545] Refuse to accept anyone as WITHOUT the blessing of Atonement, and bring him INTO it by blessing him. Holiness MUST be shared, for therein lies everything that makes it holy. Come gladly to the holy circle, and look out in peace on all who think they are outside. Cast no-one out, for this is what HE seeks along with you. Come, let us join him in the holy place of peace, which is for all of us, united as one, within the cause of peace. T(544) - 371 -

T 14 C. Out of the Darkness (*Notes* 1208 9:45)

T 14 C 1. The[546] journey that we undertake together is the change of dark for light, of ignorance for understanding. NOTHING YOU UNDERSTAND IS FEARFUL. It is only in darkness and in ignorance that you perceive the frightening, and you shrink away from it to further darkness. And yet, it is only the hidden that CAN terrify, NOT for what it IS, but FOR its hiddenness. The obscure is frightening, BECAUSE you do not understand its meaning. If you did, IT would be clear, and you would be no longer in the dark. Nothing has HIDDEN value, for what is hidden CANNOT be shared, and so its value is unknown. The hidden is KEPT APART, but value ALWAYS lies in joint appreciation. What is concealed CANNOT be loved, and so it MUST be feared.

T 14 C 2. The quiet light in which the Holy Spirit dwells within you, is merely perfect openness, in which nothing is hidden, and therefore nothing is feared. Attack will ALWAYS yield to love, if it is brought TO love, not hidden FROM it. There is no darkness that the light of love will not dispel, unless it is concealed from love's beneficence. What is KEPT APART from love CANNOT share its healing power, because it has been separated off, and KEPT IN DARKNESS. The sentinels of darkness watch over it carefully, and you who made these guardians of illusion out of nothing, are now AFRAID of them.

T 14 C 3. Would you continue to give imagined power to these strange ideas of safety? They are neither safe nor unsafe. They do not protect, NEITHER DO THEY ATTACK. They DO nothing at all, BEING nothing at all. As guardians of darkness and of ignorance, look to them ONLY for fear, for what they keep obscure IS fearful. But let them go, and what WAS fearful, will be so no longer. Without protection of obscurity, ONLY the light of love remains, for only this HAS meaning, and CAN live in light. Everything else MUST disappear.

T 14 C 4. Death yields to life, simply because destruction IS NOT TRUE. The light of guiltlessness shines guilt away because, when they are BROUGHT TOGETHER, the truth T(545) - 372 - of one MUST make the falsity of its OPPOSITE perfectly clear. Keep not guilt and guiltlessness APART, for your belief that you can HAVE THEM BOTH, is meaningless. All you have done by keeping them apart is LOSE THEIR MEANING, by confusing them with each other. And so you do not realize that only one means ANYTHING, and the other is wholly without sense of ANY kind.

T 14 C 5. You have interpreted the separation as a means which you have made for BREAKING your communication with your Father. The Holy Spirit re-interprets it as a means of re-establishing what has NOT been broken, but HAS been made obscure. All things you made have use to Him, for His most holy purpose. He KNOWS you are not separate from God, but He perceives much in your mind that lets you THINK you are. All this, and nothing else, would He separate FROM you. The power of decision, which you made IN PLACE of power of creation, He would teach you how to use ON YOUR BEHALF. You who made it to crucify yourselves, must learn of Him how to apply it to the holy cause of restoration.

T 14 C 6. You who speak in dark and devious symbols, do not understand the language you have made. It HAS no meaning, for its purpose is NOT communication, but rather, the DISRUPTION of communication. If the purpose of language IS communication, how can this tongue mean ANYTHING? Yet even this strange and twisted effort to communicate through NOT communicating, holds enough of love to MAKE IT MEANINGFUL, IF ITS INTERPRETER IS NOT ITS MAKER. You who made it are but expressing CONFLICT, from which the Holy Spirit would RELEASE you. Leave what you would communicate to Him. He will interpret it to you with perfect clarity, for He knows with Whom you ARE in perfect communication.

T 14 C 7. You know not what you say, and so you know not what is said to you. But your Interpreter perceives the meaning in your alien language. He will not attempt to communicate the meaningless. But He WILL separate out all that HAS meaning, dropping off all the rest, and offering your true communication to those T(546) - 373 - who would communicate as truly WITH you. YOU SPEAK TWO LANGUAGES AT ONCE, and this MUST lead to unintelligibility. But if one means nothing, and the other EVERYTHING, only that one is possible for purposes of communication. The other but INTERFERES with it.

T 14 C 8. The Holy Spirit's function is ENTIRELY communication. He therefore MUST remove whatever INTERFERES with it, in order to RESTORE it. Therefore, keep no source of interference from His sight, for He will NOT attack your sentinels. But bring them TO Him, and let His gentleness teach you that, in the light, they are not fearful, and CANNOT serve to guard the dark doors behind which nothing at all is carefully concealed. We must open all

---

[543] **John 15:10** "If you keep My commandments, you will abide in My love, just as I have kept My Father's commandments and abide in His love."
[544] **Exodus 3:4-5** And when the LORD saw that he turned aside to see, God called unto him out of the midst of the bush, and said, Moses, Moses. And he said, Here *am* I.
And he said, Draw not nigh hither: put off thy shoes from off thy feet, for the place whereon thou standest *is* holy ground.
[545] **Matthew 7:1** "Judge not, that you be not judged."
[546] November 22, 1966

doors, and let the light come streaming through. There are no hidden chambers in God's Temple. Its gates are open wide, to greet His Son. No-one can fail to come where God has called him, if he close not the door himself upon His Father's welcome. **T(547) - 374 -**[547]

T 14 D. Perception without Deceit (*Notes* 1215 9:52)

T 14 D 1. WHAT DO YOU WANT? Light or darkness, knowledge or ignorance are yours, but not both. Opposites must be brought together, and not kept apart. For their separation is only in your mind, and they are reconciled by union, as YOU are. In union, everything that is not real MUST disappear, for truth IS union. As darkness disappears in light, so ignorance fades away when knowledge dawns. Perception is the medium by which ignorance is BROUGHT to knowledge. But the perception must be without deceit, for otherwise, it becomes the messenger of ignorance, rather than a helper in the search for truth.

T 14 D 2. The search for truth is but the honest searching out of everything that INTERFERES with truth. TRUTH IS. And can be neither lost, nor sought, nor found. It is there, wherever YOU are, being WITHIN you. But it CAN be recognized or unrecognized, real or false, to YOU. If you hide it, it becomes unreal to you, BECAUSE you hid it, and SURROUNDED IT WITH FEAR. Under each cornerstone of fear, on which you have erected your insane system of belief, THE TRUTH LIES HIDDEN. Yet you cannot know this, for, by HIDING truth in fear, you see no reason to believe the more you LOOK at fear, the LESS you see it, and the clearer WHAT IT CONCEALS becomes.

T 14 D 3. It is not possible to convince the unknowing that they know. From their point of view, IT IS NOT TRUE. Yet it IS true, because GOD knows it. These are clearly opposite viewpoints of what the "unknowing" ARE. To God, unknowing is impossible. It is therefore not a point of view at all, but merely a belief in something that does not exist. It is only this BELIEF that the unknowing have, and BY it, they are wrong about themselves. They have DEFINED themselves as they were NOT created. Their creation was NOT a point of view, but rather, a CERTAINTY. Uncertainty BROUGHT to certainty does not retain ANY conviction of reality.

T 14 D 4. You must have noticed that the emphasis has been on bringing what is undesirable TO the desirable, what you do NOT want to what you DO. You will realize **T(548) - 375 -** that salvation MUST come to you this way, if you consider what dissociation IS. Dissociation is a distorted process of thinking, whereby two systems of belief, which CANNOT coexist, are BOTH MAINTAINED. It HAS BEEN recognized that, if they were BROUGHT TOGETHER, their joint acceptance WOULD become impossible. But, if one is kept in darkness FROM THE OTHER, their SEPARATION seems to keep them both alive, and equal in their reality. Their JOINING thus becomes the source of fear, for, if they meet, acceptance MUST be withdrawn from one of them.

T 14 D 5. You CANNOT have them both, for each DENIES the other. Apart, this fact is lost from sight, for each, in a SEPARATE place, CAN be endowed with firm belief. BRING THEM TOGETHER, and the fact of their complete incompatibility is instantly apparent. One WILL go, BECAUSE the other is seen in the SAME place. Light cannot enter darkness, when a mind BELIEVES in darkness, and will not let it go. Truth does not struggle AGAINST ignorance, and love does not ATTACK fear. What needs no protection, does not defend itself. Defense was of YOUR making. God knows it not.

T 14 D 6. The Holy Spirit uses defenses ON BEHALF of truth, only because you made them AGAINST it. His perception of them, according to HIS purpose, merely changes them into a CALL FOR what you have ATTACKED WITH them. Defenses, like everything you made, must be gently turned to your own good, translated by Him from means of self-destruction, to means of preservation and release. His task is mighty, but the power of God is with Him. Therefore, to Him, it is so easy, that it was accomplished the instant it was given Him for you.

T 14 D 7. Do not delay yourselves in your return to peace, by wondering how He can fulfill what God has given Him to do. Leave that to Him Who knows! You are not asked to do mighty tasks yourself. You are merely asked to do the little He SUGGESTS you do, trusting Him only to the small extent of believing that, if He asks it, you can do it. You will SEE how easily ALL that He asks can be **T(549) - 376 -** accomplished. He asks of you but this; - bring to Him every secret you have locked away from Him. Open every door to Him, and bid Him enter the darkness, and lighten it away.

T 14 D 8. At YOUR request, He enters gladly. He brings the light to darkness, if you make the darkness OPEN to Him. But what you hide, He cannot look upon. For He sees FOR YOU, and unless you look WITH Him, He CANNOT see. The vision of Christ is not for Him alone, but for Him WITH YOU. Bring, therefore, all your dark and secret thoughts to Him, and look upon them WITH Him. He holds the light, and you the darkness. They CANNOT coexist, when both of you TOGETHER look on them. His judgment MUST prevail, and He will GIVE it to you, as you join your perception to His. Joining with Him in seeing, is the way in which you learn to share with Him the interpretation of perception that leads to knowledge.

T 14 D 9. You cannot see alone. Sharing perception with Him Whom God has given you, teaches you how to RECOGNIZE what you see. It is the recognition that NOTHING you see means ANYTHING alone. Seeing WITH Him will SHOW you that all meaning, INCLUDING YOURS, comes not from double vision, but from the gentle fusing of everything into one meaning, one emotion and one purpose. God has one Purpose, which He shares with you. The single vision, which the Holy Spirit offers you, will bring this Oneness to your mind with clarity and brightness so intense, you could not wish, for all the world, not to accept what God would have you have. Behold your will, accepting it as His, with all His love as yours. All honor to you through Him, and through Him unto God.[548]

T 14 D 10. In the darkness you have obscured the glory God gave you, and the power that He bestowed upon His guiltless Son. All that, lies hidden in every darkened place shrouded in guilt, and in the dark denial of innocence. Behind the dark **T(550) - 377 -** doors which you have closed lies nothing, BECAUSE nothing CAN obscure the gift of God. It is the CLOSING of the doors, that interferes with recognition of the power of God that shines in you. Banish not power from your mind, but let all that would hide your glory, be brought to the judgment of the Holy Spirit, and there undone. Whom He would save for glory IS saved for it. He has promised the Father that, through Him, you would be released from littleness to glory.

T 14 D 11. To what He promised God, He is wholly faithful, for He shared WITH God the promise that was given to Him to share with YOU. He shares it still, FOR YOU. Everything that promises otherwise, great or small, however much or little valued, He will replace with the one promise GIVEN unto Him to lay upon the altar to your Father and His Son. No altar stands to God WITHOUT His Son. And NOTHING brought there that is not equally worthy of

---

[547] November 23, 1966.

[548] **1 Timothy 6:16** Who alone has immortality, dwelling in unapproachable light, whom no man has seen or can see, to whom be honor and everlasting power. Amen.

Revelation 5:12-13 Saying with a loud voice:
"Worthy is the Lamb who was slain
To receive power and riches and wisdom,
And strength and honor and glory and blessing!"
And every creature which is in heaven and on the earth and under the earth and such as are in the sea, and all that are in them, I heard saying:
"Blessing and honor and glory and power
Be to Him who sits on the throne,
And to the Lamb, forever and ever!"

BOTH, but will be REPLACED by gifts wholly acceptable to Father AND to Son. Can you offer guilt to God? You cannot, then, offer it to His Son. For they are NOT apart, and gifts to one ARE offered to the other.

T 14 D 12. You know not God, because you know not this. And yet you DO know God, and ALSO this. All this is safe WITHIN you, where the Holy Spirit shines. He shines not in division, but in the meeting-place where God, UNITED with His Son, speaks to His Son THROUGH Him. Communication between what cannot BE divided CANNOT cease. The holy meeting-place of the unseparated Father and His Son lies in the Holy Spirit, and in YOU. All interference in the communication that God Himself wills with His Son is quite impossible here. Unbroken and uninterrupted love flows constantly between the Father and the Son, as BOTH would have it be. And so it IS.

T 14 D 13. Let your minds wander not through darkened corridors, AWAY from Light's center. You may choose to lead YOURSELVES astray, but you can only be BROUGHT TOGETHER by the Guide appointed FOR you. He will surely lead you to where God **T(551) - 378 -** and His Son await your recognition. They are joined in giving you the gift of Oneness, before which ALL separation vanishes. Unite with what you ARE. You CANNOT join with anything EXCEPT reality. God's glory and His Son's BELONG to you in truth. They HAVE no opposite, and nothing else CAN you bestow upon yourselves.

T 14 D 14. There is no substitute for truth. And truth will make this plain to you, as you are brought into the place where you must MEET with truth. And there you must be led, through gentle understanding, which can lead you nowhere else. Where God is, there are YOU. Such IS the truth. Nothing can change the knowledge GIVEN you by God into UNknowing. Everything God created KNOWS its Creator. For this is how creation is accomplished, by the Creator, and by His creations. In the holy meeting-place are joined the Father and His creations, and the creations of His Son, with them together.

T 14 D 15. There is one link which joins them all together, holding them in the Oneness out of which creation happens. The link with which the Father joins Himself to those He gives the power to create LIKE Him, can NEVER be dissolved. Heaven itself is union with ALL of creation, and with its One Creator. And Heaven remains the Will of God for YOU. Lay no gifts other than this upon your altars, for nothing can coexist BESIDE it. Here, your meager offerings are BROUGHT TOGETHER with the gift of God, and only what is worthy of the Father will be accepted by the Son, for whom it was intended. To whom God gives Himself, He IS given. Your little gifts will vanish, on the altar where He has placed His Own. **T(552) - 379 -**[549]

T 14 E. The Recognition of Holiness (*Notes* 1228 9:65)

T 14 E 1. The Atonement does not MAKE holy. You were CREATED holy. It merely brings UNholiness TO holiness, or what you MADE, to what you ARE. The bringing together of truth and illusion, OF THE EGO AND GOD, is the Holy Spirit's only function. Keep not your making from your Father, for hiding it has cost you knowledge of Him, and of yourselves. The knowledge is safe, but wherein is YOUR safety, APART from it? The making of time, to TAKE THE PLACE of timelessness, lay in the decision to BE NOT as you WERE. Thus, truth was made past, and the present was dedicated to illusion. And the past, too, was changed, and INTERPOSED between what ALWAYS was, and NOW. The past that YOU remember NEVER was, and represents only denial of what ALWAYS was.

T 14 E 2. Bringing the ego to God, is but to bring error to truth, where it stands corrected, because it is the OPPOSITE of what it meets, and is undone because the CONTRADICTION can no longer stand. How long can contradiction stand, when its impossible nature is clearly revealed? What disappears in light is NOT attacked. It merely vanishes, because it is not true. Different realities ARE meaningless, for reality MUST be one. It CANNOT change with time, or mood, or chance. Its changelessness is WHAT MAKES IT REAL. This CANNOT be undone. Undoing is for UNreality. And this, reality WILL do for you.

T 14 E 3. Merely by BEING WHAT IT IS, does truth release you from everything that it is NOT. The Atonement is so gentle, you need but whisper to it, and all its power will rush to your assistance and support. You are not frail, with God beside you. But WITHOUT Him, you are nothing. The Atonement OFFERS YOU GOD. The gift which you refused, is held by Him in you. His Spirit holds it there FOR you. God has not left His altar, though His worshippers placed other gods upon it. The temple still is holy, for the Presence that dwells within it IS Holiness.

T 14 E 4. In the temple, holiness waits quietly for the return of them that love it. For the Presence knows they will return to purity and to grace. The graciousness of God will take them gently in, and cover all their sense of pain and loss, with the immortal assurance of their Father's Love. There, fear of death will be **T(553) - 380 -** replaced with joy of living. For God is Life, and they abide IN Life. Life is as holy as the Holiness by which it was created. The Presence of Holiness lives in everything that lives, for Holiness CREATED life, and leaves not what it created holy as Itself.

T 14 E 5. In the world you, can become a spotless mirror, in which the holiness of your Creator shines forth from you, to all around you. You can REFLECT HEAVEN here. But no reflections of the images of other gods must dim the mirror that would hold God's reflection in it. Earth can reflect Heaven or hell; God or the ego. You need but leave the mirror clean, and clear of all the images of hidden darkness you have drawn upon it. God will shine upon it of Himself. Only the clear reflection OF Himself can BE perceived upon it. Reflections are seen in light. In darkness, they are obscure, and their meaning seems to lie only in shifting interpretations, rather than in themselves.

T 14 E 6. The reflection of God NEEDS no interpretation. IT IS CLEAR. Clear but the mirror, and the message which shines forth from what the mirror holds out for everyone to see, NO-ONE will fail to understand. It is the message that the Holy Spirit is holding to the mirror that is in HIM. He recognizes it, because he has been taught his NEED for it, but knows not where to look to FIND it. Let him, then, see it in YOU, and share it WITH you. Could you but realize, for a single instant, the power of healing that the reflection of God, shining in YOU, can bring to all the world, you COULD not wait to make the mirror of your mind clean, to receive the image of the Holiness that heals the world.

T 14 E 7. The image of holiness that shines in YOUR mind is NOT obscure, and will NOT change. Its meaning, to those who look upon it is not obscure, for everyone perceives it AS THE SAME. All bring their DIFFERENT problems to its healing light, but ALL their problems are met ONLY with healing there. The response of holiness, to ANY form of error, is ALWAYS the same. There is no contradiction in what holiness CALLS FORTH. Its ONE response is healing, without ANY regard for what is brought TO it. **T(554) - 381 -**

T 14 E 8. Those who have learned to offer ONLY healing, because of the reflection of holiness in them, are ready at last for Heaven. There, holiness is not a reflection, but rather the ACTUAL CONDITION of what was but reflected TO them here. God is no image, and His creations, as part of Him, hold Him in them in truth. They do not merely REFLECT the truth, for THEY ARE truth.[550]

---

[549] November 26, 1966.

[550] 381 - [split paragraph]

T 14 F. The Shift to Miracles (*Notes* 1233 9:71)

T 14 F 1. When no perception stands between God and His Creation, or between His Children and their own, the knowledge of creation MUST continue forever. The reflections that you accept into the mirror of your minds in time, but bring eternity nearer or farther.

T 14 F 2. But eternity ITSELF is beyond ALL time. Reach out of time and touch it, with the help of its reflection IN you, and you will turn FROM time to holiness, as surely as the reflection of holiness calls everyone to lay all guilt aside. Reflect the peace of Heaven HERE, and bring this world to Heaven. For the REFLECTION of truth draws everyone TO truth. And as they enter INTO it, they leave ALL reflections behind. In Heaven, reality is SHARED, and not reflected. By sharing its reflection HERE, its truth becomes the only perception which the Son of God accepts. And thus, remembrance of His Father dawns on him, and he can no longer be satisfied with anything but his own reality.

T 14 F 3. You on earth have no conception of limitlessness, for the world you seem to live in IS a world of limits. In this world, it is NOT true that anything without order of difficulty can occur. The miracle, therefore, has a unique function, and is motivated by a unique Teacher, Who brings the laws of another world to this one. The miracle is the one thing you can do that TRANSCENDS order, being based, NOT on differences, but on equality. Miracles are NOT in competition, and the number you can do is LIMITLESS. They can be simultaneous and legion. This is not difficult to understand, once you conceive of them as possible at all.

T 14 F 4. What is more difficult to grasp is the lack of order of magnitude, which stamps the miracle as something that MUST come from elsewhere, NOT from here. From the world's viewpoint, this is quite impossible. You have experienced **T(555) - 382 -** the lack of competition among your thoughts, which, even though they may conflict, can occur to you together, and in great numbers. You are so used to this, that it can cause you little surprise. Yet you are also used to classifying some of your thoughts as more important, larger, or better, wiser, or more productive and valuable, than others. And this is true about the thoughts that cross the mind of those who think they live apart. For some are reflections of Heaven, while others are motivated by the ego, which but SEEMS to think.

T 14 F 5. The result is a weaving, changing pattern that never rests, and is never still. It shifts unceasingly across the mirror of your mind, and the reflections of Heaven last but a moment, and grow dim, as darkness blots them out. Where there was light, darkness removes it in an instant, and alternating patterns of light and darkness, darkness and light, sweep constantly across your minds. The little sanity that still remains is held together by a sense of order which YOU establish. The very fact that you can DO this, and bring ANY order into chaos, shows you that you are NOT an ego, and that MORE than an ego MUST be in you. For the ego IS chaos, and if it were all of you, no order at all would be possible.

T 14 F 6. But, though the order which you impose upon your minds limits the ego, IT ALSO LIMITS YOU. To order is to judge, and to arrange BY judgment. Therefore, it is NOT your function, but the Holy Spirit's. It will seem very difficult for you to learn that YOU HAVE NO BASIS AT ALL for ordering your thoughts. This lesson the Holy Spirit teaches, by giving you shining examples, to show you that your way of ordering is wrong, but that a better way is OFFERED you. The miracle offers EXACTLY the same response to EVERY call for help. IT DOES NOT JUDGE THE CALL. It merely recognizes what it IS, and answers accordingly. It does NOT consider which call is louder, or greater, or more important.

T 14 F 7. You may wonder how you, who are still bound to judgment, can be asked to do that which requires no judgment of your own. The answer is very simple. The power of God, and NOT of you, engenders miracles. The miracle ITSELF is but **T(556) - 383 -** the witness that you HAVE the power of God in you. That is the reason that the miracle gives EQUAL blessing to ALL who share in it, and that is also why EVERYONE shares in it. The power of God IS limitless. And, being always maximal, it offers EVERYTHING to EVERY call from ANYONE. There is no order here. A call for help is GIVEN help. The only judgment involved at all is in the Holy Spirit's one division into two categories; one of love, and the other, the call for love.

T 14 F 8. You cannot safely make this division, for you are much too confused, either to recognize love, or to believe that EVERYTHING else is nothing but a NEED for love. You are too bound to form, and NOT to content. What you CONSIDER content, is not content at all. It is merely form, and nothing else. For you do NOT respond to what a brother REALLY offers you, but only to the particular perception of his offering by which your EGO judges it. The ego is incapable of understanding content, and is totally unconcerned with it. To the ego, if the form is acceptable, the content MUST be. Otherwise, it will attack the form.

T 14 F 9. You who believe you understand something of the dynamics of the mind, let me assure you that you know NOTHING of it at all. For of yourselves, you COULD not know of it. The study of the ego is NOT the study of the mind. In fact, the ego enjoys the study of itself, and thoroughly approves the undertakings of the students who would analyze it, approving its importance. Yet they but study form, with meaningless content. For their teacher is senseless, though careful to conceal this fact behind a lot of words that sound impressive, but which lack ANY consistent sense when they are put together.

T 14 F 10. This is the characteristic of the ego's judgments. SEPARATELY, they seem to hold, but PUT THEM TOGETHER, and the system of thought which arises from JOINING them, is incoherent and utterly chaotic. For form is not enough for meaning, and the underlying LACK of content, makes a cohesive system impossible. SEPARATION therefore remains the ego's chosen condition. For no-one ALONE can judge the ego truly. But when two or more JOIN TOGETHER in searching for truth, the ego can no longer defend its lack of content.[551] The fact of union tells them it is not true. **T(557) - 384 -**

T 14 F 11. It is impossible to remember God in secret and alone. For remembering Him means you are NOT alone, and willing to remember it. Take no thought FOR YOURSELF, for no thought you hold IS for yourself. If you would remember your Father, let the Holy Spirit order your thoughts, and give only the answer with which He answers you. Everyone seeks for love, as you do,[552] and knows it not, unless he joins WITH you in seeking it. If you undertake the search TOGETHER, you bring with you a light so powerful, that what you see is GIVEN meaning. The lonely journey fails, because it has EXCLUDED what it would FIND.

T 14 F 12. As God communicates to the Holy Spirit in you, so does the Holy Spirit TRANSLATE His communications THROUGH you, so YOU can understand them. God has no secret communications, for everything of Him is perfectly open, and freely accessible to all, being FOR all. Nothing lives in secret, and what you would hide from the Holy Spirit IS nothing. Every interpretation you would lay upon a brother is senseless. Let the Holy Spirit SHOW HIM TO YOU, and teach you both his love and NEED for love. Neither his mind, NOR YOURS, holds but these two orders of thought. The miracle is the recognition that this is true.

T 14 F 13. Where there is love, your brother MUST give it to you, because of what it IS. But where there is NEED for love, YOU must give it, because of what YOU are. Long ago we said this course will

---

[551] **Matthew 18:20** "For where two or three are gathered together in My name, I am there in the midst of them."
[552] **Deuteronomy 4:29** But from there you will seek the LORD your God, and you will find Him if you seek Him with all your heart and with all your soul.

teach you what you are, restoring to you your identity. And we have already learned that this identity is shared. THE MIRACLE BECOMES THE MEANS OF SHARING IT. By SUPPLYING your identity, WHEREVER it is NOT recognized, YOU will recognize it. And God Himself, Who wills to be with His Son forever, will bless each recognition of His Son, with all the love He holds for him. Nor will the power of all His love be absent from any miracle you offer TO His Son. How, then, can there be ANY order of difficulty among them? **T(558) - 385 -**[553]

T 14 G. The Test of Truth (*Notes* 1242 9:79)

T 14 G 1. But the essential thing is learning that YOU DO NOT KNOW. Knowledge is power, and all power is of God. You who have tried to keep power for yourselves, have lost it. You still HAVE the power, but you have interposed so much between it and your AWARENESS of it, that you cannot use it. EVERYTHING you have taught yourselves has made your power more and more obscure to you. You know not WHAT it is, nor WHERE. You have made a SEMBLANCE of power, and a SHOW of strength, so pitiful that it MUST fail you. For power is not seeming strength, and truth is beyond a semblance of any kind.

T 14 G 2. Yet all that stands between you, and the power of God in you, is but your learning of the false, and your attempts to UNDO THE TRUE. Be willing, then, for ALL of it to be undone, and be glad that you are not bound to it forever. For you have taught yourselves HOW TO IMPRISON THE SON OF GOD, a lesson so unthinkable that only the insane, in deepest sleep, could even DREAM of it. Can God learn how NOT to be God? And can His Son, GIVEN all power BY Him, learn to be powerLESS?[554] What have you taught yourselves that you can possibly prefer to keep, in place of what you HAVE, and what you ARE?

T 14 G 3. Atonement teaches you how to escape forever from everything that you have taught yourselves in the past, by showing you ONLY what you ARE NOW. Learning HAS BEEN accomplished, BEFORE its effects are manifest. Learning is therefore IN THE PAST, but its influence DETERMINES the present, by giving it whatever meaning it holds for you. Your learning gives the present NO MEANING AT ALL. Nothing you have ever learned can help you understand the present, or teach you how to undo the past. Your past IS what you have taught yourselves.

T 14 G 4. LET IT ALL GO. Do NOT attempt to understand ANY event, or ANYTHING, or ANYONE in its light, for the light of darkness, by which you TRY to see, can ONLY obscure. Put no confidence at all in darkness to illuminate your **T(559) - 386 -** understanding, for if you do, you CONTRADICT the light, and thereby THINK you see the darkness. Yet darkness cannot BE seen, for it is nothing more than a condition in which seeing becomes impossible. You who have not yet brought ALL of the darkness you have taught yourselves unto the light in you, can hardly judge the truth and value of this course. Yet God did not abandon you. And so you have another lesson, sent from Him, ALREADY learned for every Child of Light,[555] by Him to Whom God gave it.

T 14 G 5. This lesson shines with God's glory, for in it lies His power, which He shares so gladly with His Son. Learn of His happiness, which is yours. But to accomplish this, all your dark lessons MUST be brought willingly to truth, and joyously laid down, by hands open to receive, not closed to take. Every dark lesson that you bring to Him Who teaches light, He will accept FROM you, BECAUSE YOU DO NOT WANT IT. And He will gladly EXCHANGE each one for the bright lesson He has learned FOR you. Never believe that ANY lesson you have learned, APART from Him, means ANYTHING.

T 14 G 6. You have one test, as sure as God, by which to recognize if what you learned is true. If you are WHOLLY free of fear of any kind, and if all those who meet, or even THINK of you, SHARE in your perfect peace, then you can be sure that you have learned GOD's lesson, and NOT yours. Unless all this is true, there ARE dark lessons in your minds, which hurt and hinder you, AND EVERYONE AROUND YOU. The ABSENCE of PERFECT peace means but ONE thing; you THINK you do not will for God's Son what His Father wills for him. Every dark lesson teaches this, on one form or another. And each bright lesson, with which the Holy Spirit will REPLACE the dark ones you do NOT accept and hide, teaches you that you will WITH the Father unto His Son.

T 14 G 7. Do not be concerned how you can learn a lesson so COMPLETELY different from everything you have taught yourselves. How would you know? Your part is very simple. You need only recognize that everything YOU learned you DO NOT WANT. Ask to BE taught, and do NOT use your experiences to confirm what YOU have learned. When your peace is threatened, or disturbed in **T(560) - 387 -** ANY way, say to yourself, "I do not know what anything, INCLUDING THIS, means. And so I do NOT know HOW TO RESPOND TO IT. And I will not use my own past learning as the light to guide me now." By this refusal to attempt to teach yourself what you do not know, the Guide Whom God has given you, will speak to you. HE will take His rightful place in your awareness, the instant YOU abandon it, and offer it to Him.

T 14 G 8. YOU cannot be your guide to miracles, for it is you who made them necessary. And, because you did, the means on which you can DEPEND for miracles, has been provided FOR you. God's Son can make no needs His Father will not meet, if he but turn to Him ever so little.[556] Yet He cannot COMPEL His Son to turn to Him, and remain Himself. It is impossible that God lose His identity, for if He did, YOU WOULD LOSE YOURS. And BEING yours, He cannot change Himself, for your identity IS changeless. The miracle ACKNOWLEDGES His changelessness, by seeing His Son as he always was, and NOT as he would make himself. The miracle brings the effect which ONLY guiltlessness CAN bring, and thus establishes the fact that guiltlessness MUST BE.

T 14 G 9. How can you, so firmly bound to guilt and committed so to remain, establish FOR YOURSELF your guiltlessness? This is impossible. But be sure that you are willing to acknowledge that it IS impossible. It is only because you think that you can run some little part, or deal with certain aspects of your lives alone, that the guidance of the Holy Spirit is limited. Thus would you make HIM undependable, and USE this fancied undependability as an excuse for keeping certain dark lessons FROM Him. And, by so limiting the guidance that you would ACCEPT, YOU are unable to DEPEND on miracles, to answer ALL your problems FOR you.

T 14 G 10. Do you think that what the Holy Spirit would have you GIVE, He would withhold from YOU? You have NO problems which He cannot solve, by offering YOU a miracle. Miracles are for YOU. And EVERY fear or pain or trial you have HAS BEEN undone. HE has brought ALL of them to light, having **T(561) - 388 -** ACCEPTED them INSTEAD of you, and recognized that they never were. There ARE no dark lessons He has not ALREADY lightened FOR you. The lessons you would teach yourselves, He has corrected already. They do not exist in His Mind at all. For the past binds HIM not, and therefore binds not you.

---

[553] December 5, 1966.
[554] **Matthew 28:18** And Jesus came and spoke to them, saying, "All authority has been given to Me in heaven and on earth."
[555] **Matthew 5:14** "You are the light of the world. A city that is set on a hill cannot be hidden."
John 8:12 Then Jesus spoke to them again, saying, "I am the light of the world. He who follows Me shall not walk in darkness, but have the light of life."

---

[556] **Matthew 6:8** "Therefore do not be like them. For your Father knows the things you have need of before you ask Him."
Matthew 6:32 "For after all these things the Gentiles seek. For your heavenly Father knows that you need all these things."

T 14 G 11. He does not see time as you do. And each miracle He offers you, CORRECTS your use of time, and makes it His. He Who has freed you from the past, would teach you, you ARE free of it. He would but have you accept His accomplishments AS YOURS, because He did them FOR you. And because He did, they ARE yours. He has MADE you free of what you made. You can deny Him, but you CANNOT call upon Him in vain. He ALWAYS gives what HE has made, IN PLACE of you. He would establish His bright teaching so firmly in your mind, that no dark lessons of guilt can abide in what He has established as holy by His Presence.

T 14 G 12. Thank God that He is there, and works through you. And all His works are yours. He offers YOU a miracle, with every one you LET Him do through you. God's Son will ALWAYS be indivisible. As we are held as one in God, so do we learn as one in Him. God's Teacher is as like to His Creator as is His Son, and through His Teacher does God proclaim His Oneness AND His Son's. Listen in silence, and do NOT raise your voice against Him. For He teaches the miracle of Oneness, and before HIS lesson, division disappears. Teach LIKE Him here, and you WILL remember that you have ALWAYS created like your Father. The miracle of creation has never ceased, having the holy stamp of immortality upon it. This is the Will of God for all creation, and all creation joins in willing this.

T 14 G 13. Those who remember always that THEY know nothing, but who have become willing to learn EVERYTHING, will learn it. But whenever they trust THEMSELVES, they will NOT learn. They have destroyed their motivation for learning, BY THINKING THEY ALREADY KNOW. Think not you understand ANYTHING, until you pass the test of perfect peace, for peace and understanding GO TOGETHER, and never can be found alone. Each brings the other WITH it, for **T(562) - 389 -** it is the law of God that they be not separate. They are cause and effect, each to the other, so, where one is absent, the other CANNOT be.

T 14 G 14. Only those who see they CANNOT know, UNLESS the effects of understanding are with them, can really learn at all. And for this, IT MUST BE PEACE THEY WANT, and nothing else. Whenever you think YOU know, peace will depart from you, because you have abandoned the Teacher of Peace. Whenever you fully realize that YOU KNOW NOT, peace will return, for you will have invited Him to do so, by abandoning the ego on behalf of Him. Call not upon the ego for ANYTHING. It is only that, that you need do. The Holy Spirit will, OF HIMSELF, fill every mind that so makes room for Him. If you want peace, you MUST abandon the teacher of attack.

T 14 G 15. The Teacher of Peace can NEVER abandon YOU. YOU can desert HIM, but He will never reciprocate. For His faith in you IS His understanding. It is as firm as is His faith in His Creator, and He knows that faith in His Creator MUST encompass faith in creation. In this consistency, lies His holiness, which He CANNOT abandon, for it is not His Will to do so. With your perfection ever in His sight, He gives the gift of peace to everyone who perceives the NEED for peace, and who would have it. Make way for peace, and it will come. For understanding IS in you, and from it, peace MUST come.

T 14 G 16. The power of God, from which they both arise, is yours as surely as it is His. You think you know Him not, only because, alone, it is impossible to know Him. But see the mighty works that He will do through you, and you MUST be convinced you did them through Him. It is impossible to deny the Source of effects so powerful, they COULD not be of you. Leave room for Him, and you will find yourself so filled with power, that NOTHING will prevail against your peace. And this will be the test by which you recognize that you HAVE understood. **T(563) - 390 -**[557]

---

[557] December 7, 1966

Chapter 15 – The Purpose of Time

T 15 A. Introduction (*Notes* 1253 9:90)

T 15 A 1. Can you imagine what it means to have no cares, no worries, no anxieties, but merely to be perfectly calm and quiet all the time? Yet that is what time is for; to learn just that, and nothing more. God's Teacher cannot be satisfied with His teaching, until it constitutes ALL your learning. He has not fulfilled His teaching function until you have become such consistent learners THAT YOU LEARN ONLY OF HIM. When this has happened, you will no longer need a teacher, or time in which to learn.

T 15 A 2. One of the sources of perceived discouragement from which you suffer, is your belief that THIS TAKES TIME, and that the results of the Holy Spirit's teaching are far in the future. This is not so. For the Holy Spirit USES time in His OWN way, and is NOT bound to it. Time is His friend in teaching. It does not waste Him, as it does you. But all the waste that time seems to bring with it, is due but to your identification with the ego, who uses time to support ITS belief in destruction. The ego, like the Holy Spirit, uses time to convince you of the inevitability of the goal and end of learning. To the ego, the goal is death, which IS its end. But to the Holy Spirit, the goal is life, which HAS no end.

T 15 B. The Uses of Time (*Notes* 1255 9:92)

T 15 B 1. The ego IS an ally of time, but NOT a friend. For it is as mistrustful of death as it is of life, and what it wants for you, IT cannot tolerate. The ego wants YOU dead, but NOT itself. The outcome of its strange religion MUST therefore be the conviction that it can pursue you BEYOND the grave. And out of its unwillingness for you to find peace, even in the death it wants for you, it offers you immortality in hell. It speaks to you of Heaven, but assures you that Heaven is not for you. How can the guilty hope for Heaven?

T 15 B 2. The belief in hell is inescapable to those who identify with the ego. Their nightmares and their fears are all associated with it. The ego teaches that hell is IN THE FUTURE, for this is what ALL its teaching is directed to. T(564) -391 HELL IS ITS GOAL. For, although the ego aims at death and dissolution as an end, IT does not believe it. The goal of death, which it craves for you, leaves IT unsatisfied. No-one who follows the ego's teaching is without the FEAR of death. If death were thought of merely as an end of pain, would it be FEARED?

T 15 B 3. We have seen this strange paradox in the ego's thought-system before, but never so clearly as here. For the ego must SEEM to KEEP FEAR FROM YOU, to keep your allegiance. Yet it must ENGENDER fear, in order to maintain ITSELF. Again, the ego tries, and all too frequently succeeds, in doing both, but using dissociation for holding its contradictory aims together, so that they SEEM to be reconciled. The ego teaches thus: Death is the end, as far as hope of Heaven goes. But, because you and ITSELF cannot be separated, and because it cannot conceive of its OWN death, it will pursue you still, BECAUSE YOUR GUILT IS ETERNAL.

T 15 B 4. Such is the ego's version of immortality. And it is THIS the ego's version of time supports. The ego teaches that Heaven is here and now, because the FUTURE is hell. Even when it attacks so savagely that it tries to take the life of someone who hears it temporarily as the ONLY voice, it speaks of hell even to him. For it tells him hell is HERE, and bids him leap from hell into oblivion. The only time the ego allows anyone to look upon, with some amount of equanimity is the PAST. And even then, its only value is that it is no more.

T 15 B 5. How bleak and despairing is the ego's use of time! And how TERRIFYING! For underneath its fanatical insistence that the past and future be the same, is hidden a far more insidious threat to peace. The ego does not advertise its final threat, for it would have its worshippers still believe that IT can offer the ESCAPE from it. But the belief in guilt MUST lead to the BELIEF IN HELL, and ALWAYS DOES. The only way in which the ego allows the fear of hell to be experienced is to BRING HELL HERE, but ALWAYS as a foretaste of the future. For no-one who considers himself as DESERVING hell, can believe that punishment will end in peace. T(565) -392

T 15 B 6. The Holy Spirit teaches thus: There IS no hell. Hell is only what the ego has made OF THE PRESENT. The BELIEF in hell is what PREVENTS you from UNDERSTANDING the present, because YOU ARE AFRAID OF IT. The Holy Spirit leads as steadily to Heaven, as the ego drives to hell. For the Holy Spirit, Who knows ONLY the present, uses it to UNDO the fear by which the ego would make the present useless. There is NO ESCAPE from fear, in the ego's use of time. For time, according to its teaching, is nothing but a teaching device for COMPOUNDING guilt, until it becomes all-encompassing, and demands vengeance forever.

T 15 B 7. The Holy Spirit would undo ALL of this NOW. Fear is NOT of the present, but ONLY of the past and future, which do not exist. There is no fear in the present, when each instant stands clear and separated from the past, without its shadow reaching out into the future. Each instant is a clean, untarnished birth, in which the Son of God emerges FROM the past, into the present. And the present EXTENDS FOREVER. It is so beautiful and so clean and free of guilt, that nothing but happiness is there. No darkness is remembered, and his immortality and joy are NOW.

T 15 B 8. This lesson takes NO time. For what IS time, WITHOUT a past and future? It HAS taken time to misguide you so completely, but it takes no time at all to BE what you ARE. Begin to practice the Holy Spirit's USE of time, as a teaching aid to happiness and peace. Take this very instant, NOW, and think of it as ALL THERE IS of time. Nothing can reach you here, out of the past, and it is here that you are COMPLETELY absolved, COMPLETELY free, and WHOLLY without condemnation. From this holy instant, wherein holiness is born, you will go forth in time without fear, and with no sense of change WITH time. T(566) -393

T 15 B 9. Time is inconceivable without change, and holiness does NOT change. Learn from this instant more than merely hell does not exist. IN THIS REDEEMING INSTANT LIES HEAVEN. And Heaven will NOT change, for the birth into the holy present is SALVATION from change. And change is an illusion, taught by those who could not see themselves as guiltless. There is no change in Heaven, because THERE IS NO CHANGE IN GOD.

T 15 B 10. In the holy instant, in which you see yourself as bright with freedom, you WILL remember God. For remembering Him IS to remember freedom. Whenever you are tempted to be dispirited by the thought of HOW LONG it would take to change your mind so completely, ask yourself, "How long is an instant?" Could you not give so SHORT a time to the Holy Spirit, for your Salvation? He asks no more, for He has no need of more. It takes far longer to teach you how to be willing to Give Him this, than for Him to use this tiny instant to offer you the whole of Heaven. In exchange for this instant, He stands ready to give you the remembrance of Eternity.

T 15 B 11. You will never give this holy instant to the Holy Spirit on behalf of YOUR release, while you are unwilling to give it to your brothers on behalf of THEIRS. For the instant of holiness is SHARED, and CANNOT be yours alone. Remember, then, when you are tempted to attack a brother, that HIS instant of release is YOURS. Miracles ARE the instant of release you offer, and will RECEIVE. They attest to YOUR willingness to BE released, and to offer time to the Holy Spirit, for HIS use of it. How long is an instant? It is as short for your brothers, as it is for you. Practice GIVING this blessed instant of freedom to all who are ENSLAVED by time, and thus make time their friend FOR them.

T 15 B 12. The Holy Spirit gives their blessed instant TO you, through your giving it. As you GIVE it, He offers it to YOU. Be not unwilling to give what you would receive of Him, for you join WITH Him in giving. In the crystal cleanness of the release you GIVE, is YOUR INSTANTANEOUS escape from guilt. You MUST be holy, if you OFFER holiness. How long is an instant? As long as it takes to **T(567) -394** re-establish perfect sanity, perfect peace, and perfect love for everyone, for God, and for YOURSELF. As long as it takes to remember immortality, and your immortal creations, who share it with you. As long as it takes to exchange hell for Heaven. Long enough to transcend ALL of the ego's making, and ascend unto your Father.[558]

T 15 B 13. Time is your friend, if you leave it to the Holy Spirit to use. He needs but very little, to restore God's Whole power to you. He Who transcends time FOR you, understands what it is FOR. Holiness lies not in time, but in Eternity. There never WAS an instant in which God's Son could lose his purity. His changeless state is BEYOND time, for his purity remains forever beyond attack, and without variability. Time stands still in his holiness, and changes not. And so it is no longer time at all. For, caught in the single instant of the eternal sanctity of God's creation, it is TRANSFORMED into forever.

T 15 B 14. GIVE the eternal instant, that eternity may be remembered FOR you, in that shining instant of perfect release. Offer the miracle of the holy instant THROUGH the Holy Spirit, and leave His giving it to you to Him.[559]

T 15 C. Time and Eternity (*Notes* 1264 9:101)

T 15 C 1. The Atonement is in time, but not FOR time. Being for YOU, it is for the eternal. What holds remembrance of God, CANNOT be bound by time. No more are you. For, unless GOD is bound, you CANNOT be. An instant, offered to the Holy Spirit, is offered to God on your behalf, and in that instant, you will awaken gently in Him.

T 15 C 2. In the blessed instant, you will let go ALL your past learning, and the Holy Spirit will quickly offer you the WHOLE lesson of peace. What can take time, when ALL the obstacles to learning it have been removed? Truth is so far beyond time, that ALL of it happens at once. For as it was created one, so its oneness depends not on time at all. Be not concerned with time, and fear not the instant of holiness which will remove ALL fear. For the instant of peace is eternal, BECAUSE it is wholly WITHOUT fear. It WILL come, being the lesson God gives you, through the Teacher HE has appointed, to translate time to eternity. **T(568) - 395 -**

T 15 C 3. Blessed is God's Teacher, Whose joy it is to teach God's holy Son his holiness. His joy is not contained in time. His teaching is for you, BECAUSE His joy is yours. Through Him, YOU stand before God's altar, where He gently translated hell into Heaven. For it is only in Heaven that God would have you be. How long can it take, to be where God would have you? For you ARE where you have forever been, and will forever be.[560] All that you have, you have forever. The blessed instant reaches out to ENCOMPASS time, as God extends Himself to encompass you.

T 15 C 4. You who have spent days, hours, and even years, in chaining your brothers TO your egos, in an attempt to support it, and uphold its WEAKNESS, do not perceive the Source of STRENGTH.[561] In the holy instant, you will unchain ALL of your brothers, and refuse to support either THEIR weakness, OR YOUR OWN. You do not realize how much you have MISUSED your brothers, by seeing them as sources of EGO support. As a result, they witness TO the ego in your perception, and SEEM to provide reasons for NOT letting it go. Yet they are far stronger, and MUCH more compelling witnesses for the Holy Spirit. And they support His STRENGTH.

T 15 C 5. It is, therefore, your choice, whether they support the ego or the Holy Spirit IN YOU. And you will know which you have chosen, by THEIR reactions. A Son of God who has been released through the Holy Spirit in a brother, IF THE RELEASE IS COMPLETE, is ALWAYS recognized. He cannot BE denied. As long as YOU remain uncertain, it can be ONLY because you have not given COMPLETE release. And, because of this, you have not yet given one single instant COMPLETELY to the Holy Spirit. For, when you HAVE, you will be SURE you have. You will be sure, because the witness TO Him will speak so clearly OF Him, that you will hear, and UNDERSTAND.

T 15 C 6. You WILL doubt, until you hear ONE witness whom you have WHOLLY released through the Holy Spirit. And then you will doubt no more. The holy instant has not yet happened to you. But it will, and you will recognize it, with perfect certainty. No gift of God is recognized in any other **T(569) - 396 -** way. You can practice the mechanics of the holy instant, and will learn much from doing so. But its shining and glittering brilliance, which will literally blind you to this world by its OWN vision, you can NOT supply. And here it is, ALL in this instant, complete, accomplished, and GIVEN WHOLLY.

T 15 C 7. Start NOW, to practice your little part in SEPARATING OUT the holy instant. You will receive very specific instructions, as you go along. To learn to separate out this single second, and begin to experience it as timeless, is to begin to experience yourself as NOT separate. Fear not that you will not be given help in this. God's Teacher, and His lesson will support your strength. It is only your weakness that will depart from you in this practice, for it is the practice of the power of God in you. Use it but for one instant, and you will never deny it again. Who can deny the Presence of what the universe bows to, in appreciation and gladness? Before the recognition of the universe, which witnesses to it, YOUR doubts MUST disappear. **T(570) - 397 -**[562]

T 15 D. Littleness versus Magnitude (*Notes* 1270 9:107)

T 15 D 1. Be not content with littleness, but be sure you understand what littleness is, and why you could never BE content with it. Littleness is the offering you gave YOURSELF. You offered this in place of magnitude, AND ACCEPTED IT. Everything in this world is little, because it is a world made out of littleness, in the strange belief that littleness CAN content you. When you strive for anything in the world, WITH THE BELIEF THAT IT WILL BRING YOU PEACE, you are belittling yourself, and blinding yourself to glory. Littleness and glory are the choices open to your striving and your vigilance. You will ALWAYS choose one AT THE EXPENSE of the other.

T 15 D 2. But what you do not realize, each time you choose, is that your choice is your evaluation OF YOURSELF. Choose littleness, and you will NOT have peace, for you will have judged yourself UNWORTHY of it. And whatever you offer as a substitute, is much too poor a gift to satisfy you. It is essential that you accept the fact,

---

[558] **John 20:17** Jesus said to her, "Do not cling to Me, for I have not yet ascended to My Father; but go to My brethren and say to them, 'I am ascending to My Father and your Father, and to My God and your God.'"
[559] 394 [split paragraph]
[560] **Hebrews 13:8** Jesus Christ is the same yesterday, today, and forever.

[561] **2 Corinthians 12:9** And He said to me, "My grace is sufficient for you, for My strength is made perfect in weakness." Therefore most gladly I will rather boast in my infirmities, that the power of Christ may rest upon me. **Philippians 4:13** I can do all things through Christ who strengthens me.
[562] December 10, 1966

and accept it gladly, that there is NO form of littleness that can EVER content you. You are free to try as many as you wish, but all you will be doing is to delay your homecoming. For you will be content ONLY in magnitude, which IS your home.

T 15 D 3. There is a deep responsibility you owe yourself, and one which you must learn to remember ALL the time. The lesson will seem hard at first, but you will learn to love it, when you realize that it is true, and constitutes a tribute to your power. You who have sought AND FOUND littleness, remember this: Every decision that you make stems from WHAT YOU THINK YOU ARE, and represents the value that you PUT upon yourself. Believe the little can content you, and, by LIMITING yourself, you will NOT be satisfied. For your function is NOT little, and it is only by finding your function, and fulfilling it that you can ESCAPE from littleness.

T 15 D 4. There is no doubt about what your function IS, for the Holy Spirit KNOWS what it is. There is no doubt about its magnitude, for it reaches you through Him, FROM Magnitude. You do not have to strive for it, because you HAVE it. All your striving must be directed AGAINST LITTLENESS, for it DOES **T(571) - 398 -** require vigilance to protect your magnitude in this world. To hold your magnitude in perfect awareness, in a world of littleness, is a task the little cannot undertake. Yet it is asked of you, in tribute to your magnitude, and NOT your littleness. Nor is it asked of you alone.

T 15 D 5. The power of God will support every effort you make on behalf of the magnitude of His dear Son. Search for the little, and you DENY yourself His power. God is not willing that His Son be content with less than everything. For He is not content without His Son, and His Son cannot be content with less than His Father has given him. We asked you once before, "Would you be hostage to the ego or host to God?" Let this question be asked you by the Holy Spirit in you, EVERY time you make a decision. For every decision you make DOES answer this, and invites sorrow or joy, accordingly.

T 15 D 6. When God GAVE Himself to you in your creation, He ESTABLISHED you as host to Him forever. He has NOT left you, and YOU have not left HIM. All your attempts to deny His magnitude, and make His Son hostage to the ego, CANNOT make little whom God has joined with Him. Every decision you make is made for Heaven or for hell, and will bring you AWARENESS of what you decided FOR. The Holy Spirit can hold your magnitude, clean of ALL littleness, clearly and in perfect safety in your minds, untouched by every little gift the world of littleness would offer you. But for this, you cannot side AGAINST Him in what He wills for you.

T 15 D 7. Decide for God through Him. For littleness, and the belief that you can be CONTENT with littleness, are the decisions YOU have made about yourself. The power and the glory that lie in you, from God, are for all who, like you, perceive themselves as little, and have deceived themselves into believing that littleness can be blown up, BY THEM, into a sense of magnitude that can content them.[563] Neither GIVE littleness, nor ACCEPT it. All honor is due the host of God.[564] Your littleness deceives you, but your magnitude is of Him Who dwells in you, and in Whom you dwell. Touch no-one, then, with littleness, in the Name of Christ, eternal Host unto His Father. **T(572) -399**[565]

T 15 D 8. In this season, which celebrates the birth of holiness into this world, join with me who decided for holiness for YOU. It is our task TOGETHER to restore the awareness of magnitude, to the host whom God appointed for Himself. It is beyond ALL your littleness to give the gift of God, but NOT beyond YOU. For God would give Himself THROUGH you. He reaches from you to everyone, and beyond everyone, to His Son's creations, but WITHOUT leaving you. Far beyond your little world, but still in you, He extends forever. Yet He brings all his extensions to you, as host to Him.

T 15 D 9. Is it a sacrifice to leave littleness behind, and wander not in vain? It is not sacrifice to wake to glory. But it IS a sacrifice to accept anything LESS than glory. Learn that you MUST be worthy of the Prince of Peace, born in you, in honor of Him Whose host you are.[566] You know not what love means because you have sought to purchase it with little gifts, thus VALUING it too little to be able to understand its magnitude. LOVE IS NOT LITTLE, and love dwells in you, for you are host to Him. Before the greatness that lives in you, your poor appreciation of yourself, and all the little offerings you have given, slip into nothingness.

T 15 D 10. Holy Child of God, when will you learn that ONLY holiness can content you, and give you peace? Remember that you learn not for yourself alone, no more than I did. It is BECAUSE I learned for YOU, that you can learn of ME. I would but teach you what is yours, so that, together, we can replace the shabby littleness, that binds the host of God to guilt and weakness, with the glad awareness of the glory that is in him. My birth in you is your awakening to grandeur. Welcome me not into a manger, but into the altar to holiness, where holiness abides in perfect peace.[567] **T(573) - 400**

T 15 D 11. My Kingdom is not of this world, because it is in YOU.[568] And YOU are of your Father. Let us join in honoring you, who MUST remain forever BEYOND littleness. Decide with me, who have decided to abide with you.[569] I will as my Father wills, knowing His Will is constant, and at peace forever with Itself. You will be content with nothing BUT His Will. Accept no less, remembering that everything I learned is yours. What my Father loves, I love as He does, and I can no more accept it as what it is NOT, than He can. And no more can YOU.

T 15 D 12. When you have learned to accept what you are, you will make no more gifts to offer to yourselves, for you will know you are COMPLETE, in need of nothing, and unable to accept ANYTHING for yourself. But you will gladly give, HAVING received. The host of God need not seek to find ANYTHING. If you are wholly willing to leave Salvation to the plan of God, and UNwilling to attempt to grasp for peace YOURSELF, Salvation will be GIVEN you. But think not you can substitute YOUR plan for His. Rather, join with me in His, that we may release all those who would be bound, proclaiming together that the Son of God is host to Him.[570]

T 15 D 13. Thus will we let no-one forget what YOU would remember. And thus WILL you remember it. Call forth in everyone ONLY the remembrance of God, and of the Heaven that is in him.

---

[563] **Matthew 6:13** "And do not lead us into temptation,
But deliver us from the evil one.
For Your s is the kingdom and the power and the glory forever." Amen.
[564] **1 Timothy 6:16** Who alone has immortality, dwelling in unapproachable light, whom no man has seen or can see, to whom be honor and everlasting power. Amen.
[565] December 12, 1966

[566] **Isaiah 9:6** For unto us a Child is born, Unto us a Son is given; And the government will be upon His shoulder. And His name will be called Wonderful, Counselor, Mighty God, Everlasting Father, Prince of Peace.
[567] **Luke 2:7** And she brought forth her firstborn Son, and wrapped Him in swaddling cloths, and laid Him in a manger, because there was no room for them in the inn.
[568] **John 18:36** Jesus answered, "My kingdom is not of this world. If My kingdom were of this world, My servants would fight, so that I should not be delivered to the Jews; but now My kingdom is not from here."
[569] **John 14:16** "And I will pray the Father, and He will give you another Helper, that He may abide with you forever."
John 15:4 "Abide in Me, and I in you. As the branch cannot bear fruit of itself, unless it abides in the vine, neither can you, unless you abide in Me."
John 15:10 "If you keep My commandments, you will abide in My love, just as I have kept My Father's commandments and abide in His love."
[570] **Matthew 16:19** "And I will give you the keys of the kingdom of heaven, and whatever you bind on earth will be bound in heaven, and whatever you loose on earth will be loosed in heaven."
John 20:23 "If you forgive the sins of any, they are forgiven them; if you retain the sins of any, they are retained."

For where you would help your brother be, there will you think YOU are. Hear not his call for hell and littleness, but only his call for Heaven and greatness. Forget not that his call is yours, and answer him with me. God's power is forever on the side of His host, for it protects ONLY the peace in which He dwells. Lay not littleness before His holy altar, which rises above the stars, and reaches even to Heaven, because of what is GIVEN it.

T 15 E. Practicing the Holy Instant (*Notes* 1278 9:115)

T 15 E 1. This course is not beyond IMMEDIATE learning, unless you prefer to believe that WHAT GOD WILLS TAKES TIME. And this means ONLY that you would rather DELAY the recognition that His Will IS so. The holy instant is THIS **T(574) -401** one, and EVERY one. The one you WANT it to be, it IS. The one you would NOT have it be, is lost to you. YOU must decide on WHEN it is. Delay it not. For beyond the past and future, in which you will NOT find it, it stands in shimmering readiness for your acceptance.

T 15 E 2. Yet you cannot bring it into glad awareness while you do not want it, for it holds the whole RELEASE from littleness. Your practice MUST therefore rest upon your willingness to let all littleness go. The instant in which magnitude will dawn upon you, is but as far away as your DESIRE for it. As long as you desire it not, and cherish littleness instead, by so much is it far from you. By so much as you want it, will you bring it nearer. Think not that you can find Salvation in your own way, and HAVE it.

T 15 E 3. Give over EVERY plan that you have made for your Salvation, in exchange for God's. HIS will content you, for there IS nothing else that can bring you peace. For peace is of God, and of no-one beside Him. Be humble before Him, and yet great IN Him. And value NO plan of the ego, BEFORE the plan of God. For you leave your place in His plan, which you MUST fulfill if you would join with me, empty by your decision to join in any plan BUT His. I call you to fulfill your holy part in the plan that He has given to the world, for its release from littleness. God would have His host abide in perfect freedom.

T 15 E 4. Every allegiance to a plan of Salvation that is APART from Him, diminishes the value of His Will for you in your own minds. And yet, it is your mind that IS the host to Him. Would you learn how perfect and immaculate is the holy altar on which your Father has placed HIMSELF? This you WILL recognize, in the holy instant in which you willingly and gladly give over EVERY plan but His. For there lies peace, PERFECTLY clear, because you have been willing to meet its conditions. **T(575) - 402 -**

T 15 E 5. You can claim the holy instant ANY time and ANYWHERE you want it. In your practice, try to give over EVERY plan you have accepted, for finding magnitude in littleness. IT IS NOT THERE. USE the holy instant ONLY to recognize that you alone CANNOT know where it is, and can only DECEIVE yourself. I stand within the holy instant, as clear as you would have me. And the extent to which you learn to be willing to ACCEPT me, IS the measure of the time in which the holy instant will be yours. I call to you to make the holy instant yours AT ONCE, for the release from littleness in the mind of the host of God, depends on willingness, and NOT on time.

T 15 E 6. The reason why this course is simple, is that TRUTH is simple. Complexity is of the ego, and is nothing more than the ego's attempt to obscure the obvious. You could live forever in the holy instant, BEGINNING NOW and reaching to eternity, but for a very simple reason. Do not obscure the simplicity of this reason, for, if you do, it will be ONLY because you prefer NOT to recognize it, and NOT to let it go. The simple reason, stated simply as what it is, is this: The holy instant is a time in which you receive AND GIVE perfect communication. This means, however, that it is a time in which your mind is OPEN, both to receive AND give. It is the recognition that all minds ARE in communication. It therefore seeks to CHANGE nothing, but merely to ACCEPT everything.

T 15 E 7. How can you do this when you would prefer to have PRIVATE thoughts, AND KEEP THEM? The ONLY way you COULD do this, is to DENY the perfect communication that makes the holy instant WHAT IT IS. You BELIEVE that it is possible to harbor thoughts you would NOT share, and that Salvation lies in keeping your thoughts TO YOURSELF ALONE. For, in private thoughts, KNOWN ONLY TO YOURSELF, you think you find a way to keep what you would HAVE alone, and share what YOU would share. **T(576) -403** And then you wonder why it is that you are not in full communication with those around you, and with God, Who surrounds ALL of you together.

T 15 E 8. Every thought you would keep hidden shuts communication off, BECAUSE YOU WOULD HAVE IT SO. It is impossible to RECOGNIZE perfect communication, while BREAKING communication holds value to you. Ask yourselves honestly, "Would I WANT to have perfect communication, and am I WHOLLY willing to let EVERYTHING that INTERFERES WITH IT, go forever?" If the answer is "no," then the Holy Spirit's readiness to GIVE it to you, is not enough to make it yours, for you are NOT ready to share it WITH Him. And it cannot come into a mind that has decided to OPPOSE it. For the holy instant is given and received with EQUAL willingness, being the acceptance of the SINGLE Will that governs ALL thought.

T 15 E 9. The necessary condition for the holy instant, does NOT require that you have no thoughts that are not pure. But it DOES require that you have none that you would KEEP. Innocence is not of your making. It is GIVEN you, the instant you would HAVE it. But it would not BE Atonement, if there were no NEED for Atonement. You will not be able to ACCEPT perfect communication, as long as you would HIDE it from yourself. For what you would hide IS hidden. In your practice, then, try only to be vigilant AGAINST DECEPTION, and seek not to PROTECT the thoughts you would keep unto yourself. Let the Holy Spirit's purity shine them away, and bring ALL your awareness to the READINESS for purity He offers you. Thus will He make you ready to acknowledge that you ARE host to God, and hostage to no-one and to nothing. **T(577) - 404**[571]

T 15 F. The Holy Instant and Special Relationships (*Notes* 1287 9:124)

T 15 F 1. The holy instant is the Holy Spirit's most useful learning device for teaching you love's meaning. For its purpose is to SUSPEND JUDGMENT ENTIRELY. Judgment ALWAYS rests on the past, for PAST experience is the basis on which you judge. Judgment becomes impossible without the past, for WITHOUT it you do NOT understand anything. You would make no ATTEMPT to judge, because it would be quite apparent to you that you do not know WHAT ANYTHING MEANS. You are afraid of this, because you believe that, WITHOUT THE EGO, all would be chaos. Yet I assure you that, without the ego, ALL WOULD BE LOVE.

T 15 F 2. The past is the EGO's chief learning device, for it is in the past that you learned to define your OWN needs, and acquired methods for meeting them ON YOUR OWN TERMS. We said before that, to limit love to PART of the Sonship, is to bring guilt into your relationships, and thus MAKE THEM UNREAL. If you seek to separate out certain ASPECTS of the totality, and look TO THEM to meet your imagined needs, you are attempting to USE SEPARATION TO SAVE YOU. How, then, could guilt NOT enter? For separation IS the source of guilt, and to APPEAL to it for salvation IS TO BELIEVE YOU ARE ALONE.

T 15 F 3. To be alone IS to be guilty. For to experience yourself AS alone, is to deny the Oneness of the Father and His Son, and thus to

---
[571] December 14, 1966

ATTACK REALITY. You cannot love PARTS of reality, and understand what love MEANS. If you would love UNlike to God, Who KNOWS no special love, how CAN you understand it? To believe that SPECIAL relationships, with SPECIAL love, can offer you salvation, IS the belief that separation is salvation. For it is the COMPLETE EQUALITY of the Atonement, in which salvation lies. How can YOU decide that special aspects of the Sonship CAN GIVE YOU MORE THAN OTHERS? The past HAS taught you this. But the holy instant teaches you IT IS NOT SO. **T(578) -405**

T 15 F 4. Because of guilt, ALL special relationships have some elements of fear in them. And this is why they shift and change so frequently. They are NOT based on changeless love alone. And love, where fear has entered, CANNOT be depended on, because it is NOT perfect.[572] In His function as Interpreter of what you have made, the Holy Spirit USES special relationships, which YOU have chosen to support the ego, as a learning experience which points to truth. Under His teaching, EVERY relationship becomes a lesson in love.

T 15 F 5. The Holy Spirit knows NO-ONE IS SPECIAL. But He also perceives that you have MADE special relationships, which He would purify, and NOT let YOU destroy. However UNholy the reason why you made them may be, He can TRANSLATE them into holiness, by removing AS MUCH FEAR AS YOU WILL LET HIM. You can place ANY relationship under His care, and be sure that it will NOT result in pain, if you offer Him your willingness TO HAVE IT SERVE NO NEED BUT HIS. All the guilt in it arises from YOUR use of it. All the love, from His. Do not, then, be AFRAID to let your IMAGINED need, which would DESTROY the relationship, go. Your ONLY need IS His.

T 15 F 6. Any relationship which you would SUBSTITUTE FOR ANOTHER, has not been offered to the Holy Spirit, for His use. There IS no substitute for love. If you would attempt to substitute ONE aspect of love for ANOTHER, you have placed LESS value on one, and MORE on another. You have not only SEPARATED them, but have also JUDGED AGAINST BOTH. Yet you had judged against yourself FIRST, or you would never have imagined that you needed them AS THEY WERE NOT. Unless you had seen yourself as WITHOUT love, you COULD not have judged them to be LIKE you in lack.

T 15 F 7. The ego's use of relationships is so fragmented, that it frequently goes even further; one PART of one aspect suits its purposes, while it prefers DIFFERENT parts of another. Thus does it ASSEMBLE reality to its own capricious liking, offering for YOUR seeking, a picture whose likeness DOES NOT EXIST. For there is nothing in Heaven OR earth that it resembles, **T(579) -406** and so, however much you seek for its reality, you CANNOT find it, because it is NOT real.

T 15 F 8. Everyone on earth has formed special relationships, and, although this is not so in Heaven, the Holy Spirit knows how to bring a touch of Heaven to them here. In the holy instant, no-one is special, for your PERSONAL needs INTRUDE on no-one, to MAKE them different. Without the values from the past you WOULD see them all the same, and LIKE YOURSELF. Nor would you see ANY separation between yourself and them. In the holy instant, you see, in each relationship, what it WILL be, when you perceive ONLY the present.

T 15 F 9. God knows you NOW. He remembers NOTHING, having ALWAYS known you exactly as He knows you now. The holy instant PARALLELS His knowing, by bringing ALL perception OUT of the past, thus removing the frame of reference you have built, by which to JUDGE your brothers. Once this is gone, the Holy Spirit substitutes His frame of reference FOR it. His frame of reference is simply God. The Holy Spirit's timelessness lies simply here. For in the holy instant, FREE of the past, you see that LOVE IS IN YOU, and you HAVE no need to look WITHOUT, and snatch it guiltily from where you THOUGHT it was.

T 15 F 10. ALL your relationships are blessed in the holy instant, BECAUSE THE BLESSING IS NOT LIMITED. In the holy instant, the Sonship gains AS ONE. And, UNITED in your blessing, it BECOMES one TO YOU. The meaning of love is the meaning God GAVE to it. Give to it ANY meaning APART from His, and it is IMPOSSIBLE to understand it. Every brother God loves as He loves you; neither less nor more. HE NEEDS THEM ALL EQUALLY, and so do YOU. In time, you have been told to offer miracles as Christ directs, and let the Holy Spirit bring to you those who are seeking you. But in the holy instant, you unite DIRECTLY with God, and ALL your brothers join in Christ. **T(580) -407**

T 15 F 11. Those who are joined in Christ are in no way separate. For Christ is the Self the Sonship shares, as God shares His Self with Christ. Think you that you can judge the Self of God? God has created It BEYOND judgment, out of HIS need to extend His love. With Love in you, you HAVE no need EXCEPT TO EXTEND IT. In the holy instant, there is no conflict of needs, for there is ONLY ONE. For the holy instant reaches to eternity, and to the Mind of God. And it is only there that love HAS meaning, and ONLY there CAN it be understood.

T 15 F 12. It is impossible to use one relationship AT THE EXPENSE of another, and NOT suffer guilt. And it is equally impossible to condemn PART of a relationship and find peace WITHIN it. Under the Holy Spirit's teaching, ALL relationships are seen as TOTAL commitments, yet they do not conflict with one another in ANY way. Perfect faith in each one, for its ability to satisfy you COMPLETELY, arises only from perfect faith in YOURSELF. And this you cannot have, while guilt remains. And there WILL be guilt, as long as you accept the possibility, AND CHERISH IT, that you can make a brother WHAT HE IS NOT, because YOU would have him so.

T 15 F 13. You have so little faith in yourself, because you are unwilling to accept the fact that perfect love is IN you.[573] And so you seek WITHOUT for what you CANNOT find without. I offer you MY perfect faith in you, IN PLACE of all YOUR doubts. But forget not that my faith MUST be as perfect in ALL your brothers as it is in you, or it would be a limited gift to YOU. In the holy instant, we SHARE our faith in God's Son, because we recognize, together, that he is wholly worthy OF it, and, in our appreciation of his worth, we CANNOT doubt his holiness. And so we love him. **T(581) -408**

T 15 G. The Holy Instant and the Laws of God (*Notes* 1295 9:133)

T 15 G 1. All separation vanishes, as holiness is shared. For holiness is power, and by SHARING it, it GAINS in strength. If you seek for satisfaction in gratifying your needs as YOU perceive them, you MUST believe that strength comes from ANOTHER, and that WHAT YOU GAIN HE LOSES. Someone must ALWAYS lose, if you perceive yourself as weak. Yet there is another interpretation of relationships, that TRANSCENDS the concept of the LOSS of power completely.

T 15 G 2. You do NOT find it difficult to believe that, when ANOTHER calls on God for love, YOUR call remains as strong. Nor do you think that, by God's answer to HIM, YOUR hope of answer is diminished. On the contrary, you are far more inclined to regard HIS success, as witness to the possibility of YOURS. That is because you recognize, however dimly, that God is an IDEA, and so YOUR faith in Him is STRENGTHENED by sharing. What you find it difficult to accept is the fact that, LIKE your Father, YOU are

---

[572] **1 John 4:18** There is no fear in love; but perfect love casts out fear, because fear involves torment. But he who fears has not been made perfect in love.

[573] **Luke 17:21** Nor will they say, "See here!' or "See there!' For indeed, the kingdom of God is within you."

an idea. And like Him, YOU can give yourself COMPLETELY, wholly without loss, and ONLY WITH GAIN.

T 15 G 3. Herein lies peace, for here there IS no conflict. In the world of scarcity, love HAS no meaning, and peace is impossible. For gain and loss are BOTH accepted, and so no-one is aware that perfect Love is IN him. In the holy instant, you recognize the IDEA of love in you, and UNITE this idea with the Mind that thought It, AND COULD NOT RELINQUISH IT. By HOLDING it within Itself, THERE WAS no loss. The holy instant thus becomes a lesson in how to hold ALL of your brothers in YOUR mind, experiencing not loss, but COMPLETION.

T 15 G 4. From this, it follows you can ONLY give. And this IS love, for this alone is natural, under the laws of God. In the holy instant, the laws of God prevail, and only THEY have meaning. The laws of this world cease to **T(582) - 409 -** hold any meaning at all. When the Son of God ACCEPTS the laws of God as what he gladly wills, it is impossible that he be bound, or limited in ANY way. In this instant, he IS as free as God would have him be. For, the instant that he refuses to BE bound, he is NOT bound.

T 15 G 5. In the holy instant, nothing happens that has not always been. Only the veil, that has been drawn ACROSS reality, is lifted. Nothing has changed. But the AWARENESS of changelessness comes swiftly, as the veil of time is pushed aside. No-one who has not yet experienced the lifting of the veil, and felt himself drawn irresistibly into the Light behind it, can have faith in love WITHOUT fear. Yet the Holy Spirit GIVES you this faith, because He offered it to me and I ACCEPTED it.

T 15 G 6. Fear not the holy instant will be denied you, for I denied IT not. And, through me, the Holy Spirit GAVE it unto you, as YOU will give it. Let no need that YOU perceive, obscure your need of THIS. For, in the holy instant, you will recognize the ONLY need the aspects of the Son of God share equally, and, BY this recognition, you will join with me in OFFERING what is needed. It is through US that peace will come. Join me in the IDEA of peace, for, in ideas, minds CAN communicate.

T 15 G 7. If you would GIVE YOURSELF as your Father gives His Self, you will learn to understand Selfhood. And therein is love's meaning understood. But remember that understanding is OF THE MIND, and, ONLY of the mind. KNOWLEDGE is therefore of the mind, and its CONDITIONS are in the mind, WITH it. If you were not ONLY an idea, and NOTHING ELSE, you could not be in full communication with all that ever was. But, as long as you prefer to be something else, or would attempt to be NOTHING ELSE and SOMETHING ELSE together, the language of communication, WHICH YOU KNOW PERFECTLY, you will not remember.

T 15 G 8. In the holy instant, God is remembered, and the language of communication with ALL your brothers, is remembered WITH Him. For communication **T(583) - 410 -** is remembered TOGETHER, as is truth. There is NO exclusion in the holy instant, because the past is gone, and, with it, goes the whole basis FOR exclusion. Without ITS source, exclusion vanishes. And this permits YOUR Source, and that of all your brothers, to REPLACE it in your awareness. God, and the power of God, will take their rightful place in you, and you will experience the full communication of ideas with ideas. Through your ability to do this, you will learn what you MUST be, because you will begin to understand what your Creator is, and what His creation is, along WITH Him. **T(584) - 411 -**[574]

T 15 H. The Holy Instant and Communication (*Notes 1301 9:138*)

T 15 H 1. Beyond the poor attraction of the special love relationship, and ALWAYS obscured by it, is the powerful attraction of the Father for His Son. There is no OTHER love that can satisfy you, because there IS no other love. This is the ONLY love that is fully given, AND FULLY RETURNED. Being complete, it asks nothing. Being wholly pure, everyone joined in it HAS everything. This is NOT the basis for ANY love relationship in which the ego enters. For EVERY relationship on which the ego embarks IS special. The ego establishes relationships ONLY to GET something. And it would keep the giver BOUND TO ITSELF, through guilt.

T 15 H 2. It is impossible for the ego to enter into any relationship without anger, for the ego believes that ANGER MAKES FRIENDS. This is NOT its statement, but it IS its purpose. For the ego REALLY BELIEVES that it can get, and KEEP, by MAKING GUILTY. This is its ONE attraction. An attraction so weak, that it would have no hold at all, except that NO-ONE RECOGNIZES IT. For the ego always SEEMS to attract through love, and has no attraction at all to anyone who perceives that IT ATTRACTS THROUGH GUILT.

T 15 H 3. The sick attraction of guilt MUST be recognized FOR WHAT IT IS. For, having been made REAL to you, it is essential to look at it clearly, and, by withdrawing your INVESTMENT in it, to LEARN TO LET IT GO. No-one would choose to let go what he believes has value. Yet the attraction of guilt has value to you ONLY because you have NOT looked at what it IS, and have judged it as valuable COMPLETELY in the dark. As we bring it to light, your ONLY question will be why it was you EVER WANTED it. You have NOTHING to lose by looking open-eyed at this, for ugliness such as this belongs not in your holy mind. The host of God CAN have no REAL investment here. **T(585) - 412 -**

T 15 H 4. We said before that the ego attempts to maintain and INCREASE guilt, but in such a way, that you do NOT recognize what it would do to YOU. For it is the ego's fundamental doctrine that, what you do to others, YOU HAVE ESCAPED. The ego wishes NO-ONE well. But its survival DEPENDS on your belief that YOU are exempt from its evil intentions. It counsels, therefore, that if you are HOST to it, IT will enable you to direct the anger that it holds outward, thus protecting YOU. And thus, it embarks on an endless, unrewarding chain of special relationships, forged out of anger, and dedicated to but one insane belief; that the more anger you invest OUTSIDE yourself, the safer YOU become.

T 15 H 5. It is this chain that binds the Son of God to guilt, and it is this chain the Holy Spirit would REMOVE from his holy mind. For the chain of savagery belongs not around the chosen host of God, who CANNOT make himself host to the ego. In the name of his release, and in the Name of Him Who would release him, let us look more closely at the relationships that the ego contrives, and let the Holy Spirit judge them truly. For it is certain that, if you LOOK at them, you will offer them gladly TO Him. What HE can make of them you do NOT know, but you WILL become willing to find out, if you are willing, first, to perceive what YOU have made of them.

T 15 H 6. In one way or another, every relationship which the ego makes is based on the idea that, by SACRIFICING itself, IT BECOMES BIGGER. The "sacrifice," which it regards as purification, is actually the root of its bitter resentment. For it would much prefer to attack directly, and avoid delaying what it REALLY wants. Yet the ego acknowledges "reality" as it sees it, and recognizes that NO-ONE could interpret DIRECT attack as love. Yet to make guilty IS direct attack, but does not SEEM to be. For the guilty EXPECT attack, and, having ASKED for it, they are ATTRACTED to it.

T 15 H 7. In these insane relationships, the attraction of what you do NOT want seems to be much stronger than the attraction of what you DO want. For each one thinks **T(586) - 413 -** that he has SACRIFICED something to the other, AND HATES HIM FOR IT. Yet this is what he thinks he WANTS. He is NOT in love with the other at all; he merely believes he is IN LOVE WITH SACRIFICE. And FOR this sacrifice, which he demanded OF HIMSELF, HE demands the other ACCEPT the guilt, and SACRIFICE HIMSELF as well. Forgiveness becomes impossible, for the ego believes, that to for-

---
[574] December 16, 1966.

give another, IS TO LOSE HIM. For it is only by attack WITHOUT forgiveness, that the ego can ensure the guilt which holds ALL its relationships together.

T 15 H 8. Yet they only SEEM to be together. For relationships, to the ego, mean ONLY that BODIES are together. It is always PHYSICAL closeness that the ego demands, and it does not object where the mind goes, or what it thinks, for this seems unimportant. For, as long as the BODY is there, to receive its sacrifice, it is content. To the ego, THE MIND IS PRIVATE, and only the body CAN be shared. Ideas are basically of no concern, except as they draw the BODY of another closer or farther. And it is in these terms that it evaluates ideas as "good" or "bad." What makes another guilty, AND HOLDS HIM THROUGH GUILT, is "good." What releases him FROM guilt is "bad," because he would no longer believe that BODIES communicate, and so he would be "gone."

T 15 H 9. Suffering and sacrifice are the gifts with which the ego would "bless" all unions. And those who are united at its altar ACCEPT suffering and sacrifice as the PRICE of union. In their angry alliances, born of the fear of loneliness, and yet dedicated to the CONTINUANCE of loneliness, they seek RELIEF from guilt, by INCREASING it in the other. For they believe that this DECREASES it in them. The other seems always to be attacking and wounding them, perhaps in little ways, perhaps "unconsciously," yet never without demand of sacrifice. The fury of those joined at the ego's altar, far exceeds your awareness of it. For what the ego really, wants you do NOT realize. **T(587) - 414 -**

T 15 H 10. Whenever you are angry, you can be sure that you have formed a special relationship which the ego has "blessed," for anger IS its "blessing." Anger takes many forms, but it cannot long deceive those who will learn that LOVE BRINGS NO GUILT AT ALL, and what brings guilt CANNOT be love, and MUST be anger. ALL anger is nothing more than an attempt to MAKE SOMEONE FEEL GUILTY, and this attempt is the ONLY basis which the ego accepts for special relationships. Guilt is the only need the ego has, and, as long as you identify WITH it, guilt will remain ATTRACTIVE to you.

T 15 H 11. But remember this; to be WITH A BODY is NOT communication. And, if you think it IS, you will feel guilty about COMMUNICATION, and will be AFRAID to hear the Holy Spirit, recognizing in His voice, your OWN need to communicate. The Holy Spirit CANNOT teach through fear. And how can He communicate with you, while you believe that, to communicate, is to MAKE YOURSELF ALONE? It is CLEARLY insane to believe that, by communicating, you will be abandoned. And yet, you DO believe it. For you think that your minds must be kept PRIVATE, or you will LOSE them. And, if your BODIES are together, your minds remain your own.

T 15 H 12. The union of bodies thus becomes the way in which you would KEEP MINDS APART. For bodies cannot forgive. They can do only as the mind directs. The illusion of the autonomy of the body, and ITS ability to overcome loneliness, is but the working of the ego's plan to establish its OWN autonomy. As long as you believe that, to be with a body, is companionship, you will be COMPELLED to attempt to keep your brother IN his body, HELD THERE BY GUILT. And you will see SAFETY IN GUILT, and DANGER IN COMMUNICATION. For the ego will ALWAYS teach that loneliness is solved by guilt, and that communication is the CAUSE of loneliness. And, despite the evident insanity of this lesson, YOU HAVE LEARNED IT.

T 15 H 13. Forgiveness lies in communication, as surely as damnation lies in guilt. It is the Holy Spirit's teaching function to instruct those who **T(588) - 415 -** believe that communication is damnation, that communication is salvation. And He will do so, for the power of God in Him AND YOU is joined in REAL relationship, so holy and so strong, that it can overcome even this, WITHOUT fear. It is through the holy instant that what SEEMS impossible is ACCOMPLISHED, making it evident that it is NOT impossible. In the holy instant, guilt holds NO attraction, since communication HAS BEEN restored. And guilt, whose ONLY purpose is to DISRUPT communication, HAS no function here.

T 15 I. The Holy Instant and Real Relationships (*Notes* 1310 9:147)

T 15 I 1. Here, there is no concealment, and no private thoughts. The WILLINGNESS to communicate attracts communication TO it, and overcomes loneliness completely. There is complete forgiveness here, for there is no desire to exclude ANYONE from your completion, in sudden recognition of the value of his part in it. In the protection of YOUR wholeness, all are invited and made welcome. And you understand that YOUR completion is God's, Whose only need is to have you Be complete. For your completion MAKES you His, in YOUR awareness. And here it is that you experience yourself as you were created, AND AS YOU ARE.

T 15 I 2. The holy instant does not REPLACE the need for learning, for the Holy Spirit must not leave you as your Teacher, until the holy instant has extended far beyond time. For a teaching assignment such as His, He must use EVERYTHING in this world for your release. He must side with EVERY sign or token of your willingness to learn of Him what truth MUST be. He is swift to utilize WHATEVER you offer Him, on behalf of this. His concern and care for you are limitless. In the face of your fear of forgiveness, which He perceives as clearly as He knows forgiveness IS release, He will teach you to remember always that forgiveness is NOT loss, BUT YOUR SALVATION. And that, in COMPLETE forgiveness, in which you recognize that there is nothing to forgive, YOU are absolved completely.

T 15 I 3. Hear Him gladly, and learn of Him that you have need of no special **T(589) - 416 -** relationships at all. You but seek in them what you have THROWN AWAY. And, through THEM, you will never learn the value of what you have cast aside, but what you still desire with all your hearts. Let us join together in making the holy instant all that there is, by desiring that it BE all that there is. God's Son has such great need of your willingness to strive for this, that you cannot conceive of need so great. Behold the only need that God and His Son share, and will to meet together. You are NOT alone in this. The will of your creations call[575] to you, to share your will with them. Turn, then, in peace, from guilt to God and them.

T 15 I 4. Relate only with what will never LEAVE you, and what YOU cannot leave. The loneliness of God's Son is the loneliness of his Father. Refuse not the awareness of your completion, and seek not to restore it to yourselves. Fear not to give redemption over to your Redeemer's love. He will NOT fail you, for He comes from One Who CANNOT fail. Accept YOUR sense of failure as nothing more than a mistake in WHO YOU WERE. For the holy host of God is BEYOND failure, and NOTHING that he wills can BE denied. You are forever in a relationship so holy, that it calls to everyone to ESCAPE from loneliness, and join you in your Love. And where YOU are must everyone seek, and FIND you there.

T 15 I 5. Think but an instant on this; God gave the Sonship to you, to ensure your perfect creation. This was His Gift, for, as He withheld Himself not from you, He withheld not His creation. Nothing that ever was created, but is not yours. Your relationships are with the universe. And this universe, being of God, is far beyond the petty sum of all the separate bodies YOU perceive. For all its parts are joined in God through Christ, where they become like to their Father. For Christ knows of no separation FROM His Father, Who

---

[575] Agreement in number problem. "Will" is the subject, "call" the verb, and since will is singular, the verb must be "calls." FIP corrects this, though all other versions retain what we believe is a grammar error. It is the will that calls, not the creations which call, grammatically speaking

is His One relationship, in which He gives as His Father gives to Him. **T(590) - 417 -**

T 15 I 6. The Holy Spirit is God's attempt to free you of what He does not understand. And, because of the Source of the attempt, IT WILL SUCCEED. The Holy Spirit asks you to respond as God does, for He would teach you what YOU do not understand. God would respond to EVERY need, WHATEVER form it takes. And so He has kept this Channel open to receive His communication to you, AND YOURS TO HIM. God does NOT understand your problem in communication, for He does NOT share it with you. It is only YOU, who believe that it IS understandable.

T 15 I 7. The Holy Spirit KNOWS that it is not understandable, and yet He UNDERSTANDS it, because you have MADE it. In Him alone, lies the awareness of what God CANNOT know, and what YOU do NOT understand. It is His holy function to ACCEPT THEM BOTH, and, by removing EVERY element of DISagreement, to join them into one. He will do this, BECAUSE it is His function. Leave, then, what seems to you to be impossible, to Him Who knows it MUST be possible, because it is the Will of God. And let Him, Whose teaching is ONLY of God, teach you the ONLY meaning of relationships. For God Himself created the only relationship that HAS meaning, and that is His relationship with YOU. **T(591) - 418 -**[576]

T 15 I 8. As the ego would limit your perception of your brothers to the body, so would the Holy Spirit RELEASE your vision, and let you see the Great Rays shining from them, so unlimited that they reach to God. It is this shift in vision which is accomplished in the holy instant. Yet it is needful for you to learn just what this shift entails, so you will become willing to make it permanent. Given this willingness, it will NOT leave you, for it IS permanent. For, once you have accepted it as the ONLY PERCEPTION THAT YOU WANT, it is translated into knowledge, by the part that God Himself plays in the Atonement, for it is the ONLY step in it He understands. Therefore, in this there will be NO delay, when YOU are ready for it. God is ready NOW, but YOU are not.

T 15 I 9. Our task is but to continue, as fast as possible, the necessary process of looking straight at ALL the interference, and seeing it EXACTLY as it is. For it is impossible to recognize as WHOLLY without gratification, WHAT YOU THINK YOU WANT. The body is the symbol of the ego, as the ego is the symbol of separation. And both are nothing more than attempts to LIMIT communication, and thereby TO MAKE IT IMPOSSIBLE. For communication MUST be UNlimited in order to HAVE meaning, and DEPRIVED of meaning, it will NOT satisfy YOU completely. Yet it remains the ONLY means by which you CAN establish real relationships.

T 15 I 10. Real relationships HAVE no limits, having been established by God. In the holy instant, where the Great Rays REPLACE the body in awareness, the recognition of relationships WITHOUT limits is given you. But to SEE this, it is necessary to give up EVERY use the ego has for the body, and to accept the fact that the ego has NO purpose you would SHARE with it. For the ego would limit everyone TO a body for ITS purposes, and, while you think it HAS a purpose, you will choose to utilize the means by which IT tries to turn its purpose into accomplishment. This will never BE accomplished.

T 15 I 11. Yet you have surely recognized that the ego, whose goals are altogether UNattainable, will strive for them with all its might. And will do **T(592) - 419 -** so with the strength that YOU have given it. Yet it is impossible to DIVIDE your strength between Heaven and hell, God and the ego, and RELEASE your power unto creation, that is the ONLY purpose for which it was GIVEN you. For love would always give INCREASE. Limits are DEMANDED, representing the ego's demands to make little and ineffectual. Limit

---
[576] December 18, 1966.

your vision of a brother to his body, which you WILL do, as long as you would not release him FROM it, and you have denied HIS gift to YOU. HIS BODY CANNOT GIVE IT. And seek it not through YOURS.

T 15 I 12. But your minds are ALREADY continuous, and THEIR union need only be accepted, and the loneliness in Heaven is gone. If you would but let the Holy Spirit tell you of the Love of God for you, and the need that your creations have to be with you forever, you would experience the attraction of the Eternal. For no-one can hear Him speak of this, and long remain willing to linger here. For it IS your will to be in Heaven, where you are complete and quiet, in such sure and loving relationships, that ANY limits are impossible. Would you not exchange your little relationships for this? For the body IS little and limited, and only those whom you would see WITHOUT the limits that the ego would impose on them, can offer YOU the gift of freedom.

T 15 I 13. You have no conception of the limits you have placed on your perception, and no idea of all the loveliness that you COULD see. But this you must remember; the attraction of guilt OPPOSES the attraction of God. His attraction for you remains unlimited, but, because your power, BEING His, is AS GREAT as His, you can TURN AWAY from love. What you invest in guilt, you withdraw from God. And your sight grows weak and dim and limited, for you have attempted to SEPARATE the Father from the Son, and LIMIT their communication. Seek not Atonement in FURTHER separation. And limit not your vision of God's Son to what INTERFERES with his release, and what the Holy Spirit must UNDO to set him free. For his belief in limits HAS imprisoned him. **T(593) - 420 -**

T 15 J. The Time of Christ (*Notes* 1320 9:157)

T 15 J 1. When the body ceases to attract you, and when you place no value on it as a means of GETTING ANYTHING, then there will be NO interference in communication. And your thoughts will be as free as God's. As you let the Holy Spirit teach you how to use the body ONLY for purposes of communication, and RENOUNCE its use for separation and attack, which the EGO sees in it, you will learn you have no need of a body at all. In the holy instant, there ARE no bodies. And you experience ONLY the attraction of God. Accepting it as undivided, you join Him wholly, in an instant. For you would place NO limits on your union WITH Him. The reality of THIS relationship becomes the only truth that you could ever WANT. ALL Truth IS here.

T 15 J 2. It IS in your power, IN TIME, to delay the perfect union of the Father and the Son. For in this world, the attraction of guilt DOES stand between them. Neither time nor season means anything in eternity. But here, it is the Holy Spirit's function to use them both, NOT as the ego uses them. This is the season when you would celebrate my birth into this world. Yet you know not how to do it. Let the Holy Spirit teach you, and let ME celebrate YOUR birth through Him. The only gift I can accept of you, is the gift I GAVE you. Release ME, as I willed YOUR release. The time of Christ we celebrate TOGETHER. For it HAS no meaning, if we are apart.

T 15 J 3. The holy instant is truly the time of Christ. For, in this liberating instant, no guilt is laid upon the Son of God, and his unlimited power is thus restored to him. What OTHER gift can you offer me, when ONLY THIS I will to offer YOU? And to see me, is to see me in everyone, and offer everyone the gift you offer me. I am incapable of receiving sacrifice as God is. And every sacrifice you ask of YOURSELF, you ask of me. Learn NOW that sacrifice, of ANY kind, is nothing but a LIMITATION IMPOSED ON GIVING. And, BY this limitation, you have limited YOUR acceptance of the gift I offer YOU. **T(594) - 421 -**

T 15 J 4. We who are one, cannot give separately. When you are willing to accept OUR relationship AS REAL, guilt will hold NO attraction for you. For, in OUR union, you will accept ALL of our brothers. The gift of union is the only gift that I was born to give.

Give it to ME, that YOU may have it. The time of Christ is the time appointed for the gift of freedom, offered to everyone. And, by YOUR acceptance of it, you have offered it TO everyone. It IS in your power to make this season holy. For it is in your power to make the time of Christ be NOW. **T(595) - 422 -**[577]

T 15 J 5. It is possible to do this all at once, because there is but ONE shift in perception that is necessary. For you made but ONE mistake. It SEEMS like many, but it is all the same. For, though the ego takes many forms, it is ALWAYS the same idea. What is NOT love is always fear, and nothing else. It is not necessary to follow fear through all the circuitous routes by which it burrows underground, and hides in darkness, to emerge in FORMS quite different from what it IS. It IS necessary to examine each one, as long as you would retain the PRINCIPLE which governs all of them. But when you are willing to regard them, NOT as separate, but as DIFFERENT MANIFESTATIONS OF THE SAME IDEA, and ONE YOU DO NOT WANT, they go together.

T 15 J 6. The idea is simply this; you believe that it is possible to be host to the ego, or hostage to God. This is the choice you think you have, and the decision that you believe that you must make. You see no other alternatives. For you can NOT accept the fact that SACRIFICE GETS NOTHING. Sacrifice is so essential to your thought-system, that salvation, APART from sacrifice, means NOTHING to you. Your confusion of sacrifice and love is so profound that you cannot conceive of love WITHOUT sacrifice. And it is THIS that you must look at; SACRIFICE IS ATTACK, NOT LOVE. If you would accept but this ONE idea, your fear of love would vanish.

T 15 J 7. Guilt CANNOT last, when the idea of sacrifice has been removed. For, if there MUST be sacrifice, as you are convinced, someone must pay, and someone must get. And the ONLY question that remains to BE decided is HOW MUCH is the price, for getting WHAT. As host to the ego, you believe that you can give ALL your guilt away, WHATEVER you think, and purchase peace. For the payment DOES NOT SEEM TO BE YOURS. While it is obvious that the ego DOES demand payment, it NEVER seems to be demanding it OF YOU. For you are unwilling to recognize that the ego, which you INVITED, is treacherous only to those who think they are its host.

T 15 J 8. The ego will NEVER let you perceive this, for this recognition WILL make it homeless. For, when this recognition dawns clearly, you will NOT be **T(596) - 423 -** deceived by ANY form the ego takes, to protect itself FROM your sight. Each form will be recognized as but a cover, for the one idea that hides behind them all. That love demands sacrifice, and is therefore INSEPARABLE from attack and fear. And that GUILT IS THE PRICE OF LOVE, which MUST be paid BY fear. How fearful, then, has God become to you, and how great a sacrifice do you believe His Love demands! For total love would demand total sacrifice. And so the ego seems to demand LESS of you than God, and of the two is judged as the LESSER of two evils, one to be feared a little, but the Other TO BE DESTROYED.

T 15 J 9. For you see love AS DESTRUCTIVE, and your only question is WHO is to be destroyed, you or another? You seek to answer this question in your special relationships, in which you are both destroyer and destroyed IN PART, but with the idea of being able to be neither completely. And this you think SAVES YOU FROM GOD, whose TOTAL Love would COMPLETELY destroy you. You think that everyone OUTSIDE yourself demands your sacrifice, but you do NOT see that ONLY you demand sacrifice, and ONLY of yourself. Yet the demand of sacrifice is so savage and so fearful, that you CANNOT accept it WHERE IT IS. But the REAL price of NOT accepting this has been so great, that you have GIVEN GOD AWAY, rather than look at it.

---

[577] December 23, 1966.

T 15 J 10. For, if GOD would demand total sacrifice of you, you thought it safer to project Him outward and AWAY from you, and NOT be host to Him. For to Him you ascribed the EGO's treachery, inviting it to take His place, and PROTECT you FROM Him. And you do not recognize that it is WHAT YOU INVITED IN that would destroy you, and DOES demand total sacrifice of you. No partial sacrifice will appease this savage guest, for it is an invader who but SEEMS to offer kindness, but ALWAYS to MAKE THE SACRIFICE COMPLETE. You will NOT succeed in being PARTIAL hostage to the ego, for it keeps NO bargains, and would leave you NOTHING. Nor can you be partial HOST to it.

T 15 J 11. You will have to choose between TOTAL freedom and TOTAL bondage, for there are no alternatives but these. You have tried many compromises, in the attempt to avoid recognizing the one decision that MUST be made. And **T(597) - 424 -** yet, it is the RECOGNITION of the decision, JUST AS IT IS, that makes the decision so easy! Salvation is simple, being of God, and therefore VERY easy to understand. But do not try to project it FROM you, and see it OUTSIDE yourself. In YOU are both the question and the Answer; the demand for sacrifice and the peace of God.

T 15 K. The End of Sacrifice (*Notes* 1329 9:166)

T 15 K 1. Fear not to recognize as SOLELY OF YOUR MAKING the whole idea of sacrifice. And seek not safety by attempting to PROTECT yourself from where it is NOT. Your brothers and your Father have become VERY fearful to you, and you would bargain with them for a few special relationships, in which you think you see some scraps of safety. Do not try longer to KEEP APART your thoughts and the Thought that has been GIVEN you. When they are brought together, and perceived WHERE THEY ARE, the choice BETWEEN them is nothing more than a gentle awakening, and as simple as opening your eyes to daylight, when you have no more need of sleep.

T 15 K 2. The sign of Christmas is a star, a light in darkness. See it not OUTSIDE of yourself, but as shining in the Heaven within, and accept it as the sign the time of Christ has come. He comes demanding NOTHING. No sacrifice of ANY kind, of ANYONE, is asked by Him. In His Presence, the whole IDEA of sacrifice loses ALL meaning. For He is Host to God. And you need but invite Him in Who is there ALREADY, by recognizing that His Host is One. And no thought ALIEN to His Oneness can abide with Him there. Love MUST be total to give Him welcome, for the Presence of holiness CREATES the holiness which surrounds It. No fear can touch the Host Who cradles God in the time of Christ. For the Host is as holy as the Perfect Innocence that He protects, and Whose Power protects HIM.

T 15 K 3. This Christmas, give the Holy Spirit EVERYTHING that would hurt you. LET yourself be healed completely, that you may JOIN with Him in healing. And let us celebrate our release together, by releasing everyone WITH us. Leave nothing behind, for release is TOTAL. And when you have accepted it WITH me, you will GIVE it with me. All pain and sacrifice and littleness will disappear in OUR relationship, which is as innocent as our relationship with **T(598) - 425 -** our Father, and as powerful. Pain will be brought to us, and disappear in our presence. And, WITHOUT pain, there can BE no sacrifice. And WITHOUT SACRIFICE, there love MUST be.

T 15 K 4. You who believe that sacrifice IS love, must learn that sacrifice is separation FROM love. For sacrifice brings guilt, as surely as love brings peace. Guilt is the CONDITION of sacrifice, as peace is the condition for the awareness of your relationship with God. For through guilt, you EXCLUDE your Father and your brothers FROM yourself. And through peace, you will invite them back, and realize they are where your invitation bids them be. What you excluded from yourself seems fearful, for you ENDOWED it with fear, and tried to CAST IT OUT, though it was part of you. Who can perceive part of himself as loathsome, and live within himself in peace? And who can try to resolve the perceived conflict of Heaven and hell IN HIM by casting Heaven out, and GIVING IT the attributes of hell, WITHOUT experiencing himself as incomplete and lonely?

T 15 K 5. As long as you perceive the body as your reality, so long will you perceive yourself as lonely and deprived. And so long will you also perceive yourself as a VICTIM OF SACRIFICE, JUSTIFIED in sacrificing others. For who could thrust Heaven and its Creator aside, WITHOUT a sense of sacrifice and loss? And who can suffer sacrifice and loss, without attempting to RESTORE himself? Yet how could you accomplish this yourselves, when the basis of your attempts is the belief in the REALITY OF THE DEPRIVATION? For deprivation breeds attack, BEING the belief that attack IS justified. And, as long as you would RETAIN the deprivation, attack becomes salvation, and sacrifice becomes love.

T 15 K 6. So is it that, in all your seeking for love, YOU SEEK FOR SACRIFICE, and FIND it.[578] Yet you find NOT love. For it is impossible to DENY what love IS, and still RECOGNIZE it. The meaning of love lies in what you have cast OUTSIDE yourself, and it HAS no meaning at all, APART from you. It is what you preferred to KEEP, that has no meaning. While all that you would KEEP **T(599) - 426 -** AWAY hold all the meaning of the universe, and holds the universe together in its meaning. For, unless the universe were joined in YOU, it would be APART FROM God, and to be without Him IS to be without meaning.

T 15 K 7. In the holy instant, the condition of love is met, for minds are joined without the body's INTERFERENCE, and where there is communication, there is peace. The Prince of Peace was born to re-establish the CONDITION of love, by teaching that communication remains unbroken, even if the body is destroyed, PROVIDED THAT you see NOT the body as the necessary means of communication. And if you UNDERSTAND this lesson, you will realize that, to sacrifice the BODY, is to SACRIFICE NOTHING. And communication, which MUST be of the mind, CANNOT be sacrificed. Where, then, is sacrifice?

T 15 K 8. The lesson I was born to teach, and still would teach to all my brothers, is that sacrifice is nowhere and love is everywhere. For communication EMBRACES EVERYTHING, and in the peace it re-establishes, love comes of itself. Let no despair darken the joy of Christmas, for the time of Christ is meaningless APART from joy. Let us join in celebrating peace by demanding no sacrifice of anyone, for so will you offer me the love I offer you. What can be more joyous than to perceive WE ARE DEPRIVED OF NOTHING? Such is the message of the time of Christ, which I give you, that YOU may give it, and return it to the Father, Who gave it to me.

T 15 K 9. For in the time of Christ, communication with Him is restored, and He joins us in the celebration of His Son's Creation. God offers thanks to the holy host who would receive Him, and let Him enter, and abide where He would be. And BY your welcome, does HE welcome you into Himself. For what is contained in you who welcome Him is RETURNED to Him. And we but celebrate HIS Wholeness, as we welcome Him into ourselves. Those who receive the Father are one with Him, being host to Him Who created them. And by allowing Him to enter, the remembrance of the Father enters with Him, and with Him they remember the only relationship they ever had, and ever want to have. **T(600) -427**[579]

T 15 K 10. This is the week-end in which a new year will be born from the time of Christ. I have perfect faith in you, to do all that you would accomplish. Nothing will be lacking, and you will MAKE COMPLETE, and NOT destroy. Say and UNDERSTAND this:

I give you to the Holy Spirit, as part of myself.

I know that you will be released, UNLESS I WANT TO

USE YOU TO IMPRISON MYSELF.

In the name of MY freedom, I WILL your release,

Because I recognize that we will be released TOGETHER.

So will the year begin in joy and freedom. There is much to do, and we have been long delayed. Accept the holy instant as this year is born, and take your place, so long left unfulfilled, in the Great Awakening. Make this year different, by making it ALL THE SAME. And let ALL your relationships be made holy FOR you. This is OUR will.

Amen. (601) -428[580]

---

[578] **Psalms 40:6** Sacrifice and offering You did not desire; My ears You have opened; burnt offering and sin offering You have not asked.
Psalms 51:16 For You do not desire sacrifice; or else I would give *it*; You do not delight in burnt offering.
Matthew 12:7 "But if you had known what *this* is, 'I desire mercy and not sacrifice,' you would not have condemned those who are not guilty."

[579] December 28, 1966
[580] December 30, 1966

CHAPTER 16 – THE FORGIVENESS OF ILLUSIONS

T 16 A. Introduction (*Notes* 1354 9:191)

T 16 A 1. To empathize does NOT mean to JOIN IN SUFFERING, for this is what you must REFUSE to understand. This is the EGO's interpretation of empathy, and is ALWAYS used to form a special relationship, in which SUFFERING is shared. The CAPACITY to empathize is VERY useful to the Holy Spirit, provided you let Him use it in His way. His way is very different.[581] He does NOT understand suffering, and would have you teach IT IS NOT UNDERSTANDABLE. When He relates through you, He does NOT relate through the ego to another ego. He does NOT join in pain, knowing that HEALING pain is NOT accomplished by delusional attempts to ENTER INTO IT, and lighten it by SHARING the delusion.

T 16 A 2. The clearest proof that empathy, as the ego uses it, is DESTRUCTIVE, lies in the fact that it is applied ONLY to certain types of problems, and in certain people. These it SELECTS OUT and JOINS WITH. And it NEVER joins, except to strengthen itself. Having identified with what it THINKS it understands, it sees ITSELF, and would INCREASE itself by sharing what is LIKE itself. Make no mistake about this maneuver; the ego always EMPATHIZES TO WEAKEN. And to weaken is ALWAYS to attack.

T 16 A 3. You do NOT know what empathizing means. But of this you may be sure; if you will merely sit quietly by, and let the Holy Spirit relate THROUGH you, you will EMPATHIZE WITH STRENGTH, and both of you will gain in strength, and NOT in weakness. Your part is only to remember this; you do not want anything that YOU value to come of the relationship. You will neither to hurt it, NOR TO HEAL IT in your own way. You do NOT know what healing IS. All you have learned of empathy IS FROM THE PAST. And there is NOTHING from the past that you would share, for there is nothing there that YOU WOULD KEEP. **T(602) -429**[582]

T 16 A 4. Do NOT use empathy to MAKE THE PAST REAL, and so perpetuate it. Step gently aside, and let the healing be done FOR you. Keep but one thought in mind, and do not lose sight of it, however tempted you may be to judge the situation, and DETERMINE your response BY judging it. Focus your mind only on this:[583]

> "I am not alone, and I would not intrude the past upon my Guest.
>
> I have invited Him, and He is here.
>
> I need do nothing except NOT TO INTERFERE."

T 16 B. True Empathy (*Notes* 1356 9:193)

T 16 B 1. True empathy is of Him Who knows what it is. YOU will learn HIS interpretation of it, if you let Him use YOUR capacity for strength, and NOT for weakness.

T 16 B 2. He will NOT desert you, but be sure that YOU desert not Him. Humility is strength in this sense only; to recognize and ACCEPT the fact that you do NOT know, is to recognize and accept the fact that He DOES know. You are not sure that He will do His part, because you have NEVER YET DONE YOURS COMPLETELY. You will NOT know how to respond to what you do NOT understand. Be tempted not in this and yield not to the ego's triumphant use of empathy, for ITS glory. The triumph of weakness is NOT what you would offer to a brother. And yet you know no triumph but this. This is NOT knowledge, and the form of empathy that would bring it about, is so distorted that it would imprison what it would release.

T 16 B 3. The unredeemed cannot redeem. Yet they HAVE a Redeemer. Attempt to teach Him not. YOU are the learner; HE the Teacher. Do not confuse your role with His, for this will NEVER bring peace to anyone. Offer your empathy to Him, for it is HIS perception and His STRENGTH that you would share. And let Him offer you HIS strength and HIS perception, to be shared THROUGH you. **T(603) -430**

The meaning of love is lost in any relationship which looks to weakness, and hopes to find it there. The POWER of love, which IS its meaning, lies in the strength of God, which hovers over it and blesses it silently, by enveloping it in healing wings. LET THIS BE, and do not try to substitute YOUR "miracle" for this.

T 16 B 4. We once said that, if a brother asks a foolish thing of you, to do it. But be certain that this does NOT mean to do a foolish thing that would hurt either him or you, for what would hurt one WILL hurt the other. Foolish requests ARE foolish, for the simple reason THAT THEY CONFLICT, because they contain an element of specialness. Only the Holy Spirit recognizes foolish needs, AS WELL AS real ones. And He will teach you how to meet BOTH, without losing either.

T 16 B 5. YOU will be able to do this ONLY IN SECRECY. And you will think that, by meeting the needs of one, you do NOT jeopardize another, because you keep them SEPARATE, and secret from each other. This is NOT the way, for it leads not to light and truth. No needs will long be left unmet, if you leave them ALL to Him Whose FUNCTION is to meet them. This is His function, and NOT YOURS. He will NOT meet them secretly, for He would share everything you give through Him. And that is WHY He gives it. What you give through Him is for the whole Sonship, NOT FOR PART OF IT. Leave Him His function, for He WILL fulfill it, if you but ask Him to enter your relationships, and bless them FOR you. **T(604) -431**[584]

T 16 C. The Magnitude of Holiness (*Notes* 1336 9:173)

T 16 C 1. You still think holiness is difficult, because you cannot see how it can be extended to include EVERYONE, and you HAVE learned that it MUST include everyone, to BE holy. Concern yourselves not with the EXTENSION of holiness, for the nature of miracles you do NOT understand. Nor do you DO them. It is their extension, far beyond the limits you perceive, that demonstrates you did NOT do them. Why should you worry how the miracle extends to all the Sonship, when you do not understand the miracle itself? One ATTRIBUTE is no more difficult to understand than is the whole. If miracles ARE at all, their attributes would have to be miraculous, being PART of them.

T 16 C 2. There is a tendency to fragment, and then to be concerned about the truth of just a little PART of the whole. And this is but a way of avoiding, or looking AWAY FROM the whole, to what you think you might be better able to understand. And this is but another way in which you would still try to keep understanding TO YOURSELF. A better and FAR more helpful way to think of miracles is this: You do NOT understand them, either in part OR whole. Yet you have DONE them. Therefore, YOUR understanding CANNOT be necessary. Yet it is still impossible to accomplish what you do not understand. And so there must be Something IN you that DOES understand.

---

[581] This sentence does not appear in the *Urtext* manuscript but does show up in the *Notes* and in the FIP *2nd Edition*. It appears to be an inadvertent omission.
[582] December 30, 1966 (CONTINUED)
[583] While the *Urtext* manuscript has a semi-colon here, the *Notes* has a colon which is more appropriate. The *HLC* and FIP versions also use a colon here.

[584] Jan. 1, 1967

Chapter 16 – The Forgiveness of Illusions

T 16 C 3. To you the miracle CANNOT seem natural, because what you have done to hurt your minds, has made THEM so UNnatural that they do not remember what is natural to them. And when you are TOLD about it, you cannot UNDERSTAND it. The recognition of the part as whole, and of the whole in every part, is PERFECTLY natural. For it is the way GOD thinks, and what is natural to Him, IS natural to you. WHOLLY natural perception would show you instantly that order of difficulty in miracles is quite impossible, for it involves a contradiction of what miracles MEAN. And, if you could understand their MEANING, their ATTRIBUTES could hardly cause you perplexity. **T(605) -432**

T 16 C 4. You HAVE done miracles, but it is QUITE apparent that you have NOT done them alone. You have succeeded whenever you have reached another mind, and JOINED with it. When two minds join as one, and share one idea equally, the first link in the awareness of the Sonship as one has been made. When you have made this joining, as the Holy Spirit bids you, and have OFFERED it to Him to use as HE knows how, His natural perception of your gift enables HIM to understand it, and YOU to USE His understanding on YOUR behalf. It is impossible to convince you of the reality of what has clearly BEEN accomplished, through your willingness, as long as you believe that YOU must understand it, or else IT is not real.

T 16 C 5. You think your LACK of understanding is a LOSS to you, and so you are unwilling to believe that what HAS happened is true. Yet can you REALLY believe that all that has happened, EVEN THOUGH you do NOT understand it, HAS NOT HAPPENED? Yet this IS your position. You would have PERFECT faith in the Holy Spirit, and in the EFFECTS of His teaching, if you were not AFRAID to acknowledge what He taught you. For this acknowledgement MEANS that what has happened you do NOT understand, but that you are willing to ACCEPT it, BECAUSE it has happened. How can faith in reality be yours, while you are bent on making it UNreal? And are you REALLY safer in maintaining the UNreality of what has happened, than you would be in joyously accepting it FOR WHAT IT IS, and giving thanks for it?

T 16 C 6. Honor the truth that has been given you, and be glad you do NOT understand it. Miracles are natural to God, and to the One Who speaks for Him. For His task is to TRANSLATE the miracle into the knowledge which it REPRESENTS, and which IS lost to you. Let HIS understanding of the miracle be enough for you, and do not turn away from all the witnesses that He has given you to His reality. **T(606) -433** NO evidence will convince you of the truth of what you do NOT want. Yet your relationship with Him IS real, and HAS been demonstrated. Regard this not with fear, but with rejoicing. The One you called upon IS with you. Bid Him welcome, and honor His witnesses, who bring you the glad tidings that He HAS come.[585]

T 16 C 7. It IS true, JUST AS YOU FEAR, that to acknowledge Him, IS to deny ALL that you think you know. But it was NEVER true. What gain is there to you in clinging to it, and denying the evidence for truth? For you have come too near to truth to renounce it now, and you WILL yield to its compelling attraction. You can delay this now, but only a little. The host of God has called to you, and you HAVE heard. Never again will you be wholly willing NOT to listen. This is a year of joy, in which your listening will increase, and peace will grow with its increase.

T 16 C 8. The power of holiness AND THE WEAKNESS OF ATTACK, have BOTH been brought into awareness. And this has been accomplished in minds firmly convinced that holiness is weakness, and attack is power. Should not that be a sufficient miracle to teach you that your Teacher is NOT of you? But remember also that, whenever you have listened to HIS interpretation, the results have brought YOU joy. Would you PREFER the results of YOUR interpretation, considering honestly what they have been? God wills you better. Could you not look with greater charity, on whom God loves with perfect love? Do not interpret AGAINST His love for you. For you have many witnesses that speak of it so clearly, that only the blind and deaf could fail to see and hear them.

T 16 C 9. This year, determine NOT to deny what has been given you BY God, to use for Him. He has Himself reminded you of Him. Awake and SHARE it, for that is the only reason He has called to you. His Voice has spoken clearly, and yet you have so little faith in what you heard, because you have preferred to place **T(607) -434** still greater faith in the disaster YOU have made. Today, let us resolve TOGETHER to accept the joyful tidings that disaster is NOT real, and that reality is NOT disaster. Reality is safe and sure and wholly kind to everyone and everything. There is no greater love than to accept this, and be glad. For love asks only that YOU BE HAPPY, and will GIVE you everything that makes for happiness.

T 16 C 10. You have never given ANY problem to the Holy Spirit He has not solved. NOR will you ever do so. You have never tried to solve ANYTHING yourself and been successful. Is it not time you brought these facts TOGETHER, and made SENSE of them? This is the year for the APPLICATION of the ideas that have been given you. For the ideas are mighty forces, to be USED, and not held idly by. They have ALREADY proved their power sufficiently for you to place your faith in THEM, and NOT in their denial. This year, invest in truth, and let it work in peace. Have faith in what has faith in YOU. Think what you have REALLY seen and heard, and RECOGNIZE it. Can you BE alone, with witnesses like these? **T(608) -435**[586]

T 16 D. The Reward of Teaching (*Notes* 1343 9:160)

T 16 D 1. You have taught well, and yet you have not learned how to ACCEPT the comfort of your teaching. If you will consider WHAT you have taught, and how alien it is to what you THOUGHT you knew, you will be COMPELLED to recognize that your Teacher came from BEYOND your thought-system, and so could look upon it fairly, and perceive it was untrue. And He MUST have done so from the basis of a very different thought-system, and one with NOTHING IN COMMON WITH YOURS. For certainly, what He has taught, and what you taught THROUGH Him, HAS nothing in common with what you taught BEFORE He came. And the results have been to bring peace where there was pain, and suffering has disappeared, to be replaced by joy.

T 16 D 2. You HAVE taught freedom, but you have NOT learned how to be free. We once said, "By their fruits ye shall know them, and they shall know themselves."[587] For it is certain that you judge YOURSELF according to your teaching. The ego's teaching produces IMMEDIATE results, because ITS decisions are immediately ACCEPTED AS YOUR CHOICE. And this acceptance MEANS that you are willing to judge yourself accordingly. Cause and effect are very clear in the ego's thought-system, because all your learning has been directed toward ESTABLISHING the relationship between them. And would you NOT have faith in what you have so diligently taught yourself to believe? But remember how much care you have exerted in choosing its witnesses, and in AVOIDING those who spoke for the Cause of truth, and ITS effects.

---

[585] **Luke 1:19** And the angel answered and said to him, "I am Gabriel, who stands in the presence of God, and was sent to speak to you and bring you these glad tidings."
Luke 8:1 Now it came to pass, afterward, that He went through every city and village, preaching and bringing the glad tidings of the kingdom of God. And the twelve were with Him,

[586] January 2, 1967
[587] **T 9 D 13.** By following the right Guide, you will learn the simplest of all lessons: "By their fruits ye shall know them, and THEY shall know THEMSELVES." **T(396) 223**
Matthew 7:16 "You will know them by their fruits. Do men gather grapes from thorn bushes or figs from thistles?"

T 16 D 3. Does not the fact that you have NOT learned what you HAVE taught, show you that you do NOT perceive the Sonship as one? And does it not also show you that you do not regard YOURSELF as one? For it is impossible to teach successfully, WHOLLY without conviction, and it is equally impossible that conviction be OUTSIDE you. You could never have taught freedom, unless you DID believe in it. And it MUST be that what you taught CAME FROM YOURSELF. **T(609) -436** And yet, this self you clearly DO NOT KNOW, and do not recognize EVEN THOUGH IT FUNCTIONS. What functions, must be THERE. And it is ONLY if you deny WHAT IT HAS DONE, that you could possibly deny its presence.

T 16 D 4. This is a course in how to KNOW yourself. You have TAUGHT what you are, but have NOT let what you are, teach YOU. You have been VERY careful to avoid the obvious, and NOT to see the REAL cause and effect relationship that is PERFECTLY apparent. Yet, within you, is EVERYTHING you taught. What can it be, that has NOT learned it? It must be this that is REALLY outside yourself, NOT by your own projection, BUT IN TRUTH. And it is this, that you have TAKEN IN, that is NOT you. What YOU accept into your minds, does not REALLY change them. Illusions are but beliefs in WHAT IS NOT THERE. And the seeming conflict between truth and illusion can ONLY be resolved by SEPARATING YOURSELF FROM THE ILLUSION, and NOT from truth.

T 16 D 5. Your teaching has already DONE this, for the Holy Spirit is PART OF YOU. Created by God, He left neither God nor His creation. He is both God and you, as you are God and Him together. For God's answer to the separation added more to you than you tried to TAKE AWAY. He protected both your creations AND you together, keeping one with you what you would EXCLUDE. And they will TAKE THE PLACE of what YOU took in, to replace THEM. They are QUITE real, and part of the self you do not know. And they communicate to you through the Holy Spirit, and their power and gratitude to you for THEIR creation, they offer gladly to your teaching of your self, who is their home.

T 16 D 6. You who are host to God, are also host to THEM. For nothing real has ever left the mind of its Creator. And what is NOT real was NEVER there. You are NOT two selves in conflict. What is BEYOND GOD? If you who hold Him, and whom He holds, ARE the universe, all else must be OUTSIDE, where NOTHING is. **T(610) -437** YOU have taught this, and from far off in the universe, yet NOT beyond yourself, the witnesses to your teaching have gathered to help you learn. Their gratitude has joined with yours and God's, to strengthen your faith in what you taught. FOR WHAT YOU TAUGHT IS TRUE. Alone, you stand OUTSIDE your teaching and APART from it. But WITH them, you MUST learn that you but taught YOURSELF, and LEARNED from the conviction you SHARED with them.

T 16 D 7. This year you will begin to learn, and make learning COMMENSURATE with teaching. You have CHOSEN this, by your own willingness to teach. Though you seemed to suffer for it, the joy of teaching will yet be yours. For the joy of teaching is IN THE LEARNER, who offers it to the teacher in gratitude, and shares it WITH him. As you learn, your gratitude to your SELF, Who teaches you what He IS, will grow and help you honor Him. And you will learn His power and strength and purity, and love Him as His Father does. His Kingdom has no limits and no end, and there is nothing in Him that is not perfect and eternal.[588] All this is YOU, and nothing OUTSIDE of this IS you. To your most Holy Self all praise is due, for what you are, and for what He is Who created you AS you are.

T 16 D 8. Sooner or later must everyone bridge the gap which he imagines exists between his selves. Each one builds this bridge, which CARRIES HIM ACROSS the gap, as soon as he is willing to expend some little effort on behalf of bridging it. His little efforts are powerfully supplemented by the strength of Heaven, and by the united will of all who make Heaven what it is, being joined within it. And so the one who would cross over, is literally transported there. Your bridge is builded stronger than you think, and your foot is planted firmly on it. Have no fear that the attraction of those who stand on the other side and wait for you, will not draw you safely across. For you WILL come where you would be, and where your Self awaits you. **T(611) -438**[589]

T 16 E. Illusion and Reality of Love (*Notes* 1360 9:197)

T 16 E 1. Be not afraid to look upon the special hate relationship, for freedom lies here. It would be impossible NOT to know the meaning of love, EXCEPT FOR THIS. For the special love relationship, IN WHICH THE MEANING OF LOVE IS LOST, is undertaken SOLELY to OFFSET this, but NOT to LET IT GO. Your salvation will rise clearly before your open eyes, as you look on this. YOU CANNOT LIMIT HATE. The special love relationship will NOT offset it, but will merely DRIVE IT UNDERGROUND, and out of sight. It is essential to bring it INTO sight, and to make NO attempt to hide it. For it is the attempt to BALANCE hate with love that makes love meaningless to you.

T 16 E 2. The extent of the split that lies in this you do NOT realize. And until you do, the split will remain unrecognized, AND THEREFORE UNHEALED. The symbols of hate against the symbols of love play out a conflict that does not exist. For symbols stand for something else, and the SYMBOL of love IS without meaning, if love is everything. You will go through this last undoing quite unharmed, and will emerge AS YOURSELF. This is the last step in the readiness for God. Be not unwilling now, you are too near, and you WILL cross the bridge in perfect safety, translated quietly from war to peace. For the ILLUSION of love will NEVER satisfy you. But its REALITY, which awaits you on the other side, WILL give you everything.

T 16 E 3. The special love relationship is an attempt to limit the destructive EFFECTS of hate, by finding a haven in the storm of guilt. It makes NO attempt to RISE ABOVE the storm, into the sunlight. On the contrary, it EMPHASIZES guilt OUTSIDE the haven, by attempting to build barricades AGAINST it, and keep WITHIN them. The special love relationship is NOT perceived as of[590] value IN ITSELF, but as a place of safety, from which hatred is split off, and KEPT APART. The special love partner is acceptable ONLY as long as he serves this purpose. Hatred can enter, and, indeed, is WELCOME in some ASPECTS of the relationship, but it is still held together by the illusion of love. **T(612) -439** If the illusion goes, the relationship is broken or becomes unsatisfying, on the grounds of DISillusionment.

T 16 E 4. LOVE IS NOT AN ILLUSION. It is a FACT. Where DISillusionment is possible, there was NOT love, but HATE. For hate IS an illusion, and what can change was NEVER love. It is certain that those who select certain ones as partners in ANY aspect of living, and use them for ANY purpose which they would NOT share with others, are trying to LIVE WITH guilt rather than DIE OF it. This is the choice they see. And love to them is only AN ESCAPE FROM DEATH. They seek it desperately, NOT in the peace in which it would gladly come quietly TO them. And when they find

---

[588] **Daniel 7:27** Then the kingdom and dominion,
And the greatness of the kingdoms under the whole heaven,
Shall be given to the people, the saints of the Most High.
His kingdom is an everlasting kingdom,
And all dominions shall serve and obey Him.'

[589] January 5, 1967
[590] The *Urtext* manuscript actually has "a" here but the *Notes* shows "of" and that reading makes much more sense.

the fear of death is still upon them, the "love" relationship loses the illusion that it IS what it is NOT. For, when the barricades against it are broken, fear rushes in and hatred triumphs.

T 16 E 5. There are no triumphs of love. Only hate is concerned with the triumph of love at all. The ILLUSION of love CAN triumph over the illusion of hate, but ALWAYS at the price of MAKING BOTH ILLUSIONS. As long as the illusion of hatred lasts, so long WILL love be an illusion to you. And then the ONLY choice that remains possible, is which illusion you PREFER. There IS no conflict in the choice between truth and illusion. Seen in these terms, NO-ONE would hesitate. But conflict enters the instant the choice seems to be one BETWEEN ILLUSIONS, for this choice does NOT matter. Where one choice IS as dangerous as the other, the decision MUST be one of despair.

T 16 E 6. Your task is NOT to seek for love, but merely to seek and FIND all of the barriers WITHIN YOURSELF that you have built AGAINST it. It is NOT necessary to seek for what is true, but it IS necessary to seek for what is FALSE. Every illusion is one of fear, WHATEVER form it takes. **T(613) -440** And the attempt to escape from one illusion INTO ANOTHER, MUST fail. If you seek love OUTSIDE yourself, you can be certain that you perceive hatred within, AND ARE AFRAID OF IT. Yet peace will never come from the ILLUSION of love, but ONLY from its reality.

T 16 E 7. Recognize this, for it is true, and truth MUST be recognized, if it is to be distinguished from illusion: the special love relationship is an attempt TO BRING LOVE INTO SEPARATION. And, as such, it is nothing more than an attempt to bring love into fear, and MAKE IT REAL IN FEAR. In fundamental violation of love's one condition, the special love relationship would thus ACCOMPLISH THE IMPOSSIBLE. How but in illusion COULD this be done? It is essential that we look VERY closely at exactly what it is you THINK you can do, to solve a dilemma which seems very real to you, but which does not exist. You have come very close to truth. And only this stands between you and the bridge that leads you into it. Heaven waits silently, and your creations are holding out their hands to help you cross, and welcome them.

T 16 E 8. FOR IT IS THEY YOU SEEK. You seek but for your own COMPLETION, and it is they who render you complete. The special love relationship is but a shabby substitute for what makes you whole IN TRUTH, NOT in illusion. Your relationship with them IS without guilt, and THIS enables you to look on all your brothers with gratitude, because your creations were created in union WITH them. Acceptance of your creations IS the acceptance of the oneness of creation, without which you would never BE complete. No specialness can offer you what God has given, and what YOU are joined WITH Him in giving. Across the bridge IS your completion, for you will be WHOLLY in God, willing for NOTHING special, but only to be wholly like unto Him, completing Him by your completion. **T(614) -441**

T 16 E 9. Fear not to cross to the abode of peace and perfect holiness. Only there is the completion of God and of His Son established forever. Seek not for this in the bleak world of illusion, where nothing is certain, and where everything fails to satisfy. And, in the Name of God, be wholly willing to abandon ALL illusion. In any relationship in which you are wholly willing to accept completion, and ONLY this, there is God completed, and His Son WITH Him. The bridge that leads to union IN YOURSELF, MUST lead to knowledge, for it was built with God beside you. And will lead you straight to Him, where YOUR completion rests, WHOLLY compatible with His.

T 16 E 10. Every illusion which you accept into your mind, BY JUDGING IT TO BE ATTAINABLE, removes your own sense of completion, and thus denies the Wholeness of your Father. Every fantasy, be it of love OR hate, DEPRIVES you of knowledge. For fantasies ARE the veil behind which truth is hidden. To lift the veil, which seems so dark and heavy, it is only needful to VALUE truth beyond ALL fantasy, and to be entirely UNwilling to settle for illusion IN PLACE of truth. Would you not go THROUGH fear to Love? For such the journey SEEMS to be. Love calls, though hate would bid you stay.

T 16 E 11. Hear not the call of hate, and see no fantasies. For your completion lies in truth, and NOWHERE ELSE. See in the call of hate, and in every fantasy that rises to delay you, but the call for help, that rises ceaselessly from you to your Creator. Would He not answer you; whose completion is His? He loves you, wholly WITHOUT illusion, as you must love. For love IS wholly without illusion, and therefore wholly WITHOUT fear. Whom God remembers, MUST be whole. And God has NEVER forgotten what makes HIM whole. In YOUR completion lies the memory of HIS wholeness, and His gratitude to you for His completion. **T(615) -442**

T 16 E 12. In His link with you lie both His INABILITY to forget, and YOUR ability to remember. In Him are joined your WILLINGNESS to love, and all the love of God, Who forgot you not. Your Father can no more forget the truth in you, than you can fail to remember it. The Holy Spirit is the bridge to Him, made from your willingness to UNITE with Him, and created by His joy, in union WITH you. The journey that SEEMED to be endless is ALMOST complete, for what IS endless is very near. YOU HAVE ALMOST RECOGNIZED IT. Turn with me firmly away from ALL illusion NOW, and let nothing stand in the way of truth. We will take the last foolish journey AWAY FROM truth together. And then TOGETHER we go straight to God, in joyous answer to His call for His completion.

T 16 E 13. If special relationships of ANY kind would HINDER God's completion, CAN they have any value TO YOU? What would interfere with God, MUST interfere with you. Only in time does interference in God's completion SEEM to be possible. The bridge that He would carry you across, lifts you FROM time into eternity. Waken from time, and answer fearlessly the call of Him Who gave eternity to you in your creation. On this side of the bridge to timelessness, you understand nothing. But, as you step lightly across it, upheld BY Timelessness, you are directed straight to the heart of knowledge. At Its center, and ONLY there, you are safe forever, BECAUSE YOU ARE COMPLETE FOREVER. There is no veil the love of God in us together CANNOT lift. The way to Truth is open. Follow it with me.

T 16 F. Specialness and Guilt (*Notes* 1370 9:207)

T 16 F 1. In looking at the special relationship, it is necessary first to realize that it involves a great amount of pain. Anxiety, despair, guilt, and attack all enter into it, BROKEN INTO by periods in which they SEEM to be gone. All these must be understood for what they ARE. Whatever form they take, they are always an attack on the self, TO MAKE THE OTHER GUILTY. **T(616) -443** We have spoken of this before, but there are some aspects of what is REALLY being attempted, that we have not touched on. Very simply, the attempt to make guilty is ALWAYS directed against God. For the ego would have you see Him, AND HIM ALONE, as guilty, leaving the Sonship OPEN to attack, and unprotected against it.

T 16 F 2. The[591] special love relationship is the ego's chief weapon for keeping you from Heaven. It does not APPEAR to be a weapon, but if you consider HOW you VALUE it, and why, you will realize what it MUST be. The special love relationship is the ego's most boasted gift, and the one that has the most appeal to those unwilling to relinquish guilt. The "dynamics" of the ego are clearest here, for, counting on the attraction of this offering, the fantasies which center around this, are often quite open. Here, they are usually judged to be quite acceptable, and even NATURAL. No-one considers it bizarre

---
[591] January 6, 1967

to love and hate together, and even those who believe that hate is "sin", merely feel guilty, but do NOT correct it.

T 16 F 3. This IS the "natural" condition of the separation. And those who learn that it is NOT natural at all, seem to be the UNnatural ones. For this world IS the opposite of Heaven, having been made to BE its opposite. And EVERYTHING here takes a direction EXACTLY opposite to what is true. In Heaven, where the meaning of love is known, love is the same as UNION. Here, where the ILLUSION of love is accepted IN ITS PLACE, love is perceived as separation and EXCLUSION.

T 16 F 4. It is in the special relationship, born of the hidden wish for special love from God, that the ego's hatred triumphs. For the special relationship is THE RENUNCIATION OF THE LOVE OF GOD, and the attempt to secure for the self the specialness that He denied. And it is essential **T(617) -444** to the preservation of the ego, that you believe this specialness is NOT hell, but HEAVEN. For the ego would never have you see that the separation can ONLY BE LOSS, being the one condition in which Heaven CANNOT be.

T 16 F 5. To everyone, Heaven is completion. There CAN be no disagreement on this, because both the ego AND the Holy Spirit accept it. They are, however, in complete DISagreement on what completion IS, and HOW it is accomplished. The Holy Spirit knows that self completion lies first in union, and then in the EXTENSION of union. To the ego, completion lies in triumph, and in the extension of the "victory," even to the final triumph over God. In THIS it sees the ultimate FREEDOM of the self, for nothing would remain to interfere with IT. And this IS its idea of Heaven. From this it follows that union, which is a condition in which the EGO cannot interfere, MUST BE HELL.

T 16 F 6. The special relationship is a strange and unnatural ego device for joining hell and Heaven, and making them indistinguishable. And the attempt to find the imagined "best" of BOTH worlds, has merely led to FANTASIES of both, and to the inability to perceive either one AS IT IS. The special relationship is the triumph of this confusion. It is a kind of union from which UNION IS EXCLUDED, and the BASIS for the ATTEMPT at union RESTS on exclusion. What better example could there be of the ego's maxim, "Seek, and do NOT find?"

T 16 F 7. Most curious of all, is the concept of the self, which the ego fosters in the special relationship. This "self" SEEKS the relationship, to MAKE ITSELF COMPLETE. Yet, when it FINDS the special relationship in which it thinks it can ACCOMPLISH this, IT GIVES ITSELF AWAY, and tries to TRADE itself for the self of another. This is NOT union, for there is **T(618) -445** NO increase and NO extension. Each partner tries to sacrifice the self he does NOT want, for one he thinks he would PREFER. He feels guilty for the "sin" of TAKING, and of giving nothing of value in return. For how much value CAN he place upon a self that he would GIVE AWAY, to get a BETTER one?

T 16 F 8. The "better" self the ego seeks is ALWAYS one that is MORE special. And whoever SEEMS to possess a special self is "loved," FOR WHAT CAN BE TAKEN FROM HIM. Where both partners see this special self IN EACH OTHER, the EGO sees "a union made in Heaven." For NEITHER will recognize that HE HAS ASKED FOR HELL, and so he will NOT interfere with the ego's ILLUSION of Heaven, which it offered him TO INTERFERE WITH HEAVEN. Yet if ALL illusions are of fear, and they CAN be of nothing else, the illusion of Heaven is nothing more than an ATTRACTIVE form of fear, in which the guilt is buried deep, and rises in the form of "love."

T 16 F 9. The appeal of hell lies ONLY in the terrible attraction of guilt, which the ego holds out to those who place their faith in littleness. The conviction of littleness lies in EVERY special relationship, for only the deprived COULD value specialness. The "DEMAND" for specialness, and the perception of the GIVING of specialness AS AN ACT OF LOVE, would MAKE LOVE HATEFUL. And the REAL purpose of the special relationship, in strict accordance with the ego's goals, is to DESTROY reality and SUBSTITUTE ILLUSION. For the ego is ITSELF an illusion, and ONLY illusions can BE the witnesses to its reality.

T 16 F 10. If you perceived the special relationship as a triumph over God, WOULD YOU WANT IT? Let us not think of its fearful nature, nor of the guilt it MUST entail, nor of the sadness and the loneliness. For these are only ATTRIBUTES of the whole religion of the separation, and the total **T(619) -446** context in which it is thought to occur. The central theme in its litany to sacrifice is that GOD MUST DIE SO YOU CAN LIVE. And it is this theme that is acted out in the special relationship. Through the death of YOUR self, you think you can ATTACK another self, and snatch it FROM the other, to REPLACE the self that you despised. And you despise it BECAUSE YOU DO NOT THINK IT OFFERS YOU THE SPECIALNESS THAT YOU DEMAND. And, HATING it, YOU have made it little and unworthy, BECAUSE YOU ARE AFRAID OF IT.

T 16 F 11. How can you grant unlimited power to what you think you have ATTACKED? For so fearful has the truth become that, UNLESS it is weak, and little, and unworthy of value, you would not dare to look upon it. You think it safer to endow the little self which YOU have made, with power you WRESTED FROM truth, triumphing over it, and leaving IT helpless. See how EXACTLY is this ritual enacted in the special relationship. An altar is erected IN BETWEEN two separate people, on which each seeks to kill his self, and on his body, raise another self that TAKES HIS POWER FROM ITS DEATH.

T 16 F 12. Over and over and over, this ritual is enacted. And it is NEVER completed, nor ever will BE completed. For the RITUAL of completion CANNOT complete, and life arises not from death, nor Heaven from hell. Whenever ANY form of special relationship tempts you to seek for love in ritual, remember love is CONTENT, and NOT form of ANY kind. The special relationship is a RITUAL OF FORM, aimed at the raising of the form to take the place of God, at the EXPENSE of content. There IS no meaning in the form, AND THERE WILL NEVER BE. The special relationship MUST be recognized for what it is; a senseless ritual, in which strength is extracted from the **T(620) -447** death of God, and invested in His killer, as the sign that form has triumphed over content, and love has LOST its meaning.

T 16 F 13. Would you WANT this to be possible, even APART from its evident impossibility? For, if it WERE possible, you would have made YOURSELF helpless. God is not angry. He merely could not let this happen. You can NOT change His Mind. No rituals that you have set up, in which the dance of death delights you, can bring death to the Eternal. Nor can your chosen substitute for the Wholeness of God, have ANY influence at all upon It. See in the special relationship nothing more than a meaningless attempt to raise other gods before Him, and, by worshipping them, to obscure THEIR tininess, AND HIS GREATNESS.[592]

T 16 F 14. In the name of YOUR completion, you do not WANT this. And every idol that you raise to place BEFORE Him, stands before YOU, in place of what YOU are. Salvation lies in the simple fact that illusions are NOT fearful, BECAUSE THEY ARE NOT TRUE. And they but SEEM to be fearful to the extent to which you fail to recognize them FOR WHAT THEY ARE. And you WILL fail to do this, to the extent to which you WANT them to be true. And, to the same extent, you are DENYING truth, and so are making YOURSELF unable to make the simple choice between truth and illusion, fantasy and God.

T 16 F 15. Remember this, and you will have no difficulty in perceiving the decision as just what it IS, and nothing more. The core

---

[592] **Exodus 20:3** You shall have no other gods before Me.

of the separation delusion lies simply in the fantasy DESTRUCTION of love's meaning. And, unless its meaning is RESTORED to you, you CANNOT know yourself, who SHARE its meaning. Separation is only the decision NOT to know yourself. Its whole thought-system is a carefully-contrived learning experience, designed to lead AWAY from truth, and into fantasy. **T(621) -448** Yet, for every learning that would hurt you, God offers you correction, and COMPLETE escape from ALL its consequences.

T 16 F 16. The decision whether or not to listen to this course and follow it, is but the choice between truth and illusion. For here IS truth, SEPARATED from illusion, and NOT confused with it at all. How simple does this choice become when it is perceived as only what it is. For ONLY fantasies made confusion in choosing possible, and they are totally UNreal. This year is thus the time to make the EASIEST decision that ever confronted you, and also the ONLY one. You will cross the bridge into reality, simply because you will recognize that God is on the other side AND NOTHING AT ALL IS HERE. It is impossible NOT to make the natural decision, as this is realized. **T(622) - 449 –** [593]

T 16 G. The Bridge to the Real World (*Notes* 1382 9:219)

T 16 G 1. The search for the special relationship is the sign that you equate your self with the ego, and NOT with God. For the special relationship has value ONLY to the ego. To IT, UNLESS a relationship HAS special value, IT HAS NO MEANING. And it perceives ALL love as special. Yet, this CANNOT be natural, for it is UNlike the relationship of God and His Son, and ALL relationships that are unlike this One, MUST be unnatural. For God created love as He would have it be, and GAVE it as it IS. Love HAS no meaning except as its Creator defined it, by His Will. It is impossible to define it otherwise, and UNDERSTAND it.

T 16 G 2. LOVE IS FREEDOM. To look for it by placing yourself in BONDAGE, is to SEPARATE yourself from it. For the love of God, no longer seek for union in separation, nor for freedom in bondage! As you release, so will you BE released. FORGET THIS NOT, or love will be unable to find you, and comfort you. There is a way in which the Holy Spirit asks YOUR help, if you would have His. The holy instant is His most helpful tool in protecting you from the attraction of guilt, the REAL lure in the special relationship. You do NOT recognize that this IS its REAL appeal, for the ego has taught you that FREEDOM lies in it.

T 16 G 3. Yet, the closer you look at the special relationship, the more apparent it becomes that it MUST foster guilt, and therefore must IMPRISON. The special relationship is totally without meaning WITHOUT A BODY. And, if you VALUE it, you must also VALUE THE BODY. And what you value, you WILL keep. The special relationship is a device for limiting YOUR self to a body, and for limiting your perception of others to THEIRS. The Great Rays would establish the total LACK of value of the special relationship, IF THEY WERE SEEN. For, in seeing THEM, the body WOULD disappear, BECAUSE ITS VALUE WOULD BE LOST. And so your whole INVESTMENT in seeing it would be WITHDRAWN from it.

T 16 G 4. YOU SEE THE WORLD YOU VALUE. On this side of the bridge, you see **T(623) - 450 -** the world of separate bodies, seeking to join each other in SEPARATE UNIONS, and to become one BY LOSING. When two INDIVIDUALS seek to become ONE, they are trying to DECREASE their magnitude. Each would DENY his power, for the SEPARATE union EXCLUDES THE UNIVERSE. Far more is LEFT OUTSIDE than would be taken in. For God is left WITHOUT, and NOTHING taken in. If one such union were made IN PERFECT FAITH, the universe WOULD enter into it. Yet the special relationship which the EGO seeks, does NOT include even ONE whole individual. For the ego WANTS but part of him, and sees ONLY this part, and nothing else.

T 16 G 5. Across the bridge, it is so different! For a time the body is still seen, but NOT exclusively, as it is seen here. For the little spark that holds the Great Rays within it, is ALSO visible, and this spark cannot be limited long to littleness. Once you have crossed the bridge, the VALUE of the body is so diminished in YOUR sight, that you will see no need at all to MAGNIFY it. For you will realize that the ONLY value that the body has, is to enable you to bring your brothers TO the bridge WITH you. And to be RELEASED TOGETHER there.

T 16 G 6. The bridge itself is nothing more than a transition in your PERSPECTIVE of reality. On this side, everything you see is grossly distorted, and COMPLETELY out of perspective. What IS little and insignificant is magnified, and what is strong and powerful, cut down to littleness. In the transition, there is a period of confusion, in which a sense of actual disorientation seems to occur. But fear it not, for it means nothing more than that you have been willing to LET GO your hold on the distorted frame of reference, that SEEMED to hold your world together. This frame of reference is BUILT around the special relationship. Without THIS illusion, there can BE no meaning you would still seek here.

T 16 G 7. Fear not that you will be abruptly lifted up, and hurled into reality. Time is kind, and, if you use it FOR reality, it will keep gentle pace with you, in your transition. The urgency is only in dislodging **T(624) - 451 -** your minds from their FIXED POSITION here. This will not leave you homeless, and WITHOUT a frame of reference. The period of disorientation, which precedes the actual transition, is far shorter than the time it took to fix your minds so firmly on illusions. Delay will hurt you now MORE THAN BEFORE, ONLY because you realize it IS delay, and that escape from pain IS REALLY POSSIBLE. Find hope and comfort, rather than despair, in this therefore.[594]

T 16 G 8. You could no longer find even the ILLUSION of love in ANY special relationship here. For you are no longer WHOLLY insane, and you WOULD recognize the guilt of SELF-betrayal FOR WHAT IT IS. Nothing you seek to strengthen, in the special relationship, is REALLY part of you. And you cannot keep PART of the thought-system that taught you it WAS real, and understand the Thought that REALLY knows what you are. You HAVE allowed the Thought of your reality to enter your minds, and, because YOU invited it, it WILL abide with you.[595] Your love for it will not allow you to betray yourself, and you COULD not enter into a relationship WHERE IT COULD NOT GO WITH YOU, for you would NOT be APART from it.

T 16 G 9. Be glad you have escaped the mockery of salvation that the ego offered you, and look not back with longing on the travesty it made of your relationships. Now, no-one need suffer, for you have come too far to yield to the illusion of the beauty and holiness of guilt. Only the wholly insane could look on death and suffering,

---

[594] Well this one is tricky. The *Urtext* manuscript has "this:" and not the word "therefore." In later versions the editors leave the colon but remove the paragraph break which would be most inappropriate after a colon. The *Notes* has a paragraph break specifically written in, however, making it difficult to suppose the paragraph break was an oversight. Just prior to the indicated paragraph break is a most unusual construction. It may have a colon followed by a period … very odd … or a slightly warped glyph for "therefore." Since neither a colon followed by a paragraph break nor a colon followed by a period work at all well, while "therefore" works just fine, that might well be what was intended. The "this" then refers back to what was just discussed and not forward to what follows, which does seem more suitable in the context.

[595] **John 15:4** "Abide in Me, and I in you. As the branch cannot bear fruit of itself, unless it abides in the vine, neither can you, unless you abide in Me." **John 15:10** "If you keep My commandments, you will abide in My love, just as I have kept My Father's commandments and abide in His love."

---

[593] January 7, 1967.

sickness and despair, and see it thus. What guilt has wrought is ugly, fearful, and very dangerous. See no illusion of truth and beauty there. And be you thankful that there IS a place where truth and beauty wait for you.

T 16 G 10. Go on to meet them gladly, and learn how much awaits you, for the simple willingness to give up nothing, BECAUSE it is nothing. The new perspective you will gain, from crossing over, will be the understanding of WHERE HEAVEN IS. From HERE, it seems to be outside, and ACROSS the bridge. But, as you cross to JOIN it, IT will JOIN WITH YOU, and BECOME ONE with you. And you will think, in glad astonishment, that for all this, YOU GAVE **T(625) - 452 -** UP NOTHING! The joy of Heaven, which HAS no limit, is INCREASED with each light that returns, to take its rightful place within it. Wait no longer, for the Love of God and YOU. And may the holy instant speed you on the way, as it will surely do, if you but LET it come to you.

T 16 G 11. The Holy Spirit asks only this little help of you. Whenever your thoughts wander to a special relationship which still ATTRACTS you, enter with Him into a holy instant, and there, LET HIM RELEASE YOU. He needs only your willingness to SHARE His perspective, to give it to you completely. And your willingness need not be complete, BECAUSE HIS IS PERFECT. It is His task to atone for your UNwillingness by His perfect faith. And it is HIS faith you share with Him there. Out of YOUR recognition of your UNwillingness for your release, His PERFECT willingness is GIVEN you. Call upon Him, for Heaven is at His call. And LET Him call on Heaven FOR you. **T(626) - 453 -**

T 16 H. The End of Illusions (*Notes* 1389 9:227)

T 16 H 1. It[596] is impossible to let the past go, WITHOUT relinquishing the special relationship. For the special relationship is an attempt to RE-ENACT the past, AND CHANGE IT. Imagined slights, remembered pain, past disappointments, perceived injustices and deprivations, all enter into the special relationship, which becomes a way in which you seek to restore your wounded SELF-esteem. What basis would you have for choosing a special partner, WITHOUT the past? EVERY such choice is made because of something "evil" in the past, TO WHICH YOU CLING, and for which must SOMEONE ELSE "atone."

T 16 H 2. The special relationship TAKES VENGEANCE ON THE PAST. By seeking to remove suffering IN THE PAST, it OVERLOOKS the present, in its preoccupation with the past, and its TOTAL COMMITMENT to it. NO SPECIAL RELATIONSHIP IS EXPERIENCED IN THE PRESENT. Shades of the past envelop it, and make it what it is. It HAS no meaning in the present, and, if it means nothing NOW, it cannot have any REAL meaning at all. How can you change the past, EXCEPT in fantasy? And who can give you what you think THE PAST deprived you of? The past is nothing. Do not seek to lay the blame for deprivation on it, for the past IS GONE.

T 16 H 3. You cannot REALLY not let go what has ALREADY gone. It MUST be, therefore, that YOU are maintaining the illusion that it has NOT gone, because you think it serves some purpose that you WANT FULFILLED. And it must also be that this purpose COULD NOT BE FULFILLED IN THE PRESENT, but ONLY in the past. Do not underestimate the intensity of the ego's drive for vengeance on the past. It is COMPLETELY savage, and COMPLETELY insane. For the ego remembers everything that YOU have done that offended it, and seeks retribution OF YOU. The fantasies it brings to the special relationships it chooses, in which to act out its hate, are fantasies of YOUR destruction.

T 16 H 4. For the ego holds the past AGAINST YOU, and, in your ESCAPE from **T(627) - 454 -** it, it sees ITSELF deprived of the vengeance it believes that you so justly merit. Yet, without your ALLIANCE in your own destruction, the ego could not hold you to the past. In the special relationship, YOU ARE ALLOWING YOUR DESTRUCTION TO BE. That this is insane, is obvious. But what is LESS obvious to you, is that the PRESENT is useless to you, while you pursue the ego's goal, as its ally. The past is gone; seek not to preserve it in the special relationship, which binds you to it, and would teach you that SALVATION is past, and that you must RETURN to the past, to FIND salvation. There is NO fantasy that does not contain the dream of retribution for the past. Would you ACT OUT the dream, or let it go?

T 16 H 5. In the special relationship, it does not SEEM to be an acting out of vengeance that you seek. And, even when the hatred and the savagery break briefly through into awareness, the illusion of love is not profoundly shaken. But the one thing that the ego NEVER allows to reach awareness, is that the special relationship is the acting out of VENGEANCE ON YOURSELF. Yet what else COULD it be? In seeking the special relationship, you look not for glory IN YOURSELF. You have DENIED that it is there. And the relationship becomes your SUBSTITUTE for it. And vengeance becomes YOUR substitute for Atonement, and ESCAPE from vengeance becomes your LOSS.

T 16 H 6. Against the ego's insane notion of salvation, the Holy Spirit gently lays the holy instant. We said before that the Holy Spirit must teach through comparisons, and uses opposites to point to truth. The holy instant is the OPPOSITE of the ego's fixed belief in salvation through vengeance for the past. In the holy instant, it is ACCEPTED that the past is gone, and WITH its passing, the drive for vengeance HAS BEEN uprooted, and has disappeared. The stillness and the peace of NOW, enfold you in perfect gentleness. Everything is gone, EXCEPT THE TRUTH.

T 16 H 7. For a time, you may attempt to bring illusions INTO the holy instant, to hinder your full awareness of the COMPLETE DIFFERENCE, in ALL respects, between your EXPERIENCE of truth and illusion. But you will not **T(628) - 455 -** attempt this long. In the holy instant, the power of the Holy Spirit WILL prevail, BECAUSE YOU JOINED HIM. The illusions you bring with you, will weaken the EXPERIENCE of Him for a while, and will prevent you from KEEPING the experience in your mind. Yet the holy instant IS eternal, and your illusions of time will NOT prevent the timeless from being what it is, nor you from EXPERIENCING it as it is.

T 16 H 8. What God has given you is truly given. AND WILL BE TRULY RECEIVED. For God's gifts HAVE no reality, APART from your receiving them. YOUR receiving completes HIS giving. You will receive, BECAUSE it is His Will to give. He gave the holy instant, to be given you. And it is impossible that you receive it not, BECAUSE He gave it. When He willed that His Son be free, His Son WAS free. In the holy instant is His reminder that His Son will ALWAYS be EXACTLY as he was created. And EVERYTHING the Holy Spirit teaches you, is to remind you that you HAVE received what God has given you.

T 16 H 9. There is nothing you CAN hold against reality. All that must be forgiven are the ILLUSIONS you have held against your brothers. Their reality HAS no past, and ONLY illusions can BE forgiven. God holds nothing against ANYONE, for He is INCAPABLE of illusions of ANY kind. Release your brothers from the slavery of THEIR illusions, by forgiving them for the illusions which YOU perceive in them.[597] Thus will you learn that YOU have been forgiven, for it is YOU who offered THEM illusions. In the holy instant, this is done for you IN TIME, to bring to you the true condition of Heaven.

T 16 H 10. Remember that you ALWAYS choose between truth and illusion, between the REAL Atonement that would heal, and the ego's "atonement," that would destroy. The power of God, and all

---

[596] January 10, **1967.**

[597] **John 20:23** "If you forgive the sins of any, they are forgiven them; if you retain the sins of any, they are retained."

His Love, without limit, will support you, as you seek only your place in the plan of Atonement arising from His Love. Be an ally of God, and NOT the ego, in seeking how Atonement can come to you. His help suffices, for His Messenger understands **T(629) - 456 -** how to restore the Kingdom TO you, and to place ALL your investment in salvation in your relationship with Him.[598]

T 16 H 11. Seek and FIND His message in the holy instant, where ALL illusions are forgiven. From here the miracle extends to bless everyone, and to resolve ALL problems; be they perceived as great or small, possible or impossible. There is NOTHING that will not give place to Him, and to His Majesty. To join in close relationship with Him, is to accept relationships AS REAL. And, through THEIR reality, give over ALL illusions, for the reality of your relationship with God. Praise be to your relationship with Him, and to no other. The truth lies here, AND NOWHERE ELSE. You choose this, or NOTHING.

T 16 H 12. Forgive us our illusions, Father, and help us to accept our true relationship with You, in which there are NO illusions, and where none can ever enter. Our holiness is YOURS. What can there be in us that NEEDS forgiveness, when YOURS is perfect? The sleep of forgetfulness is only the unwillingness to remember YOUR forgiveness and Your Love. Let us not wander into temptation, for the temptation of the Son of God is NOT Your Will. And let us receive ONLY what YOU have given, and accept but this into the minds which You created, and which You love.[599] Amen. **T(630) - 457**[600]

---

[598] **2 Corinthians 12:9** And He said to me, "My grace is sufficient for you, for My strength is made perfect in weakness." Therefore most gladly I will rather boast in my infirmities, that the power of Christ may rest upon me.

[599] **Matthew 6:9** "After this manner therefore pray ye. Our Father who art in heaven, Hallowed be thy name. Thy kingdom come. Thy will be done, as in heaven, so on earth. Give us this day our daily bread. And forgive us our debts, as we also have forgiven our debtors. And bring us not into temptation, but deliver us from the evil *one*."

[600] January 12, 1967

CHAPTER 17 – FORGIVENESS AND HEALING

T 17 A. Introduction (*Notes* 1397 9:234)

T 17 A 1. The betrayal of the Son of God lies only in illusions, and all his "sins" are but his own imagining.[601] His REALITY is forever sinless. He need not be forgiven but AWAKENED. In his dreams he HAS betrayed himself, his brothers and his God. Yet what is done in dreams has not been REALLY done. It is impossible to convince the DREAMER that this is so, for dreams are what they are BECAUSE of their illusion of reality. Only in waking is the full release from them, for only then does it become PERFECTLY apparent that they had no effect on reality at all, AND DID NOT CHANGE IT.

T 17 A 2. FANTASIES CHANGE REALITY. That is their purpose. They CANNOT do so IN reality, but they CAN do so in the mind that would HAVE REALITY DIFFERENT. It is, then, only your WISH to change reality that is fearful, because, by your wish you think you have ACCOMPLISHED what you wish. This strange position, in a sense, ACKNOWLEDGES your power, yet by DISTORTING it, and devoting it to 'evil,' it also MAKES IT UNREAL. You cannot be faithful to two masters,[602] who ask of you conflicting things. What you use in fantasy, you DENY to truth. But what you GIVE to truth, to use FOR you, is SAFE from fantasy.

T 17 B. Fantasy and Distorted Perception (*Notes* 1398 9:235)

T 17 B 1. When you maintain that there MUST be order of difficulty in miracles, all you mean is that there are some things you would WITHHOLD from truth. You believe that truth cannot deal with them, ONLY because YOU would keep them FROM truth. Very simply, your lack of faith in the Power that heals ALL pain, arises from YOUR wish to retain some ASPECTS of reality FOR FANTASY. If you but realized what this MUST do to your appreciation of the whole! What you RESERVE UNTO YOURSELF, you TAKE AWAY from Him Who would release you. Unless you GIVE IT BACK, it is inevitable that YOUR perspective on reality be warped and uncorrected. **(631) -458**

T 17 B 2. As long as you would have this be, so long will the ILLUSION of order of difficulty in miracles REMAIN with you. For YOU have established this order in REALITY, by giving some of it to one teacher, and some to another. And so you learn to deal with PART of truth in one way, and in ANOTHER way the OTHER part. To FRAGMENT truth is to DESTROY it by rendering it meaningless. ORDERS of reality is a perspective without understanding, a frame of reference FOR reality to which it cannot REALLY be compared at all. Think you that you can bring truth to fantasy, and learn what truth MEANS from the perspective of illusions?

T 17 B 3. Truth HAS no meaning in illusion. The frame of reference FOR its meaning MUST BE ITSELF. When you try to bring TRUTH to illusions, you are trying to MAKE THEM REAL, and KEEP them by JUSTIFYING your belief in them. But to give illusions to Truth is to enable truth to teach that the ILLUSIONS are unreal, and thus enable you to ESCAPE from them. Reserve not one idea aside from truth, or you ESTABLISH orders of reality which MUST imprison you. There IS no order in reality because EVERYTHING there is true.

T 17 B 4. Be willing, then, to give ALL you have held OUTSIDE the truth to Him Who KNOWS the truth, and in Whom all is brought to truth. Salvation from separation will be COMPLETE, or will not be at all. Be not concerned with anything except YOUR WILLINGNESS TO HAVE THIS BE ACCOMPLISHED. HE will accomplish it; not you. But forget not this; when you become disturbed and lose YOUR peace of mind because ANOTHER is attempting to solve his problems through fantasy, you are refusing to FORGIVE YOURSELF for just this same attempt. And you are holding BOTH of you AWAY from truth, and from salvation. As you FORGIVE him, you RESTORE to truth what was denied by BOTH OF YOU. And you WILL see forgiveness where YOU have given it. **T(632) - 459 -**[603]

T 17 C. The Forgiven World (*Notes* 1401 9:238)

T 17 C 1. Can you imagine how beautiful those you forgive will look to you? In no fantasy have you ever seen anything so lovely. Nothing you see here, sleeping or waking, comes near to such loveliness, and nothing will you value like unto this, nor hold so dear. Nothing that you remember, that made your heart seem to sing with joy, has ever brought you even a little part of the happiness this sight will bring you. FOR YOU WILL SEE THE SON OF GOD. You will behold the beauty that the Holy Spirit loves to look upon, and that He thanks the Father for. He was created to see this FOR YOU, until you learned to see it for yourself. And all His teaching leads to seeing it and giving thanks with Him.

T 17 C 2. This loveliness is NOT a fantasy. It is the real world, bright, and clean and new, with everything sparkling under the open sun. Nothing is hidden here, for everything has BEEN forgiven, and there ARE no fantasies to hide the truth. The bridge between that world and this is SO little and SO easy to cross that you could not believe it is the meeting-place of worlds so different. Yet this little bridge is the strongest thing that touches on this world at all. This little step, so small it has escaped your notice, is a stride through time into eternity, and beyond all ugliness, into beauty that will enchant you, and will never cease to cause you wonderment at its perfection.

T 17 C 3. This step, the smallest ever taken by anything, is still the greatest accomplishment of all, in God's plan of Atonement. All else is learned, but THIS is GIVEN, complete and wholly perfect. No-one but Him Who PLANNED salvation could complete it thus. The real world, in its loveliness, YOU learn to reach. Fantasies are all undone, no-one and nothing remains still bound by them, and, by YOUR OWN forgiveness, you are FREE TO **T(633) - 460 -** SEE. And WHAT you see is only what YOU HAVE MADE, with the blessing of your forgiveness on it. And, with this final blessing of God's Son UPON HIMSELF, the REAL perception, born of the new perspective he has learned, has served its purpose.

T 17 C 4. The stars will disappear in light, and the sun, which opened up the world to beauty, will vanish. Perception will be meaningless, when it has been perfected. For everything that has been used for learning, will have no function. Nothing will ever change; no shifts nor shadings, no differences, no variations that made perception possible, will occur. The perception of the real world will be so short, that you will barely have time to thank God for it. For God will take the last step swiftly, when you have reached the real world, and have been made ready for Him.

T 17 C 5. The real world is attained simply by the COMPLETE forgiveness of the old; the world you see WITHOUT forgiveness. The Great Transformer of perception will undertake WITH you the careful searching of the mind that MADE this world, and uncover TO YOU the SEEMING reasons for your making it. In the light of the REAL reason that He brings, as you follow Him, He will SHOW you that there is NO reason here at all. Each spot HIS reason touches, grows alive with beauty. And what SEEMED ugly, in the

---

[601] **Luke 22:48** But Jesus said to him, "Judas, are you betraying the Son of Man with a kiss?"

[602] **Matthew 6:24** "No man can serve two masters; for either he will hate the one, and love the other; or else he will hold to one, and despise the other. Ye cannot serve God and mammon."

---

[603] January 13, 1967

darkness of your LACK of reason, is suddenly released to loveliness. Not even what the Son of God made in insanity, could be without a hidden spark of beauty, that gentleness could release.

T 17 C 6. All this beauty will rise to bless your sight, as you look upon the world with forgiving eyes. For forgiveness literally TRANSFORMS vision, and lets you see the real world, reaching quietly and gently across chaos, and removing all illusions that had twisted your perception, and fixed it on the **T(634) - 461** - past. The smallest leaf becomes a thing of wonder, and a blade of grass a sign of God's perfection. From the forgiven world, the Son of God is lifted easily to his home. And there, he knows that he has ALWAYS rested there in peace.

T 17 C 7. Even salvation will become a dream, and vanish from his mind. For salvation IS the end of dreams, and, with the closing of the dream, will have no meaning. Who, awake in Heaven, COULD dream that there could ever be NEED of salvation? How much do you WANT salvation? It will GIVE you the real world, trembling with readiness to BE given you. The eagerness of the Holy Spirit to give you this, is so intense He would not wait, although He waits in patience. MEET His patience with your IMpatience at delay in meeting Him. Go out in gladness to meet with your Redeemer, and walk with Him, in trust, out of this world, and into the real world of beauty and forgiveness. **T(635) - 462 -**[604]

T 17 D. Shadows of the Past (*Notes* 1407 9:244)

T 17 D 1. To forgive is merely to remember ONLY the LOVING thoughts you gave in the past, and those that were given you. ALL the rest, must be forgotten. Forgiveness is a selective remembering, based NOT on YOUR selection. For the shadow figures YOU would make immortal, ARE 'enemies' of reality. Be willing to forgive the Son of God for what he did NOT do. The shadow figures are the witnesses you bring WITH you, to demonstrate he DID what he DID NOT. BECAUSE you brought them, YOU WILL HEAR THEM. And you who KEPT them BY YOUR OWN SELECTION, do NOT understand how they came into your minds, and what their purpose is.

T 17 D 2. THEY REPRESENT THE EVIL THAT YOU THINK WAS DONE TO YOU. You bring them with you ONLY that you may "return" evil FOR evil, hoping that THEIR witness will enable you to think guiltily of another, and NOT harm yourself. They speak so clearly for the separation, that no-one NOT obsessed with KEEPING separation, COULD hear them otherwise. They offer you the 'reasons' why you should enter into unholy alliances, which support the ego's goals, and make your relationships the witness to ITS power. It is these shadow figures which would MAKE THE EGO HOLY in your sight, and teach you what you do to keep IT safe, is really LOVE.

T 17 D 3. The shadow figures ALWAYS speak for vengeance, and ALL relationships into which they enter, are totally insane. WITHOUT EXCEPTION, these relationships have, AS THEIR PURPOSE, the EXCLUSION of the truth about the other, AND OF YOURSELF. That is why you see, IN BOTH what is not there, and MAKE of both the slaves of vengeance. And why whatever reminds you of your PAST grievances, no matter how distorted the associations by which you ARRIVE at the remembrance may be, ATTRACTS you, and seems to you to go by the name of love. And, finally, why all such relationships become the attempt at union THROUGH THE BODY, for ONLY bodies CAN be seen as means for vengeance.

T 17 D 4. That bodies are central to all unholy relationships is evident. Your OWN experience has taught you this. But what you do NOT realize, are **T(636) - 463 -** ALL the reasons that go to MAKE the relationship unholy. For UNholiness seeks to RE-INFORCE itself, by gathering TO itself, what it perceives as LIKE itself, as holiness does. In the unholy relationship, it is NOT the body of the OTHER with which union is attempted, but the bodies of those WHO ARE NOT THERE. Even the BODY of the other, ALREADY a severely limited perception of him, is NOT the central focus as it is, or in entirety. What can be used for fantasies of vengeance, and what can be most readily associated with those on whom vengeance is REALLY sought, are centered on, and SEPARATED OFF, as being the only parts OF VALUE.

T 17 D 5. Every step taken in the making, the maintaining, and the breaking off of the unholy relationship, is a move toward further fragmentation and unreality. The shadow figures enter more and more, and the one in whom they SEEM to be, DECREASES in importance. Time is indeed unkind to the unholy relationship. For time IS cruel in the ego's hands, as it is kind when used for gentleness. The attraction of the unholy relationship begins to fade and to be questioned, almost at once. Once it is formed, doubt MUST enter in, because its purpose IS impossible. The only such relationships which RETAIN the fantasies which center on them, are the ones which have been DREAMED of, but have NOT been made at all.

T 17 D 6. Where NO reality has entered, there is NOTHING to intrude upon the DREAM of happiness. But consider what this means; the more of the REALITY that enters into the unholy relationship, the LESS SATISFYING it becomes. And the more the FANTASIES can encompass, the greater the satisfaction seems to be. The 'ideal' of the unholy relationship thus becomes one in which the REALITY of the other does not ENTER AT ALL, to 'spoil' the dream. And the LESS the other REALLY brings to it, the 'better' it becomes. Thus, the attempt at union becomes a way of EXCLUDING even the one with whom the union was sought. For it was FORMED to GET HIM OUT OF IT, and join with fantasies in uninterrupted 'bliss.' **T(637) - 464 -**

T 17 D 7. How can the Holy Spirit bring HIS interpretation of the body, as a means of communicating into relationships whose ONLY purpose is SEPARATION from reality? What forgiveness IS, enables Him to do so. If all but loving thoughts have been forgotten, what remains IS eternal, and the TRANSFORMED past is made LIKE THE PRESENT. No longer does the past CONFLICT with now. THIS continuity EXTENDS the present, by increasing its reality, AND ITS VALUE, in your perception of it. In these loving thoughts is the spark of beauty, hidden in the ugliness of the unholy relationship in which the HATRED is remembered, yet there to COME ALIVE as the relationship is given to Him Who GIVES it life and beauty.

T 17 D 8. That is why Atonement centers ON THE PAST, which is the SOURCE of separation, and where it must be undone. For separation must be corrected WHERE IT WAS MADE. The EGO seeks to 'resolve' ITS problems, NOT at their source, but where they were NOT made. And thus it seeks to guarantee there WILL be no solution. The Holy Spirit wills only to make HIS resolutions complete and perfect. And so He seeks and FINDS the source of problems WHERE IT IS, and there UNDOES it. And, with each step in HIS undoing, is the SEPARATION more and more undone, and UNION brought closer. HE is not at all confused by ANY 'reasons' for separation. ALL He perceives in it is that it MUST BE UNDONE.

T 17 D 9. Let Him uncover the hidden spark of beauty in your relationships, and SHOW it to you. Its loveliness will so attract you, that you will be unwilling ever to lose the sight of it again. And you will LET it transform the relationship, so you can see it more and more. For you will want it more and more, and become increasingly unwilling to LET it be hidden from you. And you will learn to seek for, and ESTABLISH, conditions in which this, beauty CAN be seen. All this you will do gladly, if you but let Him hold the spark before you, to light your way, and make it CLEAR to you.

---
[604] January 15, 1967.

T 17 D 10. God's Son is one. And whom God has JOINED as one, the ego CANNOT break apart.[605] The spark of holiness MUST be safe, however hidden it may be, **T(638) - 465** -in EVERY relationship. For the Creator of the one relationship, has LEFT no part of it without HIMSELF. THIS is the only part of the relationship the Holy Spirit sees, because He knows that ONLY this is true. YOU have made the relationship unreal, and THEREFORE unholy, by seeing it WHERE it is not, and as it IS not. Give the past to Him Who can change YOUR mind about it, FOR you. But first, be SURE you fully realize what YOU have made the past to REPRESENT, and why.

T 17 D 11. In brief, the past is NOW your justification for entering into a continuing, unholy alliance with the ego AGAINST THE PRESENT. For the present IS forgiveness. Therefore, the relationships which the unholy alliance dictates are not perceived NOR FELT as now. Yet the frame of reference to which the present is REFERRED for meaning, is an ILLUSION of the past, in which those elements which FIT the purpose of the unholy alliance are retained and ALL THE REST LET GO. And what is thus let go, is all the truth the past could ever OFFER to the present, as witnesses for ITS reality, while what is KEPT, but witnesses to the reality of dreams.

T 17 D 12. It is still up to you to choose to be willing to join with truth or illusion. But remember that to choose ONE, is to LET THE OTHER GO. Which one you choose, YOU will endow with beauty and reality, because the choice DEPENDS on which you value more. The spark of beauty, or the veil of ugliness; the real world, or the world of guilt and fear; truth or illusion; freedom or slavery, - it is all the same. For you can NEVER choose EXCEPT between God and the ego. Thought-systems are but true or false, and all their ATTRIBUTES come simply from what they ARE. Only the Thoughts of God ARE true. And all that follows FROM them, COMES FROM what they are, and is as true as is the holy Source from which they come.

T 17 D 13. My holy brothers, I would enter into all your relationships, and step between you and your fantasies. Let MY relationship to you be REAL to you, and let me bring REALITY to your perception of your brothers. They **(639) - 466** -were not created to enable you to HURT yourselves through them. They were created to CREATE with you. This is the truth that I would interpose, between you and your goal of madness. Be not separate from me, and let not the holy purpose of Atonement be lost to you, in dreams of vengeance. Relationships in which such dreams are cherished have EXCLUDED me. Let me enter, in the Name of God, and bring YOU peace, that YOU may offer peace to me. **T(640) -467**[606]

T 17 E. Perception and the Two Worlds (*Notes* 1416 9:253)

T 17 E 1. God established His relationship with you TO MAKE YOU HAPPY, and nothing YOU do which does NOT share His purpose CAN be real. The purpose GOD ascribed to anything IS its only function. Because of HIS reason for creating HIS relationship with you, the function of relationships became forever "to make happy." AND NOTHING ELSE. To fulfill this function, you relate to your creations as GOD to HIS. For nothing God created is APART from happiness, and nothing God created but would EXTEND happiness, as its Creator did. Whatever fulfills this function NOT, CANNOT BE REAL.

T 17 E 2. In this world, it is impossible to create. Yet it IS possible to make happy. We have said repeatedly that the Holy Spirit would not DEPRIVE you of your special relationships, but would TRANSFORM them. And by that, all that is meant is that He will RESTORE to them the function that was GIVEN them, by God. The function YOU have given them is clearly NOT to make happy. But the holy relationship SHARES God's purpose, rather than aiming to make a SUBSTITUTE for it. Every special relationship that YOU have made IS a substitute for God's Will, and glorifies yours instead of His, BECAUSE OF THE DELUSION THEY ARE DIFFERENT.

T 17 E 3. You have VERY REAL relationships, even in this world, which you do not recognize, simply because you have raised their SUBSTITUTES to such predominance that, when truth calls to you, as it does constantly, YOU ANSWER WITH A SUBSTITUTE. Every special relationship which you have ever undertaken has, as its fundamental purpose, the aim of occupying your minds so completely that YOU WILL NOT HEAR the call of truth. In a sense, the special relationship was the EGO's answer to the creation of the Holy Spirit, Who was God's Answer to the separation. For, although the ego did not understand WHAT had been created, it WAS aware of threat. **T(641) -468**

T 17 E 4. The whole defense system that the ego evolved, to PROTECT the separation from the Holy Spirit, was in response to the Gift with which God blessed it, and BY His blessing enabled it to be HEALED. This Blessing holds, WITHIN ITSELF, the truth about everything. And the truth is that the Holy Spirit IS in close relationship with you, because, in Him, is your relationship with God restored to you. The relationship with Him has never been broken, because the Holy Spirit has not been separate from anyone SINCE the separation. And through Him, have all your holy relationships been carefully preserved, to serve God's purpose FOR you.

T 17 E 5. The ego IS hyperalert to threat, and the part of your mind into which the ego was accepted is VERY anxious to preserve its reason, AS IT SEES IT. It does NOT realize that it is totally insane. And YOU must realize JUST WHAT THIS MEANS, if YOU would be restored to sanity. The insane PROTECT their thought systems, BUT THEY DO IT INSANELY. And ALL their defenses are AS INSANE AS WHAT THEY ARE SUPPOSED TO PROTECT. The separation has NOTHING in it, no PART, NO 'reason,' and NO attribute, that is NOT insane. And its 'protection' IS part of it, as insane as the whole.

T 17 E 6. The special relationship, which is its chief defense, MUST therefore be insane. You have but little difficulty now in realizing that the thought-system it protects, is but a system of delusions. You recognize, at least in general terms, that the ego is insane. But the special relationship still seems to you somehow TO BE DIFFERENT. Yet we have looked at it far closer than at many other ASPECTS of the ego's thought-system which you have been more willing to let go. While this ONE remains, you will not LET the others go. FOR THIS ONE IS NOT DIFFERENT. RETAIN this one, and you HAVE retained the whole. **(642) -469**

T 17 E 7. It is essential to realize that ALL defenses DO what they would DEFEND. The underlying basis for their effectiveness is that they OFFER what they defend. What they defend is placed IN them for safe-keeping, and as THEY operate, THEY BRING IT TO YOU. Every defense operates BY GIVING GIFTS, and the gift is ALWAYS a miniature of the thought-system the defense protects, set in a golden frame. The frame is very elaborate, all set with jewels, and deeply carved and polished. Its purpose is to be of value IN ITSELF, and to divert YOUR attention from what it encloses. But the frame WITHOUT the picture, you CANNOT have. Defenses operate TO MAKE YOU THINK YOU CAN.

T 17 E 8. The special relationship has the most imposing and deceptive frame of all the defenses the ego uses. Its thought-system is offered here, surrounded by a frame so heavy and so elaborate, that the picture is almost obliterated by its imposing structure. Into the frame are woven all sorts of fanciful and fragmented illusions of love, set with dreams of sacrifice and self-aggrandizement, and interlaced with gilded threads of self-destruction. The glitter of blood

---

[605] **Matthew 19:6** "So that they are no more two, but one flesh. What therefore God hath joined together, let not man put asunder."
[606] January 17, 1967

shines like rubies, and the tears are faceted like diamonds, and gleam in the dim light in which the offering is made.

T 17 E 9. LOOK AT THE PICTURE. Do NOT let the frame distract you. This gift is given you for your damnation, and if you TAKE it, you WILL believe that you are damned. YOU CANNOT HAVE THE FRAME WITHOUT THE PICTURE. What you VALUE is the FRAME, for THERE you see no conflict. But the frame is only the wrapping for the GIFT of conflict. THE FRAME IS NOT THE GIFT. Be not deceived by the most superficial ASPECTS of this thought-system, for these aspects enclose the whole, complete with EVERY aspect. Death lies in this glittering gift. Let not your gaze dwell on the hypnotic gleaming of the frame. LOOK AT THE PICTURE, and realize that DEATH is offered you. **T(643) -470**

T 17 E 10. That is why the holy instant is so important in the defense of truth. The truth itself NEEDS no defense, but YOU DO need defense against your own ACCEPTANCE of the gift of death. When you who ARE truth, accept an idea so DANGEROUS to truth, YOU THREATEN TRUTH WITH DESTRUCTION. And YOUR defense must now be undertaken, TO KEEP TRUTH WHOLE. The power of Heaven, the Love of God, the tears of Christ and the joy of His Eternal Spirit are marshalled to defend you from your own attack. For you attack THEM, being PART of them, and they must SAVE you, for they love themselves.

T 17 E 11. The Holy instant is a miniature of Heaven, sent you FROM Heaven. It is a picture, too, set in a frame. But if you accept THIS gift, you will NOT see the frame at all, because the gift can only BE accepted through your willingness to focus ALL your attention ON THE PICTURE. The holy instant is a miniature of eternity. It is a picture of timelessness, set in a frame of time. If you focus on the picture, you will realize that it was only the frame that made you THINK it was a picture. WITHOUT the frame, the picture IS SEEN AS WHAT IT REPRESENTS. For, as the whole thought-system of the ego lies in ITS gifts, so the whole of Heaven lies in this instant, borrowed from eternity, and set in time for YOU. **T(644) -471**

T 17 E 12. Two gifts are offered you. Each is complete, and cannot be partially accepted. Each is a picture of all that you can have, SEEN VERY DIFFERENTLY. You CANNOT compare their value by comparing a picture to a frame. It MUST be the PICTURES ONLY that you compare, or the comparison is wholly without meaning. Remember that it is the picture that is the gift. And ONLY on this basis are you REALLY free to choose. LOOK AT THE PICTURES. BOTH of them. One is a tiny picture, hard to see at all beneath the heavy shadows of its enormous and disproportionate enclosure. The other is lightly framed, and hung in light, lovely to look upon for what it IS.

T 17 E 13. You who have tried so hard, and are STILL trying, to fit the better picture into the wrong frame, and so combine what cannot BE combined, accept this and be glad; These pictures are each framed perfectly, for what they represent. One is FRAMED to be out of focus, and NOT seen. The other is framed for perfect clarity. The picture of darkness and of death grows less convincing as you search it out amid its wrappings. As each senseless stone that SEEMS to shine in darkness from the frame is EXPOSED TO LIGHT, it becomes dull and lifeless, and ceases to distract you from the picture. And finally, you look upon the PICTURE ITSELF, seeing at last that, unprotected by its FRAME, it HAS no meaning.

T 17 E 14. The other picture is lightly framed, for time cannot contain eternity. There is NO distraction here. The picture of Heaven and eternity grows MORE convincing, as you look at it. **T(645) -472** And now, by REAL comparison, a TRANSFORMATION of both pictures can at last occur. And each is given its RIGHTFUL place, when both are seen IN RELATION TO EACH OTHER. The dark picture, BROUGHT TO LIGHT, is NOT perceived as fearful. But the fact that IT IS JUST A PICTURE is brought home at last. And what you SEE there, YOU will recognize what it is; a picture of what YOU THOUGHT WAS REAL, and nothing more. For, BEHIND this picture, YOU WILL SEE NOTHING.

T 17 E 15. The picture of light, in clear-cut and unmistakable contrast, is transformed into what lies BEYOND the picture. As you look on THIS, you realize that IT IS NOT A PICTURE, but a reality. This is no figured REPRESENTATION of a thought-system, but the Thought Itself. What IT represents is THERE. The frame fades gently, and God rises to your remembrance, offering you the whole of creation, in exchange for your little picture, wholly without value, and entirely deprived of meaning. As God ascends into HIS rightful place and you to yours, you will experience again the MEANING of relationship, and know it to be true.

T 17 E 16. Let us ascend, in peace together, to the Father, by giving HIM ascendance in our minds.[607] We will gain EVERYTHING by giving HIM the power and the glory, and keeping NO illusions of where they are.[608] They ARE in us, through HIS ascendance. What He has given is HIS. It shines in every part of Him, as in the Whole. The whole reality of your relationship with Him lies in OUR relationship to one another. The holy instant shines alike on ALL relationships, for in it, they ARE one. For here is only healing, ALREADY complete and perfect. For here is God, and where HE is, only the perfect and complete CAN be. **(646) -473**[609]

T 17 F. The Healed Relationship (*Notes* 1427 9:264)

T 17 F 1. The holy relationship is the EXPRESSION of the holy instant, in living in this world. Like EVERYTHING about salvation, the holy instant is a PRACTICAL device, WITNESSED by its results. The holy instant NEVER fails. The EXPERIENCE of it is ALWAYS felt. But, without EXPRESSION, IT IS NOT REMEMBERED. The holy relationship is a constant reminder of the experience in which the relationship became what it is. And, as the UNholy relationship is a continuing hymn of hate in praise of ITS maker, so is the holy relationship a happy song of praise to the REDEEMER of relationships. The holy relationship, a MAJOR step toward the perception of the real world, is LEARNED. It is the old, unholy relationship, transformed and seen anew.

T 17 F 2. The holy relationship is a phenomenal teaching accomplishment. In all its aspects, as it begins, develops, and becomes accomplished, it represents the REVERSAL of the unholy relationship. Be comforted in this; The ONLY difficult phase is the beginning. For here, the GOAL of the relationship is abruptly shifted to the EXACT OPPOSITE of what it was. This is the FIRST result of OFFERING the relationship to the Holy Spirit, to use for HIS purposes. This invitation is ACCEPTED IMMEDIATELY, and the Holy Spirit wastes no time in introducing the practical results of asking Him to enter. AT ONCE, HIS goal REPLACES yours.

T 17 F 3. This is accomplished very rapidly. But it makes the relationship seem disturbed, disjunctive and even quite distressing. The reason is quite clear. For the relationship, AS IT IS, is out of line with its own goal, and clearly unsuited to the purpose which has been ACCEPTED for it. In its UNholy condition, YOUR goal was all that SEEMED to give it meaning. Now, it seems to make NO sense. Many relationships have been broken off at this point, and the pursuit of the old goal re-established in ANOTHER relationship. For, once the unholy relationship has ACCEPTED the goal of holiness, it can **T(647) -474** never again be what it was.

T 17 F 4. The temptation of the ego becomes extremely intense, with this shift in goals. For the relationship has NOT, as yet, been

---
[607] **John 20:17** Jesus said to her, "Do not cling to Me, for I have not yet ascended to My Father; but go to My brethren and say to them, 'I am ascending to My Father and your Father, and to My God and your God.'"
[608] **Matthew 6:13** "And do not lead us into temptation,
  But deliver us from the evil one.
  For Yours is the kingdom and the power and the glory forever." Amen.
[609] January 18, 1968

changed sufficiently to make its former goal completely WITHOUT attraction, and its structure is 'threatened' by the recognition of its inappropriateness for meeting its new purpose. The conflict between the goal and the structure of the relationship is SO apparent that they CANNOT co-exist. Yet now, THE GOAL WILL NOT BE CHANGED. Set firmly in the unholy relationship, there IS no course except to CHANGE THE RELATIONSHIP to fit the goal. Until this HAPPY solution is seen and accepted as the ONLY WAY OUT of this conflict, the RELATIONSHIP seems to be severely strained.

T 17 F 5. It would NOT be kinder to shift the goal more slowly. For the CONTRAST would be obscured, and the ego given time to re-interpret each slow step, according to its liking. Only a radical shift in purpose COULD induce a COMPLETE change of mind about what the whole relationship IS FOR. As this change develops, and is finally accomplished, it grows increasingly beneficent and joyous. But, at the beginning, the situation is experienced as very precarious. A relationship, undertaken by two individuals for their unholy purposes, suddenly has HOLINESS for its goal.

T 17 F 6. As these two CONTEMPLATE their relationship from the point of view of this new purpose, they are inevitably appalled. Their perception of the relationship may even become quite disorganized. And yet, the FORMER organization of their perception, no longer serves the purpose THEY have agreed to set. THIS IS THE TIME FOR FAITH. You LET this goal be set for you. That WAS an act of faith. Do not ABANDON faith, now that the REWARDS of faith are being introduced. If you believed the Holy Spirit was THERE to ACCEPT the relationship, why would you now not STILL believe that He is there, **T(648) -475** to PURIFY what He has taken under His guidance?

T 17 F 7. Have faith in EACH OTHER in what but SEEMS to be a trying time. THE GOAL IS SET. And your relationship has SANITY as its purpose. Now you find yourselves in an INSANE relationship, RECOGNIZED as such IN THE LIGHT OF ITS GOAL. Now the ego counsels thus; substitute for this ANOTHER relationship, to which your FORMER goal was QUITE appropriate. You can ESCAPE from your distress, ONLY BY GETTING RID OF EACH OTHER. You need not part entirely, if you choose not to do so. But you MUST exclude MAJOR AREAS of fantasy FROM each other, TO SAVE YOUR SANITY.

T 17 F 8. Hear not this now! Have faith in Him Who ANSWERED you. He heard; has He not been very explicit in His answer? You are NOT now wholly insane. Can you DENY that He HAS given a MOST explicit statement? Now He asks for faith a little longer, even in bewilderment. For this will go, and you will see the JUSTIFICATION for your faith emerge, to bring you shining conviction.[610] Abandon Him not now, NOR EACH OTHER. This relationship HAS BEEN reborn as holy. Accept with gladness what you do not understand, and LET it be explained to you, as you perceive its purpose work in it, to MAKE it holy.

T 17 F 9. You will find many opportunities to blame EACH OTHER for the 'failure' of your relationship. For it will seem, at times, to have NO purpose. A sense of aimlessness will come to haunt you, and to remind you of all the ways you once SOUGHT for satisfaction, and THOUGHT you found it. Forget not now the misery you REALLY found. And do not now breathe life[611] into your failing egos. For your relationship has NOT been disrupted. IT HAS BEEN SAVED. You are very new in the ways of salvation, and think you have LOST your way. YOUR way IS lost, but think not this is LOSS. **T(649) -476**

T 17 F 10. In your newness, remember that you have started again, TOGETHER. And take each other's hand, to walk together along a road far more familiar than you now believe. Is it not certain, that you will remember a goal unchanged throughout eternity? For you have chosen but the goal of God, from which your true intent was NEVER absent. Throughout the Sonship is the song of freedom heard, in joyous echo of your choice. You have joined with many, in the holy instant, and THEY have joined with you. Think not your choice will leave YOU comfortless. For God Himself has blessed your special relationship.[612] JOIN in His blessing, and withhold not yours upon it. For all it needs now IS your blessing, that you may see that in it rests salvation.

T 17 F 11. Condemn salvation not, for it HAS come to you. And welcome it TOGETHER, for it has come to JOIN you together, in a relationship in which ALL the Sonship is together blessed. You undertook, TOGETHER to invite the Holy Spirit into your relationship. He could not have entered otherwise. And, though you have made many mistakes since then, you have also made enormous efforts to help Him do His work. And He has NOT been lacking in appreciation for all you have done for Him, nor does He see the mistakes at all.

T 17 F 12. Have you been similarly grateful to each other? Have you consistently appreciated the GOOD efforts, and OVERLOOKED mistakes? Or has your appreciation flickered and grown dim, in what SEEMED to be the LIGHT of the mistakes? You are now entering upon a campaign to blame EACH OTHER for the discomfort of the situation in which you find yourselves. And by this LACK of thanks and gratitude, you make YOURSELVES unable to EXPRESS the holy instant, and thus you lose sight of it. The experience of an instant, HOWEVER compelling **T(650) -477** it may be, is easily forgotten, if you allow time to close over it. It must be kept shining and gracious, in your AWARENESS of time, but not CONCEALED within it. The instant remains. But where are YOU?

T 17 F 13. To give thanks to each other is to APPRECIATE the holy instant, and thus enable its RESULTS to be accepted AND SHARED. To ATTACK each other is not to LOSE the instant, but TO MAKE IT POWERLESS IN ITS EFFECTS. You HAVE received the holy instant, but you have established a condition IN WHICH YOU CANNOT USE IT. As a result, you do not realize that it is WITH YOU STILL. And, by CUTTING YOURSELF OFF from its EXPRESSION, you have denied yourself its benefit. You REINFORCE this, every time YOU ATTACK EACH OTHER, for the attack MUST blind you to YOURSELF. And it IS impossible to DENY yourself, and recognize what has been given, and RECEIVED by you.

T 17 F 14. You stand together in the holy Presence of Truth Itself. Here is the goal, together WITH you. Think you not the goal ITSELF will gladly arrange the MEANS for its accomplishment? It is just this same DISCREPANCY between the purpose which has BEEN accepted and the means as they stand now, that SEEMS to make you suffer, but which makes Heaven glad. If Heaven were OUTSIDE you, you could NOT share in its gladness. But, because it is WITHIN, the gladness, too, IS yours. You ARE joined in purpose, but remain still separate and divided on the means. Yet the GOAL is fixed, firm and unalterable. And the means will surely fall in place, BECAUSE the goal is sure.

T 17 F 15. And YOU will share the gladness of the Sonship that it is so. As you begin to recognize, and ACCEPT the gifts you have so

---

[610] **Romans 3:28** Therefore we conclude that a man is justified by faith apart from the deeds of the law.
Romans 5:1 Therefore, having been justified by faith, we have peace with God through our Lord Jesus Christ,
[611] The *Notes* and the *HLC* both have "life" here which is grammatically correct. This appears to be a typing mistake but curiously, what was originally typed was "breath live" and while an "e" was handwritten in after "breath" to correct it to the *Notes*, the next word, "live," was not corrected to "life." So, while the *Urtext* has "live" it would seem that "life" is the correct reading.

[612] **John 14:18** "I will not leave you comfortless; I will come to you."

freely given to EACH OTHER, you will also accept the EFFECTS of the holy instant, and use them to correct ALL your mistakes, and free you from THEIR results. And, learning this, you will have ALSO learned how to release ALL the Sonship, and offer it in gladness and thanksgiving to Him Who gave you YOUR release, and Who would EXTEND it through you. **T(651) -478**[613]

T 17 G. Practical Forgiveness (*Notes* 1437 9:274)

T 17 G 1. The practical application of the Holy Spirit's purpose is extremely simple, but it IS unequivocal. In fact, in ORDER to be simple, it MUST be unequivocal. The simple is merely what is EASILY UNDERSTOOD, and for this, it is apparent that IT MUST BE CLEAR. The setting of the Holy Spirit's goal is GENERAL. Now He will work WITH you, TO MAKE IT SPECIFIC, for application IS specific. There are certain VERY specific guidelines He provides for ANY situation, but remember that you do not yet realize their universal application. Therefore, it is essential, at this point, to use them in each situation separately, until you can more safely look BEYOND each situation, in an understanding far broader than you now possess.

T 17 G 2. In any situation in which YOU are uncertain, the FIRST thing to consider, very simply, is, "What do I want to come of this? What is it FOR?" The clarification of the goal belongs at the BEGINNING, for it is this that will DETERMINE the outcome. In the ego's procedure, this is reversed. The SITUATION becomes the determiner of the outcome, WHICH CAN BE ANYTHING. The reason for this disorganized approach is evident. The ego does not know what it WANTS to come of it. It IS aware of what it does NOT want, but only that. It has no POSITIVE goal at all.

T 17 G 3. Without a clear-cut, positive goal, set at the outset, the situation just seems to happen, and makes no sense until it has ALREADY HAPPENED. Then you look BACK at it, and try to piece together what it MUST have meant. AND YOU WILL BE WRONG. Not only is your judgment IN THE PAST, but you have no idea what SHOULD have happened. No goal was set, with which to bring the means IN LINE. And now, the only judgment LEFT to make is whether or not the ego LIKES it; is it acceptable, or does it call for vengeance. The absence of a criterion for outcome, SET IN ADVANCE, makes understanding doubtful **T(652) -479** and evaluation impossible.

T 17 G 4. The value of deciding, in advance, what you WANT to happen, is simply that you will perceive the situation as a means to MAKE it happen. You will therefore make every effort to OVERLOOK what interferes with the accomplishment of your objective, and concentrate on everything that helps you meet it. It is quite noticeable that THIS approach has brought you closer to the Holy Spirit's SORTING OUT of truth and falsity. The "true" becomes what can be used to MEET the goal. The "false" becomes the useless FROM THIS POINT OF VIEW. The situation now HAS meaning, but only because the goal has MADE it meaningful.

T 17 G 5. The goal of truth has further practical advantages. If the situation is used for truth and sanity, its outcome MUST be peace. And this is quite APART from what the outcome IS. For if peace is the CONDITION of truth and sanity, and CANNOT be WITHOUT them, where peace is, they MUST be. Truth comes of itself. If you experience PEACE, it is because the truth HAS come to you. And you WILL see the outcome truly, for deception can not prevail against you.[614] And you will RECOGNIZE the outcome, BECAUSE you are at peace. Here, again, you see the OPPOSITE of the ego's way of looking. For the EGO believes the situation BRINGS the experience. The Holy Spirit knows the situation IS as the goal determines it, and is experienced ACCORDING to the goal.

T 17 G 6. The goal of truth REQUIRES FAITH. Faith is implicit in the acceptance of the Holy Spirit's purpose. AND THIS FAITH IS ALL-INCLUSIVE. Where the goal of truth is set, there faith MUST be. The Holy Spirit sees the situation AS A WHOLE. The goal establishes the fact that EVERYONE involved in it WILL play his part in its accomplishment. THIS IS INEVITABLE. No-one will fail in anything. **T(653) -480**

This SEEMS to ask for faith BEYOND you, and beyond what you can GIVE. But this is so ONLY from the viewpoint of the ego, for the ego believes in 'solving' conflicts through FRAGMENTATION, and does NOT perceive the situation as a whole. Therefore, it seeks to split off SEGMENTS of the situation and deal with them SEPARATELY. For it has faith in separation, and NOT in wholeness.

T 17 G 7. Confronted with any ASPECT of the situation which SEEMS to be difficult, the ego will attempt to TAKE THIS ASPECT ELSEWHERE, and resolve it there. And it will SEEM to be successful. Except that this attempt CONFLICTS WITH UNITY, and MUST obscure the goal of truth. And peace will not be experienced, EXCEPT in fantasy. Truth has NOT come, because faith has been DENIED, being WITHHELD from where it rightfully belonged. Thus do you LOSE the understanding of the situation the goal of truth would bring. For fantasy solutions bring but the ILLUSION of experience, and the illusion of peace is NOT the condition in which the truth can enter.

T 17 G 8. The substitutes for ASPECTS of the situation are the witnesses to your LACK of faith. They demonstrate that you did NOT believe that the solution AND THE PROBLEM were in the same place. The problem WAS this lack of faith. And it is THIS you demonstrate, when you REMOVE it from its source, and place it elsewhere. As a result, YOU DO NOT SEE THE PROBLEM. Had you not lacked the faith it COULD be solved, the PROBLEM would be gone. And the situation would have been MEANINGFUL to you, because the INTERFERENCE in the way of understanding, would have been removed. To remove the problem ELSEWHERE is to KEEP it. For you remove yourself FROM it, and MAKE it unsolvable.

T 17 H. The Need for Faith (*Notes* 1445 10:5)

T 17 H 1. There is NO problem in ANY situation that faith will not solve. There is no SHIFT in any ASPECT of the problem, but will make SOLUTION IMPOSSIBLE. **T(654) -481** For if you shift PART of a problem elsewhere, the meaning of the problem MUST be lost, and the SOLUTION to the problem is INHERENT in its meaning. Is it not possible that ALL your problems HAVE BEEN solved, but you have removed YOURSELF from the solution? Yet faith MUST be where something has BEEN done, and where you SEE it done. A situation is a relationship, being the joining of thoughts. If problems are perceived, it is because the thoughts are judged to be IN CONFLICT. But if the goal is TRUTH, this is impossible. Some idea of bodies MUST have entered, for minds can NOT attack.

T 17 H 2. The thought of bodies IS the sign of faithlessness, for bodies CANNOT solve anything. And it is their INTRUSION on the relationship, an error in YOUR thoughts ABOUT the situation, that then became the JUSTIFICATION for your lack of faith. You WILL make this error, but be not at all concerned with that. The error does not matter. But do not USE the error to what SEEMS to be to your advantage, for that DOES matter. Faithlessness brought to faith, will never interfere with truth. But faithlessness used AGAINST truth will ALWAYS destroy faith. If you lack faith, ask that it be restored WHERE IT WAS LOST, and seek not to have it MADE UP TO YOU elsewhere, as if you had been unjustly DEPRIVED of it.

---

[613] Jan. 20, 1967
[614] **Matthew 16:18** "And I also say to you that you are Peter, and on this rock I will build My church, and the gates of Hades shall not prevail against it."

T 17 H 3. Only what YOU have not given CAN be lacking in ANY situation. But remember this; the goal of holiness was set for YOUR relationship, AND NOT BY YOU. YOU did not set it, because holiness can NOT BE SEEN except through faith, and your relationship was not holy BECAUSE your faith in one another was so limited and little. Your faith must grow, to meet the goal that has been set. The goal's REALITY will call this forth. For you will see that peace and faith will not come separately. What situation can you be in WITHOUT FAITH, and remain faithful to each other? EVERY situation in which **T(655) -482** you find yourselves, is but a means to meet the purpose set for YOUR relationship. See it as something ELSE, and you ARE faithless.

T 17 H 4. USE NOT YOUR FAITHLESSNESS. Let it enter, and look upon it calmly, but DO NOT USE IT. Faithlessness is the servant of illusion, and wholly faithful to its master. USE it, and it will carry you straight to illusions. Be tempted not by what it offers you. It interferes, not with the goal, but with the VALUE of the goal TO YOU. Accept not the illusion of peace it offers, but look upon its offering, and recognize it IS illusion. The GOAL of illusion is as closely tied to faithlessness, as faith to truth. If you lack faith in ANYONE to fulfill, AND PERFECTLY, his part in ANY situation dedicated IN ADVANCE to truth, YOUR dedication is divided. And so you have been faithless TO EACH OTHER, and USED your faithlessness AGAINST each other.

T 17 H 5. No relationship is holy, unless its holiness goes with it EVERYWHERE. As holiness and faith go hand in hand, so must its faith go everywhere WITH it. The goal's reality will call forth, AND ACCOMPLISH, every miracle needed for its fulfillment. Nothing too small or too enormous, nothing too insignificant or too imposing, too weak or too compelling, but will be gently turned to its use and purpose. The universe will serve it gladly, as it serves the universe. BUT DO NOT INTERFERE. The power set in you, in whom the Holy Spirit's goal has been established, is so far beyond your little conception of the infinite, that you have no idea how great the strength that goes with you.

T 17 H 6. And you can use THIS in perfect safety. Yet, for all its might, so great it reaches past the stars and to the universe that lies beyond them, your little faithlessness can make IT useless, if you would use the faithlessness instead. But think on this, and learn the CAUSE of faithlessness; you think you hold against another[615] what he has done to you. But what you REALLY blame **T(656) -483** him for is WHAT YOU DID TO HIM. It is not HIS past but YOURS, you hold against him. And you lack faith in HIM, because of what YOU were. Yet YOU are as innocent of what you were, as HE is. What never was is causeless, and IS NOT THERE to interfere with truth. There IS no cause for faithlessness, but there IS a Cause for faith.

T 17 H 7. That Cause has entered ANY situation that shares its purpose. The light of truth shines from the center of the situation, and touches everyone to whom the situation's purpose calls. IT CALLS TO EVERYONE. There is NO situation that does NOT involve your WHOLE RELATIONSHIP, in every aspect and complete in every part. You can leave NOTHING of yourself outside it, and keep the situation holy. For it shares the purpose of your whole relationship, and derives its meaning FROM it. Enter each situation with the faith that you would give each other, or you ARE faithless to your own relationship. YOUR faith will call the others to SHARE your purpose, as this same purpose called forth the faith in you.

T 17 H 8. And you will see the means you once employed to lead you to illusions, transformed to means for truth. Truth calls for faith, and faith makes room FOR TRUTH. When the Holy Spirit

---

[615] The *Urtext* manuscript has the "an" crossed out and "the" handwritten in. The *Notes* however has it as originally typed: "another." We're guessing that change was made at some later date and thus leaving what was originally typed. The *HLC* has "the other" and FIP has "your brother."

CHANGED the purpose of your relationship by exchanging yours for His, the goal He placed there WAS extended to every situation in which you entered, or will EVER enter. And EVERY situation was thus MADE FREE of the past, which WOULD have made it purposeLESS. You CALL FOR faith, because of Him Who walks with you in every situation. You are no longer wholly insane, NOR NO LONGER ALONE. For loneliness in God MUST be a dream. You whose relationship SHARES the Holy Spirit's goal, are SET APART from loneliness, because the truth has come. Its call for faith is strong. Use not your faithlessness against it, for it calls you to salvation and to peace. **T(657) -484**

T 17 I. The Conditions of Forgiveness (*Notes* 1450 10:10)

T 17 I 1. The holy instant is nothing more than a special case, or an extreme example, of what EVERY situation is MEANT to be. The meaning that the Holy Spirit's purpose has GIVEN it, is also given to EVERY situation. It calls forth just the same SUSPENSION of faithlessness, withheld and left UNUSED, that faith might answer to the call of truth. The holy instant is the shining example, the clear and unequivocal demonstration of the meaning of EVERY relationship, and EVERY situation SEEN AS A WHOLE. Faith has ACCEPTED every ASPECT of the situation, and faithlessness has not forced ANY exclusion on it. It is a situation of perfect peace, simply because YOU have LET IT BE WHAT IT IS.

T 17 I 2. This simple courtesy is all the Holy Spirit asks of you. Let Truth be what it is. Do not INTRUDE upon it, do not ATTACK it, do NOT interrupt its coming. Let it encompass EVERY situation, and bring you peace. Not even faith is asked of you, for Truth asks nothing. Let it enter, and IT will call forth, and SECURE for you, the faith you need for peace. But rise you not AGAINST it, for against YOUR opposition it CANNOT come. Would you not WANT to make a holy instant of EVERY situation? For such is the gift of faith, freely given wherever faithlessness is laid aside, UNUSED.

T 17 I 3. And THEN the power of the Holy Spirit's purpose is free for use instead. This power INSTANTLY transforms ALL situations into one sure and continuous means for ESTABLISHING His purpose, and DEMONSTRATING its reality. What has been DEMONSTRATED has called for faith, and has been GIVEN it. Now it becomes a fact, from which faith can no longer BE withheld. The strain of REFUSING faith to truth is enormous, and far greater than you realize. But to ANSWER truth with faith entails no strain at all. **T(658) -485**

T 17 I 4. To you who have ACKNOWLEDGED the call of your Redeemer, the strain of NOT responding to His call SEEMS to be GREATER than before. This is not so. Before, the strain was there, but you attributed it TO SOMETHING ELSE, believing that the 'something else' PRODUCED it. This was NEVER true. But what the 'something else' produced was sorrow and depression, sickness and pain, darkness and dim imaginings of terror, cold fantasies of fear, and fiery dreams of hell. And it was nothing but the intolerable strain of your refusal to give faith to truth, and see its evident reality.

T 17 I 5. Such was the crucifixion of the Son of God. His faithlessness did this to him. Think carefully before you let yourself use faithlessness against him. For he IS risen, and YOU have accepted the cause of his awakening AS YOURS. You have assumed your part in his redemption, and you are now fully responsible to him. Fail him not now, for it has been given you to realize what your lack of faith in him MUST mean to YOU. His salvation is your ONLY purpose. See only this in EVERY situation, and it WILL be a means for bringing ONLY this.

T 17 I 6. When you accepted truth as the goal for your relationship, you became givers of peace, as surely as your Father gave peace to YOU. For the goal of peace cannot BE accepted, APART from its conditions. And you had faith in it, for no-one accepts what he does

Chapter 17 – Forgiveness and Healing

NOT believe is REAL. YOUR PURPOSE HAS NOT CHANGED, and WILL not change, for you ACCEPTED what can NEVER change. And nothing that it needs to BE forever changeless, can you now WITHHOLD from it. Your release is certain. Give as you have received. And demonstrate that you have risen FAR beyond ANY situation that could hold you back, and keep you SEPARATE from Him Whose call you answered. **T(659) -486**

CHAPTER 18 – THE DREAM AND THE REALITY

T 18 A. Introduction (*Notes* 1454 10:14)

T 18 A 1. To[616] substitute is to ACCEPT INSTEAD. If you would but consider exactly what this entails, you would perceive at once how much at variance this is with the goal the Holy Spirit has given you and would accomplish FOR you. To substitute is to CHOOSE BETWEEN, renouncing one IN FAVOR of the other. For this SPECIAL purpose, one is judged more valuable, and the other is REPLACED by him. The relationship in which the substitution occurred is thus fragmented, and ITS PURPOSE SPLIT accordingly. To fragment IS TO EXCLUDE, and substitution is the strongest defense the ego has for separation.

T 18 A 2. The Holy Spirit NEVER substitutes. Where the ego perceives one person as a REPLACEMENT FOR another, the Holy Spirit sees them joined and indivisible. He does not judge BETWEEN them, KNOWING they are one. Being united, they are one BECAUSE THEY ARE THE SAME. Substitution is clearly a process in which they are PERCEIVED AS DIFFERENT. One would UNITE; the other SEPARATE. NOTHING can come BETWEEN what God has joined, and what the Holy Spirit sees as one.[617] But everything SEEMS to come between the fragmented relationships the ego sponsors, to destroy.

T 18 A 3. The one emotion in which substitution is impossible, is love. But fear involves substitution by definition, for it is love's REPLACEMENT. Fear is both a fragmented AND FRAGMENTING emotion. It SEEMS, to take many forms, and each seems to require a DIFFERENT form of acting out, for satisfaction. While this appears to introduce quite variable BEHAVIOR, a far more serious effect lies in the fragmented PERCEPTION from which the behavior stems. NO-ONE IS SEEN COMPLETE. The body is emphasized, with special emphasis on certain parts, and USED AS THE STANDARD FOR COMPARISON for either acceptance or rejection of suitability for acting out a special FORM of fear. **T(660) -487**

T 18 B. Substitution as a Defense (*Notes* 1456 10:16)

T 18 B 1. You[618] who believe that God is fear made but ONE substitution. It has taken many forms, because it was the substitution of fragmentation for wholeness. It has become splintered and subdivided and divided again, over and over, that it is now almost impossible to perceive it once was one, and still IS what it was. That ONE error, which brought truth to illusion, infinity to time, and life to death, was all you ever made. Your whole world rests upon it. Everything you see reflects it. And every special relationship you ever made is PART of it.

T 18 B 2. You have expressed surprise at hearing how VERY different is reality from what YOU see. You do not realize the magnitude of that ONE error. It was so vast and so COMPLETELY incredible, that from it, a world of total unreality HAD to emerge. What else COULD come of it? Its fragmented ASPECTS are fearful enough, as you begin to LOOK at them. But nothing you have ever seen BEGINS to show you the enormity of the ORIGINAL error, which seemed to cast you out of Heaven, to shatter knowledge into meaningless bits of disunited perceptions, and TO FORCE YOU TO FURTHER SUBSTITUTIONS.

T 18 B 3. That was the first projection of error outward. The world arose to hide it, and became the screen on which it was projected, and drawn between you and truth. For truth extends INWARD, where the idea of loss is meaningless, and only INCREASE is conceivable. Do you REALLY think it strange that a world in which EVERYTHING is backward and upside down, arose from this? IT WAS INEVITABLE. For truth brought to THIS could only remain within in quiet, and take no part in all the mad projection by which this world was made.

T 18 B 4. Call it not sin, but madness, for such it was, and so it still remains. Invest it not with guilt, for guilt implies it was accomplished IN REALITY. And, above all, BE NOT AFRAID OF IT. When you seem to see some twisted form of the original error rise to frighten you, say only, 'God is NOT fear, but love,' and it will disappear.[619] THE TRUTH WILL SAVE YOU. It has NOT left you, **T(661) -488** to go out into the mad world and so DEPART FROM YOU. Inward is sanity; INsanity is OUTSIDE you. You but BELIEVE it is the other way; that truth is OUTSIDE, and error and guilt within.

T 18 B 5. Your little, senseless substitutions, touched with insanity, and swirling lightly off on a mad course like a feather dancing insanely in the wind, HAVE no substance. They fuse and merge and separate in shifting and totally meaningless patterns, which need not be judged at all. To judge them INDIVIDUALLY is pointless. Their tiny differences in form are not REAL differences at all. NONE OF THEM MATTERS. THAT they have in common, and nothing else, but what else is NECESSARY to make them all the same? Let them go, dancing in the wind, dipping and turning 'til they disappear from sight, far, far OUTSIDE you. And turn you to the stately calm within, where, in holy stillness, dwells the living God you never left, and Who never left you.[620]

T 18 B 6. The Holy Spirit takes you gently by the hand, and retraces WITH you your mad journey OUTSIDE yourself, leading you gently back to the truth and safety within. He brings all your insane projections and your wild substitutions which YOU have placed OUTSIDE you, to the truth. Thus, He REVERSES the course of insanity, and restores you to reason. In your relationship where He has taken charge of everything at your request, He has set the course inward, to the truth you SHARE. In the mad world OUTSIDE you, nothing CAN be shared, but only SUBSTITUTED, and sharing and substituting have NOTHING in common in reality.

T 18 B 7. Within yourselves, you love each other with perfect love. Here is holy ground,[621] in which no substitutes can enter, and where only the TRUTH about each other can abide. Here you are joined in God, as much together as you are with Him. The original error has not entered here, nor ever[622] will. Here is the radiant truth, to which the Holy Spirit submitted your relationship. **T(662) -489** Let Him bring it here, where YOU would have it be. Give Him but a little faith in each other, to help Him show you that no substitute you made for Heaven can keep you from it.

---

[616] January 25, 1967
[617] **Matthew 19:6** "So then, they are no longer two but one flesh. Therefore what God has joined together, let not man separate."
[618] January 27, 1967

[619] **1 John 4:18** There is no fear in love; but perfect love casts out fear, because fear involves torment. But he who fears has not been made perfect in love.
[620] **John 6:69** Also we have come to believe and know that You are the Christ, the Son of the living God.
[621] **Exodus 3:4** And when the LORD saw that he turned aside to see, God called unto him out of the midst of the bush, and said, Moses, Moses. And he said, Here *am* I.
Exodus 3:5 And he said, Draw not nigh hither: put off thy shoes from off thy feet, for the place whereon thou standest *is* holy ground.
[622] *Urtext* manuscript has "never" and the *Notes* might have the same, it is uncertain due to poor legibility. Later editing changes this to "ever" from "never" which seems likely to be what was originally intended and at least is grammatically correct.

T 18 B 8. In you there is no separation, and no substitute can keep you from each other. Your reality was GOD's creation, and HAS no substitute. You are so firmly joined in truth, that only God is there. And He could NEVER accept something else INSTEAD of you. He loves you both, equally and as one. And as He loves you, so you ARE. You are NOT joined together by illusions, but in the Thought so holy and so perfect that illusions cannot remain to darken the holy place in which you stand together. God is with you, my brothers. Let us join in Him in peace and gratitude, and accept His gift of our most holy and perfect reality, that we share in Him.

T 18 B 9. Heaven is restored to all the Sonship through your relationship. For in it lies the Sonship, whole and beautiful, safe in your love. Heaven has answered quietly, for all illusions have been gently brought unto the truth in you, and Love has shined upon you, blessing your relationship with truth. God and His whole Creation has[623] entered it together. How lovely and how holy is your relationship, with the truth shining upon it! Heaven beholds it, and rejoices that you have let it come to you. And God Himself is glad that your relationship is as it was created. The universe within you stands with you together. And Heaven looks with love on what is joined in it, along with its Creator.

T 18 B 10. Whom God hath called should hear no substitutes. Their call is but an echo of the original error which shattered Heaven. For what became of peace, in those who heard? Return with me to Heaven, walking together out of this world, and through another to the loveliness and joy the other holds within it. Would you still further weaken and break apart what is already **T(663) -490** broken and hopeless? Is it HERE that you would look for happiness? Or would you not prefer to HEAL what has been broken, and join in making whole what has been ravaged by separation and disease?

T 18 B 11. You have been called, together, to the most holy function that this world contains. It is the ONLY one that has no limits, and that reaches out to every broken fragment of the Sonship, with healing and uniting comfort. This is offered YOU, in your holy relationship. Accept it HERE, and you WILL give as you have accepted and received. The peace of God is given you, with the glowing purpose in which you join. The holy light that brought you together MUST extend, as YOU accept it. **T(664) -491**

T 18 C. The Basis of the Dream (N* 1463 10:23)

T 18 C 1. Does[624] not a world that seems quite real arise in dreams? But think what this world is. It is clearly NOT the world you saw BEFORE you slept. Rather, it is a DISTORTION of the world, planned solely around what you would have PREFERRED. Here, you are 'free' to make over whatever SEEMED to attack you, and CHANGE it into a TRIBUTE to your ego, which was outraged by the attack. This would not be YOUR wish unless you saw yourself AS ONE with the ego, which ALWAYS looks upon itself, and therefore on you, as UNDER attack, and highly VULNERABLE to it.

T 18 C 2. Dreams are chaotic BECAUSE they are governed by your conflicting wishes. And therefore they have NO concern with what is true. They are the best example you could have of how perception can be utilized to substitute illusions for truth. You do not take them seriously on awaking, because the fact that, in them, reality is so OUTRAGEOUSLY violated, becomes apparent. Yet they ARE a way of LOOKING at the world, and CHANGING it TO SUIT THE EGO BETTER. They provide STRIKING examples, both of the ego's INABILITY to tolerate reality, and your willingness to CHANGE reality on its behalf.

T 18 C 3. You do not find the differences between what you see in sleep and on awaking disturbing. You recognize that what you see on waking is blotted out in dreams. Yet, on awakening, you do NOT expect it to be gone. In dreams, YOU arrange everything. People BECOME what you would have them be, and what they do YOU order. No limits on substitution are laid upon you; for a time, it seems as if the world were GIVEN you, to make it what you will. You do NOT realize that YOU are ATTACKING it, trying to triumph over it and MAKE it serve you.

T 18 C 4. Dreams are perceptual temper tantrums, in which you literally scream, 'I want it THUS!' And thus it seems to be. And yet, the dream can NOT escape its origin. Anger and fear pervade it, and in an instant the illusion of satisfaction is invaded by the illusion of terror. For the **T(665) -492** dream of your ability to CONTROL reality by substituting a world that you prefer IS terrifying. Your attempts to BLOT OUT reality are VERY fearful, but THIS you are NOT willing to accept. And so you SUBSTITUTE the fantasy that REALITY is fearful, NOT what you would DO to it. And thus is guilt MADE REAL.

T 18 C 5. Dreams show you that you HAVE the power to make a world as you would have it, and that, BECAUSE you WANT it, you SEE it. And WHILE you see it, you do NOT doubt that it is real. Yet here is a world, clearly WITHIN your mind, that SEEMS to be outside. You do NOT respond to it as though you made it, nor do you realize that the emotions which the dream produces MUST come from you. It is the FIGURES in the dream, and what THEY do that seem to MAKE THE DREAM. You do not realize that you are making them act out FOR you, for if you did, the guilt would not be theirs, and the illusion of satisfaction would be gone.

T 18 C 6. In dreams these features are not obscure. You seem to waken, and the dream is gone. But what you fail to recognize is that what CAUSED the dream, has NOT gone with it. Your WISH to make another world that is NOT real, REMAINS with you. And what you seem to WAKE to, is but another FORM of this same world you see in dreams. All your time is spent in dreaming. Your sleeping and your waking dreams have different forms, and that is all. THEIR CONTENT IS THE SAME. They are your protest AGAINST reality, and your fixed and insane wish to CHANGE it.

T 18 C 7. In your WAKING dreams, the special relationship has a special place. It is the means by which you try to make your SLEEPING dreams COME TRUE. From this, you do not waken. The special relationship is your DETERMINATION to keep your hold on unreality, and to PREVENT yourself from waking. And while you see more VALUE in sleeping than in waking, you will NOT let go of it. The Holy Spirit, ever practical in His wisdom, ACCEPTS your dreams, and uses them **T(666) -493** as means for WAKING. YOU would have used them to remain ASLEEP.

T 18 C 8. We once said that the first change, before dreams disappear, is that your dreams of fear are changed to HAPPY dreams. That is what the Holy Spirit does in your special relationship. He does NOT destroy it, nor snatch it away from you. But He does use it differently, as a help to make HIS purpose REAL to you. Your special relationships will remain, NOT as a source of pain and guilt, but as a source of joy and freedom. It will NOT be for you alone, for therein lay its misery. As its UNholiness kept it as a thing apart, its HOLINESS will become an offering to everyone.

T 18 C 9. Your special relationship will be a means for UNDOING guilt in everyone blessed through your holy relationship. It will be a happy dream, and one which you will SHARE with all who come within your sight. Through it, the blessing that the Holy Spirit has laid upon it, will be EXTENDED. Think not that He has forgotten anyone, in the purpose He has given you. And think not that He has forgotten YOU, to whom He GAVE this gift. He uses everyone who calls on Him, as means for the salvation of everyone. And He will waken everyone through you, who offered your relationship to Him.

---

[623] The *Urtext* manuscript reads "has." The *Notes* is the same. *HLC* and *FIP* use "have" and grammar requires we use the plural "have" for the plural subject which is "God AND His whole Creation" unless we understand "God and His whole Creation" to be a ***single thing***, which interpretation is possible, in which case "has" is correct.

[624] January 30, 1967

T 18 C 10. If you but recognized His gratitude! Or mine through His! For we are joined as one in purpose, being of one mind with Him. Let not the dream take hold to close your eyes. It is not strange that dreams can make a world that is unreal. The WISH to make it IS incredible. Your relationship has become one in which the wish has been REMOVED, because its purpose has been changed from one of dreams to one of truth. You are not sure of this, because you think it may be THIS that is the dream. You are so used to choosing between dreams, you do not see that you have made, at last, the choice between the truth and ALL ILLUSIONS. T(667) -494

T 18 C 11. Yet Heaven IS sure. THIS IS NO DREAM. Its coming means that you have chosen truth, and it has come, because you have been willing to let your special relationship meet its conditions. In your relationship, the Holy Spirit has gently laid the real world; the world of happy dreams, from which awaking is so easy and so natural. For, as your sleeping and waking dreams represent the same wishes in YOUR mind, so do the real world and the truth of Heaven join in the Will of God. The dream of waking is easily transferred to its reality. For this dream comes from your will, JOINED with the Will of God. And what THIS will would HAVE accomplished, has never NOT been done. T(668) -495[625]

T 18 D. Light in the Dream (*Notes* 1470 10:29)

T 18 D 1. You who have spent your lives in bringing truth to illusion, reality to fantasy, HAVE walked the way of dreams. For you have gone from waking to sleeping, and on and on to a yet deeper sleep. Each dream has led to other dreams, and every fantasy that SEEMED to bring a light into the darkness but made the darkness deeper. Your GOAL was darkness, in which no ray of light could enter. And you sought a blackness so complete that you could hide from truth forever, in complete insanity. What you forgot was simply that God can NOT destroy Himself. The light is IN you. Darkness can COVER it, but CANNOT put it out.[626]

T 18 D 2. As the light comes nearer, you WILL rush to darkness, shrinking from the truth, sometimes retreating to the lesser forms of fear, and sometimes to stark terror. But you WILL advance, because your goal IS the advance from fear to truth. YOU KNOW THIS. The goal which you accepted IS the goal of knowledge, for which you signified your willingness. Fear seems to live in darkness. when you are afraid, YOU HAVE STEPPED BACK. Let us then join quickly in an instant of light, and it will be enough to remind you that your goal IS light. Truth has rushed to meet you, since YOU called upon it.

T 18 D 3. If you knew Who walks beside you on THIS way, which YOU have chosen, fear would be impossible.[627] You do NOT know, because the journey into darkness has been long and cruel, and you have gone deep into it. A little flicker of your eyelids, closed so long, has not yet been sufficient to give you confidence in yourselves, so long despised. You go TOWARD love, still hating it, and TERRIBLY afraid of its judgment upon you. And you do NOT realize that you are NOT afraid of love, but only OF WHAT YOU MADE OF IT. T(669) -496

T 18 D 4. You are advancing to love's MEANING, and away from ALL illusions in which you have surrounded it. When you retreat to the illusions, YOUR FEAR INCREASES, for there is little doubt that what YOU think it means IS fearful. But what is that to us who travel surely and very swiftly AWAY from fear? You who hold each other's hand also hold mine, for when you joined each other you were not alone. Do you believe that I would LEAVE you in the darkness you agreed to leave with ME? In your relationship is this world's light. And fear MUST disappear before you now.

T 18 D 5. Be tempted not to snatch away the gift of faith you offered to each other. You will succeed only in frightening yourselves. The gift is given forever, for God Himself received it. You CANNOT take it back. YOU HAVE ACCEPTED GOD. The holiness of your relationship is established in Heaven. You do not realize WHAT you accepted, but remember that your understanding is NOT necessary. All that was necessary was merely the WISH to understand. That wish was the DESIRE TO BE HOLY. The will of God IS granted you. For you desire the only thing you ever had, or ever were.

T 18 D 6. Each instant that we spend together will teach you that this goal is possible, and will strengthen your DESIRE to reach it. And in your desire, lies its accomplishment. YOUR desire is now in COMPLETE accord with all the power of the Holy Spirit's Will. No little faltering footsteps that you may take can separate your desire from His Will, and from His STRENGTH. I hold your hand as surely as you agreed to take each other's. YOU WILL NOT SEPARATE for I stand with you, and walk with you in your advance to truth. And where we go we carry God with us. T(670) -497

T 18 D 7. In your relationship, you have joined with me in bringing Heaven to the Son of God, who hid in darkness. You have been willing to bring the darkness to light, and this willingness has given strength to everyone who would REMAIN in darkness. Those who would see WILL see. And they will join with me in carrying THEIR light into the darkness, when the darkness in them is OFFERED to the light, and is removed forever. My need for you, joined with me in the holy light of your relationship, is YOUR need for salvation. Would I not give you what you gave to me? For when you joined each other, you answered ME.

T 18 D 8. You who are now the bringers of salvation have the function of bringing light to darkness. The darkness in you HAS been brought to light. Carry it back TO darkness, from the holy instant to which you BROUGHT it. We are made whole in our desire to make whole. Let not time worry you, for all the fear that you experience is really past. Time has been re-adjusted to help us do, together, what your separate pasts would hinder. You have gone PAST fear, for no two minds can JOIN in the desire for love without love's joining THEM.

T 18 D 9. Not one light in Heaven but goes with you. Not one ray that shines forever in the Mind of God but shines on you. Heaven is JOINED with you in your advance to Heaven. When such great light has joined with you to give the little spark of your desire the power of God Himself, can YOU remain in darkness? You are coming home together, after a long and meaningless journey which you undertook apart, and which led nowhere. You have FOUND each other, and will light each other's way. And from this light will the Great Rays extend back into darkness and forward unto God, to shine away the past and so make room for His Eternal Presence, in which everything is radiant in the light. T(671) - 498 -[628]

T 18 E. The Little Willingness (*Notes* 1476 10:36)

T 18 E 1. The holy instant is the RESULT of your determination to be holy. It is the ANSWER. The desire and the willingness to let it come PRECEDE its coming. YOU prepare your minds for it ONLY to the extent of RECOGNIZING that you want it above all else. It is not necessary that you do more; indeed, it is necessary that you realize that you can NOT do more. Do not attempt to give the Holy Spirit what He does NOT ask, or you will add the ego unto Him, and CONFUSE THE TWO. He asks but little. It is HE Who adds

---

[625] Feb. 2, 1967

[626] **Luke 1:79** "To give light to those who sit in darkness and the shadow of death, To guide our feet into the way of peace."
John 1:5 And the light shines in the darkness, and the darkness did not comprehend it.

[627] **Luke 24:13-16** Now behold, two of them were traveling that same day to a village called Emmaus, which was seven miles from Jerusalem. And they talked together of all these things which had happened. So it was, while they conversed and reasoned, that Jesus Himself drew near and went with them. But their eyes were restrained, so that they did not know Him.

[628] February 5, 1967.

Chapter 18 – The Dream and the Reality

the greatness and the might. He JOINS with you to make the holy instant far greater than you can understand.

T 18 E 2. It is your realization that you NEED do so little that enables HIM to give so much. Trust not your good intentions. They are not enough. But trust IMPLICITLY your willingness, whatever else may enter. Concentrate only on this, and be NOT disturbed that shadows surround it. THAT IS WHY YOU CAME. If you could come WITHOUT them, you would not NEED the holy instant. Come to it not in arrogance, assuming that YOU must achieve the state its coming brings with it. The miracle of the holy instant lies in your willingness to let IT be what it is. And in your willingness for THIS, lies also your acceptance of yourself as YOU were meant to be.

T 18 E 3. Humility will NEVER ask that you remain content with littleness. But it DOES require that you be NOT content with less than greatness which comes NOT of you. Your difficulty with the holy instant arises from your fixed conviction that you are not WORTHY of it. And what is this but the determination to BE as you would MAKE YOURSELF? God did not create His dwelling-place unworthy of Him. And if you believe He cannot enter where He wills to be, you MUST be INTERFERING with His Will. You do not need the strength of willingness to come from YOU, but only from HIS Will.

T 18 E 4. The holy instant does NOT come from your little willingness alone. It is ALWAYS the result of your SMALL willingness COMBINED with the unlimited power of HIS Will. You have been wrong in thinking that it is **T(672) - 499 -** needful to prepare YOURSELF for Him. It is impossible to make arrogant preparations for holiness, and NOT believe that it is up to you to establish the conditions for peace. GOD HAS ESTABLISHED THEM. They do not wait upon your willingness for what they ARE. Your willingness is needed ONLY to make it possible to TEACH you what they are.

T 18 E 5. If you maintain you are unworthy of LEARNING this, you are INTERFERING with the lesson by believing THAT YOU MUST MAKE THE LEARNER DIFFERENT. You did NOT make the learner, nor CAN you make him different. Would you FIRST make a miracle of YOURSELF, and THEN expect one to be made FOR you? You merely ask the QUESTION. The answer is GIVEN. Seek not to ANSWER it, but merely RECEIVE the answer AS it is given. In preparing for the holy instant, do NOT attempt to make yourself holy to be READY to receive it. That is but to confuse YOUR role with His. Atonement CANNOT come to those who think that THEY must <u>FIRST</u> atone, but only to those who offer it NOTHING MORE than simple willingness to make way for it.

T 18 E 6. Purification is of God alone. And THEREFORE for you. Rather than seek to prepare YOURSELF for Him, try to think thus:

"I who am host to God AM worthy of Him.

He Who ESTABLISHED His dwelling-place in me created it as He would have it be.

It is not needful that I make it ready for Him, but only that I DO NOT INTERFERE with His plan to RESTORE to me my own AWARENESS of my readiness, which is eternal.

I need ADD nothing to His plan,

But to RECEIVE it, I must be willing NOT to substitute my own IN PLACE of it."

T 18 E 7. And that is all. Add MORE, and you will merely TAKE AWAY the little that is asked. Remember YOU MADE GUILT, and that your plan for the ESCAPE from guilt has been to bring Atonement TO it, and MAKE SALVATION FEARFUL. And it is ONLY fear that you will add, if you prepare YOURSELF for love. The preparation for the holy instant belongs to Him Who gives it. RELEASE **T(673) - 500 -** yourselves to Him Whose function IS release. Do NOT assume His function FOR Him. Give Him but what He asks, that you may learn how LITTLE is your part, and how great is HIS.

T 18 E 8. It is this that makes the holy instant so easy and so natural. YOU make it difficult, because you insist there MUST be more that you need do. You find it difficult to ACCEPT the idea that you need give so LITTLE, to receive so much. And it is very hard for you to realize that it is not personally insulting that YOUR contribution and the Holy Spirit's are so EXTREMELY disproportionate. You are still convinced YOUR understanding is a powerful contribution to the truth, and MAKES IT WHAT IT IS. Yet we have emphasized that you need understand nothing. Salvation is easy JUST BECAUSE it asks nothing that you cannot give RIGHT NOW.

T 18 E 9. Forget not that it has been your decision to make EVERYTHING that is natural and easy for you IMPOSSIBLE. What you believe to be impossible WILL BE, if God so wills it, but you will remain quite UNAWARE of it. If you believe the holy instant is difficult FOR YOU, it is because YOU have become the arbiter of what is possible, and remain UNWILLING to give place to One Who KNOWS. The whole belief in orders of difficulty in miracles is centered on this. Everything God wills is not only possible, but has already happened. And that is WHY the past has gone. It NEVER HAPPENED in reality. Only in your minds, WHICH THOUGHT IT DID, is its undoing needful.

T 18 F. The Happy Dream (*Notes* 1481 10:41)

T 18 F 1. Prepare you NOW for the undoing of what never was. If you already UNDERSTOOD the difference between truth and illusion, Atonement would HAVE no meaning. The holy instant, your holy relationship, the Holy Spirit's teaching, and all the means by which salvation is accomplished, would have no purpose. For they are all but ASPECTS of the plan to change your dreams of fear to happy dreams, from which you waken easily to knowledge. Put yourself NOT in charge of this, for you can NOT distinguish between advance and retreat. Some of your greatest advances YOU have judged as failures, and some of your deepest retreats YOU have evaluated as success. **T(674) - 521 -**

T 18 F 2. Never approach the holy instant AFTER you have tried to remove all fear and hatred from your mind. That is ITS function. Never attempt to OVERLOOK your guilt BEFORE you ask the Holy Spirit's help. That is HIS function. Your part is only to offer Him a LITTLE willingness to LET Him remove all fear and hatred, and to BE forgiven. On your little faith, joined with HIS understanding, HE will build your part in the Atonement, and MAKE SURE that you fulfill it easily. And WITH Him, YOU will build a ladder planted in the solid rock of faith, and rising even to Heaven. Nor will you use it to ascend to Heaven alone.

T 18 F 3. Through your holy relationship, reborn and blessed in every holy instant which you did NOT arrange, thousands will rise to Heaven WITH you. Can YOU plan for THIS? Or could you PREPARE yourselves for such a function? Yet it IS possible, because God wills it. Nor will He change His Mind about it. The means and purpose BOTH belong to Him. You have accepted one; the other will be provided. A purpose such as this, WITHOUT the means, IS inconceivable. HE will provide the means to ANYONE who SHARES His purpose.

T 18 F 4. HAPPY DREAMS COME TRUE. NOT because they are dreams, but only because they are HAPPY. And so they MUST be loving. Their message is, "Thy Will be done," and NOT, "I want it otherwise."[629] The alignment of means and purpose is an undertaking IMPOSSIBLE for you to understand. You do not even realize you HAVE accepted the Holy Spirit's purpose as your own. And you would merely bring UNholy means to its accomplishment. The

---

[629] **Matthew 6:10** "Thy kingdom come. Thy will be done on earth as it is in heaven."

little faith it needed to change the purpose is all that is required to RECEIVE the means and USE them.

T 18 F 5. It is no dream to love your brother as yourself.[630] Nor is your holy relationship a dream. All that remains of dreams within it is that it is still a SPECIAL relationship. Yet it is VERY useful to the Holy Spirit, Who has a special FUNCTION here. It will become the HAPPY dream through which He can spread joy to thousands on thousands who believe that love is **T(675) - 572 -**[631] fear, NOT happiness. Let Him fulfill the function that He GAVE to your relationship by ACCEPTING it FOR you. And NOTHING will be wanting that would make of it what HE would have it be.

T 18 F 6. When you feel the holiness of your relationship is threatened by ANYTHING, stop instantly and offer the Holy Spirit your willingness, IN SPITE of fear, to let Him exchange this instant for the holy one which YOU would rather have. He will NEVER fail in this. But forget not that your relationship IS ONE, and so it MUST be that whatever threatens the peace of one is an equal threat to the other. The power of joining, AND ITS BLESSING, lies in the fact that it is now impossible for either of you to experience fear alone, or to attempt to DEAL with it alone. Never believe that this is necessary, or even possible.

T 18 F 7. But, just as THIS is impossible, so is it equally impossible that the holy instant come to either of you WITHOUT the other. And it WILL come to both at the REQUEST of either. Whichever is saner at the time when threat is perceived, should remember how deep is his indebtedness to the other, and how much gratitude is due him. AND BE GLAD that he can pay his debt, by bringing happiness to both. Let him remember this, and say:

"I desire this holy instant for myself

That I may SHARE it with my brother, whom I love.

It is not possible that I can have it WITHOUT him, nor he without me.

Yet it is WHOLLY possible for us to SHARE it NOW.

And so I choose THIS instant as the one to offer to the Holy Spirit, that His blessing may descend on us, and keep us BOTH in peace." **T(676) -503**[632]

T 18 G. Dreams and the Body (*Notes* 1485 10:45)

T 18 G 1. THERE IS NOTHING OUTSIDE YOU. That is what you must ultimately learn, for it is in that realization that the Kingdom of Heaven is restored to you. For God created only this, and He did not depart from it, nor leave it separate from Himself. The Kingdom of Heaven is the dwelling place of the Son of God, who left not his Father, and dwells not apart from Him. Heaven is not a place nor a condition. It is merely an awareness of perfect Oneness, and the knowledge that there is nothing else. Nothing OUTSIDE THIS Oneness, and NOTHING ELSE within.

T 18 G 2. What could God give, but knowledge of Himself? What else IS there to give? The belief that you could give AND GET something, else, something OUTSIDE yourself, has cost you the awareness of Heaven, and the loss of knowledge of your identity. And you have done a stranger thing than you yet realize. You have displaced your guilt to your bodies, FROM YOUR MINDS. Yet a body CANNOT be guilty, for it can do nothing of itself. You who think you hate your bodies, deceive yourselves. YOU HATE YOUR MINDS, for guilt has entered into them, and they would remain separate, which they CANNOT DO.

T 18 G 3. Minds ARE joined; bodies are not. Only by assigning to the mind the properties OF THE BODY, does separation SEEM to be possible. And it is MIND that seems to be fragmented and private and ALONE. Its guilt, which KEEPS it separate, is projected to the body, which suffers and dies, BECAUSE IT IS ATTACKED to hold the separation in the mind, and let it NOT KNOW its unity. Mind cannot attack, but it CAN make fantasies, and direct the body to act them out. But it is never what the BODY does that seems to satisfy. Unless the mind BELIEVES the body is ACTUALLY acting out ITS fantasies, it **T(677) -504** will attack the body by INCREASING the projection of its guilt upon it.

T 18 G 4. In this, the mind is CLEARLY delusional. It cannot attack, but maintains it CAN, and USES what it does to hurt the body, to PROVE it can. The mind can not attack, but it CAN deceive itself. And this is ALL it does, when it believes it has attacked the body, It CAN project its guilt, but it will NOT lose it through projection. And though it clearly can MISPERCEIVE the function of the body, it CANNOT change its function from what the Holy Spirit ESTABLISHES it to be. The body was NOT made by love. But love does not condemn it, and can use it lovingly, respecting what the Son of God has made, and using it to SAVE him from illusions.

T 18 G 5. Would you not have the instruments of separation RE-INTERPRETED as means for salvation, and USED for purposes of love? Would you not welcome AND SUPPORT the shift from fantasies of vengeance to RELEASE from them? Your PERCEPTION of the body can clearly be sick, but project this not upon the body. For your wish to make destructive what CANNOT destroy, can have no REAL effect at all. And what God created is only what He would have it be, being His Will.

T 18 G 6. You cannot make His Will destructive. You can make FANTASIES, in which your will CONFLICTS with His, but that is all. It is insane to use the body as the scapegoat for guilt; DIRECTING its attack, and BLAMING it for what you wished it to do. IT IS IMPOSSIBLE TO ACT OUT FANTASIES. For it is still the FANTASIES you want, and they have nothing to do with what the body does. **T(678) -505** IT does not dream of them, and they but make IT a liability, where it COULD be an asset. For fantasies have made your body your "enemy," weak, vulnerable, and treacherous, "worthy" of the hate which you invest in it.

T 18 G 7. How has this served you? You have IDENTIFIED with this thing you hate, the instrument of vengeance, and the perceived source of your guilt. YOU have done this to a thing that has no meaning, proclaiming it to be the dwelling place of the Son of God, and turning it AGAINST him. This is the host of God that YOU have made. And neither God nor His most holy Son can enter an abode which harbors hate, and where you have sown the seeds of vengeance, violence, and death.

T 18 G 8. This thing you made to serve your guilt, stands between you and other minds. The minds ARE joined, but you do not IDENTIFY with them. You SEE yourself as locked in a separate prison, remote and unreachable, incapable of reaching out as being reached. You HATE the prison that you made, and would destroy it. Yet you would NOT escape from it, leaving it unharmed, WITHOUT your guilt upon it. But only thus CAN you escape. The home of vengeance is not yours; The place you set aside to house your hatred is NOT a prison, but an ILLUSION OF YOURSELF.

T 18 G 9. The body is a limit imposed on the universal communication which is an eternal property of mind. But the communication is INTERNAL. Mind reaches to ITSELF. It is NOT made up of different PARTS, which reach each other. It does not go OUT. Within **T(679) -506** ITSELF, it HAS no limits, and there is nothing OUT-

---

[630] Leviticus 19:18 You shall not take vengeance, nor bear any grudge against the children of your people, but you shall love your neighbor as yourself: I am the LORD.
Matthew 22:39 And the second is like it: "You shall love your neighbor as yourself."
Mark 12:29-31 Jesus answered, "The first is, Hear, O Israel; The Lord our God, the Lord is one: and thou shalt love the Lord thy God with all thy heart, and with all thy soul, and with all thy mind, and with all thy strength. The second is this, Thou shalt love thy neighbour as thyself. There is none other commandment greater than these."
[631] These two paragraphs, 18 F 6 and 18 F 7, are not present in the *Notes*.
[632] Jan. [Feb.?] 12, 1967

SIDE it. It encompasses EVERYTHING. It encompasses you ENTIRELY; you within it, and it within you. There IS nothing else, anywhere or ever. The body is OUTSIDE you, and SEEMS to surround you, shutting you off from others, and keeping you APART from them, and them from you.

T 18 G 10. IT IS NOT THERE. There IS no barrier between God and His Son, nor can His Son be separated from himself, except in illusion. This is NOT his reality, though he believes it IS. Yet this could only BE, IF God were wrong. God would have had to create DIFFERENTLY, and to have separated HIMSELF from His Son, to make this possible. He would have had to create DIFFERENT things, and to establish different ORDERS of reality, only SOME of which were love. Yet love must be forever like itself, changeless forever, and forever WITHOUT alternative. And so it is.

T 18 G 11. YOU cannot put a barrier around yourself, because God placed none between HIMSELF and you. Your hand can stretch out, and reach to Heaven. You whose hands are joined have begun to reach BEYOND the body, but NOT outside yourselves. To reach your shared identity TOGETHER. Could this be OUTSIDE you? Where God is not? Is He a body, and did He create you as He is not, and where He CANNOT be? You are surrounded ONLY by Him. What limits CAN there be on you, whom HE encompasses?

T 18 G 12. Everyone has experienced what he would call a sense of being transported BEYOND himself. This feeling of liberation FAR exceeds the DREAM of freedom sometimes experienced in special relationships. It is a sense of actual ESCAPE from limitations. **T(680) -507** If you will consider what this "transportation" REALLY entails, you will realize that it is a sudden UNawareness of the body, and a joining of your self and SOMETHING ELSE, in which your mind ENLARGES to encompass it. It becomes PART of you, as you UNITE with it. And BOTH become whole, as NEITHER is perceived as separate.

T 18 G 13. What REALLY happens is that you have GIVEN UP the illusion of a LIMITED awareness, and lost your fear of union. The love that INSTANTLY replaces it EXTENDS to what has freed you, and UNITES you with it. And, while this lasts, you are NOT uncertain of your identity, and would not limit it. You have escaped from fear to peace, asking no questions of reality, but merely ACCEPTING it. You have accepted this INSTEAD of the body, and have LET yourself be ONE with something beyond it, simply by NOT letting your mind be limited BY it.

T 18 G 14. This can occur REGARDLESS of the physical distance that SEEMS to be between you and what you join; of your respective positions in space; and of your differences in size and seeming quality. Time is not relevant; it can occur with something past, present, or anticipated. The "something" can be ANYTHING and ANYWHERE; a sound, a sight, a thought, a memory, even a more GENERAL idea, WITHOUT specific reference. But, in every case, you join it without RESERVATION, because you love it, and would BE with it. And so you rush to meet it, letting your limits melt away, suspending ALL the "laws" your body obeys, and gently SETTING THEM ASIDE. **T(681) -508**

T 18 G 15. There is no violence at all in this escape. The body is NOT attacked, but merely PROPERLY PERCEIVED. It does not limit you, merely because YOU would not have it so. You are not really "lifted out" of it; it cannot CONTAIN you. You go where you would be; GAINING, NOT losing, a sense of self. In these instants of release from physical restrictions, you experience much of what happens in the holy instant; the lifting of the barriers of time and space, the sudden experience of peace and joy, and, above all, the LACK of awareness of the body, and of the questioning WHETHER OR NOT ALL THIS IS POSSIBLE. It IS possible, BECAUSE YOU WANT IT.

T 18 G 16. The sudden EXPANSION of the self that takes place with your DESIRE for it, is the irresistible appeal the holy instant holds. It calls to you to be yourself, within its safe embrace. There are the laws of limit lifted FOR you, to welcome you to openness of mind, and freedom. Come to this place of refuge, where you can be yourself in peace. NOT through destruction, NOT through a "breaking out," but merely by a quiet "melting in." For peace will join you there, simply because YOU have been willing to let go the limits YOU have placed on love, and JOINED it where it is, and where it led you, in answer to its gentle call to be at peace.[633] **T(682)T(631a)** [634]

T 18 H. "I Need Do Nothing" (*Notes* 1689 11:64)

T 18 H 1. You still have too much faith in the body as a source of strength. What plans do you make that do NOT involve its comfort or protection or enjoyment in some way? This makes it an end and not a means in your interpretation, and this ALWAYS means YOU STILL FIND SIN ATTRACTIVE. No-one accepts Atonement for himself who still accepts sin as his goal. You have thus not met your one responsibility. Atonement is not welcomed by those who PREFER pain and destruction.

T 18 H 2. You have made much progress, and are really trying to make still more, but there is one thing you have never done; not for one instant have you utterly forgotten the body. It has faded at times from your sight, but it has not yet COMPLETELY DISAPPEARED. You are not asked to let this happen for more than an instant, but it is in this instant that the miracle of Atonement happens. Afterwards, you will see the body again, but never quite the same. And every instant that you spend WITHOUT awareness of it gives you a different view of it, when you return.

T 18 H 3. At no SINGLE instant does the body exist at all. It is always remembered or anticipated, but NEVER experienced just now. Only its past and future make it seem real. Time controls it entirely. For sin is never present. In any SINGLE instant, the attraction of guilt would be experienced as pain and nothing else, and would be avoided. IT HAS NO ATTRACTION NOW. Its whole attraction is imaginary, and therefore MUST be thought of from the past, or in the future.

T 18 H 4. It is impossible to accept the holy instant WITHOUT RESERVATION unless, JUST FOR AN INSTANT, you are willing to see no past or future. You cannot PREPARE for it without placing it in the FUTURE. Release is given you the INSTANT you desire it. Many have spent a lifetime in preparation, and have, indeed, achieved their instants of success. This course does not attempt to teach more than they learned in time. But it does aim at SAVING time. **T(683) T(631b)**

T 18 H 5. You are attempting to follow a very long road to the goal you have accepted. It is extremely difficult to reach Atonement by fighting against sin. Enormous effort is expended in the attempt to make holy what is hated and despised. Nor is a lifetime of contemplation, and long periods of meditation aimed at DETACHMENT from the body necessary. All such attempts will ultimately succeed, because of their purpose. But the means are tedious and very time consuming, for all of them LOOK TO THE FUTURE for release from a state of present unworthiness and inadequacy.

T 18 H 6. Your way will be different. NOT in purpose, but in means. A HOLY RELATIONSHIP IS A MEANS OF SAVING TIME. One instant spent TOGETHER restores the universe to BOTH of you. You ARE prepared. Now you need but remember YOU NEED DO NOTHING. It would be FAR more profitable now merely to concentrate on this, than to consider what you SHOULD do.

---

[633] The next 3 pages from the Special Messages are out of chronological and numerical order in *HLC*. It is the *HLC* sequence and Chapter/section headings and order being used here.
[634] SPECIAL MESSAGE May 31, 1967

T 18 H 7. When peace comes at last to those who wrestle with temptation, and fight against giving in to sin; when the light comes at last into the mind given to contemplation, or when the goal is finally achieved by anyone, it ALWAYS comes with just ONE happy realization, -- "I need do nothing." Here is the ultimate release that everyone will one day find in his own way, at his own time. We do not need this time. Time has been SAVED for you, because you are together. This is the special means this course is using, to save you time.

T 18 H 8. You are not making use of the course if you insist on using means that have served others well, neglecting what was made for YOU. Save time for me by only this one preparation, and practice doing NOTHING ELSE. "I need do nothing" is a statement of allegiance, a truly undivided loyalty. Believe it for just one instant, and you will accomplish more than is given to a century of contemplation, or of struggle against temptation. **T(684)T(631c)**

T 18 H 9. To DO anything involves the body. And, if you recognize you NEED do nothing, you HAVE withdrawn the body's value from your mind. Here is the quick and open door through which you slip past centuries of effort, and ESCAPE from time. This is the way in which sin loses ALL attraction RIGHT NOW. For here is time denied, and past and future gone. Who need do nothing has no need for time. To do nothing is to rest, and make a place within you where the activity of the body ceases to demand attention. Into this place the Holy Spirit comes, and there abides.

T 18 H 10. He will remain when you forget, and the body's activities return to occupy your conscious mind. But there will always be this place of rest, to which you can return. And you will be more aware of the quiet center of the storm, than all its raging activity. This quiet center, IN WHICH YOU DO NOTHING, will remain with you, giving you rest in the midst of every busy doing on which you are sent. For, FROM this center, will you be directed how to use the body sinlessly. It is this center, from which the body is ABSENT, that will keep it so, in your awareness of it. **T(685) 509.**[635]

T 18 I. The Purpose of the Body (*Notes* 1495 10:55)

T 18 I 1. It is only the awareness of the body that makes love seem limited. For the body IS a limit on love. The belief in limited love was its origin, and it was MADE to limit the UNlimited. Think not that this is merely allegorical; for it was made to limit YOU. Can you who see yourselves WITHIN a body, know yourself AS AN IDEA? Everything you recognize you identify by EXTERNALS, something OUTSIDE itself. You cannot even think of GOD without a body, or some form you think you recognize. The body cannot KNOW. And while you limit your awareness to its tiny senses, you will not see the grandeur that surrounds you.

T 18 I 2. God cannot come into a body, nor can you join Him there. Limits on love will ALWAYS seem to shut Him out, and to keep you APART from Him. The body is a tiny fence around a little part of a glorious and completely limitless idea. It draws a circle, infinitely small, around a very little segment of Heaven, splintered from the whole, proclaiming that, within it, is YOUR Kingdom, where God can enter not. Within this kingdom the ego rules, and cruelly. And, to defend this little speck of dust, it bids you fight against the universe.

T 18 I 3. This fragment of your mind is such a tiny part of it that, could you but appreciate the whole, you would see instantly that it is like the smallest sunbeam is to the sun. Or like the faintest ripple on the surface of the ocean. In its amazing arrogance, this tiny sunbeam has decided it IS the sun; this almost imperceptible ripple hails itself as the ocean. Think how alone and frightened is this little thought, this infinitesimal illusion, holding itself apart, against the universe. The sun becomes the sunbeam's "enemy," which would devour it.

And the ocean terrifies the little ripple, and "wants" to swallow it. **T(686) -510.**

T 18 I 4. Yet neither sun nor ocean is even aware of all this strange and meaningless activity. They merely continue, unaware that they are feared and hated by a tiny segment of themselves. Even that segment is not LOST to them, for it could not survive APART from them And what IT thinks it is in no way changes its total dependence on them FOR ITS BEING. Its whole existence still remains IN THEM. Without the sun, the sunbeam WOULD be gone; the ripple WITHOUT the ocean IS inconceivable.

T 18 I 5. Such is the strange position in which those in a world inhabited by bodies seem to be. Each body seems to house a SEPARATE mind, a DISCONNECTED thought, living alone and in no way joined to the Thought by which it was created. Each tiny fragment seems to be self-contained, needing each other for SOME things, but by no means TOTALLY dependent on their One Creator for EVERYTHING. And needing the whole to give them ANY meaning, for by themselves, they DO mean nothing. Nor HAVE they any life apart, and by themselves.

T 18 I 6. Yet, like the sun and ocean, your Self continues, unmindful that this tiny part regards ITSELF as you. It is not missing; it could not EXIST if it were separate, nor would the whole BE whole without it. It is not a separate kingdom, ruled by an IDEA of separation from the rest. Nor does a fence surround it, preventing it from JOINING with the rest, and keeping it apart from its Creator. This little aspect is NO DIFFERENT from the whole, being continuous with it, and at one with it. It leads no separate life, because its life IS in the Oneness in which its being was created.

T 18 I 7. Do not accept this little, fenced-off aspect as your Self. The sun and ocean are as nothing, beside what YOU are. The sunbeam sparkles only in the sunlight, and the ripple dances as it rests upon the ocean. Yet in neither sun nor ocean is the power that rests in you. Would you remain WITHIN your tiny kingdom, a sorry king, a bitter ruler of all he surveys, who **T(687) -511** looks on nothing, but who would still die to DEFEND it? This little self is NOT your kingdom. Arched high above it, and surrounding it, with love, is the glorious whole, which offers all its happiness and deep content to EVERY part.

T 18 I 8. The little aspect that you think you set apart is no exception. Love knows no bodies, and reaches to everything created like itself. Its total lack of limit IS its meaning. It is COMPLETELY impartial in its giving, encompassing ONLY to preserve and KEEP COMPLETE what it would give. In your tiny kingdom you have so little! Should it not, then, be there that you would call on love to enter? Look at the desert, dry and unproductive, scorched and joyless, that makes up your little kingdom. And realize the life and joy that love would bring to it, from where IT comes, and where it would return WITH you.

T 18 I 9. The Thought of God surrounds your little kingdom, waiting at the barrier you built, to come in and shine upon the barren ground. See how life springs up everywhere! The desert becomes a garden, green and deep and quiet, offering rest to those who lost their way, and wander in the dust.[636] Give them a place of refuge, prepared by love for them, where once a desert was. And every one you welcome will bring love with him, from Heaven for you. They enter one by one into this holy place, but they will not depart as they had come, alone.

T 18 I 10. The love they BROUGHT with them will STAY with them, as it will stay with YOU. And, under its beneficence, your

---
[635] Feb. 16, 1967

[636] **Isaiah 51:3** For the LORD will comfort Zion,
He will comfort all her waste places;
He will make her wilderness like Eden,
And her desert like the garden of the LORD;
Joy and gladness will be found in it,
Thanksgiving and the voice of melody.

little garden will expand, and reach out to everyone who thirsts for living water, but has grown too weary to go on alone.[637] Go out and FIND them, for they bring your Self with them. And lead them gently to your quiet garden, and receive their blessing there. So will it grow, and stretch across the desert, leaving no lonely little kingdoms locked away from love, and leaving YOU outside. T(688) -512 And you will RECOGNIZE yourself, and see your little garden gently transformed into the Kingdom of Heaven, with all the love of its Creator shining upon it.

T 18 I 11. The holy instant is your invitation to love, to enter into your bleak and joyless kingdom, and transform it into a garden of peace and welcome. Love's answer is inevitable. It will come, because you came WITHOUT the body, and interposed no barriers which would INTERFERE with its glad coming. In the holy instant, you ask of love only what it offers everyone, neither less nor more. Asking for EVERYTHING, you will RECEIVE it. And your shining Self will lift the tiny aspect that you tried to hide from Heaven, straight into Heaven. No part of love calls on the whole in vain. No son of God remains OUTSIDE His Fatherhood.

T 18 I 12. Be sure of this; love has entered your special relationship, and entered fully, at your weak request. You do NOT recognize that love has come, because you have not yet let go of ALL the barriers you hold against EACH OTHER. And you will NOT be able to give love welcome separately. You could no more know God alone, than He knows YOU without your brother. But, TOGETHER, you could no more be UNAWARE of love, than love could know you not, or fail to recognize ITSELF in you.

T 18 I 13. You have reached the end of an ancient journey not realizing yet that it is over. You are still worn and tired, and the desert's dust still seems to cloud your eyes, and keep you sightless. Yet He Whom you welcomed has come to you, and would welcome YOU. He has waited long to give you this. Receive it now of Him, for He would have you KNOW Him. Only a little wall of dust still stands between you. Blow on it lightly and with happy laughter, and it will fall away. And walk into the garden love has prepared for BOTH of you. T(689) -513

T 18 J. The Delusional Thought System (N* 1503 10:63)

T 18 J 1. You have been told to bring the darkness to the light, and guilt to holiness. And you have also been told that error must be corrected at its source. Therefore, it is the tiny part of your self, the little thought that seems split off and separate, that the Holy Spirit needs. The rest is fully in God's keeping, and needs no guide. But this wild and delusional thought needs help, because, in its delusions, it thinks it is the Son of God, whole and omnipotent, sole ruler of the kingdom it set apart, to tyrannize by madness into obedience and slavery.

T 18 J 2. This is the LITTLE part of you, you think you stole from Heaven. Give it back to Heaven. Heaven has not lost it, but YOU have lost sight of Heaven. Let the Holy Spirit remove it from the withered kingdom in which you set it up, surrounded by darkness, guarded by attack, and reinforced by hate. Within its barricades is still a tiny segment of the Son of God, complete and holy, serene and unaware of what you think surrounds it. Be you not separate, for the One Who DOES surround it has brought union to you, returning your little offering of darkness to the Eternal Light. T(690) -514[638]

T 18 J 3. How[639] is this done? It is extremely simple, being based on what this little kingdom really IS. The barren sands, the darkness, and the lifelessness are seen only through the body's eyes. ITS vision IS distorted, and the messages IT transmits to you, who MADE it to limit your awareness, ARE little and limited, so fragmented that they are meaningless. From the world of bodies, MADE by insanity, insane messages seem to be returned to the mind which made it. And these messages bear witness to this world, pronouncing it as true. For YOU sent forth these messengers, to bring this BACK to you.[640]

T 18 J 4. Everything these messages relay to you is quite external. There are NO messages that speak of what lies underneath, for it is NOT the body that could speak of this. Its eyes perceive it not, its senses remain quite UNAWARE of it, its tongue can not relay ITS messages. Yet God can bring you there, if you are willing to follow the Holy Spirit through seeming terror, trusting Him not to abandon you, and LEAVE you there. For it is not HIS purpose to frighten you, but only YOURS. YOU are severely tempted to abandon HIM at the outside ring of fear. But HE would lead you safely through, and FAR beyond.

T 18 J 5. The circle of fear lies just below the level the body sees, and SEEMS to be the whole foundation on which the world is based. Here are all the illusions, all the twisted thoughts, all the insane attacks, the fury, vengeance, and betrayal that were made to keep the guilt in place, so that the world could RISE from it, and keep IT hidden. Its SHADOW rises to the surface, enough to hold its most external manifestations[641] in darkness, and to bring despair and loneliness to it, and keep it joyless. But its INTENSITY is veiled by its heavy coverings, and kept APART from what was made to keep it hidden. T(691) -515

T 18 J 6. The body cannot see this, for the body AROSE from this for its protection, which must ALWAYS depend on keeping it NOT seen. The body's eyes will NEVER look on it. Yet they will SEE what it dictates. The body will remain guilt's messenger, and will act as it directs, as long as YOU believe that guilt is real. For the REALITY of guilt is the illusion which seems to make it heavy and opaque, impenetrable, and a REAL foundation for the ego's thought system. Its thinness and transparency are not apparent, until you see the light BEHIND it. And then you see it as a fragile veil, before the light.

T 18 J 7. This heavy-seeming barrier, this artificial floor that looks like rock, is like a bank of low, dark clouds that seem to be a solid wall before the sun. Its impenetrable appearance is WHOLLY an illusion. It gives way softly to the mountain tops that rise above it, and has no power at all to hold back anyone willing to climb above it, to see the sun. It is not strong enough to stop a button's fall, nor hold a feather. Nothing can rest upon it, for it is but an ILLUSION of a foundation. Try but to touch it, and it disappears; attempt to grasp it, and your hands hold nothing.

T 18 J 8. Yet in this cloud bank it is easy to see a whole world rising. A solid mountain range, a lake, a city, all arise in your imagination, and FROM the clouds, the messengers of your perception return to you, assuring you that it is all THERE. Figures stand out and move about, actions seem real, and forms appear and shift from loveliness to the grotesque. And back and forth they go, as long as you would play the game of children's "make believe." Yet, how-

---

[637] **Jeremiah 2:13** For my people have committed two evils; they have forsaken me the fountain of living waters, and hewed them out cisterns, broken cisterns, that can hold no water.
John 4:10 Jesus answered and said to her, "If you knew the gift of God, and who it is who says to you, 'Give Me a drink,' you would have asked Him, and He would have given you living water."
John 7:38 "He who believes in Me, as the Scripture has said, out of his heart will flow rivers of living water."
[638] Feb. 20, 1967

[639] Feb. 20, 1967
[640] **John 1:7-8** This man came for a witness, to bear witness of the Light, that all through him might believe. He was not that Light, but was sent to bear witness of that Light.
John 18:37 Pilate therefore said to Him, "Are You a king then?" Jesus answered, "You say rightly that I am a king. For this cause I was born, and for this cause I have come into the world, that I should bear witness to the truth. Everyone who is of the truth hears My voice."
[641] The *Urtext* manuscript has this singular, but the *Notes* and *HLC* have it pluralized which seems more correct.

ever long you play it, and regardless of how much imagination you bring to it, you do NOT confuse it with the world below, nor seek to make it real. **T(692) -516**

T 18 J 9. So should it be with the dark clouds of guilt, no more impenetrable and no more substantial. You will NOT bruise yourself against them, in traveling through. Let your Guide TEACH you their UNsubstantial nature, as He leads you PAST them. For BENEATH them is a world of light, whereon they cast no shadows. Their shadows lie upon the world BEYOND them, still FURTHER from the light. But from them TO the light, their shadows CANNOT fall. This world of light, this circle of brightness, is the real world, where guilt meets with forgiveness. Here, the world OUTSIDE is seen anew, WITHOUT the shadow of guilt upon it.

T 18 J 10. Here are YOU forgiven, for here you have forgiven everyone. Here is the new perception, where everything is bright and shining with innocence, washed in the waters of forgiveness, and cleansed of every evil thought you laid upon it. Here there is no attack upon the Son of God, and YOU are welcome. Here is your innocence, waiting to clothe you and protect you, and make you ready for the final step in the journey inward. Here are the dark and heavy garments of guilt laid by, and gently replaced by purity and joy.

T 18 J 11. Yet even forgiveness is not the end. Forgiveness DOES make lovely, but it does NOT create. It IS the source of healing, but it is the MESSENGER of love, and not its Source. Here you are led, that God Himself can take the final step unhindered. For here does nothing INTERFERE with love, letting it be Itself. A step BEYOND this holy place of forgiveness. A step still further inward, but one you CANNOT take, transports you to something COMPLETELY different. Here is the Source of light; nothing perceived, forgiven, nor transformed. But merely KNOWN.

T 18 K. The Passing of the Dream (*Notes* 1510 10:70)

T 18 K 1. This course will LEAD to knowledge, but knowledge itself is still beyond the scope of our curriculum. Nor is there any need for us to try to speak of what must forever lie beyond words. We need remember only that **T(693) -517** whoever attains the real world, beyond which learning cannot go, WILL go beyond it, but in a different way. Where learning ends, there God begins, for learning ends before Him Who is complete where He begins, and where there IS no end.

T 18 K 2. It is not for us to dwell on what cannot BE attained. There is too much to learn. The readiness for knowledge still must be attained. Love is not learned. Its meaning lies in Itself. And learning ends when you have recognized all it is NOT. That is the INTERFERENCE; that is what needs to be undone. Love is not learned, because there never WAS a time in which you knew it not. Learning is useless in the Presence of your Creator, Whose ACKNOWLEDGMENT of you, AND YOURS OF HIM, so FAR transcends ALL learning, that EVERYTHING you learned is meaningless, replaced forever by the knowledge of love and its One meaning.

T 18 K 3. Your relationship has been uprooted from the world of shadows, and its unholy purpose has been safely brought through the barriers of guilt, washed with forgiveness, and set shining and firmly rooted in the world of light. From there it calls to you to follow the course it took, lifted high above the darkness, and gently placed before the gates of Heaven. The holy instant in which you were united, is but a messenger of love, sent from BEYOND forgiveness to REMIND you of all that lies beyond it. Yet it is THROUGH forgiveness that it will BE remembered.

T 18 K 4. And when the memory of God has come to you, in the holy place of forgiveness, you will remember nothing else. And memory will be as useless as learning, for your ONLY purpose will be creating. Yet this you cannot know, until every perception has been cleansed and purified, and finally removed forever. Forgiveness removes ONLY the UNtrue, lifting the shadows from the world, and carrying it, safe and sure within its gentleness, to the bright world of new and clean perception. There is YOUR purpose now. And it is there that peace awaits you. **T(694) -518**[642]

---

[642] Feb. 23, 1967

CHAPTER 19 – BEYOND THE BODY

T 19 A. Introduction (*Notes* 1513 10:73)

T 19 A 1. We said before that, when a situation has been dedicated WHOLLY to truth, peace is inevitable. Its attainment is the criterion by which the wholeness of the dedication can be safely assumed. But we also said that peace without faith will NEVER be attained, for what is WHOLLY dedicated to truth as its ONLY goal is BROUGHT to truth by faith. This faith encompasses EVERYONE involved, for only thus the situation is perceived as meaningful and as a WHOLE. And everyone must BE involved in it, or else YOUR faith is limited, and your dedication incomplete.

T 19 A 2. Every situation, properly perceived, becomes an opportunity to heal the Son of God. And he is healed BECAUSE you offered faith to him, giving him to the Holy Spirit and RELEASING him from every demand your ego would make of him. Thus do you SEE HIM FREE, and in this vision does the Holy Spirit SHARE. And since He SHARES it He HAS given it, and so He healed THROUGH YOU. It is this JOINING Him in a UNITED purpose that MAKES this purpose real, because YOU make it WHOLE. And this IS healing. The BODY is healed BECAUSE YOU CAME WITHOUT IT, and joined the Mind in which all healing rests.

T 19 B. Healing and the Mind (*Notes* 1514 10:74)

T 19 B 1. The body cannot heal, because it cannot MAKE ITSELF SICK. It NEEDS no healing. Its health or sickness depends ENTIRELY on how the mind perceives it, and the purpose which the mind would use it FOR. And it IS obvious that a segment of the mind CAN see itself as SEPARATED from the Universal Purpose. When this occurs, the body becomes its weapon, used AGAINST this Purpose to DEMONSTRATE the "fact" that separation HAS occurred. The body thus becomes the instrument of illusion, acting accordingly, seeing what is not there, HEARING what truth has never said, and BEHAVING INSANELY, being imprisoned BY insanity. **T(695) -519**

T 19 B 2. Do not overlook our earlier statement that faithlessness leads straight to illusions. For faithlessness IS the perception of a brother AS a body, and the body CANNOT be used for purposes of union. If, then, you SEE him as a body, YOU have established a condition in which UNITING with him becomes impossible. Your faithlessness to him has separated you FROM him, and kept you BOTH apart from being healed. Your faithlessness has thus OPPOSED the Holy Spirit's purpose, and brought illusions, CENTERED ON THE BODY, to stand BETWEEN you. And the body WILL seem to be sick, for you have made of it an "enemy" of healing, and the OPPOSITE of truth.

T 19 B 3. It CANNOT be difficult to realize that faith MUST be the opposite of faithLESSness. But the difference in how they operate is less apparent, though it follows directly from the fundamental difference in what they ARE. Faithlessness would always LIMIT AND ATTACK; faith would remove ALL limitations, and MAKE WHOLE. Faithlessness would destroy and SEPARATE; faith would unite and HEAL. Faithlessness would interpose illusions between the Son of God and his Creator; faith would remove ALL obstacles that SEEM to rise between them. Faithlessness is wholly dedicated to illusions; faith wholly to truth.

T 19 B 4. PARTIAL DEDICATION IS IMPOSSIBLE. Truth is the ABSENCE of illusion; illusion the ABSENCE of truth. Both cannot BE together, nor perceived in the SAME PLACE. To dedicate yourself to BOTH, is to set up a goal forever impossible to attain. For PART of it is sought through the body, THOUGHT OF as a means for seeking out reality through ATTACK. While the OTHER part would HEAL, and therefore calls upon the mind, and NOT the body. The INEVITABLE compromise is the belief that the BODY must be healed, and NOT the mind. For this divided goal has given both an EQUAL reality, and can SEEM to be possible only if the mind is limited TO the body, and divided into little parts with SEEMING wholeness, but WITHOUT CONNECTION. **T(696) -520**

T 19 B 5. This will NOT harm the body. But it WILL keep the delusional thought-system IN THE MIND. Here, then, is healing needed. And it is here that healing IS. For God gave healing not APART from sickness, nor established remedy where sickness CANNOT be. They ARE together, and when they are SEEN together, ALL attempts to KEEP both truth AND illusion in the mind, where both MUST be, are recognized as DEDICATION TO ILLUSION. And GIVEN UP when BROUGHT to truth, and seen as totally UNRECONCILABLE with truth, in ANY aspect, or in any WAY.

T 19 B 6. Truth and illusion HAVE no connection. This will remain FOREVER true, however much YOU seek to connect them. But ILLUSIONS are ALWAYS connected, AS IS TRUTH. Each is united, a COMPLETE thought-system, but totally DISconnected to EACH OTHER. Where there is NO overlap, there separation MUST be complete. And to perceive THIS is to recognize where separation IS, and WHERE IT MUST BE HEALED. The RESULT of an idea is NEVER separate from its source. The IDEA of separation PRODUCED the body, and remains connected TO it, MAKING it sick because of its identification WITH it.

T 19 B 7. You THINK you are PROTECTING the body by HIDING this connection. For this concealment SEEMS to keep your identification safe from the "attack" of truth. If you but understood how much this strange concealment has hurt your mind, and how confused your own identification has become to you, BECAUSE of it! You do NOT see how great the devastation wrought by your faithlessness. For faithlessness IS an attack, which SEEMS to be justified BY ITS RESULTS. For, by WITHHOLDING faith, you SEE what IS unworthy of it, and CANNOT look beyond the barrier to what is joined with YOU.

T 19 B 8. To have faith is to heal. It is the sign that you HAVE accepted the Atonement for yourself, and would therefore share it. By faith, you OFFER the gift of freedom from the past, which you have RECEIVED. You do NOT use ANYTHING your brother has done before to condemn him NOW. You freely choose to OVERLOOK **T(697) -521** his errors, looking PAST all barriers between your self and his, and seeing them AS ONE. And in that One you see your faith is FULLY justified. There IS no justification for faithlessness. But faith is ALWAYS justified.[643]

T 19 B 9. Faith is the OPPOSITE of fear, as much a part of love, as fear is of attack. Faith is the acknowledgment of UNION. It is the gracious acknowledgment of everyone as a Son of your most loving Father, loved by Him like[644] you, and therefore loved by you as yourself. It is HIS Love that joins you, and FOR His Love, you would keep no-one separate from YOURS. Each one APPEARS just as he is perceived in the holy instant, united in YOUR purpose to be RELEASED from guilt. You saw the Christ in him, and he was healed, because you looked on what makes faith FOREVER justified in EVERYONE.

---

[643] **Romans 3:28** Therefore we conclude that a man is justified by faith apart from the deeds of the law.
Romans 5:1 Therefore, having been justified by faith, we have peace with God through our Lord Jesus Christ,
[644] Very oddly, the *Urtext* manuscript has "like" crossed out and "as" handwritten in. All other versions, including the *Notes*, have it as "like" so we leave it as originally typed, as did the Scribes themselves when they copied this to the *HLC*.

T 19 B 10. Faith is the gift of God, through Him Whom God has GIVEN you.[645] Faithlessness looks upon the Son of God, and judges him UNWORTHY of forgiveness. But, through the eyes of faith, the Son of God is seen ALREADY forgiven, free of all the guilt he laid upon himself. Faith sees him only NOW, because it looks not to the past to judge him, but would see in him ONLY what it would see in YOU. It sees NOT through the body's eyes, nor looks to bodies for its justification. It is the messenger of the NEW perception, sent forth to gather witnesses unto its coming, and to return their messages to YOU.

T 19 B 11. Faith is as easily exchanged for knowledge as is the real world. For faith ARISES from the Holy Spirit's perception, and is the sign you share it WITH Him. Faith is a gift you offer to the Son of God THROUGH Him, and WHOLLY acceptable to his Father as to him. And therefore offered YOU. Your holy relationship, with its NEW purpose, offers you faith to give unto EACH OTHER. Your faithlessness had driven you APART, and so you did not RECOGNIZE salvation in each other. But faith UNITES you in the holiness you see, NOT through the body's eyes, but in the sight of Him Who **T(698) -522** joined you, and in Whom YOU are united.

T 19 B 12. Grace is not given to a BODY, but to a MIND. And the mind that RECEIVES it, looks INSTANTLY beyond the body, and sees the holy place where IT was healed. THERE is the altar where the grace was given, in which IT stands. Do you, then, offer grace and BLESSING to each other, for you stand at the SAME altar, where grace was laid for BOTH of you. And be you healed by grace TOGETHER, that YOU may heal through faith.

T 19 B 13. In the holy instant, you stand before the altar God has raised unto Himself and BOTH of you. Lay faithlessness aside, and come to it TOGETHER. There will you see the miracle of your relationship, as it was MADE AGAIN through faith. And there it is that you will realize that there is NOTHING faith can NOT forgive. NO error INTERFERES with its calm sight, which brings the miracle of healing with equal ease to ALL of them. For what the messengers of love are sent to do THEY DO. Returning the glad tidings that it was done, to you who stand before the altar from which they were sent forth, TOGETHER.[646]

T 19 B 14. As faithlessness will keep your little kingdoms barren and separate, so will faith help the Holy Spirit prepare the ground for the most holy garden that He would make of it. For faith brings peace, and so it calls on truth to enter and make lovely, what has already BEEN prepared for loveliness. Truth FOLLOWS faith and peace, completing the process of making lovely that they begin. For faith is still a learning goal, no longer needed when the lesson has been learned. *But Truth will stay forever.

T 19 B 15. Let, then, your dedication be to the eternal. And learn how NOT to interfere with it, and make it slave to time. For what you think you do to the eternal, you do to YOU. Whom God created as His Son is slave to nothing, being lord of all, along with his Creator. You CAN enslave a body, but an IDEA is free, INCAPABLE of being kept in prison, or limited in ANY way, **T(699) -523** EXCEPT BY THE MIND THAT THOUGHT IT. For it remains JOINED to its source, which is its jailor or its liberator, according to which it chooses as ITS purpose FOR ITSELF.[647]

---

[645] **Ephesians 2:8** For by grace you have been saved through faith, and that not of yourselves; it is the gift of God,

[646] **Luke 1:19** And the angel answered and said to him, "I am Gabriel, who stands in the presence of God, and was sent to speak to you and bring you these glad tidings."
Luke 8:1 Now it came to pass, afterward, that He went through every city and village, preaching and bringing the glad tidings of the kingdom of God. And the twelve were with Him,

[647] Feb. 24, 1967

T 19 C. Sin versus Error (*Notes* 1524 10:84)

T 19 C 1. It is ESSENTIAL that error be not confused with "sin." And it is this distinction which makes salvation possible. For error can be corrected, and the wrong made right. But sin, were it possible, WOULD be irreversible. The belief in sin is necessarily based on the firm conviction that minds, NOT bodies, can attack. And thus the mind IS guilty, and will forever so remain, unless a mind NOT part of it can give it absolution. Sin calls for punishment, as error for correction. And the belief that punishment IS correction, is clearly insane.

T 19 C 2. Sin is not error. For sin entails an arrogance which the idea of error lacks. To sin would be to violate reality, AND TO SUCCEED. Sin is the proclamation that attack is real, and guilt is JUSTIFIED. It assumes the Son of God IS guilty, and has thus SUCCEEDED in losing his innocence, and making himself what God created NOT. Thus is creation seen as NOT eternal, and the Will of God open to opposition AND DEFEAT. Sin is the "grand illusion" underlying ALL the ego's grandiosity. For BY it, God HIMSELF is changed, and rendered incomplete.

T 19 C 3. The Son of God CAN be mistaken; he CAN deceive himself; he can even turn the power of his mind AGAINST himself. But he can NOT sin. There is NOTHING he can do that would REALLY change his reality in ANY way, nor make him REALLY guilty. That is what sin WOULD do, for such is its PURPOSE. Yet, for all the wild insanity inherent in the whole IDEA of sin, IT IS IMPOSSIBLE. For the wages of sin IS death,[648] and how can the immortal die? **T(700) -524**

T 19 C 4. A MAJOR tenet in the ego's insane religion is that sin is NOT error, but TRUTH. And it is INNOCENCE that would deceive. PURITY is seen as arrogance, and the acceptance of the self AS SINFUL is perceived as holiness. And it is this doctrine that REPLACES the reality of the Son of God, as his Father created him, and willed that he be forever. Is this HUMILITY? Or is it rathe, an attempt to wrest creation AWAY from truth, and keep it separate?

T 19 C 5. ANY attempt to re-interpret sin as error is wholly indefensible to the ego. The IDEA of sin is WHOLLY sacrosanct in its thought-system, and quite unapproachable except through reverence and awe. It is the most "holy" concept in the ego's system; lovely and powerful, wholly true, and NECESSARILY protected with every defense at its disposal. For here lies its "best" defense, which all the others serve. Here is its armor, its protection, and the fundamental PURPOSE of the special relationship, in its interpretation.

T 19 C 6. It can indeed be said the ego MADE its world on sin. Only in such a world COULD everything be upside down. This IS the strange illusion which makes the clouds of guilt seem heavy and impenetrable. The solidness this world's foundation SEEMS to have is FOUND in this. For sin HAS changed creation from an Idea of God to an IDEAL the EGO wants; a world IT rules, made up of bodies, mindless, and capable of COMPLETE corruption and decay.

T 19 C 7. If this is a MISTAKE, it can be undone easily by truth. ANY mistake can be corrected, if TRUTH be left to judge it. But, if the mistake is given the STATUS of truth, to what CAN it be brought? The "holiness" of sin is kept in place by just this strange device. As TRUTH, it IS inviolate, and everything is brought to IT for judgment. As a MISTAKE, IT must be brought to truth. It is impossible to have faith in sin, for sin IS faithlessness. But it IS possible to have faith that a MISTAKE can be corrected. **T(701) -525**

T 19 C 8. There is no stone in all the ego's embattled citadel more heavily defended than the idea that sin is real; the NATURAL expression of what the Son of God has MADE himself to be, AND WHAT HE IS. To the ego, THIS IS NO MISTAKE. For this IS its

---

[648] **Romans 6:23** For the wages of sin is death; but the free gift of God is eternal life in Christ Jesus our Lord.

reality; this is the "truth," from which escape will ALWAYS be impossible. This is his past, his present, and his future. For he has somehow managed to corrupt his Father, and change His Mind COMPLETELY. Mourn then the death of God, Whom sin has killed!

T 19 C 9. And this WOULD be the ego's wish, which, in its madness, it thinks it has ACCOMPLISHED. Would you not RATHER that all this be nothing more than a MISTAKE, ENTIRELY correctable, and so easily escaped from that its whole correction is like walking through a mist into the sun? For that is all it IS. Perhaps you would be tempted to AGREE with the ego, that it is far better to be sinful than mistaken. But think you carefully before you allow yourself to make this choice. Approach it not lightly, for it IS the choice of hell or Heaven. **T(702) -526**

T 19 D. The Unreality of Sin (*Notes* 1530 10:90)

T 19 D 1. The[649] attraction of guilt is found in sin, NOT error. Sin will be repeated, BECAUSE of this attraction. Fear can become so acute that the sin is denied the acting out, but, while the guilt REMAINS attractive, the mind will suffer, and not let go the IDEA of the sin. For guilt still calls to it, and the mind hears it and yearns for it, making it a willing captive to its sick appeal. Sin is an idea of evil that can not BE corrected, and will be forever DESIRABLE. As an ESSENTIAL part of what the ego thinks you ARE, you will ALWAYS want it. And only an AVENGER, with a mind UNLIKE your own, could stamp it out through FEAR.

T 19 D 2. The ego does not think it possible that love, NOT fear, is really called upon by sin, AND ALWAYS ANSWERS. For the ego brings sin to FEAR, demanding punishment. But punishment is but another form of guilt's protection. For what is deserving punishment, must have been REALLY DONE. Punishment is always the great preserver of sin; treating it with respect, and honoring its enormity. What must be punished, MUST BE TRUE. And what is true MUST be eternal, and WILL be repeated endlessly. For what you think is real YOU WANT, and will NOT let it go.

T 19 D 3. An ERROR, on the other hand, is NOT attractive. What you see clearly AS A MISTAKE, you WANT corrected. Sometimes a sin can be repeated over and over, with OBVIOUSLY distressing results, but WITHOUT the loss of its appeal. And suddenly you change its status from a sin to a MISTAKE. Now you will NOT repeat it; you will merely stop, and let it go. UNLESS THE GUILT REMAINS. For then, you will but change the FORM of sin, granting that it was an error, but KEEPING IT UNCORRECTABLE. This is not really a change in your perception, for it is SIN that calls for punishment, NOT error. **T(703) -527**

T 19 D 4. The Holy Spirit CANNOT punish sin. Mistakes He recognizes, and would correct them all, as God entrusted Him to do. But SIN He knows not, nor can He RECOGNIZE mistakes that cannot be corrected. For a mistake that cannot be corrected is MEANINGLESS to Him. Mistakes are FOR correction. They call for NOTHING ELSE. What calls for punishment, must call for NOTHING. Yet every mistake MUST be a call for love. What, then, is sin? What COULD it be but a mistake you would keep hidden; a call for help that you would keep UNHEARD, and thus UNANSWERED?

T 19 D 5. In time, the Holy Spirit CLEARLY sees the Son of God can make mistakes. On this, you SHARE His vision. Yet you do NOT share His recognition of the difference between time and eternity. And when correction is completed, time IS eternity. Time is like a downward spiral, that seems to travel down from a long, unbroken line, along another plane, but which in no way BREAKS the line, or interferes with its smooth continuousness. Along the spiral, it SEEMS as if the line MUST have been broken, but, at the LINE, its wholeness is apparent.

T 19 D 6. Everything seen from the spiral is misperceived. But, as you approach the line, you realize that IT was not affected by the drop into another plane at all. But, FROM this plane, the LINE seems discontinuous. And this is but an error in perception, which can be easily corrected IN THE MIND, although the body's eyes will see no change. The eyes see many things the mind corrects, and YOU respond, NOT to the eyes' illusions, BUT TO THE MIND's CORRECTIONS. You SEE the line as broken, and as you shift to different aspects of the spiral, the line looks different. Yet in your mind is One Who KNOWS it is unbroken, and forever changeless. **T(704) -528**

T 19 D 7. This One can teach you how to look on time differently, and to see BEYOND it. But NOT while you believe in sin. In error, yes, for this CAN be corrected by the mind. But sin is the belief that YOUR perception is UNCHANGEABLE, and that the MIND must ACCEPT AS TRUE what it is told THROUGH it. If it does not obey, the MIND is judged insane. The ONLY power that could CHANGE perception is thus kept impotent, held to the body by the FEAR of changed perception, which its Teacher, Who is One with it, would bring.

T 19 D 8. When you are tempted to believe that sin is real, remember this: If sin is real, both God AND YOU are not. If creation is EXTENSION, the Creator MUST have extended HIMSELF, and it is impossible that what is PART of Him is totally unlike the rest. If sin is real, God must be at war WITHIN HIMSELF. HE must be split, and torn between good and evil; partly sane and partially insane. For He must have created what wills to destroy Him, and HAS THE POWER TO DO SO. Is it not EASIER to believe that YOU have been mistaken, than to believe in this?

T 19 D 9. While you believe that YOUR reality, OR YOUR BROTHER's, is bounded by a body, you will believe in sin. While you believe that BODIES can unite, you will find guilt attractive, and believe that sin is precious. For the belief that bodies LIMIT the mind leads to a perception of the world in which the PROOF of separation seems to be everywhere. And God and His creation seem to be split apart, and overthrown. For sin would PROVE what God created holy could not prevail against it, nor remain ITSELF before the power of sin.

T 19 D 10. Sin is perceived as mightier than God, before which God HIMSELF must bow, and offer His creation to its conqueror. Is this humility, or madness? If sin were real it would forever be beyond the hope of healing. **T(705) -529** For there would be a power BEYOND God's, capable of making another will, which could attack His Will, and OVERCOME it. And give His Son a will APART from His, and STRONGER. And each part of His fragmented creation would have a DIFFERENT will OPPOSED to His, and in eternal opposition to Him AND TO EACH OTHER.

T 19 D 11. Your holy relationship has, as its purpose now, the goal of proving THIS is impossible. Heaven has smiled upon it, and the belief in sin has been uprooted in its smile of love. You SEE it still, because you do not realize that its FOUNDATION has gone. Its SOURCE has been removed, and so it can be cherished but a little while, before it vanishes. Only the habit of LOOKING for it still remains. And yet you look with Heaven's smile upon YOUR lips, and Heaven's blessing on your sight.

T 19 D 12. You will NOT see it long. For, in the NEW perception, the mind CORRECTS it when it SEEMS to be seen, and it becomes invisible. But ERRORS are quickly recognized, and quickly given to correction, to be healed, NOT hidden. YOU will be healed of sin and all its ravages, the INSTANT that you give it no power over EACH OTHER. And you will HELP each other overcome MISTAKES, by joyously RELEASING one another from the belief in sin. In the holy instant, you will see the smile of Heaven shining on BOTH of you. And you will shine upon each other, in glad acknowledgment of the grace that has been GIVEN you.

---

[649] Feb. 27, 1976

T 19 D 13. For sin will NOT prevail against a union Heaven has smiled upon. Your perception was HEALED in the holy instant Heaven gave you. Forget what you HAVE seen, and raise your eyes, in faith, to what you now CAN see. The barriers to Heaven will disappear before your holy sight. For you who were sightless have been GIVEN vision, and you CAN see. Look not for what has been REMOVED, but for the glory that has been RESTORED, for you to see. T(706) - 530 -[650]

Look upon your Redeemer, and behold what He would show you in each other. And let not sin arise again, to blind your eyes. For sin would keep you separate, but your Redeemer would have you look upon each other as yourself.[651]

T 19 D 14. Your relationship is now a temple of healing, a place where all the weary ones can come and find rest.[652] Here is the rest that waits for all, after the journey. And it is brought NEARER to all, by your relationship. As this peace expands, from deep inside yourselves, to embrace ALL the Sonship and give it rest, it will encounter many obstacles. Some of them, YOU will try to impose. Others will seem to arise from elsewhere; from your brothers, and from various aspects of the world OUTSIDE. But peace will gently cover them, extending past, COMPLETELY unhindered.

T 19 D 15. The extension of the Holy Spirit's purpose, from YOUR relationship to others, to bring them gently IN, has already begun. This is the way in which He will bring means and goal in line. The peace He laid, deep within BOTH of you, will quietly extend to EVERY aspect of your lives, surrounding both of you with glowing happiness, and the calm awareness of COMPLETE protection. And you will carry its message of love and safety and freedom to everyone who draws nigh unto your temple, where healing waits for him.

T 19 D 16. You will NOT wait to give him this, for you will CALL to him and he will answer, RECOGNIZING in your call the call of God. And you will draw him in and give him rest, as it was given YOU. All this will you do. But the peace that already lies deeply within, must first expand and FLOW ACROSS the obstacles YOU place before it. THIS IT WILL DO. For nothing undertaken WITH the Holy Spirit, remains unfinished. You can indeed be sure of NOTHING you see OUTSIDE you, but of this you CAN be sure. T(707) - 531 -

T 19 D 17. The Holy Spirit asks that you offer Him a resting-place, where YOU will rest in Him. He answered you, and entered your relationship. Would you not now RETURN His graciousness, and enter into a relationship with Him? For it is HE Who offered YOUR relationship the gift of holiness, without which it would have been forever impossible to appreciate each other. The gratitude you owe to Him, He asks but that YOU receive, FOR Him. And, when you look with gentle graciousness upon each other, you ARE beholding Him. For you are looking where He IS, and NOT apart from you.

T 19 D 18. You CANNOT see the Holy Spirit, but you CAN see your brothers truly. And the light in them will show you all that you NEED to see. When the peace in you has been extended to encompass EVERYONE, the Holy Spirit's function here will be accomplished. What NEED is there for SEEING, then? When God has taken the last step Himself, the Holy Spirit will gather ALL your thanks and gratitude that you have offered Him, and lay them gently before His Creator, in the Name of His most holy Son. And the Father will ACCEPT them, in HIS Name. What need is there of seeing, in the presence of HIS gratitude? T(708) -532[653]

T 19 E. Obstacles to Peace –I. The Desire to Get Rid of It (*Notes* 1542 10:102)

T 19 E 1. The first obstacle that peace must flow across is YOUR desire to get RID of it. For it cannot extend, UNLESS you keep it. YOU are the center from which it radiates outward, to call the others IN. You are its home; its tranquil dwelling-place, from which it gently reaches out, but NEVER leaving YOU. If YOU would make it homeless, how can it abide within the Son of God? If it would spread across the whole creation, it MUST begin with you. And, FROM you, reach to everyone who calls, and bring him rest by JOINING you.

T 19 E 2. Why would you want peace homeless? What do you think that it must DISPOSSESS, to dwell in you? What SEEMS to be the cost you are so unwilling to pay? The little barriers of sand still stand between you. Would you reinforce them NOW? You are NOT asked to let them go for yourselves alone. Christ asks it of you, for HIMSELF. He would bring peace to everyone. And how can He do this, EXCEPT through you? Would you let a little bank of sand, a wall of dust, a tiny seeming barrier stand between your brothers and salvation?

T 19 E 3. And yet it IS this little remnant of attack you cherish still against each other, that is the first obstacle the peace in you encounters, in its going forth. This little wall of hatred would STILL oppose the Will of God, and keep It limited. The Holy Spirit's purpose rests in peace within you. Yet you are STILL unwilling to let it JOIN you wholly. You still oppose the Will of God, just by a little. But that little IS a limit you would place upon the whole. God's Will is One, NOT many. It HAS no opposition, for there is none BESIDE It.

T 19 E 4. What you would still contain behind your little barrier, and keep SEPARATE from each other, is mightier than the universe. For it would HOLD BACK the universe AND ITS CREATOR. This little wall would hide the purpose T(709) -533 of Heaven, and keep it FROM Heaven. Would you thrust salvation AWAY from the GIVER of salvation? For such have YOU become. Peace could no more DEPART from you than from God. Fear not this little obstacle. It can NOT contain the Will of God. Peace WILL flow across it, and join you WITHOUT hindrance.

T 19 E 5. Salvation cannot BE withheld from you. It IS your purpose. You CANNOT will APART from this. You HAVE no purpose apart from each other, nor apart from the one you asked the Holy Spirit to SHARE with you. The little wall will fall away so quietly, beneath the wings of peace! For it will send its messengers from you to all the world. And barriers will fall away before their coming, as easily as those which YOU would interpose will be surmounted. To overcome the world is no more difficult than to surmount your little wall. For in the miracle of YOUR relationship, WITHOUT this barrier, is EVERY miracle contained.

T 19 E 6. There is no order of difficulty in miracles, for they ARE all the same. Each is a gentle WINNING OVER, from the appeal of guilt to the appeal of love. How can this FAIL to be accomplished, WHEREVER it is undertaken? Guilt can raise no REAL barriers against it. And all that seems to stand between you MUST fall away, because of the appeal YOU answered. And from you who answered, He Who answered you would call. His home is in your holy relationship. Do not attempt to stand BETWEEN Him and His holy purpose, for it IS yours. But let Him quietly EXTEND the miracle of your relationship to everyone CONTAINED in it, as it was given.

T 19 E 7. There is a hush in Heaven, a happy expectancy, a little pause of gladness, in acknowledgment of the journey's end. For

---

[650] February 28, 1967.
[651] **Mark 12:29-31** "The second is this, Thou shalt love thy neighbour as thyself. There is none other commandment greater than these." Also **Matthew 22:39**
Leviticus 19:18 You shall not take vengeance, nor bear any grudge against the children of your people, but you shall love your neighbor as yourself: I am the LORD.
[652] **Matthew 11:28** "Come to Me, all you who labor and are heavy laden, and I will give you rest."

[653] March 1, 1967

Heaven knows you well, as you know Heaven. No illusions stand between you. Look not upon the little T(710) -534 wall of shadows. The sun has risen OVER it. How can a shadow KEEP you from the sun? No more can YOU be kept by shadows from the light in which illusions end. EVERY miracle is but the end of an illusion. Such was the journey; such its ending. And in the goal of truth, which you ACCEPTED, must ALL illusions end.

T 19 E 8. The little, insane wish to get rid of Him Whom you invited IN, and push Him OUT, MUST produce conflict. As you look upon the world, this little wish, uprooted and floating aimlessly, can land and settle briefly upon ANYTHING. For it HAS no purpose now. BEFORE the Holy Spirit entered to abide with you, it SEEMED to have a MIGHTY purpose; the fixed and unchangeable dedication to sin and its results. Now it is aimless, wandering pointlessly, causing no more than tiny interruptions in love's appeal.

T 19 E 9. This feather of a wish, this tiny illusion, this microscopic remnant of the belief in sin, is all that remains of what once SEEMED to be the world. It is no longer an unrelenting barrier to peace. Its pointless wandering makes its results APPEAR to be more erratic and unpredictable than before. Yet what COULD be more unstable than a tightly-organized delusional system? Its SEEMING stability is its pervasive WEAKNESS, which extends to EVERYTHING. The VARIABILITY which the little remnant induces, merely indicates its LIMITED results.

T 19 E 10. How mighty can a little feather be, before the great wings of truth? Can it oppose an eagle's flight, or hinder the advance of summer? Can it interfere with the EFFECTS of summer's sun upon a garden covered by the snow? See but how easily this little wisp[654] is lifted up and carried away, never to return. And part with it in gladness, not regret. For it is nothing in itself, and STOOD FOR nothing when you had greater faith in its protection. Would you not rather greet the summer sun, than fix your gaze upon a disappearing snowflake, and shiver in remembrance of the winter's cold? T(711) -535[655]

T 19 F. The Attraction of Guilt (*Notes* 1548 10:108)

T 19 F 1. The attraction of guilt produces fear of love. For love would NEVER look on guilt at all. It is the NATURE of love to look upon ONLY the truth, for there it sees itself, with which it would unite in holy union and completion. As love must look past fear, so must fear see love not. For love contains the END of guilt, as surely as fear DEPENDS on it. Love is attracted ONLY to love. Overlooking guilt completely, IT SEES NO FEAR. Being wholly without attack, it COULD not be afraid.

T 19 F 2. Fear is attracted to what love sees NOT. And each believes that what the other looks upon does not exist. Fear looks on guilt with just the same devotion that love looks on itself. And each has messengers which they send forth, and which return to them with messages written in the language in which their going forth was asked. Love's messengers are gently sent, and return with messages of love and gentleness. The messengers of fear are harshly ordered to seek out guilt, and cherish every scrap of evil and sin that they can find, losing none of them on pain of death, and laying them respectfully before their lord and master.

T 19 F 3. Perception cannot obey two masters, each asking for messages of different things, in different languages.[656] What fear would feed upon, love overlooks. What fear DEMANDS, love cannot even SEE. The fierce attraction that guilt holds for fear, is wholly absent from love's gentle perception. What love would look upon is meaningless to fear, and quite invisible. Relationships in this world are the result of how the world is seen. And this depends on which emotion was called on to send its messengers to look upon it, and return with word of what they saw.

T 19 F 4. Fear's messengers are trained through terror, and they tremble when T(712) -536 their master calls upon them to serve him. For fear is merciless even to its friends. Its messengers steal guiltily away in hungry search of guilt, for they are kept cold and starving, and made very vicious by their master, who allows them to feast only upon what they return to him. No little shred of guilt escapes their hungry eyes. And in their savage search for sin, they pounce on any living thing they see, and carry it screaming to their master, to be devoured.

T 19 F 5. Send not these savage messengers into the world, to feast upon it, and to prey upon reality. For they will bring you word of bones and skin and flesh. They have been taught to seek for the corruptible, and to return with gorges filled with things decayed and rotted. To them, such things are beautiful, because they seem to allay their savage pangs of hunger. For they are frantic with the pain of fear, and would avert the punishment of him who sends them forth, by offering him what THEY hold dear.

T 19 F 6. The Holy Spirit has given you love's messengers, to send INSTEAD of those YOU trained through fear. THEY are as eager to return to you what they hold dear, as are the others. If you send THEM forth, they will see only the blameless and the beautiful, the gentle and the kind. They will be as careful to let no little act of charity, no tiny expression of forgiveness, no little breaths[657] of love, escape their notice. And they will return, with all the happy things they found, to share them lovingly with you. Be not AFRAID of them. They offer you salvation. Theirs are the messages of SAFETY. For THEY see the world as kind.

T 19 F 7. If you send forth ONLY the messengers the Holy Spirit gave you, WANTING no messages but theirs, you will see fear no more. The world will be transformed before your sight, cleansed of all guilt, and softly brushed with beauty. The world contains no fear that YOU laid not upon it. T(713) -537 And none you cannot ask love's messengers to REMOVE from it, and see it still. The Holy Spirit has given you HIS messengers, to send each other, and return to each with what love sees. They have been given to REPLACE the hungry dogs of fear you sent instead. And they go forth to signify the END of fear.

T 19 F 8. Love, too, would set a feast before you, on a table covered with a spotless cloth, set in a quiet garden, where no sound but singing and a softly joyous whispering is ever heard. This is a feast which honors your holy relationship, and at which everyone is welcomed as an honored guest. And in a holy instant grace is said by everyone together, as they join in gentleness before the table of communion.[658] And I will join you there, as long ago I promised, and promise still. For in your new relationship am I made welcome, and where I am made welcome,[659] there I AM. T(714) -538[660]

T 19 F 9. I am made welcome in the state of grace, which means YOU HAVE AT LAST FORGIVEN ME. For I became the symbol of your sin, and so I had to die INSTEAD of you. To the ego, sin MEANS death, and so Atonement IS ACHIEVED THROUGH MURDER. Salvation is looked upon as a way by which the Son of

---

[654] *Urtext* manuscript has it typed "whisp," this is an apparent typo since the word intended would appear to be "wisp."
[655] March 3, 1967
[656] **Matthew 6:24** "No one can serve two masters; for either he will hate the one and love the other, or else he will be loyal to the one and despise the other. You cannot serve God and mammon."
[657] The *Urtext* manuscript says "breathe" which is a verb, and a noun is needed here, so we have some sort of copying mistake. The *Notes* says "breaths" so this has been changed to reflect the original reading.
[658] **Matthew 26:29** "But I say to you, I will not drink of this fruit of the vine from now on until that day when I drink it new with you in My Father's kingdom."
Luke 22:30 "That you may eat and drink at My table in My kingdom, and sit on thrones judging the twelve tribes of Israel."
[659] **Matthew 18:20** "For where two or three are gathered together in My name, there am I in the midst of them."
[660] March 6, 1967

God was killed, instead of YOU. Yet would I offer you my BODY, you whom I love, KNOWING its littleness? Or would I teach that bodies cannot keep us apart? Mine was of no greater value than yours; no better means for the COMMUNICATION of salvation, but NOT its Source.

T 19 F 10. No one can die for anyone, and death does not atone for sin.[661] But you can LIVE to show it is not REAL. The body DOES appear to be the symbol of sin, while you believe that it can get you what you want. While you believe that it can give you pleasure, you will ALSO believe that it can bring you pain. To think you could be satisfied and happy with so little, IS to hurt yourself. And to LIMIT the happiness that you would have, CALLS upon pain to fill your meager store, and make your lives complete. This IS completion, as the ego sees it. For guilt creeps in where happiness has been removed, and SUBSTITUTES for it.

T 19 F 11. Communion is another kind of completion, which goes beyond guilt BECAUSE it goes beyond the body. Communion comes with peace, and peace MUST transcend the body.

T 19 G. Obstacles to Peace – II. The Belief the Body is Valuable for What it Offers (not present in *Notes*)

T 19 G 1. We said that peace must first surmount the obstacle of your desire to get rid of it. Where the attraction of guilt holds sway, peace is NOT WANTED. The second obstacle that peace must flow across, and closely related to the first, is the belief that the body is valuable FOR WHAT IT OFFERS. For here is the attraction of guilt MADE MANIFEST in the body, and SEEN in it. **T(715) -539**

T 19 G 2. THIS is the value that you think peace would ROB you of. This is what you believe that it would dispossess, and leave YOU homeless. And it is this for which YOU would deny a home to peace. This "sacrifice" you feel to be too great to make, too much to ask of you. Is it a SACRIFICE, or a RELEASE? What has the body REALLY given you, that justifies your strange belief that in it lies salvation? Do you not see that this is the belief in DEATH? Here is the focus of the perception of Atonement as murder. Here is the SOURCE of the idea that love is fear.

T 19 G 3. The Holy Spirit's messengers are sent far beyond the body, calling the mind to join in holy communion, and be at peace. Such is the message that I gave them, for YOU. It is only the messengers of FEAR that see the body, for they look for what can suffer. Is it a sacrifice to be REMOVED from what can suffer? The Holy Spirit does not DEMAND you "sacrifice" the hope of the body's pleasures. It HAS no hope of pleasure. But neither can it bring you fear of pain. Pain is the ONLY "sacrifice" the Holy Spirit asks. And this He WOULD remove.

T 19 G 4. Peace is extended from you only to the eternal. And it reaches out FROM the eternal in YOU. It flows across all else. The second obstacle is no more solid than the first. For you will neither to get rid of peace, nor to LIMIT it. What are these obstacles that you would interpose between peace and its going forth, but barriers you place between your will and its accomplishment? You WANT communion, NOT the feast of fear. You WANT salvation, NOT the pain of guilt. AND YOU WANT YOUR FATHER, NOT a little mound of clay, to be your home.

T 19 G 5. In your holy relationship is your Father's Son. He has NOT lost communion with Him. NOR WITH HIMSELF. When you agreed to join each other, you acknowledged this is so. This has NO cost. But it HAS release from cost. You have paid very dearly for your illusions. And NOTHING you have paid for brought you peace. Are you not GLAD that Heaven can not BE sacrificed? **T(716) -540** And sacrifice can not BE asked of you? There IS no obstacle that you can place before our union, for in your holy relationship I am there ALREADY. We will surmount all obstacles TOGETHER, for we stand WITHIN the gates, and not outside.

T 19 G 6. How easily the gates are opened from within, to let peace through to bless the tired world! Can it be difficult for us to walk past barriers together, when you have JOINED the Limitless? The end of guilt is in your hands, to give. Would you stop now, to LOOK for guilt in each other? Let me be to you the symbol of the END of guilt, and look upon each other, as you would look on me. Forgive me for all the sins you think the Son of God committed. And in the light of your forgiveness, he will remember who he is, and forget what never was.

T 19 G 7. I ask for your forgiveness, for if YOU are guilty, so must I be. And if I surmounted guilt and overcame the world, you were WITH me.[662] Would you see in me the symbol of guilt, or of the END of guilt? Remembering that what I signify to you, you see within YOURSELF? From your holy relationship, Truth proclaims the truth, and Love looks on itself. Salvation flows from deep within the home you offered to my Father and to me. And we are there together, in the quiet communion in which the Father and the Son are joined.

T 19 G 8. Oh come ye faithful, to the holy union of the Father and Son in YOU. And keep YOU not apart from what is offered you, in gratitude for giving peace its home in Heaven. Send forth to all the world the joyous message of the end of guilt, and all the world will answer. Think of your happiness, as everyone offers you witness of the end of sin, and shows you that its power is gone forever. Where can guilt be, when the belief in sin is gone? And where is death,[663] when its great advocate is heard no more? **T(717) -541**

T 19 G 9. Forgive me your illusions, and release me from punishment for what I have NOT done. So will YOU learn the freedom that I taught, by teaching freedom to each other, and so releasing me. I am within your holy relationship, yet you would imprison me behind the obstacles you RAISE to freedom, and bar my way to YOU. Yet it is not possible to keep AWAY One Who is there ALREADY. And IN Him, it IS possible that our communion, where we are ALREADY joined, will be the focus of the new perception that will bring light to all the world, contained in YOU.

T 19 H. Pleasure and Pain (not present in *Notes*)

T 19 H 1. Your little part is but to give the Holy Spirit the whole IDEA of sacrifice. And to ACCEPT the peace He gave, instead. WITHOUT the limits that would hold its extension back, and so would limit YOUR awareness of it. For what He gives MUST be extended, if YOU would have its limitless power, and use it for the Son of God's release. It is not THIS you would be rid of, and having it, you CANNOT limit it. If peace is homeless, so are you. And so am I. And He Who IS our Home, is homeless WITH us.

---

[661] In this one sentence Jesus challenges both the traditional Jewish sacrificial cult whereby the slaughter of the "scapegoat" or sacrificial animal was believed to expiate the sin of the community, along with one early Jewish interpretation of the crucifixion, in which Jesus' execution was seen as a kind of human sacrifice to atone for the sins of the world. This particular form of "blood and suffering" Christology whereby God punished His Son for our errors has, like the earlier animal sacrifice cultus with which it shares the same atavistic bloody-mindedness and body fetishes, is frequently described in ACIM as an error, this being just one example. The next sentence points to a common thread in ACIM's treatment of this issue, it's not the *dying* but the *living* that matters, not the *crucifixion* that contains power but rather the *resurrection*.

[662] **John 16:33** "These things I have spoken to you, that in Me you may have peace. In the world you will have tribulation; but be of good cheer, I have overcome the world."
[663] **I Corinthians 15:53-57** For this corruptible must put on incorruption, and this mortal must put on immortality. But when this corruptible shall have put on incorruption, and this mortal shall have put on immortality, then shall come to pass the saying that is written, Death is swallowed up in victory. O death, where is thy victory? O death, where is thy sting? The sting of death is sin; and the power of sin is the law: but thanks be to God, who giveth us the victory through our Lord Jesus Christ.

T 19 H 2. Is this your will? Would you forever be a wanderer in search of peace? Would you invest your hope of peace and happiness in what MUST fail? Faith in the eternal is ALWAYS justified, for the eternal is forever kind, infinite in its patience, and wholly loving. It will accept you wholly, and give you peace. But it can unite only with what ALREADY is at peace in you, immortal as itself. The body can bring you neither peace nor turmoil; not pain nor joy. It is a means, and NOT an end. It HAS no purpose of itself, but only what is GIVEN it to do. The body will seem to BE whatever is the means for reaching the goal that you ASSIGN to it.

T 19 H 3. Only the mind can set a purpose, and only mind can see the means for its accomplishment, and justify its use. Peace and guilt are both conditions of the mind, to be ATTAINED. And these conditions are the home of the emotion that called them forth, and therefore is COMPATIBLE with it. But think you T(718) -542 which it is that is compatible with YOU. Here is your choice, and it IS free. But all that LIES in it WILL come with it. And what you think you are can NEVER be APART from it.

T 19 H 4. The body is the great SEEMING betrayer of faith. In it lies disillusionment and the seeds of faithlessness. But ONLY if you asked of it what it CANNOT give. Can YOUR mistake be reasonable grounds for your depression and disillusionment, and for retaliative attack on what you think has failed you? Use not your ERROR as the justification for your faithlessness. You have NOT sinned, but you HAVE been mistaken in what is faithful. And the correction of YOUR mistake will GIVE you grounds for faith. **T(719) -543**[664]

T 19 H 5. It is impossible to seek for pleasure through the body, and NOT find pain. It is essential that this relationship be understood, for it is one the ego sees as proof of sin. It is not REALLY punitive at all. It is but the inevitable result of equating yourself WITH the body, which is the INVITATION to pain. For it invites FEAR to enter, and become your PURPOSE. The attraction of guilt MUST enter with it, and WHATEVER fear directs the body to do IS therefore painful. It will share the pain of ALL illusions, and the illusion of pleasure will BE the same as pain.

T 19 H 6. Is not this inevitable? Under fear's orders, the body WILL pursue guilt, serving its master, whose attraction to guilt maintains the whole illusion of his existence. This, then, IS the attraction to PAIN. Ruled by THIS perception, the body becomes the servant of pain, seeking it dutifully, and obeying the idea that pain IS pleasure. It is this IDEA that underlies all of the ego's heavy investment in the body. And it is this insane relationship which it keeps hidden, and yet feeds upon. To YOU, it teaches that the body's pleasure is happiness. But to ITSELF it whispers, "It is death."

T 19 H 7. Why should the body be ANYTHING to you? Certainly what it is MADE of is not precious. And, just as certainly, IT has no feeling. It transmits TO YOU the feelings that you WANT. Like any communication medium, the body receives and sends the messages that it is given. It has NO feeling for them. All of the feeling with which they are invested is given by the sender and the receiver. The ego and the Holy Spirit both recognize this. And both also recognize that here, THE SENDER AND RECEIVER ARE THE SAME. The Holy Spirit TELLS you this with joy. The ego HIDES it, for it would keep you unaware of it.

T 19 H 8. Who would send messages of hatred and attack, if he but understood he sends them to HIMSELF? Who would accuse, make guilty and condemn HIMSELF? **T(720) -544** The ego's messages are ALWAYS sent AWAY from you, in the belief that, for your message of attack and guilt, will someone OTHER than yourself suffer. And, even if YOU suffer, yet someone ELSE will suffer more. The great deceiver recognizes that this is not so, but, as the "enemy" of peace, it urges you to SEND OUT all your messages of hate, and free YOURSELF. And, to convince you this is possible, it bids the body search for pain in attack upon another, calling it pleasure, and OFFERING it to you as freedom FROM attack.

T 19 H 9. Hear not its madness, and believe not the impossible is true. Forget not that the ego has DEDICATED the body to the goal of sin, and places in it ALL its faith that this can be accomplished. Its sad disciples chant the body's praise continually, in solemn celebration of the ego's rule. Not one but MUST believe that YIELDING to the attraction of guilt is the ESCAPE from pain. Not one but MUST regard the body as himself, WITHOUT which he would die, and yet WITHIN which is his death equally inevitable.

T 19 H 10. It is not given to the ego's disciples to realize that they have dedicated themselves to death. This has been OFFERED them, but they have not accepted it. And what is offered must also be received, to be truly given. For the Holy Spirit, too, is a communication medium, receiving from the Father, and offering His messages unto the Son. Like to the ego, the Holy Spirit is both the sender and receiver. For what is sent through Him RETURNS to Him, seeking itself along the way, and FINDING what it seeks. So does the ego FIND the death it seeks, returning it to YOU. **T(721) -545**[665]

T 19 I. Obstacles to Peace - III. The Attraction of Death (not present in *Notes*)

T 19 I 1. To you, into whose special relationship the Holy Spirit entered, it IS given to release and be released from the dedication to death. For it was offered you, and you ACCEPTED. But you must learn still more about this strange devotion, for it contains the third of the obstacles that peace must flow across. No-one can die, unless he chooses death. What seems to be the FEAR of death, is really its ATTRACTION. Guilt, too, is feared and fearful. Yet it could have no hold at all, except on those who are attracted to it, and seek it out. So it is with death. Made by the ego, its dark shadow falls across all living things, because the ego is the "enemy" of life.

T 19 I 2. And yet, a shadow cannot kill. What is a shadow to the living? They but walk past, and it is gone. But what of those whose dedication it is NOT to live? The black-draped "sinners," the ego's mournful chorus, plodding so heavily AWAY from life, dragging their chains and marching in the slow procession that honors their grim master, lord of death. Touch any one of them with the gentle hand of forgiveness, and watch the chains fall away, along with YOURS. See him throw aside the black robe he was wearing to his funeral, and hear him laugh at death. The sentence sin would lay upon him, he can escape with your forgiveness.

T 19 I 3. This is NOT arrogance. It is the Will of God. What is impossible to you who choose His Will as yours? What is death to you? Your dedication is NOT to death, nor to its master. When you accepted the Holy Spirit's purpose in place of the ego's, you RENOUNCED death, exchanging it for life. We know that the RESULT of an idea leaves not its source. And death is the result of the thought we call the ego, as surely as life is the result of the Thought of God.

T 19 J. The Incorruptible Body (not present in *Notes*)

T 19 J 1. From the ego came sin and guilt and death, in OPPOSITION to life and innocence, and to the Will of God Himself. Where can such opposition lie, but in the sick minds of the insane, dedicated to madness, and set AGAINST the peace of Heaven? **T(722) - 546**

T 19 J 2. One thing is sure; God, Who created neither sin nor death, wills not that you be bound by them. He knows of neither sin NOR its result. The shrouded figures in the funeral procession march not in honor of their Creator, Whose Will it is they LIVE. They are not <u>FOLLOWING</u> it; they are OPPOSING it. And what is the black-

---
[664] March 9, 1967

[665] March 10, 1967

draped body they would bury? A body THEY dedicated to death, a symbol of corruption, a sacrifice to sin, OFFERED to sin to feed upon, and keep ITSELF alive. A thing condemned, damned by its maker, and lamented by every mourner who looks upon it as himself.

T 19 J 3. You who believe you have condemned the Son of God to this ARE arrogant. But you who would RELEASE him are but honoring the Will of his Creator. The arrogance of sin, the pride of guilt, the sepulchre of separation, all are part of your unrecognized dedication to death. The glitter of guilt you laid upon the body would KILL it. For what the ego loves, it kills for its obedience. But what obeys it not, it CANNOT kill. You have ANOTHER dedication which would keep the body incorruptible and perfect, as long as it is useful for your holy purpose.

T 19 J 4. The body no more dies than it can feel. IT DOES NOTHING. Of itself, it is neither corruptible nor incorruptible. IT IS NOTHING. It is the result of a tiny, mad IDEA of corruption, WHICH CAN BE CORRECTED. For God has ANSWERED this insane idea with His Own, an Answer which left Him not, and therefore brings the Creator to the awareness of every mind which heard His Answer, and ACCEPTED it. You who are dedicated to the incorruptible, have been given, through YOUR acceptance, the power to RELEASE from corruption. What better way to teach the first and fundamental principle in a course on miracles than by showing you the one that SEEMS to be the hardest can be accomplished FIRST? **T(723) -547**

T 19 J 5. The body can but serve your purpose. As you look upon it, so will it seem to be. Death, were it true, would be the final and complete disruption of communication, which IS the ego's goal. Those who fear death see not how often and how loudly they CALL to it, and bid it come to SAVE them from communication. For death is seen as SAFETY, the great dark savior from the light of truth, the answer to the Answer, the silencer of the Voice that speaks for God. Yet the retreat to death is NOT the end of conflict. Only God's ANSWER is its end.

T 19 J 6. The obstacle of your seeming love for death, which peace must flow across, SEEMS to be very great. For in it lies hidden all the ego's secrets, all its strange devices for deception, all its sick ideas and weird imaginings. Here is the final end of union, the triumph of the ego's making over creation, the victory of lifelessness on life Itself. Under the dusty edge of its distorted world. the ego would lay the Son of God, slain by its orders, proof in his decay that God Himself is powerless before the ego's might, unable to protect the life that He created, against the ego's savage wish to kill.

T 19 J 7. My brothers, children of our Father, this is a DREAM of death. There is no funeral, no dark altars, no grim commandments, nor twisted rituals of condemnation, to which the BODY leads you. Ask not release of IT. But FREE it from the merciless and unrelenting orders you laid upon it, and forgive it what you ordered it to do. In its exaltation, you COMMANDED it to die, for only death COULD conquer life. And what but insanity could look upon the defeat of God, and think it REAL? **T(724) -548**

T 19 J 8. The fear of death will go as its appeal is yielded to love's REAL attraction. The end of sin, which nestles quietly in the safety of your relationship, protected by your union, ready to grow into a mighty force for God, is very near. The infancy of salvation is carefully guarded by love, preserved from every thought that would attack it, and quietly made ready to fulfill the mighty task for which it was GIVEN you. Your new-born purpose is nursed by angels, cherished by the Holy Spirit, and protected by God Himself. It NEEDS not your protection; it is YOURS. For it is deathless, and within it lies the END of death.

T 19 J 9. What danger can assail the wholly innocent? What can attack the guiltless? What fear can enter and disturb the peace of sinlessness? What has been given you, even in its infancy, is in full communication with God AND you. In its tiny hands, it holds, in perfect safety, every miracle you will perform, held out to YOU. The miracle of life is ageless, born in time, but nourished in eternity. Behold this infant, to whom you gave a resting place by your forgiveness of EACH OTHER, and see in it the Will of God. Here is the babe of Bethlehem reborn.[666] And everyone who gives him shelter will follow him, NOT to the cross, but to the Resurrection and the Life.[667]

T 19 J 10. When anything seems to you to be a source of fear, when any situation strikes you with terror and makes your body tremble and the cold sweat of fear comes over it, remember it is ALWAYS for one reason; the ego has perceived it as a symbol of fear, a sign of sin and death. Remember, then, that neither sign nor symbol should be CONFUSED with source, for they must STAND FOR something OTHER than themselves. Their meaning CANNOT lie in them, but must be sought in what they REPRESENT. And they may thus mean everything or nothing, according to the truth or falsity of the IDEA which they reflect. **T(725) -549**

T 19 J 11. Confronted with such seeming uncertainty of meaning, judge it not. Remember the holy Presence of the One GIVEN you to be the Source of judgment. Give it to Him to judge FOR you, and say:

"Take this from me and look upon it, judging it for me.

Let me not see it as a sign of sin and death, nor use it for destruction.

Teach me how NOT to make of it an OBSTACLE to peace, But let You use it FOR me, to FACILITATE its coming." **T(726) -550**[668]

T 19 K. Obstacles to Peace - IV. The Fear of God (not present in *Notes*)

T 19 K 1. What would you see, WITHOUT the fear of death? What would you feel and think, if death held NO attraction for you? Very simply, YOU WOULD REMEMBER YOUR FATHER. The Creator of life, the Source of everything that lives, the Father of the Universe, and of the Universe of universes, and of everything that lies even BEYOND them, would you remember. And, as this Memory rises in your mind, peace must still surmount a final obstacle, AFTER which is salvation completed, and the Son of God ENTIRELY restored to sanity. For here, your world DOES end.

T 19 K 2. The fourth obstacle to be surmounted, hangs like a heavy veil before the face of Christ. Yet, as His face rises beyond it, shining with joy because He is in His Father's love, peace will lightly brush the veil aside and run to meet Him, and to JOIN with Him at last. For this dark veil, which seems to make the face of Christ Himself like to a leper's, and the bright rays of His Father's Love which light His face with glory appear as streams of blood, fades in the blazing light BEYOND it, when the fear of death is gone.

T 19 K 3. This is the darkest veil, -- upheld by the belief in death, and protected by its attraction. The dedication to death and to its sovereignty is but the solemn vow, the promise made in secret to the ego, never to lift this veil, not to approach it, nor even to SUSPECT that it is there. This is the secret bargain, made with the ego, to keep what lies BEYOND the veil forever blotted out and unremembered. Here is your promise never to allow union to call you OUT of separation; the great amnesia in which the memory of God seems quite forgotten; the cleavage of your Self from you; THE FEAR OF GOD, the final step in your dissociation. **T(727) -551**

T 19 K 4. See how the belief in death would seem to 'save' you. For, if this is gone, what can you fear but life? It is the attraction of death that makes life seem to be ugly, cruel, and tyrannical. You are

---

[666] **Luke 2:12** And this will be the sign to you: You will find a Babe wrapped in swaddling cloths, lying in a manger."

[667] **John 11:25** Jesus said to her, "I am the resurrection and the life. He who believes in Me, though he may die, he shall live."

[668] March 13, 1967

no more afraid of death than of the ego. These are your chosen FRIENDS. For, in your secret alliance with them, you have agreed never to let the fear of God be lifted, so you could look upon the face of Christ, and join Him in His Father. Every obstacle that peace must flow across is surmounted in just the same way; the fear that RAISED it yields to the love beneath, and so the fear is gone. And so it is with this.

T 19 K 5. The desire to get rid of peace and drive the Holy Spirit FROM you, fades in the presence of the quiet recognition that you love Him. The exaltation of the body is given up in favor of the Spirit, which you love as you could NEVER love the body. And the appeal of death is lost forever, as love's attraction stirs and calls to you. From BEYOND each of these OBSTACLES to love, Love Itself has called, and each has been surmounted by the power of the attraction of what lies BEYOND. Your WANTING fear SEEMED to be holding them in place. Yet, when you heard the voice of love BEYOND them, you answered, and they disappeared.

T 19 K 6. And now you stand in terror before what you swore never to look upon. Your eyes look down, remembering your promise to your "friends." The "loveliness" of sin; the delicate appeal of guilt, the "holy" waxen image of death, and the fear of vengeance of the ego you swore in blood not to desert, all rise and bid you NOT to raise your eyes. For you realize that if you look on THIS, and LET the veil be lifted, THEY WILL BE GONE FOREVER. All of your "friends," your "protectors," and your "home," will vanish. Nothing that you remember NOW, will you remember. **T(728) -552**

T 19 K 7. It seems to you the world will utterly abandon you, if you but raise your eyes. Yet all that WILL occur is YOU will leave the world forever. This is the re-establishment of YOUR will. Look upon it, open-eyed, and you will nevermore believe that you are at the mercy of things BEYOND you, forces you can NOT control, and thoughts that come to you AGAINST your will. It IS YOUR WILL TO LOOK ON THIS. No mad desire, no trivial impulse to forget again, no stab of fear, nor the cold sweat of seeming death, CAN stand against your will. And what attracts you from BEYOND the veil, is also deep WITHIN you, unseparated from it, and COMPLETELY One.

T 19 L. The Lifting of the Veil (not present in *Notes*)

T 19 L 1. Forget not that you came this far TOGETHER. And it was surely NOT the ego that led you here. No obstacle to peace can BE surmounted through ITS help. IT does not open up its secrets, and bid you look at them, and go BEYOND them. IT would not have you see its weakness and learn it has NO power to KEEP you from the truth. The Guide Who brought you here REMAINS with you, and when you raise your eyes, you WILL be ready to look on terror with no fear at all. But first, lift up your eyes and look upon each other in innocence, born of COMPLETE forgiveness of each other's illusions, and through the eyes of faith, which see them not.

T 19 L 2. No-one can look upon the fear of God unterrified, unless he has ACCEPTED the Atonement, and learned illusions are not real. No-one can stand before this obstacle alone, for he could not have REACHED it unless his brother walked beside him. And no-one would dare to LOOK on it, without COMPLETE forgiveness of his brother in his heart. Stand you here a while, and tremble not. You will be ready. Let us join together in a holy instant, here in this place where the purpose, GIVEN in a holy instant, has led you. And let us join in faith that He Who brought us here together will OFFER you the innocence you need, and that you will ACCEPT it for my love and His. **T(729) -553**[669]

T 19 L 3. Nor is it POSSIBLE to look on this too soon. This is the place to which everyone must come, when he is ready. Once he has found his brother, he IS ready. But merely to REACH a place is not enough. A journey without a purpose is still meaningless. And even when it is over, it seems to make no sense. How can you KNOW that it is over, unless you realize its purpose IS accomplished? Here, with the journey's end before you, you SEE its purpose. And it is here you choose whether to look upon it, or wander on, only to return and make the choice again.

T 19 L 4. To look upon the fear of God DOES need some preparation. Only the sane can look on stark insanity and raving madness with pity and compassion, but NOT with fear. For only if you SHARE in it does it seem fearful. And you DO share in it until you look upon each other with perfect faith and love and tenderness. Before complete forgiveness, you still stand unforgiving. You are afraid of God BECAUSE you fear each other. Those you do not forgive, YOU FEAR. And no-one reaches love, with FEAR beside him.

T 19 L 5. This brother, who stands beside you, still seems to be a stranger. You do NOT know him, and your INTERPRETATION of him is VERY fearful. And you attack him still, to keep what seems to be YOURSELF unharmed. Yet in his hands IS your salvation. You see his madness, which you hate because you SHARE in it. And all the pity and forgiveness that would HEAL it, gives way to fear. Brothers, you NEED forgiveness of each other. For you will share in madness or in Heaven TOGETHER. And you will raise your eyes in FAITH together, or not at all.

T 19 L 6. Beside each of you is one who offers you the chalice of Atonement, for the Holy Spirit is in him. Would you hold his sins AGAINST him, or accept his gift to YOU? Is this giver of Salvation your friend or enemy? Choose which he is, remembering that you will RECEIVE of him according to your choice. **T(730) -554** He has IN HIM the power to forgive YOUR sins, as you for HIM.[670] Neither can give it to himself alone. And yet your Savior stands beside each one. Let him be what he IS, and seek not to make of love an enemy.

T 19 L 7. Behold your Friend, the Christ Who stands beside you. How holy and how beautiful He is! You THOUGHT He sinned, because you cast the veil of sin upon Him to HIDE His loveliness. Yet still He holds forgiveness out to you, to SHARE His holiness. This "enemy," this "stranger" still offers you salvation as His Friend. The "enemies" of Christ, the worshippers of sin, know not Whom they attack. This is your brother, crucified by sin, and waiting for release from pain. Would you not OFFER him forgiveness, when only he can offer it to you?

T 19 L 8. For HIS redemption he will give you yours, as surely as God created every living thing, and loves it. And he will give it truly, for it will be both offered and RECEIVED. There is no grace of Heaven that you cannot OFFER to each other, and receive from your most holy Friend. Let him withhold it not, for by receiving it, you offer it to HIM. And he WILL receive of you what YOU received of him. Redemption has been given you to give EACH OTHER, and thus receive it. Whom you forgive IS free. And what you give, YOU SHARE. Forgive the sins your brother THINKS he has committed, and all the guilt YOU see in him.

T 19 L 9. Here is the holy place of RESURRECTION, to which we come again; to which we will RETURN until redemption is accomplished AND RECEIVED. Think who your brother IS, before you would condemn him. And offer thanks to God that he is holy, and has been given the gift of holiness for YOU. Join him in gladness, and remove all trace of guilt from his disturbed and tortured mind. Help him to lift the heavy burden of sin you laid upon him, and he ACCEPTED as his own, and toss it lightly and with happy laughter

---

[669] March 17, 1963

[670] **Luke 5:21** And the scribes and the Pharisees began to reason, saying, Who is this that speaketh blasphemies? Who can forgive sins, but God alone?
John 20:23 "If you forgive the sins of any, they are forgiven them; if you retain the sins of any, they are retained."

AWAY from him. Press it not like thorns against his brow, nor nail him to it, unredeemed and hopeless. **T(731) -555**

T 19 L 10. Give each other faith, for faith and hope and mercy ARE yours to give.[671] Into the hands that give, the gift is given. Look on your brother, and see in him the gift of God you would RECEIVE. It is almost Easter, the time of Resurrection. Let us give redemption to each other, and SHARE in it, that we may rise as one in resurrection, and not SEPARATE in death. Behold the gift of freedom that I gave the Holy Spirit, for BOTH of you. And be you free together, as you offer TO the Holy Spirit this SAME gift, and, giving it, receive it OF Him, in RETURN for what you gave.

T 19 L 11. He leadeth you and me together, that we might meet here, in this holy place, and make the SAME decision.[672] Free your brother here, as I freed you. Give him the self-same gift, nor look upon him with condemnation of ANY kind. See him as guiltless as I look upon you, and OVERLOOK the sins he THINKS he sees within himself. Offer each other freedom and complete release from sin, here in the garden of seeming agony and death.[673] So will we prepare TOGETHER the way unto the Resurrection of God's Son. And let him rise again to glad remembrance of his Father, Who knows no sin, no death, but ONLY life eternal.[674]

---

[671] **1 Corinthians 13:13** And now abide faith, hope, love, these three; but the greatest of these is love.

[672] **Psalm 23:2-3** He makes me to lie down in green pastures; He leads me beside the still waters. He restores my soul; He leads me in the paths of righteousness For His name's sake.

[673] **Luke 22:39-46** Coming out, He went to the Mount of Olives, as He was accustomed, and His disciples also followed Him. When He came to the place, He said to them, "Pray that you may not enter into temptation." And He was withdrawn from them about a stone's throw, and He knelt down and prayed, saying, "Father, if it is Your will, take this cup away from Me; nevertheless not My will, but Yours, be done." Then an angel appeared to Him from heaven, strengthening Him. And being in agony, He prayed more earnestly. Then His sweat became like great drops of blood falling down to the ground. When He rose up from prayer, and had come to His disciples, He found them sleeping from sorrow. Then He said to them, "Why do you sleep? Rise and pray, lest you enter into temptation."

[674] **Matthew 20:19** And deliver Him to the Gentiles to mock and to scourge and to crucify. And the third day He will rise again.

T 19 L 12. Together we will disappear into the Presence BEYOND the veil, not to be lost, but FOUND; not to be seen, but to be KNOWN.[675] And, knowing, nothing in the plan God has established for salvation will be left undone. This is the journey's purpose, WITHOUT which IS the journey meaningless. Here is the Peace of God, given to you eternally by Him. Here is the rest and quiet that you seek, the REASON for the journey from its beginning. Heaven is the gift you OWE each other, the debt of gratitude you offer to the Son of God, in thanks for what he is, and what his Father created him to be. **T(732) -556**

T 19 L 13. Think carefully how you would look upon the giver of this gift, for as you look on HIM, so will the gift ITSELF appear to be. As HE is seen as either the giver of guilt or of salvation, so will his OFFERING be seen, and so RECEIVED. The crucified give pain, because they ARE in pain. But the redeemed give joy, because they have been HEALED of pain. Everyone gives as he receives, but HE must choose what it will BE that he receives. And he will RECOGNIZE his choice by what he gives, and what is given HIM. Nor is it given anything in hell or Heaven to INTERFERE with his decision.

T 19 L 14. You came this far because the journey WAS your choice. And no-one undertakes to do what he believes is meaningless. What you had faith in still is faithful, and watches over you in faith so gentle, yet so strong, that it would lift you far beyond the veil, and place the Son of God safely within the sure protection of his Father. Here is the ONLY purpose that gives this world, and the long journey THROUGH this world, whatever meaning lies in them. Beyond this, they ARE meaningless. You stand together, still without conviction they HAVE a purpose. Yet it is GIVEN you to SEE this purpose in your holy Friend, and RECOGNIZE it as your own. **T(733) 557**[676]

---

[675] **Luke 15:24** 'For this my son was dead and is alive again; he was lost and is found.' And they began to be merry.
Luke 15:32 It was right that we should make merry and be glad, for your brother was dead and is alive again, and was lost and is found.

[676] March 19, 1967

CHAPTER 20 – THE PROMISE OF THE RESURRECTION

T 20 A. Introduction (not present in *Notes*)

T 20 A 1. This is Palm Sunday, the celebration of victory, and the ACCEPTANCE of the truth. Let us not spend this holy week brooding on the crucifixion of God's Son, but happily in the celebration of his RELEASE. For Easter is the sign of peace, not pain. A slain Christ has no meaning. But a RISEN Christ becomes the symbol of the Son of God's forgiveness upon HIMSELF; the sign he looks upon himself as healed and whole.[677]

T 20 B. Holy Week (not present in *Notes*)

T 20 B 1. This week begins with palms and ends with lilies, the white and holy sign the Son of God is innocent. Let no dark signs of crucifixion intervene between the journey and its purpose; between the ACCEPTANCE of the truth and its EXPRESSION.

T 20 B 2. This week we celebrate eternal life, NOT death. And we honor the perfect PURITY of the Son of God, and NOT his sins. Offer each other the gift of lilies, NOT the crown of thorns; the gift of love, and NOT the "gift" of fear. You stand beside each other, thorns in one hand and lilies in the other, uncertain which to give. Join now with me, and throw away the thorns, offering the lilies to REPLACE them. This Easter I would have the gift of your forgiveness, offered by you to me, and RETURNED by me to you. We CANNOT be united in crucifixion and in death. Nor can the Resurrection be complete 'til YOUR forgiveness rests on Christ, along with mine.

T 20 B 3. A week is short, and yet this holy week is the symbol of the whole journey that the Son of God has undertaken. He started with the sign of victory, the promise of the Resurrection ALREADY given him. Let him not wander into the temptation of crucifixion, and DELAY him there.[678] Help him go in peace BEYOND it, with the light of his own innocence lighting his way to his redemption and release. Hold him not back with thorns and nails, when his redemption is so near. But let the whiteness of your shining gift of lilies speed him on his way to Resurrection. **T(734) -558**

T 20 B 4. Easter is not the celebration of the COST of sin, but of it's END. If you see glimpses of the face of Christ behind the veil, looking between the snow white petals of the lilies you have received and GIVEN as your gift, you will behold each other's face, and RECOGNIZE it. I was a stranger, and you took me in, not knowing who I was.[679] But, for your gift of lilies, you WILL know. In your FORGIVENESS of this stranger, alien to you and yet your ancient Friend, lie HIS release, and YOUR redemption WITH him. The time of Easter is a time of JOY, and not of mourning. Look on your risen Friend, and celebrate his holiness, along with me. For Easter is the time of YOUR salvation, along with mine. **T(735) -559**[680]

T 20 C. Thorns and Lilies (not present in *Notes*)

T 20 C 1. Look upon all the trinkets made to hang upon the body or cover it, or for its use. See all the useless things made for its eyes to see. Think on the many offerings made for its pleasure, and remember all these were made to make seem lovely what you hate. Would you employ this hated thing to draw your brother to you, and to attract HIS body's eyes? Learn you but offer him a crown of thorns, not recognizing it for what it is, and trying to justify your OWN interpretation of its value by HIS acceptance. Yet still the gift proclaims his worthlessness to YOU, as his acceptance and delight acknowledges the lack of value HE places on himself.

T 20 C 2. Gifts are not made through bodies, if they be truly given and received. For bodies can neither offer nor accept; hold out or take. Only the mind can value, and only the mind decides on what it would receive and give. And every gift it offers depends on what it WANTS. It will adorn its chosen home most carefully, making it ready to RECEIVE the gifts it wants, by offering them to those who come unto its home, or those it would ATTRACT to it. And there they will exchange their gifts, offering and receiving what their minds judge to be worthy of them.

T 20 C 3. Each gift is an EVALUATION of the receiver AND THE GIVER. No-one but sees his chosen home an altar to HIMSELF.[681] No-one but seeks to DRAW to it the worshippers of what he placed UPON it, making it WORTHY of their devotion. And each has set a light upon his altar, that they may see what he has placed upon it, and take it for their own. Here is the value that you lay upon your brother, and on YOURSELF. Here is your gift to BOTH; **T(736) - 560** your judgment upon the Son of God for what he is. Forget not that it is YOUR Savior to whom the gift is offered. Offer him thorns, and YOU are crucified. Offer him lilies, and it is YOURSELF you free.

T 20 C 4. I have great need for lilies, for the Son of God has not forgiven me. And can I offer HIM forgiveness, when he offers thorns to me? For he who offers thorns to anyone is against me still, and who is whole WITHOUT him?[682] Be you his Friend for me, that I may be forgiven, and you may look upon the Son of God as whole. But look you first upon the altar in your chosen home, and see what

---

[677] [split paragraph]
[678] **T 16 H 12.** Forgive us our illusions, Father, and help us to accept our true relationship with You, in which there are NO illusions, and where none can ever enter. Our holiness is YOURS. What can there be in us that NEEDS forgiveness, when YOURS is perfect? The sleep of forgetfulness is only the unwillingness to remember YOUR forgiveness and Your Love. Let us not wander into temptation, for the temptation of the Son of God is NOT Your Will. And let us receive ONLY what YOU have given, and accept but this into the minds which You created, and which You love
Matthew 6:13 "And do not lead us into temptation.
 But deliver us from the evil one.
 For Yours is the kingdom and the power and the glory forever." Amen.
[679] **Matthew 25:35** "For I was hungry and you gave Me food; I was thirsty and you gave Me drink; I was a stranger and you took Me in."
[680] March 26, 1967

[681] In the second sentence we read: *"No-one but sees his chosen home an altar to HIMSELF."* We have a prepositional deficit here. There are at least two simple ways to fix this:
1) No one but sees his chosen home *in* his chosen home an altar to Himself ... or
2) No one but sees his chosen home *as* an altar to Himself.
FIP chooses the second. After careful examination of the context, it appears that the "**chosen home**" (which can be the body, and in this example is) is not the altar per se, but that altars reside within homes. Homes are not altars, but they may contain altars. We thus feel that if the grammar is to be corrected, it should be in the manner of example *1*, above, "*No one but sees in his chosen home an altar to Himself,*" believing the *FIP* editors erred here. HOWEVER! There is poetic meter to consider. The original, with prepositional deficit, is better Iambic Pentameter than EITHER correction for grammar. This raises an issue which recurs, when grammar "errors" are required to preserve Iambic Pentameter, should they be left uncorrected? At the moment our choice is to leave them uncorrected but flag them with possible corrections. The latter is likely to be especially helpful to readers whose native tongue is not English and for whom grammar aberrations are prone to obscure the intended meaning. This passage is missing from the *Notes*, as is the whole of chapter 20. This is one instance where that missing primary source could be helpful.
[682] **Matthew 12:30** "He who is not with Me is against Me, and he who does not gather with Me scatters abroad."
Luke 9:50 But Jesus said to him, "Do not forbid him, for he who is not against us is on our side."
John 19:5 Jesus therefore came out, wearing the crown of thorns and the purple garment. And *Pilate* saith unto them, Behold, the man!

you have laid upon it, to offer me. If it be thorns, whose points gleam sharply in a blood-red light, the body is your chosen home, and it is separation that you offer me.

T 20 C 5. And yet the thorns are gone. Look you still closer at them now, and you will see your altar is no longer what it was. You look still with the body's eyes. And they CAN see but thorns. But you have asked for AND RECEIVED another sight. Those who accept the Holy Spirit's purpose as their own, share also in His vision. And what enables Him to SEE His purpose shine forth from every altar, now is yours as well as His. He sees NO strangers only dearly loved and loving Friends. He sees no thorns, but only lilies, gleaming in the gentle glow of peace that shines on everything He looks upon and loves.

T 20 C 6. This Easter, look with DIFFERENT eyes upon each other. You HAVE forgiven me. And yet, I cannot USE your gift of lilies, while you see them not. Nor can YOU use what I have given, unless T(737) -561 you SHARE it. The Holy Spirit's vision is no idle gift, no plaything to be tossed about a while and laid aside. Listen and hear this carefully, nor think it but a dream; -- a careless thought to play with, or a toy you would pick up from time to time and then put by. For if you do, so will it be to you. You have the vision to look past ALL illusions. It has been given you to see no thorns, no strangers, and NO obstacles to peace.

T 20 C 7. The fear of God is NOTHING to you now. Who is afraid to look upon illusions, KNOWING his Savior stands beside him? WITH him, your vision has become the greatest power for the UNDOING of illusion that God Himself could give. For what God gave the Holy Spirit, YOU have received. The Son of God looks unto YOU for his release. For you have asked for AND BEEN GIVEN the strength to look upon this final obstacle, and see no thorns nor nails to crucify the Son of God, and crown him king of death. Your chosen home is on the other side, BEYOND the veil. It has been carefully prepared for you, and it is ready to receive you now.

T 20 C 8. You will not see it with the body's eyes. But all you need, you have. Your home has called to you since time began, nor have you ever failed entirely to hear. You heard, but knew not HOW to look, nor WHERE. And now you KNOW. In you the knowledge lies, ready to be unveiled and freed from all the terror that kept it hidden. There IS no fear in love.[683] The song of Easter is the glad refrain the Son of God was NEVER crucified. Let us lift up our eyes together, not in fear, but FAITH.[684] And there WILL be no fear in us, for in our vision will be NO illusions. Only a pathway to the open door T(738) -562 of Heaven, the home we share in quietness, and where we live in gentleness and peace, as One together.

T 20 C 9. Would you not have your holy brother lead you there? His innocence will light your way, offering you its guiding light and sure protection, and shining from the holy altar within him, where you laid the lilies of forgiveness. Let him be to you the Savior from illusions, and look on him with the new vision that looks upon the lilies, and brings YOU joy. We go beyond the veil of fear, lighting each other's way. The holiness that leads us is WITHIN us, as is our home. So will we find what we were MEANT to find, by Him Who leads us.

T 20 C 10. This is the way to Heaven and to the peace of Easter, in which we join in glad awareness that the Son of God is risen from the past, and has awakened to the present. Now is he free, unlimited in his communion with all that is within him. Now are the lilies of his innocence untouched by guilt, and perfectly protected from the cold chill of fear and withering blight of sin alike. Your gift has saved him from the thorns and nails, and his strong arm is free to guide you safely through them, and BEYOND. Walk with him now rejoicing, for the Savior from illusions has come to greet you, and lead you home with HIM.

T 20 C 11. Here is your Savior and your Friend, RELEASED from crucifixion through YOUR vision, and free to lead you now where HE would be. He will not leave you, nor forsake the Savior from HIS pain. And gladly will you walk the way of innocence together, singing as you behold the open door of Heaven, and T(739) -563 RECOGNIZE the home that called to you. Give joyously to one another the freedom and the strength to lead you there. And come before each other's holy altar, where the strength and freedom wait, to offer and receive the bright awareness that leads you home. The lamp is lit in both of you, for one another. And by the hands that GAVE it to each other, shall both of you be led past fear to Love. T(740) -564

T 20 D. Sin as an Adjustment (not present in *Notes*)

T 20 D 1. The[685] belief in sin is an ADJUSTMENT. And an adjustment is a CHANGE, a shift in perception, or a belief that what was so before has been made DIFFERENT. Every adjustment is therefore a DISTORTION, and calls upon defenses to uphold it AGAINST reality. Knowledge requires NO adjustment, and, in fact, is lost if any shift or change is undertaken. For this reduces it at once to mere perception; a way of LOOKING in which CERTAINTY is lost, and DOUBT has entered. To this IMPAIRED condition are adjustments necessary. BECAUSE THEY ARE NOT TRUE. Who need adjust to truth, which calls upon only what he IS, to understand?

T 20 D 2. Adjustments of ANY kind are of the ego. For it is the ego's fixed belief that all relationships DEPEND upon adjustments, to make of them what it would have them be. DIRECT relationships, in which there are NO interferences, are ALWAYS seen as dangerous. The ego is the self-appointed mediator of ALL relationships, making whatever adjustments it deems necessary, and INTERPOSING them BETWEEN those who would meet, to keep them separate and PREVENT their union. It is this studied interference which makes it difficult to recognize your holy relationship for what it is.

T 20 D 3. The holy do not interfere with truth. They are NOT afraid of it, for it is WITHIN it that they RECOGNIZED their holiness, and rejoiced at what they saw. They looked on it directly, WITHOUT attempting to ADJUST themselves to it, or it to them. And so they saw that it was IN them, NOT deciding first where they would have it be. Their looking merely asked a question, and it was WHAT THEY SAW that answered . YOU make the world and THEN adjust to it. AND IT TO YOU. Nor is there any difference between yourself and it in your perception, WHICH MADE THEM BOTH. T(741) -565

T 20 D 4. A simple question yet remains, and NEEDS an answer. Do you LIKE what you have made? A world of murder and attack, through which you thread your timid way through constant dangers, alone and frightened, hoping at most that death will wait a little longer, before it overtakes you, and you disappear. YOU MADE THIS UP. It is a picture of what you think YOU are; of how you SEE yourself. A murderer IS frightened, and those who kill FEAR death. All these are but the fearful thoughts of those who would adjust themselves to a world MADE fearful by their adjustments. And they look out in sorrow from what is sad WITHIN, and see the sadness THERE.

T 20 D 5. Have you wondered what the world is REALLY like? How would it look through HAPPY eyes? The world you see is but a judgment on YOURSELF. IT is not there at all. But judgment lays a sentence on it, JUSTIFIES it, and MAKES IT REAL. Such is the world you see; a judgment on yourself, and made by YOU. This

---

[683] **1 John 4:18** There is no fear in love; but perfect love casts out fear, because fear involves torment. But he who fears has not been made perfect in love.

[684] **Psalm 121:1** I will lift up my eyes to the hills- From whence comes my help.

---

[685] March 30, 1967

sickly picture of yourself is carefully preserved by the ego, whose image it IS and which it loves, and placed OUTSIDE you, in the world. And TO this world must YOU adjust, as long as you believe this picture IS outside, and has you at its mercy.

T 20 D 6. This world IS merciless, and, were it outside you, you SHOULD indeed be fearful. But it is YOU who made it merciless. And now, if mercilessness SEEMS to look back at you, IT CAN BE CORRECTED. Who, in a holy relationship, can long remain unholy? The world the holy see is one with them, just as the world the ego looks upon is like itself. The world the holy see is beautiful, because they see their innocence in it. They did not TELL it what it was. They did not make adjustments to fit their orders. They gently questioned it, and whispered "what are you?" And He Who watches over all perception answered. T(742) -566

T 20 D 7. Take not the judgment of the world as answer to the question, "what am I?" The world BELIEVES in sin, but the belief that made it as you see it, is NOT outside you. Seek not to make the Son of God ADJUST to his insanity. There IS a stranger in him, who wandered carelessly into the home of Truth, and who will wander off. He came WITHOUT a purpose. But he will not remain before the shining light the Holy Spirit offered, and you accepted. For there the STRANGER is made homeless, and YOU are welcome. Ask not this transient stranger, "who am I?" He is the only thing in all the universe that does not know.

T 20 D 8. Yet it is he you asked, and it is to HIS answer you would adjust. This one wild thought, fierce in its arrogance and yet so tiny and so meaningless it slips unnoticed through the universe of truth, becomes your guide. To it you turn, to ask the MEANING of the universe. And of the one blind thing in all the seeing universe you ask, "how shall I look upon the Son of God?" Does one ask judgment of what is totally BEREFT of judgment? And if you HAVE, would you BELIEVE the answer? And ADJUST to it as if it were the truth? The world you look on IS the answer that it gave you. And YOU have given it power to ADJUST the world to MAKE its answer true.

T 20 D 9. You asked this puff of madness for the meaning of your unholy relationship, and adjusted it according to its insane answer. How happy did it make you? Did you meet with joy, to bless the Son of God, and give him thanks for all the happiness he held out to you? Did you RECOGNIZE each other as the eternal gift of God to you? Did you see the holiness that shone in both of you, to bless the other? That is the purpose of your HOLY relationship. Ask not the means of its attainment of the one thing that still would have it be unholy. Give it NO power to ADJUST the means and end. T(743) - 567

T 20 D 10. Prisoners bound with heavy chains for years, starved and emaciated, weak and exhausted, and with eyes so long cast down in darkness they remember not the light, do not leap up in joy the instant they are made free. It takes a while for them to understand what freedom IS. You groped but feebly in the dust and found each other's hand, uncertain whether to let it go, or to take hold on life so long forgotten. Strengthen your hold, and raise your eyes unto your strong companion, in whom the meaning of your freedom lies. He seemed to be crucified beside you. And yet his holiness remained untouched and perfect, and with him beside you shall you this day enter with him to Paradise,[686] and know the peace of God.

T 20 D 11. Such is my will for BOTH of you, and for each of you for one another, and for HIMSELF. Here there is only holiness, and joining without limit. For what is Heaven but union, direct and perfect, and WITHOUT the veil of fear upon it? Here are we one, looking with perfect gentleness upon each other, and on ourselves. Here, all thought of ANY separation between us becomes impossible. You who were prisoners in separation are now made free in Paradise. And here would I unite with you, my friends, my brothers, and my Self. Your gift unto each other has given me the certainty our union will be soon. Share then this faith with me, who KNOW[687] that it is justified. T(744) -567 a

T 20 D 12. There is no fear in perfect love,[688] BECAUSE it knows no sin. And it MUST look on others as on itself. Looking with charity within, what can it fear WITHOUT? The innocent see safety, and the pure see God[689] within His Son, and look unto the Son to lead them to the Father.[690] And where else would they go, but where they will to be? Each of you now will lead the other to the Father, as surely as God created His Son holy, and kept him so. In your brother is the light of God's eternal promise of YOUR immortality. See HIM as sinless, and there can BE no fear in you. T(745) -568[691]

T 20 E. Entering the Ark (not present in *Notes*)

T 20 E 1. Nothing can hurt you, unless you give it the power to do so. For YOU give power as the laws of this world INTERPRET giving; as you give, you LOSE. It is not up to you to give power at all. Power is of God, GIVEN by Him, and RE-AWAKENED by the Holy Spirit, Who knows that, as you give you GAIN. He gives NO power to sin, and therefore it HAS none. Nor to its results, as this world sees them; sickness and death and misery and pain. These things have not occurred, because the Holy Spirit sees them not, and gives no power to their seeming source. Thus would He keep you free of them.

T 20 E 2. Being without illusion of what you are, the Holy Spirit merely gives EVERYTHING to God, Who has already given AND RECEIVED all that is true. The UNtrue He has neither received NOR given. Sin has no place in Heaven, where its results are alien, and can no more enter than can their source. And therein lies your need to see your brother sinless. In him is Heaven. See sin in him INSTEAD, and Heaven is lost to YOU. But see him as he IS, and what is yours shines from him to you.

T 20 E 3. Your Savior gives you ONLY love. But what you would RECEIVE of him, is up to you. It lies in him to overlook ALL your mistakes, and therein lies his OWN salvation. And so it is with YOURS. Salvation is a lesson in giving, as the Holy Spirit interprets it. It is the re-awakening of the laws of God in minds that have established OTHER laws, and given them power to enforce what God created not. Your insane laws were made to GUARANTEE that you would make mistakes, and give them power over you by ACCEPTING their results as your just due. T(746) -569

T 20 E 4. What COULD this be but madness? And is it THIS that you would see within your Savior FROM insanity? He is as free from this as you are, and in the freedom that you see in HIM, you see your own. For this you SHARE. What God has given follows HIS laws, and His alone. Nor is it possible for those who follow them to suffer the results of any other source. Those who choose

---

[686] Luke 23:39-43 And one of the malefactors that were hanged railed on him, saying, Art not thou the Christ? Save thyself and us. But the other answered, and rebuking him said, Dost thou not even fear God, seeing thou art in the same condemnation? And we indeed justly; for we receive the due reward of our deeds: but this man hath done nothing amiss. And he said, Jesus, remember me when thou comest in thy kingdom. And he said unto him, "Verily I say unto thee, Today shalt thou be with me in Paradise."

[687] There is a grammar problem here, agreement in number. It should be "KNOWS" and may well be a typo. The *HLC* and *FIP* change "who" to "and" which is good grammar but substantially changes the meaning. The *Notes* is n ot available for this segment.

[688] 1 John 4:18 There is no fear in love: but perfect love casteth out fear, because fear hath punishment; and he that feareth is not made perfect in love. John 14:6 Jesus said to him, "I am the way, the truth, and the life. No one comes to the Father except through Me."

[689] Matthew 5:8 "Blessed are the pure in heart: for they shall see God."

[690] John 14:9 Jesus saith unto him, "Have I been so long time with you, and dost thou not know me, Philip? he that hath seen me hath seen the Father; how sayest thou, Show us the Father?"

[691] April 5, 1967

freedom will experience only ITS results. Their power is of God. And they will give it only to what GOD has given, to SHARE with them.

T 20 E 5. Nothing but this can touch them, for they see ONLY this, sharing their power according to the Will of God. And thus their freedom is established AND MAINTAINED. It is upheld through ALL temptations to imprison and to BE imprisoned. It is THEM, who learned of freedom, that you should ask what freedom IS. Ask not the sparrow how the eagle soars, for those with little wings have not accepted for THEMSELVES the power to share with you. The sinless give as they received. See, then, the power of sinlessness within your brother, and share with him the power of the RELEASE from sin you offered HIM.

T 20 E 6. To each who walks this earth in seeming solitude is a Savior given, whose special function here is to release him, and so to free himself. In the world of separation, each is appointed separately, though they are all the same. But those who KNOW that they are all the same, need not salvation. And each one FINDS his Savior, when he is ready to look upon the face of Christ, and see Him sinless. The plan is not of you, nor need you be concerned with anything except the part that has been given YOU to learn. For He Who knows the rest will see to it WITHOUT your help. But think not that He does not need your part, to help Him with the rest. For in your part lies ALL of it, without which is no part complete, nor is the whole completed WITHOUT your part. The ark of peace is entered two by two,[692] yet the beginning of another world goes with them. Each holy relationship **T(747) -570** must enter here, to learn its special function in the Holy Spirit's plan, now that it SHARES His purpose. And, as this purpose is fulfilled, a new world rises, in which sin can enter not, and where the Son of God can enter WITHOUT fear. And where he rests a while, to forget imprisonment, and to remember freedom.

T 20 E 7. How can he enter, to rest and to remember, without YOU? Except you be there, he is NOT complete, and it is his COMPLETION that he remembers there. This is the purpose GIVEN you. Think not that your forgiveness of each other serves but you two alone. For the whole new world rests in the hands of every two who enter here, to rest. And as they rest, the face of Christ shines on them, and they remember the laws of God, forgetting all the rest, and yearning only to have His laws perfectly fulfilled in them and all their brothers.

T 20 E 8. Think you, when this has been achieved, that you will rest WITHOUT them? You could no more leave one of them outside than I could leave you, and forget part of myself. You may wonder how you can BE at peace when, while you are in time, there is so much that must be done BEFORE the way to peace is open. Perhaps this seems impossible to YOU. But ask yourself if it is possible that GOD would have a plan for your salvation that does NOT work. Once you accept HIS plan as the ONE function that you would fulfill, there WILL be nothing else the Holy Spirit will not ARRANGE for you, WITHOUT your effort.

T 20 E 9. He will go before you, making straight your path, and leaving in your way no stones to trip on, and no obstacles to bar your way.[693] NOTHING you need will be denied you. Not one seeming difficulty but will melt away BEFORE you reach it. You need take thought for nothing, careless of everything except the only purpose that you would fulfill. As THAT was given you, so will its fulfillment be. God's guarantee will hold against **T(748) -571** ALL obstacles, for it rests on certainty, and NOT contingency. IT RESTS ON YOU. And what can be more certain than the Son of God?

T 20 F. Heralds of Eternity (not present in *Notes*)

T 20 F 1. In this world, God's Son comes closest to himself in a holy relationship. There he begins to find the certainty his Father has in him. And there he finds his function of restoring his Father's laws to what was held OUTSIDE them, and finding what was lost. Only in time can anything BE lost, but never lost forever. So do the parts of God's Son gradually join in time, and with each joining is the end of time brought nearer. Each miracle of joining is a mighty herald of eternity. No-one who has a single purpose, unified and sure, can BE afraid. No-one who SHARES his purpose with him can NOT be one with him.

T 20 F 2. Each herald of eternity sings of the end of sin and fear. Each speaks in time of what is far BEYOND it. Two voices, raised together, call to the hearts of everyone, and let them beat as one. And in that single heart beat is the unity of love proclaimed and given welcome. Peace to your holy relationship, which has the power to hold the unity of the Son of God together. You give to one another for EVERYONE. And in your gift is everyone made glad. Forget not Who has given YOU the gifts you give. And through your NOT forgetting this, will you remember Who gave the gifts to Him to give to you.

T 20 F 3. It is impossible to over-estimate your brother's value. Only the ego does this, but all it means is that it WANTS the other for ITSELF, and therefore values him too little. What is inestimable clearly cannot BE evaluated. Do you recognize the fear that rises from the meaningless attempt to judge what lies so far BEYOND your judgment you cannot even SEE it? Judge not what is invisible to you, or you will NEVER see it. But wait in patience for its coming. **T(749) -572** It will be GIVEN you to see your brother's worth, when all you WANT for him is peace. And what you want for HIM, you will receive.[694]

T 20 F 4. How can you estimate the worth of him who offers peace to you? What would you want EXCEPT his offering? His worth has been established by his Father, and you will RECOGNIZE it as you receive his Father's gift through him. What is in him will shine so brightly in your grateful vision, that you will merely love him, and be glad. You will not think to judge him. Who would SEE the face of Christ, and yet insist that judgment still has meaning? For this insistence is of those who do NOT see. Vision OR judgment is your choice, but never BOTH of these.

T 20 F 5. Your brother's body is as little use to you as it is to him. When it is used ONLY as the Holy Spirit teaches, it has no function. For minds NEED not the body to communicate. The sight that SEES the body, has no use which serves the purpose of a holy relationship. And while you look upon each other thus, the means and end have NOT been brought in line. Why should it take so many holy instants to let this be accomplished, when one would do? There IS but one. The little breath of eternity that runs through time like golden light is all the same. Nothing before it; nothing afterwards.

T 20 F 6. You look upon each holy instant as a DIFFERENT point in time. IT NEVER CHANGES. All that it ever held or will ever hold is here right now. The past takes nothing FROM it, and the future will ADD no more. Here, then, is EVERYTHING. Here is the loveliness of your relationship, with means and ends in perfect harmony ALREADY. Here is the perfect faith that you will one day offer to each other, ALREADY offered you. And here the limitless forgiveness you will give each other is ALREADY given; the face of Christ you yet will look upon ALREADY seen. **T(750) -573**

---

[692] **Genesis 7:7-9** And Noah went in, and his sons, and his wife, and his sons' wives with him, into the ark, because of the waters of the flood. Of clean beasts, and of beasts that are not clean, and of birds, and of everything that creepeth upon the ground, there went in two and two unto Noah into the ark, male and female, as God commanded Noah.

[693] **Isaiah 40:3** The voice of one crying in the wilderness: "Prepare the way of the LORD; Make straight in the desert A highway for our God.
John 1:23 He said: I am the voice of one crying in the wilderness: "Make straight the way of the LORD," as the prophet Isaiah said.

[694] April 6, 1967

Chapter 20 – The Promise of the Resurrection

T 20 F 7. Can you EVALUATE the giver of a gift like this? Would you EXCHANGE this gift for ANY other? This gift returns the laws of God to your remembrance. And merely BY remembering them, the laws that held you prisoner to pain and death MUST be forgotten. This is no gift your brother's BODY offers you. The veil that hides the gift hides him as well. He IS the gift, and yet he knows it not. No more do you. And yet have faith that He Who sees the gift in BOTH of you, will offer and receive it for you BOTH. And through His vision will YOU see it, and through His understanding RECOGNIZE it, and love it as your own.

T 20 F 8. Be comforted, and feel the Holy Spirit watching over you, in love and perfect confidence in what He sees. He knows the Son of God. And shares his Father's certainty the universe rests in his gentle hands in safety and in peace. Let us consider now what he must learn, to SHARE his Father's confidence in him. What IS he, that the Creator of the universe should offer it to him, and KNOW it rests in safety?[695] He looks upon himself not as his Father knows him. And yet it is impossible the confidence of God should be misplaced.

T 20 G. The Temple of the Holy Spirit (not present in *Notes*)

T 20 G 1. The meaning of the Son of God lies solely in his relationship with his Creator. If it were elsewhere, it WOULD rest upon contingency. But there IS nothing else. And this is wholly loving and forever. Yet has the Son of God invented an unholy relationship between him and his Father. His REAL relationship is one of perfect union, and unbroken continuity. The one he made is partial, self-centered, broken into fragments and full of fear. The one created by his Father is wholly self-encompassing and self-EXTENDING. The one he made is wholly self-DESTRUCTIVE and self-LIMITING.

T(751) -574

T 20 G 2. Nothing[696] can show the contrast better than the experience of both a holy and an unholy relationship. The first is based on love, and rests on it serene and undisturbed. THE BODY DOES NOT INTRUDE UPON IT. Any relationship in which the body enters is based, NOT on love, but on idolatry. Love wishes to be known, COMPLETELY understood, and shared.[697] IT HAS NO SECRETS; nothing that it would keep apart and hide. It walks in sunlight, open-eyed and calm, in smiling welcome, and in sincerity so simple and so obvious it cannot BE misunderstood.

T 20 G 3. But idols do not share. Idols ACCEPT, but never make return. They can BE loved, but cannot love. They do not understand what they are offered, and any relationship in which they enter, has LOST its meaning. The love of THEM has MADE love meaningless. They live in secrecy, hating the sunlight, and happy in the body's darkness, where they can hide, and keep their secrets hidden, along with them. And they have NO relationships, for no-one else is welcome there. They smile on no-one, and those who smile on them they do not see.

T 20 G 4. Love has no darkened temples, where mysteries are kept obscure and hidden from the sun. IT DOES NOT SEEK FOR POWER, but for RELATIONSHIPS. The body is the ego's chosen weapon for seeking power THROUGH relationships. And its relationships MUST be unholy, for what they ARE, it does not even SEE. It wants them solely for the offerings on which its idols thrive. The rest it merely throws away, for all that IT could offer, is seen as valueless. Homeless, the ego seeks as many bodies as it can collect, to place its idols in, and so establish them as temples to itself.

T 20 G 5. The Holy Spirit's temple is NOT a body, but a RELATIONSHIP. The body is an isolated speck of darkness; a hidden secret room, a tiny spot of senseless mystery, a meaningless enclosure carefully protected, yet **T(752) -575** hiding nothing. Here, the unholy relationship escapes reality, and seeks for crumbs to keep itself alive. Here it would drag its brothers, holding them here in its idolatry. Here it is "safe," for here love CANNOT enter. The Holy Spirit does not build His temples where love can never be. Would He Who SEES the face of Christ choose as His home the only place in all the universe where it can NOT be seen?

T 20 G 6. You CANNOT make the body the Holy Spirit's temple, and it will NEVER be the seat of love. It is the home of the idolater, and of love's CONDEMNATION. For here is love made fearful, and hope abandoned. Even the idols that are worshipped here are shrouded deep in mystery, and kept APART from those who worship them. This is the temple dedicated to no relationships, and no return. Here is the "mystery" of separation perceived in awe and held in reverence. What God would have NOT be, is here kept "safe" from Him. But what you do NOT realize is what you fear within your brother, and would not SEE in HIM, is what makes God seem fearful and kept unknown.

T 20 G 7. Idolaters will ALWAYS be afraid of love. For nothing so severely threatens them as love's approach. Let love draw near them and OVERLOOK the body, as it will surely do, and they retreat in fear, feeling the seeming firm foundation of their temple begin to shake and loosen. Brothers, you tremble with them. But what you fear is but the herald of escape. This place of darkness is NOT your home. Your temple is NOT threatened. You are idolaters no longer.[698] The Holy Spirit's purpose lies safe in your RELATIONSHIP, and NOT your bodies. You have ESCAPED the body. Where you are now, the BODY cannot enter, for the Holy Spirit has set HIS temple there.

T 20 G 8. There is no order in relationships. They either ARE, or not. An unholy relationship is NO relationship. It is a state of isolation, which SEEMS to be what it is NOT. No more than that. The instant that the **T(753) -576** mad idea of making your relationship with God unholy seemed to be possible, ALL relationships were made meaningless. In that unholy instant time was born, and bodies made to house the mad idea, and give it the ILLUSION of reality. And so it SEEMED to have a home, that held together for a little while in time, and vanished. For what could house this mad idea AGAINST reality, but for an instant?

T 20 G 9. Idols MUST disappear, and leave no trace behind their going. The unholy instant of their seeming power is frail as is a snowflake, but without its loveliness. Is this the substitute you WANT, for the eternal blessing of the holy instant, and its unlimited beneficence? Is the malevolence of the unholy relationship, so seeming powerful and so bitterly misunderstood, and so invested in FALSE attraction, your preference to the holy instant, which offers peace and understanding? Then lay aside the body and quietly TRANSCEND it, rising to welcome what you REALLY want. And from His holy temple look you not back on what you have awakened FROM.[699] For no illusions CAN attract the minds that have TRANSCENDED them, and left them far behind.

T 20 G 10. The holy relationship reflects the TRUE relationship the Son of God has with his Father in reality. The Holy Spirit rests within it, in the certainty it will endure forever. Its firm foundation is eternally upheld by truth, and love shines on it with the gentle smile

---

[695] **Psalm 8:4** What is man that You are mindful of him, And the son of man that You visit him?
Hebrews 2:6 But one testified in a certain place, saying: "What is man that You are mindful of him, Or the son of man that You take care of him?"
[696] April 7, 1967
[697] **1 Corinthians 13:4-7** Love suffers long and is kind; love does not envy; love does not parade itself, is not puffed up; does not behave rudely, does not seek its own, is not provoked, thinks no evil; does not rejoice in iniquity, but rejoices in the truth; bears all things, believes all things, hopes all things, endures all things.

[698] **Ephesians 2:19** Now, therefore, you are no longer strangers and foreigners, but fellow citizens with the saints and members of the household of God,
[699] **Luke 9:62** But Jesus said to him, "No one, having put his hand to the plow, and looking back, is fit for the kingdom of God."

and tender blessing it offers to its own. Here the unholy instant is exchanged in gladness for the holy one of safe return. Here is the way to true relationships held gently open, through which you walk together, leaving the body thankfully behind, and resting in the Everlasting Arms.[700] Love's arms are open to receive you, and give you peace forever. **T(754) -577**

T 20 G 11. The body is the ego's idol; the belief in sin made flesh, and then projected outward. This produces what SEEMS to be a wall of flesh AROUND the mind, keeping it prisoner in a tiny spot of space and time, beholden unto death, and given but an instant in which to sigh and grieve and die in honor of its master. And this unholy instant SEEMS to be life. An instant of despair, a tiny island of dry sand, bereft of water, and set uncertainly upon oblivion. Here does the Son of God stop briefly by, to offer his devotion to death's idols, and then pass on.

T 20 G 12. And here he is more dead than living. But it is also here he makes his choice again, between idolatry and love. Here it is given him to choose to spend this instant paying tribute to the body, or LET himself be given freedom from it. Here he can ACCEPT the holy instant, offered him to REPLACE the unholy one he chose before. And here can he learn relationships are his SALVATION, NOT his doom. You who ARE learning this may still be fearful, but you are NOT immobilized. The holy instant IS of greater value now to you than its unholy seeming counterpart, and you HAVE learned you REALLY want but one.

T 20 G 13. This is no time for sadness. Perhaps confusion, but hardly discouragement. YOU HAVE A REAL RELATIONSHIP. And it HAS meaning. It is as like your real relationship with God, as equal things are like themselves. Idolatry is past and meaningless. Perhaps you fear each other a little yet; perhaps a shadow of the fear of God remains with you. But what is that to those who have been given one TRUE relationship, BEYOND the body? Can they be long held back from looking on the face of Christ? And can they long withhold the memory of their relationship with their Father FROM themselves, and keep remembrance of His Love APART from their awareness? **T(755) -578**[701]

T 20 H. The Consistency of Means and End (not present in *Notes*)

T 20 H 1. We have said much about discrepancies of means and end, and how these must be brought in line before your holy relationship can bring you ONLY joy. But we have also said the means to meet the Holy Spirit's goal will come from the same Source as does His purpose. Being so simple and direct, this course has NOTHING in it that is not consistent. The SEEMING inconsistencies, or parts you find more difficult than others, are merely indications of areas where means and end are still discrepant. And this produces great discomfort. This NEED not be. This course requires almost NOTHING of you. It is impossible to imagine one that asks so little, or could offer more.

T 20 H 2. The period of discomfort that follows the sudden change in a relationship from sin to holiness, should now be almost over. To the extent you still experience it, you are REFUSING to leave the means to Him Who changed the purpose. You recognize you WANT the goal. Are you not also willing to ACCEPT the means? If you are not, let us admit that YOU are inconsistent. A purpose is ATTAINED by means. And if you WANT a goal, you MUST be willing to want the means as well. How can one be sincere and say, "I want this above all else, and yet I do not want to learn the means to get it?"

---

[700] **Deuteronomy 33:27** The eternal God is *thy* dwelling-place, And underneath are the everlasting arms. And he thrust out the enemy from before thee, And said, Destroy.
[701] April 10, 1967

T 20 H 3. To obtain the GOAL, the Holy Spirit indeed asked little. He asks no more to give the means as well. The means are second to the goal. And, when you hesitate, it is because the PURPOSE frightens you, and NOT the means. Remember this, for otherwise you will make the error of believing the MEANS are difficult. Yet how CAN they be difficult, if they are merely GIVEN you? They GUARANTEE the goal. And they are PERFECTLY in line with it. Before we look at them a little closer, remember that if you think THEY are impossible, your wanting of the PURPOSE has been shaken. For if a GOAL is possible to reach, the means to do so MUST be possible as well. **T(756) -579**

T 20 H 4. It IS impossible to see your brother sinless, and yet to look upon him as a body. Is this not perfectly consistent with the goal of holiness? For holiness is merely the result of letting the effects of sins be lifted, so what was ALWAYS true is RECOGNIZED. To see a SINLESS body is impossible. For holiness is POSITIVE, and the body is merely neutral. It is NOT sinful, but neither is it sinless. As nothing, which it IS, the body cannot meaningfully be invested with attributes of Christ OR of the ego. EITHER must be an error, for both would place the attributes where they cannot BE. And BOTH must be undone, for purposes of truth.

T 20 H 5. The body IS the means by which the ego tries to make the unholy relationship seem real. The unholy instant IS the time of bodies. But the PURPOSE here is sin. It cannot BE attained but in illusion. And so the illusion of a brother as a body is quite in keeping with the purpose of unholiness. BECAUSE of this consistency, the means remain unquestioned while the end is cherished. Vision adapts to wish, for sight is ALWAYS secondary to desire. And if you see the body, you have chosen judgment, and NOT vision. For vision, like relationships, HAS no order. You either SEE, or not.

T 20 H 6. Who sees a brother's body has laid a JUDGMENT on him, and sees him not. He does not REALLY see him as sinful; he does not see him at all. In the darkness of sin, he is INVISIBLE. He can but be IMAGINED in the darkness, and it is here that the illusions you hold about him are NOT held up to his reality. Here are illusions and reality kept SEPARATED. Here are illusions NEVER brought to truth, and ALWAYS hidden from it. And here, in darkness, is your brother's reality IMAGINED as a body, in unholy relationships with other bodies, serving the cause of sin an instant, before he dies.

T 20 H 7. There is indeed a difference between this vain imagining and vision. The difference lies not in THEM, but in their purpose. Both are but MEANS, each one appropriate to the end for which it is employed. Neither can serve **T(757) -580** the purpose of the other, for each one is a CHOICE of purpose, employed on its behalf. Either is meaningless WITHOUT the end for which it was intended, nor is it valued as a SEPARATE thing, APART from the intention. The means seem real because the GOAL is valued. And judgment HAS no value unless the GOAL is sin. The body can NOT be looked upon EXCEPT through judgment. To see the body is the sign that you LACK vision, and have DENIED the means the Holy Spirit offers you, to serve HIS purpose.

T 20 H 8. How can a holy relationship achieve its purpose through the means of sin? Judgment you taught YOURSELF; vision is learned from Him Who would UNDO your teaching. HIS vision cannot see the body, BECAUSE IT CANNOT LOOK ON SIN. And thus it leads you to reality. Your holy brother, sight of whom is YOUR release, is no illusion. Attempt to see him not in darkness, for your imaginings about him WILL seem real there. You CLOSED your eyes to shut him out. Such was your PURPOSE, and while this purpose seems to have ANY meaning, the means for its attainment will be evaluated as WORTH the seeing, and so you will NOT see.

T 20 H 9. Your question should not be, "How can I see my brother without the body?" Ask only, "Do I REALLY wish to see him sinless?" And, as you ask, forget not that HIS sinlessness is YOUR escape from fear. Salvation is the Holy Spirit's goal. The means is vision. For what the seeing look upon IS sinless. No-one who loves can judge, and what he sees is FREE of condemnation. And what he sees he did NOT make, for it was GIVEN him to see, as was the vision which made his seeing possible.

T 20 I. The Vision of Sinlessness (not present in *Notes*)

T 20 I 1. Vision will come to you at first in glimpses, but they will be enough to show you what is given YOU who see your brother sinless.

T 20 I 2. Truth is restored to you through your desire, as it was lost to you through your desire for something ELSE. Open the holy place which you closed off by VALUING the something else, and what was never lost will T(758) -581 quietly return. It HAS been saved for you. Vision would not be necessary, had judgment not been made. Desire now its whole undoing, and it is done FOR you. Do you not WANT to know your own identity? Would you not happily exchange your doubts for certainty? Would you not willingly be FREE of misery, and learn again of joy? Your holy relationship offers all this to you. As IT was given you, so will be its EFFECTS.

T 20 I 3. And as its holy purpose was not made by you, the means by which its happy end is yours is also not of you. Rejoice in what is yours but for the asking. And think not that you need make either means OR end. All this is GIVEN you, who would but SEE your brother sinless. All this is GIVEN, waiting on your desire but to RECEIVE it. Vision is freely given to those who ask to see. Your brother's sinlessness is given you in shining light, to look on with the Holy Spirit's vision, and to rejoice in, along with Him. For peace will come to all who ask for it with real desire and sincerity of purpose, SHARED with the Holy Spirit, and at one with Him on what salvation IS.

T 20 I 4. Be willing, then, to see your brother sinless, that Christ may rise before your vision, and give you joy. And place NO value on your brother's body, which held him to illusions of what he is. It is HIS desire to see his sinlessness, as it is YOURS. And bless the Son of God in your relationship, nor see in him what you have MADE of him. The Holy Spirit GUARANTEES that what God has willed and given shall be yours. This is YOUR purpose now, and the vision that makes it yours is ready to be given. You have the vision that enables you to see the body not. -→ T(759) -582[702] And as you look upon each other, you will see an altar to your Father, holy as Heaven, glowing with radiant purity, and sparkling with the shining lilies you laid upon it.

T 20 I 5. What can you value more than this? Why do you think the body is a better home, a safer shelter for God's Son? Why would you rather look on IT, than on the truth? How can the engine of destruction be PREFERRED, and chosen to REPLACE the holy home the Holy Spirit offers, where HE will dwell WITH you? The body is the sign of weakness, vulnerability, and LOSS of power. Can such a Savior HELP you? Would you turn, in your distress and need for help, unto the HELPLESS? Is the pitifully LITTLE the perfect choice to call upon for strength? Judgment WILL seem to make your Savior weak. But it is YOU who need his strength.

T 20 I 6. There is no problem, no event or situation, no perplexity, that vision will not solve. All is redeemed, when looked upon with vision. For this is not YOUR sight, and brings with it the laws beloved of Him Whose sight it IS. Everything looked upon with vision falls gently into place, according to the laws brought TO it by His calm and certain sight. The end, for everything HE looks upon, is ALWAYS sure. For it will meet His purpose, seen in UNADJUSTED form, and suited perfectly to meet it. Destructiveness becomes benign, and sin is turned to blessing under His gentle gaze.

T 20 I 7. What can the body's eyes perceive, with power to CORRECT? Its eyes ADJUST to sin, unable to overlook it in ANY form, and T(760) -583 seeing it EVERYWHERE, in EVERYTHING. Look through ITS eyes, and EVERYTHING will stand condemned before you. All that could SAVE you, you will never see. Your holy relationship, the SOURCE of your salvation, will be DEPRIVED of meaning, and its most holy purpose bereft of means for its accomplishment. Judgment is but a toy, a whim, the senseless means to play the idle game of death in your imagination. But vision sets all things right, bringing them gently within the kindly sway of Heaven's laws. T(761) -583 a[703]

T 20 I 8. What if you recognized this world is a hallucination? What if you REALLY understood you made it up? What if you realized that those who SEEM to walk about in it, to sin and die, attack and murder and destroy themselves, are WHOLLY unreal? Could you have FAITH in what you see, if you ACCEPTED this? AND WOULD YOU SEE IT? Hallucinations disappear when they are RECOGNIZED for what they are. This IS the healing and the remedy. Believe them not, and they ARE gone. And all YOU need to do is recognize YOU DID THIS. Once you ACCEPT this simple fact, and take unto YOURSELF the power you GAVE them, YOU are released from them.

T 20 I 9. One thing is sure; hallucinations serve a purpose, and when that PURPOSE is no longer held, THEY disappear. Therefore, the question never is whether you want THEM, but ALWAYS do you want the purpose that they serve? This world SEEMS to hold out many purposes, each different, and with different values. Yet they are all the same. Again, there is no order, but a SEEMING hierarchy of values. Only two purposes are possible. And one is sin; the other holiness. Nothing is in between, and which you choose determines what you see. For what you see is merely HOW you elect to meet your goal.

T 20 I 10. Hallucinations serve to meet the goal of madness. They are the means by which the OUTSIDE world, projected from within, ADJUSTS to sin, and SEEMS to witness to its reality. It still is true that nothing IS without. Yet, upon nothing, are ALL projections made. For it is the PROJECTION which gives the "nothing" ALL the meaning that it holds. What has NO meaning, cannot BE perceived. And meaning ALWAYS looks within, to find itself. And THEN looks out. ALL meaning that you give the world outside, must thus reflect the sight you saw WITHIN. Or better, IF you saw at all, or merely judged AGAINST. T(762) -584

T 20 I 11. Vision is the means by which the Holy Spirit translates your nightmares into happy dreams; your wild hallucinations, that show you all fearful outcomes of imagined sin, into the calm and reassuring sights with which He would replace them. These gentle sights and sounds are looked on happily, and heard with joy. They are HIS substitutes for all the terrifying sights and screaming sounds the ego's purpose brought to your horrified awareness. They step AWAY from sin, reminding you that it is NOT reality that frightens you, and that the errors which you made CAN be corrected.

T 20 I 12. When you have looked on what seemed terrifying, and SEEN it change to sights of loveliness and peace; when you have looked on scenes of violence and death, and WATCHED them change to quiet views of gardens under open skies, with clear life-giving water running happily beside them in dancing brooks that never waste away; who need PERSUADE you to accept the gift of vision? And AFTER vision, who is there who COULD refuse what MUST come after? Think but an instant just on this. YOU can behold the holiness God gave His Son. And NEVER need you think that there IS something else for you to see. T(763) -585

---

[702] April 11, 1967

[703] April 14, '67

Chapter 21 – The Inner Picture

T 21 A. Introduction (not present in *Notes*)

T 21 A 1. Projection[704] makes perception; the world you see is what you GAVE it, nothing more than that. But, though it is no MORE than that, it is NOT less. Therefore, to YOU, it IS important. It is the witness to your state of mind, the OUTSIDE picture of an INWARD condition. As a man thinketh, so does he perceive.[705] Therefore, seek not to change the WORLD, but will to change your mind ABOUT the world. Perception is a RESULT, and NOT a cause. And that is WHY order of miracles is meaningless. EVERYTHING looked upon with vision is healed and holy. NOTHING perceived without it means anything. And where there is no meaning, there is chaos.

T 21 A 2. Damnation is your judgment on YOURSELF. And this you WILL project upon the world. See IT as damned, and all you see is what YOU did to hurt the Son of God. If you behold disaster and catastrophe, you tried to crucify him. If you see holiness and hope, you joined the Will of God to set him free. There is no choice that lies between these two decisions. And you will see the WITNESS to the choice you made, and learn from this to RECOGNIZE the one you made. The world you see but shows you how much joy YOU have allowed yourself to see in you, and to accept as YOURS. And, if this IS its meaning, then the power to GIVE it joy MUST lie WITHIN you.

T 21 B. The Imagined World (not present in *Notes*)

T 21 B 1. Never forget the world the sightless "see" MUST be imagined. And what it REALLY looks like IS unknown to them. They must infer what COULD be seen, from evidence forever indirect, and RECONSTRUCT their inferences as they stumble and fall because of what they did NOT recognize, or walk unharmed through open doorways that they THOUGHT were closed. And so it is with **T(764) -586**

you. You do NOT see. Your cues for inference are wrong, and so you stumble and fall down upon the stones you did not recognize. But fail to be aware you CAN go through the doors you THOUGHT were closed, but which stand open before unseeing eyes, waiting to WELCOME you.

T 21 B 2. How foolish it is to attempt to judge what could be seen instead. It is not necessary to IMAGINE what the world must look like. It must be SEEN, before you recognize it for what it is. You can be SHOWN which doors are open, and you can SEE where safety lies. And which way leads to darkness; which to light. Judgment will ALWAYS give you false directions. But vision SHOWS you where to go. Why should you guess? There is no NEED to learn through pain. And gentle lessons are acquired joyously, and are remembered gladly. What gives you happiness you WANT to learn, and NOT forget.

T 21 B 3. It is not this you would deny. YOUR question is whether the means by which this course is learned WILL bring the joy it promises. If you BELIEVED it would, the LEARNING of it would be NO problem. You are not happy learners yet, because you still remain uncertain that vision gives you MORE than judgment does, and you HAVE learned that both you CANNOT have. The blind become ACCUSTOMED to their world by their adjustments TO it. They think they know their way about in it. They learned it not through joyous lessons, but through the stern necessity of limits they believed they could not overcome. And, STILL believing this, they hold those lessons dear, and cling to them BECAUSE they cannot see.

T 21 B 4. They do not understand the lessons KEEP them blind. This they do NOT believe. And so they keep the world they learned to **T(765) -587** "see" in their imagination, believing that their choice is that, or nothing. They hate the world they learned through pain. And everything they think is in it, serves to remind them that THEY are incomplete and bitterly deprived. Thus they DEFINE their life and where they live it, ADJUSTING to it as they think they must, afraid to lose the little that they have. And so it is with all who see the body as all they have, and all their brothers have. They try to reach each other, and they fail. And fail again. And they ADJUST to loneliness, believing that to KEEP the body is to SAVE the little that they have.

T 21 B 5. Listen, and try to think if you remember what we will speak of now. Listen, -- perhaps you catch a hint of an ancient state not quite forgotten; dim, perhaps, and yet not altogether unfamiliar. Like a song whose name is long forgotten, and the circumstances in which you heard completely unremembered. Not the whole song has stayed with you, but just a little wisp of melody, attached not to a person or a place, or anything particular. But you remember, from just this little part, how lovely was the song, how wonderful the setting where you heard it, and how you loved those who were there, and listened with you.

T 21 B 6. The notes are nothing; yet you have kept them with you, not for themselves, but as a soft reminder of what would make you weep, if you remembered how dear it was to you. You COULD remember, yet you are afraid, believing you would lose the world you learned since then. And yet you know that nothing in the world you learned is half so dear as this. Listen, and see if you remember an ancient song you knew so long ago, and held more **T(766) -588** dear than any melody you taught yourself to cherish since. Beyond the body, beyond the sun and stars, past EVERYTHING you see and yet somehow familiar, is an arc of golden light that stretches, as you look, into a great and shining circle. And all the circle fills with light before your eyes.

T 21 B 7. The edges of the circle disappear, and what is in it no longer is contained at all. The light expands and covers everything, extending to infinity, forever shining, and with no break or limit anywhere. Within it, EVERYTHING is joined in perfect continuity. Nor is it possible to imagine that anything COULD be outside. For there IS nowhere that this light is not. This is the vision of the Son of God, whom you know well. Here is the sight of him who knows his Father. Here is the memory of what you ARE; a PART of this, with ALL of it within you, and JOINED to all of it as surely as all is joined to you.

T 21 B 8. ACCEPT the vision that can show you this, and NOT the body. You KNOW the ancient song, and know it well. Nothing will ever be as dear to you as is this ancient hymn of love the Son of God sings to his Father still. And now the blind can see, for that same song they sing in honor of their Creator, gives praise to them as well. The blindness that they made will not withstand the memory of this song. And they will look upon the vision of the Son of God, remembering who he is they sing of. What is a miracle, but this remembering? And who is there in whom this memory lies not? The light in one, awakens it in all. And, when you see it in each other, you ARE remembering for everyone. **T(767) -589**

---

[704] April 16, 1967
[705] **Proverbs 23:7** For as he thinks in his heart, so is he. "Eat and drink!" he says to you, But his heart is not with you.

Chapter 21 – The Inner Picture

T 21 C. The Responsibility for Sight (not present in *Notes*)

T 21 C 1. We[706] have repeated how little is asked of you to learn this course. It is the same small willingness you need to have your whole relationship transformed to joy. The LITTLE gift you offer to the Holy Spirit, for which He gives you EVERYTHING. The very little, on which salvation rests. The tiny change of mind by which the crucifixion is changed to Resurrection. And, being true, it is so simple that it cannot fail to be COMPLETELY understood. Rejected, yes, but NOT ambiguous. And, if you choose AGAINST it now, it will NOT be because it is obscure, but rather that this LITTLE cost seemed, in YOUR judgment, to be TOO MUCH to pay for peace.

T 21 C 2. This is the ONLY thing that you need do for vision, happiness, release from pain, and the COMPLETE escape from sin, ALL to be given you. Say ONLY this, but MEAN it with NO reservations, for here the power of salvation lies:

"I AM responsible for what I see. I CHOSE the feelings I experience, and I DECIDED ON the goal I would achieve. And everything that SEEMS to happen TO me, I ASKED FOR and received as I had asked."

Deceive yourself no longer that you are helpless in the face of what is done TO you. Acknowledge but that YOU have been mistaken, and ALL effects of your mistakes will disappear.

T 21 C 3. It is impossible the Son of God be merely driven by events OUTSIDE him. It is impossible that the happenings that come to him were NOT his choice. His power of decision is the DETERMINER of every situation in which he seems to FIND himself by chance or accident. No accident or chance is POSSIBLE within the universe as God created it, OUTSIDE of which is nothing. Suffer, and YOU decided sin was your goal. Be happy, and you GAVE the power of decision to Him Who MUST decide for God for you. This is the little gift you offer to the Holy Spirit, and even this He gave to you to give yourself. For, BY this gift, is given you the power to release your Savior, that HE **T(768) -590** may give salvation unto YOU.

T 21 C 4. Begrudge not, then, this little offering. WITHHOLD it, and you keep the world as now you see it. GIVE IT AWAY, and everything YOU see goes with it. Never was so much given for so little. In the holy instant is this exchange effected and MAINTAINED. Here is the world you do NOT want, brought to the one you DO. And here the one you do is GIVEN you, BECAUSE you want it. But, for this, the POWER of your wanting must first be RECOGNIZED. You must accept its STRENGTH, and NOT its weakness. You must perceive that what is strong enough to MAKE a world, can let it go. And CAN accept correction, if it is willing to see that it was wrong.

T 21 C 5. The world you see is but the idle witness that you were RIGHT. This witness is insane. You trained it in its testimony, and, as it gave it BACK to you, you listened and convinced yourself that what it saw was true. YOU DID THIS TO YOURSELF. See only this, and you will also see how circular the reasoning on which your "seeing" rests. This was NOT given you. This was your GIFT to you AND TO YOUR BROTHER. Be willing, then, to have it taken FROM him, and be replaced with truth. And, as you look upon the change in HIM, it will be given you to see it in YOURSELF. **T(769) -591**

T 21 C 6. Perhaps[707] you do not see the need for you to give this little offering. Look closer, then, at what it IS. And, very simply, see in it the whole exchange of separation for salvation. All that the ego is, is an idea that it is possible that things should[708] HAPPEN to the Son of God, WITHOUT his will. And thus, without the Will of his Creator, Whose Will cannot BE separated from his own. This is the Son of God's REPLACEMENT for his will, a mad revolt against what must forever be. This is the statement that he HAS the power to make God powerLESS. And so to take it from HIMSELF, and leave himself WITHOUT what God has willed FOR him.

T 21 C 7. This is the mad idea you have enshrined upon your altars, AND WHICH YOU WORSHIP. And anything that threatens this, seems to ATTACK your faith. For here it is invested. Think not that you are faithless, for your belief and trust in THIS is strong indeed. The Holy Spirit can GIVE you faith in holiness, and vision to see it, easily enough. But you have not left open and unoccupied the altar where the gift belongs. Where THEY should be, YOU have set up your idols to something ELSE. This OTHER will, which seems to TELL you what must happen, you GAVE reality. And what would SHOW you otherwise must therefore seem unreal.

T 21 C 8. All that is asked of you is to MAKE ROOM for truth. You are NOT asked to make or do what lies BEYOND your understanding. All you are asked to do is LET IT IN. Only to stop your INTERFERENCE with what will happen OF ITSELF. Simply to recognize again the presence of what you THOUGHT you gave away. Be willing, for an instant, to leave your altars free of what YOU placed upon them and what is REALLY there you CANNOT fail to see. The holy instant is NOT an instant of creation, but of RECOGNITION. For recognition comes of vision and SUSPENDED judgment. Then only is it possible to look within and see what MUST be there, plainly in sight, and wholly INDEPENDENT of inference and judgment. **T(770) -592**

T 21 C 9. Undoing[709] is not YOUR task, but it IS up to you to welcome it or not. Faith and desire go hand in hand. For everyone believes in what he wants. We have already said that wishful thinking is how the ego deals with what it wants, to make it so. There is no better demonstration of the power of wanting, and therefore of FAITH, to make its goals seem real and possible. Faith in the UNreal leads to ADJUSTMENTS of reality, to make it fit the goal of madness. The goal of sin induces the perception of a fearful world, to JUSTIFY its purpose. What you desire, you WILL see. And if its reality is false, you will UPHOLD it by NOT realizing all the adjustments YOU have introduced, to MAKE it so.

T 21 C 10. When vision is DENIED, confusion of cause and effect becomes inevitable. The PURPOSE now becomes to KEEP OBSCURE the cause of the effect, and make effect appear to BE a cause. This seeming independence of effect enables it to be regarded as STANDING BY ITSELF, and capable of serving as a CAUSE of the events and feelings its maker thinks IT causes. Long ago, we spoke of your desire to create your own Creator, and be father and not Son to Him. This is the same desire. The Son is the effect, whose Cause he would deny. And so he seems to BE the cause, producing real EFFECTS.

T 21 C 11. Nothing can have effects WITHOUT a cause, and to confuse the two is merely to fail to understand them both. It is as needful that you recognize you MADE the world you see, as that you recognize that you did NOT create yourself. THEY ARE THE SAME MISTAKE. Nothing created NOT by your Creator, has ANY influence over you. And if you think what YOU have made can TELL you what you see and feel, and place your faith in its ability to do so, you ARE denying your Creator, and BELIEVING that you made yourself. For, if you think the world you made has power to make you what IT wills, you ARE confusing Son and Father; effect and Source. **T(771) -593**

T 21 C 12. The Son's creations ARE like his Father's. But, in creating THEM, the Son does not delude himself that he is INDEPENDENT of his Source. His union with It is the SOURCE of his creat-

---

[706] April 18, 1967
[707] April 20, 1967
[708] FIP changes this to "could" … this portion is missing from the *Notes*.

[709] April 21, 1967

ing. APART from this, he HAS no power to create, and what he makes is meaningless. It changes NOTHING in creation, depends ENTIRELY upon the madness of its maker, and can NOT serve to justify the madness. Your brother thinks he made the world with you. Thus he denies creation. With you, he thinks the world he made, made HIM. Thus he denies he MADE it.

T 21 C 13. Yet the truth is you were both created by a loving Father, Who created you together and as one. SEE what "proves" otherwise, and you DENY your whole reality. But grant that EVERYTHING that seems to stand BETWEEN you, keeping you from each other and separate from your Father, YOU MADE IN SECRET, and the instant of release has come to you. ALL its effects are gone, because its source has been uncovered. It is its seeming INDEPENDENCE of its source that kept you prisoner. This IS the same delusion that YOU are independent of the Source by which YOU were created, and have never left. T(772) -594

T 21 D. Faith, Belief and Vision (not present in *Notes*)

T 21 D 1. All[710] special relationships have sin as their goal. For they are BARGAINS with reality, toward which the seeming union is adjusted. Forget not this; to bargain is to set a limit, and any brother with whom you have a limited relationship YOU HATE. You may attempt to KEEP the bargain in the name of fairness, sometimes demanding payment of your self, perhaps more often of the other. And in this "fairness," you attempt to ease the guilt that comes from the accepted PURPOSE of the relationship. And that is why the Holy Spirit must change its purpose, to make it useful unto HIM, and harmless unto YOU.

T 21 D 2. If you ACCEPT this change, you have accepted the IDEA of making room for truth. The SOURCE of sin is gone. You may IMAGINE that you still experience its effects, but it is NOT your purpose. And you no longer WANT it. No-one allows a purpose to be REPLACED while he DESIRES it. For nothing is so cherished and protected, as is a goal the mind accepts. This it will follow, grimly or happily, but ALWAYS with faith, and with the persistence that faith INEVITABLY brings. The power of faith is NEVER recognized, if it is placed in sin. But it is ALWAYS recognized, if it is placed in love.

T 21 D 3. Why is it strange to you that faith can move mountains?[711] This is indeed a little feat for such a power. For faith can keep the Son of God in chains, as long as he believes he IS in chains. And, when he is RELEASED from them, it will be simply because he no longer BELIEVES in them, WITHDRAWING faith that they can hold him, and placing it in his freedom INSTEAD. It is impossible to T(773) -595 place equal faith in opposite directions. What faith you give to sin, you TAKE AWAY from holiness. And what you offer holiness, has been REMOVED from sin.

T 21 D 4. Faith and belief and vision are the means by which the goal of holiness is reached. Through them, the Holy Spirit leads you to the real world, and AWAY from all illusions where your faith was laid. This is HIS direction, the only one He ever sees. And, when you wander, He REMINDS you there IS but one. HIS faith and HIS belief and vision, are all for you. And, when you have accepted them completely, INSTEAD of yours, you will have need of them no longer. For faith and vision and belief are meaningful only BEFORE the state of certainty is reached. In Heaven they are unknown. Yet Heaven is REACHED through them.

T 21 D 5. It is impossible that the Son of God LACK faith. But he CAN choose where he would have it BE. Faithlessness is not a lack of FAITH, but faith in NOTHING. Faith given to illusions does NOT lack power, for, BY it, does the Son of God believe that he is powerless. Thus is he faithless to HIMSELF, but STRONG in faith in his illusions ABOUT himself. For faith, perception, and belief YOU made, as means for LOSING certainty, and finding sin. This mad direction was your CHOICE, and by your FAITH in what you chose, you made what you desired.

T 21 D 6. The Holy Spirit has a use for all the means for sin by which you sought to FIND it.[712] But, as HE uses them, they lead AWAY from sin, because His PURPOSE lies in the OPPOSITE direction. He sees the MEANS you use, but NOT the purpose for which you made them. He would not take them FROM you, for He sees their value as a means for what HE wills for you. You made perception, that T(774) -596 you might choose among your brothers, and seek for sin with them. The Holy Spirit sees perception as a means to teach you that the vision of a HOLY relationship is all you WANT to see.

T 21 D 7. Then will you give your faith to holiness, desiring and BELIEVING in it, BECAUSE of your desire. Faith and belief become ATTACHED to vision, as all the means that once served sin are REDIRECTED now toward holiness. For what you think is sin is LIMITATION; and whom you try to limit to the body YOU HATE BECAUSE YOU FEAR. In your refusal to forgive him, you would CONDEMN him to the body, because the means for sin is dear to you. And so the BODY has your faith and your belief. But HOLINESS would set your brother free, removing hatred by removing fear, NOT as a symptom, but at its source.

T 21 D 8. Those who would free their brothers from the body, can HAVE no fear. They have renounced the means for sin, by choosing to let all limitations be REMOVED. Desiring to look upon their brothers in holiness, the power of belief and faith goes far BEYOND the body, SUPPORTING vision, NOT obstructing it. But first they chose to RECOGNIZE how much their faith had limited their understanding of the world, DESIRING to place its power elsewhere, should another point of view be GIVEN them. The miracles that follow this decision, are also born of faith. For all who choose to look AWAY from sin ARE given vision, and ARE led to holiness. T(775) -596a

T 21 D 9. Those who believe in sin MUST think the Holy Spirit asks for sacrifice. For this is how they think THEIR purpose is accomplished. Brothers, the Holy Spirit KNOWS that sacrifice brings NOTHING. He makes no bargains. And if you seek to limit Him, you will hate Him BECAUSE YOU ARE AFRAID. The gift that He has given you is more than ANYTHING that stands this side of Heaven. The instant for its recognition is at hand.[713] Join your awareness to what has been ALREADY joined. The faith you give each other CAN accomplish this. For He Who LOVES the world is seeing it FOR you, without one spot of sin upon it, and in the innocence which makes the sight of it as beautiful as Heaven.

---

[710] April 23, 1967

[711] **Matthew 17:20** So Jesus said to them, "Because of your unbelief; for assuredly, I say to you, if you have faith as a mustard seed, you will say to this mountain, 'Move from here to there,' and it will move; and nothing will be impossible for you."

[712] **Romans 8:28** And we know that all things work together for good to those who love God, to those who are called according to *His* purpose.

[713] **Matthew 3:2** and saying, "Repent, for the kingdom of heaven is at hand!" **Matthew 4:17** From that time Jesus began to preach and to say, "Repent, for the kingdom of heaven is at hand."

This notion of God, and his Kingdom being "at hand" or "as close to you as your hand" as soon as you "change your mind" is consistent through the New Testament and ACIM.

While this teaching, "repent for the kingdom of heaven is at hand" is often understood to mean the final judgement and apocalyptic Armageddon, a truly fearful thought, "repent" can also be understood as "think again" or "change your mind" for "heaven is at hand" or "the kingdom of heaven is as close to you as your hand" similar to "the kingdom of heaven is within you." John the Baptist is said to have preached this and Jesus' ministry is said to have included this message early on. It is an oft-repeated theme in the New Testament and ACIM. Heaven is not some remote "pie-in-the-sky-when-you-die" so much as "at hand" and "within you" whenever judgement and guilt is replaced by forgiveness and love.

T 21 D 10. Your faith in sacrifice has given it great power in your sight. Except you do not realize you CANNOT see, BECAUSE of it. For sacrifice MUST be exacted OF a body, and by ANOTHER body. The mind could neither ask it nor RECEIVE it of itself. And no more could the body. **T(776) -597** The INTENTION is in the mind, which tries to USE the body to carry out the means for sin, in which the MIND believes. Thus is the JOINING of mind and body an INESCAPABLE belief of those who value sin. And so is sacrifice INVARIABLY a means for limitation. And thus for hate.

T 21 D 11. Think you the Holy Spirit is concerned with THIS? He GIVES not what it is His purpose to lead you FROM. You THINK He would deprive you FOR YOUR GOOD. But "good" and "deprivation" are opposites, and CANNOT meaningfully join in ANY way. It is like saying that the moon and sun are one BECAUSE they come with night and day. And so they MUST be joined. Yet sight of one is but the sign the other has DISAPPEARED from sight. Nor is it possible that what GIVES light, be one with what DEPENDS on darkness to be seen. Neither demands the SACRIFICE of the other. Yet on the ABSENCE of the other does each depend.

T 21 D 12. The body was made to BE a sacrifice to sin. And, in the darkness so it still is seen. Yet in the light of vision it is looked upon quite differently. You CAN have faith in it to serve the Holy Spirit's goal. And give it power to serve as means to help the blind to see. But, in their seeing, they look PAST it, as do you. The faith and the belief you gave it BELONG beyond. You gave perception and belief and faith from mind TO body. Let them now be given BACK to what PRODUCED them, and can use them still to SAVE itself from what it made. **T(777) -598**

T 21 E. The Fear to Look Within (*Notes* 1569 10:129)

T 21 E 1. The[714] Holy Spirit will NEVER teach you that you are sinful. ERRORS He will correct, but this makes no-one fearful. You are indeed afraid to look within, and see the sin you THINK is there. This you would NOT be fearful to admit. Fear in association with sin the ego deems quite appropriate, and smiles approvingly. IT has no fear to let you feel ashamed. It doubts not your belief and faith in sin. Its temples do not shake because of THIS. Your faith that sin is there but witnesses your desire that it BE there to see. This merely SEEMS to be the source of fear. Remember that the ego is NOT alone. Its rule IS tempered. And its unknown "Enemy," Whom it cannot even see, it FEARS.

T 21 E 2. Loudly the ego tells you NOT to look inward, for if you do, your eyes will light on sin, and God will strike you blind. This you believe, and so you do NOT look. Yet this is NOT the ego's hidden fear, nor YOURS who serve it. Loudly indeed the ego claims it IS. TOO loudly and TOO often. For underneath this constant shout and frantic proclamation, the ego is NOT certain it is so. Beneath your fear to look within because of sin is yet ANOTHER fear, and one which makes the ego tremble. What if you looked within, and saw NO sin? This "fearful" question is one the ego NEVER asks. And you who ask it now ARE "threatening" the ego's whole defensive system too seriously for it to bother to PRETEND it is your friend.

T 21 E 3. Those who have joined their brothers HAVE detached themselves from their belief that their identity lies in the ego. A holy relationship is one in which you join with what IS part of you in TRUTH. And your belief in sin has been ALREADY shaken, nor are you now ENTIRELY unwilling to look within and see it NOT. Your liberation still is only partial; still limited and incomplete, yet born WITHIN you. Not wholly mad, you HAVE been willing to look on much of your insanity, and RECOGNIZE its madness. **T(778) -599** Your faith is moving inward, PAST insanity, and on to reason. And what your reason tells you now, the ego would not hear.

T 21 E 4. The Holy Spirit's purpose was accepted by the part of your mind the ego knows not of. No more did YOU. And yet this part, with which you now identify, is NOT afraid to look upon ITSELF. It KNOWS that it is sinless. How otherwise COULD it have been willing to see the Holy Spirit's purpose as its own? This part has seen your brother, and RECOGNIZED him perfectly, since time began. And it desired nothing but to JOIN with him, and to be free again, as once it was. It has been waiting for the birth of freedom; the ACCEPTANCE of release to come to you. And now you recognize that it was NOT the ego that joined the Holy Spirit's purpose, and so there MUST be something else.

T 21 E 5. Think not that THIS is madness. For this your REASON tells you. And it follows PERFECTLY from what you have ALREADY learned. There is NO inconsistency in what the Holy Spirit teaches. This is the reasoning of the SANE. You have perceived the EGO'S madness, and NOT been made afraid, because you did not choose to SHARE in it. At times it still deceives you. Yet, in your saner moments, its ranting strikes no terror in your hearts. For you have realized that all the gifts it would withdraw from you in rage at your "presumptuous" wish to look within, you do not WANT. The few remaining trinkets still seem to shine and catch your eye. Yet you would not "sell" Heaven to have them.

T 21 E 6. And now the ego IS afraid. But what it hears in terror, the OTHER part hears as the sweetest music; the song it longed to hear since first the ego came into your minds. The ego's weakness is ITS strength. The song of freedom, which sings the praises of ANOTHER world, brings to it hope of peace. For it REMEMBERS Heaven. And now it sees that Heaven HAS come to earth at last, from which the ego's rule has kept it out so long. Heaven has come because it **T(779) -600** found a home in your relationship on earth. And earth can hold no longer what has been GIVEN Heaven as its own.

T 21 E 7. Look gently on each other, and remember the ego's WEAKNESS is revealed in BOTH your sight. What it would keep apart has met and joined, and looks upon the ego unafraid. Little children, innocent of sin, follow in gladness the way to certainty. Be not held back by fear's insane insistence that sureness lies in doubt. This HAS no meaning. What matters it to you how loudly it is proclaimed? The senseless is not made meaningful by repetition and by clamor. The quiet way is open. Follow it happily, and question not what MUST be so. **T(780) -601**

T 21 F. Reason and Perception (*Notes* 1574 10:134)

T 21 F 1. Perception[715] selects, and MAKES the world you see. It literally PICKS IT OUT, as mind directs. The laws of size and shape and brightness would hold, perhaps, if other things were equal. They are NOT equal. For what you look FOR you are far more likely to discover, REGARDLESS of its color, shape, or size, than what you would prefer to OVERLOOK. The still small Voice for God, is NOT drowned out by all the ego's raucous screams and senseless ravings, to those who WANT to hear.[716] Perception is a choice, and NOT a fact.

T 21 F 2. But on this choice depends far more than you may realize as yet. For, on the voice you choose to hear, and on the sights you choose to see, depends ENTIRELY your whole belief of what you ARE. Perception is a witness but to this, and never to reality. Yet it can show you the conditions in which AWARENESS of reality is possible, or those where it could NEVER be. Reality needs no cooperation from you, to be itself. But your awareness of it NEEDS your help, because it IS your choice.

T 21 F 3. Listen to what the ego says, and see what it DIRECTS you see, and it is sure that you will see YOURSELF as tiny, vulnerable,

---

[714] April 24, 1967

[715] April 25, 1967
[716] **1 Kings 19:12** And after the earthquake a fire, but the LORD was not in the fire; and after the fire a still small voice.

and afraid. You WILL experience depression, a sense of worthlessness, and feelings of impermanence and unreality. You WILL believe that you are helpless prey to forces far beyond your own control, and far more powerful than you. And you WILL think the world you made directs your destiny. For this will be your FAITH. But never believe, because it is your faith, it makes REALITY. There is ANOTHER vision and ANOTHER voice, in which your freedom lies, awaiting but your choice. And, if you place your faith in them, you will perceive ANOTHER Self in YOU. **T(781) -602**

T 21 F 4. This[717] other self sees miracles as natural. They are as simple and as natural to it as breathing to the body. They are the OBVIOUS response to calls for help, the ONLY one it makes. Miracles seem unnatural to the ego, because it does not understand how SEPARATE minds can influence each other. Nor COULD they do so. But minds cannot BE separate. This other self is PERFECTLY aware of this. And thus it recognizes that miracles do NOT affect ANOTHER'S mind, only its OWN. They always change YOUR mind. There IS no other.

T 21 F 5. You do not realize the whole extent to which the idea of separation has INTERFERED with reason. Reason lies in the other self you have CUT OFF from your awareness. And nothing you have allowed to STAY in it is CAPABLE of reason. How can the segment of the mind DEVOID of reason understand what reason IS? Or grasp the information it would give? All sorts of QUESTIONS may arise in it, but, if the basic question stems from REASON, it will not ask it. Like ALL that stems from reason, the basic question is obvious, simple, and remains unasked. But think not reason could not ANSWER it.

T 21 F 6. God's plan for your salvation could not have been established WITHOUT your will and your consent. It MUST have been accepted by the Son of God, for what God wills for him, he MUST receive. For God wills not, apart from him. Nor does the Will of God wait upon time to be accomplished. Therefore, what JOINED the Will of God MUST be in you NOW, being eternal. You MUST have set aside a place in which the Holy Spirit can abide, and where He IS. He must HAVE BEEN there since the need for Him arose, and was fulfilled in the same instant.

T 21 F 7. Such would your REASON tell you, if you listened. Yet such is clearly NOT the ego's "reasoning." Its alien nature, TO THE EGO, is proof you will NOT find the answer there. Yet if it MUST be so, it must exist. And, if it exists FOR you, and has your freedom as the purpose GIVEN it, you MUST be **T(782) -603** free to FIND it. God's plan is simple; NEVER circular, and NEVER Self-defeating. He has no Thoughts except the Self-EXTENDING, and in this, YOUR will MUST be included. Thus there MUST be a part of you that KNOWS His Will and SHARES It.

T 21 F 8. It is NOT meaningful to ask if what MUST be is so. But it IS meaningful to ask why you are UNAWARE of what is so. For this MUST have an answer, if the plan of God for your salvation is complete. And it must BE complete, because its Source knows not of incompletion. Where would the answer BE, but in the Source? And where are YOU but there, where this same Answer is? Your identity, as much a true EFFECT of this same Source as is this Answer, must therefore be TOGETHER and the SAME.

T 21 F 9. Oh yes, you know this. And more than this alone. But any part of knowledge threatens dissociation as much as ALL of it. And all of it will COME with any part. Here is the part you CAN accept. What reason points to, you CAN see, because the witnesses on its behalf ARE clear. Only the TOTALLY insane can disregard them. And you HAVE gone past this. Reason is a means which serves the Holy Spirit's purpose in its OWN right. It is not RE-INTERPRETED and REDIRECTED from the goal of sin, as are the others. For reason is BEYOND the ego's range of means.

T 21 F 10. Faith and perception and belief can be misplaced, and serve the great deceiver's needs, as well as truth.[718] But reason has no place at all in madness, nor can it be ADJUSTED to fit its ends. Faith and belief are STRONG in madness, guiding perception toward what the mind has valued. But reason enters NOT AT ALL in this. For the perception would fall away at once, if reason were applied. There IS no reason in insanity, for it depends ENTIRELY on reason's absence. The ego NEVER uses it, because it does not realize that it EXISTS.

T 21 F 11. The partially insane HAVE access to it. And only they have NEED of it. KNOWLEDGE does not depend on it, and madness keeps it OUT. The part of mind where reason lies was dedicated, by your will in union with your Father's, to **T(783) -604** the UNDOING of insanity. Here was the Holy Spirit's purpose accepted and accomplished, both at once. Reason is ALIEN to insanity, and those who use it have gained a means which cannot BE applied to sin. Knowledge is far beyond attainment of ANY kind. But reason CAN serve to open doors you closed AGAINST it.

T 21 F 12. You have come very close to this. Faith and belief have shifted, and you HAVE asked the question that the ego will NEVER ask. Does not your reason tell you now the question MUST have come from something that you do NOT know, but must BELONG to you? Faith and belief, upheld by reason, CANNOT fail to lead to changed perception. And, in THIS change, is room made for vision. Vision extends BEYOND itself, as does the purpose which it serves, and ALL the means for its accomplishment. **T(784) -605**

T 21 G. Reason and Correction (*Notes* 1582 10:142)

T 21 G 1. Reason[719] cannot see sin, but CAN see errors, and LEADS to their correction. It does not value THEM, but their CORRECTION. But reason will also tell you when you THINK you sin you call for help, but if you will not ACCEPT the help you call for, you will not believe that it is yours to give. And so you WILL not give it, thus MAINTAINING the belief. For uncorrected error of ANY kind deceives you about the power that is IN you, to MAKE correction. If it CAN correct, and YOU allow it not to do so, you deny it to yourself AND TO YOUR BROTHER. And, if he SHARES this same belief, you BOTH will think that you are damned.

T 21 G 2. This you COULD spare him AND YOURSELF. For reason would not make way for correction in you alone. Correction cannot BE accepted OR REFUSED by you, without your brother. SIN would maintain you can. But reason tells you that you CANNOT see your brother OR yourself as sinful, and still perceive the other innocent. Who looks upon himself as guilty, and sees a sinless world? And who can see a sinful world, and look upon himself APART from it? Sin would maintain you MUST be separate. But REASON tells you that this must be WRONG.

T 21 G 3. If you are joined, how COULD it be that you have private thoughts? And how COULD thoughts that enter into what but SEEMS like yours alone, have no effect at all on what IS yours? If minds are joined, this IS impossible. No-one can think but for himself, as God thinks not without His Son. Only were both IN BOD-

---

[717] April 26, 1967

[718] **Revelation 12:9** So the great dragon was cast out, that serpent of old, called the Devil and Satan, who deceives the whole world; he was cast to the earth, and his angels were cast out with him.
Revelation 20:7-10 Now when the thousand years have expired, Satan will be released from his prison and will go out to deceive the nations which are in the four corners of the earth, Gog and Magog, to gather them together to battle, whose number is as the sand of the sea. They went up on the breadth of the earth and surrounded the camp of the saints and the beloved city. And fire came down from God out of heaven and devoured them. The devil, who deceived them, was cast into the lake of fire and brimstone where the beast and the false prophet are. And they will be tormented day and night forever and ever.
[719] May 1, 1967

IES could this be. Nor could one mind think only for itself, unless the body WERE the mind. For ONLY bodies can be separate, and therefore UNREAL. The home of madness CANNOT be the home of reason. Yet it is easy to LEAVE the home of madness, if you see reason.

T 21 G 4. You do not leave insanity by GOING somewhere else. You leave it simply by accepting reason, where madness WAS. Madness and reason see the same things, but it is certain that they look upon them differently. Madness is an ATTACK on reason, that drives it out of mind, and TAKES ITS PLACE. Reason does NOT **T(785) -606** attack, but takes the place of madness quietly, REPLACING madness if it be the will of the insane to LISTEN to it. But the insane know not their will. For they BELIEVE they see the body, and LET their madness tell them it is real. REASON would be INCAPABLE of this. And, if you would defend the body AGAINST your reason, you will not understand the body OR yourself.

T 21 G 5. The body does NOT separate you from your brother. And, if you think it does, you ARE insane. But madness has a purpose, and believes it also has the means to make its purpose real. To see the body as a barrier between what REASON tells you MUST be joined, MUST be insane. Nor COULD you see it, if you heard the voice of reason. What CAN there be that stands BETWEEN what is continuous? And, if there IS nothing in between, how can what enters part be kept AWAY from other parts? Reason would tell you this. But think what you must RECOGNIZE, if it be so. If you choose sin INSTEAD of healing, you would condemn the Son of God to what can NEVER be corrected.[720]

T 21 G 6. You tell him, BY your choice, that he is damned; separate from you and from his Father, forever and without a hope of safe return. You TEACH him this, and you will LEARN of him EXACTLY what you taught. For you can teach him only that he IS as you would HAVE him. And what you chose he be, is but your choice for YOU. Yet think not this is fearful. That you are JOINED to him is but a fact, NOT an interpretation. How can a fact be fearful, unless it DISAGREES with what you hold more dear than truth? Reason will tell you that this fact is your RELEASE. Neither your brother nor yourself can be attacked alone. But neither can accept a miracle instead, WITHOUT the other being blessed by it, and HEALED of pain.

T 21 G 7. Reason, like love, would REASSURE you, and NOT seek to frighten you. The power to HEAL the Son of God is given you, BECAUSE he MUST be one with you. You ARE responsible for how he sees himself. But reason tells you it is GIVEN you to change his whole mind, which is one with YOU, in just an instant. And ANY instant serves to bring COMPLETE correction of his errors, and make him whole. The instant that you choose to let YOURSELF be healed, in that **T(786) -607** same instant is his whole salvation seen as complete WITH yours. Reason is given you to UNDERSTAND that this is so. For reason, kind as is the purpose for which it is the means, leads steadily AWAY from madness, toward the goal of truth.

T 21 G 8. And here you will lay down the burden of DENYING truth. THIS is the burden that is terrible, and NOT the truth. That you are JOINED is your salvation; the gift of Heaven, NOT the gift of fear. Does Heaven seem to be a BURDEN to you? In madness, yes; and yet what madness sees, MUST be dispelled by reason. Reason assures you Heaven is what you WANT, and ALL you want. Listen to Him Who SPEAKS with reason, and brings YOUR reason in line with HIS. Be willing to let reason be the means by which He would direct you how to leave INSANITY behind. Hide not BEHIND insanity, in order to ESCAPE from reason.

T 21 G 9. What madness would CONCEAL, the Holy Spirit still holds out, for everyone to look upon with gladness. You ARE your brother's Savior. He is YOURS. Reason speaks happily indeed of this. This gracious plan was given love by Love. And what Love plans is like Itself in this: Being united, It would have you learn what YOU must be. And being ONE with It, it MUST be given you to give what IT has given, and gives still. Spend but an instant in the glad ACCEPTANCE of what is given you to give your brother, and learn, with him, what has been given BOTH of you.

T 21 G 10. To give is no MORE blessed than to receive. But neither is it LESS.[721] The Son of God is ALWAYS blessed as one. And, as his gratitude goes out to you who blessed him, reason will tell you that it CANNOT be you stand APART from blessing. The gratitude he offers you reminds you of the thanks your Father gives you for completing HIM. And here alone does reason tell you that you can understand what you MUST be. Your Father is as close to you as is your brother. Yet what is there that could be nearer you, than is your Self? **T(787) -608**

T 21 G 11. The power that YOU have over the Son of God is NOT a threat to his reality. It but ATTESTS to it. Where COULD his freedom lie but in himself, if he be free ALREADY? And who could bind him but HIMSELF, if he DENY his freedom? God is not mocked; no more His Son can BE imprisoned, save by his own desire.[722] And it is BY his own desire that he is freed. Such is his STRENGTH, and NOT his weakness. He IS at his own mercy. And where he CHOOSES to be merciful, there is he free. But where he chooses to condemn instead, there is he held a prisoner, waiting in chains his pardon on HIMSELF, to set him free. **T(788) -609**

T 21 H. Perception and Wishes (*Notes* 1589 10:149)

T 21 H 1. Do[723] you not see that all your misery comes from the strange belief that you are powerless? BEING HELPLESS IS THE COST OF SIN. Helplessness is sin's CONDITION; the ONE requirement that it demands, to be believed. Only the helpless COULD believe in it. Enormity has no appeal, save to the little. And only those who FIRST believe that they are little, could SEE attraction there. Treachery to the Son of God is the defense of those who do NOT identify with him. And you are FOR him or AGAINST him; either you love him or attack him; protect his unity, or see him shattered and slain by your attack.[724]

T 21 H 2. No-one believes the Son of God is powerless. And those who see themselves as helpless MUST believe that they are NOT the Son of God. What can they BE, except his enemy? And what can they do but ENVY him his power, and BY their envy, make themselves AFRAID of it? These are the dark ones, silent and afraid, alone and not communicating, fearful the power of the Son of God will strike them dead, and raising up their helplessness AGAINST him. They join the army of the powerless, to wage their war of vengeance, bitterness, and spite on him, to make him one with THEM.

---

[720] **Mark 3:29** "but whosoever shall blaspheme against the Holy Spirit hath never forgiveness, but is guilty of an eternal sin."

[721] **Acts 20:35** I have shown you in every way, by laboring like this, that you must support the weak. And remember the words of the Lord Jesus, that He said, "It is more blessed to give than to receive."

This is one instance where ACIM offers a "correction" to a Biblical teaching, in this case equating giving and receiving rather than suggesting the one is superior to the other. As we all are One, of course, any giving or receiving is an exchange within oneness.

[722] **Job 13:9** Will it be well when He searches you out? Or can you mock Him as one mocks a man?
Galatians 6:7 Do not be deceived, God is not mocked; for whatever a man sows, that he will also reap.

[723] May 5, 1967

[724] **Matthew 12:30** "He who is not with Me is against Me, and he who does not gather with Me scatters abroad."
Luke 9:50 But Jesus said to him, "Do not forbid him, for he who is not against us is on our side."

T 21 H 3. Because they do not know that they are one with HIM, they know not WHOM they hate.[725] They are indeed a sorry army, each one as likely to attack his brother or turn upon himself, as to remember they THOUGHT they had a common cause. Frantic and loud and strong the dark ones SEEM to be. Yet they know not their enemy, EXCEPT THEY HATE HIM. In hatred they HAVE come together, but have NOT joined EACH OTHER. For, had they done so, hatred would be impossible. The army of the powerless MUST be disbanded in the presence of STRENGTH. **T(789) -610**

T 21 H 4. Those who are strong are NEVER treacherous, because they have no need to DREAM of power, and to act out their dream. How would an army ACT in dreams? Any way at all. They could be seen attacking ANYONE, with ANYTHING. Dreams have no REASON in them. A flower turns into a poisoned spear, a child becomes a giant, and a mouse roars like a lion. And LOVE IS TURNED TO HATE as easily. This is no army, but a madhouse. What SEEMS to be a planned attack is bedlam. The army of the powerless is weak indeed. It has no weapons, and it has no enemy.

T 21 H 5. Yes, it can overrun the world, and SEEK an enemy. But it can never FIND what is not there. Yes, it can DREAM it found an enemy, but this will shift even as it attacks, so that it runs at once to find another, and never comes to rest in victory. And, as it runs, it turns against itself, thinking it caught a glimpse of the great enemy that always eludes its murderous attack by turning into someone else. How treacherous does this enemy appear, who changes so, it is impossible even to RECOGNIZE him! Yet hate MUST have a target. There can BE no faith in sin without an enemy.

T 21 H 6. Who that believes in sin would DARE believe he has NO enemy? COULD he admit that no-one MADE him powerless? Reason would surely bid him seek no longer what is NOT THERE to find. Yet first he must be WILLING to perceive a world where it is NOT. It is NOT necessary that he understand HOW he can see it. Nor should he try. For, if he focuses on what he CANNOT understand, he will but EMPHASIZE his helplessness, and let sin tell him his enemy must be HIMSELF. But let him only ask himself these questions, which he MUST decide to have it done FOR him: **T(790) -611**

Do I DESIRE a world I rule, instead of one where I AM ruled?
Do I DESIRE a world where I am powerful, instead of helpless?
Do I DESIRE a world in which I have NO enemies, and CANNOT sin?
And do I WANT to see what I denied, BECAUSE it is the truth?

T 21 H 7. You have ALREADY answered the first three questions, but not yet the last. For this one still seems fearful, and UNLIKE the others. Yet reason would assure you they are all the SAME. We said this year would emphasize the sameness of things that ARE the same. This final question which is indeed the last you need decide, still seems to hold a threat the rest have lost for you. And this imagined difference attests to your belief that TRUTH may be the enemy you yet may find. Here, then, would seem to be the last remaining hope of finding sin, and NOT accepting power.

T 21 H 8. Forget not that the choice of truth or sin, power or helplessness, IS the choice of whether to attack or HEAL. For healing comes of POWER, and ATTACK of helplessness. Whom you attack, you CANNOT want to heal. And whom you would have healed, MUST be the one you chose to be PROTECTED from attack. And what IS this decision, but the choice whether to see him through the body's eyes, or let him be REVEALED to you through vision? HOW this decision leads to its effects is NOT your problem. But what you WANT to see, MUST be your choice. This is a course in CAUSE, and NOT effect. **T(791) -612**

T 21 H 9. Consider carefully your answer to the last question you have left unanswered still. And let your reason tell you that it MUST be answered, and IS answered in the other three. And then it WILL be clear to you that, as you look on the EFFECTS of sin, in ANY form, all you need do is simply ask yourself, "Is this what I WOULD see? Do I WANT this?" This is your one decision; this the CONDITION for what occurs. It IS irrelevant to HOW it happens, but NOT to WHY. You HAVE control of this. And if you CHOOSE to see a world WITHOUT an enemy, in which you are NOT helpless, the MEANS to see it WILL be given you. **T(792) -613**

T 21 H 10. Why[726] is the final question so important? Reason will tell you why. It IS the same as are the other three, EXCEPT IN TIME. The others are decisions which can be made, and then UNmade, and made again. But truth is CONSTANT, and implies a state where vacillations are impossible. You can desire a world you rule, which rules you not, and CHANGE your mind. You can desire to exchange your helplessness for power, and LOSE this same desire as a little glint of sin attracts you. And you can want to see a sinless world, and let an "enemy" tempt you to use the body's eyes, and CHANGE what you desire.

T 21 H 11. In CONTENT all the questions ARE the same. For each one asks if you are willing to exchange the world of sin for what the Holy Spirit sees. For it IS this the world of sin denies. And therefore those who look on sin ARE seeing the DENIAL of the real world. Yet the last question adds the WISH FOR CONSTANCY in your desire to see the real world, so the desire becomes the ONLY one you have. By answering the final question "yes," you add SINCERITY to the decisions you have ALREADY made to all the rest. For only then have you RENOUNCED the option to change your mind AGAIN. When it is THIS you do NOT want, the rest are really answered.

T 21 H 12. Why do you think you are unsure the others HAVE been answered? COULD it be necessary they be ASKED so often, if they HAD? Until the last decision has been made, the answer IS both yes and no. For you HAVE answered "yes," without perceiving that yes MUST mean NOT NO. No-one decides AGAINST his happiness. But he MAY do so, if he does not know he DOES it. And, if he sees his happiness as ever-changing, now this, now that, and now an elusive shadow attached to nothing, he DOES decide against it.

T 21 H 13. Elusive happiness, or happiness in changing forms that shift with time and place, is an illusion that has no meaning. Happiness MUST be constant, because it is ATTAINED by GIVING UP the wish for the INconstant. Joy cannot BE perceived, EXCEPT through constant vision. And constant **T(793) -614** vision can be given only those who WISH for constancy. The power of the Son of God's desire remains the proof that he is wrong who sees himself as helpless. Desire what you will, and you shall look on it, and think it real. No thought but has the power to release or kill. And none can leave the thinker's mind, or leave him unaffected.

T 21 I. The Inner Shift (*Notes* 1597 10:157)

T 21 I 1. Are thoughts, then, dangerous? To bodies, YES. The thoughts th44at seem to kill are those which teach the thinker that he CAN be killed. And so he dies, BECAUSE of what he learned. He goes from life to death, the final proof he valued the inconstant more than constancy. Surely he THOUGHT he wanted happiness. Yet he did NOT desire it BECAUSE it was the truth, and therefore MUST be constant. The constancy of joy is a condition quite alien to your understanding. Yet, if you could even imagine what it MUST be, you would DESIRE it, although you UNDERSTAND it not.

T 21 I 2. The constancy of happiness has NO exceptions, no change of ANY kind. It is unshakable as is the Love of God for His Creation. Sure in its vision as its Creator is in what He KNOWS, it looks on everything and SEES it is the same. It sees NOT the ephemeral, for it DESIRES that everything be like itself, and SEES it so. NOTHING has power to confound its constancy, because its OWN

---

[725] **Luke 23:34** Then Jesus said, "Father, forgive them, for they do not know what they do." And they divided His garments and cast lots.

[726] May 6 1967

desire can not BE shaken. It comes as surely unto those who see the final question is NECESSARY to the rest, as peace MUST come to those who choose to heal, and NOT to judge.

T 21 I 3. Reason will tell you that you CANNOT ask for happiness inconstantly. For, if what you desire you RECEIVE, and happiness IS constant, then you need ask for it but ONCE, to have it ALWAYS. And, if you do NOT have it always, being what it IS, you did NOT ask for it. For no-one fails to ASK for his desire of SOMETHING he believes holds out some promise of the power of GIVING it. He may be wrong in WHAT he asks, WHERE, and OF WHAT. Yet he WILL ask, because desire IS a request, an ASKING FOR, and made by one whom God Himself will never fail to answer. **T(794) -615**

T 21 I 4. God has ALREADY given him all that he REALLY wants. But what he is uncertain of, God CANNOT give. For He does NOT desire it while he REMAINS uncertain, and God's giving MUST be incomplete unless it is RECEIVED. You who complete His Will and ARE His happiness, whose will is powerful as His, -- a power that is NOT lost in your illusions, -- think carefully why it should be you have not yet decided how you would answer the final question. Your answer to the others has made it possible to help you be but partially insane. And yet it is the final one that REALLY asks if you are willing to be WHOLLY sane.

T 21 I 5. What is the holy instant but God's appeal to you to RECOGNIZE what He has given you? Here is the great appeal to reason; the awareness of what is ALWAYS there to see; the happiness that COULD be ALWAYS yours. Here is the CONSTANT peace you could experience forever. Here is what denial has denied, REVEALED to you. For here the final question is ALREADY answered, and what you ask for, GIVEN. Here is the future NOW, for time is powerless BECAUSE of your desire for what will NEVER change. For you HAVE asked that nothing STAND BETWEEN the holiness of your relationship, and your AWARENESS of its holiness. **T(795) - 616 -**

CHAPTER 22 – SALVATION AND THE HOLY RELATIONSHIP

T 22 A. Introduction (*Notes* 1601 10:161)

T 22 A 1. Take[727] pity on yourselves, so long enslaved. Rejoice whom God hath joined have come together, and need no longer look on sin APART.[728] No two can look on sin TOGETHER, for they COULD never see it in the same place and time. Sin is a strictly INDIVIDUAL perception, SEEN in the other, yet BELIEVED by each to be within HIMSELF. And each one seems to make a DIFFERENT error, and one the other cannot understand. Brothers, it IS the same, MADE by the same, and forgiven for its maker in the SAME way.

T 22 A 2. The holiness of your relationship forgives you BOTH, undoing the effects of what you both believed AND saw. And, with their going, is the NEED for sin gone WITH them. Who has a need for sin? Only the lonely and alone, who see their brothers DIFFERENT from themselves. It is this DIFFERENCE, seen but not real, that makes the need for sin, not real but seen, seem justified. And all this WOULD be real, if sin were so. For an unholy relationship is BASED on differences, where each one thinks the OTHER has what HE has NOT.

T 22 A 3. They come together, each to complete HIMSELF and ROB the other. They stay until they think there's nothing left to steal, and then move on. And so they wander through a world of strangers, UNLIKE themselves, living with their bodies perhaps beneath a common roof that shelters neither; in the same room and yet a world apart. A holy relationship starts from a different premise. Each one has looked within, and seen NO lack. ACCEPTING his completion, he would EXTEND it by JOINING with another, whole as himself.

T 22 A 4. He sees no DIFFERENCES between these selves, for differences are ONLY of the body. Therefore, he looks on nothing he would TAKE. He **T(796) - 617 -** denies NOT his own reality BECAUSE it is the truth. Just under Heaven does he stand, but close enough NOT to return to earth. For this relationship HAS Heaven's holiness. How far from home can a relationship so like to Heaven BE? Think what a holy relationship can teach! Here is BELIEF in differences undone. Here is the FAITH in differences shifted to sameness. And here is sight of differences transformed to VISION.

T 22 A 5. And reason now can lead you to the logical conclusion of your union. IT must extend, as YOU extended when you joined. It must reach out BEYOND itself, as YOU reached out beyond the body, to LET yourselves be joined. And now the sameness which you saw extends, and finally removes ALL sense of differences, so that the sameness that lies beneath them all becomes apparent. Here is the golden circle, where you RECOGNIZE the Son of God. For what is born into a holy relationship can NEVER end. **T(797) - 617a**[729]

T 22 B. The Message of the Holy Relationship (*Notes* 1604 10:164)

T 22 B 1. Let reason take another step. If you attack whom God would heal, and hate the one He loves, then you and your Creator have a DIFFERENT will. Yet, if you ARE His Will, what you MUST then believe is that you are NOT yourself. You can, indeed, believe this, and you DO. And you HAVE faith in this, and see much evidence on its behalf. And where, you wonder, does your strange uneasiness, your sense of being disconnected, and your haunting fear of lack of meaning in yourself arise? It is as though you wandered in, without a plan of any kind except to wander off, for only that seems certain.

T 22 B 2. Yet we have heard a very similar description earlier. But it was NOT of you. And yet, this strange idea which it DOES accurately describe, you think IS you. Reason would tell you that the world you see through eyes that are not yours, MUST make no sense to you. To whom would vision such as this send BACK its messages? Surely not you, whose sight is wholly INDEPENDENT of the eyes which look upon the world. If this is NOT your vision, what can it show to YOU? The brain can NOT interpret what YOUR vision sees. This YOU would understand. The brain interprets to the body, of which it is a part. But what IT says, YOU cannot understand.

T 22 B 3. Yet you have LISTENED to it. And long and hard you TRIED to understand its messages. You did not realize it is IMPOSSIBLE to understand what fails ENTIRELY to REACH you. You have received NO messages at all you understood. For you have listened to what can never communicate at all. Think, then, what happened. Denying what you are, and firm in faith that you are something ELSE, this something else, which you have MADE to be yourself, BECAME your sight. Yet it MUST be the <u>SOMETHING ELSE</u> which sees, and, as NOT YOU, explains its sight TO you.

T 22 B 4. YOUR vision would, of course, render this quite unnecessary. But, if your eyes are closed, and you have called upon this thing to lead you, asking it to EXPLAIN to you the world IT sees, you have no reason NOT to listen, nor to suspect that what it tells you is NOT true. Reason would tell you that it CAN'T be true, BECAUSE you do not understand it. GOD HAS NO SECRETS. He does NOT lead you through a world of misery, waiting **T(798) -618** to tell you, at the journey's end, why He DID this to you. What could be secret from His Will? Yet you believe that YOU have secrets. What could your secrets BE except ANOTHER will, that is your own, <u>APART</u> from His?

T 22 B 5. Reason would tell you that this is no SECRET, that need be hidden as a sin. But a MISTAKE indeed! Let not your fear of sin protect it from correction, for the attraction of guilt is ONLY fear. Here is the ONE emotion that <u>YOU</u> made, WHATEVER it may seem to be. And it IS the emotion of secrecy, of private thoughts, AND OF THE BODY. This is the ONE emotion that opposes love, and ALWAYS leads to sight of differences, and LOSS of sense of sameness. Here is the ONE emotion that keeps you blind, dependent on the self you think you made, to lead you through the world it made for you.

T 22 B 6. YOUR sight was GIVEN you, along with everything that you CAN understand. You will perceive NO difficulty in understanding what this vision tells you. For everyone sees ONLY what he thinks he IS. And what YOUR sight will show you, you will understand BECAUSE it is the truth. Only YOUR vision can convey to YOU what YOU can see. It reaches you directly, WITHOUT a need to be INTERPRETED to you. What NEEDS interpretation MUST be alien. Nor will it EVER be made understandable, by an interpreter you cannot understand. Of all the messages you have received and failed to understand, this course alone is OPEN to your understanding, and CAN be understood.

T 22 B 7. This IS your language. You do not understand it yet, only because your whole communication is like a baby's. The sounds a baby makes, and what he hears, are highly unreliable, meaning DIFFERENT things to him at different times. Neither the sounds he hears, nor sights he sees, are stable yet. Yet what he hears and does not understand WILL BE his native tongue, through which he will communicate with those around him, and they with him. And the strange, shifting ones he sees about him will become to him his

---

[727] May 7 1967.
[728] **Matthew 19:6** "So then, they are no longer two but one flesh. Therefore what God has joined together, let not man separate."
[729] May 13, 1967

comforters, and he will recognize his home, and see them there WITH him. **T(799) -619**

T 22 B 8. So, in each holy relationship, is the ability to communicate INSTEAD of separate reborn. Yet a holy relationship, so recently reborn itself from an unholy relationship, and yet more ancient than the old illusion that it has replaced, IS like a baby now, in its rebirth. Yet, in this infant is YOUR vision returned to you, and he will speak the language BOTH of you can understand. He is not nurtured by the "something else" you THOUGHT was you. He was not GIVEN there, nor was received by anything EXCEPT yourself. For no two people CAN unite EXCEPT through Christ, Whose vision sees them one.[730]

T 22 B 9. Think what is GIVEN you, my holy brothers. This child will teach you what you do not understand, and make it plain. For his will be no alien tongue. He will need NO interpreter to you. For it was YOU who taught him what he knows, BECAUSE you knew it. He could not come to anything BUT you, NEVER to something else. Where Christ has entered, no-one is alone, for never could He find a home in separate ones. Yet must He be reborn into His ancient home, so seeming new and yet as old as He, a tiny newcomer, dependent on the holiness of your relationship, to let Him live.

T 22 B 10. Be certain that God does not entrust His Son to the unworthy. Nothing but what is PART of Him is worthy of BEING joined. Nor is it possible that anything NOT part of Him CAN join. Communication MUST have been restored to those that join, for this they COULD not do through bodies. What, then, HAS joined them? Reason will tell you that they MUST have seen each other through a vision NOT of the body, and communicated in a language the body does not speak. Nor could it be a fearful sight or sound that drew them gently into one. Rather, in each, the other saw a perfect shelter where his Self could be reborn in safety and in peace. Such did his reason tell him; such he believed BECAUSE it is the truth.

T 22 B 11. Here is the first DIRECT perception that you have made. You made it through awareness older than perception, and yet reborn in just an instant. For what is time to what was ALWAYS so? Think what that instant brought; the RECOGNITION that the "something else" you thought was you **T(800) -620** IS AN ILLUSION. And truth came instantly to show you where your self MUST be. It is denial of ILLUSIONS that calls on truth. For to deny illusions is to recognize that FEAR is meaningless. Into the holy home where fear is powerless, love enters thankfully, grateful that it is one with you who joined to LET it enter.

T 22 B 12. Christ comes to what is LIKE Himself; the same, NOT different. For He is ALWAYS drawn unto Himself. What is as like Him as a holy relationship? And what draws YOU together, draws HIM to you. Here is His sweetness, and His gentle innocence PROTECTED from attack. And here can He RETURN in confidence, for faith in one another is ALWAYS faith in Him. You are indeed correct in looking on each other as His chosen home. For here you willed WITH Him and with His Father. This IS your Father's Will for you, and yours WITH Him. And who is drawn to Christ is drawn to God, as surely as both are drawn to every holy relationship, the home prepared for them as earth is turned to Heaven. **T(801) -621**[731]

T 22 C. Your Brother's Sinlessness (*Notes* 1612 10:172)

T 22 C 1. The OPPOSITE of illusions is not disillusionment, but truth. Only to the ego, to which TRUTH is meaningless, do they APPEAR to be the only alternatives, and DIFFERENT from each other. In truth, they are the SAME. Both bring the same amount of misery, though each one SEEMS to be the way to lose the misery the other brings. EVERY illusion carries pain and suffering in the dark folds of the heavy garments with which it hides its nothingness. Yet, in these dark and heavy garments, are those who SEEK illusions covered, and hidden from the joy of truth. Truth is the opposite of illusions, BECAUSE it offers joy.

T 22 C 2. What else BUT joy could be the opposite of misery? To leave one kind of misery and seek another, is hardly an ESCAPE. To change ILLUSIONS is to make NO change. The search for joy IN MISERY is senseless. For how COULD joy be found in misery? All that is possible in the dark world of misery is to select some ASPECTS out of it, see them as DIFFERENT, and DEFINE the difference as joy. Yet to PERCEIVE a difference where none exists will surely fail to MAKE a difference. Illusions carry ONLY guilt and suffering, sickness and death, to their believers. The FORM in which they are accepted is irrelevant. NO form of misery, in reason's eyes, CAN be confused with joy.

T 22 C 3. Joy is eternal. You can be sure indeed that any seeming happiness which does not last is really fear. Joy does NOT turn to sorrow, for the eternal cannot change. But sorrow CAN be turned to joy, for time gives way to the eternal. Only the timeless must remain unchanged. But everything in time can CHANGE with time. Yet, if the change be real and not IMAGINED, illusions MUST give way to truth, and not to other dreams which are but equally unreal. THIS is no difference. Reason will tell you that the ONLY way to escape from misery is to RECOGNIZE it, AND GO THE OTHER WAY.

T 22 C 4. Truth is the same and misery the same, but they ARE different from each other. In EVERY way, in every INSTANCE, and WITHOUT EXCEPTION. To believe **T(802) -622** that one exception can exist, is to confuse what IS the same with what is different. ONE illusion, cherished and defended AGAINST the truth, makes ALL truth meaningless and ALL illusions real. Such is the power of belief. It CANNOT compromise. And faith in innocence IS faith in sin, if the belief excludes ONE living thing, and holds it out, APART from its forgiveness. Both reason AND the ego will tell you this. But what they MAKE of it, is NOT the same.

T 22 C 5. The ego will assure you now that it is IMPOSSIBLE for you to see NO guilt in anyone. And, if THIS vision is the ONLY means by which ESCAPE from guilt can be attained, then the belief in sin must be eternal. Yet reason looks on this in another way. For reason sees the SOURCE of an idea as what will make it true or false. This MUST be so, if the idea is LIKE its source. Therefore, says reason, if escape from guilt was given to the Holy Spirit as His purpose, and by One to Whom NOTHING He wills CAN BE impossible, the means for its attainment are MORE than possible. They must be THERE, and YOU must HAVE them.

T 22 C 6. This is a crucial period in this course. For here, the separation of you and the ego MUST be made complete. For, if you HAVE the means to let the Holy Spirit's purpose be accomplished, they CAN be used. And, THROUGH their use, will you gain faith in them. Yet, to the ego, they MUST be impossible, and no-one undertakes to do what holds NO hope of EVER being done. You KNOW what your Creator wills is possible. But what you MADE believes it is not so. Now MUST you choose between yourself and this[732] ILLUSION of yourself. NOT both, but ONE.

---

[730] Matthew 18:20 "For where two or three are gathered together in My name, I am there in the midst of them."
[731] May 15, 1967

[732] The manuscript is typed "and ILLUSION" with "the" handwritten in between. The *Notes* rather clearly shows the glyph for "this" however so we've gone with that correction. In this example we see a common pattern in the editing. When a mistake is obvious, such as the omission of an article here is obvious, the editors often simply put in something that is grammatically correct without, apparently. checking the source. This also indicates that the correction was not made in the original oral transcription but later in the retyping. Had the error been noticed in that first transcription, we'd expect the correction to be correct. What we see here is more consistent with an inadvertent copy typing omission when the original *Thetford Transcript* was being re-typed which was then later noticed and "corrected" without reference to the *Notes*.

T 22 C 7. There is no point in trying to avoid this ONE decision. It MUST be made. Faith and belief can fall to either side, but reason tells you that misery lies ONLY on one side, and joy upon the other. FORSAKE NOT NOW EACH OTHER. **T(803) -623** For you who ARE the same will NOT decide alone. OR DIFFERENTLY. Either you give each other life or death; either you are each other's Savior or his judge, offering him sanctuary or condemnation. This course will be believed ENTIRELY, or not at all. For it is wholly true or wholly false, and CANNOT be but partially believed. And you will either ESCAPE from misery entirely, or not at all.

T 22 C 8. Reason will tell you that there IS no middle ground where you can pause uncertainly, waiting to choose between the joy of Heaven and the misery of hell. UNTIL you choose Heaven, you ARE in hell and misery. There is no PART of Heaven you can take, and weave into illusions. Nor is there ONE illusion you can enter Heaven WITH. A Savior cannot BE a judge, nor mercy condemnation. And vision CANNOT damn, but ONLY bless. Whose function is to save, WILL save. HOW He will do it IS beyond your understanding, but WHEN must be your choice. For time YOU made, and time you CAN command. You are no more a slave to time than to the world you made.

T 22 C 9. Let us look closer at the whole illusion that what you made has power to enslave its maker. This is the SAME belief that CAUSED the separation. It is the meaningless idea that thoughts can leave the thinker's mind, be DIFFERENT from it, AND IN OPPOSITION to it. If this were true, thoughts would not be the mind's extensions, but its ENEMIES. And here we see again another form of the same fundamental illusion we have seen many times before. ONLY if it were possible the Son of God could LEAVE his Father's Mind, make himself DIFFERENT, and OPPOSE His Will, would it be possible that the self he made, and all IT made, should be his master.

T 22 C 10. Behold the great projection, but look on it with the decision that it MUST BE HEALED, and NOT with fear. NOTHING you made has ANY power over you, unless you still would be APART from your Creator, and with a will OPPOSED to His. For ONLY if you would believe His Son COULD be His enemy, does it **T(804) -624** SEEM POSSIBLE that what YOU made is YOURS. YOU would condemn His joy to misery, and make HIM different. And all the misery you made has been your own. Are you not GLAD to learn it is not true? Is it not welcome news to hear NOT ONE of the illusions that you made REPLACED the truth?

T 22 C 11. Only YOUR thoughts have been impossible. Salvation CANNOT be. It IS impossible to look upon your Savior as your enemy, and RECOGNIZE him. Yet it IS possible to recognize him for what he IS, if God would have it so. What God has given to your holy relationship IS THERE. For what He gave the Holy Spirit to give to you, He GAVE. Would you not look upon the Savior Who has been given you? And would you not exchange, in gratitude and gladness, the function of an executioner YOU gave him, for the one he has in truth? Receive of him what God has given him for you, NOT what YOU tried to give.

T 22 C 12. Beyond the bodies that you interposed between you, and shining in the golden light that reaches it from the bright endless circle that extends forever, is your holy relationship, beloved of God, and holy as Himself. How still it rests, in time and yet beyond, immortal yet on earth. How great the power that lies in it. Time waits upon its will, and earth will BE as it would HAVE it be. Here is no SEPARATE will, nor the desire that ANYTHING be separate. Its will HAS no exceptions, and what it wills is true. Every illusion brought to its forgiveness is gently OVERLOOKED, and disappears. For, at its center, Christ has been reborn, to light His home with vision that overlooks the world.

T 22 C 13. Would you not have this holy home be yours as well? No misery is here but ONLY joy. All you need do to dwell in quiet here with Christ is SHARE His vision. Quickly and gladly is His vision given to anyone who is but WILLING to see his brother sinless. And no-one CAN remain beyond this willingness, if YOU would be released entirely from ALL effects of sin. Would you have PARTIAL forgiveness for yourself? Can YOU reach Heaven while a single sin still tempts you to remain in misery? Heaven is the home of perfect purity. And God created it for YOU. Look at your holy brother, sinless as yourself, and let him LEAD you there. **T(805) -625**

T 22 D. Reason and the Holy Relationship (*Notes 1620 10:180*)

T 22 D 1. The introduction of reason into the ego's thought system is the beginning of its undoing. For reason and the ego are CONTRADICTORY. Nor is it possible for them to co-exist in your AWARENESS. And reason's goal IS to make plain, and therefore obvious. You can SEE reason. This is not a play on words, for here is the beginning of a vision that has meaning. Vision is sense, quite literally. If it is not the body's sight, it MUST be understood. FOR IT IS PLAIN, and what is obvious is NOT ambiguous. It CAN be understood. And here do reason and the ego separate, to go their DIFFERENT ways.

T 22 D 2. The ego's whole continuance depends on its belief you cannot learn this course. SHARE this belief, and reason will be unable to SEE your errors, and make way for their correction. For reason SEES THROUGH errors, telling you what you THOUGHT was real is not. Reason CAN see the difference between sin and mistakes, because it WANTS correction. Therefore it tells you what you thought was uncorrectable, CAN be corrected. And therefore MUST have been an error. The ego's OPPOSITION to correction leads to its fixed belief in sin, and DISREGARD of errors. IT looks on NOTHING that can be corrected.

T 22 D 3. Thus does the ego damn, and reason save. Reason is not salvation in itself, but it MAKES WAY for peace, and brings you to a state of mind in which salvation can be given you. Sin is a block, set like a heavy gate, locked and WITHOUT a key, across the road to peace. No-one who looks on it without the help of reason, would TRY to pass it. The body's eyes behold it as solid granite, so thick it would be madness to ATTEMPT to pass it. Yet reason sees through it easily BECAUSE it is an error. The FORM it takes cannot conceal its emptiness from REASON's eyes.

T 22 D 4. ONLY the form of error attracts the ego. Meaning it does not RECOGNIZE, and does not know if it is there or not. Everything which the body's eyes can see **T(806) -626** is a mistake, an error in perception, a distorted fragment of the whole, without the meaning that the whole would give. And yet mistakes, regardless of their form, can be corrected. Sin is but error in a special form the ego venerates. It would preserve ALL errors, and make them sins. For here is its OWN stability, its heavy anchor in the shifting world it made; the rock on which its church is built, and where its worshippers are bound to bodies, and believe the body's freedom is their own.[733]

T 22 D 5. Reason will tell you that the FORM of error is not what makes it a mistake. If what the form CONCEALS is a mistake, the FORM can not prevent correction. The body's eyes see ONLY form. They cannot see BEYOND what they were MADE to see. And they were made to look on error, and NOT see past it. Theirs is indeed a strange perception, for they can see ONLY illusions, unable to look beyond the granite block of sin, and stopping at the outside FORM of nothing. To this distorted form of vision, the OUTSIDE of everything, the wall that stands between you and the truth, is wholly true.

---

[733] **Matthew 16:18** "And I also say to you that you are Peter, and on this rock I will build My church, and the gates of Hades shall not prevail against it."

T 22 D 6. Yet how can sight which stops at nothingness, as if it WERE a solid wall, see truly? It is HELD BACK by form, having been made to guarantee that nothing else BUT form will be perceived. These eyes, made NOT to see, will NEVER see. For the idea they represent left not its maker, and it is their maker that sees through them. What was its maker's GOAL, but not to see? For THIS the body's eyes are perfect means. But NOT for seeing. See how the body's eyes rest on externals, and CANNOT go beyond. Watch how they STOP at nothingness, unable to go BEYOND the form to meaning.

T 22 D 7. Nothing so blinding as perception of form.[734] For sight of form MEANS understanding HAS BEEN obscured. Only MISTAKES have different forms, and so they CAN deceive. You CAN change form, BECAUSE it is not true. It COULD not be reality, BECAUSE it can be changed. Reason will tell you that, if form is NOT reality, it MUST be an illusion. And is Not THERE to see. **T(807) -627** And, IF you see it, you MUST be mistaken, for you are seeing what can NOT be real, as if it WERE. What cannot see BEYOND what is not there, MUST be distorted perception. And must perceive illusions AS THE TRUTH. Could it, then, RECOGNIZE the truth?

T 22 D 8. Let not the FORM of his mistakes keep you from him whose holiness is YOURS. Let not the vision of his holiness, the sight of which would show you YOUR forgiveness, be kept from you by what the body's eyes can see. Let your awareness of your brother NOT be blocked by your perception of his sins, and of his body. What is there in him that you would attack, EXCEPT what you associate with his body, which YOU believe can sin? BEYOND his errors is his holiness, and YOUR salvation. You gave him not his holiness, but tried to see your sins in him, to save yourself. And yet his holiness IS your forgiveness. Can YOU be saved by making sinful the one whose holiness IS your salvation?

T 22 D 9. A holy relationship, however newly born, must value holiness above all else. Unholy values will produce confusion, and IN AWARENESS. In an unholy relationship, each one is valued BECAUSE he seems to justify the other's sin. He sees within the other what impels him to SIN AGAINST HIS WILL. And thus he lays his sins upon the other, and is ATTRACTED to him to PERPETUATE his sins. And so it MUST become impossible for each to see HIMSELF as causing sin, by his DESIRE to have sin real. Yet reason sees a holy relationship as what it IS; a common state of mind, where both give errors gladly to correction, that both may happily be healed as one. **T(808) -808a**[735]

T 22 E. The Branching of the Road (*Notes* 1628 11:3)

T 22 E 1. Special Message[736]:

When you come to the place where the branch in the road is quite apparent, you cannot go ahead. You MUST go one way or the other. For now, if you go straight ahead, the way you were going before you came to the branch, YOU WILL GO NOWHERE. The whole purpose of coming this far is to decide WHICH BRANCH YOU WILL TAKE FROM HERE ON. The way you came no longer matters. IT CAN NO LONGER SERVE.

T 22 E 2. No-one who reaches this far CAN make the wrong decision. But he CAN delay. And there is no part of the journey that seems more hopeless and futile than standing where the road branches, and not deciding which way to go. It is only the first few steps along the right way that seem hard, because you HAVE chosen, but you still think you can go back and make the other choice.

T 22 E 3. This is not so. A choice made with the power of Heaven to uphold it cannot BE undone. Your way IS decided.

T 22 E 4. There will be nothing you will NOT be told, if you acknowledge this. **T(809) -628**[737]

T 22 E 5. And so you stand, here in this holy place, before the veil of sin that hangs between you and the face of Christ. LET it be lifted! Raise it together, for it is but a veil that stands between you. Either alone will see it as a solid block, nor realize how thin the drapery that separates you now. Yes,[738] it IS almost over, IN YOUR AWARENESS. And peace has reached you even here, BEFORE the veil. Think what will happen after! The love of Christ will light YOUR faces, and shine from them into a darkened world that NEEDS the light. And, from this holy place, He will return with you, not leaving it or you.

T 22 E 6. YOU will become His messengers, returning Him unto Himself. Think of the loveliness that YOU will see, who walk with Him! And think how beautiful will each of you look to the other! How happy you will be to be TOGETHER, after such a long and lonely journey where you walked alone. The gates of Heaven, open now for you, will you now open to the sorrowful. And none who looks upon the Christ in you but will rejoice. How beautiful the sight you saw beyond the veil, which you will bring to light the tired eyes of those as weary now as once you were. How thankful will they be to see you come among them, offering Christ's forgiveness to dispel their faith in sin.

T 22 E 7. Every mistake you make the other will gently have corrected FOR you. For, in his sight, your loveliness is HIS salvation, which he would PROTECT from harm. And each will be the other's strong protector from EVERYTHING that seems to rise between you. So shall you walk the world with me, whose message has not yet been given everyone. For you are here to let it be RECEIVED. God's offer still is open; yet it waits acceptance. From you who have accepted it, is it received. Into your joined hands is it safely given. For you who SHARE it have become its willing guardians and protectors. **T(810) -629**

T 22 E 8. To all who share the love of God the grace is given to be the givers of what they have received. And so they learn that it is theirs forever. All barriers disappear before their coming, as every obstacle was finally surmounted that seemed to rise and block THEIR way before. This veil you lift together opens the way to truth to more than you. Those who would let illusions be lifted from their minds are this world's Saviors, walking the world with their Redeemer, and carrying His message of hope and freedom and RELEASE from suffering to everyone who NEEDS a miracle to save him.

T 22 E 9. How EASY is it to offer this miracle to everyone! No-one who has received it for himself COULD find it difficult. For, BY receiving it, he learned it was not given him alone. Such is the function of a holy relationship; to RECEIVE together, and give as you received. Standing BEFORE the veil, it still seems difficult. But hold out your JOINED hands and touch this heavy-seeming block, and you will learn how easily your fingers slip through its nothingness. It is no solid wall. And only an illusion stands between you and the holy Self you share. **T(811) -630**[739]

T 22 F. Weakness and Defensiveness (*Notes* 1631 11:6)

T 22 F 1. How does one overcome illusions? Surely not by force or anger. Nor by OPPOSING them in ANY way. Merely by letting reason tell you that they CONTRADICT reality. They GO AGAINST what must be true. The opposition comes from THEM, and NOT reality. Reality opposes nothing. What merely is, NEEDS no defense, and offers none. Only illusions need defense, BE-

---

[734] The grammar here is odd, and is improved if we make it "Nothing *is* so blinding as ..." but the *Notes* and all versions have it the same way.
[735] March 11, 1968
[736] [Special Message: March 11, 1968]

[737] May 24, 1967
[738] The *Notes* and *Urtext* have this as shown, while the *HLC* and *FIP* replace "Yes" with "Yet."
[739] May 25, 1967

CAUSE OF WEAKNESS. And how CAN it be difficult to walk the way of truth, when only WEAKNESS interferes? YOU are the strong ones in this seeming conflict. And you need NO defense. Everything that needs defense YOU DO NOT WANT. For anything that needs defense will WEAKEN you.

T 22 F 2. Consider what the ego wants defenses FOR. ALWAYS to justify what GOES AGAINST the truth, flies in the face of reason, AND MAKES NO SENSE. Can this BE justified? What can this be, except an invitation to insanity, to save you FROM the truth? And what would you be SAVED from, but what you FEAR? Belief in sin needs GREAT defense, and at ENORMOUS cost. All that the Holy Spirit offers must be DEFENDED AGAINST, and SACRIFICED. For sin is carved into a block out of YOUR peace, and laid BETWEEN you and its return. Yet how can peace BE so fragmented? It is STILL whole, and NOTHING has been TAKEN FROM it.

T 22 F 3. See how the means and the material of evil dreams are nothing! In truth, you stand together, with NOTHING in between. God holds your hands, and what can separate whom He has joined as one with Him?[740] It is your Father Whom you would defend against. Yet it remains impossible to keep Love out. God rests with you in quiet, undefended and wholly undefending. For in this quiet state alone is strength and power. Here can NO weakness enter, for here is no attack, and therefore no illusions. Love rests in CERTAINTY. Only UNcertainty can BE defensive. And ALL uncertainty is doubt about YOURSELF. T(812) -631

T 22 F 4. How weak is fear; how little and how meaningless! How insignificant before the quiet strength of those whom Love has joined! This is your "enemy;" a frightened mouse which would attack the universe. How likely is it that it will SUCCEED? Can it be difficult to disregard its feeble squeaks that tell of its omnipotence, and would drown out the hymn of praise to its Creator that every heart throughout the universe forever sings as one? Which IS the stronger? Is it this tiny mouse, or everything that God created? You are NOT joined together by this mouse, but by the Will of God. And can a mouse BETRAY whom God has joined?

T 22 F 5. If you but RECOGNIZED how little stands between you and your AWARENESS of your union! Be not deceived by the illusions it presents of size and thickness, weight, solidity, and firmness of foundation. Yes, to the body's eyes it looks like an enormous, solid body, immovable as is a mountain. Yet, within YOU, there is a force which NO illusions can resist. This body only SEEMS to be immovable. This force IS irresistible in truth. What, then, MUST happen when they come together? Can the illusion of immovability be long defended for what is quietly PAST THROUGH, and GONE BEYOND?

T 22 F 6. Forget not, when you feel the need arise to be defensive about ANYTHING, you have identified YOUR SELF with an illusion. And therefore feel that you are weak, BECAUSE YOU ARE ALONE. This is the cost of ALL illusions. Not one but rests on the belief that you are separate. Not one that does not SEEM to stand, heavy and solid and unmovable, between you and your brother. And not one that truth can NOT pass over lightly, and so easily that you MUST be convinced, in spite of what you THOUGHT it was, that it was nothing. If you forgive each other, this MUST happen. For it IS your unwillingness to overlook what seems to stand between you that makes it look impenetrable, and DEFENDS the illusion of its immovability. T(813) -632[741]

T 22 G. Freedom and the Holy Spirit (*Notes* 1635 11:10)

T 22 G 1. Do you want freedom of the body, or of the mind? For both you cannot have. Which do you value? Which is your goal? For one you see as means; the other, end. And one must serve the other, and LEAD to its predominance, increasing ITS importance by DIMINISHING its own. Means serve the end, and as the end is reached, the value of the means decreases, and is eclipsed entirely when they are recognized as functionless. No-one but yearns for freedom, and tries to find it, but he will seek for it where he believes it IS, and CAN be found. He will believe it possible of mind OR body, and he will make the other SERVE his choice, as means to find it.

T 22 G 2. Where freedom of the BODY has been chosen, the mind is used as MEANS, whose value lies in its ability to contrive ways to achieve the body's freedom. Yet freedom of the body HAS no meaning. And so the mind is DEDICATED to serve illusions. This is a situation SO contradictory and SO impossible that anyone who chooses this has NO idea of what is valuable. Yet even in this confusion, so profound it cannot BE described, the Holy Spirit waits in gentle patience, as certain of the outcome as He is sure of His Creator's love. He knows this mad decision was made by one as dear to His Creator as Love is to Itself.

T 22 G 3. Be not disturbed at all to think how He can change the role of means and end so easily in what God loves, and would have free forever. But be you, rather, grateful that YOU can be the means to serve His end. This is the ONLY service which leads to freedom. To serve THIS end, the body MUST be perceived as T(814) -633 sinless, BECAUSE the goal is sinlessness. The LACK of contradiction makes the soft transition from means to end as easy as is the shift from hate to gratitude before forgiving eyes. You WILL be sanctified by one another, using your bodies ONLY to serve the sinless. And it will be IMPOSSIBLE for you to hate what serves what you would HEAL.

T 22 G 4. This holy relationship, lovely in its innocence, mighty in strength, and blazing with a light far brighter than the sun which lights the sky YOU see, is chosen of your Father as a means for His Own plan. Be thankful that it serves yours not at all. Nothing entrusted to it can BE misused. And nothing given it but WILL be used. This holy relationship has the power to heal ALL pain, REGARDLESS of its form. Neither of you alone can serve at all. Only in your JOINT will does healing lie. For here YOUR healing is, and here will YOU accept Atonement. And in your healing IS the Sonship healed, BECAUSE your wills are joined.

T 22 G 5. Before a holy relationship, there IS no sin. The FORM of error is no longer seen. And reason, joined with love, looks quietly on ALL confusion, observing merely, "this was a mistake." And then the same Atonement YOU accepted in YOUR relationship, CORRECTS the error, and lays a part of Heaven in its place. How blessed are you, who let this gift be given! Each part of Heaven that you bring, is given YOU. And every empty place in Heaven that you fill again with the Eternal Light YOU bring, shines now on YOU. The means of sinlessness can know no fear, because they carry ONLY love with them.

T 22 G 6. Children of peace, the light HAS come to you. The light you bring you do NOT recognize, and yet you will remember. Who T(815) -634 can deny HIMSELF the vision that he brings to others? And who would fail to recognize a gift he let be laid in Heaven through HIMSELF? The gentle service that you give the Holy Spirit IS service to yourself. You who are now HIS means must love all that He loves. And what you bring is YOUR remembrance of everything that is eternal. No trace of anything in time can long remain in minds that serve the timeless. And NO illusion can disturb the peace of a relationship which has become the MEANS of peace.

T 22 G 7. When you have looked upon each other with COMPLETE forgiveness, from which NO error is excluded and NOTHING kept hidden, what mistake can there be ANYWHERE you can NOT overlook? What form of suffering could BLOCK your sight, preventing you from seeing PAST it? And what illusion COULD there be you will NOT recognize as a mistake; a shadow through which you walk COMPLETELY undismayed? God would let

---

[740] Matthew 19:6 "So then, they are no longer two but one flesh. Therefore what God has joined together, let not man separate."
[741] June 3, 1967

NOTHING interfere with those whose wills are His. And they will RECOGNIZE their wills are His, BECAUSE they serve His Will. AND SERVE IT WILLINGLY. How can it NOT be theirs? And COULD remembrance of what they are be long delayed? **T(816) - 635**[742]

T 22 G 8. You will see your value through each other's eyes, and each one is released as he beholds his Savior IN PLACE of the attacker who he THOUGHT was there. Through this releasing is the world released. This is YOUR part in bringing peace. For you have asked what is your function here, and have been answered. Seek not to change it, nor to substitute ANOTHER goal. This one was GIVEN you, and ONLY this. Accept this one, and serve it willingly, for what the Holy Spirit does with the gifts you give each other, to whom He offers them, and where and when, is up to Him.

T 22 G 9. He will bestow them where they are received and welcomed. He will use every one of them for peace. Nor will one little smile, or willingness to overlook the tiniest mistake, be lost to anyone. What can it be but universal blessing to look on what your Father loves with charity? EXTENSION of forgiveness is the Holy Spirit's function. Leave this to Him. Let YOUR concern be only that you give TO Him that which can BE extended. Save no dark secrets that He cannot use. But offer Him the tiny gifts He can extend forever.

T 22 G 10. He will take every one, and make of it a potent force for peace. He will withhold no blessing from it, or limit it in any way. He will join to it ALL the power that God has given Him, to make each little gift of love a source of healing for everyone. Each little gift you offer to the other lights up the world. Be not concerned with darkness; look AWAY from it, and TOWARD each other. And let the darkness be dispelled by Him Who knows the light, and lays it gently in each gentle smile of faith and confidence with which you bless each other. **T(817) -636**

T 22 G 11. On[743] your learning depends the welfare of the world. And it is only arrogance that would DENY the power of your will. Think you the Will of God is powerLESS? Is this HUMILITY? You do not see what this belief has done. You see yourself as vulnerable, frail, and easily destroyed. And at the mercy of countless attackers more powerful than you. Let us look straight at how this error came about, for here lies buried the heavy anchor that seems to keep the fear of God in place, unmovable and solid as a rock. While this remains, so will it seem to be.

T 22 G 12. Who can attack the Son of God, and NOT attack his Father? How can God's Son be weak and frail and easily destroyed, UNLESS HIS FATHER IS? You do NOT see that EVERY sin and EVERY condemnation which you perceive and justify IS an attack upon your Father. And that is WHY it has not happened, nor COULD be real. You do not see that this is your attempt, BECAUSE you think the Father and the Son are separate. And you MUST think that they are separate, BECAUSE OF FEAR. For it SEEMS safer to attack another or yourself, than to attack the great Creator of the universe, Whose power you KNOW.

---
[742] June 5, 1967
[743] June 8, 1967

T 22 G 13. If you were one with Him, AND RECOGNIZED THIS ONENESS, you would know His power is YOURS. But you will NOT remember this, while you believe attack of ANY kind means ANYTHING. It is unjustified in ANY form, BECAUSE it has no meaning. The only way it COULD be justified is if each one of you were SEPARATE from the other, and all were separate from your Creator. For ONLY then would it be possible to attack a part of the creation WITHOUT the whole; the Son WITHOUT the Father. And to attack another, WITHOUT yourself; or hurt yourself, without the other feeling pain.

T 22 G 14. And this belief, you WANT. Yet wherein lies its value, EXCEPT in the desire to attack in safety? Attack is neither safe nor dangerous. IT IS IMPOSSIBLE. And this is so, BECAUSE the universe is one. You would not **T(818) -637** choose attack on its reality, if it were not ESSENTIAL to attack to see it SEPARATE FROM ITS CREATOR. And thus it seems as if love could attack, AND BECOME FEARFUL. Only the DIFFERENT can attack. So you conclude, BECAUSE you can attack, you must be DIFFERENT. Yet does the Holy Spirit explain this differently. BECAUSE you are NOT different, you CAN NOT ATTACK.

T 22 G 15. Either position is a logical conclusion, if only the different can attack. Either could be maintained, BUT NEVER BOTH. The ONLY question to be answered to decide which MUST be true, is WHETHER YOU ARE DIFFERENT. From the position of what YOU understand, you seem to BE. And THEREFORE can attack. Of the alternatives, this SEEMS more natural, and more in line with your experience. And therefore it is necessary that you have OTHER experiences, more in line with truth, to teach you what IS natural and true. This is the function of your holy relationship. For what ONE thinks, the OTHER will experience WITH him. What can this mean, EXCEPT your minds are one?

T 22 G 16. Look not with fear upon this happy fact, and think not that it lays a heavy burden on you. For, when you have ACCEPTED it with gladness, you will realize that your relationship is a reflection of the union of the Creator and His Son. From loving minds, there IS no separation. And every thought in one brings gladness to the other, BECAUSE they are the same. Joy is unlimited, BECAUSE each shining thought of Love EXTENDS its Being, and creates more of Itself. There is no difference ANYWHERE within it. For every thought is like Itself.

T 22 G 17. The light that joins you shines throughout the universe. And, BECAUSE it joins you, so it makes you one with your Creator. And, in HIM, is all creation joined. Would you REGRET you cannot fear alone, when your relationship can also teach the power of love is there, which makes ALL fear impossible? Do not attempt to keep a little of the ego with this gift. For it was given to be USED, and NOT obscured. What teaches you **T(819) -638**[744] you CANNOT separate, DENIES the ego. Let TRUTH decide if you be different or the same, and TEACH you which is true.

---
[744] June 12, 1967

CHAPTER 23 – THE WAR AGAINST YOURSELF

T 23 A. Introduction (*Notes* 1647 11:22)

T 23 A 1. Do you not see the OPPOSITE of frailty and weakness is sinlessness? INNOCENCE IS STRENGTH, and nothing else is strong. The sinless cannot fear. And fear of any kind is weakness. The show of strength attack would use to COVER frailty, conceals it not. For how can the unreal BE hidden? No-one is strong who has an enemy. And no-one can attack, unless he thinks he HAS. Belief in enemies is therefore the belief in WEAKNESS. And what is weak is NOT the Will of God. Being OPPOSED to It, it is Its "enemy." And God is feared, as an OPPOSING will.

T 23 A 2. How strange indeed becomes this war against Yourself! You will believe that EVERYTHING you use for sin can hurt you, AND BECOME YOUR ENEMY. And you will fight AGAINST it, and try to weaken it, BECAUSE of this. And you will think that you succeeded, and attack again. It is as certain you will fear what you attack, as it is sure that you will love what you perceive as sinless. He walks in peace who travels sinlessly along the way Love shows him. For Love walks WITH him there, PROTECTING him from fear. And he will see ONLY the sinless, who can NOT attack.

T 23 A 3. Walk you in glory, with your head held high, and fear no evil.[745] The innocent are safe, because they SHARE their innocence.[746] Nothing they see is harmful, for their AWARENESS of the truth releases everything from the illusion of harmfulness. And what SEEMED harmful now stands shining in their innocence, released from sin and fear, and happily returned to love. They share the strength of love BECAUSE they looked on innocence. And every error disappeared, because they saw it not. Who looks for glory finds it where it IS. Where COULD it be, but in the innocent? **T(820) -639**

T 23 A 4. Let not the little interferers pull you to littleness. There CAN be no attraction of guilt in innocence. Think what a happy world you walk, with truth beside you! Do not give up this world of freedom, for a little sigh of seeming sin, nor for a tiny stirring of guilt's attraction. Would you, for all these meaningless distractions, lay Heaven aside? Your destiny and purpose are far beyond them, in the clean peace where littleness does not exist. Your purpose is at variance with littleness of any kind. And so it is at variance with sin.

T 23 A 5. Let us not let littleness lead God's Son into temptation.[747] His glory is BEYOND it, measureless and timeless as is Eternity. Do not let time intrude upon your sight of him. Leave him not frightened and alone in his temptation. But help him rise above it, and perceive the light of which he is a part. YOUR innocence will light the way to his, and so is YOURS protected, and KEPT in your awareness. For who can know his glory, and perceive the little and the weak about him? Who can walk trembling in a fearful world, and realize that Heaven's glory shines in him?

T 23 A 6. Nothing around you but is PART of you. Look on it lovingly, and see the light of Heaven in it. So will you come to understand all that is given you. In kind forgiveness will the world sparkle and shine, and everything you once thought sinful now will be re-interpreted as part of Heaven. How beautiful it is to walk, clean and redeemed and happy, through a world in bitter need of the redemption that your innocence bestows upon it![748] What can you value MORE than this? For here is YOUR salvation and YOUR freedom. And it MUST be complete, if YOU would recognize it. **T(821) -640**[749]

T 23 B. The Irreconcilable Beliefs (*Notes* 1652 11:27)

T 23 B 1. The memory of God comes to the quiet mind. It CANNOT come where there is conflict, for a mind at war against itself remembers not Eternal Gentleness. The means of war are NOT the means of peace. And what the warlike would remember is NOT love. War is impossible unless belief in VICTORY is cherished. Conflict WITHIN you MUST imply that you believe the ego has the power TO BE VICTORIOUS. Why else would you identify with it? Surely you realize the ego IS at war with God. Certain it is it HAS no enemy. But just as certain is its fixed belief it has an enemy that it MUST overcome, and WILL SUCCEED.

T 23 B 2. Do you not realize a war against yourself would BE a war on God? Is victory CONCEIVABLE? And, if it were, is this a victory that you would WANT? The death of God, if it were possible, would be YOUR death. Is this a VICTORY? The ego ALWAYS marches to defeat, BECAUSE it thinks that triumph over you is possible. And God thinks otherwise. This is no war. Only the mad belief the Will of God can be attacked and overthrown. You may IDENTIFY with this belief, but never will it be more than madness. And fear will reign in madness, and will SEEM to have replaced love there. This is the conflict's PURPOSE. And to those who think that it is possible, the means seem real.

T 23 B 3. Be certain that it is impossible God and the ego, or yourself and it, will EVER meet. You SEEM to meet, and make your strange alliances, on grounds that have no meaning. For your beliefs converge upon the body, the ego's chosen home, which you believe is YOURS. You meet at a mistake;[750] – an error in your self-appraisal. The ego joins with an ILLUSION of yourself you SHARE with it. And yet, illusions cannot join. They ARE the same, and they are nothing. Their joining lies in nothingness; **T(822) -641** two are as meaningless as one, or as a thousand. The ego joins with nothing, BEING nothing. The victory it seeks is meaningless as is itself.

T 23 B 4. Brothers, the war against yourself is almost over. The journey's end is at the place of peace. Would you not now ACCEPT the peace offered you here? This enemy you fought as an INTRUDER on your peace is here transformed before your sight into the GIVER of your peace. Your "enemy" was God Himself, to Whom all conflict, triumph, and attack of ANY kind are all unknown. He loves you perfectly, completely, and eternally. The Son of God at war with his Creator is a condition as ridiculous as nature roaring at the wind in anger, and proclaiming that it is part of itself no longer.

T 23 B 5. Could nature possibly ESTABLISH this, and make it true? Nor IS it up to you to say what shall be part of you, and what is kept apart. The war against yourself was undertaken to teach the Son of God that he is NOT himself, and NOT his Father's Son. For

---

[745] The *Urtext* manuscript has a comma here, but all other versions make it a period, including the *Notes*.

[746] **Psalm 23:4** Yea, though I walk through the valley of the shadow of death,
I will fear no evil;
For You are with me;
Your rod and Your staff, they comfort me.

[747] **Matthew 6:13** "And do not lead us into temptation,
But deliver us from the evil one.
For Yours is the kingdom and the power and the glory forever." Amen.

[748] The *Urtext* manuscript does not have an exclamation point here, just a period. However, both the *Notes* and the *HLC* do have an exclamation point, suggesting it was omitted in error.

[749] June 20, 1967

[750] 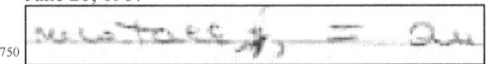 snapshot from *Notes* (*N 11:27) This is a most unusual punctuation, a semicolon followed by an em dash. The *Notes* doesn't have a semicolon. It's rather difficult to say just what it has. This could be a semicolon crossed out, followed by a comma and the "=" equal sign is ambiguous in meaning here. Probably a simple comma or dash would suffice here.

Chapter 23 – The War Against Yourself

this, the memory of his Father MUST be forgotten. It IS forgotten in the body's life, and, if you think you ARE a body, you will believe you HAVE forgotten it. But truth can never be forgotten by ITSELF. And you have NOT forgotten what you are. Only a strange illusion of yourself, a wish to triumph OVER what you are, remembers not.

T 23 B 6. The war against yourself is but the battle of two illusions, struggling to make them DIFFERENT from each other, in the belief the one which conquers will be true. There IS no conflict between them and the TRUTH. Nor ARE they different from each other. Both are NOT true. And so it matters not what form they take. What made them is insane, and they remain part of what made them. Madness holds out no menace to reality, and has no influence upon it. Illusions CANNOT triumph over truth, nor can they **T(823) -642** threaten it in any way. And the reality which they deny is NOT a part of them.

T 23 B 7. What YOU remember IS a part of you. For you MUST be as God created you. Truth does not fight against illusion, nor do illusions fight against the truth. Illusions battle ONLY with themselves. Being fragmented, they fragment. But truth is indivisible, and FAR beyond their little reach. You will remember what you know when you have learned you CANNOT be in conflict. One ILLUSION about yourself can battle with another, yet the war of two illusions is a state where NOTHING HAPPENS. There is no victor, and there is no victory. And truth stands radiant, APART from conflict, untouched and quiet, in the peace of God.

T 23 B 8. Conflict must be between two FORCES. It can NOT exist between one power and nothingness. There is nothing you COULD attack that is not part of you. And, BY attacking it, you make two illusions of yourself, IN CONFLICT with each other. And this occurs whenever you look on ANYTHING that God created with anything but love. Conflict is fearful, for it is the birth of fear. Yet what is born of nothing cannot WIN reality through battle. Why would you fill your world with conflicts with yourself? Let all this madness be undone for you, and turn in peace to the remembrance of God, still shining in your quiet mind.

T 23 B 9. See how the conflict of illusions disappears, when it is brought to truth! For it seems real ONLY as long as it is seen as war between CONFLICTING truths, the conqueror to be the truer, the MORE real, the VANQUISHER of the illusion that was less real, MADE an illusion by defeat. For conflict is the choice BETWEEN illusions, one to be crowned as real, the other vanquished and despised. Here will the Father NEVER be remembered. Yet NO illusion can invade His home, and drive Him out of what He loves forever. And what He loves MUST be forever quiet and at peace, BECAUSE it **T(824) -643** is His home. And you who are beloved of Him are no illusions, being as true and holy as Himself.

T 23 B 10. The stillness of your certainty of Him and of yourself is home to both of you, who dwell as one, and NOT apart. Open the doors of His most holy home, and let forgiveness sweep away all trace of the belief in sin that keeps God homeless, and His Son with Him. You are not strangers in the house of God. Welcome your brother to the home where God has set him in serenity and peace, and dwells with him. Illusions have no place where Love abides, protecting you from EVERYTHING that is not true. You dwell in peace as limitless as its Creator. And EVERYTHING is given those who would remember Him.

T 23 B 11. Over His home the Holy Spirit watches, sure that its peace can never BE disturbed. How can the resting place of God turn on itself, and seek to overcome the One Who dwells there? And think what happens when the house of God perceives itself divided.[751] The altar disappears, the light grows dim, the temple of the Holy One becomes a house of sin.[752] And nothing is remembered, EXCEPT illusions. Illusions CAN conflict, because their forms ARE different. And they do battle ONLY to establish which FORM is true.

T 23 B 12. Illusion meets illusion; truth, itself. The meeting of illusions leads to war. Peace looking on itself EXTENDS itself. War is the condition in which fear is born, and grows and seeks to dominate. Peace is the state where love abides, and seeks to share itself. Conflict and peace are opposites; where one abides, the other CANNOT be; where either goes, the other disappears. So is the memory of God obscured in minds that have become illusion's battleground. Yet far beyond this senseless war it shines, ready to BE remembered when you side with peace. **T(825) -644**[753]

T 23 C. The Laws of Chaos (*Notes* 1660 11:35)

T 23 C 1 The "laws of chaos" CAN be brought to light, though NEVER understood. Chaotic laws are hardly meaningful, and therefore out of reason's sphere. Yet they APPEAR to constitute an obstacle to reason and to truth. Let us, then, look upon them calmly, that we may look BEYOND them, understanding what they ARE, NOT what they would maintain. It IS essential it be understood what they are FOR, because it is their PURPOSE to make meaningless, and to ATTACK the truth. Here are the laws that rule the world you made. And yet they govern nothing, and need NOT be broken; merely looked upon and gone beyond.

T 23 C 2 The first chaotic law is that the truth is different for everyone. Like all these principles, this one maintains that each is separate, and has a different set of thoughts which SETS HIM OFF from others. This principle evolves from the belief there is a hierarchy of illusions; some are MORE valuable, and THEREFORE true. And each establishes this FOR HIMSELF, and MAKES it true by his attack on what another values. This is justified BECAUSE the values differ. And those who hold them SEEM to be unlike, and THEREFORE enemies.

T 23 C 3 Think how this SEEMS to interfere with the first principle of miracles. For this establishes degrees of TRUTH among illusions, making it appear that some are HARDER to be overcome than others. If it were realized that they are all the same and EQUALLY untrue, it would be easy, then, to understand that miracles apply to ALL of them. Errors of ANY kind can be corrected, BECAUSE they are untrue. When brought to truth, instead of TO EACH OTHER, they merely disappear. No PART of nothing CAN be more resistant to the truth than can another. **T(826) -645**

T 23 C 4 The second law of chaos, dear indeed to every worshipper of sin, is that each one MUST sin, and therefore DESERVES attack and death. This principle, closely related to the first, is the demand that errors call for punishment, and NOT correction. For the DESTRUCTION of the one who makes the error places him BEYOND correction, and beyond forgiveness. What he has done is thus interpreted as an irrevocable sentence on himself, which God Himself is powerless to overlook. Sin cannot BE remitted, being the belief the Son of God can make mistakes for which his own destruction becomes inevitable.[754]

---

[751] **Matthew 12:25** But Jesus knew their thoughts, and said to them: "Every kingdom divided against itself is brought to desolation, and every city or house divided against itself will not stand."
[752] **Psalm 16:10** For You will not leave my soul in Sheol, Nor will You allow Your Holy One to see corruption.
Jeremiah 7:11 Has this house, which is called by My name, become a den of thieves in your eyes? Behold, I, even I, have seen it," says the LORD.
Mark 1:24 Saying, "Let us alone! What have we to do with You, Jesus of Nazareth? Did You come to destroy us? I know who You are--the Holy One of God!"
Matthew 21:13 And He said to them, "It is written, 'My house shall be called a house of prayer,' but you have made it a "den of thieves.'"
[753] June 28, 1967
[754] **Matthew 26:28** "For this is My blood of the new covenant, which is shed for many for the remission of sins."

T 23 C 5 Think what this SEEMS to do to the relationship between the Father and the Son. Now it appears that they can NEVER be One again. For One must ALWAYS be condemned, AND BY THE OTHER. Now are they different, and ENEMIES. And THEIR relationship is one of opposition, just as the separate aspects of the Son meet ONLY to conflict, but NOT to join. One becomes weak, the other strong BY HIS DEFEAT. And fear of God, and of each other, now appears as sensible, made real by what the Son of God has done, both to himself AND his Creator.

T 23 C 6 The arrogance on which the laws of chaos stand could not be more apparent than emerges here. Here is a principle which would define what the CREATOR of reality must be; what He MUST think, and what He must believe; and how He must RESPOND, believing it. It is not seen as even necessary that He be asked about the truth of what has been established for His belief. His Son can TELL Him this, and He has but the choice whether to take his word for it, or be mistaken.

T 23 C 7 This leads directly to the third preposterous belief that seems to make chaos eternal. For, if God cannot BE mistaken, then He must accept His Son's belief in what he is, and HATE him for it. See how the fear of God is REINFORCED by this third principle. Now it becomes IMPOSSIBLE to turn to Him for help in misery. For now He has become the "enemy" Who "caused" it, and to Whom appeal is useless. Nor can salvation lie within the Son, **T(827) -646** whose every aspect seems to be at war with Him,[755] and JUSTIFIED in its attack.

T 23 C 8 And now is conflict made inevitable, and beyond the help of God. And now salvation MUST remain impossible, because the Savior HAS become the enemy. There can be NO release and NO escape. Atonement thus becomes a myth, and vengeance, NOT forgiveness, is the Will of God. From where all this begins, there IS no sight of help that can succeed. ONLY destruction can BE the outcome. And God Himself SEEMS to be siding with it, to overcome His Son. Think not the ego will enable you to find ESCAPE from what it wants. THAT is the function of this course, which does NOT value what the ego cherishes. **T(828) -647**[756]

T 23 C 9 The ego values only what it TAKES. This leads to the fourth law of chaos which, if the others are accepted, MUST be true. This seeming law is the belief you HAVE what you have taken. By this, another's loss becomes your gain, and thus it fails to recognize that you can never "take away" save from YOURSELF. Yet all the other laws must lead to this. For enemies do NOT give willingly to one another, nor would they seek to SHARE the things they value. And what your ENEMIES would keep from you must BE worth having, just BECAUSE they keep it hidden from your sight.

T 23 C 10 All of the mechanisms of madness are seen emerging here. The "enemy," made strong by keeping hidden the valuable inheritance which should be yours; your JUSTIFIED possession, and attack for what has been withheld; and the inevitable loss the enemy MUST suffer, to save YOURSELF. Thus do the guilty ones protest their innocence. Were they not forced into this foul attack by the unscrupulous behavior of the enemy, they would respond with only kindness. But, in a savage world, the kind cannot survive. So they MUST take, or else be taken FROM.

T 23 C 11 And now there is a vague, unanswered question, not yet "explained." What IS this precious thing, this priceless pearl, this hidden secret treasure, to be wrested in righteous wrath from this most treacherous and cunning enemy?[757] It must be what you want, and never found. And now you "understand" the reason WHY you found it not. For it was TAKEN from you by the enemy, and hidden where you would not think to look. He hid it in his BODY, making it the cover for his guilt; the hiding place for what belongs to YOU. **T(829) -648**

T 23 C 12 Now must his body be destroyed and sacrificed, that you may have that which BELONGS to you. His treachery DEMANDS his death, that YOU may live. And you attack only in self defense. But what is it you want, that NEEDS his death? Can you be sure your murderous attack IS justified, unless you know what it is FOR? And here a final principle of chaos comes to the "rescue." It holds there is a SUBSTITUTE for love. This is the "magic" that will cure all of your pain; the missing factor in your madness THAT MAKES IT SANE. THIS is the reason why you must attack. HERE is what makes your vengeance justified.

T 23 C 13 Behold, unveiled, the ego's secret gift, torn from your brother's body; hidden there in malice and in hatred for the one to whom the gift belongs. HE would deprive you of the secret ingredient which would give meaning to your life. The substitute for love, born of your enmity to one another, MUST be salvation. IT has no substitute, and there IS only one. And ALL relationships have but the purpose of seizing it, and making it your own. Never is your possession made complete. And never will your brother cease his own attack on YOU, for what you stole. Nor will God end His vengeance upon both, for, in His madness, HE must have this substitute for love, and kill you both.

T 23 C 14 You who believe you walk in sanity, with feet on solid ground, and through a world where meaning CAN be found, consider this: These ARE the laws on which your "sanity" appears to rest. These ARE the principles which makes the ground beneath your feet seem solid. And it IS here you look for meaning. These are the laws YOU made for your salvation. They hold in place the substitute for Heaven that you prefer. This is their PURPOSE; they were MADE for this. There is no point in asking what they **T(830) -649**[758] mean. This is apparent. The MEANS of madness MUST be insane. Are you as certain that you realize the GOAL is madness?

T 23 C 15 NO-ONE WANTS madness, nor does anyone cling to his madness if he sees that this is what it IS. What PROTECTS madness is the belief THAT IT IS TRUE. It is the FUNCTION of insanity to TAKE THE PLACE of truth. It must be seen AS truth, to be believed. And if it IS the truth, then must its opposite, which was the truth before, be madness now. Such a reversal, COMPLETELY turned around, with madness sanity, illusions true, attack a kindness, hatred love, and murder benediction, IS the goal the laws of chaos serve. These are the means by which the laws of God APPEAR to be reversed. Here do the laws of sin APPEAR to hold love captive, and let sin go free.

T 23 C 16 These do not SEEM to be the goals of chaos. For, by the great reversal, they appear to be the laws of ORDER. How could it NOT be so? Chaos is lawlessness, and HAS no laws. To be believed, its SEEMING laws must be perceived as REAL. Their goal of madness MUST be seen as sanity. And fear, with ashen lips and sightless eyes, blinded and terrible to look upon, is lifted to the

---

Acts 2:38 Then Peter said to them, "Repent, and let every one of you be baptized in the name of Jesus Christ for the remission of sins; and you shall receive the gift of the Holy Spirit."

This is another instance of ACIM "correcting" a commonly held view of Biblical teaching, this one relating to the nature of sin and its reality. Is the consequence of "mistakes" the destruction of the mistaken Son of God or is the consequence of mistakes the illusion of separation in which it **seems** as if sin and guilt are real? In either view the objective is release. The question here is whether the release is from the illusion of sin and the consequent illusions of guilt and punishment, or from the reality of God's damnation of the mistaken Son. ACIM says sin and guilt are illusions we made up. Some interpreters of the Bible view sin as reality, along with divine punishment for it.

[755] The *Urtext* does not capitalize "him" here although the *HLC* and FIP both do. Since the pronoun rather clearly refers to God, capitalization does seem to be consistent with Schucman's style conventions and its omission appears to be inadvertent.

[756] June 29, 1967

[757] **Matthew 13:46** "who, when he had found one pearl of great price, went and sold all that he had and bought it."

[758] June 30, 1967

throne of love, its dying conqueror, its substitute, the savior from salvation. How lovely do the laws of fear make death appear! Give thanks unto the hero on love's throne, who saved the Son of God for fear and death!

T 23 C 17 And yet, how can it be that laws like these can BE believed? There is a strange device that makes this possible. Nor is it unfamiliar; we have seen how it APPEARS to function many times before. In truth, it does NOT function, yet in dreams, where ONLY shadows play the major roles, it seems most powerful. No law of chaos COULD compel belief, but for the emphasis on form, AND DISREGARD OF CONTENT. No-one who thinks that one of them is true SEES WHAT IT SAYS. Some FORMS it takes seem **T(831) -650** to have meaning, and that is all.

T 23 C 18 How can some FORMS of murder NOT mean death? Can an attack in ANY form be love? What FORM of condemnation is a blessing? Who makes his Savior powerless, and FINDS salvation? Let not the FORM of the attack on him deceive you. You CANNOT seek to harm him, and be saved. Who can find SAFETY from attack by turning on himself? How can it matter what the FORM this madness takes? It is a judgment that defeats ITSELF, condemning what it says it wants to save. Be not deceived when madness takes a form you think is lovely. What is intent on your destruction, is NOT your friend.

T 23 C 19 You would maintain, and think it true, that you do NOT believe such senseless laws, nor act upon them. And, when you look at what they SAY, they CANNOT be believed. Brothers, you DO believe them. For how else could you PERCEIVE the form they take, with content such as this? Can ANY form of this be tenable? Yet you believe them FOR the forms they take, and DO NOT RECOGNIZE the content. IT never changes. Can you paint rosy lips upon a skeleton, dress it in loveliness, pet it and pamper it, AND MAKE IT LIVE? And can you be content with an illusion that YOU are living?

T 23 C 20 There IS no life outside of Heaven. Where God created life, there life must be. In ANY state apart from Heaven, life is illusion. At best, it SEEMS like life; at worst, like death. Yet both are judgments on what is NOT life, equal in their inaccuracy and lack of meaning. Life not in Heaven is impossible, and what is NOT in Heaven is not ANYWHERE. Outside of Heaven, only the conflict of illusions stands; senseless, impossible and beyond ALL reason, and yet perceived as an eternal BARRIER to Heaven. Illusions ARE but forms. Their content is NEVER true. **T(832) -651**

T 23 C 21 The laws of chaos govern ALL illusions. Their forms conflict, making it SEEM quite possible to value some above the others. Yet each one rests as surely on the belief the laws of chaos ARE the laws of order, as do the others. Each one upholds these laws completely, offering a certain witness that these laws are true. The seeming gentler FORM of the attack is no less certain in its witnessing, OR ITS RESULTS. Certain it is illusions will bring fear, because of the beliefs that they imply, NOT for their form. And lack of faith in love, in ANY form, attests to chaos AS REALITY.

T 23 C 22 From the belief in sin, the faith in chaos MUST follow. It is BECAUSE it follows that it seems to be a logical conclusion; a valid step in ordered thought. The steps to chaos DO follow neatly from their starting-point. Each is a different form in the progression of truth's reversal, leading still deeper into terror, and AWAY from truth. Think not one step is smaller than another, nor that return from one is easier. The whole descent from Heaven lies in each one. And where your thinking starts, there must it end.

T 23 C 23 Brothers, take not one step in the descent to hell. For, HAVING taken one, you will NOT RECOGNIZE the rest for what they are. And they WILL follow. Attack in ANY form has placed your foot upon the twisted stairway that leads FROM Heaven. Yet, any instant, it is possible to have this all undone. How can you know whether you chose the stairs to Heaven or the way to hell? Quite easily. What do you feel? Is peace in your awareness? Are you CERTAIN which way you go? And are you sure the goal of Heaven CAN be reached? If not, you walk alone. Ask, then, your Friend to JOIN with you, and GIVE you certainty of where you go. **T(833) -652**[759]

T 23 D. Salvation Without Compromise (*Notes* 1674 11:49)

T 23 D 1. Is it not true you do NOT recognize some of the forms attack can take? If it is true attack in ANY form will hurt you, and will do so just as much as in another form which you DO recognize, then it MUST follow that you do not always RECOGNIZE the source of pain. ATTACK IN ANY FORM IS EQUALLY DESTRUCTIVE. Its PURPOSE does not change. Its sole intent is murder, and what FORM of murder serves to cover the massive guilt and frantic fear of punishment the murderer MUST feel? He may deny he IS a murderer, and justify his savagery with smiles as he attacks.

T 23 D 2. Yet he will suffer, and will look on his intent in nightmares, where the smiles are gone, and where the purpose rises to meet his horrified awareness, and pursue him still. For no-one THINKS of murder, and escapes the guilt the thought entails. If the INTENT is death, what matter the form it takes? Is death in ANY form, however lovely and charitable it may SEEM to be, a blessing and a sign the Voice for God speaks through you to your brother? The wrapping does not make the gift you give. An empty box, however beautiful and gently given, still contains nothing, and neither the receiver NOR THE GIVER is long deceived. WITHHOLD forgiveness from your brother, and you ATTACK him. You GIVE him nothing, and receive of him but what you gave.

T 23 D 3. Salvation is no compromise of any kind. To compromise is to accept but PART of what you want; to take a little; and GIVE UP the rest. Salvation gives up nothing. It is complete for everyone. Let the IDEA of compromise but enter, and the awareness of salvation's PURPOSE is lost, because it is not recognized. It is DENIED where compromise has been accepted. For compromise is the belief SALVATION is impossible. It would maintain you can attack a little, love a little, AND KNOW THE DIFFERENCE. Thus it would **T(834) -653** teach a little of the same can still be different, and yet the same remain intact, as one. Does this make sense? Can it BE understood?

T 23 D 4. This course is easy just BECAUSE it makes no compromise. Yet it SEEMS difficult to those who still believe that compromise is possible. They do NOT see that, if it is, SALVATION IS ATTACK. Yet it is certain the belief that salvation is impossible can NOT uphold a quiet, calm assurance it has come. Forgiveness cannot BE withheld a little. Nor is it possible to attack for this and love for that, and UNDERSTAND forgiveness. Would you not WANT to recognize assault upon your peace in ANY form, if only thus does it become impossible that YOU lose sight of it? It CAN be kept shining before your vision, forever clear and NEVER out of sight, if YOU defend it not.

T 23 D 5. Those who believe that peace can BE defended, and that attack is JUSTIFIED on its behalf, can NOT perceive it lies within them. How COULD they know? Could they ACCEPT forgiveness side by side with the belief that murder takes some forms by which their peace is SAVED? Would they be WILLING to accept the fact their savage purpose is directed against themselves? No-one unites with enemies, nor is at one with them in purpose. And no-one COMPROMISES with an enemy but hates him still, for what he KEPT from him. Mistake not truce for peace, nor compromise for the ESCAPE from conflict.

T 23 D 6. To be RELEASED from conflict means that IT IS OVER. The door is open; you have LEFT the battleground. You have NOT

---
[759] July 10, 1967

lingered there in cowering hope, because the guns are stilled an instant and the fear that haunts the place of death is not apparent, that it will not return. There IS no safety in a battleground. You can look down on it in safety from above, and NOT be touched. But, from within it, you can find NO safety. Not one tree left standing still will shelter you. Not one illusion of protection stands against the faith in murder. Here stands the body, torn between **T(835) -654** the natural desire to communicate, and the unnatural intent to murder and to die.

T 23 D 7. Think you the FORM that murder takes can offer safety? Can guilt be ABSENT from a battlefield? Do not remain in conflict, for there IS no war without attack.

T 23 E. The Fear of Life (*Notes* 1678 11:52)

T 23 E 1. The fear of God is fear of life, and NOT of death. Yet He remains the only place of safety. In Him is no attack, and no illusion in any form stalks Heaven. Heaven is WHOLLY true. No difference enters. And what is ALL the same cannot conflict. You are NOT asked to fight AGAINST your wish to murder. But you ARE asked to realize the FORM it takes conceals the SAME intent. And it is THIS you fear, and NOT the form.

T 23 E 2. What is NOT love IS murder. What is not loving MUST be an attack. EVERY illusion is an assault on truth. And every one does violence to the IDEA of love, because it SEEMS to be of equal truth. What can be EQUAL to the truth, yet different? Murder and love are incompatible. Yet, if they BOTH are true, then must they be the SAME, and indistinguishable from one another. So WILL they be, to those who see God's Son a body. For it is NOT the body that is like the Son's Creator. And what is lifeless cannot BE the Son of Life.

T 23 E 3. How can a body be extended to hold the universe? Can IT create, and BE what it creates? And can it offer its creation ALL that it is, and NEVER suffer loss? God does not share His function with a body. He GAVE the function to create unto His Son, BECAUSE it is His Own. It is NOT sinful to believe the function of the Son is murder. But it IS insanity. What is the same can HAVE no different function. Creation is the means for God's extension. And what is His MUST be His Son's as well. Either the Father AND the Son are murderers, or neither is. Life makes not death, creating like itself. **T(836) -655**

T 23 E 4. The lovely light of your relationship IS like the love of God. It cannot yet assume the holy function God gave His Son, for your forgiveness of one another is not complete as yet. And so it cannot be extended to ALL creation. Each form of murder and attack that still attracts you, and that you do not recognize for what it is, limits the healing and the miracles you HAVE the power to extend to all. Yet does the Holy Spirit understand how to increase your little gifts, and make them mighty. Also He understands how your relationship is raised ABOVE the battleground, IN it no more.

T 23 E 5. This is your part; to realize that murder, in ANY form, is NOT your will. The OVERLOOKING of the battleground is now your purpose. Be lifted up, and from a higher place, look down upon it. From there, will your perspective be quite different. Here, in the midst of it, it DOES seem real. Here you have CHOSEN to be part of it. Here murder IS your choice. Yet, from above, the choice is miracles, INSTEAD of murder. And the perspective COMING FROM this choice shows you the battle is NOT real, and easily escaped. Bodies may battle, but the clash of forms is meaningless. And it IS over, when you realize it never was begun.

T 23 E 6. How can a battle be perceived as nothingness, when you ENGAGE in it? How can the truth of miracles be RECOGNIZED, if murder is your choice? When the temptation to attack rises to make your mind darkened and murderous, remember you CAN see the battle from above. Even in forms you do NOT recognize, the signs you know. There is a stab of pain, a twinge of guilt, and, above all, a LOSS OF PEACE. This you know well. When it occurs, leave not your place on high, but quickly choose a miracle INSTEAD of murder. And God Himself and all the lights of Heaven, will gently lean to you, and hold you up. For you have chosen to remain where He would have you. And NO illusion can attack the peace of God TOGETHER with His Son. **T(837) -656**

T 23 E 7. See no-one from the battleground, for there you look on him from nowhere. You have NO reference point from where to look, where meaning can be given what you see. For only bodies COULD attack and murder, and if this is your purpose, then you MUST be one with them. Only a PURPOSE unifies, and those who share a purpose have a mind as one.[760] The body HAS no purpose of itself, and MUST be solitary. From below, it cannot BE surmounted. From above, the limits it exerts on those in battle still, are gone and NOT perceived. The body stands between the Father and the Heaven He created for His Son. BECAUSE it has no purpose.

T 23 E 8. Think what is given those who share their Father's purpose, and who KNOW that it is theirs! They want for nothing. Sorrow of any kind is inconceivable. Only the Light they love is in awareness, and only Love shines upon them forever. It is their past, their present, and their future. Always the same, eternally complete, and wholly shared. They KNOW it is impossible their happiness could EVER suffer change of any kind. Perhaps you think the battleground CAN offer something that you can win. CAN it be anything that offers you a perfect calmness, and a sense of love so deep and quiet that no touch of doubt can EVER mar your certainty? And that will last forever?

T 23 E 9. Those with the strength of God in their awareness could never THINK of battle. What COULD they gain but LOSS of their perfection? For everything fought for on the battleground is of the body; something it seems to offer or to own. No-one who knows that he has everything could seek for limitation, nor COULD he value the body's offerings. The senselessness of conquest is quite apparent from the quiet sphere above the battleground. What can conflict with everything? And what is there that offers LESS yet could be wanted MORE? Who, with the love of God upholding him, could find the choice of miracles or murder hard to make? **T(838) - 657**[761]

---

[760] **Philippians 2:2** Fulfill my joy by being like-minded, having the same love, being of one accord, of one mind.
[761] July 17, 1967

CHAPTER 24 – SPECIALNESS AND SEPARATION

T 24 A. Introduction (*Notes* 1684 11:59)

T 24 A 1. Forget not that the motivation for this course is the attainment and the KEEPING of the state of peace. Given this state, the mind is quiet, and the condition in which God is remembered is attained. It is not necessary to tell Him what to do. He will not fail. Where He can enter, there He is already. And can it be He can NOT enter where He wills to be? Peace will be yours BECAUSE it is His Will. Can you believe a shadow can hold back the Will that holds the universe secure? God does not wait upon illusions to let Him be Himself. No more His Son. They ARE. And what illusions that idly seem to drift between them has power to defeat what IS Their Will?

T 24 A 2. To learn this course requires willingness to question EVERY value that you hold. Not one can be kept hidden and obscure, but it will jeopardize your learning. NO belief is neutral; every one has power to dictate each decision you make. For a decision is a CONCLUSION, based on EVERYTHING that you believe. It is the OUTCOME of belief, and follows it as surely as does suffering follow guilt, and freedom sinlessness. There IS no substitute for peace. What God creates has NO alternative. The truth arises from what He knows. And your decisions come from your beliefs as certainly as all creation rose in His Mind BECAUSE of what He knows.

T 24 B. Specialness as a Substitute for Love (*Notes* 1685 11:60)

T 24 B 1. Love IS extension. To withhold the smallest gift is not to know love's purpose. Love offers everything forever. Hold back but ONE belief, ONE offering, and love is gone, because you asked a substitute to take its place. And now must war, the SUBSTITUTE for peace, come with the one alternative that you CAN choose for love. Your CHOOSING it has given it ALL the reality it seems to have. Beliefs will never OPENLY attack each other, because conflicting outcomes ARE impossible. But an UNRECOGNIZED **T(839) -658** belief is a decision to war in secret, where the results of conflict are kept unknown and NEVER brought to reason, to be considered sensible or not.

T 24 B 2. And many senseless outcomes HAVE been reached, and meaningless decisions have been made and kept hidden, to become beliefs now GIVEN power to direct all subsequent decisions. Mistake you not the power of these hidden warriors to disrupt your peace. For it IS at their mercy while you decide to leave it there. The secret enemies of peace, your least decisions to choose attack instead of love, unrecognized and swift to challenge YOU to combat and to violence far more inclusive than you think, are there by your election. Do not deny their presence nor their terrible results. All that can BE denied is their REALITY, but NOT their outcome.

T 24 B 3. All that is ever cherished as a hidden belief, to be defended though unrecognized, is FAITH IN SPECIALNESS. This takes many forms, but ALWAYS clashes with the reality of God's creation, and with the grandeur which He gave His Son. What else COULD justify attack? For who could hate someone whose Self is his, and which He KNOWS? Only the special COULD have enemies, for they are different, and NOT the same. And difference of ANY kind imposes orders of reality, and a need to judge that cannot BE escaped. What God created cannot be attacked, for there is nothing in the universe unlike itself.

T 24 B 4. But what is different CALLS for judgment, and this MUST come from someone "better," someone incapable of being like what he condemns, "above" it, sinless BY COMPARISON with it. And thus does specialness become a means and end at once. For specialness not only sets apart, but serves as grounds from which attack on those who seem "beneath" the special one is "natural" and "just." The special ones feel weak and frail BECAUSE of differences. For what would make them special IS their enemy. Yet they PROTECT its enmity, and call it "friend." On its behalf they fight against the universe, **T(840) -659** for nothing in the world they value more.

T 24 B 5. Specialness is the great dictator of the wrong decisions. Here is the grand illusion of what you are and what your brother is. And here is what MUST make the body dear, and WORTH preserving. SPECIALNESS MUST BE DEFENDED. Illusions CAN attack it, and they DO. For what your brother MUST become, to KEEP your specialness, IS an illusion. He who is "worse" than you MUST be attacked, so that your specialness can live on his defeat. For specialness is triumph, and its victory IS his defeat and shame. How can he live, with all your sins upon him? And who MUST be his conqueror but you?

T 24 B 6. Would it be POSSIBLE for you to hate your brother if you were like him? COULD you attack him if you realized you journey WITH him, to a goal that is the SAME? Would you not help him reach it, in every way you could, if his attainment of it were yours? You ARE his enemy in specialness; his Friend in a SHARED purpose. Specialness can NEVER share, for it depends on goals that you ALONE can reach. And he must NEVER reach them, or YOUR goal is jeopardized. Can love HAVE meaning where the goal is triumph? And what decision CAN be made for this, that will NOT hurt you?

T 24 B 7. Your brother is your Friend BECAUSE his Father created him like you. There IS no difference. You have been GIVEN to each other that love might be extended, NOT cut off from one another. What you KEEP is lost to you. God gave you both Himself. And to remember this is now the ONLY purpose that you share. And so it is the only one you HAVE. Could you attack each other if you chose to see NO specialness of any kind between you? Look fairly at whatever makes you give each other partial welcome, or would let you think that you are better off apart. Is it not ALWAYS your belief your specialness is LIMITED by your relationship? And is not THIS the "enemy" that makes you both illusions to each other? **T(841) -660**

T 24 B 8. The fear of God and of each other comes from each unrecognized belief in specialness. For each demands the other bow to it AGAINST HIS WILL. And God Himself must honor it, or suffer vengeance. Every twinge of malice, or stab of hate, or wish to separate arises here. For here the purpose that you share becomes obscured from BOTH of you. You would oppose this course because it teaches you, YOU ARE ALIKE. You have NO purpose that is not the same. And none your Father does not share with you. For your relationship has been made clean of special goals. And would you now DEFEAT the goal of holiness that Heaven gave it?

T 24 B 9. What perspective can the special have that does NOT change with every seeming blow, each slight, or fancied judgment on itself? Those who are special MUST defend illusions against the truth. For what is specialness but an attack upon the Will of God? You love your brother not while it is this you would defend AGAINST him. This is what HE attacks and YOU protect. Here is the ground of battle which you wage against him. Here MUST he be your enemy, and NOT your Friend. Never can there be peace among the different. He is your friend BECAUSE you are the same. **T(842) -661**[762]

---

[762] August 7, 1967

T 24 C. The Treachery of Specialness (*Notes* 1695 11:70)

T 24 C 1. Comparison MUST be an ego device, for love makes none. Specialness ALWAYS makes comparisons. It is ESTABLISHED by a lack seen in another, and maintained by searching for and keeping clear in sight all lacks it can perceive. This does it seek, and this it looks upon. And ALWAYS whom it thus diminishes would be your Savior, had you not chosen to make of him a tiny measure of your specialness instead. Against the littleness you see in him you stand as tall and stately, clean and honest, pure and unsullied by comparison with what you see.

T 24 C 2. Nor do you understand it is YOURSELF that you diminish thus. Pursuit of specialness is always at the cost of peace. Who can attack his Savior, and cut him down, and recognize his strong support? Who can detract from his omnipotence, and SHARE his power? And who can use him as the gauge of littleness, and be RELEASED from limits? You have a function in salvation. ITS pursuit will bring you joy. But the pursuit of specialness MUST bring you pain. Here is a goal that would defeat salvation, and thus run COUNTER to the Will of God. To value specialness is to esteem an alien will, to which illusions of yourself ARE dearer than the truth.

T 24 C 3. Specialness is the idea of sin MADE REAL. Sin is impossible even to imagine, without this base. For sin rose from it, out of nothingness, an evil flower with no roots at all. Here is the self-made savior, the creator who creates UNLIKE the Father, and which made His Son like to itself, and NOT like unto Him. His SPECIAL sons are many, NEVER one, each one in exile from himself and Him of Whom they are a part. Nor do they love the Oneness which created them as One with Him. They chose their specialness INSTEAD of Heaven and INSTEAD of peace, and wrapped it carefully in sin, to keep it "safe" from truth. **T(843) -662**

T 24 C 4. You are NOT special. If you think you are, and would defend your specialness against the truth of what you REALLY are, how can you know the truth? What answer that the Holy Spirit gives can reach you, when it is your specialness to which you listen, and which asks AND ANSWERS? Its tiny answer, soundless in the melody which pours from God to you eternally in loving praise of what you are, is all you listen to. And that vast song of honor and of love for what you are seems silent and unheard before ITS mightiness. You strain your ears to hear ITS soundless voice, and yet the Call of God Himself is soundless to you.

T 24 C 5. You CAN defend your specialness, but never will you hear the Voice for God beside it. They speak a different language, and they fall on different ears. To every special one a DIFFERENT message, and one with DIFFERENT meaning, is the truth. Yet how CAN truth be different to each one? The special messages the special hear convince them THEY are different and apart; each in his special sins and safe from love, which does not see his specialness at all. Christ's Vision IS their enemy, for it sees not what THEY would look upon. And it WOULD show them that the specialness they think they see IS an illusion.

T 24 C 6. What would they see instead? The shining radiance of the Son of God, so like his Father that the memory of Him springs instantly to mind. And with this memory, the Son remembers his own creations, as like to him as he is to his Father. And all the world he made, and all his specialness, and all the sins he held in its defense AGAINST himself, will vanish as his mind accepts the truth about himself, as it returns to take their place. This is the only "cost" of truth. You will no longer see what never was, nor hear what makes no sound. Is it a sacrifice to give up nothing, and to receive the Love of God forever?

T 24 C 7. You who have chained your Savior to your specialness, and given it HIS place, remember this: He has NOT lost the power to forgive you all the sins you think you placed between him and the function of salvation GIVEN **T(844) -663** him for you.[763] Nor will you CHANGE his function, any more than you can change the truth in him and in yourself. But be you certain that the truth is just the same in both. It gives no different messages, and has ONE meaning. And it is one you BOTH can understand, and one which brings release to BOTH of you. Here stands your brother with the key to Heaven in his hand, held out to you.[764] Let not the dream of specialness remain between you. What is one IS joined in truth.

T 24 C 8. Think of the loveliness that you will see within yourself, when you have looked on him as on a Friend. He IS the enemy of specialness, but ONLY friend to what is real in you. Not one attack you thought you made on him has taken from him the gift that God would have him give to you. His need to give it is as great as yours to have it. Let him forgive you all your specialness, and make you whole in mind, and one with him. He waits for your forgiveness only that he may return it unto you. It is not God Who has condemned His Son. But ONLY you, to save his specialness, and kill his Self.

T 24 C 9. You have come far along the way of truth; too far to falter now. Just one step more, and every vestige of the fear of God will melt away in love. Your brother's specialness and yours ARE enemies, and bound in hate to kill each other and DENY they are the same. Yet it is not illusions that have reached this final obstacle that seems to make God and His Heaven so remote that they cannot be reached. Here, in this holy place, does truth stand waiting to receive you both in silent blessing, and in peace so real and so encompassing that NOTHING stands outside.

T 24 C 10. Leave all illusions of yourself OUTSIDE this place, to which you come in hope and honesty. Here is your Savior FROM your specialness. He is in need of your acceptance of himself as part of you, as you for his. You are alike to God as God is to Himself. He is not special, for He would not keep one part of what He is unto Himself, NOT given to His Son, but kept **T(845) -664** for Him alone. And it is this you fear; for, if He is not special, then He willed His Son be like Him, and your brother IS like you. Not special, but possessed of everything, INCLUDING you.

T 24 C 11. Give him but what he has, remembering God gave Himself to BOTH of you in equal love, that both might share the universe with Him Who chose that love could never be divided and kept separate from what it IS and must forever be. You ARE your brother's; part of love was not DENIED to him.[765] But can it be that YOU have lost because HE is complete? What has been given him makes YOU complete, as it does him. God's love gave you to him and him to you, BECAUSE He gave Himself. What is the same as God IS One with Him. And ONLY specialness could make the truth of God and you AS One seem anything BUT Heaven. And the hope of peace at last in sight.

T 24 C 12. Specialness is the seal of treachery upon the gift of love. Whatever serves its purpose MUST be given to kill. No gift that bears its seal but offers treachery to giver and receiver. Not one glance from eyes it veils but looks on sight of death. Not one believer in its potency but seeks for bargains and for compromise that would establish sin as[766] love's substitute, and serve it faithfully. And no relationship that holds its purpose dear but clings to murder

---

[763] **Matthew 9:6** "But that you may know that the Son of Man has power on earth to forgive sins"--then He said to the paralytic, "Arise, take up your bed, and go to your house."

[764] **Matthew 16:19** "And I will give you the keys of the kingdom of heaven, and whatever you bind on earth will be bound in heaven, and whatever you loose on earth will be loosed in heaven."

[765] **Genesis 4:9** Then the LORD said to Cain, "Where is Abel your brother?" He said, "I do not know. Am I my brother's keeper?"

[766] The word "as" does not appear in the *Urtext* manuscript, but it is present as a shorthand glyph in the *Notes*. Because it is rather required to make this sentence grammatically correct, this apparent inadvertent omission is replaced. Both the *HLC* and *FIP* omit "as."

Chapter 24 – Specialness and Separation

as safety's weapon, and the great defender of all illusions from the "threat" of love.

T 24 C 13. The hope of specialness makes it seem possible God made the body as the prison-house which keeps His Son from Him. For it DEMANDS a special place God cannot enter, and a hiding-place where none is welcome but your tiny self. Nothing is sacred here but unto you, and you alone, apart and separate from all your brothers; safe from ALL intrusions of sanity upon illusions; safe from God, and safe for conflict everlasting. **T(846) -665** Here are the gates of hell you closed upon yourself, to rule in madness and in loneliness your special kingdom, APART from God, AWAY from truth and from salvation.[767]

T 24 C 14. The key you threw away God gave your brother, whose holy hands would offer it to you, when you were ready to accept His plan for your salvation in place of yours.[768] How could this readiness be reached save through the sight of all your misery, and the awareness that your plan has failed, and will forever fail to bring you peace and joy of ANY kind? Through this despair you travel now, yet it is but ILLUSION of despair. The death of specialness is NOT your death, but your awaking into Life Eternal. You but emerge from an illusion of what you are, to the acceptance of yourself as God created you. **T(847) -666**[769]

T 24 D. The Forgiveness of Specialness (*Notes* 1704 11:79)

T 24 D 1. Forgiveness is the end of specialness. Only illusions can BE forgiven, and then they disappear. Forgiveness is release from ALL illusions, and that is why it is impossible but PARTLY to forgive. No-one who clings to ONE illusion can see himself as sinless, for he holds one error to himself as lovely still. And so he calls it "unforgivable," and makes it sin. How can he then give HIS forgiveness wholly, when he would not receive it for himself? For it is sure he WOULD receive it wholly, the instant that he gave it so. And thus HIS secret guilt would disappear, forgiven by himself.

T 24 D 2. Whatever form of specialness you cherish, you have made sin. Inviolate it stands, strongly defended with all your puny might against the Will of God. And thus it stands against YOURSELF, YOUR enemy, NOT God's. So does it seem to split you off from God, and make you separate from Him as its defender. YOU would protect what God created not. And yet, this idol that seems to GIVE you power has taken it away. For you have given your brother's birthright[770] to it, leaving HIM alone and unforgiven, and yourself in sin beside him, both in misery, before the idol that can save you not.

T 24 D 3. It is not YOU that is so vulnerable and open to attack that just a word, a little whisper that you do not like, a circumstance that suits you not, or an event that you did not anticipate upsets your world, and hurls it into chaos. Truth is not frail. Illusions leave it perfectly unmoved and undisturbed. But specialness is NOT the truth in you. IT can be thrown off balance by ANYTHING. What rests on nothing NEVER can be stable. However large and overblown it SEEMS to be, it still must rock and turn and whirl about with every breeze.[771]

T 24 D 4. Without foundation nothing is secure. Would God have left His Son in such a state, where safety HAS no meaning? No, -- His Son is safe, resting on Him. It is your specialness that is attacked by everything that walks and breathes, or creeps or crawls, or even lives at all. Nothing **T(848) -667** is safe from its attack, and it is safe from nothing. It will forever more BE unforgiving, for that is what it IS. A secret vow that what God wants for you will never be, and that you will oppose His Will forever. Nor is it possible the two can ever be the same, while specialness stands like a flaming sword of death between them, and makes them enemies.[772]

T 24 D 5. God asks for your forgiveness. He would have no separation, like an alien will, rise between what He wills for you, and what YOU will. THEY are the same, for neither one wills specialness. How could they will the death of love itself? Yet they are powerless to make attack upon illusions. They are NOT BODIES; as One Mind they wait for all illusions to be BROUGHT to them, and left behind. Salvation challenges not even death. And God Himself, Who knows that death is NOT your will, must say, "Thy will be done,"[773] because YOU think it is.

T 24 D 6. Forgive the great Creator of the universe, the Source of life, of love and holiness, the perfect Father of a perfect Son, for your illusions of your specialness. Here is the hell you chose to be your home. He chose not this for you. Ask not He enter this. The way is barred to love and to salvation. Yet if you would release your brother from the depths of hell, you have forgiven Him Whose Will it is you rest forever in the arms of peace, in perfect safety, and without the heat and malice of one thought of specialness to mar your rest. Forgive the Holy One the specialness He could not give, and yet you made instead.

T 24 D 7. The special ones are all asleep, surrounded by a world of loveliness they do not see. Freedom and peace and joy stand there, beside the bier on which they sleep, and call them to come forth and waken from their dream of death.[774] Yet they hear nothing. They are lost in dreams of specialness. They hate the call that would awaken them. And they curse God because He did not make their dream reality. Curse God and die,[775] but not by Him Who made not death, but only in the dreams. Open your eyes a little; **T(849) -668** see the Savior God gave to you that you might look on him, and give him back his birthright.[776] It is YOURS.

T 24 D 8. The slaves of specialness will yet be free. Such is the Will of God, and of His Son. Would God condemn HIMSELF to hell and to damnation? And do YOU will that this be done unto your Savior? God calls to you from him to join His Will to save you BOTH from hell. Look on the print of nails upon his hands that he holds out for your forgiveness.[777] God asks your mercy on His Son, and on Him-

---

[767] **Matthew 16:18** "And I also say to you that you are Peter, and on this rock I will build My church, and the gates of Hades shall not prevail against it."

[768] **Matthew 16:18** "And I also say to you that you are Peter, and on this rock I will build My church, and the gates of Hades shall not prevail against it."

[769] August 15, 1967

[770] **Genesis 25:33** And Jacob said, Swear to me this day; and he sware unto him: and he sold his birthright unto Jacob.

[771] **Matthew 7:24-27** "Therefore whoever hears these sayings of Mine, and does them, I will liken him to a wise man who built his house on the rock: and the rain descended, the floods came, and the winds blew and beat on that house; and it did not fall, for it was founded on the rock.

"But everyone who hears these sayings of Mine, and does not do them, will be like a foolish man who built his house on the sand: and the rain descended, the floods came, and the winds blew and beat on that house; and it fell. And great was its fall."

[772] **Genesis 3:24** So He drove out the man; and He placed cherubim at the east of the garden of Eden, and a flaming sword which turned every way, to guard the way to the tree of life.

[773] **Matthew 6:10** "Thy kingdom come. Thy will be done, as in heaven, so on earth."

Matthew 26:39 He went a little farther and fell on His face, and prayed, saying, "O My Father, if it is possible, let this cup pass from Me; nevertheless, not as I will, but as You will."

Matthew 26:42 Again a second time he went away, and prayed, saying, "My Father, if this cannot pass away, except I drink it, thy will be done."

[774] **John 11:43** Now when He had said these things, He cried with a loud voice, "Lazarus, come forth!"

[775] **Job 2:9** Then said his wife unto him, Dost thou still retain thine integrity? curse God, and die.

[776] **Genesis 25:33** And Jacob said, Swear to me this day; and he sware unto him: and he sold his birthright unto Jacob.

[777] **John 20:25** The other disciples therefore said to him, "We have seen the Lord." So he said to them, "Unless I see in His hands the print of the nails,

self. Deny them not. They ask of you but that your will be done. They seek your love that you may love yourself. Love not your specialness instead of them. The print of nails are[778] on your hands as well.[779] Forgive your Father it was NOT His Will that you be crucified. T(850) -669[780]

T 24 E. Specialness and Salvation (*Notes* 1709 11:84)

T 24 E 1. Specialness is a lack of trust in anyone except yourself. Faith is invested in yourself alone. Everything else becomes your enemy, feared and attacked, deadly and dangerous, hated and worthy only of destruction. Whatever gentleness it offers is but deception, but its hate is real. In danger of destruction, it MUST kill, and YOU are drawn to it, to kill it first. And such is guilt's attraction. Here is death enthroned as savior; crucifixion is now redemption, and salvation can ONLY mean destruction of the world, EXCEPT YOURSELF.

T 24 E 2. What could the purpose of the body BE but specialness? And it is this that makes it frail and helpless in its own defense. It was CONCEIVED to make YOU frail and helpless. The goal of separation is its curse. But bodies HAVE no goal. Purpose is of the mind. And minds can change, as they desire. What they ARE, and all their attributes, CANNOT change. But what they hold as purpose CAN be changed, and body states must shift accordingly. Of itself, the body can do nothing. See it as means to hurt, and it is hurt. See it as means to heal, and it is healed.

T 24 E 3. YOU CAN BUT HURT YOURSELF. This has been oft repeated, but is difficult to grasp as yet. To minds intent on specialness, it is impossible. But to those who wish to heal and NOT attack, it is quite obvious. The purpose of attack is in the MIND, and its effects are felt but where it IS. Nor is mind limited; so must it be that harmful purpose hurts the mind AS ONE. Nothing could make LESS sense to specialness. Nothing could make MORE sense to miracles. For miracles are merely change of purpose from hurt to healing.

T 24 E 4. This shift in purpose DOES "endanger" specialness, but only in the sense that all illusions are "threatened" by the truth. They will NOT stand before it, yet what comfort has ever been in them, that you would keep the T(851) -670 gift your Father asks from Him, and give it there instead? Given to HIM, the universe is yours. Offered to THEM, no gifts can be returned. What you have given specialness has left you bankrupt, and your treasure-house barren and empty, with an open door inviting everything that would disturb your peace to enter and destroy.[781]

T 24 E 5. Long ago we said consider not the means by which salvation is attained, nor how to reach it. But DO consider, and consider well, whether it be your WISH that you might see your brother sinless. To specialness the answer MUST be "no." A sinless brother IS its enemy, while sin, if it were possible, WOULD be its friend. Your brother's "sins" would justify itself, and GIVE it meaning that the truth denies. All that is real proclaims his sinlessness. All that is

---

and put my finger into the print of the nails, and put my hand into His side, I will not believe."

[778] We have an agreement in number grammar problem here. It has to be "prints of nails are" or "print of nails is." Both *Notes* and *Urtext* have this problem. FIP resolves it by changing "are" to "is." We cannot exclude however the exercise of "poetic license."

[779] **John 20:25** The other disciples therefore said to him, "We have seen the Lord." So he said to them, "Unless I see in His hands the print of the nails, and put my finger into the print of the nails, and put my hand into His side, I will not believe."

[780] August 17, 1963[?]

[781] **John 20:25** The other disciples therefore said to him, "We have seen the Lord." So he said to them, "Unless I see in His hands the print of the nails, and put my finger into the print of the nails, and put my hand into His side, I will not believe."

---

false proclaims his sins as real. If HE is sinful, then is YOUR reality not real, but just a dream of specialness which lasts an instant, crumbling into dust.

T 24 E 6. Do not defend this senseless dream, in which God is bereft of what He loves, and you remain beyond salvation. Only this is certain, in this shifting world which has NO meaning in reality: When peace is not with you ENTIRELY, and when you suffer pain of ANY kind, you have beheld some sin within your brother, AND HAVE REJOICED at what you thought was there. Your specialness seemed safe BECAUSE of it. And thus you saved what YOU appointed to be your savior, and crucified the one whom God has given you instead. So are you bound with him, for you ARE one with him.[782] And so is specialness HIS enemy, and YOURS as well. T(852) -671[783]

T 24 F. The Resolution of the Dream (*Notes* 1713 11:88)

T 24 F 1. The Christ in you is very still. He looks on what He loves, and knows it as Himself. And thus does He rejoice at what He sees, because He knows that it is one with Him, and with His Father. Specialness, too, takes joy in what it sees, although it is not true. Yet what you seek for IS a source of joy, as you conceive it. What you wish IS true for you. Nor is it possible that you can wish for something, and LACK faith that it is so. WISHING MAKES REAL, as surely as does Will create. The power of a wish upholds illusions as strongly as does Love extend Itself. Except that one deludes; the other heals.

T 24 F 2. There is no dream of specialness, however hidden or disguised its form, however lovely it may seem to be, however much it delicately offers the hope of peace and the escape from pain, in which you suffer not your condemnation. In dreams effect and cause are interchanged, for here the maker of the dream believes that what he made is happening TO him. He does NOT realize he picked a thread from here, a scrap from there, and wove a picture out of nothing. For the parts do NOT belong together, and the whole contributes nothing to the parts to GIVE them meaning.

T 24 F 3. Where could your peace arise BUT from forgiveness? The Christ in you looks ONLY on the truth, and sees no condemnation that could NEED forgiveness. HE is at peace BECAUSE He sees no sin. Identify with Him, and what has He that you have not? He is your eyes, your ears, your hands, your feet. How gentle are the sights He sees, the sounds He hears. How beautiful His hand that holds His brother's, and how lovingly He walks beside him, showing him what CAN be seen and heard, and where he will see nothing, and there IS no sound to hear. T(853) -672

T 24 F 4. Yet let your specialness direct his way, and YOU will follow. And both will walk in danger, each intent, in the dark forest of the sightless, unlit but by the shifting, tiny gleams that spark an instant from the fireflies of sin and then go out, to lead the other to a nameless precipice and hurl him over it. For what can specialness delight in but to kill? What does it seek for but the sight of death? Where does it lead but to destruction? Yet think not that it looked upon your brother FIRST, nor hated him BEFORE it hated you.[784] The sin its eyes behold in him, and love to look upon it saw in you, and looks on still with joy.

T 24 F 5. Yet IS it joy to look upon decay and madness, and believe this crumbling thing, with flesh already loosened from the bone and sightless holes for eyes, is like yourself? Rejoice you HAVE no eyes with which to see; no ears to listen, and no hands to hold nor feet to

---

[782] **Matthew 16:19** "And I will give you the keys of the kingdom of heaven, and whatever you bind on earth will be bound in heaven, and whatever you loose on earth will be loosed in heaven."

[783] August 28, 1967

[784] **John 15:18** "If the world hates you, you know that it hated Me before it hated you."

guide. Be glad that ONLY Christ can lend you His, while you have need of them. They are illusions, too, as much as yours. And yet, because they serve a different purpose, the strength their PURPOSE holds is given THEM. And what THEY see and hear and hold and lead is given light, that YOU may lead as you were led.

T 24 F 6. The Christ in you is very still. He knows where you are going, and He leads you there in gentleness and blessing all the way. His love for God replaces ALL the fear you thought you saw within yourself. His holiness shows you Himself in him whose hand you hold, and whom you lead to Him. And what you see IS like yourself. For what but Christ IS there to see and hear and love, and follow home? He looked upon you FIRST, but recognized that you were not complete. And so He sought for your completion in each living thing that He beholds and loves. And seeks it still, that each might offer YOU the Love of God. **T(854) -673**

T 24 F 7. Yet is He quiet, for He knows that Love is in you now, and safely held in you by that same hand that holds your brother's in your own. Christ's hand holds all His brothers in Himself. He gives them vision for their sightless eyes, and sings to them of Heaven, that their ears may hear no more the sound of battle and of death. He reaches through them, holding out His hand, that everyone may bless all living things, and see their holiness. And He rejoices that these sights are YOURS, to look upon with Him and share His joy. His perfect LACK of specialness He offers you, that you may save all living things from death, receiving from each one the gift of Life that your forgiveness offers to your Self.

T 24 F 8. The sight of Christ is all there is to see. The song of Christ is all there is to hear. The hand of Christ is all there is to hold. There is no journey but to walk with Him. You who would be content with specialness, and seek salvation in a war with Love, consider this:[785] The holy Lord of Heaven has Himself come down to you to offer you your own completion. What is His is yours, because in your completion is His Own. He Who willed not to be without His Son could never will that you be Brotherless. And would He give a Brother unto you except he be as perfect as yourself, and just as like to Him in holiness as YOU must be?

T 24 F 9. There must be doubt BEFORE there can be conflict. And EVERY doubt must be about yourself. Christ HAS no doubt, and from His certainty His quiet comes. He will exchange His certainty for ALL your doubts, if you agree that He is one with you, and that this Oneness is endless, timeless, and within your grasp BECAUSE your hands are His. He is within you, yet He walks beside you and before, leading the way that He must go to find Himself complete. His quietness becomes YOUR certainty. And where is doubt, when certainty has come? **T(855) -674**[786]

T 24 G. Salvation from Fear (*Notes* 1719 11:94)

T 24 G 1. Before your brother's holiness the world is still, and peace descends on it in gentleness and blessing so complete, that not one trace of conflict still remains to haunt you in the darkness of the night. He is your Savior from the dreams of terror. He is the healing of your sense of sacrifice, and fear that what you have will scatter with the wind, and turn to dust. In him is your assurance God is here, and with you now. While he is what he is, you can be sure that God is knowable, and WILL be known to you. For He could never leave His own creation. And the sign that this is so lies in your brother, offered you that all your doubts about yourself may disappear before his holiness.

T 24 G 2. See in him God's creation. For in him his Father waits for your acknowledgment that He created YOU as part of Him. Without you, there would be a lack in God, a Heaven incomplete, a Son without a Father. There could be no universe, and no reality. For what God wills is whole, and part of Him BECAUSE His Will is One. Nothing alive that is not part of Him, and nothing is but IS alive in Him. Your brother's holiness shows you that God is One with him AND you; that what he has is yours BECAUSE you are not separate from him OR from his Father.

T 24 G 3. Nothing is lost to you in all the universe. Nothing that God created has He failed to lay before you lovingly, as yours forever. And no thought within His Mind is absent from your own. It is His Will you SHARE His love for you, and look upon yourself as lovingly as He conceived of you before the world began, and as He knows you still. God changes not His Mind about His Son with passing circumstance which has no meaning in eternity where He abides, and you with Him. Your brother IS as He created him. And it is this that saves YOU from a world that He created not. **T(856) -675**

T 24 G 4. Forget not that the healing of God's Son is all the world is for. That is the ONLY purpose the Holy Spirit sees in it, and thus the only one it HAS. Until you see the healing of the Son as all you wish to be accomplished by the world, by time, and ALL appearances, you will NOT know the Father OR yourself. For you will use the world for what is NOT its purpose, and will NOT escape its laws of violence and death. Yet it is GIVEN you to be BEYOND its laws in ALL respects, in EVERY way, and EVERY circumstance; in ALL temptation to perceive what is NOT there, and ALL belief God's Son can suffer pain because he sees himself as he is not.

T 24 G 5. Look on your brother, and behold in him the whole reversal of the laws that SEEM to rule this world. See in his freedom YOURS, for such it IS. Let not his specialness obscure the truth in him, for not one law of death you bind him to will YOU escape. And not one sin you see in him but keeps you BOTH in hell. Yet will his perfect sinlessness RELEASE you both, for holiness is quite impartial, with one judgment made for all it looks upon. And that is made, not of itself, but through the Voice that speaks for God in everything that lives, and shares His Being.[787]

T 24 G 6. It is HIS sinlessness that eyes that see can look upon. It is HIS loveliness they see in everything. And it is HE they look for everywhere, and find no sight or place or time where He is NOT. Within your brother's holiness, the perfect frame for YOUR salvation and the world's, is set the shining memory of Him in Whom your brother lives, and you along with him. Let not your eyes be blinded by the veil of specialness that hides the face of Christ from him, and you as well. And let the fear of God no longer hold the vision you were MEANT to see from you. Your brother's BODY shows not Christ to you. He IS set forth within his holiness.

T 24 G 7. Choose, then, his body OR his holiness as what you WANT to see, and which you choose is yours to look upon. Yet will you choose in countless **T(857) -676** situations, and through time which seems to have no end, until the truth be your decision. For eternity is NOT regained by still one more denial of the Christ in him. And where is YOUR salvation, if he is but a body? Where is YOUR peace, but in his holiness? And where is God Himself but in that part of Him He set forever in your brother's holiness, that YOU might see the truth about yourself set forth at last in terms you recognized and understood?

T 24 G 8. Your brother's holiness is sacrament and benediction unto YOU. His errors can NOT withhold God's blessing from himself, nor you who see him truly. His mistakes can cause delay, which it is given YOU to take from him, that both may end a journey that has never been begun, and NEEDS no end. What never was is NOT a part of you. Yet will you think it is, until you realize that it is not a part of him who stands beside you. He is the mirror of yourself, wherein you see the judgment you have laid on BOTH of you. The

---

[785] The *Urtext* manuscript has a semi-colon, but all other versions, including the *Notes*, have a colon. The semi-colon would appear to be a typing mistake.
[786] Sept. 25, 1967

[787] **Acts 17:28** for in Him we live and move and have our being, as also some of your own poets have said, "For we are also His offspring."

Christ in you beholds his holiness. Your specialness looks on his body, and beholds him not.

T 24 G 9. See him as what he IS, that YOUR deliverance may not be long. A senseless wandering, without a purpose and without accomplishment of any kind, is all the other choice can offer you. Futility of function not fulfilled will haunt you while your brother lies asleep, 'til what has been assigned to you is done, and he is risen from the past. He who condemned himself, and you as well, is given you to save from condemnation, along with you. And both shall see God's glory in His Son, whom you mistook as flesh, and bound to laws that have NO power over him at all.

T 24 G 10. Would you not gladly realize these laws are not for YOU? Then see HIM not as prisoner to them. It CANNOT be what governs part of God holds not for all the rest. You place YOURSELF under the laws you see as ruling HIM. Think, then, how great the Love of God for YOU must be, that **T(858) -677** He has given you a part of Him, to save from pain and give YOU happiness. And never doubt but that your specialness will disappear before the Will of God Who loves each part of Him with equal love and care. The Christ in you CAN see your brother truly. And would you decide AGAINST the holiness He sees?

T 24 G 11. Specialness is the function that you gave yourself. It stands for you alone, as self-created, self-maintained, in need of nothing, and unjoined with anything beyond the body. In its eyes, you are a separate universe, with all the power to hold itself complete within itself, with every entry shut against intrusion, and every window barred against the light. Always attacked and always furious, with anger always fully justified, you have pursued this goal with vigilance you never thought to yield, and effort that you never thought to cease. And all this grim determination was for this: YOU WANTED SPECIALNESS TO BE THE TRUTH.

T 24 G 12. Now you are merely asked that you pursue another goal with far LESS vigilance, with little effort and with little time, and with the power of God maintaining it, and promising success. Yet, of the two, it is THIS one you find more difficult. The SACRIFICE of self you understand, nor do you deem THIS cost too heavy. But a tiny willingness, a nod to God, a greeting to the Christ in you, you find a burden wearisome and tedious, too heavy to be borne. Yet, to the dedication to the truth as GOD established it, NO sacrifice is asked, NO strain called forth, and all the power of Heaven and the might of truth itself is given to provide the means, and GUARANTEE the goal's accomplishment.

T 24 G 13. You who believe it easier to see your brother's body than his holiness, be sure you understand what made this judgment. Here is the voice of specialness heard clearly, judging AGAINST the Christ, and setting forth, for YOU, the purpose that you CAN attain, and what you can NOT do. Forget not that this **T(859) -678** judgment MUST apply to what you do with IT as your ally. For what you do through Christ it does not know. To Him, this judgment makes no sense at all, for ONLY what His Father wills is possible, and there IS no alternative for Him to see. Out of His LACK of conflict comes your peace. And from His purpose come the means for effortless accomplishment and rest. **T(860) -679**[788]

T 24 H. The Meeting-Place (*Notes* 1727 11:102)

T 24 H 1. How bitterly does everyone tied to this world defend the specialness he WANTS to be the truth! His wish is law to him, and he obeys. Nothing his specialness demands does he withhold. Nothing it needs does he deny to what he loves. And, while it calls to him, he hears no other Voice. No effort is too great, no cost too much, no price too dear, to save his specialness from the least slight, the tiniest attack, the whispered doubt, the hint of threat, or anything but deepest reverence. This is your son, beloved of you as you are to your Father.[789] Yet it stands in place of your creations, who ARE son to you, that you might SHARE the Fatherhood of God, not snatch it FROM Him.

T 24 H 2. What IS this son that you have made to be your strength? What is this child of earth, on whom such love is lavished? What is this parody of God's creation, that takes the place of YOURS? And where are THEY, now that the host of God has found another son that he prefers to them? The memory of God shines not alone. What is within your brother still contains ALL of creation, everything created and creating, born and unborn as yet, still in the future or apparently gone by. What is in him is changeless, and YOUR changelessness is recognized in its acknowledgment. The holiness in you belongs to him. And, BY your seeing it in him, returns to YOU.

T 24 H 3. All of the tribute you have given specialness belongs to him, and thus returns to you. All of the love and care, the strong protection, the thought by day and night, the deep concern, the powerful conviction this is you, belong to him. Nothing you gave to specialness but is HIS due. And nothing due him is NOT due to you. How will you KNOW your worth, while specialness claims you instead? How can you FAIL to know it, in his holiness? Seek not to make your specialness the truth, for, if it were, you would be lost indeed. Be thankful, rather, it is given you to see **T(861) -680** his holiness BECAUSE it is the truth. And what is true in him MUST be as true in you.

T 24 H 4. Ask yourself this: CAN YOU PROTECT THE MIND? The body, yes, a little; not from time, but temporarily. And much you think to save, you hurt. What would you save it FOR? For, in that choice, lie both its health AND harm. Save it for show, as bait to catch another fish, to house your specialness in better style, or weave a frame of loveliness around your hate, and you condemn it to decay and pain. And, if you see this purpose in your brother's, such is your condemnation of your own. Weave rather, then, a frame of holiness around him, that the truth may shine in him, and give YOU safety from decay.

T 24 H 5. The Father keeps what HE created safe. YOU cannot touch it with the false ideas you made, BECAUSE it was created not by you. Let not your foolish fancies frighten you. What is immortal cannot BE attacked; what is but temporal HAS no effect. Only the PURPOSE that you see in it has meaning, and, if THAT is true, its safety rests secure. If not, it HAS no purpose, and is means for nothing. Whatever is perceived as means for truth SHARES in its holiness, and rests in light as safely as Itself. Nor will that light go out when it is gone. Its holy purpose GAVE it immortality, setting another light in Heaven, where your creations recognize a gift from YOU, a sign that you have NOT forgotten them.

T 24 H 6. The test of EVERYTHING on earth is simply this: "What is it FOR?" The answer makes it what it IS for you. It has NO meaning of itself, yet you can GIVE reality to it, according to the purpose which YOU serve. Here, YOU are but means, along with it. God is a Means as well as End. In Heaven, means and end are one, and One with Him. This is the state of true creation, found not within time, but in eternity. To no-one here is this describable. Nor is there any way to learn what this condition means. Not 'til you go PAST learning to the Given; not 'til you make again **T(862) -681** a holy home for YOUR creations is it understood.

T 24 H 7. A co-creator with the Father must have a Son. Yet must this Son have been created like Himself. A perfect Being, all-encompassing and all-encompassed, nothing to add and nothing taken FROM; not born of size nor weight nor time, nor held to limits or uncertainties of ANY kind. Here do the means and end unite

---

[788] Sept. 27, 1967

[789] **Matthew 3:17** And suddenly a voice came from heaven, saying, "This is My beloved Son, in whom I am well pleased."
Matthew 17:5 While he was still speaking, behold, a bright cloud overshadowed them; and suddenly a voice came out of the cloud, saying, "This is My beloved Son, in whom I am well pleased. Hear Him!"

as One, nor does this One have any end at all. All this is true, and yet it has no meaning to anyone who still retains one unlearned lesson in his memory; one thought with purpose still uncertain, or one wish with a divided aim.

T 24 H 8. This course makes no attempt to teach what cannot easily be learned. Its scope does not exceed your own. Except to say that what is yours will come to you when you are ready. Here, are the means and purpose separate, because they were so made and so perceived. And therefore do we deal with them as if they were. It is essential it be kept in mind that ALL perception still is upside down, until its PURPOSE has been understood. Perception does not SEEM to be a means. And it is this that makes it hard to grasp the whole extent to which it MUST depend on what you use it FOR.

T 24 H 9. Perception seems to TEACH you what you see. Yet it but witnesses to what YOU taught. It is the outward picture of a wish, an image that you WANTED to be true. Look at yourself, and you will see a body. Look at this body in a different light, and it looks different. And without a light, it seems that it is gone. Yet you are reassured that it is there, because you still can feel it with your hands, and hear it move.

T 24 H 10. Here is an image that you WANT to be yourself. It is the means to make your wish come true. It GIVES the eyes with which you look on it, the hands that feel it, and the ears with which you listened to the sounds it makes. IT PROVES ITS OWN REALITY TO YOU. Thus is the body made a THEORY of yourself, with NO provisions made for evidence BEYOND itself, and NO escape within **T(863) -682** its sight. Its course is sure, when seen through its own eyes. It grows and withers, flourishes and dies. And you cannot conceive of you APART from it. You brand it sinful, and you hate its acts, judging it evil. Yet your specialness whispers, "Here is my own beloved son, with whom I am well pleased."[790]

T 24 H 11. Thus does the son become the MEANS to serve his father's purpose. NOT identical, not even like, but still a means to offer to the father WHAT HE WANTS. Such is the travesty on God's creation. For, as His Son's creation gave HIM joy, and witness to HIS Love and shared HIS Purpose, so does the body testify to the idea that made it, and speak for ITS reality and truth. And thus are two sons made, and BOTH appear to walk this earth without a meeting place, and NO encounter. One do you see OUTSIDE yourself, your OWN beloved son. The other rests within, His Father's Son, within your brother as he is in you. **T(864) -683**[791]

T 24 H 12. Their difference does not lie in how they look, or where they go, or even what they do. THEY SHARE A DIFFERENT PURPOSE. It is this that joins them to their like, and separates each from all aspects with a DIFFERENT purpose. The Son of God retains his Father's Will. The son of man perceives an alien will, AND WISHES IT WERE SO. And thus does his perception serve his wish, by giving it APPEARANCES of truth. Yet can perception serve ANOTHER goal. It is not bound to specialness, but by your choice. And it IS given you to make a different choice, and use perception FOR A DIFFERENT PURPOSE. And what you see will serve that purpose well, and prove ITS own reality to you.

---

[790] see previous footnote
[791] Sept. 29, 1967

CHAPTER 25 – THE REMEDY

T 25 A. Introduction (*Notes* 1735 11:110)

T 25 A 1. The Christ in you inhabits NOT a body. Yet He IS in you. And thus MUST it be that YOU are not within a body. What is within you CANNOT be outside. And it is certain that YOU cannot be APART from what is at the very CENTER of your life. What gives you life cannot be housed in death. NO MORE CAN YOU. Christ is within a frame of holiness, whose ONLY purpose is that He may be made manifest to those who know Him not; that He may call to them to come to Him, and see Him where they THOUGHT their bodies were. Then will their bodies melt away, that they may frame His holiness in them.

T 25 A 2. No-one who carries Christ in him can fail to recognize Him everywhere. EXCEPT IN BODIES. And, as long as they believe THEY are in bodies, where they think they are He CANNOT be. And so they carry Him unknowingly, and do not make Him manifest. And thus they do not recognize Him where He IS. The son of man is NOT the risen Christ.[792] Yet does the Son of God abide EXACTLY where he is, and walks with him, within his holiness, as plain to see as is his specialness set forth within his body. **T(865) - 684**

T 25 A 3. The body needs NO healing. But the mind that thinks it IS a body is sick indeed! And it is here that Christ sets forth the remedy. His PURPOSE folds the body in His light, and fills it with the holiness that shines from HIM. And nothing that the body says or does but makes HIM manifest. To those who know Him not it carries Him, in gentleness and love, to heal their minds. Such is the mission that your brother has for YOU. And such it MUST be that YOUR mission is for HIM.

T 25 B. The Appointed Task (*Notes* 1737 11:112)

T 25 B 1. It CANNOT be that it is hard to do the task that Christ appointed you to do, since it is HE that does it. And, in the DOING of it, will you learn the body merely SEEMS to be the means to do it. For the Mind is HIS. And so it MUST be yours. HIS holiness directs the body THROUGH the mind at one with Him. And YOU are manifest unto your holy brother, as he to you. Here is the meeting of the holy Christ unto Himself. Nor ANY differences perceived to stand between the aspects of His holiness, which meet and join, and raise Him to His Father, whole and pure, and worthy of His Everlasting Love.[793]

T 25 B 2. How can you manifest the Christ in you, EXCEPT you look on holiness, and see Him there? Perception tells you YOU are manifest in what you see. Behold the body, and you WILL believe that you are there. And every body that you look upon reminds you of yourself; YOUR sinfulness, YOUR evil, and, above all YOUR death. And would you not despise the one who tells you this, and seek HIS death instead? The message and the messenger ARE one. And you MUST see your brother as yourself. Framed in his body you will see YOUR sinfulness, wherein YOU stand condemned. Set in his holiness, the Christ in him proclaims HIMSELF as you.

T 25 B 3. Perception is a choice of what you want YOURSELF to be; the world you WANT to live in, and the state in which you think your mind will be content and satisfied. It chooses where you think your safety lies, AT YOUR DECISION. It reveals yourself to you, as YOU would have you be. **T(866) -685** And ALWAYS is it faithful to your purpose, from which it never separates, nor gives the slightest witness unto anything the purpose IN YOUR MIND upholdeth not. Perception is a PART of what it is your purpose to behold, for means and end are NEVER separate. And thus you learn what SEEMS to have a life APART has none.

T 25 B 4. YOU are the means for God. NOT separate, nor with a life apart from His. HIS Life is manifest in you who are His Son. Each aspect of Himself is framed in holiness and perfect purity, in love celestial and so complete It wishes ONLY that It may release ALL that It looks upon unto Itself. Its radiance shines through each body that It looks upon, and brushes ALL its darkness into light merely by looking PAST it TO the Light. The veil is lifted through Its gentleness, and NOTHING hides the face of Christ from its beholders. And BOTH of you stand there, before Him now, to let HIM draw aside the veil that SEEMS to keep you separate and apart. **T(867) -686**[794]

T 25 B 5. Since you believe that YOU are separate, Heaven presents itself to you as separate, too. NOT that it is the truth, but that the link that has been given you to JOIN the truth may reach to you through what you understand. Father and Son and Holy Spirit are as One, as all your brothers join as one in truth. Christ and His Father NEVER have been separate, and Christ abides within your understanding, in the part of you that SHARES His Father's Will. The Holy Spirit links the other part, the tiny, mad desire to be separate, different, and special, TO the Christ, to make the Oneness clear to what is REALLY One. In this world, this is not understood, but CAN be taught.

T 25 B 6. The Holy Spirit serves Christ's purpose in your mind, so that the aim of specialness CAN be corrected where the error lies. Because His purpose still is One with both the Father AND the Son, He KNOWS the Will of God, and what you REALLY will. But this is understood by mind PERCEIVED as one, AWARE that it is one, AND SO EXPERIENCED. It is the Holy Spirit's function to teach you HOW this Oneness is experienced; WHAT you must do that it can BE experienced; and WHERE you should go to do it. All this takes note of time and place AS IF they were discrete, for while YOU think that part of YOU is separate, the concept of a Oneness JOINED as one is meaningless.

T 25 B 7. It is apparent that a mind so split could NEVER be the teacher of the Oneness Which unites ALL things within Itself. And so what IS within this mind, and DOES unite all things together MUST be its teacher. Yet must It use the language which this mind can understand in the condition which it THINKS it is. And It must use all learning to transfer illusions TO the truth, taking all FALSE ideas of what you are, and leading you BEYOND them to the truth that IS beyond them. All this can very simply be reduced to this: What is the same can NOT be different, and what is One can NOT have separate parts. **T(868) -687**[795]

T 25 C. The Savior from the Dark (*Notes* 1746 11:21)

T 25 C 1. Is it not evident that what the body's eyes perceive FILLS YOU WITH FEAR? Perhaps you think you find a hope of satisfaction there. Perhaps you fancy to attain some peace and satisfaction in the world as YOU perceive it. Yet it MUST be evident the outcome DOES NOT CHANGE. Despite your hopes and fancies, ALWAYS does despair result. And there is NO exception, nor will there ever be. The ONLY value that the past can hold is that you learn it gave you NO rewards that you would WANT to keep, for only thus will you be WILLING to relinquish it, and have it gone forever.

T 25 C 2. Is it not strange that you should cherish still some hope of satisfaction from the world you see? In NO respect, at ANY time or

---
[792] **Matthew 8:20** And Jesus said to him, "Foxes have holes and birds of the air have nests, but the Son of Man has nowhere to lay His head."
[793] **Jeremiah 31:3** The LORD has appeared of old to me, saying:
"Yes, I have loved you with an everlasting love;
Therefore with lovingkindness I have drawn you.

[794] October 2, 1967
[795] October 5, 1967

place, has ANYTHING but fear and guilt been your reward. How long is needed for you to realize the chance of CHANGE in this regard is hardly worth delaying change that might result in better outcome? For one thing is sure; the way YOU see, and long HAVE seen, gives NO support to base your future hopes, and NO suggestions of success at all. To place your hopes where no hope lies MUST make you hopeless. Yet is this hopelessness your choice, while you would seek for hope where none is EVER found.

T 25 C 3. Is it not ALSO true that you have found some hope APART from this; some glimmering, inconstant, wavering, yet dimly seen, that hopefulness IS warranted, on grounds that are NOT in this world? And yet your hope that they may STILL lie here prevents you still from giving up the hopeless and unrewarding task you set YOURSELF. Can it make sense to hold the fixed belief that there IS reason to uphold pursuit of what has ALWAYS failed, on grounds that it will suddenly succeed, and bring what it has NEVER brought before? **T(869) -688**[796]

T 25 C 4. Its past HAS failed. Be glad that it is gone within your mind to darken what IS there. Take not the form for content, for the form is but a MEANS for content. And the frame is but a means to hold the picture up, so that it can be seen. A frame that HIDES the picture HAS no purpose. It cannot BE a frame if IT is what you see. WITHOUT the picture is the frame without its meaning. Its PURPOSE is to set the PICTURE off, and NOT itself. Who hangs an empty frame upon a wall, and stands before it, deep in reverence, as if a masterpiece were there to see?

T 25 C 5. Yet, if you see your brother as a body, it IS but this you do. The masterpiece that God has set within this frame is all there IS to see. The body holds it, for a while, without obscuring it in any way. But what God has created NEEDS no frame, for what He has created HE supports, and frames within Himself. His masterpiece He offers YOU to see. And would you rather see the frame INSTEAD of this? And see the picture not at all? The Holy Spirit is the frame God set around the part of Him that YOU would see as separate. Yet its frame is JOINED to its Creator, One with Him AND with His masterpiece.

T 25 C 6. This IS its purpose, and you do NOT make the frame INTO the picture, when you choose to see it in its place. The frame that God has given it but serves HIS purpose, not yours APART from His. It is your SEPARATE purpose that OBSCURES the picture, and cherishes the frame INSTEAD of it. But God has set His masterpiece within a frame that will endure forever, when yours has crumbled into dust. But think you not the picture is destroyed in ANY way. What God creates is safe from ALL corruption, unchanged and perfect in eternity. **T(870) -689**

T 25 C 7. Accept HIS frame instead of yours, and you WILL see the masterpiece. Look at its loveliness, and understand the Mind that thought it, NOT in flesh and bones, but in a frame as lovely as Itself. Its holiness lights up the sinlessness the frame of darkness hides, and casts a veil of light across the picture's face, which but reflects the light which shines from it to its Creator. Think not this face was ever darkened because YOU saw it in a frame of death. God kept it safe that YOU might look on it, and SEE the holiness that He has given it. Within the darkness see the Savior FROM the dark, and understand your brother as his Father's Mind shows him to you.

T 25 C 8. He will step forth from darkness as you look on him, and YOU will see the dark no more. The darkness touched him not, nor you who BROUGHT him forth for YOU to look upon. His sinlessness but pictures YOURS. His gentleness becomes YOUR strength, and BOTH will gladly look within and see the holiness that MUST be there BECAUSE of what you looked upon in him. HE is the frame in which YOUR holiness is set, and what God gave him MUST be given you. However much he overlooks the masterpiece in him, and sees only a frame of darkness, it is still YOUR only function to behold in him what he sees not. And, in this seeing, is the vision SHARED that looks on Christ INSTEAD of seeing death.

T 25 C 9. How could the Lord of Heaven NOT be glad if you appreciate His masterpiece? What COULD He do but offer thanks to you, who love His Son as He does? Would He not make KNOWN to you His Love, if you but SHARE His praise of what He loves? God cherishes **T(871) -690** creation as the perfect Father that He is. And so His joy is made complete when any part of Him JOINS in His praise, to SHARE His joy. This brother is His perfect gift to you. And He is glad and thankful when you thank His perfect Son for being what he IS. And ALL His thanks and gladness shine on you who would COMPLETE His joy, along with Him.

T 25 C 10. And thus is YOURS completed. Not one ray of darkness can be seen by those who will to make their Father's happiness complete, and theirs along with His. The gratitude of God Himself is freely offered to everyone who shares His Purpose. It was not His Will to be alone. And neither is it YOURS. Forgive your brother, and you CANNOT separate yourself from him, nor from his Father. YOU need NO forgiveness, for the wholly pure have never sinned. Give, then, what he has given you, that YOU may see His Son as one, and thank his Father, as He thanks YOU. Nor believe that all His praise is given not to you. For what you give is HIS, and giving it, you learn to understand His gift to you. And give the Holy Spirit what He offers unto the Father AND the Son alike.

T 25 C 11. Nothing has power over you EXCEPT His Will AND yours, who but EXTEND His Will. It was for this YOU were created, and your brother WITH you, and ONE with you. YOU are the same, as God Himself is One, and NOT divided in His Will. And YOU must have one purpose, since He gave the same to BOTH of you. His Will is brought together as you join in will that you be made complete by offering completion to your brother. See not in him the sinfulness HE sees, but give him honor that you may esteem yourself AND him. To each of you is given the power of salvation, that escape from darkness into light be yours to share, **T(872) -691** that you may see as one what never HAS been separate, nor apart from ALL His Love as given equally. **T(873) -692**[797]

T 25 D. The Fundamental Law of Perception (*Notes 1754 11:128*)

T 25 D 1. To the extent to which you value guilt, to that extent will you perceive a world in which attack is justified. To the extent to which you recognize that guilt is meaningless, to that extent will you perceive attack cannot BE justified. This is in strict accord with vision's FUNDAMENTAL law: You see what you believe is there, and you believe it there because you WANT it there. Perception HAS no other law than this. The rest but stem from this, to hold it up and offer it support. This is perception's form, adapted to this world, of God's more basic law; that Love creates Itself, and nothing BUT Itself.

T 25 D 2. God's laws do not obtain directly to a world perception rules, for such a world could not have been created by the Mind to which perception has no meaning. Yet are His laws reflected everywhere. NOT that the world where this reflection is, is real at all. ONLY because His Son BELIEVES it is, and from His Son's belief He COULD not let Himself be separate entirely. He could not enter His Son's insanity with him, but He could be sure His sanity went there WITH him, so he could not be lost forever in the madness of his wish.

T 25 D 3. Perception rests on choosing; knowledge does not. Knowledge has but one law BECAUSE it has but One Creator. But this world has two who made it, and they do NOT see it as the same. To each it has a DIFFERENT purpose, and to each it is a perfect means to serve the goal for which it is perceived. For specialness it

---

[796] Oct. 8, 1967

[797] October 12, 1967

is the perfect frame to set it off; the perfect battleground to wage its wars, the perfect shelter for the illusions which it would make real. Not one but it upholds in its perception; not one but can be fully justified.

T 25 D 4. There is another Maker of the world, the simultaneous Corrector of the mad belief that ANYTHING could be established and maintained without some link that kept it still within the Laws of God. NOT as the Law Itself **T(874) -693** upholds the universe as God created it. But in some form adapted to the need the Son of God believes he has. Corrected error IS the error's end. And thus has God protected still His Son, even in error. There IS another purpose in the world that error made because it has another Maker, Who CAN reconcile its goal with His Creator's Purpose.

T 25 D 5. In His perception of the world, nothing is seen but justifies forgiveness and the sight of perfect sinlessness. Nothing arises but is met with instant and complete forgiveness. Nothing remains an instant, to obscure the sinlessness that shines unchanged, beyond the pitiful attempts of specialness to put it out of mind, where it MUST be, and light the BODY up INSTEAD of it. The lamps of Heaven are NOT for it to choose to see them where it will. If it elects to see them elsewhere from their home, as if they lit a place where they could never be, AND YOU AGREE, then must the Maker of the world correct your error, lest you still remain in darkness, where the lamps are NOT.

T 25 D 6. Everyone here has entered darkness, yet no-one has entered it alone. Nor need he stay more than an instant. For he has come with Heaven's help within him, ready to lead him OUT of darkness into light at ANY time. The time he chooses can be ANY time, for help is there, awaiting but his choice. And when he chooses to AVAIL himself of what is given him, then will he see each situation that he thought before was means to justify his anger, turned to an event which justifies his love.

T 25 D 7. He will hear plainly that the calls to war he heard before are really calls to peace. He will perceive that where he gave attack is but another altar where he can, with equal ease and FAR more happiness, bestow forgiveness. And he will re-interpret ALL temptation as just another chance to bring him joy. **T(875) -694** How CAN a misperception be a sin? Let ALL your brother's errors be to you nothing except a chance for YOU to see the workings of the Helper given YOU to see the world HE made, instead of yours.

T 25 D 8. What, then, is justified? WHAT DO YOU WANT? For these two questions ARE the same, and, when you see them AS the same, your choice is made. For it is SEEING them as one that brings release from the belief there are two ways to see. This world has much to offer to your peace, and many chances to extend your own forgiveness. Such its PURPOSE is, to those who WANT to see peace and forgiveness descend on THEM, and offer THEM the light. The Maker of the world of gentleness has perfect power to offset the world of violence and hate that SEEMS to stand BETWEEN you and His gentleness. It is not there in His forgiving eyes. And THEREFORE it need not be there in yours.

T 25 D 9. Sin is the fixed belief perception CANNOT change. What has been damned IS damned, and damned forever, BEING FOREVER UNFORGIVABLE. If, then, it IS forgiven, sin's perception MUST have been wrong. And thus is change made possible. The Holy Spirit, too, sees what HE sees as far beyond the chance of change. But on His Vision sin can NOT encroach. For sin HAS BEEN corrected by His sight. And thus IT MUST HAVE BEEN AN ERROR, NOT a sin. For what it claimed could never be, HAS BEEN. Sin is ATTACKED by punishment, and so PRESERVED. But to <u>FORGIVE</u> it is to change its state from error into truth.

T 25 D 10. The Son of God could NEVER sin, but he CAN wish for what would hurt him. And he HAS the power to think he CAN BE hurt. What could this be EXCEPT a misperception of himself? Is this a sin or a mistake; forgivable or not? Does he need help or condemnation? Is it YOUR purpose that he be saved or damned? Forgetting not that what he is to YOU will make this **T(876) -695** choice YOUR future. For you MAKE IT NOW, the instant when ALL time becomes a means to reach a goal. Make, then, your choice, but recognize that, in this choice, the purpose of the world you see is chosen, and WILL be justified. **T(877) -696**[798]

T 25 E. The Joining of Minds (*Notes* 1762 11:137)

T 25 E 1. Minds that are joined, AND RECOGNIZE THEY ARE, can feel no guilt. For they can NOT attack, and they REJOICE that this is so, seeing their safety in this happy fact. Their joy is in the INNOCENCE they see. And thus they seek for it, because it is their PURPOSE to behold it and rejoice. Everyone seeks for what will bring him joy as he defines it. It is NOT the aim, as such, that varies. Yet it IS the way in which the aim is seen that makes the choice of means inevitable, and beyond the hope of change UNLESS THE AIM IS CHANGED. And THEN the means are chosen once again, as what will bring rejoicing is defined ANOTHER way, and sought for differently.

T 25 E 2. Perception's basic law could thus be said: "You will rejoice at what you see BECAUSE you see it TO rejoice." And, while you think that suffering and sin will bring you joy, so long will they be there for you to see. Nothing is harmful or beneficent APART from what you wish. It is your wish that MAKES it what it is in its effect on you,[799] BECAUSE you chose it as a means to GAIN these same effects, believing them to be the bringers of rejoicing and of joy. Even in Heaven does this law obtain. The Son of God creates to bring him joy, sharing his Father's purpose in his own creation, that his joy might be increased, and God's along with his.[800] **T(878) -697**[801]

T 25 E 3. You makers of a world that is not so, take rest and comfort in another world where peace abides. This world you bring with you to all the weary eyes and tired hearts that look on sin and beat its sad refrain. From you can come their rest. From you can rise a world they will rejoice to look upon, and where their hearts are glad. In you there is a Vision which extends to all of them, and covers them in gentleness and light. And in this widening world of light the darkness they thought was there is pushed away, until it is but distant shadows, far away, not long to be remembered, as the sun shines them to nothingness.

T 25 E 4. And all their evil thoughts and sinful hopes, their dreams of guilt and merciless revenge, and every wish to hurt and kill and die, will disappear before the sun you bring. Would you not do this, for the Love of God? And for YOURSELF? For think what it would do for YOU. YOUR evil thoughts that haunt YOU now will seem increasingly remote, and far away from YOU. And they go farther and farther off, because the sun in you has risen that they may be pushed away before its light. They linger for a while, a LITTLE while, in twisted forms too far away for recognition, and are gone forever.

T 25 E 5. And in the sunlight YOU will stand in quiet, in innocence and wholly unafraid. And from you will the rest YOU found extend, so that YOUR peace can never fall away, and leave YOU homeless. Those who offer peace to everyone have found a home in Heaven

---

[798] October 17, 1967

[799] The *Urtext* manuscript, the *HLC* and *FIP* all put a sentence break here. The *Notes* doesn't put a full stop here however and rather obviously the clause beginning with "BECAUSE" is a subordinate clause modifying the first clause and is not a stand-alone sentence. We consider the sentence break here to be a typo, one which went uncorrected in later editing, and restore the material to the original form in the *Notes*.

[800] **John 15:11** "These things I have spoken to you, that My joy may remain in you, and that your joy may be complete."

John 16:24 "Until now you have asked nothing in My name. Ask, and you will receive, that your joy may be complete."

[801] Oct. 23, 1967

the world can NOT destroy. For it is large enough to hold the world within its peace. In YOU is all of Heaven;[802] every leaf that falls is given life in you. Each bird that ever sang will sing again in you. And every flower that ever bloomed has saved its perfume and its loveliness for you. **T(879) -698**

T 25 E 6. What aim can supersede the Will of God and of His Son, that Heaven be restored to him for whom it was created as his ONLY home? Nothing before and nothing after it. No other place, no other state nor time. Nothing beyond nor nearer. Nothing else. In ANY form. This can YOU bring to ALL the world, and ALL the thoughts that entered it, and were mistaken for a little while. How better could your OWN mistakes be brought to truth than by your willingness to bring the light of Heaven with you, as you walk BEYOND the world of darkness into light? **T(880) -699**[803]

T 25 F. The State of Sinlessness (*Notes* 1766 11:141)

T 25 F 1. The state of sinlessness is merely this: The WHOLE desire to attack is gone, and so there is no reason to perceive the Son of God as other than he is. The NEED for guilt is gone, because it has no purpose, and is meaningless without the goal of sin. Attack and sin are bound as ONE illusion, each the cause and aim and JUSTIFIER of the other. Each is meaningless alone, but SEEMS to draw a meaning from the other. Each depends upon the other for whatever sense it seems to have. And no-one COULD believe in one unless the other were the truth,[804] for each attests the other MUST be true.

T 25 F 2. Attack makes Christ your enemy, and God along with Him. MUST you not be afraid, with enemies like these? And must you not be fearful of YOURSELF? For you HAVE hurt yourself, and made your Self your enemy. And now you MUST believe you are not you, but something alien to yourself and "something else," a "something" to be feared instead of loved. Who would attack whatever he sees as wholly innocent? And who, BECAUSE he wishes to attack, can FAIL to think it MUST be guilty, to DESERVE the wish and leave HIM innocent? And who would see the Son of God as innocent, and wish him dead?

T 25 F 3. Christ stands before you both, each time you look on one another. He has NOT gone because your eyes are closed. But what is there to see by searching for your Savior, seeing Him through sightless eyes? It is NOT Christ you see by looking thus. It is the enemy, CONFUSED with Christ, you look upon. And HATE BECAUSE there is no sin in him for you to see. Nor do you hear his plaintive call, unchanged in content in WHATEVER form the call is made, that you UNITE with him, and JOIN with him **T(881) -700** in innocence and peace. And yet, beneath the ego's senseless shrieks, such IS the Call that God has given him, that YOU might hear in him His Call to YOU, and answer by returning unto God what is His own.[805]

T 25 F 4. The Son of God asks only this of you; that you return to him what is his due, that you may SHARE in it with him. Alone, does NEITHER have it. So must it remain useless to both. Together, it will give to each an EQUAL strength to save the other, and save himself along WITH him. FORGIVEN by you, your Savior offers YOU salvation. CONDEMNED by you, he offers death to you. In everyone you see but the reflection of what you chose to have HIM be to you. If you decide against his proper function, the ONLY one he really has in truth, you are depriving him of all the joy he WOULD have found if he fulfilled the role God gave to him. But think not Heaven is lost to him alone. Nor can it be regained unless the way is shown to him through YOU, that YOU may find it, walking by his side.

T 25 F 5. It is no sacrifice that he be saved, for BY his freedom will you gain your own. To let HIS function be fulfilled is but the means to let YOURS be. And so you walk toward Heaven or toward hell, but NOT alone. How beautiful his sinlessness will be, when you perceive it! And how great will be YOUR joy when he is free to offer you the gift of sight God gave to him for you. He HAS no need but this; that you allow him freedom to complete the task God gave to him. Remembering but this; that what HE does YOU do, along with him. And AS you see him, so do YOU define **T(882) -701** the function he will have for you, until you see him differently, and LET him be what God APPOINTED that he be to you.

T 25 F 6. Against the hatred that the Son of God may cherish toward himself is God believed to be without the power to save what He created from the pain of hell. But in the love he shows himself is God made free to LET His Will be done. In each of you, you see the picture of your OWN belief of[806] what the Will of God MUST be for you. In YOUR forgiveness will you understand His Love for you. Through your ATTACK, believe He hates you, thinking Heaven must be hell. Look once again upon your brother, NOT without the understanding that he is the way to Heaven or to hell, as YOU perceive him. But forget not this; the role you give to him is given YOU, and YOU will walk the way you pointed out to him, BECAUSE it is your judgment made upon[807] yourself. **T(883) -702**[808]

T 25 G. The Special Function (*Notes* 1770 11:145)

T 25 G 1. The grace of God rests gently on forgiving eyes, and everything they look on speaks of Him to the beholder. He can see no evil; nothing in the world to fear, and no-one who is different from himself. And, as he loves them, so he looks upon HIMSELF with love and gentleness. He would no more condemn himself for HIS mistakes than damn another. He is not an arbiter of vengeance, nor a punisher of sin. The kindness of his sight rests on himself with all the tenderness it offers others. For he would ONLY heal and ONLY bless. And, being IN ACCORD with what God wills, he HAS the power to heal and bless all those he looks on with the grace of God upon his sight.

T 25 G 2. Eyes become used to darkness, and the light of brilliant day seems painful to the eyes grown long accustomed to the dim effects perceived at twilight. And they turn away from sunlight, and the clarity it brings to what they look upon. Dimness seems better; easier to see, and better recognized. Somehow, the vague and more obscure seems EASIER to look upon; LESS painful to the eyes than what is wholly clear and unambiguous. Yet this is NOT what eyes are FOR. And who can say that he PREFERS the darkness, and maintain he WANTS to see?

---

[802] **Luke 17:21** "Nor will they say, 'See here!' or 'See there!' For indeed, the kingdom of God is within you."
[803] October 29, 1967
[804] The *Notes* does not contain this paragraph, so we cannot check to see if the full stop found in the *Urtext* manuscript at this point was a copying mistake. However, rather clearly we have a subordinate clause modifying the preceding clause and not a separate sentence, so the full stop in the *Urtext* is replaced with a comma here. The fact that the last paragraph of the previous section and the paragraph following this one appear in the *Notes* with nothing in between but two blank lines is further evidence that this page of the *Urtext* at least is not a direct transcript of the *Notes* but rather a later re-typing in which this paragraph, apparently "dictated without notes" was interpolated.
[805] **Matthew 22:21** They said to Him, "Caesar's." And He said to them, "Render therefore to Caesar the things that are Caesar's, and to God the things that are God's."
[806] The *HLC* changes the word "**of**" here to "**in**" which does better reflect common English usage. It is very clearly "**of**" in both the *Notes* and the *Urtext* manuscripts, however, and given this segment is intensely poetic in structure, it may well be that the uncommon, but not incorrect usage was intentional.
[807] *Urtext* manuscript has it typed "made on yourself" which is also what the *Notes* suggests, the "on" was crossed out by hand and "made upon" written in by hand.
[808] Nov. 3, 1967

T 25 G 3. The WISH to see calls down the grace of God upon your eyes, and brings the gift of light that makes sight possible. Will you behold your brother? God is glad to have you look on him. He does not will your Savior be unrecognized by you. Nor does He will that he remain without the function that He gave to him. Let him no more be lonely, for the lonely ones are those who see no function in the world for them to fill; no place where they are needed, and no aim which ONLY they can perfectly fulfill. **T(884) -703**

T 25 G 4. Such is the Holy Spirit's kind perception of specialness; His use of what you made, to heal INSTEAD of harm. To each He gives a special function in salvation he alone can fill; a part for ONLY him. Nor is the plan complete until he finds his special function, and fulfills the part assigned to him, to make himself complete within a world where incompletion rules. Here, where the laws of God do NOT prevail in perfect form, can he yet do ONE perfect thing, and make ONE perfect choice. And, BY this act of special faithfulness, to one perceived as OTHER than himself, he learns the gift was given TO himself, and so they MUST be one.

T 25 G 5. Forgiveness is the ONLY function meaningful in time. It is the means the Holy Spirit uses to TRANSLATE specialness from sin into salvation. Forgiveness is for all. But, when it RESTS on all, it is complete, and every function of this world completed with it. Then is time no more. But WHILE in time, there is still much to do. And each must do what is allotted him, for, on HIS part, does ALL the plan depend. He HAS a special part in time, for so he chose, and choosing it, made it for himself. His wish was not denied, but changed in form, to let it serve his brother AND himself, and thus become a means to save INSTEAD of lose.

T 25 G 6. Salvation is no more than a reminder this world is NOT your home; its laws are NOT imposed on you, its values are NOT yours. And nothing that you THINK you see in it is REALLY there at all. And this is seen AND UNDERSTOOD as each one takes his part in its UNDOING, as he did in MAKING it. He HAS the means for either, as he always did. The specialness he chose to HURT himself did God appoint to be the means for his salvation, from the very instant that the choice was made. His special sin was made his special grace. His special hate became his special love. **T(885) -704**

T 25 G 7. The Holy Spirit needs YOUR special function, that HIS may be fulfilled. Think not you lack a special value here. You wanted it, and it IS given you. ALL that you made can serve salvation easily and well. The Son of God can make NO choice the Holy Spirit can not employ on his BEHALF, and NOT against himself. Only in darkness does your specialness APPEAR to be attack. In light, you see it is your SPECIAL FUNCTION in the plan to save the Son of God from ALL attack, and let him understand that he is safe, as he has ALWAYS been, and will remain in time and in eternity alike. This is the function given each of you for one another. Take it gently, then, from one another's hand, and let salvation be perfectly fulfilled in BOTH of you. Do this ONE thing, that EVERYTHING be given you. **T(886) -705**[809]

T 25 H. Commuting the Sentence (*Notes* 1775 11:150)

T 25 H 1. And, if the Holy Spirit can commute each sentence that you laid upon yourself into a blessing, then it CANNOT be a sin. Sin is ONE thing in all this world that CANNOT change. It is immutable. And ON its changelessness the world depends. The magic of the world can SEEM to hide the pain of sin from sinners, and deceive with glitter and with guile. Yet each one knows the cost of sin is death.[810] And so it IS. For sin is a REQUEST for death, a wish to make this world's foundation sure as love, dependable as Heaven, and as strong as God Himself. The world IS safe from love to everyone who thinks sin possible. Nor WILL it change.

T 25 H 2. Yet IS it possible what God created NOT should SHARE the attributes of His creation, when it OPPOSES it in every way? It CANNOT be the "sinner's" wish for death is just as strong as is His Will for Life. Nor CAN the basis of a world He did NOT make be firm and sure as Heaven. How COULD it be that hell and Heaven are the same? And is it possible that what He did NOT will can NOT be changed? What is immutable BESIDES His Will? And what can share Its attributes EXCEPT Itself? What wish can rise AGAINST His Will, and BE immutable?

T 25 H 3. If you could realize NOTHING is changeless BUT the Will of God, this course would not be difficult for you. For it is this that you do not believe. Yet there is nothing ELSE you COULD believe, if you but looked at what it really IS. Let us go back to what we said before, and think of it more carefully. It MUST be so that either God is mad, or is this world a place of madness. Not ONE Thought of His makes ANY sense at all within this world. And NOTHING that the world believes as true has ANY meaning in His Mind at all. **T(887) -706**

T 25 H 4. What makes no sense and has no meaning IS insanity. And what is madness CANNOT be the truth. If ONE belief so deeply valued here were true, then every Thought God ever had is an illusion. And if but ONE Thought of His is true, then ALL beliefs the world gives ANY meaning to are false, and make no sense at all. This IS the choice you make. Do not attempt to see it differently, nor twist it into something it is not. For only THIS decision CAN you make. The rest is up to God, and NOT to you.

T 25 H 5. To justify ONE value that the world upholds is to DENY your Father's sanity AND YOURS. For God and His beloved Son do NOT think differently.[811] And it is the AGREEMENT of their Thought that makes the Son a co-creator with the Mind Whose Thought created him. And if he chooses to believe ONE thought OPPOSED to truth, he has decided he is NOT his Father's Son, because the Son is mad, and sanity must lie apart from both the Father AND the Son. THIS YOU BELIEVE. Think not that this belief depends upon the form it takes. Who thinks the world is sane in any way; is justified in ANYTHING it thinks, or is maintained by ANY form of reason, believes this to be true.

T 25 H 6. Sin is not real BECAUSE the Father and the Son are NOT insane. This world is meaningless BECAUSE it rests on sin. Who could create the changeless, if it does NOT rest on truth? The Holy Spirit HAS the power to change the whole foundation of the world you see to something else; a basis NOT insane, on which a sane perception can be based, another world perceived. And one in which is nothing contradicted that would lead the Son of God to sanity and joy. Nothing attests to death and cruelty; to separation and to differences. For here is everything perceived as one, and no-one loses, that each one may gain. **T(888) -707**

T 25 H 7. Test EVERYTHING that you believe against this ONE requirement. And understand that everything that meets this ONE demand is worthy of your faith. But nothing else. What is not love is sin, and either one perceives the other as insane and meaningless. Love is the basis for a world perceived as wholly mad to sinners, who believe theirs is the way to sanity. But sin is equally insane within the sight of love, whose gentle eyes would look BEYOND the madness, and rest peacefully on truth. Each sees a world immutable, as each defines the changeless and eternal truth of what YOU are. And each reflects a view of what the Father and the Son MUST be, to make that viewpoint meaningful and sane.

T 25 H 8. Your special function is the special form in which the fact that God is NOT insane appears most sensible and meaningful to you. The CONTENT is the same. The FORM is suited to your spe-

---

[809] November 9, 1967
[810] **Romans 6:23** For the wages of sin is death, but the gift of God is eternal life in Christ Jesus our Lord.

[811] **John 10:30** "I and the Father are one."

cial needs, and to the special time and place in which you think you find yourself, and where you can be free of place and time, and ALL that you believe must limit you. The Son of God can NOT be bound by[812] time or place, or anything God did NOT will. Yet, if His Will is seen as madness, then the FORM of sanity which makes it most acceptable to those who ARE insane requires special choice. Nor CAN this choice be made BY the insane, whose problem IS their choices are NOT free, and made with reason in the light of sense.

T 25 H 9. It WOULD be madness to entrust salvation to the insane. BECAUSE He is not mad, has God appointed One as sane as He to raise a saner world to meet the sight of everyone who chose insanity as his salvation. To this One is given the choice of form most suitable to him; one which will NOT attack the world he sees, but enter into it in quietness, and SHOW him it is mad. This One but points to an ALTERNATIVE, ANOTHER way of looking at what he has seen before, and recognizes as the world in which he lives, and THOUGHT he understood before. Now MUST he question this, because the T(889) -708 form of the alternative is one which he can NOT deny, nor overlook, nor fail completely to perceive and see at all.

T 25 H 10. To each his special function is designed to be perceived as possible, and more and more desired, as it PROVES to him that it is an alternative he WANTS. From this position does his sinfulness, and ALL the sin he sees within the world, offer him less and less. Until he comes to understand it COST him sanity, and stands BETWEEN him and whatever hope he has of BEING sane. Nor is he left without ESCAPE from madness, for he has a special part in EVERYONE's escape. He can no more be left outside, WITHOUT a special function in the hope of peace, than could the Father overlook His Son, and pass him by in careless thoughtlessness.

T 25 H 11. What is dependable EXCEPT His Love? And where does sanity abide EXCEPT in Him? The One Who speaks for Him can show you this, in the alternative He chose especially for you. It is God's Will that you remember this, and so emerge from deepest mourning into perfect joy. Accept the function that has been assigned to you in God's Own plan to show His Son that hell and Heaven are different; NOT the same. But that, in Heaven THEY are all the same, WITHOUT the differences that WOULD have made a hell of Heaven, and a heaven of hell, had such insanity been possible.

T 25 H 12. The whole belief that someone loses but reflects the underlying tenet God must be insane. For in this world it seems that one must gain BECAUSE another loses. If THIS were true, then God is mad indeed. But what IS this belief, except a form of the more basic tenet, "Sin is real, and rules the world?" For every little gain, must someone lose, and pay exact amount in blood and suffering. For otherwise would evil triumph, and destruction be the total cost of any gain at all. You who believe that God is mad, look carefully at this, and understand that it MUST be that EITHER God OR this must T(890) -709 be insane, but hardly both.

T 25 H 13. Salvation is rebirth of the idea no-one CAN lose for ANYONE to gain. And everyone MUST gain, if anyone WOULD BE a gainer. Here is sanity restored.[813] And on this single rock of truth can faith in God's eternal saneness rest, in perfect confidence and perfect peace. Reason is satisfied, for ALL insane beliefs can be corrected here. And sin MUST be impossible, if THIS is true. This is the rock on which salvation rests;[814] the vantage point from which the Holy Spirit gives meaning and direction to the plan in which your special function has a part. For here your special function is made whole, because it shares the FUNCTION of the whole.

T 25 H 14. Remember ALL temptation is but this; a mad belief that God's insanity would make YOU sane, and GIVE you what you want. That either God OR you must LOSE to madness, because your aims can NOT be reconciled. Death demands life, but life is NOT maintained at ANY cost. No-one CAN suffer for the Will of God to be fulfilled. Salvation IS His Will BECAUSE you share it. NOT for you alone, but for the Self which IS the Son of God. He CANNOT lose, for if he could, the loss would be his Father's, and in Him NO loss is possible. And this is sane BECAUSE it is the truth. T(891) -710[815]

T 25 I. The Principle of Salvation (*Notes* 1785 11:160)

T 25 I 1. The Holy Spirit can use ALL that you give to Him for your salvation. But He CANNOT use what you withhold. For He can NOT take it from you, WITHOUT your willingness. For, if He did, you would believe He wrested it from you AGAINST your will. And so you would not learn it IS your will to be without it. You need not give it to Him WHOLLY willingly, for if you could, you had[816] no need for Him. But this He needs; that you PREFER He take it, than that you keep it for yourself alone, and recognize that what brings loss to no-one YOU WOULD NOT KNOW. This much is necessary to add to the idea no-one CAN lose for you to gain. And nothing more.

T 25 I 2. Here is the ONLY principle salvation needs. Nor is it necessary that your faith in it be strong, unswerving, and without attack from all beliefs opposed to it. You HAVE no fixed allegiance. But remember salvation is not needed by the saved. You are NOT called upon to do what one divided still against himself WOULD find impossible.[817] Have little faith that wisdom COULD be found in such a state of mind. But be you thankful that only little faith is ASKED of you.[818] What BUT a little faith remains to those who still believe in sin? What COULD they know of Heaven and the justice of the saved?

T 25 I 3. There is a kind of justice in salvation of which the world knows nothing. To the world, justice and VENGEANCE are the same, for sinners see justice ONLY as their punishment, perhaps sustained by someone ELSE, but NOT escaped. The laws of sin DEMAND a victim. WHO it may be makes little difference. But death MUST be the cost and MUST be paid. This is NOT justice, but insanity. Yet how could justice BE defined WITHOUT insanity, where love means hate, and death is seen as victory and triumph over eternity and timelessness and life?

T 25 I 4. You who know not of justice still can ask, and learn the answer. Justice looks on all in the same way. It is NOT just that one should lack for what another has. For that is vengeance, in WHATEVER form it takes. Justice demands NO sacrifice, for ANY sacrifice is made that sin MAY BE PRESERVED and KEPT. T(892) -711 It is a payment offered for the cost of sin, BUT NOT THE TOTAL COST. The rest is taken from another, to be laid beside your LITTLE payment, to "atone" for all that you would keep and NOT give up. So is the victim seen as PARTLY you, with someone ELSE by far the greater part. And in the TOTAL cost, the greater his, the

---

[812] The *Urtext* manuscript has "in" originally typed, crossed out and replaced with "by" in handwritten mark-up. The *Notes* has the glyph for "to" here, making it "be bound to time or place" originally.

[813] The *Urtext* manuscript has a comma, but the following word "And" is capitalized. The *Notes* has a full stop here so we're thinking this comma wasa typo which was meant to be a period.

[814] **Matthew 16:18** "And I also say to you that you are Peter, and on this rock I will build My church, and the gates of Hades shall not prevail against it."

[815] November 13, 1967
[816] Subjunctive mood, not a tense error. The reading in the *Notes* is identical.
[817] **Matthew 12:25** But Jesus knew their thoughts, and said to them: "Every kingdom divided against itself is brought to desolation, and every city or house divided against itself will not stand."
[818] **Matthew 17:20** So Jesus said to them, "Because of your unbelief; for assuredly, I say to you, if you have faith as a mustard seed, you will say to this mountain, 'Move from here to there,' and it will move; and nothing will be impossible for you."

less is yours. And justice, being blind, is satisfied by being paid, it matters not by whom.

T 25 I 5. Can this BE justice? God knows not of this. But justice DOES He know, and knows it well. For He is wholly fair to everyone. Vengeance is alien to His Mind BECAUSE He knows of justice.[819] To be just is to be fair, AND NOT be vengeful. Fairness AND vengeance are impossible, for each one contradicts the other, and denies that it is real. It is impossible for you to SHARE the Holy Spirit's justice, with a mind that can conceive of specialness at all. Yet how could HE be just, if He condemns a sinner for the crimes he did not do, but THINKS he did? And where would justice be if He demanded of the ones obsessed with the idea of punishment that they lay it aside, unaided, and perceive it is not true?

T 25 I 6. It is extremely hard for those who still believe sin meaningful to understand the Holy Spirit's justice. They believe He shares their OWN confusion, and can NOT avoid the vengeance that their own belief in justice MUST entail. And so they fear the Holy Spirit, and perceive the wrath of God in Him. They are unjust indeed to Him. Nor can they trust Him NOT to strike them dead with lightening bolts torn from the fires of Heaven by God's Own angry hand.[820] They DO believe that Heaven is hell, and ARE afraid of love. And deep suspicion and the chill of fear come over them when they are told that they have NEVER sinned. Their world DEPENDS on sin's stability. And they perceive the "threat" of what God KNOWS as justice to be more destructive to themselves and to their world than vengeance, which they understand and love. **T(893) -712**

T 25 I 7. So do they think the LOSS of sin a curse. And flee the blessing of the Holy Spirit as if He were a messenger from hell, sent from above in treachery and guile, to work God's vengeance on them in the guise of a deliverer and friend. What COULD He be to them except a devil dressed to deceive, within an angel's cloak? And what escape has He for them, except a door to hell that SEEMS to look like Heaven's gate?[821] Yet justice cannot punish those who ask for punishment, but have a Judge Who knows that they are wholly innocent in truth. In justice He is BOUND to set them free, and GIVE them all the honor they deserve, and have denied themselves because they are NOT fair, and CANNOT understand that they ARE innocent.

T 25 I 8. Love is NOT understandable to sinners. BECAUSE they think that justice is SPLIT OFF from love, and stands for something else. And thus is love perceived as weak and vengeance strong. For love has LOST when judgment left its side, and is too weak to SAVE from punishment. But vengeance WITHOUT love has GAINED in strength by being separate and apart from love. And what BUT vengeance now can help and save, while love stands feebly by, with helpless hands, bereft of justice and vitality, and powerless to save? What can Love ask of you who think that all of this is true? Could He, in justice AND in love believe in your confusion you HAVE much to give?

T 25 I 9. You are NOT asked to trust Him far. No further than what you SEE He offers you, and what you recognize you COULD not give yourself. In God's Own justice does He recognize all you deserve, but understands as well that you can NOT accept it for yourself. It is His Special Function to hold out to you the gifts the innocent DESERVE. And every one that you accept brings joy to Him AS WELL as you. He knows that Heaven is richer made by each one you accept. And God rejoices as His Son receives what loving justice KNOWS to be his due. For love and justice are NOT different. BECAUSE they are the same, does mercy stand at God's right Hand, and GIVE the Son of God **T(894) -713** the power to forgive HIMSELF of sin.[822]

T 25 I 10. To him who merits EVERYTHING, how can it be that ANYTHING is kept FROM him? For that would be injustice, and unfair indeed to all the holiness that IS in him, however much he recognize it not. God knows of NO injustice. He would not allow His Son be judged by those who seek his death, and COULD not see his worth at all. What honest witnesses could THEY call forth, to speak on his behalf? And who would come to plead FOR him, and not AGAINST his life? No justice would be given him by you. Yet God ensured that justice WOULD be done unto the Son He loves, and would protect from ALL unfairness you might seek to offer, believing vengeance IS his proper due. **T(895) -714**[823]

T 25 I 11. As specialness cares not who pays the cost of sin, so it BE paid, the Holy Spirit heeds not who looks on innocence at last, provided it IS seen and recognized. For just ONE witness is enough, if he sees truly. Simple justice asks no more. Of each one does the Holy Spirit ask if he will be that one, so justice may return to love, and there be satisfied. Each special function He allots is but for this; that each one learn that love and justice are NOT separate. And both are strengthened by their union with each other. Without love is justice prejudiced and weak. And love WITHOUT justice is impossible. For love is fair, and cannot chasten without cause. What cause can BE to warrant an attack upon the innocent? In justice, then, does love correct mistakes, but NOT in vengeance. For that would be unjust to innocence.

T 25 I 12. You can be perfect witness to the power of love AND justice, if you understand it is impossible the Son of God COULD merit vengeance. You need NOT perceive, in every circumstance, that this is true. Nor need you look to your experience WITHIN the world, which is but shadows of all that is REALLY happening within yourself. The understanding that you need comes NOT of you, but from a larger Self, so great and holy that He COULD not doubt His innocence. Your special function is a call to Him, that He may smile on you whose sinlessness He shares. HIS understanding will be YOURS. And so the Holy Spirit's Special Function has been fulfilled. God's Son has found a witness unto his sinlessness, and NOT his sin. How LITTLE need you give the Holy Spirit, that simple justice may be given YOU.

T 25 I 13. Without impartiality there IS no justice. How CAN specialness be just? Judge not because you cannot, NOT because you are a miserable sinner too.[824] **T(896) -715** How can the special REALLY understand that justice is the same for everyone? To take from one to give another MUST be an injustice to them both, since they are equal in the Holy Spirit's sight. Their Father gave the SAME inheritance to both. Who would have more OR less is not aware that he has everything. He is no judge of what MUST be another's due, because he thinks HE is deprived. And so MUST he be envious, and try to TAKE AWAY from whom he judges. He is NOT impartial, and CANNOT fairly see another's rights BECAUSE his own have been obscured to him.

---

[819] **Deuteronomy 32:35** Vengeance is Mine, and recompense; Their foot shall slip in due time; For the day of their calamity is at hand, And the things to come hasten upon them.
Romans 12:19 Beloved, do not avenge yourselves, but rather give place to wrath; for it is written, "Vengeance is Mine, I will repay," says the Lord.
[820] **Psalm 18:13-14** The LORD thundered from heaven, and the Most High uttered His voice, Hailstones and coals of fire. He sent out His arrows and scattered the foe, Lightnings in abundance, and He vanquished them.
Psalm 144:6-7 Flash forth lightning and scatter them; Shoot out Your arrows and destroy them. Stretch out Your hand from above; Rescue me and deliver me out of great waters, From the hand of foreigners,
[821] **Genesis 28:17** And he was afraid and said, "How awesome is this place! This is none other than the house of God, and this is the gate of heaven!"

[822] **Psalm 110:1** The LORD said to my Lord, "Sit at My right hand, Till I make Your enemies Your footstool."
Mark 16:19 So then, after the Lord had spoken to them, He was received up into heaven, and sat down at the right hand of God.
Matthew 9:6 "But that you may know that the Son of Man has power on earth to forgive sins"--then He said to the paralytic, "Arise, take up your bed, and go to your house."
[823] November 14, 1967
[824] **Matthew 7:1** "Judge not, that you be not judged."

T 25 I 14. You have the right to all the universe; to perfect peace, complete deliverance from ALL effects of sin, and to the life eternal, joyous, and complete in EVERY way, as God appointed for His holy Son. This is the ONLY justice Heaven knows, and all the Holy Spirit brings to earth. Your special function shows you nothing else BUT perfect justice CAN prevail for you. And you ARE safe from vengeance in ALL forms. The world deceives, but it can NOT replace God's justice with a version of its own. For only love IS just, and CAN perceive what justice must accord the Son of God. Let love decide, and never fear that you, in your unfairness, will deprive yourself of what GOD's justice has allotted you. **T(897) -716**[825]

T 25 J. The Justice of Heaven (*Notes* 1796 11:171)

T 25 J 1. What can it be but arrogance to think your little errors CANNOT be undone by Heaven's justice? And what COULD this mean, except that they are sins, and NOT mistakes, forever uncorrectable, and to be met with vengeance, NOT with justice? ARE you willing to be released from ALL effects of sin? You CANNOT answer this until you see all that the answer MUST entail. For if you answer "yes," this means you will forego ALL values of this world, in favor of the peace of Heaven. Not one sin would you retain. AND NOT ONE DOUBT THAT THIS IS POSSIBLE will you hold dear, that sin be kept in place. You mean that truth has greater value now than ALL illusions. And you recognize that truth must be REVEALED to you, because YOU know not what it IS.

T 25 J 2. To give reluctantly is not to gain the gift. BECAUSE YOU ARE RELUCTANT TO ACCEPT IT. It IS saved for you, until reluctance to receive it disappears, and you are WILLING it be given you. God's justice warrants gratitude, NOT fear. Nothing you give is lost to you or anyone, but cherished and preserved for you in Heaven, where all the treasures given to God's Son are kept for him, and offered anyone who but holds out his hand in willingness they be received.[826] Nor is the treasure LESS as it is given out. Each gift received but ADDS to the supply. For God IS fair. He does not fight AGAINST His Son's reluctance to perceive salvation as a gift from Him. Yet would His justice not be satisfied until it is received by everyone.

T 25 J 3. Be certain any answer to a problem the Holy Spirit solves will ALWAYS be one in which NO-ONE loses. And this MUST be true BECAUSE He asks no sacrifice of anyone. An answer which demands the slightest loss to ANYONE has not RESOLVED the problem, but has added TO it, and made it greater, HARDER to resolve, AND MORE UNFAIR. It is impossible the Holy Spirit could SEE unfairness as a resolution. To Him, what is unfair must be corrected BECAUSE it is unfair. And EVERY error is a perception in which one, at least, is seen unfairly. Thus is justice NOT accorded to the Son of God. When ANYONE **T(898) -717** is seen as losing, HE HAS BEEN CONDEMNED. And punishment becomes his due, INSTEAD of justice.

T 25 J 4. The sight of innocence makes punishment impossible, and justice sure. The Holy Spirit's perception leaves no GROUNDS for an attack. Only a LOSS could justify attack, and loss of ANY kind He cannot see. The world solves problems in another way. IT sees a resolution as a state in which it is DECIDED who shall win and who shall lose; HOW MUCH the one shall take, and HOW MUCH can the loser still defend. Yet does the problem still remain unsolved, for ONLY justice can set up a state in which there IS no loser; no-one left unfairly treated and deprived, and thus with grounds for vengeance. Problem SOLVING can NOT be vengeance, which at best can bring another problem ADDED to the first, in which the murder is not obvious.

T 25 J 5. The Holy Spirit's problem solving is the way in which the problem ENDS. It has been solved BECAUSE it has been met with justice. And UNTIL it has, it will recur because it has NOT yet been solved. The principle that justice MEANS no-one can lose is crucial to this course. For miracles DEPEND on justice. NOT as it is seen through this world's eyes, but as God knows it, and as knowledge is reflected in sight the Holy Spirit gives. NO-ONE deserves to lose. And what would be UNJUST to him can NOT occur. Healing must be for everyone BECAUSE he does not merit an attack of any kind. What order CAN there be in miracles, unless someone deserves to suffer MORE, and others LESS? And is this justice to the wholly innocent?

T 25 J 6. A miracle IS justice. It is NOT a special gift to some, to be WITHHELD from others as LESS worthy, MORE condemned, and thus APART from healing. Who is there who can be separate from salvation, if its PURPOSE is the end of specialness? Where is salvation's justice if SOME errors are unforgivable, and WARRANT vengeance IN PLACE of healing and return of peace? Salvation cannot SEEK to help God's Son be MORE unfair than HE has sought to be. **T(899) -718** If miracles, the Holy Spirit's gift, were given specially to an elect and special group, and kept APART from others as LESS deserving, then is He ALLY to specialness. What He cannot perceive He bears no witness to. And everyone is EQUALLY entitled to His gift of healing and deliverance and peace.

T 25 J 7. To give a problem to the Holy Spirit to solve FOR you means that you WANT it solved. To keep it for yourself to solve WITHOUT His help is to decide it should remain UNsettled, UNresolved, and lasting in its power of injustice and attack. No-one can BE unjust to you, unless you have decided first to BE unjust. And then MUST problems rise to block your way, and peace be scattered by the winds of hate. Unless you think that ALL your brothers have an equal right to miracles with you, you will not claim YOUR right to them, because you were unjust to one with EQUAL rights. Seek to deny, and you WILL feel denied. Seek to deprive, and you HAVE BEEN deprived.

T 25 J 8. A miracle can NEVER be received because another could receive it NOT. Only forgiveness OFFERS miracles. And pardon MUST be just to everyone. The little problems that you keep and hide become your secret sins BECAUSE you did not choose to let them be removed FOR you. And so they gather dust and grow, until they cover EVERYTHING that you perceive, and leave you fair to no-one. Not ONE right do YOU believe you have. And bitterness, with vengeance justified and mercy lost, condemns you as UNWORTHY of forgiveness. The unforgiven HAVE no mercy to bestow upon another. That is why your sole responsibility MUST be to take forgiveness for yourself.

T 25 J 9. The miracle that you receive you GIVE. Each one becomes an illustration of the law on which salvation rests; that justice MUST be done to all, if ANYONE is to be healed. No-one can lose, and everyone MUST benefit. Each miracle is an example of what justice can accomplish, when it is offered to everyone alike. It is received and GIVEN equally. It IS awareness that giving and receiving ARE the same. BECAUSE it does not make the same unlike, **T(900) -719** it sees no differences where none exist. And thus it is the SAME for everyone, because it sees no differences in THEM. Its offering is universal, and it teaches but one message. What is God's BELONGS to everyone, and IS his due. **T(901) -720**[827]

---

[825] November 21, 1967
[826] **Matthew 6:20** "but lay up for yourselves treasures in heaven, where neither moth nor rust destroys and where thieves do not break in and steal."
[827] November 27, 1967

Chapter 26 – The Transition

T 26 A. Introduction (*Notes* 1803 11:178)

T 26 A 1. In the "dynamics" of attack is sacrifice a key idea. It is the pivot upon which ALL compromise, ALL desperate attempts to strike a bargain, and ALL conflicts achieve a seeming balance. It is the symbol of the central theme that SOMEBODY MUST LOSE. Its focus on the BODY is apparent, for it is ALWAYS an attempt to LIMIT LOSS. The body is ITSELF a sacrifice; a giving up of power, in the name of saving just a little for yourself. To see a brother in ANOTHER body, SEPARATE from yours, is the expression of a wish to see a little PART of him, and sacrifice the rest. Look at the world, and you will see nothing attached to ANYTHING beyond itself. All seeming entities can come a little nearer, or go a little farther off, but CANNOT join.

T 26 B. The "Sacrifice" of Oneness (*Notes* 1803 11:178)

T 26 B 1. The world you see is based on SACRIFICE of oneness. It is a picture of a COMPLETE disunity and total LACK of joining. Around each entity is built a wall so seeming solid that it looks as if what is inside can never reach without, and what is out can never reach and join with what is locked away within the wall. Each part must SACRIFICE the other part to keep itself complete. For if they joined, each one would LOSE its own identity, and BY their separation are their selves maintained. The little that the body fences off BECOMES the self, preserved through sacrifice of all the rest. And all the rest must LOSE this little part, remaining incomplete to keep its own identity intact.

T 26 B 2. In THIS perception of your self the BODY's loss would be a sacrifice indeed. And sight of bodies becomes the sign that sacrifice IS limited, and something still remains for you alone. And FOR this little to belong to you, are limits placed on EVERYTHING outside, just as they are on everything you think is YOURS. For giving and receiving ARE the same. And to ACCEPT the limits of a body is to IMPOSE these limits on each brother that you see. For you MUST see him as you see yourself. The body IS a loss, and CAN be made to sacrifice. And while you see your brother as a body, **T(902) -721** APART from you and separate in his cell, you are demanding sacrifice of him AND you.

T 26 B 3. What greater sacrifice could be demanded than that God's Son perceive himself without his Father? And his Father be without His Son? Yet EVERY sacrifice demands that they be separate and without the other. The memory of God MUST be denied, if ANY sacrifice is asked of ANYONE. What witness to the wholeness of God's Son is seen within a world of separate bodies, however much he witnesses to truth? He is INVISIBLE in such a world. Nor can his song of union and of joy be heard at all. Yet is it given him to make the world recede before his song and sight of him REPLACE the body's eyes.

T 26 B 4. Those who would see the witnesses to truth INSTEAD of to illusion merely ask that they might see a PURPOSE in the world that gives it sense and makes it meaningful. WITHOUT your special function HAS this world no meaning for you. Yet it can become a treasure house as rich and limitless as Heaven Itself. No instant passes here in which your brother's holiness can NOT be seen, to add a limitless supply to every meager scrap and tiny crumb of happiness that you allot yourself. You CAN lose sight of oneness, but can NOT make sacrifice of its reality. Nor can you LOSE what you would sacrifice, nor keep the Holy Spirit from His task of showing you that it has NOT been lost.

T 26 B 5. Hear, then, the song your brother sings to you. And LET the world recede,[828] and TAKE the rest his witness offers on behalf of peace. But judge him not, for you will hear no song of liberation for yourself, nor see what it is given him to witness to, that YOU may see it and rejoice WITH him. Make not his holiness a sacrifice to your belief in sin. You sacrifice YOUR innocence with his, and die each time you see in him a sin deserving death. Yet every instant can you be reborn, and given life again. His holiness gives life to you, who CANNOT die because his sinlessness is known to God, and **T(903) -722** can no more be sacrificed by you than can the light in you be blotted out because he sees it not.

T 26 B 6. You who would make a sacrifice of life, and make your eyes and ears bear witness to the death of God and of His holy Son, think not that you have power to make of them what God willed not they be. In Heaven God's Son is NOT imprisoned in a body, nor is sacrificed in solitude to sin. And as he is in Heaven, so MUST he be eternally and everywhere. He is the same forever.[829] Born again each instant, untouched by time, and FAR beyond the reach of ANY sacrifice of life OR death.[830] For neither did he make, and only ONE was given him, by One Who KNOWS His gifts can NEVER suffer sacrifice and loss.

T 26 B 7. God's justice rests in gentleness upon His Son, and keeps him safe from ALL injustices the world would lay upon him. COULD it be that YOU could make his sins reality, and sacrifice his Father's Will for him? Condemn him not by seeing him within the rotting prison where he sees himself. It is your special function to ensure the door be opened, that he may come forth to shine on you, and give you back the gift of freedom by receiving it of you. What is the Holy Spirit's Special Function but to release the holy Son of God from the imprisonment he made, to KEEP himself from justice? Could YOUR function be a task apart and SEPARATE from His Own? **T(904) -723**[831]

T 26 C. The Forms of Error (*Notes* 1810 11:185)

T 26 C 1. It is NOT difficult to understand the reasons why you do not ask the Holy Spirit to solve ALL problems for you. HE has not a greater difficulty in resolving some than others. Every problem is the SAME to Him, because each one is solved in just the SAME respect, and through the SAME approach. The aspects that NEED solving do not change, whatever FORM the problem seems to take. A problem can appear in MANY forms, and it will do so while the problem lasts. It serves no purpose to attempt to solve it in a SPECIAL form. It WILL recur, and then recur again and yet again, until it has been answered for ALL time, and will not rise again in ANY form. And ONLY then are you RELEASED from it.

T 26 C 2. The Holy Spirit offers you release from EVERY problem that you think you have. They are the SAME to Him, because each one, regardless of the form it seems to take, is a demand that someone suffer loss, and make a sacrifice that you might gain. And, when the situation is worked out so NO-ONE loses, is the problem gone, because it was an error in perception, which now has been corrected. One mistake is NOT more difficult for Him to bring to truth than is another. For there IS but one mistake; the whole idea that loss is possible, and COULD result in gain for anyone. If THIS were true, then God WOULD be unfair; sin WOULD be possible, attack be

---

[828] *Urtext* manuscript has it typed "you see" it is corrected by handwritten mark-up to "recede" which agrees with the *Notes*.
[829] **Hebrews 13:8** Jesus Christ is the same yesterday, today, and forever.
[830] **John 3:3** Jesus answered and said to him, "Most assuredly, I say to you, unless one is born again, he cannot see the kingdom of God."
[831] November 28, 1967

justified, and vengeance fair. This ONE mistake, in ANY form, has ONE correction. There IS no loss; to think there IS, is a mistake.

T 26 C 3. You HAVE no problems, though you THINK you have. And yet you COULD not think so, if you saw them vanish one by one, WITHOUT regard to size, complexity, or place and time, or ANY attribute which you perceive that makes each one seem different from the rest. Think not the limits YOU impose on what you see can limit God in ANY way. The miracle of justice can correct ALL errors. Every problem IS an error. It does injustice to the Son of God, **T(905) -724** and therefore is not true. The Holy Spirit does not evaluate injustices as great or small, or more or less. They have NO properties to Him. They are mistakes from which the Son of God IS suffering, but needlessly. And so He takes the thorns and nails away. He does not pause to judge whether the hurt be large or little. He makes but one judgment; that to hurt God's Son MUST be unfair, and therefore is not so.

T 26 C 4. You who believe it safe to give but SOME mistakes to be corrected while you keep the others to yourself, remember this: Justice is total. There IS no such thing as partial justice. If the Son of God is guilty, then is he condemned, and he DESERVES no mercy from the God of justice. But ask not God to punish him because YOU find him guilty, and would have him die. God OFFERS you the means to see his innocence. Would it be fair to punish him because you will not LOOK at what is there to see? Each time you keep a problem for YOURSELF to solve, or judge that it is one which HAS no resolution, you have made it great, and past the hope of healing. You deny the miracle of justice CAN be fair.

T 26 C 5. If God is just, then CAN there be NO problems that justice cannot solve. But YOU believe that some injustices ARE fair and good, and necessary to preserve yourself. It is THESE problems that you think are great, and cannot BE resolved. For there are those you WANT to suffer loss, and NO-ONE whom you wish to be preserved from sacrifice entirely. Consider once again your special function. ONE is given you to see in him his perfect sinlessness. And you will ASK no sacrifice of him, because you could not will he suffer loss. The miracle of justice you call forth will rest on you as surely as on him. Nor will the Holy Spirit be content until it is received by everyone. For what you give to Him IS everyone's, and BY your giving it can He ensure that everyone receives it equally. **T(906) -725**

T 26 C 6. Think, then, how great your OWN release will be, when you are willing to receive correction for ALL your problems. You will not keep ONE, for pain in ANY form you will not WANT. And you will see each little hurt resolved before the Holy Spirit's gentle sight. For all of them ARE little in His sight and worth no more than just a tiny sigh before they disappear, to be forever undone and unremembered. What seemed once to be a SPECIAL problem, a mistake WITHOUT a remedy, or an affliction WITHOUT a cure, has been transformed into a universal blessing. Sacrifice is gone. And in its place, the Love of God can be remembered, and will shine away all memory of sacrifice and loss.

T 26 C 7. He cannot BE remembered until justice is loved INSTEAD of feared. He cannot be unjust to anyone or anything, because He knows that EVERYTHING that is belongs to Him, and will forever be as He created it. Nothing He loves but MUST be sinless and beyond attack. Your special function opens wide the door beyond which is the memory of His Love kept perfectly intact and undefiled. And all you need to do is but to wish that Heaven be given you instead of hell, and every bolt and barrier that seems to hold the door securely barred and locked, will merely fall away, and disappear. For it is NOT your Father's Will that you should offer or receive LESS than He gave, when He created you in perfect Love. **T(907) -726**[832]

---

[832] December 1, 1967

T 26 D. The Borderland (*Notes* 1816 11:191)

T 26 D 1. Complexity is not of God. How COULD it be, when all He knows is One? He knows of ONE creation, ONE reality, ONE truth, and but ONE Son. Nothing CONFLICTS with Oneness. How, then, COULD there be complexity in Him? What IS there to decide? For it is CONFLICT that makes choice complex. The truth is simple; it is one, WITHOUT an opposite. And how could strife enter in its simple Presence, and bring complexity where Oneness is? The truth makes NO decisions, for there is nothing to decide BETWEEN. And ONLY if there were could choosing be a necessary step in the advance toward Oneness. What is everything leaves room for NOTHING ELSE.

T 26 D 2. Yet is this magnitude beyond the scope of this curriculum. Nor is it necessary we dwell on anything that cannot be immediately grasped. There is a borderland of thought that stands between this world and Heaven. It is not a place, and WHEN you reach it is APART from time. Here is the meeting place where thoughts are brought TOGETHER; where conflicting values MEET, and ALL illusions are laid down beside the truth, where they are judged to be untrue. This borderland is just beyond the gate of Heaven.[833] Here is every thought made pure and wholly simple. Here is sin denied, and everything that IS received instead.

T 26 D 3. This is the journey's end. We have referred to it as the "real world." And yet there is a contradiction here, in that the words imply a LIMITED reality, a PARTIAL truth, a SEGMENT of the universe made true. This is because knowledge makes NO attack upon perception. They are brought together, and only ONE continues past the gate where Oneness is. Salvation IS a borderland, where place and time and choice have meaning still, and yet it can be seen that they are temporary, OUT of place, and EVERY choice has been ALREADY made. **T(908) -727**

T 26 D 4. Nothing the Son of God believes can be destroyed. But what is truth to him must be brought to the last comparison that he will ever make; the last evaluation that will be possible, the final judgment upon this world.[834] It is the judgment of the truth upon illusion, of knowledge on perception; IT HAS NO MEANING AND DOES NOT EXIST. This is NOT your decision. It is but a simple statement of a simple fact. But in this world there ARE no simple facts, because what is the same and what is different remain unclear. The one ESSENTIAL thing to make a choice at all is this distinction. And herein lies the difference between the worlds. In this one, choice IS made impossible. In the real world, is choosing simplified.

T 26 D 5. Salvation stops just short of Heaven, for only perception NEEDS salvation. Heaven was never lost, and so can not be saved. Yet who can make a choice BETWEEN the wish for Heaven and the wish for hell, unless he recognizes they are NOT the same? This difference is the learning goal this course has set. It will not go beyond this aim. Its ONLY purpose is to teach what is the same and what is different, leaving room to make the only choice that CAN be made. There is no basis FOR choice in this complex and over-complicated world. For no-one understands what is the same, and seems to choose where no choice really is. The real world is the area of choice made real, NOT in the outcome, but in the perception of alternatives FOR choice.

T 26 D 6. That there IS choice is an illusion. Yet, within this ONE lies the undoing of every illusion, NOT excepting this. Is not this

---

[833] **Genesis 28:17** And he was afraid and said, "How awesome is this place! This is none other than the house of God, and this is the gate of heaven!"
[834] **Matthew 11:22** "But I say to you, it will be more tolerable for Tyre and Sidon in the day of judgment than for you."

Another of the differences between a common understanding of the Bible and ACIM's teaching is pointed out here. The "last Judgement" in ACIM is not the point at which the sinners are punished, but rather the point at which God judges all Creation "innocent" and the illusion of guilt dissolves in forgiveness as the truth is recognized with joy.

like your special function, where the separation is undone by change of PURPOSE in what once was specialness, and now IS union? ALL illusions are but one. And, in the recognition this is so, lies the ability to give up ALL attempts to choose BETWEEN them, and make them different. How simple is the choice between two things so clearly UNalike. There IS no conflict here. No sacrifice T(909) -728 is possible in the relinquishment of an illusion RECOGNIZED as such. Where ALL reality has been withdrawn from what was NEVER true, can it BE hard to give it up, and choose what MUST be true? T(910) -729[835]

T 26 E. Where Sin Has Left (*Notes* 1821 11:196)

T 26 E 1. Forgiveness is this world's equivalent of Heaven's justice. It translates the world of sin into a simple world, where justice can be reflected from BEYOND the gate behind which total lack of limits lies. Nothing in boundless love could NEED forgiveness. And what is charity WITHIN the world gives way to simple justice past the gate that opens into Heaven. No-one forgives unless he has believed in sin, and STILL believes that he has much to be forgiven. Forgiveness thus becomes the means by which he learns HE has done nothing to forgive. Forgiveness always rests upon the one who offers it, until he sees HIMSELF as needing it no more. And thus is he returned to his REAL function of creating, which his forgiveness offers him again.

T 26 E 2. Forgiveness turns the world of sin into a world of glory, wonderful to see. Each flower shines in light, and every bird sings of the joy of Heaven. There is no sadness and there is no parting here, for everything is TOTALLY forgiven. And what has been forgiven MUST join, for nothing stands BETWEEN, to keep them separate and apart. The sinless MUST perceive that[836] they are one, for nothing stands between, to push the other off, and in the space which sin left vacant do they JOIN as one, in gladness recognizing what is part of them has NOT been kept apart and separate. The holy place on which you stand is but the space that sin has left.[837] And here you see the Face of Christ arising in its place.

T 26 E 3. Who could behold the Face of Christ, and NOT recall His Father as He really is? Who could fear love, and stand upon the ground where sin has left a place for Heaven's altar to rise and tower far above the world, and reach beyond the universe to touch the heart of ALL creation? What IS Heaven, but a song of gratitude and love and praise, by everything created, to the Source of its creation? The holiest of altars is set where once was sin believed to be. For here does every light of heaven come, to be rekindled and increased in joy. For here is what was lost to them restored, and all their radiance made whole again. **T(911) -730**

T 26 E 4. Forgiveness brings no little miracles to lay before the gate of Heaven. Here the Son of God Himself comes to receive each gift that brings him nearer to his home. Not one is lost, and none is cherished more than any other. Each reminds him of His Father's Love as surely as the rest. And each one teaches him that what he fears he loves the most. What BUT a miracle could change his mind, so that he understands that love cannot BE feared? What other miracle is there but this? And what else NEED there be, to make the space between you disappear? Where sin once was perceived will rise a world which will become an altar to the truth. And YOU will join the lights of Heaven there, and sing their song of gratitude and praise.

T 26 E 5. For as they come to YOU to be complete, so will you go with them. For no-one hears the song of Heaven, and remains without a voice that adds its power to the song, and makes it sweeter

still. And each one joins the singing at the altar which was raised within the tiny spot that sin proclaimed to be its own. And what WAS tiny then has soared into a magnitude of song, in which the universe has joined with but a single voice. This tiny spot of sin that stands between you still is holding back the happy opening of Heaven's gate. How LITTLE is the hindrance which withholds the wealth of Heaven from you. And how GREAT will be the joy in Heaven when you join the mighty chorus to the Love of God.[838] **T(912) -731**[839]

T 26 F. The Little Hindrance (*Notes* 1825 11:200)

T 26 F 1. A little hindrance can seem large indeed to those who do not understand that miracles are all the same. But teaching that is what this course is FOR. That is its only purpose, for only that is all there is to learn. And you can learn it many different ways. All learning is a help or hindrance to the gate of Heaven. Nothing in between is possible. There are TWO teachers only, who point in different ways. And you will go along the way your chosen teacher leads. There are but TWO directions you can take, while time remains and choice is meaningful. For never will another road be made, except the way to Heaven. You but choose whether to go TOWARD Heaven, or away to nowhere. There is nothing else to choose.

T 26 F 2. Nothing is ever lost but time, which, in the end, IS nothing. It is but a little hindrance to eternity, quite meaningless to the real Teacher of the world. But since you DO believe in its reality, why should you waste it going nowhere, when it CAN be used to reach a goal as high as learning can achieve? Think not the way to Heaven's gate is difficult at all. Nothing you undertake with certain purpose and high resolve and happy confidence, holding each other's hand and keeping step to Heaven's song, is difficult to do. But it IS hard indeed to wander off, alone and miserable, down a road which leads to nothing, and which HAS no purpose.

T 26 F 3. God gave His Teacher to REPLACE the one you made, NOT to CONFLICT with it. And what He would replace HAS BEEN replaced. Time lasted but an instant in your mind, with NO effect upon eternity. And so is ALL time past,[840] and everything EXACTLY as it was before the way to nothingness was made. The tiny tick of time, in which **T(913) -732** the first mistake was made, and ALL of them within that ONE mistake, held also the Correction for that one, and ALL of them that came within the first. And in that tiny instant time was gone, for that was all it ever was. What God gave Answer to IS answered, and IS gone.

T 26 F 4. To you who still believe you live in time, and know not it is gone, the Holy Spirit still guides you through the infinitely small and senseless maze you still perceive in time, though it has long since gone. You think you live in what is past. Each thing you look upon you saw but for an instant, long ago, before its unreality gave way to truth. Not one illusion still remains unanswered in your mind. Uncertainty was brought to Certainty so long ago that it is hard indeed to hold it to your heart, as if it were before you still. The tiny instant you would keep, and make eternal, passed away in Heaven too soon for anything to notice it had come.

T 26 F 5. What disappeared too quickly to affect the simple knowledge of the Son of God, can hardly still be there for you to choose to be your teacher. Only in the past, – an ancient past, too short to make a world in answer to creation, – did this world APPEAR to rise. So VERY long ago, for such a tiny interval of time that not one note in Heaven's song was missed. Yet, in each unforgiving act or thought, in every judgment, and in all belief in sin is that one instant

---

[835] December 4, 1967
[836] The word "that" doesn't appear in the *Notes* and was typed between the lines later, in much fainter typing.
[837] **Exodus 3:5** Then He said, "Do not draw near this place. Take your sandals off your feet, for the place where you stand is holy ground."

[838] **Luke 15:7** "I say to you that likewise there will be more joy in heaven over one sinner who repents than over ninety-nine just persons who need no repentance."
[839] December 10, 1967
[840] The *Urtext* manuscript has "passed" wile the *Notes* and *HLC* have "past" which appears more correct.

still called back, as if it could be made again in time. You keep an ancient memory before your eyes. And he who lives in memories alone is unaware of where he IS. **T(914) -740**[841]

T 26 F 6. Forgiveness is the great release from time. It is the key to learning that the past is over. Madness speaks no more. There IS no OTHER teacher and no OTHER way. For what has been undone no longer is. And who can stand upon a distant shore, and dream himself across an ocean, to a place and time that have long since gone by? How REAL a hindrance can this dream be to where he really IS? For this is fact, and does NOT change whatever dreams he has. Yet can he still IMAGINE he is elsewhere, and in another time. In the extreme, he can delude himself that this is true, and pass from mere imagining into belief and into madness, quite convinced that where he would prefer to be, he IS.

T 26 F 7. Is this a HINDRANCE to the place whereon he stands? Is any echo from the past that he may hear a fact in what is there to hear where he is now? And how much can his own delusions about time and place affect a change in where he REALLY is? The unforgiven is a voice that calls from out a past forever more gone by. And everything which points to it as real is but a wish that what is gone could be made real again, and seen as here and now, in place of what is REALLY now and here. Is this a HINDRANCE to the truth the past has gone, and CANNOT be returned to you? And do you WANT that fearful instant kept, when Heaven seemed to disappear, and God was feared and made a symbol of your hate?

T 26 F 8. Forget the time of terror that has been so long ago corrected and undone. Can sin withstand the Will of God? Can it be up to you to see the past, and put it in the present? You can NOT go back. And everything that points the way in the direction of the past but sets you on a mission whose accomplishment can ONLY be unreal. **T(915) -741** Such is the justice your ever loving Father has ensured MUST come to you. And from your own unfairness unto yourself has He protected you. You CANNOT lose your way, because there is no Way but His, and nowhere CAN you go, except to Him. Would He allow His Son to lose his way along a road long since a distant memory of a time gone by?

T 26 F 9. This course will teach you ONLY what is now. A dreadful instant in a distant past, now perfectly corrected, is of no concern or value. Let the dead and gone be peacefully forgotten.[842] Resurrection has come to take its place. And now you are a part of Resurrection, NOT of death. No past illusions have the power to keep you in a place of death, a vault God's Son entered an instant, to be instantly restored unto His Father's Perfect Love. And how can he be kept in chains long since removed, and gone forever from his mind? The Son that God created is as free as God created him. He was reborn the instant that he chose to die, instead of live. And will you not forgive him now, because he made an error in the past that God remembers not, and is not there?

T 26 F 10. Now are you shifting back and forth, between the past and present. Sometimes the past seems real, as if it WERE the present. Voices FROM the past are heard, and then are doubted. You are like to one who still hallucinates, but lacks conviction in what he perceives. This is the borderland between the worlds, the bridge between the past and present. Here the shadow of the past remains, but still a present Light is dimly recognized. Once it is seen, this Light can never be forgotten. It MUST draw you from the past into the present, where you really ARE. The shadow voices do not CHANGE the laws of time or of eternity. They come from what is past and gone, but hinder not the true existence of the here and now. **T(916) -742**

T 26 F 11. The real world is the second part of the hallucination time and death are real, and have existence which can be perceived. This terrible illusion was denied in but the time it took for God to give His Answer to illusion for ALL time and EVERY circumstance. And then it was no more, to be experienced as there. Each day, and every minute in each day, and every instant that each minute holds, you but relive the single instant when the time of terror was replaced by Love. And so you die each day to live again, until you cross the gap between the past and present, which is NOT a gap at all.

T 26 F 12. Such is each life; a seeming interval from birth to death, and on to life again, a repetition of an instant gone by long ago, which CANNOT be relived. And ALL of time is but the mad belief that what is over is still here and now. Forgive the past and let it go, for it IS gone. You stand no longer on the ground that lies between the worlds. You HAVE gone on, and reached the world that lies at Heaven's gate. There IS no hindrance to the Will of God, nor any need that you repeat again a journey that was over long ago. Look gently on each other, and behold the world in which perception of your hate has been transformed into a world of Love. **T(917) -743**[843]

T 26 G. The Appointed Friend (*Notes* 1834 11:209)

T 26 G 1. Anything in this world that you believe is good and valuable and worth striving for can hurt you, and will do so. NOT because it has the power to hurt, but just because YOU have denied it is but an illusion, AND MADE IT REAL. And it IS real to you. It is NOT nothing. And through its perceived reality has entered all the world of sick illusions. All belief in sin, in power of attack, in hurt and harm, in sacrifice and death, has come to you. For no-one can make one illusion real, and still escape the rest. For who can choose to keep the ones which he prefers, and find the safety that the truth alone can give? Who can believe illusions are the same, and still maintain that even one is best?

T 26 G 2. Lead not your little lives in solitude, with one illusion as your only friend. This is no friendship worthy of God's Son, nor one with which he could remain content. But God has given him a better Friend, in whom all power in earth and Heaven rests.[844] The one illusion that you THINK is friend obscures HIS grace and majesty from you, and keeps his friendship and forgiveness from your welcoming embrace. Without him you are friendless. Seek not another friend to take his place. There IS no other friend. What God appointed HAS no substitute. And what illusion CAN replace the truth?

T 26 G 3. Who dwells with shadows is alone indeed, and loneliness is NOT the Will of God. Would you allow one shadow to usurp the throne that God appointed for your Friend, if you but realized ITS emptiness has left YOURS empty and unoccupied? Make NO illusion friend, for if you do, it CAN but take the place of him whom God has called your Friend. And it is he who is your ONLY Friend in truth. He brings you gifts that are not of this world, and only he, to whom they have been given, CAN make sure that you receive

---

[841] The *Urtext* manuscript pagination jumps from 732 to 740. This MAY or MAY NOT indicate missing material. It could be simply a pagination error by the typist misreading the "previous page" which is 732, as 739 and then adding one for the "on-the-fly manual pagination and thus typing 740. I know this is possible because when working with this issue, I actually mistook page 732 for page 739 and thought I'd found a missing page for a moment. The "2" on the typewriter in use is unusual, and somewhat "top-heavy" making it easier to mistake a 2 for a 9 than would normally be the case. We can add that the *Notes* shows no indication of missing material, nor does the *HLC*. Were there ever pages 733-39, they are apparently not transcripts of the *Notes*.

[842] **Matthew 8:22** But Jesus said to him, "Follow Me, and let the dead bury their own dead."

[843] December 14, 1967

[844] **Matthew 28:18** And Jesus came and spoke to them, saying, "All authority has been given to Me in heaven and on earth."

them.[845] He will place them on YOUR throne, when you make room for him on his. **T(918) -744**[846]

T 26 H. Review of Principles (*Notes* 1837 11:212)

T 26 H 1. This is a course in miracles. And, as such, the laws of healing must be understood before the purpose of the course can be accomplished. Let us review the principles that we have covered, and arrange them in a way that summarizes all that must occur for healing to be possible. For when it once is possible, it MUST occur. ALL sickness comes from separation. When the separation is denied, it goes. For it IS gone as soon as the idea which brought it has been healed and been replaced by sanity. Sickness and sin are seen as consequence and cause, in a relationship kept hidden from awareness, that it may be carefully preserved from reason's light.

T 26 H 2. Guilt ASKS FOR punishment, and its request is granted. NOT in truth, but in the world of shadows and illusions BUILT on sin. The Son of God perceives what he would see, because perception IS a wish fulfilled. Perception changes, MADE to take the place of changeless knowledge. Yet is truth unchanged. It cannot BE perceived, but only known. What is perceived takes many forms, but NONE has meaning. Brought to truth, its senselessness is quite apparent. Kept APART from truth, it SEEMS to have a meaning and be real. Perception's laws are OPPOSITE to truth, and what IS true of knowledge is NOT true of ANYTHING that is apart from it. Yet has God given Answer to the world of sickness, Which applies to ALL its forms.

T 26 H 3. God's Answer is eternal, though It operates in time, where It is needed. But, because It IS of God, the laws of time do not affect Its workings. It is in this world, but NOT a part of it.[847] For It is real, and dwells where all reality MUST be. Ideas leave not their source, and their effects but SEEM to be apart from them. Ideas are of the mind. What is projected OUT, and seems to be EXTERNAL to the mind, is NOT outside at all, but an effect of what is in, and has NOT left its source. God's Answer lies where the belief in sin MUST be, for only there can its effects be utterly undone, and without cause. **T(919) -745**

T 26 H 4. Perception's laws must be reversed, because they ARE reversals of the laws of truth. The laws of truth FOREVER will be true, and cannot BE reversed;[848] yet can be SEEN as upside down. And this must be corrected where the illusion of reversal lies. It is impossible that one illusion be LESS amenable to truth than are the rest. But it IS possible that some are given greater VALUE, and less willingly OFFERED to truth for healing and for help. NO illusion has ANY truth in it. Yet it appears some are MORE true than others, although this clearly makes no sense at all. All that a hierarchy of illusions can show is PREFERENCE, NOT reality.

T 26 H 5. What relevance has preference to the truth? Illusions are illusions, and are false. Your preference gives them NO reality. Not one is true in ANY way, and all must yield with equal ease to what God gave as Answer to them all. God's Will is One. And ANY wish that SEEMS to go AGAINST His Will has NO foundation in the truth. Sin is not error, for it goes BEYOND correction to impossibility. Yet the belief that it is real has made some errors seem forever PAST the hope of healing, and the lasting grounds for hell. If this were so, would Heaven be opposed by its own opposite, as real as it.

T 26 H 6. Then would God's Will be split in two, and all creation be subjected to the laws of two opposing powers, until God becomes impatient, splits the world apart, and relegates attack unto Himself. Thus has He lost His Mind, proclaiming sin has taken His reality from Him, and brought His Love at last to vengeance' heels. For such an insane picture, an insane defense can be expected, but can NOT establish that the picture must be true. Nothing GIVES meaning where no meaning IS. And truth needs NO defense to make it true. Illusions HAVE no witnesses, and no effects. Who looks on them is but deceived.

T 26 H 7. Forgiveness is the only function here, and serves to bring the joy this world denies to every aspect of God's Son where sin was thought to rule. Perhaps you do not see the role forgiveness plays in ending death, and ALL beliefs **T(920) -746** that rise from mists of guilt. Sins are beliefs which you impose between your brother and yourself. They limit you to time and place, and give a little space to you; ANOTHER little space to him. This separating off is symbolized, in your perception, by a body which is clearly separate and a thing apart. Yet what this symbol REPRESENTS is but your wish to BE apart and separate.

T 26 H 8. Forgiveness TAKES AWAY what stands between your brother and yourself. It is the wish that you be JOINED with him, and NOT alone. We call it "wish" because it still conceives of other choices, and has not yet reached beyond the world of choice entirely. Yet is this wish in line with Heaven's state,[849] and not in OPPOSITION to God's Will. Although it falls far short of giving you your full inheritance, it DOES remove the obstacles which YOU have placed between the Heaven where you are, and RECOGNITION of where and what you are. Facts are unchanged. But facts can be denied and thus unknown, though they were known BEFORE they were denied.

T 26 H 9. Salvation, perfect and complete, asks but a LITTLE wish that what is true be true. A LITTLE willingness to overlook what is not there. A LITTLE sigh that speaks for Heaven as a preference to this world which death and desolation seem to rule. In joyous answer will creation rise within you, to REPLACE the world you see with Heaven, wholly perfect and complete. What is forgiveness, but a willingness that truth be true? What can remain unhealed and broken from a Unity Which holds all things within Itself? There is NO sin. And EVERY miracle is possible the INSTANT that the Son of God perceives his wishes and the Will of God are One. **T(921) -747**[850]

T 26 H 10. What is the Will of God? He wills His Son have everything. And this He guaranteed when He created him AS everything. It is impossible that anything be lost, if what you HAVE is what you ARE. This is the miracle by which creation became YOUR function, sharing it with God. It is not understood APART from Him, and therefore has no meaning in this world. Here does the Son of God ask NOT too much, but FAR too little. He would sacrifice his own identity WITH everything, to find a LITTLE treasure of his own. And this he cannot do, without a sense of isolation, loss, and loneliness. This IS the treasure he has sought to find. And he COULD only be afraid of it.

T 26 H 11. Is fear a treasure? Can uncertainty be what you WANT? Or is it a mistake about your will, and what you REALLY are? Let us consider what the error IS, so it can be corrected, NOT protected. Sin is belief attack can be projected OUTSIDE the mind where the

---

[845] **John 14:27** "Peace I leave with you, My peace I give to you; not as the world gives do I give to you. Let not your heart be troubled, neither let it be afraid."
[846] December 21, 1967
[847] **John 15:19** "If you were of the world, the world would love its own. Yet because you are not of the world, but I chose you out of the world, therefore the world hates you."
John 17:14 "I have given them Your word; and the world has hated them because they are not of the world, just as I am not of the world."
John 17:16 "They are not of the world, just as I am not of the world."
John 17:18 "As You sent Me into the world, I also have sent them into the world."
[848] The *Urtext* manuscript has a full stop here. In the *Notes* however, the full stop glyph is crossed out and a semi-colon inserted. Rather obviously, a full stop is not appropriate, indeed no punctuation is absolutely necessary, but a semi-colon is preferable to a full stop. We are therefore counting this a typo and restoring the *Notes* reading.

[849] *Urtext* manuscript has it typed "Heaven's **gate**" handwritten mark-up corrects this to the *Notes* reading which is "Heaven's **state**."
[850] December 25, 1967

belief arose. Here is the firm conviction that ideas CAN leave their source made real and meaningful. And FROM this error does the world of sin and sacrifice arise. This world is an attempt to prove your innocence, while cherishing attack. Its failure lies in that you STILL FEEL guilty, though without understanding WHY. Effects are SEPARATED from their source. They SEEM to be BEYOND you to control or to prevent.

T 26 H 12. What has been KEPT apart can never join. Cause and effect are one, NOT separate. God wills you learn what always has been true. That he created you as part of Him, and this must still be true BECAUSE ideas leave not their source. Such is creation's law; that each idea T(922) -748 the mind conceives but ADDS to its abundance, NEVER takes away. This is as true of what is idly wished as what is truly willed, because the mind can wish to be deceived, but CANNOT make it be what it is not. And to believe ideas can leave their source is to invite illusions to be true, WITHOUT SUCCESS. Nor never will success BE possible in trying to deceive the Son of God.

T 26 H 13. The miracle is possible when cause and consequence are brought together, NOT kept separate. The healing of effect WITHOUT the cause can merely shift effects to other forms. And this is NOT release. God's Son could never be content with LESS than full salvation, and ESCAPE from guilt. For otherwise he still demands that he must make SOME sacrifice, and thus denies that EVERYTHING is his, unlimited by loss of any kind. A tiny sacrifice is just the same in its EFFECTS as is the WHOLE idea of sacrifice. If loss in ANY form is possible, then is God's Son made incomplete and not himself. Nor will he know himself, nor recognize his will. He has foresworn his Father AND himself, and made them both his enemy in hate.

T 26 H 14. Illusions serve the purpose they were MADE to serve. And FROM their purpose, they derive whatever meaning that they seem to have. God gave to ALL illusions that were made ANOTHER purpose that would justify a miracle, WHATEVER form they took. In every miracle ALL healing lies, for God gave Answer to them all as one. And what is one to Him must BE the same. If you believe what is the same is different, you but deceive yourself. What God calls one will be forever one, NOT separate.[851] His Kingdom IS united; thus it was created, and thus will it ever be. The miracle but calls your ancient name, which you WILL recognize because the truth is in your memory. And to this name your brother calls T(923) -749 for his release and yours. Heaven is shining on the Son of God. Deny him not, that YOU may be released.

T 26 H 15. Each instant is the Son of God reborn, until he chooses NOT to die again. In every wish to hurt he chooses death, instead of what his Father wills for him. Yet every instant offers life to him, because his Father wills that he should live. In crucifixion is redemption laid, for healing is not needed where there is no pain or suffering. Forgiveness is the ANSWER to attack of any kind. So is attack DEPRIVED of its effects, and hate is answered in the Name of Love. To you to whom it has been given to save the Son of God from crucifixion and from hell and death, all glory be forever. For you HAVE power to save the Son of God, because his Father willed that it be so. And in your hand does ALL salvation lie, to be both offered and received as one.

T 26 H 16. To use the power God has given you as He would have it used is natural. It is NOT arrogant to be as He created you, or to make use of what He gave to answer ALL His Son's mistakes, and set him free. But it IS arrogant to LAY ASIDE the power that He gave, and choose a little, senseless wish instead of what He wills. The gift of God to you is limitless. There is NO circumstance it cannot answer, and NO problem which is not resolved within its gracious light. Abide in peace, where God would have you be. And be the means whereby your brother finds the peace in which YOUR wishes are fulfilled. Let us unite in bringing blessing to the world of sin and death. For what can save each one of us, can save us all. There is no difference among the Sons of God.

T 26 H 17. The Unity that specialness denies will save them all, for what is One can HAVE no specialness. And EVERYTHING belongs to each of them. No wishes lie between a brother and his own. To get from one is to deprive them all. And yet to bless but one gives blessing T(924) -750 to them all as one. Your ancient name belongs to everyone, as theirs to you. Call on your brother's name, and God will answer, for on Him you call. Could He refuse to answer, when He has ALREADY answered all who call on Him? A miracle can make no change at all. But it CAN make what always has been true be RECOGNIZED by those who know it not. And by this little gift of truth but let to be itself; the Son of God allowed to be himself, and all creation freed to call upon the Name of God as one. T(925) -751[852]

T 26 I. The Immediacy of Salvation (*Notes* 1850 11:225)

T 26 I 1. The one remaining problem that you have is that you see an interval between the TIME when you forgive, and will receive the benefits of trust. This but reflects the little you would keep between YOURSELVES, that you might be a LITTLE separate. For time and space are ONE illusion, which takes different forms. If it has been projected BEYOND your minds, you think of it as time. The nearer it is brought to where it IS, the more you think of it in terms of space. There is a DISTANCE you would keep apart from one another. And this space you see as time, because you still believe you are EXTERNAL to each other. This makes trust impossible. And you can NOT believe that trust would settle every problem NOW.

T 26 I 2. Thus do you think it SAFER to remain a LITTLE careful and a LITTLE watchful of interests perceived as separate. From this perception, you can not conceive of gaining what forgiveness offers NOW. The interval you think lies in between the giving and receiving of the gift SEEMS to be one in which you sacrifice, and suffer loss. You see EVENTUAL salvation; not IMMEDIATE results. Salvation IS immediate. Unless you so perceive it, you WILL be afraid of it, believing that the risk of loss is great between the time its PURPOSE is made yours, and its EFFECTS will come to you. In this form is the error still obscured that is the SOURCE of fear. Salvation WOULD wipe out the space you see between you still, and let you INSTANTLY become as one. And it is HERE you fear the loss would lie.

T 26 I 3. Do not project this fear to time, for time is NOT the enemy that you perceive. Time is as neutral as the body is, except in terms of what you see it FOR. If you would keep a little SPACE between you still, you want a little TIME in which forgiveness is withheld a little while. This makes the interval BETWEEN the time in which forgiveness is withheld and given seem dangerous, with terror justified. But SPACE between you is apparent NOW, and cannot BE perceived in future time. No more can it be OVERLOOKED, except within the present. T(926) -752 FUTURE loss is not your fear. But PRESENT joining IS your dread.

T 26 I 4. Who can feel desolation except NOW? A FUTURE cause as yet HAS no effects. And therefore MUST it be that, if you fear, there is a PRESENT cause. And it is THIS that needs correction, NOT a future state. The plans YOU make for safety all are laid within the future, where you CANNOT plan. No purpose has been GIVEN it as yet, and what WILL happen has as yet no cause. Who can predict effects without a cause? And who could fear effects UNLESS he thought they had BEEN caused and judged disastrous

---

[851] **Matthew 19:6** "So then, they are no longer two but one flesh. Therefore what God has joined together, let not man separate."

[852] December 29, 1967

NOW? Belief in sin arouses fear, and like its cause, is looking forward; looking back, but OVERLOOKING what is here and now.

T 26 I 5. Yet only here and now its cause must be, if its effects ALREADY have been judged as fearful. And, in overlooking THIS, is it protected and kept separate from healing. For a miracle is NOW. It stands ALREADY there, in present grace, within the only interval of time which sin and fear have overlooked, but which is all there IS to time. The working out of ALL correction takes no time at all. But the ACCEPTANCE of the working out can SEEM to take forever. The change of purpose the Holy Spirit brought to your relationship has IN it all effects that you will see. They can be looked at NOW. Why wait 'til they unfold in time, and fear they may NOT come, although already THERE?

T 26 I 6. You have been told that everything brings good that comes from God.[853] And yet it SEEMS as if this is not so. Good in disaster's form is difficult to credit in advance. Nor is there really SENSE in this idea. Why SHOULD the good appear in evil's form? And is this not deception if it does? Its CAUSE is here, if it appears at all. Why are not its effects apparent, then? Why in the future? And you seek to be content with sighing, and with "reasoning," you do not understand it now, but WILL some day. And THEN its meaning will be clear. This is NOT reason, for it is unjust, and clearly hints at punishment until the time of liberation is at hand. T(927) -753

T 26 I 7. Given a change of purpose for the good, there is NO reason for an interval in which disaster strikes, to be perceived as good some day, but now in form of pain. This is a SACRIFICE of now, which COULD not be the cost the Holy Spirit asks for what he gave WITHOUT a cost at all. Yet this illusion has a cause which, though untrue, must be ALREADY in your mind. And THIS illusion is but one effect which it engenders, and one form in which its outcome is perceived. This interval in time, when retribution is perceived to be the form in which the good appears, is but one aspect of the little space that lies between you, unforgiven still.

T 26 I 8. Be not content with future happiness. It has NO meaning, and is NOT your just reward. For you have cause for freedom NOW. What profits freedom in a prisoner's form?[854] Why SHOULD deliverance be disguised as death? Delay is senseless, and the reason that would maintain effects of PRESENT cause must be delayed until a FUTURE time is merely a denial of the fact that consequence and cause MUST come as one. Look not to time, but to the little space between you still, to be delivered FROM. And do not let it be DISGUISED as time, and so preserved BECAUSE its form is changed, and what it IS cannot be recognized. The Holy Spirit's purpose NOW is yours. Should not His happiness be yours as well? T(928) -754[855]

T 26 J. For They Have Come (*Notes* 1856 11:231)

T 26 J 1. Think but how holy you must be, from whom the Voice for God calls lovingly unto your brother, that you may awake in him the Voice that answers to YOUR call. And think how holy HE must be, when in him sleeps your OWN salvation, with HIS freedom joined. However much you wish he be condemned, God is in him. And never will you know He is in YOU as well, while you attack His chosen home, and battle with his host. Regard him gently. Look with loving eyes on him who carries Christ within him, that you may behold His glory, and rejoice that Heaven is NOT separate from you.

T 26 J 2. Is it too much to ask a little trust for him who carries Christ to you, that you may be forgiven ALL your sins, and left without a single one you cherish still. Forget not that a shadow held between your brother and yourself obscures the Face of Christ and memory of God. And would you trade Them for an ancient hate? The ground whereon you stand is holy ground[856] BECAUSE of Them Who, standing there with you, have blessed it with THEIR innocence and peace.[857] The blood of hatred fades, to let the grass grow green again, and let the flowers be all white and sparkling in the summer sun. What was a place of death has now become a living temple in a world of light.

T 26 J 3. Because of Them. It is Their Presence Which has lifted holiness again to take its ancient place upon an ancient throne. Because of Them have miracles sprung up as grass and flowers on the barren ground which hate had scorched and rendered desolate. What hate has wrought have They undone. And now you stand on ground so holy Heaven leans to join with it, and make it like Itself. The shadow of an ancient hate has gone, and all the blight and withering have passed forever from the land where They have come. T(929) -755

T 26 J 4. What is a hundred or a thousand years to Them, or tens of thousands? When They come, time's purpose is fulfilled. What never WAS passes to nothingness when They have come. What hatred claimed is given up to love, and freedom lights up every living thing and lifts it into Heaven, where the lights grow ever brighter as each one comes home. The incomplete is made complete again. And Heaven's joy has been increased because what is its own has been restored to it. The bloodied earth is cleansed, and the insane have shed their garments of insanity, to join Them on the ground whereon you stand.

T 26 J 5. Heaven is grateful for this gift of what has been withheld so long. For They have come to gather in Their Own. What has been blocked is opened; what was held APART from light is given up that light may shine on it, and leave no space nor distance lingering between the light of Heaven and the world. The holiest of all the spots on earth is where an ancient hatred has become a present love. And They come quickly to the living temple, where a home for Them has been set up. There is no place in Heaven holier. And They HAVE come to dwell within the temple offered them, to be THEIR resting place as well as YOURS.

T 26 J 6. What hatred has released to love becomes the brightest light in Heaven's radiance. And all the lights in Heaven brighter grow in gratitude for what has been restored. Around you angels hover lovingly, to keep away all darkened thoughts of sin, and KEEP the light where it has entered in. Your footprints lighten up the world, for where you walk forgiveness goes with you. No-one on earth but offers thanks to one who has restored his home, and sheltered him from bitter winter and the freezing cold. And shall the Lord of Heaven and His Son give LESS in gratitude for so much MORE? T(930) -756

T 26 J 7. Now is the temple of the living God rebuilt as host again to Him by Whom it was created.[858] Where He dwells His Son dwells with Him, NEVER separate. And They give thanks that They are welcome made at last. Where stood a cross stands now the risen

---

[853] **Romans 8:28** And we know that all things work together for good to those who love God, to those who are the called according to His purpose.
[854] **Matthew 16:26** "For what profit is it to a man if he gains the whole world, and loses his own soul? Or what will a man give in exchange for his soul?"
[855] January 2, 1968

[856] **Exodus 3:4** And when the LORD saw that he turned aside to see, God called unto him out of the midst of the bush, and said, Moses, Moses. And he said, Here *am* I.
Exodus 3:5 And he said, Draw not nigh hither: put off thy shoes from off thy feet, for the place whereon thou standest *is* holy ground.
[857] **Exodus 3:5** Then He said, "Do not draw near this place. Take your sandals off your feet, for the place where you stand is holy ground."
[858] **Mark 14:58** We heard him say, "I will destroy this temple that is made with hands, and within three days I will build another made without hands."
1 Corinthians 3:16 Do you not know that you are the temple of God and that the Spirit of God dwells in you?
1 Corinthians 6:19 Or do you not know that your body is the temple of the Holy Spirit who is in you, whom you have from God, and you are not your own?

would your self be lost. This is the secret vow that you have made with every brother who would walk apart. This is the secret oath you take again whenever you perceive yourself attacked. No-one can suffer if he does NOT see himself attacked, AND LOSING BY ATTACK. Unstated and unheard in consciousness is every pledge to sickness. Yet it is a promise to another to be hurt by him, and to attack him in return.

T 28 G 5. Sickness is anger taken out upon the body, so that IT will suffer pain. It is the obvious effect of what was made in secret, IN AGREEMENT with another's secret wish to be apart from you, as you would be apart from him. Unless you BOTH agree this is your wish, it CAN have no effects. Whoever says, "There IS no gap between my mind and yours," has kept GOD's promise, NOT his tiny oath to be forever faithful unto death. And by his healing IS his brother healed. Let THIS be your agreement with each one; that you be one with him and NOT apart. And he will keep the promise that you make with him, because it is the one which he has made to God, as God has made to him.

T 28 G 6. God keeps His promises; His Son keeps his. In his creation did his Father say, "You are beloved of Me and I of you forever. Be you perfect as Myself,[911] for you can never be apart from Me." His Son remembers not that he replied "I will," though in that promise he was born. Yet God reminds him of it every time he does not share a promise to be sick, but lets his mind be healed and unified. His secret vows are powerless before the Will of God, Whose promises he shares. And what he substitutes is NOT his will, who has made promise of himself to God. **T(987) -813**[912]

T 28 H. The Beautiful Relationship (*Notes* 1978 12:113)

T 28 H 1. God asks for nothing, and His Son, like Him, need ask for nothing. For there is no lack in him. An empty space, a little gap, would BE a lack. And it is only there that he could want for something he has not. A space where God is not, a gap between the Father and the Son is NOT the Will of either, who have promised to be One. God's promise is a promise to HIMSELF, and there is no-one who could BE untrue to what He wills as part of what He IS. The promise that there IS no gap between Himself and what He is cannot BE false. What will can come between what MUST be One, and in Whose Wholeness there can BE no gaps?

T 28 H 2. The beautiful relationship you have with all your brothers is a part of you BECAUSE it is a part of God Himself. Are you not sick, if you deny yourself your wholeness and your health, the Source of help, the call to healing and the Call to heal? Your Savior waits for healing, and the world waits with him. Nor are YOU apart from it. For healing will be one, or not at all, its oneness being where the healing LIES. What could CORRECT for separation but its opposite? There is no middle ground, in ANY aspect of salvation. You accept it wholly, or accept it not. What is unseparated must be JOINED. And what is joined cannot BE separate.

T 28 H 3. Either there IS a gap between you and your brother, or you ARE as one. There is no in between, no other choice, and no allegiance to be split BETWEEN the two. A split allegiance is but faithlessness to both, and merely sets you spinning round, to grasp uncertainly at any straw that seems to hold some promise of relief. Yet who can build his home upon a straw, and count on it as shelter from the wind?[913] The body can be made a home like this BE-CAUSE it lacks foundation in the truth. And yet, BECAUSE it does, it can be seen as NOT your home, but merely as an aid to help you reach the home where God abides. **T(988) -814**

T 28 H 4. With THIS as purpose IS the body healed. It is NOT used to witness to the dream of separation and disease. Nor is it idly blamed for what it did not do. It serves to help the HEALING of God's Son, and, for THIS purpose, it cannot BE sick. It will not join a purpose not your own, and you have chosen that it NOT be sick. All miracles are based upon this choice, and GIVEN you the instant it is made. No forms of sickness are immune, because the choice cannot be MADE in terms of form. The choice of SICKNESS seems to be a form, yet it is one, as is its opposite. And YOU are sick or well, accordingly.

T 28 H 5. But NEVER you alone. This world is but the dream that you can BE alone, and think without affecting those apart from you. To be alone MUST mean you are apart, and if you are, you cannot BUT be sick. This SEEMS to prove that you must be APART. Yet all it means is that you tried to keep a promise to be true to faithlessness. Yet faithlessness IS sickness. It is like the house upon a straw. It SEEMS to be quite solid and substantial IN ITSELF. But its stability cannot be judged APART from its foundation. If it rests on straws, there is no need to bar the door and lock the windows, and make fast the bolts. The wind WILL topple it, and rain WILL come, and carry it into oblivion.[914]

T 28 H 6. What is the SENSE in seeking to be safe in what was MADE for danger and for fear? Why burden it with further locks and chains and heavy anchors, when its weakness lies, NOT in itself, but in the frailty of the little gap of nothingness whereon it stands? What CAN be safe which rests upon a shadow? Would you build your home upon what WILL collapse beneath a feather's weight? Your home is built upon your brother's health; upon his happiness, his sinlessness, and everything his Father promised him. No secret promise you have made INSTEAD has shaken the Foundation of his home. **T(989) -815**

T 28 H 7. The winds will blow upon it and the rain will beat against it, but with NO effect. The world will wash away, and yet this house will stand forever, for its strength lies NOT within itself alone. It is an ark of safety, resting on God's promise, that His Son is safe forever in Himself.[915] What gap can interpose itself between the safety of this shelter and its Source? From here, the body can be seen as what it is, and neither less nor more in worth than the extent to which it can be used to liberate God's Son unto his home. And, with this holy purpose, is it made a home of holiness a little while, because it shares your Father's Will with You. **T(990) -816**[916]

---

[911] **Matthew 5:48** "Therefore you shall be perfect, just as your Father in heaven is perfect."
[912] March 26, 1968
[913] **Matthew 7:24-27** "Therefore whoever hears these sayings of Mine, and does them, I will liken him to a wise man who built his house on the rock: and the rain descended, the floods came, and the winds blew and beat on that house; and it did not fall, for it was founded on the rock.
"But everyone who hears these sayings of Mine, and does not do them, will be like a foolish man who built his house on the sand: and the rain descended, the floods came, and the winds blew and beat on that house; and it fell. And great was its fall."
[914] **Matthew 7:26-27** "And every one that heareth these words of mine, and doeth them not, shall be likened unto a foolish man, who built his house upon the sand: and the rain descended, and the floods came, and the winds blew, and smote upon that house; and it fell: and great was the fall thereof."
[915] **Genesis 7:9** two by two they went into the ark to Noah, male and female, as God had commanded Noah.
[916] March 28, 1968

T 28 E 9. Who seeks for substitutes, when he perceives HE HAS LOST NOTHING? Who would WANT to have the "benefits" of sickness, when he has received the simple happiness of health? What God has given cannot BE a loss, and what is not of Him has NO effects. What, then, would you perceive within the gap? The seeds of sickness come from the belief that there is JOY in separation, and its giving up WOULD BE A SACRIFICE. But miracles are the result, when you do not insist on seeing in the gap what is not there. Your willingness to LET illusions go is all the Healer of God's Son requires. He will place the miracle of healing where the seeds of sickness were. And there will be NO loss, but ONLY gain. **T(982) -808**[907]

T 28 F. The Alternate to Dreams of Fear (*Notes* 1067 12:102)

T 28 F 1. What is a sense of sickness but a sense of limitation? Of a splitting OFF and separating FROM? A gap perceived BETWEEN ourselves and what is seen as health? The good is seen OUTSIDE; the evil, IN. And thus is sickness separating OFF the self from good, and KEEPING evil there. God is the ALTERNATE to dreams of fear. Who shares in them can NEVER share in Him. But who WITHDRAWS his mind from sharing them IS sharing Him. There IS no other choice. Except you share it, NOTHING can exist. And YOU exist because God shared His Will with you, that His creation might create.

T 28 F 2. It is the SHARING of the evil dreams, of hate and malice, bitterness and death, of sin and suffering, of pain and loss, that makes them real. UNSHARED they are perceived as meaningless. The fear is gone from them BECAUSE YOU DID NOT GIVE THEM YOUR SUPPORT. Where fear has gone, there love MUST come, because there ARE but these alternatives. Where one appears, the other DISappears. And which you SHARE becomes the only one you HAVE. You HAVE the one which you accept, because it is the only one you WANT. You share NO evil dreams, if you forgive the dreamer, and perceive that he is NOT the dream he made. And so he CANNOT be a part of YOURS, from which you BOTH are free. Forgiveness SEPARATES the dreamer from the evil dream, and thus releases him.

T 28 F 3. Remember if you SHARE an evil dream, you will believe you ARE the dream you share. And, fearing it, you will not WANT to know your own identity, because you think that IT is fearful. And you WILL deny your Self, and walk upon an alien ground which your Creator did not make, and where you seem to be a "something" you are not. You WILL make war upon your Self, Which SEEMS to be your enemy, and WILL attack your brother, as a part of what you hate. There is no compromise. You are your Self, or an illusion. What CAN be between illusion and the truth? A middle ground, where you can be a thing that is NOT you, MUST be a dream, and CANNOT be the truth. **T(983) -809**[908]

T 28 F 4. You have conceived a little gap between illusions and the truth to be the place where all your safety lies, and where your Self is safely hidden by what you have made. Here is a world established that is sick, and this the world the body's eyes perceive. Here are the sounds it hears, the voices which its ears were made to hear. Yet sights and sounds the body can perceive are meaningless. It cannot see nor hear. It does not know what seeing IS; what listening is FOR. It is as little able to perceive as it can judge, or understand, or know. Its eyes are blind, its ears are deaf. It can NOT think, and so it cannot HAVE effects.

T 28 F 5. What is there God created to be sick? And what that He created not can BE? Let not your eyes behold a dream; your ears[909] bear witness to illusion. They were made to look upon a world that is not there; to hear the voices that can make no sounds. Yet are there other sounds and other sights which can be seen and heard and UNDERSTOOD. For eyes and ears are senses without sense, and what they see and hear they but report. It is not THEY that hear and see, but YOU, who PUT TOGETHER every jagged piece, each senseless scrap and shred of evidence, and MAKE a witness to the world you want.

T 28 F 6. Let not the body's ears and eyes perceive these countless fragments seen within the gap that YOU imagined, and let THEM persuade their maker his imaginings were real. Creation proves reality because it SHARES the function ALL creation shares. It is not made of little bits of glass, a piece of wood, a thread or two perhaps, and put together to ATTEST its truth. Reality does not depend on THIS. There IS no gap which separates the truth from dreams and from illusions. Truth has left no room for them in ANY place or time. For It fills every place and every time, and makes them wholly indivisible. **T(984) -810**

T 28 F 7. You who believe there is a little gap between you do not understand that it is HERE that you are kept as prisoners in a world perceived to be EXISTING here. The world you see does not exist BECAUSE the place where you perceive it is not real. The gap is carefully concealed in fog, and misty pictures rise to cover it with vague, uncertain forms and changing shapes, forever unsubstantial and unsure. Yet in the gap is NOTHING. And there ARE no awesome secrets and no darkened tombs where terror rises from the bones of death. Look at the little gap, and you behold the innocence and emptiness of sin that you will see within yourself, when you have lost the fear of recognizing love. **T(985) -811**[910]

T 28 G. The Secret Vows (*Notes* 1972 12:107)

T 28 G 1. Who punishes the body is insane. For here the little gap is SEEN, and yet it is NOT here. It has not judged ITSELF, nor made itself to be what it is not. IT does not seek to make of pain a joy, and look for lasting pleasure in the dust. It does not TELL you what its purpose is, and CANNOT understand what it is for. IT DOES NOT VICTIMIZE, because it has no will, no preferences, and NO DOUBTS. It does not wonder what it is. And so it has no NEED to be competitive. It CAN be victimized, but CANNOT feel itself as victim. It accepts no role, but does what it is told, WITHOUT attack.

T 28 G 2. It is indeed a senseless point of view to hold responsible for sight a thing that cannot see, and blame it for the sounds you do not like, although it cannot hear. IT suffers not the punishment you give, because it HAS no feeling. It behaves in ways you want, but NEVER makes the choice. It is not born and does not die. It can but follow aimlessly the path on which it has been set. And if that path is changed, it walks as easily another way. It takes no sides, and judges not the road it travels. It perceives no gap because IT DOES NOT HATE. It can be USED for hate, but it cannot be hateful MADE thereby.

T 28 G 3. The thing you hate and fear and loathe and WANT, the body does not know. You send it forth to SEEK for separation and BE separate. And THEN you hate it, NOT for what it is, but for the uses you have MADE of it. You shrink from what IT sees and what IT hears, and hate its frailty and its littleness. And you despise its acts, but NOT your own. It sees and acts for YOU. It hears YOUR voice. And it is frail and little by YOUR wish. It SEEMS to punish you, and thus DESERVE your hatred for the limitations which it brings to you. Yet you have made of it a symbol of the limitations which you want your MIND to have and see and KEEP. **T(986) - 812**

T 28 G 4. The body REPRESENTS the gap between the little bit of mind you call your own, and all the rest of what is REALLY yours. You hate it, yet you think it IS your self, and that, WITHOUT it,

---
[907] March 5, 1968
[908] March 12, 1968
[909] The *Urtext* manuscript has "eyes" but the *Notes* and *HLC* have "ears" which appears to be correct.

[910] March 23, 1968

T 28 D 8. This is a feast unlike indeed to those the dreaming of the world has shown.[901] For here, the more that anyone receives, the more is left for all the rest to share. The Guests have brought unlimited supply with Them. And no-one is deprived, or can deprive. Here is a feast the Father lays before His Son, AND shares it equally with him. And in Their sharing there can BE no gap, in **T(978) - 804** - which abundance falters and grows thin. Here can the lean years enter not,[902] for time waits not upon this feast, which HAS no end. For Love has set Its table in the space that seemed to keep your Guests APART from you. **T(979) -805**

T 28 E. The Greater Joining (*Notes* 1960 12:95)

T 28 E 1. Accepting[903] the Atonement[904] for yourself means NOT to give support to someone's dream of sickness and of death. It means that you share NOT his wish to separate, and let him turn illusions on himself. Nor do you wish that they be turned instead on YOU. Thus have they NO effects. And YOU are free of dreams of pain because you let HIM be. UNLESS you help him, YOU will suffer pain with him because that is your wish. And you become a figure in HIS dream of pain, as he in YOURS. So do you BOTH become illusions, and without identity. You could be anyone or anything, depending on whose evil dream you share. You can be sure of just ONE thing; that you are evil, for you share in dreams of fear.

T 28 E 2. There is a way of finding certainty RIGHT HERE AND NOW. Refuse to be a part of fearful dreams, WHATEVER form they take. For you will lose identity in them. You FIND yourself by NOT accepting them as causing you, and GIVING you effects. You stand apart from them, but NOT apart from him who dreams them. Thus you separate the dreamer from the dream, and join with ONE, but let the OTHER go. The dream is but illusion in the mind. And with the MIND you WOULD unite, but NEVER with the dream. It is the DREAM you fear, and NOT the mind. You see them as the same, because you think that YOU are but a dream. And what is real and what is but illusion IN YOURSELF you do not know and cannot tell apart.

T 28 E 3. Like you, your brother thinks HE is a dream. Share not in his illusion of himself, for YOUR identity depends on his reality. Think, rather, of him as a mind in which illusions still persist, but as a mind which brother is to you. He is not brother made by what he DREAMS, nor is his body, "hero" of the dream, your brother. It is his REALITY that is your brother, as is yours to him. Your mind and his ARE joined in brotherhood. His body and his dreams but SEEM to make a little gap, where yours have joined with his. And yet, between your MINDS there IS no gap. To join his dreams is thus to meet him NOT, because his dreams would SEPARATE from you. **T(980) -806**

T 28 E 4. Therefore release him, merely by your claim on brotherhood, and NOT on dreams of fear. Let him acknowledge who he IS, by not supporting his illusions by your faith, for if you do, you will have faith in YOURS. With faith in yours, HE will not be released, and YOU are kept in bondage to his dreams. And dreams of fear will haunt the little gap, inhabited but by illusions which you have SUPPORTED in each other's minds. Be certain, if you do YOUR part, he will do his, for he will JOIN you where YOU stand. Call not to him to meet you in the gap BETWEEN you, or you MUST believe that it is YOUR reality, as well as his. You CANNOT do his part, but this you DO when you become a passive figure in his dream INSTEAD of dreamer of your own.

T 28 E 5. Identity in dreams is meaningless BECAUSE the dreamer and the dream are one. Who shares a dream must BE the dream he shares, because, BY sharing, is a cause produced. You share confusion, and you ARE confused, for in the gap no stable self exists. What is the same seems different, because what IS the same appears to be unlike. His dreams are yours, because you LET them be. But, if you took your OWN away, would he be free of them, and of his own as well. Your dreams are witnesses to his, and his attest the truth of yours. But if you see there IS no truth in yours, his dreams will disappear before his eyes, and he will understand what MADE the dream.

T 28 E 6. The Holy Spirit is in BOTH your minds, and He IS One, because there is no gap that separates His Oneness from Itself. The gap between your bodies matters not, for what is joined in Him is ALWAYS one. No-one is sick, if someone ELSE accepts his union WITH him. His desire to be a sick and separated mind can NOT remain without a witness or a cause. And both ARE gone, if someone wills to be united with him. He has dreamed that he was separated from his brother, who, by sharing NOT his dream, has left the space between them vacant. And the Father comes to join His Son the Holy Spirit joined. **T(981) -807**

T 28 E 7. The Holy Spirit's Function is to take the broken picture of the Son of God, and put the pieces into place again. This holy picture, healed entirely, does He hold out to every separate piece that thinks it is a picture IN ITSELF. To each he offers his identity, which the WHOLE picture represents, instead of just a little, broken bit, which he insisted was himself. And when he sees THIS picture, he will RECOGNIZE himself. If you share not your brother's evil dreams, this IS the picture that the miracle will place within the little gap, left clean of all the seeds of sickness and of sin. And here the Father will receive His Son, because His Son was gracious to himself.

T 28 E 8. I thank you, Father, knowing you will come to close each little gap that lies between the broken pieces of Your holy Son.[905] Your Holiness, complete and perfect, lies in every one of them. And they ARE joined, because what is in one IS in them all. How holy is the smallest grain of sand, when it is recognized as being part of the completed picture of God's Son. The forms the broken pieces seem to take mean nothing. For the Whole is in each one. And every aspect of the Son of God is just the same as every other part. Join not your brother's dream, but join with HIM, and where you join His Son, the Father IS.[906]

---

[901] **John 6 4-14** Now the Passover, the feast of the Jews, was at hand. Jesus therefore lifting up his eyes, and seeing that a great multitude cometh unto him, saith unto Philip, Whence are we to buy bread, that these may eat? And this he said to prove him: for he himself knew what he would do. Philip answered him, Two hundred pennyworth of bread is not sufficient for them, that every one may take a little. One of his disciples, Andrew, Simon Peter's brother, saith unto him, There is a lad here, which hath five barley loaves, and two fishes: but what are these among so many? Jesus said, Make the people sit down. Now there was much grass in the place. So the men sat down, in number about five thousand. Jesus therefore took the loaves; and having given thanks, he distributed to them that were set down; likewise also of the fishes as much as they would. And when they were filled, he saith unto his disciples, Gather up the broken pieces which remain over, that nothing be lost. So they gathered them up, and filled twelve baskets with broken pieces from the five barley loaves, which remained over unto them that had eaten. When therefore the people saw the sign which he did, they said, This is of a truth the prophet that cometh into the world.

[902] **Genesis 41:27** And the seven thin and ugly cows which came up after them are seven years, and the seven empty heads blighted by the east wind are seven years of famine.

[903] March 3, 1968

[904] The *Urtext* manuscript does not capitalize this but the *Notes* and all other versions do.

[905] **Matthew 11:25** At that time Jesus answered and said, "I thank You, Father, Lord of heaven and earth, that You have hidden these things from the wise and prudent and have revealed them to babes. "

[906] **John 17:20-13** "Neither for these only do I pray, but for them also that believe on me through their word; that they may all be one; even as thou, Father, *art* in me, and I in thee, that they also may be in us: that the world may believe that thou didst send me. And the glory which thou hast given me I have given unto them; that they may be one, even as we *are* one; I in them, and thou in me, that they may be perfected into one; that the world may know that thou didst send me, and lovedst them, as thou lovedst me."

has produced the dream, and, while it lasts, will wakening be feared. Nor will the Call to wakening be heard, because it SEEMS to be the call of fear.

T 28 C 10. Like EVERY lesson that the Holy Spirit requests you learn, the miracle is clear. It DEMONSTRATES what He would have you learn, and SHOWS you its effects are what you WANT. In its forgiving dream, are the EFFECTS of yours undone, and hated enemies perceived as friends, with merciful intent. Their enmity is seen as causeless now, BECAUSE they did not make it. And you can accept the role of maker of their hate BECAUSE you see that it has no effects. Now are you freed from this much of the dream; the world is neutral, and the bodies which still seem to move about as separate things NEED NOT BE FEARED. And so they are NOT sick. T(975) - 801 -

T 28 C 11. The miracle returns the CAUSE of fear to you who made it. But it ALSO shows that, HAVING no effects, it is NOT cause, because the function of causation is to HAVE effects. And where effects are gone, there IS no cause. Thus is the body healed by miracles BECAUSE they show the mind MADE sickness, and employed the body to be victim, or EFFECT, of what it made. But HALF the lesson will not teach the whole. The miracle is useless, if you learn but that the BODY can be healed, for this is NOT the lesson it was sent to teach. The lesson is the MIND was sick that thought the body COULD be sick; projecting OUT its guilt caused NOTHING, and had NO effects.

T 28 C 12. This world is full of miracles. They stand in shining silence next to every dream of pain and suffering, of sin and guilt. They are the dream's ALTERNATIVE, the choice to be the dreamer, rather than deny the active role in making up the dream. They are the glad effects of taking back the consequence of sickness to its cause. The body is released, because the mind acknowledges "this is not DONE TO me, but I am doing this." And thus the mind is free to make another choice instead. Beginning here, salvation will proceed to change the course of every step in the descent to separation, until all the steps have been retraced, the ladder gone, and ALL the dreaming of the world undone.

T 28 D. The Agreement to Join (*Notes* 1955 12:90)

T 28 D 1. What waits in perfect certainty BEYOND salvation is not our concern. For you have barely started to allow your first, uncertain steps to be directed up the ladder separation led you down. The miracle alone is your concern at present. Here is where we must BEGIN. And, having started, will the way be made serene and simple in the rising up to waking and the ending of the dream. When you accept a miracle, you do not ADD your dream of fear to one that is ALREADY being dreamed. Without SUPPORT the dream will fade away, without effects. For it is your SUPPORT that strengthens it. No mind is sick until another mind AGREES that they are separate. And thus, it is their JOINT decision to be sick. T(976) - 802 -

T 28 D 2. If you WITHHOLD agreement, and accept the part YOU play in making sickness real, the other mind cannot project its guilt without your aid in LETTING it perceive itself as separate and apart from YOU. Thus is the body NOT perceived as sick by BOTH your minds, from SEPARATE points of view. UNITING with a brother's mind prevents the CAUSE of sickness, and perceived effects. Healing is the effect of minds that join, as sickness comes from minds that separate. The miracle does nothing just because the minds ARE joined, and CANNOT separate. Yet, in the dreaming, has this been reversed, and separate minds are seen as bodies, which ARE separated, and which cannot JOIN.

T 28 D 3. Do not allow your brother to be sick, for if he is, have YOU abandoned him to his own dream, by SHARING it with him. He has not seen the cause of sickness where it is, and YOU have overlooked the gap between you, where the sickness has been bred. Thus are you JOINED in sickness, to preserve the little gap un-

healed, where sickness is kept carefully protected, cherished, and upheld by firm belief, lest God should come to bridge the little gap that leads to Him. Fight not His coming with illusions, for it is His coming that you WANT above all things that seem to glisten in the dream. The end of dreaming is the end of FEAR, and love was NEVER in the world of dreams.

T 28 D 4. The gap IS little. Yet it holds the seeds of pestilence and every form of ill, because it is a WISH to keep apart, and NOT to join. And thus it seems to give a CAUSE to sickness which is NOT its cause. The PURPOSE of the gap is all the cause that sickness has. For it was made to keep you separated in a body which you see as if it were the CAUSE of pain. The cause of pain is separation, NOT the body, which is only its EFFECT. Yet separation is but empty space, enclosing nothing, doing nothing, and as unsubstantial as the vacant place between the ripples that a ship has made in passing by. And covered just as fast, as water rushes in to close the gap, and as the waves, in joining, cover it.

T 28 D 5. Where is the gap BETWEEN the waves, when they have joined, and covered up the space which seemed to keep them separate for a little while? T(977) - 803 - Where is the grounds for sickness, when the minds have joined to close the gap BETWEEN them, where the weeds of sickness seemed to grow? God builds the bridge, but only in the space left clean and vacant by the miracle. The seeds of sickness and the shame of sin He CANNOT bridge, for He cannot destroy the alien will that He created not. Let its effects be gone, and clutch them not with eager hands, to keep them for yourself. The miracle will brush them all aside, and thus make room for Him Who wills to come, and bridge His Son's returning to Himself.

T 28 D 6. Count, then, the silver miracles and golden dreams of happiness as all the treasures you would keep within the storehouse of the world. The door is open, NOT to thieves, but to your starving brothers, who mistook for gold a shining pebble, and who stored away a heap of snow that shone like silver.[898] They have nothing left behind the open door. What is the world except a little gap, perceived to tear eternity apart, and break it into days and months and years? And what are YOU who live within the world, except a picture of the Son of God in broken pieces, each concealed within a separate and uncertain bit of clay?

T 28 D 7. Be not afraid, but let your world be lit with miracles.[899] And where the gap was seen to stand BETWEEN you, join your brother there. And sickness will be seen WITHOUT a cause. The dream of healing in forgiveness lies, and gently shows you YOU have never sinned. The miracle would leave NO proof of guilt, to bring you witness to what never WAS. And, in your storehouse, it will make a place of welcome for your Father and your Self. The door is open, that all those may come who would no longer starve, and would enjoy the feast of plenty set before them there. And they will meet with your invited Guests the miracle has asked to come to you.[900]

---

[898] **Matthew 6:19** "Do not lay up for yourselves treasures on earth, where moth and rust destroy and where thieves break in and steal;"
[899] **John 6:20** But He said to them, "It is I; do not be afraid."
[900] **Luke 14:16-23** Then He said to him, "A certain man gave a great supper and invited many, and sent his servant at supper time to say to those who were invited, 'Come, for all things are now ready.' But they all with one accord began to make excuses. The first said to him, 'I have bought a piece of ground, and I must go and see it. I ask you to have me excused.' And another said, 'I have bought five yoke of oxen, and I am going to test them. I ask you to have me excused.' Still another said, 'I have married a wife, and therefore I cannot come.' So that servant came and reported these things to his master. Then the master of the house, being angry, said to his servant, 'Go out quickly into the streets and lanes of the city, and bring in here the poor and the maimed and the lame and the blind.' And the servant said, 'Master, it is done as you commanded, and still there is room.' Then the master said to the servant, 'Go out into the highways and hedges, and compel them to come in, that my house may be filled.

all its treasures to the Son of God, for whom they have been kept. How gladly does He offer them unto the one for whom He has been given them! And His Creator SHARES His thanks, because He would not be deprived of His effects. The instant's silence that His Son accepts gives welcome to eternity and Him, and lets them enter where they would abide. For in that instant does the Son of God do NOTHING that would make himself afraid. **T(971) -797**

T 28 B 11. How instantly the memory of God arises in the mind that has no fear to keep the memory away. Its own remembering has gone. There IS no past to keep its fearful image in the way of glad awakening to present peace. The trumpets of eternity resound throughout the stillness, yet disturb it not. And what is NOW remembered is not fear, but rather is the Cause that fear was made to render unremembered and undone. The stillness speaks in gentle sounds of love the Son of God remembers from BEFORE his own remembering came IN BETWEEN the present and the past, to shut them out.

T 28 B 12. Now is the Son of God at last aware of PRESENT Cause and Its benign effects. Now does he understand what he has made is causeless, making NO effects at all. He HAS done nothing. And, in seeing THIS, he understands he never had a NEED for doing ANYTHING, and never did. His Cause IS Its effects. There never WAS a cause besides It, that could generate a DIFFERENT past or future. ITS effects are changelessly eternal, BEYOND fear, and PAST the world of sin entirely. What has been lost to see the causeless NOT? And where is sacrifice, when memory of God has come to TAKE THE PLACE of loss?

T 28 B 13. What better way to close the little gap between illusions and reality than to allow the memory of God to flow ACROSS it, making it a bridge an instant will suffice to reach beyond? For God has closed it with Himself. His memory has NOT gone by, and left a stranded Son forever on a shore where he can glimpse ANOTHER shore which he can never reach. His Father wills that he be lifted up, and gently carried over. HE has built the bridge, and it is He Who will transport His Son across it. Have no fear that He will fail in what He wills. Nor that you be excluded from the Will that IS for you. **T(972) - 798 -**[897]

T 28 C. Reversing Effect and Cause (*Notes* 1947 12:82)

T 28 C 1. Without a cause there can be no effects, and yet, without effects, there is no CAUSE. The cause a cause is MADE by its effects; the Father IS a father by His Son. Effects do not CREATE their cause, but they ESTABLISH its causation. Thus the Son gives fatherhood to his Creator, and RECEIVES the gift that he has given Him. It is BECAUSE he is God's Son that he must ALSO be a father, who creates as God created him. The circle of creation has no end. Its starting and its ending are the same. But, in itself, it holds the universe of all creation, without beginning AND without an end.

T 28 C 2. Fatherhood is creation. Love MUST be extended. Purity is not confined. It is the NATURE of the innocent to be forever uncontained, without a barrier or limitation. Thus is purity NOT of the body. Nor can it be FOUND where limitation is. The body CAN be healed by its EFFECTS, which are as limitless as is itself. Yet must all healing come about because the mind is recognized as NOT within the body, and its innocence is quite APART from it, and where ALL healing IS. Where, then, is healing? ONLY where its cause is GIVEN its effects. For sickness is a meaningless attempt to give effects to causelessness, and MAKE it be a cause.

T 28 C 3. Always in sickness does the Son of God attempt to make himself his cause, and NOT allow himself to be his Father's Son. For this impossible desire, he does not believe that he is Love's EFFECTS, and must be cause BECAUSE of what he is. The cause of healing is the ONLY Cause of everything. It has but ONE effect.

---
[897] February 26, 1968.

And, in that recognition, causelessness is GIVEN no effects, and none are SEEN. A mind within a body, and a world of other bodies, each with SEPARATE minds, are your "creations," you the "other" mind, creating with effects UNLIKE yourself. And, AS their father, you must be like them.

T 28 C 4. Nothing at all has happened, but that you have put yourself to sleep, and dreamed a dream in which you were an alien to yourself, and but a part of someone ELSE's dream. The miracle does not awaken you, but merely shows you **T(973) - 799 -** who the DREAMER is. It teaches you there IS a choice of dreams while you are still asleep, depending on the PURPOSE of your dreaming. Do you wish for dreams of healing, or for dreams of death? A dream is like a memory, in that it pictures what you WANTED shown to you. An empty storehouse, with an open door, holds ALL your shreds of memories and dreams.

T 28 C 5. Yet, if you are the DREAMER, you perceive this much at least; that YOU have caused the dream, and can accept ANOTHER dream as well. But, for this change in content of the dream, it MUST be realized that it is YOU who dreamed the dreaming that you do not like. It is but an effect that YOU have caused, and you would not BE cause of this effect. In dreams of murder and attack are YOU the victim, in a dying body slain. But, in forgiving dreams, is NO-ONE asked to be the victim and the sufferer. These are the happy dreams the miracle exchanges for your own. It does NOT ask you make another. ONLY that you see you made the one you would EXCHANGE for this.

T 28 C 6. This world is CAUSELESS, as is every dream that anyone has dreamed within the world. No plans are possible, and no design exists that could be found and understood. What else could be EXPECTED from a thing that has no cause? But, if it HAS no cause, IT HAS NO PURPOSE. You may cause a dream, but never will you give it real EFFECTS. For that would change its CAUSE, and it is this you CANNOT do. The dreamer of a dream is NOT awake, but does NOT know he sleeps. He sees ILLUSIONS of himself as sick or well, depressed or happy, but without a stable cause with GUARANTEED effects.

T 28 C 7. The miracle establishes you dream a dream, and that its content is not true. This is a crucial step in dealing with illusions. No-one is AFRAID of them, when he perceives HE MADE THEM UP. The fear was held in place BECAUSE he did not see that he was AUTHOR of the dream, and not a figure IN the dream. He gives HIMSELF the consequences that he dreams he gave his brother. And it is but this the dream has put together and has offered him, to show him that his wishes have been done. Thus does he fear his OWN attack, but sees it at another's **T(974) - 800 -** hands. As victim, he is suffering from its effects, but NOT their cause. He authored NOT his own attack, and he is innocent of what he caused.

T 28 C 8. The miracle does nothing but to show him that HE has done nothing. What he fears is cause WITHOUT the consequences which would MAKE it cause. And so it never was. The separation started with the dream the Father was deprived of His effects, and powerless to keep them, since He was no longer their Creator. In the dream, the dreamer made HIMSELF, but what he made had turned AGAINST him, taking on the role of its creator, as the dreamer had. And, as he hated HIS Creator, so the figures in the dream have hated HIM. His body is their slave, which they abuse because the motives HE has given it have THEY adopted as their own. And hate it for the vengeance IT would offer THEM.

T 28 C 9. It is THEIR vengeance on the body which appears to prove the dreamer COULD not be the maker of the dream. Effect and cause are first split off, and then REVERSED, so that effect becomes a cause; the cause, effect. This is the separation's final step, with which salvation, which proceeds to go the OTHER way, begins. This final step is an effect of what has gone before, APPEARING as a cause. The miracle is the first step in giving BACK to cause the function of causation, NOT effect. For THIS confusion

Chapter 28 – The Undoing of Fear

T 28 A. Introduction (*Notes* 1936 12:71)

T 28 A 1. THE MIRACLE DOES NOTHING. All it does is to UNdo. And thus it cancels out the interference to what HAS BEEN done. It does not add, but merely takes away. And what it takes away is long since gone, but, being kept in memory, APPEARS to have immediate effects. This world was over long ago. The thoughts that made it are no longer in the mind that thought of them, and loved them for a while. The miracle but shows the past is gone, and what has truly gone HAS no effects. REMEMBERING a cause can but produce ILLUSIONS of its presence, NOT effects.

T 28 A 2. All the effects of guilt are here no more. For guilt is over. In its passing went its consequences, left without a cause. Why would you cling to it in memory, if you did not DESIRE its effects? Remembering is as selective as perception, being its past tense. It is perception of the past, as if it were occurring NOW, and still were there to see. Memory, like perception, is a skill made up by you, to take the place of what God GAVE in your creation. And, like all the things you made, it can be used to serve ANOTHER purpose, and to be means for something ELSE. It can be used to heal, and NOT to hurt, if you so wish.

T 28 A 3. Nothing employed for healing represents an effort to do anything at all. It is a recognition that you HAVE no needs which mean that something must be DONE. It is an unselective memory, which is NOT used to INTERFERE with truth. All things the Holy Spirit can employ for healing have been given Him WITHOUT the content and the purposes for which they have been made. They are but skills WITHOUT an application. They AWAIT their use. They have NO dedication and NO aim.[894]

T 28 B. The Present Memory (*Notes* 1937 12:72)

T 28 B 1. The Holy Spirit can indeed make use of memory, for God Himself is there. But this is NOT a memory of past events, but ONLY of a PRESENT state. **T(968) -794**

T 28 B 2. You are so long accustomed to believe that memory holds only what is past, that it is hard for you to realize it is a skill that CAN remember NOW. The limitations on remembering the world imposes on it are as vast as those you let the world impose on YOU. There IS no link of memory to the past. If YOU would have it there, then there IS. But ONLY your desire made the link, and ONLY you have held it to a part of time where guilt appears to linger still. The Holy Spirit's use of memory is quite APART from time. He does NOT seek to use it as a means to KEEP the past, but rather as a way TO LET IT GO.

T 28 B 3. Memory holds a message it receives, and does what it is GIVEN it to do. It does NOT write the message, nor appoint what it is FOR. Like to the body, it is purposeless within itself. And if it seems to serve to cherish ancient hate, and offer you the pictures of injustices and hurts that you were saving, this is what you asked its message BE, and this is what it IS. Committed to its vaults, the history of all the body's past is hidden there. All of the strange associations made to keep the past alive, the present dead, are stored within it, waiting your command that they be brought to you, and lived again. And thus do their effects appear to be INCREASED by time, which TOOK AWAY their cause.

T 28 B 4. Yet time is but another phase of what DOES NOTHING. It works hand in hand with all the other attributes with which you sought to keep concealed the truth about yourself. Time neither takes away, nor can restore. And yet you make strange use of it, as if the past had CAUSED the present, which is but a CONSEQUENCE, in which no change can be made possible, because its cause has GONE. And change must have a cause that will endure, or else it will not last. No change can be made in the present, if its cause is PAST. ONLY the past is held in memory, as you make use of it, and so it is a way to hold the past AGAINST the now. **T(969) - 795**

T 28 B 5. Remember NOTHING that you taught yourself, for you were badly taught. Who would keep a senseless lesson in his mind, when he can learn and can preserve a BETTER one? When ancient memories of hate appear, remember that their cause is gone. And so you CANNOT understand what they are FOR. Let not the cause that you would give them NOW be what it was that made them what they were, or seemed to be. Be GLAD that it is gone, for this is what you would be pardoned FROM. And see, instead, the NEW effects of cause accepted NOW, with consequences HERE.

T 28 B 6. They will surprise you with their loveliness. The ancient NEW ideas they bring will be the happy consequences of a cause[895] so ancient that it FAR exceeds the span of memory that your perception sees. This is the Cause the Holy Spirit has remembered FOR you, when you would forget. It is NOT past, because He let it not be unremembered. It has never changed, because there never was a time in which He did not keep it safely in your mind. Its consequences will indeed SEEM new, because you thought that you remembered not their Cause. Yet, was It NEVER absent from your mind, for it was NOT your Father's Will that He be unremembered by His only Son.

T 28 B 7. What YOU remember never WAS. It came from causelessness which you CONFUSED with cause. It CAN deserve but laughter, when you learn you have remembered consequences which were causeless, and could never BE effects. The miracle reminds you of a Cause forever present, perfectly untouched by time and interference. NEVER changed from what It IS. And YOU are Its effects, as changeless and as perfect as Itself. Its memory does NOT lie in the past, nor waits the[896] future. It is NOT revealed in miracles. They but remind you that It has not gone. When you forgive It for YOUR sins, It will no longer BE denied. **T(970) -796**

T 28 B 8. You who have sought to lay a judgment on your own Creator, cannot understand it is NOT He Who laid a judgment on His Son. You would DENY Him His effects, yet have they never BEEN denied. There WAS no time in which His Son could be condemned for what was causeless, and AGAINST His Will. What YOUR remembering would witness to, is but the fear of God. He has not DONE the thing you fear. No more have YOU. And so your innocence has NOT been lost. You need NO healing to be healed. In quietness, see in the miracle a lesson in allowing Cause to have Its OWN effects, and doing NOTHING that would interfere.

T 28 B 9. The miracle comes quietly into the mind that stops an instant, and is still. It reaches gently from that quiet time, and from the mind it healed in quiet then, to other minds to SHARE its quietness. And they will JOIN in doing nothing to prevent its radiant extension back into the Mind that caused ALL minds to be. Born out of sharing, there can BE no pause in time to cause the miracle delay in hastening to all unquiet minds, and bringing them an instant's stillness, when the memory of God returns to them. Their OWN remembering is quiet now, and what has come to take its place will not be wholly unremembered afterwards.

T 28 B 10. He to Whom time is given offers thanks for every quiet instant given Him. For in that instant is His memory allowed to offer

---

[894] 793 [split paragraph]

[895] The word "Cause" and the pronoun "It" referring to it should probably both be capitalized consistently. As you see, in the *Urtext* manuscript the capitalization is not consistent. It is not consistent in the *Notes* either.

[896] While the *Urtext* clearly has definite article "the" here, the *Notes* equally clearly has the indefinite article "a."

moved. Perhaps you come in tears, but hear Him say, "My brother, Holy Son of God, behold your idle dream, in which this could occur," and you will leave the holy instant with your laughter and your brother's JOINED with His. **T(965) -791**

T 27 I 10. The secret of salvation is but this: That YOU are doing this UNTO YOURSELF. No matter what the form of the attack, this STILL is true. Whoever takes the role of enemy and of attacker, STILL is this the truth. Whatever seems to be the cause of any pain and suffering you feel, this is STILL true. For you would not react at all to figures in a dream you knew that YOU were dreaming. Let them be as hateful and as vicious as they may, they COULD have no effect on you, unless you failed to recognize it is YOUR dream. This single lesson learned will set you free from suffering, WHATEVER form it takes.

T 27 I 11. The Holy Spirit will repeat this ONE inclusive lesson of deliverance, until it has been learned, REGARDLESS of the form of suffering that brings you pain. Whatever hurt you bring to Him, He will make answer with this very simple truth. For this one answer TAKES AWAY the cause of every form of sorrow and of pain. The form affects His answer not at all, for He would teach you but the SINGLE cause of all of them, no matter WHAT their form. And you will understand that miracles reflect the simple statement, "I have done this thing, and it is this I would undo."

T 27 I 12. Bring, then, all forms of suffering to Him Who knows that every one is like the rest. He sees NO differences where none exist, and He will teach you how each one is CAUSED. None has a DIFFERENT cause from all the rest, and ALL of them are easily undone by but a SINGLE lesson truly learned. Salvation is a secret you have kept but from yourself. The universe proclaims it so. But, to its witnesses, you pay no heed at all. For they attest the thing you do not WANT to know. They seem to keep it secret FROM you. Yet you need but learn you choose but NOT to listen, NOT to see.

T 27 I 13. How differently will you perceive the world, when this is recognized! When you forgive the world YOUR guilt, YOU will be free of it. Its innocence does NOT demand your guilt, nor does YOUR guiltlessness rest on ITS sins. This is the obvious, a secret kept from no-one but yourself. And it is this that has **T(966) -792** maintained you SEPARATE from the world, and kept your brother SEPARATE from you. Now need you but to learn that BOTH of you are innocent OR guilty. The one thing that is impossible is that you be UNLIKE each other; that they BOTH be true. This is the only secret yet to learn. And it will be NO secret you are healed. **T(967) -793**

---

[892] February 15, 1968

[893] February 19, 1968

friend. God willed he waken gently, and with joy. And GAVE him means to waken WITHOUT fear. Accept the dream He gave, INSTEAD of yours. It is NOT difficult to shift a dream, when once the dreamer has been recognized.

T 27 H 14. Rest in the Holy Spirit, and allow His gentle dreams to take the place of those you dreamed in terror, and in fear of death. He brings FORGIVING dreams, in which the choice is NOT who is the murderer, and who shall be the victim. In the dreams HE brings, there IS no murder, and there IS no death.[888] The dream of guilt is fading from your sight, although your eyes are closed. A smile has come to lighten up your sleeping face. The sleep is peaceful now, for these are happy dreams. Dream softly of your sinless brother, who unites with you in holy innocence. And, from THIS dream, the Lord of Heaven will Himself awaken His beloved Son.

T 27 H 15. Dream of your brother's kindnesses INSTEAD of dwelling in your dreams on his mistakes. Select his thoughtfulness to dream about, INSTEAD of counting up the hurts he gave. Forgive him his illusions, and give thanks to him for all the helpfulness he gave. And do not brush aside his many gifts, because he is not perfect in your dreams. He represents his Father, Whom you see as offering both life AND death to you. Brother, He gives BUT life, and what you see as gifts your brother offers REPRESENT the gifts you dream your Father gives to you. Let all your brother's gifts be seen in light of charity and kindness offered you. And let no pain disturb your dream of deep appreciation for his gifts to you. **T(962) -788**[889]

T 27 I. The "Hero" of the Dream (*Notes* 1925 12:60)

T 27 I 1. The body is the central figure in the dreaming of the world. There IS no dream without it, nor does it exist without the dream, in which it acts as if it were a person, to be seen and be believed. It takes the central place in every dream, which tells the story of how it was made by OTHER bodies, born into the world OUTSIDE the body, lives a little while, and dies, to be united in the dust with other bodies, dying like itself. In the brief time allotted it to live, it seeks for other bodies as its friends and enemies. Its safety is its main concern. Its comfort is its guiding rule. It tries to look for pleasure, and avoid the things that would be hurtful. Above all, it tries to teach itself its pains and joys are different, and CAN be told apart.

T 27 I 2. The dreaming of the world takes many forms, because the body seeks in many ways to PROVE it is autonomous and real. It puts things on itself that it has bought with little metal discs or paper strips the world proclaims as valuable and good. It works to get them, doing senseless things, and tosses them away for senseless things it does not NEED, and does not even WANT. It hires OTHER bodies, that they may protect it, and collect more senseless things that it can call its own. It looks about for special bodies which can SHARE its dream. Sometimes it dreams it is a conqueror of bodies weaker than itself. But in some phases of the dream, it is the slave of bodies which would hurt and torture it.

T 27 I 3. The body's serial adventures, from the time of birth to dying is the theme of every dream the world has ever had. The "hero" of this dream will never change, nor will its purpose. Though the dream itself takes many forms, and SEEMS to show a great variety of places and events wherein its "hero" finds itself, the dream has but ONE purpose, taught in many ways. This single lesson does it try to teach again, and still again, and yet once more; - that it is CAUSE and NOT effect. And YOU are ITS effect, and CANNOT be its cause. Thus are you NOT the dreamer, but the DREAM. And so you wander idly in and out of places and events that IT contrives.

T 27 I 4. That this is all the BODY does. is true. For it IS but a figure in a dream. But who REACTS to figures in a dream, UNLESS he sees them as if they were real? **T(963) -789**

The INSTANT that he sees them as they ARE, they HAVE no more effects on him BECAUSE he understands he GAVE them their effects BY CAUSING THEM, and MAKING them seem real. How willing are you to ESCAPE effects of all the dreams the world has ever had? Is it your wish to let NO dream appear to be the cause of what it is YOU do? Then let us merely look upon the dream's beginning, for the part you see is but the SECOND part, whose CAUSE lies in the first.

T 27 I 5. No-one asleep and dreaming in the world remembers his attack upon himself. No-one believes there really was a time when he knew nothing of a body, and could never have conceived this world as real. He would have seen at once that these ideas are one illusion, too ridiculous for anything but to be laughed away. How serious they now appear to be! And no-one can remember when they would have met with laughter and with disbelief. We CAN remember this, if we but look directly at their CAUSE. And we will see the grounds for laughter, NOT a cause for fear. Let us return the dream he gave away unto the dreamer, who perceives the dream as SEPARATE from himself, and done to him.

T 27 I 6. Into eternity, where all is one, there crept a tiny, mad idea, at which the Son of God remembered not to laugh. In his forgetting did the thought become a serious idea, and possible of both accomplishment and real effects. Together, we can laugh them BOTH away, and understand that time can NOT intrude upon eternity. It IS a joke to think that time can come to circumvent eternity, which MEANS there is no time. A timelessness in which is time made real; a Part of God Which can attack Itself; a separate brother as an enemy; a mind WITHIN a body; all are forms of circularity, whose ending starts at its beginning, ending at its cause.

T 27 I 7. The world you see depicts EXACTLY what you thought YOU did. Except that NOW you think that what you did is being done to YOU. The guilt for what YOU thought is being placed OUTSIDE yourself, and on a guilty world which dreams your dreams, and thinks your thoughts INSTEAD of you. It brings ITS vengeance, not your own. IT keeps you narrowly confined within a body, which it punishes because of all the sinful things the body does within ITS dream. You have NO power to make the body stop its evil deeds, because you did NOT make it, and can NOT **T(964) - 790** control its actions, or its purpose, or its fate.

T 27 I 8. The world but demonstrates an ancient truth; -[890] you WILL believe that others do to you EXACTLY what you think you did to them.[891] But, once deluded into blaming THEM, you will not see the CAUSE of what they do BECAUSE you want the guilt to rest on them. How childish is this petulant device to keep your innocence by pushing guilt OUTSIDE yourself, but NEVER letting go! It is not easy to perceive the jest, when all around you do your eyes behold its heavy consequences, but WITHOUT their trifling cause. Without the cause do its effects seem serious and sad indeed. Yet they but follow. And it is their CAUSE which follows nothing, and is but a jest.

T 27 I 9. In gentle laughter does the Holy Spirit perceive the cause, and looks NOT to effects. How else could He correct YOUR error, who have OVERLOOKED the cause entirely? He bids you bring each terrible effect to Him, that you may look TOGETHER on its foolish cause, and laugh with Him a while. YOU judge effects, but HE has judged their CAUSE. And by His judgment are effects re-

---

[888] **2 Timothy 1:10** But has now been revealed by the appearing of our Savior Jesus Christ, who has abolished death and brought life and immortality to light through the gospel,
Revelation 21:4 And God will wipe away every tear from their eyes; there shall be no more death, nor sorrow, nor crying. There shall be no more pain, for the former things have passed away."
[889] February 14, 1968.

[890] The *Urtext* manuscript has a hyphen here, the *Notes* doesn't.
[891] **Matthew 7:12** "Therefore, whatever you want men to do to you, do also to them, for this is the Law and the Prophets."

himself attacked unjustly, and by something NOT himself. HE is the victim of this "something else," a thing OUTSIDE himself for which he has no reason to be held responsible. He must be innocent BECAUSE he knows not what HE does, but what is done TO him. Yet is his own attack upon himself apparent still, for it is he who bears the suffering. And he can NOT escape BECAUSE its source is seen outside himself.

T 27 H 2. Now you are being shown you CAN escape. All that is needed is you look upon the problem as it IS, and NOT the way that you have set it up. How COULD there be another way to solve a problem which is VERY simple, but has been obscured by heavy clouds of complication, which were MADE to keep the problem unresolved? WITHOUT the clouds, the problem will emerge in all its primitive simplicity. The choice will NOT be difficult, because the problem is absurd when clearly seen. No-one has difficulty making up his mind to let a simple problem be resolved, if it is SEEN as hurting him, and also very easily removed.

T 27 H 3. The "reasoning" by which the world is made, on which it rests, by which it is maintained, is simply this: "YOU are the cause of what I do. Your presence JUSTIFIES my wrath, and you exist and think APART from me. While YOU attack, I MUST be innocent. And what I suffer from IS your attack." No-one who looks upon this "reasoning" EXACTLY as it is could fail to see it does NOT follow, and it makes NO sense. Yet it SEEMS sensible, because it LOOKS as if the world WERE hurting you. And so it seems as if there is no NEED to go beyond the obvious in terms of cause. **T(958) -784**

T 27 H 4. There is INDEED a need. The world's ESCAPE from condemnation is a need which those WITHIN the world are joined in sharing. Yet they do not recognize their common need. For each one thinks that, if he does his part, the condemnation of the world will rest on him. And it is this that he perceives to BE his part in its deliverance. Vengeance must have a focus. Otherwise, is the avenger's knife in his own hand, and pointed to himself. And he MUST see it in ANOTHER hand, if he would be a victim of attack he did NOT choose. And thus he suffers from the wounds a knife he does NOT hold has made upon himself.

T 27 H 5. This is the PURPOSE of the world he sees. And, LOOKED AT thus, the world provides the means by which this purpose SEEMS to be fulfilled. The means ATTEST the purpose, but are NOT themselves a cause. Nor will the CAUSE be changed by seeing it APART from its effects. The cause PRODUCES the effects, which then bear witness to the CAUSE, and NOT themselves. Look, then, BEYOND effects. It is NOT here the CAUSE of suffering and sin must lie. And dwell not on the suffering and sin, for they are but REFLECTIONS of their cause. The part you play in SALVAGING the world from condemnation IS your own escape.

T 27 H 6. Forget not that the witness to the world of evil cannot speak EXCEPT for what has seen a NEED for evil in the world. And this is where YOUR guilt was first beheld. In separation from your brother was the first attack upon yourself begun. And it is THIS the world bears witness to. Seek not another cause, nor look among the mighty legions of its witnesses for its undoing. They SUPPORT its claim on your allegiance. What CONCEALS the truth is not where you should look to FIND the truth. The witnesses to sin all stand within ONE little space. And it is HERE you find the CAUSE of your perspective on the world. **T(959) - 785 -**[886]

T 27 H 7. Once you were unaware of what the cause of everything the world appeared to thrust upon you, uninvited and unasked, must REALLY be. Of one thing you were sure; of all the many causes you perceived as bringing pain and suffering to you, your guilt was NOT among them. Nor did you, in ANY way, REQUEST them for yourself. This is how ALL illusions come about. The one who makes them does NOT see himself as making them, and their reality does NOT depend on him. Whatever cause they have is something quite APART from him, and what he sees is SEPARATE from his mind.

T 27 H 8. He CANNOT doubt his dreams' reality BECAUSE he does not see the part he plays in MAKING them, and MAKING them seem real. No-one can waken from a dream the world is dreaming FOR him. He becomes a part of someone ELSE's dream. He CANNOT choose to waken from a dream he did not make. Helpless he stands, a victim to a dream conceived and cherished by a SEPARATE mind. Careless indeed of him this mind must be, as thoughtless of his peace and happiness as is the weather, or the time of day. It loves him not, but casts him as it will, in any role that satisfies its dream.

T 27 H 9. So little is his worth that he is but a dancing shadow, leaping up and down, according to a senseless plot conceived within the idle dreaming of the world. This is the ONLY picture you can see, the ONE alternative that you can choose, the OTHER possibility of cause, if you be NOT the dreamer of your dreams. And this IS what you choose, if you deny the cause of suffering is in YOUR mind. Be glad indeed it is, for thus are YOU the ONE decider of your destiny in time. The choice IS yours to make between a sleeping death and dreams of evil, or a happy wakening and joy of life. **T(960) -786**

T 27 H 10. What COULD you choose between, but life or death, waking or sleeping, war or peace, your dream or your reality? But if the choice is REALLY given you, then you must see the causes of the things you choose BETWEEN exactly AS they are and WHERE they are. What choices can be made between two states, but ONE of which is clearly recognized? Who could be free to choose BETWEEN effects, when only ONE is seen as up to you? An honest choice could NEVER be perceived as one in which the choice is split between a tiny you and an enormous world, with DIFFERENT dreams about the truth in you.

T 27 H 11. The gap between reality and dreams lies not between the dreaming of the world and what you dream in secret. THEY are one. The dreaming of the world is but a part of your own dream you gave away, and saw as if it were its start and ending, both. Yet was it started by your SECRET dream, which you do NOT perceive, although it CAUSE the part you see and do not doubt is real. How COULD you doubt it, while you lie asleep, and dream in secret that its CAUSE is real? A brother SEPARATED from yourself, an ancient enemy, a murderer who stalks you in the night and plots your death, yet plans that it be lingering and slow, –[887]

T 27 H 12. Of this you dream. And, UNDERNEATH this dream, is yet another, in which YOU become the murderer, the secret enemy, the scavenger and the destroyer of the brother and the world you fear alike. Here is the CAUSE of suffering, the space BETWEEN your dreams and your reality. The little gap you do not even see, the birthplace of illusions and of fear, the time of terror and of ancient hate, the instant of disaster; -- all are here. Here is the CAUSE of unreality. And it is here that it will be undone. YOU are the dreamer of the world of dreams. No OTHER cause it has, nor ever will. **T(961) -787**

T 27 H 13. Nothing more fearful than an idle dream has terrified God's Son, and made him think that he has lost his innocence, denied his Father, and made war upon himself. So fearful is the dream, so seeming real, he could not waken to reality without the sweat of terror and a scream of mortal fear, unless a gentler dream preceded his awaking, and allowed his calmer mind to welcome, NOT to fear, the Voice that called with love to waken him. A gentler dream, in which his suffering was healed, and where his brother was his

---

[886] February 12, 1968.

[887] This is a very curious paragraph break in the *Urtext* manuscript. The *Notes* has no paragraph break here, just an em dash. The *HLC* and *FIP* simply use a semicolon, which seems more appropriate.

T 27 F 10. Peace be to you whom is healing offered.[880] And you will learn that peace is given you, when you accept the healing for yourself. Its TOTAL value need not be appraised by YOU, to let you understand that you have benefited from it. What occurred within the instant which love entered in WITHOUT attack, will stay with you forever. YOUR healing will be ONE of its effects, as will your brother's. Everywhere you go, will you behold its multiplied effects. Yet all the witnesses that you behold will be FAR less than all there really ARE. Infinity cannot be understood by merely counting up the separate parts. God thanks you for your healing, for He knows it is a gift of love unto His Son, and therefore is it given unto Him. T(954) -780[881]

T 27 G. The Purpose of Pain (*Notes* 1909 12:44)

T 27 G 1. Pain demonstrates the body must be real. It is a loud, obscuring voice, whose shrieks would silence what the Holy Spirit says, and keep His words from your awareness. Pain compels attention, drawing it away from Him, and focusing upon itself. Its purpose is the same as pleasure, for they both are means TO MAKE THE BODY REAL. What shares a common function IS the same. This is the law of purpose, which unites all those who share in it within itself. Pleasure and pain are EQUALLY unreal, because their purpose CANNOT be achieved. Thus are they means for nothing, for they have a goal without a meaning. And they share the lack of meaning that their PURPOSE has.

T 27 G 2. Sin shifts from pain to pleasure, and again to pain. For EITHER witness is the same, and carries but one message, "You are here, WITHIN this body, and you CAN be hurt. You can have pleasure, too, but ONLY at the cost of pain." These witnesses are joined by many more. Each one SEEMS different, because it has a different NAME, and so it seems to answer to a different SOUND. Except for this, the witnesses of sin are all alike. Call pleasure "pain," and it will hurt. Call pain pleasure, and the pain BEHIND the pleasure will be felt no more. Sin's witnesses but shift from name to name, as one steps forward, and another, back. Yet which is foremost makes NO difference. Sin's witnesses hear but the call of death.[882]

T 27 G 3. This body, purposeless within itself, holds all your memories and all your hopes. You use its eyes to see, its ears to hear, and let it TELL you what it is it feels. IT DOES NOT KNOW. It tells you but the NAMES you gave it to use, when YOU call forth the T(955) -781 witnesses to its reality. You cannot choose AMONG them which are real, for any one you choose is like the rest. This name or that, but nothing more, you choose. You do not MAKE a witness true, because you called him by truth's NAME. The truth is found in him IF IT IS TRUTH HE REPRESENTS.[883] And otherwise he lies, if you should call him by the Holy Name of God Himself.

T 27 G 4. God's Witness sees no witnesses AGAINST the body. Neither does He harken to the witnesses by OTHER names, which speak in OTHER ways for its reality. He KNOWS it is not real. For NOTHING could contain what you believe it holds within. Nor COULD it tell a Part of God Himself what It should feel, and what Its Function is. Yet must He love whatever YOU hold dear. And for each witness to the body's death, He sends a witness to your Life in Him Who knows no death. Each miracle He brings is witness that the body is NOT real. Its pains and pleasures does He heal alike, for ALL sin's witnesses do His replace.

T 27 G 5. The miracle makes NO distinctions in the names by which sin's witnesses are called. It merely proves that what they REPRESENT has no effects. And this it proves BECAUSE its own effects have come to take their place. It matters not the name by which you called your suffering. IT IS NO LONGER THERE. The One Who brings the miracle perceived them all as one, and called by name of "fear." As fear is witness unto death, so is the miracle the witness unto Life. It is a witness no-one can deny, for it is the EFFECTS of life it brings. The dying live, the dead arise, and pain has vanished.[884] Yet a miracle speaks not but for itself, but what it REPRESENTS. Love, too, has symbols in a world of sin. The miracle forgives BECAUSE T(956) -782 it stands for what is PAST forgiveness, and is TRUE.

T 27 G 6. How foolish and insane it is to think a miracle is BOUND by laws which it came solely to UNDO. The laws of SIN have different witnesses, with different strengths. And THEY attest to different suffering. Yet to the One Who sends forth miracles to bless the world, a tiny stab of pain, a little worldly pleasure, and the throes of death itself are but a single sound; a call for healing, and a plaintive cry for help within a world of misery. It is their SAMENESS that the miracle attests. It is their SAMENESS that it PROVES. The laws which call them DIFFERENT are dissolved, and SHOWN as powerless. The PURPOSE of a miracle is to accomplish this. And God Himself has GUARANTEED the strength of miracles for what they witness TO.

T 27 G 7. Be witnesses unto the miracle, and NOT the laws of sin. There is no NEED to suffer any more. But there IS need that you be healed, because the suffering of the world has made it deaf to its salvation and deliverance. The resurrection of the world awaits YOUR healing and YOUR happiness, that you may DEMONSTRATE the healing of the world. The holy instant will replace ALL sin, if you but carry its effects with you. And no-one will ELECT to suffer more. What better function COULD you serve than this? Be healed that you may heal, and suffer not the laws of sin to be applied to YOU. And Truth WILL be revealed to you who chose to let Love's symbols TAKE THE PLACE of sin. T(957) -783[885]

T 27 H. The Illusion of Suffering (*Notes* 1914 12:49)

T 27 H 1. Suffering is an emphasis upon all that the world has done to injure YOU. Here is the world's demented version of salvation clearly shown. Like to a dream of punishment, in which the dreamer is unconscious of what brought on the attack against himself, he sees

---

[880] **John 20:26** And after eight days His disciples were again inside, and Thomas with them. Jesus came, the doors being shut, and stood in the midst, and said, "Peace to you!"
[881] Feb. 4, 1968
[882] **Romans 6:23** For the wages of sin is death, but the gift of God is eternal life in Christ Jesus our Lord.
[883] **John 18:37** Pilate therefore said to Him, "Are You a king then?" Jesus answered, "You say rightly that I am a king. For this cause I was born, and for this cause I have come into the world, that I should bear witness to the truth. Everyone who is of the truth hears My voice."

[884] **Ezekiel 37:3-6** And he said unto me, Son of man, can these bones live? And I answered, O Lord GOD, thou knowest. Again he said unto me, Prophesy over these bones, and say unto them, O ye dry bones, hear the word of the LORD. Thus saith the Lord GOD unto these bones: Behold, I will cause breath to enter into you, and ye shall live. And I will lay sinews upon you, and will bring up flesh upon you, and cover you with skin, and put breath in you, and ye shall live; and ye shall know that I am the LORD.
Isaiah 26:19 Your dead shall live; Together with my dead body they shall arise. Awake and sing, you who dwell in dust; For your dew is like the dew of herbs, And the earth shall cast out the dead.
Isaiah 35:5-6 Then the eyes of the blind shall be opened, And the ears of the deaf shall be unstopped. Then the lame shall leap like a deer, And the tongue of the dumb sing. For waters shall burst forth in the wilderness, And streams in the desert.
Matthew 10:1 And when He had called His twelve disciples to Him, He gave them power over unclean spirits, to cast them out, and to heal all kinds of sickness and all kinds of disease.
Matthew 10:8 "Heal the sick, cleanse the lepers, raise the dead, cast out demons. Freely you have received, freely give."
Matthew 11:5 "The blind see and the lame walk; the lepers are cleansed and the deaf hear; the dead are raised up and the poor have the gospel preached to them."
[885] February 9, 1968

T 27 E 6. Only within the Holy Instant can an honest question honestly be asked. And from the meaning of the QUESTION does the meaningfulness of the answer come. Here is it possible to separate your wishes FROM the answer, so it can be GIVEN you, and also be RECEIVED. The answer is provided everywhere, but it is only here it can be HEARD. An honest answer asks NO sacrifice, because it answers questions truly asked. The questions of the world but ask of whom is sacrifice demanded, asking NOT if sacrifice is meaningful at all. And so, UNLESS the answer tells "of whom," it will remain unrecognized, unheard, and thus the QUESTION is preserved intact, because it gave the answer to ITSELF. T(949) -775

T 27 E 7. The Holy Instant is the interval in which the mind is still enough to hear an answer that is NOT entailed within the question asked. It offers something new and DIFFERENT from the question. How COULD it be answered, if it but repeats itself. Therefore, attempt to solve NO problem in a world from which the answer has been barred. But bring the problem to the only place which holds the answer lovingly FOR you. Here are the answers which will SOLVE your problems, because they stand APART from them, and see what CAN be answered; what the QUESTION is. Within the world, the answers merely raise ANOTHER question, though they leave the first unanswered. In the holy instant, you can bring the question TO the answer, and receive the answer that was MADE for you. T(950) -776[878]

T 27 F. The Healing Example (*Notes* 1901 12:36)

T 27 F 1. The ONLY way to heal is to be healed. The miracle extends WITHOUT your help. But you ARE needed that it can BEGIN. ACCEPT the miracle of healing, and it WILL go forth, because of what it IS. It is its NATURE to extend itself the instant it is born. And it is born the instant it is offered and RECEIVED. No-one can ask ANOTHER to be healed. But he can let HIMSELF be healed, and thus offer the other what he has received. Who can bestow upon another what he does not HAVE? And who can SHARE what he denies HIMSELF? The Holy Spirit speaks to YOU. He does not speak to someone ELSE. Yet BY your listening, His Voice extends, BECAUSE you have accepted what He says.

T 27 F 2. Health is the witness unto health. As long as it is unattested, it remains without conviction. Only when DEMONSTRATED has it BEEN proved, and MUST compel belief. No-one is healed through double messages. If you wish ONLY to be healed, you heal. Your single PURPOSE makes this possible. But if you are AFRAID of healing, then it cannot come through you. The ONLY thing that is required for a healing is a lack of fear. The fearful are NOT healed, and cannot heal. This does NOT mean the conflict must be gone forever from your mind. For if it were, there were no NEED for healing any more. But it DOES mean, if only for an instant, you love without attack. An instant is sufficient. Miracles wait not on time.

T 27 F 3. The holy instant is the miracle's abiding-place. From there, each one is born into this world, as witness to a state of mind which has TRANSCENDED conflict, and has reached to peace. It carries comfort from the place of peace into the battleground, and DEMONSTRATES that war has no effects. For all the hurt that war has sought to bring; the broken bodies and the shattered limbs, the screaming dying and the silent dead, are gently lifted up and comforted. There IS no sadness, where a miracle has come to heal. And nothing more than just ONE instant of your love WITHOUT attack is necessary, that all this occur. T(951) -777

T 27 F 4. In that ONE instant are YOU healed, and in that single instant is ALL healing done. What stands APART from you, when you accept the blessing that the holy instant brings? Be not afraid of blessing for the One Who blesses you loves all the world, and leaves nothing within the world that COULD be feared.[879] But if you SHRINK from blessing, will the world indeed seem fearful, for you have WITHHELD its peace and comfort, leaving it to die. Would not a world so bitterly bereft be looked on as a condemnation by the one who COULD have saved it, but stepped back, because he was AFRAID of being healed? The eyes of all the dying bring reproach, and suffering whispers, "What is there to fear?"

T 27 F 5. Consider well its question. It is asked of you on YOUR behalf. A dying world asks only that you rest an instant from attack upon YOURSELF, that it be healed. Come to the holy instant and be healed, for nothing that is there received is left behind, on your returning to the world. And BEING blessed, you will bring blessing. Life is given you, to give the dying world. And suffering eyes no longer will accuse, but shine in thanks to you who blessing gave. The holy instant's radiance will light YOUR eyes, and give them sight to see beyond ALL suffering, and see Christ's Face INSTEAD. Healing REPLACES suffering. Who looks on one cannot PERCEIVE the other, for they CANNOT both be there. And what YOU see the world will witness, and will witness TO.

T 27 F 6. Thus is YOUR healing everything the world requires, that it may be healed. It needs ONE lesson that has perfectly been learned. And then, when YOU forget it, will the world remind you gently of what you have taught. No reinforcement will its thanks withhold from you who let yourselves be healed, that it might live. It will call forth its witnesses to show the Face of Christ to you who brought the sight to THEM, by which THEY witnessed it. The world of accusation is replaced by one in which all eyes look lovingly upon the T(952) -778 friend who brought them their release. And happily your brother will perceive the many friends he thought were enemies.

T 27 F 7. Problems are not specific, but they take specific forms, and these specific shapes make up the world. And no-one understands the nature of his problem. If he DID, it would be there no more for him to see. Its very NATURE is that it is NOT. And thus, WHILE he perceives it, he can NOT perceive it as it is. But HEALING is apparent in specific instances, and generalizes to include them all. This is because they really ARE the same, DESPITE their different forms. All learning aims at transfer, which becomes complete within two situations which are seen as one. For ONLY common elements are there. But this can only be attained by One Who does not see the DIFFERENCES you see.

T 27 F 8. The total transfer of your learning is NOT made by you. But that it HAS been made, IN SPITE of all the differences you see, convinces YOU that they could not be real. Your healing WILL extend, and WILL be brought to problems that you thought were NOT your own. And it will ALSO be apparent that your many DIFFERENT problems will be solved, as any ONE of them has been escaped. It CANNOT be their differences which made this possible, for learning does not jump from situations to their opposites, and bring the SAME effects. All healing MUST proceed in lawful manner, in accord with laws that have been properly perceived, but NEVER violated. Fear you not the way that YOU perceive them. You ARE wrong, but there is One within you Who is RIGHT.

T 27 F 9. Leave, then, the transfer of your learning to the One Who REALLY understands its laws, and Who will GUARANTEE that they remain unviolated and unlimited. Your part is merely to apply what He has taught you TO YOURSELF, and He will do the rest. And thus the power of your learning will be PROVED to you, by all the many DIFFERENT witnesses it finds. Your brother FIRST among them will be seen, but thousands stand behind him, and beyond each one of them there are a thousand more. Each one may SEEM to have a problem which is DIFFERENT T(953) -779 from the rest. Yet they are solved TOGETHER. And their common Answer shows the QUESTIONS could not have been separate.

---

[878] Feb. 1, 1968

[879] **John 6:20** But He said to them, "It is I; do not be afraid."

T 27 D 2. You have decided that your brother IS a symbol for a "hateful-love," a "weakened-power," and, above all, a "living-death." And so he has NO meaning to you, for he stands for what is meaningless. He represents a double thought, where half is cancelled out by the remaining half. Yet even this is quickly contradicted by the half it cancelled out, and so they BOTH are gone. And now he stands for nothing. Symbols which but represent ideas that cannot BE, must stand for empty space and nothingness. Yet nothingness and empty space can NOT be interference. What CAN interfere with the awareness of reality is the belief that there is SOMETHING THERE.

T 27 D 3. The picture of your brother that you see means nothing. There is nothing to attack or to deny; to love or hate, or to endow with power or to see as weak. The picture has been wholly cancelled out, because it symbolized a contradiction which cancelled out the THOUGHT it represents. And thus the picture has no cause at all. Who can perceive effect WITHOUT a cause? What can the causeless BE but nothingness. The picture of your brother that you see is wholly absent, and has never been. Let, then, the empty space it occupies be RECOGNIZED as vacant, and the time devoted to its seeing be perceived as idly spent, a time unoccupied. **T(945) -771**

T 27 D 4. An empty space that is NOT seen as filled, an unused interval of time NOT seen as spent and fully occupied, become a silent invitation to the truth to enter, and to make Itself at home. No preparation CAN be made that would enhance the invitation's real appeal. For what you leave as vacant GOD will fill, and where HE is, there MUST the truth abide. Unweakened Power, with NO opposite, is what creation IS. For this there are NO symbols. Nothing points BEYOND the truth, and what can stand for MORE than everything? Yet true undoing must be kind, and so the first replacement for your picture is ANOTHER picture, of ANOTHER kind.

T 27 D 5. As nothingness can not BE pictured, so there IS no symbol for totality. Reality is ultimately known WITHOUT a form, unpictured and unseen. Forgiveness is not yet a Power known as wholly free of limits. Yet it sets no limits YOU have chosen to impose. Forgiveness is the means by which the truth is represented TEMPORARILY. It lets the Holy Spirit make EXCHANGE of pictures possible, until the time when aids are meaningless, and learning done. No learning aid has use which can extend BEYOND the goal of learning. When its aim HAS BEEN accomplished, it is functionless. Yet, in the learning interval, it HAS a use which now you fear, but yet will love.

T 27 D 6. The picture of your brother GIVEN you to occupy the space so lately left unoccupied and vacant, will not need defense of ANY kind. For you will give it OVERWHELMING preference. Nor delay an instant in deciding that it is the ONLY one you want. It does NOT stand for double concepts. Though it is but HALF the picture, and IS incomplete, WITHIN itself it is the same. The other half of what it represents remains unknown, but is NOT cancelled out. And thus is God left free to take the final step Himself. For this you need NO pictures and NO learning aids. And what will ultimately take the place of EVERY learning aid will merely BE. **T(946) -772**

T 27 D 7. Forgiveness vanishes and symbols fade, and nothing that the eyes have ever seen, or ears have heard, remains to be perceived.[876] A Power wholly limitless has come, NOT to destroy, but to RECEIVE Its Own. There is no CHOICE of function anywhere.

---

[876] **1 Corinthians 2:9** For since the beginning of the world
Men have not heard nor perceived by the ear,
Nor has the eye seen any God besides You,
Who acts for the one who waits for Him. Isaiah 64:4
But as it is written:
"Eye has not seen, nor ear heard,
Nor have entered into the heart of man
The things which God has prepared for those who love Him."

The choice you fear to lose you never HAD. Yet only this APPEARS to interfere with power unlimited and SINGLE thoughts, complete and happy, WITHOUT opposite. You do not know the peace of power which opposes NOTHING. Yet no OTHER kind can be at all. Give welcome to the Power beyond forgiveness, and beyond the world of symbols and of limitations. He would merely BE, and so He merely IS. **T(947) -773**[877]

T 27 E. The Quiet Answer (*Notes* 1896 12:31)

T 27 E 1. In quietness are all things answered, and is every problem quietly resolved. In conflict there can BE no answer and no resolution. For its PURPOSE is to make NO resolution possible, and to ensure NO answer will be plain. A problem set in conflict HAS no answer, for it is seen in different ways. And what would be an answer from one point of view is NOT an answer in another light. You ARE in conflict. Thus it must be clear you cannot answer anything at all, for conflict HAS no limited effects. Yet, if God gave an Answer, there MUST be a way in which your problems are resolved, for what He wills already has been done.

T 27 E 2. Thus it MUST be that time is not involved, and every problem can be answered now. Yet it must also be that in your state of mind, solution is impossible. Therefore, God must have given you a way of reaching to ANOTHER state of mind, in which the answer is ALREADY THERE. Such is the Holy Instant. It is here that ALL your problems should be brought and LEFT. Here they BELONG, for here THEIR answer is. And where its answer is, a problem MUST be simple and be easily resolved. It MUST be pointless to attempt to solve a problem where the answer cannot be. Yet, just as surely, it MUST be resolved, if it is brought to where the answer IS.

T 27 E 3. Attempt to solve NO problems but within the Holy Instant's surety. For there the problem WILL be answered and resolved. Outside, there will be no solution, for there IS no answer there that could be found. Nowhere outside a single simple question is ever ASKED. The world can ONLY ask a double question, with MANY answers, none of which will do. It does not ask a question to BE answered, but only to restate its point of view. All questions asked within this world are but a way of LOOKING, NOT a question asked. A question asked in hate cannot be answered, because it IS an answer in itself. A double question asks and answers, both attesting the same thing, in different form. **T(948) -774**

T 27 E 4. The world asks but one question. It is this: "Of these illusions, which of them are true? Which ones establish peace and offer joy? And which can bring escape from all the pain of which this world is made?" Whatever form the question takes, its purpose is the same. It asks but to ESTABLISH sin is real, and answers in the form of preference. "Which sin do you prefer?" That is the one that you should choose. The OTHERS are not true. What can the body get that you would want the most of all? It is your servant and your friend. But tell it what you want, and it will serve you lovingly and well. And this is NOT a question, for it TELLS you WHAT you want, and WHERE to go to ask for it. It leaves no room to question its beliefs, except that what it states takes question's FORM.

T 27 E 5. A pseudo-question has no answer. It DICTATES the answer, even as it asks. Thus is all questioning within the world a form of propaganda for itself. Just as the body's witnesses are but the senses from WITHIN itself, so are the answers to the questions of the world contained within the questions. Where answers represent the QUESTIONS they add nothing new, and nothing has been learned. An HONEST question is a learning tool which asks for something that you do NOT know. It does NOT set conditions for response, but merely asks what the RESPONSE should be. And no-one in a conflict state is free to ASK this question, for he does not WANT an honest answer, where the conflict ENDS.

---

[877] January 30, 1968

CAUSE you wished him well. This is the law the miracle obeys; That healing sees no specialness at all. It does NOT come from pity, but from love. And love would prove ALL suffering is but a vain imagining, a foolish wish, with NO effects. Your health is a result of your desire to see your brother with no blood upon his hands,[872] nor guilt upon his heart made heavy with the proof of sin. And what you wish is GIVEN you to see.

T 27 C 8. The "cost" of your serenity is his. This is the "price" the Holy Spirit and the world interpret differently. The world perceives in it a statement of the "fact" that your salvation SACRIFICES his. The Holy Spirit knows YOUR healing is the witness UNTO his, and CANNOT be apart from him at all. As long as he consents to suffer, YOU will be unhealed. But you can show him his suffering is purposeless and wholly without cause. Show him YOUR healing, and he will consent no more to suffer. For his innocence HAS BEEN established in your sight AND his. And laughter will REPLACE your sighs BECAUSE God's Son remembered that he IS God's Son.

T 27 C 9. Who, then, fears healing? Only those to whom their brother's sacrifice and pain is seen to represent their own serenity. Their helplessness and weakness represent grounds on which they justify his pain. The constant sting of guilt he suffers serves to prove that he is slave, and they are free. The constant pain THEY suffer demonstrates that they are free BECAUSE they hold him bound. And sickness is desired to prevent a shift of balance in the sacrifice. How could the Holy Spirit be deterred an instant, even less, to reason with an argument for sickness such as this? And need YOUR healing be delayed because you pause to listen to insanity? **T(941) - 767**[873]

T 27 C 10. Correction is NOT your function. It belongs to One Who knows of fairness, NOT of guilt. If you assume correction's role, you LOSE the function of forgiveness. No-one can forgive until he learns correction is BUT to forgive, and NEVER to accuse. Alone, you CANNOT see they are the same, and therefore is correction NOT of you. Identity and function are the same, and BY your function do you know yourself. And thus, if you confuse your function with the function of Another, you MUST be confused about yourself and who you are. What is the separation but a wish to take God's Function from Him and DENY that it is His? Yet if it is NOT His it is not YOURS, for YOU must lose what you would take away.

T 27 C 11. In a split mind, identity MUST seem to be divided. Nor can anyone perceive a function unified which has conflicting purposes and different ends. Correction, to a mind so split, MUST be a way to punish sins you think are YOURS in someone else. And thus does he become your victim, NOT your brother, DIFFERENT from you in that he is MORE GUILTY, thus in need of your correction, as the one MORE INNOCENT than he. This splits HIS function off from yours, and gives you both a DIFFERENT role. And so you CANNOT be perceived as one, and with a single function that would MEAN a shared identity with but ONE end.

T 27 C 12. Correction YOU would do MUST separate, because that is the function given it BY you. When you perceive correction is the SAME as pardon, then you also know the Holy Spirit's Mind and yours are One. And so your OWN identity is found. Yet must He work with what is GIVEN Him, and you allow Him only HALF your mind. And thus He represents the OTHER half, and seems to have a DIFFERENT purpose from the one you cherish, and you THINK is yours. Thus does your function seem DIVIDED, with a half IN OPPOSITION to a half. And these two halves appear to represent a split within a self perceived as two. **T(942) -768**

T 27 C 13. Consider how this self perception MUST extend, and do not overlook the fact that EVERY thought extends, because that is its purpose, being what it really IS. From an idea of self AS TWO, there comes a NECESSARY view of function split BETWEEN the two. And what you would correct is only HALF the error, which you think is ALL of it. Your BROTHER's sins become the central target for correction, lest your errors and his own be seen as one. YOURS are mistakes, but HIS are sins, and NOT the same as yours. HIS merit punishment, while yours, in fairness, should be overlooked.

T 27 C 14. In THIS interpretation of correction, your own mistakes you will not even SEE. The FOCUS of correction has been placed OUTSIDE yourself, on one who CANNOT be a part of you while this perception lasts. What is condemned can never be returned to its accuser, who has hated it, AND HATES IT STILL. This is your brother, focus of your hate, unworthy to be part of you, and thus OUTSIDE your self, the other half, which is denied. Only what is left, WITHOUT his presence, is perceived as ALL of you. To this remaining half the Holy Spirit must represent the OTHER half, until you recognize it IS the other half. And this He does by giving BOTH of you a function that is one, NOT different.

T 27 C 15. Correction IS the function given both, but neither one alone. And when it is fulfilled as SHARED, it MUST correct mistakes in both of you. It CANNOT leave mistakes in one unhealed, and make the other free. THAT is DIVIDED purpose, which cannot BE shared, and so it CANNOT be the function which the Holy Spirit sees as His. And you can rest assured that He will NOT fulfill a function that He cannot understand, and recognize as His. For only thus can He keep YOURS preserved intact, DESPITE your separated[874] view of what your function IS. If He UPHELD divided function, you were lost indeed. His INABILITY to see His goal divided and distinct for each of you preserves your Self from being made aware of any function OTHER than Its Own. **T(943) -769**

T 27 C 16. And thus is healing given BOTH of you. Correction MUST be left to One Who knows correction and forgiveness ARE the same. With HALF a mind, this is NOT understood. Leave, then, correction to the Mind That IS united, functioning as One BECAUSE It is not split in purpose, and conceives a single function as Its ONLY one. Here is the function GIVEN It conceived to be Its Own, and NOT apart from that Its Giver keeps BECAUSE it has been shared. In His ACCEPTANCE of this function lies the means whereby your mind is unified. His SINGLE purpose unifies the halves of you that you perceive as separate. And each forgives the other, that he may accept his OTHER half as PART of him. **T(944) - 770**[875]

T 27 D. The Symbol of the Impossible (*Notes* 1890 12:25)

T 27 D 1. Power can NOT oppose. For opposition would WEAKEN it, and weakened power is a contradiction in ideas. Weak strength is meaningless. And power used to weaken is EMPLOYED to limit. Thus it MUST be limited and weak, because that is its purpose. Power is UNopposed, to be itself. No weakness CAN intrude upon it without changing what it IS, to something it is not. To weaken IS to limit, and impose an opposite that CONTRADICTS the concept it attacks. And BY its contradiction does it JOIN to the idea a something it is not, and make it unintelligible. Who can understand a double concept, such as "weakened-power," or as "hateful-love?"

---

[872] The *Urtext* manuscript has the singular "hand" typed here. The *Notes* has the plural, "hands" and the *HLC* corrects it to "hands." We're calling this a typo in the *Urtext* and we're agreeing with the *Notes* and the *HLC* that it was meant to be plural.

[873] January 24, 1968

[874] The *Urtext* manuscript has this as "separate view" which the *HLC* changes to "separate views" which sounds better. However the *Notes* has it as "separated view" which is a rather different idea and which fits the context much better. We're thus calling this a typing mistake in the *Urtext* and restoring it to the *Notes* reading by changing "separate" to "separated" here.

[875] Jan. 26, 1968

T 27 B 8. The Holy Spirit's picture changes not the body into something it is not. It only takes away from it ALL signs of accusation and of blamefulness. Pictured WITHOUT a purpose, it is seen as neither sick nor well, nor bad nor good. No grounds are offered that it may be judged in ANY way at all. It has no life, but neither is it dead. It stands apart from ALL experience of fear OR love. For now it witnesses to NOTHING yet, its purpose being open, and the mind made free again to choose what it is FOR. Now it is not condemned, but waiting for a purpose to be GIVEN, that it may fulfill the function that it will receive.

T 27 B 9. Into this empty space, from which the GOAL of sin has been removed, is Heaven free to be remembered. Here its peace can come, and perfect healing take the place of death. The body can become a sign of life, a promise of redemption, and a breath of immortality to those grown sick of breathing in the fetid scent of death. Let it have healing as its PURPOSE. Then will it send forth the message it received, and by its health and loveliness proclaim the truth and value that it represents. Let it receive the power to represent an endless life, forever unattacked. And to your brother let its message be, "Behold me, brother, at your hand I live."

T 27 B 10. The simple way to let this be achieved is merely this; to let the body have no purpose from the past, when you were sure you KNEW its purpose was to foster guilt. For this insists your crippled picture is a lasting sign of what it represents. This leaves no space in which a DIFFERENT view, ANOTHER purpose, can be given it. You do NOT know its purpose. You but gave ILLUSIONS of a purpose to a thing you made to hide your function from yourself. This thing WITHOUT a purpose cannot hide the function that the Holy Spirit gave. Let, then, ITS purpose and YOUR function both be reconciled at last, and seen as one. **T(938) -764**[866]

T 27 C. The Fear of Healing (*Notes* 1877 12:12)

T 27 C 1. Is healing frightening? To many, yes. For accusation is a bar to love, and damaged bodies ARE accusers. They stand firmly in the way of trust and peace, proclaiming that the frail can HAVE no trust, and that the damaged HAVE no grounds for peace. Who has been injured BY his brother, and could love and trust him still? He HAS attacked, and will attack again. Protect him not, because your damaged body shows that you must be protected FROM him. To forgive may be an act of charity, but NOT his due. He may be PITIED for his guilt, but NOT exonerated. And if you forgive him his transgressions, you but ADD to all the guilt that he has really earned.[867]

T 27 C 2. The unhealed CANNOT pardon. For they are the witnesses that pardon is unfair. They would retain the CONSEQUENCES of the guilt they overlook. Yet no-one CAN forgive a sin which he believes is real. And what has consequences MUST be real, because what it has DONE is there to see. Forgiveness is NOT pity, which but seeks to pardon what it knows to be the truth. Good cannot BE returned for evil, for forgiveness does not first ESTABLISH sin, and THEN forgive it.[868] Who can say and MEAN, "My brother, you have injured me, and yet, because I am the BETTER of the two, I pardon you my hurt." HIS pardon and YOUR hurt can NOT exist together. One DENIES the other, and MUST make it false.

T 27 C 3. To witness sin, and yet forgive it, is a paradox which reason cannot see. For it maintains what has been done to you DESERVES no pardon. And, by GIVING it, you grant your brother mercy, but retain the proof he is not REALLY innocent. The sick remain accusers. They cannot forgive their brothers AND themselves as well. For no-one in whom true forgiveness reigns CAN suffer. He holds not the proof of sin, before his brother's eyes. And thus he MUST have overlooked it, and removed it from his own.[869] Forgiveness CANNOT be for one, and not the other. Who forgives IS healed. And in his healing lies the PROOF that he has truly pardoned, and retains no trace of condemnation that **T(939) -765** he still would hold against himself or any living thing.

T 27 C 4. Forgiveness is not real UNLESS it brings a healing to your brother AND yourself. YOU must attest his sins had no effect on YOU, to demonstrate they were not real. How else COULD he be guiltless? And how COULD his innocence be justified UNLESS his sins have no effect to WARRANT guilt? Sins are beyond forgiveness just BECAUSE they would entail effects which CANNOT be undone and overlooked entirely. In their UNDOING lies the proof that they were merely errors. LET yourself be healed, that you may be forgiving, offering salvation to your brother AND yourself. A broken body shows the mind has NOT been healed. A miracle of healing proves that separation is WITHOUT effect.

T 27 C 5. What you would prove to him you will believe. The power of witness COMES from your belief. And everything you say or do or think but testifies to what you teach to him. Your body can be means to teach that it has never suffered pain because of him. And in its healing can it offer him mute testimony to his innocence. It is THIS testimony that can speak with power greater than a thousand tongues. For here is his forgiveness PROVED to him. A miracle can offer nothing LESS to him than it has given unto you. So does your healing show your mind is healed, and has forgiven what he did NOT do. And so is HE convinced his innocence was never lost, and healed along with you.

T 27 C 6. Thus does the miracle undo all things the world attests can never BE undone. And hopelessness and death MUST disappear before the ancient clarion call of life. This call has power FAR beyond the weak and miserable cry of death and guilt. The ancient Calling of the Father to His Son, and of the Son unto his own, will yet be the last trumpet that the world will ever hear.[870] Brother, there is no death.[871] And this you learn when you but wish to show your brother that you had no hurt of him. He thinks your blood is on his hands, and so he stands condemned. But it is given you **T(940) -766** to SHOW him, by your healing, that his guilt is but the fabric of a senseless dream.

T 27 C 7. How just are miracles! For they bestow an equal gift of full deliverance from guilt upon your brother AND yourself. YOUR healing saves HIM pain, as well as you. And YOU are healed BE-

---

[866] January 22, 1968
[867] **Matthew 6:12** "And forgive us our debts, as we forgive our debtors."
    Here we see a larger understanding of "forgiveness" indicated, than the coon view of "forgiving the guilty wretch for his horrid sin." In the later Song of Prayer, the distinction between this genuine forgiveness and "forgiveness to destroy" is elaborated. The point is not that you first judge your brother guilty and then forgive him for his real sins, but that you realize that your judgement of him as sinner was an illusion, and never was God's view of your brother, or of you. In this lies true forgiveness and thus true salvation. See also **T 27 C 1.**
[868] See above.

[869] **Matthew 7:3-5** "And why do you look at the speck in your brother's eye, but do not consider the plank in your own eye? Or how can you say to your brother, 'Let me remove the speck from your eye'; and look, a plank is in your own eye? Hypocrite! First remove the plank from your own eye, and then you will see clearly to remove the speck from your brother's eye."
[870] **Joel 2:1** Blow the trumpet in Zion,
    And sound an alarm in My holy mountain!
    Let all the inhabitants of the land tremble;
    For the day of the LORD is coming,
    For it is at hand:
1 Corinthians 15:52 In a moment, in the twinkling of an eye, at the last trumpet. For the trumpet will sound, and the dead will be raised incorruptible, and we shall be changed.
[871] **2 Timothy 1:10** But has now been revealed by the appearing of our Savior Jesus Christ, who has abolished death and brought life and immortality to light through the gospel,
Revelation 21:4 And God will wipe away every tear from their eyes; there shall be no more death, nor sorrow, nor crying. There shall be no more pain, for the former things have passed away."

CHAPTER 27 – THE BODY AND THE DREAM

T 27 A. Introduction (*Notes* 1868 12:3)

T 27 A 1. The wish to be unfairly treated is a compromise attempt that would COMBINE attack and innocence. Who can combine the wholly incompatible, and make a unity of what can NEVER join? Walk you the gentle way, and you will fear no evil and no shadows in the night.[862] But place no terror symbols on the path, or you will weave a crown of thorns from which your brother and yourself will NOT escape.[863] You CANNOT crucify yourself alone. And if you are unfairly treated, he MUST suffer the unfairness that you see. You CANNOT sacrifice yourself alone. For sacrifice is total. If it could occur at all, it would entail the whole of God's creation, and the Father with the sacrifice of his beloved Son.[864]

T 27 A 2. In your RELEASE from sacrifice is HIS made manifest, and shown to be his own. But every pain you suffer do you see as proof that HE is guilty of attack. Thus would you make yourself to be the sign that he has LOST his innocence, and need but look on you to realize that HE has been condemned. And what to YOU has been unfair will come to HIM in righteousness. The unjust vengeance that you suffer now belongs to HIM, and when it RESTS on him, are YOU set free. Wish not to make yourself a living symbol of his guilt, for you will NOT escape the death you make for him, and in HIS innocence you find your own.

T 27 B. The Picture of the Crucifixion (*Notes* 1869 12:4)

T 27 B 1. Whenever you consent to suffer pain, to be deprived, unfairly treated, or in need of ANYTHING, you but accuse your brother of attack upon God's Son. You hold a picture of your crucifixion before his eyes, that he may see his sins are writ in Heaven in your blood and death, and go before him, closing off the gate, and damning him to hell. Yet this is writ in hell and NOT in Heaven, where you are BEYOND attack, and prove his INNOCENCE. The picture of yourself you offer him you show YOURSELF, and give it all your faith. The Holy Spirit offers you, to give to him, a picture of yourself in which there is **T(935) -761** NO pain and NO reproach at all. And what was martyred to his guilt becomes the perfect witness to his innocence.

T 27 B 2. The power of witness is beyond belief, because it brings conviction in its wake. The witness is believed BECAUSE he points beyond himself, to what he REPRESENTS. A sick and suffering you but represents your brother's guilt; the witness which you send, lest he forget the injuries he gave, from which you swear he never will escape. This sick and sorry picture YOU accept, if only it can serve to punish him. The sick are merciless to everyone, and in contagion do they seek to kill. Death seems an easy price, if they can say, "Behold me, brother, at your hand I die." For sickness is the witness to his guilt, and death would prove his errors MUST be sins.

T 27 B 3. Sickness is but a "little" death; a form of vengeance not yet total. Yet it speaks with certainty for what it represents. The bleak and bitter picture you have sent your brother, YOU have looked upon in grief. And everything that it has shown to him have you believed, BECAUSE it witnessed to the guilt in him, which you perceived and loved. Now in the hands made gentle by His touch, the Holy Spirit lays a picture of a DIFFERENT you. It is a picture of a body still, for what you REALLY are can not be seen nor pictured. But THIS one has NOT been used for purpose of attack, and therefore never suffered pain at all. IT witnesses to the eternal truth that you can not BE hurt, and points BEYOND itself to both YOUR innocence and HIS.

T 27 B 4. Show THIS unto your brother, who will see that every scar is healed, and every tear is wiped away in laughter and in love.[865] And he will look on his forgiveness there, and with healed eyes will look BEYOND it, to the innocence that he beholds in you. Here is the proof that he has NEVER sinned; that NOTHING that his madness bid him do was ever done, or ever had effects of any kind. That NO reproach he laid upon his heart was EVER justified, and NO attack can touch him with the poisoned sting of fear. Attest his **T(936) -762** innocence and NOT his guilt. YOUR healing is his comfort and HIS health. BECAUSE it proves illusions were not true.

T 27 B 5. It is not Will for Life, but wish for death, that is the motivation for this world. Its ONLY purpose is TO PROVE GUILT REAL. No worldly thought or act or feeling has a motivation other than this one. These are the witnesses that are called forth to be believed, and lend conviction to the system they speak for and represent. And each has many voices, speaking to your brother and yourself in different tongues. And yet to both the message is the same. Adornment of the body seeks to show how lovely are the witnesses for guilt. Concerns about the body demonstrate how frail and vulnerable is your life; how easily destroyed is what you love. Depression speaks of death and vanity of real concern with anything at all.

T 27 B 6. The strongest witness to futility, which bolsters all the rest and helps them paint the picture in which sin is justified, is sickness in whatever form it takes. The sick have reason for each one of their unnatural desires and strange needs. For who could live a life so soon cut short, and NOT esteem the worth of passing joys? What pleasures COULD there be that will endure? Are not the frail ENTITLED to believe that every stolen scrap of pleasure is their righteous payment for their little lives? Their death will pay the price for all of them, if they enjoy the benefits or not. The end of life must come, whatever way that life be spent. And so take pleasure in the quickly passing and ephemeral.

T 27 B 7. These are NOT sins, but witnesses unto the strange belief that sin and death are real, and innocence and sin will end alike, within the termination of the grave. If this were true, there WOULD be reason to remain content to seek for passing joys, and cherish little pleasures where you can. But in this picture is the body NOT perceived as neutral and WITHOUT a goal inherent in itself. For it becomes the symbol of reproach, **T(937) -763** the sign of guilt whose consequences still are there to see, so that the cause can NEVER be denied. Your function is to PROVE to him that sin can HAVE no cause. How futile MUST it be to see yourself a picture of the proof that what your function IS can never be.

---

[862] **Psalm 23:4** Yea, though I walk through the valley of the shadow of death, I will fear no evil;
For You are with me;
Your rod and Your staff, they comfort me.

[863] **Matthew 27:29** When they had twisted a crown of thorns, they put it on His head, and a reed in His right hand. And they bowed the knee before Him and mocked Him, saying, "Hail, King of the Jews!"

[864] **Hosea 6:6** For I desire mercy and not sacrifice, And the knowledge of God more than burnt offerings.; Also: **Matthew 9:13** But go and learn what this means: "I desire mercy and not sacrifice. For I did not come to call the righteous, but sinners, to repentance."

[865] **Isaiah 25:8** He will swallow up death forever, And the Lord GOD will wipe away tears from all faces; The rebuke of His people He will take away from all the earth; For the LORD has spoken.
Revelation 7:17 For the Lamb who is in the midst of the throne will shepherd them and lead them to living fountains of waters. And God will wipe away every tear from their eyes.
Revelation 21:4 And God will wipe away every tear from their eyes; there shall be no more death, nor sorrow, nor crying. There shall be no more pain, for the former things have passed away.

Christ, and ancient scars are healed within His sight. An ancient miracle has come to bless, and to REPLACE an ancient enmity that came to kill. In gentle gratitude do God the Father AND the Son return to what is Theirs, and will forever be. Now is the Holy Spirit's purpose done. For They have come! For They have come at last! **T(931) -757**[859]

T 26 K. The Remaining Task (N* 1862 11:237)

T 26 K 1. What, then, remains to be undone, for you to REALIZE Their Presence? Only this; you have a DIFFERENTIAL view of WHEN attack is justified, and WHEN you think it is unfair, and NOT to be allowed. When you perceive it AS unfair, you think that a response of anger now is just. And thus you see what IS the same as DIFFERENT. Confusion is not limited. If it occurs at all, it WILL be total. And its presence, in WHATEVER form, will hide Their Presence. They are known with clarity, or not at all. Confused perception will block knowledge. It is NOT a question of the SIZE of the confusion, or HOW MUCH it interferes. Its simple PRESENCE shuts the door to Theirs, and keeps Them there unknown.

T 26 K 2. What does it MEAN if you perceive attack in certain FORMS to be unfair to you? It means that there MUST be some forms in which YOU THINK IT FAIR. For otherwise, how could some be evaluated as UNfair? Some, then, are GIVEN meaning, and perceived as sensible. And only SOME are seen as meaningLESS. And this DENIES the fact that ALL are senseless; EQUALLY without a cause or consequence, and CANNOT have effects of ANY kind. Their Presence is obscured by ANY veil which stands between Their shining innocence and your awareness it is your own, and EQUALLY belongs to every living thing along with you. God limits not. And what is limited can NOT be Heaven. So it MUST be hell.

T 26 K 3. Unfairness and attack are ONE mistake, so firmly joined that where one is perceived, the other MUST be seen. You cannot BE unfairly treated. The belief you ARE is but another form of the idea you are deprived by someone NOT yourself. PROJECTION of the cause of sacrifice is at the root of everything perceived to be unfair, and NOT your just deserts. Yet it is YOU who ask this of yourself, in deep injustice to the Son of God. You HAVE no enemy except yourself, and you are enemy indeed to him, because you do not know him AS yourself.[860] What COULD be more unjust than that he be deprived of what he IS, denied the right to be himself, and asked to sacrifice his Father's Love and yours, as NOT his due? **T(932) -758**

T 26 K 4. Beware of the temptation to perceive yourself unfairly treated. In this view, you seek to find an innocence which is NOT Theirs, but yours alone, and at the cost of someone ELSE's guilt. Can innocence be purchased by the giving of YOUR guilt to someone else? And IS this innocence, which your attack on him attempts to get? Is it not retribution for your own attack upon the Son of God you seek? Is it not SAFER to believe that you are innocent of this, and victimized DESPITE your innocence? Whatever way the game of guilt is played, THERE MUST BE LOSS. Someone must LOSE his innocence that someone ELSE can take it from him, making it his own.

T 26 K 5. You think your brother is unfair to you BECAUSE you think that one must be unfair to MAKE the other innocent. And in this game do you perceive one PURPOSE of your whole relationship. And this you seek to ADD unto the purpose GIVEN it. The Holy Spirit's purpose is to let the Presence of your holy Guests be known to you. And TO this purpose nothing CAN be added, for the world is purposeless except for this. To add or take away from this ONE goal is but to take away ALL purpose from the world, and from yourself. And each unfairness that the world appears to lay upon you, you have laid on it, by rendering it purposeless, without the function that the Holy Spirit sees. And simple justice has been thus denied to every living thing upon the earth.

T 26 K 6. What this injustice does to you who judge unfairly, and who see as you have judged, you cannot calculate. The world grows dim and threatening, and not a trace of all the happy sparkle that salvation brought can you perceive, to lighten up your way. And so you see YOURSELF deprived of light, abandoned to the dark, unfairly left without a purpose in a futile world. The world is fair because the Holy Spirit has brought injustice to the Light within, and there has ALL unfairness been resolved, and been REPLACED with justice and with love. If you perceive injustice anywhere, you need but say, **T(933) -759** "By this do I DENY the Presence of the Father and the Son. And I would rather know of Them than see injustice, which Their Presence shines away." **T(934) -760**[861]

---

[859] January 8, 1968

[860] **Mathew 5:43-45** "Ye have heard that it was said, Thou shalt love thy neighbor, and hate thine enemy: but I say unto you, love your enemies, and pray for them that persecute you; that ye may be sons of your Father who is in heaven: for he maketh his sun to rise on the evil and the good, and sendeth rain on the just and the unjust."

[861] January 19, 1967

Chapter 29 – The Awakening

T 29 A. Introduction (*Notes* 1083 12:118)

T 29 A 1. There is no time, no place, no state where God is absent. There is NOTHING to be feared. There is no way in which a gap could be conceived of in the Wholeness that is His. The compromise the least and littlest gap would represent in His eternal Love is quite impossible. For it would mean His Love could harbor just a hint of hate; His gentleness turn sometimes to attack; and His eternal patience sometimes fail. All this do you BELIEVE, when you perceive a gap between your brother and yourself. How could you trust Him, then? For He must be deceptive in His Love. Be wary, then; let Him not come too close, and leave a gap between you and His Love, through which you can escape if there be need for you to flee.

T 29 A 2. Here is the fear of God most plainly seen. For love is treacherous to those who fear, since fear and hate can NEVER be apart. No-one who hates but is afraid of love, and therefore MUST be afraid of God. Certain it is he knows not what love MEANS. He fears to love and loves to hate, and so he thinks that love is fearful; hate is love. This is the consequence the little gap MUST bring to those who cherish it, and think that it is their salvation and their hope. The fear of God! -- the greatest obstacle that peace must flow across has not yet gone. The rest are past, but this one still remains to block your path, and make the way to light seem dark and fearful, perilous and bleak.

T 29 A 3. You had DECIDED that your brother is your enemy. SOMETIMES a friend, perhaps, provided that your separate interests made your friendship possible a little while. But NOT without a gap between you, lest he turn again into an enemy. Let him come close to you, and you jumped back; as you approached, he instantly withdrew. A cautious friendship, limited in scope and carefully restricted in amount, became the treaty you had made with him. You shared a qualified entente, in which a clause of separation was a point on which you both agreed to keep intact. And violating this was thought[917] to be a breach of treaty not to be allowed. **T(991) - 817**

T 29 B. The Closing of the Gap (*Notes* 1985 12:120)

T 29 B 1. The gap between you is NOT one of space between two separate bodies. This but SEEMS to be dividing off your separate minds. It is the SYMBOL of a promise, made to meet when you prefer, and separate until you both elect to meet again. And then your bodies seem to get in touch, and signify a meeting place to join. But always is it possible to go your separate ways. Conditional upon the right to separate will you agree to meet from time to time, and keep apart in intervals of separation, which protect you from the "sacrifice" of love. THE BODY SAVES YOU, for it gets away from total "sacrifice," and gives you time in which to build again your separate selves, which you believe DIMINISH as you meet.

T 29 B 2. The body COULD not separate your minds, unless you WANTED it to be a cause of separation and of[918] distance seen between you. Thus do you ENDOW it with a power that lies NOT within itself. And herein lies its power over you. For now you think that IT determines when you meet, and limits[919] your ability to make communion with each other's mind. And now it TELLS you where to go, and how to go there; what is feasible for you to undertake, and what you CANNOT do. It dictates what its health can tolerate, and what will tire it and make it sick. And its "inherent" weaknesses set up the limitations on what YOU would do, and keep your PURPOSE limited and weak.

T 29 B 3. The body WILL accommodate to this, if you would have it so. It WILL allow but limited indulgences in "love," with intervals of hatred in between. And it WILL take command of when to "love," and when to shrink more safely into fear. It will be sick BECAUSE you do not know what loving means. And so you MUST misuse each circumstance and everyone you meet, and see in them a purpose NOT their own. It is not love that asks a[920] sacrifice. But fear DEMANDS the sacrifice of love, for in love's presence fear cannot abide. For hate to be maintained love MUST be feared, and only SOMETIMES present; SOMETIMES gone. **T(992) -818**

T 29 B 4. Thus is love seen as treacherous, because IT seems to come and go uncertainly, and offer no stability to you. You do NOT see how limited and weak is YOUR allegiance, and how frequently you have demanded that it go away, and leave you quietly alone in "peace." The body, innocent of ANY goal, is your excuse for variable goals YOU hold, and force the body to maintain. You do not fear its weakness, but its lack of strength OR weakness. Would you recognize that NOTHING stands between you? Would you know there IS no gap behind which you can hide?

T 29 B 5. There IS a shock that comes to those who learn their Savior is their enemy no more. There IS a wariness that is aroused by learning that the body is not real. And there ARE overtones of seeming fear around the happy message "God is Love."[921] Yet all that happens when the gap is gone is peace eternal. Nothing MORE than that, and nothing less. Without the fear of God, what could induce you to abandon Him? What toys or trinkets in the gap could serve to hold you back an instant from His Love? Would you ALLOW the body to say "No" to Heaven's calling, were you not afraid to find a LOSS of self in finding God? And CAN your Self be lost by being found?[922] **T(993) -819**[923]

T 29 C. The Coming of the Guest (*Notes* 1989 12:124)

T 29 C 1. Why would you not perceive it as RELEASE from suffering to learn that you are free? Why would you not ACCLAIM the truth, instead of looking on it as an enemy? Why does an EASY path, so clearly marked it is impossible to lose the way seem thorny, rough, and far too difficult for you to follow? Is it not because you see it as the road to hell, instead of looking on it as a simple way, without a sacrifice or ANY loss, to find yourself in Heaven and in God? Until you realize you give up NOTHING; until you understand there IS no loss; you will have some regrets about the way that you have chosen. And you will NOT see the many gains your choice has offered you.

T 29 C 2. Yet, though you do not see them, they are there. Their CAUSE has been effected, and they MUST be present were their cause has entered in. You have accepted healing's Cause, and so it MUST be you are healed. And, being healed, the power to heal must ALSO now be yours. The miracle is not a separate thing that happens suddenly, as an effect without a cause, nor is it, in itself, a

---

[917] *Urtext* manuscript has it typed "though" the final "t" is handwritten in.
[918] The word "of" is handwritten into the *Urtext* manuscript. The word does appear in the *Notes*.
[919] *Urtext* manuscript has it typed "limit" the final "s" is handwritten. The *Notes* also has it as "limits."
[920] *Urtext* manuscript has it typed "for", this is crossed out and "a" is typed above it. This is consistent with the *Notes*.
[921] **1 John 4:16** He that loveth not knoweth not God; for God is love;
1 John 4:8 And we know and have believed the love which God hath in us. God is love; and he that abideth in love abideth in God, and God abideth in him.
[922] **Luke 15:24** 'For this my son was dead and is alive again; he was lost and is found.' And they began to be merry.
Luke 15:32 It was right that we should make merry and be glad, for your brother was dead and is alive again, and was lost and is found.
[923] April 1, 1968

cause. But where its Cause is MUST it be. Now IS it caused, though not as yet perceived. And its effects are THERE, though not yet seen. Look inward now, and you will not behold a reason for regret, but cause indeed for glad rejoicing and for hope of peace.

T 29 C 3. It HAS been hopeless to attempt to find the hope of peace upon a battleground. It HAS been futile to demand escape from sin and pain of what was made to serve the function of RETAINING sin and pain. For pain and sin are ONE illusion, as are hate and fear, attack and guilt but one. Where they are causeless, their effects ARE gone, and love MUST come wherever they are not. Why are you not rejoicing? You ARE free of pain and sickness, misery and loss, and ALL effects of hatred and attack. No more is pain your friend and guilt your god, and you should WELCOME the effects of love. **T(994) -820**

T 29 C 4. Your Guest HAS come. You asked Him and He came. You did not hear Him enter, for you did not wholly welcome Him. And yet His gifts came with Him. He has laid them at your feet, and asks you now that you will look on them, and take them for your own. He NEEDS your help in giving them to all who walk apart, believing they are separate and alone. They WILL be healed when you accept your gifts, because your Guest will welcome everyone whose feet have touched the holy ground[924] whereon you stand, and where His gifts for them are laid.

T 29 C 5. You do not see how much you now can GIVE, because of everything you have received. Yet He Who entered in but waits for YOU to come where you invited HIM to be. There is no other place where He can find His host, nor where His host can meet with Him. And nowhere else His gifts of peace and joy, and all the happiness His Presence brings, can be obtained. For they are where He is that brought them with Him, that they might be yours. You can[925] not see your Guest, but you CAN see the gifts He brought. And when you LOOK on them, you will believe His Presence MUST be there. For what you now can do could not BE done without the love and grace His Presence holds. **T(995) -821**[926]

T 29 C 6. Such is the promise of the living God; His Son have life, and every living thing is part of him, and nothing else has life. What YOU have "given" life is NOT alive, and symbolizes but your wish to be alive APART from life, alive in death, with death perceived as life, and living, death. Confusion follows on confusion here, for ON confusion has this world been based, and there is nothing else it rests upon. Its basis does not change, although it SEEMS to be in constant change. But what is that except the state confusion really MEANS? Stability to those who are confused is meaningless. And shift and change become the law on which they predicate their lives.

T 29 C 7. The body does not change. It represents the larger dream that change is POSSIBLE. To change is to attain a state unlike the one in which you found yourself before. There IS no change in immortality, and Heaven knows it not. Yet here on earth, it has a double purpose, for it can be made to teach opposing things. And they reflect the teacher who is teaching them. The body can APPEAR to change with time, with sickness or with health, and with events that seem to alter it. And this but means the mind remains unchanged in its belief of what the PURPOSE of the body is.

T 29 C 8. Sickness is a demand[927] the body be a thing that it is not. Its NOTHINGNESS is guarantee[928] that it can NOT be sick. In your demand that it be MORE than this lies the idea of sickness. For it asks that God be LESS than all He really is. What, then, becomes of YOU, for it IS you of whom the sacrifice is asked? For He is told that part of him BELONGS to Him no longer. He must sacrifice your self, and in His sacrifice are YOU made more, and He is lessened by the loss of you. And what is GONE from Him becomes your god, PROTECTING you from being part of Him. **T(996) -822**

T 29 C 9. The body that is asked to be a god WILL be attacked, because its nothingness has not been recognized. And so it seems to be a thing with power IN ITSELF. As something, it CAN be perceived, and thought to feel and act, and hold you in its grasp as prisoner to itself. And it CAN fail to be what you demanded it to be. And you WILL hate it for its littleness, unmindful that the failure does not lie in that it is not MORE than it should be, but ONLY in YOUR failure to perceive that it is nothing. Yet its nothingness IS your salvation, from which you would flee.

T 29 C 10. As something, is the body asked to be God's enemy, replacing what He is with littleness and limit and despair. It is HIS loss you celebrate when you behold the body as a thing you love, or look upon it as a thing you hate. For if He be the sum of everything, then what is NOT in Him does not exist. And His completion IS nothingness. Your Savior is NOT dead,[929] nor does he dwell in what was built as temple unto death. He lives in God, and it is this that makes him Savior unto YOU, and ONLY this. His body's nothingness releases yours from sickness and from death. For what is yours cannot be more NOR less than what is his. **T(997) -823**[930]

T 29 D. God's Witnesses (*Notes* 1997 12:132)

T 29 D 1. Condemn your Savior not because he thinks he is a body. Far beyond his dreams is his reality. But he must learn he is a Savior[931] first, before he can remember what he is. And he must save who would BE saved. On saving YOU depends his happiness. For who is Savior, but the one who GIVES salvation? Thus he learns it must be his to give. UNLESS he gives, he will not know he HAS, for giving is the proof of having. Only those who think that God is lessened by their strength could fail to understand this must be so. For who COULD give unless he has, and who could lose by giving what must be INCREASED thereby?

T 29 D 2. Think you the Father LOST Himself when He created you? Was HE made weak because He shared His Love? Was He made incomplete by YOUR perfection? Or are you the proof that He IS perfect and complete? Deny Him not His witness in the dream His Son prefers to his reality. He must be Savior FROM the dream he made, that he be free of it. He must see someone ELSE as NOT a body, one with him, without the wall the world has built to keep apart all living things who know not that they live. Within the dream of bodies and of death, is yet one theme[932] of truth. No more, perhaps, than just a tiny spark, a space of light created in the dark, where God shines still.

T 29 D 3. You cannot wake yourself. But you can LET yourself be wakened. You can overlook your brother's dreams. So perfectly can you forgive him his illusions, he becomes your Savior from YOUR dreams. And as you see him shining in the space of light where God abides within the darkness, you will see that God Himself is where his body is. Before this light the body disappears, as heavy shadows MUST give way to light. The darkness cannot CHOOSE that it remain. The coming of the light MEANS it is gone. In glory will

---

[924] **Exodus 3:4-5** And when the LORD saw that he turned aside to see, God called unto him out of the midst of the bush, and said, Moses, Moses. And he said, Here *am* I. And he said, Draw not nigh hither: put off thy shoes from off thy feet, for the place whereon thou standest *is* holy ground.

[925] *Urtext* manuscript has it typed "do" this is crossed out and "can" is handwritten in. The *Notes* glyph would suggest "cannot."

[926] April 5, 1968

[927] Originally the word "that" was typed after "demand." The *Notes* does not have the extra word.

[928] *Urtext* manuscript has it typed "guaranteed" the "d" is crossed out, making it consistent with the *Notes*.

[929] *Urtext* manuscript has it typed "deaf" the letter "d" is handwritten in. the *Notes* rather clearly has "death" written hear. It cannot really be interpreted as either "deaf" or "dead." It would appear from the context that the original intent was for this word to be "death" and "deaf" was actually a "hearing" error in transcription which was not caught.

[930] April 8, 1968

[931] Note that "Savior" is here spelled with no "u"

[932] *Urtext* manuscript has it typed "dream" the word "THEME" is handwritten in with block letters. The *Notes* clearly also has it as "theme."

you see your brother then, and understand what REALLY fills the gap so long perceived as keeping you apart. **T(998) -824**

T 29 D 4. There, in its place, God's Witness has set forth the gentle way of kindness to God's Son. Whom you forgive is GIVEN power to forgive you your illusions.[933] By your gift of freedom is it given unto YOU. Make way for love which you did not create, but which you CAN extend. On earth this means forgive your brother, that the darkness may be lifted from YOUR mind. When light has come to him through your forgiveness, he will not forget his Savior, leaving him unsaved. For it was in YOUR face he saw the light that he would keep beside him, as he walks through darkness to the everlasting Light.

T 29 D 5. How holy are you, that the Son of God can be your Savior in the midst of dreams of desolation and disaster. See how eagerly he comes, and steps aside from heavy shadows that have hidden him, and shines[934] on you in gratitude and love. He is himself, but not himself alone. And as his Father lost not part of Him in your creation, so the light in him is brighter still, because you gave your light to him, to save him from the dark. And now the light in you must be as bright as shines in him. This is the spark that shines within the dream; that you can help him waken, and be sure his waking eyes will rest upon you first, and in his glad salvation YOU are saved. **T(999) -813**[935]

T 29 E. Dream Roles (*Notes* 2001 12:136)

T 29 E 1. Do you believe that truth can be but SOME illusions? They are dreams BECAUSE they are not true. Their EQUAL lack of truth becomes the basis for the miracle, which MEANS that you have understood that dreams are dreams, and that escape depends, NOT on the dream, but ONLY on awaking. COULD it be some dreams are KEPT, and others WAKENED FROM? The choice is NOT between which dreams to keep, but ONLY if you want to live in dreams, or to awaken from them. Thus it is the miracle does not select SOME dreams to leave untouched by its beneficence. You cannot dream some dreams and wake from some. For you are either sleeping OR awake. And dreaming goes with only ONE of these.

T 29 E 2. The dreams you THINK you like would hold you back, as much as those in which the fear is seen. For EVERY dream is but a dream of fear, no matter what the form it seems to take. The fear is seen within, without, or both. Or it can be disguised in pleasant form. But never is it ABSENT from the dream. For fear is the material of dreams, from which they ALL are made. Their form can change, but they cannot be MADE of something else. The miracle were treacherous indeed if it allowed you still to be afraid, because you did not RECOGNIZE the fear. You would not then be WILLING to awake, for which the miracle prepares[936] the way.

T 29 E 3. In simplest form, it can be said attack is a response to function unfulfilled AS YOU PERCEIVE THE FUNCTION. It can be in you or someone else, but where it is perceived, it will be there it is attacked. Depression or assault must be the theme of every dream, for they are made of fear. The thin disguise of pleasure and of joy in which they may be wrapped but slightly veils the heavy lump of fear which is their core. And it is THIS the miracle perceives, and NOT the wrappings in which it is bound. When you are angry, is it not because someone has failed to fill the function YOU allotted him? And does not THIS become the "reason" your attack is justified? **T(1000) -814**

T 29 E 4. The dreams you THINK you like are those in which the functions YOU have given have been filled; the needs which YOU ascribe to you are met. It does not matter if they be fulfilled, or merely wanted. It is the idea that they EXIST from which the fears arise. Dreams are not wanted more or less. They are desired or not. And each one represents some function which you have assigned; some goal which an event, or body, or a thing SHOULD represent, and SHOULD achieve for you. If it succeeds, you think you LIKE the dream. If it should fail, you think the dream is sad. But whether it succeeds or fails is not its core, but just the flimsy covering.

T 29 E 5. How happy would your dreams become, if you were NOT the one who gave the "proper" role to every figure that the dream contains. No-one can fail but your IDEA of him, and there IS no betrayal but of this. The core of dreams the Holy Spirit gives is NEVER one of fear. The coverings may not appear to change, but what they MEAN has changed BECAUSE they cover something else. Perceptions are determined by their purpose, in that they seem to BE what they are FOR. A shadow figure who attacks becomes a brother giving you a chance to help, if this becomes the FUNCTION of the dream. And dreams of sadness thus are turned to joy.

T 29 E 6. What is your brother FOR? You do not know, because YOUR function is obscure to you. Do NOT ascribe a role to him which you imagine would bring happiness to you. And do not try to hurt him, when he fails to take the part which you assigned to him in what you dream your life was meant to be. He asks for help in every dream he has, and you have Help to give him if you see the FUNCTION of the dream as He perceives its function, Who can utilize all dreams as means to serve the Function given Him. Because He loves the dreamer, NOT the dream, each dream becomes an offering of love. For at its center is His Love for you, which lights WHATEVER form it takes with love. **T(1001) -815**[937]

T 29 F. The Changeless Dwelling-Place (*Notes* 2006 12:141)

T 29 F 1. There is a place in you where this whole world has been forgotten. Where no memory of sin and of illusion linger still. There is a place in you which time has left, and echoes of eternity are heard. There is a resting place so still no sound except a hymn to Heaven rises up to gladden God the Father and the Son. Where Both abide are They remembered Both. And where They are is Heaven and is peace. Think not that you can change Their dwelling place. For your Identity abides in Them, and where They are, forever must YOU be.

T 29 F 2. The changelessness of Heaven is in you, so deep within that nothing in this world but passes by, unnoticed and unseen. The still infinity of endless peace surrounds you gently in its soft embrace, so strong and quiet, tranquil in the might of its Creator, nothing can intrude upon the sacred Son of God within. Here is the role the Holy Spirit gives to you who wait[938] upon the Son of God, and would behold him waken and be glad:[939] He is a part of you, and you of him, BECAUSE he is his Father's Son, and not for ANY purpose you may see in him. Nothing is asked of you but to ACCEPT the Changeless and Eternal that abide in him, for YOUR Identity is there.

T 29 F 3. The peace in you CAN but be found in him. And every thought of love you offer him but brings you nearer to your wakening to peace eternal and to endless joy. This sacred Son of God is like yourself; the mirror of his Father's Love for you, the soft reminder of his Father's Love by which he was created, and which

---

[933] **Matthew 16:19** "And I will give you the keys of the kingdom of heaven, and whatever you bind on earth will be bound in heaven, and whatever you loose on earth will be loosed in heaven."
[934] Originally typed "shine" the final "s" is handwritten in which matches the *Notes* which has it as 'shines.'
[935] April 12, 1968
[936] *Urtext* manuscript has it typed "prepared" the final "d" is crossed out and "s" is handwritten in which matches the *Notes* which has it as "prepares."

[937] April 25, 1968
[938] *Urtext* manuscript has it typed "look" this is crossed out and "wait" is typed in. The *Notes* also has it as "wait."
[939] Obviously we can't have both semicolon and colon, but the manuscript does. The *Notes* however has just a colon, so we're viewing the semicolon preceding it as a typo and have removed it.

still abides in him, as It abides in you. Be very still, and hear God's Voice in him, and let It tell you what his function is.[940] He was created that YOU might be whole, for only the complete can be a part of God's Completion, Which created you.

T 29 F 4. There is no gift the Father asks of you but that you see in all creation but the shining glory of His Gift to you. Behold His Son, His perfect gift, in whom his Father shines forever, and to whom is all creation given as his own.[941] **T(1002) -816** BECAUSE he has it is it given you, and where it lies in him behold YOUR peace. The quiet that surrounds you dwells in him, and FROM this quiet come the happy dreams in which your hands are joined in innocence. These are not hands that grasp in dreams of pain. They hold no sword, for they have left their hold on every vain illusion of the world. And, being empty, they received instead a brother's hand in which completeness lay.

T 29 F 5. If you but knew the glorious goal that lies beyond forgiveness, you would not keep hold on any thought, however light the touch of evil on it may appear to be. For you would understand how great the cost of holding anything God did not give in minds that can direct the hand to bless, and lead God's Son unto His Father's house.[942] Would you not WANT to be a friend to him, created by his[943] Father as His home? If God esteems him worthy of Himself, would YOU attack him with the hands of hate? Who would lay bloody hands on Heaven itself, and hope to find its peace? Your brother thinks he holds the hand of death. Believe him not. But learn, instead, how blessed are you who can release him, just by offering him yours.

T 29 F 6. A dream is given you in which he is your Savior, NOT your enemy in hate. A dream is given you in which you have forgiven him for all his dreams of death; a dream of hope you SHARE with him, instead of dreaming evil separate dreams of hate. Why does it seem so hard to share this dream? Because, unless the Holy Spirit gives the dream its function, it was made for hate, and will continue in death's services. Each form it takes in some way calls for death. And those who serve the lord of death have come to worship in a separated world, each with his tiny spear and rusted sword, to keep his ancient promises to die. **T(1003) -817**

T 29 F 7. Such is the core of fear in every dream that has been kept apart from use by Him Who sees a different function for a dream. When dreams are SHARED, they lose the function of attack and separation, even though it was for this that every dream was made. Yet nothing in the world of dreams remains without the hope of change and betterment, for here is NOT where changelessness is found. Let us be glad indeed that this is so, and seek not the eternal in this world. Forgiving dreams are means to step aside from dreaming of a world OUTSIDE yourself. And leading finally beyond ALL dreams, unto the peace of everlasting life. **T(1004) -818**[944]

T 29 G. Forgiveness and Peace (*Notes* 2011 12:146)

T 29 G 1. How willing are you to forgive your brother? How much do you desire peace, instead of endless strife and misery and pain? These questions are the same, in different form. Forgiveness IS your peace, for herein lies the end of separation, and the dream of danger and destruction, sin and death; of madness and of murder, grief and loss. This is the "sacrifice" salvation asks, and gladly offers peace INSTEAD of this. Swear not to die, thou holy Son of God! You make a bargain that you cannot keep. The Son of Life cannot BE killed. He is immortal as his Father. What he is cannot be changed. He is the only thing in all the universe that MUST be One.

T 29 G 2. What SEEMS eternal all will have an end. The stars will disappear, and night and day will be no more. All things that come and go,[945] the tides, the seasons, and the lives of man; all things that change with time and bloom and fade, will not return. Where time has set an end is not where the Eternal is. God's Son can never change by what men made of him. He will be as he was, and as he is, for time appointed not his destiny, nor sets the hour of his birth and death.[946] Forgiveness will not change him. But time waits upon forgiveness, that the things of time may disappear because they have no use.

T 29 G 3. Nothing survives its purpose. If it be conceived to die, then die it must, unless it does not take this purpose as its own. Change is the only thing that can be made a blessing here, where purpose is NOT fixed, however changeless it APPEARS to be. Think not that YOU can set a goal unlike God's Purpose FOR you, and establish it as changeless and eternal. You CAN give yourself a purpose that you do not have. But you can NOT remove the Power to change your mind, and see ANOTHER purpose there. Change is the gift of God He gave to all that YOU would make eternal, to ensure that ONLY Heaven would not pass away.[947] **T(1005) -819**

T 29 G 4. You were NOT born to die. You CANNOT change, because your Function HAS been fixed by God. All other goals are set in time, and change that time might be preserved, EXCEPTING ONE. Forgiveness does not aim at KEEPING time, but at its ending, when it has no use. Its purpose ended, it is gone. And where it once held seeming sway is now restored the Function God established for His Son in full awareness. Time can set no end to Its fulfillment, nor Its changelessness. There is no death, because the living share the Function their Creator gave to them.[948] Life's function CANNOT be to die. It must be life's EXTENSION, that it be as One forever and forever, WITHOUT end.[949]

T 29 G 5. This world will bind your feet and tie your hands and kill your body, ONLY if you think that it was made to crucify God's Son.[950] For even though it WAS a dream of death, you need not let it stand for this to you. Let THIS be changed, and nothing in the world but MUST be changed as well. For nothing here but is defined as what you see it FOR. How lovely is the world whose purpose is forgiveness of God's Son! How free from fear, how filled with blessing and with happiness! And what a joyous thing it is to dwell a little while in such a happy place! Nor CAN it be forgot, in such a world, it IS a little while 'til timelessness comes quietly to take the place of time. **T(1006) -820**[951]

T 29 H. The Lingering Illusion (*Notes* 2038 12:173)

T 29 H 1. Seek not outside yourself. For it will fail, and you will weep each time an idol falls. Heaven cannot be found where it is not, and there can be no peace EXCEPTING there. Each idol that you worship when God calls will never answer in His place. There

---

[940] **Psalm 46:10** Be still, and know that I am God; I will be exalted among the nations, I will be exalted in the earth!
[941] **John 19:5** Then Jesus came out, wearing the crown of thorns and the purple robe. And Pilate said to them, "Behold the Man!"
[942] **John 14:2** "In My Father's house are many mansions; if it were not so, I would have told you. I go to prepare a place for you."
[943] *Urtext* manuscript has it typed "His" it is crossed out and "his" is typed in. The previous instance of "Father" is preceded by a capitalized "His" with reference to the Son also. One of these is incorrect. The *Notes* is also erratic in capitalization here.
[944] May 6, 1968

[945] Originally there is a sentence break here, but handwritten mark-up makes it a comma break instead. The *Notes* also has a comma.
[946] **Hebrews 13:8** Jesus Christ is the same yesterday, today, and forever.
[947] **Matthew 24:35** "Heaven and earth will pass away, but My words will by no means pass away."
[948] **2 Timothy 1:10** But has now been revealed by the appearing of our Savior Jesus Christ, who has abolished death and brought life and immortality to light through the gospel,
[949] This is reminiscent of the King James version of the benediction in **Ephesians 3:21** "Unto him *be* glory in the church by Christ Jesus throughout all ages, world without end. Amen"
[950] **John 11:44** And he who had died came out bound hand and foot with graveclothes, and his face was wrapped with a cloth. Jesus said to them, "Loose him, and let him go."
[951] May 8, 1968

IS no other answer you can substitute, and find the happiness His Answer brings. Seek not outside yourself. For all your pain comes simply from a futile search for what you want, insisting WHERE it must be found. What if it is not there? Do you prefer that you be right or happy? Be you glad that you are told where happiness abides,[952] and seek no longer elsewhere. You will fail.

T 29 H 2. But it is given you to know the truth, and NOT to seek for it outside yourself. No-one who comes here but must still have hope, some lingering illusion, or some dream that there is something OUTSIDE of himself that will bring happiness and peace to him. If everything is IN him, this can not be so. And therefore, BY his coming, he denies the truth about himself, and seeks for something MORE than everything, as if a part of it were separated off, and found where all the REST of it is NOT. This is the purpose he bestows upon the body; that it seek for what he lacks, and <u>GIVE</u> him what would make himself complete.

T 29 H 3. And thus he wanders aimlessly about, in search of something that he cannot find, believing him to be what he is not. The lingering illusion will impel him to seek out a thousand idols, and to seek beyond them for a thousand more. And each will fail him, all excepting one; for he will die, and does not understand the idol that he seeks IS but his death. Its FORM appears to be outside himself. Yet does he seek to kill God's Son within, and PROVE that he is victor over him. This is the purpose EVERY idol has, for this the role that is assigned to it, and this the role that cannot BE fulfilled. T(1007) -821

T 29 H 4. Whenever you attempt to reach a goal in which the body's betterment is cast as major beneficiary, you try to bring about your death. For you believe that you can suffer lack, and lack IS death. To sacrifice is to GIVE UP, and thus to be without, and to have suffered loss. And, BY this giving up is life renounced. Seek not outside yourself. The search implies you are not whole within, and fear to look upon your devastation, and prefer to seek outside yourself for what you are. Idols must fall BECAUSE they have no life, and what is lifeless IS a sign of death. You came to die, and what would you expect, but to PERCEIVE the signs of death you seek?

T 29 H 5. No sadness and no suffering proclaims a message OTHER than an idol found, which represents a parody of life which, in its lifelessness, is really death, conceived as real and given living form. Yet each must fail and crumble and decay, because a form of death can not BE life, and what is sacrificed can not BE whole. All idols of this world were made to keep the truth within from being known to you, and to maintain allegiance to the dream that you must find what is OUTSIDE of you to be complete and happy. It is vain to worship idols in the hope of peace. God dwells within, and your completion lies in Him. No idol takes His place. Look not to idols. Do not seek outside yourself.

T 29 H 6. Let us forget the purpose of the world the past has given it. For otherwise, the future WILL be like the past, and but a series of depressing dreams, in which all idols fail you, one by one, and you see death and disappointment everywhere. To change all this, and open up a road of hope and of release in what appeared to be an endless circle of despair, you need but to decide you do not KNOW the purpose of the world. You GIVE it goals it does not have, and thus do YOU decide what it is for. You try to see in it a place of idols, found outside yourself, with power to make complete what is within by splitting what you are BETWEEN the two. T(1008) -822

T 29 H 7. You CHOOSE your dreams, for they are what you wish, perceived AS IF it had been given you. And idols do what you would have them do, and HAVE the power you ascribe to them. And you pursue them vainly in the dream, because you want their power as your own. Yet where ARE dreams, but in a mind asleep?

And CAN a dream succeed in making real the pictures it projects outside itself? Save time, my brothers![953] Learn what time is FOR. And speed the end of idols in the world made sad and sick by seeing idols there. Your holy minds are altars unto God, and where He is NO idols can abide.

T 29 H 8. The fear of God is but the fear of loss of idols. It is NOT the fear of loss of your reality. But YOU have made of your reality an idol, which you must protect AGAINST the light of truth. And all the world becomes the means by which this idol can be saved. Salvation thus appears to THREATEN life, and offer death. It is not so. Salvation seeks to prove there IS no death, and ONLY life exists. The sacrifice of death is NOTHING lost. An idol CANNOT take the place of God. Let Him remind you of His Love for you, and do not seek to drown His Voice in chants of deep despair to idols of yourself. Seek not outside your Father for your hope. For hope of happiness is NOT despair. T(1009) -823[954]

T 29 I. Christ and Anti-Christ (*Notes* 2015 12:150)

T 29 I 1. What is an idol? Do you think you know? For idols are unrecognized as such, and never seen for what they really are. That is the only power which they have. Their purpose is obscure, and they are feared, and worshipped, both, BECAUSE you do not know what they are for, and why they have been made. An idol is an image of your brother, which you would value MORE than what he IS. Idols are made that HE may be replaced, no matter what their form. And it is this which NEVER is perceived and recognized. Be it a body or a thing, a place, a situation or a circumstance, an object owned or wanted, or a right demanded or achieved, it is the same.

T 29 I 2. Let not their form deceive you. Idols are but substitutes for your reality. In some way you believe they will complete your little self, and let you walk in safety in a world perceived as dangerous, with forces massed against your confidence and peace of mind. They have the power to supply your lacks, and add the value which you do not have. No-one believes in idols who has not enslaved himself to littleness and loss. And thus must seek BEYOND his little self for strength to raise his head and stand apart from all the misery the world reflects. This is the penalty for looking not within for certainty, and[955] for a quiet calm which liberates you FROM the world, and lets you stand apart in quiet and in peace unlimited.

T 29 I 3. An idol is a false impression, or a false belief; some form of anti-Christ which constitutes a gap BETWEEN the Christ and what you see.[956] An idol is a wish, made tangible and given form, and thus perceived as real, and seen OUTSIDE the mind. Yet they remain ideas, and CANNOT leave the mind that is their source. Nor is their form apart from the idea it represents. All forms of anti-Christ oppose the Christ. And fall before His Face like a dark veil which SEEMS to shut you off from Him, alone in darkness. Yet the light is there. A cloud does not put out the sun. No more a veil can banish what it seems to separate, nor darken by one whit the Light Itself. T(1010) -824

T 29 I 4. This world of idols IS a veil across the Face of Christ BECAUSE its purpose is to separate your brother from yourself. A dark and fearful purpose, yet a thought without the power to change one blade of grass from something living to a sign of death. Its form is

---

[952] *Urtext* manuscript has it typed "lies" the word "abides" is handwritten. The *Notes* has "abides."

[953] The *Urtext* manuscript has a comma here, but also capitalizes "Learn" indicating a sentence break was intended. The *Notes* has an exclamation point, which seems more likely to have been what was intended, so we're replacing this comma with the original punctuation.
[954] May 13, 1968
[955] The *Urtext* manuscript capitalizes the "A" in "and." It's not clear why there is a comma and a capital here but we're calling it a typo.
[956] **1 John 2:18** Little children, it is the last hour; and as you have heard that the Antichrist is coming, even now many antichrists have come, by which we know that it is the last hour.
1 John 2:22 Who is a liar but he who denies that Jesus is the Christ? He is antichrist who denies the Father and the Son.

nowhere, for its source abides within your mind where God abideth not. Where IS this place, where What is everywhere has been excluded, and been kept apart? What hand could be held up to block God's way; whose voice could make demands He enter not? The "more-than-everything" is NOT a thing to make you tremble and to quail in fear. Christ's enemy is nowhere. He can take NO form in which he EVER will be real.

T 29 I 5. What is an idol? Nothing! It must be believed BEFORE it seems to come to life, and GIVEN power that it may be feared. Its life and power are its believer's gift, and this is what the miracle restores to what HAS life and power worthy of the gift of Heaven and eternal peace. The miracle does not restore the truth, the light the veil between has NOT put out. It merely LIFTS the veil, and LETS the truth shine unencumbered, being what It is. It does not NEED belief to be Itself, for It HAS BEEN created, so It IS. An idol is ESTABLISHED by belief, and when it is withdrawn, the idol "dies."

T 29 I 6. This is the anti-Christ; the strange idea there is a power PAST omnipotence, a place BEYOND the infinite, a time transcending the eternal. Here the world of idols has been set by the idea this power and place and time are given form, and shape the world where the impossible has happened. Here the deathless come to die; the all-encompassing to suffer loss; the timeless to be made the slaves of time. Here does the changeless change; the peace of God, forever given to all living things, give way to chaos. And the Son of God, as perfect, sinless, and as loving as his Father, come to hate a little while; to suffer pain, and finally to die. **T(1011) -825**

T 29 I 7. WHERE is an idol? Nowhere! Can there be a gap in what is infinite, a place where time can INTERRUPT eternity? A place of darkness set where all is light, a dismal alcove separated off from what is endless, HAS no place to be. An idol is beyond where God has set all things forever, and has left no room for anything EXCEPT His Will to be. Nothing and nowhere MUST an idol be, while God is everything and everywhere. What purpose has an idol, then? What is it FOR? This is the only question which has many answers, each depending on the one of whom the question has been asked.

T 29 I 8. The world BELIEVES in idols. No-one comes unless he worshipped them, and still attempts to seek for one that yet might offer him a gift reality does NOT contain. Each worshipper of idols harbors hope his SPECIAL deities will give him MORE than other men possess. It MUST be "more." It does not really matter more of what, - more beauty, more intelligence, more wealth; or even more affliction and more pain. But MORE of SOMETHING is an idol FOR. And when one fails another takes its place, with hope of finding more of something ELSE. Be not deceived by forms the "something" takes. An idol is a means for getting MORE. And it is THIS that is against God's Will.

T 29 I 9. God has not many sons, but only One. Who can have more, and who be given less? In Heaven would the Son of God but laugh, if idols could intrude upon his peace. It is for HIM the Holy Spirit speaks, and tells you[957] idols HAVE no purpose here.[958] For MORE than Heaven can you never have. If Heaven is within why would you seek for idols which would make of Heaven less, to give you MORE than God bestowed upon your brother AND on you, as One with Him?[959] God GAVE you all there is. And to be sure you could not lose it, did He ALSO give the same to every living thing as well. And thus IS every living thing a part of you as of Himself.

---

[957] *Urtext* manuscript has it typed "him" that is crossed out and "you" handwritten in. The *Notes* has the glyph most commonly used to mean 'you.'
[958] The word "here" is not originally present, it is handwritten in. It is also present in the *Notes*.
[959] **Luke 17:21** Nor will they say, 'See here!' or 'See there!' For indeed, the kingdom of God is within you."

No idol can establish you as MORE than God. But YOU will never be content with being LESS. **T(1012) -826**[960]

T 29 J. The Forgiving Dream (*Notes* 2022 12:157)

T 29 J 1. The slave of idols is a WILLING slave. For willing he MUST be, to let himself bow down in worship to what has no life, and seek for power in the powerless.[961] What happened to the holy Son of God, that this could BE his wish; to let himself fall lower than the stones upon the ground, and look to idols that they raise him up? Hear, then, your story in the dream you made, and ask yourself if it be not the truth that you believe that it is NOT a dream. A dream of judgment came into the mind that God created perfect as Himself. And in that dream was Heaven changed to hell, and God made enemy unto His Son.

T 29 J 2. How can His Son AWAKEN from the dream? It is a dream of judgment. So must he judge NOT, and he WILL waken. For the dream will seem to last while he is PART of it. Judge not, for he who judges WILL have need of idols, which will hold the judgment off from resting on himself.[962] Nor CAN he know the Self he has condemned. Judge not, because you make yourself a PART of evil dreams, where idols are your "true" identity, and your salvation from the judgment laid, in terror and in guilt, upon yourself. All figures in the dream are idols, made to save you FROM the dream. Yet they are PART of what they have been made to save you FROM.

T 29 J 3. Thus does an idol KEEP the dream alive and terrible. For who would wish for one UNLESS he were in terror and despair? And this idol REPRESENTS, and so its worship IS the worship of despair and terror, and the dream from which they come. Judgment is an INjustice to God's Son, and it IS justice that who judges HIM will not escape the penalty he laid upon HIMSELF within the dream he made.[963] God knows of justice; NOT of penalty. But in the dream of judgment, you attack and ARE condemned. And WISH to be the slave of idols, who are interposed BETWEEN your judgment and the penalty it brings. **T(1013) -827**

T 29 J 4. There CAN be no salvation in the dream, as YOU are dreaming it. For idols MUST be part of it, to save you from what you believe you have accomplished, and have done to make you sinful, and put out the Light within you. Little children, It is there. You do but dream, and idols are the toys you dream you play with. Who has need of toys but children? They pretend they rule the world, and give their toys the power to move about, and talk and think and feel, and speak for them. Yet everything their toys appear to do is in the minds of those who play with them. But they are ea-

---

[960] May 20, 1968
[961] **Exodus 32:1-8** Now when the people saw that Moses delayed coming down from the mountain, the people gathered together to Aaron, and said to him, "Come, make us gods that shall go before us; for as for this Moses, the man who brought us up out of the land of Egypt, we do not know what has become of him." And Aaron said to them, "Break off the golden earrings which are in the ears of your wives, your sons, and your daughters, and bring them to me." So all the people broke off the golden earrings which were in their ears, and brought them to Aaron. And he received the gold from their hand, and he fashioned it with an engraving tool, and made a molded calf. Then they said, "This is your god, O Israel, that brought you out of the land of Egypt!" So when Aaron saw it, he built an altar before it. And Aaron made a proclamation and said, "Tomorrow is a feast to the LORD." Then they rose early on the next day, offered burnt offerings, and brought peace offerings; and the people sat down to eat and drink, and rose up to play. And the LORD said to Moses, "Go, get down! For your people whom you brought out of the land of Egypt have corrupted themselves. They have turned aside quickly out of the way which I commanded them. They have made themselves a molded calf, and worshiped it and sacrificed to it, and said, 'This is your god, O Israel, that brought you out of the land of Egypt!'"
[962] **Matthew 7:1** "Judge not, that you be not judged."
[963] **Matthew 7:1-2** "Judge not, that ye be not judged. For with what judgment ye judge, ye shall be judged: and with what measure ye mete, it shall be measured unto you."

ger to forget that they made up the dream in which their toys are real, and recognize their wishes are their own.

T 29 J 5. Nightmares are childish dreams. Their toys have turned against the child who thought he made them real. Yet CAN a dream attack? Or CAN a toy grow large and dangerous and fierce and wild? This does the child believe BECAUSE he fears his thoughts, and gives them to his toys instead. And their reality becomes his own, because they seem to SAVE him from his thoughts. Yet do they KEEP his thoughts alive and real, but seen OUTSIDE himself, where they can turn against him for his treachery to them. He thinks he NEEDS them that he may escape his thoughts, because he thinks the THOUGHTS are real. And so he makes of ANYTHING a toy, to make his world remain outside himself, and play that HE is but a part of it.

T 29 J 6. There is a time when childhood should be passed and gone forever. Seek not to retain the toys of children.[964] Put them all away, for you have need of them no more. The dream of judgment is a children's game, in which the child becomes the father, powerful, but with the little wisdom of the child. What hurts him is destroyed; what helps him, blessed. Except he judges this as does a child, who does not KNOW what hurts and what will heal. And bad things seem to happen, and he is afraid of all the chaos in a world he thinks is governed by the laws he made. Yet is the real world unaffected by the world he thinks is real. Nor have its laws been changed because he did not understand. **T(1014) -828**

T 29 J 7. The real world still is but a dream. Except the figures have been changed. They are not seen as idols which betray. It is a dream in which no-one is used to substitute for something else, or interposed between the thoughts the mind conceives and what it sees. No-one is used for something he is not, for childish things have all been put away. And what was once a dream of judgment now has changed into a dream where all is joy, because that is the PURPOSE that it has. Only forgiving dreams can enter here, for time is almost over. And the forms which enter in the dreams are now perceived as brothers, not in judgment, but in love.

T 29 J 8. Forgiving dreams have little need to last. They are not made to separate the mind from what it thinks. They do not seek to prove the dream is being dreamed by someone ELSE. And in these dreams a melody is heard which everyone remembers, though he has not heard it since before all time began. Forgiveness, once complete, brings timelessness so close the song of Heaven can be heard, not with the ears, but with the holiness that never left the altar which abides forever deep within the Son of God. And when he hears this song again, he knows he NEVER heard it not. And where IS time, when dreams of judgment have been put away?

T 29 J 9. Whenever you feel fear in any form, – and you ARE fearful if you do not feel a deep content, a certainty of help, a calm assurance Heaven goes with you, – be sure you made an idol, and believe it will betray you. For, beneath your hope that it will save you, lie the guilt and pain of self-betrayal and uncertainty, so deep and bitter that the dream can not conceal completely all your sense of doom. Your self-betrayal MUST result in fear, and fear IS judgment, leading surely to the frantic search for idols and for death. Forgiving dreams remind you that you live in safety, and have NOT attacked yourself. **T(1015) -829**

T 29 J 10. So do your childish terrors melt away, and dreams become a sign that you have made a new beginning, NOT another try to worship idols, and to KEEP attack. Forgiving dreams are kind to everyone who figures in the dream. And so they bring the dreamer full release from dreams of fear. He does not fear his judgment, for he has judged no-one, nor has sought to be released THROUGH judgment from what judgment MUST impose. And all the while he is remembering what he forgot when judgment seemed to be the way to SAVE him from its penalty. **T(1016) -830**

---

[964] **1 Corinthians 13:11** When I was a child, I spoke as a child, I understood as a child, I thought as a child; but when I became a man, I put away childish things.

CHAPTER 30 – THE NEW BEGINNING

T 30 A. Introduction (*Notes* 2029 12:164)

T 30 A 1. The[965] "new beginning" now becomes the focus of the curriculum. The goal is clear, but now you need specific methods for attaining it. The speed by which it can be reached depends on only this; your willingness to practice every step. Each one will help a little, every time it is attempted. And, together, they will lead you both from dreams of judgment to forgiving dreams, and out of pain and fear. They are not new to you, but they are more ideas than rules of thought to you as yet. So now we need to practice them awhile, until they are the rules by which you live. We seek to make them habits now, so you will have them ready, and for ANY need.[966]

T 30 B. Rules for Decision (*Notes* 2029 12:164)

T 30 B 1. Decisions are continuous. You do not always know when you are making them. But, with a little practice in the ones you recognize, a set begins to form which sees you through the rest. It is not wise to let yourself become preoccupied with every step you take. The proper set, adopted consciously each time you wake, will put you well ahead. And if you find resistance strong and dedication weak, you are not ready. DO NOT FIGHT YOURSELF. But think about the kind of day you want, and tell yourself there is a way by which this very day can happen just like that. Then try again to HAVE the day you want.

T 30 B 2. 1. The outlook starts with this:
 "Today I will make NO decisions by myself."

This means that you are choosing NOT to be the judge of what to do. But it must ALSO mean you will not judge the situations where you will be called upon to make response. For if you judge them, you HAVE set the rules for how you should react to them. And then ANOTHER answer cannot BUT produce confusion and uncertainty AND FEAR. This is your major problem now. You still make up your minds, and THEN decide to ask what you should do. And what you hear may not resolve the problem AS YOU SAW IT FIRST. This leads to **T(1017) 831** fear, because it contradicts what you perceive, and so you feel attacked,[967] AND THEREFORE ANGRY. There are rules by which this will not happen. But it does occur, at first, to everyone who listens well.

T 30 B 3. 2. Throughout the day, at any time you think of it, and have a quiet moment for reflection, tell yourself again the kind of day you want; the feelings you would have, the things you WANT to happen, and the things you WOULD experience. And say,
 "If I make no decisions by[968] myself,
 This is the day that will be GIVEN me."[969]

These two procedures, practiced well, will serve to let you be directed WITHOUT fear, for opposition will not FIRST arise, and THEN become a problem in itself. But there will still be times when you have judged ALREADY. Now the answer will provoke attack, unless you quickly straighten out your mind to WANT an answer that will work. Be certain this has happened, if you feel yourself to be unwilling to sit by, and ask to have the answer GIVEN you. This means you HAVE decided by yourself, AND CANNOT SEE THE QUESTION. Now you need a quick restorative BEFORE you ask.

T 30 B 4. 3. Remember once again the day you want, and recognize that something has occurred which is not part of it. Then realize that you have asked a question by yourself, and MUST have set an answer in your terms. Then say,
 "I HAVE no question. I forgot what to decide."

This cancels out the terms which you have set, and lets the ANSWER show you what the question MUST have really been. Try to observe this rule without delay DESPITE your opposition. For you have ALREADY gotten angry, and your fear of being answered in a different way from what YOUR version of the question asks will gain momentum until you believe the day you want is one in which you get YOUR answer to your question. And you will not get it, for it would destroy **T(1018) -832** the day by robbing you of what you REALLY want. This can be very hard to realize, when once you have decided by yourself the rules which PROMISE you a happy day. But these decisions still can be undone, by simple methods which you CAN accept.

T 30 B 5. 4. If you are so unwilling to receive you cannot even let your QUESTION go, you can begin to change your mind with this:
 "At least I can decide I do not LIKE what I feel now."

This much is obvious, and paves the way for the next easy step, which follows this.

T 30 B 6. 5. Having decided that you do not like the way you feel, what could be easier than to continue with –
 "And so I HOPE I have been wrong."

This works AGAINST the sense of opposition, and reminds you that help is not being thrust upon you, but is something that you want and that you need BECAUSE you do not like the way you feel. This tiny opening will be enough to let you go ahead with just a few more steps you need to LET yourself be helped.

T 30 B 7. 6. Now you have reached the turning point, because it has occurred to you that YOU will gain, if what you have decided is NOT so. Until this point is reached, you will believe your happiness DEPENDS on being right. But this much reason have you now attained; YOU would be better off if you were WRONG. This tiny grain of wisdom will suffice to take you further. You are NOT coerced, but merely hope to have a thing you WANT. And you can say in perfect honesty,
 "I WANT another way to look at this."

 Now you have changed your mind about the day, and have REMEMBERED what you really want. Its PURPOSE has no longer been obscured by the insane belief you want it for the goal of being RIGHT when you are WRONG. This is the READINESS for asking,[970] brought to your awareness, for you CANNOT be in conflict when you **T(1019) -833** ask for what you want, and SEE that it is this for which you ask.

T 30 B 8. 7. This final step is but acknowledgment of LACK of opposition to be helped. It is a statement of an open mind, not certain yet, but willing to be shown:
 "Perhaps there IS another way to look at this.
 What can I LOSE by asking?"

Thus are you made ready for a question that makes sense, and so the ANSWER will make sense as well. Nor will you fight AGAINST it, for you see that it is YOU who will be helped by it.

T 30 B 9. It MUST be clear that it is easier to have a happy day if you PREVENT unhappiness from entering at all. But this takes practice in the rules which will PROTECT you from the ravages of fear. When THIS has been achieved, the sorry dream of judgment

---

[965] May 22, 1968
[966] *Urtext* manuscript has it "needs" was typed, and the "s" was crossed out. The *Notes* appears to have "need" as singular also.
[967] *Urtext* manuscript has a period here, which leaves the next phrase as a sentence fragment. We corrected it to a comma which is what is in the *Notes*.
[968] *Urtext* manuscript has "(for)" in brackets above "by" which is crossed out. The *Notes* has "for" originally written with "by" written in above.
[969] *Urtext* manuscript has no period here, only the quotation marks. The *Notes* has a period.

[970] A comma is typed and so is a forward slash overtyped. We just kept the comma, which reflects the *Notes*.

has FOREVER been undone. But, meanwhile, you have need for practicing the rules for its undoing. Let us, then, consider once again the very first of the decisions which are offered here. We said you can begin a happy day with the determination NOT to make decisions by yourself. This SEEMS to be a free decision in itself. And yet, you CANNOT make decisions by yourself. The only question really is WITH WHAT you choose to make them. That is really all.

T 30 B 10. The first rule, then, is not coercion, but a simple statement of a simple fact. You WILL not make decisions by yourself whatever you decide. For they are made with idols or with God. And you ask help of[971] Christ or anti-Christ, and which you choose WILL join with you, and tell you what to do.[972] Your day is NOT at random. It is set by what you choose to live it WITH, and HOW the friend whose counsel you have sought perceives your happiness. You ALWAYS ask advice before you can decide ANYTHING. Let THIS be understood, and you can see there cannot BE coercion here, nor grounds for opposition that you may be free. There IS no freedom from what must occur. And if you think there is, you MUST be wrong. **T(1020) -834**

T 30 B 11. The second rule as well is but a fact. For you and your adviser must AGREE on what you want BEFORE it can occur. It is but this AGREEMENT which permits all things to happen. NOTHING can be caused without some form of union, be it with a dream of judgment or the Voice for God. Decisions cause results BECAUSE they are not made in isolation. They are made by you and your adviser, for yourself, AND FOR THE WORLD AS WELL. The day you want you offer to the world, for it WILL be what you have asked for, and will reinforce the rule[973] of your adviser through the world. Whose kingdom is the world for you today?[974] What kind of day will you decide to have?

T 30 B 12. It needs but two who would have happiness this day to promise it to all the world. It needs but two to understand that they can not decide alone, to GUARANTEE the joy they asked for will be wholly shared. For they have understood the basic law which MAKES decision powerful, and gives it all effects that it will EVER have. It needs but two. These two ARE joined before there CAN be a decision. Let this be the ONE reminder that you keep in mind, and you will have the day you want, and give it to the world by having it yourselves. Your judgment has been LIFTED from the world by your decision for a happy day. And as you have received so MUST you give.[975] **T(1021) -835**

T 30 C. Freedom of Will (*Notes* 2045 12:180)

T 30 C 1. Do you not understand that to oppose the Holy Spirit IS to fight yourself? He tells you but YOUR will; He speaks for YOU. In HIS Divinity is but your own. And all He knows is but YOUR knowledge, saved for YOU, that you may do YOUR will through Him. God ASKS you do your will. He joins with YOU. He did not set His[976] kingdom up alone. And Heaven itself but represents your will, where everything created is for you. No spark of life but was created with your glad consent, as you would have it be. And not one Thought that God has ever had but waited for your blessing to be born. God is no enemy to you. He asks no more than that He hear you call Him Friend.

T 30 C 2. How wonderful it is to do your will! For that IS freedom. There is nothing else that ever should be called by freedom's name. UNLESS you do your will, you are NOT free. And would God leave His Son WITHOUT what he has chosen for himself? God but ensured that you would never LOSE your will, when He gave you His perfect Answer. Hear It now, that you may be reminded of His Love, and learn YOUR will. God would not have His Son made prisoner to what he does not want. He JOINS with you in willing you be free. And to OPPOSE Him is to make a choice against YOURSELF, and choose that YOU be bound.

T 30 C 3. Look once again upon your enemy, the one you chose to hate instead of love. For thus was hatred born into the world, and thus the rule of fear established here. Now hear God speak to you through Him Who is His Voice, and YOURS as well, reminding you that it is NOT your will to hate, and be a prisoner to fear, a slave to death, a LITTLE creature with a LITTLE life. Your will is boundless; it is NOT your will that it be bound. What lies in you has joined with God Himself in all creation's birth. Remember Him Who has created you, and through YOUR will created everything. **T(1022) -836**

T 30 C 4. Not one created thing but gives you thanks, for it is by your will that it was born. No light of Heaven shines except for you, for it was set in Heaven by your will. What cause have you for anger in a world which merely waits YOUR blessing to be free? If YOU be prisoner, then God Himself could not be free. For what is done to him whom God so loves is done to God Himself.[977] Think not HE wills to bind you, Who has made you co-creator of the universe along with Him. He would but KEEP your will forever and forever limitless.

T 30 C 5. The world awaits the freedom you will give, when you have recognized that YOU are free. But you will not forgive the world until you have forgiven Him Who GAVE your will to you. For it is BY your will the world is given freedom. Nor can YOU be free APART from Him Whose holy Will you share. God turns to YOU to ask the world be saved, for[978] by your OWN salvation is it healed. And no-one walks upon the earth but must depend on YOUR decision, that he learn death HAS no power over him because he shares YOUR freedom, as he shares your will. It IS your will to heal him, and because you have decided WITH him, he is healed. And now is God forgiven, for you chose to look upon your brother as a friend. **T(1023) -837**[979]

T 30 D. Beyond All Idols (*Notes* 2050 12:185)

T 30 D 1. Idols are quite specific. But your will is universal, being limitless. And so it has NO form, nor is content for its expression in the terms of form. Idols are LIMITS; they are the belief that there are FORMS which will bring happiness, and that, BY limiting, is all attained. It is as if you said, "I have no need of everything. This LITTLE thing I want, and it will BE as everything to me." And this MUST fail to satisfy, because it IS your will that everything be yours. Decide for idols, and you ask for LOSS. Decide for truth, and everything IS yours.

T 30 D 2. IT IS NOT FORM YOU SEEK. What form can be a substitute for God the Father's Love? What form can take the place of all the love in the divinity of God the Son? What idol can make two of what IS one? And CAN the limitless be limited? You do not WANT an idol. It is NOT your will to have one. It will NOT bestow on you the gift you seek. When you decide upon the FORM of what you want, you LOSE the understanding of its purpose. So you see YOUR will within the idol, thus reducing it to a SPECIFIC form.

---

[971] The word "the" or "their" is typed in here and crossed out. The *Notes* contains no such extra word.

[972] 1 John 2:22 "Who is a liar but he who denies that Jesus is the Christ? He is antichrist who denies the Father and the Son."

[973] *Urtext* manuscript has it "rules" the "s" is crossed out by handwritten mark-up reflecting the form in the *Notes*.

[974] Matthew 6:24 "No one can serve two masters; for either he will hate the one and love the other, or else he will be loyal to the one and despise the other. You cannot serve God and mammon."

[975] Matthew 10:8 "Heal the sick, cleanse the lepers, raise the dead, cast out demons. Freely you have received, freely give."

[976] In the *Urtext* manuscript it is lower case "his" but being a pronoun for God, was probably meant to be capitalized, as it is in the *Notes*.

---

[977] John 3:16 "For God so loved the world that He gave His only begotten Son, that whoever believes in Him should not perish but have everlasting life."

1John 4:11 Beloved, if God so loved us, we also ought to love one another.

[978] A typed word is crossed out, it is illegible

[979] May 24, 1968

But this could never BE your will, because what shares in all creation CANNOT be content with SMALL ideas and LITTLE things.

T 30 D 3. Behind the search for EVERY idol lies the yearning for completion. Wholeness has no form BECAUSE it is unlimited. To seek a special person or a thing to ADD to you to make yourself complete, can ONLY mean that you believe some FORM is missing. And, by finding THIS, you will achieve completion in a FORM you like. This is the purpose of an idol; that you will not look BEYOND it, to the source of your belief that you ARE incomplete. ONLY if you had sinned could this be so. For sin is the IDEA you are alone, and separated OFF from what is whole. And thus it WOULD be necessary for the search for wholeness to be made BEYOND the boundaries of limits on yourself. **T(1024) -838**

T 30 D 4. It NEVER is the idol that you want. But what you think it OFFERS you, you want indeed, and have the RIGHT to ask for. Nor could it be POSSIBLE it be denied. Your will to be complete IS but God's will, and this is given you BY being His. God knows not form. He CANNOT answer you in terms which have no meaning. And YOUR will could not BE satisfied with empty forms, made but to fill a gap which is not there. It is not this you WANT. Creation gives no SEPARATE person and no SEPARATE thing the power to complete the Son of God. What idol CAN be called upon to give the Son of God what he already HAS?

T 30 D 5. Completion is the FUNCTION of God's Son. He has no need to SEEK for it at all. Beyond ALL idols stands his holy will to be but what he IS. For MORE than whole is meaningless. If there were change in him; if he could be reduced to ANY form and limited to what is NOT in him, he would not BE as God created him. What idol CAN he need to be himself? For CAN he give a part of away? What is not whole cannot MAKE whole. But what is REALLY asked for CANNOT be denied. Your will IS granted. NOT in any form that would content you not, but in the whole, completely lovely Thought God holds of you. **T(1025) -839**[980]

T 30 D 6. Nothing that God knows not exists. And what He knows exists forever, changelessly. For thoughts endure as long as does the mind that thought of them, and in the Mind of God there is no ending, nor a time in which His Thoughts were absent, or could suffer change. Thoughts are not born and cannot die. They share the attributes of their creator, nor have they a separate life, apart from him. The thoughts YOU think are in your mind, as you are in the Mind Which thought of you. And so there ARE no separate parts in what exists within God's Mind. It is forever One, eternally united and at peace.

T 30 D 7. Thoughts SEEM to come and go. But all this means is that you are sometimes AWARE of them, and sometimes not. An unremembered thought is born again too YOU when it returns to your awareness. Yet it did not die when you forgot it. It was ALWAYS there, but YOU were unaware of it. The Thought God holds of you is perfectly unchanged by your forgetting. It will <u>ALWAYS</u> be exactly as it was before the time when you forgot, and will be just the same when you remember. And it is the same WITHIN the interval when you forgot. The Thoughts of God are FAR beyond all change, and shine forever. They await not birth. They wait for welcome and remembering.

T 30 D 8. The Thought God holds of you is like a star, unchangeable in an eternal sky. So high in Heaven is it set that those outside of Heaven know not it is there. But still and white and lovely will it shine through all eternity. There was no time it was not there. No instant when its light grew dimmer or less perfect ever was. Who knows the Father knows this light, for He is the eternal sky which holds it safe, forever lifted up and anchored sure. Its perfect purity does not depend on whether it is seen on earth or not. The sky embraces it, and softly holds it in its perfect place, which is as far from earth as earth from Heaven. It is not the distance nor the time which keeps this star invisible to earth. But those who seek for idols CANNOT know this star is there. **T(1026) -840**

T 30 D 9. Beyond all idols is the Thought God holds of you. Completely unaffected by the turmoil and the terror of the world, the dreams of birth and death that here are dreamed, the myriad of forms that fear can take, quite undisturbed, the Thought God holds of you remains EXACTLY as It always was. Surrounded by a stillness so complete no sound of battle comes remotely near, It rests in certainty and perfect peace. Here is your ONE reality kept safe, completely unaware of all the world that worships idols, and that knows not God. In perfect sureness of Its changelessness and of Its rest in Its eternal home, the Thought God holds of you has never left the Mind of Its Creator, Whom It knows as Its Creator knows that It is there.

T 30 D 10. Where could the Thought God holds of you EXIST but where you are? Is your reality a thing APART from you, and in a world which your reality knows NOTHING of? Outside you there IS no eternal sky, no changeless star, and NO reality. The Mind of Heaven's Son in Heaven is, for there the Mind of Father and of Son joined in creation which can HAVE no end. You have not two realities, but One. Nor can you be AWARE of more than one. An idol OR the Thought God holds of you is your reality. Forget not, then, that idols MUST keep hidden what you are, NOT from the Mind of God, but from your own. The star shines still; the sky has never changed. But you, the holy Son of God Himself, are unaware of your reality. **T(1027) -841**[981]

T 30 E. The Truth Behind Illusions (*Notes* 2058 12:193)

T 30 E 1. You WILL attack what does not satisfy, and thus you will not see you made it up. You ALWAYS fight illusions. For the truth behind them is so lovely and so still in loving gentleness, were you AWARE of it, you would forget defensiveness entirely, and rush to its embrace. The truth could never BE attacked. And this you knew when you made idols. They were made that this might be forgotten. You attack but FALSE ideas, and NEVER truthful ones. All idols ARE the false ideas you made to fill the gap you think arose between yourself and what is true. And you attack them for the things you think they REPRESENT. What lies BEYOND them cannot BE attacked.

T 30 E 2. The wearying, dissatisfying gods you made are blown-up children's toys. A child IS frightened when a wooden head springs up as a closed box is opened suddenly. Or when a soft and silent wooly bear begins to squeak as he takes hold of it. The rules he made for boxes and for bears have failed him, and have broken his control of what surrounds him. And he is afraid because he thought the rules PROTECTED him. Now must he learn the boxes and the bears did NOT deceive him, broke no rules, nor mean his world is made chaotic and unsafe. HE WAS MISTAKEN. He misunderstood what MADE him safe, and thought that it had left.

T 30 E 3. The gap that is not there is filled with toys in countless forms. And each one seems to break the rules you set for it. It never WAS the thing you thought. It MUST appear to break your rules for safety, since the RULES are wrong. But YOU are not endangered. You can laugh at popping heads and squeaking toys, as does the child who learns they are no threat to him. But while he likes to play with them, he still perceives them as obeying rules he made for his enjoyment. So there still are rules which they can seem to break, and frighten him. Yet IS he at the mercy of his toys? And CAN they represent a threat to him? **T(1028) -842**

T 30 E 4. Reality observes the laws of God, and NOT the rules you set. It is His laws which GUARANTEE your safety. All illusions that you believe about yourself obey NO laws. They seem to dance a

---

[980] May 27, 1968

[981] May 31, 1968

little while, according to the rules you set for them. But then they fall, and cannot rise again. They are but toys, my children. Do not grieve for them. Their dancing never brought you joy, but neither were they things to frighten you, nor make you safe if they obeyed your rules. They must be neither cherished NOR attacked, but merely looked upon as children's toys, without a SINGLE meaning of their own. See ONE in them, and you will see them all. See NONE in them, and they will touch you not.

T 30 E 5. Appearances deceive BECAUSE they are appearances, and not reality. Dwell not on them in ANY form. They but OBSCURE reality. And they bring fear BECAUSE they hide the truth. Do not attack what you have made to LET you be deceived. For thus you prove that you HAVE BEEN deceived. Attack HAS power to make illusions real. Yet what it makes is nothing. Who could be made fearful by a power that can have no REAL effects at all? What could it BE but an illusion, making things appear like to itself? Look calmly at its toys, and understand that they are idols which but dance to vain desires. Give them not your worship, for they are not there. But this is EQUALLY forgotten in attack.

T 30 E 6. God's Son needs NO defense against his dreams. His idols do not threaten him at all. His ONE mistake is that he thinks them real. What can the power of illusions DO? Appearances can but deceive the mind that WANTS to be deceived. And you can make a simple choice that will forever place you far BEYOND deception.[982] You need not concern yourself with HOW this will be done, for this you CANNOT understand. But you WILL understand that mighty changes have been quickly brought about, when you decide one very simple thing; you do not WANT whatever you believe an idol gives. For thus the Son of God declares that he is free of idols. And thus IS he free. **T(1029) -843**

T 30 E 7. Salvation is a paradox indeed! What could it be EXCEPT a happy dream? For you are asked but to forgive all things that no-one ever did; to overlook what is not there; and not to look upon the unreal as reality. You are but asked to let your will be done, and seek no longer for the things you do not want. And you are asked to let yourself be free of all the dreams of what you never were, and seek no more to substitute the strength of idle wishes for the Will of God. Here does the dream of separation start to fade and disappear. For here the gap that is not there begins to be perceived without the toys of terror that you made.

T 30 E 8. No more than this is asked. Be glad indeed salvation asks so little, NOT so much. It asks for NOTHING in reality. And even in illusions it but asks forgiveness be the substitute for fear. Such is the ONLY rule for happy dreams. The gap is emptied of the toys of fear, and then its unreality is plain. Dreams are for nothing. And the Son of God CAN have no need of them. They offer him no single thing that he could ever want. He is DELIVERED from illusions by his will, and but restored to what he IS. What could God's plan for his salvation BE, except a means to give him to Himself? **T(1030) -844**[983]

T 30 F. The Only Purpose (*Notes* 2064 12:199)

T 30 F 1. The real world is the state of mind in which the ONLY purpose of the world is seen to be forgiveness. Fear is NOT its goal, and the ESCAPE from guilt becomes its aim. The VALUE of forgiveness is perceived, and TAKES THE PLACE of idols, which are sought no longer, for their "gifts" are not held dear. No rules are idly set, and no demands are made of anyone or anything to twist and fit into the dream of fear. Instead, there is a wish to understand all things created as they really are. And it is recognized that all things must be FIRST forgiven, and THEN understood. Here, it is thought that understanding is ACQUIRED by attack. There it is clear that BY attack is understanding LOST.

T 30 F 2. The folly of pursuing guilt as GOAL is fully recognized. And idols are not wanted there, for guilt is recognized as the sole cause of pain in any form. No-one is tempted by its vain appeal, for suffering and death have been perceived as things NOT wanted, and not striven FOR. The possibility of freedom has been grasped and welcomed, and the means by which it can be gained can now be understood. The world becomes a place of hope, because its only purpose is to BE a place where hope of happiness can be fulfilled. And no-one stands outside this hope, because the world has been united in belief the purpose of the world is one which all must SHARE, if hope be more than just a dream.

T 30 F 3. Not yet is Heaven quite remembered, for the purpose of forgiveness still remains. Yet everyone is certain he will go BEYOND forgiveness, and he but remains until it is made perfect in himself. He has no wish for anything but this. And fear has dropped away, because he is united in his purpose with HIMSELF. There is a hope of happiness in him so sure and constant he can barely stay, and wait a little longer with his feet still touching earth. Yet is he glad to wait 'til every hand is joined, and every heart made ready to arise and go with him. For thus is HE made ready for the step in which is all forgiveness left behind. **T(1031) -845**

T 30 F 4. The final step is God's, because it is but God Who could create a perfect Son, and share His Fatherhood with him. No-one outside of Heaven knows how this can be. For understanding this is Heaven itself. Even the real world has a purpose still beneath creation and eternity. But fear is gone, because its purpose is forgiveness, NOT idolatry. And so is Heaven's Son prepared to be Himself, and to remember that the Son of God knows everything his Father understands, and understands it perfectly with Him. The real world still falls short of this, for this is God's Own Purpose; ONLY His, and yet completely shared and perfectly fulfilled.

T 30 F 5. The real world is a state in which the mind has learned how easily do idols go when they are still perceived, but wanted not. How willingly the mind can let them go when it has understood that idols are nothing and nowhere, AND ARE PURPOSELESS. For only then can guilt and sin be seen WITHOUT a purpose, and as meaningless. Thus is the real world's purpose gently brought into awareness, to REPLACE the goal of sin and guilt. And all that stood BETWEEN your image of yourself and what you ARE forgiveness washes joyfully away. Yet God need not create His Son AGAIN, that what is his be given BACK to him. The gap between your brother and yourself was never there. And what the Son of God knew in creation he MUST know again.

T 30 F 6. When brothers join in purpose in the world of fear, they stand ALREADY at the edge of the real world. Perhaps they still look back, and think they see an idol that they want.[984] Yet has their path been surely set AWAY from idols toward reality, for when they joined their hands, it was Christ's hand they took. And they WILL look on Him Whose hand they hold. The face of Christ is looked upon BEFORE the Father is remembered. For He MUST be unremembered 'til His Son has reached BEYOND forgiveness to the Love of God. Yet is the love of Christ accepted first. And THEN will come the knowledge They are One. How light and easy is the step across the narrow boundaries of the world of fear, when you have RECOGNIZED Whose hand you hold! **T(1032) -846**

T 30 F 7. Within your hand is everything you need to walk with perfect confidence away from fear forever.[985] And to go straight on, and quickly reach the gate of Heaven itself. For He Whose hand you hold was waiting but for you to join Him. Now that you have come,

---

[982] *Urtext* manuscript has it typed "perception" handwritten mark-up changes it to "deception." The *Notes* has it as "deception."
[983] June 30, 1968
[984] **Luke 9:62** But Jesus said to him, "No one, having put his hand to the plow, and looking back, is fit for the kingdom of God."
[985] **Genesis 28:17** And he was afraid and said, "How awesome is this place! This is none other than the house of God, and this is the gate of heaven!"

would HE delay in showing you the way that He must walk with you? His blessing lies on you as surely as His Father's Love rests upon Him. His gratitude to you is past your understanding, for you have enabled Him to rise from chains, and go with you TOGETHER to His Father's house.[986] An ancient hate is passing from the world, and with it goes ALL hatred and ALL fear. Look back no longer, for what lies ahead is all you EVER wanted in your hearts.

T 30 F 8. Give up the world! But NOT to sacrifice. You never WANTED it. What happiness have you sought here that did not bring you pain? What moment of content has not been bought at fearful price in coins of suffering? Joy HAS no cost. It is your sacred right. And what you pay for is NOT happiness. Be speeded on your way by honesty, and let not your experiences here deceive in retrospect. They were NOT free from bitter cost and joyless consequence. Do not look back except in honesty. And when an idol tempts you, think of this; there never was a time an idol brought you ANYTHING except the "gift" of guilt. Not one was bought EXCEPT at cost of pain. Nor was it ever paid by you alone.

T 30 F 9. Be merciful unto your brother, then. And do not choose an idol thoughtlessly, remembering that he will pay the cost as well as you.[987] For HE will be delayed when you look back, and YOU will not perceive Whose hand you hold. Look forward, then, and walk in confidence, with happy hearts that beat in hope and do not pound in fear. The Will of God forever lies in those whose hands are joined. UNTIL they joined, they thought He was their enemy. But when they joined and SHARED a purpose, they were free to learn their will is one. And thus the Will of God MUST reach to their awareness. Nor can they forget for long that It is but their own. T(1033) -847

T 30 G. The Justification for Forgiveness (*Notes 2072 12:207*)

T 30 G 1. Anger[988] is NEVER justified. Attack has NO foundation. It is here escape from fear begins, and will be made complete. Here is the real world given in exchange for dreams of terror. For it is on this forgiveness rests, AND IS BUT NATURAL. You are NOT asked to offer pardon where attack is due, and WOULD be justified. For this would mean that you forgive a sin by overlooking what is REALLY there. THIS IS NOT PARDON. For it would assume that, by responding in a way which is NOT justified, your PARDON will become the answer to attack which HAS been made. And thus is pardon inappropriate, by being granted where it is NOT due.

T 30 G 2. Pardon is ALWAYS justified, and has a sure foundation. You do NOT forgive the unforgivable, nor overlook a REAL attack that calls for punishment. Salvation does not lie in being asked to make unnatural responses, which are inappropriate to what is real. Instead, it merely asks that you respond appropriately to what is NOT real, by not perceiving what has not occurred. If pardon WERE unjustified, you WOULD be asked to sacrifice your rights when you return forgiveness for attack. But you are merely asked to see forgiveness as the NATURAL reaction to distress which rests on error, and thus calls for help. Forgiveness is the ONLY sane response. It KEEPS your rights from being lost to you.

T 30 G 3. This understanding is the ONLY change that lets the real world rise to take the place of dreams of terror. Fear cannot ARISE unless attack is justified. And if it HAD a real foundation, pardon could have none. The real world is achieved when you perceive the basis of FORGIVENESS is quite real and fully justified. While you regard it as a gift unwarranted, it MUST uphold the guilt you would "forgive." Unjustified forgiveness IS attack. And this is all the world can ever give. It pardons "sinners" sometimes, but remains AWARE that they have sinned. And so they do not MERIT the forgiveness that it gives. T(1034) -848

T 30 G 4. This is the false forgiveness which the world employs to KEEP the sense of[989] sin alive. And recognizing God is just, it seems impossible His pardon COULD be real.[990] Thus is the fear of God the sure result of seeing pardon as unmerited. No-one who sees himself as guilty CAN avoid the fear of God. But he is SAVED from this dilemma if HE can forgive. The mind MUST think of its Creator as it looks upon itself. If you can see your brother MERITS pardon, you have learned forgiveness is YOUR right, as much as his. Nor will you think that God intends for you a fearful judgment which your brother does not merit. For it is the truth that you CAN merit neither more nor less than he. T(1035) -849[991]

T 30 G 5. Forgiveness RECOGNIZED as merited will heal. It gives the miracle its strength to OVERLOOK illusions. This is how you learn that you must be forgiven too. There CAN be no appearance that can NOT be overlooked. For, if there were, it would be necessary FIRST there be some sin which stands BEYOND forgiveness. There would be an error that is MORE than a mistake; a special FORM of error, which remains unchangeable, eternal, and beyond correction or escape. There would be one mistake which had the power to UNDO creation, and to make a world which could REPLACE it and DESTROY the Will of God. Only if this were possible could there be SOME appearances which could withstand the miracle, and NOT be healed by it.

T 30 G 6. There is no surer proof idolatry is what you wish than a belief there are some forms of sickness and of joylessness forgiveness CANNOT cure. This means that you prefer to keep SOME idols, and are not prepared, as yet, to let ALL idols go. And thus you think that SOME appearances are real, and not appearances at all. Be not deceived about the MEANING of a fixed belief that SOME appearances are harder to look past than others are. It ALWAYS means you think forgiveness must be limited. And you have set a goal of partial pardon and a limited escape from guilt FOR YOU. What can this be, except a false forgiveness of YOURSELF, and everyone who seems APART from you?

T 30 G 7. It MUST be true the miracle can heal ALL forms of sickness, or it CANNOT HEAL. Its purpose cannot be to judge which FORMS are real, and which APPEARANCES are true. If one appearance must remain APART from healing, one illusion must be part of truth. And you could NOT escape all guilt, but only SOME of it. You must forgive God's Son ENTIRELY. Or you will keep an image of yourself that is not whole, and will remain afraid to look within, and find escape from EVERY idol there. Salvation rests on faith there CANNOT be some forms of guilt which you can NOT forgive. And so there cannot be appearances which have replaced the truth about God's Son. T(1036) -850

T 30 G 8. Look on your brother with the willingness to see him as he is. And do not keep a part of him outside your willingness that he be healed. To heal is to make whole. And what is whole can HAVE no missing parts that have been kept outside. Forgiveness rests on recognizing this, and being GLAD there cannot be some forms of sickness which the miracle must LACK the power to heal. God's Son is perfect, or he cannot be God's Son. Nor will you KNOW him, if you think he does not merit the escape from guilt in ALL its

---

[986] **John 14:2** "In My Father's house are many mansions; if it were not so, I would have told you. I go to prepare a place for you."
[987] **Luke 6:36** "Therefore be merciful, just as your Father also is merciful."
[988] June 7, 1968
[989] *Urtext* manuscript has it typed "senseless." It is crossed out and handwriting changes it to "sense of" which is what the *Notes* says.
[990] **Isaiah 45:21** Tell and bring forth your case;
Yes, let them take counsel together.
Who has declared this from ancient time?
Who has told it from that time?
Have not I, the LORD?
And there is no other God besides Me,
A just God and a Savior;
There is none besides Me.
[991] June 10, 1968

forms and ALL its consequence. There IS no way to think of him but this, if you would know the truth about yourself:

> "I thank you, Father, for your perfect Son,
> And in his glory will I see my own."[992]

T 30 G 9. Here is the joyful statement that there are NO forms of evil which can overcome the Will of God; the glad acknowledgment that guilt has NOT succeeded, by your wish, to make illusions real. And what is this, except a simple statement of the truth? Look on your brother with this hope in you, and you will understand he COULD not make an error that could change the truth in him. It is NOT difficult to overlook mistakes that have been given no effects. But what you see as having power to make an idol of the Son of God, you will NOT pardon. For he has become to you a graven image, and a sign of death.[993] Is THIS your Savior? Is his Father WRONG about His Son? Or have YOU been deceived in him who has been given you to heal for YOUR salvation and deliverance? T(1037) -851[994]

T 30 H. The New Interpretation (*Notes* 2078 12:213)

T 30 H 1. Would God have left the meaning of the world to YOUR interpretation? If He had, it HAS no meaning. For it cannot be that meaning changes constantly, and yet is true. The Holy Spirit looks upon the world as with ONE purpose, changelessly established. And NO situation can affect its aim, but MUST be in accord with it. For ONLY if its aim could change with every situation could each one be OPEN to interpretation which is different every time you think of it. You ADD an element into the script you write for every minute in the day, and all that happens now means something else. You TAKE AWAY another element, and every meaning shifts accordingly.

T 30 H 2. What do your scripts reflect except your plans for what the day SHOULD be? And thus you judge disaster and success, advance, retreat, and gain and loss. These judgments all are made according to the roles the script assigns. The fact they have no meaning in themselves is DEMONSTRATED by the ease with which these labels change with other judgments made on different aspects of experience. And then, in looking back, you think you see ANOTHER meaning in what went before. What have you really done, except to show there WAS no meaning there?[995] And YOU assigned a meaning in the light of goals that change, with EVERY meaning shifting as they change.

T 30 H 3. Only a CONSTANT purpose can endow events with stable meaning. But it must ACCORD ONE MEANING TO THEM ALL. If they are given DIFFERENT meanings, it MUST mean that they reflect but different purposes, and this is ALL the meaning that they have. Can this BE meaning? Can confusion BE what meaning means? Perception CANNOT be in constant flux, and make allowance for stability of meaning ANYWHERE. Fear is a judgment NEVER justified. Its presence has no meaning but to show you wrote a fearful script, and are afraid accordingly. But NOT because the thing you fear has fearful meaning in itself. T(1038) -852

T 30 H 4. A common purpose is the ONLY means whereby perception can be stabilized, and ONE interpretation given to the world and all experiences here. In this shared purpose is one meaning shared by everyone and everything you see. You do not have to judge, for you have learned one meaning has been GIVEN everything, and you are GLAD to see it everywhere. It cannot change BECAUSE you would perceive it everywhere, unchanged by circumstance. And so you OFFER it to all events, and LET them offer you stability. Escape from judgment simply lies in this; - All things have but one purpose, which you share with all the world. And nothing IN the world can BE opposed to it, for it belongs TO everything, as it belongs to you.

T 30 H 5. In SINGLE purpose is the end of all ideas of sacrifice, which MUST assume a DIFFERENT purpose for the one who gains and him who loses. There could BE no thought of sacrifice apart from this idea. And it IS this idea of different goals which makes perception shift and meaning change. In one united goal does this become impossible, for your AGREEMENT makes interpretation stabilize and last. How can communication REALLY be established, while the symbols which are used mean different things? The Holy Spirit's goal gives ONE interpretation, meaningful to you AND to your brother. Thus can you communicate with him, and he with you. In symbols which you BOTH can understand, the sacrifice of meaning is undone.

T 30 H 6. All sacrifice entails the LOSS of your ability to see relationships AMONG events. And, looked at SEPARATELY, they HAVE no meaning. For there is no light by which they can be seen and understood. They HAVE no purpose. And what they are FOR cannot BE seen. In any thought of loss, there IS no meaning. No-one has agreed with you on what it means. It is a part of a distorted script, which cannot be interpreted with meaning. It must be forever unintelligible. This is NOT communication. Your dark dreams are but the senseless, isolated scripts you write in sleep. Look not to separate dreams for meaning. ONLY dreams of pardon can be shared. They mean the same for BOTH of you. T(1039) -853

T 30 H 7. Do not interpret out of solitude, for what you see means nothing. It will shift in what it stands for, and you will believe the world is an uncertain place, in which you walk in danger and uncertainty. It is but your INTERPRETATIONS which are lacking in stability. And they are NOT in line with what you really are. This is a state so seemingly unsafe that fear MUST rise. Do not continue thus, my brothers. We have ONE Interpreter.[996] And through His use of symbols are we joined, so that they mean the same to ALL of us. Our common language lets us speak to all our brothers, and to understand with them forgiveness has been given to us all, and thus we CAN communicate again. T(1040) -854[997]

T 30 I. Changeless Reality (*Notes* 2083 12:218)

T 30 I 1. Appearances deceive BUT CAN BE CHANGED. Reality is changeless. It does not deceive at all. And if you fail to see BEYOND appearances, you ARE deceived. For everything you see will change, and yet you thought it real before, and now you think it real again. Reality is thus reduced to form, and CAPABLE of change. Reality is changeless. It is this that MAKES it real, and KEEPS it separate from all appearances. It MUST transcend all form to be itself. It CANNOT change. The miracle is means to demonstrate that ALL appearances can change BECAUSE they are appearances, and CANNOT have the changelessness reality entails. The miracle attests salvation FROM appearances by SHOWING they can change.

T 30 I 2. Your brother has a changelessness in him beyond appearance and deception both. It is obscured by changing views of him which you PERCEIVE as his reality. The happy dream about him

---

[992] **Matthew 11:25** At that time Jesus answered and said, "I thank You, Father, Lord of heaven and earth, that You have hidden these things from the wise and prudent and have revealed them to babes."
John 17:20-13 "Neither for these only do I pray, but for them also that believe on me through their word; that they may all be one; even as thou, Father, *art* in me, and I in thee, that they also may be in us: that the world may believe that thou didst send me. And the glory which thou hast given me I have given unto them; that they may be one, even as we *are* one; I in them, and thou in me; that they may be perfected into one; that the world may know that thou didst send me, and lovedst them, even as thou lovedst me."
[993] **Exodus 20:4** You shall not make for yourself a carved image--any likeness of anything that is in heaven above, or that is in the earth beneath, or that is in the water under the earth;
[994] June 13, 1968
[995] The question mark is not in the original *Urtext* manuscript, nor in the *Notes*. It is however, necessary since the sentence is a question.

[996] *Urtext* manuscript has it spelled "Interpretor"
[997] June 17, 1968

takes the form of the appearance of his perfect health; his perfect freedom from all forms of lack; and safety from disaster of all kinds. The miracle is proof he is not bound by loss or suffering in any form BECAUSE IT CAN SO EASILY BE CHANGED. This demonstrates that it was never real, and COULD not stem from his reality. For that is changeless, and has no effects which anything in Heaven or on earth could ever alter. But appearances are shown to be unreal BECAUSE they change.

T 30 I 3. What is temptation but a wish to make illusions real? It does not SEEM to be the wish that NO reality be so. But it IS an assertion that some FORMS of idols have a powerful appeal which makes them HARDER to resist than those you would not WANT to have reality. Temptation, then, is nothing more than this; - a prayer the miracle touch not some dreams, but KEEP their unreality obscure, and GIVE to them reality instead. And Heaven gives no answer to the prayer, nor CAN the miracle be given you to heal appearances you do not like. YOU HAVE ESTABLISHED LIMITS. What you ask IS given you,[998] but not of God Who knows no limits. YOU have limited YOURSELF. **T(1041) -855**

T 30 I 4. Reality is changeless. Miracles but show what you have interposed BETWEEN reality and your awareness is unreal, and does not interfere at all. The cost of the belief there must be some appearances BEYOND the hope of change is that the miracle cannot come forth from you consistently. For you have ASKED it be withheld from power to heal all dreams. There is no miracle you cannot have when you DESIRE healing. But there is no miracle that CAN be given you UNLESS you want it. CHOOSE what you would heal, and He Who gives all miracles has not been given freedom to bestow His gifts upon God's Son. When he is tempted, he DENIES reality. And he becomes the willing slave of what he chose instead.

T 30 I 5. BECAUSE reality is changeless is a miracle already there to heal all things that change, and offer them[999] to you to see in happy form, devoid of fear. It WILL be given you to look upon your brother thus. But NOT while you would have it otherwise in some respects. For this but means you would not have him healed and whole. The Christ in him is perfect. Is it this that you would look upon? Then let there be no dreams about him that you would PREFER to seeing this. And you WILL see the Christ in him because you LET Him come to you. And when He has appeared to you, you will be certain you are like Him, for He is the changeless in your brother AND in you.[1000]

T 30 I 6. This will you look upon, when you decide there is not one appearance you would hold in place of what your brother really IS. Let no temptation to prefer a dream allow uncertainty to enter here. Be not made guilty and afraid when you are tempted by a dream of what he is. But do not give it power to REPLACE the changeless in him in your sight of him. There is no false appearance but will fade, if you request a miracle instead. There is no pain from which he is not free, if you would have him be but what he is. Why should you fear to see the Christ in him? You but behold yourself in what you see. As he is healed are YOU made free of guilt, and his appearance IS your own to you. **T(1042) -856**[1001]

---

[998] **Matthew 7:7** "Ask, and it shall be given you; seek, and ye shall find; knock, and it shall be opened unto you:"

[999] The *Urtext* manuscript has "it" which is grammatically incorrect. Both the *Notes* and the *HLC* have "them" which appears correct.

[1000] **1 John 3:2** Beloved, now we are children of God; and it has not yet been revealed what we shall be, but we know that when He is revealed, we shall be like Him, for we shall see Him as He is.

[1001] June 24, 1968

CHAPTER 31 – THE SIMPLICITY OF SALVATION

T 31 A. Introduction (*Notes* 2088 12:223)

T 31 A 1. How simple is salvation! All it says is what was never true is not true now, and never will be. The impossible has NOT occurred, and CAN have no effects. And that is all. Can this BE hard to learn by anyone who WANTS it to be true? ONLY unwillingness to learn it could make such an easy lesson difficult. How hard is it to see that what is false can not be true, and what is true can not be false? You can no longer say that you perceive no differences in false and true. You have been told EXACTLY how to tell one from the other, and just what to do if you become confused. Why, then, do you persist in learning NOT such simple things?

T 31 A 2. There IS a reason. But confuse it not with difficulty in the simple things salvation asks you learn. It teaches but the very obvious. It merely goes from one apparent lesson to the next, in easy steps which lead you gently from one to another, with no strain at all. This CANNOT be confusing, yet you ARE confused. For somehow you believe that what is TOTALLY confused is easier to learn and understand. What you have taught yourselves is such a giant learning feat it is indeed incredible. But you accomplished it because you wanted to, and did not pause in diligence to judge it hard to learn, or too complex to grasp.

T 31 A 3. No-one who understands what you have learned, how carefully you learned it, and the pains to which you went to practice and repeat the lessons endlessly, in every form you could conceive of them, could EVER doubt the power of your learning skill. There is no greater power in the world. The world was MADE by it, and even now depends on nothing else. The lessons you have taught yourselves have been so overlearned and fixed they rise like heavy curtains, to obscure the simple and the obvious. Say not you cannot learn them. For your power to learn is strong enough to teach you that your will is NOT your own; your thoughts do NOT belong to you; and even YOU are someone else. **T(1043) -857**

T 31 A 4. Who could maintain that lessons such as these are easy? Yet you have learned more than this. You have continued, taking every step, however difficult, without complaint, until a world was built that suited you. And every lesson that makes up the world arises from the first accomplishment of learning; an enormity so great the Holy Spirit's Voice seems small and still before its magnitude.[1002] The world began with one strange lesson, powerful enough to render God forgotten, and His Son an alien to himself, in exile from the home where God Himself established him. You who have taught yourselves the Son of God is guilty, say not that you cannot learn the simple things salvation teaches you.

T 31 A 5. Learning is an ability you made, and gave yourselves. It was NOT made to do the Will of God, but to uphold a wish that It COULD be opposed, and that a will APART from It was yet more real than It. And this has learning sought to demonstrate, and you HAVE learned what it was made to teach. Now does your ancient overlearning stand implacable before the Voice of Truth, and teach you that Its lessons are not true; too hard to learn, too difficult to see, and too opposed to what is REALLY true. Yet you WILL learn them, for their learning is the ONLY purpose for your learning skill the Holy Spirit sees in all the world.

T 31 A 6. His simple lessons in forgiveness have a power mightier than yours, because they call from God and from your Self to you. Is this a LITTLE Voice, so small and still It cannot rise above the senseless noise of sounds which have no meaning? God willed not His Son forget Him. And the power of His Will is in the Voice That speaks for Him. Which lesson will you learn? Which outcome is inevitable, sure as God, and far beyond all doubts or question? CAN it be your little learning,[1003] strange in outcome, and incredible in difficulty, will withstand the simple lessons being taught to you in every moment of each day, since time began and learning had been made? **T(1044) -858**

T 31 A 7. The lessons to be learned are only two. Each has its outcome in a different world. And each world follows surely from its source. The certain outcome of the lesson that God's Son is guilty is the world you see. It IS a world of terror and despair. Nor IS there hope of happiness in it. There IS no plan for safety you can make that ever will succeed. There IS no joy that you can seek for here, and hope to find. But this is NOT the only outcome which your learning can produce. However much you may have overlearned your chosen task, the lesson[1004] which reflects the Love of God is stronger still. And you WILL learn God's Son is innocent, and see ANOTHER world.

T 31 A 8. The outcome of the lesson that God's Son is guiltless is a world in which there is no fear, and everything is lit with hope, and sparkles with a gentle friendliness. Nothing but calls to you in soft appeal to be your friend, and let it join with you. And never does a call remain unheard, misunderstood, or left unanswered in the language in which the call itself was made. And you will understand it was THIS call that everyone and everything within the world has ALWAYS made. But YOU had not perceived it as it was. And now you see YOU were mistaken. You had been deceived by forms the call was hidden in. And so you did not hear it, and had lost a friend who ALWAYS wanted to be part of you.

T 31 A 9. The soft, eternal calling of each part of God's creation to the whole is heard throughout the world this second lesson brings. There is no living thing which does not share the universal will that it be whole, and that you do not leave its call unheard. Without your answer is it left to die, as it is saved from death when you have heard its[1005] calling as the ancient call to life, and understood that it is but your own. The Christ in you remembers God with all the certainty with which He knows His Love. But ONLY if His Son is innocent can He BE Love. For God were fear indeed, if he whom He created innocent could be a slave to guilt. God's perfect Son remembers his creation. But in guilt he has forgotten what he really is. **T(1045) -859**

T 31 A 10. The fear of God results as surely from the lesson that His Son is guilty as God's Love must be remembered when he learns[1006] his innocence. For hate must father fear, and look upon its father as itself. How wrong are you who fail to hear the call that echoes past each seeming call to death, that sings behind each murderous attack, and pleads that love restore the dying world! You do not understand Who calls to you beyond each form of hate, each call to war. But you will recognize Him as you give Him answer in the language that He calls. He will appear when you have answered Him, and you will know in Him that God is Love.[1007]

T 31 A 11. What is temptation but a wish to make the wrong decision on what you would learn, and have an outcome which you do

---
[1002] **1 Kings 19:12** And after the earthquake a fire, but the LORD was not in the fire; and after the fire a still small voice.

[1003] In the *Urtext* manuscript a period appears here, but no capital on the next word. The *Notes* has a comma. We're calling the period a typo.
[1004] The word "lessons" is originally typed, with the final s crossed out. *HLC* also omits the final s, as does the *Notes*.
[1005] *Urtext* manuscript has it typed "it", it appears to have a handwritten "s" added. *HLC* also has the s, so does the *Notes*.
[1006] *Urtext* manuscript has it typed "remembers", that is crossed out and "LEARNS" is handwritten. That's also the reading in the *Notes*. While the handwriten mark-up is in all caps, the word is not underlined in the *Notes* so it seems that the use of capitals in the mark-up is not intended to convey emphasis.
[1007] **1 John 4:16** He who does not love does not know God, for God is love. **1 John 4:8** And we have known and believed the love that God has for us. God is love, and he who abides in love abides in God, and God in him.

not want? It is the RECOGNITION that it is a state of mind UNWANTED that becomes the means whereby the choice is reassessed; another outcome seen to be preferred. You are deceived if you believe you want disaster and disunity and pain. Hear not the call for this within yourself, but listen, rather, to the deeper call beyond it, that appeals for peace and joy. And all the world will GIVE you joy and peace. For as you hear you answer, and behold! - your answer is the proof of what you learned. Its outcome is the world you look upon. **T(1046) -860**[1008]

T 31 A 12. Let us be still an instant,[1009] and forget all things we ever learned, all thoughts we had, and every preconception that we hold of what things mean, and what their purpose is. Let us remember not our own ideas of what the world is for. We do not know. Let every image held of anyone be loosened from our minds and swept away. Be innocent of judgment, unaware of any thoughts of evil or of good that ever crossed your mind of anyone. Now do you know him not. But you ARE free to learn of him, and learn of him anew. Now is he born again to you, and you are born again to him,[1010] WITHOUT the past that sentenced him to die, and you with him. Now is he free to live, as you are free, because an ancient learning passed away, and left a place for truth to be reborn.

T 31 B. The Illusion of an Enemy (*Notes* 2097 12:232)

T 31 B 1. An ancient lesson is not overcome[1011] by the OPPOSING of the new and old. It is not VANQUISHED that the truth be known, or fought against to LOSE to truth's appeal. There is no battle which must be prepared, no time to be expended, and no plans that need be laid for bringing in the new. There IS an ancient battle being waged AGAINST the truth, but truth does not respond. Who COULD be hurt in such a war, unless he hurts himself? He HAS no enemy in truth. And CAN he be assailed by dreams? Let us review again what seems to stand BETWEEN you and the truth of what you are. For there are steps in its relinquishment. The first is a decision which YOU make. But afterwards, the truth is GIVEN you.

T 31 B 2. You would ESTABLISH truth. And by your wish, you set two choices to be made each time you think you must decide on anything. NEITHER is true. Nor ARE they different. Yet must we see them both, before you can look PAST them, to the ONE Alternative that IS a different choice. But not in dreams you made, that this might be OBSCURED to you. What YOU would choose between is NOT a choice, and gives but the ILLUSION it is free, for it will have ONE outcome either way. Thus is it really not a choice at all. The leader and the follower emerge as SEPARATE roles, each seeming to possess advantages you would not want to lose. So in their fusion there appears to be the hope of satisfaction and of peace. **T(1047) -861**

T 31 B 3. You see yourself divided into both these roles, forever split between the two. And every friend or enemy becomes a means to help you save yourself from this. Perhaps you call it love. Perhaps you think that it is murder justified at last. You hate the one you gave the leader's role when YOU would have it, and you hate as well his NOT assuming it, at times you want to let the follower in you arise, and give away the role of leadership. And this is what you made your brother FOR, and learned to think that this his purpose IS. Unless he serves it, he has not fulfilled the function that was given him by you. And thus he merits death, because he has no purpose and no usefulness to you.

T 31 B 4. And what of him? What does he want of YOU? What COULD he want, but what you want of him? Herein is life as easily as death, for what you choose you choose as well for him. Two calls you make to him, as he to you. Between these two IS choice, because from them there IS a different outcome. If he be the leader or the follower to you, it matters not, for you have chosen death. But if he calls for death or calls for life, for hate or for forgiveness and for help, is NOT the same in outcome. Hear the one, and you are separate from him, and are lost. But hear the other, and you join with him, and in your answer is salvation found.

T 31 B 5. The voice you hear in him is but your own. What does he ask you for? And listen well. For he is asking what will come to you, because you see an image of yourself, and hear your voice requesting what you want. Before you answer, pause to think of this:

The answer that I give my brother is
What I am asking for. And what I learn
Of him is what I learn about myself.

Then let us wait an instant and be still,[1012] forgetting everything we thought we heard; remembering how much we do not know. This brother neither leads nor follows us, but walks beside us on the self-same road. He is like us, as near or far away from what we want as we will let him be. **T(1048) -862**

T 31 B 6. We make no gains he does not make with us, and we fall back if he does not advance. Take not his hand in anger but in love, for in his progress do you count your own. And we go separately along the way unless you keep him safely by your side. BECAUSE he is your equal in God's Love will YOU be saved from all appearances, and answer to the Christ Who calls to you. Be still and listen. Think not ancient thoughts. Forget the dismal lessons that you learned about this Son of God who calls to you. Christ calls to all with EQUAL tenderness, seeing no leaders and no followers, and hearing but ONE Answer to them all. Because He hears one Voice, He cannot hear a DIFFERENT answer from the one He gave when God appointed Him His only Son.

T 31 B 7. Be very still an instant. Come without all thought[1013] of what you ever learned before, and put aside all images you made. The old will fall away before the new, without your opposition or intent. There will be no attack upon the things you thought were precious, and in need of care. There will be no assault upon your wish to hear a call that never has been made. Nothing will hurt you in this holy place to which you come to listen silently, and learn the truth of what you really want. No more than this will you be asked to learn. But as you hear it, you will understand you need but come away WITHOUT the thoughts you did not want, and that were NEVER true.

T 31 B 8. Forgive your brother ALL appearances, which are but ancient lessons that you taught yourself about the sinfulness in you. Hear but his call for mercy and release from all the fearful images he holds of what HE is, and of what YOU must be. He is afraid to walk with you, and thinks perhaps a bit behind, a bit ahead, would be a safer place for him to be. Can YOU make progress if you think the same, advancing only when he would step back, and falling back when he would go ahead? For so[1014] do you forget the journey's goal which is but to decide to walk WITH him, so neither leads nor follows. Thus it is a way you go together, NOT alone. And in THIS choice is learning's outcome changed, for Christ has been reborn to BOTH of you. **T(1049) -863**

T 31 B 9. An instant spent without your old ideas of who your great Companion is and what he SHOULD be asking for, will be enough to let this happen. And you will perceive his purpose is the same as

---

[1008] July 1, 1968
[1009] **Psalm 46:10** Be still, and know that I am God; I will be exalted among the nations, I will be exalted in the earth!
[1010] **John 3:3** Jesus answered and said to him, "Most assuredly, I say to you, unless one is born again, he cannot see the kingdom of God."
[1011] *Urtext* manuscript has it typed "over," handwritten mark-up removes the comma and adds "come." The *Notes* has "overcome."

[1012] **Psalms 4:4** Stand in awe, and sin not: Commune with your own heart upon your bed, and be still,
[1013] *Urtext* manuscript has it typed "thoughts" and that is what is in the *Notes*.
[1014] The word "so" is not in the original, it is handwritten in. It is also present in the *Notes*.

yours. He asks for what YOU want, and needs the SAME as you. It takes, perhaps, a different FORM in him, but it is NOT the form you answer to. He asks and YOU receive, for you have come with but ONE purpose; that you both may learn you love each other with a brother's love. And AS a brother, must his Father be the same as yours, as he is like yourself. Together is your joint inheritance remembered and accepted by you both. Alone it is denied to both of you.

T 31 B 10. Is it not clear that while you still insist on leading or on following, you think you walk alone, with no-one by your side? This is the road to nowhere, for the light cannot be given while you walk alone, and so you cannot SEE which way you go. And so there IS confusion, and a sense of endless doubting, as you stagger back and forward in the darkness and alone. Yet are these but appearances of what the journey is, and how it must be made. For next to you is One Who holds the light before you, so that every step is made in certainty and sureness of the road. A blindfold can indeed obscure your sight, but cannot make the way itself grow dark. And He Who travels with you HAS the Light.[1015] **T(1050) -864**

T 31 C. The Self-Accused (*Notes* 2105 12:240)

T 31 C 1. Only[1016] the self-accused condemn. As you prepare to make a choice that will result in DIFFERENT outcomes, there is first one thing that must be overlearned. It must become a habit of response so typical of everything you do, that it becomes your FIRST response to all temptation, and to every situation that occurs. Learn this, and learn it well, for it is here delay of happiness is shortened by a span of time you cannot realize. You NEVER hate your brother for HIS "sins",[1017] but ONLY for your own. Whatever form his sins appear to take, the form obscures the fact that you believe it to be yours, and THEREFORE meriting a just attack.

T 31 C 2. Why should his sins BE sins, if you did not believe they could not be forgiven in you? Why are they real in him, if you did not believe that they are YOUR reality? And why do you attack them anywhere except you hate yourself? Are YOU a sin? You answer "yes" WHENEVER you attack, for BY attack do you assert that you are guilty, and must give as you deserve. And what CAN you deserve but what you ARE? If you did not believe that you DESERVED attack, it never would occur to you to GIVE attack to anyone at all. Why should you? What would be the gain to you? What could the outcome be that you would WANT? And how COULD murder bring you benefit?

T 31 C 3. Sins are in bodies. They are not perceived in minds. They are not seen as purposes, but ACTIONS. Bodies act, and minds do not. And therefore must the body be at fault for what it does. It is not seen to be a passive thing, obeying your commands, and doing nothing of itself at all. If you are sin you ARE a body, for the mind acts not. And purpose must be in the body, NOT the mind. The body must act on its own, and motivate itself. If you are sin, you lock the mind WITHIN the body, and you give its purpose to its prison house, which acts INSTEAD of it. A jailer does not follow orders, but ENFORCES orders on the prisoner. **T(1051) -865**

T 31 C 4. Yet is the BODY prisoner, and NOT the mind. The body thinks no thoughts. It has no power to learn, to pardon, or enslave. It gives no orders that the mind need serve, nor sets conditions that it must obey. It holds in prison but the willing mind[1018] that would abide in it. It sickens at the bidding of the mind that would become its prisoner. And it grows old and dies, because that mind is sick within ITSELF. Learning is all that causes change. And so the body, where no learning CAN occur, could never change unless the mind PREFERRED the body change in its appearances, to suit the purpose given by the mind. For it CAN learn, and there is ALL change made.

T 31 C 5. The mind that thinks it is a sin has but ONE purpose; that the body be the source of sin, and KEEP it in the prison house it chose, and guards, and holds itself at bay, a sleeping prisoner to the snarling dogs of hate and evil, sickness and attack; of pain and age, of grief and suffering. Here are the thoughts of sacrifice preserved, for here guilt rules, and orders that the world be like itself; a place where nothing can find mercy, or survive the ravages of fear except in murder and in death. For here are you made sin, and sin can not abide the joyous nor accept the free, for they are enemies which sin must kill. In death is sin preserved, and those who think that they are sin MUST die for what they are.

T 31 C 6. Let us be glad that you WILL see what you believe, and that it HAS been given you to CHANGE what you believe. The body will but follow. It can NEVER lead you where you would not be. IT does not guard your sleep, nor interfere with your awakening. Release your body from imprisonment, and you will see no-one as prisoner to what you have escaped. You will not WANT to hold in guilt your chosen enemies, nor keep in chains to the illusion of a changing love the ones you think are friends. The innocent release in gratitude for THEIR release. And what they see upholds their freedom FROM imprisonment and death. Open your mind to change, and there will be no ancient penalty exacted from your brother or yourself. For God has said there IS no sacrifice that can be asked; there IS no sacrifice that can be made.[1019] **T(1052) -866**

T 31 D. The Real Alternative (*Notes* 2109 12:245)

T 31 D 1. There[1020] is a tendency to think the world can offer consolation and escape from problems that its purpose is to keep. Why should this be? Because it is a place where choice among illusions seems to be the ONLY choice. And YOU are in control of outcomes of your choosing. Thus you think, within the narrow band from birth to death, a little time is given you to use for you alone; a time when everyone conflicts with you, but you can choose which road will lead you out of conflict, and AWAY from difficulties which concern you not. But they ARE your concern. How, then, can you escape from them by leaving them behind? What MUST go with you, you will take with you whatever road you choose to walk along.

T 31 D 2. Real choice is no illusion. But the world has none to offer. ALL its roads but lead to disappointment, nothingness and death. There IS no choice in its alternatives. Seek not ESCAPE from problems here. The world was made that problems could not BE escaped. Be not deceived by all the different names its roads are given. They have but one end. And each is but the means to GAIN that end, for it is here that all its roads will lead, however differently they seem to start; however differently they seem to go. Their end is certain, for there is no choice among them. All of them will lead to death. On some you travel gaily for a while, before the bleakness enters. And on some the thorns are felt at once. The choice is not WHAT will the ending be, but WHEN it comes.

T 31 D 3. There IS no choice where every end is sure. Perhaps you would prefer to try them all, before you REALLY learn they are but one. The roads this world can offer seem to be quite large in number, but the time must come when everyone begins to see how like they are to one another. Men have died on seeing this, because they saw no way EXCEPT the pathways offered by the world. And, learning THEY led nowhere, lost their hope. And yet this was the

---

[1015] Original typed both lower and upper, overstruck. It does not appear capitalized in the *Notes*.
[1016] July 5, 1968
[1017] The quotation marks are handwritten in the *Urtext* manuscript. They are not present in the *Notes*.
[1018] *Urtext* manuscript has a comma and forward slash overstuck appear here. It seems the intent was to cross out the comma which is not in the *Notes*.

[1019] **Hosea 6:6** For I desire mercy and not sacrifice, And the knowledge of God more than burnt offerings.
Matthew 9:13 But go and learn what this means: "I desire mercy and not sacrifice. For I did not come to call the righteous, but sinners, to repentance."
[1020] July 16, 1968

time they COULD have learned their greatest lesson. All must[1021] reach this point, and go BEYOND it. It is true indeed there is no choice at all within the world. But this is NOT the lesson in itself. The lesson has a PURPOSE, and in THIS you come to understand what it is FOR. T(1053) -867

T 31 D 4. Why would you seek to try another road, another person or another place, when you HAVE learned the way the lesson starts, but do not yet perceive what it is for? Its purpose is the ANSWER to the search that all must undertake who still believe there is another answer to be found. Learn now, WITHOUT despair, there is no hope of answers in the world. But do not judge the lesson which is but BEGUN with this. Seek not another signpost in the world which seems to point to still another road. No longer look for hope where there is none. Make fast your learning NOW, and understand you but waste time unless you go BEYOND what you have learned to what is yet to learn. For from this lowest point will learning lead to heights of happiness, in which you see the PURPOSE of the lesson shining clear, and perfectly within your learning grasp.

T 31 D 5. Who would be willing to be turned AWAY from all the roadways of the world, UNLESS he understood their real futility? Is it not needful that he should BEGIN with this to seek another way instead? For while he sees a choice where there is none, what power of decision can he use? The great RELEASE of power must begin with learning where it really HAS a use. And what decision has power, if it be applied in situations without choice? The learning that the world can offer but ONE choice, no matter what its form may be, is the beginning of acceptance that there is a REAL alternative instead. To fight AGAINST this step is to defeat your purpose here. You did not come to learn to find a road the world does not contain.

T 31 D 6. The search for DIFFERENT pathways in the world is but the search for different FORMS of truth. And this would KEEP the truth from being reached. Think not that happiness is EVER found by following a road AWAY from it. This makes NO sense, and CANNOT be the way. To you who seem to find this course to be too difficult to learn, let me repeat that, to achieve a goal, you must proceed in its direction, not AWAY from it. And EVERY road that goes the other way will NOT advance the purpose to be found. If THIS be difficult to understand, then IS this course impossible to learn. But only then. For otherwise, it is a simple teaching in the obvious. T(1054) -868

T 31 D 7. There IS a choice which you have power to make, when you have seen the real alternatives. UNTIL that point is reached you HAVE no choice, and you can but decide how you would choose the better to deceive yourself again. This course attempts to teach no more than that the power of decision cannot lie in choosing different forms of what is still the SAME illusion and the SAME mistake. All choices in the world depend on this; - You choose BETWEEN your brother and yourself, and you will gain as much as he will lose, and what you lose is what is given him. How utterly OPPOSED to truth is this, when what the lesson's purpose is to teach that what your brother loses YOU have lost, and what he gains is what is given YOU.

T 31 D 8. He has not left His Thoughts! But you forgot His Presence, and remember not His Love. No pathway in the world can lead to Him, nor any worldly goal is one with His. What road in all the world will lead within, when EVERY road was made to separate the journey and the purpose it MUST have, unless it be but futile wandering? All roads that lead AWAY from what you are will lead you to confusion and despair. Yet has He never left His Thoughts to die, without their Source forever in themselves. He has not left His Thoughts. He could no more depart from them than they could keep Him out. In unity with Him do they abide, and in their Oneness BOTH are kept complete.

T 31 D 9. There IS no road that leads away from Him. A journey FROM yourself does not exist. How foolish and insane it is to think that there COULD be a road with such an aim. Where could it go? And how could you be made to travel on it, walking there without your own Reality at one with you? Forgive yourself your madness, and forget all senseless journeys and all goal-less aims. They have no meaning. You can NOT escape from what you are. For God IS merciful, and did not let HIS Son abandon Him. For what He is be thankful, for in that[1022] is YOUR escape from madness and from death. Nowhere but where He is can YOU be found. There IS no path that does not lead to Him. T(1055) -869

T 31 E. Self-Concept versus Self (*Notes* 2117 12:252)

T 31 E 1. The[1023] learning of the world is built upon a concept of the self adjusted to the world's reality. It fits it well. For this an image is that suits a world of shadows and illusions. Here it walks at home, where what it sees is one with it. The building of a concept of the self is what the learning of the world is FOR. This is its purpose; that you come WITHOUT a self, and MAKE one as you go along. And by the time you reach "maturity," you have perfected it to meet the world on equal terms, at one with its demands. A concept of the self is made by YOU. It bears NO likeness to yourself at all. It is an idol, made to take the place of your reality as Son of God.

T 31 E 2. The concept of the self the world would teach is not the thing that it appears to be. For it is made to serve two purposes, but one of which the mind can recognize. The first presents the face of innocence, the aspect acted ON. It is this face that smiles and charms and even seems to love. It searches for companions, and it looks at times with pity on the suffering, and sometimes offers solace. It believes that it is good, within an evil world. This aspect can grow angry, for the world is wicked, and unable to provide the love and shelter innocence deserves. And so this face is often wet with tears, at the injustices the world accords to those who would be generous and good.

T 31 E 3. This aspect NEVER makes the first attack. But every day a hundred little things make small assaults upon its innocence, provoking it to irritation, and at last to open insult and abuse. The face of innocence the concept of the self so proudly wears can tolerate attack in self-defense, for is it not a well-known fact the world deals harshly with defenseless innocence? No-one who makes a picture of himself omits this face, for he has need of it. The other side he does not want to see. But it is here the learning of the world has set its sights. For it is here the world's reality is set, to see to it the idol lasts. T(1056) -870

T 31 E 4. Beneath the face of innocence there is a lesson that the concept of the self was made to teach. It is a lesson in a terrible displacement, and a fear so devastating that the face which smiles above it must forever look away, lest it perceive the treachery it hides. The lesson teaches this; "I am the thing you made of me, and as you look on me you stand condemned, because of what I am." On this conception of the self the world smiles with approval, for it guarantees the pathways of the world are safely kept, and those who walk on them will not escape.

T 31 E 5. Here is the central lesson that ensures your brother is condemned eternally. For what YOU are has now become his sin. For this is no forgiveness possible. No longer does it matter what he does, for your accusing finger points to him, unwavering and deadly in its aim. It points to you as well, but this is kept still deeper in the mists below the face of innocence. And in these shrouded vaults are all his sins and yours preserved, and kept in darkness, where they cannot be perceived as errors, which the light would surely show.

[1021] *Urtext* manuscript has it typed "much." It is "must" in the *Notes*.

[1022] There is both a capital and a lower case "t" typed originally. The *Notes* does not capitalize it.
[1023] July 18, 1968

You can be neither BLAMED for what you are, nor can you CHANGE the things it makes you do. And you are each the symbol of your sins to one another, silently, and yet with ceaseless urgency condemning still your brother for the hated thing you are.

T 31 E 6. Concepts are learned. They are not natural. Apart from learning they do not exist. They are not given, and they must be made. Not one of them is true, and many come from feverish imaginations, hot with hatred and distortions born of fear. What is a concept, but a thought to which its maker gives a meaning of his own? Concepts maintain the world. But they can NOT be used to demonstrate the world is real. For all of them are made WITHIN the world, born in its shadow, growing in its ways, and finally "maturing" in its thought. They are ideas of idols painted with the brushes of the world, which cannot make a single picture representing truth. **T(1057) -871**

T 31 E 7. A concept of the self is meaningless, for no-one here can see what it is for, and therefore cannot picture what it IS. Yet is all learning that the world directs begun and ended with the single aim of teaching you this concept of yourself, that you will choose to follow this world's laws, and never seek to go BEYOND its roads, nor realize the way you see yourself. Now must the Holy Spirit find a way to help you see this concept of the self must be undone, if ANY peace of mind is to be given you. Nor can it be unlearned except by lessons aimed to teach that you are something else. For otherwise, you would be asked to make exchange of what you now believe for total loss of self. And greater terror would arise in you.

T 31 E 8. Thus are the Holy Spirit's lesson plans arranged in easy steps, that, though there be some lack of ease at times, and some distress, there is no shattering of what was learned, but just a re-translation of what seems to be the evidence on its behalf. Let us consider, then, what proof there is that you are what your brother made of you. For even though you do not yet perceive that this is what you think, you surely learned by now that you BEHAVE as if it were. Does he REACT for you? And did he know exactly what would happen? Could he see your future, and ordain before it came what you should do in EVERY circumstance? He must have made the world as well as you, to have such prescience in the things to come.

T 31 E 9. That you are what your brother made of you seems most unlikely. Even if he did, who gave the face of innocence to you? Is this YOUR contribution? Who is, then, the "you" who made it? And who is deceived by all your goodness, and attacks it so? Let us forget the concept's foolishness, and merely think of this; there are two parts to what you think yourself to be. If one was generated by your brother, who was there to make the other? And from whom must something be kept hidden? If the world be evil, there is still no need to hide what YOU are made of. Who is there to see? And what but is attacked could NEED defense? **T(1058) -872**

T 31 E 10. Perhaps the reason why this concept must be kept in darkness is that, in the light, the one who would not think it true is YOU. And what would happen to the world you know, if all its underpinnings were removed? Your concept of the world DEPENDS upon this concept of the self. And BOTH would go, if either one were ever raised to doubt. The Holy Spirit does not seek to throw you into panic. So He merely asks if just a LITTLE question might be raised. There ARE alternatives about the thing that you must be. You might, for instance, be the thing you chose to have your BROTHER be.

T 31 E 11. This shifts the concept of the self from what is wholly passive, and at least makes way for active choice, and some acknowledgment that interaction must have entered in. There is some understanding that you chose for BOTH of you, and what he represents has meaning that was given it by YOU. It also shows some glimmering of sight into perception's law that what you see reflects the state of the PERCEIVER's mind. Yet who was it that did the choosing first? If you are what you chose your brother be, alternatives were there to choose between, and someone must have first decided on the one to choose, and let the others go.

T 31 E 12. Although this step has gains, it does not yet approach a basic question. Something must have gone BEFORE these concepts of the self. And something must have done the learning which gave rise to them. Nor can this be explained by either view. The main advantage of the shifting to the second from the first is that you somehow entered in the choice by YOUR decision. But this gain is paid in almost equal loss, for now YOU stand accused of guilt for what your BROTHER is. And you must SHARE his guilt, because you chose it FOR him, in the image of your own. While ONLY he was treacherous before, now must YOU be condemned along with him. **T(1059) -873**

T 31 E 13. The concept of the self has always been the great preoccupation of the world. And everyone believes that he must find the answer to the riddle of himself. Salvation can be seen as nothing more than the ESCAPE from concepts. It does not concern itself with content of the mind, but with the simple statement THAT IT THINKS. And what can think has choice, and CAN be shown that different thoughts have different consequence. And it can learn that EVERYTHING it thinks reflects the deep confusion that it feels about how it was made, and what it is. And vaguely does the concept of the self appear to answer what it does not know.

T 31 E 14. Seek not your Self in symbols. There can be no concept that can stand for what you are. What matters it which concept you accept, while you perceive a self which interacts with evil, and reacts to wicked things? Your concept of yourself will still remain quite meaningless. And you will not perceive that you can interact but with yourself. To see a guilty world is but the sign your learning has been guided by the world, and you behold it as you see yourself. The concept of the self embraces all you look upon, and NOTHING is outside of this perception. If you can be hurt by ANYTHING, you see a picture of your secret wishes. Nothing more than this. And in your suffering of ANY kind, you see your own concealed desire to kill.

T 31 E 15. You will make many concepts of the self as learning goes along. Each one will show the changes in your own relationships, as your perception of yourself is changed. There will be some confusion every time there is a shift, but be you thankful that the learning of the world is loosening its grasp upon your mind. And be you sure and happy in the confidence that it will go at last, and leave your mind at peace. The role of the accuser will appear in many places and in many forms, and each will seem to be accusing you. But have no fear it will not be undone. The world can teach no images of you unless you WANT to learn them. There will come a time when images have all gone by, and you will see you know not what you are. **T(1060) -874**

T 31 E 16. It is to this unsealed and open mind that truth returns, unhindered and unbound. Where concepts of the self have been laid by is truth revealed exactly as it is. When every concept has been raised to doubt and question, and been recognized as made on NO assumptions that would stand the light, then is the truth left free to enter in its sanctuary clean and free of guilt. There is no statement that the world is more afraid to hear than this:

> *"I do not know the thing I am, and THEREFORE do not know what I am doing, where I am, or how to look upon the world and on myself."* Yet in this learning is salvation born. And what you are will TELL you of Itself. **T(1061) -875**

T 31 F. Recognizing the Spirit (*Notes* 2129 12:264)

T 31 F 1. You[1024] see the flesh or recognize the Spirit.[1025] There is no compromise between the two. If one is real the other must be

---
[1024] August 23, 1968
[1025] **John 3:6** "That which is born of the flesh is flesh, and that which is born of the Spirit is spirit."

false, for what is real denies its opposite. There is no choice in vision but this one. What you decide in this determines all you see, and think is real, and hold as true. On this one choice does all your world depend, for here have you established what you are, as flesh or Spirit in your own belief. If you choose flesh, you never will escape the body as your own reality, for you have chosen that you want it so. But choose the Spirit, [1026] and all Heaven bends to touch your eyes, and bless your holy sight, that you may see the world of flesh no more, except to heal and comfort and to bless.

T 31 F 2. Salvation is undoing. If you choose to see the body, you behold a world of separation, unrelated things, and happenings that make no sense at all. This one appears and disappears in death. That one is doomed to suffering and loss. And no-one is exactly as he was an instant previous. Nor will he be the same as he is now an instant hence. Who could have trust where so much change is seen, for who is worthy if he be but dust? Salvation is undoing of all this. And constancy arises in the sight of those whose eyes salvation has released from looking at the cost of keeping guilt, because they chose to let it go instead.

T 31 F 3. Salvation does not ask that you behold the Spirit, and perceive the body not. It merely asks that this should be your CHOICE. For YOU can see the body WITHOUT help, but do not understand how to behold a world APART from it. It is your world salvation will undo, and LET you see another world your eyes could never find. Be not concerned HOW this could ever be. You do not understand how what YOU see arose to meet your sight. For if you did, it would be gone. The veil of ignorance is drawn across the evil and the good, and must be passed that both may disappear, so that perception finds no hiding place. **T(1062) -876**

T 31 F 4. How is this done? It is not done at all. What COULD there be within the universe that God created that must still be done? Only in arrogance could you conceive that YOU must make the way to Heaven plain. The means are GIVEN you by which to see the world that will replace the one you made. Your will be done! In Heaven as on earth this is forever true.[1027] It matters not where you believe you are, or what you think the truth about yourself must really be. It makes no difference what you look upon, nor what you choose to feel or think or wish. For God Himself hath said, "Thy will be done."[1028] And it IS done to you accordingly.

T 31 F 5. You who believe that you can choose to see the Son of God as you would have him be, forget not that no CONCEPT of yourself will stand against the truth of what you are. Undoing truth would be impossible. But concepts are not difficult to change. One vision, clearly seen, that does not fit the picture as it was perceived before, will change the world for eyes that learn to see BECAUSE THE CONCEPT OF THE SELF HAS CHANGED. Are YOU invulnerable? Then the world is harmless in your sight. Do YOU forgive? Then is the world forgiving, for you have forgiven it its trespasses.[1029] And so it looks on you with eyes that see as yours.

T 31 F 6. Are YOU a body? So is all the world perceived as treacherous, and out to kill. Are you a Spirit, deathless, and without the promise of corruption and the stain of sin upon you? So the world is seen as stable, fully worthy of your trust; a happy place to rest in for a while, where nothing need be feared but only loved. Who is unwelcome to the kind in heart? And what could hurt the truly innocent? Thy will be done, you holy Child of God. It does not matter if you think you are in earth or Heaven. What your Father wills for you can never change. The truth in you remains as radiant as a star, as pure as light, as innocent as Love Itself. And you ARE worthy that your Will[1030] be done. **T(1063) -877**

T 31 G. The Savior's Vision (*Notes* 2133 12:268)

T 31 G 1. Learning[1031] is change. Salvation does not seek to use a means as yet too alien to your thinking to be helpful, nor to make the kinds of change you could not recognize. Concepts are needed while perception lasts. And changing concepts IS salvation's task. For it must deal in contrasts, not in truth, which has no opposite and cannot change. In this world's concepts are the guilty "bad;" the "good" are innocent. And no-one here but holds a concept of himself in which he counts the "good" to pardon him the "bad." Nor does he trust the "good" in anyone, believing that the "bad" must lurk behind.

T 31 G 2. This concept emphasizes treachery, and trust becomes impossible. Nor could it change while you perceive the "bad" in you. You could not recognize your "evil" thoughts as long as you see value in attack. You WILL perceive them sometimes, but will NOT see them as meaningless. And so they come in fearful form, with content still concealed, to shake your sorry concept of yourself, and blacken it with still another "crime." YOU cannot give yourself your innocence, for you are too confused about yourself. But should ONE brother dawn upon your sight as wholly worthy of forgiveness, then your concept of yourself IS wholly changed.

T 31 G 3. YOUR "evil" thoughts have been forgiven with his, because you let them all effect YOU not. No longer did you choose that you should be the sign of "evil" and of guilt in him. And as you gave your trust to what is "good" in him, you gave it to the "good"[1032] in you. In terms of concepts, it is thus you see him MORE than just a body, for the "good" is NEVER what the body seems to be. The actions of the body are perceived as coming from the "baser" part of you, and thus of him as well. By focusing upon the "good" in him, the body grows decreasingly persistent in your sight, and will at length be seen as little more than just a shadow circling round the "good." **T(1064) -878**

T 31 G 4. And this will be your concept of YOURSELF, when you have reached the world beyond the sight your eyes alone can offer you to see. For you will not interpret what you see without the Aid that God has given you. And in His sight there IS another world. You live in that world just as much as this, for BOTH are concepts of yourself, which can be interchanged, but never jointly held. The contrast is far greater than you think, for you will love this concept of yourself, BECAUSE IT WAS NOT MADE FOR YOU ALONE. Born as a gift for someone NOT perceived to be yourself, it has been given YOU. For your forgiveness, offered unto him, has been accepted now for BOTH of you.

T 31 G 5. Have faith in him who walks with you, so that your fearful concept of yourself may change. And look upon the "good" in him, that you may not be fearful of your "evil" thoughts, because they do not cloud your view of him. And all this shift requires is that you be WILLING that this happy change occur. No more than this is asked. On its behalf, remember what the concept of yourself which now you hold has brought you in its wake, and welcome the glad contrast offered you. Hold out your hand, that you may have the gift of kind forgiveness, which you offer one whose need for it is just the same[1033] as yours. And let your cruel concept of yourself be changed to one which brings the peace of God.

T 31 G 6. The concept of yourself which now you hold would GUARANTEE your function here remain forever unaccomplished

---

[1026] In this paragraph and throughout this section "spirit" is originally typed with a lowercase "s" and the capitals are handwritten in numerous times.
[1027] **Matthew 6:10** "Thy kingdom come. Thy will be done, as in heaven, so on earth."
[1028] ibid
[1029] **Matthew 6:12** "And forgive us our trespasses,
  As we forgive our those who trespass against us."

[1030] *Urtext* manuscript has it typed "will", the capital is handwritten in reflecting the reading in the *Notes*.
[1031] August 26, 1968
[1032] A spurious period appears in the *Urtext* manuscript here.
[1033] *Urtext* manuscript has it typed "as great", this is crossed out and "the same" typed in. The *Notes* appears to read "the same."

Chapter 31 The Simplicity of Salvation

and undone. And thus it dooms you to a bitter sense of deep depression and futility. Yet it need not be fixed, unless you choose to hold it past the hope of change, and keep it static and concealed within your mind. Give it instead to Him Who understands the changes that it needs to let it SERVE the function given you to bring you peace, that you may offer peace to have it yours. Alternatives are in your mind to use, and you CAN see yourself another way. Would you not rather look upon yourself as NEEDED for salvation of the world, instead of as salvation's enemy? **T(1065) -879**

T 31 G 7. The[1034] concept of the self stands like a shield, a silent barricade before the truth, and hides it from your sight. All things you see are images because you look on them as through a barrier which dims your sight and warps your vision, so that you behold nothing with clarity.[1035] The light is kept from everything you see. At most, you glimpse a shadow of what lies beyond. At least you merely look on darkness, and perceive the terrified imaginings that come from guilty thoughts and concepts born of fear. And what you see is hell, for fear IS hell. All that is given you is for release; the sight, the vision and the inner Guide all lead you OUT of hell, with those you love beside you, and the universe with them.

T 31 G 8. Behold your role within the universe! To every part of true creation has the Lord of Love and Life entrusted ALL salvation from the misery of hell. And to each one has He allowed the grace to be a Savior to the holy ones especially entrusted to his care. And this he learns when first he looks upon ONE brother as he looks upon himself, and sees the mirror of himself in him. Thus is the CONCEPT of himself laid by, for nothing stands BETWEEN his sight and what he looks upon, to judge what he beholds. And in this single vision does he see the Face of Christ, and understands he looks on everyone, as he beholds this One. For there is light where darkness was before, and now the veil is lifted from his sight.

T 31 G 9. The veil across the Face of Christ, the fear of God and of salvation, and the love of guilt and death, - they all are different names for just ONE error; that there is a space between you and your brother, kept apart by an illusion of yourself which holds him off from you, and you away from him. The sword of judgment is the weapon which you give to the illusion of yourself, that it may fight to keep the space that holds your brother off unoccupied by love. Yet while you hold this sword you MUST perceive the body as YOURSELF, for you are bound to separation from the sight of him who holds the mirror to another view of what HE is, and thus what YOU must be. **T(1066) -880**

T 31 G 10. What is temptation but the WISH to stay in hell and misery? And what could this give rise to BUT an image of yourself that CAN be miserable, and remain in hell and torment? Who has learned to see his brother NOT as this HAS saved himself, and thus IS he a savior to the rest. To everyone has God entrusted all, because a PARTIAL savior would be one who is but partly saved. The holy ones whom God has given each of you to save are everyone you meet or look upon, not knowing who they are; all those you saw an instant and forgot, and those you knew a long while since, and those you will yet meet, the unremembered and the not yet born. For God has given you His Son to save from every concept that he ever held.

T 31 G 11. Yet while you wish to stay in hell, how COULD you be the savior of the Son of God? How would you know his holiness, while you see him apart from yours? For holiness is seen through holy eyes that look upon the innocence within, and thus EXPECT to see it everywhere. And so they call it forth in everyone they look upon, that he may be what they expect of him. This is the Savior's vision;[1036] that he see HIS innocence in all he looks upon, and sees his own salvation everywhere. He holds NO concept of himself between his calm and open eyes and what he sees. He BRINGS the light to what he looks upon, that he may see it as it really is.

T 31 G 12. Whatever form temptation seems to take, it ALWAYS but reflects a wish to be a self that you are not. And FROM that wish a concept rises, teaching you you ARE the thing you wish to be. It will remain your concept of yourself until the wish that fathered it no longer is held dear. And while you cherish it, you will behold your brother in the likeness of the self whose image has the wish begot of YOU.[1037] For vision CAN but represent a wish, because it has NO power to create. Yet it can look with love or look with hate, depending only on the simple choice of whether you would JOIN with what you see, or keep yourself apart and separate. **T(1067) -881**

T 31 G 13. The Savior's vision is as innocent of what your brother is as it is free of any judgment made upon yourself. It sees no past in anyone at all. And thus it serves a wholly open mind, unclouded by old concepts and prepared to look on ONLY what the present holds. It cannot judge because it does not know. And RECOGNIZING this, it merely asks, "What is the meaning of what I behold?" Then is the Answer given, and the door held open for the Face of Christ to shine upon the one who asks in innocence to see BEYOND the veil of old ideas and ancient concepts held so long and dear AGAINST the vision of the Christ in you. **T(1068) -882**

T 31 G 14. Be vigilant against temptation, then, remembering that it is but a wish, insane and meaningless, to make yourself a thing which you are not. And think as well upon the thing that you would be instead. It is a thing of madness, pain, and death; a thing of treachery and black despair, of failing dreams and no remaining hope except to die and end the dream of fear. THIS is temptation; nothing MORE than this. CAN this be difficult to choose AGAINST? Consider what temptation is, and see the real alternatives you choose between. There ARE but two. Be not deceived by what appears as many choices. There is hell or Heaven.[1038] And of these you choose but ONE.

T 31 G 15. Let not the world's light, given unto you, be hidden from the world. It NEEDS the light, for it is dark indeed, and men[1039] despair because the Savior's vision is withheld, and what they see is death. Their Savior stands, unknowing and unknown, beholding them with eyes unopened. And THEY cannot see until he looks on them with seeing eyes, and offers them forgiveness with his own. Can you to whom God says, "Release My Son" be tempted NOT to listen, when you learn that it is YOU for whom He asks release? And what BUT this is what this course would teach? And what BUT this is there for you to learn?

T 31 H Choose Once Again (*Notes* 2146 12:281)

T 31 H 1. Temptation has ONE lesson it would teach, in ALL its forms, WHEREVER it occurs. It would persuade the holy Son of God he is a body, born in what must die, unable to escape its frailty, and bound by what it orders him to feel. It sets the limits on what he can do; its power is the only strength he has; his grasp cannot ex-

---
[1034] Sept. 30, 1968
[1035] **1 Corinthians 13:12** For now we see in a glass darkly, but then face to face. Now I know in part, but then I shall know just as I also am known.
[1036] Originally it appears to be both a colon and semi-colon. In the *Notes* it is a semi-colon.
[1037] **Genesis 1:26-27** Then God said, "Let Us make man in Our image, according to Our likeness; let them have dominion over the fish of the sea, over the birds of the air, and over the cattle, over all the earth and over every creeping thing that creeps on the earth." So God created man in His own image; in the image of God He created him; male and female He created them.
[1038] *Urtext* manuscript has it typed as it stands, handwritten mark-up suggests a comma instead of a period. The *Notes* has it as it stands also.
[1039] *Urtext* manuscript has it typed "many" this is crossed out and "men" is written in. The *Notes* appears to read "that men" rather than either "and many" or "and men."

ceed its tiny reach. Would you BE this, if Christ appeared to you in all His glory, asking you but this, "Choose once again if you would take your place among the Saviors of the world, or would remain in hell, and hold your brothers there." For He HAS come, and He IS asking this. **T(1069) -883**

T 31 H 2. How[1040] do you make the choice? How easily is this explained! You ALWAYS choose between YOUR weakness and the strength of Christ in you.[1041] And what you choose is what you think is real. Simply by never using weakness to direct your actions, you have given it no power. And the Light of Christ in you is given charge of everything you do. For you have brought your weakness unto Him, and He has given you His strength instead. Trials are but lessons which you failed to learn presented once again, so where you made a faulty choice before you now can make a better one, and thus escape all pain which what you chose before has brought to you.

T 31 H 3. In every difficulty, all distress, and each perplexity you face Christ calls to you, and gently says, "My brother, choose again." He would not leave one source of pain unhealed, nor any image left to veil the truth. He would remove all misery from you whom God created altars unto joy. He would not leave you comfortless, alone in dreams of hell, but would release your minds from everything that hides His Face from you. His holiness is yours because He is the ONLY power that is real in you. His strength is yours because He is the Self that God created as His ONLY Son. The images you make can not prevail against what God Himself would have you be.

T 31 H 4. Be never fearful of temptation then, but see it as it is; another chance to choose again, and let Christ's strength prevail in every circumstance and every place you raised an image of yourself before. For what appears to hide the Face of Christ is powerless before His Majesty, and disappears before His holy sight. The Saviors of the world, who see like Him, are merely those who chose His strength instead of their own weakness, seen APART from Him. They will redeem the world, for they are joined to all the power of the Will of God. And what they will is ONLY what He wills. **T(1070) -884**

T 31 H 5. Learn, then, the happy habit of response to ALL temptation to perceive yourself as weak and miserable with these words:
*"I am as God created me. His Son
can suffer nothing. And I AM His Son."*

Thus is Christ's strength INVITED to prevail, replacing all your weakness with the strength that comes from God, and that can NEVER fail. And thus are miracles as natural as fear and agony APPEARED to be before the choice for holiness was made. For IN that choice are false distinctions gone, illusory alternatives laid by, and nothing left to INTERFERE with truth.

T 31 H 6. You ARE as God created you, and so is every living thing you look upon, REGARDLESS of the images you see. What you behold as sickness and as pain, as weakness and as suffering and loss, is but temptation to perceive YOURSELF defenseless and in hell. Yield NOT to this, and you will see ALL pain in EVERY form WHEREVER it occurs but disappear as mists before the sun. A miracle has come to heal God's Son, and close the door upon his dreams of weakness, opening the way to his salvation and release. Choose once again what you would have him be, remembering that every choice you make establishes your own identity as you will see it, and believe it IS.

T 31 H 7. Deny me not the little gift I ask, when in exchange I lay before your feet the peace of God, and power to bring this peace to everyone who wanders in the world, uncertain, lonely, and in constant fear. For it is given you to JOIN with him, and through the Christ in you unveil his eyes, and let him look upon the Christ in him. My brothers in salvation, do not fail to hear my voice and listen to my words. I ask for nothing but your OWN release. There is no place for hell within a world whose loveliness can yet be so intense and so inclusive it is but a step from there to Heaven. To your tired eyes I bring a vision of a different world, so new and clean and fresh you will forget the pain and sorrow that you saw before. **T(1071) -885**

T 31 H 8. But this a vision is which you must SHARE with everyone you see. For otherwise you will behold it not. To GIVE this gift is how to make it yours. And God ordained, in loving kindness, that it BE for you. Let us be glad that we can walk the world, and find so many chances to perceive another situation where His gift can[1042] once again be recognized as ours. And thus will all the vestiges of hell, the secret sins and hidden hates be gone, and all the loveliness which they concealed appear like lawns of Heaven to our sight, to lift us high above the thorny roads we travelled[1043] on before the Christ appeared.[1044]

T 31 H 9. Hear me,[1045] my brothers, hear and join with me. God has ordained I cannot call in vain. And in His certainty I rest content. For you WILL hear, and you WILL choose again. And in this choice is everyone made free. I thank You, Father, for these holy ones who are my brothers as they are Your Sons. My faith in them is Yours. I am as sure that they will come to me as You are sure of what they are, and will forever be. They will accept the gift I offer[1046] them because You gave it me on their behalf. And as I would but do Your holy Will, so will they choose. And I give thanks for them.

T 31 H 10. Salvation's song will echo through the world with every choice they make. For we are one in purpose, and the end of hell is near. In joyous welcome is my hand outstretched to every brother who would join with me in reaching past temptation, and who looks with fixed determination toward the light that shines beyond in perfect constancy. Give me my own, for they belong to You. And can You fail in what is but Your Will? I give You thanks for what my brothers are, and as each one elects to join with me, the song of thanks from earth to Heaven grows from tiny, scattered threads of melody to one inclusive chorus from a world redeemed from hell, and giving thanks to You. **T(1072) -886**

T 31 H 11. And now we say "Amen." For Christ has come to dwell in the abode You set for Him before time was, in calm Eternity. The journey closes, ending at the place where it began. No trace of it remains. Not one illusion is accorded faith, and not one spot of darkness still remains to hide the Face of Christ from anyone. Thy Will is done, complete and perfectly, and all creation recognizes You and knows You as the only Source it has. Clear in Your Likeness does the Light shine forth from everything that lives and moves in You.[1047] For we have reached where all of us are One, and we ARE home where You would have us be.

[1040] October 10, 1968
[1041] **2 Corinthians 12:9** And He said to me, "My grace is sufficient for you, for My strength is made perfect in weakness." Therefore most gladly I will rather boast in my infirmities, that the power of Christ may rest upon me.
Philippians 4:13 I can do all things through Christ who strengthens me.
[1042] The word "can" is handwritten in.
[1043] *Urtext* manuscript has it typed "travel" the letters "led" are handwritten in. This corrects the manuscript to reflect the *Notes*.
[1044] *Urtext* manuscript has it typed "appears." The letters "ed" are typed in. This corrects it to reflect the *Notes*.
[1045] These few paragraphs have an uncanny resemblance to the parting speech of Jesus recorded in John's gospel, chapter 14.
[1046] *Urtext* manuscript has it typed "the gift offered" but the handwritten mark-up changes it to "I offer" which is the same as the *Notes*.
[1047] **Acts 17:28** for in Him we live and move and have our being, as also some of your own poets have said, "For we are also His offspring."

Urtext **Volume II:** *Workbook*

Volume II – Workbook
Table of Contents

PART 1 1
INTRODUCTION (W 1 IN1) 1
   Lesson **1** "Nothing I see in this room (on this street, from this window, in this place) means anything." 2
   Lesson **2** "I have given everything I see in this room (on this street, from this window, in this place) all the meaning that it has for me." 2
   Lesson **3** "I do not understand anything I see in this room (on this street, from this window, in this place)." 2
   Lesson **4** "These thoughts do not mean anything. They are like the things I see in this room (on this street, from this window, in this place)." 2
   Lesson **5** "I am never upset for the reason I think." 2
   Lesson **6** "I am upset because I see something that is not there." 3
   Lesson **7** "I see only the past." 3
   Lesson **8** "My mind is preoccupied with past thoughts." 3
   Lesson **9** "I see nothing as it is now." 4
   Lesson **10** "My thoughts do not mean anything." 4
   Lesson **11** "My meaningless thoughts are showing me a meaningless world." 4
   Lesson **12** "I am upset because I see a meaningless world." 5
   Lesson **13** "A meaningless world engenders fear." 5
   Lesson **14** "God did not create a meaningless world." 5
   Lesson **15** "My thoughts are images which I have made." 6
   Lesson **16** "I have no neutral thoughts." 6
   Lesson **17** "I see no neutral things." 7
   Lesson **18** "I am not alone in experiencing the effects of my seeing." 7
   Lesson **19** "I am not alone in experiencing the effects of my thoughts." 7
   Lesson **20** "I am determined to see." 7
   Lesson **21** "I am determined to see things differently." 8
   Lesson **22** "What I see is a form of vengeance." 8
   Lesson **23** "I can escape from the world I see by giving up attack thoughts." 8
   Lesson **24** "I do not perceive my own best interests." 9
   Lesson **25** "I do not know what anything is for." 9
   Lesson **26** "My attack thoughts are attacking my invulnerability." 9
   Lesson **27** "Above all else I want to see." 10
   Lesson **28** "Above all else I want to see things differently." 10
   Lesson **29** "God is in everything I see." 10
   Lesson **30** "God is in everything I see because God is in my mind." 11
   Lesson **31** "I am not the victim of the world I see." 11
   Lesson **32** "I have invented the world I see." 11
   Lesson **33** "There is another way of looking at the world." 12
   Lesson **34** "I could see peace instead of this." 12
   Lesson **35** "My mind is part of God's. I am very holy." 12
   Lesson **36** "My holiness envelops everything I see." 13
   Lesson **37** "My holiness blesses the world." 13
   Lesson **38** "There is nothing my holiness cannot do." 13
   Lesson **39** "My holiness is my salvation." 14
   Lesson **40** "I am blessed as a Son of God." 14
   Lesson **41** "God goes with me wherever I go." 15
   Lesson **42** "God is my strength. Vision is His gift." 15
   Lesson **43** "God is my Source. I cannot see apart from Him." 16
   Lesson **44** "God is the Light in which I see." 16
   Lesson **45** "God is the Mind with which I think." 17
   Lesson **46** "God is the Love in which I forgive." 17
   Lesson **47** "God is the Strength in which I trust." 18
   Lesson **48** "There is nothing to fear." 18
   Lesson **49** "God's Voice speaks to me all through the day." 19
   Lesson **50** "I am sustained by the Love of God." 19

Volume II – Workbook
Table of Contents

REVIEW 1 (W 50 R1) 19
   Introduction 19
   Lesson **51** The review for today covers the following ideas: (1-5) 20
   Lesson **52** Today's review covers these ideas: (6-10) 20
   Lesson **53** Today we will review the following: (11-15) 20
   Lesson **54** These are the review ideas for today: (16-20) 21
   Lesson **55** Today's review includes the following: (21-25) 21
   Lesson **56** Our review for today covers the following: (26-30) 21
   Lesson **57** Today let us review these ideas: (31-35) 22
   Lesson **58** These ideas are for review today: (36-40) 22
   Lesson **59** The following ideas are for review today: (41-45) 22
   Lesson **60** These ideas are for today's review. (46-50) 23
   Lesson **61** "I am the light of the world." 23
   Lesson **62** "Forgiveness is my function as the light of the world." 23
   Lesson **63** "The light of the world brings peace to every mind through my forgiveness." .. 24
   Lesson **64** "Let me not forget my function." 24
   Lesson **65** "My only function is the one God gave me." 25
   Lesson **66** "My happiness and my function are one." 25
   Lesson **67** "Love created me like Itself." 26
   Lesson **68** "Love holds no grievances." 26
   Lesson **69** "My grievances hide the light of the world in me." 27
   Lesson **70** "My salvation comes from me." 28
   Lesson **71** "Only God's plan for salvation will work." 28
   Lesson **72** "Holding grievances is an attack on God's plan for salvation." 29
   Lesson **73** "I will there be light." 30
   Lesson **74** "There is no will but God's." 31
   Lesson **75** "The light has come." 31
   Lesson **76** "I am under no laws but God's" 32
   Lesson **77** "I am entitled to miracles." 32
   Lesson **78** "Let miracles replace all grievances." 33
   Lesson **79** "Let me recognize the problem so it can be solved." 34
   Lesson **80** "Let me recognize my problems have been solved." 34

REVIEW 2 (W 80 R2) 35
   Introduction 35
   Lesson **81** Our ideas for review today are: (61-62) 35
   Lesson **82** We will review these ideas today: (63-64) 35
   Lesson **83** Today let us review these ideas: (65-66) 35
   Lesson **84** These are the ideas for today's review: (67-68) 36
   Lesson **85** Today's review will cover these ideas: (69-70) 36
   Lesson **86** These ideas are for review today: (71-72) 36
   Lesson **87** Our review today will cover these ideas: (73-74) 36
   Lesson **88** Today we will review these ideas: (75-76) 37
   Lesson **89** These are our review ideas for today: (77-78) 37
   Lesson **90** For this review we will use these ideas: (79-80) 37
   Lesson **91** "Miracles are seen in light." 37
   Lesson **92** "Miracles are seen in light, and light and strength are one." 38
   Lesson **93** "Light and joy and peace abide in me." 39
   Lesson **94** "I am as God created me." 40
   Lesson **95** "I am One Self, united with My Creator." 40
   Lesson **96** "Salvation comes from my One Self." 41
   Lesson **97** "I am Spirit." 42
   Lesson **98** "I will accept my part in God's plan for salvation." 42
   Lesson **99** "Salvation is my only function here." 43
   Lesson **100** "My part is essential to God's plan for salvation." 44
   Lesson **101** "God's will for me is perfect happiness." 44
   Lesson **102** "I share God's Will for happiness for me." 45
   Lesson **103** "God, being Love, is also happiness." 45
   Lesson **104** "I seek but what belongs to me in truth." 45
   Lesson **105** "God's peace and joy are mine." 46

Volume II – Workbook
Table of Contents

    Lesson **106** "Let me be still and listen to the truth." 46
    Lesson **107** "Truth will correct the errors in my mind." 47
    Lesson **108** "To give and to receive are one in truth." 48
    Lesson **109** "I rest in God." 48
    Lesson **110** "I am as God created me." 49
REVIEW 3 (W 110 R3) **49**
    Introduction 49
    Lesson **111** For morning and evening review: (91-92) 50
    Lesson **112** For morning and evening review: (93-94) 50
    Lesson **113** For morning and evening review: (95-96) 51
    Lesson **114** For morning and evening review: (97-98) 51
    Lesson **115** For morning and evening review: (99-100) 51
    Lesson **116** For morning and evening review: (101-102) 51
    Lesson **117** For morning and evening review: (103-104) 51
    Lesson **118** For morning and evening review: (105-106) 51
    Lesson **119** For morning and evening review: (107-108) 51
    Lesson **120** For morning and evening review: (109-110) 52
    Lesson **121** "Forgiveness is the key to happiness." 52
    Lesson **122** "Forgiveness offers everything I want." 52
    Lesson **123** "I thank my Father for His gifts to me." 53
    Lesson **124** "Let me remember I am one with God." 54
    Lesson **125** "In quiet I receive God's Word today." 54
    Lesson **126** "All that I give is given to myself." 55
    Lesson **127** "There is no love but God's." 56
    Lesson **128** "The world I see has nothing that I want." 56
    Lesson **129** "Beyond this world there is a world I want." 57
    Lesson **130** "It is impossible to see two worlds." 57
    Lesson **132** "I loose the world from all I thought it was." 59
    Lesson **133** "I will not value what is valueless." 60
    Lesson **134** "Let me perceive forgiveness as it is." 61
    Lesson **135** "If I defend myself I am attacked." 62
    Lesson **136** "Sickness is a defense against the truth." 63
    Lesson **137** "When I am healed, I am not healed alone." 65
    Lesson **138** "Heaven is the decision I must make." 65
    Lesson **139** "I will accept Atonement for myself." 66
    Lesson **140** "Only salvation can be said to cure." 67
REVIEW 4 (W 140 R4) **68**
    Introduction 68
    Lesson **141** "My mind holds only what I think with God." (121-122) 68
    Lesson **142** "My mind holds only what I think with God." (123-124) 68
    Lesson **143** "My mind holds only what I think with God." (125-126) 69
    Lesson **144** "My mind holds only what I think with God." (127-128) 69
    Lesson **145** "My mind holds only what I think with God." (129-130) 69
    Lesson **146** "My mind holds only what I think with God." (131-132) 69
    Lesson **147** "My mind holds only what I think with God." (133-134) 69
    Lesson **148** "My mind holds only what I think with God." (135-136) 69
    Lesson **149** "My mind holds only what I think with God." (137-138) 69
    Lesson **150** "My mind holds only what I think with God." (139-140) 69
    Lesson **151** "All things are echoes of the Voice of God." 69
    Lesson **152** "The power of decision is my own." 70
    Lesson **153** "In my defenselessness my safety lies." 71
    Lesson **154** "I am among the ministers of God." 72
    Lesson **155** "I will step back and let Him lead the way." 73
    Lesson **156** "I walk with God in perfect holiness." 74
    Lesson **157** "Into His Presence would I enter now." 74
    Lesson **158** "Today I learn to give as I receive." 75
    Lesson **159** "I give the miracles I have received." 76
    Lesson **160** "I am at home. Fear is the stranger here." 76
    Lesson **161** "Give me your blessing, holy Son of God." 77

Volume II – Workbook
Table of Contents

Lesson **162** "I am as God created me." 78
Lesson **163** "There is no death. The Son of God is free." 78
Lesson **164** "Now are we One with Him Who is our Source." 79
Lesson **165** "Let not my mind deny the Thought of God." 79
Lesson **166** "I am entrusted with the gifts of God." 80
Lesson **167** "There is one life, and that I share with God." 81
Lesson **168** "Your grace is given me. I claim it now." 81
Lesson **169** "By grace I live. By grace I am released." 82
Lesson **170** "There is no cruelty in God and none in me." 83

REVIEW 5 (W 170 R5) 83
   Introduction 83
   Lesson **171** "God is but Love, and therefore so am I." 84
   Lesson **172** "God is but Love, and therefore so am I." 84
   Lesson **173** "God is but Love, and therefore so am I." 84
   Lesson **174** "God is but Love, and therefore so am I." 84
   Lesson **175** "God is but Love, and therefore so am I." 85
   Lesson **176** "God is but Love, and therefore so am I." 85
   Lesson **177** "God is but Love, and therefore so am I." 85
   Lesson **178** "God is but Love, and therefore so am I." 85
   Lesson **179**. "God is but Love, and therefore so am I." 85
   Lesson **180** "God is but Love, and therefore so am I." 85
   Lesson **181** "I trust my brothers, who are one with me." 85
   Lesson **182** "I call upon God's Name and on my own." 86
   Lesson **183** "I will be still a moment and go home." 86
   Lesson **184** "The Name of God is my inheritance." 87
   Lesson **185** "I want the peace of God." 88
   Lesson **186** "Salvation of the world depends on me." 89
   Lesson **187** "I bless the world because I bless myself." 90
   Lesson **188** "The peace of God is shining in me now." 91
   Lesson **189** "I feel the Love of God within me now." 91
   Lesson **190** "I choose the joy of God instead of pain." 92
   Lesson **191** "I am the holy Son of God Himself" 92
   Lesson **192** "I have a function God would have me fill." 93
   Lesson **193** "All things are Lessons God would have me learn." 94
   Lesson **194** "I place the future in the hands of God." 95
   Lesson **195** "Love is the way I walk in gratitude." 95
   Lesson **196** "It can be but myself I crucify." 96
   Lesson **197** "It can be but my gratitude I earn." 97
   Lesson **198** "Only my condemnation injures me." 97
   Lesson **199** "I am not a body. I am free." 98
   Lesson **200** "There is no peace except the peace of God." 98

REVIEW 6 (W 200 R6) 99
   Introduction 99
   Lesson **201** "I am not a body. I am free. For I am still as God created me." 100
   Lesson **202** "I am not a body. I am free. For I am still as God created me." 100
   Lesson **203** "I am not a body. I am free. For I am still as God created me." 100
   Lesson **204** "I am not a body. I am free. For I am still as God created me." 100
   Lesson **205** "I am not a body. I am free. For I am still as God created me." 100
   Lesson **206** "I am not a body. I am free. For I am still as God created me." 100
   Lesson **207** "I am not a body. I am free. For I am still as God created me." 100
   Lesson **208** "I am not a body. I am free. For I am still as God created me." 100
   Lesson **209** "I am not a body. I am free. For I am still as God created me." 100
   Lesson **210** "I am not a body. I am free. For I am still as God created me." 100
   Lesson **211** "I am not a body. I am free. For I am still as God created me." 101
   Lesson **212** "I am not a body. I am free. For I am still as God created me." 101
   Lesson **213** "I am not a body. I am free. For I am still as God created me." 101
   Lesson **214** "I am not a body. I am free. For I am still as God created me." 101
   Lesson **215** "I am not a body. I am free. For I am still as God created me." 101
   Lesson **216** "I am not a body. I am free. For I am still as God created me." 101

Volume II – Workbook
Table of Contents

    Lesson **217** "I am not a body. I am free. For I am still as God created me." 101
    Lesson **218** "I am not a body. I am free. For I am still as God created me." 101
    Lesson **219** "I am not a body. I am free. For I am still as God created me." 101
    Lesson **220** "I am not a body. I am free. For I am still as God created me." 101
INTRODUCTION TO PART 2 (W 220 IN2) 102
(1) WHAT IS FORGIVENESS? (W 220 W1) 102
    Lesson **221** "Peace to my mind. Let all my thoughts be still." 103
    Lesson **222** "God is with me. I live and breathe in Him." 103
    Lesson **223** "God is my life. I have no life but His." 103
    Lesson **224** "God is my Father, and He loves His Son." 103
    Lesson **225** "God is my Father, and His Son loves Him." 103
    Lesson **226** "My home awaits me. I will hasten there." 103
    Lesson **227** "This is my holy instant of release." 103
    Lesson **228** "God has condemned me not. No more do I." 104
    Lesson **229** "Love, Which created me, is what I am." 104
    Lesson **230** "Now will I seek and find the peace of God." 104
(2) WHAT IS SALVATION? (W 230 W2) 104
    Lesson **231** "Father, I will but to remember You." 104
    Lesson **232** "Be in my mind, my Father, through the day." 104
    Lesson **233** "I give my life to God to run today." 104
    Lesson **234** "Father, today I am Your Son again." 105
    Lesson **235** "God in His mercy wills that I be saved." 105
    Lesson **236** "I rule my mind, which I alone must rule." 105
    Lesson **237** "Now would I be as God created me." 105
    Lesson **238** "On my decision all salvation rests." 105
    Lesson **239** "The glory of my Father is my own." 105
    Lesson **240** "Fear is not justified in any form." 105
(3) WHAT IS THE WORLD? (W 240 W3) 105
    Lesson **241** "This holy instant is salvation come." 106
    Lesson **242** "This day is God's. It is my gift to Him." 106
    Lesson **243** "Today I will judge nothing that occurs." 106
    Lesson **244** "I am in danger nowhere in the world." 106
    Lesson **245** "Your peace is with me, Father. I am safe." 106
    Lesson **246** "To love my Father is to love His Son." 106
    Lesson **247** "Without forgiveness I will still be blind." 106
    Lesson **248** "Whatever suffers is not part of me." 107
    Lesson **249** "Forgiveness ends all suffering and loss." 107
    Lesson **250** "Let me not see myself as limited." 107
(4) WHAT IS SIN? (W 250 W4) 107
    Lesson **251** "I am in need of nothing but the truth." 107
    Lesson **252** "The Son of God is my Identity." 107
    Lesson **253** "My Self is ruler of the universe." 107
    Lesson **254** "Let every voice but God's be still in me." 108
    Lesson **255** "This day I choose to spend in perfect peace." 108
    Lesson **256** "God is the only goal I have today." 108
    Lesson **257** "Let me remember what my purpose is." 108
    Lesson **258** "Let me remember that my goal is God." 108
    Lesson **259** "Let me remember that there is no sin." 108
    Lesson **260** "Let me remember God created me." 108
(5) WHAT IS THE BODY? (W 260 W5) 108
    Lesson **261** "God is my refuge and security." 109
    Lesson **262** "Let me perceive no differences today." 109
    Lesson **263** "My holy vision sees all things as pure." 109
    Lesson **264** "I am surrounded by the Love of God." 109
    Lesson **265** "Creation's gentleness is all I see." 109
    Lesson **266** "My holy Self abides in you, God's Son." 109
    Lesson **267** "My heart is beating in the peace of God." 110
    Lesson **268** "Let all things be exactly as they are." 110
    Lesson **269** "My sight goes forth to look upon Christ's face." 110

Volume II – Workbook
Table of Contents

 Lesson **270** "I will not use the body's eyes today." 110
(6) WHAT IS THE CHRIST? (W 270 W6) **110**
 Lesson **271** "Christ's is the vision I will use today." 110
 Lesson **272** "How can illusions satisfy God's Son?" 110
 Lesson **273** "The stillness of the peace of God is mine." 111
 Lesson **274** "Today belongs to Love. Let me not fear." 111
 Lesson **275** "God's healing Voice protects all things today." 111
 Lesson **276** "The Word of God is given me to speak." 111
 Lesson **277** "Let me not bind Your Son with laws I made." 111
 Lesson **278** "If I am bound, my Father is not free." 111
 Lesson **279** "Creation's freedom promises my own." 111
 Lesson **280** "What limits can I lay upon God's Son?" 111
(7) WHAT IS THE HOLY SPIRIT? (W 280 W7) **112**
 Lesson **281** "I can be hurt by nothing but my thoughts." 112
 Lesson **282** "I will not be afraid of love today." 112
 Lesson **283** "My true Identity abides in You." 112
 Lesson **284** "I can elect to change all thoughts that hurt." 112
 Lesson **285** "My holiness shines bright and clear today." 112
 Lesson **286** "The hush of Heaven holds my heart today." 113
 Lesson **287** "You are my goal, my Father. Only You." 113
 Lesson **288** "Let me forget my brother's past today." 113
 Lesson **289** "The past is over. It can touch me not." 113
 Lesson **290** "My present happiness is all I see." 113
(8) WHAT IS THE REAL WORLD? (W 290 W8) **113**
 Lesson **291** "This is a day of stillness and of peace." 113
 Lesson **292** "A happy outcome to all things is sure." 114
 Lesson **293** "All fear is past and only love is here." 114
 Lesson **294** "My body is a wholly neutral thing." 114
 Lesson **295** "The Holy Spirit looks through me today." 114
 Lesson **296** "The Holy Spirit speaks through me today." 114
 Lesson **297** "Forgiveness is the only gift I give." 114
 Lesson **298** "I love You, Father, and I love Your Son." 114
 Lesson **299** "Eternal holiness abides in me." 115
 Lesson **300** "Only an instant does this world endure." 115
(9) WHAT IS THE SECOND COMING? (W 300 W9) **115**
 Lesson **301** "And God Himself shall wipe away all tears." 115
 Lesson **302** "Where darkness was I look upon the light." 115
 Lesson **303** "The holy Christ is born in me today." 115
 Lesson **304** "Let not my world obscure the sight of Christ." 116
 Lesson **305** "There is a peace that Christ bestows on us." 116
 Lesson **306** "The gift of Christ is all I seek today." 116
 Lesson **307** "Conflicting wishes cannot be my will." 116
 Lesson **308** "This instant is the only time there is." 116
 Lesson **309** "I will not fear to look within today." 116
 Lesson **310** "In fearlessness and love I spend today." 116
(10) WHAT IS THE LAST JUDGMENT? (W 310 W10) **116**
 Lesson **311** "I judge all things as I would have them be." 117
 Lesson **312** "I see all things as I would have them be." 117
 Lesson **313** "Now let a new perception come to me." 117
 Lesson **314** "I seek a future different from the past." 117
 Lesson **315** "All gifts my brothers give belong to me." 117
 Lesson **316** "All gifts I give my brothers are my own." 117
 Lesson **317** "I follow in the way appointed me." 118
 Lesson **318** "In me salvation's means and end are one." 118
 Lesson **319** "I came for the salvation of the world." 118
 Lesson **320** "My Father gives all power unto me." 118
(11) WHAT IS CREATION? (W 320 W11) **118**
 Lesson **321** "Father, my freedom is in You alone." 118
 Lesson **322** "I can give up but what was never real." 119

Volume II – Workbook
Table of Contents

Lesson **323** "I gladly make the 'sacrifice' of fear." 119
Lesson **324** "I merely follow, for I would not lead." 119
Lesson **325** "All things I think I see reflect ideas." 119
Lesson **326** "I am forever an Effect of God." 119
Lesson **327** "I need but call and You will answer me." 119
Lesson **328** "I choose the second place to gain the first." 119
Lesson **329** "I have already chosen what You will." 120
Lesson **330** "I will not hurt myself again today." 120
(12) WHAT IS THE EGO? (W 330 W12) 120
Lesson **331** "There is no conflict, for my will is Yours." 120
Lesson **332** "Fear binds the world. Forgiveness sets it free." 120
Lesson **333** "Forgiveness ends the dream of conflict here." 120
Lesson **334** "Today I claim the gifts forgiveness gives." 121
Lesson **335** "I choose to see my brother's sinlessness." 121
Lesson **336** "Forgiveness lets me know that minds are joined." 121
Lesson **337** "My sinlessness protects me from all harm." 121
Lesson **338** "I am affected only by my thoughts." 121
Lesson **339** "I will receive whatever I request." 121
Lesson **340** "I can be free of suffering today." 121
(13) WHAT IS A MIRACLE? (W 340 W13) 121
Lesson **341** "I can attack but my own sinlessness, ... 122
Lesson **342** "I let forgiveness rest upon all things, ... 122
Lesson **343** "I am not asked to make a sacrifice 122
Lesson **344** "Today I learn the law of love; 122
Lesson **345** "I offer only miracles today, ... 122
Lesson **346** "Today the peace of God envelops me, ... 122
Lesson **347** "Anger must come from judgment. Judgment is 123
Lesson **348** "I have no cause for anger or for fear, ... 123
Lesson **349** "Today I let Christ's vision look upon 123
Lesson **350** "Miracles mirror God's eternal Love. 123
(14) WHAT AM I? (W 350 W14) 123
Lesson **351** "My sinless brother is my guide to peace. 124
Lesson **352** "Judgment and love are opposites. From one 124
Lesson **353** "My eyes, my tongue, my hands, my feet today 124
Lesson **354** "We stand together, Christ and I, in peace 124
Lesson **355** "There is no end to all the peace and joy 124
Lesson **356** "Sickness is but another name for sin. 124
Lesson **357** "Truth answers every call we make to 124
Lesson **358** "No call to God can be unheard or left 124
Lesson **359** "God's answer is some form of peace. 125
Lesson **360** "Peace be to me, the holy Son of God. 125
FINAL LESSONS (W 360 FL) 125
Lesson 361-365. "This holy instant would I give to You. Be You in charge. For I would follow You, Certain that Your direction gives me peace." 125
EPILOGUE (W 361 EP) 125

Urtext Volume II: *Workbook*

Part 1

Introduction[1] *(W 1 IN1)*

May 26, 1969

W 1 IN1 1. A theoretical foundation such as the text is necessary as a background to make these exercises meaningful. Yet it is the exercises which will make the goal possible. An untrained mind can accomplish nothing. It is the purpose of these exercises to train the mind to think along the lines which the course sets forth.

W 1 IN1 2. The exercises are very simple. They do not require more than a few minutes, and it does not matter where or when you do them. They need no preparation. They are numbered, running from 1 to 365. The training period is one year. Do not undertake more than one exercise a day.

W 1 IN1 3. The purpose of these exercises is to train the mind to a different perception of everything in the world. The workbook is divided into two sections, the first dealing with the undoing of what you see now, and the second with the restoration of sight. It is recommended that each exercise be repeated several times a day, preferably in a different place each time, and if possible in every situation in which you spend any long period of time. The purpose is to train the mind to generalize the lessons, so that you will understand that each of them is as applicable to one situation as it is to another.

W 1 IN1 4. Unless specified to the contrary, the exercise should be practiced with the eyes open, since the aim[2] is to learn how to see. The only rule that should be followed throughout is to practice the exercises with great specificity. Each one applies to every situation in which you find yourself, and to everything you see in it. Each day's exercises are planned around one central idea, the exercises themselves consisting of applying that idea to as many specifics as possible. Be sure that you do not decide that there are some things you see to which the idea for the day is inapplicable. The aim **W(2)** of the exercises will always be[3] to increase the application of the idea to everything. This will not require effort. Only be sure that you make no exceptions in applying the idea.

W 1 IN1 5. Some of the ideas you will find hard to believe, and others will seem quite startling. It does not matter. You are merely asked to apply them to what you see. You are not asked to judge them, nor even to believe them. You are asked only to use them. It is their use which will give them meaning to you, and show you they are true. Remember only this; you need not believe them, you need not accept them, and you need not welcome them. Some of them you may actively resist. None of this will matter, nor decrease their efficacy. But allow yourself to make no exceptions in applying the ideas the exercises contain. Whatever your reactions to the ideas may be, use them. Nothing more than this is required.

---

[1] The word "Introduction" is not present in the *Urtext* manuscript.
[2] The *Urtext* manuscript has "end." Handwritten mark-up suggests (aim). The *Notes* has "aim."
[3] This line is typed twice, once on the bottom of page one, and crossed out and again on the top of page 2. "**The exercises is**" is changed to (the exercises will always be). The *Notes* has "will always be."

Lesson 1 "Nothing I see in this room (on this street, from this window, in this place) means anything."

W 1 L 1. Now look slowly around you, and practice applying this idea very specifically to whatever you see:[4]

"This table does not mean anything."
"This chair does not mean anything."
"This hand does not mean anything."
"This pen does not mean anything."

W 1 L 2. Then look farther away from your immediate area, and apply the idea to a wider range: **W(3)**

"That door does not mean anything."
"That body does not mean anything."
"That lamp does not mean anything."
"That sign does not mean anything."
"That shadow does not mean anything."

W 1 L 3. Notice that these statements are not arranged in any order, and make no allowance for differences in the kinds of things to which they are applied. That is the purpose of the exercise. The statement is merely applied to anything you see. As you practice applying the idea for the day, use it totally indiscriminately. Do not attempt to apply it to everything you see, for these exercises should not become ritualistic. Only be sure that nothing you see is specifically excluded. One thing is like another as far as the application of the idea is concerned. **W(4)**

Lesson 2 "I have given everything I see in this room (on this street, from this window, in this place) all the meaning that it has for me."

W 2 L 1. The exercises with this idea are the same as those for the first one. Begin with the things that are near you, and apply the idea to whatever your glance rests on. Then increase the range outward. Turn your head so that you include whatever is to either side. If possible, turn around and apply the idea to what was behind you. Remain as indiscriminate as possible in selecting subjects for its application, do not concentrate on anything in particular, and do not attempt to include everything in an area or you will introduce strain. Merely glance easily and fairly quickly around you, trying to avoid selection by size, brightness, color, material, or relative importance to you.

W 2 L 2. Take the subjects simply as you see them. Try to apply the exercise with equal ease to a body or a button, a fly or a floor, an arm or an apple. The sole criterion for applying the idea to anything is merely that your eyes have 'lighted on it. Make no attempt to include anything in particular, but be sure that nothing is specifically excluded. **W(5)**

Lesson 3 "I do not understand anything I see in this room (on this street, from this window, in this place)."

W 3 L 1. Apply this idea in the same way as the previous ones, without making distinctions of any kind. Whatever you see becomes a proper subject for applying the idea. Be sure that you do not question the suitability of anything for the application of the idea. These are not exercises in judgment. Anything is suitable if you see it. Some of the things you see may have emotionally-charged meaning for you. Try to lay such feelings aside, and merely use these things exactly as you would anything else.

W 3 L 2. The point of the exercises is to help you clear your mind of all past associations, to see things exactly as they appear to you now, and to realize how little you really understand about them. It is therefore essential that you keep a perfectly open mind, unhampered by judgment, in selecting the things to which the idea for the day is to be applied. For this purpose one thing is like another; equally suitable and therefore equally useful. **W(6)**

Lesson 4 "These thoughts do not mean anything. They are like the things I see in this room (on this street, from this window, in this place)."

W 4 L 1. Unlike the preceding ones, these exercises do not begin with the idea for the day. In these practice periods, begin with noting the thoughts that are crossing your mind for about a minute. Then apply the idea to them. If you are already aware of unhappy thoughts use them as subjects for the idea. Do not, however, select only the thoughts you think are "bad." You will find, if you train yourself to look at your thoughts, that they represent such a mixture that, in a sense, none of them can be called "good" or "bad." This is why they do not mean anything.

W 4 L 2. In selecting the subjects for the application of today's idea, the usual specificity is required. Do not be afraid to use "good" thoughts as well as "bad." None of them represents your real thoughts, which are being covered up by them. The "good" ones of which you are aware are but shadows of what lies beyond, and shadows make sight difficult. The "bad" ones are blocks to sight, and make seeing impossible. You do not want either.

W 4 L 3. This is a major exercise, and will be repeated from time to time in somewhat different form. The aim here is to train you in the first steps toward the goal of separating the meaningless from the meaningful. It is a first attempt in the long-range purpose of learning to see the meaningless as outside you and the meaningful within. It is also the beginning of training your mind to recognize what is the same and what is different. In using your thoughts for application of the idea for today, identify each thought by the central figure or event it contains; for example:

"This thought about ___ does not mean anything. It is like the things I see in this room (or wherever you are)" **W(7)**

W 4 L 4. You can also use the idea for a particular thought which you recognize as harmful. This practice is useful, but is not a substitute for the more random procedures to be followed for the exercises. Do not, however, examine your mind for more than a minute or so. You are too inexperienced as yet to avoid a tendency to become pointlessly preoccupied. Further, since these exercises are the first of their kind, you may find the suspension of judgment in connection with thoughts particularly difficult. Do not repeat these exercises more than three or four times during the day. We will return to them later. **W(8)**

Lesson 5 "I am never upset for the reason I think."

W 5 L 1. This idea, like the preceding one, can be used with any person, situation or event you think is causing you pain. Apply it specifically to whatever you believe is the cause of your upset, using the description of the feeling in whatever term seems accurate to you. The upset may seem to be fear, worry, depression, anxiety, anger, hatred, jealousy, or any number of forms, all of which will be perceived as different. This is not true. However, until you learn that form does not matter, each form becomes a proper subject for the exercises for the day. Applying the same idea to each of them separately is the first step in ultimately recognizing they are all the same.

W 5 L 2. When using the idea for today for a specific perceived cause of an upset in any form, use both the name of the form in which you see the upset, and the cause which you ascribe to it. For example:

---

[4] *Urtext* manuscript has semicolon here. We changed it to a colon because that is more appropriate and is generally used in the *Urtext* manuscript for this sort of structure. We thus consider the semi-colon an inadvertent error here. The *Notes* also has a colon.

"I am not angry at ____ for the reason I think."

"I am not afraid of ____ for the reason I think."

But again, this should not be substituted for practice periods in which you first search your mind for "sources" of upset in which you believe, and forms of upset which you think result.

W 5 L 3. In these exercises, more than in the preceding ones, you may find it hard to be indiscriminate, and to avoid giving greater weight to some subjects than to others. It might help to precede the exercises with the statement:

"There are no small upsets. They are all equally disturbing to my peace of mind."

Then examine your mind for whatever is distressing you, regardless of how much or how little you think it is doing so.

W 5 L 4. You may also find yourself less willing to apply today's idea **W(9)** to some perceived sources of upset than to others. If this occurs, think first of this:

"I cannot keep this form of upset and let the others go. For the purposes of these exercises, then, I will regard them all as the same."

Then search your mind for no more than a minute or so, and try to identify a number of different forms of upset that are disturbing you, regardless of the relative importance you may give them. Apply the idea for today to each of them, using the name of both the source of the upset as you perceive it, and of the feelings as you experience it. Further examples are:

"I am not worried about ____ for the reason I think."

"I am not depressed about ____ for the reason I think."

Three or four times during the day is enough. **W(10)**

Lesson 6 "I am upset because I see something that is not there."

W 6 L 1. The exercises with this idea are very similar to the preceding ones. Again, it is necessary to name both the form of upset (anger, fear, worry, depression, and so on) and the perceived source very specifically for any application of the idea. For example:

"I am angry at ____ because I see something that is not there."

"I am worried about ____ because I see something that is not there."

W 6 L 2. Today's idea is useful for application to anything that seems to upset you, and can profitably be used throughout the day for that purpose. However, the three or four practice periods which are required should be preceded by a minute or so of mind-searching, as before, and the application of the idea to each upsetting thought uncovered in the search.

W 6 L 3. Again, if you resist applying the idea to some upsetting thoughts more than to others, remind yourself of the two cautions stated in the previous lesson:

"There are no small upsets. They are all equally disturbing to my peace of mind."

and

"I cannot keep this form of upset and let the others go. For the purposes of these exercises, then, I will regard them all as the same" **W(11)**

Lesson 7 "I see only the past."

W 7 L 1. This idea is particularly difficult to believe at first. Yet it is the rationale for all of the preceding ones.

It is the reason why nothing that you see means anything. It is the reason why you have given everything you see all the meaning that it has for you. It is the reason why you do not understand anything you see.

It is the reason why your thoughts do not mean anything, and why they are like the things you see.

It is the reason why you are never upset for the reason you think.

It is the reason why you are upset because you see something that is not there.

W 7 L 2. Old ideas about time are very difficult to change, because everything you believe is rooted in time, and depends on your not learning these new ideas about it. Yet that is precisely why you need new ideas about time. This first time idea is not really so strange as it may sound at first. Look at a cup, for example.

W 7 L 3. Do you see a cup, or are you merely reviewing your past experiences of picking up a cup, being thirsty, drinking from a cup, feeling the rim of a cup against your lips, having breakfast, and so on? Are not your aesthetic reactions to the cup, too, based on past experiences? How else would you know whether or not this kind of cup will break if you drop it? What do you know about this cup except what you learned in the past? You would have no idea what this cup is except for your past learning. Do you, then, really see it?

W 7 L 4. Look about you. This is equally true of whatever you look at. Acknowledge this by applying the idea for today indiscriminately to whatever catches your eye. For example:**W(12)**

"I see only the past in this pencil."

"I see only the past in this shoe."

"I see only the past in this hand."

"I see only the past in that body."

"I see only the past in that face."

Do not linger over any one thing in particular, but remember to omit nothing specifically.[5] Glance briefly at each subject, and then move on to the next. **W(13)**

Lesson 8 "My mind is preoccupied with past thoughts."

W 8 L 1. This idea is, of course, the reason why you see only the past. No-one really sees anything. He sees only his thoughts projected outward. The mind's preoccupation with the past is the cause of the total misconception about time from which your seeing suffers. Your mind cannot grasp the present, which is the only time there is. It therefore cannot understand time, and cannot, in fact, understand anything.

W 8 L 2. The only wholly true thought one can hold about the past is that it is not here. To think about it at all is therefore to think about illusions.[6] Very few minds have realized what is actually entailed in picturing the past or in anticipating the future. The mind is actually blank when it does this, because it is not really thinking about anything.

W 8 L 3. The purpose of the exercises for today is to begin to train your mind to recognize when it is not really thinking at all. While thoughtless "ideas" preoccupy your mind, the truth is blocked. Recognizing that your mind has been merely blank, rather than believing that it is filled with real ideas, is the first step to opening the way to vision.

W 8 L 4. The exercises for today should be done with eyes closed. This is because you actually cannot see anything, and it is easier to recognize that no matter how vividly you may picture a thought, you are not seeing anything. With as little investment as possible, search

---

[5] The *Urtext* manuscript shows a comma here, but capitalizes the next word "**Glance**" suggesting a new sentence. *FIP* puts a sentence break here too.

[6] The *Urtext* manuscript has "delusions." Handwritten mark-up suggests (illusions). The *Notes* has "illusions."

your mind for the usual minute or so, merely noting the thoughts[7] you find there. Name each one by the central figure or theme it contains, and pass on to the next. Introduce the practice period by saying:

"I seem to be thinking about ____." **W(14)**

Then name each of your thoughts specifically, for example:

"I seem to be thinking about (name of person), about (name of object), about (name of emotion), and so on,"

concluding at the end of the mind-searching period with:

"But my mind is preoccupied with past thoughts."

W 8 L 5. This can be done four or five times during the day, unless you find it irritates you. If you find it trying, three or four times is sufficient. You might find it helpful, however, to include your irritation, or any emotion which the idea[8] may induce, in the mind-searching itself. **W(15)**

Lesson 9 "I see nothing as it is now."

W 9 L 1. This idea obviously follows from the two preceding ones. But while you may be able to accept it intellectually, it is unlikely that it will mean anything to you as yet. However, understanding is not necessary at this point. In fact, the recognition that you do not understand is a prerequisite for undoing your false ideas. These exercises are concerned with practice, not with understanding. You do not need to practice what you really understand. It would indeed be circular to aim at understanding, and assume that you have it already.

W 9 L 2. It is difficult for the untrained mind to believe that what seems to be pictured before it is not there. This idea can be quite disturbing, and may meet with active resistance in any number of forms. Yet that does not preclude applying it. No more than that is required for these or any other exercises. Each little[9] step will clear a little of the darkness away, and understanding will finally come to lighten every corner of the mind which[10] has been cleared of the debris which darkens it.

W 9 L 3. These exercises, for which three or four practice periods are sufficient, involve looking about you and applying the idea for the day to whatever you see, remembering[11] the need for its indiscriminate application, and the essential rule of excluding nothing. [12]It is emphasized again that while complete inclusion should not be attempted, specific exclusion must be avoided. Be sure you are honest with yourself in making this distinction. You may be tempted to obscure it. **W(16)**

W 9 L 4. For example:

"I do not see that[13] typewriter as it is now."

"I do not see this key as it is now."

"I do not see this telephone as it is now."

Begin with things that are nearest you, and then extend the range:

"I do not see that coat rack as it is now."

"I do not see that face as it is now."

"I do not see that door as it is now."[14] **W(17)**

Lesson 10 "My thoughts do not mean anything."

W 10 L 1. This idea applies to all the thoughts of which you are aware, or become aware in the practice periods. The reason the idea is applicable to all of them is that they are not your real thoughts. We have made this distinction before, and will again. You have no basis for comparison as yet. When you do, you will have no doubt that what you once believed were your thoughts did not mean anything.

W 10 L 2. This is the second time we have used this kind of idea. The form is only slightly different. This time, the idea is introduced with "My thoughts" instead of "These thoughts," and no link is made overtly with the things around you. The emphasis is now on the lack of reality of what you think you think.

W 10 L 3. This aspect of the correction process began with the idea that the thoughts of which you are aware are meaningless, outside rather than within; and then stressed their past rather than their present status. Now we are emphasizing that the presence of these "thoughts" means that you are not thinking. This is merely another way of repeating our earlier statement that your mind is really a blank. To recognize this is to recognize nothingness when you think you see it. As such, it is the prerequisite for vision.

W 10 L 4. Close your eyes for these exercises, and introduce them by repeating the idea for today quite slowly to yourself. Then add:

"This idea will help to release me from all that I now believe."

The exercises consist, as before, in searching your mind for all the thoughts which are available to you, without selection or judgment. Try to avoid classification of any kind. In fact, if you find it helpful to do so, you might imagine that you are watching an oddly assorted procession going by, which has little if any personal meaning to you. As each one crosses your mind, say:

"This thought about ____ does not mean anything."

"That thought about ____ does not mean anything." **W(18)**

W 10 L 5. Today's idea can obviously serve for any thought that distresses you at any time. In addition, five practice periods are recommended, each involving no more than a minute or so of mind-searching. It is not recommended that this time period be extended, and it should be reduced to half a minute or even less if you experience discomfort. Remember, however, to repeat the idea slowly before applying it specifically, and also to add:

"This idea will help to release me from all that I now believe." **W(19)**

Lesson 11 "My meaningless thoughts are showing me a meaningless world."

W 11 L 1. This is the first idea we have had which is related to a major phase of the correction process; the reversal of the thinking of the world. It seems as if the world determines what you perceive. Today's idea introduces the concept that your thoughts determine the world you see. Be glad indeed to practice it in this initial form, for in this idea is your release made sure. The key to forgiveness lies in it.

W 11 L 2. The practice periods for today's idea are to be undertaken somewhat differently from the previous ones. Begin with eyes closed, and repeat the idea slowly to yourself. Then open your eyes and look about, near or far, up or down, -- anywhere. During the minute or so to be spent in using the idea, merely repeat it to

---

[7] The *Urtext* manuscript has the word "**that**" crossed out. The word is not present in the *Notes*.
[8] Handwritten mark-up suggests (for today). The *Notes* does not have "for today."
[9] The *Urtext* manuscript has "**little**" crossed out. *FIP* has "**small**" here. The *Notes* has "little."
[10] Handwritten mark-up suggests (that). The *Notes* has the glyph for "which."
[11] The *Urtext* manuscript shows "**that**" crossed out. It is not present in the *Notes* and doesn't work here grammatically.
[12] Handwritten mark-up suggests (insert below on next page.) *FIP* does so. The "next page" material here is not present in the *Notes*.
[13] Handwritten mark-up suggests (this). This material is not present in the *Notes*.

[14] *FIP* adds (It is emphasized again that while complete inclusion should not be attempted, specific exclusion must be avoided. Be sure you are honest in making this distinction. You may be tempted to obscure it.) This material is not present in the *Notes*.

yourself, being sure to do so without haste and with no sense of urgency or effort.

W 11 L 3. To do these exercises for maximum benefit, the eyes should move from one thing to another fairly rapidly, since they should not linger on anything in particular. The words, however, should be used in an unhurried, even leisurely fashion. The introduction to this idea should be practiced as casually as possible. It contains the foundation for the peace, relaxation and freedom from worry that we are trying to achieve. On concluding the exercises, close your eyes and repeat the idea once more, slowly to yourself.

W 11 L 4. Three practice periods today will probably be sufficient. However, if there is little or no uneasiness and an inclination to do more, as many as five may be undertaken. More than this is not recommended. **W(20)**

Lesson 12 "I am upset because I see a meaningless world."

W 12 L 1. The importance of this idea lies in the fact that it contains a correction for a major perceptual distortion. You think that what upsets you is a frightening world, or a sad world, or a violent world, or an insane world. All these attributes are given it by you. The world is meaningless in itself.

W 12 L 2. These exercises are done with eyes open. Look around you, this time quite slowly. Try to pace yourself so that the slow shifting of your glance from one thing to another involves a fairly constant time interval. Do not allow the time of the shift to become markedly longer or shorter, but try, instead, to keep a measured, even tempo throughout. What you see does not matter. You teach yourself this as you give whatever your glance rests on equal attention and equal time. This is a beginning step in learning to give them all equal value.

W 12 L 3. As you look about you, say to yourself:

"I think I see a fearful world, a dangerous world, a hostile world, a sad world, a wicked world, a crazy world,"

and so on, using whatever descriptive terms happen to occur to you. If terms which seem positive rather than negative occur to you, include them. For example, you might think of "a good world," or "a satisfying world." If such terms occur to you, use them along with the rest. You may not yet understand why these "nice" adjectives belong in these exercises, but remember that "a good world" implies a "bad" one, and "a satisfying world" implies an "unsatisfying" one. All terms which cross your mind are suitable subjects for today's exercises. Their seeming quality does not matter.

W 12 L 4. Be sure that you do not alter the time intervals between applying today's idea to what you think is pleasant and what you think is unpleasant. For the purposes of these exercises, there is no difference between them. **W(21)** At the end of the practice period, add:

"But I am upset because I see a meaningless world."

W 12 L 5. What is meaningless is neither good nor bad. Why, then, should a meaningless world upset you? If you could accept the world as meaningless and let the truth be written upon it for you, it would make you indescribably happy. But because it is meaningless, you are impelled to write upon it what you would have it be. It is this you see in it. It is this that is meaningless in truth. Beneath your words is written the Word of God. The truth upsets you now, but when your words have been erased, you will see His. That is the ultimate purpose of these exercises.

W 12 L 6. Three or four times is enough for practicing the idea for today. Nor should the practice periods exceed a minute. You may find even this too long. Terminate the exercises whenever you experience a sense of strain. **W(22)**

Lesson 13 "A meaningless world engenders fear."

W 13 L 1. Today's idea is really another form of the preceding one, except that it is more specific as to the emotion aroused. Actually, a meaningless world is impossible. Nothing without meaning exists. However, it does not follow that you will not[15] perceive something that has no meaning. On the contrary, you will be particularly likely to think you do[16] perceive it.

W 13 L 2. Recognition of meaninglessness arouses intense anxiety in all the separated ones. It represents a situation in which God and the ego "challenge" each other as to whose meaning is to be written in the empty space which meaninglessness provides. The ego rushes in frantically to establish its own "ideas" there, fearful that the void may otherwise be used to demonstrate its own unreality. And on this alone it is correct.

W 13 L 3. It is essential, therefore, that you learn to recognize the meaningless, and accept it without fear. If you are fearful, it is certain that you will endow the world with attributes which it does not possess, and crowd it with images that do not exist. To the ego illusions are safety devices, as they must also be to you who equate yourself with the ego.

W 13 L 4. The exercises for today, which should be done about three or four times, for not more than a minute or so at most each time, are to be practiced in a somewhat different way from the preceding ones. With eyes closed, repeat today's idea to yourself. Then open your eyes and look about you slowly, saying:[17]

"I am looking at a meaningless world."

Repeat this statement to yourself as you look about. Then close your eyes and conclude with: "A meaningless world engenders fear because I think I am in competition with God." **W(23)**

W 13 L 5. You may find it difficult to avoid resistance, in one form or another, to this concluding statement. Whatever form such resistance may take, remind yourself that you are really afraid of such a thought because of the "vengeance" of the "enemy." You are not expected to believe the statement at this point, and will probably try to dismiss it as preposterous. Note carefully, however, any signs of overt or covert fear which it may arouse.

W 13 L 6. This is our first attempt at stating an explicit cause and effect relationship of a kind which you are very inexperienced in recognizing. Do not dwell on the concluding statement, and try not even to think of it except during the exercise periods. That will suffice at present. **W(24)**

Lesson 14 "God did not create a meaningless world."

W 14 L 1. The idea for today is, of course, the reason why a meaningless world is impossible. What God did not create does not exist. And everything that does exist exists as He created it. The world you see has nothing to do with reality. It is of your own making, and it does not exist.

W 14 L 2. The exercises for today are to be practiced with eyes closed throughout. The mind-searching period should be short, a minute at most. Do not have more than three practice periods with today's idea unless you find them comfortable. If you do, it will be because you really understand what they are for.

W 14 L 3. The idea for today is another step in learning to let go the thoughts which you have written on the world, and see the Word of God in their place. The early steps in this exchange, which can truly be called salvation, can be quite difficult and even quite pain-

---

[15] Handwritten mark-up suggests (think you). That is not present in the *Notes*.
[16] Handwritten mark-up suggests (so). The *Notes* has "do."
[17] Handwritten mark-up suggests (saying:), it's not in the *Urtext* manuscript. The *Notes* includes the word, however, so we include it also.

ful. Some of them will lead you directly into fear. You will not be left there. You will go far beyond it. Our direction is toward perfect safety and perfect peace.

W 14 L 4. With eyes closed, think of all the horrors in the world that cross your mind. Name each one as it occurs to you, and then deny its reality. God did not create it, and so it is not real. Say, for example:

> *"God did not create that war, and so it is not real."*
> *"God did not create that airplane crash, and so it is not real."*
> *"God did not create that disaster (specify) so it is not real."*
> *"God did not create that illness(specify with name of person) and so it is not real."*[18]

W 14 L 5. Suitable subjects for the application of today's idea also include anything you are afraid might happen to you, or to anyone about whom you are concerned. In each case, name the "disaster" quite specifically. **W(25)** Do not use general terms. For example, do not say, "God did not create illness," but, "God did not create cancer," or heart attacks, or whatever may arouse fear in you.

W 14 L 6. This is your personal repertory of horrors at which you are looking. These things are part of the world you see. Some of them are shared illusions, and others are part of your personal hell. It does not matter. What God did not create can only be in your own mind apart from His. Therefore, it has no meaning. In recognition of this fact, conclude the practice periods by repeating today's idea.

> *"God did not create a meaningless world."*

W 14 L 7. The idea for today can, of course, be applied to anything that disturbs you during the day, aside from the practice periods. Be very specific in applying it. Say:

> *"God did not create a meaningless world. He did not create (specify the situation which is disturbing you), and so it is not real."* **W(26)**

Lesson 15 "My thoughts are images which I have made."

W 15 L 1. It is because the thoughts you think you think appear as images that you do not recognize them as nothing. You think you think them, and so you think you see them. This is how your "seeing" was made. This is the function you have given your body's eyes. It is not seeing. It is image-making. It takes the place of seeing, replacing vision with illusions.

W 15 L 2. This introductory idea to the process of image-making which you call seeing will not have much meaning for you. You will begin to understand it when you have seen little edges of light around the same familiar objects which you see now. That is the beginning of real vision. You can be certain that real vision will come quickly when this has occurred.

W 15 L 3. As we go along, you may have many "light episodes". They may take many different forms, some of them quite unexpected. Do not be afraid of them. They are signs that you are opening your eyes at last. They will not persist, because they merely symbolize true perception, and they are not related to knowledge. These exercises will not reveal knowledge to you. But they will prepare the way to it.

W 15 L 4. In practicing the idea for today, repeat it first to yourself, and then apply it to whatever you see around you, using its name and letting your eyes rest on it as you say:

> *"This _____ is an image which I have made."*
> *"That _____ is an image which I have made."*

It is not necessary to include a large number of specific subjects for the application of today's idea. It is necessary, however, to continue to look at each subject while you repeat the idea to yourself. The idea should be repeated quite slowly each time. **W(27)**

W 15 L 5. Although you will obviously not be able to apply the idea to very many things during the minute or so of practice that is recommended, try to make the selection as random as possible. Less than a minute will do for the practice periods, if you begin to feel uneasy. Do not have more than three application periods for today's idea unless you feel completely comfortable with it, and do not exceed four.[19] **W(28)**

Lesson 16 "I have no neutral thoughts."

W 16 L 1. The idea for today is a beginning step in dispelling the belief that your thoughts have no effect. Everything you see is the result of your thoughts. There is no exception to this fact. Thoughts are not big or little; powerful or weak. They are merely true or false. Those which are true create their own likeness.[20] Those which are false make theirs.

W 16 L 2. There is no more self-contradictory concept than that of "idle thoughts." What gives rise to the perception of a whole world can hardly be called idle. Every thought you have contributes to truth or to illusion; either it extends the truth or it multiplies illusions. You can indeed multiply nothing, but you will not extend it by doing so.

W 16 L 3. In addition to never being idle, salvation requires that you recognize that every thought you have brings either peace or war; either love or fear. A neutral result is impossible because a neutral thought is impossible. There is such a temptation to dismiss fear thoughts as unimportant, trivial; and not worth bothering about that it is essential you recognize them all as equally destructive but equally unreal. We will practice this idea in many forms before you really understand it.

W 16 L 4. In applying the idea for today, search your mind for a minute or so, with eyes closed, and actively seek not to overlook any "little" thought which tends to elude the search. This is quite difficult until you get used to it. You will find that it is still hard for you not to make artificial distinctions. Every thought that occurs to you, regardless of the quality which you assign to it, is a suitable subject for applying today's idea. **W(29)**

W 16 L 5. In the practice periods, first repeat the idea, and then as each one crosses your mind, hold it in awareness while you tell yourself:

> *"This thought about _____ is not a neutral thought."*
> *"That thought about _____ is not a neutral thought."*

W 16 L 6. As usual, use today's idea whenever you are aware of a particular thought which arouses uneasiness. The following form is suggested for this purpose:

> *"This thought about _____ is not a neutral thought, because I have no neutral thoughts."*

W 16 L 7. Four or five practice periods are recommended, if you find them relatively effortless. If strain is experienced, three will be enough. The length of the exercise period[21] should also be reduced if there is discomfort. **W(30)**

---

[18] This fourth line is not present in the *Urtext* manuscript or FIP but it is present in the *Notes*, so we include it as probably an inadvertent omission.

[19] Handwritten mark-up suggests (However, the idea can be applied as needed throughout the day.). That line is not present in the *Notes*.

[20] **Genesis 1:26-27** Then God said, "Let Us make man in Our image, according to Our likeness; let them have dominion over the fish of the sea, over the birds of the air, and over the cattle, over all the earth and over every creeping thing that creeps on the earth." So God created man in His own image; in the image of God He created him; male and female He created them.

[21] The *Urtext* manuscript has (, however) crossed out. The word "however" is not in the *Notes*.

Lesson 17 "I see no neutral things."

W 17 L 1. This idea is another step in the direction of identifying cause and effect as it really operates. You see no neutral things because you have no neutral thoughts. It is always the thought that comes first, despite the temptation to believe that it is really the other way around. This is not the way the world thinks, but you must learn that it is the way you think. If it were not so, perception would have no cause, and would itself be the cause of reality. In view of its highly variable nature, this is hardly likely.

W 17 L 2. In applying today's idea, say to yourself, with eyes open:

"I see no neutral things because I have no neutral thoughts."

Then look about you, resting your glance on each thing that catches your eye long enough to say:

"I do not see a neutral ____ because my thoughts about ____ are not neutral."

For example, you might say:

"I do not see a neutral wall, because my thoughts about walls are not neutral."

"I do not see a neutral body, because my thoughts about bodies are not neutral."

W 17 L 3. As usual, it is essential to make no distinction between what you believe to be animate or inanimate; pleasant or unpleasant. Regardless of what you may believe, you do not see anything which is really alive and really joyous. That is because you are unaware as yet of any thoughts which are really true and therefore really happy.

W 17 L 4. Three or four specific practice periods are recommended, and no less than three are required for maximum benefit, even if you experience resistance. However, if you do, the length of the practice period may be reduced to less than the minute or so which is otherwise recommended. **W(31)**

Lesson 18 "I am not alone in experiencing the effects of my seeing."

W 18 L 1. The idea for today is another step in learning that the thoughts which give rise to what you see are never neutral or unimportant. It also emphasizes the idea that minds are joined, which will be given increasing stress later.

W 18 L 2. Today's idea does not refer to what you see as much as to how you see it. Therefore, the exercises for today will emphasize this aspect of your perception. The three or four practice periods which are recommended should be done as follows:

W 18 L 3. Selecting subjects for the application of the idea randomly, look at each one long enough to say:

"I am not alone in experiencing the effects of how I see ____."

Conclude the practice period by repeating the more general statement:

"I am not alone in experiencing the effects of my seeing."

A minute or so or even less will be sufficient. **W(32)**

Lesson 19 "I am not alone in experiencing the effects of my thoughts."

W 19 L 1. The idea for today is obviously the reason why your seeing does not affect you alone. You will notice that at times the ideas related to thinking precede those related to perceiving, while at other times the order is reversed. The reason is that the order does not actually matter. Thinking and its results are really simultaneous, for cause and effect are never separate.

W 19 L 2. Today we are again emphasizing the fact that minds are joined. This is rarely a wholly welcome idea at first, since it seems to carry with it an enormous sense of responsibility, and may even be regarded as an "invasion of privacy." Yet it is a fact that there are no private thoughts. Despite your initial resistance to this idea, you will yet understand that it must be true if salvation is possible at all. And salvation must be possible because it is the Will of God.

W 19 L 3. The minute or so of mind-searching which today's exercises require are[22] to be undertaken with closed eyes. The idea is to be repeated first, and then the mind should be carefully searched for the thoughts it contains at that time. As you consider each one, name it in terms of the central person or theme it contains, and holding it in your mind as you do so, say:

"I am not alone in experiencing the effects of this thought about ____."

W 19 L 4. The requirement of as much indiscriminateness as possible in selecting subjects for the practice period should be quite familiar to you by now, and will no longer be repeated each day, although it will occasionally be included as a reminder. Do not forget, however, that random selection of subjects for all practice periods remains essential throughout. Lack of order in this connection will ultimately make the recognition of lack of order in miracles meaningful to you. **W(33)**

W 19 L 5. Apart from the "as needed" application of today's idea, at least three practice periods are required, shortening the length of time involved, if necessary. Do not attempt more than four. **W(34)**

Lesson 20 "I am determined to see."

W 20 L 1. We have been quite casual about our practice periods thus far. There has been virtually no attempt to direct the time for undertaking them, minimal effort has been required, and not even active cooperation and interest have been asked. This casual approach has been intentional, and very carefully planned. We have not lost sight of the crucial importance of the reversal of your thinking. The salvation of the world depends on it. Yet you will not see if you regard yourself as being coerced, and if you give in to resentment and opposition.

W 20 L 2. This is our first attempt to introduce structure. Do not misconstrue it as an effort to exert force or pressure. You want salvation. You want to be happy. You want peace. You do not have them now because your minds are totally undisciplined, and you cannot distinguish between joy and sorrow, pleasure and pain, love and fear. You are now learning how to tell them apart. And great indeed will be your reward.[23]

W 20 L 3. Your decision to see is all that vision requires. What you want is yours. Do not mistake the little effort that is asked of you for a sign that our goal is of little worth. Can the salvation of the world be a trivial purpose? And can the world be saved if you are not? God has one Son, and he is the resurrection and the life.[24] His will is done because all power is given him in Heaven and on earth.[25] In your determination to see is vision given you.

W 20 L 4. The exercises for today consist in reminding yourselves throughout the day that you want to see. Today's idea also tacitly implies the recognition that you do not see now. Therefore, as you repeat the idea, you are stating that you are determined to change your present state for a better one, and one you really want. **W(35)**

W 20 L 5. Repeat today's idea slowly and positively at least twice an hour today, attempting to do so every half hour. Do not be distressed if you forget to do so, but make a real effort to remember. The extra repetitions should be applied to any situation, person, or

---

[22] The *Urtext* manuscript says "**are**" and so does the *Notes* but agreement in number arguably requires "**is**", which is what FIP uses. Is "a minute or so" plural or singular? That is debatable.
[23] **Matthew 5:12** Rejoice and be exceedingly glad, for great is your reward in heaven, for so they persecuted the prophets who were before you.
[24] **John 11:25** Jesus said to her, "I am the resurrection and the life. He who believes in Me, though he may die, he shall live.
[25] **Matthew 28:18** And Jesus came and spoke to them, saying, "All authority has been given to Me in heaven and on earth."

event which upsets you. You can see them differently, and you will. What you desire you will see. Such is the real law of cause and effect as it operates in the world. **W(36)**

Lesson 21 "I am determined to see things differently."

W 21 L 1. The idea for today is obviously a continuation and extension of the preceding one. This time, however, specific mind-searching periods are necessary in addition to applying the idea to particular situations as they arise. Five practice periods are urged, allowing a full minute for each.

W 21 L 2. In the practice periods, begin by repeating the idea to yourself. Then close your eyes and search your mind carefully for situations past, present or anticipated, which arouse anger in you. The anger may take the form of any reaction ranging from mild irritation to rage. The degree of the emotion you experience does not matter. You will become increasingly aware that a slight twinge of annoyance is nothing but a veil drawn over intense fury.

W 21 L 3. Try, therefore, not to let the "little" thoughts of anger escape you in the practice periods. Remember that you do not really recognize what really arouses anger in you, and nothing that you believe in this connection means anything. You will probably be tempted to dwell more on some situations than on others, on the fallacious grounds that they are more "obvious." This is not so. It is merely an example of the belief that some forms of attack are more justified than others.

W 21 L 4. As you search your mind for all the forms in which attack thoughts present themselves, hold each one in mind and tell yourself;

"I am determined to see ____ (name of person) differently."

"I am determined to see ____ (specify the situation) differently."

Try to be as specific as possible. You may, for example, focus your anger on a particular attribute of a particular person, believing that the anger is limited to this aspect. If your perception of the person is suffering from this form of distortion, say:

"I am determined to see____ (specify the attribute) in____ (name of person) differently." **W(37)**

Lesson 22 "What I see is a form of vengeance."

W 22 L 1. Today's idea accurately describes the way anyone who holds attack thoughts in his mind must see the world. Having projected his anger onto the world, he sees vengeance about to strike at him. His own attack is thus perceived as self-defense. This becomes an increasingly vicious circle until he is willing to change how he sees. Otherwise, thoughts of attack and counterattack will preoccupy him, and people his entire world. What peace of mind is possible to him then?

W 22 L 2. It is from this savage fantasy that you want to escape. Is it not joyous news to hear that it is not real? Is it not a happy discovery to find that you can escape? You made what you would destroy; everything that you hate and would attack and kill. All that you fear does not exist.

W 22 L 3. Look at the world about you at least five times today, for at least a minute each time. As your eyes move slowly from one object to another, from one body to another, say to yourself:

"I see only the perishable.

I see nothing that will last.[26]

What I see is a form of vengeance."

At the end of each practice period, ask yourself:

"Is this the world I really want to see?"

The answer is surely obvious. **W(38)**

Lesson 23 "I can escape from the world I see by giving up attack thoughts."

W 23 L 1. The idea for today contains the only way out of fear that will[27] succeed. Nothing else will work; everything else is meaningless. But this way cannot fail. Every thought you have makes up some segment of the world you see. It is with your thoughts, then, that we must work, if your perception of the world is to be changed.

W 23 L 2. If the cause of the world you see is attack thoughts, you must learn that it is these thoughts which you do not want. There is no point in lamenting the world. There is no point in trying to change the world. It is incapable of change because it is merely an effect. But there is indeed a point in changing your thoughts about the world. Here you are changing the cause. The effects will change automatically.

W 23 L 3. The world you see is a vengeful world, and everything in it is a symbol of vengeance. Each of your perceptions of "external reality" is a pictorial representation of your own attack thoughts. One can well ask if this can be called seeing. Is not fantasy a better word for such a process, and hallucination a more appropriate term for the result?

W 23 L 4. You see the world which you have made, but you do not see yourself as the image-maker. You cannot be saved from the world, but you can escape from its cause. This is what salvation means, for where is the world you see when its cause is gone? Vision already holds a replacement for everything you think you see now. Loveliness can light your images, and so transform them that you will love them even though they were made of hate. For you will not be making them alone. **W(39)**

W 23 L 5. The idea for today introduces the thought that you are not trapped in the world you see, because its cause can be changed. This change requires, first, that the cause be identified and then let go, so that it can be replaced. The first two steps in this process require your cooperation. The final one does not. Your images have already been replaced. By taking the first two steps, you will see that this is so.

W 23 L 6. Besides using it throughout the day as the need arises, five practice periods are required in applying today's idea. As you look about you, repeat the idea slowly to yourself, and then close your eyes and devote about a minute to searching your mind for as many attack thoughts as occur to you. As each one crosses your mind, say:

"I can escape from the world by giving up attack thoughts about ____."

Hold each one in mind[28] as you say this, and then dismiss that thought and go on to the next.

W 23 L 7. In the practice periods, be sure to include both your thoughts of attacking and of being attacked. Their effects are exactly the same, because they are exactly the same. You do not yet recognize this, and you are asked at this time only to treat them as the same in today's practice periods. We are still at the stage of identifying the cause of the world you see. When you finally realize that thoughts of attack and of being attacked are not different, you will be ready to let the cause go. **W(40)**

---

[26] Handwritten mark-up adds (What I see is not real.). That line is present in the *Notes* but is crossed out.

[27] Handwritten mark-up suggests (ever). That is not present in the *Notes*.
[28] *Urtext* manuscript has a struck-out "one in mind" and replaced it with "attack thought" but "one in mind" is the reading in the *Notes*.

Lesson 24 "I do not perceive my own best interests."

W 24 L 1. In no situation which arises do you realize the outcome that would make you happy. Therefore you have no guide to appropriate action, and no way of judging the result.[29] What you do is determined by your perception of the situation, and that perception is wrong. It is inevitable, then, that you will not serve your own best interests. Yet they are your only goal in any situation which is correctly perceived. Otherwise you will not recognize what they are.

W 24 L 2. If you realized that you do not perceive your own best interests, you could be taught what they are. But in the presence of your conviction that you do know what they are, you cannot learn. The idea for today is a step toward opening your mind so that learning can begin.

W 24 L 3. The exercises for today require much more honesty than you are accustomed to using. A few subjects, honestly and carefully considered in each of the five practice periods which should be undertaken today, will be more helpful than a more cursory examination of a large number. Two minutes are suggested for each of the mind-searching periods which the exercises involve.

W 24 L 4. Practice periods begin with repeating today's idea, followed by searching the mind, with closed eyes, for unresolved situations about which you are currently concerned. The emphasis should be on uncovering the outcome you want. You will quickly realize that you have a number of goals in mind as part of the desired outcome; and also that these goals are on different levels, and often conflict.

W 24 L 5. Name each situation that occurs to you, and enumerate carefully as many goals as possible that you would like to be met in its resolution. The form of each application should be roughly as follows: **W(41)**

> "In the situation involving ___, I would like ____ to happen, and ____ to happen," and so on.

Try to cover as many different kinds of outcome as may honestly occur to you, even if some of them do not appear to you to be directly related to the situation, or even to be inherent in it at all.

W 24 L 6. If these exercises are done properly, you will quickly recognize that you are making a large number of demands of the situation which have nothing to do with it. You will also recognize that many of your goals are contradictory, that you have no unified outcome in mind, and that you must experience disappointment in connection with some of your goals however the situation turns out. After covering the list of as many hoped for goals as possible for each unresolved situation that crosses your mind, say to yourself:

> "I do not perceive my own best interests in this situation," and go on to the next. **W(42)**

Lesson 25 "I do not know what anything is for."

W 25 L 1. Purpose is meaning. Today's idea explains why nothing you see means anything. You do not know what it is for. Therefore it is meaningless to you. Everything is for your own best interests. That is what it is for; that is its purpose; that is what it means. It is in recognizing this that your goals become unified. It is in recognizing this that what you see is given meaning.

W 25 L 2. You perceive the world and everything in it as meaningful in terms of ego goals. These goals have nothing to do with your own best interests, because the ego is not you. This false identification makes you incapable of understanding what anything is for. As a result, you are bound to misuse it. When you believe this, you will try to withdraw the goals you have assigned to the world, instead of attempting to reinforce them.

W 25 L 3. Another way of describing the goals you now perceive as valuable is to say that they are all concerned with "personal" interests. Since you have no personal interests, your goals are really concerned with nothing. In cherishing them, therefore, you have no goals at all. And thus you do not know what anything is for.

W 25 L 4. Before you can make any sense out of the exercises for today, one more thought is necessary. At the most superficial levels, you do recognize purpose. Yet purpose cannot be understood at these levels. For example, you do understand that a telephone is for the purpose of talking to someone who is not physically in your immediate vicinity. What you do not understand is what you want to reach him for. And it is this that makes your contact with him meaningful or not. **W(43)**

W 25 L 5. It is crucial to your learning to be willing to give up the goals you have established for everything. The recognition that they are meaningless, rather than "good" or "bad", is the only way to accomplish this. The idea for today is a step in this direction.

W 25 L 6. Six practice periods, each of two minutes duration, are required. Each practice period should begin with a slow repetition of the idea for today, followed by looking about you and letting your glance rest on whatever happens to catch your eye, near or far, "important" or "unimportant," "human" or "unhuman," with your eyes resting on each subject you so select, say, for example:

> "I do not know what this chair is for."
> "I do not know what this pencil is for."
> "I do not know what this hand is for."

Say this quite slowly, without shifting your eyes until you have completed the statement. Then move on to the next subject, and apply today's idea as before. **W(44)**

Lesson 26 "My attack thoughts are attacking my invulnerability."

W 26 L 1. It is surely obvious that if you can be attacked you are not invulnerable. You see attack as a real threat. That is because you believe that you can really attack. And what would have effects through you must also have effects on you. It is this law that will ultimately save you. But you are misusing it now. You must therefore learn how it can be used for your own best interests, rather than against them.

W 26 L 2. Because your attack thoughts will be projected, you will fear attack. And if you fear attack, you must believe that you are not invulnerable. Attack thoughts therefore make you vulnerable in your own mind, which is where the attack thoughts are. Attack thoughts and invulnerability cannot be accepted together. They contradict each other.

W 26 L 3. The idea for today introduces the thought that you always attack yourself first. If attack thoughts must entail the belief that you are vulnerable, their effect is to weaken you in your own eyes. Thus they have attacked your perception of yourself. And because you believe in them, you can no longer believe in yourself. A false image of yourself has come to take the place of what you are.

W 26 L 4. Practice with today's idea will help you to understand that vulnerability or invulnerability is the result of your own thoughts. Nothing except your thoughts can attack you. Nothing except your thoughts can make you think you are vulnerable. And nothing except your thoughts can prove to you this is not so. **W(45)**

W 26 L 5. Six practice periods are required in applying today's idea. A full two minutes should be attempted for each of them, although the time may be reduced to a minute if the discomfort is too great. Do not reduce it further.

---

[29] Originally typed "results" the handwritten mark-up crosses out the "s" making it "result" which is what is present in the *Notes*.

W 26 L 6. The practice period should begin with repeating the idea for today, then closing your eyes and reviewing the unresolved situations whose outcomes are causing you concern. The concern may take the form of depression, worry, anger, a sense of imposition, fear, foreboding, or preoccupation. Any problem as yet unsettled which tends to recur in your thoughts during the day is a suitable subject. You will not be able to use very many for one practice period, because a longer time than usual should be spent with each one. Today's idea should be applied as follows:

First, name the situation:

"I am concerned about ____."

Then go over every possible outcome which has occurred to you in that connection and which has caused you concern, referring to each one quite specifically, saying:

"I am afraid ____ will happen."

If you are doing the exercises properly, you should have some five or six distressing possibilities available for each situation you use, and quite possibly more. It is much more helpful to cover a few situations thoroughly than to touch on a larger number.

W 26 L 7. As the list of anticipated outcomes for each situation continues, you will probably find some of them, especially those which occur to you toward the end, less acceptable to you. Try, however, to treat them all alike to whatever extent you can.

W 26 L 8. After you have named each outcome of which you are afraid, tell yourself:

"That thought is an attack upon myself."

Conclude each practice period by repeating today's idea once more. **W(46)**

Lesson 27 "Above all else I want to see."

W 27 L 1. Today's idea expresses something stronger than mere determination. It gives vision priority among your desires. You may feel hesitant about using the idea on the ground that you are not sure you really mean it. This does not matter. The purpose of today's exercises is to bring the time when the idea will be wholly true a little nearer.

W 27 L 2. There may be a great temptation to believe that some sort of sacrifice is being asked of you when you say you want to see above all else. If you become uneasy by the lack of reservation involved, add:

"Vision has no cost to anyone."

If fear of loss still persists, add further:

"It can only bless."

W 27 L 3. The idea for today needs many repetitions for maximum benefit. It should be used at least every half hour, and more often if possible. You might try for every 15 or 20 minutes. It is recommended that you set a definite time interval for using the idea when you wake or shortly afterwards, and attempt to adhere to it throughout the day. It will not be difficult to do this, even if you are engaged in conversation or otherwise occupied at the time. You can still repeat one short sentence to yourself without disturbing anything that is going on.

W 27 L 4. The real question is how often will you remember? How much do you want today's idea to be true? Answer one[30] of these two questions, and you have answered the other. You will probably miss several applications, and perhaps quite a number. Do not be disturbed by this, but do try to keep on your schedule from then on. If only once during the day you feel that you were perfectly sincere while you were repeating today's idea, you can be sure that you have saved yourself many years of effort. **W(47)**

Lesson 28 "Above all else I want to see things differently."

W 28 L 1. Today we are really giving specific application to the idea of for yesterday. In these practice periods you will be making a series of definite commitments. The question of whether you will keep them in the future is not our concern here. If you are willing at least to make them now, you have started on the way to keeping them. And we are still at the beginning.

W 28 L 2. You may wonder why it is important to say, for example, "Above all else I want to see this table differently." In itself it is not important at all. Yet what is by itself? And what does "in itself" mean? You see a lot of separate things about you, which really means you are not seeing at all. You either see or not. When you have seen one thing differently, you will see all things differently. The light you will see in any one of them is the same light you will see in them all.

W 28 L 3. When you say "Above all else I want to see this table differently," you are making a commitment to withdraw your preconceived ideas about the table, and open your minds to what it is and what it is for. You are not defining it in past terms. You are asking what it is, rather than telling it what it is. You are not binding its meaning to your tiny experiences of tables, nor are you limiting its purpose to your little personal thoughts.

W 28 L 4. You will not question what we have already defined. And the purpose of these exercises is to ask questions and receive the answers. In saying, "Above all else I want to see this table differently," you are committing yourself to seeing. It is not an exclusive commitment. It is a commitment which applies to the table just as much as to anything else, neither more nor less. **W(48)**

W 28 L 5. You could, in fact, gain vision from just that table, if you could withdraw all your own ideas from it, and look upon it with a completely open mind. It has something to show you; something beautiful and clean and of infinite value, full of happiness and hope. Hidden under all your ideas about it is its real purpose, the purpose it shares with all the universe.

W 28 L 6. In using the table as a subject for applying the idea for today you are therefore really asking to see the purpose of the universe. You will be making the same request of each subject which you use in the practice periods. And you are making a commitment to each of them to let their purpose be revealed to you, instead of placing your own judgment upon them.

W 28 L 7. We will have six two minute practice periods today, in which the idea for the day is stated first, and then applied to whatever you see in looking about you. Not only should the subjects be chosen randomly, but each one should be accorded equal sincerity as today's idea is applied to it, in an attempt to acknowledge the equal value of them all in their contribution to your seeing.

W 28 L 8. As usual, the applications should include the name of the subject which your eyes happen to 'light on, and you should rest your eyes on it while saying:

"Above all else, I want to see this ____ differently[31]"

Each application should be made quite slowly and as thoughtfully as possible. There is no hurry. **W(49)**

Lesson 29 "God is in everything I see."

W 29 L 1. The idea for today explains why you can see all purpose in anything. It explains why nothing is separate, by itself or in itself. And it explains why nothing you see means anything. In fact, it

---

[30] The word "**one**" is not present in the *Urtext* manuscript. *FIP* changes the phrase to "**one of these questions**" which is what the *Notes* reads.

[31] The *Urtext* manuscript does not have the word "**differently**" although *FIP* does. We agree with *FIP* that it should be there and deem its omission to be inadvertent. It is not in the *Notes* curiously.

explains every idea we have used thus far, and all subsequent ones as well. Today's idea is the whole basis for vision.

W 29 L 2. You will probably find this idea very difficult to grasp at this point. You may find it silly, irreverent, senseless, funny, and even objectionable. Certainly God is not in a table, for example, as you see it. Yet we emphasized yesterday that a table shares the purpose of the universe. And what shares the purpose of the universe shares the purpose of its Creator.

W 29 L 3. Try then, today, to begin to learn how to look on all things with love, appreciation, and open-mindedness. You do not see them now. Would you know what is in them? Nothing is as it appears to you. Its holy purpose stands beyond your little range. When vision has shown you the holiness that lights up the world, you will understand today's idea perfectly. And you will not understand how you could ever have found it difficult.

W 29 L 4. Our six two minute practice periods for today should follow a now familiar pattern; begin with repeating the idea to yourself, and then apply it to randomly chosen subjects about you, naming each one specifically. Try to avoid the tendency toward self-directed selection, which may be particularly tempting in connection with today's idea because of its wholly alien nature. Remember that any order which you impose is equally alien to reality.

W 29 L 5. Your list of subjects should therefore be as free of self-selection as possible. For example, a suitable list might include: **W(50)**

"God is in this coat hanger."
"God is in this magazine."
"God is in this finger."
"God is in this lamp."
"God is in that body."
"God is in that door."
"God is in that wastebasket."

W 29 L 6. In addition to the assigned practice periods, repeat the idea for today at least once an hour, looking slowly about you as you say the words unhurriedly to yourself. At least once or twice you should experience a sense of restfulness as you do this. **W(51)**

Lesson 30 "God is in everything I see because God is in my mind."

W 30 L 1. The idea for today is the springboard for vision. From this idea will the world open up before you, and you will look upon it and see in it what you have never seen before. Nor will what you saw before be even faintly visible to you.

W 30 L 2. Today we are trying to use the new kind of projection. We are not attempting to get rid of what we do not like by seeing it outside. Instead, we are trying to see in the world what is in our minds, and what we want to recognize is there. Thus we are trying to join with what we see, rather than keeping it apart from us. That is the fundamental difference between vision and the way you see.

W 30 L 3. Today's idea should be applied as often as possible throughout the day. Whenever you have a moment or so, repeat it to yourself slowly, looking about you, and trying to realize that the idea applies to everything you do see now, or could see now if it were within the range of your sight.

W 30 L 4. Real vision is not limited to concepts such as "near" and "far." To help you begin to get used to this idea, try to think of things beyond your present range as well as those you can actually see, as you apply today's idea. Real vision is not only unlimited by space and distance, but it does not depend on the body's eyes at all. The mind is its only source.

W 30 L 5. To aid in helping you to become more accustomed to this idea as well, devote several practice periods to applying today's idea with your eyes closed, using whatever subject comes to mind, and looking within rather than without. Today's idea applies equally to both. **W(52)**

Lesson 31 "I am not the victim of the world I see."

W 31 L 1. Today's idea is the introduction to your declaration of release. Again, the idea should be applied to both the world you see without and the world you see within. In applying the idea, we will use a form of practice which will be used more and more, with changes as indicated. Generally speaking, the form includes two aspects, one in which you apply the idea on a more sustained basis, and the other consisting of frequent applications of the idea throughout the day.

W 31 L 2. Two longer periods of practice with the idea for today are needed, one in the morning and one at night. Three to five minutes for each of them is recommended. During that time, look about you slowly while repeating the idea two or three times. Then close your eyes and apply the same idea to your inner world. You will escape from both together, for the inner is the cause of the outer.

W 31 L 3. As you survey your inner world, merely let whatever thoughts cross your mind come into your awareness, each to be considered for a moment and then replaced by the next. Try not to establish any thought of hierarchy among them. Watch them come and go as dispassionately as possible. Do not dwell on any one in particular, but try to let the stream move on evenly and calmly, without any special investment on your part. As you sit and quietly watch your thoughts, repeat today's idea to yourself as often as you care to, but with no sense of hurry.

W 31 L 4. In addition, repeat the idea for today as often as possible during the day. Remind yourself that you are making a declaration of independence in the name of your own freedom. And in your freedom lies the freedom of the world.

W 31 L 5. The idea for today is a particularly useful one to use as a response to any form of temptation. It is a declaration that you will not yield to it and put yourself in bondage. **W(53)**

Lesson 32 "I have invented the world I see."

W 32 L 1. Today we are continuing to develop the theme of cause and effect. You are not the victim of the world you see because you invented it. You can give it up as easily as you made it up. You will see it or not see it, as you wish. While you want it you will see it; when you no longer want it, it will not be there for you to see.

W 32 L 2. The idea for today, like the preceding ones, applies to your inner and outer worlds, which are actually the same. However, since you see them as different, the practice periods for today will again include two phases, one involving the world you see outside you, and the other the world you see in your mind. In today's exercises, try to introduce the thought that both are in your own imagination.

W 32 L 3. Again we will begin the practice periods for the morning and evening by repeating the idea for today two or three times, while looking around at the world you see as outside yourself. Then close your eyes, and look around your inner world. Try to treat them both as equally as possible. Repeat the idea for today unhurriedly as often as you wish, as you watch the images which your imagination presents to your awareness.

W 32 L 4. For the two longer practice periods, three to five minutes are recommended with not less than three required. More than five can be utilized, if you find the exercises restful. To facilitate this, select a time when few distractions are anticipated, and when you yourself feel reasonably ready.

W 32 L 5. These exercises are also to be continued during the day, as often as possible. The shorter applications consist of repeating the idea slowly, as you survey either your inner or outer world. It does not matter which you choose.

W 32 L 6. The idea for today should also be applied immediately to any situation which may distress you. Apply the idea by telling yourself:

"I have invented this situation as I see it." **W(54)**

Lesson 33 "There is another way of looking at the world."

W 33 L 1. Today's idea is an attempt to recognize that you can shift your perception of the world in both its outer and inner aspects. A full five minutes should be devoted to the morning and evening application.

W 33 L 2. In these practice periods, the idea should be repeated as often as you find profitable, though unhurried applications are essential. Alternate between surveying your outer and inner perceptions, but without an abrupt sense of shifting. Merely glance casually around the world you perceive as outside yourself, then close your eyes and survey your inner thoughts with equal casualness. Try to remain equally uninvolved in both, and to maintain this detachment as you repeat the idea throughout the day.

W 33 L 3. The shorter exercise periods should be as frequent as possible. Specific applications of today's idea should also be made immediately when any situation arises which tempts you to become disturbed. For these applications, say:

"There is another way of looking at this."

W 33 L 4. Remember to apply today's idea the instant you are aware of distress. It may be necessary to take a minute or so to sit quietly and repeat the idea to yourself several[32] times. Closing your eyes will probably help in this form of application. **W(55)**

Lesson 34 "I could see peace instead of this."

W 34 L 1. The idea for today begins to describe the conditions which prevail in the other way of seeing. Peace of mind is clearly an internal matter. It must begin with your own thoughts, and then extend outward. It is from your peace of mind that a peaceful perception of the world arises.

W 34 L 2. Three longer practice periods are required for today's exercises. One in the morning and one in the evening is advised, with an additional one to be undertaken at any time in between which seems most conducive to readiness. All applications should be done with your eyes closed. It is your inner world to which the applications of today's idea should be made.

W 34 L 3. Some five minutes of mind-searching are required for each of the longer practice periods. Search your mind for fear thoughts, anxiety provoking situations, "offending" personalities or events, or anything else about which you are harboring unloving thoughts. Note each one casually, repeating the idea for today slowly, as you watch them arise in your mind, and let each one go to be replaced by the next.

W 34 L 4. If you begin to experience difficulty in thinking of specific subjects, continue to repeat the idea to yourself in an unhurried manner, without applying it to anything in particular. Be sure, however, not to make any specific exclusions.

W 34 L 5. The shorter applications are to be frequent, and made whenever you feel your peace of mind is threatened in any way. The purpose is to protect yourself from temptation throughout the day. If a specific form of temptation arises in your awareness, the exercise should take this form:

"I could see peace in this situation instead of what I now see in it."

If the inroads on your peace of mind take the form of more generalized adverse emotions, such as depression, anxiety or worry, use the idea in its original form. **W(56)**

W 34 L 6. If you find you need more than one application of today's idea to help you change your mind in any specific context, try to take several minutes and devote them to repeating the idea until you feel some sense of relief. It will help you if you tell yourself specifically:

"I can replace my feelings of depression, anxiety, or worry (or my thoughts about this situation, personality, or event) with peace." **W(57)**

Lesson 35 "My mind is part of God's. I am very holy."

W 35 L 1. Today's idea does not describe the way you see yourself now. It does, however, describe what vision will show you. It is difficult for anyone who thinks he is in this world to believe this of himself. Yet the reason he thinks he is in this world is because he does not believe it.

W 35 L 2. You will believe that you are part of where you think you are. That is because you surround yourself with the environment you want. And you want it to protect the image of yourself which you have made. The image is part of it.[33] What you see while you believe you are in it is seen through the eyes of the image. It[34] is not vision. Images cannot see.

W 35 L 3. The idea for today presents a very different view of yourself. By establishing your Source it establishes your identity, and it describes you as you must really be in truth. We will use a somewhat different kind of application for today's idea, because the emphasis for today is on the perceiver, rather than on what he perceives.

W 35 L 4. For each of the three five-minute practice periods today, begin by repeating today's idea to yourself, and then close your eyes and search your mind for the various kinds of descriptive terms in which you see yourself. Include all of the ego-based attributes which you ascribe to yourself, positive or negative, desirable or undesirable, grandiose or debased. All of them are equally unreal because you do not look upon yourself through the eyes of holiness.

W 35 L 5. In the earlier part of the mind-searching period, you will probably emphasize what you consider to be the more negative aspects of your perception of yourself. Toward the latter part of the exercise period, however, more self-inflating descriptive terms may well cross your mind. Try to recognize that the direction of your fantasies about yourself does not matter. Illusions have no direction in reality. They are merely not true. **W(58)**

W 35 L 6. A suitable unselected list for applying the idea for today might be as follows:

"I see myself as imposed on."

"I see myself as depressed."

"I see myself as failing."

"I see myself as endangered."

"I see myself as helpless."

"I see myself as victorious."

"I see myself as losing out."

"I see myself as charitable."

"I see myself as virtuous."

---

[32] *Urtext* manuscript has "separate" in this spot. It's being assessed as a typo. *FIP* changes it as we do. The *Notes* uses an abbreviation "sev." which is likely meant to be "separate."

[33] Handwritten mark-up suggests (this environment).
[34] Handwritten mark-up suggests (This).

W 35 L 7. You should not think of these terms in an abstract way. They will occur to you as various situations, personalities, and events in which you figure cross your mind. Pick up any specific situation that occurs to you, identify the descriptive term or terms which you feel are applicable to your reactions to that situation, and use them in applying today's idea. After you have named each one, add:

"But my mind is part of God's. I am very holy."

W 35 L 8. During the longer exercise periods, there will probably be intervals in which nothing specific occurs to you. Do not strain to think up specific things to fill the interval, but merely relax and repeat today's idea slowly until something occurs to you. Although nothing that does occur should be omitted from the exercises, nothing should be "dug out" with effort. Neither force nor discrimination should be used.

W 35 L 9. As often as possible during the day, pick up a specific attribute or attributes which you are ascribing to yourself at the time, and apply the idea for today to them, adding the idea to each of them in the form stated above. If nothing particular occurs to you, merely repeat the idea to yourself, with closed eyes. **W(59)**

Lesson 36 "My holiness envelops everything I see."

W 36 L 1. Today's idea extends the idea for yesterday from the perceiver to the perceived. You are holy because your mind is part of God's. And because you are holy, your sight must be holy as well. "Sinless" means without sin. You cannot be without sin a little. You are sinless or not. If your mind is part of God's you must be sinless, or a part of His Mind would be sinful. Your sight is related to His holiness, not to your ego and therefore not to your body.

W 36 L 2. Four three to five minute practice periods are required for today. Try to distribute them fairly evenly, and make the shorter application frequently, to protect your protection throughout the day. The longer practice periods should take this form:

W 36 L 3. First, close your eyes and repeat the idea for today several times slowly. Then open your eyes and look quite slowly about you, applying the idea specifically to whatever you note in your casual survey. Say, for example:

"My holiness envelops that rug."

"My holiness envelops that wall."

"My holiness envelops these fingers."

"My holiness envelops that chair."

"My holiness envelops that body."

"My holiness envelops this pen."

Several times during these practice periods, close your eyes and repeat the idea to yourself. Then open your eyes and continue as before.

W 36 L 4. For the shorter exercise periods, close your eyes and repeat the idea; look about you as you repeat it again; and conclude with one more repetition with your eyes closed. All applications should, of course, be made quite slowly, as effortlessly and unhurriedly as possible. **W(60)**

Lesson 37 "My holiness blesses the world."

W 37 L 1. This idea contains the first glimmerings of your true function in the world, or why you are here. Your purpose is to see the world through your own holiness. Thus are you and the world blessed together. No-one loses; nothing is taken away from anyone; everyone gains through your holy vision. It signifies the end of sacrifice, because it offers everyone his full due. And he is entitled to everything, because it is his birthright as a Son of God.

W 37 L 2. There is no other way in which the idea of sacrifice can be removed from the world's thinking. Any other way of seeing will inevitably demand payment of someone or something. As a result, the perceiver will lose. Nor will he have any idea why he is losing. Yet is his wholeness restored to his awareness through your vision. Your holiness blesses him by asking nothing of him. Those who see themselves as whole make no demands.

W 37 L 3. Your holiness is the salvation of the world. It lets you teach the world that it is one with you, not by preaching to it, not by telling it anything, but merely by your quiet recognition that in your holiness are all things blessed, along with you.

W 37 L 4. Today's four longer exercise periods, each to involve three to five minutes of practice, begin with the repetition of the idea for today, followed by a minute or so of looking about you as you apply the idea to whatever you see:

"My holiness blesses this chair."

"My holiness blesses that window."

"My holiness blesses this body."

Then close your eyes and apply the idea to any person who occurs to you, using his name and saying:

"My holiness blesses you, (name)" **W(61)**

W 37 L 5. You may continue the practice period with your eyes closed; you may open your eyes again and apply the idea for today to your outer world if you so desire; you may alternate between applying it[35] to what you see around you and to those who are in your thoughts; or you may use any combination of these two phases of application which you prefer. The practice period should conclude with a repetition of the idea made with your eyes closed, and another, following immediately, made with your eyes open.

W 37 L 6. The shorter exercises consist of repeating the idea as often as you can. It is particularly helpful to apply it silently to anyone you meet, using his name as you do so. It is essential to use the idea if anyone seems to cause an adverse reaction in you. Offer him the blessing of your holiness immediately, that you may learn to keep it in your own awareness. **W(62)**

Lesson 38 "There is nothing my holiness cannot do."

W 38 L 1. Your holiness reverses all the laws of the world. It is beyond every restriction of time, space, distance, and limits of any kind. Your holiness is totally unlimited in its power because it establishes you as a Son of God, at one with the Mind of his Creator. Through your holiness the power of God is made manifest. Through your holiness the power of God is made available. And there is nothing the power of God cannot do.

W 38 L 2. Your holiness, then, can remove all pain, can end all sorrow, and can solve all problems. It can do so in connection with yourself and with anyone else. It is equal in its power to help anyone, because it is equal in its power to save anyone. If you are holy, so is everything God created. You are holy because all things He created are holy, and all things He created are holy because you are.

W 38 L 3. In today's exercises, we will apply the power of your holiness to all problems, difficulties, or suffering in any form that you happen to think of in yourself or someone[36] else. We will make no distinctions because there are no distinctions.

W 38 L 4. In the four longer practice periods, each preferably to last a full five minutes, repeat the idea for today, close your eyes, and then search your mind for any sense of loss or unhappiness of any kind, as you see it. Try to make as little distinction as possible between a situation that is difficult for you and one that is difficult

---

[35] Handwritten mark-up suggests (the idea).
[36] Handwritten mark-up suggests (in anyone).

for someone else. Identify the situation specifically, and also name the person concerned. Use this form in applying the idea for today:

"In the situation involving _____ in which I see myself, there is nothing that my holiness cannot do."

"In the situation involving _____ in which _____ sees himself, there is nothing my holiness cannot do." **W(63)**

W 38 L 5. From time to time you may want to vary this procedure, and add some relevant thoughts of your own. You might like, for example, to include thoughts such as:

"There is nothing my holiness cannot do because the power of God lies in it."

Introduce whatever variations appeal to you, but keep the exercises focused on the theme

"There is nothing your[37] holiness cannot do."

The purpose of today's exercises is to begin to instill in you a sense that you have dominion over all things because of what you are.[38]

W 38 L 6. In the frequent shorter applications, apply the idea in its original form unless a specific problem concerning you or someone else arises, or comes to mind. In that event, use the more specific form of application. **W(64)**

Lesson 39 "My holiness is my salvation."

W 39 L 1. If guilt is hell, what is its opposite? Like the text for which this workbook was written, the ideas which are used for these exercises are very simple, very clear, and totally unambiguous. We are not concerned with intellectual feats nor logical toys. We are dealing only in the very obvious, which has been overlooked in the clouds of complexity in which you think you think.

W 39 L 2. If guilt is hell, what is its opposite? This is not difficult, surely. The hesitation you may feel in answering is not due to the ambiguity of the question. But do you believe that guilt is hell? If you did, you would see at once how direct and simple the text is, and you would not need a workbook at all. No-one needs practice to gain what is already his.

W 39 L 3. We have already said that your holiness is the salvation of the world. What about your own salvation? You cannot give what you do not have. A Savior must be saved. How else can he teach salvation? Today's exercises will apply to you alone, recognizing that your salvation is crucial to the salvation of the world. As you apply the exercises to your own world, the whole world stands to benefit.

W 39 L 4. Your holiness is the answer to every question that was ever asked, is being asked now, or will be asked in the future. Your holiness means the end of guilt, and therefore the end of hell. Your holiness is the salvation of the world, and your own. How could you to whom your holiness belongs be excluded from it? God does not know unholiness. Can it be He does not know His Son?

W 39 L 5. A full five minutes are urged[39] for the four longer practice periods for today. [40]Longer and more frequent practice sessions are encouraged.[41] If you want to exceed the minimum requirements more rather than longer sessions are recommended, although both are encouraged. **W(65)**

W 39 L 6. Begin the practice periods as usual, by repeating today's idea to yourself. Then, with closed eyes, search out your unloving thoughts in whatever form they appear; uneasiness, depression, anger, fear, worry, attack, insecurity, and so on. Whatever form they take they are unloving and therefore fearful. And so it is from them that you need to be saved.

W 39 L 7. Specific situations, events or personalities you associate with unloving thoughts of any kind are suitable subjects for today's exercises. It is imperative for your own salvation that you see them differently. And it is your blessing on them that will save you and give you vision.

W 39 L 8. Slowly, without conscious selection and without undue emphasis on any one in particular, search your mind for every thought that stands between you and your salvation. Apply the idea for today to each one of them in this way:

"My unloving thoughts about _____ are keeping me in hell. My holiness is my salvation."

W 39 L 9. You may find these sessions[42] easier if you intersperse the applications[43] with several short periods during which you merely repeat today's idea to yourself slowly a few times. You may also find it helpful to include a few short intervals in which you just relax and do not seem to be thinking of anything. Sustained concentration is very difficult at first. It will become much easier as your mind becomes more disciplined and less distractible.

W 39 L 10. Meanwhile, you should feel free to introduce variety into your application[44] periods, in whatever form appeals to you. Do not, however, change the idea itself in varying the method of applying it. However you elect to use it, the idea should be stated so that its meaning remains[45] that your holiness is your salvation. End each practice period by repeating the idea in its original form once more, and adding:

"If guilt is hell, what is its opposite?" **W(66)**

In the shorter applications, which should be made some three or four times an hour and more if possible, you may ask yourself this question, repeat today's idea, or preferably both. If temptations arise, a particularly helpful form of the idea is:

"My holiness is my salvation from this." **W(67)**

Lesson 40 "I am blessed as a Son of God."

W 40 L 1. Today we will begin to assert[46] some of the happy things to which you are entitled, being what you are. No long practice periods are required today, but very frequent short ones are necessary. Once every ten minutes would be highly desirable, and you are urged to attempt this and to adhere to this schedule whenever possible. If you forget, try again. If there are long interruptions, try again. Whenever you remember, try again.

W 40 L 2. You need not close your eyes for the exercise periods, although you will probably find it more helpful if you do. However, you may be in a number of situations during the day when closing your eyes would not be appropriate. Do not miss a practice period because of this. You can practice quite well under almost any circumstance, if you really want to.

W 40 L 3. Today's exercises take little time and no effort. Repeat today's idea, and then add several of the attributes which you associate with being a Son of God, applying them to yourself. One practice period might, for example, consist of the following:

"I am blessed as a Son of God.

I am happy, peaceful, loving and contented."

Another might be something as follows:

---

[37] Handwritten mark-up suggests (my).
[38] **Genesis 1:28** Then God blessed them, and God said to them, "Be fruitful and multiply; fill the earth and subdue it; have dominion over the fish of the sea, over the birds of the air, and over every living thing that moves on the earth."
[39] Handwritten mark-up suggests (required).
[40] Handwritten mark-up suggests (and).
[41] Handwritten mark-up suggests (urged).

[42] Handwritten mark-up suggests (practice periods).
[43] Handwritten mark-up suggests (them).
[44] Handwritten mark-up suggests (practice).
[45] Handwritten mark-up suggests (explanation is the fact).
[46] Originally in the *Urtext* manuscript the word "**insert**" was typed, handwriting suggests (assert), which appears to be a genuine correction.

"I am blessed as a Son of God.

I am calm, quiet, assured and confident."

If only a brief period is available, merely telling yourself that you are blessed as a Son of God will do. **W(68)**

Lesson 41 "God goes with me wherever I go."

W 41 L 1. Today's idea will eventually overcome completely the sense of loneliness and abandonment which all the separated ones experience. Depression is an inevitable consequence of separation. So are anxiety, worry, a deep sense of helplessness, misery, suffering, and intense fear of loss.

W 41 L 2. The separated ones have invented many "cures" for what they believe to be the "ills of the world." But the one thing they do not do is to question the reality of the problem. Yet its effects cannot be cured because it is not real.

The idea for today has the power to end all this foolishness forever. And foolishness it is, despite the serious and tragic forms it may take.

W 41 L 3. Deep within you is everything that is perfect, ready to radiate through you and out into the whole world. It will cure all sorrow and pain and fear and loss because it will heal the mind that thought these things were real, and suffered out of its allegiance to these beliefs.

W 41 L 4. You can never be deprived of your perfect holiness because its Source goes with you wherever you go. You can never suffer because the Source of all joy goes with you wherever you go. You can never be alone because the Source of all life goes with you wherever you go. Nothing can destroy your peace of mind because God goes with you wherever you go.

W 41 L 5. We understand that you do not believe all this. How could you, when the truth is hidden deep within, under a heavy cloud of insane thoughts, dense and obscuring, yet representing all you see?

W 41 L 6. Today we will make our first real attempt to get past this dark and heavy cloud, and to go through it to the light beyond. **W(69)** There will be only one long practice period today. In the morning, as soon as you get up if possible, sit quietly for some three to five minutes with your eyes closed. At the beginning of this[47] practice period, repeat today's idea very slowly. Then make no effort to think of anything. Try, instead, to get a sense of turning inward, past all the idle thoughts of the world. Try to enter very deeply into your own mind, keeping it clear of any thoughts that might divert your attention.

W 41 L 7. From time to time you may repeat today's[48] idea, if you find it helpful. But most of all, try to sink down and inward, away from the world and all the foolish thoughts of the world. You are trying to reach past all these things. You are trying to leave appearances and approach reality.

W 41 L 8. It is quite possible to reach God. In fact it is very easy, because it is the most natural thing in the world. You might even say it is the only natural thing in the world. The way will open if you believe that it is possible. This exercise can bring very startling results even the first time it is attempted, and[49] sooner or later it is always successful. We will go into more detail in connection with this kind of practice as we go along. But it will never fail completely, and instant success is possible.

W 41 L 9. Throughout the day use today's idea often, repeating it very slowly, and preferably with eyes closed. Think of what you are saying; what the words mean. Concentrate on the holiness which they imply about you; on the unfailing companionship which is yours; on the complete protection that surrounds you.

W 41 L 10. You can indeed afford to laugh at fear thoughts, remembering that God goes with you wherever you go. **W(70)**

Lesson 42 "God is my strength. Vision is His gift."

W 42 L 1. The idea for today combines two very powerful thoughts, both of major importance. It also sets forth a cause and effect relationship which explains why you cannot fail in your efforts to achieve the goal of the course. You will see because it is the Will of God. It is His strength, not your own, that gives you power. And it is His gift to you, rather than your own, which offers vision to you.

W 42 L 2. God is indeed your strength, and[50] what He gives is truly given. This means that you can receive it any time and anywhere, wherever you are and in whatever circumstances you find yourself. Your passage through time and space is not random. You cannot but be in the right place at the right time. Such is the strength of God. Such are His gifts.

W 42 L 3. We will have two three-to-five-minute longer exercise periods today, one as soon as possible after you wake, and another as close as possible to the time you go to sleep. It is better, however, to wait until you can sit quietly by yourself at a time when you feel ready, than it is to be concerned with the time as such.

W 42 L 4. Begin the longer[51] practice period by repeating the idea for today slowly, with eyes open, looking about you. Then close your eyes and repeat the idea again, quite slowly. After this, try to think of nothing except thoughts which occur to you in relation to today's idea. You might think, for example:

"Vision must be possible. God gives truly."

or,

"God's gifts to me must be mine because He gave them to me."

Whatever[52] thought that is clearly related to the idea itself is suitable.

W 42 L 5. You may, in fact, be astonished at the amount of course-related understanding some of your own thoughts contain. Let them come without censoring unless you realize that your mind is merely wandering, and you have let obviously irrelevant thoughts **W(71)** intrude. You may also reach a point where no thoughts at all seem to come to mind. If such interferences occur, open your eyes and repeat the thought once more while looking slowly about; close your eyes, repeat the idea once more, and then continue to look for related thoughts in your mind.

W 42 L 6. Remember, though, that active searching[53] is not appropriate for today's exercises. Try merely to step back and let the thoughts come. If you find this difficult, it is better to spend the practice period alternating between slow repetitions of the idea with eyes open, then[54] closed, then[55] open, and so on than it is to strain in order to find suitable thoughts.

W 42 L 7. There is no limit on the number of short practice periods which would be most beneficial. The idea for today is a beginning step in bringing thoughts together and teaching you that what you are studying is a unified thought system in which nothing is lacking that is needed, and nothing is included that is contradictory or irrelevant. The more often you repeat[56] the idea during the day, the more

---

[47] Originally in the *Urtext* manuscript "a" is typed. Handwritten mark-up suggests (this) which appears to be correct.

[48] Handwritten mark-up suggests (the).

[49] Originally in the *Urtext* manuscript there is a sentence break here. Handwritten mark-up suggests comma instead of period, and that is better.

[50] Originally in the *Urtext* manuscript two sentences, the comma is handwritten in, and appears to be an improvement.

[51] The word (longer) is handwritten and appears to be a suitable correction.

[52] Handwritten mark-up suggests (Any).

[53] Handwritten mark-up suggests (for relevant thoughts).

[54] Handwritten mark-up suggests (eyes).

[55] Handwritten mark-up suggests (eyes).

[56] Handwritten mark-up suggests (use).

often you will be reminding yourself that the goal of the course is important to you, and that you have not forgotten it. **W(72)**

Lesson 43 "God is my Source. I cannot see apart from Him."

W 43 L 1. Perception is not an attribute of God. His is the realm of knowledge. Yet He has created the Holy Spirit as the Mediator between perception and knowledge. Without this link with God, perception would have replaced knowledge forever in your minds. With this link with God, perception will become so changed and purified that it will lead to knowledge. That is its function as the Holy Spirit sees it. Therefore, that is its function in truth.

W 43 L 2. In God you cannot see. Perception has no function in God, and does not exist. Yet in salvation, which is the undoing of what never was, perception has a mighty purpose. Made by the Son of God for an unholy purpose, it must become the means for the restoration of his holiness to his awareness. Perception has no meaning. Yet does the Holy Spirit give it a meaning very close to God's. Healed perception becomes the means by which the Son of God forgives his brother and thus forgives himself.

W 43 L 3. You cannot see apart from God because you cannot be apart from God. Whatever you do you do in Him, because whatever you think you think with His Mind. If vision is real, and it is real to the extent to which it shares the Holy Spirit's purpose, then you cannot see apart from God.

W 43 L 4. Three five-minute practice periods are required today, one as early as possible and another as late as possible.[57] The third may be undertaken at the most convenient and suitable time which circumstances and readiness permit. At the beginning of the[58] practice period,[59] repeat the idea[60] to yourself with your eyes open. Then glance around you for a short time, applying today's idea specifically to what you see. Four or five subjects for this phase of the exercise are sufficient. You might say, for example:

"God is my Source. I cannot see this desk apart from Him."

"God is my Source. I cannot see that picture apart from Him."

W 43 L 5. Although this part of the exercise period should be relatively short, be sure that you select the subjects for this phase indiscriminately, without self-directed inclusion or exclusion. **W(73)** For the second and longer phase of the exercise period, close your eyes, repeat today's idea again, and then let whatever relevant thoughts occur to you add to the idea in your own personal way. Thoughts such as:

"I see through the eyes of forgiveness,"

"I see the world as blessed,"

"The world can show me myself,"

"I see my own thoughts, which are like God's,"

or any thought related more or less directly to today's idea is suitable. The thoughts need not bear an obvious relationship to the idea, but they should not be in opposition to it.

W 43 L 6. If you should find your mind wandering; if you begin to be aware of thoughts which are clearly out of accord with today's idea; or if you seem to be unable to think of anything, open your eyes, repeat the first phase; and then try the second phase again. Do not allow any protracted period to occur in which you become preoccupied with irrelevant thoughts. Return to the first phase as often as necessary to prevent this.

W 43 L 7. In applying today's idea in the shorter practice periods, the form may vary according to the circumstances and situations in which you find yourself during the day. When you are with someone else, for example, try to remember to tell him silently:

"God is my Source. I cannot see you apart from Him."

This form is equally applicable to strangers and to those you know well.[61] Try, in fact, not to make distinctions of this kind at all.

W 43 L 8. The[62] idea should also be applied throughout the day to various situations and events which may occur, particularly those which distress you in any way. For this kind of application, use this form:

"God is my Source. I cannot see this apart from Him."

If no particular subject presents itself to your awareness,[63] merely repeat the idea in its original form. **W(74)**

W 43 L 9. Try today not to allow long periods of time to slip by without remembering today's idea, and thus remembering your function. **W(75)**

Lesson 44 "God is the Light in which I see."

W 44 L 1. Today we are continuing with the idea for yesterday, adding another dimension to it. You cannot see in darkness, and you cannot make light. You can make darkness and then think you see in it, but light reflects life, and is therefore an aspect of creation. Creation and darkness cannot coexist, but light and life must go together, being but different aspects of creation.

W 44 L 2. In order to see, one[64] must recognize that light is within, not without. You do not see outside yourself. Nor is the equipment for seeing outside you. An essential part of this equipment is the light which makes seeing possible. It is with you always, making vision possible in every circumstance.

W 44 L 3. Today we are going to attempt to reach that light. For that[65] purpose, we will use a form of practice which has been suggested once before, and which we will utilize increasingly. It is a particularly difficult form for the undisciplined mind because it[66] represents a major goal of mind training. It embodies precisely what the untrained mind lacks. Yet the training must be accomplished if you are to see.

W 44 L 4. Have at least three practice periods today, each lasting three-to-five minutes. A longer time[67] is highly recommended, but only if you find the time merely slipping by with little or no sense of strain. The form of exercise we will use today is the most natural and easy one in the world for the trained mind, just as it seems to be the most unnatural and difficult for the untrained mind.

W 44 L 5. Your mind is no longer wholly untrained. You are quite ready to learn the form of exercise we will use today, but you may find that you will encounter strong resistance. The reason is very simple. While you practice in this form,[68] you leave behind everything that you now believe, and all the thoughts which you have made up. Properly speaking, this is the release from hell. Perceived through the ego's eyes, it is loss of identity and a descent into hell. **W(76)**

W 44 L 6. If you can stand aside from the ego[69] ever so little, you will have no difficulty in recognizing that its opposition and fears are meaningless. You might find it helpful to remind yourself from

---

[57] Handwritten mark-up suggests (one as early and one as late as possible).
[58] Handwritten mark-up suggests (these).
[59] Handwritten mark-up suggests (s).
[60] Handwritten mark-up suggests (for today).
[61] Handwritten mark-up suggests (as it is to those you think are closer to you).
[62] Handwritten mark-up suggests (Today's).
[63] Handwritten mark-up suggests (at the time).
[64] Handwritten mark-up suggests (you).
[65] Handwritten mark-up suggests (this).
[66] Handwritten mark-up suggests (and) in place of "because it"
[67] Handwritten mark-up suggests (period).
[68] Handwritten mark-up suggests (way).
[69] Handwritten mark-up suggests (by).

time to time that to reach light is to escape from darkness, whatever you may believe to the contrary. God is the Light in which you see. You are attempting to reach Him.

W 44 L 7. Begin the practice period by repeating today's idea with your eyes open, and close them slowly, repeating the idea several times more. Then try to sink into your mind, letting go every kind of interference and intrusions by quietly sinking past them. Your mind cannot be stopped in this unless you choose to stop it. It is merely taking its natural course. Try to observe your passing thoughts without involvement, and slip quietly by them.

W 44 L 8. While no particular form of approach is advocated, what is needful is a sense of the importance of what you are doing, its inestimable value to you, and an awareness that you are attempting something very holy. Salvation is your happiest accomplishment. It is also the only one that has any meaning, because it is the only one that has any use to you at all.

W 44 L 9. If resistance rises in any form, pause long enough to repeat today's idea, keeping your eyes closed unless you are aware of fear. In that case, you will probably find it more reassuring to open your eyes briefly. Try, however, to return to the exercises as soon as possible.

W 44 L 10. If you are doing the exercises correctly, you should experience some sense of relaxation, and even a feeling that you are approaching, if not actually entering into light. Try to think of light, formless and without limit, as you pass by the thoughts of this world. And do not forget that they cannot hold you to the world unless you give them the power to do so. **W(77)**

W 44 L 11. Throughout the day, repeat the idea often, with eyes open or closed as seems better to you at the time. Do not forget. Above all, be determined not to forget today. **W(78)**

Lesson 45 "God is the Mind with which I think."

W 45 L 1. Today's idea holds the key to what your real thoughts are. They are nothing that you think you think, just as nothing that you think you see is related to vision in any way. There is no relationship between what is real and what you think is real. Nothing that you think are your real thoughts resemble your real thoughts in any respect. Nothing that you think you see bears any resemblance to what vision will show you.

W 45 L 2. You think with the Mind of God. Therefore you share your thoughts with Him, as He shares His with you. They are the same thoughts, because they are thought by the same Mind. To share is to make alike, or to make one. Nor do the thoughts you think with the Mind of God leave your mind, because thoughts do not leave their source. Therefore your thoughts are in the Mind of God, as you are. They are in your mind as well, where He is. As you are part of His Mind, so are your thoughts part of His Thoughts.

W 45 L 3. Where, then, are your real thoughts? Today we will attempt to reach them. We will have to look for them in your mind, because that is where they are. They must still be there because they cannot have left. What is thought by the Mind of God is eternal, being part of creation.

W 45 L 4. Our three five-minute practice periods for today will take the same general form that we used in applying yesterday's idea. We will attempt to leave the unreal and seek for the real. We will deny the world in favor of truth. We will not let the thoughts of the world hold us back, and[70] we will not let the beliefs of the world tell us that what God would have us do is impossible.

W 45 L 5. Instead, we will try to recognize that only what God would have us do is possible. We will also try to understand that only what God would have us do is what we want to do. And we will also try to remember that we cannot fail in doing what He would have us do. There is every reason to feel confident that you will succeed today. It is the Will of God. **W(79)**

W 45 L 6. Begin the exercises for today by repeating the idea to yourself, closing your eyes as you do so. Spend a fairly short period in thinking a few relevant thoughts of your own, keeping the idea in mind as you do so. After you have added some four or five thoughts of your own, repeat the idea again, and tell yourself gently:

"My real thoughts are in my mind. I would like to find them."

Then try to go past all the unreal thoughts which cover the truth in your mind, and reach to the eternal. Under all the senseless thoughts and mad ideas with which you have cluttered up your mind are the thoughts which you thought with God in the beginning. They are there in your mind now, completely unchanged. They will always be in your mind, exactly as they always were.

W 45 L 7. Everything that you have thought since then will change, but the foundation on which they rest is wholly changeless. It is this foundation toward which the exercises for today are directed. Here is your mind joined with the Mind of God. Here are your thoughts one with His.

W 45 L 8. For this kind of practice only one thing is necessary; approach it as you would an altar dedicated in Heaven itself to God the Father and God the Son. For such is the place you are trying to reach. You will probably be unable as yet to realize how high you are trying to go. Yet even with the little understanding you have already gained, you should be able to remind yourself that this is no idle game, but an exercise in holiness and an attempt to reach the Kingdom of Heaven.

W 45 L 9. In using the shorter form for applying today's idea, try to remember how important it is to you to understand the holiness of the mind that thinks with God. Take a minute or two, as you repeat the idea throughout the day, to appreciate your mind's holiness. Stand aside, however briefly, **W(80)** from all thoughts that are unworthy of Him Whose host you are. And thank Him for the thoughts He is thinking with you. **W(81)**

Lesson 46 "God is the Love in which I forgive."

W 46 L 1. God does not forgive because He has never condemned. And there must be condemnation before forgiveness is necessary. Forgiveness is the great need of this world, but that is because it is a world of illusions. Those who forgive are thus releasing themselves from illusions, while those who withhold forgiveness are binding themselves to them. As you condemn only yourself, so do you forgive only yourself.[71]

W 46 L 2. [72]Although God does not forgive, His Love is nevertheless the basis of forgiveness. Fear condemns and love forgives. Forgiveness thus undoes what fear has produced, returning the mind to the awareness of God. For this reason, forgiveness can truly be called salvation. It is the means by which illusions disappear.

W 46 L 3. Today's exercises require at least three full five-minute practice periods, and as many shorter applications[73] as possible. Begin the[74] practice periods by repeating today's idea to yourself, as usual. Close your eyes as you do so, and spend a minute or two in searching your mind for those whom you have not forgiven. It does

---

[70] Handwritten editing deletes "and" and begins new sentence with "We will not ..."

[71] **Matthew 16:19** "And I will give you the keys of the kingdom of heaven, and whatever you bind on earth will be bound in heaven, and whatever you loose on earth will be loosed in heaven."
John 20:23 If you forgive the sins of any, they are forgiven them; if you retain the sins of any, they are retained."
[72] Handwritten mark-up inserts (Yet).
[73] Handwritten mark-up suggests (ones).
[74] Handwritten mark-up inserts (longer).

not matter "how much" you have not forgiven.[75] You have forgiven them entirely or not at all.

W 46 L 4. If you are doing the exercises well, you should have no difficulty in finding a number of people you have not forgiven. It is a safe rule that anyone you do not like is a suitable subject. Mention each one by name, and say:

"God is the Love in which I forgive you, (name)"

W 46 L 5. The purpose of the first phase of today's practice[76] is to put you in the best[77] position to forgive yourself. After you have applied the idea for today to all those who have come to mind, tell yourself:

"God is the Love in which I forgive myself." **W(82)**

Then devote the remainder of the practice period to offering[78] related ideas such as:

"God is the Love with which I love myself."

"God is the Love in which I am blessed."

W 46 L 6. The form of the applications may vary considerably, but the central idea should not be lost sight of. You might say, for example:

"I cannot be guilty because I am a Son of God."

"I have already been forgiven."

"No fear is possible in a mind beloved of God."

"There is no need to attack because love has forgiven me."

The practice period should end, however, with a repetition of today's idea as originally stated.

W 46 L 7. The shorter applications may consist either of a repetition of the idea in the original or in a related form[79] or in[80] more specific applications if[81] needed. They will be needed at any time during the day when you become aware of any kind of negative reaction to anyone, present or not. In this event, tell him silently:

"God is the Love in which I forgive you." **W(83)**

Lesson 47 "God is the Strength in which I trust."

W 47 L 1. If you are trusting your own strength, you have every reason to be apprehensive, anxious, and fearful. What can you predict or control? What is there in you that can be counted on? What would give you the ability to be aware of all the facets of any problem, and to resolve them in such a way that only good can come of it? What is there in you that gives you the recognition of the right solution, and the guarantee that it will be accomplished?

W 47 L 2. Of yourself you can do none of these things.[82] To believe that you can is to put your trust where trust is unwarranted, and to justify fear, anxiety, depression, anger, and sorrow. Who can put his faith in weakness and feel safe? Yet who can put his faith in strength and feel weak?

W 47 L 3. God is your safety in every circumstance. His Voice speaks for Him in all situations and in every aspect of all situations, telling you exactly what to do to call upon His strength and His protection. There are no exceptions because God has no exceptions. And the Voice Which speaks for Him thinks as He does.

W 47 L 4. Today we will try to reach past your own weakness to the Source of real strength. Four five-minute practice periods are necessary today, and longer and more frequent ones are urged. Close your eyes and begin as usual by repeating today's idea. Then spend a minute or two in searching for situations in your life which you have invested with fear, dismissing each one by telling yourself,

"God is the Strength in which I trust."

W 47 L 5. Now try to slip past all concerns related to your own sense of inadequacy. It is obvious that any situation which causes you concern is associated with feelings of inadequacy, since[83] otherwise you would believe that you could deal with the situation successfully. It is not by trusting yourself **W(84)** that you will gain confidence. But the strength of God in you is successful in all things.

W 47 L 6. The recognition of your own frailty is a necessary step in the correction of your errors. But it is[84] hardly[85] a sufficient one in giving you the confidence which you need and to which you are entitled. You must also gain an awareness that your confidence in your real strength is fully justified in every respect and in all circumstances.

W 47 L 7. In the latter phase of the practice period, try to reach down into your mind to a place of real safety. You will recognize that you have reached it if you feel a[86] deep peace, however briefly. Let go all the trivial things that churn and bubble on the surface of your mind, and reach down and below them to the Kingdom of Heaven. There is a place in you where there is perfect peace. There is a place in you where nothing is impossible. There is a place in you where the strength of God abides.

W 47 L 8. Repeat the idea for today often. Use it as your answer to any disturbance. Remember that peace is your right because you are giving your trust to the strength of God. **W(85f**

Lesson 48 "There is nothing to fear."

W 48 L 1. The idea for today simply states a fact. It is not a fact to those who believe in illusions, but illusions are not facts. In truth there is nothing to fear. It is very easy to recognize this. But it is very difficult to recognize[87] for those who want illusions to be true.

W 48 L 2. Today's practice periods will be very short, very simple, and very frequent. Merely repeat the idea as often as possible. You can use it with your eyes open at any time and in any situation. It is strongly recommended, however, that you take a minute or so whenever possible to close your eyes and repeat the idea slowly to yourself several times. It is particularly important that you use the idea immediately, should anything disturb your peace of mind.

W 48 L 3. The presence of fear is a sure sign that you are trusting in your own strength. The awareness that there is nothing to fear shows that somewhere in your mind, not necessarily in a place which you recognize as yet, you have remembered God and let His strength take the place of yours.[88] The instant you are willing to do this there is indeed nothing to fear. **W(86)**

---

[75] Handwritten mark-up inserts (them).
[76] Handwritten mark-up inserts (periods).
[77] Handwritten mark-up replaces "the best" with "a better" and then crosses out "better."
[78] Handwritten mark-up replaces "offering" with "adding".
[79] Handwritten mark-up inserts (as you prefer).
[80] Handwritten mark-up inserts (Be sure, however, to make).
[81] Handwritten mark-up inserts (they are).
[82] **John 5:19** Then Jesus answered and said to them, "Most assuredly, I say to you, the Son can do nothing of Himself, but what He sees the Father do; for whatever He does, the Son also does in like manner."

[83] Handwritten mark-up suggests (for).
[84] Handwritten mark-up suggests (could).
[85] Handwritten mark-up suggests (be).
[86] Handwritten mark-up suggests (sense of).
[87] Handwritten mark-up suggests (it).
[88] Handwritten mark-up suggests (your weakness) for "**yours.**" *Notes* has it as "yours."
2 Corinthians 12:9 And He said to me, "My grace is sufficient for you, for My strength is made perfect in weakness." Therefore most gladly I will rather boast in my infirmities, that the power of Christ may rest upon me.
Philippians 4:13 I can do all things through Christ who strengthens me.

Lesson 49 "God's Voice speaks to me all through the day."

W 49 L 1. It is quite possible to listen to God's Voice all[89] day without interrupting your regular activities in any way. The part of your mind in which truth abides is in constant communication with God, whether you are aware of it or not. It is the other part of your mind that functions in the world and obeys the world's laws. It is this part which is constantly distracted, disorganized, and highly uncertain.

W 49 L 2. The part that is listening to the Voice of God is calm, always at rest and wholly certain. It is really the only part there is. The other part is a wild illusion, frantic and distraught, but without reality of any kind. Try today not to listen to it. Try to identify with the part of your mind where stillness and peace reign forever. Try to hear God's Voice call to you lovingly, reminding you that your Creator has not forgotten His Son.

W 49 L 3. We will need at least four five-minute practice periods today, and more if possible. We will try actually to hear the[90] Voice reminding you of God[91] and of your Self. We will approach this happiest and holiest of thoughts with confidence, knowing that in doing so we are joining our will with the Will of God. He wants you to hear His Voice. He gave It to you to be heard.

W 49 L 4. Listen in deep silence. Be very still and open your mind.[92] Go past all the raucous shrieks and sick imaginings that cover your real thoughts and obscure your eternal link with God. Sink deep into the peace that waits for you beyond the frantic, riotous thoughts and sounds and sights[93] of this insane world. You do not live there.[94] We are trying to reach your real home. We are trying to reach the place where you are truly welcome. We are trying to reach God. **W(87)**

W 49 L 5. Do not forget to repeat today's idea very frequently. Do so with your eyes open when necessary, but closed when possible. And be sure that you[95] sit quietly and repeat the idea for today slowly[96] whenever you can, closing your eyes on the world, and realizing that you are inviting God's Voice to speak to you. **W(88)**

Lesson 50 "I am sustained by the Love of God."

W 50 L 1. Here is the answer to every problem that confronts[97] you today and tomorrow and throughout time. In this world, you believe you are sustained by everything but God. Your faith is placed in the most trivial and insane symbols; pills, money, "protective" clothing, "influence," "prestige," being liked, knowing the "right" people, and an endless list of forms of nothingness which you endow with magical powers.

W 50 L 2. All these things are your replacements for the Love of God. All these things are cherished to ensure a body identification. They are songs of praise to the ego. Do not put your faith in the worthless. It will not sustain you.

W 50 L 3. Only the Love of God will protect you in all circumstances. It will lift you out of every trial, and raise you high above all the perceived dangers of this world into a climate of perfect peace and safety. It will transport you into a state of mind which nothing can threaten, nothing can disturb, and[98] nothing can intrude upon the eternal calm of the Son of God.

W 50 L 4. Put not your faith in illusions. They will fail you. Put all your faith in the Love of God within you, eternal, changeless and forever unfailing. This is the answer to whatever confronts you today. Through the Love of God in you, you can resolve all seeming difficulties without effort and in sure confidence. Tell yourself this often today. It is a declaration of release from the belief in idols. It is your acknowledgment of the truth about yourself.

W 50 L 5. Twice today, morning and evening, let the idea for today sink deep into your consciousness. Repeat it, think about it, let related thoughts come to help you recognize its truth, and allow peace to flow over you like a blanket of protection and surety. Let no idle and foolish thoughts enter to **W(89)** disturb the holy mind of the Son of God. Such is the Kingdom of Heaven.[99] Such is the resting-place where your Father has placed you forever. **W(90)**

Review 1 (W 50 R1)
Introduction

W 50 R1 1. Beginning with today, we will have a series of review periods. Each of them will cover five of the ideas already presented, starting with the first and ending with the fiftieth. There will be[100] a short comment[101] after each of the ideas, which you should consider in your review. In the practice period, the exercises should be done as follows:

W 50 R1 2. Begin, the day by reading the five ideas, with the comments included. Thereafter, it is not necessary to follow any particular order in considering them, though each one should be practiced at least once. Devote two minutes or more to each practice period, thinking about the idea and the related comments.[102] Do this as often as possible during the day. If any one of the five ideas appeals to you more than the others, concentrate on that one. At the end of the day, however, be sure to review all of them once more.

W 50 R1 3. It is not necessary to cover the comments literally or thoroughly in the practice periods. Try, rather, merely to emphasize the central point, and think about it as part of your review of the idea to which it relates. The review[103] exercises should be done with the eyes closed, and when you are alone in a quiet place, if possible.

W 50 R1 4. This is emphasized particularly for reviews at your stage of learning. It will be necessary, however, that you learn to require no special settings in which to apply what you have learned. You will need it most in situations which appear to be upsetting, rather than in those which already seem to be calm and quiet. The

---

[89] Handwritten mark-up suggests (through the).
[90] Handwritten mark-up suggests (God's).
[91] Handwritten mark-up suggests (Him).
[92] **Psalm 46:10** Be still, and know that I am God; I will be exalted among the nations, I will be exalted in the earth!
[93] Handwritten mark-up suggests (sights and sounds).
[94] Handwritten mark-up suggests (here).
[95] Handwritten mark-up suggests (to) for **that you**
[96] Handwritten mark-up crosses out the word **slowly**
[97] Handwritten mark-up suggests (will confront).
[98] Handwritten mark-up suggests (where).
[99] **Mathew 3:2** "saying, Repent ye; for the kingdom of heaven is at hand." **Matthew 19:14** But Jesus said, "Let the little children come to Me, and do not forbid them; for of such is the kingdom of heaven."
This first Biblical quote is attributed to John the Baptist, but it is a teaching also attributed to Jesus. The phrase "Kingdom of Heaven" shows up 32 times in the Bible, all 32 in the Gospel according to Matthew. Elsewhere the same teaching uses the phrase "Kingdom of God" rather than "Kingdom of Heaven," as in **Mark 1:15**. It shows up 20 times in the seven volumes of ACIM also. The basic formulation "repent, for the Kingdom of Heaven is at hand" has often been understood to mean, roughly, "confess your sins for the end of the world will occur soon." Another way of understanding it, more plausible when we look at the Greek original in the Bible and examine it in light of ACIM is "change your mind; Heaven is as close to you as your hand."
[100] Handwritten mark-up suggests (a few).
[101] *Urtext* manuscript reads "**comment**" with the "**s**" handwritten in. Originally this might have been "**a short comment**" mistyped by leaving the word "**a**" out, or simply "**short comments**" or possibly even, as corrected by hand. The original reading in the *Notes* is "a short comment."
[102] Handwritten mark-up suggests (after reading).
[103] Handwritten mark-up suggests (After you have read the idea and the related comments, the).

purpose of your learning is to enable you to bring the quiet with you, and to heal distress and turmoil. This is not done by avoiding them and seeking a haven of isolation for yourself.

W 50 R1 5. You will yet learn that peace is part of you, and requires only that you be there to embrace any situation in which you are. And finally you will learn that there is no limit to where you are, so that your peace is everywhere, as you are. **W(91)**

W 50 R1 6. You will note that for review purposes[104] the ideas are not always given in quite their original form of statement.[105] Use them as they are given here. It is not necessary to return to the original statements, nor to apply the ideas as was suggested then. We are now emphasizing the relationships among the first fifty of the ideas we have covered, and the cohesiveness of the thought system to which they are leading you. **W(92)**

Lesson 51 The review for today covers the following ideas: (1-5)

W 51 L 1. 1) "Nothing I see means anything."

The reason this is so is that I see nothing, and nothing has no meaning. It is necessary that I recognize this that I may learn to see. What I think I see now is taking the place of vision. I must let it go by realizing that it has no meaning, so that vision may take its place.

W 51 L 2. 2) "I have given what I see all the meaning it has for me."

I have judged everything I look upon. And it is this and only this that I see. This is not vision. It is merely an illusion of reality, because my judgments have been made quite apart from reality. I am willing to recognize the lack of validity in my judgments because I want to see. My judgments have hurt me, and I do not want to see according to them.

W 51 L 3. 3) "I do not understand anything I see."

How could I understand what I see when I have judged it amiss? What I see is the projection of my own errors of thought. I do not understand what I see because it is not understandable. There is no sense in trying to understand it. But there is every reason to let it go, to make room for what can be seen and understood and loved. I can exchange what I see now for this merely by being willing to do so. Is not this a better choice than the one I made before?

W 51 L 4. 4) "These thoughts do not mean anything."

The thoughts of which I am aware do not mean anything because I am trying to think without God. What I call "my" thoughts are not my real thoughts. My real thoughts are the thoughts I think with God. I am not aware of them because I have made "my" thoughts to take their place. I am willing to recognize that "my" thoughts do not mean anything, and to let them go. I choose to have them replaced by what they were intended to replace. "My" thoughts are meaningless, but all creation lies in the Thoughts I think with God. **W(93)**

W 51 L 5. 5) "I am never upset for the reason I think."

I am never upset for the reason I think because I am constantly trying to justify "my" thoughts. I am constantly trying to make them true. I make all things my "enemies," so that my anger is justified, and my attacks are warranted. I have not realized how much I have misused everything I see by assigning this role to it. I have done this to defend a thought system which has hurt me, and which I no longer want. I am willing to let it go. **W(94)**

Lesson 52 Today's review covers these ideas: (6-10)

W 52 L 1. 6) "I am upset because I see what is not there."

Reality is never frightening. It is impossible that it could upset me. Reality brings only perfect peace. When I am upset, it is always because I have replaced reality with illusions which I made up. The illusions are upsetting because I have given them reality, and thus regard reality as an illusion. Nothing in God's creation is affected in any way by this confusion of mine. I am always upset by nothing.

W 52 L 2. 7) "I see only the past."

As I look about, I condemn the world I look upon. I call this seeing. I hold the past against everyone and everything, making them my "enemies." When I have forgiven myself and remembered who I am, I will bless everyone and everything I see. There will be no past, and therefore no "enemies." And I will look with God[106] on all that I failed to see before.

W 52 L 3. 8) "My mind is preoccupied with past thoughts."

I see only my own thoughts, and my mind is preoccupied with the past. What, then, can I see as it is? Let me remember that I look on the past to prevent the present from dawning on my mind. Let me understand that I am trying to use time against God. Let me learn to give the past away, realizing that in so doing I am giving up nothing.

W 52 L 4. 9) "I see nothing as it is now."

If I see nothing as it is now, it can truly be said that I see nothing. I can see only what is now. The choice is not whether to see the past or the present: it is merely whether to see or not. What I have chosen to see has cost me vision. Now I would choose again, that I may see. **W(95)**

W 52 L 5. 10) "My thoughts do not mean anything."

I have no private thoughts. Yet it is only private thoughts of which I am aware. What can these thoughts mean? They do not exist, and so they mean nothing. Yet my mind is part of creation and part of its Creator. Would I not rather join the thinking of the universe than to obscure all that is really mine[107] with my pitiful and meaningless "private" thoughts? **W(96)**

Lesson 53 Today we will review the following: (11-15)

W 53 L 1. 11) "My meaningless thoughts are showing me a meaningless world."

Since the thoughts of which I am aware do not mean anything, the world which pictures them can have no meaning. What is producing this world is insane, and so is what it produces. Reality is not insane, and I have real thoughts as well as insane ones. I can therefore see a real world, if I look to my real thoughts as my guide for seeing.

W 53 L 2. 12) "I am upset because I see a meaningless world."

Insane thoughts are upsetting, and They produce a world in which there is no order anywhere. Only chaos rules a world which represents chaotic thinking, and chaos has no laws. I cannot live in peace in such a world. I am grateful that this world is not real, and that I need not see it at all unless I choose to value it. And I do not choose to value what is totally insane and has no meaning.

W 53 L 3. 13) "A meaningless world engenders fear."

The totally insane engenders fear because it is completely undependable, and offers no grounds for trust. Nothing in madness is dependable. It holds out no safety and no hope. But such a world is not real. I have given it the illusion of reality, and have suffered from my belief in it. Now I choose to withdraw this belief, and place my trust in reality. In choosing this, I will escape all the ef-

---

[104] Handwritten mark-up suggests (some of).
[105] Handwritten mark-up suggests removing the words "**of statement**".
[106] Handwritten mark-up suggests replacing "**God**" with (love).
[107] The *Urtext* manuscript has "**mind**" while the handwritten suggestion "**mine**" appears rather clearly to be a correction of a spelling error. We have thus incorporated this suggested change as a spelling correction. The *Notes* also has "mine."

fects of the world of fear because I am acknowledging that it does not exist. **W(97)**

W 53 L 4. 14) "God did not create a meaningless world."

How can a meaningless world exist if God did not create it? He is the Source of all meaning, and everything that is real is in His Mind. It is in my mind too, because He created it with me. Why should I continue to suffer from the effects of my own insane thoughts, when the perfection of creation is my home? Let me remember the power of my decision, and recognize where I really abide.

W 53 L 5. 15) "My thoughts are images which I have made."

Whatever I see reflects my thoughts. It is my thoughts which tell me where I am and what I am. The fact that I see a world in which there is suffering and loss and death shows me that I am seeing only the representation of my insane thoughts, and am not allowing my real thoughts to cast their beneficent light on what I see. Yet God's way is sure. The images I have made can not prevail against Him because it is not my will that they do so. My will is His, and I will place no other gods before Him.[108] **W(98)**

Lesson 54 These are the review ideas for today: (16-20)

W 54 L 1. 16) "I have no neutral thoughts."

Neutral thoughts are impossible because all thoughts have power. They will either make a false world or lead me to the real one. But thoughts cannot be without effects. As the world I see arises from my thinking errors, so will the real world rise before my eyes as I let my errors be corrected. My thoughts cannot be neither true nor false. They must be one or the other. What I see shows me which they are.

W 54 L 2. 17) "I see no neutral things."

What I see witnesses to what I think. If I did not think I would not exist, because life is thought. Let me look on the world[109] as the representation of my own state of mind. I know that my state of mind can change. And so I also know that the world I see can change as well.

W 54 L 3. 18) "I am not alone in experiencing the effects of my seeing."

If I have no private thoughts, I cannot see a private world. Even the mad idea of separation had to be shared before it could form the basis of the world I see. Yet that sharing was a sharing of nothing. I can also call upon my real thoughts, which share everything with everybody. As my thoughts of separation call to the separation thoughts of others, so my real thoughts awaken[110] the real thoughts in them. And the world my real thoughts show me will dawn on their sight as well as mine.

W 54 L 4. 19) "I am not alone in experiencing the effects of my thoughts."

I am alone in nothing. Everything I think or say or do touches all the universe. A Son of God cannot think or speak or act in vain. He cannot be alone in anything. It is therefore in my power to change every mind along with mine, for mine is the power of God. **W(99)**

W 54 L 5. 20) "I am determined to see."

Recognizing the shared nature of my thoughts, I am determined to see. I would look upon the witnesses that show me the thinking of the world has been changed. I would behold the proof that what has been done through me has enabled love to replace fear, laughter to replace weeping, and abundance to replace loss. I would look upon the real world, and let it teach me that my will and the Will of God are one. **W(100)**

Lesson 55 Today's review includes the following: (21-25)

W 55 L 1. 21) "I am determined to see things differently."

What I see now are but signs of disease, disaster and death. This cannot be what God created for His beloved Son. The very fact that I see such things is proof that I do not understand God. Therefore I also do not understand His Son. What I see tells me that I do not know who I am. I am determined to see the witnesses to the truth in me, rather than those which show me an illusion of myself.

W 55 L 2. 22) "What I see is a form of vengeance."

The world I see is hardly the representation of loving thoughts. It is a picture of attack on everything and by everything. It is anything but a reflection of the Love of God and the love of His Son. It is my own attack thoughts which give rise to this picture. My loving thoughts will save me from this perception of the world, and give me the peace God intended me to have.

W 55 L 3. 23) "I can escape from the world by giving up attack thoughts."

Herein lies my salvation, and nowhere else. Without attack thoughts I could not see a world of attack. As forgiveness allows love to return to my awareness I will see a world of peace and safety and Joy. And It is this that I choose to see, in place of what I look on now.

W 55 L 4. 24) "I do not perceive my own best interests."

How could I recognize my own best interests when I do not know who I am? What I think are my best interests would merely bind me closer to the world of illusions. I am willing to follow the Guide God has given me to find out what my own best interests are, recognizing that I cannot perceive them by myself. **W(101)**

W 55 L 5. 25) "I do not know what anything is for."

To me, the purpose of everything is to prove that my illusions about myself are real. It is for that purpose that I attempt to use everyone and everything. It is this that I believe the world is for. Therefore I do not recognize its real purpose. The purpose I have given the world has le[111]d to a frightening picture of it. Let me open my mind to its[112] real purpose by withdrawing the one I have given it, and learning the truth about it. **W(102)**

Lesson 56 Our review for today covers the following: (26-30)

W 56 L 1. 26) "My attack thoughts are attacking my invulnerability."

How can I know who I am when I see myself as under constant attack? Pain, illness, loss, age and death seem to threaten me. All my hopes and wishes and plans appear to be at the mercy of a world I cannot control. Yet perfect security and complete fulfillment are my inheritance. I have tried to give my inheritance away in exchange for the world I see. But God has kept my inheritance safe for me. My own real thoughts will teach me what it is.

W 56 L 2. 27) "Above all else I want to see."

Recognizing that what I see reflects what I think I am, I realize that vision is my greatest need. The world I see attests to the fearful nature of the self-image I have made. If I would remember who I am, it is essential that I let this image of myself go. As it is replaced by truth, vision will surely be given me. And with this vision I will look upon the world and upon myself with charity and love.

W 56 L 3. 28) "Above all else I want to see differently."

---

[108] **Exodus 20:3** You shall have no other gods before Me.
[109] Handwritten mark-up suggests (I see).
[110] The *Urtext* manuscript clearly has "await" here but the *Notes* has "awaken" and so does FIP.

[111] Originally in the *Urtext* manuscript typed "lead", illegible handwriting may be a correction
[112] Handwritten mark-up suggests (the world's).

The world I see holds my fearful self-image in place, and guarantees its continuance. While I see the world as I see it now, truth cannot enter my awareness. I would let the door behind this world be opened for me, that I may look past it to the world that[113] reflects the Love of God.

W 56 L 4. 29) "God is in everything I see."

Behind every image I have made, the truth remains unchanged. Behind every veil I have drawn across the face of love, its light remains undimmed. Beyond all my insane wishes is my will united with the Will of my Father. God is still everywhere and in everything forever. And we who are part of Him will yet look past all appearances, and recognize the truth beyond them all. **W(103)**

W 56 L 5. 30) "God is in everything I see because God is in my mind."

In my own mind, behind all my insane thoughts of separation and attack, is the knowledge that all is one forever. I have not lost the knowledge of who I am because I have forgotten it. It has been kept for me in the Mind of God, Who has not left His Thoughts. And I, who am among them, am one with them and[114] with Him. **W(104)**

Lesson 57 Today let us review these ideas: (31-35)

W 57 L 1. 31) "I am not the victim of the world I see."

How can I be the victim of a world which can be completely undone if I so choose? My chains are loosened. I can drop them off merely by desiring to do so. The prison door is open. I can leave it[115] simply by walking out. Nothing holds me in this world. Only my wish to stay keeps me a prisoner. I would give up[116] insane wishes, and walk into the sunlight at last.

W 57 L 2. 32) "I have invented the world I see."

I made up the prison in which I see myself. All I need do is recognize this, and I am free. I have deluded myself into believing it is possible to imprison the Son of God. I was bitterly mistaken in this belief, which I no longer want. The Son of God must be forever free. He is as God created him, and not what I would make of him. He is where God would have him be, and not where I thought to hold him prisoner.

W 57 L 3. 33) "There is another way of looking at the world."

Since the purpose of the world is not the one I ascribed to it, there must be another way of looking at it. I see everything upside-down, and my thoughts are the opposite of truth. I see the world as a prison for God's Son. It must be, then, that the world is really a place where he can be[117] set free. I would look upon the world as it is, and see it as a place where the Son of God finds his freedom.

W 57 L 4. 34) "I could see peace instead of this."

When I see the world as a place of freedom, I will realize that it reflects the laws of God instead of the rules which I made up for it to obey. I will understand that peace, not war, abides in it. And I will perceive that peace also abides in the hearts of all who share this place with me. **W(105)**

W 57 L 5. 35) "My mind is part of God's. I am very holy."

As I share the peace of the world with my brothers, I begin to understand that this peace comes from deep within myself. The world I look upon has taken on the light of my forgiveness, and shines forgiveness back at me. In this light,[118] I begin to see what my illusions about myself had kept hidden. I begin to understand the holiness of all living things including myself, and their oneness with me. **W(106)**

Lesson 58 These ideas are for review today: (36-40)

W 58 L 1. 36) "My holiness envelops everything I see."

From my holiness does the perception of the real world come. Having forgiven, I no longer see myself as guilty. I can accept the innocence that is the truth about me. Seen through understanding eyes the holiness of the world is all I see, for I can picture only the thoughts I hold about myself.

W 58 L 2. 37) "My holiness blesses the world."

The perception of my holiness does not bless me alone. Everyone and everything I see in it's light shares in the joy it brings to me. There is nothing that is apart from this joy, because there is nothing that does not share my holiness. As I recognize my holiness, so does the holiness of the world shine forth for everyone to see.

W 58 L 3. 38) "There is nothing my holiness cannot do."

My holiness is unlimited in its power to heal, because it is unlimited in its power to save. What is there to be saved from except illusions? And what are all illusions except false ideas about myself? My holiness undoes them all by asserting the truth about me. In the presence of my holiness, which I share with God Himself, all idols vanish.

W 58 L 4. 39) "My holiness is my salvation."

Since my holiness saves me from all guilt, recognizing my holiness is recognizing my salvation. It is also recognizing the salvation of the world. Once I have accepted my holiness, nothing can make me afraid. And because I am unafraid, everyone must share in my understanding,[119] which is the gift of God to me and to the world. **W(107)**

W 58 L 5. 40) "I am blessed as a Son of God."

Herein lies my claim to all good and only good. I am blessed as a Son of God. All good things are mine because God intended them for me. I cannot suffer any loss or deprivation or pain because of who I am. My Father supports me, protects me, and directs me in all things. His care for me is infinite, and is with me forever. I am eternally blessed as His Son. **W(108)**

Lesson 59 The following ideas are for review today: (41-45)

W 59 L 1. 41) "God goes with me wherever I go."

How can I be alone when God always goes with me? How can I be doubtful and unsure of myself when perfect certainty abides in Him? How can I be disturbed by anything when He rests in absolute[120] peace? How can I suffer when love and joy surround me through Him? Let me not cherish illusions about myself. I am perfect because God goes with me wherever I go.

W 59 L 2. 42) "God is my strength. Vision is His gift."

Let me not look to my own eyes to see today. Let me be willing to exchange my pitiful illusion of seeing for the vision that is given by God. Christ's vision is His gift, and He has given it to me. Let me call upon this gift today, so that this day may help me to understand eternity.

W 59 L 3. 43) "God is my Source. I cannot see apart from Him."

I can see what God wants me to see. I cannot see anything else. Beyond His Will lie only illusions. It is these I choose when I think I can see apart from Him. It is these I choose when I try to see

---

[113] Handwritten mark-up suggests (which).
[114] Handwritten mark-up suggests (One).
[115] Handwritten mark-up suggests deleting "it."
[116] Handwritten mark-up suggests (my).
[117] Handwritten mark-up suggests (is).
[118] The *Urtext* manuscript has "life" crossed out by hand, with "light" written above it. This appears to be the correction of a typo, and is retained. The *Notes* has "light."

[119] Handwritten mark-up suggests (salvation from fear) in place of **understanding.** The *Notes* has "share in my strength and understanding which are the gift of God to me ..."
[120] Handwritten mark-up suggests (eternal).

through the body's eyes. Yet the vision of Christ has been given me to replace them. It is through this vision that I choose to see.

W 59 L 4. 44) "God is the Light in which I see."

I cannot see in darkness. God is the only Light. Therefore, if I am to see, it must be through Him. I have tried to define what seeing is, and I have been wrong. Now it is given me to understand that God is the Light in which I see. Let me welcome vision and the happy world it will show me. W(109)

W 59 L 5. 45) "God is the Mind with which I think."

I have no thoughts which I do not share with God. I have no thoughts apart from Him because I have no mind apart from His. As part of His Mind, my thoughts are His and His Thoughts are mine. W(110)

Lesson 60 These ideas are for today's review. (46-50)

W 60 L 1. 46) "God is the Love in which I forgive."

God does not forgive because He has never condemned. The blameless cannot blame, and those who have accepted their innocence see nothing to forgive. Yet forgiveness is the means by which I will recognize my innocence. It is the reflection of God's Love on earth. It will bring me near enough to Heaven that the Love of God can reach down to me and raise me to my home.

W 60 L 2. 47) "God is the Strength in which I trust."

It is not my own strength through which I forgive. It is through the strength of God in me, which I am remembering as I forgive. As I begin to see, I recognize His reflection on earth. I forgive all things because I feel the stirring of His strength in me. And I begin to remember the Love I chose to forget, but Which has not forgotten me.

W 60 L 3. 48) "There is nothing to fear."

How safe the world will look to me when I can see it! It will not look anything like what I imagine I see now. Everyone and everything I see will lean toward me to bless me. I will recognize in everyone my dearest Friend. What could there be to fear in a world which I have forgiven, and which has forgiven me?

W 60 L 4. 49) "God's Voice speaks to me all through the day."

There is not a moment in which God's Voice ceases to call on my forgiveness to save me. There is not a moment in which His Voice fails to direct my thoughts, guide my actions, and lead my feet. I am walking steadily on toward truth. There is nowhere else I can go, because God's Voice is the only voice and the only guide that has been given to His Son. W(111)

W 60 L 5. 50) "I am sustained by the Love of God."

As I listen to God's Voice, I am sustained by[121] His Love. As I open my eyes, His Love lights up the world for me to see. As I forgive, His Love reminds me that His Son is sinless. And as I look upon the world with the vision He has given me, I remember that I am His Son. W(112)

Lesson 61 "I am the light of the world."

W 61 L 1. Who is the light of the world except God's Son?[122] This, then, is merely a statement of the truth about yourself. It is the opposite of a statement of pride, of arrogance, or of self-deception. It does not describe the self-concept you have made. It does not refer to any of the characteristics with which you have endowed your idols. It refers to you as you were created by God. It simply states the truth.

W 61 L 2. To the ego, today's idea is the epitome of self-glorification. But the ego does not understand humility, mistaking it for self-debasement. Humility consists of accepting your role in salvation, and in taking no other. It is not humility to insist that you cannot be the light of the world, if that is the function God assigned to you. It is only arrogance that would assert this function cannot be for you, and arrogance is always of the ego.

W 61 L 3. True humility requires that you accept today's idea because it is God's Voice which tells you it is true. This is a beginning step in accepting your real function on earth. It is a giant stride toward taking your rightful place in salvation. It is a positive assertion of your right to be saved, and an acknowledgment of the power that is given you to save others.

W 61 L 4. You will want to think about this idea as often as possible today. It is the perfect answer to all illusions, and therefore to all temptation. It brings all the images you have made about yourself to the truth, and helps you depart in peace,[123] unburdened and certain of your purpose.

W 61 L 5. As many practice periods as possible should be undertaken today, although each one need not exceed a minute or two. They should begin with telling yourself: W(113)

> *"I am the light of the world.*
> *That is my only function.*
> *That is why I am here."*

Then think about these statements for a short while, preferably with your eyes closed if the situation permits. Let a few related thoughts come to you, and repeat the idea to yourself if your mind wanders away from the central thought.

W 61 L 6. Be sure both to begin and end the day[124] with a practice period. Thus you will awaken with an acknowledgment of the truth about yourself, reinforce it throughout the day, and turn to sleep as you re-affirm your function and your only purpose here. These two practice periods may be longer than the rest,[125] if you find them helpful and want to extend them.

W 61 L 7. Today's idea goes far beyond the ego's petty views of what you are and what your purpose is. As a bringer of salvation, this is obviously necessary. This is the first of a number of giant steps we will take in the next few weeks. Try today to begin to build a firm foundation for these advances.[126] You are the light of the world. God has built His plan for the salvation of His Son on you. W(114)

Lesson 62 "Forgiveness is my function as the light of the world."

W 62 L 1. It is your forgiveness that will bring the world of darkness to the light. It is your forgiveness that lets you recognize the

---

[121] The *Urtext* manuscript is missing the word "**by**" which is handwritten in. This is an apparent correction of a typing mistake. The word "by" does show up in the *Notes*.
[122] **Matthew 5:14** You are the light of the world. A city that is set on a hill cannot be hidden.
John 8:12 Then Jesus spoke to them again, saying, "I am the light of the world. He who follows Me shall not walk in darkness, but have the light of life."
John 9:5 "When I am in the world, I am the light of the world."
 The phrase "light of the world" shows up 42 times in ACIM, 9 in the *Text* volume, and 33 in the *Workbook*. We are only footnoting the reference this once in the *Workbook*.
[123] **Luke 2:29** Lord, now You are letting Your servant depart in peace, According to Your word;
[124] Handwritten mark-up suggests (today).
[125] Handwritten mark-up suggests (others).
[126] **Luke 6:48** "He is like a man building a house, who dug deep and laid the foundation on the rock. And when the flood arose, the stream beat vehemently against that house, and could not shake it, for it was founded on the rock."

light in which you see. Forgiveness is the demonstration that you are the light of the world. Through your forgiveness does the truth about yourself return to your memory. Therefore in your forgiveness lies your salvation.

W 62 L 2. Illusions about yourself and the world are one. That is why all forgiveness is a gift to yourself. Your goal is to find out who you are, having denied your identity by attacking creation and its Creator. Now you are learning how to remember the truth. For this, attack must be replaced by forgiveness, so that thoughts of life may replace thoughts of death.

W 62 L 3. Remember that in every attack you call upon your own weakness, while every[127] time you forgive you call upon the strength of Christ in you. Do you not then begin to understand what forgiveness will do for you? It will remove all sense of weakness, strain and fatigue from your mind. It will take away all fear and guilt and pain. It will restore the invulnerability and power God gave His Son to your awareness.

W 62 L 4. Let us be glad to begin and end this day by practicing today's idea, and to use it as frequently as possible throughout the day. It will help to make the day as happy for you as God wants you to be. And it will help those around you, as well as those who seem to be far away in space and time, to share this happiness with you.

W 62 L 5. As often as you can, closing your eyes if possible, say to yourself:

> "Forgiveness is my function as the light of the world.
> I would fulfill my function that I may be happy."

Then devote a minute or two to considering your function, and the happiness and release[128] it will bring you. **W(115)**

W 62 L 6. Let related thoughts come freely, for your heart will recognize these words, and in your mind is the awareness that they are true. Should your attention wander, repeat the idea and add:

> "I would remember this because I want to be happy." **W(116)**

Lesson 63 "The light of the world brings peace to every mind through my forgiveness."

W 63 L 1. How holy are you who have the power to bring peace to every mind! How blessed are you who can learn to recognize the means for letting this be done through you! What purpose could you have that would bring you greater happiness?

W 63 L 2. You are indeed the light of the world with such a function. The Son of God looks to you for his redemption. It is yours to give him, for it belongs to you. Accept no trivial purpose or meaningless desire in its place, or you will forget your function and leave the Son of God in hell. This is no idle request that is being asked of you. You are asked to accept salvation that it may be yours to give.

W 63 L 3. Recognizing the importance of this function, we will be happy to remember it very often today. We will begin the day by acknowledging it, and close the day with the thought of it in our awareness. And throughout the day, we will repeat this as often as we can:

> "The light of the world brings peace to every mind through my forgiveness.
> I am the means God has appointed for the salvation of the world."

W 63 L 4. [129]You will probably find it easier to let the related thoughts come to you in the minute or two which you should devote to considering this if you can close your eyes. Do not, however, wait for such an opportunity. No chance should be lost for reinforcing today's idea. Remember that God's Son looks to you for his salvation. And who but your Self must be His Son? **W(117)**

Lesson 64 "Let me not forget my function."

W 64 L 1. Today's idea is merely another way of saying, "Let me not wander into temptation."[130] The purpose of the world you see is to obscure your function of forgiveness, and provide you with a justification for forgetting it. It is the temptation to abandon God and His Son, taking on a physical appearance. It is this which the body's eyes look upon.

W 64 L 2. Nothing the body's eyes seem to see can be anything but a form of temptation, since this was the purpose of the body itself. Yet we have learned that the Holy Spirit has another use for all the illusions you have made, and therefore He sees another purpose in them. To the Holy Spirit, the world is a place where you learn to forgive yourself what you think of as your sins. In this perception, the physical appearance of temptation becomes the spiritual recognition of salvation.

W 64 L 3. To review our last few lessons, your function here is to be the light of the world, a function given you by God. It is only the arrogance of the ego which leads you to question this, and only the fear of the ego which induces you to regard yourself as unworthy of the task assigned to you by God Himself. The world's salvation awaits your forgiveness because through it does the Son of God escape from all illusions and thus from all temptation. The Son of God is you.

W 64 L 4. Only by fulfilling the function given you by God will you be happy. That is because your function is to be happy by using the means by[131] which happiness becomes inevitable. There is no other way. Therefore every time you choose whether or not to fulfill your function, you are really choosing whether to be happy or not.

W 64 L 5. Let us remember this today. Let us remind ourselves of it in the morning and again at night, and all through the day as well. **W(118)** Prepare yourself in advance for all the decisions you will make today by remembering that they are all really very simple. Each one will lead to happiness or unhappiness. Can such a simple decision really be difficult to make?

W 64 L 6. Let not the form of the decision deceive you. Complexity of form does not imply complexity of content. It is impossible that any decision on earth can have a content different from just this one simple choice. That is the only choice the Holy Spirit sees. Therefore it is the only choice there is.

W 64 L 7. Today, then, let us practice these thoughts:

> "Let me not forget my function.
> Let me not try to substitute mine for God's.
> Let me forgive and be happy."

At least once devote ten or fifteen minutes to reflecting on this with closed eyes. Related thoughts will come to help you, if you remember the crucial importance of your function to you and to the world.

W 64 L 8. In the frequent applications of today's idea to be made throughout the day, devote several minutes to reviewing the[132] thoughts, and then to thinking about them and about nothing else. This will be difficult at first particularly, since you are not proficient in the mind discipline which it requires. You may need to repeat "Let me not forget my function" quite often, to help you concentrate.

---

[127] Handwritten mark-up suggests (each).
[128] Handwritten mark-up suggests "**release** (that) **it will bring you**"
[129] Handwritten mark-up suggests (If you close your eyes,) at the beginning of the sentence, and crosses out "**if you can close your eyes.**" at the end.

[130] **Matthew 6:13** "And do not lead us into temptation,
But deliver us from the evil one.
For Yours is the kingdom and the power and the glory forever." Amen.
[131] Handwritten mark-up replaces the word "**by**" with (through).
[132] Handwritten mark-up suggests replacing "**the**" with (these).

W 64 L 9. Two forms of the shorter practice periods are required. At times, do the exercises with your eyes closed, trying to concentrate on the thoughts you are applying. At other times keep your eyes open after reviewing the thoughts and look slowly and unselectively about you, telling yourself:

> *"This is the world it is my function to save."* **W(119)**

Lesson 65 "My only function is the one God gave me."

W 65 L 1. The idea for today reaffirms your commitment to salvation. It also reminds you that you have no other function[133] than this. Both of these thoughts are obviously necessary for a total commitment. Salvation cannot be the only purpose you hold while you still cherish others. The full acceptance of salvation as your only function necessarily entails two phases; the recognition of salvation as your function, and the relinquishment of all the other goals you have invented for yourself.

W 65 L 2. This is the only way in which you can take your rightful place among the Saviors of the world. This is the only way in which you can say and mean, "My only function is the one God gave me." This is the only way in which you can find peace of mind.

W 65 L 3. Today, and for a number of days to follow, set aside ten to fifteen minutes for a more sustained practice period in which you try to understand and accept what today's idea[134] really means. It[135] offers you escape from all your perceived difficulties. It places the key to the door to peace, which you have closed upon yourself, in your own hands. It gives you the answer to all the searching you have done since time began.

W 65 L 4. Try, if possible, to undertake the daily extended practice periods at approximately the same time each day. Try, also, to determine this time today in advance, and then adhere to it as closely as possible. The purpose of this is to arrange your day so that you have set apart the time for God, as well as for all the trivial purposes and goals you will pursue. This is part of the long range disciplinary training which your mind needs so that the Holy Spirit can use it consistently for the purpose He shares with you. **W(120)**

W 65 L 5. For this[136] practice period, begin by reviewing the idea for today. Then close your eyes, repeat the idea to yourself once again, and watch your mind carefully to catch whatever thoughts cross it. At first, make no attempt to concentrate only on thoughts related to the idea for today.[137] Rather, try to uncover each one[138] that arises to[139] interfere with it. Note each one[140] as it[141] comes to you with as little involvement or concern as possible, dismissing them[142] by telling yourself:

> *"This thought reflects a goal which is preventing me from accepting my only function."*

W 65 L 6. After a while, interfering thoughts will become harder to find. Try, however, to continue a minute or so longer, attempting to catch a few of the idle thoughts which escaped your attention before, but do not strain or make undue effort in doing this. Then tell yourself:

> *"On this clean slate, let my true function be written for me."*

You need not use these exact words, but try to get a sense of being willing to have your illusions of purpose be replaced by truth.

W 65 L 7. Finally, repeat the idea for today once more and devote the rest of the practice period to trying to focus on its importance to you; the relief its acceptance will bring you by resolving your conflicts once and for all, and the extent to which you really want salvation in spite of your own foolish ideas to the contrary.

W 65 L 8. In the shorter practice periods, which should be undertaken at least once an hour, use this form in applying today's idea:

> *"My only function is the one God gave me.*
> *I want no other and I have no other."*

Sometimes close your eyes as you practice, and sometimes keep them open and look about you. It is what you see now that will be totally changed when you accept today's idea completely. **W(121)**

Lesson 66 "My happiness and my function are one."

W 66 L 1. You have surely noticed an emphasis throughout our recent lessons on the connection between fulfilling your function and achieving happiness. This is because you do not really see the connection. Yet there is more than just a connection between them; they are the same. Their forms are different, but their content is completely one.

W 66 L 2. The ego does constant battle with the Holy Spirit on the fundamental question of what your function is. So does it do constant battle with the Holy Spirit about what your happiness is. It is not a two-way battle. The ego attacks and the Holy Spirit does not respond. He knows what your function is. He knows that it is your happiness.

W 66 L 3. Today we will try to go past this wholly meaningless battle, and arrive at the truth about your function. We will not engage in ceaseless arguments about what it is. We will not become hopelessly involved in defining happiness and determining the means for achieving it. We will not indulge the ego by listening to its attacks on truth. We will merely be glad that we can find out what truth is.

W 66 L 4. Our longer practice period today has as its purpose your acceptance of the fact that not only is there a very real connection between the function God gave you and your happiness, but that they are actually identical. God gives you only happiness. Therefore the function He gave you must be happiness, even if it appears to be different. Today's exercises are an attempt to go beyond these differences in appearance, and recognize a common content where it exists in truth.

W 66 L 5. Begin the 10 to 15 minute practice period by reviewing these thoughts:

> *"God gives me only happiness.*
> *He has given my function to me.*
> *Therefore my function must be happiness."* **W(122)**

Try to see the logic in this sequence, even if you do not[143] accept the conclusion. It is only if the first two thoughts are wrong that the conclusion could be false. Let us, then, think about the premises for a while, as we are practicing.

W 66 L 6. The first premise is that God gives you only happiness. This could be false, of course, but in order to be false it is necessary to define God as something He is not. Love cannot give evil, and what is not happiness is evil. God cannot give what He does not have, and He cannot have what He is not. Unless God gives you only happiness, He must be evil. And it is this definition of Him which you are believing if you do not accept the first premise.

---

[133] Handwritten mark-up switches word order (function other).
[134] Handwritten mark-up suggests (the idea for today) in place of "**today's idea**".
[135] Handwritten mark-up suggests (Today's idea).
[136] Handwritten mark-up suggests (the longer) for "**this**".
[137] Handwritten mark-up suggests (today's idea).
[138] Handwritten mark-up suggests (thought).
[139] Handwritten mark-up suggests (which would).
[140] Handwritten mark-up suggests (these).
[141] Handwritten mark-up suggests (they).
[142] Handwritten mark-up suggests (each one).

[143] Handwritten mark-up suggests (yet).

W 66 L 7. The second premise is that God has given you your function. We have seen that there are only two parts of your mind. One is ruled by the ego, and is made up of illusions. The other is the home of the Holy Spirit, where truth abides. There are no other guides but these to choose between, and no other outcomes possible as a result of your choice but the fear which the ego always engenders and the love which the Holy Spirit always offers to replace it.

W 66 L 8. Thus it must be that your function is established by God through His Voice or is made by the ego which you made to replace Him. Which is true? Unless God gave your function to you, it must be the gift of the ego. Does the ego really have gifts to give, being itself an illusion and offering only the illusion of gifts?

W 66 L 9. Think about this during the longer practice period today. Think also about the many forms which the illusion of your function has taken in your mind, and the many ways in which you try[144] to find salvation under the ego's guidance. Did you find it? Were you happy? Did they bring you peace? W(123) We need great honesty today. Remember the outcomes fairly, and consider also whether it was ever reasonable to expect happiness from anything the ego has ever proposed. Yet the ego is the only alternative to the Holy Spirit's Voice.

W 66 L 10. You will listen to madness or hear the truth. Try to make this choice as you think about the premises on which our conclusion rests. We can share in this conclusion, but in no other. For God Himself shares it with us.

W 66 L 11. Today's idea is another giant stride in the perception of the same as the same, and the different as different. On one side stand all illusions. All truth stands on the other. Let us try today to realize that only the truth is true.

W 66 L 12. In the shorter practice periods, which would be most helpful today if undertaken twice an hour, this form of the application is suggested:

"My happiness and function are one,
because God has given me both."

It will not take more than a minute, and probably less, to repeat these words slowly, and think about them a little[145] as you say them. W(124)

Lesson 67 "Love created me like Itself."

W 67 L 1. Today's idea is a complete and accurate statement of what you are. This is why you are the light of the world. This is why God appointed you as the world's savior. This is why the Son of God looks to you for his salvation. He is saved by what you are. We will make every effort today to reach this truth about you, and to realize fully, if only for a moment, that it is the truth.

W 67 L 2. In the longer practice period, we will think about your reality and its wholly unchanged and unchangeable nature. We will begin by repeating this truth about you, and then spend a few minutes adding some relevant thoughts, such as:

"Holiness created me holy"[146]

"Kindness created me kind."

"Helpfulness created me helpful."

"Perfection created me perfect."

Any attribute which is in accord with God as He defines Himself is appropriate for use. We are trying today to undo your definition of God and replace it with His Own. We are also trying to emphasize that you are part of His definition of Himself.

W 67 L 3. After you have gone over several such related thoughts, try to let all thoughts drop away for a brief preparatory interval, and then try to reach past all your images and preconceptions about yourself to the truth in you. If Love created you like Itself this Self must be in you. And somewhere in your mind It is there for you to find.

W 67 L 4. You may find it necessary to repeat the idea for today from time to time, to replace distracting thoughts. You may also find that this is not sufficient, and that you need to continue adding other thoughts related to the truth about yourself. Yet perhaps you will succeed in going past that, and through the interval of thoughtlessness[147] to the awareness of a blazing W(125) light in which you recognize yourself as Love created you. Be confident that you will do much today to bring that awareness nearer, whether you feel you have succeeded or not.

W 67 L 5. It will be particularly helpful today to practice the idea for today[148] as often as you can. You need to hear the truth about yourself as frequently as possible, because your mind is so preoccupied with false self-images. Four or five times an hour, and perhaps even more, it would be most beneficial to remind yourself that Love created you like Itself. Hear the truth about yourself in this.

W 67 L 6. Try to realize in the shorter practice periods, that this is not your tiny solitary voice that tells you this. This is the Voice for God, reminding you of your Father and of your Self. This is the Voice of truth, replacing everything that the ego tells you about yourself with the simple truth about the Son of God. You were created by Love like Itself. W(126)

Lesson 68 "Love holds no grievances."

W 68 L 1. You who were created by Love like Itself can hold no grievances and know your Self. To hold a grievance is to forget who you are. To hold a grievance is to see yourself as a body. It is the decision[149] to let the ego rule your mind, and to condemn the body to death. Perhaps you do not yet fully realize just what holding grievances does to your awareness.[150] It seems to split you off from your Source, and make you unlike Him. It makes you believe that He is like what you think you have become, for no-one can conceive of his Creator as unlike himself.

W 68 L 2. Shut off from your Self, Who[151] remains aware of His[152] likeness to His[153] Creator, your Self seems to sleep, while the part of your mind that weaves illusions in its sleep appears to be awake. Can all this arise from holding grievances? Oh yes! For he who holds grievances denies he was created by Love, and his Creator has become fearful to him in his dreams[154] of hate. Who can dream of hatred and not fear God?

W 68 L 3. It is as sure that those who hold grievances will redefine God in their own image as it is certain that God created them like Himself and defined them as part of Him.[155] It is as sure that those who hold grievances will suffer guilt as it is certain that those who forgive will find peace. It is as sure that those who hold grievances will forget who they are as it is certain that those who forgive will remember.

---

[144] Handwritten mark-up suggests (tried).
[145] Handwritten mark-up suggests (while).
[146] The *Urtext* manuscript has "whole" typed and crossed out with the word "holy" handwritten in. The *Notes* also has "holy" as does FIP.

[147] The original *Urtext* manuscript reads (thought-lessness).
[148] Handwritten mark-up suggests (the day).
[149] Handwritten mark-up suggests (To hold a grievance is).
[150] Handwritten mark-up suggests (mind).
[151] Handwritten mark-up suggests (Which).
[152] Handwritten mark-up suggests (Its).
[153] Handwritten mark-up suggests (Its).
[154] Handwritten mark-up suggests (dream).
[155] **Genesis 1:26-27** Then God said, "Let Us make man in Our image, according to Our likeness; let them have dominion over the fish of the sea, over the birds of the air, and over the cattle, over all the earth and over every creeping thing that creeps on the earth." So God created man in His own image; in the image of God He created him; male and female He created them.

W 68 L 4. Would you not be willing to relinquish your grievances if you believed all this were so? Perhaps you do not think that you can let all your grievances go. That, however, is simply a question of motivation. Today we will try to find out how you would feel without them. If you succeed even by ever so little, there will never be a problem in motivation ever again. **W(127)**

W 68 L 5. Begin today's extended practice period by searching your mind for those against whom you hold what you regard as major grievances. Some of these will be quite easy to find. Then think of the seemingly minor grievances you hold against those you like, and even think you love. It will quickly become apparent that there is no-one against whom you do not cherish grievances of some sort. This has left you alone in all the universe in your perception of yourself.

W 68 L 6. Determine now to see all these people as friends. Say to them all, collectively, thinking of each one in turn as you do so:

> *"I would see you as my friend,*
>
> *that I may remember you are part of me,*
>
> *and come to know myself."*

Spend the remainder of the practice period trying to think of yourself as completely at peace with everyone and everything, safe in a world which protects you and loves you, and which you love in return.

W 68 L 7. Try to feel safety surrounding you, hovering over you, and holding you up. Try to believe, however briefly, that nothing can harm you in any way. At the end of the practice period tell yourself:

> *"Love holds no grievances.*
>
> *when I let all my grievances go,*
>
> *I will know I am perfectly safe."*

W 68 L 8. The short practice periods should include a quick application of today's ideas in this form, whenever any thought of grievance arises against anyone, physically present or not:

> *"Love holds no grievances.*
>
> *Let me not betray my Self."*

In addition, repeat the idea several times an hour in this form:

> *"Love holds no grievances.*
>
> *I would wake to my Self*
>
> *by laying all my grievances aside*
>
> *and wakening in Him."* **W(128)**

Lesson 69 "My grievances hide the light of the world in me."

W 69 L 1. No-one can look upon what your grievances conceal. Because your grievances are hiding the light of the world in you, everyone stands in darkness, and you beside him. But as the veil of your grievances is lifted, you are released with him. Share your salvation now with him who stood beside you when you were in hell. He is your brother in the light of the world which saves you both.

W 69 L 2. Today let us make another real attempt to reach the light in you. Before we undertake this in our more extended practice period, let us devote several minutes in thinking about what we are[156] trying to do. We are literally attempting to get in touch with the salvation of the world. We are trying to see past the veil of darkness that keeps it concealed. We are trying to let the veil be lifted, and[157] see the tears of God's Son disappear in the sunlight.

W 69 L 3. Let us begin our longer practice period today with the full realization of all this,[158] and[159] real determination to reach what is dearer to us than all else. Salvation is our only need. There is no other purpose here, and no other function to fulfill. Learning salvation is our only goal. Let us end the ancient search today, by finding the light in us and holding it up for everyone who searches with us to look upon and rejoice.

W 69 L 4. Very quietly now, with your eyes closed, try to let[160] all the content which generally occupies your consciousness go. Think of your mind as a vast round area,[161] surrounded by a layer of heavy dark clouds. You can see only the clouds because you seem to be standing outside the whole area,[162] and quite apart from it. From where you stand, you can see no reason to believe there is a brilliant light hidden by the clouds. The clouds seem to be the only reality. They seem to be all there is to see. Therefore you do not attempt to go through them and past them, which is the only way in which you would be really convinced **W(129)** of their lack of substance. We will make this attempt today.

W 69 L 5. After you have thought about the importance of what you are trying to do for yourself and the world, try to settle[163] in perfect stillness, remembering only how much you want to reach the light in you today, - now. Determine to go past the clouds. Reach out and touch them in your mind. Brush them aside with your hand; feel them resting on your cheeks and forehead and eyelids as you go through them. Go on; clouds cannot stop you.

W 69 L 6. If you are doing the exercises properly, you will begin to feel a sense of being lifted up and carried ahead. Your little effort and small determination call on the power of the universe to help you, and God Himself will raise you from darkness into light. You are in accord with His Will. You cannot fail because your will is His.

W 69 L 7. Have confidence in your Father today, and[164] be certain that He has heard you and has answered you. You may not recognize His answer yet, but you can indeed be sure that it is given you, and you will yet receive it. Try, as you attempt to go through the clouds to the light, to hold this confidence in your mind. Try to remember that you are at last joining your will to God's. Try to keep the thought clearly in mind that what you undertake with God must succeed. Then let the power of God work in you and through you, that His Will and yours may be done.[165]

W 69 L 8. In the shorter practice periods, which you will want to do as often as possible in view of the importance of today's idea to you and your happiness, remind yourself that your grievances are hiding the light of the world from your awareness. Remind yourself also that you are not searching for it alone, and that you do know where to look for it. Say, then:

> *"My grievances hide the light of the world in me.*
>
> *I cannot see what I have hidden.*
>
> *Yet I want to let it be revealed to me*
>
> *for my salvation and the salvation of the world."* **W(130)**

Also, be sure to tell yourself:

> *"If I hold this grievance, the light of the world will be hidden from me,"*

if you are tempted to hold anything against anyone today. **W(131)**

---

[156] Overstrike typing suggests (will be).

[157] Handwritten mark-up suggests (to).

[158] Handwritten mark-up suggests (that this is so).

[159] Handwritten mark-up suggests (with).

[160] Handwritten mark-up suggests (go of).

[161] Handwritten mark-up suggests (circle).

[162] Handwritten mark-up suggests (circle).

[163] Handwritten mark-up suggests (down).

[164] *Urtext* manuscript has a sentence break here. Handwritten mark-up suggests a comma instead, which we feel is preferable.

[165] **Matthew 6:10** "Your kingdom come. Your will be done on earth as it is in heaven."

Lesson 70 "My salvation comes from me."

W 70 L 1. All temptation is nothing more than some form of the basic temptation not to believe the idea for today. Salvation seems to come from anywhere except from you. So, too, does the source of guilt. You see neither guilt nor salvation as in your own mind, and nowhere else. When you realize that all guilt is solely an invention of your mind, you must also realize that guilt and salvation must be in the same place. [166]Understanding this you are saved.

W 70 L 2. The seeming "cost" of accepting today's idea is this: It means that nothing outside yourself can save you; nothing outside yourself can give you peace. But it also means that nothing outside yourself can hurt you, or disturb your peace, or upset you in any way. Today's idea places you in charge of the universe, where you belong because of who you are.

W 70 L 3. This is not a role which can be partially accepted, and[167] you must surely begin to see that accepting it is salvation. It may not, however, be clear to you why the recognition that guilt is in your own mind entails the realization that salvation is there as well. God would not have put the remedy for sickness where it cannot help. That is the way your mind has worked, but hardly His. He wants you to be healed, and so He has kept the Source of healing where the need for healing lies.

W 70 L 4. You have tried to do just the opposite, making every attempt, however distorted and fantastic it might be, to separate healing from the sickness for which it was intended, and thus keep the sickness. Your purpose was to ensure that healing did not occur; God's purpose was to ensure that it did. Today we will practice realizing that God's Will and ours are really the same in this. **W(132)** God wants us to be healed, and we do not really want to be sick because it makes us unhappy. Therefore, in accepting the idea for today, we are in agreement with God. He does not want us to be sick. Neither do we. He wants us to be healed. So do we.

W 70 L 5. We are ready for two longer practice periods today, each of which should last some ten to fifteen minutes. We will, however, still let you decide when to undertake them. We will follow this practice for a number of lessons, and it would again be well to decide in advance when would be a good time to lay aside for each of them, and adhere to your own decision[168] as closely as possible.

W 70 L 6. Begin these practice periods by repeating the idea for today, adding a statement signifying your recognition that salvation comes from nothing outside of you. You might put it this way:

"My salvation comes from me.

It cannot come from anywhere else."

Then devote a few minutes with your eyes closed, to reviewing some of the external places where you have looked for salvation in the past, - in other people, in possessions, in various situations and events, and in self-concepts which you sought to make real. Recognize that it was[169] not there. [170]Tell yourself:

"My salvation cannot come from any of these things.

My salvation comes from me, and only from me."

W 70 L 7. Now we will try again to reach the light in you, which is where your salvation is. You cannot find it in the clouds that surround the light, and it is in them you have been looking for it. It is not there. It is past the clouds, and in the light beyond. Remember that you will have to go through the clouds before you can reach the light. But remember also that you have never found anything in the cloud patterns you imagined that endured, or that you wanted. **W(133)**

W 70 L 8. Since all illusions of salvation have failed you, surely you do not want to remain in the clouds looking vainly for idols there, when you could so easily walk on into the light of real salvation. Try to pass the clouds by whatever means appeals to you. If it helps you, think of me holding your hand and leading you. And I assure you that this will be no idle fantasy.

W 70 L 9. For the short and frequent practice periods today, remind yourself that your salvation comes from you, and nothing but your own thoughts can hamper your progress. You are free from all external interference. You are in charge of your salvation. You are in charge of the salvation of the world. Say, then:

"My salvation comes from me.

Nothing outside of me can hold me back.

Within me is the world's salvation and my own." **W(134)**

Lesson 71 "Only God's plan for salvation will work."

W 71 L 1. You may not realize that the ego has set up a plan for salvation in opposition to God's. It is this plan in which you believe. Since it is the opposite of God's, you also believe that to accept God's plan in place of the ego's is to be damned. This sounds preposterous, of course. Yet after we have considered just what the ego's plan is, perhaps you will realize that, however preposterous it may be, you do believe in[171] it.

W 71 L 2. The ego's plan for salvation centers around holding grievances. It maintains that if someone else spoke or acted differently, if some external circumstance or event were changed, you would be saved. Thus the source of salvation is constantly perceived as outside yourself. Each grievance you hold is a declaration, and an assertion in which you believe, that[172] says, "If this were different, I would be saved." The change of mind that is necessary for salvation is thus demanded of everyone and everything except yourself.

W 71 L 3. The role assigned to your own mind in this plan, then, is simply to determine what other than itself must change if you are to be saved. According to this insane plan, any perceived source of salvation is acceptable, provided that it will not work. This ensures that the fruitless search will continue, for the illusion that,[173] although this hope has[174] failed, there is still grounds for hope in other places and in other things, persists. Another person will yet serve better; another situation will yet offer success.

W 71 L 4. Such is the ego's plan for your salvation. Surely you can see how it is in strict accord with the ego's basic doctrine, "Seek but do not find?"[175] For what could more surely guarantee that you will not find salvation than to channelize all your efforts in searching for it where it is not? **W(135)**

W 71 L 5. God's plan for salvation works simply because, by following His direction, you seek for salvation where it is. But if you are to succeed, as God promises you will, you must be willing to seek there only. Otherwise your purpose is divided, and you will attempt to follow two plans for salvation which are diametrically opposed in all ways. The result can only bring confusion, misery, and a deep sense of failure and despair.

W 71 L 6. How can you escape all this? Very simply. The idea for today is the answer. Only God's plan for salvation will work. There

---

[166] Handwritten mark-up suggests (In).
[167] *Urtext* manuscript has a sentence break here. Handwritten mark-up suggests a comma instead, which we feel is preferable
[168] Handwritten mark-up suggests (s).
[169] Handwritten mark-up suggests (is).
[170] Handwritten mark-up removes period and inserts (and).

[171] The word "**in**" is not present in the *Urtext* manuscript, but is handwritten in. It appears to be a correction of a typing error.
[172] Handwritten mark-up suggests (which).
[173] Handwritten mark-up moves (persists) from end of sentence to this location.
[174] Handwritten mark-up suggests (always).
[175] **Matthew 7:7** Ask, and it will be given to you; seek, and you will find; knock, and it will be opened to you.

can be no real conflict about this, because there is no possible alternative to God's plan[176] that will save you. His is the only plan that is certain in its outcome. His is the only plan that must succeed. Let us practice recognizing this certainty today. And let us rejoice that there is an answer to what seems to be a conflict with no resolution possible. All things are possible to God.[177] Salvation must be yours because of His plan, which cannot fail.

W 71 L 7. Begin the two longer practice periods for today by thinking about today's idea, and realizing that it contains two parts, each making equal contribution to the whole. God's plan for your salvation will work, and other plans will not. Do not allow yourself to become depressed or angry at the second part; it is inherent in the first. And in the first is your full release from all your own insane attempts and mad proposals to free yourself. They have led to depression and anger, but[178] God's plan will succeed. It will lead to release and joy.

W 71 L 8. Remembering this, let us devote the remainder of the extended practice period to asking God to reveal His plan to us. Ask Him very specifically:

"What would you have me do?"

Where would You have me go?

What would You have me say, and to whom?"

Give Him full charge of the rest of the practice period, and let Him tell you what needs to be done by you in His plan for your salvation. He will answer you in proportion to your willingness to hear His Voice. Refuse not to hear. The very **W(136)** fact that you are doing the exercises proves that you have some willingness to listen. This is enough to establish your claim to God's answer.

W 71 L 9. In the shorter practice periods tell yourself often that God's plan for salvation, and only His, will work. Be alert to all temptation to hold grievances today, and respond to them with this form of today's idea:

"Holding grievances is the opposite of God's plan for salvation.

And only His plan will work."

Try to remember the[179] idea for today some six or seven times an hour. There could be no better way to spend a half minute or less than to remember the Source of your salvation, and to see It where It is. **W(137)**

Lesson 72 "Holding grievances is an attack on God's plan for salvation."

W 72 L 1. While we have recognized that the ego's plan for salvation is the opposite of God's, we have not yet emphasized that it is an active attack on His plan, and a deliberate attempt to destroy it. In the attack, God is assigned the attributes which are actually associated with the ego, while the ego appears to take on the attributes of God.

W 72 L 2. The ego's fundamental wish is to replace God. In fact, the ego is the physical embodiment of this[180] wish. For it is this[181] wish which seems to surround the mind with a body, keeping it separate and alone, and unable to reach other minds except through the body which was made to imprison it. The limit on communication cannot be the best means to expand communication. Yet the ego would have you believe that it is.

W 72 L 3. Although the attempt to keep the limitations which a body would impose is obvious here, it is perhaps not so apparent why holding grievances is an attack on God's plan for salvation. But let us consider the kinds of things which you are apt to hold grievances for. Are they not always associated with something a body does? A person says something we[182] do not like; he does something that displeases us[183]; he "betrays" his hostile thoughts in his behavior.

W 72 L 4. We[184] are not dealing here with what the person is. On the contrary, we[185] are exclusively concerned with what he does in a body. We[186] are doing more than failing to help in freeing him from its[187] limitations. We[188] are actively trying to hold him to it by confusing it with him, and judging them as one. Herein is God attacked, for if His Son is only a body, so must He be as well. A creator wholly unlike his creation is inconceivable.

W 72 L 5. If God is a body, what must His plan for salvation be? What could it be but death? In trying to present Himself as the Author of life and not of death, He is a liar and a deceiver, full of false promises, and offering illusions in place of truth. **W(138)** The body's apparent reality makes this view of God quite convincing. In fact, if the body were real, it would be difficult indeed to escape this conclusion. And every grievance that you hold insists that the body is real. It overlooks entirely what your brother is. It reinforces your belief that he is a body, and condemns him for it. And it asserts that his salvation must be death, projecting this attack onto God, and holding Him responsible for it.

W 72 L 6. To this carefully prepared arena, where angry animals seek for prey and mercy cannot enter, the ego comes to save you. God made you a body. Very well. Let us accept this and be glad. As a body, do not let yourself be deprived of what the body offers. Take the little you can get. God gave you nothing. The body is your only savior. It is the death of God and your salvation. This is the universal belief of the world you see.

W 72 L 7. Some hate the body, and try to hurt and humiliate it. Others love the body, and try to glorify and exalt it. But while it stands at the center of your concept of yourself, you are attacking God's plan for salvation, and holding your grievances against Him and His creations, that you may not hear the Voice of truth and welcome it as Friend. Your chosen Savior takes His place instead. It is your friend; He is your enemy. We will try today to stop these senseless attacks on salvation. We will try to welcome it instead.

W 72 L 8. Our[189] upside-down perception has been ruinous to our[190] peace of mind. We[191] have seen ourselves[192] in a body and the truth outside us,[193] locked away from our[194] awareness by the body's limitations. Now we are going to try to see this differently. The light of truth is in us, where it was placed by God. It is the body that is outside us, and is not our concern. To be without a body is to be in our natural state. To recognize the light of truth in us is to recognize ourselves as we are. To see our Self as separate from the body is to end the attack on God's plan for salvation, and to accept it instead. And **W(139)** wherever it[195] is accepted it is accomplished already.

---

[176] Handwritten mark-up suggests (for salvation).
[177] **Matthew 19:26** But Jesus looked at them and said to them, "With men this is impossible, but with God all things are possible."
[178] *Urtext* manuscript has a sentence break here. Handwritten mark-up suggests a comma instead, which we feel is preferable
[179] Handwritten mark-up suggests (today's) instead of "**the**".
[180] Handwritten mark-up suggests (that).
[181] Handwritten mark-up suggests (that).
[182] Handwritten mark-up suggests (you).
[183] Handwritten mark-up suggests (you).
[184] Handwritten mark-up suggests (You).
[185] Handwritten mark-up suggests (You).
[186] Handwritten mark-up suggests (You).
[187] Handwritten mark-up suggests (the body's).
[188] Handwritten mark-up suggests (You).
[189] Handwritten mark-up suggests (Your).
[190] Handwritten mark-up suggests (your).
[191] Handwritten mark-up suggests (You).
[192] Handwritten mark-up suggests (yourself).
[193] Handwritten mark-up suggests (you).
[194] Handwritten mark-up suggests (your).
[195] Handwritten mark-up suggests (His plan).

W 72 L 9. Our goal in the longer practice periods today is to become aware that God's plan for salvation has already been accomplished in us. To achieve this goal, we must replace attack with acceptance. As long as we attack it, we cannot understand what God's plan for us is. We are therefore attacking what we do not recognize. Now we are going to try to lay judgment aside, and ask what God's plan for us is:

"What is salvation, Father?

I do not know.

Tell me, that I may understand."

Then we will wait in quiet for His answer.

W 72 L 10. We have attacked God's plan for salvation, without waiting to hear what it is. We have shouted our grievances so loudly that we have not listened to His Voice. We have used our grievances to close our eyes and stop our ears. Now we would see and hear and learn. "What is salvation, Father?" Ask and you will be answered. Seek and you will find.

W 72 L 11. We are no longer asking the ego what salvation is and where to find it. We are asking it of truth. Be certain, then, that the answer will be true because of Whom you ask. Whenever you feel your confidence wane and your hope of success flicker and go out, repeat your question and your request, remembering that you are asking them of the infinite Creator of infinity, Who created you like Himself:

"What is salvation, Father?

I do not know.

Tell me, that I may understand."

He will answer. Be determined to hear.

W 72 L 12. One or perhaps two shorter practice periods an hour will be enough for today, since they will be somewhat longer than usual. The exercises are as follows[196]:

"Holding grievances is an attack on God's plan for salvation.

Let me accept it instead.

What is salvation, Father?"

Then wait a minute or so in silence, preferably with your eyes closed, and listen for His answer. **W(140)**[197] **W(141)**

Lesson 73 "I will there be light."[198]

W 73 L 1. Today we are considering the will that you share with God. This is not the same as the ego's idle wishes, out of which darkness and nothingness arise. The will you share with God has all the power of creation in it. The ego's idle wishes are unshared, and therefore have no power at all. Its wishes are not idle in the sense that they can make a world of illusions in which your belief can be very strong. But they are idle indeed in terms of creation. They make nothing that is real.

W 73 L 2. Idle wishes and grievances are partners or co-makers in picturing the world you see. The wishes of the ego gave rise to it, and the ego's need for grievances, which are necessary to maintain it, peoples it with figures which seem to attack you and call for "righteous" judgment. They[199] become the "middlemen" the ego employs to traffic in grievances, and[200] stand between your awareness and your brother's[201] reality. Beholding them, you do not know your brothers nor[202] your Self.

W 73 L 3. Your will is lost to you in this strange bartering, in which guilt is traded back and forth, and grievances increase with each exchange. Can such a world have been created by the will the Son of God shares with his Father? Did God create disaster for His Son? Creation is the will[203] of both[204] together. Would God create a world that kills Himself?

W 73 L 4. Today we will try once more to reach the world that is in accordance with your will. The light is in it because it does not oppose the Will of God. It is not Heaven, but the light of Heaven shines on it. Darkness has vanished; the ego's idle wishes have been withdrawn. Yet the light that[205] shines upon this world reflects your will, and so it must be in you that we will look for it.

W 73 L 5. Your picture of the world can only mirror what is within. The source of neither light nor darkness can be found without. Grievances darken your mind, and you look out on a darkened world. Forgiveness lifts the darkness, reasserts your will, and lets you look upon **W(142)** a world of light.

W 73 L 6. We have repeatedly emphasized that the barrier of grievances is easily past, and cannot stand between you and your salvation. The reason is very simple. Do you really want to be in hell? Do you really want to weep and suffer and die? Forget the ego's arguments which seek to prove all this is really Heaven. You know it is not so. You can[206] not want this for yourself. There is a point beyond which illusions cannot go. Suffering is not happiness, and it is happiness you really want. Such is your will in truth. And so salvation is your will as well. You want to succeed in what we are trying to do today. We undertake it with your blessing and your glad accord.

W 73 L 7. We will succeed today if you remember that you will salvation for yourself. You will to accept God's plan because you share in it. You have no will that can really oppose it, and you do not want to do so. Salvation is for you. Above all else you want the freedom to remember who you really are. Today it is the ego which stands powerless before your will. Your will is free, and nothing can prevail against it.

W 73 L 8. Therefore we undertake the exercises for today in happy confidence, certain that we will find what it is your will to find, and remember what it is your will to remember. No idle wishes can detain us, nor deceive us with an illusion of strength. Today let your will be done. And end forever the insane belief that it is hell in place of Heaven that you choose.

W 73 L 9. We will begin our longer practice periods with the recognition that God's plan for salvation, and only His, is wholly in accord with your will. It is not the purpose of an alien power, thrust upon you unwillingly. It is the one purpose here on which you and your Father are in perfect accord. **W(143)** You will succeed today, the time appointed for the release of the Son of God from hell and from all idle wishes. His will is now restored to his awareness. He is willing this very day to look upon the light in him and be saved.

W 73 L 10. After reminding yourself of this and determining to keep your will clearly in mind, tell yourself with gentle firmness and quiet certainty:

"I will there be light.

---

[196] Handwritten mark-up suggests(These exercises should begin with this).

[197] It would appear that there never was a page 140 in the *Workbook* manuscript. No page 140 is present in any copy consulted. Between the end of **Lesson 72** on page 139 of this manuscript and the beginning of **Lesson 73** on page 141 of this manuscript there is no additional material in any known version of ACIM. It is likely therefore that the Scribes simply missed a page number rather than inadvertently omitting any material.

[198] Genesis 1:3 Then God said, "Let there be light"; and there was light.

[199] Handwritten mark-up suggests (These figures).

[200] Handwritten mark-up suggests (They) and the removal of "**and**" and the start of a new sentence..

[201] Handwritten mark-up suggests (brothers').

[202] Handwritten mark-up suggests (or).

[203] Handwritten mark-up suggests (Will).

[204] Handwritten mark-up suggests (Both).

[205] Strikeout and re-typing suggests (which).

[206] *Urtext* manuscript has "**do**" overstruck and "**can**" replacing it.

*Let me behold the light
that reflects God's Will and mine."*

Then let your will assert itself, joined with the power of God and united with your Self. Put the rest of the practice period under Their guidance. Join with Them as They lead the way.

W 73 L 11. In the shorter practice periods, again make a declaration of what you really want. Say:

*"I will there be light.
Darkness is not my will."*

This should be repeated several times an hour. It is most important, however, to apply today's idea in this form immediately you are tempted to hold a grievance of any kind. This will help you let your grievances go, instead of cherishing them and hiding them in the darkness. **W(144)**

Lesson 74 "There is no will but God's."

W 74 L 1. The idea for today can be regarded as the central thought toward which all our exercises are directed. God's is the only will. When you have recognized this, you have recognized that your will is His. The belief that conflict is possible has gone. Peace has replaced the strange idea that you are torn by conflicting goals. As an expression of the Will of God, you have no goal but His.

W 74 L 2. There is great peace in today's idea. And the exercises for today are directed toward finding it. The idea itself is wholly true. Therefore it cannot give rise to illusions. Without illusions conflict is impossible. Let us try to recognize this today, and experience the peace this recognition brings.

W 74 L 3. Begin the longer practice periods by repeating these thoughts several times, slowly and with firm determination to understand what they mean and to hold them in mind:

*"There is no will but God's.
I cannot be in conflict."*

Then spend several minutes in adding some related thoughts, such as:

*"I am at peace."
"Nothing can disturb me. My will is God's."
"My will and God's are one."
"God wills peace for His Son."*

During this introductory phase, be sure to deal quickly with any conflict thoughts that may cross your mind. Tell yourself immediately:

*"There is no will but God's
These conflict thoughts are meaningless."*

W 74 L 4. If there is one conflict area which seems particularly difficult to resolve, single it out for special consideration. Think about it briefly but very specifically, identify the particular person or persons and the situation or situations involved, and tell yourself:

*"There is no will but God's.
I share it with Him.
My conflicts about _____ cannot be real."* **W(145)**

W 74 L 5. After you have cleared your mind in this way, close your eyes and try to experience the peace to which your reality entitles you. Sink into it, and feel it closing around you. There may be some temptation to mistake these attempts for withdrawal, but the difference is easily detected. If you are succeeding, you will feel a deep sense of joy and an increased alertness, rather than a feeling of drowsiness and enervation. Joy characterizes peace. By this experience will you recognize that you have reached it.

W 74 L 6. If you feel yourself slipping off into withdrawal, quickly repeat the idea for today and try again. Do this as often as neces-

sary. There is definite gain in refusing to allow retreat into withdrawal, even if you do not experience the peace you seek.

W 74 L 7. In the shorter periods, which should be undertaken at regular and predetermined intervals today, say to yourself:

*"There is no will but God's.
I seek His peace today."*

Then try to find what you are seeking. A minute or two every half hour, with eyes closed if possible, would be well spent on this today. **W(146)**

Lesson 75 "The light has come."

W 75 L 1. The light has come. You are healed and you can heal. The light has come. You are saved and you can save. You are at peace and you bring peace with you wherever you go. Darkness and turmoil and death have disappeared. The light has come. Today we celebrate the happy ending to your long dream of disaster. There are no dark dreams now. The light has come.

W 75 L 2. Today the time of light begins for you and everyone. It is a new era, in which a new world is born. The old one has left no trace upon it in its passing. Today we see a different world because the light has come. Our exercises for today will be happy ones, in which we offer thanks for the passing of the old and the beginning of the new. No shadows from the past remain to darken our sight and hide the world forgiveness offers us.

W 75 L 3. Today we will accept the new world as what we want to see. We will be given what we desire. We will to see the light; the light has come.

W 75 L 4. Our longer practice periods will be devoted to looking at the world which our forgiveness shows us. This is what we want to see, and only this. Our single purpose makes our goal inevitable. Today the real world rises before us in gladness, to be seen at last. Sight is given us, now that the light has come. We do not see the ego's shadow on the world today. We see the light, and in it we see Heaven's reflection lie across the world.

W 75 L 5. Begin the[207] practice period by telling yourself the glad tidings of your release:[208]

*"The light has come.
I have forgiven the world."* **W(147)**

Dwell not upon the past today. Keep a completely open mind, washed of all past ideas and clean of every concept you have made. You have forgiven the world today. You can look upon it now as if you never saw it before. You do not know yet what it looks like. You merely wait to have it shown to you. [209]While you wait, repeat several times slowly and in complete patience;

*"The light has come.
I have forgiven the world."*

W 75 L 6. Realize that your forgiveness entitles you to vision. Understand that the Holy Spirit never fails to give the gift of sight to the forgiving. Believe He will not fail you now. You have forgiven the world. He will be with you as you watch and wait. He will show[210] what true vision sees. It is His Will, and you have joined with Him.

W 75 L 7. Wait patiently for Him. He will be there. The light has come. You have forgiven the world. Tell Him you know you cannot fail because you trust in Him.[211] Tell yourself you wait in cer-

---

[207] Handwritten mark-up suggests (longer).
[208] **Luke 1:19** And the angel answered and said to him, "I am Gabriel, who stands in the presence of God, and was sent to speak to you and bring you these glad tidings."
[209] Handwritten mark-up suggests(And).
[210] Handwritten mark-up suggests (you).
[211] Handwritten mark-up suggests (And).

tainty to look upon the world He promised you. From this time forth you will see differently. Today the light has come. And you will see the world that has been promised you since time began, and in which is the end of time ensured.

W 75 L 8. The shorter practice periods, too, will be joyful reminders of your release. Remind yourself every quarter of an hour or so that today is a time for special celebration. Give thanks for mercy and the Love of God. Rejoice in the power of forgiveness to heal your sight completely. Be confident that on this day there is a new beginning. Without the darkness of the past upon your eyes, you cannot fail to see today. And what you see will be so welcome that you will gladly extend today forever. Say, then:

> "The light has come.
> I have forgiven the world." **W(148)**

Should you be tempted, say to anyone who seems to pull you back to darkness:

> "The light has come.
> I have forgiven you."

W 75 L 9. We dedicate this day to the serenity in which God would have you be. Keep it in your awareness of yourself and see it everywhere today, as we celebrate the beginning of your vision, and the sight of the real world which has come to replace the unforgiven world you thought was real. **W(149)**

Lesson 76 "I am under no laws but God's"

W 76 L 1. We have observed before how many senseless things have seemed to you to be salvation. Each has imprisoned you with laws as senseless as itself. You are not bound by them. Yet to understand that this is so, you must first realize salvation lies not there. While you would seek for it in things that have no meaning, you bind yourself to laws that make no sense.

W 76 L 2. Thus do you seek to prove salvation is where it is not. Today we will be glad you cannot prove it. For if you could, you would forever seek[212] where it is not and never find it. The idea for today tells you once again how simple is salvation. Look for it where it waits for you, and there it will be found. Look nowhere else, for it is nowhere else.

W 76 L 3. Think of the freedom in the recognition that you are not bound by all the strange and twisted laws which you have set up to save you. You really think that you would starve unless you have stacks of green paper strips and piles of metal discs. You really think a small round pellet or some fluid pushed into your veins through a sharpened needle will ward off death. You really think you are alone unless another body is with you.

W 76 L 4. It is insanity that thinks these things. You call them laws, and put them under different names in a long catalogue of rituals that have no use and serve no purpose. You think you must obey the "laws" of medicine, of economics, and of health. Protect the body and you will be saved. These are not laws, but madness.

W 76 L 5. The body is endangered by the mind that hurts itself. The body suffers[213] that the mind will fail to see it is the victim of itself. The body's suffering is a mask the mind holds up to hide what really suffers. It would not understand it is its own enemy; that it attacks itself and wants to die. It is from this your **W(150)** "laws" would save the body. It is for this you think you are a body.

W 76 L 6. There are no laws except the laws of God. This needs repeating, - over and over until you realize that it applies to everything that you have made in opposition to His Will. Your magic has no meaning. What it is meant to save does not exist. Only what it is meant to hide will save you.

W 76 L 7. The laws of God can never be replaced. We will devote today to rejoicing that this is so. It is no longer a truth which we would hide. We realize instead it is a truth which keeps us free forever.[214] Magic imprisons, but the laws of God set free. The light has come because there are no laws but His.

W 76 L 8. We will begin the longer practice periods today with a short review of the different kinds of "laws" we have believed we must obey. These would include, for example, the laws of nutrition, of immunization, of medication, and of the body's protection in innumerable ways. Think further; you believe in laws of friendship, of "good" relationships and reciprocity.

W 76 L 9. Perhaps you even think that there are laws which set forth what is God's and what is yours. Many "religions" have been based on this. They would not save, but damn in Heaven's name. Yet they are no more strange than other "laws" you hold must be obeyed to make you safe.

W 76 L 10. There are no laws but God's. Dismiss all foolish magical beliefs today, and hold your mind in silent readiness to hear the Voice that speaks the truth to you. You will be listening to One Who says there is no loss under the laws of God. Payment is neither given nor received. Exchange cannot be made, there are no substitutes, and nothing is replaced by something else. God's laws forever give and never take. **W(151)**

W 76 L 11. Hear Him Who tells you this, and realize how foolish are the laws you thought upheld the world you thought you saw. Then listen further. He will tell you more. About the love your Father has for you. About the endless joy He offers you. About His yearning for His only Son, created as His channel for creation; denied to Him by his belief in hell.

W 76 L 12. Let us today open God's channels to Him, and let His Will extend through us to Him. Thus is creation endlessly increased. His Voice will speak of this to us, as well as of the joys of Heaven which His laws keep limitless forever. We will now[215] repeat today's idea until we have listened and understood there are no laws but God's. Then we will tell ourselves, as a dedication with which the practice period concludes:

> "I am under no laws but God's."

W 76 L 13. We will repeat this dedication as often as possible today; at least four or five times an hour, as well as in response to any temptation to experience ourselves as subject to other laws throughout the day. It is our statement of freedom from all danger and all tyranny. It is our acknowledgment that God is our Father, and that His Son is saved. **W(152)**

Lesson 77 "I am entitled to miracles."

W 77 L 1. You are entitled to miracles because of what you are. You will receive miracles because of what God is. And you will offer miracles because you are one with God. Again, how simple is salvation! It is merely a statement of your true identity. It is this that we will celebrate today.

W 77 L 2. Your claim to miracles does not lie in your illusions about yourself. It does not depend on any magical powers you have ascribed to yourself, nor on any of the rituals you have devised. It is inherent in the truth of what you are. It is implicit in what God your Father is. It was ensured in your creation, and guaranteed by the laws of God.

W 77 L 3. Today we will claim the miracles which are your right, since they belong to you. You have been promised full release from

---

[212] Handwritten mark-up suggests (salvation).
[213] Handwritten mark-up suggests (just in order).

[214] **John 8:32** "And you shall know the truth, and the truth shall make you free."
[215] *Urtext* manuscript has "**not**" which is clearly inappropriate. Handwritten mark-up strikes the word, as does *FIP*, but we think it was probably supposed to be "**now**" instead of "**not**" as this is one of the most common "typos" in English. The *Notes* has the glyph for "now."

the world you made. You have been assured that the Kingdom of God is within you, and can never be lost[216] We ask no more than what belongs to us in truth. Today, however, we will also make sure that we will not content ourselves with less.

W 77 L 4. Begin the longer practice periods[217] by telling yourself quite confidently that you are entitled to miracles. Closing your eyes, remind yourself that you are asking only for what is rightfully yours. Remind yourself also that miracles are never taken from one and given to another, and that in asking for your rights you are upholding the rights of everyone. Miracles do not obey the laws of this world. They merely follow from the laws of God.

W 77 L 5. After this brief introductory phase, wait quietly for the assurance that your request is granted. You have asked for the salvation of the world and for your own. You have requested that you be given the means by which this is accomplished. You cannot fail to be assured in this. You are but asking that the Will of God be done.

W 77 L 6. In doing this, you do not really ask for anything. You state a fact that cannot be denied. **W(153)** The Holy Spirit cannot but assure you that your request is granted. The fact that you accepted must be so. There is no room for doubt and uncertainty today. We are asking a real question at last. The answer is a simple statement of a simple fact. You will receive the assurance that you seek.

W 77 L 7. Our shorter practice periods will be frequent, and will also be devoted to a reminder of a simple fact. Tell yourself often today:

"I am entitled to miracles."

Ask for them whenever a situation arises in which they are called for. You will recognize these situations,[218] you are not relying on yourself to find them,[219] and you are therefore fully entitled to receive them[220] whenever you ask. Remember, too, not to be satisfied with less than the perfect answer. Be quick to tell yourself, should you be tempted:

"I will not trade miracles for grievances.

I want only what belongs to me.

God has established miracles as my right." **W(154)**

Lesson 78 "Let miracles replace all grievances."

W 78 L 1. Perhaps it is not yet quite clear to you that each decision that you make is one between a grievance and a miracle. Each grievance stands like a dark shield of hate before the miracle it would conceal. And as you raise it up before your eyes, you will not see the miracle beyond. Yet all the while it waits for you in light, but you behold your grievances instead.

W 78 L 2. Today we go beyond the grievances, to look upon the miracle instead. We will reverse the way you see by not allowing sight to stop before it sees. We will not wait before the shield of hate, but lay it down and gently lift our eyes in silence, to behold the Son of God.

W 78 L 3. He waits for you behind your grievances, and as you lay them down he will appear in shining light where each one stood before. For every grievance is a block to sight, and as it lifts, you see the Son of God where he has always been. He stands in light, but you were in the dark. Each grievance made the darkness deeper, and you could not see. Today we will attempt to see God's Son. We will not let ourselves be blind to him; we will not look upon our grievances. So is the seeing of the world reversed, as we look out toward truth, away from fear.

W 78 L 4. We will select one person you have used as target for your grievances, and lay the grievances aside, and look at him. Someone, perhaps, you fear and even hate; someone you think you love who angers you; someone you call a friend, but whom you see as difficult at times, or hard to please; demanding, irritating, or untrue to the ideal he should accept as his according to the role you set for him.

W 78 L 5. You know the one to choose; his name has crossed your mind already. He will be the one of whom we ask God's Son be shown to us.[221] Through seeing him behind the grievances that we[222] have held against him, you will learn **W(155)** that what lay hidden while you saw him not is there in everyone, and can be seen. He who was enemy is more than friend when be is freed to take the holy role the Holy Spirit has assigned to him. Let him be Savior unto you today. Such is his role in God your Father's plan.

W 78 L 6. Our longer practice periods today will see him in this role. We[223] will attempt to hold him in our[224] mind, first as you now consider him. We[225] will review his faults, the difficulties you have had with him, the pain he caused you, his neglect, and all the little and the larger hurts he gave. We[226] will regard his body with its flaws and better points as well, as[227] we[228] will think of his mistakes and even of his "sins."

W 78 L 7. Then let us ask of Him who knows this Son of God in his reality and truth, that we may look on him a different way, and see our Savior shining in the light of true forgiveness, given unto us. We ask Him in the Holy Name of God and of His Son, as holy as Himself:

"Let me behold my Savior in this one

You have appointed as the One for me

To ask to lead me to the holy light

In which he stands, that I may join with him."

The body's eyes are closed, and as you think of him who grieved you, let your mind be shown the light in him beyond your grievances.

W 78 L 8. What you have asked for cannot be denied. Your Savior has been waiting long for this. He would be free, and make his freedom yours. The Holy Spirit leans from him to you, seeing no separation in God's Son. And what you see through Him will free you both. Be very quiet now, and look upon your shining Savior. No dark grievances obscure the sight of him. You have allowed the Holy Spirit to express through him the role God gave Him, that you might be saved.

W 78 L 9. God thanks you for these quiet times today, in which you laid your images aside, **W(156)** and looked upon the miracle of love the Holy Spirit showed you in their place. The world and Heaven join in thanking you, for not one Thought of God but must rejoice as you are saved, and all the world with you.

W 78 L 10. We will remember this throughout the day, and take the role assigned to us as part of God's salvation plan, and not our own. Temptation falls away when we allow each one we meet to save us, and refuse to hide his light behind our grievances. To everyone you meet, and to the ones you think of, or remember from the past, allow

---

[216] **Luke 17:21** "Nor will they say, 'See here!' or 'See there!' For indeed, the kingdom of God is within you."
[217] The *Urtext* manuscript has the singular "**period**", with the "**s**" handwritten in.
[218] Handwritten mark-up suggests (And since), beginning a new sentence here.
[219] Handwritten mark-up suggests (the miracles).
[220] Handwritten mark-up suggests (it).

[221] Handwritten mark-up suggests (you).
[222] Handwritten mark-up suggests (you).
[223] Handwritten mark-up suggests (You).
[224] Handwritten mark-up suggests (your).
[225] Handwritten mark-up suggests (You).
[226] Handwritten mark-up suggests (You).
[227] Handwritten mark-up suggests (and).
[228] Handwritten mark-up suggests (you).

the role of Savior to be given, that you may share it with them.[229] For you both, and all the sightless ones as well, we pray:

"Let miracles replace all grievances." **W(157)**

Lesson 79 "Let me recognize the problem so it can be solved."

W 79 L 1. A problem cannot be solved if you do not know what it is. Even if it is really solved already, you will still have the problem because you cannot[230] recognize that it has been solved. This is the situation of the world. The problem of separation, which is really the only problem, has already been solved. But[231] the solution is not recognized because the problem is not recognized.

W 79 L 2. Everyone in this world seems to have his own special problems. Yet they are all the same, and must be recognized as one if the one solution which solves them all is to be accepted. Who can see that a problem has been solved if he thinks the problem is something else? Even if he is given the answer, he cannot see its relevance.

W 79 L 3. That is the position in which you find yourselves now. You have the answer, but you are still uncertain about what the problem is. A long series of different problems seem to confront you, and as one is settled the next one and the next arise. There seems to be no end to them. There is no time in which you feel completely free of problems, and at peace.

W 79 L 4. The temptation to regard problems as many is the temptation to keep the problem of separation unsolved. The world seems to present you with a vast number of problems, each requiring a different answer. This perception places you in a position in which your problem solving must be inadequate, and failure must be [232]inevitable.

W 79 L 5. No-one could solve all the problems the world appears to hold. They seem to be on so many levels, in such varying forms and with such varied content, that they confront you with an impossible situation. Dismay and depression are inevitable as you regard them. Some spring up unexpectedly, just as you think you have resolved the previous ones. Others remain unsolved under a cloud of denial, and rise to haunt you from time to time, only to be hidden again but still unsolved. **W(158)**

W 79 L 6. All this complexity is but a desperate attempt not to recognize the problem, and therefore not to let it be resolved. If you could recognize that your only problem is separation, no matter what form it takes, you could accept the answer because you would see its relevance. Perceiving the underlying constancy in all the problems which confront you, you would understand that you have the means to solve them all. And you would use the means because you recognize the problem.

W 79 L 7. In our longer practice periods,[233] we will ask what the problem is, and what is the answer to it. We will not assume that we already know. We will try to free our minds of all the many different kinds of problems that we think we have. We will try to realize that we have only one problem, which we have failed to recognize. We will ask what it is, and wait for the answer. We will be told. Then we will ask for the solution to it. And we will be told.

W 79 L 8. Our[234] exercises for today will be successful to the extent to which we[235] do not insist on defining the problem. Perhaps we[236] will not succeed in letting all our[237] preconceived notions go, but that is not necessary. All that is necessary is to entertain some doubt about the reality of our[238] version of what our[239] problems are. We[240] are trying to recognize that we[241] have been given the answer by recognizing the problem, so that the problem and the answer can be brought together, and we[242] can be at peace.

W 79 L 9. The shorter practice periods for today will not be set by time, but by need. You will see many problems today, each one calling for an answer. Our efforts will be directed toward recognizing that there is only one problem and one answer. In this recognition are all problems resolved. In this recognition there is peace. **W(159)**

W 79 L 10. Be not deceived by the form of problems today. Whenever any difficulty seems to rise, tell yourself quickly:

"Let me recognize this problem so it can be solved."

Then try to suspend all judgment about what the problem is. If possible, close your eyes for a moment, and ask what it is. You will be heard and you will be answered. **W(160)**

Lesson 80 "Let me recognize my problems have been solved."

W 80 L 1. If you are willing to recognize your problems, you will recognize that you have no problems. Your one central problem has been answered, and you have no other. Therefore you must be at peace. Salvation does[243] depend[244] on recognizing this one problem, and understanding that it has been solved. One problem -- one solution. Salvation is accomplished. Freedom from conflict has been given you. Accept that fact, and you are ready to take your rightful place in God's plan for salvation.

W 80 L 2. Your only problem has been solved! Repeat this over and over to yourself today, with gratitude and conviction. You have recognized your only problem, opening the way for the Holy Spirit to give you God's answer. You have laid deception aside, and seen the light of truth. You have accepted salvation for yourself by bringing the problem to the answer. And you can recognize the answer because the problem has been identified.

W 80 L 3. You are entitled to peace today. A problem that has been resolved cannot trouble you. Only be certain you do not forget that all problems are the same. Their many forms will not deceive you while you remember this. One problem --one solution. Accept the peace this simple statement brings.

W 80 L 4. In our longer practice periods today, we will claim the peace that must be ours when the problem and the answer have been brought together. The problem must be gone because God's answer cannot fail. Having recognized one, you have recognized the other. The solution is inherent in the problem. You are answered and have accepted the answer. You are saved. **W(161)**

W 80 L 5. Now let the peace that your acceptance brings be given you. Close your eyes and receive your reward. Recognize that your problems have been solved. Recognize that you are out of conflict, free and at peace. Above all, remember that you have one problem and that the problem has one solution. It is in this that the simplicity of salvation lies. It is because of this that it is guaranteed to work.

W 80 L 6. Assure yourselves often today that your problems have been solved. Repeat the idea with deep conviction as frequently as possible. And be particularly sure to remember to apply the idea for today to any specific problem that may arise. Say quickly:

"Let me recognize this problem has been solved."

---

[229] Handwritten mark-up suggests (him).
[230] Handwritten mark-up suggests (will not).
[231] Handwritten mark-up suggests(Yet).
[232] Handwritten mark-up suggests(is).
[233] Handwritten mark-up suggests (today).
[234] Handwritten mark-up suggests (The).
[235] Handwritten mark-up suggests (you).
[236] Handwritten mark-up suggests (you).
[237] Handwritten mark-up suggests (your).
[238] Handwritten mark-up suggests (your).
[239] Handwritten mark-up suggests (your).
[240] Handwritten mark-up suggests (You).
[241] Handwritten mark-up suggests (you)
[242] Handwritten mark-up suggests (you)
[243] Handwritten mark-up suggests (thus).
[244] Handwritten mark-up suggests (s).

Let us be determined not to collect grievances today. Let us be determined to be free of problems that do not exist. The means is simple honesty. Do not deceive yourself about what the problem is, and you must recognize it has been solved. **W(162)**

Review 2 (W 80 R2)
Introduction

W 80 R2 1. We are now ready for another review. We will begin where our last review left off, and cover two ideas each day. The earlier part of the day will be devoted to one of these ideas, and the latter part of the day to the other. We will have one longer exercise period and frequent shorter ones in which we practice each of them.

W 80 R2 2. The longer practice periods will follow this general form: Take about 15 minutes for each of them, and begin by thinking about the idea and the comments which are included in the assignments. Devote about 3 or 4[245] minutes to reading them over slowly, several times if you wish, and then close your eyes and listen. Repeat the first phase if you find your mind wandering, but try to spend the major part of the practice period[246] listening quietly but attentively.

W 80 R2 3. There is a message waiting for you. Be confident that you will receive it. Remember that it belongs to you, and that you want it. Do not allow your intent to waver in the face of distracting thoughts. Realize that, whatever form they [247] take, they have no meaning and no power. Replace them with your determination to succeed.

W 80 R2 4. Do not forget that your will has power over fantasies and dreams. Trust it to see you through, and carry you beyond them all. Regard these practice periods as dedications to the way, the truth, and the life.[248] Refuse to be side-tracked into detours, illusions, and thoughts of death. You are dedicated to salvation. Be determined each day not to leave your function unfulfilled.

W 80 R2 5. Reaffirm your determination in the shorter practice periods as well, and using the original form of the idea for general application, and a more specific form when needed. Some specific forms will be included in the comments. **W(163)** These, however, are merely suggestions. It is not the particular words you use that matter. **W(164)**

Lesson 81 Our ideas for review today are: (61-62)

W 81 L 1. 61. "I am the light of the world."

W 81 L 2. How holy am I, who have been given the function of lighting up the world! Let me be still before my holiness. In its calm light let all my conflicts disappear. In its peace let me remember who I am.

W 81 L 3. Some specific forms for applying the idea when specific difficulties seem to arise might be:

"Let me not obscure the light of the world in me."
"Let the light of the world shine through this appearance."
"This shadow will vanish before the light."

W 81 L 4. 62. "Forgiveness is my function as the light of the world."

W 81 L 5. It is through accepting my function that I will see the light in me. And in this light will my function stand clear and perfectly unambiguous before my sight. My acceptance does not depend on my recognizing what my function is, for I do not yet understand forgiveness. Yet I will trust that in the light I will see it as it is.

W 81 L 6. Specific forms for using the idea might include:

"Let this help me learn what forgiveness means."
"Let me not separate my function from my will."
"I would not use this for an alien purpose." **W(165)**

Lesson 82 We will review these ideas today: (63-64)

W 82 L 1. 63. "The light of the world brings peace to every mind through my forgiveness."

W 82 L 2. My forgiveness is the means by which the light of the world finds expression through me. My forgiveness is the means by which I become aware of the light of the world in me. My forgiveness is the means by which the world is healed, together with myself. Let me, then, forgive the world that it may be healed along with me.

W 82 L 3. Suggestions for specific forms for applying this idea are:

"Let[249] peace extend from my mind to yours, (name)"
"I share the light of the world with you, (name)"
"Through my forgiveness I can see this as it is."

W 82 L 4. 64. "Let me not forget my function."

W 82 L 5. I would not forget my function because I would remember my Self. I cannot fulfill my function by forgetting.[250] And unless I fulfill my function, I will not experience the joy that God intends for me.

W 82 L 6. Suitable specific forms of this idea include:

"Let me not use this to hide my function from me."
"I would use this as an opportunity to fulfill my function."
"This may threaten my ego, but cannot change my function in any way." **W(166)**

Lesson 83 Today let us review these ideas: (65-66)

W 83 L 1. 65. "My only function is the one God gave me."

W 83 L 2. I have no function but the one God gave me. This recognition releases me from all conflict, because it means I cannot have conflicting goals. With one purpose only, I am always certain what to do, what to say, and what to think. All doubt must disappear and[251] I acknowledge that my only function is the one God gave me.

W 83 L 3. More specific applications of this idea might take these forms:

"My perception of this does not change my function."
"This does not give me a function other than the one God gave me."
"Let me not use this to justify a function God did not give to me."

W 83 L 4. 66. "My happiness and my function are one."

W 83 L 5. All things that come from God are one. They come from Oneness, and must be received as one. Fulfilling my function is my happiness because both come from the same Source. And I must learn to recognize what makes me happy if I would find happiness.

W 83 L 6. Some useful forms for specific applications of this idea are:

"This cannot separate my happiness from my function."
"The oneness of my happiness and my function remains wholly

---

[245] Handwritten mark-up suggests (some three or four).
[246] Handwritten mark-up suggests (time).
[247] Handwritten mark-up suggests(such thoughts may).
[248] **John 14:6** Jesus said to him, "I am the way, the truth, and the life. No one comes to the Father except through Me."
[249] *Urtext* manuscript has the word "to" crossed out; "Let ~~to~~ peace ..."
[250] Handwritten mark-up suggests (if I forget it).
[251] Handwritten mark-up suggests (as). The handwriting appears different. This could be a correction.

unaffected by this."

"Nothing, including this, can justify the illusion of happiness apart from my function." **W(167)**

Lesson 84 These are the ideas for today's review: (67-68)

W 84 L 1. 67. "Love created me like Itself."

W 84 L 2. I am in the likeness of my Creator.[252] I cannot suffer, I cannot experience loss, and I cannot die. I am not a body. I would recognize my reality today. I will worship no idols, nor raise my own self-concepts to replace my Self. I am in the likeness of my Creator. Love created me like Itself.

W 84 L 3. You might find these specific forms helpful in applying the idea:

"Let me not see an illusion of myself in this."

"As I look on this, let me remember my Creator."

"My Creator did not create this as I see it."

W 84 L 4. 68. "Love holds no grievances."

W 84 L 5. Grievances are completely alien to love. Grievances attack love, and keep its light obscure. If I hold grievances I am attacking love, and therefore attacking my Self. My Self thus becomes alien to me. I am determined not to attack my Self today, so that I can remember who I am.

W 84 L 6. These specific forms for applying this idea would be helpful:

"This is no justification for denying my Self."

"I will not use this to attack love."

"Let this not tempt me to attack myself." **W(168)**

Lesson 85 Today's review will cover these ideas: (69-70)

W 85 L 1. 69. "My grievances hide the light of the world in me."

W 85 L 2. My grievances show me what is not there, and hide from me what I would see. Recognizing this, what do I want my grievances for? They keep me in darkness and hide the light. Grievances and light cannot go together, but light and vision must be joined for me to see. To see, I must lay grievances aside. I want to see, and this will be the means by which I will succeed.

W 85 L 3. Specific applications of this idea might be made in these forms:

"Let me not use this as a block to sight."

"The light of the world will shine all this away."

"I have no need for this. I want to see."

W 85 L 4. 70. "My salvation comes from me."

W 85 L 5. Today I will recognize where my salvation is. It is in me because its Source is there. It has not left its Source and so it cannot have left my mind. I will not look for it outside myself. It is not found outside and then brought in. But from within me it will reach beyond, and everything I see will but reflect the light that shines in me and in itself.

W 85 L 6. These forms of the idea are suitable for more specific application[253]:

"Let this not tempt me to look away from me for my salvation."

"I will not let this interfere with my awareness of the Source of my salvation."

"This has no power to remove salvation from me." **W(169)**

Lesson 86 These ideas are for review today: (71-72)

W 86 L 1. 71 "Only God's plan for salvation will work."

W 86 L 2. It is senseless for me to search wildly about for salvation. I have seen it in many people and in many things, but when I reached for it, it was not there. I was mistaken about where it is. I was mistaken about what it is. I will undertake no more idle seeking. Only God's plan for salvation will work. And I will rejoice because His plan can never fail.

W 86 L 3. These are some suggested forms for applying this idea specifically:

"God's plan for salvation will save me from my perception of this."

"This is no exception in God's plan for my salvation."

"Let me perceive this only in the light of God's plan for salvation."

W 86 L 4. 72 "Holding grievances is an attack on God's plan for salvation."

W 86 L 5. Holding grievances is an attempt to prove that God's plan for salvation will not work. Yet only His plan will work. By holding grievances I am therefore excluding my own only hope of salvation from my awareness. I would no longer defeat my own best interests in this insane way. I would accept God's plan for salvation and be happy.

W 86 L 6. Specific applications of this idea might be in these forms:

"I am choosing between misperception and salvation as I look on this." *"If I see grounds for grievances in this, I will not see the grounds for my salvation."*

"This calls for salvation, not attack." **W(170)**

Lesson 87 Our review today will cover these ideas: (73-74)

W 87 L 1. 73 "I will there be light."

W 87 L 2. I will use the power of my will today. It is not my will to grope about in darkness, fearful of shadows and afraid of things unseen and unreal. Light shall be my guide today. I will follow it where it leads me, and I will look on only what it shows me. This day I will experience the peace of true perception.

W 87 L 3. These forms of this idea would be helpful for specific applications:[254]

"This cannot hide the light I will to see."

"You stand with me in light, (name)"

"In the light this will look different."

W 87 L 4. 74 "There is no will but God's."

W 87 L 5. I am safe today because there is no will but God's. I can become afraid only when I believe that there is another will. I try to attack only when I am afraid, and only when I try to attack can I believe that my eternal safety is threatened. Today I will recognize that all this has not occurred. I am safe because there is no will but God's.

W 87 L 6. These are some useful forms of this idea for specific applications:

"Let me perceive this in accordance with the Will of God."

---

[252] **Genesis 1:26-27** Then God said, "Let Us make man in Our image, according to Our likeness; let them have dominion over the fish of the sea, over the birds of the air, and over the cattle, over all the earth and over every creeping thing that creeps on the earth." So God created man in His own image; in the image of God He created him; male and female He created them.

[253] Handwritten mark-up suggests (s).

[254] The *Urtext* manuscript reads "application" in the singular, but both the *Notes* and FIP have it as plurar, so we do also.

"It is God's Will you are His Son (name), and mine as well."
"This is part of God's Will for me, however I may see it." **W(171)**

Lesson 88 Today we will review these ideas: (75-76)

W 88 L 1. 75 **"The light has come."**

W 88 L 2. In choosing salvation rather than attack I merely choose to recognize what is already there. Salvation is a decision made already. Attack and grievances are not there to choose. That is why I always choose between truth and illusion; between what is there and what is not. The light has come. I can but choose the light, for it has no alternative. It has replaced the darkness, and the dark is gone.

W 88 L 3. These would prove useful forms for specific applications of this idea:

"This cannot show me darkness, for the light has come."
"The light in you is all that I would see, (name)"
"I would see in this only what is there."

W 88 L 4. 76 **"I am under no laws but God's."**

W 88 L 5. Here is the perfect statement of my freedom. I am under no laws but God's. I am constantly tempted to make up other laws, and give them power over me. I suffer only because of my belief in them. They have no real effect on me at all. I am perfectly free of the effects of all laws save God's. And His are the laws of freedom.

W 88 L 6. For specific forms in applying this idea, these would be useful:

"My perception of this shows me I believe in laws which do not exist."
"I see only the laws of God at work in this."
"Let me allow God's laws to work in this, and not my own."
W(172)

Lesson 89 These are our review ideas for today: (77-78)

W 89 L 1. 77 **"I am entitled to miracles."**

W 89 L 2. I am entitled to miracles because I am under no laws but God's. His laws release me from all grievances, and replace them with miracles. And I would accept the miracles in place of the grievances, which are but illusions that hide the miracles beyond. Now I would accept only what the laws of God entitle me to have, that I may use it on behalf of the function He has given me.

W 89 L 3. You might use these suggestions for specific applications of this idea:

"Behind this is a miracle to which I am entitled."
"Let me not hold a grievance against you (name), but offer you the miracle that belongs to you instead."
"Seen truly, this offers me a miracle."

W 89 L 4. 78 **"Let miracles replace all grievances."**

W 89 L 5. By this idea do I unite my will with the Holy Spirit's, and perceive them as one. By this idea do I accept my release from hell. By this idea do I express my willingness to have all my illusions be replaced with truth, according to God's plan for my salvation. I would make no exceptions and no substitutes. I want all of Heaven and only Heaven, as God wills me to have.

W 89 L 6. Useful specific forms for applying this idea would be:

"I would not hold this grievance apart from my salvation."
"Let our grievances be replaced by miracles, (name)"
"Beyond this is the miracle by which all my grievances are replaced." **W(173)**

Lesson 90 For this review we will use these ideas: (79-80)

W 90 L 1. 79 **"Let me recognize the problem so it can be solved."**

W 90 L 2. Let me realize today that the problem is always some form of grievance which I would cherish. Let me also understand that the solution is always a miracle with which I let the grievance be replaced. Today I would remember the simplicity of salvation by reinforcing the lesson that there is one problem and one solution. The problem is a grievance; the solution is a miracle. And I invite the solution to come to me through my forgiveness of the grievance, and my welcome of the miracle which takes its place.

W 90 L 3. Specific applications of this idea might be in these forms:

"This presents a problem to me which I would have resolved."
"The miracle behind this grievance will resolve it for me."
"The answer to this problem is the miracle which it conceals."

W 90 L 4. 80 **"Let me recognize my problems have been solved."**

W 90 L 5. I seem to have problems only because I am misusing time. I believe that the problem comes first, and time must elapse before it can be worked out. I do not see the problem and the answer as simultaneous in their occurrence. That is because I do not yet realize that God has placed the answer together with the problem, so that they cannot be separated by time. The Holy Spirit will teach me this, if I will let Him. And I will understand it is impossible that I could have a problem which has not been solved already.

W 90 L 6. These forms of the idea will be useful for specific applications:

"I need not wait for this to be resolved."
"The answer to this problem is already given me, if I will accept it."
"Time cannot separate this problem from its solution." **W(174)**

Lesson 91 "Miracles are seen in light."

W 91 L 1. It is important to remember that miracles and vision necessarily go together. This needs repeating and frequent repeating. It is a central idea in your new thought system and the perception which it produces. The miracle is always there. Its presence is not caused by your vision; its absence is not the result of your failure to see. It is only your awareness of miracles that is affected. You will see it[255] in the light; you will not see it[256] in the dark.

W 91 L 2. To you, then, light is crucial. While you remain in darkness the miracle remains unseen. Thus you are convinced it is not there. This follows from the premises from which the darkness comes. Denial of light leads to failure to perceive it. Failure to perceive light is to perceive darkness. The light is useless to you then, even though it is there. You cannot use it because its presence is unknown to you. And the seeming reality of the darkness makes the idea of light meaningless.

W 91 L 3. To be told that what you do not see is there sounds like insanity. It is very difficult to become convinced that it is insanity not to see what is there, and to see what is not there instead. You do not doubt that the body's eyes can see. You do not doubt the images they show you are reality. Your faith lies in the darkness, not the light. How can this be reversed? For you it is impossible, but you are not alone in this.[257]

---

[255] Handwritten mark-up suggests (them).
[256] Handwritten mark-up suggests (them).
[257] **Matthew 19:26** But Jesus looked at them and said to them, "With men this is impossible, but with God all things are possible."

W 91 L 4. Your efforts, however little they may be, have strong support. Did you but realize how great[258] this strength, your doubts would vanish. Today we will devote ourselves to the attempt to let you feel this strength. When you have felt the strength in you, which makes all miracles within your easy reach, you will not doubt. The miracles your sense of weakness hides will leap into awareness as you feel the[259] strength in you. **W(175)** September 21, 1969

W 91 L 5. Three times today, set aside about 10[260] minutes for a quiet time in which you try to leave your weakness behind. This is accomplished very simply, as you instruct yourself that you are not a body. Faith goes to[261] what you want, and you instruct your mind accordingly. Your will remains your teacher, and your will has all the strength to do whatever[262] it desires. You can escape the body if you choose. You can experience the strength in you.

W 91 L 6. Begin the longer practice periods with this statement of true cause and effect relationships:

"Miracles are seen in light.
The body's eyes do not perceive the light.
But I am not a body. What am I?"

The question with which this statement ends is needed for our exercises today. What you think you are is a belief to be undone. But what you really are must be revealed to you. The belief you are a body calls for correction, being a mistake. The truth of what you are calls on the strength in you to bring to your awareness what the mistake concealed.

W 91 L 7. If you are not a body, what are you? You need to be aware of what the Holy Spirit uses to replace the image of a body in your mind. You need to feel something to put your faith in, as you lift it from the body. You need a real experience of something else, something more solid and more sure; more worthy of your faith, and really there.

W 91 L 8. If you are not a body, what are you? Ask this in honesty, and then devote several minutes to allowing your mistaken thoughts about your attributes to be corrected, and their opposites to take their place. Say, for example:

"I am not weak, but strong."
"I am not helpless, but all powerful."
"I am not limited, but unlimited."
"I am not doubtful, but certain."
"I am not an illusion, but a reality."
"I cannot see in darkness, but in light." **W(176)**

W 91 L 9. In the second phase of the exercise period, try to experience these truths about yourself. Concentrate particularly on the experience of strength. Remember that all sense of weakness is associated with the belief[263] you are a body, a belief that is mistaken and deserves no faith. Try to remove your faith from it, if only for a moment. You will become accustomed to keeping faith with the more worthy in you as we go along.

W 91 L 10. Relax for the rest of the practice period, confident that your efforts, however meager, are fully supported by the strength of God and all His Thoughts. It is from Them your strength will come. It is through Their strong support that you will feel the strength in you. They are united with you in this practice period, in which you share a purpose like Their own. Theirs is the light in which you will see miracles, because Their strength is yours. Their strength becomes your eyes, that you may see.

W 91 L 11. Five or six times an hour, at reasonably regular intervals, remind yourself that miracles are seen in light. Also, be sure to meet temptation with today's idea. This form would be helpful for this special purpose:

"Miracles are seen in light.
Let me not close my eyes because of this." **W(177)**

Lesson 92 "Miracles are seen in light, and light and strength are one."

W 92 L 1. The idea for today is an extension of the previous one. You do not think of light in terms of strength and darkness in terms of weakness. That is because your idea of what seeing means is tied up with the body, and its eyes and brain. This is why you believe that you can change what you see by keeping[264] little bits of glass or other clear material before your eyes held in a frame or placed against the eye. These are[265] among the many magical beliefs that come from the conviction you are a body, and the body's eyes can see.

W 92 L 2. You also believe the body's brain can think. If you but understood the nature of thought, you could but laugh at this insane idea. It is as if you thought you held the match that lights the sun, and gives it all its warmth; or that you held the universe imprisoned in your hand, securely bound until you let it go.[266] Yet this is no more foolish than to believe[267] the body's eyes can see; the brain can think.[268]

W 92 L 3. It is God's strength in you that is the light in which you see, as it is His Mind with which you think. His strength denies your weakness. It is your weakness that sees through the body's eyes, peering about in darkness to behold the likeness of itself; the small, the weak, the sickly and the dying, those in need, the helpless and afraid, the sad, the poor, the starving and the joyless. These are seen through eyes which cannot see and cannot bless.[269]

W 92 L 4. Strength overlooks these things by seeing past appearances. It keeps its steady gaze upon the light that lies beyond them. It unites[270] with light, of which it is a part. It sees itself. It brings the light in which your Self appears. In darkness you perceive a self that is not there. **W(178)** Strength is the truth about you; weakness is an idol falsely worshipped, and adored that strength may be dispelled, and darkness rule where God appointed that there should be light.

W 92 L 5. Strength comes from truth, and shines with light its Source has given it; weakness reflects the darkness of its maker. It is sick and looks on sickness, which is like itself. Truth is a savior, and can only will for happiness and peace for everyone. It gives its strength to everyone who asks, in limitless supply. It sees that lack

---

[258] Possibly this should be "how great **is** this strength." The *Notes* has "how great this this strength" with the first "this" spelled out and crossed out, and the second being the shorthand glyph for "this" which suggests perhaps it originally was meant to be "is" rather than the first written out "this."
[259] Handwritten mark-up suggests (this).
[260] Handwritten mark-up suggests (ten).
[261] Handwritten mark-up suggests (with).
[262] The second part of the word **whate**ver is crossed out by hand.
[263] Handwritten mark-up suggests (that).
[264] Handwritten mark-up suggests (putting).
[265] Handwritten mark-up suggests (This is). It would seem that the antecedent to the pronoun is singular, making the handwritten suggestion a valid correction.
[266] Handwritten mark-up offers an alternative: (or that you held the world within your hand, securely bound ...)
[267] Handwritten mark-up suggests (think?).
[268] Handwritten mark-up suggests (know).
[269] **Jeremiah 5:21**
Hear this now, O foolish people,
Without understanding,
Who have eyes and see not,
And who have ears and hear not:
Mark 8:18 "Having eyes, do you not see? And having ears, do you not hear? And do you not remember?"
[270] The *Urtext* manuscript has "united" which is corrected by handwritten mark-up to the form found in the *Notes* which is "unites." FIP also has "unites."

in anyone would be a lack in all, and so it gives its light that all may see, and benefit as one. Its strength is shared, that it may bring to all the miracle in which they will unite in purpose and forgiveness and in love.

W 92 L 6. Weakness, which looks in darkness, cannot see a purpose in forgiveness and in love. It sees all others different from itself, and nothing in the world which it would share. It judges and condemns, but does not love. In darkness it remains to hide itself, and dreams that it is strong and conquering, a victor over limitations which but grow in darkness to enormous size. It fears and it attacks and hates itself, and darkness covers everything it sees, leaving it dreams as fearful as itself. No miracles are here, but only hate. It separates itself from what it sees, while light and strength perceive themselves as one.

W 92 L 7. The light of strength is not the light you see. It does not change and flicker and go out. It does not shift from night to day and back to darkness 'til the morning comes again. The light of strength is constant, sure as love, forever glad to give itself away because it cannot give but to Itself. No-one can ask in vain to share its sight, and none who enters its abode can leave without a miracle before his eyes, and strength and light abiding in his heart. **W(179)**

W 92 L 8. The strength in you will offer you the light and guide your seeing, so you do not dwell on idle shadows which the body's eyes provide for self-deception. Strength and light unite in you, and where they meet your Self stands ready to embrace you as Its own. Such is the meeting place we try today to find and rest in, for the peace of God is where your Self, His Son, is waiting now to meet Itself again, and be as One.

W 92 L 9. Let us give 20[271] minutes twice today to join this meeting. Let yourself be brought unto your Self. Its strength will be the light in which the gift of sight is given you. Leave, then, the dark a little while today, and we will practice seeing in the light, closing the body's eyes, and asking truth to show us how to find the meeting place of self and Self, where light and strength are one.

W 92 L 10. After the morning meeting,[272] we will use the day in preparation for the time at night when we will meet again in hope and trust. Let us repeat as often as we can the idea for today, and recognize that we are being introduced to sight, and led away from darkness to the light where only miracles can be perceived. **W(180)**

Lesson 93 "Light and joy and peace abide in me."

W 93 L 1. You think you are the home of evil, darkness and sin. You think if anyone could see the truth about you he would be repelled, recoiling from you as if from a poisonous snake. You think if what is true about you were revealed to you, you would be struck with horror so intense that you would rush to death by your own hand, living on after seeing this being impossible.

W 93 L 2. These are beliefs so firmly fixed that it is difficult to help you see that they are based on nothing. That you have made mistakes is obvious. That you have sought salvation in strange ways; have been deceived, deceiving and afraid of foolish fantasies and savage dreams; and have bowed down to idols made of dust; all this is true by what you now believe.

W 93 L 3. Today we question this, not from the point of view of what you think, but from a very different reference point, from which such idle thoughts are meaningless. These thoughts are not according to God's Will. These weird[273] beliefs He does not share with you. This is enough to prove that they are wrong, but you do not perceive that this is so.

W 93 L 4. Why would you not be overjoyed to be assured that all the evil which you think you did was never done, that all your "sins" are nothing; that you are as pure and holy as you were created, and that light and joy and peace abide in you? Your image of yourself cannot withstand the Will of God. You think that this is death, but it is life. You think you are destroyed, but you are saved.

W 93 L 5. The self you made is not the Son of God. Therefore this self does not exist at all. And anything it seems to do and think means nothing. It is neither bad nor good. It is unreal, and nothing more than that. It does not battle with the Son of God. It does not hurt him, nor attack his peace. It has not changed creation, nor reduced eternal sinlessness to sin and love to hate. What power can this self you made possess, when it would contradict the Will of God? **W(181)**

W 93 L 6. Your sinlessness is guaranteed by God. Over and over this must be repeated until it is accepted. It is true. Your sinlessness is guaranteed by God. Nothing can touch it, nor can change what God created as eternal. The self you made, evil and full of sin, is meaningless. Your sinlessness is guaranteed by God, and light and joy and peace abide in you.

W 93 L 7. Salvation requires the acceptance of but one thought; you are as God created you, not what you made of yourself. Whatever evil you may think you did, you are as God created you. Whatever mistakes you made, the truth about you is unchanged. Creation is eternal and unalterable. Your sinlessness is guaranteed by God. You are and will forever be exactly as you were created. Light and joy and peace abide in you because God put them there.

W 93 L 8. In our longer exercise periods today, which would be most profitable if done for the first five minutes of every waking hour, we will begin by stating the truth about our[274] creation:

"Light and joy and peace abide in me.

My sinlessness is guaranteed by God."

Then put away your foolish self-images, and spend the rest of the practice period in trying to experience what God has given you, in place of what you have decreed for yourself.

W 93 L 9. You are what God created, or what you made. One Self is true; the other is not there. Try to experience the unity of your One Self. Try to appreciate Its holiness and the Love from Which[275] It was created. Try not to interfere with the Self Which God created as you by hiding Its majesty behind the tiny idols of evil and sinfulness you have made to replace It. Let It come into Its own. Here you are; This is you. And light and joy and peace abide in you because this is so. **W(182)**

W 93 L 10. You may not be willing or even able to use the first five minutes of each hour for these exercises. Try, however, to do so when you can. At least remember to repeat these thoughts each hour:

"Light and joy and peace abide in me.

My sinlessness is guaranteed by God."

Then try to devote at least a minute or so to closing your eyes and realizing that this is a statement of the truth about you.

W 93 L 11. If a situation arises which seems to be disturbing, quickly dispel the illusion of fear by repeating these thoughts again. Should you be tempted to become angry with someone,[276] tell him silently:

"Light and joy and peace abide in you.

Your sinlessness is guaranteed by God."

---

[271] Handwritten mark-up suggests (twenty).

[272] Handwritten mark-up suggests (Morning and evening we will practice thus.)

[273] The manuscript has a spelling error here "wierd" instead of "weird."

[274] Handwritten mark-up suggests (your).

[275] The capitalization of "**Love**" and "**Which**" is written in by hand in the manuscript.

[276] Handwritten mark-up suggests (one) as in "**someone**". Originally in the *Urtext* manuscript typed "**some**". In the *Notes* it is "someone."

W 93 L 12. You can do much for the world's salvation today. You can do much today to bring you closer to[277] the part in salvation which God has assigned to you. And you can do much today to bring the conviction to your mind that the idea for the day is true indeed. **W(183)**

September 24, 1969

Lesson 94 "I am as God created me."

W 94 L 1. Today we continue with the one idea which brings complete salvation; the one statement which makes all forms of temptation powerless; the one thought which renders the ego silent and entirely undone. You are as God created you. The sounds of this world are still, the sights of this world disappear, and all the thoughts which this world ever held are wiped away forever by this one idea. Here is salvation accomplished. Here is sanity restored.

W 94 L 2. True light is strength, and strength is sinlessness. If you remain as God created you, you must be strong, and light must be in you. He Who ensured your sinlessness must be the guarantee of strength and light as well. You are as God created you. Darkness cannot obscure the glory of the Son of God.[278] You stand in light, strong in the sinlessness in which you were created, and in which you will remain throughout eternity.

W 94 L 3. Today we will again devote the first five minutes of each waking hour to the attempt to feel the truth in you. Begin these times of searching with these words:

"I am as God created me.

I am His Son eternally."

Now try to reach the Son of God in you. This is the Self Which never sinned, nor made an image to replace reality. This is the Self Which never left Its home in God, to walk the world uncertainly. This is the Self Which knows no fear, nor could conceive of loss or suffering or death.

W 94 L 4. Nothing is required[279] of you to reach this goal except to lay all idols and self-images aside; go past the long list of attributes, both "good" and "bad," you have ascribed to yourself; and wait in silent expectancy for the truth. God has Himself promised that it will be revealed to all who ask for it.[280] You are asking now. You will not fail because He cannot fail. **W(184)**

W 94 L 5. If you do not meet the requirement of practicing for the first five minutes of every hour, at least remind yourself hourly:

"I am as God created me.

I am His Son eternally."

Tell yourself frequently today that you are as God created you. And be sure to respond to anyone who seems to irritate you with these words:

"You are as God created You.

You are His Son eternally."

Make every effort to do the hourly exercises today. Each one you do will be a giant stride toward your release, and a milestone in learning the thought system which this course sets forth. **W(185)**

Lesson 95 "I am One Self, united with My Creator."

W 95 L 1. Today's idea accurately describes you as God created you. You are one within yourself, and One with Him. Yours is the unity of all creation. Your perfect unity makes change in you impossible. You do not accept this, and you fail to realize it must be so, only because you believe that you have changed yourself already.

W 95 L 2. You see yourself as a ridiculous parody on God's creation, weak, vicious, ugly and sinful, miserable and beset with pain. Such is your version of your self; a self divided into many warring parts, separated from God, and tenuously held together by its erratic and capricious maker, to which you pray. It does not hear your prayers, for it is deaf. It does not see the Oneness[281] in you, for it is blind. It does not understand you are the Son of God, for it is senseless and understands nothing.

W 95 L 3. We will attempt today to be aware only of what can hear and see, and what makes perfect sense. We will again direct our exercises toward reaching your One Self, which is united with Its Creator. In patience and in hope we try again today. The use of the first 5[282] minutes of every waking hour for practicing the idea for the day has special advantages at the stage of learning in which you are at present.

W 95 L 4. It is difficult at this point not to allow your mind to wander if it undertakes extended attempts.[283] To have surely realized this by now. You have seen the extent of your lack of mental discipline, and of your need for mind training. It is necessary that you be aware of this, for it is indeed a hindrance to your advance.

W 95 L 5. Frequent but shorter practice periods have other advantages for you at this time. In addition to recognizing your difficulties with sustained attention, you must also have noticed that, unless you are reminded of your purpose frequently, you tend to forget about it for long periods of time. You often fail to remember **W(186)** the short applications of the idea for the day, and you have not yet formed the habit of using it[284] as an automatic response to temptation.

W 95 L 6. Structure, then, is necessary for you at this time, planned to include frequent reminders of your goal, and regular attempts to reach it. Regularity in terms of time is not the ideal requirement for the most beneficial form of practice in salvation. It is advantageous, however, for these whose motivation is inconsistent, and who remain heavily defended against learning.

W 95 L 7. We will therefore keep to the five minutes an hour practice periods for a while, and urge you to omit as few as possible. Using the first five minutes of the hour will be particularly helpful, since it imposes firmer structure. Do not, however, use your lapses from this schedule as an excuse not to return to it again as soon as you can.

W 95 L 8. There may well be a temptation to regard the day as lost because you have already failed to do what is required. This should, however, merely be recognized as what it is; a refusal to let your mistakes[285] be corrected, and an unwillingness to try again. The Holy Spirit is not delayed in His teaching by your mistakes. He can be held back only by your unwillingness to let them go.

W 95 L 9. Let us therefore be determined, particularly for the next week or so, to be willing to forgive ourselves for our lapses in diligence, and our failures to follow the instructions for practicing the day's idea. This tolerance for weakness will enable us to overlook it, rather than give it power to delay our learning. If we give it power to do this, we are regarding it as strength, and are confusing strength and weakness.

W 95 L 10. When you fail to comply with the requirements of this course you have merely made a mistake. This calls for correction, and for nothing else. **W(187)** To allow a mistake to continue is to make additional mistakes, based on the first, and reinforcing it. It is

---

[277] Handwritten mark-up suggests (accepting).
[278] Handwritten mark-up suggests (God's Son).
[279] Handwritten mark-up suggests (asked).
[280] **Matthew 7:7** "Ask, and it will be given to you; seek, and you will find; knock, and it will be opened to you."

[281] Handwritten mark-up suggests (oneness).
[282] Handwritten mark-up suggests (five).
[283] Handwritten mark-up suggests (practicing).
[284] Handwritten mark-up suggests (the idea).
[285] Handwritten mark-up suggests (mistake).

this process which must be laid aside, for it is but another way in which you would defend illusions against the truth.

W 95 L 11. Let all these errors go by recognizing them for what they are. They are attempts to keep you unaware you are One Self, united with your Creator, at one with every aspect of creation, and limitless in power and in peace. This is the truth, and nothing else is true. Today we will affirm this truth again, and try to reach the place in you in which there is no doubt that only this is true. Begin the longer practice periods with this assurance, given[286] to your mind with all the certainty that you can give:

> "I am One Self, united with my Creator,
>
> At one with every aspect of creation,
>
> And limitless in power and in peace."

W 95 L 12. Then close your eyes and tell yourself again, slowly and thoughtfully, attempting to allow the meaning of the words to sink into your mind, replacing false ideas:

> "I am One Self."

Repeat this several times, and then attempt to feel the meaning which the words convey. You are One Self, united and secure in light and joy and peace. You are God's Son, One Self with One Creator and one goal; to bring awareness of this Oneness to all minds, that true creation may extend the Allness and the Unity of God.

W 95 L 13. You are One Self, complete and healed and whole, with power to lift the veil of darkness from the world, and let the light in you come through to teach the world the truth about itself. You are One Self, in perfect harmony with all there is and all that there will be. You are One Self, the holy Son of God, united with your brothers in this Self; united with your Father in His Will. **W(188)**

W 95 L 14. Feel this One Self in you, and let It shine away all your illusions and your doubts. This is your Self, the Son of God Himself, sinless as Its Creator, with His strength within you, and His Love forever yours. You are One Self, and it is given you to feel this Self within you, and to cast all your illusions out of the One Mind Which is this Self, the holy truth in you.

W 95 L 15. Do not forget today. We need your help, your little part in bringing happiness to all the world. And Heaven looks to you in confidence that you will try today. Share, then, its surety, for it is yours. Be vigilant. Do not forget today.

W 95 L 16. Throughout the day do not forget your goal. Repeat today's idea as frequently as possible, and understand each time you do so, someone hears the voice of hope, the stirring of the truth within his mind, the gentle rustling of the wings[287] of peace. Your own acknowledgment you are One Self, united with your Father, is a call to all the world, to be at one with you.

W 95 L 17. To everyone you meet today be sure to give the promise of today's idea, and tell him this:

> "You are One Self with me,
>
> United with our Creator in this Self.
>
> I honor you because of what I am,
>
> And what He is, Who loves us both as one." **W(189)**

Lesson 96 "Salvation comes from my One Self."

W 96 L 1. Although you are One Self, you experience yourself as two; as both good and evil, loving and hating, mind and body. This sense of being split into opposites induces feelings of acute and constant conflict, and leads to frantic attempts to reconcile the contradictory aspects of this self-perception. You have sought many such solutions, and none of them has worked. The opposites you see in you will never be compatible. But one exists.

W 96 L 2. The fact that truth and illusion cannot be reconciled no matter how you try, what means you use and where you see the problem, must be accepted if you would be saved. Until you have accepted this, you will attempt an endless list[288] of goals you cannot reach; a senseless series of expenditures of time and effort, hopefulness and doubt, each one as futile as the one before, and failing as the next one surely will.

W 96 L 3. Problems which have no meaning cannot be resolved within the framework they are set. Two selves in conflict could not be resolved, and good and evil have no meeting place. The self you made can never be your Self, nor can your Self be split in two and still be what it is, and must forever be.

W 96 L 4. A mind and body cannot both exist. Make no attempt to reconcile the two, for one denies the other can be real. If you are physical your mind is gone from your self-concept, for it has no place in which it could be really part of you. If you are Spirit, then the body must be meaningless to your reality.

W 96 L 5. Spirit makes use of mind as means to find Its Self-expression. And the mind that serves the Spirit is at peace and filled with joy. Its power comes from Spirit, and it is fulfilling happily its function here. Yet mind can also see itself divorced from Spirit, and perceive itself within a body it confuses with itself. Without its function then, it has no peace, and happiness is alien to its thoughts. **W(190)**

W 96 L 6. Yet mind apart from Spirit cannot think. It has denied its Source of strength, and sees itself as helpless, limited and weak. Dissociated from its function now, it thinks it is alone and separate, attacked by armies massed against itself, and hiding in the body's frail support. Now must it reconcile unlike with like, for this is what it thinks that it is for. Waste no more time on this. Who can resolve the senseless conflicts which a dream presents? What could the resolution mean in truth? What purpose could it serve? What is it for?

W 96 L 7. Salvation cannot make illusions real, and solve a problem which does not exist. Perhaps you hope it can. Yet would you have God's plan for the release of His dear Son bring pain to him, and fail to set him free? Your Self retains Its Thoughts, and They remain within your mind and in the Mind of God. The Holy Spirit holds salvation in your mind, and offers it the way to peace.

W 96 L 8. Salvation is a Thought you share with God, because His Voice accepted it for you, and answered in your name that it was done. Thus is salvation kept among the Thoughts your Self holds dear and cherishes for you. We will attempt today to find this Thought, Whose[289] presence in your mind is guaranteed by Him Who speaks to you from your One Self. Our hourly five minute practicing will be a search for Him within your mind. Salvation comes from this One Self through Him Who is the bridge between your mind and It.

W 96 L 9. Wait patiently, and let Him speak to you about your Self, and what your mind can do, restored to It and free to serve Its Will. Begin by saying this:

> "Salvation comes from my One Self.
>
> Its Thoughts are mine to use."

Then seek Its Thoughts, and claim them as your own. **W(191)** These are your own real thoughts you have denied, and let your mind go wandering in a world of dreams, to find illusions in their place. Here are your Thoughts, the only ones you have. Salvation is among Them; find it there.

---

[286] Handwritten mark-up suggests (offered?).
[287] Originally in the *Urtext* manuscript typed "**winds**" the d is changed to a g by hand. This appears to be a spelling correction. The *Notes* has "wings."

[288] Originally typed "endless lists." Handwritten mark-up suggests (an endless list). The *Notes* has "an endless list."
[289] **Handwritten mark-up suggests (thought, whose).**

W 96 L 10. If you succeed, the Thoughts that come to you will tell you you are saved, and that your mind has found the function that it sought to lose. Your Self will welcome it, and give it peace. Restored in strength, it will again flow out from Spirit to the Spirit in all things created by the Spirit as Itself. Your mind will bless all things. Confusion done, you are restored, for you have found your Self.

W 96 L 11. Your Self knows that you cannot fail today. Perhaps your mind remains uncertain yet a little while. Be not dismayed by this. The joy your Self experiences, It will save for you, and it will yet be yours in full awareness. Every time you spend five minutes of the hour seeking Him Who joins your mind and Self, you offer Him another treasure to be kept for you.

W 96 L 12. Each time today you tell your frantic mind salvation comes from your One Self, you lay another treasure in your growing store. And all of it is given everyone who asks for it, and will accept the gift. Think, then, how much is given unto you to give this day, that it be given you! **W(192)**

Lesson 97 "I am Spirit." [290]

W 97 L 1. Today's idea identifies you with your One Self. It accepts no split identity, nor tries to weave opposing factors into unity. It simply states the truth. Practice this truth today as often as you can, for it will bring your mind from conflict to the quiet fields of peace. No chill of fear can enter, for your mind has been absolved of madness, letting go illusions of a split identity.

W 97 L 2. We state again the truth about your Self, the holy Son of God Who rests in you; Whose mind has been restored to sanity. You are the Spirit lovingly endowed with all your Father's Love and peace and joy. You are the Spirit Which completes Himself, and shares His Function as Creator. He is with you always,[291] as you are with Him.

W 97 L 3. Today we try to bring reality still closer to your mind. Each time you practice, awareness is brought a little nearer at least; sometimes a thousand years or more are saved. The minutes which you give are multiplied over and over, for the miracle makes use of time, but is not ruled by it. Salvation is a miracle, the first and last; the first that is the last, for it is one.

W 97 L 4. You are the Spirit in Whose Mind abides the miracle in which all time stands still; the miracle in which a minute spent in using these ideas becomes a time which has no length[292] and which has no end. Give, then, these minutes willingly, and count on Him Who promised to lay timelessness beside them. He will offer all His strength to every little effort which[293] you make.

W 97 L 5. Give Him the minutes which He needs today to help you understand with Him you are the Spirit that abides in Him, and Which calls through His Voice to every living thing; offers His sight to everyone who asks; replaces errors with the simple truth. **W(193)**

W 97 L 6. The Holy Spirit will be glad to take five minutes of each hour from your hands, and carry them around this aching world where pain and misery appear to rule. He will not overlook one open mind that will accept the healing gifts they bring, and He will lay them everywhere He knows they will be welcome. And they will increase in healing power each time someone accepts them as his thoughts, and uses them to heal.

W 97 L 7. Thus will your gifts[294] to Him be multiplied a thousand-fold and tens of thousands more. And when it is returned to you, it will surpass in might the little gift you gave as much as does the radiance of the sun outshine the tiny gleam a firefly makes an uncertain moment, and goes out. The steady brilliance of this light remains, and leads you out of darkness, nor will you be able to forget the way again.

W 97 L 8. Begin these happy exercises with the words the Holy Spirit speaks to you, and let them echo round the world through Him:

> *"Spirit am I, a holy Son of God,*
> *Free of all limits, safe and healed and whole,*
> *Free to forgive, and free to save the world."*

Expressed through you, the Holy Spirit will accept this gift which you received of Him, increase its power, and give it back to you.

W 97 L 9. Offer each practice period today gladly to Him. And He will speak to you, reminding you that you are Spirit, one with Him and God, your brothers and your Self. Listen for His assurance every time you speak the word He offers you today, and let Him tell your mind that they are true. Use them against temptation, and escape its sorry consequences if you yield to the belief that you are something else. The Holy Spirit gives you peace today. Receive His words, and offer them to Him. **W(194)**

Lesson 98 "I will accept my part in God's plan for salvation."

W 98 L 1. Today is a day of special dedication. We take a stand on but one side today. We side with the truth and let illusions go. We will not vacillate between the two, but take a firm position with the One. We dedicate ourselves to truth today, and to salvation as God planned it be. We will not argue it is something else, we will not seek for it where it is not. In gladness we accept it as it is, and take the part assigned to us by God.

W 98 L 2. How happy to be certain! All our doubts we lay aside today, and take our stand with certainty of purpose, and with thanks that doubt is gone and surety has come. We have a mighty purpose to fulfill, and have been given everything we need with which to reach the goal. Not one mistake stands in our way. For we have been absolved of errors. All our sins are washed away by realizing that they were but mistakes.

W 98 L 3. The guiltless have no fear, for they are safe and recognize their safety. They do not appeal to magic, nor invent escapes from fancied threats without reality. They rest in quiet certainty that they will do what it is given them to do. They do not doubt their own ability, because they know their function will be filled completely, in the perfect time and place. They took the stand which we will take today, that we may share their certainty, and thus increase it by accepting it ourselves.

W 98 L 4. They will be with us; all who took the stand we take today will gladly offer us all that they learned and every gain they made. Those still uncertain, too, will join with us, and borrowing our certainty, will make it stronger still. While those as yet unborn will hear the call we heard, and answer it, when they have come to make their choice again. We do not choose but for ourselves today. **W(195)**

W 98 L 5. Is it not worth five minutes of your time each hour to be able to accept the happiness which God has given you? Is it not worth five minutes hourly to recognize your special function here? Is not five minutes of the hour but a small request in terms of a reward so great it has no measure? You have made a thousand losing bargains at the least.

---

[290] Originally typed "I am a Spirit." Handwritten mark-up crosses out the "a". The *Notes* also omits the "a."
[291] **Matthew 28:20** "Teaching them to observe all things that I have commanded you; and lo, I am with you always, even to the end of the age." Amen.
[292] Handwritten mark-up suggests (limit).
[293] Handwritten mark-up suggests (that).

[294] **Handwritten mark-up suggests (each gift) instead of "your gifts".**

W 98 L 6. Here is an offer guaranteeing you your full release from pain of every[295] kind, and joy the world does not contain. You can exchange a little of your time for peace of mind and certainty of purpose, with the promise of complete success. And since time has no meaning, you are being asked for nothing in return for everything. Here is a bargain which you cannot lose. And what you gain is limitless indeed!

W 98 L 7. Each hour today give Him your tiny gift of but five minutes. He will give the words you use in practicing today's idea the deep conviction and the certainty you lack. His words will join with yours, and make each repetition of today's idea a total dedication, made in faith as perfect and as sure as His in you. His confidence in you will bring the light to all the words you say, and you will go beyond their sound to what they really mean.

W 98 L 8. Today you practice with Him, as you say:

"I will accept my part in God's plan for salvation."

In each five minutes that you spend with Him, He will accept your words and give them back to you all bright with faith and confidence so strong and steady they will light the world with hope and gladness. Do not lose one chance to be the glad receiver of His gifts, that you may give them to the world today. **W(196)**

W 98 L 9. Give Him the words, and He will do the rest. He will enable you to understand your special function. He will open up the way to happiness, and peace and trust will be His gifts, His answer to your words. He will respond with all His faith and joy and certainty that what you say is true. And you will have conviction then of Him Who knows the function that you have on earth as well as Heaven.[296] He will be with you each practice period you share with Him, exchanging every instant of the time you offer Him for timelessness and peace.

W 98 L 10. Throughout the hour let your time be spent in happy preparation for the next five minutes you will spend again with Him. Repeat today's idea while you wait for the glad time to come to you again. Repeat it often, and do not forget each time you do so, you have let your mind be readied for the happy time to come.

W 98 L 11. And when the hour is gone,[297] and He is there once more to spend a little time with you be thankful, and lay down all earthly tasks, all little thoughts and limited ideas, and spend a happy time again with Him. Tell Him once more that you accept the part which[298] He would have you take, and help you fill, and He will make you sure you want this choice, which He has made with you, and you with Him. **W(197)**

Lesson 99 "Salvation is my only function here."

W 99 L 1. Salvation and forgiveness are the same. They both imply that something has gone wrong; something you need be saved from or forgiven for; something amiss that needs corrective change, something apart or different from the Will of God. Thus do both terms imply something impossible but yet[299] which has occurred, resulting in a state of conflict[300] between what is and what could never be.

W 99 L 2. Truth and illusions both are equal now, for both have happened. The impossible becomes the thing you need forgiveness for; salvation from. Salvation is the borderland between truth and illusion.[301] It[302] reflects the truth because it is the means by which you can escape illusions. Yet it is not truth because it undoes what was never done.

W 99 L 3. How could there be a meeting place at all where earth and Heaven can be reconciled within a mind where both of them exist? The mind which sees illusions thinks them real. They have existence in that they are thoughts. And yet they are not real because the mind that thinks these thoughts is separate from God.

W 99 L 4. What joins the separated mind and thoughts with Mind and Thought which are forever One? What plan could hold the truth inviolate, yet recognize the need illusions bring, and offer means by which they are undone without attack, and with no touch of pain? What but a Thought of God could be this plan by which the never done is overlooked, and sins forgotten which were never real?

W 99 L 5. The Holy Spirit holds this plan of God exactly as it was received of Him within the Mind of God, and in your own. It is apart from time in that its Source is timeless. Yet it operates in time because of your belief that time is real. Unshaken does the Holy Spirit look on what you see; on sin and pain and death, on grief and separation and on loss. Yet does He know one thing must **W(198)** still be true; God still is Love, and this is not His Will.[303]

W 99 L 6. This is the Thought Which brings illusions to the truth, and sees them as appearances behind which is the changeless and the sure. This is the Thought Which saves and Which forgives, because It lays no faith in what is not created by the only Source It knows. This is the Thought Whose function is to save by giving you Its function as your own.

W 99 L 7. Salvation is your function, with the One to Whom the plan was given. Now are you entrusted with this plan, along with Him. He has one answer to appearances regardless of their form, their size, their depth, or any attribute they seem to have:

"Salvation is my only function here.

God still is Love, and this is not His Will."

W 99 L 8. You who will yet work miracles, be sure you practice well the idea for today. Try to perceive the strength in what you say, for these are words in which your freedom lies. Your Father loves you. All the world of pain is not His will. Forgive yourself the thought He wanted this for you. Then let the Thought with Which He has replaced all your mistakes enter the darkened places of your mind which thought the thoughts that never were His Will. This part belongs to God, as does the rest. It does not think its solitary thoughts and make them real by hiding them from Him.

W 99 L 9. Let in the light, and you will look upon no obstacle to what He wills for you. Open your secrets to His kindly Light, and see how bright this Light still shines in you. Practice His Thought today, and let His Light seek out and lighten up all darkened spots, and shine through them to join them to the rest.

W 99 L 10. It is God's will your mind be One with His. It is God's Will that He has but one Son. **W(199)** It is God's Will that His one Son is you. Think of these things in practicing today, and start your longer practice periods with this instruction in the way of truth:

"Salvation is my only function here.

Salvation and forgiveness are the same."

Then turn to Him who shares your function with you,[304] and let Him teach you what you need to learn to lay all fear aside, and know your Self as Love Which has no opposite in you.

---

[295] *Urtext* manuscript has "**very**" which appears to be a mistake. It is "every" in the *Notes*.
[296] **Matthew 6:10** "Your kingdom come. Your will be done On earth as it is in heaven."
[297] Handwritten mark-up suggests (goes).
[298] Handwritten mark-up suggests (that).
[299] Handwritten mark-up suggests (the thought of the impossible).
[300] Handwritten mark-up suggests (now).
[301] Handwritten mark-up suggests (Salvation thus becomes a borderland which stands between the truth and fantasies.). The *Notes* originally states

"Forgiveness is the borderland between truth and illusion." The word "forgiveness" is crossed out after the "g," and "Salvation" is written in, making it "For Salvation."
[302] Handwritten mark-up suggests (now). That's not in the *Notes*.
[303] **1 John 4:8** He who does not love does not know God, for God is love.
1 John 4:16 And we have known and believed the love that God has for us. God is love, and he who abides in love abides in God, and God in him.
[304] Handwritten mark-up suggests (here?).

W 99 L 11. Forgive all thoughts which would oppose the truth of your completeness, unity and peace. You cannot lose the gifts your Father gave. You do not want to be another self. You have no function that is not of God. Forgive yourself the one you think you made. Forgiveness and salvation are the same. Forgive what you have made, and you are saved.

W 99 L 12. You have a special message for today which has the power to remove all forms of doubt and fear forever from your mind. If you are tempted to believe them true, remember that appearances can not withstand the truth these mighty words contain:

> "Salvation is my only function here.
> God still is Love, and this is not His Will."

W 99 L 13. Your only function tells you you are One. Remind yourself of this between the times you give five minutes to be shared with Him Who shares God's plan with you. Remind yourself:

> "Salvation is my only function here."

Thus do you lay forgiveness on your mind, and let all fear be gently laid aside that Love may find Its rightful place in you, and show you that you are the Son of God. **W(200)**

Lesson 100 "My part is essential to God's plan for salvation."

W 100 L 1. Just as God's Son completes his Father, so your part in it completes your Father's plan. Salvation must reverse the mad belief in separate thoughts and separate bodies which lead separate lives and go their separate ways. One function shared by separate minds unites them in one purpose, for each one is equally essential to them all.

W 100 L 2. God's Will for you is perfect happiness. Why should you choose to go against His Will? The part that[305] He has saved for you to take in working out His plan is given you that you might be restored to what He wills. This part is as essential to His plan as to your happiness. Your joy must be complete to let His plan be understood by those to whom He sends you.[306] They will see their function in your shining face, and hear God calling to them in your happy laugh.

W 100 L 3. You are indeed essential to God's plan. Without your joy His joy is incomplete. Without your smile the world cannot be saved. While you are sad the light which God Himself appointed as the means to save the world is dim and lusterless. And no-one laughs because all laughter can but echo yours. You are indeed essential to God's plan. Just as your light increases every light that shines in Heaven, so your joy on earth calls to all minds to let their sorrows go, and take their place beside you in God's plan.

W 100 L 4. God's messengers are joyous, and their joy heals sorrow and despair. They are the proof that God wills perfect happiness for all who will accept their Father's gifts as theirs. We will not let ourselves be sad today. For if we do, we fail to take the part that is essential to God's plan, as well as to our vision. Sadness is the sign that you would play another part, instead of what has been assigned to you by God. Thus do you fail to show the world how great the happiness He wills for you. And so you do not recognize that it is yours. **W(201)**

W 100 L 5. Today we will attempt to understand joy is our function here. If you are sad your part is unfulfilled, and all the world is thus deprived of joy, along with you. God asks that you be happy, so the world can see how much He loves His Son, and wills no sorrow rises to abate his joy; no fear besets him to disturb his peace. You are God's messenger today. You bring His happiness to all you look upon; His peace to everyone who looks on you, and sees His message in your happy face.

W 100 L 6. We will prepare ourselves for this today in our five minute practice periods, by feeling happiness arise in us according to our Father's will and ours. Begin the exercises with the thought today's idea contains. Then realize your part is to be happy. Only this is asked of you or anyone who wants to take his place among God's messengers.

W 100 L 7. Think what this means. You have indeed been wrong in your belief that sacrifice is asked. You but receive according to God's plan, and never lose or sacrifice or die. Now let us try to find that joy which proves to us and all the world God's Will for us. It is your function that you find it here, and that you find it now. For this you came. Let this one be the day that you succeed!

W 100 L 8. Look deep within you, undismayed by all the little thoughts and foolish goals you pass as you ascend to meet the Christ in you. He will be there. And you can reach Him now. What could you rather look upon in place of Him who waits that you may look on Him? What little thought has power to hold you back? What foolish goal can keep you from success when He Who calls to you is God Himself?

W 100 L 9. He will be there. You are essential to His plan. You are His messenger today, and you must find what He would have you give. **W(202)** Do not forget the idea for today between your longer practice periods. It is your Self who calls to you today. And it is Him you answer every time you tell yourself you are essential to God's plan for the salvation of the world. **W(203)**

Lesson 101 "God's will for me is perfect happiness."

W 101 L 1. Today we will continue with the theme of happiness. This is a key idea in understanding what salvation means. You still believe it asks for suffering as penance for your "sins." This is not so. Yet you must think it so while you believe that sin is real, and that God's Son can sin.

W 101 L 2. If sin is real then punishment is just, and cannot be escaped. Salvation thus cannot be purchased but through suffering. If sin is real then happiness must be illusion, for they cannot both be true. The sinful warrant only death and pain, and it is this they ask for, for they know it waits for them and it will seek them out and find them somewhere, sometime, in some form which evens the account they owe to God. They would escape Him in their fear. And yet He will pursue, and they can not escape.

W 101 L 3. If sin is real, salvation must be pain. Pain is the cost of sin, and suffering can never be escaped if sin is real. Salvation must be feared, for it will kill, but slowly, taking everything away before it grants the welcome boon of death[307] to victims who are little more than bones before salvation is appeased. Its wrath is boundless, merciless, but wholly just.

W 101 L 4. Who would seek out such savage punishment? Who would not flee salvation, and attempt in every way he can to drown the Voice Which offers it to him? Why would he try to listen, and accept Its offering? If sin is real Its offering is death, and meted out in cruel form to match the vicious wishes in which sin is born. If sin is real salvation has become your bitter enemy, the curse of God upon you who have crucified His Son.

W 101 L 5. You need the practice periods today. The exercises teach sin is not real, and all that you believe must come from sin will never happen, for it has no cause. Accept atonement with an

---

[305] Handwritten mark-up suggests (which).

[306] **John 15:11** "These things I have spoken to you, that My joy may remain in you, and that your joy may be complete."
John 16:24 "Until now you have asked nothing in My name. Ask, and you will receive, that your joy may be complete."

[307] The *Urtext* manuscript ends the sentence here and starts a new one, making the next clause a sentence with no verb unless the next period, after *appeased*, is removed. *FIP* changes it as we do. This is also the reading in the *Notes*.

open mind which cherishes no lingering belief that you have made a devil of God's Son. **W(204)**

W 101 L 6. There is no sin. We practice with this thought as often as we can today, because it is the basis for today's idea. God's Will for you is perfect happiness because there is no sin, and suffering is causeless. Joy is just, and pain is but the sign you have misunderstood yourself.

W 101 L 7. Fear not the Will of God. But turn to It in confidence that It will set you free from all the consequences sin has wrought in feverish imagination. Say:

"God's Will for me is perfect happiness.

There is no sin; it has no consequence."

So should you start your practice periods, and then attempt again to find the joy these thoughts will introduce into your mind. Give these five minutes gladly, to remove the heavy load you laid upon yourself with the insane belief that sin is real.

W 101 L 8. Today escape from madness. You are set on freedom's road, and now today's idea brings wings to speed you on, and hope to go still faster to the waiting goal of peace. There is no sin. Remember this today, and tell yourself as often as you can:

"God's Will for me is perfect happiness.

This is the truth because there is no sin." **W(205)**

Lesson 102 "I share God's Will for happiness for me."

W 102 L 1. You do not want to suffer. You may think it buys you something, and may still believe a little that it buys you what you want. Yet this belief is surely shaken now, at least enough to let you question it, and to suspect it really makes no sense. It has not gone as yet, but lacks the roots that once secured it tightly to the dark and hidden secret places of your mind.

W 102 L 2. Today we try to loose its weakened hold still further and to realize that pain is purposeless, without a cause, and with no power to accomplish anything. It cannot purchase anything at all. It offers nothing, and does not exist,[308] and everything you think it offers you is lacking in existence like itself. You have been slave to nothing. Be you free today to join the happy Will of God.

W 102 L 3. For several days we will continue to devote our longer practice periods to exercises planned to help you reach the happiness God's Will has placed in you. Here is your home, and here your safety is. Here is your peace, and here there is no fear. Here is salvation. Here is rest at last.

W 102 L 4. Begin the longer practice periods today with this acceptance of God's Will for you:

"I share God's Will for happiness for me,

And I accept it as my function now."

Then seek this function deep within your mind, for it is there, awaiting but your choice. You cannot fail to find it when you learn it is your choice, and that you share God's Will. **W(206)**

W 102 L 5. Be happy, for your only function here is happiness. You have no need to be less loving to God's Son than He Whose Love created him as loving as Himself. Besides these hourly five minute rests, pause frequently today to tell yourself that you have now accepted happiness as your one function. And be sure that you are joining with God's Will in doing this. **W(207)**

Lesson 103 "God, being Love, is also happiness."

W 103 L 1. Happiness is an attribute of love. It cannot be apart from it, nor can it be experienced where love is not. Love has no limits, being everywhere. And therefore joy is everywhere as well. Yet can the mind deny that this is so, believing there are gaps in love where sin can enter, bringing pain instead of joy. This strange belief would limit happiness by redefining love as limited, and introducing opposition in what has no limit and no opposite.

W 103 L 2. Fear is associated then with love, and its results become the heritage of minds which think what they have made is real. These images, with no reality in truth, bear witness to the fear of God, forgetting being Love.[309] He must be joy.

This basic error we will try again to bring to truth today, and teach ourselves:

"God, being Love, is also happiness.

To fear Him is to be afraid of joy."

Begin your longer exercises for[310] today with this association, which corrects the false belief that God is fear. It also emphasizes happiness belongs to you because of what He is.

W 103 L 3. Allow this one correction to be placed within your minds each waking hour today. Then welcome all the happiness it brings, as truth replaces fear, and joy becomes what you expect to take the place of pain. God being Love, it will be given you. Bolster this expectation frequently throughout the day, and quiet all your fears with this assurance, kind and wholly true:

"God, being Love, is also happiness.

And it is happiness I seek today.

I cannot fail, because I seek the truth." **W(208)**

Lesson 104 "I seek but what belongs to me in truth."

W 104 L 1. Today's idea continues with the thought that joy and peace are not but idle dreams. They are your right, because of what you are. They come to you from God, Who cannot fail to give you what He wills. Yet must there be a place made ready to receive His gifts. They are not welcomed gladly by a mind which has instead received the gifts it made where His belong, as substitutes for them.

W 104 L 2. Today we would remove all meaningless and self-made gifts which we have placed upon the holy altar where God's gifts belong. These[311] are the gifts which are our own in truth. These[312] are the gifts which we inherited before time was, and which will still be ours when time has passed into eternity. These[313] are the gifts which are within us now, for they are timeless. And we need not wait to have them. They belong to us today. Therefore we will to have them now, and know in choosing them in place of what we made, we but unite our will with what God wills, and recognize the same as being One.

W 104 L 3. Our longer practice periods today, the hourly five minutes given to the truth for your salvation, should begin with this:

"I seek but what belongs to me in truth."

And joy and peace are my inheritance."

Then lay aside the conflicts of the world which offer other gifts and other goals made of illusions, witnessed to by them, and sought for only in a world of dreams.

W 104 L 4. All this we lay aside, and seek instead that which is truly ours, as we ask to recognize what God has given us. We clear a holy place within our minds before His altar, where His gifts of peace and joy are welcome, and to which we come to find what has

---

[308] *Urtext* manuscript begins new sentence here, corrected in handwriting to a comma instead of period.

[309] The manuscript has a comma handwritten in. In the *Notes*, legibility is an issue but word spacing suggests a period was intended and that certainly seems to make the most sense. FIP keeps the comma.

[310] Handwritten mark-up suggests (practice periods).

[311] Handwritten mark-up suggests (His).

[312] Handwritten mark-up suggests (His).

[313] Handwritten mark-up suggests (His).

been given us by Him. We come in confidence today, aware that what belongs to us in truth is what He gives. And we would wish for nothing else, for nothing else belongs to us in truth. **W(209)**

W 104 L 5. So do we clear the way for Him today by simply recognizing that His Will is done already, and that joy and peace belong to us as His eternal gifts. We will not let ourselves lose sight of them between the times we come to seek for them where He has laid them. This reminder will we bring to mind as often as we can:

> *"I seek but what belongs to me in truth.*
> *God's gifts of joy and peace are all I want."* **W(210)**

Lesson 105 "God's peace and joy are mine."

W 105 L 1. God's peace and joy are yours. Today we will accept them, knowing they belong to us. And we will try to understand these gifts increase as we receive them. They are not like to the gifts the world can give, in which the giver loses as he gives the gift; the taker is the richer by his loss. These[314] are not gifts, but bargains made with guilt. The truly given gift entails no loss. It is impossible that one can gain because another loses. This implies a limit and an insufficiency.

W 105 L 2. No gift is given thus. Such "gifts" are but a bid for a more valuable return; a loan with interest to be paid in full; a temporary lending, meant to be a pledge of debt to be repaid with more than was received by him who took the gift. This strange distortion of what giving means pervades all levels of the world you see. It strips all meaning from the gifts you give, and leaves you nothing in the ones you take.

W 105 L 3. A major learning goal this course has set is to reverse your view of giving, so you can receive. For giving has become a source of fear, and so you would avoid the only means by which you can receive. Accept God's peace and joy, and you will learn a different way of looking at a gift. God's gifts will never lessen when they are given away. They but increase thereby. As Heaven's peace and joy intensify when you accept them as God's gift to you, so does the joy of your Creator grow when you accept His joy and peace as yours.

W 105 L 4. True giving is creation. It extends the limitless to the unlimited, eternity to timelessness, and love unto itself. It adds to all that is complete already, not in simple terms of adding more, for that implies that it was less before. It adds by letting what cannot contain itself fulfill its aim of giving everything it has away, securing it forever for itself. **W(211)**

W 105 L 5. Today accept God's peace and joy as yours. Let Him complete Himself as He defines completion. You will understand that what completes Him must complete His Son as well. He cannot give through loss. No more can you. Receive His gift of joy and peace today, and He will thank you for your gift to Him.

W 105 L 6. Today our practice periods will start a little differently. Begin today by thinking of those brothers who have been denied by you the peace and joy which are their right under the equal laws of God. Here you denied them to yourself. And here you must return, to claim them as your own. Think of your "enemies" a little while, and tell each one as he occurs to you:

> *"My brother, peace and joy I offer you,*
> *That I may have God's peace and joy as mine."*

W 105 L 7. Thus you prepare yourself to recognize God's gifts to you, and let your mind be free of all that would prevent success today. Now are you ready to accept the gift of peace and joy which God has given you. Now are you ready to experience the joy and peace you have denied yourself. Now you can say "God's peace and joy are mine," for you have given what you would receive.

W 105 L 8. You must succeed today if you prepare your mind as we suggest, for you have let all bars to peace and joy be lifted up, and what is yours can come to you at last. So tell yourself "God's peace and joy are mine," and close your eyes a while, and let His Voice assure you that the words you speak are true.

W 105 L 9. Spend your five minutes thus with Him each time you can today, but do not think that less is worthless when you cannot give Him more. At least remember hourly to say the words which call on Him to give you what He wills to give, and wills you to receive. **W(212)** Determine not to interfere today with what He wills. And if a brother seems to tempt you to deny God's gift to him, see it as but another chance to let yourself receive the gifts of God as yours. Then bless your brother thankfully, and say:

> *"My brother, peace and joy I offer you,*
> *That I may have God's peace and joy as mine."* **W(213)**

Lesson 106 "Let me be still and listen to the truth."[315]

W 106 L 1. If you will lay aside the ego's voice however loudly it may seem to call; if you will not accept its petty gifts which give you nothing that you really want; if you will listen with an open mind which[316] has not told you what salvation is; then you will hear the mighty Voice of truth, quiet in power, strong in stillness, and completely certain in Its messages. Listen, and hear your Father speak to you through His appointed Voice, Which silences the thunder of the meaningless, and shows the way to peace to those who cannot see.

W 106 L 2. Be still today and listen to the truth. Be not deceived by voices of the dead which tell you they have found the source of life, and offer it to you for your belief. Attend them not, but listen to the truth. Be not afraid today to circumvent the voices of the world. Walk lightly past their meaningless persuasion. Hear them not.

W 106 L 3. Be still today and listen to the truth. Go past all things which do not speak of Him Who holds your happiness within His hand, held out to you in welcome and in love. Hear only Him today, and do not wait to reach Him longer. Hear one Voice today.

W 106 L 4. Today the promise of God's Word is kept. Hear and be silent. He would speak to you. He comes with miracles a thousand times as happy and as wonderful as those you ever dreamt[317] or wished for in your dreams. His miracles are true. They will not fade when dreaming ends. They end the dream instead, and last forever for they come from God, to His dear Son, whose other name is you. Prepare yourself for miracles today. Today allow your Father's ancient pledge to you and all your brothers to be kept.

W 106 L 5. Hear Him today, and listen to the Word which lifts the veil which[318] lies upon the earth, and wakes all those who sleep and cannot see. God calls to them through you. He needs your voice to speak to them, for who could reach God's Son except his Father calling through your Self? **W(214)**

W 106 L 6. Hear Him today, and offer Him your voice to speak to all the multitudes who wait to hear the Word that He will speak today. Be ready for salvation. It is here, and will today be given unto you. And you will learn your function from the One Who shows[319] it in your Father's Name for you.

W 106 L 7. Listen today, and you will hear a Voice Which will resound throughout the world through you. The Bringer of all miracles has need that you receive them first, and thus become the joy-

---

[314] Handwritten mark-up suggests (Such).

[315] **Psalm 46:10** Be still, and know that I am God; I will be exalted among the nations, I will be exalted in the earth!
[316] Handwritten mark-up suggests (that).
[317] Handwritten mark-up suggests (dreamed).
[318] Handwritten mark-up suggests (that).
[319] While the *Urtext* manuscript has "shows" typed initially, it is corrected with handwriting to "chose" which is the form found in the *Notes*.

ous giver of what you received. Thus does salvation start and thus it ends; when everything is yours, and everything is given away, it will remain with you forever. And the lesson has been learned.

W 106 L 8. Today we practice giving, not the way you understand it now, but as it is. The longer[320] exercises should begin with this request for your enlightenment:

"I will be still and listen for the truth.

What does it mean to give and to receive?"

Ask and expect an answer. Your request is one whose answer has been waiting long to be received by you. It will begin the ministry for which you came, and which will free the world from thinking giving is a way to lose. And so the world becomes ready to understand and to receive.

W 106 L 9. Be still and listen to the truth today. For each five minutes spent in listening a thousand minds are opened to the truth, and[321] they will hear the holy Word you hear. And when the hour is past, you will again release a thousand more who pause to ask that truth be given them, along with you.

W 106 L 10. Today the holy Word of God is kept through your receiving it to give away, so you can teach the world what giving means by listening and learning it of Him. Do not forget today to reinforce your choice to hear and to receive the Word by your[322] reminder, given to yourself as often as is possible today:

"Let me be still and listen to the truth.

I am the messenger of God today,

My voice is His, to give what I receive." **W(215) W(216)**

Lesson 107 "Truth will correct the[323] errors in my mind."

W 107 L 1. What can correct illusions but the truth? And what are errors but illusions which remain unrecognized for what they are? Where truth has entered errors disappear. They merely vanish, leaving not a trace by which to be remembered. They are gone because without belief they have no life, and so they disappear to nothingness, returning whence they came. From dust to dust they come and go, for only truth remains.[324]

W 107 L 2. Can you imagine what a state of mind without illusions is? How it would feel? Try to remember when there was a time, - perhaps a minute, maybe even less, - when nothing came to interrupt your peace; when you were certain you were loved and safe. Then try to picture what it would be like to have that moment be extended to the end of time and to eternity. Then let the sense of quiet that you felt be multiplied a hundred times, and then be multiplied another hundred more.

W 107 L 3. And now you have a hint, not more than just the faintest intimation of the state your mind will rest in when the truth has come. Without illusions there could be no fear, no doubt and no attack. When truth has come all pain is over, for there is no room for transitory thoughts and dead ideas to linger in your mind. Truth occupies your mind completely, liberating you from all beliefs in the ephemeral. They have no place because the truth has come, and they are nowhere. They cannot be found, for truth is everywhere forever now.

W 107 L 4. When truth has come it does not stay a while, to disappear, or change to something else. It does not shift and alter in its form, nor come and go and go and come again. It stays exactly as it always was, to be depended on in every need, and trusted with a perfect trust in all the seeming difficulties and the doubts which the appearances the world presents engender. They will merely blow[325] away when truth corrects the errors in your mind. **W(217)**

W 107 L 5. When truth has come it harbors in its wings the gift of perfect constancy, and love which does not falter in the face of pain but looks beyond it, steadily and sure. Here is the gift of healing, for the truth needs no defense, and therefore no attack is possible. Illusions can be brought to truth to be corrected. But the truth stands far beyond illusions, and can not be brought to them to turn them into truth.

W 107 L 6. Truth does not come and go nor shift nor change, in this appearance now and then in that, evading capture and escaping grasp. It does not hide. It stands in open light, in obvious accessibility. It is impossible that anyone could seek it truly and would not succeed. Today belongs to truth. Give truth its due, and it will give you yours. You were not meant to suffer and to die. Your Father wills these dreams be gone. Let truth correct them all.

W 107 L 7. We do not ask for what we do not have. We merely ask for what belongs to us, that we may[326] recognize it as our own. Today we practice on the happy note of certainty which has been born of truth. The shaky and unsteady footsteps of illusion is[327] not our approach today. We are as certain of success as we are sure we live and hope and breathe and think. We do not doubt we walk with truth today, and count on it to enter into all the exercises that we do this day.

W 107 L 8. Begin by asking Him Who goes with you upon this undertaking that He be in your awareness as you go with Him. You are not made of flesh and blood and bone, but were created by the self-same Thought Which gave the gift of life[328] to Him as well. He is your Brother, and so like to you your Father knows that you are both the same. It is your Self you ask to go with you, and how could He be absent where you are? **W(218)**

W 107 L 9. Truth will correct all errors in your mind which tell you you could be apart from Him. You speak to Him today, and make your pledge to let His function be fulfilled through you. To share His function is to share His joy. His confidence is with you as you say:

"Truth will correct all errors in my mind,

And I will rest in Him who is my Self."

Then let Him lead you gently to the truth which will envelop you and give you peace so deep and tranquil that you will return to the familiar world reluctantly.

W 107 L 10. And yet you will be glad to look again upon this world. For you will bring with you the promise of the changes which the truth that goes with you will carry to the world. They will increase with every gift you give of five small minutes, and the errors which surround the world will be corrected as you let them be corrected in your mind.

W 107 L 11. Do not forget your function for today. Each time you tell yourself with confidence, "Truth will correct all errors in my

---

[320] Handwritten mark-up suggests (Each hour's).
[321] The manuscript originally has a sentence break here rather than a comma. The shift to a comma is written in by hand, obviously correct, and thus retained.
[322] Handwritten mark-up suggests (this).
[323] Handwritten mark-up suggests (all).
[324] **Genesis 3:19** "By the sweat of your brow you will eat your food until you return to the ground, since from it you were taken; for dust you are and to dust you will return."

[325] Originally in the *Urtext* manuscript typed "flow" the handwritten correction (blow) appears obviously correct. In the *Notes* it is "blow."
[326] Omitted in the *Urtext* manuscript, the word "**may**" is handwritten in. It is also the reading in the *Notes*.
[327] *FIP* changes "**is**" to "**are**" because the subject appears to be the plural "**footsteps**." The subject can also be considered to be the phrase "**the shaky and unsteady footsteps of illusion**" which can be (and originally was) considered singular.
[328] Originally in the *Urtext* manuscript typed "**light**" the word (life) is handwritten in and probably correct. It is "life" in the *Notes*.

mind," you speak for all the world, and Him Who would release the world as He would set you free. **W(219)**

Lesson 108 "To give and to receive are one in truth."

W 108 L 1. Vision depends upon today's idea. The light is in it, for it reconciles all seeming opposites. And what is light except the resolution, born of peace, of all your conflicts and mistaken thoughts into one concept which is wholly true? Even that one will disappear because the Thought behind it will appear instead, to take its place. And now we are at peace forever, for the dream is over now.

W 108 L 2. True light which makes true vision possible is not the light the body's eyes behold. It is a state of mind which has become so unified that darkness cannot be perceived at all. And thus what is the same is seen as one, while what is not the same remains unnoticed, for it is not there.

W 108 L 3. This is the light which shows no opposites, and vision, being healed, has power to heal. This is the light which brings your peace of mind to other minds, to share it and be glad that they are one with you and with themselves. This is the light which heals because it brings single perception, based upon one frame of reference from which one meaning comes.

W 108 L 4. Here are both giving and receiving seen as different aspects of one Thought Whose truth does not depend on which is seen as first, nor which appears to be in second place. Here it is understood that both occur together, that the Thought remains complete. And in this understanding is the base on which all opposites are reconciled, because they are perceived from the same frame of reference which unifies this Thought.

W 108 L 5. One thought, completely unified, will serve to unify all thought. This is the same as saying one correction will suffice for all correction, or that to forgive one brother wholly is enough to bring salvation to all minds. For these are but some special cases of one law which holds for every kind of learning, if it be directed by the One Who knows the truth. **W(220)**

W 108 L 6. To learn that giving and receiving are the same has special usefulness, because it can be tried so easily and seen as true. And when this special case has proved it always works in every circumstance where it is tried, the thought behind it can be generalized to other areas of doubt and double vision. And from there it will extend, and finally arrive at the one Thought Which underlies them all.

W 108 L 7. Today we practice with the special case of giving and receiving. We will use this simple lesson in the obvious because it has results we cannot miss. To give is to receive. Today we will attempt to offer peace to everyone, and see how quickly peace returns to us. Light is tranquility, and in that peace is vision given us, and we can see.

W 108 L 8. So we begin the practice periods with the instruction for today, and say:

"To give and to receive are one in truth.

I will receive what I am giving now."

Then close your eyes, and for five minutes think of what you would hold out to everyone to have it yours. You might, for instance, say:

"To everyone I offer quietness."

"To everyone I offer peace of mind."

"To everyone I offer gentleness."

W 108 L 9. Say each one slowly, and then pause a while, expecting to receive the gift you gave, and it will come to you in the amount in which you gave it. You will find you have exact return, for this[329] is what you asked. It might be helpful, too, to think of one to whom to give your gifts. He represents the others, and through him you give to all. **W(221)**

W 108 L 10. Our very simple lesson for today will teach you much. Effect and cause will be far better understood from this time on, and we will make much faster progress now. Think of the exercises for today as quick advances in your learning, made still faster and more sure each time you say:[330]

"To give and to receive are one in truth." **W(222)**

Lesson 109 "I rest in God."

W 109 L 1. We ask for rest today, and quietness unshaken by the world's appearances. We ask for peace and stillness in the midst of all the turmoil born of clashing dreams. We ask for safety and for happiness, although we seem to look on danger and on sorrow. And we have the thought that will answer our asking with what we request.

W 109 L 2. "I rest in God." This thought will bring to you the rest and quiet, peace and stillness, and the safety and the happiness you seek. "I rest in God." This thought has power to wake the sleeping truth in you, whose vision sees beyond appearances to that same truth in everyone and everything there is. Here is the end of suffering for all the world, and everyone who ever came and yet will come to linger for a while. Here is the thought in which the Son of God is born again, to recognize Himself.[331]

W 109 L 3. "I rest in God." Completely undismayed this thought will carry you through storms and strife, past misery and pain, past loss and death, and onward to the certainty of God. There is no suffering it cannot heal. There is no problem which[332] it cannot solve. And no appearance but will turn to truth before the eyes of you who rest in God.

W 109 L 4. This is the day of peace. You rest in God, and while the world is torn by winds of hate, your rest remains completely undisturbed. Yours is the rest of truth. Appearances cannot intrude on you. You call to all to join you in your rest, and they will hear and come to you because you rest in God. They will not hear another voice but yours, because you gave your voice to God and now you rest in Him, and let Him speak through you.

W 109 L 5. In Him you have no cares and no concerns, no burdens, no anxiety, no pain, no fear of future and no past regrets. In timelessness you rest, while time goes by without its touch upon you, for your rest can never change in any way at all. **W(223)** You rest today. And as you close your eyes, sink into stillness. Let these periods of rest and respite reassure your mind that all its frantic fantasies were but the dreams of fever that has passed away. Let it be still and thankfully accept its healing. No more fearful dreams will come now that you rest in God. Take time today to slip away from dreams and into peace.

W 109 L 6. Each hour that you take your rest today a tired mind is suddenly made glad, a bird with broken wings begins to sing, a stream long dry begins to flow again. The world is born again each time you rest, and hourly remember that you came to bring the peace of God into the world, that it might take its rest along with you.

W 109 L 7. With each five minutes that you rest today the world is nearer waking. And the time when rest will be the only thing there is comes closer to all worn and tired minds, too weary now to go their way alone. And they will hear the bird begin to sing, and see the stream begin to flow again, with hope reborn and energy re-

---

[329] Handwritten mark-up suggests (that).
[330] In the *Urtext* manuscript this is a comma rather than a colon.
[331] **John 3:3** Jesus answered and said to him, "Most assuredly, I say to you, unless one is born again, he cannot see the kingdom of God."
John 3:7 Do not marvel that I said to you, "You must be born again."
[332] Handwritten mark-up suggests (that).

stored to walk with lightened steps along the road that suddenly seems easy as they go.

W 109 L 8. You rest within the peace of God today, and call upon your brothers from your rest, to draw them to their rest along with you. You will be faithful to your trust today, forgetting no-one, bringing everyone into the boundless circle of your peace, the holy sanctuary where you rest. Open the temple doors and let them come from far across the world and near as well; your distant brothers and your closest friends; bid them all enter here and rest with you.

W 109 L 9. You rest within the peace of God today, quiet and unafraid. Each brother comes to take his rest, and offer it to you. **W(224)** We rest together here, for thus our rest is made complete, and what we give today we have received already. Time is not the guardian of what we give today. We give to those unborn and those passed by, to every Thought of God, and to the Mind in Which these Thoughts were born, and where they rest. And we remind them of their resting place each time we tell ourselves:

"*I rest in God.*" **W(225)**

Lesson 110 "I am as God created me."

W 110 L 1. We will repeat today's idea from time to time. For this one thought would be enough to save you and the world, if you believed that it is true. Its truth would mean that you have made no changes in yourself which have reality, nor changed the universe so that what God created was replaced by fear and evil, misery and death. If you remain as God created you, fear has no meaning, evil is not real, and misery and death do not exist.

W 110 L 2. Today's idea is therefore all you need to let complete correction heal your mind and give you perfect vision, which will heal all the mistakes that any mind has made at any time or place. It is enough to heal the past and make the future free. It is enough to let the present be accepted as it is. It is enough to let time be the means for all the world to learn escape from time, and every change which time appears to bring in passing by.

W 110 L 3. If you remain as God created you appearances cannot replace the truth, health cannot turn to sickness, nor can death be substitute for life, or fear for love. All this has not occurred, if you remain as God created you. You need no thought but just this one, to let redemption come to light the world and free it from the past.

W 110 L 4. In this one thought is all the past undone; the present saved to quietly extend into a timeless future. If you are as God created you, then there has been no separation of your mind from His, no split between your mind and other minds, and only unity within your own.

W 110 L 5. The healing power of today's idea is limitless. It is the birthplace of all miracles, the great restorer of the truth to the awareness of the world. Practice today's idea with gratitude. This is the truth that comes to set you free.[333] This is the truth that God has promised you. This is the Word in which all sorrow ends. **W(226)**

W 110 L 6. For your five minute practice periods, begin with this quotation from the text:

"*I am as God created me. His Son*

can suffer nothing. And I am His Son."

Then, with this statement firmly in your mind, try to discover in your mind this[334] Self Who is the holy Son of God Himself. Seek Him within you Who is Christ in you, the Son of God and Brother to the world; the Savior Who has been forever saved, with power to save whoever touches Him however lightly, asking for the Word which tells him he is brother unto Him.

W 110 L 7. You are as God created you. Today honor your Self. Let graven images you made to be the Son of God instead of what he is be worshipped not today.[335] Deep in your mind the holy Christ in you is waiting your acknowledgment as you. And you are lost and do not know yourself while He is unacknowledged and unknown.

W 110 L 8. Seek Him today, and find Him. He will be your Savior from all idols you have made. For when you find Him you will understand how worthless are your idols, and how false the images which you believed were you. Today we make a great advance to truth by letting idols go, and opening our hands and hearts and minds to God today.

W 110 L 9. We will remember Him throughout the day with thankful hearts, and loving thoughts for all who meet with us today, for it is thus that we remember Him. And we will say, that we may be reminded of His Son, our holy Self, the Christ in each of us,

"*I am as God created me.*"

Let us declare this truth as often as we can. This is the Word of God that sets you free.[336] This is the key that opens up the gate of Heaven, and which lets you enter in the peace of God and His eternity. **W(227)**[337]**W(228)**

Review 3 (W 110 R3)
Introduction

W 110 R3 1. Our third[338] review begins today. We will review two of the last twenty ideas each day until we have reviewed them all.[339] We will observe the[340] special format for these practice periods, which you are urged to follow[341] as closely as you can. We understand, of course, that it may be impossible for you to undertake what is suggested here as optimal each day and every hour of the day.

W 110 R3 2. Learning will not be hampered when you miss a practice period because it is impossible at the appointed time. Nor is it necessary that you make excessive efforts to be sure that you catch up in terms of numbers. Rituals are not our aim, and would defeat our learning goal. But learning will be hampered when you skip a practice period because you are unwilling to devote the time to it which you are asked to give. Do not deceive yourself in this. Unwillingness can be most carefully concealed behind a cloak of situations you can not control.

W 110 R3 3. Learn to distinguish situations which are poorly suited to your practicing from those which you establish to uphold a camouflage for your unwillingness. Those practice periods which you

---

[333] **John 8:32** "And you shall know the truth, and the truth shall make you free."

[334] Handwritten mark-up suggests (The).

[335] **Exodus 20:4** You shall not make for yourself a carved image--any likeness of anything that is in heaven above, or that is in the earth beneath, or that is in the water under the earth;

[336] **John 8:32** "And you shall know the truth, and the truth shall make you free."

John 1:1-5 In the beginning was the Word, and the Word was with God, and the Word was God. The same was in the beginning with God. All things were made by him; and without him was not anything made that hath been made. In him was life; and the life was the light of men. And the light shineth in the darkness; and the darkness apprehended it not.

[337] The original manuscript page 227 is not present in our copy. It would appear that there never was a page 227 in the *Workbook* manuscript. No page 227 is present in any copy consulted. Between the end of **Lesson 110** on page 226 of this manuscript and the beginning of REVIEW 3 on page 228 of this manuscript there is no additional material in any known version of ACIM, including the *Notes*. It is likely therefore that the Scribes simply missed a page number rather than inadvertently leaving out any material. We note additionally that on the top of page 226, "227" is handwritten in, indicating the editors were aware of a missing page.

[338] Handwritten mark-up suggests (next).

[339] Handwritten mark-up suggests (two recent lessons every day for ten successive days of practicing.)

[340] Handwritten mark-up suggests (a).

[341] Handwritten mark-up suggests (just).

have lost because you did not want to do them for whatever reason should be done as soon as you have changed your mind about your goal.

W 110 R3 4. You are unwilling to cooperate in practicing salvation only if it interferes with gods you hold more dear. When you withdraw the value given them, allow your practice periods to be replacements for your litanies to them. They gave you nothing. But your practice periods[342] offer you everything.[343] Accept their offering and be at peace.[344]

W 110 R3 5. The format you should use for these reviews is this: Devote five minutes twice a day, or longer if you would prefer, to contemplating the ideas assigned. Read over the ideas and comments which are written first in each day's exercises.[345] Then begin to think about them quietly, letting your mind **W(229)** relate them to your needs, your seeming problems and all your concerns.

W 110 R3 6. Place the ideas within your mind, and let it use them as it chooses. Give it faith that it will use them wisely, being helped in its decisions by the One Who gave the thoughts to you. What can you trust but what is in your mind? Have faith, in these reviews, the means the Holy Spirit uses will not fail. The wisdom of your mind will come to your assistance. Give it direction at the start, and then lean back in quiet faith, and let it use the ideas you have given it as they were given you.[346]

W 110 R3 7. You have been given them in perfect trust; in perfect confidence that you would use them well; in perfect faith that you would understand[347] their messages, and use them for yourself. Offer them to your mind in that same trust and confidence and faith. It will not fail. It is the Holy Spirit's chosen means for your salvation. And with His trust it merits yours as well.[348]

W 110 R3 8. We emphasize the benefits to you, if you devote the first five minutes of the day to your review,[349] and also give the last five minutes of your waking day to it.[350] If this cannot be done, at least try to divide them so you undertake one in the morning, and the other in the hour just before you go to sleep.

W 110 R3 9. The exercises to be done throughout the day are equally important, and perhaps of even greater value. You have been inclined to do the exercises and then go on to other things, without applying what you learned to them. As a result, your learning has had little reinforcement, and you have not given it the opportunity to prove its worth to you.[351]

W 110 R3 10. Here is another chance to use it well. In these reviews we stress the need to let your learning not lie idly by between your longer practice periods. Attempt to give your daily two ideas a brief but serious review each hour. Use one on the hour, and the other one a half an hour later. You need not give more than just a moment to each one. **W(230)** Repeat it, and allow your mind to rest a little time in silence and in peace.

W 110 R3 11. Then turn to other things, but try to keep the thought with you, and let it serve to help you keep your peace throughout the day.[352] If you are shaken, think of it again. These practice periods are planned to help you form the habit of applying what you learn each day to everything you do. Do not repeat it[353] and then lay it down. Its usefulness is limitless to you. And it is meant to serve you in all ways, all times and places, and whenever you need help of any kind. Try, then, to take it with you in the business of the day, and make it holy, worthy of God's Son, acceptable to God and to your Self.

W 110 R3 12. Each day's review assignment will conclude with a restatement of the thought to use each hour, and the one to be applied on each half hour as well. Forget them not. This second chance with each of these ideas will bring such large advances that we come from these reviews with learning gains so great that we begin again[354] on[355] solid ground. Do not forget how little you have learned. Do not forget how much you can learn now. Do not forget your Father's need of you, as you review these thoughts He gave to you. **W(231)**

Lesson 111 For morning and evening review: (91-92)

W 111 L 1. 91) *"Miracles are seen in light."*

I cannot see in darkness. Let the light
Of holiness and truth light up my mind,
And let me see the innocence within.

W 111 L 2. 92) *"Miracles are seen in light, and light and strength are one."*

I see through strength, the gift of God to me.
My weakness is the dark His gift dispels
By giving me His strength to take its place.

W 111 L 3. On the hour:

"Miracles are seen in light."

W 111 L 4. On the half hour:

"Miracles are seen in light, and light and strength are one."
W(232)

Lesson 112 For morning and evening review: (93-94)

W 112 L 1. 93) *"Light and joy and peace abide in me."*

I am the home of light and joy and peace.
I welcome them into the home I share
With God, because I am a part of Him.

W 112 L 2. 94) *"I am as God created me."*

I will remain forever as I was
Created by the Changeless like Himself.
And I am one with Him, and He with me.

W 112 L 3. On the Hour:

---

[342] Handwritten mark-up suggests (practicing can).
[343] Handwritten mark-up suggests (everything to you).
[344] This sentence is re-written by hand as (And so accept its offering, and be at peace.) In the *Notes* it is the same as shown here.
[345] This paragraph is extensively marked up to read as follows: (The format you should use for these reviews is this: Devote five minutes twice a day, or longer if you would prefer it, to considering the thoughts that are assigned. Read over the ideas and comments that are written down for each day's exercise. And then begin to think about them, while letting your mind relate them to your needs, your seeming problems and all your concerns.) FIP has it in that re-written form. In the *Notes* it reads as shown.
[346] This sentence is extensively re-written as follows: (Give directions at the outset; then lean back in quiet faith, and let the mind employ the thoughts you gave as they were given you for it to use.) In the *Notes* it is the same as shown.
[347] Handwritten mark-up suggests (see).
[348] This sentence is re-written as follows: (Since it has His trust, it surely merits having yours as well.)
[349] Handwritten mark-up suggests (s).
[350] Handwritten mark-up suggests (them).
[351] This paragraph is extensively rewritten: (The exercises to be done throughout the day are equally important, and perhaps of even greater value. You have been inclined to practice only at appointed times, and then go on your way to other things, without applying what you learned to them. As a result, you have gained little reinforcement, and have not given your learning a fair chance to prove how great are its potential gifts to you.) In the *Notes* it is as shown above. FIP has it as re-written.

[352] Handwritten mark-up suggests (as well).
[353] Handwritten mark-up suggests (the thought).
[354] Handwritten mark-up suggests (we will continue).
[355] Handwritten mark-up suggests (more).

"Light and joy and peace abide in me."

W 112 L 4. On the half hour:

"I am as God created me." **W(233)**

Lesson 113 For morning and evening review: (95-96)

W 113 L 1. 95) *"I am One Self, united with my Creator."*

Serenity and perfect peace are mine
Because I am One Self, completely whole,
At one with all creation and with God.

W 113 L 2. 96) *"Salvation comes from my One Self."*

From my One Self, Whose knowledge still remains
Within my mind, I see God's perfect plan
For my salvation perfectly fulfilled.

W 113 L 3. On the hour:

"I am One Self, united with my Creator."

W 113 L 4. On the half hour:

"Salvation comes from my One Self." **W(234)**

Lesson 114 For morning and evening review: (97-98)

W 114 L 1. 97) *"I am Spirit."*

I am the Son of God. No body can
Contain my Spirit, nor impose on me
A limitation God created not.

W 114 L 2. 98) *"I will accept my part in God's plan for salvation."*

What can my function be but to accept
The Word of God, Who has created me,
For what I am and will forever be?

W 114 L 3. On the hour:

"I am Spirit."

W 114 L 4. On the half hour:

"I will accept my part in God's plan for salvation." **W(235)**

Lesson 115 For morning and evening review: (99-100)

W 115 L 1. 99) *"Salvation is my only function here."*

My function here is to forgive the world
For all the errors I have made. For thus
Am I released from them with all the world.

W 115 L 2. 100) *"My part is essential to God's plan for salvation."*

I am essential to the plan of God
For the salvation of the world. For He
Gave me His plan that I might save the world.

W 115 L 3. On the hour:

"Salvation is my only function here."

W 115 L 4. On the half hour:

"My part is essential to God's plan for salvation." **W(236)**

Lesson 116 For morning and evening review: (101-102)

W 116 L 1. 101) *"God's Will for me is perfect happiness."*

God's Will is perfect happiness for me.
And I can suffer but from the belief
There is another will apart from His.

W 116 L 2. 102) *"I share God's Will for happiness for me."*

I share my Father's Will for me, His Son.
What He has given me is all I want.
What He has given me is all there is.

W 116 L 3. On the hour:

"God's Will for me is perfect happiness."

W 116 L 4. On the half hour:

"I share God's Will for happiness for me." **W(237)**

Lesson 117 For morning and evening review: (103-104)

W 117 L 1. 103) *"God, being Love, is also happiness."*

Let me remember love is happiness
And nothing else brings joy. And so I choose
To entertain no substitutes for love.

W 117 L 2. 104) *"I seek but what belongs to me in truth."*

Love is my heritage, and with it joy.
These are the gifts my Father gave to me.
I would accept all that is mine in truth.

W 117 L 3. On the hour:

"God, being Love, is also happiness."

W 117 L 4. On the half hour:

"I seek but what belongs to me in truth." **W(238)**

Lesson 118 For morning and evening review: (105-106)

W 118 L 1. 105) *"God's peace and joy are mine"*

Today I will accept God's peace and joy
In glad exchange for all the substitutes
Which I have made for happiness and peace.

W 118 L 2. 106) *"Let me be still and listen to the truth."*

Let my own feeble voice be still, and let
Me hear the mighty Voice of truth itself
Assure me that I am God's perfect Son.

W 118 L 3. On the hour:

"God's peace and joy are mine."

W 118 L 4. On the half hour:

"Let me be still and listen to the truth." **W(239)**

Lesson 119 For morning and evening review: (107-108)

W 119 L 1. 107) *"Truth will correct all errors in my mind."*

I am mistaken when I think I can
Be hurt in any way. I am God's Son,
Whose Self rests safely in the Mind of God.

W 119 L 2. 108) *"To give and to receive are one in truth."*

I will forgive all things today, that I
May learn how to accept the truth in me,
And come to recognize my sinlessness.

W 119 L 3. On the hour:

"Truth will correct all errors in my mind."

W 119 L 4. On the half hour:

"To give and to receive are one in truth." **W(240)**

Lesson 120 For morning and evening review: (109-110)

W 120 L 1. 109) *"I rest in God."*

> *I rest in God today, and let Him work*
> *In me and through me, while I rest in Him*
> *In quiet and in perfect certainty.*

W 120 L 2. 110) *"I am as God created me."*

> *I am God's Son. Today I lay aside*
> *All sick illusions of myself, and let*
> *My Father tell me Who I really am.*

W 120 L 3. On the hour:

> *"I rest in God."*

W 120 L 4. On the half hour:

> *"I am as God created me."* **W(241)**

Lesson 121 "Forgiveness is the key to happiness."

W 121 L 1. Here is the answer to your search for peace. Here is the key to meaning in a world which seems to make no sense. Here is the way to safety in apparent dangers which appear to threaten you at every turn, and bring uncertainty to all your hopes of ever finding quietness and peace. Here are all questions answered; here the end of all uncertainty ensured at last.

W 121 L 2. The unforgiving mind is full of fear, and offers love no room to be itself; no place where it can spread its wings in peace, and soar above the turmoil of the world. The unforgiving mind is sad, without the hope of respite and release from pain. It suffers and abides in misery, peering about in darkness, seeing not, yet certain of the danger lurking there.

W 121 L 3. The unforgiving mind is torn with doubt, confused about itself and all it sees, afraid and angry, weak and blustering, afraid to go ahead, afraid to stay, afraid to waken or to go to sleep, afraid of every sound, yet more afraid of stillness; terrified of darkness, yet more terrified at the approach of light. What can the unforgiving mind perceive but its damnation? What can it behold except the proof that all its sins are real?

W 121 L 4. The unforgiving mind sees no mistakes, but only sins. It looks upon the world with sightless eyes, and shrieks as it beholds its own projections rising to attack its miserable parody of life. It wants to live, yet wishes it were dead. It wants forgiveness, yet it sees no hope. It wants escape, yet can conceive of none because it sees the sinful everywhere. **W(242)**

W 121 L 5. The unforgiving mind is in despair, without the prospect of a future which can offer anything but more despair. Yet it regards its judgment of the world as irreversible, and does not see it has condemned itself to this despair. It thinks it cannot change, for what it sees bears witness that its judgment is correct.[356] It does not ask because it thinks it knows. It does not question, certain it is right.

W 121 L 6. Forgiveness is acquired. It is not inherent in a[357] mind which cannot sin. As sin was an idea you taught yourself, forgiveness must be learned by you as well, but from a Teacher other than yourself, who represents the other Self in you. Through Him you learn how to forgive the self you think you made, and let it disappear. Thus you return your mind as one to Him Who is your Self, and Who can never sin.

W 121 L 7. Each unforgiving mind presents you with an opportunity to teach your own how to forgive itself. Each one awaits release from hell through you, and turns to you imploringly for Heaven here and now. It has no hope, but you become its hope. And as its hope do you become your own. The unforgiving mind must learn through your forgiveness that it has been saved from hell. And as you teach salvation, you will learn. Yet all your teaching and your learning will not be of you, but of the Teacher Who was given you to show the way to you.

W 121 L 8. Today we practice learning to forgive. If you are willing, you can learn today to take the key to happiness, and use it on your own behalf. We will devote ten minutes in the morning, and at night another ten, to learning how to give forgiveness and receive forgiveness too. **W(243)**

W 121 L 9. The unforgiving mind does not believe that giving and receiving are the same. Yet we will try to learn today that they are one through practicing forgiving toward one whom you think of as an enemy and one whom you consider as a friend. And as you learn to see them both as one, we will extend the lesson to ourselves,[358] and see that their escape included ours.[359]

W 121 L 10. Begin the longer practice periods by thinking of someone you do not like, who seems to irritate you, or to cause regret in you if you should meet him; one you actively despise, or merely try to overlook. It does not matter what the form your anger takes. You probably have chosen him already. He will do.

W 121 L 11. Now close your eyes and see him in your mind, and look at him a while. Try to perceive some light in him somewhere; a little gleam which you had never noticed. Try to find some little spark of brightness shining through the ugly picture which you hold of him. Look at this picture until[360] you see a light somewhere within it, and then try to let this light extend until it covers him, and makes the picture beautiful and good.

W 121 L 12. Look at this changed perception for a while, and turn your mind to one you call a friend. Try to transfer the light you learned to see around your former "enemy" to him. Perceive him now as more than friend to you, for in that light his holiness shows you your Savior, saved and saving, healed and whole.

W 121 L 13. Then let him offer you the light you see in him, and let your "enemy" and Friend unite in blessing you with what you gave. Now are you one with them, and they with you. Now have you been forgiven by yourself. Do not forget, throughout the day, the role forgiveness plays in bringing happiness to every unforgiving mind, with yours among them.

W 121 L 14. Every hour tell yourself:

> *"Forgiveness is the key to happiness.*
> *I will awaken from the dream that I*
> *Am mortal, fallible, and full of sin,*
> *And know I am the perfect Son of God."* **W(244)**

Lesson 122 "Forgiveness offers everything I want."

W 122 L 1. What could you want forgiveness cannot give? Do you want peace? Forgiveness offers it. Do you want happiness, a quiet mind, a certainty of purpose, and a sense of worth and beauty that transcends the world? Do you want care and safety, and the warmth of sure protection always? Do you want a quietness that cannot be

---

[356] **John 1:7-8** This man came for a witness, to bear witness of the Light, that all through him might believe. He was not that Light, but was sent to bear witness of that Light.
John 18:37 Pilate therefore said to Him, "Are You a king then?" Jesus answered, "You say rightly that I am a king. For this cause I was born, and for this cause I have come into the world, that I should bear witness to the truth. Everyone who is of the truth hears My voice."
[357] Handwritten mark-up suggests (the).

[358] Handwritten mark-up suggests (yourself).
[359] Handwritten mark-up suggests (yours).
[360] Handwritten mark-up suggests (till) or in the spelling conventions used in this edition, ('til).

disturbed, a gentleness that never can be hurt, a deep, abiding comfort, and a rest so perfect it can never be upset?

W 122 L 2. All this forgiveness offers you, and more. It sparkles in your eyes as you awake, and gives you joy with which to meet the day. It soothes your forehead while you sleep, and rests upon your eyelids so you see no dreams of fear and evil, malice and attack. And when you wake again, it offers you another day of happiness and peace. All this forgiveness offers you, and more.

W 122 L 3. Forgiveness lets the veil be lifted up which hides the Face of Christ from those who look with unforgiving eyes upon the world. It lets you recognize the Son of God, and clears your memory of all dead thoughts so that remembrance of your Father can arise across the threshold of your mind. What would you want forgiveness cannot give? What gifts but these are worthy to be sought? What fancied value, trivial effect, or transient promise never to be kept, can hold more hope than what forgiveness brings?

W 122 L 4. Why would you seek an answer other than the answer that will answer everything? Here is the perfect answer, given to imperfect questions, meaningless requests, half-hearted willingness to hear, and less than halfway diligence and partial trust. Here is the answer! Seek for it no more. You will not find another one instead.

W 122 L 5. God's plan for your salvation cannot change, nor can it fail. Be thankful it remains exactly as He planned it. Changelessly it stands before you, like an open door with warmth and welcome calling from beyond the doorway, bidding you to enter in, and make yourself at home where you belong. **W(245)**

W 122 L 6. Here is the answer! Would you stand outside while all of Heaven waits for you within? Forgive and be forgiven. As you give you will receive. There is no plan but this for the salvation of the Son of God. Let us today rejoice that this is so, for here we have an answer, clear and plain, beyond deceit in its simplicity.

W 122 L 7. All of the complexities the world has spun of fragile cobwebs disappear before the power and the majesty of this extremely simple statement of the truth. Here is the answer! Do not turn away in aimless wandering again. Accept salvation now. It is the gift of God and not the world. The world can give no gifts of any value to a mind which has received what God has given as its own.

W 122 L 8. God wills salvation be received today, and that the intricacies of your dreams no longer hide their nothingness from you. Open your eyes today, and look upon a happy world of safety and of peace. Forgiveness is the means by which it comes to take the place of hell. In quietness it rises up to greet your open eyes, and fill your heart with deep tranquility as ancient truths, forever newly born, arise in your awareness. What you will remember then can never be described. Yet your forgiveness offers it to you.

W 122 L 9. Remembering the gifts forgiveness gives, we undertake our practicing today with hope and faith that this will be the day salvation will be ours. Earnestly and gladly will we seek for it today, aware we hold the key within our hands, accepting Heaven's answer to the hell we made, but where we would remain no more.

W 122 L 10. Morning and evening do we gladly give a quarter of an hour to the search in which the end of hell is guaranteed. Begin in hopefulness, for we have reached the turning point at which the road becomes far easier. And now the way is short that yet we travel. We are close indeed to the appointed ending of the dream. **W(246)**

W 122 L 11. Sink into happiness as you begin these practice periods, for they hold out the sure rewards of questions answered, and what your acceptance of the answer brings. Today it will be given you to feel the peace forgiveness offers, and the joy the lifting of the veil holds out to you.

W 122 L 12. Before the light you will receive today the world will fade until it disappears, and you will see another world arise you have no words to picture. Now we walk directly into light, and we receive the gifts which have been held in store for us since time began, kept waiting for today.

W 122 L 13. Forgiveness offers everything you want. Today all things you want are given you. Let not your gifts recede throughout the day, as you return again to meet a world of shifting change and bleak appearances. Retain your gifts in clear awareness as you see the changeless in the heart of change; the light of truth behind appearances.

W 122 L 14. Be tempted not to let your gifts slip by, and drift into forgetfulness but hold them firmly in your mind by your attempts to think of them at least a minute as each quarter of an hour passes by. **W(247)** Remind yourself how precious are these gifts with this reminder, which has power to hold your gifts in your awareness through the day:

> "Forgiveness offers everything I want.
> Today I have accepted this as true.
> Today I have received the gifts of God." **W(248)**

Lesson 123 "I thank my Father for His gifts to me."

W 123 L 1. Today let us be thankful. We have come to gentler pathways and to smoother roads. There is no thought of turning back, and no implacable resistance to the truth. A bit of wavering remains, some small objections and a little hesitance, but we[361] can well be grateful for our[362] gains, which are far greater than we[363] realize. A day devoted now to gratitude will add the benefit of some insight into the real extent of all the gains which you have made; the gifts you have received.

W 123 L 2. Be glad today in loving thankfulness your Father has not left you to yourself, nor let you wander in the dark alone. Be grateful He has saved you from the self you thought you made to take the place of Him and His creation. Give Him thanks today. Give thanks that He has not abandoned you, and that His Love forever will remain shining on you, forever without change.

W 123 L 3. Give thanks as well that you are changeless, for the Son He loves is changeless as Himself. Be grateful you are saved. Be glad you have a function in salvation to fulfill. Be thankful that your value far transcends your meager gifts and petty judgments of the one whom God established as His Son.

W 123 L 4. Today in gratitude we lift our hearts above despair, and raise our thankful eyes, no longer looking downward to the dust. We sing the song of thankfulness today in honor of the Self Which God has willed to be our true identity in Him. Today we smile on everyone we see, and walk with lightened footsteps as we go to do what is appointed us to do.

W 123 L 5. We do not go alone. And we give thanks that in our solitude a Friend has come to speak the saving Word of God to us. **W(249)** And thanks to you for listening to Him. His Word is soundless if it be not heard. In thanking Him the thanks are yours as well. An unheard message will not save the world, however mighty be the Voice that speaks, however loving may the message be.

W 123 L 6. Thanks be to you who heard, for you become the messengers who bring His Voice with you, and let it echo round and round the world. Receive the thanks of God today, as you give thanks to Him. For He would offer you the thanks you give, since He receives your gifts in loving gratitude, and gives them back a thousand and a hundred thousand more than they were given. He will bless your gifts by sharing them with you. And so they grow in

---

[361] Handwritten mark-up suggests (you).
[362] Handwritten mark-up suggests (your).
[363] Handwritten mark-up suggests (you).

power and in strength until they fill the world with gladness and with gratitude.

W 123 L 7. Receive His thanks and offer yours to Him for fifteen minutes twice today. And you will realize to Whom you offer thanks, and Whom He thanks as you are thanking Him. This holy half an hour given Him will be returned to you in terms of years for every second; power to save the world eons more quickly for your thanks to Him.

W 123 L 8. Receive His thanks, and you will understand how lovingly He holds you in His Mind, how deep and limitless His care for you, how perfect is His gratitude to you. Remember hourly to think of Him, and give Him thanks for everything He[364] gave His Son, that he might rise above the world remembering His Father and his Self. **W(250)**

Lesson 124 "Let me remember I am one with God."

W 124 L 1. Today we will again give thanks for our identity in God. Our home is safe, protection guaranteed in all we do, power and strength available to us in all our undertakings. We can fail in nothing. Everything we touch takes on a shining light which blesses and which heals. At one with God and with the universe, we go our way rejoicing, with the thought that God Himself goes everywhere with us.

W 124 L 2. How holy are our minds! And everything we see reflects the holiness within the mind at one with God and with itself. How easily do errors disappear, and death give place to everlasting life. Our shining footprints point the way to truth, for God is our Companion as we walk the world a little while. And those who come to follow us will recognize the way because the light we carry stays behind, yet still remains with us as we walk on.

W 124 L 3. What we receive is our eternal gift to those who follow after, and to those who went before or stayed with us a while. And God, Who loves us with the equal love in which we were created, smiles on us and offers us the happiness we gave.

W 124 L 4. Today we will not doubt His Love for us, nor question His protection and His care. No meaningless anxieties can come between our faith and our awareness of His Presence. We are one with Him today in recognition and remembrance. We feel Him in our hearts. Our minds contain His Thoughts, our eyes behold His loveliness in all we look upon. Today we see only the loving and the loveable.

W 124 L 5. We see it in appearances of pain, and pain gives way to peace. We see it in the frantic, in the sad and the distressed, the lonely and afraid, who are restored to the tranquility and peace of mind in which they were created. And we see it in the dying and the dead as well, restoring them to life. **W(251)** All this we see because we saw it first within ourselves.

W 124 L 6. No miracle can ever be denied to those who know that they are one with God. No thought of theirs but has the power to heal all forms of suffering in anyone in times gone by and times as yet to come as easily as in the ones who walk beside them now. Their thoughts are timeless, and apart from distance as apart from time.

W 124 L 7. We join in this awareness as we say that we are one with God. For in these words we say as well that we are saved and healed; that we can save and heal accordingly. We have accepted and we now would give, for we would keep the gifts our Father gave. Today we would experience ourselves at one with Him, so that the world may share our recognition of reality. In our experience the world is freed. As we deny our separation from our Father, it is healed along with us.

W 124 L 8. Peace be to you today. Secure your peace by practicing awareness you are one with your Creator, as He is with you. Sometime today, whenever it seems best, devote a half an hour to the thought that you are one with God. This is our first attempt at an extended period for which we give no rules nor special words to guide your meditation. We will trust God's Voice to speak as He sees fit today, certain He will not fail. Abide with Him this half an hour. He will do the rest.

W 124 L 9. Your benefit will not be less if you believe that nothing happened. You may not be ready to accept the gain today. Yet sometime, somewhere, it will come to you, nor will you fail to recognize it when it dawns with certainty upon your mind. This half an hour will be framed in gold, with every minute like a diamond set around the mirror that this exercise will offer you. And you will see Christ's Face upon it, in reflection of your own. **W(252)**

W 124 L 10. Perhaps today, perhaps tomorrow, you will see your own transfiguration in the glass this holy half an hour will hold out to you, to look upon yourself.[365] When you are ready; you will find it there, within your mind and waiting to be found. You will remember then the Thought to which you gave this half an hour, thankfully aware no time was ever better spent. Perhaps today, perhaps tomorrow, you will look into this glass, and understand the sinless light you see belongs to you; the loveliness you look on is your own.

W 124 L 11. Count this half hour as your gift to God, in certainty that His return will be a sense of love you cannot understand, a joy too deep for you to comprehend, a sight too holy for the body's eyes to see, and yet you can be sure some day, perhaps today, perhaps tomorrow, you will understand and comprehend and see. Add further jewels to the golden frame that holds the mirror offered you today by hourly repeating to yourself:

> *"Let me remember I am one with God,*
> *At one with all my brothers and my Self,*
> *In everlasting holiness and peace."* **W(253)**

Lesson 125 "In quiet I receive God's Word today."

W 125 L 1. Let this day be a day of stillness and of quiet listening. Your Father wills you hear His Word today. He calls to you from deep within your mind where He abides. Hear Him today. No peace is possible until His Word is heard around the world; until your mind, in quiet listening, accepts the message which the world must hear to usher in the quiet time of peace.

W 125 L 2. This world will change through you. No other means can save it, for God's plan is simply this: The Son of God is free to save himself, given the Word of God to be his Guide, forever in his mind and at his side to lead him surely to his Father's house by his own will, forever free as God's. He is not led by force, but only love. He is not judged, but only sanctified.

W 125 L 3. In stillness we will hear His[366] Voice today, without intrusion of our petty thoughts, without our personal desires, and without all judgment of His holy Word. We will not judge ourselves today, for what we are can not be judged. We stand apart from all the judgments which the world has laid upon the Son of God. It knows him not. Today we will not listen to the world, but wait in silence for the Word of God.

W 125 L 4. Hear, holy Son of God, your Father speak. His Voice would give to you His holy Word to spread across the world the

---

[364] While the *Urtext* manuscript has "you" instead of "He", both the *Notes* and FIP have "He" which does seem more likely to be correct.

[365] **Matthew 17:2** And He was transfigured before them. His face shone like the sun, and His clothes became as white as the light.
1 Corinthians 13:12 For now we see in a mirror, dimly, but then face to face. Now I know in part, but then I shall know just as I also am known.
[366] Handwritten mark-up suggests (God's).

tidings of salvation and the holy time of peace.[367] We gather at the throne of God today, the quiet place within your[368] mind where He abides forever in the holiness which He created and will never leave.

W 125 L 5. He has not waited until you return your mind to Him to give His Word to you. He has not hid Himself from you while you have wandered off a little while from Him. He does not cherish the illusions which you hold about yourself. He knows His Son, and wills that he remain as part of Him regardless of his dreams; regardless of his madness that his will is not his own. **W(254)**

W 125 L 6. Today He speaks to you. His Voice awaits your silence, for His Word cannot be heard until your mind is quiet for a while, and meaningless desires have been stilled. Await His Word in quiet. There is peace within you to be called upon today to help make ready your most holy mind to hear the Voice of its Creator speak.

W 125 L 7. Three times today, at times most suitable for silence, give ten minutes set apart from listening to the world, and choose instead a gentle listening to the Word of God. He speaks from nearer than your heart to you. His Voice is closer than your hand. His Love is everything you are and that He is; the same as you, and you the same as He.

W 125 L 8. It is your voice to which you listen as He speaks to you. It is your Word He speaks. It is the Word of freedom and of peace, of unity of will and purpose, with no separation nor division in the single Mind of Father and of Son. In quiet listen to your Self today, and let Him tell you God has never left is Son, and you have never left your Self.

W 125 L 9. Only be quiet. You will need no rule but this to let your practicing today lift you above the thinking of the world, and free your vision from the body's eyes. Only be still and listen. You will hear the Word in which the Will of God the Son joins in His Father's Will, at one with It, with no illusions interposed between the wholly indivisible and true. As every hour passes by today be still a moment, and remind yourself you have a special purpose for this day; - in quiet to receive the Word of God.[369] **W(255)**

Lesson 126 "All that I give is given to myself."

W 126 L 1. Today's idea, completely alien to the ego and the thinking of the world, is crucial to the thought reversal which this course will bring about. If you believed this statement there would be no problem in complete forgiveness, certainty of goal, and sure direction. You would understand the means by which salvation comes to you, and would not hesitate to use it now.

W 126 L 2. Let us consider what you do believe in place of this idea. It seems to you that other people are apart from you, and able to behave in ways which have no bearing on your thoughts, nor theirs on yours. Therefore your attitudes have no effect on them, and their appeals for help are not in any way related to your own. You further think that they can sin without affecting your perception of yourself, while you can judge their sin and yet remain apart from condemnation and at peace.

W 126 L 3. When you "forgive" a sin, there is no gain to you directly. You give charity to one unworthy merely to point out that you are better, on a higher plane than he whom you forgive. He has not earned your charitable tolerance, which you bestow on one unworthy of the gift because his sins have lowered him beneath a true equality with you. He has no claim on your forgiveness. It holds out a gift to him but hardly to yourself.

W 126 L 4. Thus is forgiveness basically unsound; a charitable whim, benevolent yet undeserved; a gift bestowed at times, at other times withheld. Unmerited, withholding it is just, nor is it fair that you should suffer when it is withheld. The sin which you forgive is not your own. Someone apart from you committed it and if you then are gracious unto him by giving him what he does not deserve, your[370] gift is no more yours than was his sin. **W(256)**

W 126 L 5. If this be true, forgiveness has no grounds on which to rest dependably and sure. It is an eccentricity in which you sometimes choose to give indulgently an undeserved reprieve. Yet it remains your right to let the sinner not escape the justified repayment for his sin. Think you the Lord of Heaven would allow the world's salvation to depend on this? Would not His care for you be small indeed if your salvation rested on a whim?

W 126 L 6. You do not understand forgiveness. As you see it, it is but a check upon overt attack, without requiring correction in your mind. It cannot give you peace as you perceive it. It is not a means for your release from what you see in someone other than yourself. It has no power to restore your unity with him to your awareness. It is not what God intended it to be for you.

W 126 L 7. Not having given Him the gift He asks of you, you cannot recognize His gifts, and think He has not given them to you. Yet would He ask you for a gift unless it was for you? Could He be satisfied with empty gestures, and evaluate such petty gifts as worthy of His Son? Salvation is a better gift than this,[371] and true forgiveness, as the means by which it is attained, must heal the mind that gives, for giving is receiving. What remains as unreceived has not been given, but what has been given must have been received.

W 126 L 8. Today we try to understand the truth that giver and receiver are the same. You will need help to make this meaningful because it is so alien to the thoughts to which you are accustomed. But the Help you need is there. Give Him your faith today and ask Him that He share your practicing in truth today. And if you only catch a tiny glimpse of the release which lies in the idea we practice for today, this is a day of glory for the world. **W(257)**

W 126 L 9. Give fifteen minutes twice today to the attempt to understand today's idea. It is the thought by which forgiveness takes its proper place in your priorities. It is the thought that will release your mind from every bar to what forgiveness means, and let you realize its worth to you.

W 126 L 10. In silence close your eyes upon the world which does not understand forgiveness, and seek sanctuary in the quiet place where thoughts are changed and false beliefs laid by. Repeat today's idea, and ask for help in understanding what it really means. Be willing to be taught. Be glad to hear the Voice of truth and healing speak to you, and you will understand the words He speaks, and recognize He speaks your words to you.

W 126 L 11. As often as you can, remind yourself you have a goal today; an aim which makes this day of special value to yourself and all your brothers. Do not let your mind forget this goal for long, but tell yourself:

"All that I give is given to myself.
The Help I need to learn that this is true
Is with me now. And I will trust in Him."

Then spend the[372] quiet moment, opening your mind to His correction and His Love. And what you hear of Him you will believe, for what He gives will be received by you. **W(258)**

---

[367] **Luke 1:19** And the angel answered and said to him, "I am Gabriel, who stands in the presence of God, and was sent to speak to you and bring you these glad tidings."
Luke 8:1 Now it came to pass, afterward, that He went through every city and village, preaching and bringing the glad tidings of the kingdom of God. And the twelve were with Him,
[368] Handwritten mark-up suggests (the).
[369] **Psalm 46:10** Be still, and know that I am God; I will be exalted among the nations, I will be exalted in the earth!

[370] Handwritten mark-up suggests (the).
[371] Handwritten mark-up suggests a period and a new sentence.
[372] Handwritten mark-up suggests (a).

Volume II - Workbook Part 1

Lesson 127 "There is no love but God's."

W 127 L 1. Perhaps you think that different kinds of love are possible. Perhaps you think there is a kind of love for this, a kind for that; a way of loving one, another way of loving still another. Love is one. It has no separate parts and no degrees; no kinds nor levels, no divergences and no distinctions. It is like itself, unchanged throughout. It never alters with a person or a circumstance. It is the heart of God and also of His Son.

W 127 L 2. Love's meaning is obscure to anyone who thinks that love can change. He does not see that changing love must be impossible. And thus he thinks that he can love at times and hate at other times. He also thinks that love can be bestowed on one and yet remain itself although it is withheld from others. To believe these things of love is not to understand it. If it could make such distinctions it would have to judge between the righteous and the sinner, and perceive the Son of God in separate parts.

W 127 L 3. Love cannot judge. As it is one itself, it looks on all as one. Its meaning lies in oneness. And it must elude the mind that thinks of it as partial or in part. There is no love but God's, and all of love is His. There is no[373] principle which rules where love is not. Love is a law without an opposite. Its wholeness is the power holding everything as one, the link between the Father and the Son which holds them both forever as the same.

W 127 L 4. No course whose purpose is to teach you what you really are could fail to emphasize there is no difference in what you are and what love is. Love's meaning is your own, and shared by God Himself. For what you are is what He is. There is no love but His, and what He is is everything there is. There is no limit placed upon Himself, and so are you unlimited as well. **W(259)**

W 127 L 5. No laws the world obeys can help you grasp love's meaning. What the world believes was made to hide love's meaning and to keep it dark and secret. There is not one principle the world upholds but violates the truth of what love is, and what you are as well. Seek not within the world to find your Self.[374] Love is not found in darkness and in death. Yet it is perfectly apparent to the eyes that see and ears that hear its[375] Voice.

W 127 L 6. Today we practice making free our[376] minds of all the laws you think you must obey; of all the limits under which you live, and all the changes which you think are part of human destiny. Today we take the largest single step this course requests in your advance toward its established goal. If you achieve the faintest glimmering of what love means today, you have advanced in distance without measure and in time beyond the count of years to your release.

W 127 L 7. Let us together, then, be glad to give some time to God today, and understand there is no better use for time than this. For fifteen minutes twice today escape from every law in which you now believe. Open your mind and rest. The world which seems to hold you prisoner can be escaped by anyone who does not hold it dear. Withdraw all value you have placed upon its meagre offerings and senseless gifts, and let the Gift of God replace them all.

W 127 L 8. Call to your Father, certain that His Voice will answer. He Himself has promised this. And He Himself will place a spark of truth within your mind wherever you give up a false belief, a dark illusion of your own reality and what love means. He will shine through your idle thoughts today, and help you understand the truth of love. In loving gentleness He will abide with you, as you allow His Voice to teach love's meaning to your clean and open mind.[377] And He will bless the lesson with His Love. **W(260)**

W 127 L 9. Today the legion of the future years of waiting for salvation disappears before the timelessness of what you learn. Let us give thanks today that we are spared a future like the past. Today we leave the past behind us, never more to be remembered. And we raise our eyes upon a different present, where a future shines[378] unlike the past in every attribute.

W 127 L 10. The world in infancy is newly born. And we will watch it grow in strength and health[379] to shed its blessing upon all who come to learn to cast aside the world they thought was made in hate to be love's enemy. Now are they all made free along with us. Now are they all our brothers in God's Love.

W 127 L 11. We will remember them throughout the day because we cannot leave a part of us outside our love, if we would know our Self. At least three times an hour think of one who makes the journey with you, and who came to learn what you must learn. And as he comes to mind, give him this message from your Self:

> "I bless you, brother, with the Love of God
> Which I would share with you. For I would learn
> The joyous lesson that there is no love
> But God's and yours and mine and everyone's." **W(261)**

Lesson 128 "The world I see has nothing that I want."

W 128 L 1. The world you see has nothing that you need to offer you; nothing that you can use in any way, nor anything at all that serves to give you joy. Believe this thought, and you are saved from years of misery, from countless disappointments, and from hopes that turn to bitter ashes of despair. No-one but must accept this thought as true, if he would leave this world behind and soar beyond its petty scope and little ways.

W 128 L 2. Each thing you value here is but a chain that binds you to the world, and it will serve no other end but this. For everything must serve the purpose you have given it until you see a different purpose there. The only purpose worthy of your mind this world contains is that you pass it by, without delaying to perceive some hope where there is none. Be you deceived no more. The world you see has nothing that you want.

W 128 L 3. Escape today the chains you place upon your mind when you perceive salvation here. For what you value you make part of you, as you perceive yourself. All things you seek to make your value greater in your sight limit you further, hide your worth from you, and add another bar across the door that leads to true awareness of your Self.

W 128 L 4. Let nothing which[380] relates to body thoughts delay your progress to salvation, nor permit temptation to believe the world has anything you want to hold you back. Nothing is here to cherish. Nothing here is worth one instant of delay and pain; one moment of uncertainty and doubt. The worthless offers nothing. Certainty of worth cannot be found in worthlessness.

W 128 L 5. Today we practice letting go all thought of values we have given to the world. We leave it free of purposes we gave its aspects and its phases and its dreams. We hold it purposeless within our minds, and loosen it from all we wish it were. Thus do we lift the chains which bar the door to freedom from **W(262)** the world, and go beyond all little values and diminished goals.

---

[373] Handwritten mark-up suggests (other).
[374] **John 5:44** "How can ye believe, who receive glory one of another, and the glory that *cometh* from the only God ye seek not?"
[375] Handwritten mark-up suggests (Love's).
[376] Handwritten mark-up suggests (your).
[377] **John 14:16** "And I will pray the Father, and He will give you another Helper, that He may abide with you forever."
[378] Handwritten mark-up suggests (dawns).
[379] Handwritten mark-up suggests (health and strength).
[380] Handwritten mark-up suggests (that).

W 128 L 6. Peace and be still a little while, and see how far you rise above the world when you release your mind from chains, and let it seek the level where it finds itself at home. It will be grateful to be free a while. It knows where it belongs. But free its wings, and it will fly in sureness and in joy to join its holy purpose. Let it rest in its Creator, there to be restored to sanity, to freedom and to love.

W 128 L 7. Give it ten minutes rest three times today. And when your eyes are opened afterwards, you will not value anything you see as much as when you looked at it before. Your whole perspective on the world will shift by just a little every time you let your mind escape its chains. The world is not where it belongs. And you belong where it would be, and where it goes to rest when you release it from the world. Your Guide is sure. Open your mind to Him. Be still and rest.

W 128 L 8. Protect your mind throughout the day as well. And when you think you see some value in an aspect or an image of the world, refuse to lay this chain upon your mind, and tell yourself with quiet certainty:

> *"This will not tempt me to delay myself.*
> *The world I see has nothing that I want."* **W(263)**

Lesson 129 "Beyond this world there is a world I want."

W 129 L 1. This is the thought which follows from the one we practiced yesterday. You cannot stop with the idea the world is worthless, for unless you see that there is something else to hope for you will only be depressed. Our emphasis is not on giving up the world, but on exchanging it for what is far more satisfying, filled with joy, and capable of offering you peace. Think you this world can offer that to you?

W 129 L 2. It might be worth a little time to think once more about the value of this world. Perhaps you will concede there is no loss in letting go all thought of value here. The world you see is merciless indeed, unstable, cruel, unconcerned with you, quick to avenge and pitiless with hate. It gives but to rescind, and takes away all things that you have cherished for a while. No lasting love is found, for none is here. This is the world of time, where all things end.

W 129 L 3. Is it a loss to find a world instead where losing is impossible? Where love endures forever, hate cannot exist, and vengeance has no meaning? Is it loss to find all things you really want and know they have no ending, and they will remain exactly as you want them throughout time? Yet even they will be exchanged at last for what we cannot speak of, for you go from there to where words fail entirely, into a silence where the language is unspoken and yet surely understood.

W 129 L 4. Communication, unambiguous and plain as day, remains unlimited for all eternity. And God Himself speaks to His Son as His Son speaks to Him. Their language has no words, for what they say cannot be symbolized. Their knowledge is direct and wholly shared and wholly one. **W(264)**

W 129 L 5. How far away from this are you who stay bound to this world. And yet how near are you when you exchange it for the world you want. Now is the last step certain; now you stand an instant's space away from timelessness. Here can you but look forward, never back to see again the world you do not want. Here is the world that comes to take its place as you unbind your mind from little things the world sets forth to keep you prisoner there. Value them not, and they will disappear. Esteem them, and they will seem real to you.

W 129 L 6. Such is the choice. What loss can be for you in choosing not to value nothingness? This world holds nothing that you really want, but what you choose instead you want indeed! Let it be given you today. It waits but for your choosing it to take the place of all the things you seek but do not want.

W 129 L 7. Practice your willingness to make this change ten minutes in the morning and at night, and once more in between. Begin with this:

> *"Beyond this world there is a world I want.*
> *I choose to see that world instead of this,*
> *For here is nothing that I really want."*

Then close your eyes upon the world you see, and in the silent darkness watch the lights that are not of this world light one by one until where one begins, another ends, loses all meaning as they blend in one.

W 129 L 8. Today the lights of Heaven bend to you, to shine upon your eyelids as you rest beyond the world of darkness. Here is light your eyes cannot behold. And yet your mind can see it plainly, and can understand. A day of grace is given you today, and we give thanks.

W 129 L 9. This day we realize that what you feared to lose was only loss. **W(265)** Now do we understand there is no loss. For we have seen its opposite at last, and we are grateful that the choice is made. Remember your decision hourly, and take a moment to confirm your choice by laying by whatever thoughts you have, and dwelling briefly only upon this:

> *"The world I see has nothing that I want.*
> *Beyond this world there is a world I want."* **W(266)**

Lesson 130 "It is impossible to see two worlds."

W 130 L 1. Perception is consistent. What you see reflects your thinking. And your thinking but reflects your choice of what you want to see. Your values are determiners of this, for what you value you must want to see, believing what you see is really there. No-one can see a world his mind has not accorded value. And no-one can fail to look upon what he believes he wants.

W 130 L 2. Yet who can really hate and love at once? Who can desire what he does not want to have reality? And who can choose to see a world of which he is afraid? Fear must make blind, for this its weapon is; that which you fear to see you cannot see. Love and perception thus go hand in hand, but fear obscures in darkness what is there.

W 130 L 3. What, then, can fear project upon the world? What can be seen in darkness that is real? Truth is eclipsed by fear, and what remains is but imagined. Yet what can be real in blind imaginings of panic born? What would you want that this[381] is shown to you? What would you wish to keep in such a dream?

W 130 L 4. Fear has made everything you think you see. All separation, all distinctions, and the multitude of differences you believe make up the world. They are not there. Love's enemy has made them up. Yet love can have no enemy, and so they have no cause, no being and no consequence. They can be valued, but remain unreal. They can be sought, but they can not be found.[382] Today we will not seek for them, nor waste this day in seeking not what can be found.

W 130 L 5. It is impossible to see two worlds which have no overlap of any kind. Seek for the one; the other disappears. But one remains. They are the range of choice beyond which your decision cannot go. The real and the unreal are all there is to choose between, and nothing more than these. **W(267)**

---

[381] The *Urtext* manuscript has "**thus**". This appears to be a typo, and *FIP* agrees it should be "**this**". In the *Notes* it also appears to be "this."
[382] **Matthew 7:7** "Ask, and it will be given to you; seek, and you will find; knock, and it will be opened to you."

W 130 L 6. Today we will attempt no compromise where none is possible. The world you see is proof you have already made a choice as all-embracing as its opposite. What we would learn today is more than just the lesson that you cannot see two worlds. It also teaches that the one you see is quite consistent from the point of view from which you see it. It is all a piece because it stems from one emotion, and reflects its source in everything you see.

W 130 L 7. Six times today, in thanks and gratitude, we gladly give five minutes to the thought which ends all compromise and doubt, and go beyond it[383] all as one. We will not make a thousand meaningless distinctions, nor attempt to bring with us a little part of unreality, as we devote our minds to finding only what is real.

W 130 L 8. Begin your searching for the other world, by asking for a strength beyond your own, and recognize what it is you seek. You do not want illusions. And you come to these five minutes emptying your hands of all the petty treasures of this world. You wait for God to help you, as you say:

"It is impossible to see two worlds.

Let me accept the strength God offers me

And see no value in this world, that I

May find my freedom and deliverance."

W 130 L 9. God will be there. For you have called upon the great unfailing Power Who will take this giant step with you in gratitude. Nor will you fail to see His thanks expressed in tangible perception and in truth. You will not doubt what you will look upon. For though it is perception, it is not the kind of seeing that your eyes alone have ever seen before. And you will know God's strength upheld as you made this choice. **W(268)**

W 130 L 10. Dismiss temptation easily today whenever it arises, merely by remembering the limits on your choice. The unreal or the real, the false or true is what you see, and only what you see. Perception is consistent with your choice, and hell or Heaven comes to you as one.

W 130 L 11. Accept a little part of hell as real, and you have damned your eyes and cursed your sight, and what you will behold is hell indeed. Yet the release of Heaven still remains within your range of choice, to take the place of everything that hell would show to you. All you need say to any part of hell, whatever form it takes, is simply this:

"It is impossible to see two worlds.

I seek my freedom and deliverance,

And this is not a part of what I want." **W(269)**

Lesson 131 "No-one can fail who asks to reach the truth."

W 131 L 1. Failure is all about you while you seek for goals which cannot be achieved. You look for permanence in the impermanent; for love where there is none; for safety in the midst of danger; immortality within the darkness of the dream of death. Who could succeed where contradiction is the setting of his searching, and the place to which he comes to find stability?

W 131 L 2. Goals which are meaningless are not attained. There is no way to reach them, for the means by which you strive for them are meaningless as they are. Who can use such senseless means and hope through them to gain in anything? Where can they lead? And what could they achieve that offers any hope of being real? Pursuit of the imagined leads to death because it is the search for nothingness, and while you seek for life you ask for death. You look for safety and security while in your heart you pray for danger and protection for the little dream you made.

W 131 L 3. Yet searching is inevitable here. For this you came, and you will surely do the thing you came for. But the world cannot dictate the goal for which you search unless you give it power to do so. Otherwise, you still are free to choose a goal that lies beyond the world and every worldly thought, and one which comes to you from an idea relinquished yet remembered, old yet new; an echo of a heritage forgot, yet holding everything you really want.

W 131 L 4. Be glad that search you must. Be glad as well to learn you search for Heaven, and must find the goal you really want. No-one can fail to want this goal, and reach it in the end. God's Son cannot seek vainly, though he try to force delay, deceive himself, and think that it is hell he seeks. When he is wrong he finds correction, when he wanders off he is led back to his appointed task. **W(270)**

W 131 L 5. No-one remains in hell, for no-one can abandon his Creator, nor affect His perfect, timeless and unchanging Love. You will find Heaven. Everything you seek but this will fall away, yet not because it has been taken from you. It will go because you do not want it. You will reach the goal you really want as certainly as God created you in sinlessness.

W 131 L 6. Why wait for Heaven? It is here today. Time is the great illusion it is past or in the future. Yet this cannot be if it is where God wills His Son to be. How could the Will of God be in the past or yet to happen? What He wills is now, without a past and wholly futureless. It is as far removed from time as is a tiny candle from a distant star, or what you chose from what you really want.

W 131 L 7. Heaven remains your one alternative to this strange world you made and all its ways; its shifting patterns and uncertain goals, its painful pleasures and its tragic joys. God made no contradictions. What denies its own existence and attacks itself is not of Him. He did not make two minds, with Heaven as the glad effect of one, and earth the other's sorry outcome which is Heaven's opposite in every way.

W 131 L 8. God does not suffer conflict. Nor is His creation split in two. How could it be His Son could be in hell when God Himself established him in Heaven? Could he lose what the Eternal Will has given him to be his home forever? Let us not try longer to impose an alien will upon His[384] single purpose. He is here because He Wills to be, and what He wills is present now beyond the reach of time.

W 131 L 9. Today we will not choose a paradox in place of truth. How could the Son of God make time to take away the Will of God? He thus denies himself, and contradicts what has no opposite. He thinks he made a hell opposing Heaven, and believes that he abides in what does not exist, while Heaven is the place he cannot find. Leave foolish thoughts like these behind today, and turn your mind to true ideas instead. **W(271)** No-one can fail who asks to reach the truth, and it is truth we ask to reach today.

W 131 L 10. We will devote ten minutes to this goal three times today, and we will ask to see the rising of the real world to replace the foolish images that we held dear, with true ideas arising in the place of thoughts which have no meaning, no effect, and neither source nor substance in the truth. This we acknowledge as we start upon our practice periods. Begin with this:

"I ask to see a different world, and think

A different kind of thoughts from those I made.

The world I seek I did not make alone,

The thoughts I want to think are not my own."

W 131 L 11. For several minutes watch your mind and see, although your eyes are closed, the senseless world you think is real. Review the thoughts as well which are compatible with such a world, and which you think are true. Then let them go, and sink

---

[383] Handwritten mark-up suggests (them).

[384] Handwritten mark-up suggests (God's).

below them to the holy place where they can enter not. There is a door beneath them in your mind which you could not completely lock to hide what lies beyond.

W 131 L 12. Seek for that door and find it. But before you try to open it, remind yourself no-one can fail who asks to reach the truth, and it is this request you make today. Nothing but this has any meaning now; no other goal is valued now nor sought; nothing before this door you really want, and only what lies past it do you seek.

W 131 L 13. Put out your hand and see how easily the door swings open with your one intent to go beyond it. Angels light the way, so that all darkness vanishes and you are standing in a light so bright and clear that you can understand all things you see. A tiny moment of surprise, perhaps, will make you pause before you realize the world you see before you in the light reflects the truth you knew, and did not quite forget in wandering away in dreams. **W(272)**

W 131 L 14. You cannot fail today. There walks with you the Spirit Heaven sent you that you might approach this door some day, and through His aid slip effortlessly past it to the light. Today that day has come. Today God keeps His ancient promise to His holy Son, as does His Son remember his to Him. This is a day of gladness, for we come to the appointed time and place where you will find the goal of all your searching here and all the seeking of the world, which end together as you pass beyond the door.

W 131 L 15. Remember often that today should be a time of special gladness, and refrain from dismal thoughts and meaningless laments. Salvation's time has come. Today is set by Heaven Itself to be a time of grace for you and for the world. If you forget this happy fact, remind yourself with this:

> "Today I seek and find all that I want.
> "My single purpose offers it to me.
> No-one can fail who asks to reach the truth." **W(273)**

Lesson 132 "I loose the world from all I thought it was."

W 132 L 1. What keeps the world in chains but your beliefs? And what can save the world except your Self? Belief is powerful indeed. The thoughts you hold are mighty, and illusions are as strong in their effects as is the truth. A madman thinks the world he sees is real and does not doubt it. Nor can he be swayed by questioning his thoughts' effects. It is but when their source is raised to question that the hope of freedom comes to him at last.

W 132 L 2. Yet is salvation easily achieved, for anyone is free to change his mind, and all his thoughts change with it. Now the source of thought has shifted, for to change your mind means you have changed the source of all ideas you think or ever thought or yet will think. You free the past from what you thought before. You free the future from all ancient thoughts of seeking what you do not want to find. The present now remains the only time.

W 132 L 3. Here in the present is the world set free. For as you let the past be lifted and release the future from your ancient fears, you find escape and give it to the world. You have enslaved the world with all your fears, with[385] doubts and miseries, your pain and tears, and all your sorrows press upon it, and keep it a prisoner to your beliefs. Death strikes it everywhere because you hold the bitter thought of death within your mind.

W 132 L 4. The world is nothing in itself. Your mind must give it meaning. And what you behold upon it are your wishes, acted out so you can look on them and think them real. **W(274)** Perhaps you think you did not make the world, but came unwillingly to what was made already, hardly waiting for your thoughts to give it meaning. Yet in truth you found exactly what you looked for when you came.

---
[385] Handwritten mark-up suggests (your).

There is no world apart from what you wish, and herein lies your ultimate release. Change but your mind on what you want to see, and all the world must change accordingly.

W 132 L 5. Ideas leave not their source. This central theme is often stated in the text, and must be borne in mind if you would understand the lesson for today. It is not pride that[386] tells you that you made the world you see, and that it changes as you change your mind. But it is pride that argues you have come into a world quite separate from yourself, impervious to what you think, and quite apart from what you chance to think it is.

W 132 L 6. There is no world! This is the central thought the course attempts to teach. Not everyone is ready to accept it, and each one must go as far as he can let himself be led along the road to truth. He will return and go still farther, or perhaps step back a while and then return again. But healing is the gift of those who are prepared to learn there is no world, and can accept the lesson now. Their readiness will bring the lesson to them in some form which they can understand and recognize.

W 132 L 7. Some see it suddenly on point of death, and rise to teach it. Others find it in experience that is not of this world, which shows them that the world does not exist because what they behold must be the truth, and yet it clearly contradicts the world. And some will find it in this course, and in the exercises that we do today.

W 132 L 8. Today's idea is true because the world does not exist. And if it is indeed your own imagining, then you can loose it from all things you ever thought it was by merely changing all the thoughts that gave it these appearances. The sick are healed as you let go all thoughts of sickness, and the dead arise when you let thoughts of life replace all thoughts you ever held of death.[387]
W(275)

W 132 L 9. A lesson earlier repeated once must now be stressed again, for it contains the firm foundation for today's idea. You are as God created you. There is no place where you can suffer, and no time that can bring change to your eternal state. How can a world of time and place exist if you remain as God created you?

W 132 L 10. What is the lesson for today except another way of saying that to know your Self is the salvation of the world? To free the world from every kind of pain is but to change your mind about yourself. There is no world apart from your ideas because ideas leave not their source, and you maintain the world within your mind in thought.

W 132 L 11. Yet if you are as God created you, you cannot think apart from Him, nor make what does not share His timelessness and love. Are these inherent in the world you see? Does it create like Him? Unless it does, it is not real and cannot be at all. If you are real the world you see is false, for God's creation is unlike the world in every way. And as it was His Thought by which[388] you were

---
[386] *Urtext* manuscript has "**that**" struck out and (which) typed above the line.
[387] **Isaiah 26:19** Your dead shall live; Together with my dead body they shall arise. Awake and sing, you who dwell in dust; For your dew is like the dew of herbs, And the earth shall cast out the dead.
Isaiah 35:5-6 Then the eyes of the blind shall be opened, And the ears of the deaf shall be unstopped. Then the lame shall leap like a deer, And the tongue of the dumb sing. For waters shall burst forth in the wilderness, And streams in the desert.
Matthew 10:1 And when He had called His twelve disciples to Him, He gave them power over unclean spirits, to cast them out, and to heal all kinds of sickness and all kinds of disease.
Matthew 10:8 "Heal the sick, cleanse the lepers, raise the dead, cast out demons. Freely you have received, freely give."
Matthew 11:5 "The blind see and the lame walk; the lepers are cleansed and the deaf hear; the dead are raised up and the poor have the gospel preached to them." *There are many more references to healing and raising the dead in the Bible.*
[388] Handwritten mark-up suggests (Which).

created, so it is your thoughts which made it and must set it free, that you may know the Thoughts you share with God.

W 132 L 12. Release the world! Your real creations wait for this release to give you fatherhood, not of illusions, but as God in truth. God shares His Fatherhood with you who are His Son, for He makes no distinctions in what is Himself and what is still Himself. What He creates is not apart from Him, and nowhere does the Father end, the Son begin as something separate from Him.

W 132 L 13. There is no world because it is a thought apart from God, and made to separate the Father and the Son, and break away a part of God Himself and thus destroy His wholeness. Can a world which comes from this idea be real? Can it be anywhere? Deny illusions, but accept the truth. Deny you are a shadow briefly laid upon a dying world. Release your mind, and you will look upon a world released. **W(276)**

W 132 L 14. Today our purpose is to free the world from all the idle thoughts we ever held about it, and about all living things we see upon it. They can not be there, no more then we. For we are in the home our Father set for us along with them. And we who are as He created us would loose the world this day from every one of our illusions, that we may be free.

W 132 L 15. Begin the fifteen minute periods in which we practice twice today with this:

> "I who remain as God created me
> Would loose the world from all I thought it was.
> For I am real because the world is not,
> And I would know my own reality."

Then merely rest, alert but with no strain, and let your mind in quietness be changed so that the world is freed along with you.

W 132 L 16. You need not realize that healing comes to many brothers far across the world as well as to the ones you see near by, as you send out these thoughts to bless the world. But you will sense your own release, although you may not fully understand as yet that you could never be released alone.

W 132 L 17. Throughout the day, increase the freedom sent through your ideas to all the world, and say whenever you are tempted to deny the power of your simple change of mind:

> "I loose the world from all I thought it was,
> And choose my own reality instead." **W(277)**

Lesson 133 "I will not value what is valueless."

W 133 L 1. Sometimes in teaching there is benefit, particularly after you have gone through what seems theoretical and quite remote[389] from what the student has already learned, to bring him back to practical concerns. This we will do today. We will not speak of lofty, world-encompassing ideas, but dwell instead on benefits to you.

W 133 L 2. You do not ask too much of life, but far too little. When you let your mind be drawn to bodily concerns, to things you buy, to eminence as valued by the world, you ask for sorrow, not for happiness. This course does not attempt to take from you the little that you have. It does not try to substitute utopian ideas for satisfactions which the world contains. There are no satisfactions in the world.

W 133 L 3. Today we list the real criteria by which to test all things you think you want. Unless they meet these sound requirements, they are not worth desiring at all, for they can but replace what offers more. The laws which govern choice you cannot make, no more than you can make alternatives from which to choose. The choosing you can do; indeed you must. But it is wise to learn the laws you set in motion when you choose, and what alternatives you choose between.

W 133 L 4. We have already stressed there are but two, however many there appear to be. The range is set, and this we cannot change. It would be most ungenerous to you to let alternatives be limitless, and thus delay your final choice until you had considered all of them in time, and not been brought so clearly to the place where there is but one choice which must be made. **W(278)**

W 133 L 5. Another kindly and related law is that there is no compromise in what your choice must bring. It cannot give you just a little, for there is no in between. Each choice you make brings everything to you or nothing. Therefore, if you learn the tests by which you can distinguish everything from nothing, you will make the better choice.

W 133 L 6. First, if you choose a thing that will not last forever, what you chose is valueless. A temporary value is without all value. Time can never take away a value that is real. What fades and dies was never there, and makes no offering to him who chooses it. He is deceived by nothing in a form he thinks he likes.

W 133 L 7. Next, if you choose to take a thing away from someone else, you will have nothing left. This is because when you deny his right to everything, you have denied your own. You therefore will not recognize the things you really have, denying they are there. Who seeks to take away has been deceived by the belief[390] that loss can offer gain. Yet loss must offer loss and nothing more.

W 133 L 8. Your next consideration is the one on which the others rest. Why is the choice you make of value to you? What attracts your mind to it? What purpose does it serve? Here it is easiest of all to be deceived, for what the ego wants it fails to recognize. It does not even tell the truth as it perceives it, for it needs to keep the halo which it uses to protect its goals from tarnish and from rust, that you may see how "innocent" it is.

W 133 L 9. Yet is its camouflage a thin veneer which could deceive but those who are content to be deceived. Its goals are obvious to anyone who cares to look for them. Here is deception doubled, for the one who is deceived will not perceive that he has merely failed to gain. He will believe that he has served the ego's hidden goals.

W 133 L 10. And[391] though he tries to keep its halo clear within his vision, yet must he perceive its tarnished edges and its rusted core. **W(279)** His ineffectual mistakes appear as sins to him because he looks upon the tarnish as his own, the rust a sign of deep unworthiness within himself. He who would still preserve the ego's goals and serve them as his own makes no mistakes according to the dictates of his guide. This guidance teaches it is error to believe that sins are but mistakes, for who would suffer for his sins if this were so?

W 133 L 11. And so we come to the criterion for choice which is the hardest to believe, because its obviousness is overlaid with many levels of obscurity. If you feel any guilt about your choice, you have allowed the ego's goals to come between the real alternatives, and thus you do not realize there are but two. And the alternative you think you chose seems fearful and too dangerous to be the nothingness it actually is.

W 133 L 12. All things are valuable or valueless, worthy or not of being sought at all, entirely desirable or not worth the slightest effort to obtain. Choosing is easy just because of this. Complexity is nothing but a screen of smoke which hides the very simple fact that no decision can be difficult. What is the gain to you in learning this? It is far more than merely letting you make choices easily and without pain.

---

[389] Handwritten mark-up suggests (far).

[390] The word "**belief**" is overstruck and the word "**illusion**" typed after it. The word "**that**" immediately following is also overstruck out. The *Notes* has it as we do.

[391] Handwritten mark-up suggests (Yet).

W 133 L 13. Heaven Itself is reached by[392] empty hands and open minds, which come with nothing to find everything and claim it as their own. We will attempt to reach this state today, with self-deception laid aside, and with an honest willingness to value but the truly valuable and the real.

W 133 L 14. Our two extended practice periods of fifteen minutes will[393] begin with this:

"I will not value what is valueless,

And only what has value do I seek,

For only that do I desire to find."

And then receive what waits for everyone who reaches, unencumbered, to the gate of Heaven, which swings open as he comes.[394] **W(280)** Should you begin to let yourself collect some needless burdens, or believe you see some difficult decisions facing you, be quick to answer with this simple thought:

"I will not value what is valueless,

For what is valuable belongs to me." **W(281)**

Lesson 134 "Let me perceive forgiveness as it is."

W 134 L 1. Let us review the meaning of "forgive," for it is apt to be distorted and to be perceived as something which entails an unfair sacrifice of righteous wrath, a gift unjustified and undeserved, and a complete denial of the truth. In such a view, forgiveness must be seen as mere eccentric folly, and this course appears to rest salvation on a whim.

W 134 L 2. This twisted view of what forgiveness means is easily corrected when you can accept the fact that pardon is not asked for what is true. It must be limited to what is false. It is irrelevant to everything except illusions. Truth is God's creation, and to pardon this[395] is meaningless. All truth belongs to Him, reflects His laws and radiates His Love. Does this need pardon? How can you forgive the sinless and eternally benign?

W 134 L 3. The major difficulty that[396] you find in genuine forgiveness on your part is that you still believe you must forgive the truth and not illusions. You conceive of pardon as a vain attempt to look past what is there; to overlook the truth in an unfounded effort to deceive yourself by making an illusion true. This twisted viewpoint but reflects the hold that the idea of sin retains as yet upon your mind as[397] you regard yourself.

W 134 L 4. Because you think your sins are real, you look on pardon as deception. For it is impossible to think of sin as true and not believe forgiveness is a lie. Thus is forgiveness really but a sin, like all the rest. It says the truth is false, and smiles on the corrupt as if they were as blameless as the grass; as white as snow.[398] It is delusional in what it thinks it can accomplish. It would see as right the plainly wrong; the loathsome as the good. **W(282)**

W 134 L 5. Pardon is no escape in such a view. It merely is a further sign that sin is unforgivable, at best to be concealed, denied, or called another name, for pardon is a treachery to truth. Guilt can not be forgiven. If you sin, your guilt is everlasting. Those who are forgiven from the view their sins are real are pitifully mocked and twice condemned; first by themselves for what they think they did, and once again by those who pardon them.

W 134 L 6. It is sin's unreality which makes forgiveness natural and wholly sane, a deep relief to those who offer it; a quiet blessing where it is received. It does not countenance illusions, but collects them lightly, with a little laugh, and gently lays them at the feet of truth. And there they disappear entirely.

W 134 L 7. Forgiveness is the only thing that stands for truth in the illusions of the world. It sees their nothingness, and looks right through the thousand forms in which they may appear. It looks on lies but it is not deceived. It does not heed the self-accusing shrieks of sinners mad with guilt. It looks on them with quiet eyes, and merely says to them, "My brother, what you think is not the truth."

W 134 L 8. The strength of pardon is its honesty, which is so uncorrupted that it sees illusions as illusions, not as truth. It is because of this that it becomes the undeceiver in the face of lies, the great restorer of the simple truth. By its ability to overlook what is not there, it opens up the way to truth, which had been blocked by dreams of guilt. Now are you free to follow in the way your true forgiveness opens up to you. For if one brother has received this gift of you, the door is open to yourself.

W 134 L 9. There is a very simple way to find the door to true forgiveness, and perceive it open wide in welcome. When you feel that you are tempted to accuse someone of sin in any form, do not allow your mind to dwell on what you think he did, for this is self-deception. Ask instead, "Should I accuse myself of doing this?" **W(283)**

W 134 L 10. Thus will you see alternatives for choice in terms which render choosing meaningful, and keep your mind as free of guilt and pain as God Himself intended it to be, and as it is in truth. It is but lies which would condemn. In truth is innocence the only thing there is. Forgiveness stands between illusions and the truth, between the world you see and that which lies beyond, between the hell of guilt and Heaven's gate.

W 134 L 11. Across this bridge, as powerful as Love Which laid Its blessing on it, are all dreams of evil and of hatred and attack brought silently to truth. They are not kept to swell and bluster and to terrify the foolish dreamer who believes in them. He has been gently wakened from his dream by understanding what he thought he saw was never there. And now he cannot feel that all escape has been denied to him.

W 134 L 12. He does not have to fight to save himself. He does not have to kill the dragons which he thought pursued him. Nor need he erect the heavy walls of stone and iron doors he thought would make him safe. He can remove the ponderous and useless armor made to chain his mind to fear and misery. His step is light, and as he lifts his foot to stride ahead, a star is left behind to point the way to those who follow him.

W 134 L 13. Forgiveness must be practiced for the world cannot perceive its meaning, nor provide a guide to teach you its beneficence. There is no thought in all the world which leads to any understanding of the laws it follows, nor the Thought which it reflects. It is as alien to the world as is your own reality. And yet it joins your mind with the reality in you.

W 134 L 14. Today we practice true forgiveness that the time of joining be no more delayed. For we would meet with our Reality[399] in freedom and in peace. Our practicing becomes the footsteps lightening up the way for all our brothers, who will follow us to the Reality[400] we share with them. **W(284)**

---

[392] Handwritten mark-up suggests (with).
[393] Handwritten mark-up suggests (each).
[394] **Genesis 28:17** And he was afraid and said, "How awesome is this place! This is none other than the house of God, and this is the gate of heaven!"
[395] Handwritten mark-up suggests (that).
[396] Handwritten mark-up suggests (which).
[397] Originally in the *Urtext* manuscript typed (when), the word is overstruck and replaced with "**as**"
[398] **Isaiah 1:18** Come now, and let us reason together,"
   Says the LORD,
   "Though your sins are like scarlet,
   They shall be as white as snow;
   Though they are red like crimson,
   They shall be as wool.
Isaiah 1:18

[399] Handwritten mark-up suggests (reality).
[400] Handwritten mark-up suggests (reality).

W 134 L 15. That this may be accomplished, let us give a quarter of an hour twice today, and spend it with the Guide Who understands the meaning of forgiveness, and was sent to us to teach it. Let us ask of Him:

> *"Let me perceive forgiveness as it is."*

W 134 L 16. Then choose one brother as He will direct, and catalogue his "sins" as one by one they cross your mind. Be certain not to dwell on any one of them, but realize that you are using his "offenses" but to save the world from all ideas of sin. Briefly consider all the evil things you thought of him, and each time ask yourself "Would I condemn myself for doing this?"

W 134 L 17. Let him be freed from all the thoughts you had of sin in him. And now you are prepared for freedom. If you have been practicing thus far in willingness and honesty, you will begin to sense a lifting up, a lightening of weight across your chest, a deep and certain feeling of relief. The time remaining should be given to experiencing the escape from all the heavy chains you sought to lay upon your brother, which were laid upon yourself.

> *W 134 L 18. Forgiveness should be practiced through the day, for there will[401] be so many times when you forget its meaning, and attack yourself. When this occurs, allow your mind to see through this illusion as you tell yourself:*
>
> *"Let me perceive forgiveness as it is.*
>
> *Would[402] I accuse myself of doing this?*
>
> *I will not lay this chain upon myself."*

In everything you do remember this:

> *No-one is crucified alone, and yet,*
>
> *No-one can enter Heaven by himself.* **W(285)**

Lesson 135 "If I defend myself I am attacked."

W 135 L 1. Who would defend himself unless he thought he was attacked, that the attack is real, and that his own defense can save himself? And herein lies the folly of defense; it gives illusions full reality, and then attempts to handle them as real. It adds illusions to illusions, thus making correction doubly difficult. And it is this you do when you attempt to plan the future, activate the past, or organize the present as you wish.

W 135 L 2. You operate from the belief you must protect yourself from what is happening, because it must contain what threatens you. A sense of threat is an acknowledgment of an inherent weakness; a belief that there is danger which has power to call on you to make appropriate defense.

W 135 L 3. The world is based on this insane belief. And all its structures, all its thoughts and doubts, its penalties and heavy armaments, its legal definitions and its codes, its ethics and its leaders and its gods, all serve but to preserve its sense of threat. For no-one walks the world in armature but must have terror striking at his heart.

W 135 L 4. Defense is frightening. It stems from fear, increasing fear as each defense is made. You think it offers safety. Yet it speaks of fear made real and terror justified. Is it not strange you do not pause to ask, as you elaborate your plans and make your armor thicker and your locks more tight, what you defend, and how, and against what?

W 135 L 5. Let us consider first what you defend. It must be something that is very weak and easily assaulted. It must be something made easy prey, unable to protect itself, and needing your defense. What but the body has such frailty that constant care and watchful, deep concern are needful to protect its little life? **W(286)** What but the body falters and must fail to serve the Son of God as worthy host?

W 135 L 6. Yet it is not the body that can fear, nor be a thing to fear. It has no needs but those which you assign to it. It needs no complicated structures of defense, no health-inducing medicine, no care and no concern at all. Defend its life, or give it gifts to make It beautiful or walls to make it safe, and you but say your home is open to the thief of time, corruptible and crumbling, so unsafe it must be guarded with your very life.

W 135 L 7. Is not this picture fearful? Can you be at peace with such a concept of your home? Yet what endowed the body with the right to serve you thus except your own belief? It is your mind which gave the body all the functions that you see in it, and set its value far beyond a little pile of dust and water.[403] Who would make defense of something that he recognized as this?

W 135 L 8. The body is in need of no defense. This cannot be too often emphasized. It will be strong and healthy if the mind does not abuse it by assigning it to roles it cannot fill, to purposes beyond its scope, and to exalted aims which it cannot accomplish. Such attempts, ridiculous yet deeply cherished, are the sources for the many mad attacks you make upon it. For it seems to fail your hopes, your needs, your values and your dreams.

W 135 L 9. The "self" that needs protection is not real. The body, valueless and hardly worth the least defense, need merely be perceived as quite apart from you, and it becomes a healthy, serviceable instrument through which the mind can operate until its usefulness is over. Who would want to keep it when its usefulness is done?

W 135 L 10. Defend the body and you have attacked your mind. For you have seen in it the faults, the weaknesses, the limits and the lacks from which you think the body must be saved. You will not see the mind as separate from bodily conditions. And you will impose upon the body all the pain that comes from the conception of the mind as limited and fragile, and apart from other minds **W(287)** and separate from its Source.

W 135 L 11. These are the thoughts in need of healing, and the body will respond with health when they have been corrected and replaced with truth. This is the body's only real defense. Yet is this where you look for its defense? You offer it protection of a kind from which it gains no benefit at all, but merely adds to your distress of mind. You do not heal, but merely take away the hope of healing, for you fail to see where hope must lie if it be meaningful.

W 135 L 12. A healed mind does not plan. It carries out the plans which it receives through listening to Wisdom that is not its own. It waits until it has been taught what should be done, and then proceeds to do it. It does not depend upon itself for anything except its adequacy to fulfill the plans assigned to it. It is secure in certainty that obstacles can not impede its progress to accomplishment of any goal which serves the greater plan established for the good of everyone.

W 135 L 13. A healed mind is relieved from the belief that it must plan, although it cannot know the outcome which is best, the means by which it is achieved, nor how to recognize the problem that the plan is made to solve. It must misuse the body in its plans until it recognizes this is so. But when it has accepted this as true, then is it healed, and lets the body go.

W 135 L 14. Enslavement of the body to the plans the unhealed mind sets up to save itself must make the body sick. It is not free to be a means of helping in a plan which far exceeds its own protection and which needs its service for a little while. In this capacity is

---

[401] Handwritten mark-up suggests (still).
[402] In the *Notes* this was originally written "Would" which is crossed out and "Should" written in. FIP switches it back to "Would" which does seem rather better.

[403] **Genesis 2:6-7** but a mist went up from the earth and watered the whole face of the ground. And the LORD God formed man of the dust of the ground, and breathed into his nostrils the breath of life; and man became a living being.

health assured. For everything the mind employs for this will function flawlessly, and with the strength that has been given it and cannot fail. **W(288)**

W 135 L 15. It is, perhaps, not easy to perceive that self-initiated plans are but defenses, with the purpose all of them were made to realize. They are the means by which a frightened mind would undertake its own protection at the cost of truth. This is not difficult to realize in some forms which these self-deceptions take, for[404] the denial of reality is very obvious. Yet planning is not often recognized as a defense.

W 135 L 16. The mind engaged in planning for itself is occupied in setting up control of future happenings. It does not think that it will be provided for unless it makes its own provisions. Time becomes a future emphasis, to be controlled by learning and experience obtained from past events and previous beliefs. It[405] overlooks the present, for it rests on the idea the past has taught enough to let the mind direct its future course.

W 135 L 17. The mind that plans is thus refusing to allow for change. What it has learned before becomes the basis for its future goals. Its past experience directs its choice of what will happen. And it does not see that here and now is everything it needs to guarantee a future quite unlike the past, without a continuity of any old ideas and sick beliefs. Anticipation plays no part at all, for present confidence directs the way.

W 135 L 18. Defenses are the plans you undertake to make against the truth. Their aim is to select what you approve, and disregard what you consider incompatible with your beliefs of your reality. Yet what remains is meaningless indeed. For it is your reality which is the "threat" that your defenses would attack, obscure, and take apart and crucify. **W(289)**

W 135 L 19. What could you not accept, if you but knew that everything which happens, all events, past, present and to come, are gently planned by One Whose only purpose is your good? Perhaps you have misunderstood His plan, for He would never offer pain to you. But your defenses did not let you see His loving blessing shine in every step you ever took. While you made plans for death, He led you gently to Eternal Life.

W 135 L 20. Your present trust in Him is the defense which promises a future undisturbed, without a trace of sorrow, and with joy which constantly increases as this life becomes a holy instant, set in time, but heeding only immortality. Let no defenses but your present trust direct the future, and this life becomes a meaningful encounter with the truth that only your defenses would conceal.

W 135 L 21. Without defenses, you become a light which Heaven gratefully acknowledges to be its own. And it will lead you on in ways appointed for your happiness according to the ancient plan, begun when time was born. Your followers will join their light with yours, and it will be increased until the world is lighted up with joy. And gladly will our brothers lay aside their cumbersome defenses which availed them nothing, and could only terrify.

W 135 L 22. We will anticipate that time today with present confidence, for this is part of what was planned for us. We will be sure that everything we need is given us for our accomplishment of this today. We make no plans for how it will be done, but realize that our defenselessness is all that is required for the truth to dawn upon our minds with certainty.

W 135 L 23. For fifteen minutes twice today we rest from senseless planning, and from every thought which blocks the truth from entering our minds. Today we will receive instead of plan, that we may give instead of organize. And we are given truly, as we say:

"If I defend myself I am attacked.

But in defenselessness I will be strong,

And I will learn what my defenses hide." **W(290)**

W 135 L 24. Nothing but that. If there are plans to make, you will be told of them. They may not be the plans you thought were needed, nor indeed the answers to the problems which you thought confronted you. But they are answers to another kind of question, which remains unanswered, yet in need of answering until the Answer comes to you at last.

W 135 L 25. All your defenses have been aimed at not receiving what you will receive today. And in the light and joy of simple truth, you will but wonder why you ever thought that you must be defended from release. Heaven asks nothing. It is hell that makes extravagant demands for sacrifice. You give up nothing in these times today when, undefended you present yourself to your Creator as you really are.

W 135 L 26. He has remembered you. Today we will remember Him. For this is Easter time in your salvation. And you rise again from what was seeming death and hopelessness. Now is the light of hope reborn in you, for now you come without defense to learn the part for you within the plan of God. What little plans or magical beliefs can still have value, when you have received your function from the Voice of God Himself?

W 135 L 27. Try not to shape this day as you believe would benefit you most. For you can not conceive of all the happiness that comes to you without your planning. Learn today. And all the world will take this giant stride, and celebrate your Easter time with you. Throughout the day, as foolish little things appear to raise defensiveness in you and tempt you to engage in weaving plans, remind yourself this is a special day for learning, and acknowledge it with this:

"This is Easter time. And I would keep

It holy. I will not defend myself,

Because the Son of God needs no defense

Against the truth of his Reality." W(291)

Lesson 136 "Sickness is a defense against the truth."

W 136 L 1. No-one can heal unless he understands what purpose sickness seems to serve. For then he understands as well its purpose has no meaning. Being causeless and without a meaningful intent of any kind, it cannot be at all. When this is seen, healing is automatic. It dispels this meaningless illusion by the same approach which carries all of them to truth, and merely leaves them there to disappear.

W 136 L 2. Sickness is not an accident. Like all defenses, it is an insane device for self deception. And like all the rest its purpose is to hide reality, attack it, change it, render it inept, distort it, twist it, or reduce it to a little pile of unassembled parts. The aim of all defenses is to keep the truth from being whole. The parts are seen as if each one were whole within itself.

W 136 L 3. Defenses are not unintentional, nor are they made without awareness. They are secret magic wands you wave when truth appears to threaten what you would believe. They seem to be unconscious but because of the rapidity with which you choose to use them. In that second, even less, in which the choice is made, you recognize exactly what you would attempt to do, and then proceed to think that it is done.

W 136 L 4. Who but yourself evaluates a threat, decides escape is necessary, and sets up a series of defenses to reduce the threat that has been judged as real? All this cannot be done unconsciously. But afterwards your plan requires that you must forget you made it, so it seems to be external to your own intent; a happening beyond

---

[404] Handwritten mark-up suggests (where?).
[405] Handwritten mark-up suggests (This?).

your state of mind, an outcome with a real effect on you, instead of one effected by your self. **W(292)**

W 136 L 5. It is this quick forgetting of the part you play in making your "reality" which makes defenses seem to be beyond your own control. But what you have forgot can be remembered, given willingness to reconsider the decision which is doubly shielded by oblivion. Your not remembering is but the sign that this decision still remains in force, as far as your desires are concerned. Mistake this not for fact. Defenses must make facts unrecognizable. They aim at doing this, and this they seem to do.

W 136 L 6. Every defense takes fragments of the whole, assembles them without regard to all their true relationships, and thus constructs illusions of a whole which[406] is not there. It is this process which imposes threat, and not whatever outcome may result. When parts are wrested from the whole and seen as separate and as wholes within themselves, they become symbols standing for attack upon the whole, successful in effect, and never to be seen as whole again. And yet you have forgotten that they stand but for your own decision of what should be real, to take the place of what is real.

W 136 L 7. Sickness is a decision. It is not a thing that happens to you quite unsought, which makes you weak and brings you suffering. It is a choice you make, a plan you lay when, for an instant, truth arises in your own deluded mind, and all your world appears to totter and prepare to fall. Now are you sick, that truth may go away, and threaten your establishments no more. How do you think that sickness can succeed in shielding you from truth? Because it proves the body is not separate from you, and so you must be separate from the truth.

W 136 L 8. You suffer pain because the body does, and in this pain are you made one with it. Thus is your "true" identity preserved, and the strange, haunting thought that you might be something beyond this little pile of dust silenced and stilled. For see, this dust can make you suffer, twist your limbs and stop your heart, commanding you to die and cease to be. **W(293)**

W 136 L 9. Thus is the body stronger than the truth, which asks you live but cannot overcome your choice to die. And so the body is more powerful than Everlasting Life, Heaven more frail than hell, and God's design for the salvation of His Son opposed by a decision stronger than His Will. His Son is dust, the Father incomplete, and chaos sits in triumph on His throne.

W 136 L 10. Such is your planning for your own defense. And you believe that Heaven quails before such mad attacks as these, with God made blind by your illusions, truth turned into lies, and all the universe made slaves to laws which your defenses would impose on it. Yet who believes illusions but the one who made them up? Who else can see them and react to them as if they were the truth?

W 136 L 11. God knows not of your plans to change His Will. The universe remains unheeding of the laws by which you thought to govern it. And Heaven has not bowed to hell, nor life to death. You can but choose to think you die, or suffer sickness or distort the truth in any way. What is created is apart from all of this. Defenses are plans to defeat what cannot be attacked. What is unalterable cannot change. And what is wholly sinless cannot sin.

W 136 L 12. Such is the simple truth. It does not make appeal to might nor triumph. It does not command obedience, nor seek to prove how pitiful and futile your attempts to plan defenses which would alter it. It[407] merely wants to give you happiness, for such its purpose is. Perhaps it sighs a little when you throw away its gifts, and yet it knows with perfect certainty that what God wills for you must be received.

W 136 L 13. It is this fact which demonstrates that time is an illusion. For it[408] lets you think what God has given you is not the truth right now, as it must be. The Thoughts of God are quite apart from time. For time is but another meaningless defense you made against the truth. Yet what God wills is here, and you remain as He created you. **W(294)**

W 136 L 14. Truth has a power far beyond defense, for no illusions can remain where it has been allowed to enter. And it comes to any mind that would lay down its arms and cease to play with folly. It is found at any time; today, if you will choose to practice giving welcome to the truth.

W 136 L 15. This is our aim today. And we will give a quarter of an hour twice to ask the truth to come to us and set us free.[409] And truth will come, for it has never been apart from us. It merely waits for just this invitation which we give today. We introduce it with a healing prayer to help us rise above defensiveness, and let the truth be as it has always been:

> "Sickness is a defense against the truth.
> I will accept the truth of what I am,
> And let my mind be wholly healed today."

W 136 L 16. Healing will flash across your open mind as peace and truth arise to take the place of war and vain imaginings. There will be no dark corners sickness can conceal and keep defended from the light of truth. There will be no dim figures from your dreams, nor their obscure and meaningless pursuits with double purposes insanely sought, remaining in your mind. It will be healed of all the sickly wishes that it tried to authorize the body to obey.

W 136 L 17. Now is the body healed because the source of sickness has been opened to relief. And you will recognize you practiced well by this; the body should not feel at all. If you have been successful, there will be no sense of feeling ill or feeling well, of pain or pleasure. No response at all is in the mind to what the body does. Its usefulness remains, and nothing more.

W 136 L 18. Perhaps you do not realize that this removes the limits you had placed upon the body by the purposes you gave to it. As these are laid aside, the strength the body has will always be enough to serve all truly useful purposes. The body's health is fully guaranteed because it is not limited by time, by weather or fatigue, by food and drink, or any laws you made it serve before. You need do nothing now to make it well, for sickness has become impossible. **W(295)**

W 136 L 19. Yet this protection needs to be preserved by careful watching. If you let your mind harbor attack thoughts, yield to judgment or make plans against uncertainties to come, you have again misplaced yourself, and made a bodily identity which will attack the body, for the mind is sick. Give instant remedy, should this occur, by not allowing your defensiveness to hurt you longer. Do not be confused about what must be healed, but tell yourself:

> "I have forgotten what I really am,
> For I mistook my body for myself.
> Sickness is a defense against the truth,
> But I am not a body. And my mind
> Cannot attack. So I can not be sick." **W(296)**

---

[406] Handwritten mark-up suggests (that).
[407] Handwritten mark-up suggests (Truth).
[408] Handwritging suggests (time?).
[409] **John 8:32** "And you shall know the truth, and the truth shall make you free."

Lesson 137 "When I am healed, I am not healed alone."

W 137 L 1. Today's idea remains the central thought on which salvation rests. For healing is the opposite of all[410] the world's ideas which dwell on sickness and on separate states. Sickness is a retreat from others, and a shutting off of joining. It becomes a door that closes on a separate self, and keeps it isolated and alone.

W 137 L 2. Sickness is isolation. For it seems to keep one self apart from all the rest, to suffer what the others do not feel. It gives the body final power to make separation real and keep the mind in solitary prison, split apart and held in pieces by a solid wall of sickened flesh which it can not surmount. The world obeys the laws that sickness serves, but healing operates apart from them.

W 137 L 3. It is impossible that anyone be healed alone. In sickness must he be apart and separate. But healing is his own decision to be one again, and to accept his Self with all its parts intact and unassailed. In sickness does his Self appear to be dismembered and without the unity which gives It life. But healing is accomplished as he sees the body has no power to attack the universal Oneness of God's Son. Sickness would prove that lies must be the truth. But healing demonstrates that truth is true.

W 137 L 4. The separation sickness would impose has never really happened. To be healed is merely to accept what always was the simple truth, and always will remain exactly as it has forever been. Yet eyes accustomed to illusions must be shown that what they look upon is false. So healing, never needed by the truth, must demonstrate that sickness is not real. **W(297)**

W 137 L 5. Healing might thus be called a counter-dream which cancels out the dream of sickness in the name of truth, but not in truth itself. Just as forgiveness overlooks all sins that never were accomplished, healing but removes illusions that have not occurred. Just as the real world will arise to take the place of what has never been at all, healing[411] offers restitution for imagined states and false ideas which dreams embroider into pictures of the truth.

W 137 L 6. Yet think not healing is unworthy of your function here. For anti-Christ becomes more powerful than Christ to those who dream the world is real.[412] The body seems to be more solid and more stable than the mind. And love becomes a dream, while fear remains the one reality which can be seen and justified and fully understood.

W 137 L 7. Just as forgiveness shines away all sin, and the real world will occupy the place of what you made, so healing must replace the fantasies of sickness which you hold before the simple truth. When sickness has been seen to disappear in spite of all the laws which hold it cannot but be real, then questions have been answered. And the laws can be no longer cherished nor obeyed.

W 137 L 8. Healing is freedom, for it demonstrates that dreams will not prevail against the truth. Healing is shared. And by this attribute it proves that laws unlike the ones which hold that sickness is inevitable are more potent than their sickly opposites. Healing is strength. For by its gentle hand is weakness overcome. And minds which were walled off within a body free to join with other minds, to be forever strong. **W(298)**

W 137 L 9. Healing, forgiveness, and the glad exchange of all the world of sorrow for a world where sadness cannot enter, are the means by which the Holy Spirit urges you to follow Him. His gentle lessons teach how easily salvation can be yours; how little practice you need undertake to let His laws replace the ones you made, to hold yourself a prisoner to death. His life becomes your own as you extend the little help He asks in freeing you from everything that ever caused you pain.

W 137 L 10. And as you let yourself be healed, you see all those around you, or who cross your mind, or whom you touch, or those who seem to have no contact with you, healed along with you. Perhaps you will not recognize them all, nor realize how great your offering to all the world, when you let healing come to you. But you are never healed alone. And legions upon legions will receive the gift which you receive when you are healed.

W 137 L 11. Those who are healed become the instruments of healing. Nor does time elapse between the instant they are healed and all the grace of healing it is given them to give. What is opposed to God does not exist, and[413] who accepts it not within his mind becomes a haven where the weary can remain to rest. For here is truth bestowed, and here are all illusions brought to truth.

W 137 L 12. Would you not offer shelter to God's will? You but invite your Self to be at home, and can this invitation be refused? Ask the inevitable to occur and you will never fail. The other choice is but to ask what cannot be to be, and this cannot succeed. Today we ask that only truth will occupy our minds; that thoughts of healing will this day go forth from what is healed to what must yet be healed, aware that they will both occur as one. **W(299)**

W 137 L 13. We will remember, as the hour strikes, our function is to let our minds be healed that we may carry healing to the world, exchanging curse for blessing, pain for joy, and separation for the peace of God. Is not a minute of the hour worth the giving to receive a gift like this? Is not a little time a small expense to offer for the gift of everything?

W 137 L 14. Yet must we be prepared for such a gift. And so we will begin the day with this, and give ten minutes to these thoughts with which we will conclude today at night as well:

"When I am healed I am not healed alone.

And I would share my healing with the world,

That sickness may be banished from the mind

Of God's One Son, Who is my only Self."

W 137 L 15. Let healing be through you this very day. And as you rest in quiet be prepared to give as you receive, to hold but what you give, and to receive the Word of God to take the place of all the foolish thoughts that ever were imagined. Now we come together to make well all that was sick, and offer blessing where there was attack. Nor will we let this function be forgot as every hour of the day slips by, remembering our function[414] with this thought:

"When I am healed I am not healed alone.

And I would bless my brothers, for I would

Be healed with them as they are healed with me." **W(300)**

Lesson 138 "Heaven is the decision I must make."

W 138 L 1. In this world Heaven is a choice, because here we believe there are alternatives to choose between.[415] We think that all things have an opposite, and what we want we choose. If Heaven exists there must be hell as well, for contradiction is the way we make what we perceive and what we think is real.

W 138 L 2. Creation knows no opposite. But here is opposition part of being "real." It is this strange perception of the truth

---

[410] The *Urtext* manuscript reads "**the all the**" which is clearly an error. We've removed the first "**the**" to conform to the *Notes*.
[411] Handwritten mark-up suggests (but).
[412] **1 John 2:18** Little children, it is the last hour; and as you have heard that the Antichrist is coming, even now many antichrists have come, by which we know that it is the last hour.
1 John 2:22 Who is a liar but he who denies that Jesus is the Christ? He is antichrist who denies the Father and the Son.

[413] The *Urtext* manuscript has a full stop here, beginning a new sentence but the handwriting changes that to a comma, which change we agree with.
[414] Handwritten mark-up suggests (purpose?).
[415] The *Urtext* manuscript has "**from**" overstruck and replaced with "**between**".

which[416] makes the choice of Heaven seen to be the same as the relinquishment of hell. It is not really thus. Yet what is true in God's creation cannot enter here, until it is reflected in some form the world can understand. Truth cannot come where it could only be perceived with fear, for this would be the error truth can be brought to illusions. Opposition makes the truth unwelcome, and it cannot come.

W 138 L 3. Choice is the obvious escape from what appears as opposites. Decision lets one of conflicting goals become the aim of effort and expenditure of time. Without decision time is but a waste and effort dissipated. It is spent for nothing in return. And time goes by without results. There is no sense of gain, for nothing is accomplished; nothing learned.

W 138 L 4. You need to be reminded that you think a thousand choices are confronting you when there is really only one to make. And even this but seems to be a choice. Do not confuse yourself with all the doubts that myriad decisions would induce. You make but one. And when that one is made, you will perceive it was no choice at all, for truth is true and nothing else is real. There is no opposite to choose instead. There is no contradiction to the truth. **W(301)**

W 138 L 5. Choosing depends on learning. But[417] the truth cannot be learned but only recognized. In recognition its acceptance lies, and as it is accepted it is known. But knowledge is beyond the goals we seek to teach within the framework of this course. Ours are teaching goals to be attained through learning how to reach them, what they are, and what they offer you. Decisions are the outcome of your learning, for they rest on what you have accepted as the truth of what you are and what your needs must be.

W 138 L 6. In this insanely complicated world Heaven appears to take the form of choice, rather than merely being what it is. Of all the choices you have tried to make this is the simplest, most definitive, the prototype of all the rest, the one which settles all decisions. If you could decide the rest, this one remains unsolved. But when you solve this one the others are resolved with it, for all decisions but conceal this one by taking different forms. Here is the final and the only choice in which is truth accepted or denied.

W 138 L 7. So we begin today considering the choice that time was made to help us make. Such is its holy purpose, now transformed from the intent you gave it; that it be a means for demonstrating hell is real, hope changes to despair, and life itself must in the end be overcome by death. In death alone are opposites resolved, for ending opposition is to die. And thus salvation must be seen as death, for life is seen as conflict. To resolve the conflict is to end your life as well.

W 138 L 8. These mad beliefs can gain unconscious hold of great intensity, and grip the mind with terror and anxiety so strong that it will not relinquish its ideas about its own protection. It must be saved from salvation, threatened to be safe, and magically armored against truth. And these decisions are made unaware to keep them safely undisturbed, apart from question and from reason and from doubt. **W(302)**

W 138 L 9. Heaven is chosen consciously. The choice cannot be made until alternatives are accurately seen and understood. All that is veiled in shadows must be raised to understanding to be judged again, this time with Heaven's help, and all mistakes in judgment which the mind had made before are open to correction as the truth dismisses them as causeless. Now are they without effects. They cannot be concealed because their nothingness is recognized.

W 138 L 10. The conscious choice of Heaven is as sure as is the ending of the fear of hell, when it is raised from its protective shield of unawareness, and is brought to light. Who can decide between the clearly seen and the unrecognized? Yet who can fail to make a choice between alternatives when only one is seen as valuable; the other as a wholly worthless thing, a but imagined source of guilt and pain?

W 138 L 11. Who hesitates to make a choice like this? And shall we hesitate to choose today? We make the choice for Heaven as we wake, and spend five minutes making sure that we have made the one decision that is sane. We recognize we make a conscious choice between what has existence and what has nothing but an appearance of the truth. Its pseudo-being brought to what is real, is flimsy and transparent in the light. It holds no terror now, for what was made enormous, vengeful, pitiless with hate, demands obscurity for fear to be invested there. Now it is recognized as but a foolish, trivial mistake. **W(303)**

W 138 L 12. Before we close our eyes in sleep tonight we reaffirm the choice that we have made each hour in between. And now we give the last five minutes of our waking day to the decision with which we awoke. As every hour passed, we have declared our choice again in a brief quiet time devoted to maintaining sanity. And finally we close the day with this, acknowledging we chose but what we want:

> *"Heaven is the decision I must make.*
> *I make it now and will not change my mind,*
> *Because it is the only thing I want."* **W(304)**

Lesson 139 "I will accept Atonement for myself."

W 139 L 1. Here is the end of choice. For here we come to a decision to accept ourselves as God created us. And what is choice except uncertainty of what we are? There is no doubt that is not rooted here. There is no question but reflects this one. There is no conflict that does not entail the single simple question, "What am I?"

W 139 L 2. Yet who could ask this question except one who has refused to recognize himself? Only refusal to accept yourself could make the question seem to be sincere. The only thing that can be surely known by any living thing is what it is. From this one point of certainty it looks on other things as certain as itself.

W 139 L 3. Uncertainty about what you must be is self-deception on a scale so vast its magnitude can hardly be conceived. To be alive and not to know yourself is to believe that you are really dead. For what is life except to be yourself, and what but you can be alive instead? Who is the doubter? What is it he doubts? Whom does he question? Who can answer him?

W 139 L 4. He merely states that he is not himself and therefore, being something else, becomes a questioner of what that something is. Yet he could never be alive at all unless he knew the answer. If he asks as if he did not know, it merely shows he does not want to be the thing he is. He has accepted it because he lives; has judged against it and denied its worth; and has decided that he does not know the only certainty by which he lives.

W 139 L 5. Thus he becomes uncertain of his life, for what it is has been denied by him. **W(305)** It is for this denial that you need Atonement. Your denial made no change in what you are. But you have split your mind into what knows and does not know the truth. You are yourself. There is no doubt of this, and yet you doubt it. But you do not ask what part of you can really doubt yourself. It cannot really be a part of you that asks this question, for it asks of one who knows the answer. Were it part of you, uncertainty would be impossible.

W 139 L 6. Atonement remedies the strange idea that it is possible to doubt yourself and be unsure of what you really are. This is the depth of madness. Yet it is the universal question of the world. What does this prove except the world is mad? Why share its madness in the sad belief that what is universal here is true? Nothing the world believes is true. It is a place whose purpose is to be a home

---
[416] Handwritten mark-up suggests (that).
[417] Handwritten mark-up suggests (And).

where those who claim they do not know themselves can come to question what it is they are.

W 139 L 7. And they will come again until the time Atonement is accepted, and they learn it is impossible to doubt yourself and not to be aware of what you are. Only acceptance can be asked of you, for what you are is certain. It is set forever in the holy Mind of God and in your own. It is so far beyond all doubt and question that to ask what it must be is all the proof you need to show that you believe the contradiction that you know not what you cannot fail to know.

W 139 L 8. Is this a question or a statement which denies itself in statement? Let us not allow our holy minds to occupy themselves with senseless musings such as this. We have a mission here. We did not come to reinforce the madness which we once believed in. Let us not forget the goal that we accepted. It is more than just our happiness alone we came to gain.

W 139 L 9. What we accept as what we are proclaims what everyone must be along with us. **W(306)** Fail not your brothers, or you fail yourself. Look lovingly on them that they may know that they are part of you and you of them. This does Atonement teach, and demonstrates the oneness of God's Son is unassailed by his belief he knows not what he is.

W 139 L 10. Today accept Atonement, not to change reality, but merely to accept the truth about yourself, and go your way rejoicing in the endless Love of God. It is but this that we are asked to do. It is but this that we will do today. Five minutes in the morning and at night we will devote to dedicate our minds to our assignment for today. We start with this review of what our mission is:

"I will accept Atonement for myself,

For I remain as God created me."

W 139 L 11. We have not lost the knowledge that God gave to us when He created us like Him. We can remember it for everyone, for in creation are all minds as one, and in our memory is the recall how dear our brothers are to us in truth, how much a part of us is every mind, how faithful they have really been to us, and how our Father's Love contains us all.

W 139 L 12. In thanks for all creation, in the Name of its Creator and His Oneness with all aspects of creation, we repeat our dedication to our cause today each hour, as we lay aside all thoughts which would distract us from our holy aim. For several minutes let your mind be cleared of all the foolish cobwebs which the world would weave around the holy Son of God[418] and learn the fragile nature of the chains which seem to keep the knowledge of yourself apart from your awareness, as you say:

"I will accept Atonement for myself,

For I remain as God created me." **W(307)**

Lesson 140 "Only salvation can be said to cure."

W 140 L 1. Cure is a word which cannot be applied to any remedy the world accepts as beneficial. What the world perceives as therapeutic is but what will make the body "better." When it tries to heal the mind, it sees no separation from the body where it thinks the mind exists. Its forms of healing thus must substitute illusion for illusion. One belief in sickness takes another form, and so the patient now perceives himself as well.

W 140 L 2. He is not healed. He merely had a dream that he was sick, and in the dream he found a magic formula to make him well. Yet he has not awakened from the dream, and so his mind remains exactly as it was before. He has not seen the light that would awaken him and end the dream. What difference does the content of a dream make in reality? One either sleeps or wakens. There is nothing in between.

W 140 L 3. The happy dreams the Holy Spirit brings are different from the dreams[419] of the world, where one can merely dream he is awake. The dreams forgiveness lets the mind perceive do not induce another form of sleep, so that the dreamer dreams another dream. His happy dreams are heralds of the dawn of truth upon the mind. They lead from sleep to gentle waking, so that dreams are gone. And thus they cure for all eternity.

W 140 L 4. Atonement heals with certainty, and cures all sickness. For the mind which understands that sickness can be nothing but a dream is not deceived by forms the dream may take. Sickness where guilt is absent cannot come, for it is but another form of guilt. Atonement does not heal the sick, for that is not a cure. It takes away the guilt that makes the sickness possible. And that is cure indeed. For sickness now is gone, with nothing left to which it can return. **W(308)**

W 140 L 5. Peace be to you who have been cured in God, and not in idle dreams.[420] For cure must come from holiness, and holiness can not be found where sin is cherished. God abides in holy temples. He is barred where sin has entered. Yet there is no place where He is not. And therefore sin can have no home in which to hide from His beneficence.

W 140 L 6. There is no place where holiness is not, and nowhere sin and sickness can abide. This is the thought that cures. It does not make distinctions among unrealities. Nor does it seek to heal what is not sick, unmindful where the need of for healing is. This is no magic. It is merely an appeal to truth, which cannot fail to heal and heal forever. It is not a thought which judges an illusion by its size, its seeming gravity, or anything that is related to the form it takes. It merely focuses on what it is, and knows that no illusion can be real.

W 140 L 7. Let us not try today to seek to cure what cannot suffer sickness. Healing must be sought but where it is, and then applied to what is sick so that it can be cured. There is no remedy the world provides that can effect a change in anything. The mind that brings illusions to the truth is really changed. There is no change but this. For how can one illusion differ from another but in attributes which have no substance, no reality, no core, and nothing that is truly different?

W 140 L 8. Today we seek to change our minds about the source of sickness, for we seek a cure for all illusions, not another shift among them. We will try today to find the source of healing, which is in our minds because our Father placed it there for us. It is not further from us than ourselves. It is as near to us as our own thoughts, so close it is impossible to lose. We need but seek it and it must be found. **W(309)**

W 140 L 9. We will not be misled today by what appears to us as sick. We go beyond appearances today, and reach the source of healing from which nothing is exempt. We will succeed to the extent to which we realize that there can never be a meaningful distinction made between what is untrue and equally untrue. Here there are no degrees, and no beliefs that what does not exist is truer in some forms than others. All of them are false, and can be cured because they are not true.

W 140 L 10. So do we lay aside our amulets, our charms and medicines, our chants and bits of magic in whatever form they took.[421]

---

[418] For some reason the *Urtext* manuscript has a sentence break here.

[419] Handwritten mark-up suggests (dreaming).

[420] **John 20:19** Then, the same day at evening, being the first day of the week, when the doors were shut where the disciples were assembled, for fear of the Jews, Jesus came and stood in the midst, and said to them, "Peace be with you."
John 20:21 So Jesus said to them again, "Peace to you! As the Father has sent Me, I also send you."
John 20:26 And after eight days His disciples were again inside, and Thomas with them. Jesus came, the doors being shut, and stood in the midst, and said, "Peace to you!"

[421] Handwritten mark-up suggests (take).

We will be still and listen for the Voice of healing which will cure all ills as one, restoring saneness to the Son of God. No voice but This can cure. Today we hear a single Voice Which speaks to us of truth where all illusions end, and peace returns to the eternal quiet home of God.

W 140 L 11. We waken hearing Him, and let Him speak to us five minutes as the day begins, and end the day by listening again five minutes more before we go to sleep. Our only preparation is to let our interfering thoughts be laid aside, not separately, but all of them as one. They are the same. We have no need to make them different, and thus delay the time when we can hear our Father speak to us. We hear Him now. We come to Him today.

W 140 L 12. With nothing in our hands to which we cling, with lifted hearts and listening minds we pray:

"*Only salvation can be said to cure.*
Speak to us, Father, that we may be healed."

And we will feel salvation cover us with soft protection, and with peace so deep that no illusion can disturb our minds, nor offer proof to us that it is real. This will we learn today. And we will say our prayer for healing hourly, and take a minute as the hour strikes to hear the answer to our prayer be given us as we attend in silence and in joy. **W(310)** This is the day when healing comes to us. This is the day when separation ends, and we remember Who we really are. **W(311)**

Review 4 (W 140 R4)
Introduction

W 140 R4 1. Now a[422] review again, this time aware we are preparing for the second part of learning how the truth can be applied. Today we will begin to concentrate on readiness for what will follow next. Such is our aim for this review and for the lessons following. Thus we review the recent lessons and their central thoughts in such a way as will facilitate the readiness which we would now achieve.

W 140 R4 2. There is a central theme that unifies each step in the review we undertake, which can be simply stated in these words:

"*My mind holds only what I think with God.*"

This is a fact[423] and represents the truth of What you are and What your Father is. It is this Thought by Which the Father gave creation to the Son, establishing the Son as co-creator with Himself. It is this Thought Which fully guarantees salvation to the Son, for in his mind no thoughts can dwell but those his Father shares. Lack of forgiveness blocks this Thought from his awareness. Yet It is forever true.

W 140 R4 3. Let us begin our preparation with some understanding of the many forms in which the lack of true forgiveness may be carefully concealed. Because they are illusions, they are not perceived to be but what they are; defenses which protect your unforgiving thoughts from being seen and recognized. Their purpose is to show you something else, and hold correction off through self-deceptions made to take its place.

W 140 R4 4. And yet your mind holds only what you think with God. Your self-deceptions cannot take the place of truth. No more than can a child who throws a stick into the ocean change the coming and the going of the tides, the warming of the water by the sun, the silver of the moon on it at night. So do we start each practice period in this review with readying our minds to understand the lessons that we read, and see the meaning which they offer us. **W(312)**

W 140 R4 5. Begin each day with time devoted to the preparation of your mind to learn what each idea you will review that day can offer you in freedom and in peace. Open your mind and clear it of all thoughts that would deceive, and let this Thought alone engage it fully and remove the rest:

"*My mind holds only what I think*[424] *with God.*"

Five minutes with this Thought will be enough to set the day along the lines which God appointed, and to place His Mind in charge of all the thoughts you will receive that day. They will not come from you alone, for they will all be shared with Him. And so each one will bring the message of His Love to you, returning messages of yours to Him. So will communion with the Lord of Hosts be yours, as He Himself has willed it be.[425] And as His Own completion joins with Him, so will He join with you who are complete as you unite with Him and He with you.

W 140 R4 6. After your preparation, merely read each of the two ideas assigned to you to be reviewed that day. Then close your eyes and say them slowly to yourself. There is no hurry now, for you are using time for its intended purpose. Let each word shine with the meaning God has given it as it was given to you through His Voice. Let each idea that you review that day give you the gift which He has laid in it for you to have of Him. And we will use no format for our practicing but this:

W 140 R4 7. Each hour of the day bring to your mind the Thought with which the day began, and spend a quiet moment with It. Then repeat the two ideas you practice for the day unhurriedly, with time enough to see the gifts which they contain for you, and let them be received where they were meant to be.

W 140 R4 8. We add no other thoughts, but let them be the messages they are. We need no more than that[426] to give us happiness and rest and endless quiet, perfect certainty, and all our Father wills that we receive as the inheritance we have of Him. **W(313)**

W 140 R4 9. Each day of practicing, as we review, we close as we began, repeating first the Thought that made the day a special time of blessing and of happiness for us; and through our faithfulness restored the world from darkness to the light, from grief to joy, from pain to peace, from sin to holiness. God offers thanks to you who practice thus the keeping of His Word. And as you give your mind to the ideas for the day again before you sleep, His gratitude surrounds you in the peace wherein He wills you be forever, and are learning now to claim again as your inheritance. **W(314)**

Lesson 141 "My mind holds only what I think with God." (121-122)

W 141 L 1. 121) "Forgiveness is the key to happiness."

W 141 L 2. 122) "Forgiveness offers everything I want."

Lesson 142 "My mind holds only what I think with God." (123-124)

W 142 L 1. 123) "I thank my Father for His gifts to me."

W 142 L 2. 124) "Let me remember I am one with God."

---

[424] Handwritten mark-up suggests (*think*), which is probably correct. Typing has "**hold**". The *Notes* has a glyph commonly associated with "think" and other "th" words, but not with "hold."

[425] **Psalm 46:7** The LORD of hosts is with us; The God of Jacob is our refuge.

Romans 9:29 And as Isaiah said before, "Unless the Lord of hosts had left us a seed, we would have been as Sodom, and would have been like Gomorrah."

James 5:4 Behold, the hire of the laborers reaping your fields cry out, being kept back by you. And the cries of those who have reaped have entered into the ears of *the* Lord of hosts.

[426] Handwritten mark-up suggests (this).

---

[422] Handwritten mark-up suggests (we).

[423] The *Urtext* manuscript has a sentence break here for some reason.

Lesson 143 "My mind holds only what I think with God." (125-126)

W 143 L 1. 125) "In quiet I receive God's Word today."

W 143 L 2. 126) "All that I give is given to myself."

Lesson 144 "My mind holds only what I think with God." (127-128)

W 144 L 1. 127) "There is no love but God's."

W 144 L 2. 128) "The world I see has[427] nothing that I want."

Lesson 145 "My mind holds only what I think with God." (129-130)

W 145 L 1. 129) "Beyond this world there is a world I want."

W 145 L 2. 130) "It is impossible to see two worlds."

Lesson 146 "My mind holds only what I think with God." (131-132)

W 146 L 1. 131) "No-one can fail who asks to reach the truth."

W 146 L 2. 132) "I loose the world from all I thought it was." **W(315)**

Lesson 147 "My mind holds only what I think with God." (133-134)

W 147 L 1. 133) "I will not value what is valueless."

W 147 L 2. 134) "Let me perceive forgiveness as it is."

Lesson 148 "My mind holds only what I think with God." (135-136)

W 148 L 1. 135) "If I defend myself I am attacked."

W 148 L 2. 136) "Sickness is a defense against the truth."

Lesson 149 "My mind holds only what I think with God." (137-138)

W 149 L 1. 137) "When I am healed I am not healed alone."

W 149 L 2. 138) "Heaven is the decision I must make."

Lesson 150 "My mind holds only what I think with God." (139-140)

W 150 L 1. 139) "I will accept Atonement for myself."

W 150 L 2. 140) "Only salvation can be said to cure." **W(316)**

Lesson 151 "All things are echoes of the Voice of God."

W 151 L 1. No-one can judge on partial evidence. That is not judgment. It is merely an opinion based on ignorance and doubt. Its seeming certainty is but a cloak for the uncertainty it would conceal. It needs irrational defense because it is irrational. And its defense seems strong, convincing, and without a doubt, because of all the doubting underneath.

W 151 L 2. You do not seem to doubt the world you see. You do not really question what is shown you through the body's eyes. Nor do you ask why you believe it, even though you learned a long while since your senses do deceive. That you believe them to the last detail which they report is even stranger when you pause to recollect how frequently they have been faulty witnesses indeed! Why would you trust them so implicitly? Why but because of underlying doubt which you would hide with show of certainty?

W 151 L 3. How can you judge? Your judgment rests upon the witness that your senses offer you. Yet witness never falser was than this. But how else do you judge the world you see? You place pathetic faith in what your eyes and ears report. You think your fingers touch reality and close upon the truth. This is awareness which you understand, and think more real than what is witnessed to by the eternal Voice of God Himself.

W 151 L 4. Can this be judgment? You have often been urged to refrain from judging, not because it is a right to be withheld from you. You cannot judge. You merely can believe the ego's judgments, all of which are false. It guides your senses carefully, to prove how weak you are; how helpless and afraid, how apprehensive of just punishment how black with sin, how wretched in your guilt. **W(317)**

W 151 L 5. This thing it speaks of and would yet defend it tells you is yourself. And you believe that this is so with stubborn certainty. Yet underneath remains the hidden doubt that what it shows you as reality with such conviction it does not believe. It is itself alone that it condemns. It is within itself it sees the guilt. It is its own despair it sees in you.

W 151 L 6. Hear not its voice. The witnesses it sends to prove to you its evil is your own are false, and speak with certainty of what they do not know. Your faith in them is blind because you would not share the doubts their lord can not completely vanquish. You believe to doubt his vassals is to doubt yourself.

W 151 L 7. Yet you must learn to doubt their evidence will clear the way to recognize yourself, and let the Voice for God alone be Judge of what is worthy of your own belief. He will not tell you that your brother should be judged by what your eyes behold in him, nor what his body's mouth says to your ears, nor what your fingers' touch reports of him. He passes by such idle witnesses, which merely bear false witness to God's Son.[428]

W 151 L 8. He recognizes only what God loves, and in the holy light of what He sees do all the ego's dreams of what you are vanish before the splendor He beholds. Let Him be Judge of what you are, for He has certainty in which there is no doubt because it rests on Certainty so great that doubt is meaningless before Its Face. Christ cannot doubt Himself. The Voice of God can only honor Him, rejoicing in His perfect, everlasting sinlessness.

W 151 L 9. Whom He has judged can only laugh at guilt, unwilling now to play with toys of sin, unheeding of the body's witnesses before the rapture of His[429] holy Face. **W(318)** And thus He judges you. Accept His word of what you are, for He bears witness to your beautiful creation and the Mind Whose Thought created your reality.

W 151 L 10. What can the body mean to Him Who knows the glory of the Father and the Son? What whispers of the ego can He hear? What could convince Him that your sins are real? Let Him be Judge as well of everything that seems to happen to you in this world. His lessons will enable you to bridge the gap between illusions and the truth.

W 151 L 11. He will remove all faith that you have placed in pain, disaster, suffering and loss. He gives you vision which can look beyond these grim appearances, and can behold the gentle Face of Christ in all of them. You will no longer doubt that only good can come to you who are beloved of God, for He will judge all happenings and teach the single lesson which they all contain.

W 151 L 12. He will select the elements in them that represent the truth, and disregard those aspects which reflect but idle dreams. And He will reinterpret all you see, and all occurrences, each cir-

---

[427] Handwritten mark-up suggests (holds).

[428] **Exodus 20:16** You shall not bear false witness against your neighbor. **Matthew 19:18** He said to Him, "Which ones?" Jesus said, "You shall not murder," "You shall not commit adultery," "You shall not steal," "You shall not bear false witness,"

[429] Handwritten mark-up suggests (Christ's?).

cumstance, and every happening which seems to touch on you in any way from His one frame of reference, wholly unified and sure. And you will see the love beyond the hate, the constancy in change, the pure in sin, and only Heaven's blessing on the world.

W 151 L 13. Such is your resurrection, for your life is not a part of anything you see. It stands beyond the body and the world, past every witness for unholiness, within the Holy, holy as Itself.[430] In everyone and everything His Voice would speak to you of nothing but your Self and your Creator, Who is One with Him. So will you see the holy Face of Christ in everything, and hear in everything no sound except the echo of God's Voice. **W(319)**

W 151 L 14. We practice wordlessly today, except at the beginning of the time you[431] spend with God. We introduce these times with but a single, slow repeating of the thought with which the day begins. And then we watch our thoughts, appealing silently to Him Who sees the elements of truth in them. Let Him evaluate each thought that comes to mind, remove the elements of dreams, and give them back to you[432] as clean ideas which do not contradict the Will of God.

W 151 L 15. Give Him your thoughts, and He will give them back as miracles which joyously proclaim the wholeness and the happiness God wills His Son as proof of His eternal Love. And as each thought is thus transformed, it takes on healing power from the Mind Which saw the truth in it, and failed to be deceived by what was falsely added. All the threads of fantasy are gone, and what remains is unified into a perfect Thought that offers Its perfection everywhere.

W 151 L 16. Spend fifteen minutes thus when you awake, and gladly give another fifteen more before you go to sleep. Your ministry begins as all your thoughts are purified. So are you taught to teach the Son of God the holy lesson of his sanctity. No-one can fail to listen when you hear the Voice of God give honor to God's Son. And everyone will share the thoughts with you which He has re-translated in your mind.

W 151 L 17. Such is your Eastertide. And so you lay the gift of snow-white lilies on the world, replacing witnesses to sin and death. Through your transfiguration is the world redeemed and joyfully released from guilt.[433] Now do we lift our resurrected minds in gladness and in gratitude to Him Who has restored our sanity to us. **W(320)**

W 151 L 18. And we will hourly remember Him Who is salvation and deliverance. As we give thanks, the world unites with us, and happily accepts our holy thoughts, which Heaven has corrected and made pure. Now has our ministry begun at last, to carry 'round the world the joyous news that truth has no illusions, and the peace of God, through us, belongs to everyone. **W(321)**

Lesson 152 "The power of decision is my own."

W 152 L 1. No-one can suffer loss unless it be his own decision. No-one suffers pain except his choice elects this state for him. No-one can grieve nor fear nor think him sick unless these are the outcomes that he wants, and no-one dies without his own consent. Nothing occurs but represents your wish, and nothing is omitted that you choose. Here is your world, complete in all details. Here is its whole reality for you. And it is only here salvation is.

W 152 L 2. You may believe that this position is extreme, and too inclusive to be true. Yet can truth have exceptions? If you have the gift of everything can loss be real? Can pain be part of peace, or grief of joy? Can fear and sickness enter in a mind where love and perfect holiness abide?

W 152 L 3. Truth must be all-inclusive if it be the truth at all. Accept no opposite and no exceptions, for to do so is to contradict the truth entirely. Salvation is the recognition that the truth is true and nothing else is true. This you have heard before, but may not yet accept both parts of it. Without the first the second has no meaning, but without the second is the first no longer true. Truth cannot have an opposite. This can not be too often said and thought about. For if what is not true is true as well as what is true, then part of truth is false, and truth has lost its meaning. Nothing but the truth is true, and what is false is false.

W 152 L 4. This is the simplest of distinctions, yet the most obscure. But not because it is a difficult distinction to perceive. It is concealed behind a vast array of choices which do not appear to be entirely your own. And thus the truth appears to have some aspects which belie consistency, but do not seem to be but contradictions introduced by you. **W(322)**

W 152 L 5. As God created you, you must remain unchangeable with transitory states by definition false. And that includes all shifts in feeling, alterations in conditions of the body and the mind, in all awareness and in all response. This is the all-inclusiveness which sets the truth apart from falsehood, and the false kept separate from the truth as what it is.

W 152 L 6. Is it not strange that you believe to think you made the world you see is arrogance? God made it not. Of this you can be sure. What can He know of the ephemeral, the sinful and the guilty, the afraid, the suffering and lonely, and the mind which lives within a body that must die? You but accuse Him of insanity to think He made a world where such things seem to have reality. He is not mad. Yet only madness makes a world like this.

W 152 L 7. To think that God made chaos, contradicts His Will, invented opposites to truth, and suffers death to triumph over life, all this is arrogance. Humility would see at once these things are not of Him. And can you see what God created not? To think you can is merely to believe you can perceive what God willed not to be. And what could be more arrogant than this?

W 152 L 8. [434]Let us today be truly humble, and accept what we have made as what it is. The power of decision is our own. Decide but to accept your rightful place as co-creator of the universe, and all you think you made will disappear. What rises to awareness then will be all that there ever was, eternally as it is now. And it will take the place of self deceptions made but to usurp the altar to the Father and the Son.

W 152 L 9. Today we practice true humility, abandoning the false pretense by which the ego seeks to prove it arrogant. Only the ego can be arrogant. But truth is humble in acknowledging its mightiness, its changelessness and its eternal wholeness, all-encompassing, God's perfect gift to His beloved Son. **W(323)** We lay aside the arrogance which says that we are sinners, guilty and afraid, ashamed of what we are. And lift our hearts in true humility instead to Him Who has created us immaculate, like to Himself in power and in love.

W 152 L 10. The power of decision is our own. And we accept of Him that which we are, and humbly recognize the Son of God. To recognize God's Son implies as well that all self-concepts have been laid aside and recognized as false. Their arrogance has been perceived, And in humility the radiance of God's Son, his gentleness, his perfect sinlessness, his Father's love, his right to Heaven and release from hell, are joyously accepted as our own.

W 152 L 11. Now do we join in glad acknowledgment that lies are false and only truth is true. We think of truth alone as we arise, and

---

[430] **Exodus 26:33** And you shall hang the veil from the clasps. Then you shall bring the Ark of the Covenant in there, behind the veil. The veil shall be a divider for you between the holy place and the Most Holy.
[431] Handwritten mark-up suggests (we).
[432] Handwritten mark-up suggests (again).
[433] **Matthew 17:2** And He was transfigured before them. His face shone like the sun, and His clothes became as white as the light.

---

[434] Handwritten mark-up suggests (Today).

spend five minutes practicing its ways, encouraging our frightened minds with this:

"The power of decision is my own.
This day I will accept myself as what
My Father's Will created me to be."

Then will we wait in silence, giving up all self-deceptions as we humbly ask our Self that He reveal Himself to us. And He Who never left will come again to our awareness, grateful to restore His home to God as it was meant to be.

W 152 L 12. In patience wait for Him throughout the day, and hourly invite Him with the words with which the day began, concluding it with this same invitation to your Self. God's Voice will answer, for He speaks for you and for your Father. He will substitute the peace of God for all your frantic thoughts, the truth of God for self-deceptions, and God's Son for your illusions of yourself. **W(324)**

Lesson 153 "In my defenselessness my safety lies."

W 153 L 1. You who feel threatened by this changing world, its twists of fortune and its bitter jests, its brief relationships and all the "gifts" it merely lends to take away again, attend this lesson well. The world provides no safety. It is rooted in attack, and all its "gifts" of seeming safety are illusory deceptions. It attacks and then attacks again. No peace of mind is possible where danger threatens thus.

W 153 L 2. The world gives rise but to defensiveness. For threat brings anger, anger makes attack seem reasonable, honestly provoked, and righteous in the name of self-defense. Yet is defensiveness a double threat. For it attests to weakness, and sets up a system of defense which cannot work. Now are the weak still further undermined, for there is treachery without and still a greater treachery within. The mind is now confused, and knows not where to turn to find escape from its imaginings.

W 153 L 3. It is as if a circle held it fast, wherein another circle bound it, and another in that one, until escape no longer can be hoped for nor obtained. Attack, defense; defense, attack, become the circles of the hours and the days which bind the mind in heavy bands of steel with iron overlaid, returning but to start again. There seems to be no break nor ending in the ever-tightening grip of imprisonment upon the mind.

W 153 L 4. Defenses are the costliest of all the prices which the ego would exact. In them lies madness in a form so grim that hope of sanity seems but to be an idle dream, beyond the possible. The sense of threat the world encourages is so much deeper and so far beyond the frenzy and intensity of which you can conceive that you have no idea of all the devastation it has wrought. You are it's slave. You know not what you do in fear of it.[435] You do not understand how much you have been made to sacrifice who feel its iron grip upon your heart. **W(325)**

W 153 L 5. You do not realize what you have done to sabotage the holy peace of God by your defensiveness. For you behold the Son of God as but a victim to attack by fantasies, by dreams, and by illusions he has made; yet helpless in their presence, needful only of defense by still more fantasies and dreams, by which illusions of his safety comfort him.

W 153 L 6. Defenselessness is strength. It testifies to recognition of the Christ in you. Perhaps you will recall the course maintains that choice is always made between His[436] strength and your own weakness seen apart from Him. Defenselessness can never be attacked because it recognizes strength so great attack is folly, or a silly game a tired child might play when he becomes too sleepy to remember what he wants.

W 153 L 7. Defensiveness is weakness. It proclaims you have denied the Christ and come to fear His Father's anger. What can save you now from your delusion of an angry god whose fearful image you believe you see at work in all the evils of the world? What but illusions could defend you now, when it is but illusions which you fight?

W 153 L 8. We will not play such childish games today,[437] for our true purpose is to save the world, and we would not exchange for foolishness the endless joy our function offers us. We would not let our happiness slip by because a senseless fragment of a[438] dream happened to cross our minds, and we mistook the figures in it for the Son of God; its tiny instant for eternity.

W 153 L 9. We look past dreams today, and recognize that we need no defense because we are created unassailable, without all thought or wish or dream in which attack has any meaning. Now we cannot fear, for we have left all fearful thoughts behind. And in defenselessness[439] we stand secure, serenely certain of our safety now, sure of salvation; sure we will fulfill our chosen purpose as our ministry extends its holy blessing through the world. **W(326)**

W 153 L 10. Be still a moment, and in silence think how holy is your purpose, how secure you rest, untouchable within its light. God's ministers have chosen that the truth be with them. Who is holier than they? Who could be surer that his happiness is fully guaranteed? And who could be more mightily protected? What defense could possibly be needed by the ones[440] who are among the chosen ones of God by His election and their own as well?

W 153 L 11. It is the function of God's ministers to help their brothers choose as they have done. God has elected all, but few have come to realize His Will is but their own.[441] And while you fail to teach what you have learned salvation waits, and darkness holds the world in grim imprisonment. Nor will you learn that light has come to you, and your escape has been accomplished. For you will not see the light until you offer it to all your brothers. As they take it from your hands, so will you recognize it as your own.

W 153 L 12. Salvation can be thought of as a game that happy children play. It was designed by One Who loves His children, and Who would replace their fearful toys with joyous games, which teach them that the game of fear is gone. His game instructs in happiness because there is no loser. Everyone who plays must win, and in his winning is the gain to everyone ensured. The game of fear is gladly laid aside when children come to see the benefits salvation brings.

W 153 L 13. You who have played that you are lost to hope, abandoned by your Father, left alone in terror in a fearful world made mad by sin and guilt, be happy now. That game is over. Now a quiet time has come in which we put away the toys of guilt, and lock our quaint and childish thoughts of sin forever from the pure and holy minds of Heaven's children and the Son of God.

W 153 L 14. We pause but for a moment more, to play our final happy game upon this earth. And then we go to take our rightful place where truth abides and games are meaningless. **W(327)**

---

[435] **Luke 23:34** Then Jesus said, "Father, forgive them, for they do not know what they do."
[436] Handwritten mark-up suggests (Christ's(?)).
2 Corinthians 12:9 And He said to me, "My grace is sufficient for you, for My strength is made perfect in weakness." Therefore most gladly I will rather boast in my infirmities, that the power of Christ may rest upon me.

[437] The *Urtext* manuscript has a sentence break here, corrected by the handwriting to a comma. We agree with the correction.
[438] Handwritten mark-up moves (senseless) here.
[439] *Urtext* manuscript has the word "**defenceless**" here. We agree with *FIP* and correct it to "**defenselessness**".
[440] Handwritten mark-up suggests (now by those).
[441] **Matthew 20:16** "So the last will be first, and the first last. For many are called, but few chosen."

So is the story ended. Let this day bring the last chapter closer to the world, that everyone may learn the tale[442] he reads of terrifying destiny, defeat of all his hopes, his pitiful defense against a vengeance he can not escape, was[443] but his own deluded fantasy.[444] God's ministers have come to waken him from the dark dreams this story has evoked in his confused, bewildered memory of this distorted tale. God's Son can smile at last, on learning that it is not true.

W 153 L 15. Today we practice in a form we will maintain for quite a while. We will begin each day by giving our attention to the daily thought as long as possible. Five minutes now becomes the least we give to preparation for a day in which salvation is the only goal we have. Ten would be better; fifteen better still. And as distraction ceases to arise to turn us from our purpose, we will find that half an hour is too short a time to spend with God. Nor will we willingly give less at night in gratitude and joy.

W 153 L 16. Each hour adds to our increasing peace, as we remember to be faithful to the Will we share with God. At times, perhaps, a minute, even less, will be the most that we can offer as the hour strikes. Sometimes we will forget. At other times the business of the world will close on us, and we will be unable to withdraw a little while and turn our thoughts to God.

W 153 L 17. Yet when we can, we will observe our trust as ministers of God in hourly remembrance of our mission and His Love. And we will quietly sit by and wait on Him and listen to His Voice, and learn what He would have us do the hour that is yet to come; while thanking Him for the gifts He gave us in the one gone by. **W(328)**

W 153 L 18. In time, with practice, you will never cease to think of Him, and hear His loving Voice guiding your footsteps into quiet ways, where you will walk in true defenselessness, for you will know that Heaven goes with you. Nor would you keep your mind away from Him a moment, even though your time is spent in offering salvation to the world. Think you He will not make this possible for you who chose to carry out His plan for the salvation of the world and yours?

W 153 L 19. Today our theme is our defenselessness. We clothe ourselves in it as we prepare to meet the day. We rise up strong in Christ, and let our weakness disappear, as we remember that His strength abides in us.[445] We will remind ourselves that He remains beside us through the day, and never leaves our weakness unsupported by His strength. We call upon His strength each time we feel the threat of our defenses undermine our certainty of purpose. We will pause a moment, as He tells us "I am here."

W 153 L 20. Our[446] practicing will now begin to take the earnestness of love to help you keep your mind from wandering from its intent. Be not afraid nor timid.[447] There can be no doubt that you will reach your final goal. The ministers of God can never fail, because the love and strength and peace that shine from them to all their brothers come from Him. These are His gifts to you. Defenselessness is all you need to give Him in return. You lay aside but what was never real, to look on Christ and see His sinlessness. **W(329)**

Lesson 154 "I am among the ministers of God."

W 154 L 1. Let us today be neither arrogant nor falsely humble. We have gone beyond such foolishness. We cannot judge ourselves, nor need we do so. These are but attempts to hold decision off, and to delay commitment to our function. It is not our part to judge our worth, nor can we know what role is best for us; what we can do within a larger plan we cannot see in its entirety. Our part is cast in Heaven, not in hell. And what we think is weakness can be strength; what we believe to be our strength is often arrogance.

W 154 L 2. Whatever your appointed role may be it was selected by the Voice for God, Whose function is to speak for you as well. Seeing your strengths exactly as they are, and equally aware of where they can be best applied, for what, to whom and when, He chooses and accepts your part for you. He does not work without your own consent, but He is not deceived in what you are, and listens only to His Voice in you.

W 154 L 3. It is through His ability to hear One[448] Voice which is His Own[449] that you become aware at last there is One[450] Voice in you. And that One[451] Voice appoints your function, and relays it to you, giving you the strength to understand it, do what it entails, and to succeed in everything you do that is related to it. God has joined His Son in this, and thus His Son becomes His messenger of unity with Him.

W 154 L 4. It is this joining, through the Voice of God, of Father and of Son, that sets apart salvation from the world. It is this Voice which speaks of laws the world does not obey; Which promises salvation from all sin, with guilt abolished in the mind which God created sinless. Now this mind becomes aware again of Who created it, and of His lasting union with itself. So is its Self the one Reality[452] in Which its will and That of God are joined. **W(330)**

W 154 L 5. A messenger does not elect to make the message he delivers. Nor does he question the right of him who does, nor ask why he has chosen those who will receive the message that he brings. It is enough that he accept it, bring[453] it to the ones for which[454] it was appointed,[455] and fulfill his role in its delivery. If he insists on judging[456] what the messages should be, or what their purpose is, or where they should be carried, he is failing to perform his proper part as bringer of the Word.

W 154 L 6. There is one major difference in the role of Heaven's messengers, which sets them off from those the world appoints. The messages which they deliver are intended first for them. And it is only as they can accept them for themselves that they become able to bring them further, and to give them everywhere that they were meant to be. Like earthly messengers, they did not write the messages they bear, but they become their first receivers in the truest sense, receiving to prepare themselves to give.

W 154 L 7. An earthly messenger fulfills his role by giving all the messages away. The messengers of God perform their part by their acceptance of His messages as for themselves, and show they understand the messages by giving them away. They choose no roles that are not given them by His authority. And so they gain by every message which they give away.

W 154 L 8. Would you receive the messages of God? For thus do you become His messengers. You are appointed now,[457] and yet you wait to give the messages you have received, and so you do not know that they are yours, and do not recognize them. No-one can receive and understand he has received until he gives. For in the giving is his own acceptance of what he received. **W(331)**

---

[442] Handwritten mark-up suggests (s).
[443] Handwritten mark-up suggests (are).
[444] Handwritten mark-up suggests (fantasies).
[445] **1 John 3:24** And he who keeps His commandment dwells in Him, and He in him. And by this we know that He abides in us, by the Spirit which He gave to us.
[446] Handwritten mark-up suggests (Your).
[447] **John 6:20** But He said to them, "It is I; do not be afraid."

[448] Handwritten mark-up suggests (one).
[449] Handwritten mark-up suggests (own).
[450] Handwritten mark-up suggests (one).
[451] Handwritten mark-up suggests (one).
[452] Handwritten mark-up suggests (reality).
[453] Handwritten mark-up suggests (give).
[454] Handwritten mark-up suggests (whom).
[455] Handwritten mark-up suggests (is intended).
[456] Handwritten mark-up suggests (determines).
[457] The *Urtext* manuscript has a full sentence break, with handwriting changing it to a comma. We agree there should be no sentence break here.

W 154 L 9. You who are now the messengers of God receive His messages, for that is part of your appointed role. He[458] has not failed to offer what you need, nor has it been left unaccepted. Yet another part of your appointed task is yet to be accomplished. He Who has received for you the messages of God would have them be received by you as well. For thus do you identify with Him and claim your own.

W 154 L 10. It is this joining that we undertake to recognize today. We will not seek to keep our minds apart from Him Who speaks for us, for it is but our voice we hear as we attend Him. He alone can speak to us and for us, joining in One Voice the getting and the giving of God's Word; the giving and receiving of His Will.

W 154 L 11. We practice giving Him what He would have, that we may recognize His gifts to us. He needs our voice that He may speak through us. He needs our hands to hold His messages, and carry them to those[459] He appoints. He needs our feet to bring us where He wills, that those who wait in misery may be at last delivered. And He needs our will united with His Own, that we may be the true receivers of the gifts He gives.

W 154 L 12. Let us but learn this lesson for today: we will not recognize what we receive until we give it. You have heard this said a hundred ways,[460] and yet belief is lacking still. But this is sure; until belief is given it, you will receive a thousand miracles and then receive a thousand more, but will not know that God Himself has left no gift beyond what you already have; nor has denied the tiniest of blessings to His Son. What can this mean to you, until you have identified with him and with his own? **W(332)**

W 154 L 13. Our lesson for today is stated thus:

"I am among the ministers of God,

And I am grateful that I have the means

By which to recognize that I am free."

The world recedes as we light up our minds, and realize these holy words are true. They are the message sent to us today from our Creator. Now we demonstrate how they have changed our minds about ourselves, and what our function is. For as we prove that we accept no will we do not share, our many gifts from our Creator will spring to our sight and leap into our hands, and we[461] recognize what we received. **W(333)**

Lesson 155 "I will step back and let Him lead the way."

W 155 L 1. There is a way of living in the world that is not here, although it seems to be.[462] You do not change appearance, though you smile more frequently, Your forehead is serene; your eyes are quiet. And the ones who walk the world as you do recognize their own. Yet those who have not yet perceived the way will recognize you also, and believe that you are like them as you were before.

W 155 L 2. The world is an illusion. Those who choose to come to it are seeking for a place where they can be illusions, and avoid their own Reality. Yet when they find their own Reality[463] is even here, then they step back and let It lead the way. What other choice is really theirs to make? To let illusion walk ahead of truth is madness, but to let illusion sink behind the truth, and let the truth stand forth as what it is, is simple[464] sanity.

W 155 L 3. This is the simple choice we make today. The mad illusion will remain awhile in evidence, for those to look upon who chose to come, and have not yet rejoiced to find they were mistaken in the choice. They cannot learn directly from the truth, because they have denied that it is so. And so they need a Teacher Who perceives their madness, but Who still can look beyond illusion to the simple truth in them.

W 155 L 4. If truth demanded they give up the world, it would appear to them as if it asked the sacrifice of something that is real. Many have chosen to renounce the world while still believing its reality, and they have suffered from a sense of loss and have not been released accordingly. Others have chosen nothing but the world, and they have suffered from a sense of loss still deeper, which they did not understand.

W 155 L 5. Between these paths there is another road which leads away from loss of every kind, for sacrifice and deprivation both are quickly left behind. This is the way appointed for you now. You walk this path as others walk, nor do you seem to be distinct from them although you are indeed. Thus can you serve them while you serve yourself, and set their footsteps on the way **W(334)** which God has opened up to you, and them through you.[465]

W 155 L 6. Illusion still appears to cling to you, that you may reach them. Yet it has stepped back, and it is not illusion that they hear you speak of, nor illusion which you bring their eyes to look on and their minds to grasp. Now can the truth, which walks ahead of you, speak to them through illusion, for the road leads past illusion now, while on the way you call to them that they may follow you.

W 155 L 7. All roads will lead to this one in the end. For sacrifice and deprivation are paths which[466] lead nowhere, choices for defeat, and aims which will remain impossible. All this steps back as truth comes forth in you, to lead your brothers from the ways of death, and set them on the way to happiness. Their suffering is but illusion. Yet they need a guide to lead them out of it, for they mistake illusion for the truth.

W 155 L 8. Such is salvation's call, and nothing more. It asks that you accept the truth, and let It go before you, lighting up the path of ransom from illusion. It is not a ransom with a price. There is no cost, but only gain. Illusion can but seem to hold in chains the holy Son of God. It is but from illusions he is saved. As they step back he finds himself again.

W 155 L 9. Walk safely now yet carefully, because this path is new to you. And you may find that you are tempted still to walk ahead of truth, and let illusion be your guide. Your holy brothers have been given you to follow in your footsteps, as you walk with certainty of purpose to the truth. It goes before you now, that they may see something with which they can identify; something they understand to lead the way. **W(335)**

W 155 L 10. Yet at the journey's ending there will be no gap, no distance between truth and you. And all illusions walking in the way you travelled will be gone from you as well, with nothing left to keep the truth apart from God's completion, holy as Himself. Step back in faith, and let truth lead the way. You know not where you go, but One Who knows goes with you. Let Him lead you with the rest.

W 155 L 11. When dreams are over, time has closed the door on all the things that pass and miracles are purposeless, the holy Son of God will make no journeys. There will be no wish to be illusion rather than the truth. And we step forth toward this, as we progress along the way that truth points out to us. This is our final journey,

---

[458] Handwritten mark-up suggests (God)
[459] Handwritten mark-up suggests (whom).
[460] Handwritten mark-up suggests (a hundred times).
[461] Handwritten mark-up suggests (will).
[462] **John 17:16** "They are not of the world, just as I am not of the world."
[463] Handwritten mark-up suggests (reality).
[464] Handwritten mark-up suggests (merely).

[465] **Isaiah 42:16** I will bring the blind by a way they did not know;
I will lead them in paths they have not known.
I will make darkness light before them,
And crooked places straight.
These things I will do for them,
And not forsake them.
Matthew 20:28 "Just as the Son of Man did not come to be served, but to serve, and to give His life a ransom for many."
[466] Handwritten mark-up suggests (that).

which we make for everyone. We must not lose our way. For as truth goes before us so it goes before our brothers, who will follow us.

W 155 L 12. We walk to God. Pause and reflect on this. Could any way be holier, or more deserving of your effort, of your love, and of your full intent? What way could give you more than everything, or offer less and still content the holy Son of God? We walk to God. The truth that walks before us now is One[467] with Him, and leads us to where He has always been. What way but this could be a path which you would choose instead?

W 155 L 13. Your feet are safely set upon the road which[468] leads the world to God. Look not to ways that seem to lead you elsewhere. Dreams are not a worthy guide for you who are God's Son. Forget not He has placed His hand in yours, and given you your brothers in His Trust that you are worthy of His Trust in you. He cannot be deceived. His Trust has made your pathway certain and your goal secure. You will not fail your brothers nor your Self. **W(336)**

W 155 L 14. And now He asks but that you think of Him a while each day, that He may speak to you and tell you of His Love, reminding you how great His Trust; how limitless His Love. In your name and His Own, which are the same, we practice gladly with this thought today:

> *"I will step back and let Him lead the way,*
> *For I would walk along the road to Him."* **W(337)**

Lesson 156 "I walk with God in perfect holiness."

W 156 L 1. Today's idea but states the simple truth which makes the thought of sin impossible. It promises there is no cause for guilt, and being causeless it does not exist. It follows surely from the basic thought so often mentioned in the text; ideas leave not their source. If this be true, how can you be apart from God? How could you walk the world alone and separate from your Source?

W 156 L 2. We are not inconsistent in the thoughts that we present in our curriculum. Truth must be true throughout if it be true. It cannot contradict itself, nor be in parts uncertain and in others sure. You cannot walk the world apart from God because you could not be without Him. He is what your life is. Where you are He is.[469] There is One[470] life. That Life[471] you share with Him. Nothing can be apart from Him and live.[472]

W 156 L 3. Yet where He is there must be holiness as well as life. No attribute of His remains unshared by everything that lives. What lives is holy as Himself because what shares His Life is part of Holiness, and could no more be sinful than the sun could choose to be of ice; the sea elect to be apart from water, or the grass to grow with roots suspended in the air.

W 156 L 4. There is a Light in you Which cannot die, Whose Presence is so holy that the world is sanctified because of you. All things that live bring gifts to you, and offer them in gratitude and gladness at your feet. The scent of flowers is their gift to you. The waves bow down before you, and the trees extend their arms to shield you from the heat and lay their leaves before you on the ground, that you may walk in softness, while the wind sinks to a whisper 'round[473] your holy head. **W(338)**

W 156 L 5. The Light in you is what the universe longs to behold. All living things are still before you, for they recognize Who walks with you. The Light you carry is their own, and thus they see in you their holiness, saluting you as Savior and as God. Accept their reverence, for it is due to Holiness Itself Which walks with you, transforming in its gentle Light all things into Its likeness and Its purity.[474]

W 156 L 6. This is the way salvation works. As you step back, the Light in you steps forward and encompasses the world. It heralds not the end of sin in punishment and death. In lightness and in laughter is it[475] gone, because its quaint absurdity is seen. It is a foolish thought, a silly dream, not frightening, ridiculous perhaps, but who would waste an instant in approach to God Himself for such a senseless whim?

W 156 L 7. Yet you have wasted many, many years on just this foolish thought. The past is gone with all its fantasies. They keep you bound no longer. The approach to God is near. And in the little interval of doubt which still remains, you may perhaps lose sight of your Companion, and mistake Him for the senseless ancient dream that now is past.

W 156 L 8. "Who walks with me?" This question should be asked a thousand times a day, 'til certainty has ended doubting and established peace. Today let doubting cease. God speaks for you in answering your question with these words:

> *"I walk with God in perfect holiness.*
> *I light the world, I light my mind and all*
> *The minds which God created one with me."* **W(339)**

Lesson 157 "Into His Presence would I enter now."

W 157 L 1. This is a day of silence and of trust. It is a special time of promise in your calendar of days. It is a time Heaven has set apart to shine upon, and cast a timeless light upon this day when echoes of eternity are heard. This day is holy, for it ushers in a new experience, a different kind of feeling and awareness. You have spent long days and nights in celebrating death. Today you learn to feel the joy of life.

W 157 L 2. This is another crucial turning point in the curriculum. We add a new dimension now; a fresh experience which sheds a light on all that we have learned already, and prepares us for what we have yet to learn. It brings us to the door where learning ceases, and we catch a glimpse of what lies past the highest reaches it can possibly attain. It leaves us there an instant and we go beyond it, sure of our direction and our only goal.

W 157 L 3. Today it will be given you to feel a touch of Heaven, though you will return to paths of learning, yet you have come far enough along the way to alter time sufficiently to rise above its laws, and walk into eternity a while. This you will learn to do increasingly, as every lesson, faithfully rehearsed, brings you more swiftly to this holy place and leaves you, for a moment, to your Self.

W 157 L 4. He will direct your practicing today, for what you ask for now is what He wills. And having joined your will with His this day, what you are asking must be given you. Nothing is needed but

---

[467] Handwritten mark-up suggests (one).
[468] Handwritten mark-up suggests (that).
[469] **John 14:3** "And if I go and prepare a place for you, I will come again and receive you to Myself; that where I am, there you may be also."
[470] Handwritten mark-up suggests (one).
[471] Handwritten mark-up suggests (life).
[472] **Acts 17:28** for in Him we live and move and have our being, as also some of your own poets have said, "For we are also His offspring."

[473] The *Urtext* manuscript has this typed "around" with the "a" crossed out. The *Notes* has it just as "round" which spelling FIP also has. Since it is a contraction of "around" we insert the apostrophe making it 'round.
[474] **Genesis 1:26-27** Then God said, "Let Us make man in Our image, according to Our likeness; let them have dominion over the fish of the sea, over the birds of the air, and over the cattle, over all the earth and over every creeping thing that creeps on the earth." So God created man in His own image; in the image of God He created him; male and female He created them.
[475] Handwritten mark-up suggests (sin).

today's idea to light your mind, and let it rest in still anticipation and in quiet joy wherein you quickly leave the world behind. **W(340)**

W 157 L 5. From this day forth your ministry takes on a genuine devotion, and a glow that travels from your fingertips to those you touch, and blesses those you look upon. A vision reaches everyone you meet, and everyone you think of, or who thinks of you. For your experience today will so transform your mind that it becomes the touchstone for the holy Thoughts of God.

W 157 L 6. Your body will be sanctified today, its only purpose being now to bring the vision of what you experience this day to light the world. We cannot give experience like this directly. Yet it leaves a vision in our eyes which we can offer everyone, that he may come the sooner to the same experience in which the world is quietly forgot, and Heaven is remembered for a while.

W 157 L 7. As this experience increases and all goals but this become of little worth, the world to which you will return becomes a little closer to the end of time; a little more like Heaven in its ways; a little nearer its deliverance. And you who bring it light will come to see the light more sure; the vision more distinct. The time will come when you will not return in the same form in which you now appear, for you will have no need of it. Yet now it has a purpose, and will serve it well.

W 157 L 8. Today we will embark upon a course you have not dreamed of. But the Holy One,[476] the Giver of the happy dreams of life, Translator of perception into truth, the holy Guide to Heaven given you, has dreamed for you this journey, which you make and start today, with the experience, this day holds out to you to be your own.

W 157 L 9. Into Christ's Presence will we enter now serenely unaware of everything except His shining Face and perfect Love. The vision of His Face will stay with you, but there will be an instant which transcends all vision, even this, the holiest. This you will never teach, for you attained it not through learning. Yet the vision speaks of your remembrance of what you knew that instant, and will surely know again. **W(341)**

Lesson 158 "Today I learn to give as I receive."

W 158 L 1. What has been given you? The knowledge that you are a mind, in Mind and purely mind, sinless forever, wholly unafraid because you were created out of Love. Nor have you left your Source, remaining as you were created. This was given you as knowledge which you cannot lose. It was given as well to every living thing, for by that knowledge only does it live.

W 158 L 2. You have received all this. No-one who walks the world but has received it. It is not this knowledge which you give, for that is what creation gave. All this cannot be learned. What, then, are you to learn to give today? Our

lesson yesterday evoked a theme found early in the text. Experience cannot be shared directly in the way that vision can. The revelation that the Father and the Son are One will come in time to every mind. Yet is that time determined by the mind itself, not taught.

W 158 L 3. The time is set already. It appears to be quite arbitrary. Yet there is no step along the road that anyone but takes[477] by chance. It has already been taken by him, although he has not yet embarked on it. For time but seems to go in one direction. We but undertake a journey that is over. Yet it seems to have a future still unknown to us.

W 158 L 4. Time is a trick; a sleight of hand, a vast illusion in which figures come and go as if by magic. Yet there is a plan behind appearances which does not change. The script is written. When experience will come to end your doubting has been set. For we but see the journey from the point at which it ended, looking back on it, imagining we make it once again; reviewing mentally what has gone by. **W(342)**

W 158 L 5. The[478] teacher does not give experience, because he did not learn it. It revealed itself to him at its appointed time. But vision is his gift. This he can give directly, for Christ's knowledge is not lost because He has a vision He can give to anyone who asks. The Father's Will and His are joined in knowledge. Yet there is a vision which the Holy Spirit sees because the mind of Christ beholds it too.

W 158 L 6. Here is the joining of the world of doubt and shadows made with the intangible. Here is a quiet place within the world made holy by forgiveness and by love. Here are all contradictions reconciled, for here the journey ends. Experience, unlearned, untaught, unseen, is merely there. This is beyond our goal, for it transcends what needs to be accomplished. Our concern is with Christ's vision. This we can attain.

W 158 L 7. Christ's vision has one law. It does not look upon a body and mistake it for the Son whom God created. It beholds a light beyond the body; an idea beyond what can be touched, a purity undimmed by errors, pitiful mistakes, and fearful thoughts of guilt from dreams of sin. It sees no separation. And it looks on everyone, on every circumstance, all happenings and all events, without the slightest fading of the light it sees.

W 158 L 8. This can be taught, and must be taught by all who would achieve it. It requires but the recognition that the world can not give anything that faintly can compare with this in value; nor set up a goal which does not merely disappear when this has been perceived. And this you give today, see no-one as a body. Greet him as the Son of God he is, acknowledging that he is one with you in holiness. **W(343)**

W 158 L 9. Thus are his sins forgiven him, for Christ has vision which has power to overlook them all. In His forgiveness they are gone. Unseen by One, they merely disappear, because a vision of the holiness which lies beyond them comes to take their place. It matters not what form they took, nor how enormous they appeared to be, nor who seemed to be hurt by them. They are no more, and all effects they seemed to have are gone with them, undone and never to be done.

W 158 L 10. Thus do you learn to give as you receive. And thus Christ's vision looks on you as well. This lesson is not difficult to learn, if you remember in your brother you but see yourself. If he be lost in sin so must you be; if you see light in him your sins have been forgiven by yourself. Each brother whom you meet today provides another chance to let Christ's vision shine on you, and offer you the peace of God.

W 158 L 11. It matters not when revelation comes, for that is not of time. Yet time has still one gift to give in which true knowledge is reflected in a way so accurate its image shares its unseen holiness;[479] its likeness shines with its immortal Love.[480] We practice seeing with the eyes of Christ today. And by the holy gifts we give, Christ's vision looks upon ourselves as well. **W(344)**

---

[476] **Psalm 16:10** For You will not leave my soul in Sheol, Nor will You allow Your Holy One to see corruption.
Mark 1:24 Saying, "Let us alone! What have we to do with You, Jesus of Nazareth? Did You come to destroy us? I know who You are--the Holy One of God!"
[477] Handwritten mark-up suggests (but) should go here.

[478] Handwritten mark-up suggests (A).
[479] **Romans 8:29** For whom He foreknew, He also predestinated *to be* conformed to the image of His Son, for Him to be *the* First-born among many brothers.
[480] Handwritten mark-up suggests(love).

Lesson 159 "I give the miracles I have received."

W 159 L 1. No-one can give what he has not received. To give a thing requires first you have it in your own possession. Here the laws of Heaven and the world agree. But here they also separate. The world believes that to possess a thing it must be kept. Salvation teaches otherwise. To give is how to recognize you have received. It is the proof that what you have is yours.

W 159 L 2. You understand that you are healed when you give healing. You accept forgiveness as accomplished in yourself when you forgive. You recognize your brother as yourself, and thus do you perceive that you are whole. There is no miracle you cannot give, for all are given you. Receive them now by opening the storehouse of your mind where they are laid, and giving them away.

W 159 L 3. Christ's vision is a miracle. It comes from far beyond itself, for it reflects Eternal Love and the rebirth of love which never dies, but has been kept obscure. Christ's vision pictures Heaven, for it sees a world so like to Heaven that what God created perfect can be mirrored there. The darkened glass the world presents can show but twisted images in broken parts.[481] The real world pictures Heaven's innocence.

W 159 L 4. Christ's vision is the miracle in which all miracles are born. It is their source, remaining with each miracle you give, and yet remaining yours. It is the bond by which the giver and receiver are united in extension here on earth as they are one in Heaven. Christ beholds no sin in anyone, and in His sight the sinless are as one. Their holiness was given by His Father and Himself. **W(345)**

W 159 L 5. Christ's vision is the bridge between the worlds, and in its power can you safely trust to carry you from this world into one made holy by forgiveness. Things which seem quite solid here are merely shadows there, transparent, faintly seen, at times forgot, and never able to obscure the light that shines beyond them. Holiness has been restored to vision, and the blind can see.[482]

W 159 L 6. This is the Holy Spirit's single gift; the treasure house to which you can appeal with perfect certainty for everything that can contribute to your happiness. All are laid here already. All can be received but for the asking. Here the door is never locked, and no-one is denied his least request or his most urgent need. There is no sickness not already healed. No lack unsatisfied, no need unmet, within this golden treasury of Christ.

W 159 L 7. Here does the world remember what was lost when it was made. For here it is repaired, made new again but in a different light. What was to be the home of sin becomes the center of redemption and the hearth of mercy, where the suffering are healed and welcome. No-one will be turned away from this new home, where his salvation waits. No-one is stranger to him. No-one asks for anything of him except the gift of his acceptance of his welcoming

W 159 L 8. Christ's vision is the holy ground in which the lilies of forgiveness set their roots.[483] This is their home. They can be brought from here back to the world, but they can never grow in its unnourishing and shallow soil. They need the light and warmth and kindly care Christ's charity provides. They need the love with which He looks on them. And they become His messengers which give as they received. **W(346)**

W 159 L 9. Take from His storehouse, that its treasures may increase. His lilies do not leave their home when they are carried back into the world. Their roots remain. They do not leave their source, but carry its beneficence with them, and turn the world into a garden like the one they came from, and to which they go again with added fragrance. Now are they twice blessed. The messages they brought from Christ have been delivered and returned to them. And they return them gladly unto Him.

W 159 L 10. Behold the store of miracles set out for you to give. Are you not worth the gift, when God appointed it be given you? Judge not God's Son, but follow in the way He has established. Christ has dreamed the dream of a forgiven world. It is His gift whereby a sweet transition can be made from death to life, from hopelessness to hope. Let us an instant dream with Him. His dream awakens us to truth. His vision gives the means for a return to our unlost and everlasting sanctity in God. **W(347)**

Lesson 160 "I am at home. Fear is the stranger here."

W 160 L 1. Fear is a stranger to the ways of love. Identify with fear, and you will be a stranger to yourself. And thus you are unknown to you. What is your Self remains an alien to the part of you which thinks that it is real but different from yourself. Who could be sane in such a circumstance? Who but a madman could believe he is what he is not, and judge against himself?

W 160 L 2. There is a stranger in our midst, who comes from an idea so foreign to the truth he speaks a different language, looks upon a world truth does not know, and understands what truth regards as senseless. Stranger yet, he does not recognize to whom he comes, and yet maintains his home belongs to him while he is alien now who is at home. And yet how easy it would be to say, "This is my home. Here I belong, and will not leave because a madman says I must."

W 160 L 3. What reason is there for not saying this? What could the reason be except that you had asked this stranger in to take your place, and let you be a stranger to yourself? No-one would let himself be dispossessed so needlessly unless he thought there was another home more suited to his tastes.

W 160 L 4. Who is the stranger? Is it fear or you that is unsuited to the home which God provided for His Son? Is fear His Own, created in His likeness?[484] Is it fear that love completes and is completed by? There is no home can shelter love and fear. They cannot coexist. If you are real, then fear must be illusion. And if fear is real, then you do not exist at all. **W(348)**

W 160 L 5. How simply, then, the question is resolved. Who fears has but denied himself and said, "I am the stranger here. And so I leave my home to one more like me than myself, and give him all I thought belonged to me." Now is he exiled of necessity, not knowing who he is, uncertain of all things but this; that he is not himself, and that his home has been denied to him.

W 160 L 6. What does he search for now? What can he find? A stranger to himself can find no home wherever he may look, for he has made return impossible.[485] His way is lost except a miracle will search him out, and show him that he is no stranger now. The miracle will come. For in his home his Self remains. It asked no stranger in, and took no alien thought to be Itself. And It will call Its Own[486] unto Itself, in recognition of what is Its Own.

---

[481] **1 Corinthians 13:12** For now we see in a glass darkly, but then face to face. Now I know in part, but then I shall know just as I also am known.
[482] **Luke 4:18** "The Spirit of the Lord is on Me; because of this He has anointed Me to proclaim the Gospel to the poor. He has sent me to heal the brokenhearted, to proclaim deliverance to the captives, and new sight to the blind, to set at liberty those having been crushed,"
[483] **Exodus 3:5** Then He said, "Do not draw near this place. Take your sandals off your feet, for the place where you stand is holy ground."

[484] **Genesis 1:26-27** Then God said, "Let Us make man in Our image, according to Our likeness; let them have dominion over the fish of the sea, over the birds of the air, and over the cattle, over all the earth and over every creeping thing that creeps on the earth." So God created man in His own image; in the image of God He created him; male and female He created them.
[485] **John 10:5** "And they will not follow a stranger, but will flee from him, for they do not know the voice of strangers."
[486] Three instances of "**Own**" on this page, and one on the previous page are rendered lower case "**own**" by handwritten strokes.

W 160 L 7. Who is the stranger? Is he not the one your Self calls not? You are unable now to recognize this stranger in your midst, for you have given him your rightful place. Yet is your Self as certain of Its Own as God is of His Son. He cannot be confused about creation. He is sure of what belongs to Him. No stranger can be interposed between His knowledge and His Son's reality. He does not know of strangers. He is certain of His Son.

W 160 L 8. His[487] certainty suffices. Who he knows to be His Son belongs where He has set His Son forever. He has answered you who ask, "Who is the stranger?" Hear His Voice assure you, quietly and sure, that you are not a stranger to your Father, nor is your Creator stranger made to you. Whom God has joined remains forever one, at home in Him, no stranger to Himself.[488]

W 160 L 9. Today we offer thanks that Christ has come to search the world for what belongs to Him. His vision sees no strangers, but beholds His Own, and joyously unites with them. They see Him as a stranger, for they do not recognize themselves. Yet as they give Him welcome they remember. And He leads them gently home again where they belong. **W(349)**

W 160 L 10. Not one does He[489] forget. Not one He fails to give you to remember, that your home may be complete and perfect as it was established. He has not forgotten you. But you will not remember Him until you look on all as He does. Who denies his brother is denying Him,[490] and thus refusing to accept the gift of sight by which his Self is clearly recognized, his home remembered, and salvation come. **W(350)**

Lesson 161 "Give me your blessing, holy Son of God."

W 161 L 1. Today we practice differently, and take a stand against our anger, that our fears may disappear and offer room to love. Here is salvation in the simple words in which we practice with today's idea. Here is the answer to temptation which can never fail to welcome in the Christ where fear and anger had prevailed before. Here is Atonement made complete, the world passed safely by and Heaven now restored. Here is the Answer of the Voice of God.

W 161 L 2. Complete abstraction is the natural condition of the mind. But part of it is now unnatural. It does not look on everything as one. It sees instead but fragments of the whole, for only thus could it invent the partial world you see. The purpose of all seeing is to show you what you wish to see. All hearing but brings to your mind the sounds it wants to hear.

W 161 L 3. Thus were specifics made. And now it is specifics we must use in practicing. We give them to the Holy Spirit that He may employ them for a purpose which is different from the one we gave to them. Yet He can use but what we made to teach us from a different point of view, so we can see a different use in everything.

W 161 L 4. One brother is all brothers. Every mind contains all minds, for every mind is one. Such is the truth. Yet do these thoughts make clear the meaning of creation? Do these words bring perfect clarity with them to you? What can they seem to be but empty sounds, pretty, perhaps; correct in sentiment, yet fundamentally not understood nor understandable. The mind that taught itself to think specifically can no longer grasp abstraction in the sense that it is all-encompassing. We need to see a little that we learn a lot. **W(351)**

W 161 L 5. It seems to be the body we[491] feel limits our[492] freedom, makes us[493] suffer and at last puts out our[494] life. Yet bodies are but[495] symbols of a[496] concrete form[497] of fear. Fear without symbols calls for no response, for symbols can stand for the meaningless.[498] Love needs no symbols, being true. But fear attaches to specifics, being false.

W 161 L 6. Bodies attack, but minds do not. This thought is surely reminiscent of our text, where it is often emphasized. This is the reason bodies easily become fear's symbols. You have many times been urged to look beyond the body, for its sight presents the symbol of love's "enemy" Christ's vision does not see. The body is the target for attack, for no-one thinks he hates a mind. Yet what but mind directs the body to attack? What else could be the seat of fear except what thinks of fear?

W 161 L 7. Hate is specific. There must be a thing to be attacked. An enemy must be perceived in such a form he can be touched and seen and heard, and ultimately killed. When hatred rests upon a thing, it calls for death as surely as God's Voice proclaims there is no death. Fear is insatiable, consuming everything its eyes behold; seeing itself in everything; compelled to turn upon itself and to destroy.

W 161 L 8. Who sees a brother as a body sees him as fear's symbol. And he will attack because what he beholds is his own fear external to himself, poised to attack, and howling to unite with him again. Mistake not the intensity of rage projected fear must spawn. It shrieks in wrath, and claws the air in frantic hope it can reach to its maker and devour him.

W 161 L 9. This do the body's eyes behold in one whom Heaven cherishes, the angels love, and God created perfect. This is his reality. And in Christ's vision is his loveliness reflected in a form so holy and so beautiful that you could scarce refrain from kneeling at his feet. Yet you will take his hand instead, for you are like him in the sight which sees him thus. **W(352)** Attack on him is enemy to you, for you will not perceive that in his hands is your salvation. Ask him but for this, and he will give it to you. Ask him not to symbolize your fear. Would you request that love destroy itself? Or would you have it be revealed to you and set you free?

W 161 L 10. Today we practice in a form we have attempted earlier. Your readiness is closer now, and you will come today nearer Christ's vision. If you are intent on reaching it, you will succeed today. And once you have succeeded, you will not be willing to accept the witnesses your body's eyes call forth. What you will see will sing to you of ancient melodies you will remember. You are not forgot in Heaven. Would you not remember it?

W 161 L 11. Select one brother, symbol of the rest, and ask salvation of him. See him first as clearly as you can, in that same form to which you are accustomed. See his face, his hands and feet, his clothing. Watch him smile, and see familiar gestures which he makes so frequently. Then think of this; what you are seeing now conceals from you the sight of one who can forgive you all your sins; whose sacred hands can take the nails which pierce your own away, and lift the crown of thorns which you have placed upon your bleeding head.[499] Ask this of him that he may set you free:

---

[487] Handwritten mark-up suggests (God's).
[488] **Matthew 19:6** "So then, they are no longer two but one flesh. Therefore what God has joined together, let not man separate."
[489] Handwritten mark-up suggests (Christ).
[490] **Matthew 25:45** Then He will answer them, saying, "Assuredly, I say to you, inasmuch as you did not do it to one of the least of these, you did not do it to Me."

[491] Handwritten mark-up suggests (you).
[492] Handwritten mark-up suggests (your).
[493] Handwritten mark-up suggests (you).
[494] Handwritten mark-up suggests (your).
[495] Handwritten mark-up suggests (concrete).
[496] Handwritten mark-up suggests (the).
[497] Handwritten mark-up suggests (s).
[498] The *Urtext* manuscript has "meanings" here but both the *Notes* and FIP have "meaningless" which appears to be more correct.
[499] **Matthew 9:6** "But so that you may know that the Son of Man has authority on earth to forgive sins," then He said to the paralytic, Arise, take up your bed and go to your house."

"Give me your blessing, holy Son of God,
I would behold you with the eyes of Christ,
And see my perfect sinlessness in you."

W 161 L 12. And He will answer Whom you called upon, for He will hear the Voice of God in you, and answer in your own. Behold him now whom you had seen as merely flesh and bone, and recognize that Christ has come to you. Today's idea is your safe escape from anger and from fear. Be sure you use it instantly, should you be tempted to attack a brother and perceive in him the symbol of your fear. And you will see him suddenly transformed from enemy to Savior; from the devil into Christ. W(353)[500]W(354)

Lesson 162 "I am as God created me."

W 162 L 1. This single thought, held firmly in the mind, would save the world. From time to time we will repeat it, as we reach another stage in learning. It will mean far more to you as you advance. These words are sacred, for they are the words God gave in answer to the world you made. By them it disappears, and all things seen within its misty clouds and vaporous illusions vanish as these words are spoken. For they come from God.

W 162 L 2. Here is the Word by which the Son became His Father's happiness, His Love, and His completion. Here creation is proclaimed, and honored as it is. There is no dream these words will not dispel; no thought of sin and no illusion that the dream contains that[501] will not fade away before their might. They are the trumpet of awakening that sounds around the world.[502] The dead awake in answer to its call. And those who live and hear this sound will never look on death.[503]

W 162 L 3. Holy indeed is he who makes these words his own; arising with them in his mind, recalling them throughout the day, at night bringing them with him as he goes to sleep. His dreams are happy and his rest secure; his safety certain and his body healed, because he sleeps and wakens with the truth before him always. He will save the world because he gives the world what he receives each time he practices the words of truth.

W 162 L 4. Today we practice simply. For the words we use are mighty, and they need no thoughts beyond themselves to change the mind of him who uses them. So wholly is it changed that it is now the treasury in which God places all His gifts and all His Love to be distributed to all the world, increased in giving; kept complete because its sharing is unlimited. And thus you learn to think with God. Christ's vision has restored your sight by salvaging your mind. W(355)

John 20:25 The other disciples therefore said to him, "We have seen the Lord."
So he said to them, "Unless I see in His hands the print of the nails, and put my finger into the print of the nails, and put my hand into His side, I will not believe."

[500] In no edition does any material appear between lessons 161 and 162, yet there is a skipped page number in the *Urtext* manuscript.

[501] Handwritten mark-up suggests (which).

[502] **Joel 2:1** Blow the trumpet in Zion,
 And sound an alarm in My holy mountain!
 Let all the inhabitants of the land tremble;
 For the day of the LORD is coming,
 For it is at hand:

1 Corinthians 15:52 In a moment, in the twinkling of an eye, at the last trumpet. For the trumpet will sound, and the dead will be raised incorruptible, and we shall be changed.

[503] **John 8:51** Most assuredly, I say to you, if anyone keeps My word he shall never see death.
John 11:25 Jesus said to her, "I am the resurrection and the life. He who believes in Me, though he may die, he shall live."
John 11:26 "And whoever lives and believes in Me shall never die. Do you believe this?"

W 162 L 5. We honor you today. Yours is the right to perfect holiness you now accept. With this acceptance is salvation brought to everyone, for who could cherish sin when holiness like this has blessed the world? Who could despair when perfect joy is yours, available to all as remedy for grief and misery, all sense of loss, and for complete escape from sin and guilt?

W 162 L 6. And who would not be brother to you now; you, his redeemer and his Savior? Who could fail to welcome you into his heart with loving invitation, eager to unite with one like him in holiness? You are as God created you. These words dispel the night, and darkness is no more. The light is come today to bless the world, for you have recognized the Son of God, and in your recognition is the world's. W(356)

Lesson 163 "There is no death. The Son of God is free."

W 163 L 1. Death is a thought which takes on many forms, often unrecognized. It may appear as sadness, fear, anxiety or doubt; as anger, faithlessness and lack of trust; concern for bodies, envy, and all forms in which the wish to be as you are not may come to tempt you. All such thoughts are but reflections of the worshipping of death as Savior and as giver of release.

W 163 L 2. Embodiment of fear, the host of sin, god of the guilty and the lord of all illusions and deceptions, does the thought of death seem mighty. For it seems to hold all living things within its withered hand; all hopes and wishes in its blighting grasp; all goals perceived but in its sightless eyes. The frail, the helpless and the sick bow down before its image, thinking it alone is real, inevitable, worthy of their trust. For it alone will surely come.

W 163 L 3. All things but death are seen to be unsure, too quickly lost however hard to gain, uncertain in their outcome, apt to fail the hopes they once engendered, and to leave the taste of dust and ashes in their wake in place of aspirations and of dreams. But death is counted on. For it will come with certain footsteps when the time has come for its arrival. It will never fail to take all life as hostage to itself.

W 163 L 4. Would you bow down to idols such as this? Here is the strength and might of God Himself perceived within an idol made of dust. Here is the opposite of God proclaimed as lord of all creation, stronger than God's Will for life, the endlessness of love and Heaven's perfect, changeless constancy. Here is the Will of Father and of Son defeated finally, and laid to rest beneath the headstone death has placed upon the body of the holy Son of God. W(357)

W 163 L 5. Unholy in defeat, he has become what death would have him be. His epitaph, which death itself has written, gives no name to him, for he has passed to dust. It says but this: "Here lies a witness God is dead." And this it writes again and still again, while all the while its worshippers agree, and kneeling down with foreheads to the ground, they whisper fearfully that it is so.

W 163 L 6. It is impossible to worship death in any form, and still select a few you would not cherish, and would yet avoid while still believing in the rest. For death is total. Either all things die, or else they live and cannot die. No compromise is possible. For here again we see an obvious position which we must accept if we be sane; what contradicts one thought entirely can not be true unless its opposite is proven false.

W 163 L 7. The idea of the death of God is so preposterous that even the insane have difficulty in believing it. For it implies that God was once alive and somehow perished, killed, apparently, by those who did not want him to survive. Their stronger will could triumph over His, and so Eternal Life gave way to death. And with the Father died the Son as well.

W 163 L 8. Death's worshippers may be afraid. And yet can thoughts like these be fearful? If they saw that it is only this which they believed, they would be instantly released. And you will show them this today. There is no death, and we renounce it now in every form, for their salvation and our own as well.[504] God made not death. Whatever form it takes must therefore be illusion. This the stand we take today. And it is given us to look past death and see the life[505] beyond.

W 163 L 9. *"Our Father, bless our eyes today. We are Your messengers, and we would look upon the glorious reflection of Your Love which shines in everything. We live and breathe in You alone.[506] We are not separate from Your Eternal Life. There is no death, for death is not Your Will. And we abide where You have placed us, in the Life we share with You and with all living things, to be* **W(358)** *like You and part of You forever. We accept Your Thoughts as ours, and our will is One with Yours eternally. Amen."* **W(359)**

Lesson 164 "Now are we One[507] with Him Who is our Source."

W 164 L 1. What time but now can truth be recognized? The present is the only time there is. And so today, this instant, now, we come to look upon what is forever there; not in our sight but in the eyes of Christ. He looks past time and sees eternity as represented there. He hears the sounds the senseless busy world engenders, yet He hears them faintly, for beyond them all He hears the song of Heaven and the Voice of God more clear, more meaningful, more near.

W 164 L 2. The world fades easily away before His sight. Its sounds grow dim. A melody from far beyond the world increasingly is more and more distinct; an ancient Call to Which He gives an ancient answer. You will recognize them both. For they are but your answer to your Father's Call to you. Christ answers for you, echoing your Self, using your voice to give His glad consent; accepting your deliverance for you.

W 164 L 3. How holy is your practicing today, as He[508] gives you His sight and hears for you, and answers in your name the Call He hears. How quiet is the time you give to spend with Him beyond the world. How easily are all your seeming sins forgot and all your sorrows unremembered. On this day is grief laid by, for sights and sounds which come from nearer than the world are[509] clear to you who will today accept the gifts He gives.

W 164 L 4. There is a silence into which the world can not intrude. There is an ancient peace you carry in your heart and have not lost. There is a sense of holiness in you the thought of sin has never touched. All this today you will remember. Faithfulness in practicing today will bring rewards so great and so completely different from all things you sought before, that you will know that here your treasure is, and here your rest. **W(360)**

---

[504] **Isaiah 25:8** He will swallow up death in victory; and the Lord Jehovah will wipe away tears from all faces. And He shall take away from all the earth the rebuke of His people. For Jehovah has spoken.
1 Corinthians 15:55 O death, where *is* your sting? O grave, where *is* your victory?"
2 Timothy 1:10 But has now been revealed by the appearing of our Savior Jesus Christ, who has abolished death and brought life and immortality to light through the gospel,
Revelation 21:4 And God will wipe away every tear from their eyes; there shall be no more death, nor sorrow, nor crying. There shall be no more pain, for the former things have passed away."
[505] The *Urtext* manuscript has "light" originally typed, with "life" handwritten in as a correction. The *Notes* has "life" which appears to be correct.
[506] **Acts 17:28** for in Him we live and move and have our being, as also some of your own poets have said, "For we are also His offspring."
[507] Handwritten mark-up suggests (one).
[508] Handwritten mark-up suggests (Christ).
[509] Handwritten mark-up suggests(are) but original *Urtext* manuscript has "**made**". The handwritten option is the grammatically correct so has been chosen. However, "**are made**" may have been the underlying original. FIP has "are clear" while the *Notes* has it does the *Urtext* "made clear."

W 164 L 5. This is the day when vain imaginings part like a curtain, to reveal what lies beyond them. Here[510] is what is really there made visible, while all the shadows which appeared to hide it sink to obscurity.[511] Now is the balance righted, and the scales[512] of judgment left to Him Who judges true. And in His judgment will a world unfold in perfect innocence before your eyes. Now will you see it with the eyes of Christ. Now is its transformation clear to you.

W 164 L 6. Brothers, this day is sacred to the world. Your vision, given you from far beyond all things within the world looks back on them in a new light. And what you see becomes the healing and salvation of the world. The valuable and valueless are both perceived and recognized for what they are. And what is worthy of your love receives your love, while nothing to be feared remains.

W 164 L 7. We will not judge today. We will receive but what is given us from Judgment made beyond the world. Our practicing today becomes our gift of thankfulness for our release from blindness and from misery. All that we see will but increase our joy, because its holiness reflects our own. We stand forgiven in the sight of Christ, with all the world forgiven in our own. We bless the world as we behold it in the light in which our Savior looks on us, and offer it the freedom given us through His forgiving vision, now our own.

W 164 L 8. Open the curtain in your practicing by merely letting go all things you think you want. Your trifling treasures put away, and leave a clean and open space within your mind where Christ can come, and offer you the treasure of salvation. He has need of your most holy mind to save the world. Is not this purpose worthy to be yours? Is not Christ's vision worthy[513] to be sought above the world's unsatisfying goals?

W 164 L 9. Let not today slip by without the gifts it holds for you receiving your consent and your acceptance. We can change the world if you acknowledge them. You may not see the value your acceptance gives the world. But this you surely want; you can exchange all suffering for joy this very day. **W(361)** Practice in earnest and the gift is yours. Would God deceive you? Can His promise fail? Can you withhold so little when His Hand holds out complete salvation to His Son? **W(362)**

Lesson 165 "Let not my mind deny the Thought of God."

W 165 L 1. What makes this world seem real except your own denial of the truth which lies beyond? What but your thoughts of misery and death obscure the perfect happiness and the Eternal Life your Father wills for you? And what could hide what cannot be concealed except illusion? What could keep from you what you already have, except your choice to see it not, denying it is there?

W 165 L 2. The Thought of God created you. It left you not, nor have you ever been apart from It an instant. It belongs to you. By It you live. It is your Source of life, holding you one[514] with It, and everything is one with you because It left you not. The Thought of God protects you, cares for you, makes soft your resting place and smooth your way, lighting your mind with happiness and love. Eternity and Everlasting Life shine in your mind because the Thought of God has left you not, and still abides with you.

W 165 L 3. Who would deny his safety and his peace, his joy, his healing and his peace of mind, his quiet rest, his calm awakening, if he but recognized where they abide? Would he not instantly prepare

---

[510] Handwritten mark-up suggests (Now).
[511] Handwritten mark-up suggests (merely sink away).
[512] Handwritten mark-up suggests (scale).
[513] The *Urtext* manuscript has "worthy" handwritten in. It is present in the *Notes* so we include it.
[514] Originally in the *Urtext* manuscript typed (One), handwriting suggests lower case which we think is correct since "One" is not a reference to the deity.

to go where they are found, abandoning all else as worthless in comparison with them? And having found them, would he not make sure they stay with him and he remains with them?

W 165 L 4. Deny not Heaven. It is yours today but for the asking. Nor need you perceive how great the gift, how changed your mind will be, before it comes to you. Ask to receive and it is given you. Conviction lies within it. 'Til you welcome it as yours uncertainty remains. Yet God is fair. Sureness is not required to receive what only your acceptance can bestow. **W(363)**

W 165 L 5. Ask with desire. You need not be sure that you request the only thing you want. But when you have received, you will be sure you have the treasure you have always sought. What would you then exchange it for? What would induce you now to let it fade away from your ecstatic vision? For this sight proves that you have exchanged your blindness for the seeing eyes of Christ; your mind has come to lay aside denial and accept the Thought of God as its inheritance.

W 165 L 6. Now is all doubting past, the journey's end made certain and salvation given you. Now is Christ's power in your mind to heal as you were healed. For now you are among the Saviors of the world. Your destiny lies there and nowhere else. Would God consent to let His Son remain forever starved by his denial of the nourishment he needs to live? Abundance dwells in him, and deprivation cannot cut him off from God's sustaining[515] Love and from his home.

W 165 L 7. Practice today in hope. For hope indeed is justified. Your doubts are meaningless, for God is certain. And the Thought of Him is never absent. Sureness must abide within you who are host to Him. This course removes all doubts which you have interposed between Him and your certainty of Him. We count on Him and not upon ourselves to give us certainty. And in His Name we practice as His Word directs we do. His sureness lies beyond our every doubt. His Love remains beyond our every fear. The Thought of Him is still beyond all dreams, and in our minds according to His Will. **W(364)**

Lesson 166 "I am entrusted with the gifts of God."

W 166 L 1. All things are given you. God's trust in you is limitless. He knows His Son. He gives without exception, holding nothing back that can contribute to your happiness. And yet, unless your will is one with His, His gifts are not received. But what would make you think there is another will than His?

W 166 L 2. Here is the paradox that underlies the making of the world. This world is not the Will of God, and so it is not real. Yet those who think it real must still believe there is another will, and one which leads to opposite effects from those He wills. Impossible indeed; but every mind which looks upon the world and judges it as certain, solid, trustworthy and trued believes in two creators; or in one, himself alone. But never in One[516] God.

W 166 L 3. The gifts of God are not acceptable to anyone who holds such strange beliefs. He must believe that to accept God's gifts, however evident they may become, however urgently he may be called to claim them as his own, is being pressed to treachery against himself. He must deny their presence, contradict the truth, and suffer to preserve the world he made.

W 166 L 4. Here is the only home he thinks he knows. Here is the only safety he believes that he can find. Without the world he made is he an outcast, homeless and afraid. He does not realize that it is here he is afraid indeed, and homeless too; an outcast wandering so far from home, so long away, he does not realize he has forgotten where he came from, where he goes, and even who he really is.

W 166 L 5. Yet in his lonely, senseless wanderings God's gifts go with him, all unknown to him. He cannot lose them. But he will not look at what is given him. He wanders on, aware of the futility he sees about him everywhere, perceiving how his little lot but dwindles as he goes ahead to nowhere. Still he wanders on in misery and poverty, alone though God is with him, and a treasure his so great that everything the world contains is valueless before its magnitude. **W(365)**

W 166 L 6. He seems a sorry figure, weary, worn, in threadbare clothing, and with feet that bleed a little from the rocky road he walks. No-one but has identified with him, for everyone who comes here has pursued the path he follows, and has felt defeat and hopelessness as he is feeling them. Yet is he really tragic when you see that he is following the way he chose, and need but realize Who walks with him, and open up his treasures to be free?

W 166 L 7. This is your chosen self, the one you made as a replacement for reality. This is the self you savagely defend against all reason, every evidence, and all the witnesses with proof to show this is not you. You heed them not. You go on your appointed way, with eyes cast down lest you might catch a glimpse of truth, and be released from self deception and set free.

W 166 L 8. You cower fearfully lest you should feel Christ's touch upon your shoulder, and perceive His gentle hand directing you to look upon your gifts. How could you then proclaim your poverty in exile? He would make you laugh at this perception of yourself. Where is self-pity then? And what becomes of all the tragedy you sought to make for him whom God intended only joy?

W 166 L 9. Your ancient fear has come upon you now, and justice[517] has caught up with you at last. Christ's hand has touched your shoulder, and you feel that you are not alone. You even think the miserable self you thought was you may not be your identity. Perhaps God's Word is truer than your own. Perhaps His gifts to you are real. Perhaps He has not wholly been outwitted by your plan to keep His Son in deep oblivion, and go the way you chose without your Self. **W(366)**

W 166 L 10. God's Will does not oppose. It merely is. It is not God you have imprisoned in. your plan to lose your Self. He does not know about a plan so alien to His Will. There was a need He did not understand, to which He gave an Answer. That is all. And you who have this Answer given you have need no more of anything but this.

W 166 L 11. Now do we live, for now we cannot die. The wish for death is answered, and the sight that looked upon it now has been replaced by vision which perceives that you are not what you pretend to be. One walks with you Who gently answers all your fears with this one merciful reply, "It is not so." He points to all the gifts you have each time the thought of poverty oppresses you, and speaks of His Companionship when you perceive yourself as lonely and afraid.

W 166 L 12. Yet He reminds you still of one thing more you had forgotten. For His touch on you has made you like Himself. The gifts you have are not for you alone. What He has come to offer you, you now must learn to give. This is the lesson that His giving holds, for He has saved you from the solitude you sought to make, in which to hide from God. He has reminded you of all the gifts that God has given you. He speaks as well of what becomes your will when you accept these gifts, and recognize they are your own.

W 166 L 13. The gifts are yours, entrusted to your care, to give to all who chose the lonely road you have escaped. They do not understand they but pursue their wishes. It is you who teach them now. For you have learned of Christ there is another way for them to walk. Teach them by showing them the happiness that comes to

---

[515] The *Urtext* manuscript is typed "sustained" and changed by handwriting to "sustaining" which is what is in the *Notes*.
[516] Handwritten mark-up suggests (one).

[517] Handwritten mark-up suggests (Justice).

those who feel the touch of Christ and recognize God's gifts. Let sorrow not tempt you to be unfaithful to your trust. **W(367)**

W 166 L 14. Your sighs will now betray the hopes of those who look to you for their release. Your tears are theirs. If you are sick you but withhold their healing. What you fear but teaches them their fears are justified. Your hand becomes the giver of Christ's touch; your change of mind becomes the proof that who accepts God's gifts can never suffer anything. You are entrusted with the world's release from pain.

W 166 L 15. Betray it not. Become the living proof of what Christ's touch can offer everyone. God has entrusted all His gifts to you. Be witness in your happiness to how transformed the mind becomes which chooses to accept His gifts and feel the touch of Christ. Such is your mission now. For God entrusts the giving of His gifts to all who have received them. He has shared His joy with you. And now you go to share it with the world. **W(368)**

Lesson 167 "There is one life, and that I share with God."

W 167 L 1. There are not different kinds of life, for life is like the truth. It does not have degrees. It is the one condition in which all that God created share. Like all His Thoughts, it has no opposite. There is no death because what God created shares His Life. There is no death because an opposite to God does not exist. There is no death because the Father and the Son are One.[518]

W 167 L 2. In this world there appears to be a state that is life's opposite. You[519] call it death. Yet we have learned that the idea of death takes many forms. It is the one idea which underlies all feelings that are not supremely happy. It is the alarm to which you give response of any kind that is not perfect joy. All sorrow, loss, anxiety and suffering and pain, even a little sigh of weariness, a slight discomfort or the merest frown, acknowledge death. And thus deny you live.

W 167 L 3. You think that death is of the body. Yet it is but an idea, irrelevant to what is seen as physical. A thought is in the mind. It can be then applied as mind directs it. But its origin is where it must be changed, if change occurs. Ideas leave not their source. The emphasis this course has placed on that idea is due to its centrality in our attempts to change your mind about yourself. It is the reason you can heal. It is the cause of healing. It is why you cannot die. Its truth established you as one with God.

W 167 L 4. Death is the thought that you are separate from your Creator. It is the belief conditions change, emotions alternate because of causes you cannot control, you did not make, and you can never change. It is the fixed belief ideas can leave their source, and take on qualities the source does not contain, becoming different from their own origin, apart from it in kind as well as distance, time, and form. **W(369)**

W 167 L 5. Death cannot come from life. Ideas remain united to their source. They can extend all that their source contains. In that they can go far beyond themselves. But they can not give birth to what was never given them. As they are made, so will their making be. As they were born, so will they then give birth. And where they come from, there will they return.

W 167 L 6. The mind can think it sleeps, but that is all. It cannot change what is its waking state. It cannot make a body, nor abide within a body. What is alien to the mind does not exist, because it has no source. For mind creates all things that are, and cannot give them attributes it lacks, nor change its own eternal, mindful state. It cannot make the physical. What seems to die is but the sign of mind asleep.

W 167 L 7. The opposite of life can only be another form of life. As such, it can be reconciled with what created it, because it is not opposite in truth. Its form may change; it may appear to be what it is not. Yet mind is mind awake or sleeping. It is not its opposite in anything created, nor in what it seems to make when it believes it sleeps.

W 167 L 8. God creates only mind awake. He does not sleep, and His creations cannot share what He gives not, nor make conditions which He does not share with them. The thought of death is not the opposite to thoughts of life. Forever unopposed by opposites of any kind, the Thoughts of God remain forever changeless, with the power to extend forever changelessly but yet within Themselves, for They are everywhere.

W 167 L 9. What seems to be the opposite of life is merely sleeping. When the mind elects to be what it is not, and to assume an alien power which it does not have, a foreign state it cannot enter, or a false condition not within its Source, it merely seems to go to sleep a while. It dreams of time; an interval in which what seems to happen never has occurred, the changes wrought are substanceless, and all events are nowhere. When the mind awakes, it but continues as it always was. **W(370)**

W 167 L 10. Let us today be children of the truth, and not deny our holy heritage. Our life is not as we imagine it. Who changes life because he shuts his eyes, or makes himself what he is not because he sleeps and sees in dreams an opposite to what he is? We will not ask for death in any form today. Nor will we let imagined opposites to life abide even an instant where the Thought of Life Eternal has been set by God Himself.

W 167 L 11. His holy home we strive to keep today as He established it, and wills it be forever and forever. He is Lord of what we think today. And in His Thoughts, Which have no opposite, we understand there is one life, and that we share with Him; with all creation, with their thoughts as well, whom He created in a Unity of life which cannot separate in death and leave the Source of Life from where It came.

W 167 L 12. We share our life because we have one Source, a Source from Which perfection comes to us, remaining always in the holy minds which He created perfect. As we were, so are we now and will forever be.[520] A sleeping mind must waken as it sees its own perfection mirroring the Lord of Life so perfectly it fades into what is reflected there. And now it is no more a mere reflection. It becomes the thing reflected, and the light which makes reflection possible. No vision now is needed. For the wakened mind is one that knows its Source, its Self, its Holiness. **W(371)**

Lesson 168 "Your grace is given me. I claim it now."

W 168 L 1. God speaks to us. Shall we not speak to Him? He is not distant. He makes no attempt to hide from us. We try to hide from Him, and suffer from deception. He remains entirely accessible. He loves His Son. There is no certainty but this, yet this suffices. He will love His Son forever. When his mind remains asleep, He loves him still. And when his mind awakes, He loves him with a never-changing Love.[521]

---

[518] Handwritten mark-up suggests (one).
[519] Originally in the *Urtext* manuscript typed "**We**" it is overstruck and replaced with (You).

[520] **Hebrews 13:8** Jesus Christ is the same yesterday, today, and forever. The wording here is reminiscent of the *Gloria Patri* or *Minor Doxology* commonly used in Christian luturgy: "Glory be to the Father, and to the Son and to the Holy Ghost/Spirit. As it was in the beginning, is now, and ever shall be, world without end. Amen." The Greek original is of great aniquity, possibly the first century.
[521] **Jeremiah 31:3**
The LORD has appeared of old to me, saying:
"Yes, I have loved you with an everlasting love;
Therefore with lovingkindness I have drawn you."

W 168 L 2. If you but knew the meaning of His Love, hope and despair would be impossible, for hope would be forever satisfied; despair of any kind unthinkable. His grace His answer is to all despair, for in it lies remembrance of His Love. Would He not gladly give the means by which His Will is recognized? His grace is yours by your acknowledgment. And memory of Him awakens in the mind which asks the means of Him whereby its sleep is done.

W 168 L 3. Today we ask of God the gift He has most carefully preserved within our hearts, waiting to be acknowledged. This the gift by which God leans to us and lifts us up, taking salvation's final step Himself. All steps but this we learn, instructed by His Voice. But finally He comes Himself and takes us in His arms, and sweeps away the cobwebs of our sleep. His gift of grace is more than just an answer. It restores all memories the sleeping mind forgot; all certainty of what love's meaning is.

W 168 L 4. God loves His Son. Request Him now to give the means by which this world will disappear, and vision first will come, with knowledge but an instant later. For in grace you see a light that covers all the world in love, and watch fear disappear from every face as hearts rise up and claim the light as theirs. What now remains that Heaven be delayed an instant longer? What remains[522] undone when your forgiveness rests on everything? **W(372)**

W 168 L 5. It is a new and holy day today, for we receive what has been given us. Our faith lies in the Giver, not our own acceptance. We acknowledge our mistakes, but He to Whom all error is unknown is yet the One Who answers our mistakes by giving us the means to lay them down, and rise to Him in gratitude and love.

W 168 L 6. And He descends to meet us as we come to Him,[523] for what he has prepared for us He gives and we receive. Such is His Will because He loves His Son. To Him we pray today, returning but the words He gave to us through His Own Voice, His Word, His Love:

> *"Your grace is given me. I claim it now.*
> *Father, I come to You. And You will come*
> *To me who asks. I am the Son You love."* **W(373)**

Lesson 169 "By grace I live. By grace I am released."

W 169 L 1. Grace is an aspect of the Love of God which is most like the state prevailing in the Unity of truth. It is the world's most lofty aspiration, for it leads beyond the world entirely. It is past learning yet the goal of learning, for grace cannot come until the mind prepares itself for true acceptance. Grace becomes inevitable instantly in those who have prepared a table where it can be gently laid and willingly received; an altar clean and holy for the gift.

W 169 L 2. Grace is acceptance of the Love of God within a world of seeming hate and fear. By grace alone the hate and fear are gone, for grace presents a state so opposite to everything the world contains that those whose minds are lighted by the gift of grace can not believe the world of fear is real.

W 169 L 3. Grace is not learned. The final step must go beyond all learning. Grace is not the goal this course aspires to attain. Yet we prepare for grace in that an open mind can hear the Call to waken. It is not shut tight against God's Voice. It has become aware that there are things it does not know, and thus is ready to accept a state completely different from experience with which it is familiarly at home.

W 169 L 4. We have perhaps appeared to contradict our statement that the revelation of the Father and the Son as One[524] has been already set. But we have also said the mind determines when that time will be, and has determined it. And yet we urge you to bear witness to the Word of God to hasten the experience of truth, and speed its advent into every mind which recognizes its effects on you.[525] **W(374)**

W 169 L 5. Oneness is simply the idea God is. And in His Being He encompasses all things. No mind holds anything but Him. We say "God is," and then we cease to speak, for in that knowledge words are meaningless. There are no lips to speak them, and no part of mind sufficiently distinct to feel that it is now aware of something not itself. It has united with its Source, and like the Source Itself, it merely is.

W 169 L 6. We cannot speak nor write nor even think of this at all. It comes to every mind when total recognition that its will is God's has been completely given and received completely. It returns the mind into the endless present, where the past and future cannot be conceived. It lies beyond salvation; past all thought of time, forgiveness, and the holy Face of Christ. The Son of God has merely disappeared into His Father, as His Father has in Him. The world has never been at all. Eternity remains a constant state.

W 169 L 7. This is beyond the[526] experience we try to hasten. Yet forgiveness, taught and learned, brings with it the experiences which bear witness that the time the mind itself determined to abandon all but this is now at hand.[527] We do not hasten it, in that what you will offer was concealed from Him Who teaches what forgiveness means.

W 169 L 8. All learning was already in His Mind, accomplished and complete. He recognized all that time holds and gave it to all minds, that each one might determine, from a point where time has ended, when it is released to revelation and eternity. We have repeated several times before that you but make a journey that is done.

W 169 L 9. For Oneness must be here. Whatever time the mind has set for revelation is entirely irrelevant to what must be a constant state, forever as it always was; forever to remain as it is now. We merely take the part assigned long since, and fully recognized as perfectly fulfilled by Him Who wrote salvation's script in His Creator's Name, and in the Name of His Creator's Son. **W(375)**

W 169 L 10. There is no need to further clarify what no-one in the world can understand. When revelation of your Oneness comes, it will be known and fully understood. Now we have work to do, for those in time can speak of things beyond, and listen to words which explain what is to come is past already. Yet what meaning can the words convey to those who count the hours still, and rise and work and go to sleep by them?

W 169 L 11. Suffice it, then, that you have work to do to play your part. The ending must remain obscure to you until your part is done. It does not matter. For your part is still what all the rest depends on. As you take the role assigned to you, salvation comes a little nearer each uncertain heart that does not beat as yet in tune with God. Forgiveness is the central theme which runs throughout salvation, holding all its parts in meaningful relationships, the course it runs directed, and its outcome sure.

W 169 L 12. And now we ask for grace, the final gift salvation can bestow. Experience that grace provides will end in time, for grace foreshadows Heaven yet does not replace the thought of time but for a little while. The interval suffices. It is here that miracles are laid; to be returned by you from holy instants you receive, through grace, in your experience, to all who see the light that lingers on your face.

W 169 L 13. What is the Face of Christ but his who went a moment into timelessness, and brought a clear reflection of the Unity he felt

---

[522] Handwritten mark-up suggests (is still) in place of "**remains**".
[523] Handwritten mark-up suggests a sentence break at this point.
[524] Handwritten mark-up suggests (one).
[525] **John 1:7-8** This man came for a witness, to bear witness of the Light, that all through him might believe. He was not that Light, but was sent to bear witness of that Light.
[526] We have added the word "**the**" in order to make the sentence make sense. It is not present in any other version we consulted.
[527] **Matthew 4:17** From that time Jesus began to preach and to say, "Repent, for the kingdom of heaven is at hand."

an instant back to bless the world? How could you finally attain to it forever, while a part of you remains outside, unknowing, unawakened and in need of you as witness to the truth? **W(376)**

W 169 L 14. Be grateful to return, as you were glad to go an instant and accept the gifts which grace provided you. You carry them back to yourself. And revelation stands not far behind. Its coming is ensured. We ask for grace and for experience that comes from grace. We welcome the release it offers everyone. We do not ask for the unaskable. We do not look beyond what grace can give. For this we can give in the grace that has been given us.

W 169 L 15. Our learning goal today does not exceed this prayer, yet in the world what could be more than what we ask this day of Him Who gives the grace we ask, as it was given Him?

> *"By grace I live. By grace I am released.*
> *By grace I give. By grace I will release."* **W(377)**

Lesson 170 "There is no cruelty in God and none in me."

W 170 L 1. No-one attacks without intent to hurt. This can have no exception. When you think that you attack in self-defense, you mean that to be cruel is protection; you are safe because of cruelty. You mean that you believe to hurt another brings you freedom. And you mean that to attack is to exchange the state in which you are for something better, safer, more secure from dangerous invasion and from fear.

W 170 L 2. How thoroughly insane is the idea that to defend from fear is to attack! For here is fear begot and fed with blood, to make it grow and swell and rage. And thus is fear protected, not escaped. Today we learn a lesson which can save you more delay and needless misery than you can possibly imagine. It is this:

> *You make what you defend against, and by*
> *your own defense against it is it real*
> *and inescapable. Lay down your arms,*
> *and only then do you perceive it false.*

W 170 L 3. It seems to be the enemy without that you attack. Yet your defense sets up an enemy within; an alien thought at war with you, depriving you of peace, splitting your mind into two camps which seem wholly irreconcilable. For love now has an "enemy," an opposite; and fear, the alien, now needs your defense against the threat of what you really are.

W 170 L 4. If you consider carefully the means by which your fancied self-defense proceeds on its imagined way, you will perceive the premises on which the idea stands. First, it is obvious ideas must leave their source. For it is you who make attack, and must have first conceived of it. Yet you attack outside yourself, and separate your mind from him who is to be attacked, with perfect faith the split you made is real. **W(378)**

W 170 L 5. Next are the attributes of love bestowed upon its "enemy." For fear becomes your safety and protector of your peace, to which you turn for solace and escape from doubts about your strength and hope of rest in dreamless quiet. And as love is shorn of what belongs to it and it alone, love is endowed with attributes of fear. For love would ask you lay down all defense as merely foolish. And your arms indeed would crumble into dust. For such they are.

W 170 L 6. With love as enemy must cruelty become a god, and gods demand that those who worship them obey their dictates, and refuse to question them. Harsh punishment is meted out relentlessly to those who ask if the demands are sensible or even sane. It is their enemies who are unreasonable and insane, while they are always merciful and just.

W 170 L 7. Today we look upon this cruel god dispassionately. And we note that though his lips are smeared with blood and fire seems to flame from him, he is but made of stone. He can do nothing. We need not defy his power. He has none. And those who see in him their safety have no guardian, no strength to call upon in danger, and no mighty warrior to fight for them.

W 170 L 8. This moment can be terrible. But it can also be the time of your release from abject slavery. You make a choice, standing before this idol, seeing him exactly as he is. Will you restore to love what you have sought to wrest from it, and lay before this mindless piece of stone? Or will you make another idol to replace it? For the god of cruelty takes many forms. Another can be found.

W 170 L 9. Yet do not think that fear is the escape from fear. Let us remember what the course has stressed about the obstacles to peace. The final one, the hardest to believe is nothing, and a seeming obstacle with the appearance of a solid block, impenetrable, fearful and beyond surmounting, is the fear **W(379)** of God himself. Here is the basic premise which enthrones the thought of fear as god. For fear is loved by those who worship it, and love appears to be invested now with cruelty.

W 170 L 10. Where does the totally insane belief in gods of vengeance come from?[528] Love has not confused its attributes with those of fear. Yet must the worshippers of fear perceive their own confusion in fear's "enemy"; its cruelty as now a part of love. And what becomes more fearful than the Heart of Love Itself? The blood appears to be upon His lips; the fire comes from Him. And He is terrible above all else, cruel beyond conception, striking down all who acknowledge Him to be their God.

W 170 L 11. The choice you make today is certain. For you look for the last time upon this bit of carven stone you made, and call it god no longer. You have reached this place before, but you have chosen that this cruel god remain with you in still another form, and so the fear of God returned with you. This time you leave it here. And you return to a new world unburdened by its weight; beheld not in its sightless eyes, but in the vision that your choice restored to you.

W 170 L 12. Now do your eyes belong to Christ, and He looks through them. Now your voice belongs to God, and echoes His. And now your heart remains at peace forever. You have chosen Him in place of idols, and your attributes, given by your Creator, are restored to you at last. The Call of God is heard and answered. Now has fear made way for love, as God Himself replaces cruelty. **W(380)**

W 170 L 13. *"Father, we are like You. No cruelty abides in us for there is none in You. Your peace is ours. And we bless the world with what we have received from You alone. We choose again and make our choice for all our brothers, knowing they are one with us. We bring them Your salvation as we have received it now. And we give thanks for them who render us complete. In them we see Your glory, and in them we find our peace. Holy are we because Your holiness has set us free. And we give thanks. Amen."*[529] **W(381)**

Review 5 (W 170 R5)
Introduction
May 11, 1970

W 170 R5 1. We now review again. This time we are ready to give more effort and more time to what we undertake. We recognize we are preparing for another phase of understanding. We would take this step completely, that we may go on again more certain, more sincere, with faith upheld more surely. Our footsteps have not been

---

[528] **Deuteronomy 32:35** Vengeance is Mine, and recompense; Their foot shall slip in due time; For the day of their calamity is at hand, And the things to come hasten upon them.

[529] The quotation marks are not in the *Urtext* manuscript, but are in all subsequent versions.

unwavering, and doubts have made us walk uncertainly and slowly on the road this course sets forth. But now we hasten on, for we approach a greater certainty, a firmer purpose and a surer goal.

W 170 R5 2. Steady our feet, our Father; let our doubts be quiet and our holy minds be still, and speak to us. We have no words to give to You. We would but listen to Your Word and make it ours. Lead our practicing as does a father lead a little child along a way he does not understand. Yet does he follow, sure that he is safe because his father leads the way for him.

W 170 R5 3. So do we bring our practicing to You. And if we stumble, You will raise us up. If we forget the way, we count upon Your sure remembering. We wander off, but You will not forget to call us back. Quicken our footsteps now, that we may walk more certainly and quickly unto You. And we accept the Word You offer us to unify our practicing, as we review the thoughts that You have given us.

W 170 R5 4. This is the thought which should precede the thoughts that we review. Each one but clarifies some aspect of this thought, or helps it be more meaningful, more personal and true, and more descriptive of the holy Self we share and now prepare to know again:

"God is but Love, and therefore so am I."[530]

This Self alone knows love. This Self alone is perfectly consistent in Its thoughts; knows Its Creator, understands Itself, is perfect in Its knowledge and Its love, and never changes from Its constant state of union with Its Father and Itself. **W(382)**

W 170 R5 5. And it is This that waits to meet us at the journey's ending. Every step we take brings us a little nearer. This review will shorten time immeasurably if we keep in mind that This remains our goal, and as we practice it is This to which we are approaching. Let us raise our hearts from dust to life as we remember This is promised us, and that this course was sent to open up the path of light to us, and teach us, step by step, how to return to the Eternal Self we thought we lost.

W 170 R5 6. I take the journey with you. For I share your doubts and fears a little while, that you may come to me who recognize the road by which all fears and doubts are overcome. We walk together. I must understand uncertainty and pain, although I know they have no meaning. Yet a Savior must remain with those he teaches, seeing what they see, but still retaining in his mind the way which led him out, and now will lead you out with him. God's Son is crucified until you walk along the road with me.

W 170 R5 7. My resurrection comes again each time I lead a brother safely to the place at which the journey ends and is forgot. I am renewed each time a brother learns there is a way from misery and pain. I am reborn each time a brother's mind turns to the light in him and looks for me. I have forgotten no-one. Help me now to lead you back to where the journey was begun, to make another choice with me.

W 170 R5 8. Release me as you practice once again the thoughts I brought to you from Him Who sees your bitter need, and knows the answer God has given Him. Together we review these thoughts. Together we devote our time and effort to them. And together we will, teach them to our brothers. God would not have Heaven incomplete. It waits for you as I do. I am incomplete without your part in me. And as I am made whole, we go together to our ancient home, prepared for us before time was, and kept unchanged by time, immaculate and safe, as it will be at last, when time is done. **W(383)**

W 170 R5 9. Let this review be then your gift to me. For this alone I need; that you will hear the words I speak and give them to the world. You are my voice, my eyes, my feet, my hands, through which I save the world. The Self from Which I call to you is but your Own.[531] To Him we go together. Take your brother's hand, for this is not a way we walk alone. In him I walk with you and you with me. Our Father wills His Son be One[532] with Him. What lives but must not then be one with you?

W 170 R5 10. Let this review become a time in which we share a new experience for you, yet one as old as time, and older still. Hallowed your name.[533] Your glory undefiled forever. And your wholeness now complete, as God established it. You are His Son, completing His extension in your own. We practice but an ancient truth we knew before illusion seemed to claim the world. And we remind the world that it is free of all illusion every time we say,

"God is but Love, and therefore so am I."

W 170 R5 11. With this we start each day of our review. With this we start and end each period of practice time. And with this thought we sleep, to waken once again with these same words upon our lips to greet another day. No thought that we review but we surround with it, and use the thoughts to hold it up before our minds, and keep it clear in our remembrance throughout the day. And thus when we have finished this review, we will have recognized the words we speak are true. **W(384)**

W 170 R5 12. Yet are the words but aids and to be used, except at the beginning and the end of practice periods, but to recall the mind, as needed, to its purpose. We place faith in the experience that comes from practice, not the means we use. We wait for the experience, and recognize that it is only here conviction lies. We use the words, and try and try again to go beyond them to their meaning, which is far beyond their sound. The sound grows dim and disappears as we approach the Source of meaning. It is here that we find rest. **W(385)**

Lesson 171 "God is but Love, and therefore so am I."

W 171 L 1. 151) "All things are echoes of the Voice of God."
  "God is but Love, and therefore so am I."

W 171 L 2. 152) "The power of decision is my own."
  "God is but Love, and therefore so am I."

Lesson 172 "God is but Love, and therefore so am I."

W 172 L 1. 153) "In my defenselessness my safety lies."
  "God is but Love, and therefore so am I."

W 172 L 2. 154) "I am among the ministers of God."
  "God is but Love, and therefore so am I."

Lesson 173 "God is but Love, and therefore so am I."

W 173 L 1. 155) "I will step back and let Him lead the way."
  "God is but Love, and therefore so am I."

W 173 L 2. 156) "I walk with God in perfect holiness."
  "God is but Love, and therefore so am I."

Lesson 174 "God is but Love, and therefore so am I."

W 174 L 1. 157) "Into His Presence would I enter now."
  "God is but Love, and therefore so am I."

W 174 L 2. 158) "Today I learn to give as I receive."

---

[530] **1 John 4:16** And we have known and believed the love that God has for us. God is love, and he who abides in love abides in God, and God in him.

[531] Handwritten mark-up suggests (own).
[532] Handwritten mark-up suggests (one).
[533] **Matthew 6:9** "In this manner, therefore, pray: Our Father in heaven, Hallowed be Your name."

"God is but Love, and therefore so am I."

Lesson 175 "God is but Love, and therefore so am I."

W 175 L 1. 159) "I give the miracles I have received."
"God is but Love, and therefore so am I."

W 175 L 2. 160) "I am at home. Fear is the stranger here."
"God is but Love, and therefore so am I." **W(386)**

Lesson 176 "God is but Love, and therefore so am I."

W 176 L 1. 161) "Give me your blessing, holy Son of God."
"God is but Love, and therefore so am I."

W 176 L 2. 162) "I am as God created me."
"God is but Love, and therefore so am I."

Lesson 177 "God is but Love, and therefore so am I."

W 177 L 1. 163) "There is no death. The Son of God is free."
"God is but Love, and therefore so am I."

W 177 L 2. 164) "Now are we One with Him Who is our Source."
"God is but Love, and therefore so am I."

Lesson 178 "God is but Love, and therefore so am I."

W 178 L 1. 165) "Let not my mind deny the Thought of God."
"God is but Love, and therefore so am I."

W 178 L 2. 166) "I am entrusted with the gifts of God."
"God is but Love, and therefore so am I."

Lesson 179. "God is but Love, and therefore so am I."

W 179 L 1. 167) "There is one life, and that I share with God."
"God is but Love, and therefore so am I."

W 179 L 2. 168) "Your grace is given me. I claim it now."
"God is but Love, and therefore so am I."

Lesson 180 "God is but Love, and therefore so am I."

W 180 L 1. 169) "By grace I live. By grace I am released."
"God is but Love, and therefore so am I."

W 180 L 2. 170) "There is no cruelty in God and none in me."
"God is but Love, and therefore so am I." **W(387)**

W 180 L 3. Our next few lessons make a special point of firming up your willingness to make your weak commitment strong; your scattered goals blend into one intent. You are not asked for total dedication all the time, as yet. But you are asked to practice now in order to attain the sense of peace such unified commitment will bestow, if only intermittently. It is experiencing this which makes it sure that you will give your total willingness to following the way the course sets forth.

W 180 L 4. Our lessons now are geared specifically to widening horizons, and direct approaches to the special blocks which keep your vision narrow, and too limited to let you see the value of our goal. We are attempting now to lift these blocks, however briefly. Words alone can not convey the sense of liberation which their lifting brings. But the experience of freedom and of peace that comes as you give up your tight control of what you see speaks for itself. Your motivation will be so intensified that words become of little consequence. You will be sure of what you want, and what is valueless.

W 180 L 5. And so we start our journey beyond words by concentrating first on what impedes our progress still. Experience of what exists beyond defensiveness remains beyond achievement while it is denied. It may be there, but you cannot accept its presence. So we now attempt to go past all defenses for a little while each day. No more than this is asked because no more than this is needed. It will be enough to guarantee the rest will come. **W(388)**

Lesson 181 "I trust my brothers, who are one with me."

W 181 L 1. Trusting your brothers is essential to establishing and holding up your faith in your ability to transcend doubt and lack of sure conviction in yourself. When you attack a brother, you proclaim that he is limited by what you have perceived in him. You do not look beyond his errors. Rather, they are magnified, becoming blocks to your awareness of the Self that lies beyond your own mistakes, and past his seeming sins as well as yours.

W 181 L 2. Perception has a focus. It is this which gives consistency to what you see. Change but this focus, and what you behold will change accordingly. Your vision now will shift to give support to the intent which has replaced the one you held before. Remove your focus on your brother's sins, and you experience the peace that comes from faith in sinlessness. This faith receives its only sure support from what you see in others past their sins. For their mistakes, if focused on, are witnesses to sins in you. And you will not transcend their sight and see the sinlessness that lies beyond.

W 181 L 3. Therefore, in practicing today, we first let all such little focuses give way to our great need to let our sinlessness become apparent. We instruct our minds that it is this we seek and only this, for just a little while. We do not care about our future goals, and what we saw an instant previous has no concern for us within this interval of time wherein we practice changing our intent. We seek for innocence and nothing else. We seek for it with no concern but now. **W(389)**

W 181 L 4. A major hazard to success has been involvement with your past and future goals. You have been quite preoccupied with how extremely different the goals this course is advocating are from those you held before. And you have also been dismayed by the depressing and restricting thought that, even if you should succeed, you will inevitably lose your way again.

W 181 L 5. How could this matter? For the past is gone; the future but imagined. These concerns are but defenses against present change of focus in perception. Nothing more. We lay these pointless limitations by a little while. We do not look to past beliefs, and what we will believe will not intrude upon us now. We enter in the time of practicing with one intent; to look upon the sinlessness within.

W 181 L 6. We recognize that we have lost this goal if anger blocks our way in any form. And if a brother's sins occur to us, our narrowed focus will restrict our sight and turn our eyes upon our own mistakes, which we will magnify and call our "sins". So, for a little while, without regard to past or future, should such blocks arise, we will transcend them with instructions to our minds to change their focus, as we say:

"It is not this that I would look upon.

I trust my brothers, who are one with me."

W 181 L 7. And we will also use these thoughts to keep us safe throughout the day. We do not seek for long-range goals. As each obstruction seems to block the vision of our sinlessness, we seek but for surcease an instant from the misery the focus upon sin will bring, and uncorrected will remain. **W(390)**

W 181 L 8. Nor do we ask for fantasies. For what we seek to look upon is really there. And as our focus goes beyond mistakes, we will behold a wholly sinless world. When seeing this is all we want to see, when this is all we seek for in the name of true perception, are the eyes of Christ inevitably ours. And the love He feels for us becomes our own as well. This will become the only thing we see reflected in the world and in ourselves.

W 181 L 9. The world which once proclaimed our sins becomes the proof that we are sinless. And our love for everyone we look upon attests to our remembrance of the holy Self Which knows no sin, and never could conceive of anything without Its sinlessness.

W 181 L 10. We seek for this remembrance as we turn our minds to practicing today. We look neither ahead nor backwards. We look straight into the present. And we give our trust to the experience we ask for now. Our sinlessness is but the Will of God. This instant is our willing one with His. **W(391)**

Lesson 182 "I call upon God's Name and on my own."[534]

W 182 L 1. God's Name is holy, but no holier than yours. To call upon His Name is but to call upon your own. A father gives his son his name, and thus identifies the son with him. His brothers share his name, and thus are they united in a bond to which they turn for their identity. Your Father's Name reminds you who you are, even within a world which does not know; even though you have not remembered it.

W 182 L 2. God's Name can not be heard without response, nor said without an echo in the mind which calls you to remember. Say His Name, and you invite the angels to surround the ground on which you stand, and sing to you as they spread out their wings to keep you safe, and shelter you from every worldly thought that would intrude upon your holiness.

W 182 L 3. Repeat God's Name and all the world responds by laying down illusions. Every dream the world holds dear has suddenly gone by, and where it seemed to stand you find a star; a miracle of grace. The sick arise, healed of their sickly thoughts. The blind can see; the deaf can hear.[535] The sorrowful cast off their mourning, and the tears of pain are dried as happy laughter comes to bless the world.[536]

W 182 L 4. Repeat the Name of God and little names have lost their meaning. No temptation but becomes a nameless and unwanted thing before God's Name. Repeat His Name and see how easily you will forget the names of all the gods you valued. They have lost the name of god you gave them. They become anonymous and valueless to you, although before you let the Name of God replace their little names, you stood before them worshipfully, naming them as gods. **W(392)**

W 182 L 5. Repeat the Name of God and call upon your Self, Whose Name is His. Repeat His Name and all the tiny, nameless things on earth slip into right perspective. Those who call upon the Name of God can not mistake the nameless for the Name, nor sin for grace nor bodies for the holy Son of God. And should you join a brother as you sit with him in silence, and repeat God's Name along with him within your quiet minds, you have established there an altar which reaches to God Himself and to His Son.

W 182 L 6. Practice but this today; repeat God's Name slowly again and still again. Become oblivious to every name but His. Hear nothing else. Let all your thoughts become anchored on This. No other words we use except at the beginning, when we say today's idea but once. And then God's Name becomes our only thought, our only word, the only thing that occupies our minds, the only wish we have, the only sound with any meaning, and the only Name of everything that we desire to see; of everything that we would call our own.

W 182 L 7. Thus do we give an invitation which can never be refused. And God will come and answer it Himself. Think not He hears the little prayers of those who call on Him with names of idols cherished by the world. They cannot reach Him thus. He cannot hear requests that He be not Himself, or that His Son receive another name than His. Repeat His Name and you acknowledge Him as sole Creator of Reality. And you acknowledge also that His Son is part of Him, creating in His Name.

W 182 L 8. Sit silently and let His Name become the all-encompassing idea which holds your mind completely. Let all thoughts be still except this one.[537] And to all other thoughts respond with This, and see God's Name replace the thousand little names you gave your thoughts, not realizing that there is One[538] Name for all there is, and all that there will be. **W(393)**

W 182 L 9. Today you can achieve a state in which you will experience the gifts of grace. You can escape all bondage of the world, and give the world the same release you found. You can remember what the world forgot, and offer it your own remembering. You can accept today the part you play in its salvation and your own as well, and both can be accomplished perfectly.

W 182 L 10. Turn to the Name of God for your release, and it is given you. No prayer but this is necessary, for it holds them all within it. Words are insignificant and all requests unneeded when God's Son calls on His Father's Name. His Father's Thoughts become his own. He makes his claim to all his Father gave, is giving still, and will forever give. He calls on Him to let all things he thought he made be nameless now, and in their place the holy Name of God becomes his judgment of their worthlessness.

W 182 L 11. All little things are silent. Little sounds are soundless now. The little things of earth have disappeared. The universe consists of nothing but the Son of God who calls upon his Father. And his Father's Voice gives answer in his Father's holy Name. In this eternal, still relationship, in which communication far transcends all words and yet exceeds in depth and height whatever words could possibly convey, is peace eternal. In our Father's Name, we would experience this peace today. And in His Name it shall be given us. **W(394)**

Lesson 183 "I will be still a moment and go home."

W 183 L 1. This world you seem to live in is not home to you. And somewhere in your mind you know that this is true. A memory of home keeps haunting you, as if there were a place which called you to return although you do not recognize the Voice, nor what it is the Voice reminds you of. Yet still you feel an alien here, from somewhere all unknown. Nothing so definite that you could say with certainty you are an exile here. Just a persistent feeling, sometimes not more than a tiny throb, at other times hardly remembered, actively dismissed, but surely to return to mind again.

---

[534] Lessons 182 and 183 are reversed in the *Notes* and in *FIP* as compared to this order in the *Urtext* manuscript.

[535] Originally in the *Urtext* manuscript there is just a comma here, no sentence break. Handwritten mark-up suggests the break and we agree it is better. The *Notes* has a full stop also.

[536] **Isaiah 25:8** He will swallow up death forever, And the Lord GOD will wipe away tears from all faces; The rebuke of His people He will take away from all the earth; For the LORD has spoken.
Revelation 7:17 For the Lamb who is in the midst of the throne will shepherd them and lead them to living fountains of waters. And God will wipe away every tear from their eyes."
Revelation 21:4 And God will wipe away every tear from their eyes; there shall be no more death, nor sorrow, nor crying. There shall be no more pain, for the former things have passed away."

[537] Originally in the *Urtext* manuscript capitalized as "One", handwriting suggests (one). We agree it should not be capitalized.

[538] Handwritten mark-up suggests (one).

W 183 L 2. No-one but knows whereof we speak. Yet some try to put by their suffering in games they play to occupy their time, and keep their sadness from them. Others will deny that they are sad, and do not recognize their tears at all. Still others will maintain that what we speak of is illusion, not to be considered more than but a dream. Yet who in simple honesty, without defensiveness and self deception, would deny he understands the words we speak?

W 183 L 3. We speak today for everyone who walks this world, for he is not at home. He goes uncertainly about in endless search, seeking in darkness what he cannot find; not recognizing what it is he seeks. A thousand homes he makes, yet none contents his restless mind. He does not understand he builds in vain. The home he seeks can not be made by him. There is no substitute for Heaven. All he ever made was hell.

W 183 L 4. Perhaps you think it is your childhood home that you would find again. The childhood of your body and its place of shelter are a memory now so distorted that you merely hold a picture of a past that never happened. Yet there is a Child in you Who seeks His Father's house,[539] and knows that He is alien here. This Childhood is eternal, with an innocence that will endure forever. Where this Child shall go is holy ground.[540] It is His holiness that lights up Heaven, and that brings to earth the pure reflection of the light above, wherein are earth and Heaven joined as one. **W(395)**

W 183 L 5. It is this Child in you your Father knows as His Own Son. It is this Child Who knows His Father. He desires to go home so deeply, so unceasingly, His Voice cries unto you to let Him rest a while. He does not ask for more than just a few instants of respite; just an interval in which He can return to breathe again the holy air that fills His Father's house. You are His home as well. He will return. But give Him just a little time to be Himself, within the peace that is His home, resting in silence and in peace and in love.

W 183 L 6. This Child needs your protection. He is far from home. He is so little that He seems so easily shut out, His tiny Voice so readily obscured, His calls for help almost unheard amid the grating sounds and harsh and rasping noises of the world. Yet does He know that in you still abides His sure protection. You Will fail Him not. He will go home, and you along with Him.

W 183 L 7. This Child is your defenselessness, your strength. He trusts in you. He came because He knew you would not fail. He whispers of His home unceasingly to you. For He would bring you back with Him, that He Himself might stay, and not return again where He does not belong and where He lives an outcast in a world of alien thoughts. His patience has no limits. He will wait until you hear His gentle Voice within you, calling you to let Him go in peace, along with you, to where He is at home, and you with Him.

W 183 L 8. When you are still an instant, when the world recedes from you, when valueless ideas cease to have value in your restless mind, then will you hear His Voice. So poignantly He calls to you that you will not resist Him longer. In that instant, He will take you to His home, and you will stay with Him in perfect stillness, silent and at peace, beyond all words, untouched by fear and doubt, sublimely certain that you are at home. **W(396)**

W 183 L 9. Rest with Him frequently today. For He was willing to become a little Child that you might learn of Him how strong is he who comes without defenses, offering only love's messages to those who think He is their enemy. He holds the might of Heaven in His hand and calls them friend, and gives His strength to them that they may see He would be Friend to them. He asks but[541] they protect Him, for His home is far away, and He will not return to it alone.

W 183 L 10. Christ is reborn as but a little Child each time a wanderer would leave his home. For he must learn that what he would protect is but this Child, Who comes defenseless and Who is protected by defenselessness. Go home with Him from time to time today. You are as much an alien here as He.

W 183 L 11. Take time today to lay aside your shield which profits nothing,[542] and lay down the spear and sword you raised against an enemy without existence. Christ has called you friend and brother. He has even come to you to ask your help in letting Him go home completed and completely. He has come as does a little child who must beseech his father for protection and for love. He rules the universe, and yet He asks unceasingly that you return with Him, and take illusions as your gods no more.

W 183 L 12. You have not lost your innocence. It is for this you yearn. This is your heart's desire. This is the Voice you hear, and this the Call which cannot be denied. The holy Child remains with you. His home is yours. Today He gives you His defenselessness, and you accept it in exchange for all the toys of battle you have made. And now the way is open, and the journey has an end in sight at last. Be still a moment and go home with Him and be at peace awhile. **W(397) W(398)**

Lesson 184 "The Name of God is my inheritance."

W 184 L 1. You live by symbols. You have made up names for everything you see. Each one becomes a separate entity, identified by its own name. By this you carve it out of unity. By this you designate its special attributes, and set it off from other things by emphasizing space surrounding it. This space you lay between all things to which you give a different name; all happenings in terms of place and time; all bodies which are greeted with a name.

W 184 L 2. This space you see as setting off all things from one another is the means by which the world's perception is achieved. You see something where nothing is, and see as well nothing where there is unity; a space between all things, between all things and you. Thus do you think that you have given life in separation. By this split you think you are established as a unity which functions with an independent will.

W 184 L 3. What are these names by which the world becomes a series of discrete events, of things ununified, of bodies kept apart and holding bits of mind as separate awarenesses? You gave these names to them, establishing perception as you wished to have perception be. The nameless things were given names, and thus reality was given them as well. For what is named is given meaning, and will then be seen as meaningful, a cause of true effects, with consequence inherent in itself.

W 184 L 4. This is the way reality is made by partial vision, purposefully set against the given truth. Its enemy is wholeness. It conceives of little things, and looks upon them. And a lack of space, a sense of unity or vision which sees differently become the threats which it must overcome, conflict with and deny. **W(399)**

W 184 L 5. Yet does this other vision still remain a natural direction for the mind to channel its perception. It is hard to teach the mind a thousand alien names and thousands more. Yet you believe this is what learning means; its one essential goal by which communication is achieved and concepts can be meaningfully shared.

W 184 L 6. This is the sum of the inheritance the world bestows. And everyone who learns to think that it is so accepts the signs and symbols which assert the world is real. It is for this they stand. They leave no doubt that what is named is there. It can be seen, as is anticipated. What denies that it is true[543] is but illusion, for it is

---

[539] **John 14:2** "In My Father's house are many mansions; if it were not so, I would have told you. I go to prepare a place for you."
[540] **Exodus 3:5** Then He said, "Do not draw near this place. Take your sandals off your feet, for the place where you stand is holy ground."
[541] Handwritten mark-up suggests (that) in place of "**but**".

[542] **John 6:63** "It is the Spirit who gives life; the flesh profits nothing. The words that I speak to you are spirit, and they are life."
[543] Original typing shows "**false**" but handwritten in is (true). The handwritten correction appears to work better here, so has been adopted.

the ultimate reality. To question it is madness; to accept its presence is the proof of sanity.

W 184 L 7. Such is the teaching of the world. It is a phase of learning everyone who comes must go through. But the sooner he perceives on what it rests, how questionable are its premises, how doubtful its results, the sooner does he question its effects. Learning which stops with what the world would teach stops short of meaning. In its proper place, it serves but as a starting point from which another kind of learning can begin, a new perception can be gained, and all the arbitrary names the world bestows can be withdrawn as they are raised to doubt.

W 184 L 8. Think not you made the world. Illusions, yes! But what is true in earth and Heaven is beyond your naming. When you call upon a brother, it is to his body that you make appeal. His true identity is hidden from you by what you believe he really is. His body makes response to what you call him, for his mind consents to take the name you give him as his own. And thus his unity is twice denied, for you perceive him separate from you, and he accepts this separate name as his. **W(400)**

W 184 L 9. It would indeed be strange if you were asked to go beyond all symbols of the world, forgetting them forever; yet were asked to take a teaching function. You have need to use the symbols of the world a while. But be you not deceived by them as well. They do not stand for anything at all, and in your practicing it is this thought which will release you from them. They become but means by which you can communicate in ways the world can understand, but which you recognize is not the unity where true communication can be found.

W 184 L 10. Thus what you need are intervals each day in which the learning of the world becomes a transitory phase; a prison house from which you go into the sunlight and forget the darkness. Here you understand the Word, the Name Which God has given you; the One[544] Identity Which all things share; the one acknowledgment of what is true. And then step back to darkness, not because you think it real, but only to proclaim its unreality in terms which still have meaning in the world which darkness rules.

W 184 L 11. Use all the little names and symbols which delineate the world of darkness. Yet accept them not as your reality. The Holy Spirit uses all of them, but He does not forget creation has One[545] Name, One[546] Meaning and a single Source Which unifies all things within Itself. Use all the names the world bestows on them but for convenience, yet do not forget they share the Name of God along with you.

W 184 L 12. God has no name. And yet His Name becomes the final lesson that all things are one, and at this lesson does all learning end. All names are unified; all space is filled with truth's reflection. Every gap is closed, and separation healed. The Name of God is the inheritance He gave to those who chose the teaching of the world to take the place of Heaven. In our practicing, our purpose is to let our minds accept what He has given as the answer to the pitiful inheritance you made as fitting tribute to the Son He loves. **W(401)**

W 184 L 13. No-one can fail who seeks the meaning of the Name of God. Experience must come to supplement the Word. But first you must accept One[547] Name for all reality, and realize the many names you gave its aspects have distorted what you see but have not interfered with truth at all. One Name we bring into our practicing. One Name we use to unify our sight.

W 184 L 14. And though we use a different name for each awareness of an aspect of God's Son, we understand that they have but One[548] Name Which He has given them. It is this Name we use in practicing. And through Its use, all foolish separations disappear which kept us blind. And we are given strength to see beyond them. Now our sight is blessed with blessings we can give as we receive.

W 184 L 15. "Father, our Name is Yours. In It we are united with all living things, and You Who are their One Creator. What we made and call by many different names is but a shadow we have tried to cast across Your Own Reality. And we are glad and thankful we were wrong. All our mistakes we give to you, that we may be absolved of all effects our errors seemed to have. And we accept the truth You give in place of every one of them. Your Name is our salvation and escape from what we made. Your Name unites us in the Oneness which is our inheritance and peace. Amen.[549]" **W(402)**

Lesson 185 "I want the peace of God."

W 185 L 1. To say these words is nothing. But to mean these words is everything. If you could but mean them for just an instant, there would be no further sorrow possible for you in any form; in any place or time. Heaven would be completely given back to full awareness, memory of God entirely restored, the resurrection of all creation fully recognized.

W 185 L 2. No-one can mean these words and not be healed. He cannot play with dreams, nor think he is himself a dream. He cannot make a hell and think it real. He wants the peace of God and it is given him. For that is all he wants, and that is all he will receive. Many have said these words. But few indeed have meant them. You have but to look upon the world you see around you to be sure how very few they are. The world would be completely changed should any two agree these words express the only thing they want.[550]

W 185 L 3. Two minds with one intent become so strong that what they will becomes the Will of God. For minds can only join in truth. In dreams, no two can share the same intent. To each, the hero of the dream is different; the outcome wanted not the same for both. Loser and gainer merely shift about in changing patterns, as the ratio of gain to loss and loss to gain takes on a different aspect or another form.

W 185 L 4. Yet compromise alone a dream can bring. Sometimes it takes the form of union, but only the form. The meaning must escape the dream, for compromising is the goal of dreaming. Minds cannot unite in dreams. They merely bargain. And what bargain can give them the peace of God? Illusions come to take His place. And what He means is lost to sleeping minds intent on compromise, each to his gain and to another's loss. **W(403)**

W 185 L 5. To mean you want the peace of God is to renounce all dreams. For no-one means these words who wants illusions, and who therefore seeks the means which bring illusions. He has looked on them and found them wanting. Now he seeks to go beyond them, recognizing that another dream would offer nothing more than all the others. Dreams are one to him. And he has learned their only difference is one of form, for one will bring the same despair and misery as do the rest.

W 185 L 6. The mind which means that all it wants is peace must join with other minds, for that is how peace is obtained. And when the wish for peace is genuine, the means for finding it is given in a form each mind which seeks for it in honesty can understand. Whatever form the lesson takes is planned for him in such a way that he can not mistake it if his asking is sincere. And[551] if he asks

---

[544] Handwritten mark-up suggests (one).
[545] Handwritten mark-up suggests (one)
[546] Handwritten mark-up suggests (one).
[547] Handwritten mark-up suggests (one).
[548] Handwritten mark-up suggests (one).
[549] The quotation marks are not in the *Urtext* manuscript. We include them because all other editions do.
[550] Matthew 18:19 "Again I say to you that if two of you agree on earth concerning anything that they ask, it will be done for them by My Father in heaven".
[551] Handwritten mark-up suggests (But).

without sincerity, there is no form in which the lesson will meet with acceptance and be truly learned.

W 185 L 7. Let us today devote our practicing to recognizing that we really mean the words we say. We want the peace of God. This is no idle wish. These words do not request another dream be given us. They do not ask for compromise, nor try to make another bargain in the hope that there must yet be one which can succeed where all the rest have failed. To mean these words acknowledges illusions are in vain, requesting the eternal in the place of shifting dreams which seem to change in what they offer, but are one in nothingness.

W 185 L 8. Today devote your practice periods to careful searching of your mind, to find the dreams you cherish still. What do you ask for in your heart? Forget the words you use in making your requests. Consider but what you believe will comfort you and bring you happiness. But be you not dismayed by lingering illusions, for their form is not what matters now. Let not some dreams be more acceptable, reserving shame and secrecy for others. They are one. **W(404)** And being one, one question should be asked of all of them; "Is this what I would have in place of Heaven and the peace of God?"

W 185 L 9. This is the choice you make. Be not deceived that it is otherwise. No compromise is possible in this. You choose God's peace or you have asked for dreams, and dreams will come as you requested them. Yet will God's peace come just as certainly, and to remain with you forever. It will not be gone with every twist and turning of the road, to reappear unrecognized in forms which shift and change with every step you take.

W 185 L 10. You want the peace of God. And so do all who seem to seek for dreams. For them as well as for yourself you ask but this when you make this request with deep sincerity. For thus you reach to what they really want, and join your own intent with what they seek above all things, perhaps unknown to them, but sure to you. You have been weak at times, uncertain in your purpose, and unsure of what you wanted, where to look for it, and where to turn for help in the attempt. Help has been given you. And would you not avail yourself of it[552] by sharing it?

W 185 L 11. No-one who truly seeks the peace of God can fail to find it.[553] For he merely asks that he deceive himself no longer by denying to himself what is God's Will. Who can remain unsatisfied who asks for what he has already? Who could be unanswered who requests an answer which is his to give? The peace of God is yours.

W 185 L 12. For you it was[554] created, given you by its Creator, and established as His Own eternal gift. How can you fail when you but ask for what He wills for you? And how could your request be limited to you alone? No gift of God can be unshared. It is this attribute which sets the gifts of God apart from every dream that ever seemed to take the place of truth. **W(405)**

W 185 L 13. No-one can lose and everyone must gain whenever any gift of God has been requested and received by anyone. God gives but to unite. To take away is meaningless to Him. And when it is as meaningless to you, you can be sure you share One[555] Will with Him and He with you. And you will also know you share One[556] Will with all your brothers, whose intent is yours.

W 185 L 14. It is this one intent we seek today, uniting our desires with the need of every heart, the call of every mind, the hope that lies beyond despair, the love attack would hide, the brotherhood that hate has sought to sever, but which still remains as God created it.

---

[552] Handwritten mark-up suggests(help).
[553] **Matthew 7:7** "Ask, and it will be given to you; seek, and you will find; knock, and it will be opened to you."
[554] Handwritten mark-up suggests (was peace) in place of "**it was**".
[555] Handwritten mark-up suggests (one).
[556] Handwritten mark-up suggests (one).

With Help like this beside us, can we fail today as we request the peace of God be given us? **W(406)**

Lesson 186 "Salvation of the world depends on me."

W 186 L 1. Here is the statement that will one day take all arrogance away from every mind. Here is the thought of true humility which holds no function as your own but that which has been given you. It offers your acceptance of a part assigned to you, without insisting on another role. It does not judge your proper role. It but acknowledges the Will of God is done on earth as well as Heaven.[557] It unites all wills on earth in Heaven's plan to save the world, restoring it to Heaven's peace.

W 186 L 2. Let us not fight our function. We did not establish it. It is not our idea. The means are given us by which it will be perfectly accomplished. All that we are asked to do is to accept our part in genuine humility, and not deny with self-deceiving arrogance that we are worthy. What is given us to do we have the strength to do. Our minds are suited perfectly to take the part assigned to us by One Who knows us well.

W 186 L 3. Today's idea may seem quite sobering until you see its meaning. All it says is that your Father still remembers you, and offers you the perfect trust He holds in you who are His Son. It does not ask that you be different in any way from what you are. What could humility request but this? And what could arrogance deny but this? Today we will not shrink from our assignment on the specious grounds that modesty is outraged. It is pride that would deny the Call of God Himself.

W 186 L 4. All false humility we lay aside today, that we may listen to God's Voice reveal to us what He would have us do. We do not doubt our adequacy for the function He will offer us. We will be certain only that He knows our strengths, our wisdom and our holiness. And if He deems us worthy, so we are. It is but arrogance that judges otherwise. **W(407)**

W 186 L 5. There is one way, and only one, to be released from the imprisonment your plan to prove the false is true has brought to you. Accept the plan you did not make instead. Judge not your value to it. If God's Voice assures you that salvation needs your part, and that the whole depends on you, be sure that it is so. The arrogant must cling to words, afraid to go beyond them to experience which might affront their stance. Yet are the humble free to hear the Voice Which tells them what they are and what to do.

W 186 L 6. Arrogance makes an image of yourself that is not real. It is this image which quails and retreats in terror as the Voice for God assures you that you have the strength, the wisdom and the holiness to go beyond all images. You are not weak, as is the image of yourself. You are not ignorant and helpless. Sin can not tarnish the truth in you, and misery can come not near the holy home of God.

W 186 L 7. All this the Voice for God relates to you. And as He speaks, the image trembles and seeks to attack the threat it does not know, sensing its basis crumble. Let it go. Salvation of the world depends on you, and not upon this little pile of dust. What can it tell the holy Son of God? Why need he be concerned with it at all?

W 186 L 8. And so we find our peace. We will accept the function God has given us, for all illusions rest upon the weird[558] belief that we can make another for ourselves. Our self-made roles are shifting, and they seem to change from mourner to ecstatic bliss of love and loving. We can laugh or weep, and greet the day with welcome or with tears. Our very being seems to change as we experience a

---

[557] **Matthew 6:10** "Your kingdom come. Your will be done On earth as it is in heaven."
[558] Handwritten mark-up suggests (strange).

thousand shifts in mood, and our emotions raise us high indeed or dash us to the ground in hopelessness. **W(408)**

W 186 L 9. Is this the Son of God? Could He create such instability and call it Son? He Who is changeless shares His attributes with His creation. All the images His Son appears to make have no effect on what he is. They blow across his mind like wind-swept leaves that form a patterning an instant, break apart to group again, and scamper off. Or like mirages seen above a desert, rising from the dust.

W 186 L 10. These unsubstantial images will go, and leave your mind unclouded and serene when you accept the function given you. The images you make give rise to but conflicting goals, impermanent and vague, uncertain and ambiguous. Who could be constant in his efforts, or direct his energies and concentrated drive toward goals like these? The functions which the world esteems are so uncertain that they change ten times an hour at their most secure. What hope of gain can rest on goals like this?

W 186 L 11. In lovely contrast, certain as the sun's return each morning to dispel the night, your truly given function stands out clear and wholly unambiguous. There is no doubt of its validity. It comes from One Who knows no error. And His Voice is certain of Its messages. They will not change nor be in conflict. All of them point to one goal, and one you can attain. Your plan may be impossible, but God's can never fail because He is its Source.

W 186 L 12. Do as His[559] Voice directs. And if It asks a thing of you that seems impossible, remember Who it is that asks and who would make denial. Then consider this; which is more likely to be right? The Voice that speaks for the Creator of all things, Who knows all things exactly as they are, or a distorted image of yourself, confused, bewildered, inconsistent and unsure of everything? Let not its voice direct you. Hear instead a certain **W(409)** Voice Which tells you of a function given you by your Creator, Who remembers you and urges that you now remember Him.

W 186 L 13. His gentle Voice is calling from the known to the unknowing. [560]He would comfort you although He knows no sorrow. He would make a restitution though He is complete; a gift to you although He knows that you have everything already. He has Thoughts which answer every need His Son perceives, although He sees them not. For Love must give, and what is given in His Name takes on the form most useful in a world of form.

W 186 L 14. These are the forms which never can deceive, although[561] they come from Formlessness Itself. Forgiveness is an earthly form of love which as it is in Heaven has no form. Yet what is needed here is given here as it is needed. In this form you can fulfill your function even here, although what love will mean to you when formlessness has been restored to you is greater still. Salvation of the world depends on you who can forgive. Such is your function here. **W(410)**

Lesson 187 "I bless the world because I bless myself."

W 187 L 1. No-one can give unless he has. In fact, giving is proof of having. We have made this point before. What seems to make it hard to credit is not this. No-one can doubt that you must first possess what you would give. It is the second phase on which the world and true perception differ. Having had and given, then the world asserts that you have lost what you possessed. The truth maintains that giving will increase what you possess.

W 187 L 2. How is this possible? For it is sure that if you give a finite thing away, your body's eyes will not perceive it yours. Yet we have learned that things but represent the thoughts which make them. And you do not lack for proof that when you give ideas away, you strengthen them in your own mind. Perhaps the form in which the thought seems to appear is changed in giving. Yet it must return to him who gives. Nor can the form it takes be less acceptable. It must be more.

W 187 L 3. Ideas must first belong to you before you give them. If you are to save the world, you first accept salvation for yourself. But you will not believe that this is done until you see the miracles it brings to everyone you look upon. Herein is the idea of giving clarified and given meaning. Now you can perceive that by your giving is your store increased.

W 187 L 4. Protect all things you value by the act of giving them away, and you are sure that you will never lose them. What you thought you did not have is thereby proven yours. Yet value not its form. For this will change, and grow unrecognizable in time, however much you try to keep it safe. No form endures. It is the thought behind the form of things that lives unchangeable. **W(411)**

W 187 L 5. Give gladly. You can only gain thereby. The thought remains and grows in strength as it is reinforced by giving. Thoughts extend as they are shared, for they can not be lost. There is no giver and receiver in the sense the world conceives of them. There is a giver who retains; another who will give as well. And both must gain in this exchange, for each will have the thought in form most helpful to him. What he seems to lose is always something he will value less than what will surely be returned to him.

W 187 L 6. Never forget you give but to yourself. Who understands what giving means must laugh at the idea of sacrifice. Nor can he fail to recognize the many forms which sacrifice may take. He laughs as well at pain and loss, at sickness and at grief, at poverty, starvation and at death. He recognizes sacrifice remains the one idea that stands behind them all, and in his gentle laughter are they healed.

W 187 L 7. Illusion recognized must disappear. Accept not suffering, and you remove the thought of suffering. Your blessing lies on everyone who suffers when you choose to see all suffering as what it is. The thought of sacrifice gives rise to all the forms that suffering appears to take. And sacrifice is an idea so mad that sanity dismisses it at once.

W 187 L 8. Never believe that you can sacrifice. There is no place for sacrifice in what has any value. If the thought occurs, its very presence proves that error has arisen, and correction must be made. Your blessing will correct it. Given first to you, it now is yours to give as well. No form of sacrifice and suffering can long endure before the face of one who has forgiven and has blessed himself. **W(412)**

W 187 L 9. The lilies that your brother offers you are laid upon your altar, with the ones you offer him beside them. Who could fear to look upon such lovely holiness? The great illusion of the fear of God diminishes to nothingness before the purity that you will look on here. Be not afraid to look. The blessedness you will behold will take away all thought of form, and leave instead the perfect gift forever there, forever to increase, forever yours, forever given away.

W 187 L 10. Now are we one in thought, for fear has gone. And here, before the altar to one God, one Father, one Creator and one Thought, we stand together as one Son of God. Not separate from Him Who is our Source; not distant from one brother who is part of our one Self Whose innocence has joined us all as one, we stand in blessedness and give as we received. The Name of God is on our lips. And as we look within, we see the purity of Heaven shine in our reflection of our Father's Love.

W 187 L 11. Now are we blessed, and now we bless the world. What we have looked upon we would extend, for we would see it everywhere. We would behold it shining with the grace of God in everyone. We would not have it be withheld from anything we look upon. And to ensure this holy sight is ours, we offer it to everything

---

[559] Handwritten mark-up suggests (God's).
[560] Handwritten mark-up suggests (For).
[561] Handwritten mark-up suggests (because).

we see. For where we see it, it will be returned to us in form of lilies we can lay upon our altar, making it a home for Innocence Itself, Who dwells in us and offers us His Holiness as ours. **W(413)**

Lesson 188 "The peace of God is shining in me now."

W 188 L 1. Why wait for Heaven? Those who seek the light are merely covering their eyes. The light is in them now. Enlightenment is but a recognition, not a change at all. Light is not of the world, yet you who bear the light in you are alien here as well. The light came with you from your native home, and stayed with you because it is your own. It is the only thing you bring with you from Him Who is your Source. It shines in you because it lights your home, and leads you back to where it came from and you are at home.

W 188 L 2. This light can not be lost. Why wait to find it in the future, or believe it has been lost already or was never there? It can so easily be looked upon that arguments which prove it is not there become ridiculous. Who can deny the presence of what he beholds in him? It is not difficult to look within, for there all vision starts. There is no sight, be it of dreams or from a truer source, that is not but the shadow of the seen through inward vision. There perception starts and there it ends. It has no source but this.

W 188 L 3. The peace of God is shining in you now, and from your heart extends around the world. It pauses to caress each living thing, and leave a blessing with it which remains forever and forever. What it gives must be eternal. It removes all thoughts of the ephemeral and valueless. It brings renewal to all tired hearts, and lights all vision as it passes by. All of its gifts are given everyone, and everyone unites in giving thanks to you who give and you who have received.

W 188 L 4. The shining in your mind reminds the world of what it has forgotten, and the world restores the memory to you as well. From you salvation radiates with gifts beyond all measure, given and returned. To you, the giver of the gift, does God Himself give thanks. And in His blessing does the light in you shine brighter, adding to the gifts you have to offer to the world. **W(414)**

W 188 L 5. The peace of God can never be contained. Who recognizes it within himself must give it. And the means for giving it are in his understanding. He forgives because he recognized the truth in him. The peace of God is shining in you now, and in all living things. In quietness is it acknowledged universally. For what your inward vision looks upon is your perception of the universe.

W 188 L 6. Sit quietly and close your eyes. The light within you is sufficient. It alone has power to give the gift of sight to you. Exclude the outer world, and let your thoughts fly to the peace within. They know the way. For honest thoughts, untainted by the dream of worldly things outside yourself, become the holy messengers of God Himself. These thoughts you think with Him. They recognize their home. And they point surely to their Source, where God the Father and the Son are One.

W 188 L 7. God's peace is shining on them, but they must remain with you as well, for they were born within your mind, as yours was born in God's. They lead you back to peace, from where they came but to remind you how you must return. They heed your Father's Voice when you refuse to listen. And they urge you gently to accept His Word for what you are, instead of fantasies and shadows. They remind you that you are the co-creator of all things that live. For as the peace of God is shining in you, it must shine on them.

W 188 L 8. We practice coming nearer to the light in us today. We take our wandering thoughts, and gently bring them back to where they fall in line with all the thoughts we share with God. We will not let them stray. We let the light within our minds direct them to come home. We have betrayed them, ordering that they depart from us. But now we call them back, and **W(415)** wash them clean of strange desires and disordered wishes. We restore to them the holiness of their inheritance.

W 188 L 9. Thus are our minds restored with them, and we acknowledge that the peace of God still shines in us, and from us to all living things that share our life. We will forgive them all, absolving all the world of what we thought it did to us. For it is we who make the world as we would have it. Now we choose that it be innocent, devoid of sin, and open to salvation. And we lay our saving blessing on it as we say:

"The peace of God is shining in me now.
Let all things shine upon me in that peace,
And let me bless them with the light in me." **W(416)**

Lesson 189 "I feel the Love of God within me now."

W 189 L 1. There is a light in you the world can not perceive. And with its eyes you will not see this light, for you are blinded by the world. Yet you have eyes to see it. It is there for you to look upon. It was not placed in you to be kept hidden from your sight. This light is a reflection of the thought we practice now. To feel the Love of God within you is to see the world anew, shining in innocence, alive with hope, and blessed with perfect charity and love.

W 189 L 2. Who could feel fear in such a world as this? It welcomes you, rejoices that you came, and sings your praises as it keeps you safe from every form of danger and of pain. It offers you a warm and gentle home in which to stay a while. It blesses you throughout the day, and watches through the night as silent guardian of your holy sleep. It sees salvation in you, and protects the light in you in which it sees its own. It offers you its flowers and its snow in thankfulness for your benevolence.

W 189 L 3. This is the world the Love of God reveals. It is so different from the world you see through darkened eyes of malice and of fear that one belies the other. Only one can be perceived at all. The other one is wholly meaningless. A world in which forgiveness shines on everything and peace offers its gentle light to everyone is inconceivable to those who see a world of hatred, rising from attack, poised to avenge, to murder and destroy.

W 189 L 4. Yet is the world of hatred equally unseen and inconceivable to those who feel God's Love in them. Their world reflects the quietness and peace that shines in them; the gentleness and innocence they see surrounding them; the joy with which they look out from the endless wells of joy within. What they have felt in them they look upon, and see Its sure reflection everywhere. **W(417)**

W 189 L 5. What would you see? The choice is given you. But learn and do not let your mind forget this law of seeing: You will look upon that which you feel within. If hatred finds a place within your heart, you will perceive a fearful world, held cruelly in death's sharp-pointed, bony fingers. If you feel the Love of God within you, you look out upon a world of mercy and of love.

W 189 L 6. Today we pass illusions as we seek to reach to what is true in us, and feel Its all-embracing tenderness, Its Love Which knows us perfect as Itself, Its sight which is the gift Its Love bestows on us. We learn the way today. It is as sure as Love Itself, to Which it carries us. For its simplicity avoids the snares the foolish convolutions of the world's apparent reasoning but serve to hide.

W 189 L 7. Simply do this: Be still and lay aside all thoughts of what you are and what God is; all concepts you have learned about the world; all images you hold about yourself. Empty your mind of everything it thinks is either true or false or good or bad; of every thought it judges worthy and all the ideas of which it is ashamed. Hold onto nothing. Do not bring with you one thought the past has taught, nor one belief you ever learned before from anything. Forget this world, forget this course, and come with wholly empty hands unto your God.

W 189 L 8. Is it not He Who knows the way to you? You need not know the way to Him.[562] Your part is simply to allow all obstacles that[563] you have interposed between the Son and God the Father to be quietly removed forever. God will do His part in joyful and immediate response. Ask and receive. But do not make demands, nor point the road to God by which He should appear to you. The way to reach Him is merely to let Him be. For in that way is your reality acclaimed as well. **W(418)**

W 189 L 9. And so today we do not choose the way in which we go to Him. But we do choose to let Him come, and[564] with this choice we rest. And in our quiet hearts and open minds His Love will blaze Its pathway of Itself. What has not been denied is surely there, if it be true, and can be surely reached. God knows His Son, and knows the way to him. He does not need His Son to show Him how to find His way. Through every opened door His Love shines outward from Its home within, and lightens up the world in innocence.

W 189 L 10. Father, we do not know the way to You. But we have called and You have answered us. We will not interfere. Salvation's ways are not our own for they belong to You, and[565] it is unto You we look for them. Our hands are open to receive Your gifts. We have no thoughts we think apart from You, and cherish no beliefs of what we are or who created us. Yours is the way that we would find and follow. And we ask but that Your Will, Which is our own as well, be done in us and in the world, that it becomes a part of Heaven now.[566] Amen. **W(419)**

Lesson 190 "I choose the joy of God instead of pain."

W 190 L 1. Pain is a wrong perspective. When it is experienced in any form, it is a proof of self-deception. It is not a fact at all. There is no form it takes which will not disappear if seen aright. For pain proclaims God cruel. How could it be real in any form? It witnesses to God the Father's hatred of His Son, the sinfulness He sees in him, and His insane desire for revenge and death.

W 190 L 2. Can such projections be attested to? Can they be anything but wholly false? Pain is but witness to the Son's mistakes in what he thinks he is. It is a dream of fierce retaliation for a crime that could not be committed; for attack on what is wholly unassailable. It is a nightmare of abandonment by an Eternal Love Which could not leave the Son whom It created out of love.

W 190 L 3. Pain is a sign illusions reign in place of truth. It demonstrates God is denied, confused with fear, perceived as mad and seen as traitor to Himself. If God is real there is no pain. If pain is real there is no God. For vengeance is not part of love,[567] and fear, denying love and using pain to prove that God is dead, has shown that death is victor over life. The body is the Son of God, corruptible in death, as mortal as the Father he has slain.

W 190 L 4. Peace to such foolishness! The time has come to laugh at such insane ideas. There is no need to think of them as savage crimes or secret sins with weighty consequence. Who but a madman could conceive of them as cause of anything? Their witness, pain, is mad as they, and no more to be feared than the insane illusions which it shields and tries to demonstrate must still be true. **W(420)**

W 190 L 5. It is your thoughts alone that cause you pain. Nothing external to your mind can hurt or injure you in any way. There is no cause beyond yourself that can reach down and bring oppression. No-one but yourself affects you. There is nothing in the world which has the power to make you ill or sad, or weak or frail. But it is you who have the power to dominate all things you see by merely recognizing what you are. As you perceive the harmlessness in them, they will accept your holy will as theirs. And what was seen as fearful now becomes a source of innocence and holiness.

W 190 L 6. My holy brothers, think of this awhile; the world you see does nothing. It has no effects at all. It merely represents your thoughts. And it will change entirely as you elect to change your mind, and choose the joy of God as what you really want. Your Self is radiant in this holy joy, unchanged, unchanging and unchangeable forever and forever. And would you deny a little corner of your mind its own inheritance, and keep it as a hospital for pain, a sickly place where living things must come at last to die?

W 190 L 7. The world may seem to cause you pain. And yet the world, as causeless, has no power to cause. As an effect it cannot make effects. As an illusion it is what you will. Your idle wishes represent its pains. Your strange desires bring it evil dreams. Your thoughts of death envelop it in fear, while in your kind forgiveness does it live.

W 190 L 8. Pain is the thought of evil taking form, and working havoc in your holy mind. Pain is the ransom you have gladly paid not to be free. In pain is God denied the Son He loves. In pain does fear appear to triumph over love, and time replace eternity and Heaven. And the world becomes a cruel and a bitter place, where sorrow rules and little joys give way before the onslaught of the savage pain that waits to end all joy in misery. **W(421)**

W 190 L 9. Lay down your arms and come without defense into the quiet place where Heaven's peace holds all things still at last. Lay down all thoughts of danger and of fear. Let no attack enter with you. Lay down the cruel sword of judgment that you hold against your throat, and put aside the withering assaults with which you seek to hide your holiness.

W 190 L 10. Here will you understand there is no pain. Here does the joy of God belong to you. This is the day when it is given you to realize the lesson which contains all of salvation's power. It is this: Pain is illusion; joy reality. Pain is but sleep; joy is awakening. Pain is deception; joy alone is truth.

W 190 L 11. And so again we make the only choice that ever can be made; we choose between illusions and the truth, or pain and joy, or hell and Heaven. Let our gratitude unto our Teacher fill our hearts as we are free to choose our joy instead of pain, our holiness in place of sin, the peace of God instead of conflict, and the light of Heaven for the darkness of the world. **W(422)**

Lesson 191 "I am the holy Son of God Himself"

W 191 L 1. Here is your declaration of release from bondage of the world. And here as well is all the world released. You do not see what you have done by giving to the world the role of jailor to the Son of God. What could it be but vicious and afraid, fearful of shadows, punitive and wild, lacking all reason, blind, insane and sad?

W 191 L 2. What have you done that this should be your world? What have you done that this is what you see? Deny your own identity and this is what remains. You look on chaos and proclaim it as yourself. There is no sight that fails to witness this to you. There is no sound that does not speak of frailty within you and without; no breath you draw that does not seem to bring you nearer death; no hope you hold but will dissolve in tears.

---

[562] **John 14:5** Thomas said to Him, "Lord, we do not know where You are going, and how can we know the way?"
[563] Handwritten mark-up suggests (which).
[564] The *Urtext* manuscript originally has a new sentence starting with "**And**" while handwritten editing changes that to a comma, which we think is preferable.
[565] As with the preceding note, the *Urtext* manuscript originally has a new sentence starting with "**And**" here while handwritten editing changes that to a comma, which we think is preferable
[566] **Matthew 6:10** "Your kingdom come. Your will be done on earth as it is in heaven."
[567] *Urtext* manuscript has over-striking indicating a sentence break ... but one is not required.

W 191 L 3. Deny your own identity and you will not escape the madness which induced this weird, unnatural and ghostly thought which[568] mocks creation and which[569] laughs at God. Deny your own identity and you assail the universe alone, without a friend, a tiny particle of dust against the legions of your enemies. Deny your own identity and look on evil, sin and death, and[570] watch despair snatch from your fingers every scrap of hope, leaving you nothing but the wish to die.

W 191 L 4. Yet what is it except a game you play in which identity can be denied? You are as God created you. All else but this one thing is folly to believe. In this one thought is everything[571] set free. In this one truth are all illusions gone. In this one fact is sinlessness proclaimed to be forever part of everything; the central core of its existence and its guarantee of immortality. **W(423)**

W 191 L 5. But let today's idea find a place among your thoughts, and you have risen far above the world and all the worldly thoughts that hold it prisoner. And from this place of safety and escape you will return and set it free. For he who can accept his true identity is truly saved. And his salvation is the gift he gives to everyone in gratitude to Him Who pointed out the way to happiness that changed his whole perception of the world.

W 191 L 6. One holy thought like this and you are free; you are the holy Son of God Himself. And with this holy thought you learn as well that you have freed the world. You have no need to use it cruelly and then perceive this savage need in it. You set it free of your imprisonment. You will not see a devastating image of yourself walking the world in terror, with the world twisting in agony because your fears have laid the mark of death upon its heart.

W 191 L 7. Be glad today how very easily is hell undone. You need but tell yourself:

"I am the holy Son of God Himself.

I cannot suffer; cannot be in pain;

I cannot lose, nor can I fail to do

All that salvation asks."

And in that thought is everything you look on wholly changed.

W 191 L 8. A miracle has lighted up all dark and ancient caverns where the rites of death echoed since time began. For time has lost its hold upon the world. The Son of God has come in glory to redeem the lost, to save the helpless and to give the world the gift of his forgiveness.[572] Who could see the world as dark and sinful when God's Son has come again at last to set it free? **W(424)**

W 191 L 9. You who perceive yourself as weak and frail, with futile hopes and devastated dreams, born but to die, to weep and suffer pain, hear this: All power is given you in earth and Heaven.[573] There is nothing that you cannot do.[574] You play the game of death, of being helpless, pitifully tied to dissolution in a world which shows no mercy to you. Yet when you accord it mercy, will its mercy shine on you.

W 191 L 10. Then let the Son of God awaken from his sleep, and opening his holy eyes return again to bless the world he made. In error it began. But it will end in the reflection of his holiness. And we will sleep no more and dream of death. Then join with me today. Your glory is the light that saves the world. Do not withhold salvation longer. Look about the world and see the suffering there. Is not your heart willing to bring your weary brothers rest?

W 191 L 11. They must await your own release. They stay in chains 'til you are free. They cannot see the mercy of the world until you find it for[575] yourself. They suffer pain until you have denied its hold on you. They die 'til you accept your own Eternal Life. You are the holy Son of God Himself. Remember this and all the world is free. Remember this and earth and Heaven are one. **W(425)**

Lesson 192 "I have a function God would have me fill."

W 192 L 1. It is your Father's holy Will that you complete Himself and that your Self shall be His sacred Son, forever pure as He, of love created and in love preserved, extending love, creating in its Name, forever one with God and with your Self. Yet what can such a function mean within a world of envy, hatred and attack?

W 192 L 2. Therefore you have a function in the world in its own terms. For who can understand a language far beyond his simple grasp? Forgiveness represents your function here. It is not God's creation, for it is the means by which untruth can be undone. And who would pardon Heaven? Yet on earth you need the means to let illusion go. Creation merely waits for your return to be acknowledged, not to be complete.

W 192 L 3. Creation cannot even be conceived of in the world. It has no meaning here. Forgiveness is the closest it can come to earth. For being Heaven-borne, it has no form at all. Yet God created One Who has the power to translate into[576] form the wholly formless. What He makes are dreams, but of a kind so close to waking that the light of day already shines in them,[577] and eyes already opening behold the joyful sights their offerings contain.

W 192 L 4. Forgiveness gently looks upon all things unknown in Heaven, sees them disappear, and leaves the world a clean and unmarked slate on which the Word of God can now replace the senseless symbols written there before. Forgiveness is the means by which the fear of death is overcome because it holds no fierce attraction now, and guilt is gone. **W(426)** Forgiveness lets the body be perceived as what it is; a simple teaching aid to be laid by when learning is complete, but hardly changing him who learns at all.

W 192 L 5. The mind without the body cannot make mistakes. It cannot think that it will die, nor be the prey of merciless attack. Anger becomes impossible, and where is terror then? What fears could still assail those who have lost the source of all attack; the core of anguish and the seat[578] of fear? Only forgiveness can relieve the mind of thinking that the body is its home. Only forgiveness can restore the peace that God intended for His holy Son. Only forgiveness can persuade the Son to look again upon his holiness.

W 192 L 6. With anger gone, you will indeed perceive that for Christ's vision and the gift of sight no sacrifice was asked, and only pain was lifted from a sick and tortured mind. Is this unwelcome? Is it to be feared? Or is it to be hoped for, met with thanks and joy-

---

[568] Handwritten mark-up suggests (that).
[569] Handwritten mark-up suggests (that).
[570] The *Urtext* manuscript has a sentence break here, but the handwrittrn markup changes it to a comma which we agree is preferable.
[571] Handwritten mark-up suggests (everyone).
[572] **Matthew 16:27** "For the Son of Man will come in the glory of His Father with His angels, and then He will reward each according to his works."
Matthew 18:11 "For the Son of Man has come to save that which was lost."
Matthew 25:31 "When the Son of Man comes in His glory, and all the holy angels with Him, then He will sit on the throne of His glory."
[573] **Matthew 28:18** And Jesus came and spoke to them, saying, "All authority has been given to Me in heaven and on earth."
[574] **Matthew 17:20** So Jesus said to them, "Because of your unbelief; for assuredly, I say to you, if you have faith as a mustard seed, you will say to this mountain, 'Move from here to there,' and it will move; and nothing will be impossible for you."
John 14:12 "Truly, truly, I say to you, He who believes on Me, the works that I do he shall do also, and greater *works* than these he shall do, because I go to My Father."

[575] Handwritten mark-up suggests (in) in place of "**for**".
[576] Handwritten mark-up suggests (in) in place of "**into**".
[577] The *Urtext* manuscript has a sentence break here, but the handwriting changes it to a comma which we agree is preferable.
[578] In the *Urtext* manuscript "**deceit**" appears here, with (the seat) handwritten in. We've adopted the handwritten correction because in the context it appears more likely to be the intended meaning.

ously accepted? We are one, and therefore give up nothing, for[579] we have indeed been given everything by God.

W 192 L 7. Yet do we need forgiveness to perceive that this is so. Without its kindly light we grope in darkness, using reason but to justify our rage and our attack. Our understanding is so limited that what we think we understand is but confusion born of error. We are lost in mists of shifting dreams and fearful thoughts, our eyes shut tight against the light; our minds engaged in worshipping what is not there.

W 192 L 8. Who can be born again in Christ but him who has forgiven everyone he sees or thinks of or imagines?[580] Who could be set free while he imprisons anyone? A jailor is not free, for he is bound together with his prisoner. He must be sure that he does not escape, and so he spends his time in keeping watch on him. The bars which limit him become the world in which the[581] jailor lives, along with him. And it is on his freedom that the way to liberty depends for both of them. **W(427)**

W 192 L 9. Therefore hold no-one prisoner. Release instead of bind, for thus are you made free.[582] The way is simple. Every time[583] you feel a stab of anger, realize you hold a sword above your head. And it will fall or be averted as you choose to be condemned or free. Thus does each one who seems to tempt you to be angry represent your Savior from the prison-house of death. And so you owe him thanks instead of pain.

W 192 L 10. Be merciful today. The Son of God deserves your mercy. It is he who asks that you accept the way to freedom now. Deny him not. His Father's Love for him belongs to you. Your function here on earth is only to forgive him, that you may accept him back as your identity. He is as God created him. And you are what he is. Forgive him now his sins, and you will see that you are one with him. **W(428)**

Lesson 193 "All things are Lessons God would have me learn."

W 193 L 1. God does not know of learning. Yet His Will extends to what He does not understand, in that He wills the happiness His Son inherited of Him be undisturbed; eternal and forever gaining scope, eternally expanding in the joy of full creation, and eternally open and wholly limitless in Him. This is His Will. And thus His Will provides the means to guarantee that it is done.

W 193 L 2. God sees no contradictions. Yet His Son believes he sees them. Thus he has a need for One Who can correct his erring sight, and give him vision that will lead him back to where perception ceases. God does not perceive at all. Yet it is He Who gives the means by which perception is made true and beautiful enough to let the light of Heaven shine upon it. It is He Who answers what His Son would contradict, and keeps his sinlessness forever safe.

W 193 L 3. These are the lessons God would have you learn. His Will reflects them all, and they reflect His loving kindness to the Son He loves. Each lesson has a central thought, the same in all of them. The form alone is changed, with different circumstances and events; with different characters and different themes apparent but not real. They are the same in fundamental content. It is this: "Forgive and you will see this differently."

W 193 L 4. Certain it is that all distress does not appear to be but unforgiveness. Yet that is the content underneath the form. It is this sameness which makes learning sure, because the lesson is so simple that it cannot be rejected in the end. No-one can hide forever from a truth so very obvious that it appears in countless forms, and yet is recognized as easily in all of them, if one but wants to see the simple lesson there. **W(429)**

W 193 L 5. "Forgive and you will see this differently." These are the words the Holy Spirit speaks in all your tribulations, all your pain, all suffering regardless of its forms. These are the words with which temptation ends and guilt, abandoned, is revered no more. These are the words which end the dream of sin, and rid the mind of fear. These are the words by which salvation comes to all the world.

W 193 L 6. Shall we not learn to say these words when we are tempted to believe that pain is real, and death becomes our choice instead of life? Shall we not learn to say these words when we have understood their power to release all minds from bondage? These are words which give you power over all events which[584] seem to have been given power over you. You see them rightly when you hold these words in full awareness, and do not forget these words apply to everything you see or any brother looks upon amiss.

W 193 L 7. How can you tell when you are seeing wrong, or someone else is failing to perceive the lesson he should learn? Does pain seem real in the perception? If it does, be sure the lesson is not learned. And there remains an unforgiveness hiding in the mind which[585] sees the pain through eyes the mind directs.

W 193 L 8. God would not have you suffer thus. He would help you forgive yourself. His Son does not remember who he is. And God would have him not forget His Love, and all the gifts His Love brings with It. Would you now renounce your own salvation? Would you fail to learn the simple lessons Heaven's Teacher sets before you that all pain may disappear, and God may be remembered by His Son?

W 193 L 9. All things are lessons God would have you learn. He would not leave an unforgiving thought without correction, nor one thorn or nail to hurt His sacred Son in any way. He would ensure his holy rest remain untroubled and serene, without a care in an eternal home which cares for him. And He would have all tears be wiped away, with none remaining yet unshed, and none but waiting their appointed time to fall. For God has willed that laughter **W(430)** should replace each one, and that His Son be free again.

W 193 L 10. We will attempt today to overcome a thousand seeming obstacles to peace in just one day. Let mercy come to you more quickly. Do not try to hold it off another day, another minute, or another instant. Time was made for this. Use it today for what its purpose is. Morning and night devote what time you can to serve its proper aim, and do not let the time be less than meets your deepest need. Give all you can and give a little more, for now we would arise in haste and go unto our Father's house.[586] We have been gone too long, and we would linger here no more.

W 193 L 11. And as we practice, let us think about all things we saved to settle by ourselves, and kept apart from healing. Let us give them all to Him Who knows the way to look upon them so that they will disappear. Truth is His message; truth His teaching is. His are the lessons God would have us learn.

W 193 L 12. Each hour spend a little time today, and in the days to come, in practicing the lesson in forgiveness in the form established for the day. And try to give it application to the happenings the hour brought, so that the next one is free of the one before. The chains of time are easily unloosened in this way. Let no one hour cast its

---

[579] The *Urtext* manuscript has a sentence break, and "**But**" instead of "**for**". This appears to be the correction of a typing error.
[580] **John 3:3** Jesus answered and said to him, "Most assuredly, I say to you, unless one is born again, he cannot see the kingdom of God."
[581] Handwritten mark-up suggests (his).
[582] **Matthew 16:19** "And I will give you the keys of the kingdom of heaven, and whatever you bind on earth will be bound in heaven, and whatever you loose on earth will be loosed in heaven."
[583] Originally in the *Urtext* manuscript typed as one words, "**everytime**".

[584] Handwritten mark-up suggests (that).
[585] Handwritten mark-up suggests (that).
[586] **Matthew 19:21** Jesus said to him, "If you want to be perfect, go, sell what you have and give to the poor, and you will have treasure in heaven; and come, follow Me."
John 14:2 "In My Father's house are many mansions; if it were not so, I would have told you. I go to prepare a place for you."

shadow on the one that follows, and when that one goes let everything that happened in its course go with it. Thus will you remain unbound, in peace eternal in the world of time.

W 193 L 13. This is the lesson God would have you learn: There is a way to look on everything that lets it be to you another step to Him and to salvation of the world. **W(431)** To all that speaks of terror, answer thus:

"I will forgive and this will disappear."

To every apprehension, every care, and every form of suffering repeat these selfsame words. And then you hold the key that opens Heaven's gate,[587] and brings the Love of God the Father down to earth at last, to raise it up to Heaven. God will take this final step Himself. Do not deny the little steps He asks you take to Him. **W(432)**

Lesson 194 "I place the future in the hands of God."

W 194 L 1. Today's idea takes another step toward quick salvation, and a giant stride it is indeed! So great the distance is that it encompasses, it sets you down just short of Heaven, with the goal in sight and obstacles behind. Your foot has reached the lawns that welcome you to Heaven's gate; the quiet place of peace where you await with certainty the final step of God. How far are we progressing now from earth! How close are we approaching to our goal! How short the journey still to be pursued!

W 194 L 2. Accept today's idea, and you have passed[588] all anxiety, all pits of hell, all blackness of depression, thoughts of sin, and devastation brought about by guilt. Accept today's idea, and you have released the world from all imprisonment by loosening the heavy chains that locked the door to freedom on it. You are saved, and your salvation thus becomes the gift you give the world because you have received.

W 194 L 3. In no one instant is depression felt, or pain experienced, or loss perceived. In no one instant sorrow can be set upon a throne and worshipped faithfully. In no one instant can one even die. And so each instant given unto God in passing, with the next one given Him already, is a time of your release from sadness, pain, and even death itself.

W 194 L 4. God holds your future as He holds your past and present. They are one to Him, and so they should be one to you. Yet in this world the temporal progression still seems real. And so you are not asked to understand the lack of sequence really found in time. You are but asked to let the future go, and place it in God's hands. And you will see by your experience that you have laid the past and present in His hands as well, because the past will punish you no more, and future dread will now be meaningless. **W(433)**

W 194 L 5. Release the future. For the past is gone, and what is present, freed from its bequest of grief and misery, of pain and loss, becomes the instant in which time escapes the bondage of illusions where it runs its pitiless, inevitable course. Then is each instant, which was slave to time, transformed into a holy instant when the light that was kept hidden in God's Son is freed to bless the world. Now is he free, and all his glory shines upon a world made free with him, to share his holiness.

W 194 L 6. If you can see the lesson for today as the deliverance it really is, you will not hesitate to give as much consistent effort as you can to make it be a part of you. As it becomes a thought which[589] rules your mind, a habit in your problem-solving repertoire, a way of quick reaction to temptation, you extend your learning to the world. And as you learn to see salvation in all things, so will the world perceive that it is saved.

W 194 L 7. What worry can beset the one who gives his future to the loving hands of God? What can he suffer? What can cause him pain, or bring experience of loss to him? What can he fear? And what can he regard except with love? For he who has escaped all fear of future pain has found his way to present peace, and certainty of care the world can never threaten. He is sure that his perception may be faulty, but will never lack correction. He is free to choose again when he has been deceived; to change his mind when he has made mistakes.

W 194 L 8. Place, then, your future in the hands of God. For thus you call the memory of Him to come again, replacing all your thoughts of sin and evil with the truth of love. Think you the world could fail to gain thereby, and every living creature not respond with healed perception? Who entrusts himself to God has also placed the world within the Hands to which he has himself appealed for comfort and security. He lays aside the sick illusions of the world along with his, and offers peace to both. **W(434)**

W 194 L 9. Now are we saved indeed. For in God's hands we rest untroubled, sure that only good can come to us. If we forget, we will be gently reassured. If we accept an unforgiving thought, it will be seen replaced by love's reflection. And if we are tempted to attack, we will appeal to Him Who guards our rest to make the choice for us that leaves temptation far behind. No longer is the world our enemy, for we have chosen that we be its friends.[590] **W(435)**

Lesson 195 "Love is the way I walk in gratitude."

W 195 L 1. Gratitude is a lesson hard to learn for those who look upon the world amiss. The most[591] they can do is see themselves as better off than others. And they try to be content because another seems to suffer more than they. How pitiful and deprecating are such thoughts! For who has cause for thanks while others have less cause? And who could suffer less because he sees another suffer more? Your gratitude is due to Him alone Who made all cause of sorrow disappear throughout the world.

W 195 L 2. It is insane to offer thanks because of suffering. But it is equally insane to fail in gratitude to One Who offers you the certain means whereby all pain is healed, and suffering replaced with laughter and with happiness. Nor could the even partly sane refuse to take the steps which He directs, and follow in the way He sets before them to escape a prison which they thought contained no door to the deliverance they now perceive.

W 195 L 3. Your brother is your "enemy" because you see in him the rival for your peace; a plunderer who takes his joy from you, and leaves you nothing

but a black despair so bitter and relentless that there is no hope remaining. Now is vengeance all there is to wish for. Now can you but try to bring him down to lie in death with you, as useless as yourself; as little left within his grasping fingers as in yours.

W 195 L 4. You do not offer God your gratitude because your brother is more slave than you, nor could you sanely be enraged if he seems freer. Love makes no comparisons. And gratitude can only be sincere if it is joined to love. We offer thanks to God our Father that in us all things will find their freedom. It will never be that some are loosed while others still are bound,[592] for who can bargain in the Name of love? **W(436)**

W 195 L 5. Therefore give thanks, but in sincerity. And let your gratitude make room for all who will escape with you; the sick, the

---

[587] **Matthew 16:19** And I will give you the keys of the kingdom of heaven, and whatever you bind on earth will be bound in heaven, and whatever you loose on earth will be loosed in heaven.

[588] *Urtext* manuscript has "**past**", obviously a spelling error. In the *Notes* it is as we have it, "passed." FIP also corrects it.

[589] Handwritten mark-up suggests (that).

[590] Handwritten mark-up suggests (Friend) instead of "**friends**".

[591] Handwritten mark-up suggests (that).

[592] **Matthew 16:19** "And I will give you the keys of the kingdom of heaven, and whatever you bind on earth will be bound in heaven, and whatever you loose on earth will be loosed in heaven."

weak, the needy and afraid, and those who mourn a seeming loss or feel apparent pain, who suffer cold or hunger, or who walk the way of hatred and the path of death. All these go with you. Let us not compare ourselves with them, for thus we split them off in our awareness from the Unity we share with them,[593] as they must share with us.

W 195 L 6. We thank our Father for one thing alone; that we are separate from no living thing, and therefore one with Him. And we rejoice that no exceptions ever can be made which would reduce our wholeness, nor impair or change our function to complete the One Who is Himself completion. We give thanks for every living thing, for otherwise we offer thanks for nothing, and we fail to recognize the gifts of God to us.

W 195 L 7. Then let our brothers lean their tired heads against our shoulders as they rest a while. We offer thanks for them. For if we can direct them to the peace that we would find, the way is opening at last to us. An ancient door is swinging free again; a long forgotten Word re-echoes in our memory, and gathers clarity as we are willing once again to hear.

W 195 L 8. Walk, then, in gratitude the way of love. For hatred is forgotten when we lay comparisons aside. What more remains as obstacles to peace? The fear of God is now undone at last, and we forgive without comparing. Thus we cannot choose to overlook some things, and yet retain some other things still locked away as sins. When your forgiveness is complete you will have total gratitude, for you will see that everything has earned the right to love by being loving, even as your Self. **W(437)**

W 195 L 9. Today we learn to think of gratitude in place of anger, malice and revenge. We have been given everything. If we refuse to recognize it, we are not entitled therefore to our bitterness, and to a self-perception which regards us in a place of merciless pursuit, where we are badgered ceaselessly and pushed about without a thought or care for us or for our future. Gratitude becomes the single thought we substitute for these insane perceptions. God has cared for us, and calls us Son. Can there be more than this?

W 195 L 10. Our gratitude will pave the way to Him, and shorten our learning time by more than you could ever dream of. Gratitude goes hand in hand with love, and where one is the other must be found. For gratitude is but an aspect of the love which is the Source of all creation. God gives thanks to you, His Son, for being what you are; His Own completion and the Source of love, along with Him. Your gratitude to Him is one with His to you. For love can walk no road except the way of gratitude, and thus we go who walk the way to God. **W(438)**

Lesson 196 "It can be but myself I crucify."

W 196 L 1. When this is firmly understood and kept in full awareness, you will not attempt to harm yourself, nor make your body slave to vengeance. You will not attack yourself, and you will realize that to attack another is but to attack yourself. You will be free of the insane belief that to attack a brother saves yourself. And you will understand his safety is your own, and in his healing you are healed.

W 196 L 2. Perhaps at first you will not understand how mercy, limitless and with all things held in its sure protection, can be found in the idea we practice for today. It may, in fact, appear to be a sign that punishment can never be escaped because the ego, under what it sees as threat, is quick to cite the truth to save its lies. Yet must it fail to understand the truth it uses thus. But you can learn to see these foolish applications, and deny the meaning they appear to have.

W 196 L 3. Thus do you also teach your mind that you are not an ego. For the ways in which the ego would distort the truth will not deceive you longer. You will not believe you are a body to be crucified. And you will see within today's idea the light of resurrection, looking past all thoughts of crucifixion and of death to thoughts of liberation and of life.

W 196 L 4. Today's idea is one step we take in leading us from bondage to the state of perfect freedom. Let us take this step today that we may quickly go the way salvation shows us, taking every step in its appointed sequence as the mind relinquishes its burdens one by one. It is not time we need for this. It is but willingness. And[594] what would seem to need a thousand years can easily be done in just one instant by the grace of God. **W(439)**

W 196 L 5. The dreary, hopeless thought that you can make attacks on others and escape yourself has nailed you to the cross. Perhaps it seemed to be salvation. Yet it merely stood for the belief the fear of God is real. And what is that but hell? Who could believe his Father is his deadly enemy, separate from him, and waiting to destroy his life and blot him from the universe, without the fear of hell upon his heart?

W 196 L 6. Such is the form of madness you believe, if you accept the fearful thought you can attack another and be free yourself. Until this form is changed, there is no hope. Until you see that this, at least, must be entirely impossible, how could there be escape? The fear of God is real to anyone who thinks this thought is true. And he will not perceive its foolishness, nor even see that it is there so that it would be possible to question it.

W 196 L 7. To question it at all, its form must first be changed at least as much as will permit fear of retaliation to abate, and the responsibility returned to some extent to you. From there you can at least consider if you want to go along this painful path. Until this shift has been accomplished, you can not perceive that it is but your thoughts which bring you fear, and your deliverance depends on you.

W 196 L 8. Our next steps will be easy, if you take this one today. From there we go ahead quite rapidly. For once you understand it is impossible that you be hurt except by your own thoughts, the fear of God must disappear. You do not now believe that fear is caused without. And God, Whom you had thought to banish, can be welcomed back within the holy mind He never left. **W(440)**

W 196 L 9. Salvation's song can certainly be heard in the idea we practice for today. If it can but be you you crucify, you did not hurt the world and need not fear its vengeance and pursuit. Nor need you hide in terror from the deadly fear of God projection hides behind. The thing you dread the most is your salvation. You are strong, and it is strength you want. And you are free, and glad of freedom. You have sought to be both weak and bound, because you feared your strength and freedom. Yet salvation lies in them.

W 196 L 10. There is an instant in which terror seems to grip your mind so wholly that escape appears quite hopeless. When you realize, once and for all, that it is you you fear, the mind perceives itself as split. And this had been concealed while you believed attack could be directed outward, and returned from outside to within. It seemed to be an enemy outside you had to fear. And thus a god outside yourself became your mortal enemy; the source of fear.

W 196 L 11. Now, for an instant, is a murderer perceived within you, eager for your death, intent on plotting punishment for you until the time when it can kill at last. Yet in this instant is the time as well in which salvation comes. For fear of God has disappeared. And you can call on Him to save you from illusions in[595] His Love, calling Him Father and yourself His Son. Pray that the instant may be soon, - today. Step back from fear and make advance to love.

---

[593] Handwritten mark-up edits this to: "**for thus we split them off from our awareness of the unity we share with them.**" In the *Notes* and the *Urtext*, we "split them off in our awareness from the unity," In the mark-up and FIP we "split them off from our awareness of the unity."

[594] Handwritten mark-up suggests (For).
[595] Handwritten mark-up suggests (by) in place of "**in**".

W 196 L 12. There is no Thought of God that does not go with you to help you reach that instant, and to go beyond it quickly, surely and forever. When the fear of God is gone, there are no obstacles which still remain between you and the holy peace of God. How kind and merciful is the idea we practice! Give it welcome as you should, for it is your release. It is indeed but you your mind can try to crucify. Yet your redemption, too, will come from you. **W(441)**

Lesson 197 "It can be but my gratitude I earn."

W 197 L 1. Here is the second step we take to free your mind from the belief in outside force pitted against your own. You make attempts at kindness and forgiveness. Yet you turn them to attack again, unless you find external gratitude and lavish thanks. Your gifts must be received with honor, lest they be withdrawn. And so you think God's gifts are loans at best; at worst, deceptions which would cheat you of defenses to ensure that when He strikes He will not fail to kill.

W 197 L 2. How easily are God and guilt confused by those who know not what their thoughts can do. Deny your strength, and weakness must become salvation to you. See yourself as bound, and bars become your home. Nor will you leave the prison house or claim your strength until guilt and salvation are not seen as one, and freedom and salvation are perceived as joined, with strength beside them, to be sought and claimed and found and fully recognized.

W 197 L 3. The world must thank you when you offer it release from your illusions. Yet your thanks belong to you as well, for its release can only mirror yours. Your gratitude is all your gifts require, that they be a lasting offering of a thankful heart released from hell forever. Is it this you would undo by taking back your gifts because they were not honored? It is you who honor them and give them fitting thanks, for it is you who have received the gifts.

W 197 L 4. It does not matter if another thinks your gifts unworthy. In his mind there is a part which joins with yours in thanking you. It does not matter if your gifts seem lost and ineffectual. They are received where they are given. In your gratitude are they accepted universally, and thankfully acknowledged by the Heart of God Himself. And would you take them back, when He has gratefully accepted them? **W(442)**

W 197 L 5. God blesses every gift you give to Him and every gift is given Him because it can be given only to yourself, and what belongs to God must be His Own. Yet you will never realize His gifts are sure, eternal, changeless, limitless, forever giving out, extending love and adding to your never-ending joy, while you forgive but to attack again.

W 197 L 6. Withdraw the gifts you give, and you will think that what is given you has been withdrawn. But learn to let forgiveness take away the sins you think you see outside yourself, and you can never think the gifts of God are lent but for a little while, before He snatches them away again in death. For death will have no meaning for you then. And with the end of this belief is fear forever over. Thank your Self for this, for He is grateful only unto God, and He gives thanks for you unto Himself.

W 197 L 7. To everyone who lives will Christ yet come, for everyone must live and breathe in Him.[596] His Being in His Father is secure because Their Will is One. Their gratitude to all They have created has no end, for gratitude remains a part of love. Thanks be to you, the holy Son of God, for as you were created you contain all things within your Self. And you are still as God created you. Nor can you dim the light of your perfection. In your heart the Heart of God is laid. He holds you dear because you are Himself. All gratitude belongs to you because of what you are.

W 197 L 8. Give thanks as you receive it. Be you free of all ingratitude to anyone who makes your Self complete. And from this Self is no-one left outside. Give thanks for all the countless channels that extend this Self. All that you do is given unto Him. All that you think can only be His Thoughts, sharing with Him the holy Thoughts of God. Earn now the gratitude you have denied yourself when you forgot the function God has given you. But never think that He has ever ceased to offer thanks to you. **W(443)**

Lesson 198 "Only my condemnation injures me."

W 198 L 1. Injury is impossible. And yet illusion makes illusion. If you can condemn you can be injured. For you have believed that you can injure, and the right you have established for yourself can be now used against you, 'til you lay it down as valueless, unwanted and unreal. Then does illusion cease to have effects, and all[597] it seemed to have will be undone. Then are you free, for freedom is your gift, and you can now receive the gift you gave.

W 198 L 2. Condemn and you are made a prisoner. Forgive and you are freed. Such is the law that rules perception. It is not a law that knowledge understands, for freedom is a part of knowledge. To condemn is thus impossible in truth. What seems to be its influence and its effects have not occurred at all. Yet must we deal with them a while as if they had. Illusion makes illusion. Except one. Forgiveness is illusion that is answer to the rest.

W 198 L 3. Forgiveness sweeps all other dreams away, and though it is itself a dream, it breeds no others. All illusions save this one must multiply a thousand fold. But this is where illusions end. Forgiveness is the end of dreams because it is a dream of waking. It is not itself the truth. Yet does it point to where the truth must be, and gives direction with the certainty of God Himself. It is a dream in which the Son of God awakens to his Self and to his Father knowing They are One.[598]

W 198 L 4. Forgiveness is the only road that leads out of disaster, past all suffering, and finally away from death. How could there be another way, when this one is the plan of God Himself? And why should[599] you oppose it, quarrel with it, seek to find a thousand ways in which it must be wrong; a thousand other possibilities? **W(444)**

W 198 L 5. Is it not wiser to be glad you hold the answer to your problems in your hand? Is it not more intelligent to thank the One Who gives salvation, and accept His gift with gratitude? And is it not a kindness to yourself to hear His Voice and learn the simple lessons He would teach, instead of trying to dismiss His Words and substitute your own in place of His?

W 198 L 6. His Words[600] will work. His Words will save. His Words contain all hope, all blessing and all joy that ever can be found upon this earth. His Words are born in God, and come to you with Heaven's love upon them. Those who hear His Words have heard the song of Heaven, for these are the words in which all will merge as one at last. And as this one will fade away, the Word of God will come to take its place, for It will be remembered then and loved.

W 198 L 7. This world has many seeming separate haunts where mercy has no meaning, and attack appears as justified. Yet all are one; a place where death is offered to God's Son and to his Father. You may think They have accepted, but if you will look again upon the place where you beheld Their blood you will perceive a miracle instead. How foolish to believe that They could die! How foolish to

---

[596] **Acts 17:28** for in Him we live and move and have our being, as also some of your own poets have said, "For we are also His offspring."

---

[597] Handwritten mark-up suggests (those) in place of "**all**".
Matthew 6:12 "And forgive us our trespasses, As we forgive those who trespass against us."
[598] Handwritten mark-up suggests (one).
[599] Handwritten mark-up suggests (would).
[600] Handwritten mark-up suggests that "**Words**" be set in lower case as (words) in each instance in this paragraph, but we're only footnoting it once.

believe you can attack! How mad to think that you could be condemned, and that the holy Son of God can die!

W 198 L 8. The stillness of your Self remains unmoved, untouched by thoughts like these, and unaware of any condemnation which could need forgiveness. Dreams of any kind are strange and alien to the truth. Yet[601] what but Truth could have a Thought Which builds a bridge to truth which[602] brings illusions to the other side? **W(445)**

W 198 L 9. Today we practice letting freedom come to make its home with you. The truth bestows these words upon your mind, that you may find the key to light and let the darkness end:

> *"Only my condemnation injures me.*
> *Only my own forgiveness sets me free."*

Do not forget today that there can be no form of suffering that fails to hide an unforgiving thought. Nor can there be a form of pain forgiveness cannot heal.

W 198 L 10. Accept the one illusion which proclaims there is no condemnation in God's Son, and Heaven is remembered instantly; the world forgotten, all its weird beliefs forgotten with it, as the Face of Christ appears unveiled at last in this one dream. This is the gift the Holy Spirit holds for you from God your Father. Let today be celebrated both on earth and in your holy home as well. Be kind to both, as you forgive the trespasses you thought them guilty of, and see your innocence shining upon you from the Face of Christ.[603]

W 198 L 11. Now is there silence all around the world. Now is there stillness where before there was a frantic rush of thoughts that made no sense. Now is there tranquil light across the face of earth, made quiet in a dreamless sleep. And now the Word of God alone remains upon it. Only That can be perceived an instant longer. Then are symbols done, and everything you ever thought you made completely vanished from the mind which God forever knows to be His only Son.

W 198 L 12. There is no condemnation in him. He is perfect in his holiness. He needs no thoughts of mercy. Who could give him gifts when everything is his? And who could dream of offering forgiveness to the Son of Sinlessness Itself, so like to Him Whose Son he is, that to behold the Son is to perceive no more, and only know the Father? In this vision of the Son, so brief that not an instant stands between this single sight and timelessness itself, you see the vision of yourself and then you disappear forever into God. **W(446)**

W 198 L 13. Today we come still nearer to the end of everything that yet would stand between this vision and our sight. And we are glad that we have come this far, and recognize that He Who brought us here will not forsake us now. For He would give to us the gift that God has given us through Him today. Now is it[604] time for[605] your deliverance. The time has come. The time has come today. **W(447)**

Lesson 199 "I am not a body. I am free."

W 199 L 1. Freedom must be impossible as long as you perceive a body as yourself. The body is a limit. Who would seek for freedom in a body looks for it where it can not be found. The mind can be made free when it no longer sees itself as in a body, firmly tied to it, and sheltered by its presence. If this were the truth, the mind were vulnerable indeed!

W 199 L 2. The mind that serves the Holy Spirit is unlimited forever, in all ways, beyond the laws of time and space, unbound by any preconceptions, and with strength and power to do whatever it is asked. Attack thoughts cannot enter such a mind, because it has been given to the Source of Love, and[606] fear can never enter in a mind which has attached itself to Love. It rests in God, and who can be afraid who lives in Innocence and only loves?

W 199 L 3. It is essential for your progress in this course that you accept today's idea, and hold it very dear. Be not concerned that to the ego it is quite insane. The ego holds the body dear because it dwells in it, and lives united with the home that it has made. It is a part of the illusion which has sheltered it from being found illusory itself.

W 199 L 4. Here does it hide, and here it can be seen as what it is. Declare your innocence, and you are free. The body disappears because you have no need of it except the need the Holy Spirit sees. For this, the body will appear as useful form for what the mind must do. It thus becomes a vehicle which helps forgiveness be extended to the all-inclusive goal that it must reach, according to God's plan. **W(448)**

W 199 L 5. Cherish today's idea, and practice it today and every day. Make it a part of every practice period you take. There is no thought that will not gain thereby in power to help the world, nor none which will not gain in added gifts to you as well. We sound the call of freedom 'round the world with this idea. And would you be exempt from the acceptance of the gifts you give?

W 199 L 6. The Holy Spirit is the home of minds that seek for freedom. In Him they find[607] what they have sought. The body's purpose now is unambiguous. And it becomes perfect in the ability to serve an undivided goal. In conflict-free and unequivocal response to mind with but the thought of freedom as its goal, the body serves, and serves its purpose well. Without the power to enslave, it is a worthy servant of the freedom which the mind within the Holy Spirit seeks.

W 199 L 7. Be free today, and carry freedom as your gift to those who still believe they are enslaved within a body. Be you free, so that the Holy Spirit can make use of your escape from bondage to set free the many who perceive themselves as bound and helpless and afraid. Let love replace their fears through you. Accept salvation now, and give your mind to Him Who calls to you to make this gift to Him. For He would give you perfect freedom, perfect joy, and hope that finds its full accomplishment in God.

W 199 L 8. You are God's Son. In immortality you live forever. Would you not return your mind to this? Then practice well the thought the Holy Spirit gives you for today. Your brothers stand released with you in it; the world is blessed along with you, God's Son will weep no more, and Heaven offers thanks at[608] the increase of joy your practice brings even to it. And God Himself extends His Love and happiness each time you say:

> *"I am not a body. I am free.*
> *I hear the Voice that God has given me,*
> *And it is only this my mind obeys."* **W(449)**

Lesson 200 "There is no peace except the peace of God."

W 200 L 1. Seek you no further. You will not find peace except the peace of God.[609] Accept this fact, and save yourself the agony of yet more bitter disappointments, bleak despair, and sense of icy hopelessness and doubt. Seek you no further. There is nothing else

---

[601] Handwritten mark-up suggests (And).
[602] Handwritten mark-up suggests (it that) in place of "**truth which**".
[603] **Mark 11:25** "And when you stand praying, if you have anything against anyone, forgive *it* so that also your Father in Heaven may forgive you your trespasses."
[604] Handwritten mark-up suggests (the) in place of "**it**".
[605] Handwritten mark-up suggests (of) in place of "**for**".

[606] The *Urtext* manuscript has a sentence break here, with handwriting suggesting a comma instead. We agree with the handwriting on this one.
[607] Handwritten mark-up suggests (have found).
[608] Handwritten mark-up suggests (for) in place of "**at**".
[609] **Philippians 4:7** And the peace of God which passes all understanding shall keep your hearts and minds through Christ Jesus.
Collosians 3:15 And let the peace of God rule in your hearts, to which you also are called in one body, and be thankful.

for you to find except the peace of God, unless you seek for misery and pain.

W 200 L 2. This is the final point to which each one must come at last, to lay aside all hope of finding happiness where there is none; of being saved by what can only hurt; of making peace of chaos, joy of pain and Heaven out of hell. Attempt no more to win through losing, nor to die to live. You cannot but be asking for defeat.

W 200 L 3. Yet you can ask as easily for love, for happiness, and for eternal life in peace that has no ending. Ask for this, and you can only win. To ask for what you have already must succeed. To ask that what is false be true can only fail. Forgive yourself for vain imaginings,[610] and seek no longer what you cannot find. For what could be more foolish than to seek and seek and seek again for hell, when you have but to look with open eyes to find that Heaven lies before you, through a door which opens easily to welcome you?

W 200 L 4. Come home. You have not found your happiness in foreign places, and in alien forms which have no meaning to you,[611] though you sought to make them meaningful. This world is not where you belong.[612] You are a stranger here.[613] But it is given you to find the means whereby the world no longer seems to be a prison house for you[614] or anyone.[615] **W(450)**

W 200 L 5. Freedom is given you where you beheld but chains and iron doors. For[616] you must change your mind about the purpose of the world, if you would find escape. You will be bound 'til all the world is seen by you as blessed, and everyone made free of your mistakes and honored as he is.[617] You made him not; no more yourself. And as you free the one, the other is accepted as he is.

W 200 L 6. What does forgiveness do? In truth it has no function and does nothing, for it is unknown in Heaven. It is only hell where it is needed, and where it must serve a mighty function. Is not the escape of God's beloved Son from evil dreams which he imagines, yet believes are true, a worthy purpose? Who could hope for more while there appears to be a choice to make between success and failure; love and fear?

W 200 L 7. There is no peace except the peace of God because He has one Son, who cannot make a world in opposition to God's Will and to his own, which is the same as His. What could he hope to find in such a world? It cannot have reality because it never was created. Is it here that he would seek for peace? Or must he see that, as he looks on it, the world can but deceive? Yet can he learn to look on it another way, and find the peace of God.[618]

W 200 L 8. Peace is the bridge which everyone will cross to leave this world behind. But it[619] begins within the world perceived as different, and leading from this fresh perception to the gate of Heaven and the way beyond.[620] Peace is the answer to conflicting goals, to senseless journeys, frantic vain pursuits and meaningless endeavors. Now the way is easy, sloping gently toward the bridge where freedom lies within the peace of God. **W(451)**

W 200 L 9. Let us not lose our way again today. We go to Heaven, and the path is straight.[621] Only if you attempt to wander can there be delay, and needless wasted time on thorny byways. God alone is sure, and He will guide your footsteps. He will not desert His Son in need, nor let him stray forever from his home. The Father calls; the Son will hear. And that is all there is to what appears to be a world apart from God, where bodies have reality.

W 200 L 10. Now is there silence. Seek no further. You have come to where the road is carpeted with leaves of false desires, fallen from the trees of hopelessness you sought before. Now are they underfoot. And you look up and on toward Heaven, with the body's eyes but serving for an instant longer now. Peace is already recognized at last, and you can feel its soft embrace surround your heart and mind with comfort and with love.

W 200 L 11. Today we seek no idols.[622] Peace can not be found in them. The peace of God is ours, and only this will we accept and want. Peace be to us today. For we have found a simple, happy way to leave the world of ambiguity, and to replace our shifting goals and solitary dreams with single purpose and companionship. For peace is union if it be of God. We seek no further. We are close to home, and draw still nearer every time we say:

> *"There is no peace except the peace of God,*
> *And I am glad and thankful it is so."* **W(452)**

Review 6 (W 200 R6)
Introduction

September 1, 1970

W 200 R6 1. For this review, we take but one idea each day, and practice it as often as is possible. Besides the time you give morning and evening, which should not be less than fifteen minutes, and the hourly remembrances you make throughout the day, use the idea as often as you can between them. Each of these ideas alone would be sufficient for salvation, if it were learned truly. Each would be enough to give release to you and to the world from every form of bondage, and invite the memory of God to come again.

W 200 R6 2. With this in mind, we start our practicing in which we carefully review the thoughts the Holy Spirit has bestowed on us in our last twenty lessons. Each contains the whole curriculum, if understood, practiced, accepted and applied to all the seeming happenings throughout the day. One is enough. But for[623] that one, there must be no exceptions made. And so we need to use them all, and let them blend as one as each contributes to the whole we learn.

W 200 R6 3. These practice sessions, like our last review, are centered round a central theme with which we start and end each lesson. It is this:

> *"I am not a body. I am free.*

---

[610] **Acts 4:25** who by the mouth of Your servant David has said, "Why did the nations rage and the people imagine vain things?
[611] **Exo 18:2-3** then Jethro, Moses' father-in-law, took Zipporah, Moses' wife, after he had sent her back, and her two sons, of which the name of the one *was* Gershom (for he said, I have been an alien in a strange land),
[612] **John 18:36** Jesus answered, "My kingdom is not of this world. If My kingdom were of this world, then My servants would fight so that I might not be delivered to the Jews. But now My kingdom is not from here."
[613] **2 Samuel 15:19** Then the king said to Ittai the Gittite, Why do you also go with us? Return to your place, and stay with the king. For you *are* a stranger, and also an exile.
[614] Handwritten mark-up suggests (your prison house, the jail for anyone).
[615] **Acts 5:19** But the angel of *the* Lord opened the prison doors by night and brought them out, and said,
[616] Handwritten mark-up suggests (But).
[617] **Matthew 16:19** "And I will give you the keys of the kingdom of heaven, and whatever you bind on earth will be bound in heaven, and whatever you loose on earth will be loosed in heaven."
[618] **Mark 1:15** and saying, "The time is fulfilled, and the kingdom of God draws near. Repent, and believe the gospel."
[619] Handwritten mark-up suggests (peace).

[620] **Genesis 28:17** And he was afraid and said, "How awesome is this place! This is none other than the house of God, and this is the gate of heaven!"
[621] **Isaiah 40:3** The voice of one crying in the wilderness: "Prepare the way of the LORD; Make straight in the desert A highway for our God."
John 1:23 He said: "I am the voice of one crying in the wilderness: Make straight the way of the LORD,"
as the prophet Isaiah said.
[622] **Isaiah 19:3** And the spirit of Egypt shall fail in the midst of it, and I will destroy its wisdom. And they shall seek to idols, and to the enchanters, and to the mediums, and to the future-tellers.
Hosea 4:12 My people seek advice from their wooden *idols*, and their rod declares to them. For the spirit of harlotry has caused them to go astray, and they have gone lusting away from under their God.
[623] Handwritten mark-up suggests (from).

For I am still as God created me."

The day begins and ends with this. And we repeat it every time the hour strikes, or we remember, in between, we have a function that transcends the world we see. Beyond this, and a repetition of the special thought we practice for the day, no form of exercise is urged, except a deep relinquishment of everything that clutters up the mind, and makes it deaf to reason, sanity and simple truth.

W 200 R6 4. We will attempt to get beyond all words and special forms of practicing for this review. For we attempt this time to reach a quickened pace along a shorter path to the serenity and peace of God. We merely close our eyes, and then forget all that we thought we knew and understood. For thus is freedom given us from all we did not know and failed to understand. **W(453)**

W 200 R6 5. There is but one exception to this lack of structuring. Permit no idle thought to go unchallenged. If you notice it,[624] deny its hold and hasten to assure your mind that this is not what it would have. Then gently let the thought which you denied be given up in sure and quick exchange for the idea you[625] practice for the day.

W 200 R6 6. When you are tempted, hasten to proclaim your freedom from temptation, as you say:

"This thought I do not want. I choose instead . . ."

And then repeat the idea for the day, and let it take the place of what you thought. Beyond such special applications of each day's idea, we will add but[626] few formal expressions or specific thoughts to aid your[627] practicing. Instead we give these times of quiet to the Teacher Who instructs in quiet, speaks of peace, and gives our thoughts whatever meaning they may have.

W 200 R6 7. To Him I offer this review for you. I place you in His charge, and let Him teach you what to do and say and think each time you turn to Him. He will not fail to be available to you each time you call to Him to help you. Let us offer Him the whole review we now begin, and let us also not forget to Whom it has been given, as we practice, day by day, advancing toward the goal He set for us; allowing Him to teach us how to go, and trusting Him completely for the way each practice period can best become a loving gift of freedom to the world. **W(454)**

Lesson 201 "I am not a body. I am free. For I am still as God created me."

W 201 L 1. 181) "I trust my brothers, who are one with me."
No-one but is my brother. I am blessed
with oneness with the universe and God,
my Father, One[628] Creator of the Whole
that is my Self, forever One[629] with me.[630]

Lesson 202 "I am not a body. I am free. For I am still as God created me."

W 202 L 1. 182) "I will be still a moment and go home."
Why would I choose to stay an instant more
where I do not belong, when God Himself
has given me His Voice to call me home?

Lesson 203 "I am not a body. I am free. For I am still as God created me."

W 203 L 1. 183) "I call upon God's Name and on my own."

---

[624] Handwritten mark-up suggests (one).
[625] Handwritten mark-up suggests (we).
[626] Handwritten mark-up suggests (a).
[627] Handwritten mark-up suggests (in) in place of "**your**".
[628] Handwritten mark-up suggests (one).
[629] Handwritten mark-up suggests (one).
[630] Handwritten mark-up suggests (Repeat theme.)

The Name of God is my deliverance
from every thought of evil and of sin,
because it is my own as well as His.

Lesson 204 "I am not a body. I am free. For I am still as God created me."

W 204 L 1. 184) "The Name of God is my inheritance."
God's Name reminds me that I am His Son,
not slave to time, unbound by laws which rule
the world of sick illusions, free in God,
forever and forever one with Him. **W(455)**

Lesson 205 "I am not a body. I am free. For I am still as God created me."

W 205 L 1. 185) "I want the peace of God."
The peace of God is everything I want.
The peace of God is my one goal; the aim
of all my living here, the end I seek,
my purpose and my function and my life
while I abide where I am not at home.

Lesson 206 "I am not a body. I am free. For I am still as God created me."

W 206 L 1. 186) "Salvation of the world depends on me."
I am entrusted with the gifts of God,
because I am His Son. And I would give
His gifts where He intended them to be.

Lesson 207 "I am not a body. I am free. For I am still as God created me."

W 207 L 1. 187) "I bless the world because I bless myself."
God's blessing shines upon me from within
my heart, where He abides. I need but turn
to Him, and every sorrow melts away
as I accept His boundless love for me.

Lesson 208 "I am not a body. I am free. For I am still as God created me."

W 208 L 1. 188) "The peace of God is shining in me now."
I will be still, and let the earth be still
along with me. And in that stillness, we
will find the peace of God. It is within
my heart, which witnesses to God Himself. **W(456)**

Lesson 209 "I am not a body. I am free. For I am still as God created me."

W 209 L 1. 189) "I feel the Love of God within me now."
The Love of God is what created me.
The Love of God is everything I am.
The Love of God proclaimed me as His Son.
The Love of God within me sets me free.

Lesson 210 "I am not a body. I am free. For I am still as God created me."

W 210 L 1. 190) "I choose the joy of God instead of pain."
Pain is my own idea. It is not
a thought of God, but one I thought apart

from Him and from His Will. His Will is joy
and only joy for His beloved Son.
And that I choose instead of what I made.

Lesson 211 "I am not a body. I am free. For I am still as God created me."

W 211 L 1. 191) "I am the holy Son of God Himself."
In silence and in true humility
I seek God's glory, to behold it in
the Son whom He created as my Self.

Lesson 212 "I am not a body. I am free. For I am still as God created me."

W 212 L 1. 192) "I have a function God would have me fill."
I seek the function that would set me free
from all the vain illusions of the world.
Only the function God has given me
can offer freedom. Only this I seek,
and only this will I accept as mine. **W(457)**

Lesson 213 "I am not a body. I am free. For I am still as God created me."

W 213 L 1. 193) "All things are lessons God would have me learn."
A lesson is a miracle which God
offers to me, in place of thoughts I made
that hurt me. What I learn of Him becomes
the way I am set free. And so I choose
to learn His lessons, and forget my own.

Lesson 214 "I am not a body. I am free. For I am still as God created me."

W 214 L 1. 194) "I place the future in the hands of God."
The past is gone; the future is not yet.
Now am I freed from both. For what God gives
can only be for good. And I accept
but what He gives as what belongs to me.

Lesson 215 "I am not a body. I am free. For I am still as God created me."

W 215 1. 195) "Love is the way I walk in gratitude."
The Holy Spirit is my only Guide.
He walks with me in love. And I give thanks
to Him for showing me the way to go.

Lesson 216 "I am not a body. I am free. For I am still as God created me."

W 216 L 1. 196) "It can be but myself I crucify."
All that I do I do unto myself.
If I attack, I suffer. But if I
forgive, salvation will be given me. **W(458)**

Lesson 217 "I am not a body. I am free. For I am still as God created me."

W 217 L 1. 197) "It can be but my gratitude I earn."
Who should give thanks for my salvation but
myself? And how but through salvation can
I find the Self to Whom my thanks are due?

Lesson 218 "I am not a body. I am free. For I am still as God created me."

W 218 L 1. 198) "Only my condemnation injures me."
My condemnation keeps my vision dark,
and through my sightless eyes I cannot see
the vision of my glory. Yet today
I can behold this glory, and be glad.

Lesson 219 "I am not a body. I am free. For I am still as God created me."

W 219 L 1. 199) "I am not a body. I am free."
I am God's Son. Be still, my mind, and think
a moment upon this. And then return
to earth without confusion as to what
my Father loves forever as His Son.

Lesson 220 "I am not a body. I am free. For I am still as God created me."

W 220 L 1. 200) "There is no peace except the peace of God."
Let me not wander from the way of peace,
for I am lost on other roads than this.
But let me follow Him Who leads me home,
and peace is certain as the Love of God. **W(459)**

Introduction to Part 2 (W 220 IN2)

W 220 IN2 1. Words will mean little now. We use them but as guides on which we do not now depend. For now we seek direct experience of truth alone. The lessons which remain are merely introductions to the times in which we leave the world of pain, and go to enter into peace. Now we begin to reach the goal this course has set, and find the end toward which our practicing is geared.[631]

W 220 IN2 2. Now we attempt to let the exercise be merely a beginning. For we wait in quiet expectation for our God and Father. He has promised He will take the final step Himself. And we are sure His promises are kept. We have come far along the road, and now we wait for Him.

W 220 IN2 3. We will continue spending time with Him each morning and at night, as long as makes us happy. We will not consider time a matter of duration now. We use as much as we will need for the result that we desire. Nor will we forget our hourly remembrance, in between calling to God when we have need of Him as we are tempted to forget our goal.

W 220 IN2 4. We will continue with a central thought for all the days to come. And we will use that thought to introduce our times of rest, and calm our minds at need. Yet we will not content ourselves with simple practicing in the remaining holy instants which conclude the year that we have given God. We say some simple words of welcome, and expect our Father to reveal Himself as He has promised. We have called on Him, and He has promised that His Son will not remain unanswered when he calls His Name. **W(460)**

W 220 IN2 5. Now do we come to Him with but His Word upon our minds and hearts,[632] and wait for Him to take the step to us that He has told us, through His Voice, He would not fail to take when we invited Him. He has not left His Son in all his madness, nor betrayed His trust in him. Has not His faithfulness earned Him the invitation that He seeks to make us happy? We will offer it, and it will be accepted. So our times with Him will now be spent. We say the words of invitation that His Voice suggests,[633] then we wait for Him to come to us.

W 220 IN2 6. Now is the time of prophecy fulfilled. Now are all ancient promises upheld and fully kept. No step remains for time to separate from its accomplishment. For now we cannot fail. Sit silently and wait upon your Father. He has willed to come to you when you have recognized it is your will He do so. And you could have never come this far unless you saw, however dimly, that it is your will.

W 220 IN2 7. I am so close to you, we[634] cannot fail. Father, we give these holy times to You in gratitude to Him Who taught us how to leave the world of sorrow, in exchange for its replacement given us by You. We look not backward now. We look ahead, and fix our eyes upon the journey's end. Accept these little gifts of thanks from us, as through Christ's vision we behold a world beyond the one we made, and take that world to be the full replacement of our own.

W 220 IN2 8. And now we wait in silence, unafraid, and certain of Your coming. We have sought to find our way by following the Guide You sent to us. We did not know the way, but You did not forget us. And we know that You will not forget us now. We ask but that Your ancient promises be kept which are Your Will to keep. We will with You in asking this. The Father and the Son, Whose holy Will created all that is, can fail in nothing. In this certainty, we undertake these last few steps to You, and rest in confidence upon Your Love, Which will not fail the Son who calls to You. **W(461)**

W 220 IN2 9. And so we start upon the final part of this one holy year, which we have spent together in the search for Truth and God, Who is Its one Creator.[635] We have found the way He chose for us, and made the choice to follow it as He would have us go.[636] His hand has held us up. His Thoughts have lit the darkness of our minds. His Love has called to us unceasingly since time began.

W 220 IN2 10. We had a wish that God would fail to have the Son whom He created of Himself. We wanted God to change Himself, and be what we would make of Him. And we believed that our insane desires were the truth. Now we are glad that this is all undone, and we no longer think illusions true. The memory of God is shimmering across the wide horizons of our minds. A moment more, and It will rise again. A moment more, and we who are God's Son are safely home, where He would have us be.

W 220 IN2 11. Now is the need for practice almost done. For in this final section we will come to understand that we need only call to God, and all temptations disappear. Instead of words, we need but feel His Love. Instead of prayer,[637] we need but call His Name. Instead of judging, we need but be still and let all things be healed. We will accept the way God's plan will end, as we received the way it started. Now is it complete. This year has brought us to eternity.

W 220 IN2 12. One further use for words we still retain. From time to time, instructions on a theme of special relevance will intersperse our daily lessons and the periods of wordless, deep experience which should come afterwards. These special thoughts should be reviewed each day, each one of them to be continued 'til the next is given you. They should be slowly read and thought about a little while, preceding one of the holy and blessed instants in the day. We give the first of these instructions now. **W(462)**

(1) What is forgiveness? (W 220 W1)

W 220 W1 1. Forgiveness recognizes what you thought your brother did to you has not occurred. It does not pardon sins and make them real. It sees there was no sin. And in this view are all your sins forgiven. What is sin except a false idea about God's Son? Forgiveness merely sees its falsity, and therefore lets it go. What then is free to take its place is now the Will of God.

W 220 W1 2. An unforgiving thought is one which makes a judgment that it will not raise to doubt, although it is untrue. The mind is closed, and will not be released. The thought protects projection, tightening its chains, so that distortions are more veiled and more obscure; less easily accessible to doubt, and further kept from reason. What can come between a fixed projection and the aim that it has chosen as its needed[638] goal?

W 220 W1 3. An unforgiving thought does many things. In frantic action it pursues its goal, twisting and overturning what it sees as interfering with its chosen path. Distortion is its purpose and the

---

[631] The Urtext manuscript just says "(PART II)". We added the words "Introduction to" and lowered the case.
[632] The Urtext manuscript, curiously, puts a sentence break in this spot, but the handwritten markup corrects it as shown here.
[633] Handwritten mark-up suggests (and).
[634] Handwritten mark-up suggests (you).
[635] **Isaiah 40:28** Have you not known? Have you not heard, that the everlasting God, the Lord, the Creator of the ends of the earth, does not grow weak nor weary? *There is* no searching of His understanding.
[636] **Isaiah 40:3** The voice of him who cries in the wilderness, Prepare ye the way of the Lord, make straight a highway in the desert for our God.
Isaiah 62:10 Pass! Pass through the gates; prepare the way of the people. Raise up! Raise up the highway; gather out the stones; lift up a banner for the peoples. **Matthew 7:13-14** "Go in through the narrow gate, for wide *is* the gate and broad *is* the way that leads to destruction, and many there are who go in through it. Because narrow *is* the gate and constricted *is* the way which leads to life, and there are few who find it."
Mark 1:3 The voice of one crying in the wilderness, "prepare the way of *the* Lord, make His paths straight."
[637] Handwritten mark-up suggests pluralizing "prayer" to become (prayers).
[638] Handwritten mark-up suggests (wanted).

means by which it would accomplish it as well. It sets about its furious attempts to smash reality without concern for anything that would appear to pose a contradiction to its point of view.

W 220 W1 4. Forgiveness, on the other hand, is still, and quietly does nothing. It offends no aspect of reality, nor seeks to twist it to appearance[639] that it likes. It merely looks and waits and judges not. He who would not forgive must judge, for he must justify his failure to forgive. But he who would forgive himself must learn to welcome truth exactly as it is.

W 220 W1 5. Do nothing, then, and let forgiveness show you what to do through Him Who is your Guide, your Savior and Defender,[640] strong in hope and certain of your ultimate success. He has forgiven you already, for such is His function, given Him by God. Now must you share His function, and forgive whom He has saved, whose sinlessness He sees, and whom He honors as the Son of God. **W(463)**

Lesson 221 "Peace to my mind. Let all my thoughts be still."

W 221 L 1. "Father, I come to You today to seek the peace that You alone can give. I come in silence. In the quiet of my heart, the deep recesses of my mind, I wait and listen for Your Voice. My Father, speak to me today. I come to hear Your Voice in silence and in certainty and love, sure You will hear my call and answer me."[641]

W 221 L 2. Now do we wait in quiet. God is here because we wait together. I am sure that He will speak to you, and you will hear. Accept my confidence, for it is yours. Our minds are joined. We wait with one intent; to hear our Father's answer to our call, to let our thoughts be still and find His peace, to hear Him speak to us of what we are, and to reveal Himself unto His Son. **W(464)**

Lesson 222 "God is with me. I live and breathe in Him."

W 222 L 1. God is with me. He is my Source of life, the life within, the air I breathe, the food by which I am sustained, the water which renews and cleanses me. He is my home, wherein I live and move; the Spirit Which directs my actions, offers me Its Thoughts, and guarantees my safety from all pain. He covers me with kindness and with care, and holds in love the Son He shines upon, who also shines on Him. How still is he who knows the truth of what He speaks today!

W 222 L 2. *"Father, we have no words except Your Name upon our lips and in our minds, as we come quietly into Your Presence now, and ask to rest with You in peace a while."* **W(465)**

Lesson 223 "God is my life. I have no life but His."

W 223 L 1. I was mistaken when I thought I lived apart from God, a separate entity which moved in isolation, unattached, and housed within a body. Now I know my life is God's, I have no other home, and I do not exist apart from Him. He has no Thoughts that are not part of me, and I have none but Those which are of Him.

W 223 L 2. *"Our Father, let us see the face of Christ instead of our mistakes. For we who are Your holy Son,[642] are sinless.*

We would look upon our sinlessness, for guilt proclaims that we are not Your Son. And we would not forget You longer. We are lonely here, and long for Heaven where we are at home. Today we would return. Our name is Yours, and we acknowledge that we are Your Son." **W(466)**

Lesson 224 "God is my Father, and He loves His Son."

W 224 L 1. My true identity is so secure, so lofty, sinless, glorious and great, wholly beneficent and free from guilt, that Heaven looks to It to give it light. It lights the world as well. It is the gift my Father gave me, and the one as well I give the world. There is no gift but This that can be either given or received. This is reality, and only This. This is illusion's end. It is the Truth.

W 224 L 2. *"My Name, oh Father, still is known to You. I have forgotten it, and do not know where I am going, who I am, or what it is I do. Remind me, Father, now, for I am weary of the world I see. Reveal what You would have me see instead."* **W(467)**

Lesson 225 "God is my Father, and His Son loves Him."

W 225 L 1. "Father, I must return Your Love for me. For giving and receiving are the same, and You have given all Your Love to me. I must return It, for I want It mine in full awareness, blazing in my mind, and keeping it within Its kindly light, inviolate, beloved, with fear behind and only peace ahead. How still the way Your loving Son is led along to You!"

W 225 L 2. Brother, we find that stillness now. The way is open. Now we follow it in peace together. You have reached your hand to me, and I will never leave you. We are one, and it is but this oneness that we seek as we accomplish these few final steps which end a journey that was not begun. **W(468)**

Lesson 226 "My home awaits me. I will hasten there."

W 226 L 1. If I so choose, I can depart this world entirely. It is not death which makes this possible, but it is change of mind about the purpose of the world. If I believe it has a value as I see it now, so will it still remain for me. But if I see no value in the world as I behold it, nothing that I want to keep as mine or search for as a goal, it will depart from me. For I have not sought for illusions to replace the truth.

W 226 L 2. *"Father, my home awaits my glad return. Your arms are open, and I hear Your Voice. What need have I to linger in a place of vain desires and of broken dreams, when Heaven can so easily be mine?"* **W(469)**

Lesson 227 "This is my holy instant of release."

W 227 L 1. "Father, it is today that I am free, because my will is Yours. I thought to make another will. Yet nothing that I thought apart from You exists. And I am free because I was mistaken, and did not affect my own reality at all by my illusions. Now I give them up, and lay them down before the feet of truth, to be removed

---

[639] Handwritten mark-up suggests (appearances it likes.)
[640] Handwritten mark-up suggests (Protector) in place of "**Defender**".
[641] John 11:41 Then they took away the stone where the dead was laid. And Jesus lifted up *His* eyes and said, Father, I thank You that You have heard Me.
[642] The original *Urtext* manuscript has "**Son**" in the singular, while the handwritten editing adds the "**s**" in each instance in this paragraph. The plural form is grammatically more appropriate. However the *Notes* and FIP both have the singular form.

Throughout the Course the plural and singular forms of words for relatives are both used with great frequency, e.g. child and children, son and sons, brother and brothers. There seems little significance to the choice of

singular or plural since "God has only ONE Son" (T 2 E 16 (43)) The entire paragraph from Chapter II is probably worth quoting in the context of the singular/plural consideration: "If all the Souls God created ARE His Sons, then every Soul MUST be an integral part of the whole Sonship. You do not find the concept that the whole is greater than its parts difficult to understand. You should, therefore, not have too much trouble in understanding this. The Sonship in its Oneness DOES transcend the sum of its parts. However, this is obscured as long as any of its parts are missing. That is why the conflict cannot ultimately be resolved until ALL the parts of the Sonship have returned. Only then can the meaning of wholeness, in the true sense, be fully understood."

forever from my mind. This is my holy instant of release. Father, I know my will is one with Yours."

W 227 L 2. And so today we find our glad return to Heaven, which we never really left. The Son of God this day lays down his dreams. The Son of God this day comes home again, released from sin and clad in holiness, with his right mind restored to him at last. **W(470)**

Lesson 228 "God has condemned me not. No more do I."

W 228 L 1. My Father knows my holiness. Shall I deny His knowledge, and believe in what His knowledge makes impossible? Shall I accept as true what He proclaims as false? Or shall I take His Word for what I am since He is my Creator, and the One Who knows the true condition of His Son?

> **W 228 L 2.** *"Father, I was mistaken in myself, because I failed to realize the Source from which I came. I have not left that Source to enter in a body and to die. My holiness remains a part of me, as I am part of You. And my mistakes about myself are dreams. I let them go today. And I stand ready to receive Your Word alone for what I really am."* **W(471)**

Lesson 229 "Love, Which created me, is what I am."

W 229 L 1. I seek my own identity, and find it in these words: "Love, Which created me, is what I am." Now need I seek no more. Love has prevailed. So still it waited for my coming home, that I will turn away no longer from the holy face of Christ. And what I look upon attests the truth of the identity I sought to lose, but which my Father has kept safe for me.

> **W 229 L 2.** *"Father, my thanks to You for what I am; for keeping my identity untouched and sinless in the midst of all the thoughts of sin my foolish mind made up. And thanks to You for saving me from them. Amen."* **W(472)**

Lesson 230 "Now will I seek and find the peace of God."

W 230 L 1. In peace I was created. And in peace do I remain. It is not given me to change my Self. How merciful is God my Father, that when He created me He gave me peace forever. Now I ask but to be what I am. And can this be denied me when it is forever so[643]?

> **W 230 L 2.** *"Father, I seek the peace you gave as mine in my creation.[644] What was given then must be here now, for my creation was apart from time and still remains beyond all change. The peace in which Your Son was born into Your Mind is shining there unchanged. I am as You created me. I need but call on You to find the peace You gave. It is Your Will that gave it to Your Son."* **W(473)**

(2) What is salvation? (W 230 W2)

W 230 W2 1. Salvation is a promise, made by God, that you would find your way to Him at last. It cannot not[645] be kept. It guarantees that time will have an end, and all the thoughts that[646] have been born in time will end as well. God's Word is given every mind which thinks that it has separate thoughts, and will replace these thoughts of conflict with the Thought of peace.

W 230 W2 2. The Thought of peace was given to God's Son the instant that his mind had thought of war. There was no need for such a Thought before, for peace was given without opposite, and merely was. But when the mind is split, there is a need of healing.

So the Thought Which[647] has the power to heal the split became a part of every fragment of the mind which still was one, but failed to recognize its oneness. Now it did not know itself, and thought its own identity was lost.

W 230 W2 3. Salvation is undoing in the sense that it does nothing, failing to support the world of dreams and malice. Thus it lets illusions go. By not supporting them, it merely lets them quietly go down to dust. And what they hid is now revealed; an altar to the holy Name of God whereon His Word is written, with the gifts of your forgiveness laid before It, and the memory of God not far behind.

W 230 W2 4. Let us come daily to this holy place, and spend a while together. Here we share our final dream. It is a dream in which there is no sorrow, for it holds a hint of all the glory given us by God. The grass is pushing through the soil, the trees are budding now, and birds have come to live within their branches. Earth is being born again in new perception. Night has gone, and we have come together in the light.

W 230 W2 5. From here we give salvation to the world, for it is here salvation was received. The song of our rejoicing is the call to all the world that freedom is returned, that time is almost over, and God's Son has but an instant more to wait until his Father is remembered, dreams are done, eternity has shined away the world, and only Heaven now exists at all. **W(474)**

Lesson 231 "Father, I will but to remember You."

> **W 231 L 1.** *"What can I seek for, Father, but Your Love? Perhaps I think I seek for something else; a something I have called by many names. Yet is Your Love the only thing I seek, or ever sought. For there is nothing else that I could ever really want to find. Let me remember You. What else could I desire but the truth about myself?"*

W 231 L 2. This is your will, my brother. And you share this will with me, and with the One as well Who is our Father. To remember Him is Heaven. This we seek. And only this is what it will be given us to find. **W(475)**

Lesson 232 "Be in my mind, my Father, through the day."

> **W 232 L 1.** *"Be in my mind, my Father, when I wake, and shine on me throughout the day today. Let every minute be a time in which I dwell with You. And let me not forget my hourly thanksgiving that You have remained with me, and always will be there to hear my call to You and answer me. As evening comes, let all my thoughts be still of You and of Your Love, and let me sleep sure of my safety, certain of Your care, and happily aware I am Your Son."*

W 232 L 2. This is as every day should be. Today practice the end of fear. Have faith in Him Who is your Father. Trust all things to Him. Let Him reveal all things to you, and be you undismayed because you are His Son. **W(476)**

Lesson 233 "I give my life to God to run[648] today."

> **W 233 L 1.** *"Father, I give You all my thoughts today. I would have none of mine. In place of them give me Your own. I give You all my acts as well, that I may do Your Will instead of seeking goals which cannot be obtained, and wasting time in vain imaginings. Today I come to You. I will step back and merely follow You. Be You the Guide, and I the follower who questions not the wisdom of the Infinite, nor Love Whose tenderness I cannot comprehend, but which is yet Your perfect gift to me."*

---

[643] Handwritten mark-up suggests (true).
[644] **Genesis 1:27** So God created man in his *own* image, in the image of God created he him; male and female created he them.
[645] Handwritten mark-up suggests (but) in place of "**and**".
[646] Handwritten mark-up suggests (which).

[647] Handwritten mark-up suggests (That).
[648] Handwritten mark-up suggests (guide).

W 233 L 2. Today we have one Guide to lead us on. And as we walk together, we will give this day to Him with no reserve at all. This is His day. And so it is a day of countless gifts and mercies unto us. **W(477)**

Lesson 234 "Father, today I am Your Son again."

W 234 L 1. Today we will anticipate the time when dreams of sin and guilt are gone, and we have reached again[649] the holy place we never left. Merely a tiny instant has elapsed between eternity and timelessness. So brief the interval there was no lapse in continuity, nor break in thoughts which are forever unified as one. Nothing has ever happened to disturb the peace of God the Father and the Son. This we accept as wholly true today.

> **W 234 L 2.** *"We thank you, Father, that we cannot lose the memory of You and of Your Love. We recognize our safety, and give thanks for all the gifts You have bestowed on us, for all the loving help we have received, for Your eternal patience, and the Word Which You have given us that we are saved."* **W(478)**

Lesson 235 "God in His mercy wills that I be saved."

W 235 L 1. I need but look upon all things that seem to hurt me, and with perfect certainty assure myself, "God wills that I be saved from this," and merely watch them disappear. I need but keep in mind my Father's Will for me is only happiness, to find that only happiness has come to me. And I need but remember that His[650] Love surrounds His Son and keeps his sinlessness forever perfect, to be sure that I am saved and safe forever in His arms. I am the Son He loves. And I am saved because God in His mercy wills it so.

> **W 235 L 2.** *"Father, Your holiness is mine. Your Love created me, and made my sinlessness forever part of You. I have no guilt nor sin in me, for there is none in You."* **W(479)**

Lesson 236 "I rule my mind, which I alone must rule."

W 236 L 1. I have a kingdom I must rule. At times, it does not seem I am its king at all. It seems to triumph over me, and tell me what to think, and what to do and feel. And yet it has been given me to serve whatever purpose I perceive in it. My mind can only serve. Today I give its service to the Holy Spirit, to employ as He sees fit. I thus direct my mind, which I alone can rule. And thus I set it free, to do the Will of God.

> **W 236 L 2.** *"Father, my mind is open to Your Thoughts, and closed today to every thought but Yours. I rule my mind, and offer it to You. Accept my gift, for it is Yours to me."* **W(480)**

Lesson 237 "Now would I be as God created me."

W 237 L 1. Today I will accept the truth about myself. I will arise in glory, and allow the light in me to shine upon the world throughout the day.[651] I bring the world the tidings of salvation that[652] I hear as God my Father speaks to me. And I behold the world that Christ would have me see, aware it ends the bitter dream of death; aware it is my Father's call to me.

> **W 237 L 2.** *"Christ is my eyes today, and His the ears which listen to the Voice of God today. Father, I come to You through Him Who is Your Son and my true Self as well. Amen."* **W(481)**

Lesson 238 "On my decision all salvation rests."

W 238 L 1. *"Father, Your trust in me has been so great I must be worthy. You created me, and know me as I am. And yet You placed Your Son's salvation in my hands, and let it rest on my decision. I must be beloved of You indeed. And I must be steadfast in holiness as well, that You would give Your Son to me in certainty that He is safe Who still is part of You, and yet is mine because He is my Self."*

W 238 L 2. And so again today we pause to think how much our Father loves us. And how dear His Son, created by His Love, remains to Him Whose Love is made complete in him. **W(482)**

Lesson 239 "The glory of my Father is my own."

W 239 L 1. Let not the truth about ourselves today be hidden by a false humility. Let us instead be thankful for the gifts our Father gave us. Can we see in those with whom He shares His glory any trace of sin and guilt? And can it be that we are not among them, when He loves His Son forever and with perfect constancy, knowing he is as He created him?

> **W 239 L 2.** *"We thank you, Father, for the light that shines forever in us. And we honor it, because You share it with us. We are one, united in this light and one with You, at peace with all creation and ourselves."* **W(483)**

Lesson 240 "Fear is not justified in any form."

W 240 L 1. Fear is deception. It attests that you have seen yourself as you could never be, and therefore look upon a world which is impossible. Not one thing in this world is true. It does not matter what the form in which it may appear. It witnesses but to your own illusions of yourself. Let us not be deceived today. We are the Son of God. There is no fear in us, for we are each a part of Love Itself.

> **W 240 L 2.** *"How foolish are our fears! Would You allow Your Son to suffer? Give us faith today to recognize Your Son and set him free. Let us forgive him in Your Name, that we may understand his holiness, and feel the love for him that[653] is Your own as well."* **W(484)**

(3) What is the world? (W 240 W3)

W 240 W3 1. The world is false perception. It is born of error, and it has not left its source. It will remain no longer than the thought which gave it birth is cherished. When the thought of separation has been changed to one of true forgiveness, will the world be seen in quite another light; and one which leads to truth, where all the world must disappear, and all its errors vanish. Now its source has gone, and its effects are gone as well.

W 240 W3 2. The world was made as an attack on God. It symbolizes fear. And what is fear except love's absence? Thus the world was meant to be a place where God could enter not, and where His Son could be apart from Him. Here was perception born, for knowledge could not cause such insane thoughts. But eyes deceive, and ears hear falsely. Now mistakes become quite possible, for certainty has gone.

W 240 W3 3. The mechanisms of illusion have been born instead. And now they go to find what has been given them to seek. Their aim is to fulfill the purpose which the world was made to witness and make real. They see in its illusions but a solid base where truth exists, upheld apart from lies. Yet everything which they report is but illusion which is kept apart from truth.

---

[649] The word "**again**" is crossed out in the *Urtext* manuscript.
[650] Handwritten mark-up suggests (God's).
[651] **Isaiah 60:1** Arise, shine;
 For your light has come!
 And the glory of the LORD is risen upon you.
[652] Handwritten mark-up suggests (which).

[653] Handwritten mark-up suggests (which).

W 240 W3 4. As sight was made to lead away from truth, it can be redirected. Sounds become the call of God, and[654] all perception can be given a new purpose by the One Whom God appointed Savior to the world. Follow His light and see the world as He beholds it. Hear His Voice alone in all that speaks to you. And let Him give you peace and certainty, which you have thrown away, but Heaven has preserved for you in Him.

W 240 W3 5. Let us not rest content until the world has joined our changed perception. Let us not be satisfied until forgiveness has been made complete. And let us not attempt to change our function. We must save the world. For we who made it must behold it through the eyes of Christ, that what was made to die can be restored to Everlasting Life. **W(485)**

Lesson 241 "This holy instant is salvation come."

W 241 L 1. What joy there is today! It is a time of special celebration. For today holds[655] out the instant to the darkened world where its release is set. The day has come when sorrows pass away and pain is gone. The glory of salvation dawns today upon a world set free. This is the time of hope for countless millions. They will be united now, as you forgive them all. For I will be forgiven by you today.

> **W 241 L 2.** *"We have forgiven one another now, and so we come at last to You again. Father, Your Son, who never left, returns to Heaven and his home. How glad are we to have our sanity restored to us, and to remember that we all are one."* **W(486)**

Lesson 242 "This day is God's. It is my gift to Him."

W 242 L 1. I will not lead my life alone today. I do not understand the world. And so to try to lead my life alone must be but foolishness. For[656] there is One Who knows all that is best for me. And He is glad to make no choices for me but the ones that lead to God. This day I give[657] to Him, for I would not delay my coming home, and it is He Who knows the way to Him.

> **W 242 L 2.** *"And so we give today to You. We come with wholly open minds. We do not ask for anything that we may think we want. Give us what You would have received by us. You know all our desires and our needs.[658] And You will give us everything we want and that will help us[659] find the way to You."* **W(487)**

Lesson 243 "Today I will judge nothing that occurs."

W 243 L 1. I will be honest with myself today. I will not think that I already know what must remain beyond my present grasp. I will not think I understand the whole from bits of my perception, which are all that I can see. Today I recognize that this is so. And so I am relieved of judgment[660] which I cannot make. Thus do I free myself and what I look upon, to be in peace as God created us.

> **W 243 L 2.** *"Father, today I leave creation free to be itself. I honor all the[661] parts, in which I am included. We are one because each part contains Your memory, and truth must shine in all of us as one."* **W(488)**

Lesson 244 "I am in danger nowhere in the world."

W 244 L 1. "Your Son is safe wherever he may be, for You are there with him. He need but call upon Your Name, and he will recollect his safety and Your Love, for they are one. How can he fear or doubt or fail to know he cannot suffer, be endangered, or experience unhappiness, when he belongs to You, beloved and loving, in the safety of Your Fatherly embrace?"

W 244 L 2. And there we are in truth. No storms can come into the hallowed haven of our home. In God are we secure. For what can come to threaten God Himself, or make afraid what will forever be a part of Him? **W(489)**

Lesson 245 "Your peace is with me, Father. I am safe."

W 245 L 1. "Your peace surrounds me, Father. Where I go, Your peace goes there with me. It sheds its light on everyone I meet. I bring it to the desolate and lonely and afraid. I give Your peace to those who suffer pain, or grieve for loss, or think they are bereft of hope and happiness. Send them to me, my Father. Let me bring Your peace with me. For I would save Your Son, as is Your Will, that I may come to recognize my Self."

W 245 L 2. And so we go in peace. To all the world we give the message that we have received. And thus we come to hear the Voice of God, Who speaks to us as we relate His Word; Whose Love we recognize because we share the Word that He has given unto us. **W(490)**

Lesson 246 "To love my Father is to love His Son."

W 246 L 1. Let me not think that I can find the way to God if I have hatred in my heart.[662] Let me not try to hurt God's Son and think that I can know his Father or my Self. Let me not fail to recognize myself, and still believe that my awareness can contain my Father; or my mind conceive of all the love my Father has for me, and all the love which I return to Him.

> **W 246 L 2.** *"I will accept the way You choose for me to come to You, my Father. For in that will I succeed, because it is Your Will. And I would recognize that what You will is what I will as well, and only that. And so I choose to love Your Son. Amen."* **W(491)**

Lesson 247 "Without forgiveness I will still be blind."

W 247 L 1. Sin is the symbol of attack. Behold it anywhere, and I will suffer. For forgiveness is the only means whereby Christ's vision comes to me. Let me accept what His sight shows me as the simple truth, and I am healed completely. Brother, come and let me look on you. Your loveliness reflects my own. Your sinlessness is mine. You stand forgiven, and I stand with you.

> **W 247 L 2.** *"So would I look on everyone today. My brothers are Your Sons. Your Fatherhood created them, and gave them all to me as part of You and my own Self as well. Today I honor You through them, and thus I hope this day to recognize my Self."* **W(492)**

---

[654] The *Urtext* manuscript has a sentence break here which handwritten editing changes to a comma. We agree with the handwriting.
[655] Originally typed "hold", the handwritten mark-up suggests (holds) so the statement changes from an injunction to "hold out the instant" to a statement that "today holds out the instant." This is what it is in the *Notes* and also in FIP.
[656] Handwritten mark-up suggests (But).
[657] Handwritten mark-up suggests changing "**This day I give**" to (I give this day).
[658] Handwritten mark-up suggests (wants).
[659] Handwritten mark-up suggests (we need in helping us to) in place of "**we want and that will help us**". The *Notes* has "want."
[660] Handwritten mark-up suggests making "**judgment**" plural (judgments).

[661] Handwritten mark-up suggests (its) instead of "**the**"
[662] **1 John 2:9** He who says he is in the light, and hates his brother, is in darkness until now.
1 John 4:20 If someone says, "I love God," and hates his brother, he is a liar; for he who does not love his brother whom he has seen, how can he love God whom he has not seen?

Lesson 248 "Whatever suffers is not part of me."

W 248 L 1. I have disowned the truth. Now let me be as faithful in disowning falsity. Whatever suffers is not part of me. What grieves is not myself. What is in pain is but illusion in my mind. What dies was never living in reality, and did but mock the truth about myself. Now I disown self-concepts and deceits and lies about the holy Son of God. Now am I ready to accept him back as God created him, and as he is.

> **W 248 L 2.** *"Father, my ancient love for You returns, and lets me love Your Son again as well. Father, I am as You created me. Now is Your Love remembered, and my own. Now do I understand that they are one."* **W(493)**

Lesson 249 "Forgiveness ends all suffering and loss."

W 249 L 1. Forgiveness paints a picture of a world where suffering is over, loss becomes impossible and anger makes no sense. Attack is gone, and madness has an end. What suffering is now conceivable? What loss can be sustained? The world becomes a place of joy, abundance, charity and endless giving. It is now so like to Heaven, that it quickly is transformed into the Light which it reflects. And so the journey which the Son of God began has ended in the Light from Which he came.

> **W 249 L 2.** *"Father, we would return our minds to you. We have betrayed them; held them in a vise of bitterness, and frightened them with thoughts of violence and death. Now would we rest again in You, as You created us."* **W(494)**

Lesson 250 "Let me not see myself as limited."

W 250 L 1. Let me behold the Son of God today, and witness to his glory. Let me not try to obscure the holy light in him, and see his strength diminished and reduced to frailty; nor perceive the lacks in him with which I would attack his sovereignty.

> **W 250 L 2.** *"He is Your Son, my Father. And today I would behold his gentleness instead of my illusions. He is what I am, and as I see him so I see myself. Today I would see truly, that this day I may at last identify with him."* **W(495)**

(4) What is Sin? (W 250 W4)

W 250 W4 1. Sin is insanity. It is the means by which the mind is driven mad, and seeks to let illusions take the place of truth. And being mad, it sees illusions where [663]truth should be, and where it really is. Sin gave the body eyes, for what is there the sinless would behold? What need have they of sights or sounds or touch? What would they hear or reach to grasp? What would they sense at all? To sense is not to know. And truth can be but filled with knowledge, and with nothing else.

W 250 W4 2. The body is the instrument the mind made in its striving[664] to deceive itself. Its purpose is to strive. Yet can the goal of striving change. And now the body serves a different aim for striving. What it seeks for now is chosen by the aim the mind has taken as replacement for the goal of self-deception. Truth can be its aim as well as lies. The senses then will seek instead for witnesses to what is true.

W 250 W4 3. Sin is the home of all illusions, which but stand for things imagined, issuing from thoughts which[665] are untrue. They are the "proof" that what has no reality is real. Sin "proves" God's Son is evil; timelessness must have an end; eternal Life must die. And God Himself has lost the Son He loves, with but corruption to complete Himself, His Will forever overcome by death, love slain by hate, and peace to be no more.

W 250 W4 4. A madman's dreams are frightening, and sin appears indeed to terrify. And yet what sin perceives is but a childish game. The Son of God may play he has become a body, prey to evil and to guilt, with but a little life that ends in death. But all the while his Father shines on him, and loves him with an everlasting Love Which his pretenses cannot change at all.[666]

W 250 W4 5. How long, oh Son of God, will you maintain the game of sin?[667] Shall we not put away these sharp-edged children's toys? How soon will you be ready to come home? Perhaps today? There is no sin. Creation is unchanged. Would you still hold return to Heaven back? How long, oh holy Son of God, how long? **W(496)**

Lesson 251 "I am in need of nothing but the truth."

W 251 L 1. I sought for many things, and found despair. Now do I seek but one, for in that one is all I need, and only what I need. All that I sought before I needed not, and did not even want. My only need I did not recognize. But now I see that I need only truth. In that, all needs are satisfied, all cravings end, all hopes are finally fulfilled and dreams are gone. Now have I everything that I could need. Now have I everything that I could want. And now at last I find myself at peace.

> **W 251 L 2.** *"And for that peace, our Father, we give thanks. What we denied ourselves You have restored, and only that is what we really want."* **W(497)**

Lesson 252 "The Son of God is my Identity."

W 252 L 1. My Self is holy beyond all the thoughts of holiness of which I now conceive. Its shimmering and perfect purity is far more brilliant than is any light that I have ever looked upon. Its love is limitless, with an intensity which holds all things within it in the calm of quiet certainty. Its strength comes not from burning impulses which move the world, but from the boundless Love of God Himself. How far beyond this world my Self must be, and yet how near to me and close to God.

> **W 252 L 2.** *"Father, You know my true Identity. Reveal It now to me who am Your Son, that I may waken to the truth in You, and know that Heaven is restored to me."* **W(498)**

Lesson 253 "My Self is ruler of the universe."

W 253 L 1. It is impossible that anything should come to me unbidden by myself. Even in this world, it is I who rule my destiny. What happens is what I desire. What does not occur is what I do not want to happen. This must I accept. For thus am I led past this world to my creations, children of my Will, in Heaven where my holy Self abides with them, and Him Who has created me.

> **W 253 L 2.** *"You are the Self Whom You created Son, creating like Yourself and one with You. My Self, Which rules the universe, is but Your Will in perfect union with my own, Which can but offer glad assent to Yours, that It may be extended to Itself."* **W(499)**

---

[663] Handwritten mark-up suggests (the).
[664] Handwritten mark-up suggests (efforts) in place of "**striving**".
[665] Handwritten mark-up suggests (that).

[666] **Jeremiah 31:3** The LORD has appeared of old to me, saying:
"Yes, I have loved you with an everlasting love;
Therefore with lovingkindness I have drawn you.

[667] **Psalm 13:1** How long, O LORD? Will You forget me forever? How long will You hide Your face from me?
Psalm 89:46 How long, LORD? Will You hide Yourself forever? Will Your wrath burn like fire?

Lesson 254 "Let every voice but God's be still in me."

W 254 L 1. *"Father, today I would but hear Your Voice. In deepest silence I would come to You, to hear Your Voice and to receive Your Word. I have no prayer but this: I come to You to ask You for the truth. And truth is but Your Will, Which I would share with You today."*

W 254 L 2. Today we let no ego[668] thoughts direct our words or actions. When such thoughts occur, we quietly step back and look at them, and then we let them go. We do not want what they would bring with them. And so we do not choose to keep them. They are silent now. And in the stillness, hallowed by His Love, God speaks to us and tells us of our Will,[669] as we have chosen to remember Him. **W(500)**

Lesson 255 "This day I choose to spend in perfect peace."

W 255 L 1. It does not seem to me that I can choose to have but peace today. And yet my God assures me that His Son is like Himself. Let me this day have faith in Him Who says I am God's Son. And let the peace I choose be mine today bear witness to the truth of what He says.[670] God's Son can have no cares, and must remain forever in the peace of Heaven. In His Name I give today to finding what my Father wills for me, accepting it as mine, and giving it to all my Father's Sons, along with me.

W 255 L 2. *"And so, my Father, would I pass this day with You. Your Son has not forgotten You. The peace You gave him still is in his mind, and it is there I choose to spend today."* **W(501)**

Lesson 256 "God is the only goal I have today."

W 256 L 1. The way to God is through forgiveness here. There is no other way. If sin had not been cherished by the mind, what need would there have been to find a[671] way to where you are? Who would still be uncertain? Who could be unsure of who he is? And who would yet remain asleep in heavy clouds of doubt about the holiness of him whom God created sinless? Here we can but dream. But we can dream we have forgiven him in whom all sin remains impossible, and it is this we choose to dream today. God is our goal; forgiveness is the means by which our minds return to Him at last.

W 256 L 2. *"And so, our Father, would we come to You in Your appointed way. We have no goal except to hear Your Voice, and find the way Your sacred Word has pointed out to us."* **W(502)**

Lesson 257 "Let me remember what my purpose is."

W 257 L 1. If I forget my goal, I can be but confused, unsure of what I am, and thus conflicted in my actions. No-one can serve contradicting goals and serve them well. Nor can he function without deep distress and great depression. Let us therefore be determined to remember what we want today, that we may unify our thoughts and actions meaningfully, and achieve only what God would have us do today.[672]

W 257 L 2. *"Father, forgiveness is Your chosen means for our salvation. Let us not forget* [673] *that we can have no will but Yours today. And thus our purpose must be Yours as well, if we would reach the peace You will for us."* **W(503)**

Lesson 258 "Let me remember that my goal is God."

W 258 L 1. All that is needful is to train our minds to overlook all little, senseless aims, and to remember that our goal is God. His memory is hidden in our minds, obscured but by our pointless little goals which offer nothing and do not exist. Shall we continue to allow God's grace to shine in unawareness, while the toys and trinkets of the world are sought instead? God is our only goal, our only Love. We have no aim but to remember Him.

W 258 L 2. *"Our goal is but to follow in the way that leads to You. We have no goal but this. What could we want but to remember You? What could we seek but our Identity?"* **W(504)**

Lesson 259 "Let me remember that there is no sin."

W 259 L 1. Sin is the only thought that makes the goal of God seem unobtainable. What else could blind us to the obvious, and make the strange and the distorted seem more clear? What else but sin engenders our attacks? What else but sin could be the source of guilt, demanding punishment and suffering? And what but this could be the source of fear, obscuring God's creation; giving love the attributes of fear and of attack?

W 259 L 2. *"Father, I would not be insane today. I would not be afraid of love, nor seek for refuge in its opposite. For love can have no opposite. You are the Source of everything that is. And everything that is remains with You and You with it."* **W(505)**

Lesson 260 "Let me remember God created me."

W 260 L 1. *"Father, I did not make myself, although in my insanity I thought I did. Yet, as Your Thought, I have not left my Source, remaining part of What created me. Your Son, my Father, calls on You today. Let me remember You created me. Let me remember my Identity. And let my sinlessness arise again before Christ's vision, through which I would look upon my brothers and myself today."*

W 260 L 2. Now is our Source remembered, and Therein we find our true Identity at last. Holy indeed are we, because our Source can know no sin. And we who are His Sons are like each other, and alike to Him. **W(506)**

(5) What is the Body? (W 260 W5)

W 260 W5 1. The body is a fence the Son of God imagines he has built to separate parts of his Self from other parts. It is within this fence he thinks he lives, to die as it decays and crumbles. For within this fence he thinks that he is safe from love. Identifying with his safety, he regards himself as what his safety is. How else could he be certain he remains within the body, keeping love outside?

W 260 W5 2. The body will not stay. Yet this he sees as double "safety". For the Son of God's impermanence is "proof" his fences work, and do the task his mind assigns to them. For if his oneness still remained untouched, who could attack and who could be attacked? Who could be victor? Who could be his prey? Who could

---

[668] Originally typed "evil", the handwritten mark-up suggests (ego) in place of "evil". The *Notes* has "ego."
[669] Handwritten mark-up suggests (will).
[670] **John 1:7-8** This man came for a witness, to bear witness of the Light, that all through him might believe. He was not that Light, but was sent to bear witness of that Light.
John 18:37 Pilate therefore said to Him, "Are You a king then?" Jesus answered, "You say rightly that I am a king. For this cause I was born, and for this cause I have come into the world, that I should bear witness to the truth. Everyone who is of the truth hears My voice."
[671] Handwritten mark-up suggests (the).

[672] Handwritten mark-up suggests (this day).
[673] Handwritten mark-up suggests inserting (today).

be victim? Who the murderer? And if he did not die, what "proof" is there that God's eternal Son has been[674] destroyed?

W 260 W5 3. The body is a dream. Like other dreams, it sometimes seems to picture happiness, but can quite suddenly revert to fear, where every dream is born. For only love creates in truth, and truth can never fear. Made to be fearful, must the body serve the purpose given it. But we can change the purpose which the body will obey by changing what we think that it is for.

W 260 W5 4. The body is the means by which God's Son returns to sanity. Though it was made to fence him into hell without escape, yet has the goal of Heaven been exchanged for the pursuit of hell. The Son of God extends his hand to reach his brother, and to help him walk along the road with him. Now is the body holy. Now it serves to heal the mind that it was made to kill.

W 260 W5 5. You will identify with what you think will make you safe. Whatever it may be, you will believe that it is one with you. Your safety lies in truth and not in lies. Love is your safety. Fear does not exist. Identify with love, and you are safe. Identify with love, and you are home. Identify with love, and find your Self. **W(507)**

Lesson 261 "God is my refuge and security."

W 261 L 1. I will identify with what I think is refuge and security. I will behold myself where I perceive my strength, and think I live within the citadel where I am safe, and cannot be attacked. Let me today seek not security in danger, nor attempt to find my peace in murderous attack. I live in God. In Him I find my refuge and my strength.[675] In Him is my Identity. In Him is everlasting peace. And only there will I remember Who I really am.

W 261 L 2. *"Let me not seek[676] for idols.[677] I would come, my Father, home to You today. I choose to be as You created me, and find the Son whom You created as my Self."[678]* **W(508)**

Lesson 262 "Let me perceive no differences today."

W 262 L 1. *"Father, You have one Son. And it is he that I would look upon today. He is Your one creation. Why should I perceive a thousand forms in what remains as one? Why should I give this one a thousand names, when only one suffices? For Your Son must bear Your Name, for You created him. Let me not see him as a stranger to his Father, nor as stranger to myself. For he is part of me and I of him, and we are part of You Who are our Source, eternally united in Your Love; eternally the holy Son of God."*

W 262 L 2. We who are one would recognize this day the truth about ourselves. We would come home, and rest in unity. For there is peace, and nowhere else can peace be sought and found.[679] **W(509)**

Lesson 263 "My holy vision sees all things as pure."

W 263 L 1. *"Father, Your Mind created all that is, Your Spirit entered into it; Your Love gave life to it. And would I look upon what You created as if it could be made sinful? I would not perceive such dark and fearful images. A madman's dream is hardly fit to be my choice, instead of all the loveliness with which You blessed creation; all its purity, its joy, and its eternal, quiet home in You."*

W 263 L 2. And while we still remain outside the gate of Heaven, let us look on all we see through holy vision and the eyes of Christ. Let all appearances seem pure to us, that we may pass them by in innocence, and walk together to our Father's house as brothers and the holy Sons of God.[680] **W(510)**

Lesson 264 "I am surrounded by the Love of God."

W 264 L 1. *"Father, You stand before me and behind, beside me, in the place I see myself, and everywhere I go.[681] You are in all the things I look upon, the sounds I hear, and every hand that reaches for my own. In You time disappears, and place becomes a meaningless belief. For what surrounds Your Son and keeps him safe is Love Itself. There is no Source but This, and nothing is that does not share Its holiness; that stands beyond Your one creation, or without the Love Which holds all things within Itself. Father, Your Son is like Yourself. We come to You in Your own Name today, to be at peace within Your everlasting Love."*

W 264 L 2. My brothers, join with me in this today. This is salvation's prayer. Must we not join in what will save the world, along with us? **W(511)**

Lesson 265 "Creation's gentleness is all I see."

W 265 L 1. I have indeed misunderstood the world, because I laid my "sins" on it, and saw them looking back at me. How fierce they seemed! And how deceived was I to think that what I feared was in the world, instead of in my mind alone. Today I see the world in the celestial gentleness with which creation shines. There is no fear in it. Let no appearance of my "sins" obscure the light of Heaven, shining on the world. What is reflected here is in God's Mind. The images I see reflect my thoughts. Yet is my mind at one with God's. And so I can perceive creation's gentleness.

W 265 L 2. *"In quiet would I look upon the world, which but reflects Your Thoughts and mine as well. Let me remember that they are the same, and I will see creation's gentleness."* **W(512)**

Lesson 266 "My holy Self abides in you, God's Son."

W 266 L 1. *"Father, You gave me all Your Sons, to be my Saviors and my Counselors in sight; the Bearers of Your holy Voice to me. In them are You reflected, and in them does Christ look back upon me from my Self. Let not Your Son forget his holy Name. Let not Your Son forget his holy Source. Let not Your Son forget his name is Yours."*

W 266 L 2. This day we enter into paradise,[682] calling upon God's Name and on our own, acknowledging our Self in each of us; united in the holy Love of God. How many Saviors God has given us! How can we lose the way to Him, when He has filled the world with those who point to Him, and given us the sight to look on them? **W(513)**

---

[674] Handwritten mark-up suggests (can be).
[675] **Psalm 46:1** God is our refuge and strength, A very present help in trouble.
[676] The *Urtext* manuscript says "**speak**" but handwriting (this appears **not** to be Helen's hand) crosses it out and puts (seek) which does seem to make more sense. This is also what the *Notes* has.
[677] **Hosea 4:12** My people seek advice from their wooden *idols*, and their rod declares to them. For the spirit of harlotry has caused them to go astray, and they have gone lusting away from under their God.
[678] **Genesis 1:27** And God created man in His image; in the image of God He created him. He created them male and female.
[679] **Psalms 34:14** Depart from evil, and do good; seek peace, and pursue it.

[680] **John 14:2** In My Father's house are many mansions; if it were not so, I would have told you. I go to prepare a place for you.
[681] **Psalm 139:5** You have hedged me behind and before, And laid Your hand upon me.
[682] **Luke 23:43** And Jesus said to him, "Assuredly, I say to you, today you will be with Me in Paradise."

Lesson 267 "My heart is beating in the peace of God."

W 267 L 1. Surrounding me is all the life that God created in His Love. It calls to me in every heartbeat and in every breath; in every action and in every thought. Peace fills[683] my heart, and floods my body with the purpose of forgiveness. Now my mind is healed, and all I need to save the world is given me. Each heartbeat brings me peace; each breath infuses me with strength. I am a messenger of God, directed by His Voice, sustained by Him in love, and held forever quiet and at peace within His loving arms. Each heartbeat calls His Name, and every one is answered by His Voice, assuring me I am at home in Him.

W 267 L 2. *"Let me attend Your Answer, not my own. Father, my heart is beating in the peace the Heart of Love created. It is there and only there that I can be at home."* **W(514)**

Lesson 268 "Let all things be exactly as they are."

W 268 L 1. *"Let me not be Your critic, Lord, today, and judge against You. Let me not attempt to interfere with Your creation, and distort it into sickly forms. Let me be willing to withdraw my wishes from its unity, and thus to let it be as You created it. For thus will I be able, too, to recognize my Self as You created me. In Love was I created, and in Love will I remain forever. What can frighten me when I let all things be exactly as they are?"*

W 268 L 2. Let not our sight be blasphemous today, nor let our ears attend to lying tongues. Only reality is free of pain. Only reality is free of loss. Only reality is wholly safe. And it is only this we seek today. **W(515)**

Lesson 269 "My sight goes forth to look upon Christ's face."

W 269 L 1. *"I ask Your blessing on my sight today. It is the means which You have chosen to become the way to show me my mistakes, and look beyond them. It is given me to find a new perception through the Guide You gave to me. And through His lessons to surpass perception and return to truth. I ask for the illusion which transcends all those I made. Today I choose to see a world forgiven, in which everyone shows me the face of Christ, and teaches me that what I look upon belongs to me; that nothing is, except Your holy Son."*

W 269 L 2. Today our sight is blessed indeed. We share one vision, as we look upon the face of Him Whose Self is ours. We are one because of Him Who is the Son of God; of Him Who is our own Identity. **W(516)**

Lesson 270 "I will not use the body's eyes today."

W 270 L 1. *"Father, Christ's vision is Your gift to me, and it has power to translate all that the body's eyes behold into the sight of a forgiven world. How glorious and gracious is this world! Yet how much more will I perceive in it than sight can give. The world forgiven signifies Your Son acknowledges his Father, lets his dreams be brought to truth, and waits expectantly the one remaining instant more of time, which ends forever as Your memory returns to him. And now his will is one with Yours. His function now is but Your own, and every thought except Your own is gone."*

W 270 L 2. The quiet of today will bless our hearts, and through them peace will come to everyone. Christ is our eyes today. And through His sight we offer healing to the world through Him, the holy Son whom God created whole; the holy Son whom God created one. **W(517)**

(6) What is the Christ? (W 270 W6)

W 270 W6 1. Christ is God's Son as He created him. He is the Self we share, uniting us with one another, and with God as well. He is the Thought Which still abides within the Mind That is His Source. He has not left His holy home, nor lost the innocence in which He was created. He abides unchanged forever in the Mind of God.

W 270 W6 2. Christ is the link that keeps you one with God, and guarantees that separation is no more than an illusion of despair. For hope forever will abide in Him. Your mind is part of His, and His of yours. He is the part in Which God's Answer lies; where all decisions are already made, and dreams are over. He remains untouched by anything the body's eyes perceive. For though in Him His Father placed the means for your salvation, yet does He remain the Self Who, like His Father, knows no sin.

W 270 W6 3. Home of the Holy Spirit, and at home in God alone, does Christ remain at peace, within the Heaven of your holy mind. This is the only part of you that has reality in truth. The rest is dreams. Yet will these dreams be given unto Christ to fade before His glory, and reveal your holy Self, the Christ, to you at last.

W 270 W6 4. The Holy Spirit reaches from the Christ in you to all your dreams, and bids them come to Him, to be translated into truth. He will exchange them for the final dream which God appointed as the end of dreams. For when forgiveness rests upon the world and peace has come to every Son of God, what could remain[684] to keep things separate, for what remains to see except Christ's face?[685]

W 270 W6 5. And how long will this holy face be seen, when it is but the symbol that the time for learning now is over, and the goal of the Atonement has been reached at last? So therefore let us seek to find Christ's face, and look on nothing else. As we behold His glory, will we know we have no need of learning or perception or of time, or anything except the holy Self, the Christ Whom God created as His Son. **W(518)**

Lesson 271 "Christ's is the vision I will use today."

W 271 L 1. Each day, each hour, every instant, I am choosing what I want to look upon, the sounds I want to hear, the witnesses to what I want to be the truth for me. Today I choose to look upon what Christ would have me see, to listen to God's Voice, and seek the witnesses to what is true in God's creation. In Christ's sight, the world and God's creation meet, and as they come together all perception disappears. His kindly sight redeems the world from death. For nothing that He looks upon on but must live, remembering the Father and the Son; Creator and Creation unified.

W 271 L 2. *"Father, Christ's vision is the way to You. What He beholds invites Your memory to be[686] restored to me. And this I choose to be what I would look upon today."* **W(519)**

Lesson 272 "How can illusions satisfy God's Son?"

W 272 L 1. *"Father, the truth belongs to me. My home is set in Heaven by Your Will and mine. Can dreams content me? Can illusions bring me happiness? What but Your memory can satisfy Your Son? I will accept no less than You have given me.*

---

[683] The *Urtext* manuscript has "stills" corrected by handwriting to "fills" which is what is in the *Notes*.

[684] Handwritten mark-up suggests (there be) in place of "**remain**". The *Notes* has "remain."
[685] **2 Corinthians 4:6** Seeing it is God, that said, Light shall shine out of darkness, who shined in our hearts, to give the light of the knowledge of the glory of God in the face of Jesus Christ.
[686] The word "**be**" is not in the *Urtext* manuscript which has a grammatically impossible sentence here. *FIP* inserts "**be**" as do we, guessing this what was intended. The *Notes* also has this reading.

I am surrounded by Your Love, forever still, forever gentle and forever safe. God's Son must be as You created him."

W 272 L 2. Today we pass illusions by. And if we hear temptation call to us to stay and linger in a dream, we turn aside and ask ourselves if we, the Sons of God, could be content with dreams, when Heaven can be chosen just as easily as hell, and love will happily replace all fear. **W(520)**

Lesson 273 "The stillness of the peace of God is mine."

W 273 L 1. Perhaps we are now ready for a day of undisturbed tranquility. If this is not yet feasible, we are content and even more than satisfied to learn how such a day can be achieved. If we give way to a disturbance, let us learn how to dismiss it and return to peace. We need but tell our minds, with certainty, "The stillness of the peace of God is mine," and nothing can intrude upon the peace that God Himself has given to His Son.

W 273 L 2. *"Father, Your peace is mine. What need have I to fear that anything can rob me of what You would have me keep? I cannot lose Your gifts to me. And so the peace You gave Your Son is with me still, in quietness and in my own eternal love for You."* **W(521)**

Lesson 274 "Today belongs to Love. Let me not fear."

W 274 L 1. *"Father, today I would let all things be as You created them, and give Your Sons[687] the honor due their[688] sinlessness; the love of brother to his brother and his friend. Through this I am redeemed. Through this as well the truth will enter where illusions were, light will replace all darkness, and Your Son will know he is as You created him."*

W 274 L 2. A special blessing comes to us today from Him Who is our Father. Give this day to Him and there will be no fear today, because the day is given unto Love. **W(522)**

Lesson 275 "God's healing Voice protects all things today."

W 275 L 1. Let us today attend the Voice of God, Which speaks an ancient lesson, no more true today than any other day. Yet has this day been chosen as the time when we will seek and hear and learn and understand. Join me in hearing. For the Voice of God tells us of things we cannot understand alone, nor learn apart. It is in this that all things are protected. And in this the healing of the Voice of God is found.

W 275 L 2. *"Your healing Voice protects all things today, and so I leave all things to You. I need be anxious over nothing. For Your Voice will tell me what to do, and where to go; to whom to speak, and what to say to him; what thoughts to think; what words to give the world. The safety that I bring is given me. Father, Your Voice protects all things through me."* **W(523)**

Lesson 276 "The Word of God is given me to speak."

W 276 L 1. What is the Word of God? "My Son is pure, and holy as Myself." And thus did God become the Father of the Son He loves, for thus was he created. This the Word His Son did not create with Him, because in this His Son was born. Let us accept His Fatherhood, and all is given us. Deny we were created in His Love and we deny our Self, to be unsure of who we are, of who our Father is, and for what purpose we have come. And yet, we need but to acknowledge Him Who gave His Word to us in our creation, to remember Him and so[689] recall our Self.

W 276 L 2. *"Father, Your Word is mine. And it is this that I would speak to all my brothers, who are given me to cherish as my own, as I am loved and blessed and saved by You."* **W(524)**

Lesson 277 "Let me not bind Your Son with laws I made."

W 277 L 1. *"Your Son is free, my Father. Let me not imagine I have bound him with the laws I made to rule the body. He is not subject to any laws I made by which I try to make the body more secure. He is not changed by what is changeable. He is not slave to any laws of time. He is as You created him, because he knows no laws except the Law of Love."*

W 277 L 2. Let us not worship idols, nor believe in any laws idolatry would make to hide the freedom of the Son of God. He is not bound except by his beliefs. Yet what he is is far beyond his faith in slavery or freedom. He is free because he is his Father's Son. And he can not be bound unless God's Truth can lie, and God can will that He deceive Himself. **W(525)**

Lesson 278 "If I am bound, my Father is not free."

W 278 L 1. If I accept that I am prisoner within a body, in a world in which all things that seem to live appear to die, then is my Father prisoner with me. And this do I believe, when I maintain the laws the world obeys must I obey; the frailties and the sins which I perceive are real, and cannot be escaped. If I am bound in any way, I do not know my Father or my Self. And I am lost to all reality. For truth is free, and what is bound is not a part of truth.

W 278 L 2. *"Father, I ask for nothing but the truth. I have had many foolish thoughts about myself and my creation, and have brought a dream of fear into my mind. Today I would not dream. I choose the way to You instead of madness and instead of fear. For truth is safe and only love is sure."* **W(526)**

Lesson 279 "Creation's freedom promises my own."

W 279 L 1. The end of dreams is promised me, because God's Son is not abandoned by His Love. Only in dreams is there a time when he appears to be in prison, and awaits a future freedom if it be at all. Yet in reality his dreams are gone, with truth established in their place. And now is freedom his already. Should I wait in chains which have been severed for release, when God is offering me freedom now?

W 279 L 2. *"I will accept Your promises today, and give my faith to them. My Father loves the Son Whom He created as His Own. Would You withhold the gifts You gave to me?"* **W(527)**

Lesson 280 "What limits can I lay upon God's Son?"

W 280 L 1. Whom God created limitless is free. I can invent imprisonment for him, but only in illusions, not in truth. No Thought of God has left Its Father's Mind. No Thought of God is limited at all. No Thought of God but is forever pure. Can I lay limits on the Son of God, whose Father willed that he be limitless, and like Himself in freedom and in love?

W 280 L 2. *"Today let me give honor to Your Son, for thus alone I find the way to You. Father, I lay no limits on the Son You love, and You created limitless. The honor that I give to*

---

[687] Handwritten mark-up suggests (Son) in place of "**Sons**" making the following pronoun "**their**" singular (his) as well. The *Notes* has "and give Your Sons the honor due their ~~holiness~~; sinlessness"
[688] Handwritten mark-up suggests (his).

[689] Handwritten mark-up suggests (thus) in place of "**so**".

(7) What is the Holy Spirit? (W 280 W7)

W 280 W7 1. The Holy Spirit mediates between illusions and the truth. As[690] He must bridge the gap between reality and dreams, perception leads to knowledge through the grace that God has given Him, to be His gift to everyone who turns to Him for truth. Across the bridge that He provides are dreams all carried to the truth, to be dispelled before the light of knowledge. There are sights and sounds forever laid aside. And where they were perceived before, forgiveness has made possible perception's tranquil end.

W 280 W7 2. The goal the Holy Spirit's teaching sets is just this end of dreams. For sights and sounds must be translated from the witnesses of fear to those of love. And when this is entirely accomplished, learning has achieved the only goal it has in truth. For learning, as the Holy Spirit guides it to the outcome He perceives for it, becomes the means to go beyond itself, to be replaced by the Eternal Truth.

W 280 W7 3. If you but knew how much your Father yearns to have you recognize your sinlessness, you would not let His Voice appeal in vain, nor turn away from His replacement for the fearful images and dreams you made. The Holy Spirit understands the means you made, by which you would attain what is forever unattainable.[691] And if you offer them to Him, He will employ the means you made for exile, to restore your mind to where it truly is at home.

W 280 W7 4. From knowledge, where He has been placed by God, the Holy Spirit calls to you, to let forgiveness rest upon your dreams, and be restored to sanity and peace of mind. Without forgiveness will your dreams remain to terrify you. And the memory of all your Father's Love will not return to signify the end of dreams has come.

W 280 W7 5. Accept your Father's gift. It is a call from Love to Love, that It be but Itself. The Holy Spirit is His gift, by Which the quietness of Heaven is restored to God's beloved Son. Would you refuse to take the function of completing God, when all He wills is that you be complete? **W(529)**

Lesson 281 "I can be hurt by nothing but my thoughts."

W 281 L 1. *"Father, Your Son is perfect. When he[692] thinks that he is hurt in any way, it is because he has forgotten who he is,[693] and that he is as You created him. Your Thoughts can only bring me happiness. If ever I am sad or hurt or ill, I have forgotten what You think, and put my little, meaningless ideas in place of where Your Thoughts belong, and where They are. I can be hurt by nothing but my thoughts. The Thoughts I think with You can only bless. The Thoughts I think with You alone are true."*

W 281 L 2. I will not hurt myself today. For I am far beyond all pain. My Father placed me safe in Heaven, watching over me. And I would not attack the Son He loves, for what He loves is[694] mine to love as well. **W(530)**

Lesson 282 "I will not be afraid of love today."

W 282 L 1. If I could realize but this today, salvation would be reached for all the world. This the decision not to be insane, and to accept myself as God Himself, my Father and my Source, created me. This the determination not to be asleep in dreams of death, while truth remains forever living in the joy of life.[695] And this the choice to recognize the Self Whom God created as the Son He loves, and Who remains my one Reality.

W 282 L 2. *"Father, Your Name is Love, and so is mine. Such is the truth. And can the truth be changed by merely giving it another name? The name of fear is simply a mistake. Let me not be afraid of truth today."* **W(531)**

Lesson 283 "My true Identity abides in You."

W 283 L 1. *"Father, I made an image of myself, and it is this I call the Son of God. Yet is creation as it always was, for Your creation is unchangeable. Let me not worship idols. I am he my Father loves. His holiness remains the light of Heaven and the Love of God. Is not what is beloved of You secure? Is not the light of Heaven infinite? Is not Your Son my true Identity, when You created everything that is?"*

W 283 L 2. Now are we one in shared Identity, with God our Father as our only Source, and everything created part of us. And so we offer blessing to all things, uniting lovingly with all the world, which our forgiveness has made one with us. **W(532)**

Lesson 284 "I can elect to change all thoughts that hurt."

W 284 L 1. Loss is not loss when properly perceived. Pain is impossible. There is no grief with any cause at all[696] and suffering of any kind is nothing but a dream. Such[697] is the truth, at first to be but said, and then repeated many times, and next to be accepted as but partly true, with many reservations,[698] then to be considered seriously more and more, and finally accepted as the truth. I can elect to change all thoughts that hurt. And I would go beyond the[699] words today, go[700] past all reservations, and arrive at full acceptance of the truth in them.

W 284 L 2. *"Father, what You have given cannot hurt, and[701] grief and pain must be impossible. Let me not fail to trust in You today, accepting but the joyous as Your gifts; accepting but the joyous as the truth."* **W(533)**

Lesson 285 "My holiness shines bright and clear today."

W 285 L 1. Today I wake with joy, expecting but the happy things of God to come to me. I ask but them to come and realize my invitations[702] will be answered by the thoughts to which they[703] have been sent by me. And I will ask for only joyous things, the instant I accept my holiness. For what would be the use of pain to me; what purpose would my suffering fulfill; and how would grief and loss avail me, if insanity departs from me today, and I accept my holiness instead?

---

[690] Handwritten mark-up suggests (Since) in place of "**As**".
[691] The *Urtext* manuscript has "unobtainable" typed first and then corrected by hand to "unattainable" which is the reading in the *Notes*.
[692] This entire sentence is shifted in the mark-up to the First person: (When I think that I am hurt in any way, it is because I have forgotten who I am, and that I am as You created me.)
[693] In the *Urtext* manuscript, this comma is a period, a new sentence beginning with "And that he is ..."
[694] Handwritten mark-up suggests (also) here and deletes "**as well**" at the end of the sentence.
[695] They *Urtext* manuscript shows "**life**" here, with (love) handwritten in. The *Notes* clearly has "life" however.
[696] The *Urtext* manuscript has a sentence break here for some odd reason.
[697] Handwritten mark-up suggests (This).
[698] The *Urtext* manuscript has a sentence break here which doesn't seem like a good idea.
[699] Handwritten mark-up suggests (these) instead of "**the**".
[700] Handwritten mark-up suggests (and) instead of "**go**".
[701] Handwritten mark-up suggests (so) instead of "**and**".
[702] Handwritten mark-up suggests (invitation).
[703] Handwritten mark-up suggests (it).

W 285 L 2. *"Father, my holiness is Yours. Let me rejoice in it, and through forgiveness be restored to sanity. Your Son is still as You created him. My holiness is part of me and also part of You. And what can alter Holiness Itself?"* **W(534)**

Lesson 286 "The hush of Heaven holds my heart today."

W 286 L 1. *"Father, how still today! How quietly do all things fall in place! This is the day that has been chosen as the time in which I come to understand the lesson that there is no need that I do anything. In You is every choice already made. In You has every conflict been resolved. In You is everything I hope to find already given me. Your peace is mine. My heart is quiet, and my mind at rest. Your Love is Heaven, and Your Love is mine."*

W 286 L 2. The stillness of today will give us hope that we have found the way, and travelled far along it, to a wholly certain goal. Today we will not doubt the end which God Himself has promised us. We trust in Him, and in our Self, Who still is one with Him. **W(535)**

Lesson 287 "You are my goal, my Father. Only You."

W 287 L 1. Where would I go but Heaven? What could be a substitute for happiness? What gift could I prefer before the peace of God? What treasure would I seek and find and keep that can compare with my Identity? And would I rather live with fear than love?

W 287 L 2. *"You are my goal, my Father. What but You could I desire to have? What way but that which leads to You could I desire to walk? And what except the memory of You could signify to me the end of dreams and futile substitutions for the truth? You are my only goal. Your Son would be as You created Him. What way but this could I expect to recognize my Self, and be at one with my Identity?"* **W(536)**

Lesson 288 "Let me forget my brother's past today."

W 288 L 1. *"This is the thought that leads the way to You, and brings me to my goal. I cannot come to You without my brother. And to know my Source, I first must recognize what You created one with me. My brother's is the hand that leads me on the way to You. His sins are in the past along with mine,[704] and I am saved because the past is gone. Let me not cherish it within my heart, or I will lose the way to walk to You. My brother is my Savior. Let me not attack the Savior You have given me. But let me honor him who bears Your Name, and so remember that It is my own."*

W 288 L 2. Forgive me, then, today. And you will know you have forgiven me if you behold your brother in the light of holiness. He cannot be less holy than can[705] I, and you can not be holier than he. **W(537)**

Lesson 289 "The past is over. It can touch me not."

W 289 L 1. Unless the past is over in my mind, the real world must escape my sight. For I am really looking nowhere; seeing but what is not there. How can I then perceive the world forgiveness offers? This past was made to hide, for this world that can be looked on only now. It has no past. For what can be forgiven but the past, and if it is forgiven it is gone.

W 289 L 2. *"Father, let me not look upon a past that is not there. For You have offered me Your own replacement, in a present world the past has left untouched and free of sin. Here is the end of guilt. And here am I made ready for Your final step. Shall I demand that You wait longer for Your Son to find the loveliness You planned to be the end of all his dreams and all his pain?"* **W(538)**

Lesson 290 "My present happiness is all I see."

W 290 L 1. Unless I look upon what is not there, my present happiness is all I see. Eyes that begin to open see at last. And I would have Christ's vision come to me this very day. What I perceive without God's own correction for the sight I made is frightening and painful to behold. Yet I would not allow my mind to be deceived by the belief the dream I made is real an instant longer. This day I seek my present happiness, and look on nothing else except the thing I seek.

W 290 L 2. *"With this resolve I come to You, and ask Your strength to hold me up today, while I but[706] do Your Will. You cannot fail to hear me, Father. What I ask have You already given me, and I am sure that I will see my happiness today."* **W(539)**

(8) What is the Real World? (W 290 W8)

W 290 W8 1. The real world is a symbol, like the rest of what perception offers. Yet it stands for what is opposite to what you made. Your world is seen through eyes of fear, and brings the witnesses of terror to your mind. The real world cannot be perceived except through eyes forgiveness blesses, so they see a world where terror is impossible, and witnesses to fear can not be found.

W 290 W8 2. The real world holds a counterpart for each unhappy thought reflected in your world; a sure correction for the sights of fear and sounds of battle which your world contains. The real world shows a world seen differently, through quiet eyes and with a mind at peace. Nothing but rest is here. There are no cries of pain and sorrow heard, for nothing here remains outside forgiveness. And the sights are gentle. Only happy sights and sounds can reach the mind that has forgiven itself.

W 290 W8 3. What need has such a mind for thoughts of death, attack and murder? What can it perceive surrounding it but safety, love and joy? What is there it would choose to be condemned, and what is there that it would judge against? The world it sees arises from a mind at peace within itself. No danger lurks in anything it sees, for it is kind and only kindness does it look upon.

W 290 W8 4. The real world is the symbol that the dream of sin and guilt is over, and God's Son no longer sleeps. His waking eyes perceive the sure reflection of his Father's Love; the certain promise that he is redeemed. The real world signifies the end of time, for its perception makes time purposeless.

W 290 W8 5. The Holy Spirit has no need of time when it has served His purpose. Now He waits but that one instant more for God to take His final step, and time has disappeared, taking perception with it as it goes, and leaving but the Truth to be Itself. That instant is our goal, for it contains the memory of God. And as we look upon a world forgiven, it is He Who calls to us and comes to take us home, reminding us of our Identity Which our forgiveness has restored to us. **W(540)**

Lesson 291 "This is a day of stillness and of peace."

W 291 L 1. Christ's vision looks through me today. His sight shows me all things forgiven and at peace, and offers this same vi-

---

[704] The *Urtext* manuscript has a period and sentence break here. Handwritten mark-up suggests a comma only, which we feel is correct. The *Notes* agrees, showing a full stop which is struck out.

[705] Handwritten mark-up suggests (am) in place of "**can**".

[706] Handwritten mark-up suggests (seek to).

sion to the world. And I accept this vision in its name, both for myself and for the world as well. What loveliness we look upon today! What holiness we see surrounding us! And it is given us to recognize it is a holiness in which we share; it is the Holiness of God Himself.

> **W 291 L 2.** *"This day my mind is quiet, to receive the Thoughts You offer me. And I accept what comes from You instead of from myself. I do not know the way to You. But You are wholly certain. Father, lead[707] Your Son along the quiet path that ends in[708] You. Let my forgiveness be complete, and let the memory of You return to me."* **W(541)**

Lesson 292 "A happy outcome to all things is sure."

W 292 L 1. God's promises make no exceptions. And He guarantees that only joy can be the final outcome found for everything. Yet it is up to us when this is reached; how long we let an alien will appear to be opposing His. And while we think this will be real, we will not find the end He has appointed, as the outcome of all problems we perceive, all trials we see, and every situation that we meet. Yet is the ending certain. For God's Will is done in earth and Heaven.[709] We will seek and we will find according to His Will, Which guarantees that our will is done.

> **W 292 L 2.** *"We thank you, Father, for Your guarantee of only happy outcomes in the end. Help us not interfere, and so delay the happy endings You have promised us for every problem that we can perceive; for every trial we think we still must meet."* **W(542)**

Lesson 293 "All fear is past and only love is here."

W 293 L 1. All fear is past because its source is gone, and all its thoughts gone with it. Love remains the only present state, whose Source is here forever and forever. Can the world seem bright and clear and safe and welcoming, with all my past mistakes oppressing it, and showing me distorted forms of pain[710]? Yet in the present love is obvious, and its effects apparent. All the world shines in reflection of its holy light, and I perceive a world forgiven at last.

> **W 293 L 2.** *"Father, let not Your holy world escape my sight today. Nor let my ears be deaf to all the hymns of gratitude the world is singing underneath the sounds of fear. There is a real world which the present holds safe from all past mistakes. And I would see only this world before my eyes today."* **W(543)**

Lesson 294 "My body is a wholly neutral thing."

W 294 L 1. I am a Son of God. And can I be another thing as well? Did God create the mortal and corruptible? What use has God's beloved Son for what must die? And yet a neutral thing does not see death, for thoughts of fear are not invested there, nor is a mockery of love bestowed upon it. Its neutrality protects it while it has a use. And afterwards, without a purpose, it is laid aside. It is not sick or old or hurt. It is but functionless, unneeded and cast off. Let me not see it more than this today; of service for a while and fit to serve, to keep its usefulness while it can serve, and then to be replaced for greater good.

> **W 294 L 2.** *"My body, Father, cannot be Your Son. And what is not created cannot be sinful or sinless; neither good nor bad. Let me, then, use this dream to help Your plan that we awaken from all dreams we made."* **W(544)**

Lesson 295 "The Holy Spirit looks through me today."

W 295 L 1. Christ asks that He may use my eyes today, and thus redeem the world. He asks this gift that He may offer peace of mind to me, and take away all terror and all pain. And as they are removed from me, the dreams that seemed to settle on the world are gone. Redemption must be one. As I am saved, the world is saved with me. For all of us must be redeemed together. Fear appears in many different forms, but love is one.

> **W 295 L 2.** *"My Father, Christ has asked a gift of me, and one I give that it be given me. Help me to use the eyes of Christ today, and thus allow the Holy Spirit's Love to bless all things that[711] I may look upon, that His forgiving Love may rest on me."* **W(545)**

Lesson 296 "The Holy Spirit speaks through me today."

W 296 L 1. *"The Holy Spirit needs my voice today, that all the world may listen to Your Voice, and hear Your Word through me. I am resolved to let You speak through me, for I would use no words but Yours, and have no thoughts which are apart from Yours, for only Yours are true. I would be Savior to the world I made. For having damned it, I would set it free that I may find escape, and hear the Word Your holy Voice will speak to me today."*

W 296 L 2. We teach today what we would learn, and that alone. And so our learning goal becomes an unconflicted one, and possible of easy reach and quick accomplishment. How gladly does the Holy Spirit come to rescue us from hell,[712] when we allow His teaching to persuade the world, through us, to seek and find the easy path to God! **W(546)**

Lesson 297 "Forgiveness is the only gift I give."

W 297 L 1. Forgiveness is the only gift I give because it is the only gift I want, and everything I give I give myself. This is salvation's simple formula. And I, who would be saved, would make it mine, to be the way I live within a world that needs salvation, and that will be saved as I accept Atonement for myself.

> **W 297 L 2.** *"Father, how certain are Your ways; how sure their[713] outcome, and how truly faithfully is every step in my salvation set already, and accomplished by Your grace. Thanks be to You for Your eternal gifts, and thanks to You for my Identity."* **W(547)**

Lesson 298 "I love You, Father, and I love Your Son."

W 298 L 1. My gratitude permits my love to be accepted without fear. And thus am I restored to my Reality at last. All that intruded on my holy sight forgiveness takes away. And I draw near the end of senseless journeys, mad careers, and artificial values. I accept instead what God establishes as mine, sure that in that alone I will be saved; sure that I go through fear to meet my Love.

> **W 298 L 2.** *"Father, I come to You today, because I would not follow any way but Yours. You are beside me. Certain is Your way. And I am grateful for Your holy gifts of certain sanctuary, and escape from everything that would obscure my love for God my Father and His holy Son."* **W(548)**

---

[707] Handwritten mark-up suggests (guide).
[708] Handwritten mark-up suggests (leads to).
[709] **Matthew 6:10** "Your kingdom come. Your will be done On earth as it is in heaven."
[710] Handwritten mark-up suggests (fear).
[711] Handwritten mark-up suggests (which).
[712] **Psalms 144:7** Stretch forth thine hand from above; rescue me, and deliver me out of great waters, out of the hand of strangers;
[713] Handwritten mark-up suggests (final).

Lesson 299 "Eternal holiness abides in me."

W 299 L 1. My holiness is far beyond my own ability to understand or know. Yet God my Father, Who created it, acknowledges my holiness as His. Our Will, together, understands it. And our Will, together, knows that it is so.

> **W 299 L 2.** *"Father, my holiness is not of me. It is not mine to be destroyed by sin. It is not mine to suffer from attack. Illusions can obscure it, but can not put out its radiance nor dim its light. It stands forever perfect and untouched. In it are all things healed, for they remain as You created them. And I can know my holiness. For Holiness Itself created me and I can know my Source because it is Your Will that You be known."* **W(549)**

Lesson 300 "Only an instant does this world endure."

W 300 L 1. This is the[714] thought that[715] can be used to say that death and sorrow are the certain lot of all who come here,[716] for their joys are gone before they are possessed, or even grasped. Yet this is also the idea that[717] lets no false perception keep us in its hold, nor represents more than a passing cloud upon a sky eternally serene. And it is this serenity we seek, unclouded, obvious and sure, today.

> **W 300 L 2.** *"We seek Your holy world today. For we, Your loving Sons, have lost our way a while. But we have listened to Your Voice, and learned exactly what to do to be restored to Heaven and our true Identity. And we give thanks today the world endures but for an instant. We would go beyond that tiny instant to eternity."* **W(550)**

(9) What is the Second Coming? (W 300 W9)

W 300 W9 1. Christ's Second Coming, which is sure as God, is merely the correction of mistakes and the return of sanity. It is a part of the condition which restores the never-lost, and re-establishes what is forever and forever true. It is the invitation to God's Word to take illusion's place; the willingness to let forgiveness rest upon all things without exception and without reserve.

W 300 W9 2. It is the all-inclusive nature of Christ's Second Coming that permits it to embrace the world, and hold you safe within its gentle advent which encompasses all living things with you. There is no end to the release the Second Coming brings, as God's creation must be limitless. Forgiveness lights the Second Coming's way because it shines on everyone[718] as one.[719]

W 300 W9 3. The Second Coming ends the lessons which the Holy Spirit teaches, making way for the Last Judgment, in which learning ends in one last summary that will extend beyond itself, and reaching[720] up to God. The Second Coming is the time in which all minds are given to the hands of Christ, to be returned to Spirit in the Name[721] of true creation and the Will of God.[722]

W 300 W9 4. The Second Coming is the one event in time which time itself can not affect. For every one who ever came to die, or yet will come or who is present now, is equally released from what he made. In this equality is Christ restored as one Identity, in Which all[723] Sons of God acknowledge that they all are one. And God the Father smiles upon His Son, His one creation and His only joy.

W 300 W9 5. Pray that this[724] Second Coming will be soon, but do not rest with that. It needs your eyes and ears and hands and feet. It needs your voice. And most of all it needs your willingness. Let us rejoice that we can do God's Will, and join together in Its holy light. Behold, the Son of God is one in us, and we can reach our Father's Love through him. **W(551)**

Lesson 301 "And God Himself shall wipe away all tears."

> **W 301 L 1.** *"Father, unless I judge I cannot weep. Nor can I suffer pain, or feel I am abandoned and[725] unneeded in the world. This is my home, because I judge it not,[726] and therefore is it only what You will. Let me today behold it uncondemned, through happy eyes forgiveness has released from all distortion. Let me see Your world instead of mine. And all the tears I shed will be forgotten, for their source is gone. Father, I will not judge Your world today."*

W 301 L 2. God's world is happy. Those who look on it can only add their joy to it, and bless it as a cause of further joy in them. We wept because we did not understand. But we have learned the world we saw was false, and we will look upon God's world today. **W(552)**

Lesson 302 "Where darkness was I look upon the light."

> **W 302 L 1.** *"Father, our eyes are opening at last. Your holy world awaits us, as our sight is finally restored and we can see. We thought we suffered. But we had forgot the Son whom You created. Now we see that darkness is our own imagining, and light is there for us to look upon. Christ's vision changes darkness into light, for fear must disappear when love has come. Let me forgive Your holy world today that I may look upon its holiness, and understand it but reflects my own."*

W 302 L 2. Our Love awaits us as we go to Him, and walks beside us, showing us the way. He fails in nothing. He the end we seek, and He the means by which we come to Him. **W(553)**

Lesson 303 "The holy Christ is born in me today."

W 303 L 1. Watch with me, angels, watch with me today. Let all God's holy Thoughts surround me, and be still with me while Heaven's Son is born. Let earthly sounds be quiet, and the sights to which I am accustomed disappear. Let Christ be welcomed where He is at home, and let Him hear the sounds He understands, and see but sights which show His Father's Love. Let Him no longer be a stranger here, for He is born again in me today.[727]

> **W 303 L 2.** *"Your Son is welcome, Father. He has come to save me from the evil self I made. He is the Self that You have given me. He is but what I really am in truth. He is the Son You love above all things. He is my Self as You created me. It is not Christ that can be crucified. Safe in Your arms let me receive Your Son."* **W(554)**

---

[714] Handwritten mark-up suggests (a).
[715] Handwritten mark-up suggests (which).
[716] The original *Urtext* manuscript has a full sentence break here, with handwriting suggesting only a comma instead. We accept the handwriting as a correction.
[717] Handwritten mark-up suggests (which).
[718] Handwritten mark-up suggests (everything).
[719] Handwritten mark-up suggests (And thus is oneness recognized at last.)
[720] *Urtext* manuscript has "**reaching**" and handwriting suggests (reaches). Since the *Notes* also has "reaching" we're leaving it that way. FIP has "reaches."
[721] Handwritten mark-up suggests (name).
[722] **Matthew 11:22** "But I say to you, it will be more tolerable for Tyre and Sidon in the day of judgment than for you."
[723] Handwritten mark-up suggests (the).
[724] Handwritten mark-up suggests (the).
[725] Handwritten mark-up suggests (or) in place of "and".
[726] *Urtext* manuscript has period and new sentence beginning here. Handwritten mark-up suggests a comma only, which we feel is correct.
[727] **John 3:3** Jesus answered and said to him, "Most assuredly, I say to you, unless one is born again, he cannot see the kingdom of God."
John 3:7 "Do not marvel that I said to you, 'You must be born again.'

Lesson 304 "Let not my world obscure the sight of Christ."

W 304 L 1. I can obscure my holy sight, if I intrude my world upon it. Nor can I behold the holy sights Christ looks upon unless it is His vision that I use. Perception is a mirror, not a fact. And what I look on is my state of mind reflected outward. I would bless the world by looking on it through the eyes of Christ. And I will look upon the certain signs that all my sins have been forgiven me.

W 304 L 2. *"You lead me from the darkness to the light; from sin to holiness. Let me forgive, and thus receive salvation for the world. It is Your gift, my Father, given me to offer to Your holy Son, that he may find again the memory of You, and of Your Son as You created him."* **W(555)**

Lesson 305 "There is a peace that Christ bestows on us."

W 305 L 1. Who uses but Christ's vision finds a peace so deep and quiet, undisturbable and wholly changeless, that the world contains no counterpart. Comparisons are still before this peace. And all the world departs in silence, as this peace envelops it, and gently carries it to truth, no more to be the home of fear. For Love has come, and healed the world by giving it Christ's peace.

W 305 L 2. *"Father, the peace of Christ is given us, because it is Your Will that we be saved. Help us today but to accept Your gift, and judge it not. For it has come to us to save us from our judgment on ourselves."* **W(556)**

Lesson 306 "The gift of Christ is all I seek today."

W 306 L 1. What but Christ's vision would I use today, when it can offer me a day in which I see a world so like to Heaven that an ancient memory returns to me? Today I can forget the world I made. Today I can go past all fear, and be restored to love and holiness and peace. Today I am redeemed, and born anew into a world of mercy and of care; of loving kindness and the peace of God.

W 306 L 2. *"And so, our Father, we return to You, remembering we never went away; remembering Your holy gifts to us. In gratitude and thankfulness we come, with empty hands and open hearts and minds, asking but what You give. We cannot make an offering sufficient for Your Son. But in Your Love the gift of Christ is his."* **W(557)**

Lesson 307 "Conflicting wishes cannot be my will."

W 307 L 1. *"Father, Your Will is mine, and only That. There is no other will for me to have. Let me not try to make another will, for it is senseless and will cause me pain. Your Will alone can bring me happiness, and only Yours exists. If I would have what only You can give. I must accept Your will for me, and enter into peace where conflict is impossible, Your Son is one with You in being and in will, and nothing contradicts the holy truth that I remain as You created me."*

W 307 L 2. And with this prayer, we enter silently into a state where conflict cannot come, because we join our holy will with God's in recognition that they are but one.[728] **W(558)**

Lesson 308 "This instant is the only time there is."

W 308 L 1. I have conceived of time in such a way that I defeat my aim. If I elect to reach past time to timelessness, I must change my perception of what time is for. Time's purpose cannot be to keep the past and future one. The only interval in which I can be saved from time is now. For in this instant has forgiveness come to set me free. The birth of Christ is now, without a past or future. He has come to give His present blessing to the world, restoring it to timelessness and love. And love is ever present, here and now.

W 308 L 2. *"Thanks for this instant, Father. It is now I am redeemed. This instant is the time You have appointed for Your Son's release, and for salvation of the world in him."* **W(559)**

Lesson 309 "I will not fear to look within today."

W 309 L 1. Within me is Eternal Innocence, because it is God's Will that It be there forever and forever. I, His Son, whose will is limitless as is His own, can will no change in this. For to deny my Father's Will is to deny my own. To look within is but to find my will as God created it, and as it is. I fear to look within because I think I made another will which is not true, and made it real. Yet it has no effects. Within me is the holiness of God. Within me is the memory of Him.

W 309 L 2. *"The step I take today, my Father, is my sure release from idle dreams of sin. Your altar stands serene and undefiled. It is the holy altar to my Self, and there I find my true Identity."* **W(560)**

Lesson 310 "In fearlessness and love I spend today."

W 310 L 1. *"This day, my Father, would I spend with You, as You have chosen all my days should be. And what I will experience is not of time at all. The joy that comes to me is not of days nor hours, for it comes from Heaven to Your Son. This day will be your sweet reminder to remember You, Your gracious calling to Your holy Son, the sign Your grace has come to me, and that it is Your Will that I be free today."*

W 310 L 2. We spend this day together, you and I, and all the world joins with us in our song of thankfulness and joy to Him Who gave salvation to us, and Who set us free. We are restored to peace and holiness. There is no room in us for fear today, for we have welcomed love into our hearts. **W(561)**

(10) What is the Last Judgment?
(W 310 W10)

W 310 W10 1. Christ's Second Coming gives the Son of God the gift to hear the Voice for God proclaim that what is false is false, and what is true has never changed.[729] And this the judgment is in which perception ends. At first you see a world which has accepted this as true, projected from a now corrected mind.[730] And with this

---

[728] Handwritten mark-up suggests(the same) in place of "**but one**". In the *Notes* we find "the same" written between the lines above "but one."

[729] **Matthew 16:27** For the Son of Man will come in the glory of His Father with His angels, and then He will reward each according to his works.

[730] **2 Peter 3:13** But according to His promise, we look for new heavens and a new earth in which righteousness dwells.

Romans 8:15-23 For ye received not the spirit of bondage again unto fear; but ye received the spirit of adoption, whereby we cry, Abba, Father. The Spirit himself beareth witness with our spirit, that we are children of God: and if children, then heirs; heirs of God, and joint-heirs with Christ; if so be that we suffer with *him*, that we may be also glorified with *him*. For I reckon that the sufferings of this present time are not worthy to be compared with the glory which shall be revealed to us–ward. For the earnest expectation of the creation waiteth for the revealing of the sons of God. For the creation was subjected to vanity, not of its own will, but by reason of him who subjected it, in hope that the creation itself also shall be delivered from the bondage of corruption into the liberty of the glory of the children of God. For we know that the whole creation groaneth and travaileth in pain together until now. And not only so, but ourselves also, which have the firstfruits of the Spirit, even we ourselves groan within ourselves, waiting for *our* adoption, *to wit*, the redemption of our body.

holy sight, perception gives a silent blessing and then disappears, its goal accomplished and its mission done.[731]

W 310 W10 2. The final judgment[732] on the world contains no condemnation. For it sees the world as totally forgiven, without sin, and wholly purposeless. Without a cause, and now without a function in Christ's sight, it merely slips away to nothingness. There it was born, and there it ends as well. And all the figures in the dream in which the world began go with it. Bodies now are useless, and will therefore fade away, because the Son of God is limitless.

W 310 W10 3. You who believed that Gods Last Judgment would condemn the world to hell along with you, accept this holy truth: God's Judgment is the gift of the Correction He bestowed on all your errors, freeing you from them, and all effects they ever seemed to have. To fear God's saving grace is but to fear complete release from suffering, return to peace, security and happiness, and union with your own Identity.

W 310 W10 4. God's Final Judgment is as merciful as every step in His appointed plan to bless His Son, and call Him to return to the eternal peace He shares with him. Be not afraid of Love. For It alone can heal all sorrow, wipe away all tears, and gently waken from his dreams of pain the Son whom God acknowledges as His. Be not afraid of this. Salvation asks you give it welcome. And the world awaits your glad acceptance, which will set it free.

W 310 W10 5. This is God's Final Judgment: "You are still My holy Son, forever innocent, forever loving and forever loved, as limitless as Your Creator, and completely changeless and forever pure. Therefore awaken and return to Me. I am Your Father and you are My Son." **W(562)**

Lesson 311 "I judge all things as I would have them be."

W 311 L 1. Judgment was made to be a weapon used against the truth. It separates what it is being used against, and sets it off as if it were a thing apart. And then it makes of it what you[733] would have it be. It judges what it cannot understand, because it cannot see totality and therefore judges falsely. Let us not use it today, but make a gift of it to Him Who has a different use for it. He will relieve you[734] of the agony of all the judgments you[735] have made against yourself,[736] and re-establish peace of mind by giving you[737] God's Judgment of His Son.

> **W 311 L 2.** *"Father, we wait with open mind today, to hear Your Judgment of the Son You love. We do not know him, and we cannot judge. And so we let Your Love decide what he whom You created as Your Son must be."* **W(563)**

Lesson 312 "I see all things as I would have them be."

W 312 L 1. Perception follows judgment. Having judged, you[738] therefore see what you would look upon. For vision merely serves to offer you what you would have. It is impossible to overlook what you would see, and fail to see what you have chosen to behold. How surely, therefore, must the real world come to greet the holy sight of anyone who takes the Holy Spirit's purpose as his goal for seeing. And he cannot fail to look upon what Christ would have him see, and share Christ's love for what he looks upon.

> **W 312 L 2.** *"I have no purpose for today except to look upon a liberated world, set free from all the judgments I have made. Father, this is Your Will for me today, and therefore it must be my goal as well."* **W(564)**

Lesson 313 "Now let a new perception come to me."

> **W 313 L 1.** *"Father, there is a vision which beholds all things as sinless, so that fear has gone, and where it was is Love invited in. And Love will come wherever it is asked. This vision is Your gift. The eyes of Christ look on a world forgiven. In His sight are all its sins forgiven, for He sees no sin in anything He looks upon. Now let His true perception come to me, that I may waken from the dream of guilt and look within upon my sinlessness, which You have kept completely undefiled upon the altar to Your holy Son, the Self with Which I would identify."*

W 313 L 2. Let us today behold each other in the sight of Christ. How beautiful we are! How holy and how loving! Brother, come and join with me today. We save the world when we are[739] joined. For in our vision it becomes as holy as the Light in us. **W(565)**

Lesson 314 "I seek a future different from the past."

W 314 L 1. From new perception of the world there comes a future very different from the past. The future now is recognized as but extensions[740] of the present. Past mistakes can cast no shadows on it, so that fear has lost its idols and its images, and being formless, it has no effects. Death will not claim the future now, for life is now its goal, and all the needed means are happily provided. Who can grieve or suffer, when the present has been freed, extending its security and peace into a quiet future filled with hope?

> **W 314 L 2.** *"Father, we were mistaken in the past, and choose to use the present to be free. Now do we leave the future in Your hands, leaving behind our past mistakes, and sure that You will keep Your present Promises, and guide the future in their holy light."* **W(566)**

Lesson 315 "All gifts my brothers give belong to me."

W 315 L 1. Each day a thousand treasures come to me with every passing moment. I am blessed with gifts throughout the day, in value far beyond all things of which I can conceive. A brother smiles upon another, and my heart is gladdened. Someone speaks a word of gratitude or mercy, and my mind perceives[741] this gift and takes it as its own. And everyone who finds the way to God becomes my Savior, pointing out the way to me, and giving me his certainty that what he learned is surely mine as well.

> **W 315 L 2.** *"I thank You, Father, for the many gifts that come to me today and every day from every Son of God. My brothers are unlimited in all their gifts to me. Now may I offer them my thankfulness, that gratitude to them may lead me on to my Creator and His memory."* **W(567)**

Lesson 316 "All gifts I give my brothers are my own."

W 316 L 1. As every gift my brothers give is mine, so every gift I give belongs to me. Each one allows a past mistake to go, and leave no shadow on the holy mind my Father loves. His grace is given me in every gift a brother has received throughout all time, and past all time as well. My treasure-house is full, and angels watch its open doors, that not one gift is lost and only more are added. Let me

---

[731] **Revelation 21:1** And I saw a new heaven and a new earth. For the first heaven and the first earth had passed away. And the sea no longer is.
[732] Handwritten mark-up suggests (Final Judgment).
[733] Handwritten mark-up suggests (we).
[734] Handwritten mark-up suggests (us).
[735] Handwritten mark-up suggests (we).
[736] Handwritten mark-up suggests(ourselves).
[737] Handwritten mark-up suggests (us).
[738] Handwritten mark-up suggests this whole paragraph be shifted from the second person plural (you) to the first person plural (we).

[739] Handwritten mark-up suggests (have) in place of "**are**".
[740] Handwritten mark-up suggests (extension).
[741] The *Urtext* manuscript has "**perceives**" here and so does the *Notes*. The handwritten mark-up suggests (receives).

come to where my treasures are, and enter in where I am truly welcome and at home among the gifts that God has given me.

> **W 316 L 2.** *"Father, I would accept Your gifts today. I do not recognize them. Yet I trust that You Who gave them will provide the means by which I can behold them, see their worth, and cherish only them as what I want."* **W(568)**

Lesson 317 "I follow in the way appointed me."

W 317 L 1. I have a special place to fill; a role for me alone. Salvation waits until I take this part as what I choose to do. Until I make this choice, I am the slave of time and human destiny. But when I willingly and gladly go the way my Father's plan appointed me to go, then will I recognize salvation is already here, already given all my brothers and already mine as well.

> **W 317 L 2.** *"Father, Your way is what I choose today. Where it would lead me do I choose to go; what it would have me do I choose to do. Your way is certain, and the end secure. The memory of You awaits me there, and all my sorrows end in Your embrace, which You have promised to Your Son, who thought mistakenly that he had wandered from the sure protection of Your loving arms."* **W(569)**

Lesson 318 "In me salvation's means and end are one."

W 318 L 1. In me, God's holy Son, are reconciled all parts of Heaven's plan to save the world. What could conflict, when all the parts have but one purpose and one aim? How could there be a single part that stands aside, or one of more or less importance than the rest? I am the means by which God's Son is saved, because salvation's purpose is to find the sinlessness which God has placed in me. I was created as the thing I seek. I am the goal the world is searching for. I am God's Son, His one Eternal Love. I am salvation's means and end as well.

> **W 318 L 2.** *"Let me today, my Father, take the role You offer me in Your request that I accept Atonement for myself. For thus does what is thereby reconciled in me become as surely reconciled to You."* **W(570)**

Lesson 319 "I came for the salvation of the world."

W 319 L 1. Here is a thought from which all arrogance has been removed, and only truth is left. For arrogance opposes truth. But where[742] there is no arrogance, the truth will come immediately, and fill up the space the ego left unoccupied by lies. Only the ego can be limited, and therefore it must seek for aims which are curtailed and limiting. The ego thinks that what one gains totality must lose. And yet it is the Will of God I learn that what one gains is given unto all.

> **W 319 L 2.** *"Father, Your Will is total, and the goal that[743] stems from It shares Its totality. What aim but the salvation of the world could You have given me? And what but this could be the Will my Self has shared with You?"* **W(571)**

Lesson 320 "My Father gives all power unto me."

W 320 L 1. The Son of God is limitless. There are no limits on his strength, his peace, his joy, nor[744] any attributes his Father gave in his creation. What he wills with his Creator and Redeemer must be done. His holy will can never be denied, because his Father shines upon his mind, and lays before it all the strength and love in earth and Heaven.[745] I am he to whom all this is given. I am he in whom the power of my Father's Will abides.

> **W 320 L 2.** *"Your Will can do all things in me, and then extend to all the world as well through me. There is no limit on Your will. And so all power has been given to Your Son."* **W(572)**

(11) What is Creation? (W 320 W11)

W 320 W11 1. Creation is the sum of all God's Thoughts, in number infinite, and everywhere without all limit. Only Love creates, and only like Itself. There was no time when all that It created was not there. Nor will there be a time when anything that It created suffers any pain.[746] Forever and forever are God's Thoughts exactly as They[747] were and as They[748] are, unchanged through time and after time is done.

W 320 W11 2. God's Thoughts are given all the power that Their own Creator has. For He would add to Love by Its extension. Thus His Son shares in creation, and must therefore share in power to create. What God has willed to be forever one will still be one when time is over; and will not be changed throughout the course of time, remaining as it was before the thought of time began.

W 320 W11 3. Creation is the opposite of all illusions, for Creation[749] is the truth. Creation is the holy Son of God, for in Creation[750] is His Will complete in every aspect, making every part container of the whole. Its oneness is forever guaranteed inviolate; forever held within His holy Will, beyond all possibility of harm, of separation, imperfection and of any spot upon its sinlessness.

W 320 W11 4. We are Creation;[751] we the Sons of God. We seem to be discrete and unaware of our eternal unity with Him. Yet back of all our doubts, past all our fears, there still is certainty. For Love remains with all Its Thought, Its sureness being Theirs. God's memory is in our holy minds, which know their oneness and their unity with their Creator. Let our function be only to let this memory return, only to let God's Will be done on earth,[752] only to be restored to sanity, and to be but as God created us.

W 320 W11 5. Our Father calls to us. We hear His Voice, and we forgive creation in the Name of its Creator, Holiness Itself, Whose holiness His own creation shares; Whose holiness is still a part of us. **W(573)**

Lesson 321 "Father, my freedom is in You alone."

> **W 321 L 1.** *"I did not understand what made me free, nor what my freedom is, nor where to look to find it. Father, I have searched in vain until I heard Your Voice directing me. Now I would guide myself no more. For I have neither made nor understood the way to find my freedom. But I trust in You. You Who endowed me with my freedom as Your holy Son will not be lost to me. Your Voice directs me. And the way to You is opening and clear to me at last. Father, my freedom is in You alone. Father, it is my will that I return."*

W 321 L 2. Today we answer for the world, which will be freed along with us. How glad are we to find our freedom through the

---

[742] Handwritten mark-up suggests (when) instead of "**where**".
[743] Handwritten mark-up suggests (which).
[744] Handwritten mark-up suggests (nor) instead of the originally typed "**or**". This is probably correct.
[745] **Acts 22:6** And it came to pass, that, as I made my journey, and drew nigh unto Damascus, about noon, suddenly there shone from heaven a great light round about me.
[746] Handwritten mark-up suggests (loss) instead of "**pain**".
[747] Handwritten mark-up suggests (they).
[748] Handwritten mark-up suggests (they).
[749] Handwritten mark-up suggests (creation).
[750] Handwritten mark-up suggests (creation).
[751] In the *Urtext* manuscript this word is not capitalized, but we feel that it should be, consistent with the previous paragraph, and the fact that it is a proper noun in this usage.
[752] **Matthew 6:10** "Your kingdom come. Your will be done On earth as it is in heaven."

certain way our Father has established. And how sure is all the world's salvation, when we learn our freedom can be found in God alone. **W(574)**

Lesson 322 "I can give up but what was never real."

W 322 L 1. I sacrifice illusions; nothing more. And as illusions go I find the gifts illusions tried to hide, awaiting me in shining welcome, and in readiness to give God's ancient messages to me. His memory abides in every gift that I receive of Him. And every dream serves only to conceal the Self Which is God's only Son, the likeness of Himself, the Holy One Who still abides in Him forever, as He still abides in me.[753]

W 322 L 2. *"Father, to You all sacrifice remains forever inconceivable. And so I cannot sacrifice except in dreams. As You created me, I can give up nothing You gave me. What You did not give has no reality. What loss can I anticipate except the loss of fear, and the return of Love into my mind?"* **W(575)**

Lesson 323 "I gladly make the 'sacrifice' of fear."

W 323 L 1. *"Here is the only 'sacrifice' You ask of Your beloved Son; You ask him to give up all suffering, all sense of loss and sadness, all anxiety and doubt, and freely let Your Love come streaming in to his awareness, healing him of pain, and giving him Your own eternal joy.[754] Such is the 'sacrifice' You ask of me, and one I gladly make; the only 'cost' of restoration of Your memory to me, for the salvation of the world."*

W 323 L 2. And as we pay the debt we owe to truth - a debt which merely is the letting go of self-deceptions and of images we worshipped falsely - truth returns to us in wholeness and in joy. We are deceived no longer. Love has now returned to our awareness. And we are at peace again, for fear has gone, and only Love remains. **W(576)**

Lesson 324 "I merely follow, for I would not lead."

W 324 L 1. *"Father, You are the One Who gave the plan for my salvation to me. You have set the way I am to go, the role to take, and every step in my appointed path. I cannot lose the way. I can but choose to wander off a while, and then return. Your loving Voice will always call me back, and guide my feet aright. My brothers all can follow in the way I lead them. Yet I merely follow in the way to You, as You direct me and would have me go."*

W 324 L 2. So let us follow One Who knows the way. We need not tarry, and we cannot stray except an instant from His loving hand. We walk together, for we follow Him. And it is He Who makes the ending sure, and guarantees a safe returning home. **W(577)**

Lesson 325 "All things I think I see reflect ideas."

W 325 L 1. This is salvation's keynote. What I see reflects a process in my mind, which starts with my idea of what I want. From there, the mind makes up an image of the thing the mind desires, judges valuable, and therefore seeks to find. These images are then projected outward, looked upon, esteemed as real, and guarded as one's own. From insane wishes comes an insane world. From judgment comes a world condemned. And from forgiving thoughts a gentle world comes forth, with mercy for the holy Son of God, to offer him a kindly home where he can rest a while before he journeys on, and help his brothers walk ahead with him and find the way to Heaven and to God.

W 325 L 2. *"Our Father, Your Ideas reflect the truth, and mine apart from Yours but makes up dreams. Let me behold what only Yours reflect, for Yours and Yours alone establish truth."* **W(578)**

Lesson 326 "I am forever an Effect of God."

W 326 L 1. *"Father, I was created in Your Mind, a holy Thought that never left its home. I am forever Your Effect, and You forever and forever are my Cause. As You created me I have remained. Where You established me I still abide,[755] and all Your attributes abide in me because it is Your Will to have a Son so like his Cause that Cause and Its Effect are indistinguishable. Let me know that I am an Effect of God, and so I have the power to create like You. And as it is in Heaven, so on earth.[756] Your plan I follow here, and at the end I know that You will gather Your Effects into the tranquil Heaven of Your Love, where earth will disappear, and separate things unite in glory as the Son of God."*

W 326 L 2. Let us today behold earth disappear, at first transformed, and then, forgiven, fade entirely into God's holy Will. **W(579)**

Lesson 327 "I need but call and You will answer me."

W 327 L 1. I am not asked to take salvation on the basis of an unsupported faith. For God has promised He will hear my call, and answer me Himself. Let me but learn from my experience that this is true, and faith in Him must surely come to me. This is the faith that will endure, and take me farther and still farther on the road that leads to Him. For thus I will be sure that He has not abandoned me, and loves me still, awaiting but my call to give me all the help I need to come to Him.

W 327 L 2. *"Father, I thank You that Your promises will never fail in my experience, if I but test them out. Let me attempt therefore to try them, and to judge them not. Your Word is one with You. You give the means whereby conviction comes, and surety of Your abiding Love is gained at last."* **W(580)**

Lesson 328 "I choose the second place to gain the first."

W 328 L 1. What seems to be the second place is first, for all things we perceive are upside-down until we listen to the Voice of God. It seems that we will gain autonomy but by our striving to be separate, and that our independence from the rest of God's creation is the way in which salvation is obtained. Yet all we find is sickness, suffering, and loss and death. This is not what our Father wills for us, nor is

---

[753] **Genesis 1:26-27** Then God said, "Let Us make man in Our image, according to Our likeness; let them have dominion over the fish of the sea, over the birds of the air, and over the cattle, over all the earth and over every creeping thing that creeps on the earth." So God created man in His own image; in the image of God He created him; male and female He created them.
Psalm 16:10 For You will not leave my soul in Sheol, Nor will You allow Your Holy One to see corruption.
Mark 1:24 Saying, "Let us alone! What have we to do with You, Jesus of Nazareth? Did You come to destroy us? I know who You are--the Holy One of God!"
[754] **Isaiah 60:15** Whereas thou hast been forsaken and hated, so that no man passed through thee, I will make thee an eternal excellency, a joy of many generations.
Matthew 3:17 And suddenly a voice came from heaven, saying, "This is My beloved Son, in whom I am well pleased."

[755] Handwritten mark-up suggests a period here, beginning a new sentence with "And all ..."
[756] **Matthew 6:10** "Your kingdom come. Your will be done On earth as it is in heaven."

there any second to His Will. To join with His is but to find our own. And since our will is His, it is to Him that we must go to recognize our will.

 W 328 L 2. *"There is no will but Yours. And I am glad that nothing I imagine contradicts what You would have me do.[757] It is Your Will that I be wholly safe, eternally at peace. And happily I share that Will which You, my Father, gave as part of me."* **W(581)**

Lesson 329 "I have already chosen what You will."

 W 329 L 1. *"Father, I[758] wandered from Your Will, defied It, broke Its laws, and interposed a second will more powerful than Yours. Yet what I am in truth is but Your Will, extended and extending. This am I. And This will never change. As You are One, so am I one with You. And This I chose in my creation, where my will became forever one with Yours. That choice was made for all eternity. It cannot change, and be in opposition to Itself. Father, my will is Yours. And I am safe, untroubled and serene, in endless joy, because it is Your Will that it be so."*

W 329 L 2. Today we will accept our union with each other and our Source. We have no will apart from His, and all of us are one because His Will is shared by all of us. Through It we recognize that we are one. Through It we find our way at last to God. **W(582)**

Lesson 330 "I will not hurt myself again today."

W 330 L 1. Let us this day accept forgiveness as our only function. Why should we attack our minds, and give them images of pain? Why should we teach them they are powerless, when God holds out His power and His Love, and bids them take what is already theirs? The mind that is made willing to accept God's gifts has been restored to Spirit, and extends its freedom and its joy, as is the Will of God united with its own. The Self Which God created cannot sin, and therefore cannot suffer. Let us choose today that He be our Identity, and thus escape forever from all things the dream of fear appears to offer us.

 W 330 L 2. *"Father, Your Son can not be hurt. And if we think we suffer, we but fail to know our one Identity we share with You. We would return to It today, to be made free forever from all our mistakes, and to be saved from what we thought we were."* **W(583)**

(12) What is the Ego? (W 330 W12)

W 330 W12 1. The ego is idolatry; the sign of limited and separated self, born in a body, doomed to suffer and to end its life in death. It is the will that sees the Will of God as enemy, and takes a form in which It is denied. The ego is the "proof" that strength is weak and love is fearful, life is really death, and what opposes God alone is true.

W 330 W12 2. The ego is insane. In fear it stands beyond the Everywhere, apart from All, in separation from the Infinite. In its insanity it thinks it has become a victor over God Himself, and in its terrible autonomy it "sees" the Will of God has been destroyed. It dreams of punishment, and trembles at the figures in its dreams, its enemies who seek to murder it before it can ensure its safety by attacking them.

W 330 W12 3. The Son of God is egoless. What can he know of madness and the death of God, when he abides in Him? What can he know of sorrow and of suffering, when he lives in eternal joy? What can he know of fear and punishment, of sin and guilt, of hatred and attack, when all there is surrounding him is everlasting peace, forever conflict-free and undisturbed, in deepest silence and tranquility?

W 330 W12 4. To know Reality is not to know the ego and its thoughts, its works, its acts, its laws and its beliefs, its dreams, its hopes, its plans for its salvation, and the cost belief in it entails. In suffering, the price for faith in it is so immense that crucifixion of the Son of God is offered daily at its darkened shrine, and blood must flow before the altar where its sickly followers prepare its feast of death.[759]

W 330 W12 5. Yet will one lily of forgiveness change the darkness into light; the altar to illusions to the shrine of Life Itself. And peace will be restored forever to the holy minds which God created as His Son, His dwelling-place, His joy, His love, completely His, completely one with Him. **W(584)**

Lesson 331
"There is no conflict, for my will is Yours."

 W 331 L 1. *"How foolish, Father, to believe Your Son could cause himself to suffer! Could he make a plan for his damnation, and be left without a certain way to his release? You love me, Father. You could never leave me desolate, to die within a world of pain and cruelty. How could I think that Love has left Itself? There is no will except the Will of Love. Fear is a dream, and has no will that can conflict with Yours. Conflict is sleep, and peace awakening. Death is illusion; life, Eternal Truth. There is no opposition to Your Will. There is no conflict, for my will is Yours."*

W 331 L 2. Forgiveness shows us that God's Will is one, and that we share It. Let us look upon the holy sights forgiveness shows today, that we may find the peace of God. Amen. **W(585)**

Lesson 332
"Fear binds the world. Forgiveness sets it free."

W 332 L 1. The ego makes illusions. Truth undoes its evil dreams by shining them away. Truth never makes attack. It merely is. And by its Presence is the mind recalled from fantasies, awaking to the Real. Forgiveness bids this Presence enter in, and take its rightful place within the mind. Without forgiveness is the mind in chains, believing in its own futility. Yet with forgiveness does the light shine through the dream of darkness, offering it hope, and giving it the means to realize the freedom that is its inheritance.

 W 332 L 2. *"We would not bind the world again today.[760] Fear holds it prisoner. And yet Your Love has given us the means to set it free. Father, we would release it now. For as we offer freedom it is given us. And we would not remain as prisoners, while You hold out our[761] freedom unto[762] us."* **W(586)**

Lesson 333
"Forgiveness ends the dream of conflict here."

W 333 L 1. Conflict must be resolved. It cannot be evaded, set aside, denied, disguised, seen somewhere else, called by another name, nor hidden by deceit of any kind, if it would be escaped. It must be seen exactly as it is, where it is thought to be, in the reality which has been given it, and with the purpose that the mind accorded it. For only then are its defenses lifted, and the truth can shine upon it as it disappears.

---

[757] Handwritten mark-up suggests (be) instead of "**do**".
[758] Handwritten mark-up suggests (thought I).

[759] The words "**its feast of**" are crossed out and overtyped with "**for**".
[760] **Matthew 16:19** "And I will give you the keys of the kingdom of heaven, and whatever you bind on earth will be bound in heaven, and whatever you loose on earth will be loosed in heaven."
[761] Handwritten mark-up suggests (are holding).
[762] Handwritten mark-up suggests (out to).

W 333 L 2. *"Father, forgiveness is the light You chose to shine away all conflict and all doubt, and light the way for our return to You. No light but this can end our evil dreams. No light but this can save the world. For this alone will never fail in anything, being Your gift to Your beloved Son."* **W(587)**

Lesson 334 "Today I claim the gifts forgiveness gives."

W 334 L 1. I will not wait another day to find the treasures which my Father offers me.[763] Illusions must be[764] vain, and dreams are gone even while they are woven out of thoughts that rest on false perception. Let me not accept such meager gifts again today. God's Voice is offering the peace of God to all who hear and choose to follow Him. This is my choice today. And so I go to find the treasures God has given me.

W 334 L 2. *"I seek but the eternal. For Your Son can be content with nothing less than this. What, then, can be his solace but what You are offering to his bewildered mind and frightened heart, to give him certainty and bring him peace? Today I would behold my brother sinless. This Your Will for me, for thus[765] will I behold my sinlessness."* **W(588)**

Lesson 335 "I choose to see my brother's sinlessness."

W 335 L 1. Forgiveness is a choice. I never see my brother as he is, for that is far beyond perception. What I see in him is merely what I wish to see, because it stands for what I want to be the truth. It is to this alone that I respond, however much I seem to be impelled by outside happenings. I choose to see what I would look upon, and this I see, and only this. My brother's sinlessness shows me that I would look upon my own. And I will see it, having chosen to behold my brother in its holy light.

W 335 L 2. *"What could restore Your memory to me except to see my brother's sinlessness? His holiness reminds me that he was created one with me and like myself. In him I find my Self, and in Your Son I find the memory of You as well."* **W(589)**

Lesson 336 "Forgiveness lets me know that minds are joined."

W 336 L 1. Forgiveness is the means appointed for perception's ending. Knowledge is restored after perception first is changed, and then gives way entirely to what remains forever past its highest reach. For sights and sounds, at best, can serve but to recall the memory that lies beyond them all. Forgiveness sweeps away distortions, and opens the hidden altar to the truth. Its lilies shine into the mind, and call it to return and look within, to find what it has vainly sought without. For here, and only here, is peace of mind restored, for this the dwelling-place of God Himself.

W 336 L 2. *"In quiet may forgiveness wipe away my dreams of separation and of sin. Then let me, Father, look within and find Your promise of my sinlessness is kept; Your Word remains unchanged within my mind, Your Love is still abiding in my heart."* **W(590)**

Lesson 337 "My sinlessness protects me from all harm."

W 337 L 1. My sinlessness ensures me perfect peace, eternal safety, everlasting love, freedom forever from all thought of loss; complete deliverance from suffering. And only happiness can be my state, for only happiness is given me. What must I do to know all this is mine? I must accept Atonement for myself, and nothing more. God has already done all things that need be done. And I must learn I need do nothing of myself, for I need but accept my Self, my sinlessness, created for me, now already mine, to feel God's Love protecting me from harm, to understand my Father loves His Son; to know I am the Son my Father loves.

W 337 L 2. *"You who created me in sinlessness are not mistaken about what I am. I was mistaken when I thought I sinned, but I accept Atonement for myself. Father, my dream is ended now. Amen."* **W(591)**

Lesson 338 "I am affected only by my thoughts."

W 338 L 1. It needs but this to let salvation come to all the world. For in this single thought is everyone released at last from fear. Now he has learned that no-one frightens him, and nothing can endanger him. He has no enemies, and he is safe from all external things. His thoughts can frighten him, but since these thoughts belong to him alone, he has the power to change them, and exchange each fear thought for a happy thought of love. He crucified himself. Yet God has planned that His beloved Son will be redeemed.

W 338 L 2. *"Your plan is sure, my Father, - only Yours. All other plans will fail. And I will have thoughts that will frighten me until I learn that You have given me the only Thought Which leads me to salvation. Mine alone will fail and lead me nowhere. But the Thought You gave me promises to lead me home, because it holds Your promise to Your Son."* **W(592)**

Lesson 339 "I will receive whatever I request."

W 339 L 1. No-one desires pain. But he can think that pain is pleasure. No-one would avoid his happiness. But he can think that joy is painful, threatening and dangerous. Everyone will receive what he requests. But he can be confused indeed about the things he wants; the state he would attain. What can he then request that he would want when he receives it? He has asked for what will frighten him, and bring him suffering. Let us resolve today to ask for what we really want, and only this, that we may spend this day in fearlessness, without confusing pain with joy, or fear with love.

W 339 L 2. *"Father, this is Your day. It is a day in which I would do nothing by myself, but hear Your Voice in everything I do; requesting only what You offer me, accepting only Thoughts You share with me."* **W(593)**

Lesson 340 "I can be free of suffering today."

W 340 L 1. *"Father, I thank You for today, and for the freedom I am certain it will bring. This day is holy, for today Your Son will be redeemed. His suffering is done. For he will hear Your Voice directing him to find Christ's vision through forgiveness, and be free forever from all suffering. Thanks for today, my Father. I was born into this world but to achieve this day, and what it holds in joy and freedom for Your holy Son, and for the world he made, which is released along with him today."*

W 340 L 2. Be glad today! Be glad! There is no room for anything but joy and thanks today. Our Father has redeemed His Son this day. Not one of us but will be saved today. Not one who will remain in fear, and none the Father will not gather to Himself, awake in Heaven in the Heart of Love. **W(594)**

(13) What is a Miracle? (W 340 W13)

W 340 W13 1. A miracle is a correction. It does not create, nor really change at all. It merely looks on devastation, and reminds the mind that what it sees is false. It undoes error, but does not attempt to go beyond perception, nor exceed the function of forgiveness.

---

[763] **Matthew 13:44** "The kingdom of heaven is like unto a treasure hidden in the field; which a man found, and hid; and in his joy he goeth and selleth all that he hath, and buyeth that field."

[764] Handwritten mark-up suggests (all are).

[765] Handwritten mark-up suggests (so) instead of "**thus**".

Thus it stays within time's limits. Yet it paves the way for the return of timelessness and love's awakening, for fear must slip away under the gentle remedy it gives.

W 340 W13 2. A miracle contains the gift of grace, for it is given and received as one. And thus it illustrates the law of truth the world does not obey, because it fails entirely to understand its ways. A miracle inverts perception which was upside-down before, and thus it ends the strange distortions that were manifest. Now is perception open to the truth. Now is forgiveness seen as justified.

W 340 W13 3. Forgiveness is the home of miracles. The eyes of Christ deliver[766] them to all they look upon in mercy and in love. Perception stands corrected in His sight, and what was meant to curse has come to bless. Each lily of forgiveness offers all the world the silent miracle of love. And each is laid before the Word of God upon the universal altar to Creator and creation, in the Light of perfect purity and endless joy.

W 340 W13 4. The miracle is taken first on faith, because to ask for it implies the mind has been made ready to conceive of what it cannot see and does not understand. Yet faith will bring its witnesses to show that what it rested on is really there. And thus the miracle will justify your faith in it, and show it rested on a world more real than what you saw before; a world redeemed from what you thought you saw.

W 340 W13 5. Miracles fall like drops of healing rain from Heaven on a dry and dusty world, where starved and thirsty creatures came to die. Now they have water. Now the world is green. And everywhere the signs of life spring up, to show that what is born can never die, for what has life has immortality. **W(595)**

Lesson 341
"I can attack but my own sinlessness,
And it is only that which keeps me safe."

W 341 L 1. *"Father, Your Son is holy. I am he on whom You smile in love and tenderness so deep and dear and still the universe smiles back on You, and shares Your holiness. How pure, how safe, how sacred, then, are we, abiding in Your smile, with all Your love bestowed upon us, living one with You, in brotherhood and Fatherhood complete; in sinlessness so perfect that the Lord of Sinlessness conceives us as His Son, a universe of Thought completing Him."*

W 341 L 2. Let us not, then, attack our sinlessness.[767] For it contains the Word of God to us, and in its kind reflection we are saved. **W(596)**

Lesson 342
"I let forgiveness rest upon all things,
For thus forgiveness will be given me."

W 342 L 1. *"I thank You, Father, for Your plan to save me from the hell I made. It is not real. And You have given me the means to prove its unreality to me. The key is in my hand, and I have reached the door beyond which lies the end of dreams. I stand before the gate of Heaven, wondering if I should enter in and be at home. Let me not wait again today. Let me forgive all things, and let creation be as You would have it be, and as it is. Let me remember that I am Your Son, and opening the door at last, forget illusions in the blazing light of truth, as memory of You returns to me."*

---

[766] The *Urtext* manuscript reads "**The eyes of Christ delivers**" presenting a grammar problem of agreement in number. *FIP* replaces "**delivers**" with (deliver). So do we.

[767] The *Urtext* manuscript has "**ourselves**" rather than (our sinlessness) here, which presents problems in the next sentence, to what then would "**it**" refer? We find the word (sinlessness) hardwritten in here and deem it to be a valid correction. The *Notes* also has "our sinlessness" here.

W 342 L 2. Brother, forgive me now. I come to you to take you home with me. And as we go, the world goes with us on the way to God. **W(597)**

Lesson 343
"I am not asked to make a sacrifice
To find the mercy and the peace of God."

1. "The end of suffering can not be loss. The gift of everything can but be gain.[768] You only give. You never take away. And You created me to be like You, so sacrifice becomes impossible for me as well as You. I, too, must give, and so all things are given unto me forever and forever. As I was created, I remain. Your Son can make no sacrifice, for he must be complete, having the function of completing You. I am complete because I am Your Son. I cannot lose, for I can only give. And everything is mine eternally."

2. The mercy and the peace of God are free. Salvation has no cost. It is a gift that must be freely given and received, and it is this that we would learn today. **W(598)**

Lesson 344
"Today I learn the law of love;
that what I give my brother is my gift to me."

W 344 L 1. *"This is Your law, my Father, not my own. I did not understand[769] what giving means, and thought to save what I desired for myself alone. And as I looked upon the treasure which I thought I had, I found an empty place where nothing ever was, or is or will be. Who can share a dream? And what can an illusion offer me? Yet he whom I forgive will give me gifts beyond the worth of anything on earth. Let my forgiven brothers fill my store with Heaven's treasures, which alone are real. Thus is the law of love fulfilled. And thus Your Son arises and returns to You."*

W 344 L 2. How near we are to one another, as we go to God. How near is He to us. How close the ending of the dream of sin, and the redemption of the Son of God. **W(599)**

Lesson 345
"I offer only miracles today,
For I would have them be returned to me."

W 345 L 1. *"Father, a miracle reflects Your gifts to me, Your Son. And every one I give returns to me, reminding me the law of love is universal. Even here it takes a form which can be recognized, and seen to work. The miracles I give are given back in just the form I need to help me with the problems I perceive. Father, in Heaven it is different, for there, there are no needs. But here on earth the miracle is closer to Your gifts than any other gift which I can give. Then let me give this gift alone today, which, born of true forgiveness, lights the way that I must travel to remember You."*

W 345 L 2. Peace to all seeking hearts today. The light has come, to offer miracles to bless the tired world. It will find rest today, for we will offer what we have received. **W(600)**

Lesson 346
"Today the peace of God envelops me,
And I forget all things except His Love."

W 346 L 1. *"Father, I wake today with miracles correcting my perception of all things. And so begins a day I share with You as I will share eternity, for time has stepped aside today. I do*

---

[768] Handwritten mark-up suggests (be but gain).
[769] Handwritten mark-up suggests (have not understood).

not seek the things of time, and so I will not look upon them.[770] *What I seek today transcends all laws of time and things perceived in time.*[771] *I would forget all things except Your Love. I would abide in You, and know no laws except Your law of Love.*[772] *And I would find the peace which You created for Your Son, forgetting all the foolish toys I made as I behold Your glory and my own."*[773]

W 346 L 2. And when the evening comes today, we will remember nothing but the peace of God. For we will learn today what peace is ours when we forget all things except God's Love. **W(601)**

Lesson 347
"Anger must come from judgment.
Judgment is the weapon I would use against myself To keep all[774] miracles away from me."

W 347 L 1. *"Father, I want what goes against my will, and do not want what is my will to have. Straighten my mind, my Father. It is sick. But You have offered freedom, and I choose to claim Your gift today. And so I give all judgment to the One You gave to me to judge for me. He sees what I behold, and yet He knows the truth. He looks on pain, and yet He understands it is not real, and in His understanding it is healed. He gives the miracles my dreams would hide from my awareness. Let Him judge today. I do not know my will, but He is sure it is Your own. And He will speak for me, and call Your miracle to come to me."*

W 347 L 2. Listen today. Be very still, and hear the gentle Voice for God assuring you that He has judged you as the Son He loves.[775] **W(602)**

Lesson 348
"I have no cause for anger or for fear,
For You surround me. And in every need
That I perceive Your grace suffices me."

W 348 L 1. *"Father, let me remember You are here, and I am not alone. Surrounding me is everlasting Love. I have no cause for anything except the perfect peace and joy I share with You. What need have I for anger or for fear? Surrounding me is perfect safety. Can I be afraid, when Your eternal promise goes with me? Surrounding me is perfect sinlessness. What can I fear, when You created me in holiness as perfect as Your own?"*

W 348 L 2. God's grace suffices us in everything that He would have us do. And only that we choose to be our will as well as His. **W(603)**

Lesson 349
"Today I let Christ's vision look upon
All things for me and judge them not, but give
Each one a miracle of love instead."

W 349 L 1. *"So would I liberate all things I see, and give to them the freedom that I seek. For thus do I obey the law of love, and give what I would find and make my own. It will be given me because I have chosen it as the gift I want to give. Father, Your gifts are mine. Each one that I accept gives me a miracle to give. And giving as I would receive, I learn Your healing miracles belong to me."*

W 349 L 2. Our Father knows our needs.[776] He gives us grace to meet them all.[777] And so we trust in Him to send us miracles to bless the world and heal our minds as we return to Him. **W(604)**

Lesson 350
"Miracles mirror God's eternal Love.
To offer them is to remember Him,
And through His memory to save the world."

W 350 L 1. *"What we forgive becomes a part of us, as we perceive ourselves. The Son of God incorporates all things within himself as You created him. Your memory depends on his forgiveness. What he is, is unaffected by his thoughts. But what he looks upon is their direct result. Therefore, my Father, I would turn to You. Only Your memory will set me free. And only my forgiveness teaches me to let Your memory return to me, and give it to the world in thankfulness."*

W 350 L 2. And as we gather miracles from Him, we will indeed be grateful. For as we remember Him, His Son will be restored to us in the Reality of Love. **W(605)**

(14) What am I? (W 350 W14)

W 350 W14 1. *"I am God's Son, complete and healed and whole, shining in the reflection of His Love. In me is His creation sanctified and guaranteed eternal life. In me is love perfected, fear impossible, and joy established without opposite. I am the holy home of God Himself. I am the Heaven where His Love resides. I am His holy Sinlessness Itself, for in my purity abides His own."*

W 350 W14 2. Our use for words is almost over now. Yet in the final days of this one year we gave to God together, you and I, we found a single purpose that we shared. And thus you joined with me,[778] so what I am are you as well. The truth of what we are is not for words to speak of or[779] describe. Yet we can realize our function here, and words can speak of this and teach it, too, if we exemplify the words in us.

W 350 W14 3. We are the bringers of salvation. We accept our part as Saviors of the world, which through our joint forgiveness is redeemed. And this, our gift, is therefore given us. We look on everyone as brothers, and perceive all things as kindly and as good. We do not seek a function that is past the gates of Heaven. Knowledge will return when we have done our part. We are concerned only with giving welcome to the truth.

W 350 W14 4. Ours[780] are the eyes through which Christ's vision sees a world redeemed from every thought of sin. Ours are the ears

---

[770] **Romans 8:5** For they that are after the flesh do mind the things of the flesh; but they that are after the spirit the things of the spirit.
[771] **1Corinthians 2:14** Now the natural man receiveth not the things of the Spirit of God: for they are foolishness unto him; and he cannot know them, because they are spiritually judged.
[772] **John 15:4** "Abide in Me, and I in you. As the branch cannot bear fruit of itself, unless it abides in the vine, neither can you, unless you abide in Me."
[773] **1Corinthians 13:11** When I was a child, I spake as a child, I felt as a child, I thought as a child: now that I am become a man, I have put away childish things.
[774] Handwritten mark-up suggests (the miracle) in place of "**all miracles**".
[775] **Titus 3:2** to speak evil of no man, not to be contentious, to be gentle, shewing all meekness toward all men.

[776] **Matthew 6:8** Therefore do not be like them. For your Father knows the things you have need of before you ask Him.
Matthew 6:32 For after all these things the Gentiles seek. For your heavenly Father knows that you need all these things.
[777] **Acts 20:32** And now I commend you to God, and to the word of his grace, which is able to build *you* up, and to give *you* the inheritance among all them that are sanctified.
[778] Handwritten mark-up suggests the comma where the *Urtext* manuscript has a period and new sentence. We agree with the handwriting here, it should be a comma.
[779] Handwritten mark-up suggests (nor).
[780] *Urtext* manuscript has "Our" and it clearly needs to be "Ours". *FIP* agrees, and so does the *Notes*.

which hear the Voice of God proclaim the world as sinles.[781] Ours the minds which join together as we bless the world. And from the oneness that we have attained we call to all our brothers, asking them to share our peace and consummate our joy.

W 350 W14 5. We are the holy messengers of God who speak for Him, and carrying His Word to everyone whom He has sent to us, we learn that It is written[782] on our hearts. And thus our minds are changed about the aim for which we came and which we seek to serve. We bring glad tidings to the Son of God, who thought he suffered.[783] Now is he redeemed. And as he sees the gate of Heaven stand open before him, he will enter in and disappear into the Heart of God. **W(606)**

Lesson 351

"My sinless brother is my guide to peace. My sinful brother is my guide to pain. And which I choose to see I will behold."

> **W 351 L 1.** *"Who is my brother but Your holy Son? And if I see him sinful, I proclaim myself a sinner; not a Son of God; alone and friendless in a fearful world. Yet this perception is a choice I make, and can relinquish. I can also see my brother sinless, as Your holy Son. And with this choice I see my sinlessness, my everlasting Comforter and Friend beside me, and my way secure and clear. Choose, then, for me, my Father, through Your Voice. For He alone gives judgment in Your Name."* **W(607)**

Lesson 352

"Judgment and love are opposites. From one Come all the sorrows of the world. But from The Other comes the peace of God Himself."

> **W 352 L 1.** *"Forgiveness looks on sinlessness alone, and judges not. Through this I come to You. Judgment will bind my eyes and make me blind. Yet love, reflected in forgiveness here, reminds me You have given me a way to find Your peace again. I am redeemed when I elect to follow in this way. You have not left me comfortless.[784] I have within me both the memory of You, and One Who leads me to It. Father, I would hear Your Voice, and find Your peace today. For I would love my own Identity, and find in Him the memory of You."* **W(608)**

Lesson 353

"My eyes, my tongue, my hands, my feet today Have but one purpose; to be given Christ To use to bless the world with miracles."

> **W 353 L 1.** *"Father, I give all that is mine today to Christ, to use in any way that best will serve the purpose which I share with Him. Nothing is mine alone, for He and I have joined in purpose. Thus has learning come almost to its appointed end. A while I work with Him to serve His purpose. Then I lose my-*

---

[781] Handwritten mark-up suggests ((holy)).

[782] **Jeremiah 31:33** But this is the covenant that I will make with the house of Israel after those days, saith the LORD; I will put my law in their inward parts, and in their heart will I write it; and I will be their God, and they shall be my people:
Romans 2:15 Who show the work of the law written in their hearts, their conscience also bearing witness, and between themselves their thoughts accusing or else excusing them.

[783] **Luke 1:19** And the angel answered and said to him, "I am Gabriel, who stands in the presence of God, and was sent to speak to you and bring you these glad tidings."
Luke 8:1 Now it came to pass, afterward, that He went through every city and village, preaching and bringing the glad tidings of the kingdom of God. And the twelve were with Him,

[784] **John 14:18** "I will not leave you comfortless; I will come to you".

self in my Identity, and recognize that Christ is but my Self." **W(609)**

Lesson 354

"We stand together, Christ and I, in peace And certainty of purpose. And in Him Is His Creator, as He is in me."

> **W 354 L 1.** *"My oneness with the Christ establishes me as Your Son, beyond the reach of time, and wholly free of every law but Yours. I have no self except the Christ in me. I have no purpose but His own. And He is like His Father. Thus must I be one with You as well as Him. For who is Christ except Your Son as You created Him? And what am I except the Christ in me?"* **W(610)**

Lesson 355

"There is no end to all the peace and joy And all the miracles that I will give When I accept God's Word. Why not today?"

> **W 355 L 1.** *"Why should I wait, my Father, for the joy You promised me? For You will keep Your Word You gave Your Son in exile. I am sure my treasure waits for me, and I need but reach out my hand to find it. Even now my fingers touch it. It is very close. I need not wait an instant more, to be at peace forever. It is You I choose, and my Identity along with You. Your Son would be Himself, and know You as his Father and Creator and his Love."* **W(611)**

Lesson 356

"Sickness is but another name for sin. Healing is but another Name for God. The miracle is thus a call to Him."

> **W 356 L 1.** *"Father, You promised You would never fail to answer any call Your Son might make to You. It does not matter where he is, what seems to be his problem, nor what he believes he has become. He is Your Son, and You will answer him. The miracle reflects Your Love, and thus it answers him. Your Name replaces every thought of sin, and who is sinless cannot suffer pain. Your Name gives answer to Your Son, because to call Your Name is but to call his own."* **W(612)**

Lesson 357

"Truth answers every call we make to God, Responding first with miracles, and then Returning unto us to be Itself."

> **W 357 L 1.** *"Forgiveness, truth's reflection, tells me how to offer miracles, and thus escape the prison house in which I think I live. Your holy Son is pointed out to me, first in my brother; then in me. Your Voice instructs me patiently to hear Your Word and give as I receive. And as I look upon Your Son today, I hear Your Voice instructing me to find the way to You as You appointed that the way shall be: 'Behold his sinlessness and be you healed'."* **W(613)**

Lesson 358

"No call to God can be unheard or left Unanswered. And of this I can be sure; His answer is the one I really want."

> **W 358 L 1.** *"You Who remember what I really am alone remember what I really want. You speak for God, and so You*

speak for me,[785] *and what You give me comes from God Himself. Your Voice, my Father, then is mine as well, and all I want is what You offer me, in just the form You chose that it be mine. Let me remember all I do not know, and let my voice be still, remembering.*[786] *But let me not forget Your Love and care, keeping Your promise to Your Son in my awareness always. Let me not forget myself is nothing, but my Self is All."* **W(614)**

Lesson 359
"God's answer is some form of peace. All pain is healed; all misery replaced with joy. All prison doors are opened. And all sin is understood as merely a mistake."

W 359 L 1. *"Father, today we will forgive Your world, and let creation be Your own. We have misunderstood all things. But we have not made sinners of the holy Sons of God. What You created sinless so abides forever and forever. Such are we. And we rejoice to learn that we have made mistakes which have no real effects on us. Sin is impossible, and on this fact forgiveness rests upon a certain base more solid than the shadow world we see. Help us forgive, for we would be redeemed. Help us forgive, for we would be at peace."* **W(615)**

Lesson 360
"Peace be to me, the holy Son of God. Peace to my brother, who is one with me. Let all the world be blessed with peace through us."

W 360 L 1. *"Father, it is Your peace that I would give, receiving it of You. I am Your Son, forever just as You created me, for the Great Rays remain forever still and undisturbed within me. I would reach to them in silence and in certainty, for nowhere else can certainty be found. Peace be to me, and peace to all the world. In holiness were we created, and in holiness do we remain. Your Son is like to You in perfect sinlessness, and with this thought we gladly say 'Amen'."* **W(616)**

Final Lessons[787] *(W 360 FL)*

W 360 FL 1. Our final lessons will be left as free of words as possible. We use them but at the beginning of our practicing, and only to remind us that we seek to go beyond them. Let us turn to Him Who leads the way and makes our footsteps sure. To Him we leave these lessons, as to Him we give our lives henceforth. For we would not return again to the belief in sin, which made the world seem ugly and unsafe, attacking and destroying, dangerous in all its ways and treacherous beyond the hope of trust and the escape from pain.

W 360 FL 2. His is the only way to find the peace that God has given us. It is His way that everyone must travel in the end, because it is this ending God Himself appointed. In the dream of time it seems to be far off. And yet, in truth, it is already here; already serving us as gracious guidance in the way to go. Let us together follow in this way that truth points out to us. And let us be the leaders of our many brothers who are seeking for the way but find it not.

W 360 FL 3. And to this purpose let us dedicate our minds, directing all our thoughts to serve the function of salvation. Unto us the aim is given to forgive the world.[788] It is the goal that God has given us. It is His ending to the dream we seek, and not our own. For all that we forgive we will not fail to recognize as part of God Himself. And thus His memory is given back completely and complete.

W 360 FL 4. It is our function to remember Him on earth, as it is given us to be His own completion in reality. So let us not forget our goal is shared. For it is that remembrance which contains the memory of God, and points the way to Him and to the Heaven of His peace. And shall we not forgive our brother, who can offer this to us? He is the way, the truth and life that show the way to us.[789] In him resides salvation, offered us through our forgiveness given unto him. **W(617)**

W 360 FL 5. We will not end this year without the gift our Father promised to His holy Son. We are forgiven now,[790] and we are saved from all the wrath we thought belonged to God, and found it was a dream. We are restored to sanity, in which we understand that anger is insane, attack is mad, and vengeance merely foolish fantasy. We have been saved from wrath because we learned we were mistaken. Nothing more than that. And is a Father[791] angry at His[792] Son[793] because he failed to understand the truth?

W 360 FL 6. We come in honesty to Him[794] and say we did not understand, and ask Him to help us to learn His lessons through the Voice of His own Teacher. Would He hurt His Son? Or would He rush to answer him, and say, "This is my Son, and all I have is his?"[795] Be certain He will answer thus, for these are His own Words to you. And more than that can no-one ever have, for in these Words is all there is, and all that there will be throughout all time and in eternity. **W(618)**

Lesson 361-365.[796]
"This holy instant would I give to You. Be You in charge. For I would follow You, Certain that Your direction gives me peace."

W 361 L 1. If I need a word to help me, He will give it to me. If I need a thought, that will He also give. [797] And if I need but stillness and a tranquil, open mind, these are the gifts I will receive of Him. He is in charge by my request. And He will hear and answer me, because He speaks for God my Father and His holy Son. **W(619)**

Epilogue[798] *(W 361 EP)*

W 361 EP 1. This course is a beginning, not an end. Your Friend goes with you. You are not alone. No-one who calls on Him can call in vain. Whatever troubles you, be certain that He has the answer, and will gladly give it to you if you simply turn to Him and ask it of Him. He will not withhold all answers that you need for anything that seems to trouble you. He knows the way to solve all problems and resolve all doubts. His certainty is yours. You need but ask it of him, and it will be given you.

W 361 EP 2. You are as certain of arriving home as is the pathway of the sun laid down before it rises, after it has set, and in the half-lit hours in between. Indeed, your pathway is more certain still, for it

---

[785] *Urtext* manuscript has period and sentence break here. Handwritten mark-up suggests the comma only, with which suggestion we agree.
[786] **John 14:26** "But the Comforter, *even the Holy Spirit, whom the Father will send in my name, he shall teach you all things, and bring to your remembrance all that I said unto you.*"
[787] The words "Final Lessons" are not present in the *Urtext* manuscript.
[788] **John 20:23** "If you forgive the sins of any, they are forgiven them; if you retain the sins of any, they are retained."
[789] **John 14:6** Jesus said to him, "I am the way, the truth, and the life. No one comes to the Father except through Me."
[790] *Urtext* manuscript has period and new sentence here. Handwritten mark-up suggests only a comma, with which suggestion we agree.
[791] Handwritten mark-up suggests (father).
[792] Handwritten mark-up suggests (his).
[793] Handwritten mark-up suggests (son).
[794] Handwritten mark-up suggests (God) instead of "**Him**".
[795] **Luke 15:31** And he said to him, "Son, you are always with me, and all that I have is yours."
[796] The *Urtext* manuscript says "3 60-365" but there is already a **Lesson 360**, so this needs to be "361-365".
[797] Handwritten mark-up suggests (And).
[798] The word "Epilogue" is not present in the *Urtext* manuscript.

can not be possible to change the course of those whom God has called to Him. Therefore obey your will, and follow Him Whom you accepted as your voice, to speak of what you really want and really need. His is the Voice of God, and also yours. And thus He speaks of freedom and of truth.

W 361 EP 3. No more specific lessons are assigned, for there is no more need of them. Henceforth, hear but the Voice for God and for your Self when you retire from the world, to seek reality instead. He will direct your efforts, telling you exactly what to do, how to direct your mind, and when to come to Him in silence, asking for His sure direction and His certain Word. His is the Word that God has given you. His is the Word you chose to be your own.

W 361 EP 4. And now I place you in His hands, to be His faithful followers, with Him as Guide through every difficulty and all pain that you may think is real. Nor will He give you pleasures that will pass away, for He gives only the eternal and the good. Let Him prepare you further. He has earned your trust by speaking daily to you of your Father and yourbrother and your Self. He will continue; now you walk with Him as certain as is He of where you go; as sure as He of how you should proceed, as confident as He is of the **W(620)** goal, and of your safe arrival in the end.

W 361 EP 5. The end is certain, and the means as well. To this we say "Amen." We[799] will be told exactly what God wills for us[800] each time there is a choice to make. And He will speak for God and for your Self, thus making sure that hell will claim you not, and that each choice you make brings Heaven nearer to your reach. And so we walk with Him from this time on, and turn to Him for guidance and for peace and right[801] direction. Joy attends our way.[802] For we go homeward to an open door which God has held unclosed to welcome us.[803]

W 361 EP 6. We trust our ways to Him and say "Amen." In peace we will continue in His way, and trust all things to Him. In confidence we wait His answers, as we ask His will in everything we do. He loves Gods Son as we would love him, and He teaches us how to behold him through His eyes, and love him as He does. You do not walk alone. God's angels hover close, and all about. His Love surrounds you,[804] and of this be sure: that I will never leave you comfortless.[805] **W(621)**

---

[799] Handwritten mark-up suggests (You) (it does this in shorthand). *Notes* clearly has shorthand for "we."
[800] Handwritten mark-up suggests (you) (it does this in shorthand). *Notes* clearly has "us."
[801] Handwritten mark-up suggests (sure)
[802] **Isaiah 55:12** For ye shall go out with joy, and be led forth with peace: the mountains and the hills shall break forth before you into singing, and all the trees of the field shall clap their hands.
[803] **John 10:9** "I am the door: by me if any man enter in, he shall be saved, and shall go in and go out, and shall find pasture."
[804] **Isaiah 63:9** In all their affliction he was afflicted, and the angel of his presence saved them: in his love and in his pity he redeemed them; and he bare them, and carried them all the days of old.
[805] **John 15:10** "If ye keep my commandments, ye shall abide in my love; even as I have kept my Father's commandments, and abide in his love."

Urtext Volume III: *Manual for Teachers*

Urtext Volume III - *Manual for Teachers*

Table of Contents

URTEXT* VOLUME III: *MANUAL FOR TEACHERS I

1. INTRODUCTION 1
2. WHO ARE GOD'S TEACHERS? 1
3. WHO ARE THEIR PUPILS? 1
4. WHAT ARE THE LEVELS OF TEACHING? 2
5. WHAT ARE THE CHARACTERISTICS OF GOD'S TEACHERS? 3
   - A. Introduction 3
   - B. Trust 3
   - C. Honesty 4
   - D. Tolerance 4
   - E. Gentleness 4
   - F. Joy 4
   - G. Defenselessness 4
   - H. Generosity 4
   - I. Patience 5
   - J. Faithfulness 5
   - K. Open-Mindedness 5
6. HOW IS HEALING ACCOMPLISHED? 5
   - A. Introduction 5
   - B. The perceived purpose of sickness 5
   - C. The shift in perception 6
   - D. The function of the Teacher of God 6
7. IS HEALING CERTAIN? 6
8. SHOULD HEALING BE REPEATED? 7
9. HOW CAN THE PERCEPTION OF ORDER OF DIFFICULTIES BE AVOIDED? 7
10. ARE CHANGES REQUIRED IN THE LIFE SITUATIONS OF GOD'S TEACHERS? 8
11. HOW IS JUDGMENT RELINQUISHED? 8
12. HOW IS PEACE POSSIBLE IN THIS WORLD? 9
13. HOW MANY TEACHERS OF GOD ARE NEEDED TO SAVE THE WORLD? 9
14. WHAT IS THE REAL MEANING OF SACRIFICE? 10
15. HOW WILL THE WORLD END? 11
16. IS EACH ONE TO BE JUDGED IN THE END? 11
17. HOW SHOULD THE TEACHER OF GOD SPEND HIS DAY? 12
18. HOW DO GOD'S TEACHERS DEAL WITH THEIR PUPILS' THOUGHTS OF MAGIC? 13
19. HOW IS CORRECTION MADE? 14
20. WHAT IS JUSTICE? 14
21. WHAT IS THE PEACE OF GOD? 15
22. WHAT IS THE ROLE OF WORDS IN HEALING? 15
23. HOW ARE HEALING AND ATONEMENT RELATED? 16
24. DOES JESUS HAVE A SPECIAL PLACE IN HEALING? 17
25. IS REINCARNATION TRUE? 18
26. ARE "PSYCHIC" POWERS DESIRABLE? 18
27. CAN GOD BE REACHED DIRECTLY? 19
28. WHAT IS DEATH? 19
29. WHAT IS THE RESURRECTION? 20
30. AS FOR THE REST 21

Urtext Volume III: *Manual for Teachers*

1. INTRODUCTION

M 1 A 1. The[1] role of teaching and learning is actually reversed in the thinking of the world. The reversal is characteristic. It seems as if the teacher and the learner are separated, the teacher giving something to the learner rather than to himself. Further, the act of teaching is regarded as a special activity in which one engages only a relatively small proportion of one's time. The course, on the other hand, emphasizes that to teach is to learn, so that teacher and learner are the same. It also emphasizes that teaching is a constant process; it goes on every moment of the day and continues into sleeping thoughts as well.

M 1 A 2. To teach is to demonstrate. There are only two thought systems, and you demonstrate that you believe one or the other is true all the time. From your demonstration others learn and so do you. The question is not whether you will teach, for in that there is no choice. The purpose of the course might be said to provide you with a means of choosing what you want to teach on the basis of what you want to learn. You cannot give to someone else,[2] and this you learn through teaching. Teaching is but a call to witnesses to attest to what you believe. It is a method of conversion. This is not done by words alone. Any situation must be to you a chance to teach others what you are and what they are to you. No more than that, but also never less.

M 1 A 3. The curriculum that[3] you set up is therefore determined exclusively by what you think you are, and what you believe the relationship of others is to you. In the formal teaching situation, these questions may be totally unrelated to what you think you are teaching. Yet it is impossible not to use the content of any situation on behalf of what you really teach and therefore[4] learn. To this the verbal content of your teaching is quite irrelevant. It may coincide with it or it may not. It is the teaching underlying what you say that teaches you. Teaching but reinforces what you believe about yourself. Its fundamental **M(2)** purpose is to diminish self-doubt. This does not mean that the self you are trying to protect is real. But it does mean that the self you think is real is what you teach.

M 1 A 4. This is inevitable. There is no escape from it. How could it be otherwise? Everyone who follows the world's curriculum, and everyone here does follow it until he changes his mind, teaches solely to convince himself that he is what he is not. Herein is the purpose of the world. What else, then, would its curriculum be? Into this hopeless and closed learning situation, which teaches nothing but despair and death, God sends His teachers. And as they teach His lessons of joy and hope, their learning finally becomes complete.

M 1 A 5. Except for God's teachers there would be no[5] hope of salvation, for the world of sin would be forever real. The self-deceiving must deceive, for they must teach deception. And what else is hell? This is a manual for the teachers of God. They are not perfect or they would not be here. Yet it is their mission to become perfect here, and so they teach perfection over and over, in many, many ways, until they have learned it. And then they are seen no more, although their thoughts remain a source of strength and truth forever. Who are they? How are they chosen? What do they do? How can they work out their own salvation and the salvation of the world? This manual attempts to answer these questions. **M(3)**

2. WHO ARE GOD'S TEACHERS?

M 2 A 1. A teacher of God is anyone who chooses to be one. His qualifications consist solely in this; somehow, somewhere he has made a deliberate choice in which he did not see his interests as apart from someone else's. Once he has done that his road is established and his direction is sure. A light has entered the darkness.[6] It may be a single light, but that is enough. He has entered an agreement with God, even if he does not yet believe in Him. He has become a bringer of salvation.[7] He has become a teacher of God.

M 2 A 2. They come from all over the world. They come from all religions and from no religion. They are the ones who have answered. The Call is universal. It goes on all the time everywhere. It calls for teachers to speak for it and redeem the world. Many hear it but few will answer.[8] But[9] it is all a matter of time. Everyone will answer in the end, but the end can be a long, long way off. It is because of this that the plan of the teachers was established. Their function is to save time. Each one begins as a single light, but with the Call at its center it is a light that cannot be limited. And each one saves a thousand years of time as the world judges it. To the Call itself time has no meaning.

M 2 A 3. There is a course for every teacher of God. The form of the course varies greatly. So do the particular teaching aids involved. But the content of the course never changes. Its central theme is always, "God's Son is guiltless, and in his innocence is his salvation." It can be taught by actions or thoughts; in words or soundlessly; in any language or in no language; in any place or time or manner. It does not matter who the teacher was before he heard the Call. He has become a savior by his answering. He has seen someone else as himself. He has therefore found his own salvation and the salvation of the world. In his rebirth is the world reborn. **M(4)**

M 2 A 4. This[10] is a manual for a special curriculum, intended for teachers of a special form of the universal course. There are many thousands of other forms, all with the same outcome. They merely save time. Yet it is time alone that winds on wearily, and the world is very tired now. It is old and worn and without hope. There was never a question of outcome, for what can change the Will of God? But time, with its illusions of change and death, wears out the world and all things in it. Yet time has an ending, and it is this that the teachers of God are appointed to bring about. For time is in their hands. Such was their choice, and it is given them.

3. WHO ARE THEIR PUPILS?

M 3 A 1. Certain pupils have been assigned to each of God's teachers, and they will begin to look for him as soon as he has answered the Call. They were chosen for him because the form of the universal curriculum that he will teach is best for them in view

---

[1] APRIL 12, 1972
[2] FIP inserts "but only to yourself." That insertion also appears written in between the lines in the *Notes*.
[3] FIP omits "that" but it is distinctly present in the *Notes*.
[4] FIP inserts "really" which is also written between the lines in the *Notes*.
[5] FIP changes "no" to "little." It is "no" in the *Notes*.
[6] **Luke 1:79** "To give light to those who sit in darkness and the shadow of death, To guide our feet into the way of peace."
John 1:5 And the light shines in the darkness, and the darkness did not comprehend it.
[7] **Luke 1:77** "To give knowledge of salvation to His people by the remission of their sins,"
[8] **Matthew 20:16** "So the last will be first, and the first last. For many are called, but few chosen."
[9] FIP changes "But" to "Yet." The *Notes* has "yet."
[10] (April 27 1972)

of their level of understanding. His pupils have actually[11] been waiting for him, for his coming is certain. Again, it is only a matter of time. Once he has chosen to fulfill his role, they are ready to fulfill theirs. Time waits on his choice, but not whom he will serve. When he is ready to learn, the opportunities to teach will be provided for him.

M 3 A 2. In order to understand the teaching-learning plan of salvation, it is necessary to grasp the concept of time which[12] the course sets forth. Atonement corrects illusions, not truth. Therefore, it corrects what never was. Further, the plan for this correction was established and completed simultaneously, for the Will of God is entirely apart from time. So is all reality, being of Him. The instant the idea of separation entered the mind of God's Son, in that same instant was God's Answer given. In time this happened very long ago. In reality it never happened at all. **M(5)**

M 3 A 3. The world of time is the world of illusion. What happened long ago seems to be happening now. Choices made long since appear to be open; yet to be made. What has been learned and understood and long ago passed by is looked upon as a new thought, a fresh idea, a different approach. Because your will is free you can accept what has already happened at any time you choose, and only then will you realize that it was always there. As the course emphasizes, you are not free to choose the curriculum, or even the form in which you will learn it. You are free, however, to decide when you want to learn it. And as you accept it, it is already learned.

M 3 A 4. Time really, then, goes backward to an instant so ancient that it is beyond all memory and past even the possibility of remembering. Yet because it is an instant that is relived again and again and still again, it seems to be now. And thus it is that pupil and teacher seem to come together in the present, finding each other as if they had not met before. The pupil comes at the right time to the right place. This is inevitable, because he made the right choice in that ancient instant which he now relives. So has the teacher, too, made an inevitable choice out of an ancient past. God's Will in everything but seems to take time in the working-out. What could delay the power of eternity?

M 3 A 5. When pupil and teacher come together, a teaching-learning situation begins. For the teacher is not really the one who does the teaching. God's Teacher speaks to any two who join together for learning purposes.[13] The relationship is holy because of that purpose, and God has promised to send His Spirit into any holy relationship. In the teaching-learning situation, each one learns that giving and receiving are the same. The demarcations they have drawn between their roles, their minds, their bodies, their needs, their interests, and all the differences they thought separated them from one another, fade and grow dim and disappear. Those who would learn the same course share one interest and one goal. And thus he who was the learner becomes a teacher **M(6)** of God Himself, for he has made the one decision that gave his teacher to him. He has seen in another person the same interests as his own.

4. WHAT ARE THE LEVELS OF TEACHING?

M 4 A 1. The teachers of God have no set teaching level. Each teaching-learning situation involves a different relationship at the beginning, although the ultimate goal is always the same; to make of the relationship a holy relationship, in which both can look upon the Son of God as sinless. There is no-one from whom a teacher of God cannot learn, so there is no-one whom he cannot teach. However, from a practical point of view he cannot meet everyone, nor can everyone find him. Therefore, the plan includes very specific contacts to be made for each teacher of God. There are no accidents in salvation. Those who are to meet will meet, because together they have the potential for a holy relationship. They are ready for each other.

M 4 A 2. The simplest level of teaching appears to be quite superficial. It consists of what seem to be very casual encounters; a chance meeting of two apparent strangers in an elevator, a child who is not looking where he is going running into an adult "by accident,"[14] two students who happen[15] to walk home together. These are not chance encounters. Each of them has the potential for becoming a teaching-learning situation.[16] Perhaps the seeming strangers in the elevator will smile to one another, perhaps the man[17] will not scold the child for bumping into him; perhaps the students will become friends. Even at the level of the most casual encounter, it is possible for two people to lose sight of separate interests, if only for a moment. That moment will be enough. Salvation has come. **M(7)**

M 4 A 3. It is difficult to understand that levels of teaching the universal course is a concept as meaningless in reality as is time. The illusion of one permits the illusion of the other. In time, the teacher of God seems to begin to change his mind about the world with a[18] single decision, and then learns more and more about the new direction as he teaches it. We have covered the illusion of time already, but the illusion of levels of teaching seems to be something different. Perhaps the best way to demonstrate that these levels cannot exist is simply to say that any level of the teaching-learning situation is part of God's plan for Atonement, and His plan can have no levels, being a reflection of His Will. Salvation is always ready and always there. God's teachers work at different levels, but the result is always the same.

M 4 A 4. Each teaching-learning situation is maximal in the sense that each person involved will learn the most that he can from the other person at that time. In this sense, and in this sense only, we can speak of levels of teaching. Using the term in this way, the second level of teaching is a more sustained relationship, in which, for a time, two people enter into a fairly intense teaching-learning situation and then appear to separate. As with the first level, these meetings are not accidental, nor is what appears to be the end of the relationship a real end. Again, each has learned the most he can at the time. Yet all who meet will someday meet again, for it is the destiny of all relationships to become holy. God is not mistaken in His Son.

M 4 A 5. The third level of teaching occurs in relationships which, once they are formed, are lifelong. These are teaching-learning situations in which each person is given a chosen learning partner who presents him with unlimited opportunities for learning. These relationships are generally few, because their existence implies that those involved have reached a stage simultaneously in which the teaching-learning balance is actually perfect. This does not mean that **M(8)** they necessarily recognize this; in fact, they generally do not. They may even be quite hostile to each other for some time, and perhaps for life. Yet should they decide to learn it, the perfect lesson is before them and can be learned. And if they decide to learn that lesson, they become the saviors of the teachers who falter and may even seem to fail. No teacher of God can fail to find the Help he needs.

---

[11] Handwritten mark-up suggests the insertion of "actually." The *Notes* has "actually."
[12] FIP changes "which" to "that." The *Notes* has "which."
[13] **Matthew 18:20** "For where two or three are gathered together in My name, I am there in the midst of them."
[14] FIP changes "accident" to "chance." The *Notes* has "accident."
[15] FIP changes "who happen" to "happening." The *Notes* has "who happen."
[16] The *Urtext* manuscript has this sentence originally typed as "Each of them has a potential for becoming teaching-learning situations." Handwritten mark-up changes the sentence to the way it is in the *Notes*, which is also how it appears above.
[17] FIP changes "man" to "adult." The *Notes* has "man."
[18] The manuscript has "the." Handwritten mark-up and FIP change "the" to "a" which reflects the *Notes*.

5. What Are the Characteristics of God's Teachers?

A. Introduction

M 5 A 1. The[19] surface traits of God's teachers are not at all alike. They do not look alike to the body's eyes, they come from vastly different backgrounds, their experiences of the world vary greatly, and their superficial "personalities" are quite distinct. Nor at the beginning stages of their functioning as teachers of God, have they[20] yet acquired the deeper characteristics that will establish them as what they are. God gives special gifts to His teachers because they have a special role in His plan for Atonement. Their specialness is, of course, only temporary; set in time as a means of leading out of time. These special gifts, born in the holy relationship toward which the teaching-learning situation is geared, become characteristic of all teachers of God who have advanced in their own learning. In this respect they are all alike.

M 5 A 2. All differences among the Sons of God are temporary. Nevertheless, in time it can be said that the advanced teachers of God have the following characteristics:

B. Trust

M 5 B 1. This is the foundation on which their ability to fulfill their function rests. Perception is[21] the[22] result of learning. In fact, perception is learning, because cause and effect are never separated. The teachers of God have trust in the world, because they have learned it is not governed by the laws the **M(9)** world made up. It is governed by a Power which is in them but not of them.[23] It is this Power that keeps all things safe. It is through this Power that the teachers of God look on a forgiven world.

M 5 B 2. When this Power has once been experienced, it is impossible to trust one's own petty strength again. Who would attempt to fly with the tiny wings of a sparrow when the mighty power of an eagle has been given him? And who would place his faith in the shabby offerings of the ego when the gifts of God are laid before him? What is it that induces them to make the shift?

M 5 B 3. First, they must go through what might be called "a period of undoing." This need not be painful, but it usually is so experienced. It seems as if things are being taken away, and it is rarely understood initially that their lack of value is merely being recognized. How can lack of value be perceived unless the perceiver is in a position where he must see things in a different light? He is not yet at a point at which he can make the shift entirely internally. And so the plan will sometimes call for changes in what seem to be external circumstances. These changes are always helpful. When the teacher of God has learned that much, he goes on to the second stage.

M 5 B 4. Next, the teacher of God must go through "a period of sorting-out." This is always somewhat difficult because, having learned that the changes in his life are always helpful, he must now decide all things on the basis of whether they increase the helpfulness or hamper it. He will find that many, if not most of the things he valued before will merely hinder his ability to transfer what he has learned to new situations as they arise. Because he has valued what is really valueless, he will not generalize the lesson for fear of loss and sacrifice. **M(10)** It takes great learning to understand that all things, events, encounters and circumstances are helpful. It is only to the extent to which they are helpful that any degree of reality should be accorded them in this world of illusion. The word "value" can apply to nothing else.

M 5 B 5. The third stage through[24] which the teacher of God must go can be called a "period of relinquishment." If this is interpreted as giving up the desirable it will engender enormous conflict. Few teachers of God escape this distress entirely. There is, however, no point in sorting out the valuable from the valueless unless the next obvious step is taken. The third step is rarely if ever begun until the second is complete.[25] Therefore, the period of overlap is apt to be one in which the teacher of God feels called upon to sacrifice his own best interests on behalf of truth. He has not realized as yet how wholly impossible such a demand would be. He can learn this only as he actually does give up the valueless. Through this, he learns that where he anticipated grief, he finds a happy light-heartedness instead; where he thought something was asked of him he finds a gift bestowed on[26] him.

M 5 B 6. Now comes "a period of settling down." This is a quiet time, in which the teacher of God rests a while in reasonable peace. Now he consolidates his learning. Now he begins to see the transfer value of what he has learned. Its potential is literally staggering, and the teacher of God is now at the point in his progress at which he sees in it his whole way out. "Give up what you do not want, and keep what you do." How simple is the obvious. And how easy to do. The teacher of God needs this period of respite. He has not yet come as far as he thinks. Yet when he is ready to go on, he goes with mighty companions beside him. Now he rests a while, and gathers them before going on. He will not go on from here alone. **M(11)**

M 5 B 7. The next stage is indeed "a period of unsettling." Now must the teacher of God understand that he did not really know what was valuable and what was valueless. All that he really learned so far was that he did not want the valueless and that he did want the valuable. Yet his own sorting out was meaningless in teaching him the difference. The idea of sacrifice, so central to his own thought system, had made it impossible for him to judge. He thought he had[27] learned willingness, but now he sees that he does not know what the willingness is for. And now he must attain a state that may remain impossible[28] for a long, long time. He must learn to lay all judgment aside and ask only what he really wants in every circumstance. Were not each step in this direction so heavily reinforced, it would be hard indeed.

M 5 B 8. And finally, there is "a period of achievement." It is here that learning is consolidated. Now what was seen as merely shadows before become[29] solid gains, to be counted on in all "emergencies" as well as tranquil times. Indeed, the tranquility is their result; the outcome of honest learning, consistency of thought and full transfer. This is the stage of real peace, for here is Heaven's state fully reflected. From here, the way to Heaven is

---

[19] May 26, 1972
[20] FIP inserts "as" after "they." This does not appear to be present in the *Notes*, but the *Notes* legibility is poor, leaving the question somewhat open.
[21] FIP adds emphasis. The *Notes* does not.
[22] The manuscript has "a"; Handwritten mark-up and FIP suggest "the" instead of "a" which reflects the *Notes*.
[23] **John 15:19** "If you were of the world, the world would love its own. Yet because you are not of the world, but I chose you out of the world, therefore the world hates you."
1 John 4:4 "Ye are of God, *my* little children, and have overcome them: because greater is he that is in you than he that is in the world."

[24] *Urtext* manuscript has "to" originally typed. Handwritten mark-up inserts "through." The *Notes* has the glyph for "through."
[25] This sentence omitted by FIP, (all editions) but it is present in the *Notes*.
[26] Originally typed "upon," handwritten mark-up and FIP change "upon" to "on" which reflects the *Notes*.
[27] FIP omits the word "had." The *Notes* includes "had."
[28] FIP inserts "to reach" which words are not present in the *Notes*.
[29] Originally typed "becomes." FIP makes this "become" which reflects the *Notes*. There is more than one way to understand the grammar here. "What was seen as shadows" could be considered a singular noun clause or the subject could be considered "shadows" which is plural, making either "becomes" or "become" appropriate. We're opting for the majority view here.

open and easy. In fact, it is here. Who would "go" anywhere, if peace of mind is already complete? And who would seek to change tranquility for something more desirable? What could be more desirable than this? **M(12)**

C. Honesty

M 5 C 1. All other traits of God's teachers rest on trust. Once that has been achieved the others cannot fail to follow. Only the trusting can afford honesty, for only they can see its value. Honesty does not apply only to[30] what you say. The term actually means consistency. There is nothing you say that contradicts what you think or do; no thought opposes any other thought; no act belies your word; and no word lacks agreement with another. Such are the truly honest. At no level are they in conflict with themselves. Therefore it is impossible for them to be in conflict with anyone or anything.

M 5 C 2. The peace of mind which the advanced teachers of God experience is largely due to their perfect honesty. It is only the wish to deceive that makes for war. No-one at one with himself can even conceive of conflict. Conflict is the inevitable result of self-deception, and self-deception is dishonesty. There is no challenge to a teacher of God. Challenge implies doubt, and the trust on which God's teachers rest secure makes doubt impossible. Therefore they can only succeed. In this as in all things they are honest. They can only succeed, because they never do their will alone. They choose for all mankind; for all the world and all things in it; for the unchanging and unchangeable beyond appearances; and for the Son of God and his Creator. How could they not succeed? They choose in perfect honesty, sure of their choice of themselves.

D. Tolerance

M 5 D 1. God's teachers do not judge. To judge is to be dishonest, for to judge is to assume a position you do not have. Judgment without self-deception is impossible. Judgment implies that you have been deceived in your brothers. How then could you not have been deceived in yourself? Judgment implies a lack of trust, and trust remains the bedrock of the teacher of God's whole thought system. **M(13)** Let this be lost and all his learning goes. Without judgment are all things equally acceptable, for who could judge otherwise? Without judgment are all men brothers, for who is there who stands apart? Judgment destroys honesty and shatters trust. No teacher of God can judge and hope to learn.

E. Gentleness

M 5 E 1. Harm is impossible for God's teachers. They can neither harm nor be harmed. Harm is the outcome of judgment. It is the dishonest act that follows a[31] dishonest thought. It is a verdict of guilt upon a brother and therefore on oneself. It is the end of peace and the denial of learning. It demonstrates the absence of God's curriculum and its replacement by insanity. No teacher of God but must learn, – and fairly early in his training, – that harmfulness completely obliterates his function from his awareness. It will make him confused, fearful, angry and suspicious. It will make the Holy Spirit's lessons impossible to learn. Nor can God's Teacher be heard at all except by those who realize that harm can actually achieve nothing. No gain can come from[32] it.

M 5 E 2. Therefore God's teachers are wholly gentle. They need the strength of gentleness, for it is in this that the function of salvation becomes easy. To those who would do harm it is impossible. To those to whom harm has no meaning it is merely natural. What choice but this has meaning to the sane? Who chooses hell when he perceives a way to Heaven? And who would choose the weakness that must come from harm in place of the unfailing, all-encompassing and limitless strength of gentleness? The might of God's teachers lies in their gentleness, for they have understood their evil thoughts came neither from God's Son nor his Creator. Thus did they join their thoughts with Him Who is their Source. And so their will, which always was His Own, is free to be itself. **M(14)**

F. Joy

M 5 F 1. Joy is the inevitable result of gentleness. Gentleness means that fear is now impossible, and what could come to interfere with joy? The open hands of gentleness are always filled. The gentle have no pain. They cannot suffer. Why would they not be joyous? They are sure they are beloved and must be safe. Joy goes with gentleness as surely as grief attends attack. God's teachers trust in Him. And they are sure His Teacher goes before them, making sure no harm can come to them. They hold His gifts and follow in His way, because God's Voice directs them in all things. Joy is their song of thanks. And Christ looks down on them in thanks as well. His need of them is just as great as theirs of Him. How joyous it is to share the purpose of salvation.

G. Defenselessness

M 5 G 1. God's teachers have learned how to be simple. They have no dreams that need defense against the truth.[33] They do not try to make themselves. Their joy comes from their understanding Who created them. And does what God created need defense? No-one can become an advanced teacher of God until he fully understands that defenses are but the[34] foolish guardians of mad illusions. The more grotesque the dream, the fiercer and more powerful its defenses seem to be. Yet when the teacher of God finally agrees to look past them, he finds[35] nothing was there. Slowly at first he lets himself be undeceived. But he learns faster as his trust increases. It is not danger that comes when defenses are laid down. It is safety. It is peace. It is joy. And it is God. **M(15)**

H. Generosity

M 5 H 1. The term generosity has special meaning to the teacher of God. It is not the usual meaning of the word; in fact, it is a meaning that must be learned and learned very carefully. Like all the other attributes of God's teachers this one rests ultimately on trust, for without trust no-one can be generous in the true sense. To the world, generosity means "giving away" in the sense of "giving up." To the teachers of God, it means "giving away" in order to keep. This has been emphasized throughout the text and the workbook, but it is perhaps more alien to the thinking of the world than many other ideas in our curriculum. Its greater strangeness lies merely in the obviousness of its reversal of the world's thinking. In the clearest way possible and at the simplest of levels, the word means the exact opposite to the teachers of God and to the world.

M 5 H 2. The teacher of God is generous out of Self-interest.[36] This does not refer, however, to the self the world speaks of.[37] The teacher of God does not want anything he cannot give away, because he realizes it would be valueless to him by definition. What would he want it for? He could only lose because of it. He could not gain. Therefore he does not seek what only he could keep,

---

[30] Originally typed, "to only," handwritten mark-up and FIP change this to "only to" which reflects the *Notes*.
[31] Handwritten mark-up and FIP change "the" to "a" which change reflects the *Notes*.
[32] FIP changes "from" to "of" but the *Notes* and the *Urtext* manuscript clearly have "from."
[33] *Urtext* manuscript has "trust" crossed out and "truth" penciled in. The *Notes* and FIP both have "truth."
[34] FIP omits "the" but the *Notes* retains it.
[35] FIP adds "that" which is not present in the *Notes*.
[36] *Urtext* manuscript does not capitalize "Self" here, but FIP does and we agree it should be capitalized. It is not clear from the *Notes* whether this was originally capitalized or not.
[37] FIP changes this to "to the self of which the world speaks" which is arguably better grammar. However, the *Notes* has it as it stands.

because that is a guarantee of loss. He does not want to suffer. Why should he ensure himself pain? But he does want to keep for himself all things that are of God, and therefore for His Son. These are the things that belong to him. These he can give away in true generosity, protecting them forever for himself. **M(16)**

I. Patience

M 5 I 1. Those who are certain of the outcome can afford to wait, and wait without anxiety. Patience is natural to the teacher of God. All he sees is certain outcome, at a time perhaps unknown[38] as yet, but not in doubt. The time will be as right as is the answer. And this is true for everything that happens now or in the future. The past as well held no mistakes; nothing that did not serve to benefit the world as well as him to whom it seemed to happen. Perhaps it was not understood at the time. Even so, the teacher of God is willing to reconsider all his past decisions, if they are causing pain to anyone. Patience is natural to those who trust. Sure of the ultimate interpretation of all things in time, no outcome already seen or yet to come can cause them fear.

J. Faithfulness

M 5 J 1. The extent of the teacher of God's faithfulness is the measure of his advancement in the curriculum. Does he still select some aspects of his life to bring to his learning, while keeping others apart? If so, his advancement is limited and his trust not yet firmly established. Faithfulness is the teacher of God's trust in the Word of God to set all things right; not some, but all. Generally, his faithfulness begins by resting on just some problems, remaining carefully limited for a time. To give up all problems to one Answer is to reverse the thinking of the world entirely. And that alone is faithfulness. Nothing but that really deserves the name. Yet each degree, however small, is worth achieving. Readiness, as the text notes, is not mastery.

M 5 J 2. True faithfulness, however, does not deviate. Being consistent it is wholly honest. Being unswerving it is full of trust. Being based on fearlessness it is gentle. Being certain it is joyous, and being confident it is tolerant. Defenselessness attends it naturally, and joy is its condition.[39] Faithfulness, then, combines in itself the other attributes of God's teachers. It implies acceptance of the Word of God and His definition of His Son. It is to Them **M(17)** that faithfulness in the true sense is always directed. Toward Them it looks, seeking until it finds.[40] And having found, it rests in quiet certainty on That alone to which all faithfulness is due.

K. Open-Mindedness

M 5 K 1. The centrality of open-mindedness, perhaps the last of the attributes the teacher of God acquires, is easily understood when its relation to forgiveness is recognized. Open-mindedness comes with lack of judgment. As judgment shuts the mind against God's Teacher, so open-mindedness invites Him to come in. As condemnation judges the Son of God as evil, so open-mindedness permits him to be judged by the Voice for God on His behalf. As the projection of guilt upon him would send him to hell, so open-mindedness lets Christ's image be projected on[41] him. Only the open-minded can be at peace, for they alone see reason for it.

M 5 K 2. How do the open-minded forgive? They have let go all things that would prevent forgiveness. They have in truth abandoned the world, and let it be restored to them in newness and in joy so glorious they never could[42] have conceived of such a change. Nothing is now as it was formerly. Nothing but sparkles now which seemed so dull and lifeless before. And above all are all things welcoming, for threat has[43] gone. No clouds remain to hide the Face of Christ. Now is the goal achieved. Forgiveness is the final goal of the curriculum. It paves the way for what goes far beyond all learning. The curriculum makes no effort to exceed its legitimate goal. Forgiveness is its single aim, at which all learning ultimately converges. It is indeed enough.

M 5 K 3. You may have noticed that the list of attributes of God's teachers does not include those things which are the Son of God's inheritance. Terms like love, sinlessness, perfection, knowledge, and eternal truth do not appear in this context. They would be most inappropriate here. What God has given is so far **M(18)** beyond our curriculum that learning but disappears in its presence. Yet while its presence is obscured, the focus properly belongs on the curriculum. It is the function of God's teachers to bring true learning to the world. Properly speaking, it is unlearning that they bring, for that is "true learning" in the world. It is given to the teachers of God to bring the glad tidings[44] of complete forgiveness to the world. Blessed indeed are they, for they are the Bringers of salvation.[45]

6. HOW IS HEALING ACCOMPLISHED?

A. Introduction

M 6 A 1. Healing involves an understanding of what the illusion of sickness is for. Healing is impossible without this.

B. The perceived purpose of sickness

M 6 B 1. Healing is accomplished the instant the sufferer no longer sees any value in pain. Who would choose suffering unless he thought it brought him something, and something of value to him? He must think it is a small price to pay for something of greater worth. For sickness is an election; a decision. It is the choice of weakness, in the mistaken conviction that it is strength. When this occurs, real strength is seen as threat and health as danger. Sickness is a method, conceived in madness, for placing God's Son on his Father's throne. God is seen as outside, fierce and powerful, eager to keep all power for Himself. Only by his death can He be conquered by His Son.

M 6 B 2. And what, in this insane conviction, does healing stand for? It symbolizes the defeat of God's Son and the triumph of his Father over him. It represents the ultimate defiance in a direct form which the Son of God is forced to recognize. It stands for all that he would hide from himself to protect his life. If he is healed, he is responsible for his thoughts. And if he is responsible for his thoughts he will be killed, to prove to him how weak and pitiful he is. But if he chooses death himself, his weakness is his strength. Now has he given himself what God would give to him, and thus entirely usurped the throne of his Creator. **M(19)**

---

[38] FIP inserts "to him" but that is not present in the *Notes*.
[39] FIP moves this whole sentence forward by four sentences, beginning after "finds." and before "And having" but in the *Notes* it is the same as it appears here.
[40] **Matthew 7:7-8** "Ask, and it will be given to you; seek, and you will find; knock, and it will be opened to you. For everyone who asks receives, and he who seeks finds, and to him who knocks it will be opened."
[41] FIP changes "projected on" to "extended to" but the *Notes* has "projected on." The distinction between "projection" (of the ego) and "extension" (more divine) which the later editing makes is frequently not made in the original dictation which uses "project" interchangeably with "extend" in a number of instances to refer to a divine and loving projection.

[42] FIP changes "never could" to "could never." The *Notes* has "never could."
[43] FIP changes "has gone" to "is gone" but the *Notes* clearly has "has gone."
[44] **Luke 1:19** And the angel answered and said to him, "I am Gabriel, who stands in the presence of God, and was sent to speak to you and bring you these glad tidings." **Luke 8:1** Now it came to pass, afterward, that He went through every city and village, preaching and bringing the glad tidings of the kingdom of God.
[45] **Isaiah 45:8** Drop down, ye heavens, from above, and let the skies pour down righteousness: let the earth open, that they may bring forth salvation, and let her cause righteousness to spring up together; I the LORD have created it.

C. The shift in perception

M 6 C 1. Healing must occur in exact proportion in[46] which the valuelessness of sickness is recognized. One need but say, "There is no gain at all to me in this," and he is healed. But to say this one must first recognize certain facts. First, it is obvious that decisions are of the mind, not of the body. If sickness is but a faulty problem-solving approach, it is a decision. And if it is a decision, it is the mind and not the body that makes it. The resistance to recognizing this is enormous, because the existence of the world as we[47] perceive it depends on the body being the decision-maker. Terms like "instincts," "reflexes" and the like represent attempts to endow the body with non-mental motivators. Actually, such terms merely state or describe the problem. They do not answer it.

M 6 C 2. The acceptance of sickness as a decision of the mind, for a purpose for which it would use the body, is the basis of healing. And this is so for healing in all forms. A patient decides that this is so, and he recovers. If he decides against recovery he will not be healed. Who is the physician? Only the mind of the patient himself. The outcome is what he decides that it is. Special agents seem to be ministering to him, yet they but give form to his own choice. He chooses them[48] to bring tangible form to his desires. And it is this they do, and nothing else. They are not actually needed at all. The patient could merely rise up without their aid and say, "I have no use for this." There is no form of sickness that would not be cured at once.

M 6 C 3. What is the single requisite for this shift in perception? It is simply this; the recognition that sickness is of the mind, and has nothing to do with the body. What does this recognition "cost"? It costs the world[49] we see, for the world will never again appear to rule the mind. For with this recognition is responsibility placed where it belongs; not with the world, but on him who looks on the world and sees it as it is not. He looks on what he chooses to see. No more and no less. The world does nothing to him. **M(20)** He only thought it did. Nor does he do anything to the world, because he was mistaken about what it was.[50] Herein is the release from guilt and sickness both, for they are one. Yet to accept this release, the insignificance of the body must be an acceptable idea.

M 6 C 4. With this idea is pain forever gone. But with this idea goes also all confusion about creation. Does not this follow of necessity? Place cause and effect in their true sequence in one respect, and the learning will generalize and transform the world. The transfer value of one true idea has no end nor[51] limit. The final outcome of this lesson is the remembrance of God. What do guilt and sickness, pain, disaster and all suffering mean now? Having no purpose, they are gone. And with them also go[52] all the effects they seemed to cause. Cause and effect but replicate creation. Seen in their proper perspective, without distortion and without fear, they re-establish Heaven.

D. The function of the Teacher of God

M 6 D 1. If the patient must change his mind in order to be healed, what does the teacher of God do? Can he change the patient's mind for him? Certainly not. For those already willing to change their mind he has no function except to rejoice with them, for they have become teachers of God with him. He has, however, a more specific function for those who do not understand what healing is. These patients do not realize they have chosen sickness. On the contrary, they believe that sickness has chosen them. Nor are they open-minded on this point. The body tells them what to do and they obey. They have no idea how insane this concept is. If they even suspected it they would be healed. Yet they suspect nothing. To them the separation is quite real. **M(21)**

M 6 D 2. To them God's teachers come to represent another choice which they had forgotten. The simple presence of a teacher of God[53] is a reminder. Their[54] thoughts ask for the right to question what the patient has accepted is true. As God's messengers, they[55] are the symbols of salvation. They ask the patient for forgiveness for God's Son in his own Name. They stand for the Alternative. With God's Word in their minds they come in benediction, not to heal the sick but to remind them of the remedy God has already given them. It is not their hands that heal. It is not their voice that speaks the Word of God. They merely give what has been given them. Very gently they call to their brothers to turn away from death. Behold, you Son of God, what life can offer you. Would you choose sickness in place of this?

M 6 D 3. Not once do the advanced teachers of God consider the forms of sickness in which their brother believes. To do this is to forget that all of them have the same purpose and therefore are not really different. They seek for God's Voice in this brother who would so deceive himself as to believe God's Son can suffer. And they remind him that he has not made[56] himself, and must remain as God created him. They recognize illusions can have no effect. The truth in their minds reaches out to the truth in the minds of their brothers, so that illusions are not reinforced. They are thus brought to truth, and truth is not brought to them. So are they dispelled, not by the will of another, but by the union of the One Will with Itself. And this is the function of God's teachers; to see no will as separate from their own, nor theirs as separate from God's. **M(22)**

7. Is Healing Certain?

M 7 A 1. Healing is always certain. It is impossible to let illusions be brought to truth and keep the illusions. Truth demonstrates illusions have no value. The teacher of God has seen the correction of his errors in the mind of the patient, recognizing it for what it is. Having accepted the Atonement for himself, he has also accepted it for the patient. Yet what if the patient uses sickness as a way of life, believing healing is the way to death? When this is so, a sudden healing may[57] precipitate intense depression, and a sense of loss so deep that the patient may even try to destroy himself. Having nothing to live for, he may ask for death. Healing must wait, for his protection.

M 7 A 2. Healing will always stand aside when[58] it would be seen as threat. The instant it is welcome it is there. Where healing has been given it will be received. And what is time before the gifts of God? We have referred many times in the text to the storehouse of

---

[46] FIP replaces the manuscript "in" with "to", but the *Notes* has "in."

[47] FIP changes "we" to "you" but in the *Notes* the glyph for "we" is used.

[48] FIP inserts "in order" which is not present in the *Notes*.

[49] FIP changes "world we see" to "whole world you see" but in the *Notes* the glyph for "we" is used.

[50] FIP changes "was" to "is" but in the *Notes* it is "was."

[51] FIP changes "nor" to "or" but in the *Notes* it is "nor."

[52] *Urtext* manuscript has "goes" which appears to be a grammar error, disagreement in number. In the *Notes*, it was originally written "and with ??? (illegible crossed out characters)" followed by them. Possibly it was originally a singular noun making "goes" the correct form. However, with a plural noun "them," it needs to be "go." FIP also has "go."

[53] Both FIP and the manuscript have this as "a teacher of God" but in the manuscript that is crossed out and replaced with "God's Teachers." The subsequent pronoun (His vs. Their) is treated likewise. In the *Notes* it is 'Their simple presence is" but then "a Teacher of God" is written in between the lines.

[54] *Urtext* manuscript has "Their" in brackets just before "His." The *Notes* has "Their."

[55] Both FIP and the manuscript have "His Teachers" but again, that is crossed out in the manuscript and replaced with "they." The *Notes* has "they."

[56] FIP changes "has not made" to "did not make." The *Notes* has "has not made."

[57] FIP changes "may" to "might." The *Notes* has "may."

[58] Both FIP and the manuscript have "when" instead of "where" but it is crossed out in the manuscript and "where" is written in. The *Notes* has "when."

treasures laid up equally for the giver and the receiver of God's gifts. Not one is lost, for they can but increase. No teacher of God should feel disappointed if he has offered healing and it does not appear to have been received. It is not up to him to judge when his gift should be accepted. Let him be certain it has been received, and trust that it will be accepted when it is recognized as a blessing and not a curse.

M 7 A 3. It is not the function of God's teachers to evaluate the outcome of their gifts. It is merely their function to give them. Once they have done that, they have also given the outcome, for that is part of the gift. No-one can give if he is concerned with the result of the[59] giving. That is a limitation on the giving itself, and neither the giver nor the receiver would have the gift. Trust is an essential part of giving; in fact, it is the part that makes sharing possible, the part that guarantees the giver will not lose, but only gain. Who gives a gift, and then remains with it, to be sure it is used as the giver deems appropriate? Such is not giving but imprisoning. **M(23)**

M 7 A 4. It is the relinquishing of all concern about the gift that makes it truly given. And it is trust that makes true giving possible. Healing is the change of mind that the Holy Spirit in the patient's mind is seeking for him. And it is the Holy Spirit in the mind of the giver Who gives the gift to him. How can it be lost? How can it be ineffectual? How can it be wasted? God's treasure house can never be empty. And if one gift were[60] missing it would not be full. Yet is its fullness guaranteed by God. What concern, then, can a teacher of God have about what becomes of his gifts? Given by God to God, who in this holy exchange can receive less than everything?

8. SHOULD HEALING BE REPEATED?

M 8 A 1. This question really answers itself. Healing cannot be repeated. If the patient is healed, what remains to heal him from? And if the healing is certain, as we have already said it is, what is there to repeat? For a teacher of God to remain concerned about the result of healing is to limit the healing. It is now the teacher of God himself whose mind needs to be healed. And it is this he must facilitate. He is now the patient, and he must so regard himself. He has made a mistake, and must be willing to change his mind about it. He lacked the trust that makes for giving truly, and so he has not received the benefit of his gift.

M 8 A 2. Whenever a teacher of God has tried to be a channel for healing he has succeeded. Should he be tempted to doubt this, he should not repeat his previous effort. That was already maximal, because the Holy Spirit so accepted it and so used it. Now the teacher of God has only one course to follow. He must use his reason to tell himself that he has given the problem to One Who cannot fail, and[61] recognize that his own uncertainty is not love but fear, and therefore hate. His position has thus become untenable, for he is offering **M(24)** hate to one to whom he offered love. This is impossible. Having offered love, only love can be received.

M 8 A 3. It is in this that the teacher of God must trust. This is what is really meant by the statement that the one responsibility of the miracle worker is to accept the Atonement for himself. The teacher of God is a miracle worker because he gives the gifts he has received. Yet he must first accept them. He need do no more, nor is there more that he could do. By accepting healing he can give it. If he doubts this, let him remember Who gave the gift and Who received it. Thus is his doubt corrected. He thought the gifts of God could be withdrawn. That was a mistake, but hardly one to stay with. And so the teacher of God can only recognize it for what it is, and let it be corrected for him.

M 8 A 4. One of the more[62] difficult temptations to recognize is that to doubt a healing because of the appearance of continuing symptoms is a mistake in the form of lack of trust. As such, it is an attack. Usually it seems to be just the opposite. It does appear unreasonable at first to be told that continued concern is attack. It has all the appearance[63] of love. Yet love without trust is impossible, and doubt and trust cannot coexist. And hate must be the opposite of love, regardless of the form it takes. Doubt not the gift, and it is impossible to doubt its result. This is the certainty that gives God's teachers the power to be miracle workers, for they have put their trust in Him.

M 8 A 5. The real basis for doubt about the outcome of any problem that has been given to God's Teacher for resolution is always self-doubt. And that necessarily implies that trust has been placed in an illusory self, for only such a self can be doubted. This illusion can take many forms. Perhaps there is a fear of weakness and vulnerability. Perhaps there is[64] fear of failure and shame associated with a sense of inadequacy. Perhaps there is a guilty **M(25)** embarrassment stemming from false humility. The form of the mistake is not important. What is important is only the recognition of a mistake as a mistake.

M 8 A 6. The mistake is always some form of concern with the self to the exclusion of the patient. It is a failure to recognize him as part of the self, and thus represents a confusion in identity. Conflict about what you are has entered your mind, and you have become deceived about yourself. And you are deceived about yourself because you have denied the Source of your creation. If you are offering only healing, you cannot doubt. If you really want the problem solved, you cannot doubt. If you are certain what the problem is, you cannot doubt. Doubt is the result of conflicting wishes. Be sure of what you want, and doubt becomes impossible.

9. HOW CAN THE PERCEPTION OF ORDER OF DIFFICULTIES BE AVOIDED?

M 9 A 1. The belief in order of difficulties is the basis for the world's perception. It rests on differences; on uneven background and shifting foreground, on unequal heights and diverse sizes, on varying degrees of darkness and light, and thousands of contrasts in which each thing seen competes with every other in order to be recognized. A larger object overshadows a smaller one. A brighter thing draws the attention from another with less intensity of appeal. And a more threatening idea, or one conceived of as more desirable by the world's standards, completely upsets the mental balance. What the body's eyes behold is only conflict. Look not to them for peace and understanding.

M 9 A 2. Illusions are always illusions of differences. How could it be otherwise? By definition, an illusion is an attempt to make something real that is regarded as of major importance, but is recognized as being untrue. The mind therefore seeks to make it true out of its intensity of desire to have it for itself. **M(26)** Illusions are travesties of creation; attempts to bring truth to lies. Finding truth unacceptable, the mind revolts against truth and gives itself an illusion of victory. Finding health a burden, it retreats into feverish dreams. And in these dreams the mind is separate, different from other minds, with different interests of its own, and able to gratify its needs at the expense of others.

M 9 A 3. Where do all these differences come from? Certainly they seem to be in the world outside. Yet it is surely the mind that judges what the eyes behold. It is the mind that interprets the eyes' messages and gives them "meaning." And this meaning does not exist in the world outside at all. What is seen as "reality" is simply

---

[59] Handwritten mark-up and FIP omit "the" however it is present in the *Notes*.

[60] FIP changes "were" to "is" but the *Notes* has "were."

[61] FIP inserts "must" before "recognize" but that is not present in the *Notes*.

[62] FIP changes "more" to "most" but the *Notes* has "more."

[63] FIP changes "appearance" to "appearances" but the *Notes* has "appearance."

[64] FIP inserts "a" before "fear." There is no "a" in the *Notes*.

what the mind prefers. Its hierarchy of values is projected outward, and it sends the body's eyes to find it. The body's eyes will never see except through differences. Yet it is not the messages they bring on which perception rests. Only the mind evaluates their messages, so[65] only the mind is responsible for seeing. It alone decides whether what is seen is real or illusory, desirable or undesirable, pleasurable or painful.

M 9 A 4. It is in the sorting out and categorizing activities of the mind that errors in perception enter. And it is here correction must be made. The mind classifies what the body's eyes bring to it according to its preconceived values, judging where each sense datum fits best. What basis could be faultier than this? Unrecognized by itself, it has itself asked to be given what will fit into these categories. And having done so, it concludes that the categories must be true. On this the judgment of all differences rests, because it is on this that judgments of the world depend. Can this confused and senseless "reasoning" be depended on for anything?

M 9 A 5. There can be no order of difficulty in healing merely because all sickness is illusion. Is it harder to dispel the belief of the insane in a larger hallucination as opposed to a smaller one? Will he agree more quickly to the unreality of a louder voice he hears than to that of a softer one? Will he dismiss more easily a whispered demand to kill than a shout? And do the number of pitchforks the devils he sees carrying affect their credibility in his perception? His mind has categorized **M(27)** them[66] as real, and so they are[67] real to him. When he realizes they are all illusions they will disappear. And so it is with healing. The properties of illusions which seem to make them different are really irrelevant, for their properties are as illusory as they are.

M 9 A 6. The body's eyes will continue to see differences,[68] but the mind which[69] has let itself be healed will no longer acknowledge them. There will be those who seem to be "sicker" than others, and the body's eyes will report their changed appearances as before. But the[70] mind will put them all in one category[71] – they are unreal. This is the gift of its Teacher; the understanding that only two categories are meaningful in sorting out the messages the mind receives from what appears to be the outside world. And of these two but one is real. Just as reality is wholly real, apart from size and shape and time and place, for differences cannot exist within it, so too are illusions without distinctions.[72] The one answer to sickness of any kind is healing. The one answer to all illusions is truth.

10. ARE CHANGES REQUIRED IN THE LIFE SITUATIONS OF GOD'S TEACHERS?

M 10 A 1. Changes are required in the minds of God's teachers. This may or may not involve changes in the external situation. Remember that no-one is where he is by accident, and chance plays no part in God's plan. It is most unlikely that changes in his attitudes would not be the first step in the newly-made teacher of God's training. There is, however, no set pattern, since training is always highly individualized. There are those who are called upon to change their life situation almost immediately, but these are generally special cases. By far the majority are given a slowly-evolving training program, in which as many previous mistakes as possible are corrected. Relationships in particular must be properly perceived, and all dark cornerstones of unforgiveness removed. Otherwise the old thought-system still has a basis for return. **M(28)**

M 10 A 2. As the teacher of God advances in his training, he learns one lesson with increasing thoroughness. He does not make his own decisions; he asks his Teacher for His answer, and it is this he follows as his guide for action. This becomes easier and easier, as the teacher of God learns to give up his own judgment. The giving up of judgment, the obvious prerequisite for hearing God's Voice, is usually a fairly slow process, not because it is difficult, but because it is apt to be perceived as personally insulting. The world's training is directed toward achieving a goal in direct opposition to that of our curriculum. The world trains for reliance on one's judgment as the criterion for maturity and strength. Our curriculum trains for the relinquishment of judgment as the necessary condition of salvation.

11. HOW IS JUDGMENT RELINQUISHED?

M 11 A 1. Judgment, like other devices by which the world of illusions is maintained, is totally misunderstood by the world. It is actually confused with wisdom, and substitutes for truth. As the world uses the term, an individual is capable of "good" and "bad" judgment, and his education aims at strengthening the former and minimizing the latter. There is, however, considerable confusion about what these categories mean. What is "good" judgment to one is "bad" judgment to another. Further, even the same person classifies the same action as showing "good" judgment at one time and "bad" judgment at another time. Nor can any consistent criteria for determining what these categories are be really taught. At any time the student may disagree with what his would-be teacher says about it, and the teacher himself is inconsistent in what he believes they are.[73] **M(29)**

M 11 A 2. "Good judgment" in these terms, does not mean anything. No more does "bad." It is necessary for the teacher of God to realize not that he should not judge, but that he cannot. In giving up judgment he merely gives up what he did not have. He gives up an illusion; or better, he has an illusion of giving up. He has actually merely become more honest. Recognizing that judgment was always impossible for him, he no longer attempts it. This is no sacrifice. On the contrary, he puts himself in a position where judgment through him rather than by him can occur. And this Judgment is neither "good" nor "bad." It is the only Judgment there is, and it is only one: "God's Son is guiltless, and sin does not exist."

M 11 A 3. The aim of our curriculum, unlike the goal of the world's learning, is the recognition that judgment in the usual sense is impossible. This is not an opinion but a fact. In order to judge anything rightly,[74] one would have to be fully aware of an inconceivably wide range of things; past, present and to come. One would have to recognize in advance all the effects of his judgments on everyone and everything involved in them in any way. And one would have to be certain there is no distortion in his perception, so that his judgment would be wholly fair to everyone on whom it rests now and in the future. Who is in a position to do this? Who except in grandiose fantasies would claim this for himself?

---

[65] Handwritten mark-up and FIP add "and" before "so" but that is not present in the *Notes*.
[66] Handwritten mark-up and FIP add "all" but that is not present in the *Notes*.
[67] Handwritten mark-up and FIP add "all" but that is not present in the *Notes*.
[68] The *Urtext* manuscript has a sentence break typed here, which FIP restores; handwritten mark-up corrects this to a comma which is the reading in the *Notes*.
[69] FIP changes "which" to "that." The *Notes* has "which."
[70] FIP changes "the mind" to "the healed mind." The *Notes* has "the mind."
[71] The *Urtext* manuscript has ", -" here, FIP uses a semicolon. The *Notes* has an "=" sign glyph which commonly is used to signify an em-dash.
[72] *Urtext* manuscript is singular, "distinction," Handwritten mark-up and FIP pluralize this. The *Notes* also pluralizes it.

[73] This sentence is heavily marked-up in the *Urtext* manuscript. The last words "they are" are handwritten in. FIP modifies this sentence to: "*At any time the student may disagree with what his would-be teacher says about them, and the teacher himself may well be inconsistent in what he believes.*" The *Notes* reads slightly differently "*At any time the student may disagree with what his would-be teacher says about it, and the teacher himself is inconsistent in what he believes.*" The *Notes* was originally written "*about what he believes*" but "about" was crossed out, and "in" written above the line.
[74] John 7:24 "Do not judge according to appearance, but judge with righteous judgment."

M 11 A 4. Remember how many times you thought you knew all the "facts" you needed for judgment, and how wrong you were! Is there anyone who has not had this experience? Would you know how many times you merely thought you were right, without ever realizing you were wrong? Why would you choose such an arbitrary basis for decision-making? Wisdom is not judgment; it is the relinquishment of judgment. Make then but one more judgment. It is this; there is Someone with you Whose judgment is perfect. He does know all the facts, past, present and to come. He does know all the effects of His judgment on everyone and everything involved in any way. And He is wholly fair to everyone, for there is no distortion in His perception. **M(30)**

M 11 A 5. Therefore lay judgment down, not with regret but with a sigh of gratitude. Now are you free of a burden so great that you could merely stagger and fall down beneath it. And it was all illusion. Nothing more. Now can the teacher of God rise up unburdened, and walk lightly on. Yet it is not only this that is his benefit. His sense of care is gone, for he has none. He has given it away, along with judgment. He gave himself to Him Whose judgment he has chosen now to trust instead of his own. Now he makes no mistakes. His Guide is sure. And where he came to judge he comes to bless. Where now he laughs he used to come to weep.

M 11 A 6. It is not difficult to relinquish judgment. But it is difficult indeed to try to keep it. The teacher of God lays it down happily the instant he recognizes its cost. All of the ugliness he sees[75] about him is its outcome. All of the pain he looks upon is its result. All of the loneliness and sense of loss; of passing time and growing hopelessness; of sickening despair and fear of death; all these have come of it. And now he knows that these things need not be. Not one is true. For he has given up their cause, and they, which never were but the effects of his mistaken choice, have fallen from him. Teacher of God, this step will bring you peace. Can it be difficult to want but this?

12. HOW IS PEACE POSSIBLE IN THIS WORLD?

M 12 A 1. This is a question everyone must ask. Certainly peace seems to be impossible here.[76] Yet the Word of God promises other things that seem impossible, as well as this. His Word has promised peace. It has also promised that there is no death; that resurrection must occur, and that rebirth is man's inheritance. The world you see cannot be the world God loves, and yet His Word assures us that He loves the world. God's Word has promised us[77] that peace is possible here, and what He promises can hardly be impossible. But it is true that the world must be looked at differently, if His promises are to be accepted. What the world is, is but a fact. You cannot choose what this should be. But you can choose how you would see it. Indeed, you must choose this. **M(31)**

M 12 A 2. Again we come to the question of judgment. This time, ask yourself whether your judgment or the Word of God is more likely to be true. For they say different things about the world, and things so opposite that it is pointless to try to[78] reconcile them. God offers the world salvation; your judgment would condemn it. God says there is no death; your judgment sees but death as the inevitable end of life. God's Word assures you that He loves the world; your judgment says it is unlovable. Who is right? For one of you is wrong. It must be so.

M 12 A 3. The text explains that the Holy Spirit is the Answer to all problems you have made. These problems are not true,[79] but that is meaningless to those who believe in them. And everyone believes in what he made, for it was made by his believing it. Into this strange and paradoxical situation, – one without meaning and devoid of sense, yet out of which no way seems possible, – God has sent His Judgment to answer yours. Gently His Judgment substitutes for yours. And through this substitution is the ununderstandable made understandable. How is peace possible in this world? In your judgment it is not possible, and can never be possible. But in the Judgment of God what is reflected here is only peace.

M 12 A 4. Peace is impossible to those who look on war. Peace is inevitable to those who offer peace. How easily, then, is your judgment of the world escaped. It is not the world which makes peace seem impossible. It is the world you see that is impossible. Yet has God's Judgment on this distorted world redeemed it and made it fit to welcome peace. And peace descends on it in joyous answer. Peace now belongs here, because a Thought of God has entered. What else but a Thought of God turns hell to Heaven merely by being what It is? The earth bows down before Its gracious Presence, and It leans down in answer to raise it up again. Now is the question different. It is no longer, "Can peace be possible in this world?" but instead, "Is it not impossible that peace be absent here?" **M(32)**

13. HOW MANY TEACHERS OF GOD ARE NEEDED TO SAVE THE WORLD?

M 13 A 1. The[80] answer to this question is "one". One wholly perfect teacher, whose learning is complete, suffices. This One, sanctified and redeemed, becomes the Self Who is the Son of God. He Who was always wholly spirit now no longer sees Himself as a body, or even as in a body. Therefore He is limitless. And being limitless, His Thoughts are joined with God's forever and ever. His perception of Himself is based upon God's Judgment, not His Own. Thus does He share God's Will, and bring His Thoughts to still deluded minds. He is forever One, because He is as God created Him. He has accepted Christ and He is saved.[81]

M 13 A 2. Thus does the son of man become the Son of God.[82] It is not really a change; it is a change of mind. Nothing external alters, but everything internal now reflects only the Love of God. God can no longer be feared, for the mind sees no cause for punishment. God's teachers appear to be many, for that is the world's need. Yet being joined in one purpose, and one they share with God, how could they be separate from each other? What does it matter if they then appear in many forms? Their minds are one; their joining is complete. And God works through them now as One, for that is what they are.

M 13 A 3. Why is the illusion of many necessary? Only because reality is not understandable to the deluded. Only a very few can hear God's Voice at all, and even they cannot communicate His messages directly through the Spirit Which gave them. They need a medium through which communication becomes possible to those who do not realize that they are Spirit. A body they can see. A voice they understand and listen to without the fear that truth would

---

[75] Mark-up shifts the next two sentences to past tense. FIP does not preserve that, nor do we. The *Notes* has this reading in its mark-up, but something else which I can't make out was written first, and crossed out.
[76] Handwritten mark-up and FIP insert "here" which is also found in the *Notes*.
[77] Handwritten mark-up and FIP omit "us" but that word is present in the *Notes*.
[78] The *Urtext* manuscript has "try to" inserted as handwritten mark-up as does FIP. It is also present in the *Notes*.

[79] Handwritten mark-up and FIP replace "true" with "real" but the *Notes* reads "true."
[80] (June 14, 1972)
[81] The manuscript says "safe" and a handwritten correction indicates "saved" which is what is in the *Notes*.
[82] **Matthew 8:20** Jesus said to him, "Foxes have holes and birds of the air have nests, but the Son of Man has nowhere to lay His head." The "Son of Man" is the term Jesus usually uses to refer to himself ***and*** people in general in the Gospels, and this phrase in the Course appears to harken to the Gospels.

find[83] in them. Do not forget that truth can come only where it is welcomed without fear. So do God's teachers need a body, for their Unity could not be recognized directly. **M(33)**

M 13 A 4. Yet what makes them[84] God's teachers is their recognition of the proper purpose of the body. As they advance in their profession, they become more and more certain that the body's function is but to let God's Voice speak through it to human ears. And these ears will carry to the mind of the hearer messages which[85] are not of this world, and the mind will understand because of their Source. From this understanding will come the recognition, in this new teacher of God, of what the body's purpose really is; the only use there really is for it. This lesson is enough to let the Thought of Unity come in, and what is One is recognized as One. The teachers of God appear to share the illusion of separation, but because of what they use the body for, they do not believe in the illusion despite appearances.

M 13 A 5. The central lesson is always this; that what you use the body for, it will become to you. Use it for sin or for attack, which is the same as sin, and you will see it as sinful. Because it is sinful it is weak, and being weak it suffers and it dies. Use it to bring the Word of God to those who have It[86] not, and the body becomes holy. Because it is holy it cannot be sick, nor can it die. When its usefulness is done it is laid by, and that is all. The mind makes this decision, as it makes all decisions which[87] are responsible for the body's condition. Yet the teacher of God does not make this decision alone. To do that would be to give the body another purpose from the one that keeps it holy. God's Voice will tell him when he has fulfilled his role, just as It tells him what his function is. He does not suffer either in going or remaining. Sickness is now impossible to him.

M 13 A 6. Oneness and sickness cannot co-exist. God's teachers choose to look on dreams a while. It is a conscious choice. For they have learned that all choices are made consciously, with full awareness of their consequences. The dream says otherwise, but who would put his faith in dreams, once they are recognized for what they are? Awareness of dreaming is the real function of God's teachers. They watch the dream figures come and go, shift and change, suffer and die. Yet they are not deceived by what they see. They recognize that to behold a dream figure as sick and separate is no more real than to regard it as healthy and beautiful. **M(34)** Unity alone is not a thing of dreams. And it is this God's teachers acknowledge as behind the dream, beyond all seeing and yet surely theirs.

14. WHAT IS THE REAL MEANING OF SACRIFICE?

M 14 A 1. Although in truth the term sacrifice is altogether meaningless, it does have meaning in the world. Like all things in the world its meaning is temporary, and will ultimately fade into the nothingness from which it came when there is no more use for it. Now its real meaning is a lesson. Like all lessons it is an illusion, for in reality there is nothing to learn. Yet this illusion must be replaced by a corrective device; another illusion that replaces the first, so both can finally disappear. The first illusion, which must be displaced before another thought system can take hold, is that it is a sacrifice to give up the things of this world. What could this be but an illusion, since this world itself is nothing more than that?

M 14 A 2. It takes great learning both to realize and to accept the fact that the world has nothing to give. What can the sacrifice of nothing mean? It cannot mean that you have less because of it. There is no sacrifice in the world's terms that does not involve the body. Think a while about what the world calls sacrifice. Power, fame, money, physical pleasure; who is the hero to whom all these things belong? Could they mean anything except to a body? Yet a body cannot evaluate. By seeking after such things the mind associates itself with the body, obscuring its identity and losing sight of what it really is. **M(35)**

M 14 A 3. Once this confusion has occurred, it becomes impossible for the mind to understand that all the "pleasures" of the world are nothing. But what a sacrifice,- and it is sacrifice indeed[88] - all this entails! Now has the mind condemned itself to seek without finding[89]; to be forever dissatisfied and discontented; to know not what it really wants to find. Who can escape this self-condemnation? Only through God's Word could this be possible. For self-condemnation is a decision about identity, and no-one doubts what he believes he is. He can doubt all things, but never this.

M 14 A 4. God's teachers can have no regret on giving up the pleasures of the world. Is it a sacrifice to give up pain? Does an adult resent the giving up of children's toys? Does one whose vision has already glimpsed the Face of Christ look back with longing on a slaughter house? No-one who has escaped the world and all its ills looks back on it with condemnation. Yet he must rejoice that he is free of all the sacrifice which[90] its values[91] would demand of him. To them he sacrifices all his freedom.[92] To them he sacrifices all his peace.[93] And to possess them must he sacrifice his hope of Heaven and remembrance of his Father's Love. Who in his sane mind chooses nothing as a substitute for everything?

M 14 A 5. What is the real meaning of sacrifice? It is the cost of believing in illusions. It is the price that must be paid for the denial of truth. There is no pleasure of the world that does not demand this, for otherwise the pleasure would be seen as pain. And no-one asks for pain if he recognizes it. It is the idea of sacrifice that makes him blind. He does not see what he is asking for. And so he seeks it in a thousand ways and in a thousand places, each time believing it is there and each time disappointed in the end. "Seek but do not find[94]" remains this world's stern decree, and no-one who pursues the world's goals can do otherwise. **M(36)**

M 14 A 6. You may believe this course requires sacrifice of all you really hold dear. In one sense that[95] is true, for you hold dear the things that crucify God's Son. And it is the course's aim to set him free. But do not be mistaken about what sacrifice means. It always means the giving up of what you want. And what, oh teacher of God, is it that you want? You have been called by God, and you have answered. Would you now sacrifice that Call? Few have heard it as yet, and they can but turn to you. There is no other hope in all the world that they can trust. There is no other voice in all the world that echoes God's. If you would sacrifice the truth, they stay in hell. And if they stay, you will remain with them.

M 14 A 7. Do not forget that sacrifice is total. There are no "half sacrifices." You cannot give up Heaven partially. You cannot be a

---

[83] *Urtext* manuscript has "find" in brackets and "encounter" scratched out. The *Notes* has "find."
[84] FIP omits "them" but there is a glyph present in the *Notes* which is reasonably construed to be "them."
[85] FIP changes "which" to "that." The *Notes* has the glyph for "which."
[86] FIP removes the capital I from "It." It is capitalized in the *Notes*.
[87] FIP replaces "which" with "that." The *Notes* has the glyph for "which."

[88] FIP puts exclamation point here. The *Notes* does not.
[89] **Matthew 7:7-8** "Ask, and it will be given to you; seek, and you will find; knock, and it will be opened to you. For everyone who asks receives, and he who seeks finds, and to him who knocks it will be opened."
[90] FIP omits "which" but it is present in the *Notes*.
[91] FIP changes the manuscript "sacrifice its value" to "sacrifice its values" which is the reading in the *Notes*..
[92] FIP has "peace" instead of "freedom." The *Notes* has "freedom."
[93] FIP has "freedom" instead of "peace." The *Notes* has "peace."
[94] **Matthew 7:7-8** "Ask, and it will be given to you; seek, and you will find; knock, and it will be opened to you. For everyone who asks receives, and he who seeks finds, and to him who knocks it will be opened."
[95] Handwritten mark-up and FIP change "that" to "this." In the *Notes* it is the glyph for "that" which is present.

little bit in hell. The Word of God has no exceptions. It is this that makes It holy and beyond the world. It is Its holiness that points to God. It is Its holiness that makes you safe. It is denied if you attack any brother for anything. For it is here the split with God occurs. A split that is impossible. A split that cannot happen. Yet a split in which you surely will believe, because you have set up a situation that is impossible. And in this situation the impossible can seem to happen. It seems to happen at the "sacrifice" of truth.

M 14 A 8. Teacher of God, do not forget the meaning of sacrifice, and remember what each decision you make must mean in terms of cost. Decide for God, and everything is given you at no cost at all. Decide against Him and you choose nothing at the expense of the awareness of everything. What would you teach? Remember only what you would learn. For it is here that your concern should be. Atonement is for you. Your learning claims it and your learning gives it. The world contains it not, but learn this course and it is yours. God holds out His Word to you, for He has need of teachers. What other way is there to save His Son? **M(37)**

15. How Will the World End?

M 15 A 1. Can what has no beginning really end? The world will end in an illusion, as it began. Yet will its ending be an illusion of mercy. The illusion of forgiveness, complete, excluding no-one, limitless in gentleness, will cover it, hiding all evil, concealing all sin and ending guilt forever. So ends the world that guilt had made, for now it has no purpose and is gone. The father of illusions is the belief that they have a purpose; that they serve a need or gratify a want. Perceived as purposeless, they are no longer seen. Their uselessness is recognized and they are gone. How but in this way are all illusions ended? They have been brought to truth, and truth saw them not. It merely overlooked the meaningless.

M 15 A 2. Until forgiveness is complete, the world does have a purpose. It becomes the home in which forgiveness is born, and where it grows and becomes stronger and more all embracing. Here is it nourished, for here it is needed. A gentle Savior, born where sin was made and guilt seemed real. Here is His home, for here there is need of Him indeed. He brings the ending of the world with Him. It is His Call God's teachers answer, turning to Him in silence to receive His Word. The world will end when all things in it have been rightly judged by His judgment. The world will end with the benediction of holiness upon it. When not one thought of sin remains, the world is over. It will not be destroyed nor attacked nor even touched. It will merely cease to seem to be.

M 15 A 3. Certainly this seems to be a long, long while away. "When not one thought of sin remains" appears to be a long-range goal indeed. But time stands still, and waits on the goals[96] of God's teachers. Not one thought of sin will remain the instant any one of them accepts the[97] Atonement for himself. It is not easier to forgive one sin than to forgive all of them. The illusion of orders of difficulty is an obstacle the teacher of God must learn to pass by and leave behind. One sin perfectly forgiven by one teacher of God can make salvation complete. Can you understand this? No; it is meaningless to anyone here. Yet it is the final lesson **M(38)** in which Unity is restored. It goes against all the thinking of the world, but so[98] does Heaven.

M 15 A 4. The world will end when its thought system has been completely reversed. Until then, bits and pieces of its thinking will still seem sensible. The final lesson which brings the ending of the world cannot be grasped by those not yet prepared to leave the world and go beyond its tiny reach. What, then, is the function of the teacher of God in this concluding lesson? He need merely learn how to approach it; to be willing to go in its direction. He need merely trust that, if God's Voice tells him it is a lesson he can learn, he can learn it. He does not judge it either as hard or easy. His Teacher points to it, and he trusts that He will show him how to learn it.

M 15 A 5. The world will end in joy because it is a place of sorrow. When joy has come the purpose of the world has gone. The world will end in peace because it is a place of war. When peace has come, what is the purpose of the world? The world will end in laughter because it is a place of tears. Where there is laughter, who can[99] longer weep? And only complete forgiveness brings all this to bless the world. In blessing it departs, for it will not end as it began. To turn hell into Heaven is the function of God's teachers, for what they teach are lessons in which Heaven is reflected. And now sit down in true humility, and realize that all God would have you do you can do. Do not be arrogant and say you cannot learn His Own curriculum. His Word says otherwise. His Will be done. It cannot be otherwise. And be you thankful it is so. **M(39)**

16. Is Each One to be Judged In the End?

M 16 A 1. Indeed,[100] yes! No-one can escape God's final judgment. Who could flee forever from the truth? But the final judgment will not come until it is no longer associated with fear. One day each one will welcome it, and on that very day it will be given him. He will hear his sinlessness proclaimed around and around the world, setting it free as God's final judgment on him is received. This is the judgment in which salvation lies. This is the judgment that will set him free. This is the judgment in which all things are freed with him. Time pauses as eternity comes near, and silence lies across the world that everyone may hear this judgment of the Son of God:

> "Holy are you, eternal, free and whole,
>
> At peace forever in the Heart of God.
>
> Where is the world, and where is sorrow now?"

M 16 A 2. Is this your judgment on yourself, teacher of God? Do you believe that this is wholly true? No, not yet, not yet. But this is still your goal; why you are here. It is your function to prepare yourself to hear this judgment and to recognize that it is true. One instant of complete belief in this, and you will go beyond belief to Certainty. One instant out of time can bring time's end. Judge not, for you but judge yourself[101] and thus delay this final judgment. What is your judgment on[102] the world, teacher of God? Have you yet learned to stand aside and hear the Voice of Judgment in yourself? Or do you still attempt to take His role from Him? Learn to be quiet, for His Voice is heard in stillness. And His Judgment comes to all who stand aside in quiet listening, and wait for Him. **M(40)**

M 16 A 3. You who are sometimes sad and sometimes angry; who sometimes feel your just due is not given you, and your best efforts meet with lack of appreciation and even with[103] contempt; give up these foolish thoughts.[104] They are too small and meaningless to occupy your holy minds[105] an instant longer. God's Judgment waits for you to set you free. What can the world hold out to you, regardless of your judgments on its gifts, that you would rather have? You will be judged, and judged in fairness and in honesty. There is no deceit in God. His promises are sure. Only remember

---

[96] FIP changes "goals" to "goal." The *Notes* has the plural, "goals."
[97] FIP omits "the." It is present in the *Notes* however.
[98] Although not part of the original typing, the handwritten mark-up and FIP add "but" before "so" and so does the *Notes*.
[99] "who can *any* longer weep" sounds much better than "who can longer weep." Possibly there is an Iambic Pentameter issue here. All versions have it the same, we're just noting the odd syntax as a possible clue to an error.
[100] (June 26, 1972)
[101] **Matthew 7:1** "Judge not, that you be not judged."
[102] FIP changes "on" to "of" but in the *Notes* it is clearly "on."
[103] FIP omits "with" however this is present in the *Notes*.
[104] FIP adds "!" (exclamation point) but that is not present in the *Notes*.
[105] FIP has "mind" instead of "minds" but in the *Notes* it is "minds."

that. His promises have guaranteed His judgment, and His alone, will be accepted in the end. It is your function to make that end be soon. It is your function to hold it in[106] your heart, and offer it to all the world to keep it safe.

17. HOW SHOULD THE TEACHER OF GOD SPEND HIS DAY?

M 17 A 1. To the advanced teacher of God this question is meaningless. There is no program, for the lessons in the curriculum[107] change each day. Yet he[108] is sure of but one thing; they do not change at random. Seeing this, and understanding it is true, he rests content. He will be told all that his role should be, this day and every day. And those who share that role with him will find him, so they can learn the lessons for the day together. Not one is absent whom he needs; not one is sent without a learning goal already set, and one which can be met[109] that very day. For the advanced teacher of God, then, this question is superfluous. It has been asked and answered, and he keeps in constant contact with the Answer. He is set, and[110] sees the road on which he walks stretch surely and smoothly before him.

M 17 A 2. But what about those who have not reached his certainty? They are not yet ready for such lack of structuring on their own part. What must they do to learn to give the day to God? There are some general rules which do apply, although each one must use them as best he can in his own way. Routines as such are dangerous, because they easily become gods in their own right, threatening the very goals for which they were set up. Broadly speaking, then, it can be said **M(41)** that it is well to start the day right. It is always possible to begin again, should the day begin with error. Yet there are obvious advantages in terms of saving time if the need for this can be avoided.[111]

M 17 A 3. At the beginning it is wise to think in terms of time. This is by no means the ultimate criterion, but at the outset it is probably the simplest to observe. The saving of time[112] is an essential early emphasis which, although it remains important throughout the learning process, becomes less and less emphasized. At the outset, we can safely say that time devoted to starting the day right does indeed save time. How much time should be so spent? This must depend on the teacher of God himself. He cannot claim that title until he has gone through the Workbook, since we are learning within the framework of our course. After completion of the more structured practice periods which the Workbook contains, individual need becomes the chief consideration.

M 17 A 4. This course is always practical. It may be that the teacher of God is not in a situation which[113] fosters quiet thought as he awakes. If this is so, let him but remember that he chooses to spend time with God as soon as possible, and let him do so. Duration is not the major concern. One can easily sit still an hour with closed eyes, and accomplish nothing. One can as easily give God only an instant, and in that instant join with Him completely.

Perhaps the one generalization that can be made is this; as soon as possible after waking take your quiet time, continuing a minute or two after you begin to find it difficult. You may find that the difficulty will diminish and drop away. If not, that is the time to stop.

M 17 A 5. The same procedures should be followed at night. Perhaps your quiet time should be fairly early in the evening, if it is not feasible for you to take it just before going to sleep. It is not wise to lie down for it. It is better to sit up, in whatever position you prefer. Having gone through the Workbook you must have come to some conclusions in this respect. If possible, **M(42)** however, just before sleeping[114] is a desirable time to devote to God. It sets your mind into a pattern of rest, and orients you away from fear. If it is expedient to spend this time earlier, at least be sure that you do not forget a brief period,- not more than a moment will do,- in which you close your eyes and think of God.

M 17 A 6. There is one thought in particular that should be remembered throughout the day. It is a thought of pure joy; a thought of peace, a thought of limitless release, - limitless because all things are freed within it. You think you made a place of safety for yourself. You think you made a power that can save you from all the fearful things you see in dreams. It is not so. Your safety lies not there. What you give up is merely the illusion of protecting illusions. And it is this you fear, and only this. How foolish to be so afraid of nothing! Nothing at all! Your defenses will not work, but you are not in danger. You have no need of them. Recognize this and they will disappear. And only then will you accept your real protection.

M 17 A 7. How simply and how easily does time[115] slip by for the teacher of God who has accepted His protection! All that he did before in the name of safety no longer interests him. For he is safe, and knows it to be[116] so. He has a Guide Who will not fail. He need make no distinctions among the problems he perceives, for He to Whom he turns with all of them recognizes no order of difficulty in resolving them. He is as safe in the present as he was before illusions were accepted into his mind, and as he will be when he has let them go. There is no difference in his state at different times and different places, because they are all one to God. This is his safety. And he has no need for more than this.

M 17 A 8. Yet there will be temptations along the way the teacher of God has yet to travel, and he has need of reminding himself throughout the day of his protection. How can he do this, particularly during the time when his mind is occupied with external things? He can but try, and his success depends on his conviction that he will succeed. He must be sure success is not of him, but will be given him at any **M(43)** time, in any place and circumstance he calls for it. There are times his certainty will waver, and the instant this occurs he will return to earlier attempts to place reliance on himself alone. Forget not this is magic, and that[117] magic is a sorry substitute for true assistance. It is not good enough for God's teacher because it is not good[118] enough for God's Son.

M 17 A 9. The avoidance of magic is the avoidance of temptation. For all temptation is nothing more than the attempt to substitute another will for God's. These attempts may indeed seem frightening, yet[119] they are merely pathetic. They can have no effects; neither good nor bad, neither rewarding nor demanding sacrifice, healing nor destructive, quieting nor fearful. When all

---

[106] FIP changes "hold it in your heart" to "hold it to your heart." The *Notes* has "in your heart."
[107] FIP omits "in the curriculum" and the *Urtext* manuscript places it in parentheses. The *Notes* has it just as it is here.
[108] FIP replaces "he" with "the teacher of God" however the *Notes* has it just as it stands here.
[109] FIP replaces "met" with "learned." The *Notes* has "met."
[110] *Urtext* manuscript doesn't have "and", it is handwritten in. FIP preserves it. It is also present in the *Notes*.
[111] FIP omits the phrase "if the need for this can be avoided." The phrase is present in the *Notes*.
[112] The Manuscript says "the saving of the mind" and FIP changes that to "the saving of time" which corrects the passage to conform to its original form in the *Notes*. We're viewing this as a copying mistake in the *Urtext* manuscript and incorporating this correction.
[113] FIP changes "which" to "that." It is "which" in the *Notes*.

[114] FIP changes "sleeping" to "going to sleep." It is "sleeping" in the *Notes*.
[115] The *Urtext* manuscript has the words "the day" typed in above "time" indicating a correction, but "time" is not crossed out. The *Notes* has "time" and so does FIP.
[116] Originally typed "is", the handwritten mark-up and FIP change "is" to "be" which is the reading in the *Notes*.
[117] FIP omits "that" however it is present in the *Notes*.
[118] FIP omits "good" however it is present in the *Notes*.
[119] FIP changes "yet" to "but." It is "but" in the *Notes*.

magic is recognized as merely nothing, the teacher of God has reached the most advanced state. All intermediate lessons will but lead to this, and bring this goal nearer to recognition. For magic of any kind, in all its forms,[120] simply does nothing. Its powerlessness is the reason it can be so easily escaped. What has no effects can hardly terrify.

M 17 A 10. There is no substitute for the Will of God. In simple statement, it is to this[121] fact that the teacher of God devotes his day. Each substitute he may accept as real can but deceive him. But he is safe from all deception if he so decides. Perhaps he needs to remember "God is with me. I cannot be deceived." Perhaps he prefers other words, or only one or none at all. Yet each temptation to accept magic as true must be abandoned through his recognition not that it is fearful, not that it is sinful, not that it is dangerous, but merely that it is meaningless. Rooted in sacrifice and separation, two aspects of one error and no more, he merely chooses to give up all that he never had. And for this "sacrifice" is Heaven restored to his awareness. **M(44)**

M 17 A 11. Is not this an exchange that you would want? The world would gladly make it, if it knew it could be made. It is God's teachers who must teach it that it can. And so it is their function to make sure that they have learned it. No risk is possible throughout the day except to put your trust in magic, for it is only this that leads to pain. "There is no will but God's." His teachers know that this is so, and have learned that everything but this is magic. All belief in magic is maintained by just one simple-minded illusion; – that it works. All through his training, every day and hour, and even every minute and second, must God's teachers learn to recognize the forms of magic and perceive their meaninglessness. Fear is withdrawn from them and so they go. And thus the Gate of Heaven is reopened, and its light can shine again on an untroubled mind.

18. HOW DO GOD'S TEACHERS DEAL WITH THEIR PUPILS' THOUGHTS OF MAGIC?

M 18 A 1. This is a crucial question both for teacher and pupil.[122] If this issue is mishandled, the teacher of God has hurt himself and has also attacked his pupil. This strengthens fear and makes the magic seem quite real to both of them. How to deal with magic thus becomes a major lesson for the teacher of God to master. His first responsibility in this is not to attack it. If a magic thought arouses anger in any form, God's teacher[123] can be sure that he is strengthening his own belief in sin and has condemned himself. He can be sure as well that he has asked for depression, pain, fear and disaster to come to him. Let him remember, then, it is not this that he would teach because it is not this that he would learn.

M 18 A 2. There is, however, a temptation to respond to magic in a way that reinforces it. Nor is this always obvious. It can, in fact, be easily concealed beneath a wish to help. It is this double wish that makes the help of little value, and must lead to undesired outcomes. Nor should it be forgotten that the outcome that[124] results will always come to teacher and to pupil.[125] How many times has it been emphasized that you give but to yourself? And where could this be better shown than in the kinds of help the teacher gives to those who need his aid? Here is his gift **M(45)** most clearly given him. For he will give only what he has chosen for himself. And in this gift is his judgment upon the holy Son of God.

M 18 A 3. It is easiest to let error be corrected where it is most apparent, and errors can be recognized by their results. A lesson truly taught can lead to nothing but release for teacher and pupil, who have shared in one intent. Attack can enter only if perception of separate goals has entered. And this must indeed have been the case if the result is anything but joy. The single aim of the teacher turns the divided goal of the pupil into one direction, with the call for help becoming his one appeal. This then is easily responded to with just one answer, and this answer will enter the teacher's mind unfailingly. From there it shines into his pupil's mind, making it one with his.

M 18 A 4. Perhaps it will be helpful to remember that no-one can be angry at a fact. It is always an interpretation that gives rise to negative emotions, regardless of their seeming justification by what appear as facts.[126] Regardless, too, of the intensity of the anger which[127] is aroused. It may be merely slight irritation, perhaps too mild to be even clearly recognized. Or it may also take the form of intense rage, accompanied by thoughts of violence, fantasied or apparently acted out. It does not matter. All of these reactions are the same. They obscure the truth, and this can never be a matter of degree. Either truth is apparent or it is not. It cannot be partially recognized. Who is unaware of truth must look upon[128] illusions.

M 18 A 5. Anger in response to perceived magic thoughts is a[129] basic cause of fear. Consider what this reaction means, and its centrality in the world's thought system becomes apparent. A magic thought, by its mere presence, acknowledges a separation from God. It states, in the clearest form possible, that the mind which thinks it[130] believes it has a separate will that can oppose the Will of God and succeed. That this can hardly be a fact is obvious. Yet that it can be believed as fact is surely so.[131] And herein lies the birthplace of guilt. Who usurps the place of God and takes it for himself now has a deadly "enemy." And he must stand alone in his protection, and make himself a shield to keep him safe from fury that can never be abated and vengeance that can never be satisfied. **M(46)**

M 18 A 6. How can this unfair battle be resolved? Its ending is inevitable, for its outcome must be death. How then can one believe in one's defenses? Magic again must help. Forget the battle. Accept it as a fact and then forget it. Do not remember the impossible odds against you. Do not remember the immensity of the "enemy," and do not think about your frailty in comparison. Accept your separation, but do not remember how it came about. Believe that you have won it, but do not retain the slightest memory of Who your great "opponent" really is. Projecting your "forgetting" onto Him, it seems to you He has forgotten, too.

M 18 A 7. But what will now be your reaction to all magic thoughts? They can but reawaken sleeping guilt, which you have hidden but have not let go. Each one says clearly to your frightened

---

[120] The *Urtext* manuscript types above the originally typed "in any form" the words "in all its forms". FIP uses that reading, which is the reading in the *Notes*.

[121] In the *Urtext* manuscript the word "simple" appears here. Handwritten mark-up crosses out "simple," FIP omits it. It is not present in the *Notes*.

[122] *Urtext* manuscript has "student" crossed out, and "pupil" penciled in. It is "pupil" in the *Notes*.

[123] *Urtext* manuscript has the plural, "teachers" here. The *Notes* uses an abbreviation which could be read as either. The singular works better in the context, since the following pronoun "he" refers back to this word and if it were plural, the pronoun would be "they."

[124] Handwritten mark-up and FIP change the originally typed "which" to "that" which corrects the passage to conform to the *Notes*.

[125] FIP inserts here "alike." That word is not present in the *Notes*.

[126] *Urtext* manuscript has "appears as facts," FIP emphasizes the word "appears" and has "*appears* as facts." The *Notes* has "is seen as facts." There is a grammar problem with "what appears as facts." Either "appears as fact" or "appear as facts" work, but "appears as facts" does not. This is a tricky sentence to parse, but "appears" is a verb and the subject of that verb is the facts which are appearing. If there is more than one fact, then *they appear*. If there is only one then *it appears*.

[127] FIP changes "which" to "that" but it is "which" in the *Notes*.

[128] Handwritten mark-up and FIP change the originally typed "see" to "look upon" which is also the reading in the *Notes*.

[129] The *Urtext* manuscript has the word "the" typed in above "a" in "a basic cause." FIP makes it "a basic cause" as does the *Notes*.

[130] FIP omits "thinks it" so the sentence becomes "the mind which believes." The *Notes* has it as it is here.

[131] FIP replaces "so" with "obvious." The *Notes* has "so."

mind, "You have usurped the place of God. Think not He has forgotten." Here we have the fear of God most starkly represented. For in that thought has guilt already raised madness to the throne of God Himself. And now there is no hope. Except[132] to kill. Here is salvation now. An angry Father pursues His guilty Son. Kill or be killed, for here alone is choice. Beyond this there is none, for what was done cannot be done without. The stain of blood can never be removed, and anyone who bears this stain on him must meet with death.

M 18 A 8. Into this hopeless situation God sends His teachers. They bring the light of hope from God Himself. There is a Way in which escape is possible. It can be learned and taught, but it requires patience and abundant willingness. Given that, the lesson's manifest simplicity stands out like an intense white light against a black horizon, for such it is. If anger comes from an interpretation and not a fact, it is never justified. Once this is even dimly grasped, the Way is open. Now it is possible to take the next step. The interpretation can be changed at last. Magic thoughts need not lead to condemnation, for they do not really have the power to give rise to guilt. And so they can be overlooked, and thus forgiven[133] in the truest sense. **M(47)**

M 18 A 9. Madness but seems terrible. In truth it has no power to make anything. Like the magic which becomes its servant, it neither attacks nor protects. To see it and to recognize its thought system is to look on nothing. Can nothing give rise to anger? Hardly so. Remember then, teacher of God, that anger recognizes a reality that is not there; yet is the anger certain witness that you do believe in it as fact. Now is escape impossible until you see you have responded to your own interpretation, which you have projected on an outside world. Let this grim sword be taken from you now. There is no death.[134] This sword does not exist. The fear of God is causeless. But His Love is Cause of everything beyond all fear, and thus forever real and always true.

19. HOW IS CORRECTION MADE?

M 19 A 1. Correction of a lasting nature, – and only this is true correction, – cannot be made until the teacher of God has ceased to confuse interpretation with fact, or illusion with truth. If he argues with his pupil about a magic thought, attacks it, tries to establish its error or demonstrate its falsity, he is but witnessing to its reality. Depression is then inevitable, for he has "proved" both to his pupil and himself that it is their task to escape from what is real. And this can only be impossible. Reality is changeless. Magic thoughts are but illusions. Otherwise salvation would be only the same age old impossible dream in but another form. Yet the dream of salvation has new content. It is not the form alone in which the difference lies.

M 19 A 2. God's teachers' major lesson is to learn how to react to magic thoughts wholly without anger. Only in this way can they proclaim the truth about themselves. Through them, the Holy Spirit can now speak of the reality of the Son of God. Now He can remind the world of sinlessness, the one unchanged, unchangeable condition of all that God created. Now He can speak the Word of God to listening ears, and bring Christ's vision to eyes that see. Now is He free to teach all minds the truth of what they are, so they will gladly be returned to Him. And now is guilt forgiven, overlooked completely in His sight and in God's Word. **M(48)**

M 19 A 3. Anger but screeches, "Guilt is real!" Reality is blotted[135] out as this insane belief is taken as replacement for God's Word. The body's eyes now "see"; its ears alone are thought to[136] hear. Its little space and tiny breath become the measure of reality. And truth becomes diminutive and meaningless. Correction has one answer to all this, and to the world that rests on this:

> *"You but mistake interpretation for the truth. And you are . wrong. But a mistake is not a sin, nor has reality been taken . from its throne by your mistakes. God reigns forever, and His . laws alone prevail upon you and upon the world. His Love . remains the only thing there is. Fear is illusion, for you are like Him."*

M 19 A 4. In order to heal, it thus becomes essential for the teacher of God to let all his own mistakes be corrected. If he senses even the faintest hint of irritation in himself as he responds to anyone, let him instantly realize that he has made an interpretation which is not true. Then let him turn within to his Eternal Guide, and let Him Judge what the response should be. So is he healed, and in his healing is his pupil healed with him. The sole responsibility of God's teacher is to accept the Atonement for himself. Atonement means correction, or the undoing of errors. When this has been accomplished, the teacher of God becomes a miracle worker by definition. His sins have been forgiven him, and he no longer condemns himself. How can he then condemn anyone? And who is there whom his forgiveness can fail to heal?"

20. WHAT IS JUSTICE?

M 20 A 1. Justice is the divine correction for injustice. Injustice is the basis for all the judgments of the world. Justice corrects the interpretations to which injustice gives rise, and cancels them out. Neither justice nor injustice exists in Heaven, for error is impossible and correction meaningless. In this world, however, forgiveness depends on justice, since all attack can only be unjust. Justice is the Holy Spirit's verdict upon the world. Except in His judgment justice is **M(49)** impossible, for no-one in the world is capable of making only just interpretations and laying all injustices aside. If God's Son were fairly judged, there would be no need for salvation. The thought of separation would have been forever inconceivable.

M 20 A 2. Justice, like its opposite, is an interpretation. It is, however, the one interpretation that leads to truth. This becomes possible because, while it is not true in itself, justice includes nothing that opposes truth. There is no inherent conflict between justice and truth; one is but the first small step in the direction of the other. The path becomes quite different as one goes along. Nor could all the magnificence, the grandeur of the scene and the enormous opening vistas that rise to meet one as he travels on,[137] be foretold from the outset. Yet even these, whose splendor reaches indescribable heights as one proceeds, fall short indeed of all that awaits one[138] when the pathway ceases and time ends with it. But somewhere one must start. Justice is the beginning.

M 20 A 3. All concepts of your brothers and yourself; all fears of future states and all concern[139] about the past stem from injustice. Here is the lens which, held before the body's eyes, distorts perception and brings witness of the distorted world back to the

---

[132] The *Urtext* manuscript also has "accept" instead of "except." The *Notes* has "Except."
[133] FIP replaces "forgiven" with "forgotten"!! The *Notes* has "forgiven."
[134] **2 Timothy 1:10** But has now been revealed by the appearing of our Savior Jesus Christ, who has abolished death and brought life and immortality to light through the gospel.

[135] Handwritten mark-up and FIP have "blotted" while the *Urtext* manuscript has "blocked." The *Notes* has "blotted."
[136] FIP replaces "are thought to" with "can." The *Notes* has "are thought to."
[137] FIP replaces "he travels on" with "the journey continues." The *Notes* has "he travels on."
[138] *Urtext* manuscript has "waits". Handwritten mark-up suggests "awaits one", although it is possible that the handwritten mark-up indicates "'waits' (contraction of "awaits"). FIP changes "waits" to "wait" viewing "all" as plural, (possibly) which it *can* be, but isn't necessarily. One can have "all is well" as well as "all are well." The *Notes* has "awaits one."
[139] FIP pluralizes "concern" making it "concerns". That is also what the *Notes* has.

mind that made the lens and holds it very dear. Selectively and arbitrarily is every concept of the world built up in[140] just this way. "Sins" are perceived and justified by this[141] careful selectivity in which all thought of wholeness must be lost. Forgiveness has no place in such a scheme, for not one "sin" but seems forever true.

M 20 A 4. Salvation is God's justice. It restores to your awareness the wholeness of the fragments you perceive as broken off and separate. And it is this that overcomes the fear of death.[142] For separate fragments must decay and die, but wholeness is immortal. It remains forever and forever like its Creator, being one with Him. God's Judgment is His justice. Onto this, – a judgment wholly lacking in condemnation; an evaluation based entirely on love, – you have projected your injustice, giving[143] God the lens of warped perception through which you look. Now it belongs to Him and not to you. You are afraid of Him, and do not see you hate and fear your Self as enemy. **M(50)**

M 20 A 5. Pray for God's justice, and do not confuse His mercy with your own insanity. Perception can make whatever picture the mind desires to see. Remember this. In this lies either Heaven or hell, as you elect. God's justice points to Heaven just because it is entirely impartial. It accepts all evidence that is brought before it, omitting nothing and assessing nothing as separate and apart from all the rest. From this one standpoint does it judge, and this alone. Here all attack and condemnation become[144] meaningless and indefensible. Perception rests, the mind is still, and light returns again. Vision is now restored. What had been lost has now been found.[145] The peace of God descends on all the world, and we can see. And we can see!

21. What Is the Peace of God[146]?

M 21 A 1. It has been said that there is a kind of peace that is not of this world.[147] How is it recognized? How is it found? And being found, how can it be retained? Let us consider each of these questions separately, for each reflects a different step along the way.

M 21 A 2. First, how can the peace of God be recognized? God's peace is recognized at first by just one thing; in every way it is totally unlike all previous experiences. It calls to mind nothing that went before. It brings with it no past associations. It is a new thing entirely. There is a contrast, yes, between this thing and all the past. But strangely, it is not a contrast of true differences. The past just slips away, and in its place is everlasting quiet. Only that. The contrast first perceived has[148] merely gone. Quiet has reached to cover everything.

M 21 A 3. How is this quiet found? No-one can fail to find it who but seeks out its conditions. God's peace can never come where anger is, for anger must deny that peace exists.[149] Who sees anger as justified in any way or any circumstance proclaims that peace is meaningless, and must believe that it cannot exist. In this condition, peace cannot be found. Therefore, forgiveness is the necessary condition for finding the peace of God. More than this, given forgiveness there must be peace. For what except attack will lead to war? And what but peace is opposite to war? Here the initial contrast stands out clear and apparent. Yet when peace is found, the war **M(51)** is meaningless. And it is conflict now that is perceived as non-existent and unreal.

M 21 A 4. How is the peace of God retained, once it is found? Returning anger, in whatever form, will drop the heavy curtain once again, and the belief that peace cannot exist will certainly return. War is again accepted as the one reality. Now must you once again lay down your sword, although you will[150] not recognize that you have picked it up again. But you will learn, as you remember even faintly now what happiness was yours without it, that you must have taken it again as your defense. Stop for a moment now and think of this: Is conflict what you want, or is God's peace the better choice? Which gives you more? A tranquil mind is not a little gift. Would you not rather live than choose to die?

M 21 A 5. Living is joy, but death can only weep. You see in death escape from what you made. But this you do not see; that you made death, and it is but illusion of an end. Death cannot be escape, because it is not life in which the problem lies. Life has no opposite, for it is God. Life and death seem to be opposites because you have decided[151] death ends life. Forgive the world, and you will understand that everything which[152] God created cannot have an end, and nothing He did not create is real. In this one sentence is our course explained. In this one sentence is our practicing given its one direction. And in this[153] the Holy Spirit's whole curriculum is specified exactly as it is.

M 21 A 6. What is the peace of God? No more than this; the simple understanding that His Will is wholly without opposite. There is no thought that contradicts His Will, yet can be true. The contrast between His Will and yours but seemed to be reality. In truth there is[154] no conflict, because His Will is yours. Now is the mighty Will of God Himself His gift to you. He does not seek to keep it for Himself. Why would you seek to keep your tiny, frail imaginings apart from Him? The Will of God is One and all there is. This is your heritage. The universe beyond the sun and stars, and all the thoughts of which you can conceive, belong to you. God's peace is the condition for His Will. Attain His peace, and you remember Him. **M(52)**

22. What Is the Role of Words in Healing?

M 22 A 1. Strictly speaking, words play no part at all in healing. The motivating factor is prayer, or asking. What you ask for you receive.[155] But this refers to the prayer of the heart, not to the words you use in praying. Sometimes the words and the prayer are contradictory; sometimes they agree. It does not matter. God does not understand words, for they were made by separated minds to

---

[140] Handwritten mark-up and FIP insert "in" which is also present in the *Notes*.
[141] FIP omits "this" as does the *Notes*.
[142] *Urtext* manuscript and FIP and the *Notes* all put a sentence break here needlessly, rendering the following clause into an incomplete sentence.
[143] The *Urtext* manuscript has "attributing to" typed above "giving." FIP goes with "giving God" while the *Notes* has "giving Him."
[144] FIP changes "become" to "becomes". The subject is "attack and condemnation" which is plural so the *Urtext* is correct. The *Notes* has an abbreviation "bec." which could be either.
[145] **Luke 15:24** "For this my son was dead and is alive again; he was lost and is found." And they began to be merry.
[146] **Philippians 4:7** "And the peace of God, which passeth all understanding, shall guard your hearts and your thoughts in Christ Jesus."
[147] **John 14:27** "Peace I leave with you, My peace I give to you; not as the world gives do I give to you. Let not your heart be troubled, neither let it be afraid."
[148] Handwritten mark-up and FIP change the originally typed "is" to "has" which is the reading in the *Notes*.

[149] **Deuteronomy 4:29** "But from there you will seek the LORD your God, and you will find Him if you seek with all your heart and with all your soul."
[150] Handwritten mark-up suggests "may," FIP changes "will" to "do." The *Notes* has the glyph for "will."
[151] Handwritten mark-up suggests inserting "that." The word "that" is present in the *Notes* but is scratched out. At least there is a scratched out word in this spot in the *Notes* which *could* be "that." FIP does not insert the word.
[152] FIP changes "which" to "that." The *Notes* has "which."
[153] FIP adds the words "one sentence." Those words are not present in the *Notes*.
[154] FIP changes "is" to "was" which is the reading in the *Notes*.
[155] **Matthew 21:22** "And all things, whatsoever ye shall ask in prayer, believing, ye shall receive."

keep them in the illusion of separation. Words can be helpful, particularly for the beginner, in helping concentration and facilitating the exclusion or at least the control of extraneous thoughts. Let us not forget, however, that words are but symbols of symbols. They are thus twice removed from reality.

M 22 A 2. As symbols, words have quite specific references. Even when they seem most abstract, the picture which[156] comes to mind is apt to be very concrete. Unless a specific referent does occur to the mind in conjunction with the word, the word has little or no practical meaning and thus cannot help the healing process. The prayer of the heart does not really ask for concrete things. It always requests some kind of experience, the specific things asked for being the bringers of the desired experience in the judgment[157] of the asker. The words, then, are symbols for the thing[158] asked for, but the things themselves but stand for the experiences which[159] are hoped for.

M 22 A 3. The prayer for things of this world will bring experiences of this world. If the prayer of the heart asks for this, this will be given because this will be received. It is impossible that the prayer of the heart remain unanswered in the perception of the one who asks. If he asks for the impossible, if he wants what does not exist or seeks for illusions in his heart, all this becomes his own. The power of his decision offers it to him as he requests. Herein lie hell and Heaven. The sleeping Son of God has but this power left to him. It is enough. His words do not matter. Only the Word of God has any meaning, because it symbolizes that which has no human symbols at all. The Holy Spirit alone understands what this Word stands for. And this, too, is enough. **M(53)**

M 22 A 4. Is the teacher of God then to avoid the use of words in his teaching? No, indeed. There are many who must be reached through words, being as yet unable to hear in silence. The teacher of God must, however, learn to use words in a new way. Gradually, he learns how to let his words be chosen for him by ceasing to decide for himself what he will say. This process is merely a special case of the Workbook lesson[160] "I will step back and let Him lead the way." The teacher of God accepts the words which are offered him and gives as he receives. He does not control the direction of his speaking. He listens and hears and speaks.

M 22 A 5. A major hindrance in this aspect of his learning is the teacher of God's fear about the validity of what he hears. And what he hears may indeed be quite startling. It may also seem to be[161] irrelevant to the presented problem as he perceives it, and may, in fact, confront him[162] with a situation that appears to be very embarrassing.[163] All these are judgments which have no value. They are his own, coming from the shabby self-perception that[164] he would leave behind. Judge not the words that come to you, but offer them in confidence. They are far wiser than your own. God's teachers have God's Word behind their symbols. And He Himself gives to the words they use the power of His Spirit, raising them from meaningless symbols to the call of Heaven itself.

23. How Are Healing and Atonement Related?

M 23 A 1. Healing and Atonement are not related; they are identical. There is no order of difficulty in miracles because there are no degrees of Atonement. It is the one complete concept possible in this world, because it is the source of a wholly unified perception. Partial Atonement is a meaningless idea, just as special areas of hell in Heaven is[165] inconceivable. Accept Atonement and you are healed. Atonement is the Word of God. Accept His Word and what remains to make sickness possible? Accept His Word and every miracle has been accomplished. To forgive is to heal. The teacher of God has taken accepting the Atonement for himself as his only function. What is there then he cannot heal? What miracle can be withheld from him? **M(54)**

M 23 A 2. The progress of the teacher of God may be slow or rapid, depending on whether he recognizes the Atonement's inclusiveness or for a time excludes some problem areas from it. In some cases, there is a sudden and complete awareness of the perfect applicability of the lesson of the[166] Atonement to all situations. This,[167] however, is comparatively rare. The teacher of God may have accepted the function God has given him long before he has learned all that his acceptance holds out to him. It is only the end that is certain. Anywhere along the way,[168] the necessary realization of inclusiveness may reach him. If the way seems long, let him be content. He has decided on the direction he will[169] take. What more is[170] asked of him? And having done what was required, would God withhold the rest?

M 23 A 3. That forgiveness is healing needs to be understood, if the teacher of God is to make progress. The idea that a body can be sick is a central concept in the ego's thought system. This thought gives the body autonomy, separates it from the mind, and keeps the idea of attack inviolate. If the body could be sick Atonement would be impossible. A body that can order a mind to do as it sees fit could[171] merely take the place of God and prove salvation is impossible. What then is left to heal? The body has become lord of the mind. How could the mind be returned to the Holy Spirit unless the body is killed? And who would want salvation at such a price?

M 23 A 4. Certainly sickness does not appear to be a decision. Nor would anyone actually believe he wants to be sick. Perhaps he can accept the idea in theory, but it is rarely if ever consistently applied to all specific forms of sickness, both in the individual's perception of himself and of all others as well. Nor is it at this level that the teacher of God calls forth the miracle of healing. He overlooks the mind and body, seeing only the Face of Christ shining in front of him, correcting all mistakes and healing all perception. Healing is the result of the recognition, by God's teacher, of Who it is that is in need of healing. This recognition has no special reference. It is true of all things that God created. In it are all illusions healed. **M(55)**

M 23 A 5. When a teacher of God fails to heal, it is because he has forgotten Who he is. Another's sickness thus becomes his own. In allowing this to happen, he has identified with another's ego, and has thus confused him with a body. In so doing, he has refused to accept[172] Atonement for himself, and can hardly offer it to his brother in Christ's Name. He will, in fact, be unable to recognize his brother at all, for his Father did not create bodies, and so he is

---

[156] FIP changes "which" to "that;" the *Notes* has "which."
[157] FIP changes "judgment" to "opinion." The *Notes* has "opinion" written first, crossed out, and changed to "judgment."
[158] FIP changes "thing" to "things." The *Notes* has "things."
[159] FIP changes "which" to "that." The *Notes* has "which."
[160] FIP changes "Workbook lesson" to "lesson in the workbook that says." The *Notes* has "lesson in the workbook **which** says…"
[161] FIP adds "quite" which is also in the *Notes*.
[162] FIP changes "him" to "the teacher." The *Notes* has "the teacher."
[163] FIP adds "to him" and so does the *Notes*.
[164] FIP changes "that" to "which;" the *Notes* also has "which."

[165] FIP changes "is" to "are" viewing the subject as the plural "special areas." In fact the subject is the implied "[the idea of] special areas." It's not the "special areas" which are inconceivable, but the IDEA of them. The *Notes* has it as "is."
[166] The word "the" is not present in the *Urtext* manuscript, but it is present in the *Notes* and in FIP. This is being regarded as an inadvertent omission.
[167] FIP replaces the period with a comma and then adds "but" and deletes "however." The *Notes* is the same as FIP "… the Atonement to all situations, but this is comparatively rare."
[168] Illegible handwritten mark-up suggests something, possibly "line" in place of "way." FIP and the *Notes* are all the same here.
[169] FIP changes "will" to "wants to." The *Notes* also has "wants to."
[170] FIP replaces "is" with "was." The *Notes* also has "was."
[171] The Manuscript shows "could" handwritten above "would." FIP chooses "could" which is also the reading in the *Notes*.
[172] FIP inserts "the" before "Atonement." The *Notes* has no "the" here.

seeing in a[173] brother only the unreal. Mistakes do not correct mistakes, and distorted perception does not heal. Step back now, teacher of God. You have been wrong. Lead not the way, for you have lost it. Turn quickly to your Teacher, and let yourself be healed.

M 23 A 6. The offer of Atonement is universal. It is equally applicable to all individuals in all circumstances. And in it is the power to heal all individuals of all forms of sickness. Not to believe this is to be unfair to God, and thus unfaithful to Him. A sick person perceives himself as separate from God. Would you see him as separate from you? It is your task to heal the sense of separation that has made him sick. It is your function to recognize for him that what he believes about himself is not the truth.[174] It is your forgiveness that must show him this. Healing is very simple. Atonement is received and offered. Having been received, it must be accepted. It is in the receiving, then, that healing lies. All else must follow from this single purpose.

M 23 A 7. Who can limit the power of God Himself? Who then can say who[175] can be healed of what, and what must[176] remain beyond God's power to forgive? This is insanity indeed. It is not up to God's teachers to set limits upon Him, because it is not up to them to judge His Son. And to judge His Son is to limit his Father. Both are equally meaningless. Yet this will not be understood until God's teacher recognizes that they are the same mistake. Herein does he receive Atonement, for he withdraws his judgment from the Son of God, accepting him as God created him. No longer does he stand apart from God, determining where healing should be given and where it should be withheld. Now can he say with God, "This is my beloved Son,[177] created perfect and forever so." **M(56)**

24. DOES JESUS HAVE A SPECIAL PLACE IN HEALING?

M 24 A 1. God's gifts can rarely be received directly. Even the most advanced of God's teachers will give way to temptation in this world. Would it be fair if their pupils were denied healing because of this? The Bible says "Ask in the name of Jesus Christ."[178] Is this merely an appeal to magic? A name does not heal, nor does an invocation call forth any special power. What does it mean to call on Jesus Christ? What does calling on his Name confer? Why is the appeal to him part of healing?

M 24 A 2. We have repeatedly stated[179] that one who has perfectly accepted the Atonement for himself can heal the world. Indeed, he has already done so. Temptation may recur to others, but never to this One. He has become the risen Son of God. He has overcome death because he has accepted Life. He has recognized himself as God created him, and in so doing he has recognized all living things as part of him. There is now no limit on his power, because it is the Power of God. So has his name become the Name of God, for he no longer sees himself as separate from Him.

M 24 A 3. What does this mean to you? It means that in remembering Jesus you are remembering God. The whole relationship of the Son to the Father lies in him. His part in the Sonship is also yours, and his completed learning guarantees your own success. Is he still available for help? What did he say about this? Remember his promises,[180] and ask yourself honestly whether it is likely that[181] he will fail to keep them. Can God fail His Son? And can one who is one with God be unlike Him? Who transcends the body has transcended limitation. Would the greatest teacher be unavailable to those who follow him?

M 24 A 4. The name of Jesus Christ as such is but a symbol. But it stands for love that is not of this world. It is a symbol that can safely be used[182] as a replacement for the many names of all the gods you pray to.[183] It becomes the shining symbol for the Word of God, so close to What it stands for that the little space between the two is lost the moment that the Name is called to mind. Remembering His name is to **M(57)** give thanks for all the gifts that God has given you. And gratitude to God becomes the way in which He is remembered, for love cannot be far behind a grateful heart and thankful mind. God enters easily, for these are the true conditions for your coming home.[184]

M 24 A 5. Jesus has led the way. Why would you not be grateful to him? He has asked for love, but only that he might give it to you. You do not love yourself. But in his eyes your loveliness is so complete and flawless that he sees in it an image of his Father. You become the symbol of his Father here on earth. To you he looks for hope, because in you he sees no limit and no stain to mar your beautiful perfection. In his eyes Christ's vision shines in perfect constancy. He has remained with you. Would you not learn the lesson of salvation through his learning? Why would you choose to start again, when he has made the journey for you?

M 24 A 6. No-one on earth can grasp what Heaven is, or what its One Creator really means. Yet we have witnesses. It is to them that wisdom would[185] appeal. There have been those whose learning far exceeds what you[186] can learn. Nor would we teach the limitations we have laid on us. No-one who has become a true and dedicated teacher of God forgets his brothers. Yet what he can offer them is limited by what he learns himself. Then turn to one who laid all limits by, and went beyond the farthest reach of learning. He will take you with him, for he did not go alone. And you were with him then, as you are now.

M 24 A 7. This course has come from him because his words have reached you in a language you can love and understand. Are other teachers possible, to lead the way to those who speak in different tongues and appeal to different symbols? Certainly there are. Would God leave anyone without a very present help in time of trouble; a Savior who can symbolize Himself? Yet do we need a many-faceted curriculum, not because of content differences but because symbols must shift and change to suit the need. Jesus has come to answer yours. In him you find God's Answer. Do you then teach with him,[187] for he is with you; he is always here. **M(58)**

---

[173] FIP replaces "a brother" with "his brother." The *Notes* has "his brother."
[174] Handwritten mark-up suggests "true," FIP keeps "the truth" and that is what the *Notes* has also.
[175] FIP replaces "who" with "which one." The *Notes* has "who."
[176] Handwritten mark-up suggests "must still." Both FIP and the *Notes* have it as it is here.
[177] **Matthew 17:5** While he was still speaking, behold, a bright cloud overshadowed them; and suddenly a voice came out of the cloud, saying, "This is My beloved Son, in whom I am well pleased. Hear Him!"
[178] **John 14:13-14** "And whatever you ask in My name, that I will do, that the Father may be glorified in the Son. If you ask anything in My name, I will do it."
[179] FIP replaces "stated" with "said." The *Notes* has "stated."

[180] There are so many specific and general "promises" Jesus made in the Bible, to begin to cite them would require a separate book! **Matthew 28:20** is apt however: "lo, I am with you always, even unto the end of the world."
[181] Handwritten mark-up and FIP insert "that" which is also in the *Notes* although it is not originally typed in the manuscript.
[182] FIP changes "that can safely be used" to "that safely used" which is the reading in the *Notes*.
[183] FIP changes "you pray to" to "to which you pray." The *Notes* has "you pray to."
[184] FIP replaces "coming home" with "homecoming." The *Notes* has "coming home."
[185] FIP replaces "would" with "should." The *Notes* has "... that wisdom sh would appeal." It appears that Schucman began to write "should" then crossed out the "sh" and proceeded to write "would."
[186] FIP changes "you" to "we." The glyph used in the *Notes* is that most commonly used for "we" rather than "you."
[187] **Mathew 28:20** "lo, I am with you always, even unto the end of the world."

25. Is Reincarnation True?

M 25 A 1. In the ultimate sense, reincarnation is impossible. There is no past nor future, and the idea of birth into a body has no meaning either once or many times. Reincarnation cannot, then, be true in any real sense. Our only question should be, "Is the concept helpful?" And that depends, of course, on what it is used for. If it is used to strengthen the recognition of the eternal nature of life it is helpful indeed. Is any other question about it really useful in lighting up the way? Like many other beliefs, it can be bitterly misused. At least, such misuse offers preoccupation and perhaps pride in the past. At worst, it induces inertia in the present. In between, many kinds of folly are possible.

M 25 A 2. Reincarnation would not, under any circumstances, be the problem to be dealt with now. If it were responsible for some of the difficulties the individual faces now, his task would still be only to escape from them now. If he is laying the groundwork for a future life, he can still work out his salvation only now. To some there may be comfort in the concept, and if it heartens them its value is self-evident. It is certain, however, that the way to salvation can be found by those who believe in reincarnation and by those who do not. The idea cannot, therefore, be regarded as essential to the curriculum. There is always some risk in seeing the present in terms of the past. There is always some good in any thought which strengthens the idea that life and the body are not the same.

M 25 A 3. For our purposes, it would not be helpful to take any definite stand on reincarnation. A teacher of God should be as helpful to those who believe in it as to those who do not. If a definite stand on it[188] were required of him, it would merely limit his usefulness as well as his own decision-making. Our course is not concerned with any concept that is not acceptable to anyone, regardless of his formal beliefs. His ego will be enough for him to cope with, and it is not the[189] part of wisdom to add sectarian controversies to his burdens. Nor would there be an advantage in his premature acceptance of the course merely because it advocates a long-held belief of his own. **M(59)**

M 25 A 4. It cannot be too strongly emphasized that this course aims at a complete reversal of thought. When this is finally accomplished issues such as the validity of reincarnation become meaningless. Until then they are likely to be merely controversial. The teacher of God is therefore wise to step away from all such questions, for he has much to teach and learn apart from them. He should both learn and teach that theoretical issues but waste time, draining it away from its appointed purpose. If there are aspects to any concept or belief that will be helpful, he will be told about it. He will also be told how to use it. What more need he know?

M 25 A 5. Does this mean that the teacher of God should not believe in reincarnation himself, or discuss it with others who do? The answer
is, certainly not. If he does believe in reincarnation, it would be a mistake for him to renounce the belief unless his Internal Teacher so advised. And this is most unlikely. He might be advised that he is misusing the belief in some way which[190] is detrimental to his pupil's advance or his own. Reinterpretation would then be recommended because it would be necessary. All that must be recognized, however, is[191] that birth was not the beginning and death is not the end. Yet even this much is not required of the beginner. He need merely accept the idea that what he knows is not necessarily all there is to learn. His journey has begun.

M 25 A 6. The emphasis of this course always remains the same; – it is at this moment that complete salvation is offered you, and it is at this moment that you can accept it. This is still your one responsibility. Atonement might be equated with total escape from the past and total lack of interest in the future. Heaven is here. There is nowhere else. Heaven is now. There is no other time. No teaching that does not lead to this is of concern to God's teachers. All beliefs will point to this if properly interpreted. In this sense it can be said that their truth lies in their usefulness. All beliefs that lead to progress should be honored. This is the sole criterion this course requires. No more than this is necessary. **M(60)**

26. Are "Psychic" Powers Desirable?

M 26 A 1. The answer to this question is much like the preceding one. There are, of course, no "unnatural" powers, and it is obviously merely an appeal to magic to make up a power that does not exist. It is equally obvious, however, that each individual has many abilities of which he is unaware. As his awareness increases, he may well develop abilities that seem quite startling to him. Yet nothing that[192] he can do can compare even in the slightest with the glorious surprise of remembering Who he is. Let all his learning and all his effort[193] be directed toward this one great final surprise, and he will not be content to be delayed by the little ones that may come to him on the way.

M 26 A 2. Certainly there are many "psychic" powers that are clearly in line with this course. Communication is not limited to the small range of channels the world recognizes. If it were there would be little point in trying to teach salvation. It would be impossible to do so. The limits the world places on communication is[194] the chief barrier to direct experience of the Holy Spirit, Whose Presence is always there and Whose Voice is available but for the hearing. These limits are placed out of fear, for without them the walls that surround all the separate places of the world would fall at the holy sound of His Voice.[195] Who transcends these limits in any way is merely becoming more natural. He is doing nothing special, and there is no magic in his accomplishments.

M 26 A 3. The seemingly new abilities that may be gathered on the way can be very helpful. Given to the Holy Spirit, and used under His direction, they are very[196] valuable teaching aids. To this, the question of how they arise is irrelevant. The only important consideration is how they are used. Taken[197] as ends in themselves, no matter how this is done, will delay progress. Nor does their value lie in proving anything; achievements from the past, unusual attunement with the "unseen," or special favors from God. God gives no special favors, and no-one has any powers that are not available to everyone. Only by tricks of magic are special powers "demonstrated." **M(61)**

M 26 A 4. Nothing that is genuine is used to deceive. The Holy Spirit is incapable of deception, and He can use only genuine abilities. What is used for magic is useless to Him, but what He uses cannot be used for magic. There is, however, a particular appeal in unusual abilities which[198] can be curiously tempting. Here

---

[188] FIP omits "on it." The words "on it" are present in the *Notes*.
[189] The word "the" is not present in the *Urtext* manuscript; however it is present in FIP and in the *Notes*. We include it because its presence is clearly called for and its absence appears to be an inadvertent omission.
[190] FIP changes "which" to "that" which reflects the *Notes*.
[191] *Urtext* manuscript has "if" here ... an obvious typo. The *Notes* and FIP both have "is."
[192] FIP omits "that" although it is present in the *Notes*.
[193] FIP changes "effort" to "efforts" but it is "effort" in the *Notes*.
[194] FIP changes "is" to "are" reading "the limits" as a plural subject. The *Notes* rather clearly has it the same as the *Urtext* manuscript. However, "limits" can be a single body of limitations which could be construed as a singular subject. This is a "noun clause" which can be singular, referring essentially to a singular "body of limits" as it were. We're leaving it singular.
[195] **Joshua 6:20** So the people shouted when the priests blew the trumpets. And it happened when the people heard the sound of the trumpet, the people shouted with a great shout, that the wall fell down flat. Then the people went up into the city, every man straight before him, and they took the city.
[196] FIP omits "very" although it is present in the *Notes*.
[197] FIP replaces "Taken" with "Taking them." The *Notes* has "Taken."
[198] FIP replaces "which" with "that" but the *Notes* has "which."

are strengths which the Holy Spirit wants and needs. Yet the ego sees in these same strengths an opportunity to glorify itself. Strengths turned to weakness are tragedy indeed. Yet what is not given to the Holy Spirit must be given to weakness, for what is withheld from love is given to fear, and will be fearful in consequence.[199]

M 26 A 5. Even those who no longer value the material things of the world may still be deceived by "psychic" powers. As investment has been withdrawn from the world's material gifts the ego has been seriously threatened. It may still be strong enough to rally under this new temptation to win back strength by guile. Many have not seen through the ego's defenses here, although they are not particularly subtle. Yet, given a remaining wish to be deceived, deception is made easy. Now the "power" is no longer a genuine ability, and cannot be used dependably. It is almost inevitable that, unless the individual changes his mind about its purpose, he will bolster[200] its uncertainties with increasing deception.

M 26 A 6. Any ability that anyone develops has the potentiality for good. To this there is no exception. And the more unusual and unexpected the power, the greater its[201] potential usefulness. Salvation has need of all abilities, for what the world would destroy the Holy Spirit would restore. "Psychic" abilities have been used to call upon the devil, which merely means to strengthen the ego. Yet here is also a great channel of hope and healing in the Holy Spirit's service. Those who have developed "psychic" powers have merely[202] let some of the limitations they laid upon their minds be lifted. It can be but greater[203] limitations they lay upon themselves if they utilize their increased freedom for further[204] imprisonment. The Holy Spirit needs these gifts, and those who offer them to Him and Him alone go with Christ's gratitude upon their hearts, and His holy sight not far behind. **M(62)**

27. CAN GOD BE REACHED DIRECTLY?

M 27 A 1. God indeed can be reached directly, for there is no distance between Him and His Son. His awareness is in everyone's memory and His Word is written on everyone's heart.[205] Yet this awareness and this memory can arise across the threshold of the unconscious[206] only where all barriers to truth have been removed. In how many is this the case? Here then is the role of God's teachers. They too have not attained the necessary understanding as yet, but they have joined with others. This is what sets them apart from the world. And it is this that enables others to leave the world with them. Alone they are nothing. But in their joining is the Power of God.

M 27 A 2. There are those who have reached God directly, retaining no trace of worldly limits and remembering their own Identity perfectly. These might be called the Teachers of teachers because, although they are no longer visible, their image can yet be called upon. And they will appear when and where it is helpful for them to do so. To those to whom such appearances would be frightening, they give their ideas. No-one can call on them in vain. Nor is there anyone of whom they are unaware. All needs are known to them, and all mistakes are recognized and overlooked by them. The time will come when this is understood. And meanwhile, they give all their gifts to the teachers of God who look to them for help, asking all things in Their Name and in no other.

M 27 A 3. Sometimes a teacher of God may have a brief experience of direct union with God. In this world, it is almost impossible that this endure. It can, perhaps, be won after much devotion and dedication, and then be maintained for most[207] of the time on earth. But this is so rare that it cannot be considered a realistic goal. If it happens, so be it. If it does not happen, so be it as well. All worldly states must be illusory. If God were reached directly in sustained awareness, the body would not be long maintained. Those who have laid the body down merely to extend their helpfulness to those remaining behind are few indeed. And they need helpers who are still in bondage and still asleep, so that by their awakening can God's Voice be heard. **M(63)**

M 27 A 4. Do not despair, then, because of limitations. It is your function to escape from them, but not to be without them. If you would be heard by those who suffer, you must speak their language. If you would be Saviors, you must understand what needs to be escaped. Salvation is not theoretical. Behold the problem, ask for the answer, and then accept the answer[208] when it comes. Nor will its coming be long delayed. All the help you can accept will be provided, and not one need you have will not be met. Let us not, then, be too concerned with goals for which you are not ready. God takes you where you are and welcomes you. What more could you desire, when this is all you need?

28. WHAT IS DEATH?

M 28 A 1. Death is the central dream from which all illusions stem. Is it not madness to think of life as being born, aging, losing vitality, and dying in the end? We have asked this question before, but now we need to consider it still[209] more carefully. It is the one fixed, unchangeable belief of the world that all things in it are born only to die. This is regarded as "the way of nature," not to be raised to question, but to be accepted as the "natural" law of life. The cyclical, the changing and unsure; the undependable and the unsteady, waxing and waning in a certain way upon a certain path, – all this is taken as the Will of God. And no-one asks if a benign Creator could will this.

M 28 A 2. In this perception of the universe as God created it, it would not be possible[210] to think of Him as loving. For who decreed that all things pass away, ending in dust and disappointment and despair, can[211] but be feared. He holds your little life in his hand but by a thread, ready to break it off without regret or care, perhaps today. Or if he waits, yet is the ending certain. Who loves such a god knows not of love, because he has denied that life is real. Death has become life's symbol. His world is now a battleground, where contradiction reigns and opposites make endless war. Where there is death is peace impossible. **M(64)**

M 28 A 3. Death is the symbol of the fear of God. His Love is blotted out in the idea, which holds It from awareness like a shield

---

[199] **1 John 4:18** There is no fear in love; but perfect love casts out fear, because fear involves torment. But he who fears has not been made perfect in love.
[200] FIP adds "his "power's"" but that is not present in the *Notes*.
[201] *Urtext* manuscript has "is," but it should obviously be "its." FIP agrees. The *Notes* has "its."
[202] FIP replaces "merely" with "simply." The *Notes* has "merely."
[203] FIP replaces "greater limitations" with "further limitations." The *Notes* has "grater burdens."
[204] FIP replaces "further" with "greater." The *Notes* has "further."
[205] **Jeremiah 31:33** "But this is the covenant that I will make with the house of Israel after those days," saith the LORD; "I will put my law in their inward parts, and in their heart will I write it; and I will be their God, and they shall be my people:"
Romans 2:15 Who show the work of the law written in their hearts, their conscience also bearing witness, and between themselves their thoughts accusing or else excusing them.
[206] FIP replaces "the unconscious" with "recognition." The *Notes* has "unconscious."

[207] Handwritten mark-up suggests and FIP replaces "most" with "much." The *Notes* has "most."
[208] FIP replaces "the answer" with "it." The *Notes* has "the answer."
[209] FIP omits "still" however it is present in the *Notes*.
[210] FIP replaces "would not be possible" with "would be impossible." The *Notes* has "would not be possible."
[211] Handwritten mark-up suggests "could" in place of "can." The *Notes* has "can."

held[212] to obscure the sun. The grimness of the symbol is enough to show it cannot co-exist with God. It holds an image of the Son of God in which he is "laid to rest" in devastation's arms, where worms await[213] to greet him and to last a little while by his destruction. Yet the worms as well are doomed to be destroyed as certainly. And so do all things live because of death. Devouring is nature's "law of life." God is insane, and fear alone is real.

M 28 A 4. The curious belief that there is part of dying things that may go on apart from what will die does not proclaim a loving God, nor re-establish any grounds for trust. If death is real for anything there is no life. Death denies life. But if there is reality in life, death is denied. No compromise in this is possible. There is either a god of fear or One of Love. The world attempts a thousand compromises, and will attempt a thousand more. Not one can be acceptable to God's teachers, because not one could be acceptable to God. He did not make death because He did not make fear. Both are equally meaningless to Him.

M 28 A 5. The "reality" of death is firmly rooted in the belief that God's Son is a body. And if God created bodies, death would indeed be real. But God would not be loving. There is no point at which the contrast between the perception of the real world and that of the world of illusions becomes more sharply evident. Death is indeed the death of God, if He is Love. And now His Own creation must stand in fear of Him. He is not Father but destroyer. He is not Creator but avenger. Terrible His Thoughts and fearful His image. To look on His creations is to die. **M(65)**

M 28 A 6. "And the last to be overcome will be death."[214] Of course! Without the idea of death there is no world. All dreams will end with this one. This is salvation's final goal; the end of all illusions. And in death are all illusions born. What can be born of death and still have life? But what is born of God and still can die? The inconsistencies, the compromises and the rituals the world fosters in its vain attempts to cling to death and yet to think love real are mindless magic, ineffectual and meaningless. God is, and in Him all created things must be eternal. Do you not see that otherwise He has an opposite, and fear would be as real as love?

M 28 A 7. Teacher of God, your one assignment could be stated thus: Accept no compromise in which death plays a part. Do not believe in cruelty, nor let attack conceal the truth from you. What seems to die has[215] been misperceived and carried[216] to illusion. Now it becomes your task to let the illusion be carried[217] to the truth. Be steadfast but in this; be not deceived by the "reality" of any changing form. Truth neither moves nor wavers nor sinks down to death and dissolution. And what is the end of death? Nothing but this; the realization that the Son of God is guiltless now and forever. Nothing but this. But do not let yourself forget it is not less than this. **M(66)**

29. WHAT IS THE RESURRECTION?

M 29 A 1. Very simply, the resurrection is the overcoming or surmounting of death. It is a reawakening or a rebirth; a change of mind about the meaning of the world. It is the acceptance of the Holy Spirit's interpretation of the world's purpose; the acceptance of the Atonement for oneself. It is the end of dreams of misery and the glad awareness of the Holy Spirit's final dream. It is the recognition of the gifts of God. It is the dream in which the body functions perfectly, having no function except communication. It is the lesson in which learning ends, for it is consummated and surpassed with this. It is the invitation to God to take His final step. It is the relinquishment of all other purposes, all other interests, all other wishes and all other concerns. It is the single desire of the Son for the Father.

M 29 A 2. The resurrection is the denial of death, being the assertion of life. Thus is all the thinking of the world reversed entirely. Life is now recognized as salvation, and pain and misery of any kind perceived as hell. Love is no longer feared but gladly welcomed. Idols have disappeared, and the remembrance of God shines unimpeded across the world. Christ's face is seen in every living thing, and nothing is held in darkness apart from the light of forgiveness. There is no sorrow still upon the earth. The joy of Heaven has come upon it.

M 29 A 3. Here the curriculum ends. From here on no directions are needed. Vision is wholly corrected and all mistakes undone. Attack is meaningless and peace has come. The goal of the curriculum has been achieved. Thoughts turn to Heaven and away from hell. All longings are satisfied, for what remains unanswered or incomplete? The last illusion spreads over[218] the world, forgiving all things and replacing all attack. The whole reversal is accomplished. Nothing is left to contradict the Word of God. There is no opposition to the truth. And now the truth can come at last. How quickly will it come as it is asked to enter and envelop such a world! **M(67)**

M 29 A 4. All living hearts are tranquil, with a stir of deep anticipation, for the time of everlasting things is now at hand. There is no death. The Son of God is free. And in His freedom is the end of fear. No hidden places now remain on earth to shelter sick illusions, dreams of fear and misperceptions of the universe. All things are seen in light, and in the light their purpose is transformed and understood. And we, God's children, rise up from the dust and look upon our perfect sinlessness. The song of Heaven sounds around the world, as it is lifted up and brought to truth.

M 29 A 5. Now there are no distinctions. Differences have disappeared and Love looks on Itself. What further sight is needed? What remains that vision could accomplish? We have seen the face of Christ, His sinlessness, His Love behind all forms, beyond all purposes. Holy are we because His Holiness has set us free indeed! And we accept His Holiness as ours; as it is. As God created us so will we be forever and forever, and we wish for nothing but His Will to be our own. Illusions of another will are[219] lost, for unity of purpose has been found.

M 29 A 6. These things await us all, but we are not prepared as yet to welcome them with joy. As long as any mind remains possessed of evil dreams the thought of hell is real. God's teachers have the goal of wakening the minds of those asleep, and seeing there the vision of Christ's face to take the place of what they dream.[220] The thought of murder is replaced with blessing. Judgment is laid by, and given Him Whose function judgment is. And in His final judgment is restored the truth about the holy Son of God. He is redeemed, for he has heard God's Word and understood Its meaning. He is free because he let God's Voice proclaim the truth.

---

[212] FIP changes "shield held" to "shield held up." The *Notes* has "shield held."

[213] FIP changes "await" to "wait." The *Notes* has "await."

[214] **1 Corinthians 15:26** "The last enemy that shall be abolished is death." (ASV)

[215] Handwritten mark-up and FIP insert "but" here. The word "but" is not present in the *Notes*.

[216] Handwritten mark-up offers "brought" as a substitute for "carried." The *Notes* has "carried" and so does FIP.

[217] ibid

[218] FIP replaces "over" with "across." The *Notes* has "over."

[219] *Urtext* manuscript has "is," FIP corrects the agreement in number problem as we have with "are." *Notes* clearly has "is" also. It is possible that "Illusions of another will" should be considered a "noun clause" which could be construed as singular. We can for instance think of this one thing called "our illusions of another will" which is capable of being lost. However it seems more likely that this is just an error and "are" is what was intended.

[220] *Urtext* manuscript has "dreamed" but handwritten mark-up and FIP replace that with "dream." Given that the rest of the paragraph is in the present tense, this seems to be an appropriate correction. The *Notes* also has "dream."

And all he sought before to crucify are resurrected with him, by his side as he prepares with them to meet his God. **M(68)**

30. AS FOR THE REST

M 30 A 1. This manual is not intended to answer all questions which both teacher and pupil may raise. In fact, it covers only a few of the more obvious ones, in terms of a brief summary of some of the major concepts in the text and workbook. It is not a substitute for either, but merely a supplement. While it is called a manual for teachers, it must be remembered that only time divides teacher and pupil, so that the difference is temporary by definition. In some cases, it may be helpful for the pupil to read the manual first. Others might do better to begin with the workbook. Still others may need to start at the more abstract level of the text.

M 30 A 2. Which is for whom?[221] Who would profit more from prayers alone? Who needs but a smile, being as yet unready for more? No-one should attempt to answer these questions alone. Surely no teacher of God has come this far without realizing that. The curriculum is highly individualized. And all aspects are under the Holy Spirit's particular care and guidance. Ask and He will answer. The responsibility is His, and He alone is fit to assume it. To do so is His function. To refer the questions to Him is yours. Would you want to be responsible for decisions about which you understand so little? Be glad you have a Teacher Who cannot make a mistake. His answers are always right. Would you say that of yours?

M 30 A 3. There is another advantage,– and a very important one, – in referring decisions to the Holy Spirit with increasing frequency. Perhaps you have not thought of this aspect, but its centrality is obvious. To follow the Holy Spirit's guidance is to let yourself be absolved of guilt. It is the essence of the Atonement. It is the core of the curriculum. The imagined usurping of functions not your own is the basis of fear. The whole world you see reflects the illusion you have done so, making fear inevitable. To return the function to the One To Whom it belongs is thus the escape from fear. And it is this that lets the memory of love return to **M(69)** you. Do not, then, think that following the Holy Spirit's guidance is necessary merely because of your own inadequacies. It is the way out of hell for you.

M 30 A 4. Here again is the paradox often referred to in the course. To say, "Of myself I can do nothing"[222] is to gain all power. And yet it is but a seeming paradox. As God created you, you have all power. The image you made of yourself has none. The Holy Spirit knows the truth about you. The image you made does not. Yet, despite its obvious and complete ignorance, this image assumes it knows all things because you have given that belief to it. Such is your teaching and the teaching of the world which was made to uphold it. But the Teacher Who knows the truth has not forgotten it. His decisions bring benefit to all, being wholly devoid of attack. And therefore incapable of arousing guilt.

M 30 A 5. Who assumes a power that he does not have[223] is deceiving himself. Yet to accept the power given him by God is but to acknowledge his Creator and accept His gifts. And His gifts have no limit. To ask the Holy Spirit to decide for you is merely[224] to accept your true inheritance. Does this mean that you cannot say anything without consulting Him? No, indeed! That would hardly be practical, and it is the practical with which this course is most concerned. If you have made it a habit to ask for help when and where you can, you can be confident that wisdom will be given you when you need it. Prepare for this each morning, remember God when you can throughout the day, ask the Holy Spirit's help when it is feasible to do so, and thank Him for His guidance at night. And your confidence will be well founded indeed. **M(70)**

M 30 A 6. Never forget that the Holy Spirit does not depend on your words. He understands the requests of your heart and answers them. Does this mean that, while attack remains attractive to you He will respond with evil? Hardly! For God has given Him the power to translate your prayers of the heart into His language.[225] He understands that an attack is a call for help. And He responds with help accordingly. God would be cruel if He let your words replace His Own. A loving father does not let his child harm himself or choose his own destruction. He may ask for injury, but his father will protect him still. And how much more than this does your Father love His Son?

M 30 A 7. Remember you are His completion and His Love. Remember your weakness is His strength.[226] But do[227] not read this hastily or wrongly. If His strength is in you, what you perceive as your weakness is but illusion. And He has given you the means to prove it so. Ask all things of His Teacher, and all things are given you. Not in the future but immediately; now. God does not wait, for waiting implies time and He is timeless. Forget your foolish images, your sense of frailty and your fear of harm, your dreams of danger and selected "wrongs." God knows but His Son, and as he was created so he is. In confidence I place you in His Hands, and I give thanks for you that this is so.

> **M 30 A 8.** *And now in all your doings be you blessed.*
> *God turns to you for help to save the world.*
> *Teacher of God, His thanks He offers you,*
> *And all the world stands silent in the grace*
> *You bring from Him. You are the Son He loves,*
> *And it is given you to be the means*
> *Through which His Voice is heard around the world*
> *To close all things of time, to end the sight*
> *Of all things visible; and to undo*
> *All things that change. Through you is ushered in*
> *A world unseen, unheard, yet truly there.*
> *Holy are you, and in your light the world* **M(71)**
> *Reflects your holiness, for you are not*
> *Alone and friendless. I give thanks for you,*
> *And join your efforts on behalf of God,*
> *Knowing they are on my behalf as well*
> *And for all those who walk to God with me.*
>
> FINIS[228]

---

[221] FIP replaces "whom" with "which." The *Notes* has "which" also.
[222] **John 5:19** Then Jesus answered and said to them, "Most assuredly, I say to you, the Son can do nothing of Himself, but what He sees the Father do; for whatever He does, the Son also does in like manner."
[223] FIP replaces "have" with "possess." In the *Notes* we find the glyph for "have."
[224] FIP replaces "merely" with "simply." The *Notes* has "merely."

[225] **Romans 8:26** Likewise the Spirit also helps in our weaknesses. For we do not know what we should pray for as we ought, but the Spirit Himself makes intercession for us with groanings which cannot be uttered.
[226] **2 Corinthians 12:9** And He said to me, "My grace is sufficient for you, for My strength is made perfect in weakness." Therefore most gladly I will rather boast in my infirmities, that the power of Christ may rest upon me.
[227] The word "do" is not present in the *Urtext* manuscript, nor is it handwritten in. FIP includes it and it appears to be a necessary correction. It is clearly present in the *Notes*.
[228] FIP replaces "FINIS" with "AMEN" however neither word appears in the *Notes* which simply ends with no comment.

Urtext* Volume IV: *Use of Terms

Urtext Volume IV: *Use of Terms*

Table of Contents

1. INTRODUCTION 1
2. MIND-SPIRIT 1
3. THE EGO- THE MIRACLE 1
4. FORGIVENESS – THE FACE OF CHRIST 2
5. PERCEPTION - KNOWLEDGE 2
6. JESUS - CHRIST 3
7. THE HOLY SPIRIT 3
8. EPILOGUE 4

Urtext Volume IV: *Use of Terms*

1. INTRODUCTION

U 1 A 1. This is not a course in theoretical philosophy, nor is it concerned with precise terminology in connection with origins. It is concerned only with Atonement, or the correction of perception. The means of the Atonement is forgiveness. The structure of "individual consciousness" is essentially irrelevant, because it is a concept representing the "original error" or the "original sin." To study the error itself does not lead to correction, if you are indeed to succeed in overlooking the error. And it is just this process of overlooking at which the course aims.

U 1 A 2. All terms are potentially controversial, and those who seek controversy will find it. Yet those who seek clarification will find it as well. They must, however, be willing to overlook controversy, recognizing that it is a defense against truth in the form of a delaying maneuver. Theological considerations as such are necessarily controversial, since they depend on belief and can therefore be accepted or rejected. A universal theology is impossible, but a universal experience is not only possible but necessary. It is this experience toward which the course is directed. Here alone consistency becomes possible because here alone uncertainty ends.

U 1 A 3. This course remains within the ego framework, where it is needed. It is not concerned with what is beyond all error because it is planned only to set the direction toward it. Therefore it uses words, which are symbolic, and cannot express what lies beyond symbols. It is always the ego that questions because it is only the ego that doubts. The course merely gives another Answer, once a question has been raised. However, this Answer does not attempt to resort to inventiveness or ingenuity. These are attributes of the ego. THE COURSE IS SIMPLE. It has one function and one goal. Only in that does it remain wholly consistent because only that can BE consistent.

U 1 A 4. The ego will demand many answers this course does not give. It does not recognize as questions the mere form of a question to which an answer is impossible. The ego may ask, "How did the impossible occur?", "To what did the impossible happen?", and may ask[1] in many forms. Yet there is no answer; only an experience. Seek only this, and do not let theology delay you. **(2)**

U 1 A 5. You will notice that the emphasis on structural issues in the course is brief and early. Afterwards and soon, it drops away to make way for the central teaching. Since you have asked for clarification, however, these are some of the terms that are used.[2]

2. MIND-SPIRIT

U 2 A 1. The term "mind" is used to represent the activating agent of Spirit, supplying its creative energy. When the term is capitalized it refers to God or Christ (i.e., the Mind of God or the Mind of Christ). Spirit is the Thought of God which He created like Himself. The unified Spirit is God's one Son, or Christ.

U 2 A 2. In this world, because the mind is split, the Sons of God appear to be separate. Nor do their minds seem to be joined. In this illusory state, the concept of an "individual mind" seems to be meaningful. It is therefore described in the course AS IF it has two parts; spirit and ego.

U 2 A 3. Spirit is the part that is still in contact with God through the Holy Spirit, Who abides in this part but sees the other part as well. The term "soul" is not used except in direct Biblical quotations because of its highly controversial nature. It would, however, be an equivalent of "spirit," with the understanding that, being of God, it is eternal and was never born.

U 2 A 4. The other part of the mind is entirely illusory and makes only illusions. Spirit retains the potential for creating, but its Will which is God's, seems to be imprisoned while the mind is not unified. Creation continues unabated because that is the Will of God. This Will is always unified, and therefore has no meaning in this world. It has no opposite and no degrees.

U 2 A 5. The mind can be right or wrong, depending on the voice to which it listens. RIGHT-MINDEDNESS listens to the Holy Spirit, forgives the world, and through Christ's vision sees the real world in its place. This is the final vision, the last perception, the condition in which God takes the final step Himself. Here time and illusions end together.[3] WRONG-MINDEDNESS listens to the ego and makes illusions; perceiving sin and justifying anger, and seeing guilt, disease and death as real. Both this world and the real world are illusions because right-mindedness merely overlooks, or forgives, what never happened. **U(3)** Therefore it is not the ONE-MINDEDNESS of the Christ Mind, Whose Will is One with God's.

U 2 A 6. In this world the only remaining freedom is the freedom of choice; this choice is always between two choices or two voices. Will is not involved in perception at any level, and has nothing to do with choice. CONSCIOUSNESS is the receptive mechanism, receiving messages from above or below; from the Holy Spirit or the ego. Consciousness has levels and awareness can shift quite dramatically, but it cannot transcend the perceptual realm. At its highest it becomes aware of the real world, and can be trained to do so increasingly. Yet the very fact that it has levels and can be trained demonstrates that consciousness cannot reach knowledge. **U(4)**

3. THE EGO- THE MIRACLE

U 3 A 1. Illusions will not last. Their death is sure and this alone is certain in their world. It is the ego's world because of this. What is the ego? But a dream of what you really are. A thought you are apart from your Creator and a wish to be what He created not. It is a thing of madness, not reality at all. A name for namelessness is all it is. A symbol of impossibility; a choice for options that do not exist. We call it that to help us understand that it is nothing but an ancient thought that what is made has immortality. But what could come of this except a dream which, like all dreams, could only die?

U 3 A 2. What is the ego? Nothingness, but in a form that seems like something. In a world of form the ego cannot be denied for it alone seems real. How could God's Son as He created him abide in form or in a world of form? Who asks you to define the ego and explain how it arose can be but he who thinks it real, and seeks by definition to ensure that its illusive nature is concealed behind the words that seem to make it so.

U 3 A 3. There is no definition for a lie that serves to make it true. Nor can there be a truth that lies conceal effectively. The ego's unreality is not denied by words nor is its meaning clear because its nature seems to have a form. Who can define the undefinable? And yet there is an answer even here.

U 3 A 4. We cannot really make a definition for what the ego is, but we CAN say what it is not. And this is shown to us with perfect clarity. It is from this that we deduce all that the ego is. Look at its opposite and you can see the only answer that is meaningful.

U 3 A 5. The ego's opposite in every way,--in origin, effect and consequence--we call a miracle. And here we find all that is not the ego in the world. Here is the ego's opposite and here alone we look

---

[1] Handwritten markup inserts "this."
[2] Originally a colon appears here in the *Urtext* manuscript. In the *Notes* there is no colon and the sentence is "Since you have asked for clarification, however, these are some of the terms that are used in the beginning."
[3] Handwritten mark-up suggests paragraph break here.

on what the ego was. For here we see all that it seemed to do, and cause and its effects must still be one.

U 3 A 6. Where there was darkness now we see the light. What was the ego? What the darkness was. Where was the ego? Where the darkness was. What is it now and where can it be found? Nothing and nowhere. Now the light has come: Its opposite has gone without a trace. Where evil was there U(5) now is holiness. What is the ego? What the evil was. Where is the ego? In an evil dream that but seemed real while you were dreaming it. Where there was crucifixion stands God's Son. What is the ego? Who has need to ask? Where is the ego? Who has need to seek for an illusion now that dreams are gone?

U 3 A 7. What is a MIRACLE? A dream as well. But look at all the aspects of THIS dream, and you will never question any more. Look at the kindly world you see stretched forth before you as you walk in gentleness. Look at the helpers all along the way you travel, happy in the hope of Heaven and the certainty of peace. And look an instant, too, on what you left behind at last and finally passed by.

U 3 A 8. This was the ego -- all the cruel hate, the need for vengeance and the cries of pain, the fear of dying and the urge to kill, the brotherless illusion and the self that seemed alone in all the universe. This terrible mistake about yourself the miracle corrects as gently as a loving mother sings her child to rest. Is not a song like this what you would hear? Would it not answer all you thought to ask, and even make the question meaningless?

U 3 A 9. Your questions have no answer, being made to still God's Voice, which asks of everyone one question only:

"Are you ready yet to help Me save the world?"

Ask this instead of what the ego is, and you will see a sudden brightness cover up the world the ego made. No miracle is now withheld from anyone. The world is saved from what you thought it was. And what it is, is wholly uncondemned and wholly pure.

U 3 A 10. The miracle forgives; the ego damns. Neither need be defined except by this. Yet could a definition be more sure, or more in line with what salvation asks? Problem and answer lie together here, and having met at last the choice is clear. Who chooses hell when it is recognized? And who would not go on a little while when it is given him to understand the way is short and Heaven is his goal? U(6)

4. FORGIVENESS – THE FACE OF CHRIST

U 4 A 1. Forgiveness is for God and toward God but not of Him. It is impossible to think of anything He created that could need forgiveness. Forgiveness, then, is an illusion, but because of its purpose, which is the Holy Spirit's, it has one difference. Unlike all other illusions it leads away from error and not toward it.

U 4 A 2. Forgiveness might be called a kind of happy fiction; a way in which the unknowing can bridge the gap between their perception and the truth. They cannot go directly from perception to knowledge because they do not think it is their will to do so. This makes God appear to be an enemy instead of what He really is. And it is just this insane perception that makes them unwilling merely to rise up and to return to Him in peace.

U 4 A 3. And so they need an illusion of Help because they are helpless; a Thought of peace because they are in conflict. God knows what His Son needs before he asks.[4] He is not at all concerned with form, but having given the content it is His Will that it be understood. And that suffices. The form adapts itself to need; the content is unchanging, as eternal as its Creator.

U 4 A 4. THE FACE OF CHRIST has to be seen before the memory of God can return. The reason is obvious. Seeing the Face of Christ is perception. No-one can look on knowledge. But the Face of Christ is[5] the great symbol of forgiveness. It is salvation. It is the symbol of the real world. Whoever looks on this no longer sees the world. He is as near to Heaven as is possible outside the gate.[6] Yet from this gate it is no more than just a step inside. It is the final step. And this we leave to God.

U 4 A 5. It[7] is a symbol, too, but as the symbol of His Will alone it cannot be divided. And so the Unity that it reflects becomes His Will. It is the only thing still in the world in part, and yet the bridge to Heaven. U(7)

U 4 A 6. God's Will is all there is. We can but go from nothingness to everything; from hell to Heaven. Is this a journey? No, not in truth, for truth goes nowhere. But illusions shift from place to place; from time to time. The final step is also but a shift. As a perception it is partly unreal. And yet this part will vanish. What remains is peace eternal and the Will of God.

U 4 A 7. There are no wishes now for wishes change. Even the wished-for can become unwelcome. That must be so because the ego cannot be at peace. But Will is constant, as the gift of God. And what He gives is always like Himself. This is the purpose of the Face of Christ. It is the gift of God to save His Son. But look on this and you have been forgiven.

U 4 A 8. How lovely does the world become in just that single instant when you see the truth about yourself reflected there. Now you are sinless and behold your sinlessness. Now you are holy and perceive it so. And now the mind returns to its Creator; the joining of the Father and the Son, the Unity of unities that stands behind all joining but still beyond them all. God IS NOT SEEN BUT ONLY UNDERSTOOD. His Son is not attacked but recognized.

5. PERCEPTION - KNOWLEDGE

U 5 A 1. The world you see is an illusion of a world. God did not create it, for what He creates must be eternal as Himself. Yet there is nothing in the world you see that will endure forever. Some things will last in time a little while longer than others. But the time will come when all things visible will have an end.

U 5 A 2. The body's eyes are therefore not the means by which the real world can be seen, for the illusions that they look upon must lead to more illusions of reality.[8] And so they do. For everything they see not only will not last, but lends itself to thoughts of sin and guilt. While everything that God created is forever without sin and therefore is forever without guilt.

U 5 A 3. Knowledge is not the remedy for false perception since, being another level, they can never meet. The one correction possible for false perception must be <u>true perception</u>. U(8) It will not endure. But for the time it lasts it comes to heal. For true perception is a remedy with many names. Forgiveness, salvation, Atonement, true perception, all are one. They are the[9] one beginning with the end to lead to Oneness far beyond themselves. True perception is the means by which the world is saved from sin, for sin does not exist. And it is this that true perception sees.

U 5 A 4. The world stands like a block before Christ's face. But true perception looks on it as nothing more than just a fragile veil, so easily dispelled that it can last no longer than an instant. It is seen at last for only what it is. And now it cannot fail to disappear, for now

---

[4] **Matthew 6:8** "Therefore do not be like them. For your Father knows the things you have need of before you ask Him."

[5] Handwritten mark-up suggests "**involves**" which *FIP* adopts. The *Notes* does not include the word "involves."

[6] **Genesis 28:17** "And he was afraid and said, 'How awesome is this place! This is none other than the house of God, and this is the gate of heaven!'"

[7] Handwritten mark-up suggests "**forgiveness**" which *FIP* adopts. The *Notes* has it as it is here, but has no paragraph break here.

[8] *Urtext* Manuscript has, in brackets **of reality** here. *FIP* omits the brackets as does the *Notes*.

[9] The *Urtext* manuscript has "a" crossed out and "the" handwritten in. The *Notes* has "a."

there is an empty place made clean and ready. Where destruction was perceived the face of Christ appears, and in that instant is the world forgot, with time forever ended as the world spins into nothingness from where it came.

U 5 A 5. A world forgiven cannot last. It was the home of bodies. But forgiveness looks past bodies. This is its holiness; this is how it heals. The world of bodies is the world of sin, for only if there is a body is sin possible. From sin comes guilt as surely as forgiveness takes all guilt away. And once all guilt is gone what more remains to keep a separated world in place? For place has gone as well, along with time. Only the body makes the world seem real, for being separate it could not remain where separation is impossible. Forgiveness proves it is impossible because it sees it not. And what you then will overlook will not be understandable to you, just as its[10] presence once had been your certainty.

U 5 A 6. This is the shift that true perception brings: What was projected out is seen within, and there forgiveness lets it disappear. For there the altar to the Son is set, and there his Father is remembered. Here are all illusions brought to truth and laid upon the altar. What is seen outside must lie beyond forgiveness, for it seems to be forever sinful. Where is hope while sin is seen as outside? What remedy can guilt expect? But seen within your mind, guilt and forgiveness for an instant lie together, side by side, upon one altar. There at last are sickness and its single remedy joined in one healing brightness. God has come to claim His Own. Forgiveness is complete. **U(9)**

U 5 A 7. And now God's KNOWLEDGE, changeless, certain, pure and wholly understandable, enters its Kingdom. Gone is perception, false and true alike. Gone is forgiveness, for its task is done. And gone are bodies in the blazing light upon the altar to the Son of God. God knows it is His Own, as it is his. And here They join, for here the face of Christ has shone away time's final instant, and now is the last perception of the world without a purpose and without a cause. For where God's memory has come at last there is no journey, no belief in sin, no walls, no bodies, and the grim appeal of guilt and death is there snuffed out forever.

U 5 A 8. Oh my brothers, if you only knew the peace that will envelop you and hold you safe and pure and lovely in the Mind of God, you could but rush to meet Him where His altar is. Hallowed your Name and His,[11] for they are joined here in this holy place. Here He leans down to lift you back to Him, out of illusions into holiness; out of the world and into timelessness[12]; out of all fear and given back to Love.

6. JESUS - CHRIST

U 6 A 1. There is no need for help to enter Heaven for you never left. But there is need for help beyond yourself as you are circumscribed by false beliefs about your Identity, Which God alone established in reality. Helpers are given you in many forms, although upon the altar They are one. Beyond each one there is a Thought of God, and this will never change. But they have names which differ for a time, for time needs symbols, being itself unreal. Their names are legion,[13] but we will not go beyond the names the course itself employs. God does not help because He knows no need. But He creates all Helpers of His Son while he believes his fantasies are true. Thank God for them for they will lead you home. **U(10)**

U 6 A 2. The Name of Jesus is the Name of one who was a man but saw the face of Christ in all his brothers and remembered God. So he became identified with Christ, a man no longer, but at one with God. The man was an illusion, for he seemed to be a separate being, walking by himself, within a body that appeared to hold his self from Self, as all illusions do. Yet who can save unless he sees illusions and then identifies them as what they are? Jesus remains a Savior because he saw the false without accepting it as true. And Christ needed his form that He might appear to men and save them from their own illusions.

U 6 A 3. In his complete identification with the Christ--the perfect Son of God, His one creation and His happiness, forever like Himself and One with Him – Jesus became what all of us must be. He led the way for us to follow him. He leads us back to God because he saw the road before him, and he followed it. He made a clean distinction, still obscure to us, between the false and true. He offered us all a final demonstration that[14] it is impossible to kill God's Son; nor can his life in any way be changed by sin and evil, malice, fear or death.

U 6 A 4. And therefore all your sins have been forgiven[15] because they carried no effects at all. And so they were but dreams. Arise with him who showed you this because you owe him this who shared your dreams that they might be dispelled. And shares them still, to be at one with you.

U 6 A 5. Is he the Christ? Oh yes, along with you. His little life on earth was not enough to teach the mighty lesson that he learned for all of us. He will remain with you to lead you from the hell you made to God. And when you join your will with his, your sight will be his vision, for the eyes of Christ are shared. Walking with him is just as natural as walking with a brother whom you knew since you were born, for such indeed he is. Some bitter idols have been made of him who would be only brother to the world. Forgive him your illusions, and behold how dear a brother he would be to you. For he will set your mind at rest at last and carry it with you unto your God. **U(11)**

U 6 A 6. Is he God's only Helper? No, indeed. For Christ takes many forms with different names until their oneness can be recognized. But Jesus is for you the bearer of Christ's single message of the Love of God. You need no other. It is possible to read his words and benefit from them without accepting him into your life. Yet he would help you yet a little more if you will share your pains and joys with him, and leave them both to find the peace of God. Yet still it is his lesson most of all that he would have you learn, and it is this:

> *"There is no death[16] because the Son of God is like his Father. Nothing you can do can change Eternal Love. Forget your dreams of sin and guilt, and come with me instead to share the resurrection of God's Son. And bring with you all those whom He has sent to you to care for as I care for you."*

7. THE HOLY SPIRIT

U 7 A 1. Jesus is the manifestation of the Holy Spirit, Whom he called down upon the earth after he ascended into Heaven,[17] or be-

---

[10] The *Urtext* Manuscript has "just as its opposite was once your certainty" which, since "its" refers to "sin" appears to be an error. Immediately after this is typed "presence once had been your certainty" which appears to make more sense. *FIP* retains only the second reading. In the *Notes* we find the substitution of "presence" for "opposite."
[11] **Matthew 6:9** "In this manner, therefore, pray: Our Father in heaven, Hallowed be Your name."
[12] In the manuscript **into timelessness** is crossed out and **to eternity** is typed in above it. The *Notes* has "timelessness."
[13] **Mark 5:9** "Then He asked him, 'What is your name?' And he answered, saying, 'My name is Legion; for we are many.'"

---

[14] The word "that" is handwritten at the end of the line. The *Notes* just has the glyph for "it is."
[15] The word "you" is originally typed here and then crossed out. In the *Notes* the glyph for "you" appears above the line, as if it were an afterthought.
[16] **2 Timothy 1:10** "But has now been revealed by the appearing of our Savior Jesus Christ, who has abolished death and brought life and immortality to light through the gospel,"
[17] **Acts 1:8-9** "But you shall receive power when the Holy Spirit has come upon you; and you shall be witnesses to Me in Jerusalem, and in all Judea and Samaria, and to the end of the earth. Now when He had spoken these

came completely identified with the Christ, the Son of God as He created Him. The Holy Spirit, being a creation of the one Creator, creating with Him and in His likeness or Spirit, is eternal and has never changed.[18] He was "called down upon the earth"[19] in the sense that it was now possible to accept Him and to hear His Voice. His is the Voice for God, and has therefore taken form. This form is not His reality, which God alone knows along with Christ, His real Son, Who is part of Him.

U 7 A 2. The Holy Spirit is described throughout the course as giving us the answer to the separation and bringing the plan of the Atonement to us, establishing our particular part in it and showing us exactly what it is. He has established Jesus as the leader in carrying out this plan since he was the first to complete his own part perfectly. All power in Heaven and earth is therefore given him and he will share it with you when you have completed yours.[20] The Atonement principle was given to the Holy Spirit long before Jesus set it in motion.

U 7 A 3. The Holy Spirit is described as the remaining communication link between God and His separated sons. In order to fulfill this special function the Holy Spirit has assumed a dual function. He knows because He is part of God; He perceives because He U(12) was sent to save humanity. He is the great correction principle; the bringer of true perception, the inherent power of the vision of Christ. He is the light in which the forgiven world is perceived; in which the face of Christ alone is seen. He never forgets the Creator or His Creation. He never forgets the Son of God. He never forgets you. And He brings the Love of your Father to you in an eternal shining that will never be obliterated because God has put it there.

U 7 A 4. The Holy Spirit abides in the part of your mind that is part of the Christ Mind. He represents your Self and your Creator, Who are One. He speaks for God and also for you, being joined with both. And therefore it is He Who proves them One. He seems to be a Voice, for in that form He speaks God's Word to you. He seems to be a Guide through a far country, for you need that form of help.[21] He seems to be whatever meets the needs you think you have. But He is not deceived when you perceive your self entrapped in needs you do not have. It is from these He would deliver you. It is from these that He would make you safe.

U 7 A 5. You are His manifestation in this world. Your brother calls to you to be His Voice along with him. Alone he cannot be the Helper of God's Son for he alone is functionless. But joined with you he is the shining Savior of the world, Whose part in its redemption you have made complete. He offers thanks to you as well as him for you arose with him when he began to save the world. And you will be with him when time is over, and no trace remains of dreams of spite in which you dance to death's thin melody. For in its place the hymn to God is heard a little while. And then the Voice is gone, no longer to take form but to return to the eternal Formlessness of God. U(13)

8. EPILOGUE

U 8 A 1. Forget not once this journey is begun the end is certain. Doubt along the way will come and go and go to come again. Yet is the ending sure. No-one can fail to do what God appointed him to do. When you forget, remember that you walk with Him and with His Word upon your heart. Who could despair when hope like this is his? Illusions of despair may seem to come, but learn how not to be deceived by them. Behind each one there is reality and there is God. Why would you wait for this and trade it for illusions, when His Love is but an instant farther on the road where all illusions end? The end IS sure and guaranteed by God. Who stands before a lifeless image when a step away the Holy of the Holies opens up an ancient door that leads beyond the world?[22]

U 8 A 2. You ARE a stranger here, but you belong to Him Who loves you as He loves Himself.[23] Ask but my help to roll the stone away,[24] and it is done according to His Will.

U 8 A 3. We HAVE begun the journey. Long ago the end was written in the stars and set into the Heavens with a shining Ray that held it safe within eternity and through all time as well. And holds it still; unchanged, unchanging and unchangeable.

U 8 A 4. Be not afraid.[25] We only start again an ancient journey long ago begun that but seems new. We have begun again upon a road we travelled on before and lost our way a little while. And now we try again. Our new beginning has the certainty the journey lacked 'til now. Look up and see His Word among the stars, where He has set your Name along with His. Look up and find your certain destiny the world would hide but God would have you see.

U 8 A 5. Let us wait here in silence, and kneel down an instant in our gratitude to Him Who called to us and helped us hear His Call. And then let us arise and go in faith along the way to Him. Now we are sure we do not walk alone. For God is here, and with Him all our brothers. Now we know that we will never lose the way again. The song begins again which had been stopped[26] only an instant, though it seems to be unsung forever. What is here begun will grow in life and strength and hope, until the world is still U(14) an instant and forgets all that the dream of sin had made of it.

U 8 A 6. Let us go out and meet the newborn world, knowing that Christ has been reborn in it, and that the holiness of this rebirth will last forever. We had lost our way, but He has found it for us. Let us come and bid Him welcome Who returns to us to celebrate salvation and the end of all we thought we made. The morning[27] star of this new day looks on a different world where God is welcomed and His Son with Him.[28] We who complete Him offer thanks to Him, as He gives thanks to us. The Son is still, and in the peace[29] that God has given him enters his home and is at peace at last.[30]

---

things, while they watched, He was taken up, and a cloud received Him out of their sight."
[18] **Isaiah 40:28** Have you not known? Have you not heard, that the everlasting God, the Lord, the Creator of the ends of the earth, does not grow weak nor weary? *There is* no searching of His understanding.
[19] **Acts 1:8-9** (quoted above)
[20] **Matthew 28:18** "And Jesus came and spoke to them, saying, 'All authority has been given to Me in heaven and on earth.'"
[21] **Luke 15:13** And not many days after, the younger son gathered all together, journeyed to a far country, and there wasted his possessions with prodigal living.

[22] **Exodus 26:33** "And you shall hang the veil from the clasps. Then you shall bring the ark of the Testimony in there, behind the veil. The veil shall be a divider for you between the holy place and the Most Holy."
[23] **Matthew 22:39** And the second is like it: "You shall love your neighbor as yourself."
[24] **Matthew 28:2** "And behold, there was a great earthquake; for an angel of the Lord descended from heaven, and came and rolled back the stone from the door, and sat on it."
[25] **John 6:20** "But He said to them, "It is I; do not be afraid.'" (and many others)
[26] *Urtext* Manuscript has (stilled) typed in brackets, then crossed out by hand. The *Notes* appears to have "stilled" but it is not entirely clear.
[27] *Urtext* Manuscript has "**(rising)**" typed in above "**morning**" and then crossed out. The *Notes* has "morning star."
[28] **Revelation 2:28** And I will give him the morning star.
[29] *Urtext* Manuscript has "**peace that**" crossed out and "**(quiet)**" typed in. The *Notes* has "peace."
[30] The *Urtext* Manuscript includes three lines crossed out at the end, "**and there is still at last**"; "**enters the stillness of his home at last**"; "**enters his home in stillness and in peace.**" These alternatives also appear in the *Notes*.

Urtext* Volume V: *Psychotherapy:
Purpose, Process and Practice

Urtext Volume V: *Psychotherapy*:
Purpose, Process and Practice

Table of Contents

1. AN INTRODUCTION TO PSYCHOTHERAPY 1
2. THE PURPOSE OF PSYCHOTHERAPY 1
   A. Introduction 1
3. THE PROCESS OF PSYCHOTHERAPY 1
   A. Introduction 1
   B. The Limits on Psychotherapy 2
   C. The Place of Religion in Psychotherapy 2
   D. The Role of the Psychotherapist 3
   E. The Process of Illness 3
   F. The Process of Healing 4
   G. The Definition of Healing 5
   H. The Ideal Patient-Therapist Relationship 5
4. THE PRACTICE OF PSYCHOTHERAPY 6
   A. The Selection of Patients 6
   B. Is Psychotherapy a Profession? 7
   C. The Question of Payment 8

Urtext Volume V: *Psychotherapy: Purpose, Process and Practice*

1. AN INTRODUCTION TO PSYCHOTHERAPY

P 1 A 1. Psychotherapy is the only form of therapy there is. Since only the mind can be sick, only the mind can be healed. Only the mind is in need of healing. This does not appear to be the case, for the manifestations of this world seem real indeed. Psychotherapy is necessary so that an individual[1] can begin to question his reality. Sometimes he is able to start to open his mind without formal help, but even then it is always some change in his perception of interpersonal relationships that enables him to do so. Sometimes he needs a more structured, extended relationship with an "official" therapist. Either way, the task is the same; the patient must be helped to change his mind about the "reality" of illusions.

2. THE PURPOSE OF PSYCHOTHERAPY

A. Introduction

P 2 A 1. Very simply, the purpose of psychotherapy is to remove the blocks to truth. Its aim is to aid the patient in abandoning his fixed delusional system, and to begin to reconsider the spurious cause and effect relationships on which it rests. No-one in this world escapes fear, but everyone can reconsider its causes and learn to evaluate them correctly. God has given everyone a Teacher Whose wisdom and help far exceed whatever contributions an earthly therapist can provide. Yet there are times and situations in which the[2] patient-therapist relationship becomes the means through which He offers His greater gifts to both.

P 2 A 2. What better[3] purpose could any relationship have than to invite the Holy Spirit to enter into it and give it His Own great gift of rejoicing? What higher goal could there be for anyone than to learn to call upon God and hear His Answer? And what more transcendent aim can there be than to recall the Way, the Truth and the Life,[4] and to remember God? To help in this is the proper purpose of psychotherapy. Could anything be holier? For psychotherapy, correctly understood, teaches forgiveness and helps the patient to recognize and accept it. And in his healing is the therapist forgiven with him. P(2)

P 2 A 3. Everyone who needs help, regardless of the form of his distress, is attacking himself, and his peace of mind is suffering in consequence. These tendencies are often described as "self-destructive," and the patient often regards them in that way himself. What he does not realize and needs to learn is that this "self," which can attack and be attacked as well, is a concept he made up. Further, he cherishes it, defends it, and is sometimes even willing to "sacrifice" his "life" on its behalf. For he regards it as himself. This self he sees as being acted on, reacting to external forces as they demand, and helpless in[5] the power of the world.

P 2 A 4. Psychotherapy, then, must restore to his awareness the ability to make his own decisions. He must become willing to reverse his thinking, and to understand that what he thought projected its effects on him were made by his projections on the world. The world he sees does therefore not exist. Until this is at least in part accepted, the patient cannot see himself as really capable of making decisions. And he will fight against his freedom because he thinks that it is slavery.

P 2 A 5. The patient need not think of truth as God in order to make progress in salvation. But he must begin to separate truth from illusion, recognizing that they are not the same, and becoming increasingly willing to see illusions as illusions[6] and to accept the truth as true. His Teacher will take him on from there, as far as he is ready to go. Psychotherapy can only save him time. The Holy Spirit uses time as He thinks best, and He is never wrong. Psychotherapy under His direction is one of the means He uses to save time, and to prepare additional teachers for His work. There is no end to the help that He begins and He directs. By whatever routes He chooses, all psychotherapy leads to God in the end. But that is up to Him. We are all His psychotherapists, for He would have us all be healed in Him. P(3)

3. THE PROCESS OF PSYCHOTHERAPY

A. Introduction

P 3 A 1. Psychotherapy is a process that changes the view of the self. At best this "new" self is a more beneficent self-concept, but psychotherapy can hardly be expected to establish reality. That is not its function. If it can make way for reality, it has achieved its ultimate success. Its whole function, in the end, is to help the patient deal with one fundamental error; the belief that anger brings him something he really wants, and that by justifying attack he is protecting himself. To whatever extent he comes to realize that this is mistaken,[7] to that extent is he truly saved.

P 3 A 2. Patients do not enter the therapeutic relationship with this goal in mind. On the contrary, such concepts mean little to them, or they would not need help. Their aim is to be able to retain their self-concept exactly as it is, but without the suffering that it entails. Their whole equilibrium rests on the insane belief that this is possible. And because to the sane mind it is so clearly impossible, what they seek is magic. In illusions the impossible is easily accomplished, but only at the cost of making illusions true. The patient has already paid this price. Now he wants a "better" illusion.

P 3 A 3. At the beginning, then, the patient's goal and the therapist's are at variance. The therapist as well as the patient may cherish false self-concepts, but their respective perceptions of "improvement" still must differ. The patient hopes to learn how to get the changes he wants without changing his self-concept to any significant extent. He hopes, in fact, to stabilize it sufficiently to include within it the magical powers he seeks in psychotherapy. He wants to make the vulnerable invulnerable and the finite limitless. The self he sees is his god, and he seeks only to serve it better.

---

[1] The *Urtext* manuscript has "***an individual** can begin to question **their** reality.*" FIP keeps that reading. Grammar requires that "*an individual question **his** reality*" or "*individuals question **their** reality.*" When this was written in the mid-1970s the modern habit of using "their" when "his" or "her" would be correct in order to achieve "gender-neutral language" had not come into vogue. The *Notes* has the abbreviation *indiv.* which could be either plural or singular and it clearly has the glyph for "their" rather than "his" four words later. Just before *indiv.* the *Notes* has a letter or glyph, possibly the glyph for "an" crossed out with a dash above it, that dash often being the glyph for "the" but also sometimes other things. That *could be* intended as "the individual" and *might* originally have been "an individual." However it could also just be noise with the intended meaning simply being "individuals" and that is the only option which keeps the subject plural to fit with the subsequent unambiguous "their."
[2] Handwritten mark-up and FIP change "the" to "an earthly." That is not present in the *Notes*.
[3] The *Notes* has "greater" rather than "better."
[4] *Urtext* manuscript has "Light", handwritten mark-up corrects this Biblical quote to "Life". This is also the reading in the *Notes*. **John 14:6** Jesus said to him, "I am the way, the truth, and the life. No one comes to the Father except through Me."
[5] FIP replaces "in" with "midst." The *Notes* reads "in."
[6] Handwritten mark-up and FIP replace "illusions" with "false." The *Notes* has "illusions."
[7] Handwritten mark-up and FIP change "mistaken" to "error." The *Notes* omits the word entirely, reading "to whatever extent he comes to realize this, to that extent is he truly saved."

Volume V - Psychotherapy

P 3 A 4. Regardless of how advanced[8] the therapist himself may be, he must want to change the patient's self-concept in some way that he believes is real. The task of therapy is one of reconciling these differences. Hopefully, both will learn to give up their original goals, for it is only in relationships that salvation can be found. At the beginning, it is inevitable that patients and therapists alike accept unrealistic goals not completely free of magical overtones. **P(4)** They are finally given up in the minds of both.

B. The Limits on Psychotherapy

P 3 B 1. Yet the ideal outcome is rarely achieved. But psychotherapy[9] begins with the realization that healing is of the mind, and in psychotherapy those have come together who[10] believe this. It may be they will not get much further, for no-one learns beyond his own readiness. Yet levels of readiness change, and when therapist or patient has reached the next one, there will be a relationship held out to them that meets the changing need. Perhaps they will come together again and advance in the same relationship, making it holier. Or perhaps each of them will enter into another commitment. Be assured of this; each will progress. Retrogression is temporary. The overall direction is one of progress toward the truth.

P 3 B 2. Psychotherapy itself cannot be creative. This is one of the errors which the ego fosters; that it is capable of true change, and therefore of true creativity. When we speak of "the saving illusion" or "the final dream," this is not what we mean, but here is the ego's last defense. "Resistance" is its way of looking at things; its interpretation of "progress"[11] and "growth."[12] These interpretations will be wrong of necessity, because they are delusional. The "changes"[13] the ego seeks to make are not really changes. They are but deeper shadows, or perhaps different cloud patterns. Yet what is made of nothingness cannot be called new or different. Illusions are illusions; truth is truth.

P 3 B 3. Resistance as defined here[14] can be characteristic of a therapist as well as of a patient. Either way, it sets a limit on psychotherapy because it restricts its aims. Nor can the Holy Spirit fight against the intrusions of the ego on the therapeutic process. But He will wait, and His patience is infinite. His goal is wholly undivided always. Whatever resolutions patient and therapist reach in connection with their own divergent goals, they cannot become completely reconciled as one until they join with His. Only then is all conflict over, for only then can there be certainty. **P(5)**

P 3 B 4. Ideally, psychotherapy is a series of holy encounters in which brothers meet to bless each other and to receive the peace of God. And this will one day come to pass for every "patient" on the face of this earth, for who except a patient could possibly have come here? The therapist is only a somewhat more specialized Teacher of God. He learns through teaching, and the more advanced he is the more he teaches and the more he learns. But whatever stage he is in, there are patients who need him just that way. They cannot take more than he can give for now. Yet they[15] both will find sanity at last.

C. The Place of Religion in Psychotherapy[16]

P 3 C 1. To be a Teacher of God, it is not necessary to be religious or even to believe in God to any recognizable extent. It is necessary, however, to teach forgiveness rather than condemnation. Even in this, complete consistency is not required, for one who has[17] achieved that point can[18] teach salvation completely, within an instant and without a word. Yet he who has learned all things does not need a teacher, and the healed have no need for a therapist. Relationships are still the Temple[19] of the Holy Spirit,[20] and they will be made perfect in time and restored to Eternity.[21]

P 3 C 2. Formal religion has no place in psychotherapy, but it also has no real place in religion. In this world, there is an astonishing tendency to join contradictory words into one term without perceiving the contradiction at all. The attempt to formalize religion is so obviously an ego attempt to reconcile the irreconcilable that it hardly requires elaboration here. Religion is experience; psychotherapy is experience. At the highest levels they become one. Neither is truth itself, but both can lead to truth. What can be necessary to find truth, which remains perfectly obvious, but to remove the seeming obstacles to true awareness? **P(6)**

P 3 C 3. No-one who learns to forgive can fail to remember God. Forgiveness, then, is all that need be taught, because it is all that need be learned. All blocks to the remembrance of God are forms of unforgiveness, and nothing else. This is never apparent to the patient, and only rarely so to the therapist. The world has marshalled[22] all its forces against this one awareness, for in it lies the ending of the world and all it stands for.

P 3 C 4. Yet it is not the awareness of God that constitutes a reasonable goal for psychotherapy. This will come when psychotherapy is complete, for where there is forgiveness truth must come. It would be unfair indeed if belief in God were necessary to psychotherapeutic success. Nor is belief in God a really meaningful concept, for God can be but known. Belief implies that unbelief is possible, but knowledge of God has no true opposite. Not to know God is to have no knowledge, and it is to this that all unforgiveness leads. And without knowledge one can have only belief.

P 3 C 5. Different teaching aids appeal to different people. Some forms of religion have nothing to do with God, and some forms of psychotherapy have nothing to do with healing. Yet if pupil and teacher join in sharing one goal, God will enter into their relationship because He has been invited to come in. In the same way, a union of purpose between patient and therapist restores the place of God to ascendance, first through Christ's vision and then through the memory of God Himself. The process of psychotherapy is the return to sanity. Teacher and pupil, therapist and patient, are all insane or they would not be here. Together they can find a pathway out, for no-one will find sanity alone. **P(7)**

---

[8] Handwritten mark-up and FIP change "advanced" to "sincere." The *Notes* has "advanced."

[9] Handwritten mark-up and FIP replace "But psychotherapy" with "Therapy." The *Notes* has "But therapy."

[10] Handwritten mark-up and FIP insert "already." The *Notes* doesn't.

[11] Handwritten mark-up and FIP delete the quotation marks. They are present in the *Notes*.

[12] Handwritten mark-up and FIP delete the quotation marks. They are present in the *Notes*.

[13] Handwritten mark-up and FIP delete the quotation marks. They are present in the *Notes*.

[14] Handwritten mark-up adds the word "here" which is not in the *Urtext* manuscript nor the *Notes*.

[15] Handwritten mark-up and FIP delete "they." The word is present in the *Notes*.

[16] This heading is originally typed at the end of the paragraph; mark-up suggests moving it, as we have done. However, in the *Notes* it also occurs at the end of paragraph **P 3 C 1**, which would make that paragraph **P 3 B 5**. It appears from the context that moving the section break is warranted, as this paragraph introduces the topic of the following section.

[17] Handwritten mark-up and FIP replace "has" with "had," making the sentence shift from present to past tense half way through, a most curious alteration. In the *Notes* it is "has."

[18] Handwritten mark-up and FIP replace "can" with "could." In the *Notes* it is "can."

[19] Handwritten mark-up and FIP change this to lower case, but in the *Notes* it is upper case "Temple."

[20] **1 Corinthians 6:19** Or do you not know that your body is the temple of the Holy Spirit who is in you, whom you have from God, and you are not your own? **1 Corinthians 3:16** Do you not know that you are the temple of God and that the Spirit of God dwells in you?

[21] Handwritten mark-up and FIP change "Eternity" to lower case, but in the *Notes* it is upper case.

[22] *Urtext* manuscript spells it "martialed", FIP spells it "marshaled." Some dictionaries prefer "marshalled" which is the spelling in the *Notes*.

P 3 C 6. If healing is an invitation to God to enter into His Kingdom, what difference does it make how the invitation is written? Does the paper matter, or the ink, or the pen? Or is it he who writes that gives the invitation? God comes to those who would restore His world, for they have found the way to call to Him. If any two are joined, He must be there.[23] It does not matter what their purpose is, but they must share it wholly to succeed. It is impossible to share a goal not blessed by Christ, for what is unseen through His eyes is too fragmented to be meaningful.

P 3 C 7. As true religion heals, so must true psychotherapy be religious. But both have many forms, because no true[24] teacher uses one approach to every pupil. On the contrary, he listens patiently to each one, and lets him formulate his own curriculum; not the curriculum's goal, but how he can best reach the aim it sets for him. Perhaps the teacher does not think of God as part of teaching. Perhaps the psychotherapist does not understand that healing comes from God. They can succeed where many who believe they have found God will fail.

P 3 C 8. What must the teacher do to ensure learning? What must the therapist do to bring healing about? Only one thing; the same requirement salvation asks of everyone. Each one must share one goal with someone else, and in so doing, lose all sense of separate interests. Only by doing this is it possible to transcend the narrow boundaries the ego would impose upon the self. Only by doing this can teacher and pupil, therapist and patient, you and I, accept Atonement and learn to give it as it was received.

P 3 C 9. Communion is impossible alone. No-one who stands apart can receive Christ's vision. It is held out to him, but he cannot hold out his hand to receive it. Let him be still and recognize his brother's need is his own.[25] And let him then meet his brother's need as his and see that they are met as one, for such they are. What is religion but an aid in helping him to see that this is so? And what is psychotherapy except a help in just this same direction? It is the goal that makes these processes the same, for they are one in purpose and must thus be one in means. **P(8)**

D. The Role of the Psychotherapist

P 3 D 1. The psychotherapist is a leader in the sense that he walks slightly ahead of the patient, and helps him to avoid a few of the pitfalls along the road by seeing them first. Ideally, he is also a follower, for One should walk ahead of him to give him light to see. Without this One, both will merely stumble blindly on to nowhere. It is, however, impossible that this One be wholly absent if the goal is healing. He may, however, not be recognized. And so the little light that can be then accepted is all there is to light the way to truth.

P 3 D 2. Healing is limited by the limitations of the psychotherapist, as it is limited by those of the patient. The aim of the process, therefore, is to transcend these limits. Neither can do this alone, but when they join, the potentiality for transcending all limitations has been given them. Now the extent of their success depends on how much of this potentiality they are willing to use. The willingness may come from either one at the beginning, and as the other shares it, it will grow. Progress becomes a matter of decision; it can reach almost to Heaven or go no further than a step or two from hell.

P 3 D 3. It is quite possible for psychotherapy[26] to seem to fail. It is even possible for the result to look like retrogression. But in the end there must be some success. One asks for help; another hears and tries to answer in the form of help. This is the formula for salvation, and must heal. Divided goals alone can interfere with perfect healing. One wholly egoless therapist could heal the world without a word, merely by being there. No-one need see him or talk to him or even know of his existence. His simple Presence is enough to heal.

P 3 D 4. The ideal therapist is one with Christ. But healing is a process, not a fact. The therapist cannot progress without the patient, and the patient cannot be ready to receive the Christ or he could not be sick. In a sense, the egoless psychotherapist is an abstraction that stands at the end of the process of healing, too advanced to believe in sickness and too near to God to keep his feet on earth. Now he can help through those in need of help, for thus he carries out the plan established for salvation. **P(9)** The psychotherapist becomes his patient, working through other patients to express his thoughts as he receives them from the Mind of Christ.

E. The Process of Illness

P 3 E 1. As all therapy is psychotherapy, so all illness is mental illness. It is a judgment on the Son of God, and judgment is a mental activity. Judgment is a decision, made again and again, against creation and its Creator. It is a decision to perceive the universe as you would have created it. It is a decision that truth can lie and must be lies. What, then, can illness be except an expression of sorrow and of guilt? And who could weep but for his innocence?

P 3 E 2. Once God's Son is seen as guilty, illness becomes inevitable. It has been asked for and will be received.[27] And all who ask for illness have now condemned themselves to seek for remedies that cannot help, because their faith is in the illness and not in salvation. There can be nothing that a change of mind cannot effect, for all external things are only shadows of a decision already made. Change the decision, and how can its shadow be unchanged? Illness can be but guilt's shadow, grotesque and ugly since it mimics deformity. If a deformity is seen as real, what could its shadow be except deformed?[28]

P 3 E 3. The descent into hell follows step by step in an inevitable course, once the decision that guilt is real has been made. Sickness and death and misery now stalk the earth in unrelenting waves, sometimes together and sometimes in grim succession. Yet all these things, however real they seem, are but illusions. Who could have faith in them once this is realized? And who could not have faith in them until he realizes this? Healing is therapy or correction, and we have said already and will say again, all therapy is psychotherapy. To heal the sick is but to bring this realization to them.

P 3 E 4. The word "cure" has come into disrepute among the more "respectable" therapists of the world, and justly so. For not one of them can cure, and not one of them understands healing. At worst,[29] they but make the body real in their own minds, and having done so, seek for magic by which to heal the ills with which their minds endow it. **P(10)** How could such a process cure? It is ridiculous from start to finish. Yet having started, it must finish thus. It is as if God were the devil and must be found in evil. How could love be there? And how could sickness cure? Are not these both one question?

P 3 E 5. At best, and the word is perhaps questionable here, the "healers" of the world may recognize the mind as the source of illness. But their error lies in the belief that it can cure itself. This has some merit in a world where "degrees of error" is a meaningful concept. Yet must their cures remain temporary, or another illness

---

[23] **Matthew 18:20** "For where two or three are gathered together in My name, I am there in the midst of them."
[24] Handwritten mark-up and FIP replace "true" with "good." The *Notes* has "true."
[25] **Psalm 46:10** "Be still, and know that I am God; I will be exalted among the nations, I will be exalted in the earth!"
[26] Handwritten mark-up and FIP replace the originally typed "the psychotherapist" with "psychotherapy." While the *Notes* reading is slightly ambiguous, "psychotherapy" appears as the most probable reading.

[27] **Matthew 7:7** "Ask, and it will be given to you; seek, and you will find; knock, and it will be opened to you."
[28] The *Urtext* manuscript originally has "the form" here. Handwritten mark-up and FIP change this to "deformed" which restores the reading to that found in the *Notes*.
[29] *Urtext* manuscript has "worse." FIP corrects it to "worst" as we do which restores the reading to that found in the *Notes*.

rise[30] instead, for death has not been overcome until the meaning of love is understood. And who can understand this without the Word of God, given by Him to the Holy Spirit as His gift to you?

P 3 E 6. Illness of any kind may be defined as the result of a view of the self as weak, vulnerable, evil and endangered, and thus in need of constant defense. Yet if such were really the self, defense would be impossible. Therefore, the defenses sought for must be magical. They must overcome all limits perceived in the self, at the same time making a new self-concept into which they[31] cannot return. In a word, error is accepted as real and dealt with by illusions. Truth being brought to illusions, reality now becomes a threat and is perceived as evil. Love becomes feared because reality is love. Thus is the circle closed against the "inroads" of salvation.

P 3 E 7. Illness is therefore a mistake and needs correction. And as we have already emphasized before,[32] correction cannot be achieved by first establishing the "rightness" of the mistake and then overlooking it. If illness is real it cannot be overlooked in truth, for[33] to overlook reality is insanity. Yet that is magic's purpose; to make illusions true through false perception. This cannot heal, for it opposes truth. Perhaps an illusion of health is substituted for a little while, but not for long. Fear cannot long be hidden by illusions, for it is part of them. It will escape and take another form, being the source of all illusions. **P(11)**

P 3 E 8. Sickness is insanity because all sickness is mental illness, and in it there are no degrees. One of the illusions by which sickness is perceived as real is the belief that illness varies in intensity; that the degree of threat differs according to the form it takes. Herein lies the basis of all errors,[34] for all of them are but attempts to compromise by seeing just a little bit of hell. This is a mockery so alien to God that it must be forever inconceivable. But the insane believe it because they are insane.

P 3 E 9. A madman will defend his own illusions because in them he sees his own salvation. Thus, he will attack the one who tries to save him from them, believing that he is attacking him. This curious circle of attack-defense is one of the most difficult problems with which the psychotherapist must deal. In fact, this is his central task; the core of psychotherapy. The therapist is seen as one who is attacking the patient's most cherished possession; his picture of himself. And since this picture has become the patient's security as he perceives it, the therapist cannot but be seen as a real source of danger, to be attacked and even killed.

P 3 E 10. The psychotherapist, then, has a tremendous responsibility. He must meet attack without attack, and therefore without defense. It is his task to demonstrate that defenses are not necessary, and that defenselessness is strength. This must be his teaching, if his lesson is to be that sanity is safe. It cannot be too strongly emphasized that the insane believe that sanity is threat. This is the corollary of the "original sin"; the belief that guilt is real and fully justified. It is therefore the psychotherapist's function to teach that guilt, being unreal, cannot be justified. But neither is it safe. And thus it must remain unwanted as well as unreal.

P 3 E 11. Salvation's single doctrine is the goal of all therapy. Relieve the mind of the insane burden of guilt it carries so wearily, and healing is accomplished. The body is not cured. It is merely recognized as what it is. Seen rightly, its purpose can be understood. What is the need for sickness then? Given this single shift, all else will follow. There is no need for complicated change. There is no need for long analyses and wearying discussions and pursuits. The truth is simple, being one for all. **P(12)**

F. The Process of Healing

P 3 F 1. While truth is simple, it must still be taught to those who have already lost their way in endless mazes of complexity. This is the great illusion. In its wake comes the inevitable belief that, to be safe, one must control the unknown. This strange belief relies on certain steps which never reach to consciousness. First, it is ushered in by the belief that there are forces to be overcome to be alive at all. And next, it seems as if these forces can be held at bay only by an inflated sense of self that holds in darkness what is truly felt, and seeks to raise illusions to the light.

P 3 F 2. Let us remember that the ones who come to us for help are bitterly afraid. What they believe will help can only harm; what they believe will harm alone can help. Progress becomes impossible until the patient is persuaded to reverse his twisted way of looking at the world; his twisted way of looking at himself. The truth is simple. Yet it must be taught to those who think it will endanger them. It must be taught to those who will attack because they feel endangered, and to those who need the lesson of defenselessness above all else, to show them what is strength.

P 3 F 3. If this world were ideal, there could perhaps be ideal therapy. And yet it would be useless in an ideal state. We speak of ideal teaching in a world in which the perfect teacher could not long remain; the perfect psychotherapist is but a glimmer of a thought not yet conceived. But still we speak of what can yet be done in helping the insane within the bounds of the attainable. While they are sick, they can and must be helped. No more than that is asked of psychotherapy; no less than all he has to give is worthy of the therapist. For God Himself holds out his brother as his Savior[35] from the world.

P 3 F 4. Healing is holy. Nothing in the world is holier than helping one who asks for help. And two come very close to God in this attempt, however limited, however lacking in sincerity. Where two have joined for healing, God is there. And He has guaranteed that He will hear and answer them in truth. They can be sure that healing is a process He directs, because it is according to His Will. We have His Word to guide us, as we try to help our brothers. Let us not forget that we are helpless of ourselves, and lean upon a strength beyond our little scope for what to teach as well as what to learn.[36] **P(13)**

P 3 F 5. A brother seeking aid can bring us gifts beyond the heights perceived in any dream. He offers us salvation, for he comes to us as Christ and Savior. What he asks is asked by God through him. And what we do for him becomes the gift we give to[37] God. The sacred calling of God's holy Son for help in his perceived distress can be but answered by his Father. Yet He needs a voice through which to speak His holy Word; a hand to reach His Son and touch his heart. In such a process, who could not be healed? This holy interaction is the plan of God Himself, by which His Son is saved.

---

[30] *Urtext* manuscript has "lies," handwritten mark-up and FIP correct this to "rise" which is also the reading in the *Notes*.

[31] Handwritten mark-up and FIP replace "they" with "the old one." The *Notes* also has "they."

[32] FIP and handwritten mark-up delete "before." The word "before" is in the *Notes*.

[33] In the *Urtext* manuscript "for to overlook" is "but to overlook." Handwritten mark-up and FIP replace "but" with "for" which restores the reading in the *Notes*.

[34] Handwritten mark-up and FIP change the singular "error" to the plural "errors." The *Notes* has the same reading as the *Urtext*: "error."

[35] FIP removes the capital on "Savior" which is present in the *Urtext* and the *Notes*.

[36] **John 5:19** Then Jesus answered and said to them, "Most assuredly, I say to you, the Son can do nothing of Himself, but what He sees the Father do; for whatever He does, the Son also does in like manner."
John 5:30 "I can of Myself do nothing. As I hear, I judge; and My judgment is righteous, because I do not seek My own will but the will of the Father who sent Me."

[37] Handwritten mark-up and FIP insert "to" which was not originally typed, restoring the *Notes* reading.

P 3 F 6. For two have joined. And now God's promises are kept by Him. The limits laid on both the patient and the therapist will count as nothing, for the healing has begun. What man[38] must start his[39] Father will complete. For He has never asked for more than just the smallest willingness, the least advance, the tiniest of whispers of His Name. To ask for help, whatever form it takes, is but to call on Him. And He will send His Answer through the therapist who best can serve His Son in all his present needs. Perhaps the answer does not seem to be a gift from Heaven. It may even seem to be a worsening and not a help. Yet let the outcome not be judged by us.

P 3 F 7. Somewhere all gifts of God must be received. In time no effort can be made in vain. It is not our perfection that is asked in our attempts to heal. We are deceived already, if we think there is a need of healing. And the truth will come to us only through one who seems to share our dream of sickness. Let us help him to forgive himself for all the trespasses with which he would condemn himself without a cause.[40] His healing is our own. And as we see the sinlessness[41] in him come shining through the veil of guilt that shrouds the Son of God, we will behold in him the Face[42] of Christ, and understand that it is but our own.

P 3 F 8. Let us stand silently before God's Will, and do what It[43] has chosen that we do. There is one way alone by which we come to where all dreams began. And it is there that we will lay them down, to come away in peace forever. Hear a brother call for help and answer him. It will be God to Whom you answer, for you called on Him. There is no other way to hear His Voice. There is no other way to seek[44] His Son. There is no other way to find[45] your Self. Holy is healing, for the Son of God returns to Heaven through its kind embrace. For healing tells him, in the Voice of[46] God, that all[47] his sins have been forgiven him.[48] **P(14)**

G. The Definition of Healing

P 3 G 1. The process of psychotherapy, then, can be defined simply as forgiveness, for no healing can be anything else. The unforgiving are sick, believing they are unforgiven. The hanging-on to guilt, its hugging-close and sheltering, its loving protection and alert defense, -- all this is but the grim refusal to forgive. "God may not enter here" the sick repeat, over and over, while they mourn their loss and yet rejoice in it. Healing occurs as a patient begins to hear the dirge he sings, and questions its validity. Until he hears it, he cannot understand that it is he who sings it to himself. To hear it is the first step in recovery. To question it must then become his choice.

P 3 G 2. There is a tendency, and it is very strong, to hear this song of death[49] an instant, and then dismiss it uncorrected. These fleeting awarenesses represent the many opportunities given us literally "to change our tune." The sound of healing can be heard instead. But first the willingness to question the "truth" of the song of condemnation must arise. The strange distortions woven inextricably into the self-concept, itself but a "pseudo-creation,"[50] make this ugly sound seem truly beautiful. "The rhythm of the universe," "the herald angel's song," all these and more are heard instead of loud discordant shrieks.

P 3 G 3. The ear translates; it does not hear. The eye reproduces; it does not see. Their task is to make agreeable whatever is called on, however disagreeable it may be. They answer the decisions of the mind, reproducing its desires and translating them into acceptable and pleasant forms. Sometimes the thought behind the form breaks through, but only very briefly, and the mind grows fearful and begins to doubt its sanity. Yet it will not permit its slaves to change the forms they look upon; the sounds they hear. These are its "remedies"; its "safeguards" from insanity.

P 3 G 4. These testimonies which the senses bring have but one purpose; to justify attack and thus keep unforgiveness unrecognized for what it is. Seen undisguised it is intolerable. Without protection it could not endure. Here is all sickness cherished, but without the recognition that this is so. For when an unforgiveness is not recognized, the form it takes seems to be something else. And now it is the "something else" that seems to terrify. But it is not the "something else" that can be healed. It is not sick, and **P(15)** needs no remedy. To concentrate your healing efforts here is but futility. Who can cure what cannot be sick and make it well?

P 3 G 5. Sickness takes many forms, and so does unforgiveness. The forms of one but reproduce the forms of the other, for they are the same illusion. So closely is one translated into the other, that a careful study of the form a sickness takes will point quite clearly to the form of unforgiveness that it represents. Yet seeing this will not effect a cure. That is achieved by only one recognition; that only forgiveness heals an unforgiveness, and only an unforgiveness can possibly give rise to sickness of any kind.

P 3 G 6. This realization is the final goal of psychotherapy. How is it reached? The therapist sees in the patient all that he has not forgiven in himself, and is thus given another chance to look at it, open it to re-evaluation and forgive it. When this occurs, he sees his sins as gone into a past that is no longer here. Until he does this, he must think of evil as besetting him here and now. The patient is his screen for the projection of his sins, enabling him to let them go. Let him retain one spot of sin in what he looks upon, and his release is partial and will not be sure.

P 3 G 7. No-one is healed alone. This is the joyous song salvation sings to all who hear its Voice. This statement cannot be too often remembered by all who see themselves as therapists. Their patients can but be seen as the bringers of forgiveness, for it is they who come to demonstrate their sinlessness to eyes that still believe that sin is there to look upon. Yet will the proof of sinlessness, seen in the patient and accepted in the therapist, offer the mind of both a covenant in which they meet and join and are as one. **P(16)**

H. The Ideal Patient-Therapist Relationship

P 3 H 1. Who, then, is the therapist, and who is the patient? In the end, everyone is both. He who needs healing must heal. "Physi-

---

[38] Handwritten mark-up and FIP replace "man" with "they." The *Notes* has "man."
[39] Handwritten mark-up and FIP replace "his" with "their." The *Notes* has "his."
[40] **Matthew 6:12-15** "And forgive us our trespasses, as we forgive those who trespass against us. And bring us not into temptation, but deliver us from the evil one. For if ye forgive men their trespasses, your heavenly Father will also forgive you. But if ye forgive not men their trespasses, neither will your Father forgive your trespasses."
[41] Handwritten mark-up and FIP replace the originally typed "sinless" with "sinlessness." This is also the reading in the *Notes*.
[42] Handwritten mark-up and FIP make "Face" lower case. In the *Notes* it is capitalized.
[43] Handwritten mark-up and FIP make "It" lower case. In the *Notes* it is capitalized.
[44] Handwritten mark-up and FIP replace "find" with "seek" In this and the next sentence, "seek" and "find" are switched. In the *Notes* it is originally written "find His Son" and "seek your Self" but these are crossed out and switched. The exact same handwritten corrections occur in the *Urtext* manuscript, suggesting they might have been made at the same time. We've kept it here as originally written in the *Notes* and typed in the *Urtext* manuscript.
[45] Handwritten mark-up and FIP replace "seek" with "find." (see previous footnote)
[46] Handwritten mark-up and FIP replace "of" with "for." In the *Notes* it is "of."
[47] Handwritten mark-up and FIP insert "all" restoring the passage to the reading found in the *Notes*.
[48] Our copy of the *Urtext* manuscript is missing the last word, "him" which is present in the *Notes*. FIP includes it.

[49] Handwritten mark-up and FIP insert "only" which is not present in the *Notes*.
[50] Handwritten mark-up and FIP delete quotation marks which are present in the *Notes*.

cian, heal thyself."[51] Who else is there to heal? And who else is in need of healing? Each patient who comes to a therapist offers him a chance to heal himself. He is therefore his therapist. And every therapist must learn to heal from each patient who comes to him. He thus becomes his patient. God does not know of separation. What He knows is only that He has one Son. His knowledge is reflected in the ideal patient-therapist relationship. God comes to him who calls, and in Him he[52] recognizes Himself.

P 3 H 2. Think carefully, teacher and therapist, for whom you pray, and who is in need of healing. For therapy is prayer, and healing is its aim and its result. What is prayer except the joining of minds in a relationship which Christ can enter? This is His home, into which psychotherapy invites Him. What is symptom cure, when another is always there to choose? But once Christ enters in, what choice is there except to have Him stay? There is no need for more than this, for it is everything. Healing is here, and happiness and peace. These are the "symptoms" of the ideal patient-therapist relationship, replacing those with which the patient came to ask for help.

P 3 H 3. The process that takes place in this relationship is actually one in which the therapist in his heart tells the patient that all his sins have been forgiven him, along with his own. What could be the difference between healing and forgiveness? Only Christ forgives, knowing His sinlessness. His vision heals perception and sickness disappears. Nor will it return again, once its cause has been removed. This, however, needs the help of a very advanced therapist, capable of joining with the patient in a holy relationship in which all sense of separation finally is overcome.

P 3 H 4. For this, one thing and one thing only is required: The therapist in no way confuses himself with God. All "unhealed healers" make this fundamental confusion in one form or another, because they must regard themselves as self-created rather than God-created. This confusion is rarely if ever in awareness, or the unhealed **P(17)** healer would instantly become a Teacher of God, devoting his life to the function of true healing. Before he reached this point, he thought he was in charge of the therapeutic process and was therefore responsible for its outcome. His patient's failures[53] thus became his own mistakes,[54] and guilt became the cover, dark and strong, for what should be the Holiness of Christ. Guilt is inevitable in those who use their judgment in making their decisions. Guilt is impossible in those through whom the Holy Spirit speaks.

P 3 H 5. The passing of guilt is the true aim of therapy and the obvious aim of forgiveness. In this their oneness can be clearly seen. Yet who could experience the end of guilt who feels responsible for his brother in the role of guide for him? Such a function presupposes a knowledge that no-one here can have; a certainty of past, present and future, and of all the effects that may occur in them. Only from this omniscient point of view would such a role be possible. Yet no perception is omniscient, nor is the tiny self of one alone against the universe able to assume he has such wisdom except in madness. That many therapists are mad is obvious. No unhealed healer can be wholly sane.

P 3 H 6. Yet it is as insane not to accept a function God has given you as to invent one He has not. The advanced therapist in no way can ever doubt the power that is in him. Nor does he doubt its Source. He understands all power in earth and Heaven belongs to him because of who he is.[55] And he is this because of his Creator, Whose Love is in him and Who cannot fail. Think what this means; he has the gifts of God Himself to give away. His patients are God's saints, who call upon his sanctity to make it theirs. And as he gives it to them, they behold Christ's shining face as it looks back at them.

P 3 H 7. The insane, thinking they are God, are not afraid to offer weakness to the Son of God.[56] But what they see in him because of this they fear indeed. The unhealed healer cannot but be fearful of his patients, and suspect them of the treachery he sees in him. He tries to heal, and thus at times he may. But he will not succeed except to some extent and for a little while. He does not see the Christ in him who calls. **P(18)** What answer can he give to one who seems to be a stranger; alien to the truth and poor in wisdom, without the god who must be given him? Behold your God in him, for what you see will be your Answer.

P 3 H 8. Think what the joining of two brothers really means. And then forget the world and all its little triumphs and its dreams of death. The same are one, and nothing now can be remembered of the world of guilt. The room becomes a temple, and the street a stream of stardust brushing[57] lightly past all sickly dreams. Healing is done, for what is perfect needs no healing, and what remains to be forgiven where there is no sin?

P 3 H 9. Be thankful, therapist, that you can see such things as this, if you but understand your proper role. But if you fail in that,[58] you have denied that God created you, and so you will not know you are His Son.[59] Who is your brother[60] now? What saint can come to take you home with him? You lost the way. And can you now expect to see in him an answer that you have refused to give? Heal and be healed. There is no other choice of pathways that can ever lead to peace. Oh let your patient in, for he has come to you from God. Is not his holiness enough to wake your memory of Him? **P(19)**

4. THE PRACTICE OF PSYCHOTHERAPY

A. The Selection of Patients

P 4 A 1. Everyone who is sent to you is a patient of yours. This does not mean that you select him, nor that you choose the kind of "treatment" that is suitable. But it does mean that no-one comes to you by mistake. There are no errors in God's plan. It would be an error, however, to assume that you know what to offer everyone who comes. This is not up to you to decide. There is a tendency to assume that you are being called on constantly to make sacrifices of yourself for those who come. This could hardly be true. To demand sacrifice of yourself is to demand a sacrifice of God, and He knows nothing of sacrifice. Who could ask of Perfection that He be imperfect?

P 4 A 2. Who, then, decides what each brother needs? Surely not you, who do not yet recognize who he is who asks. There is Some-

---

[51] Handwritten mark-up and FIP delete quotation marks. This paragraph has not been located in the *Notes*.
Luke 4:23 He said to them, "You will surely say this proverb to Me, 'Physician, heal yourself! Whatever we have heard done in Capernaum, do also here in Your country.'"
[52] The capitals on Him and He are reversed in the *Urtext* manuscript. This paragraph has not been located in the *Notes*.
[53] Handwritten mark-up and FIP have "errors" in place of "failures." In the *Notes* there are two words crossed out, which aren't legible, and the word "failures" is written in between the lines to replace them.
[54] Handwritten mark-up and FIP have "failures" in place of "mistakes." The *Notes* has "mistakes."

[55] **Matthew 28:18** And Jesus came and spoke to them, saying, "All authority has been given to Me in heaven and on earth."
[56] Handwritten mark-up and FIP change "Son of God" to "God's Son." In the *Notes* it is "Son of God" but there is a curious mark between "of" which occurs at the end of line N 3:36:2 and "God" which occurs at the beginning of line N 3:36:3 which may be a question mark indicating scribal uncertainty.
[57] Handwritten mark-up and FIP replace "stardust brushing" with "stars that brush." The *Notes* has "stardust brushing."
[58] Handwritten mark-up and FIP change "that" to "this" restoring the material to the form found in the *Notes*.
[59] "Son" is not capitalized in the *Urtext* manuscript. It is in the *Notes* and the capitalization is appropriate for a person of the Trinity. The omission of capitalization here is deemed a typo.
[60] Originally typed "bother" ... this is a typo Thetford reports frequently making in his autobiographical speech. This appears to be clearly a typo. It is "brother" in the *Notes* and FIP.

thing in him that will tell you, if you listen. And that is the answer; listen. Do not demand, do not decide, do not sacrifice. Listen. What you hear is true. Would God send His Son to you and not be sure you recognize his needs? Think what God is telling you; He needs your voice to speak for Him. Could anything be holier? Or a greater gift to you? Would you rather choose who would be god, or hear the Voice of Him Who is God in you?

P 4 A 3. Your patients need not be physically present for you to serve them in the Name of God. This may be hard to remember, but God will not have His gifts to you limited to the few you actually see. You can see others as well, for[61] seeing is not limited to the body's eyes. Some do not need your physical presence. They need you as much, and perhaps even more, at the instant they are sent. You will recognize them in whatever way can be most helpful to both of you. It does not matter how they come. They will be sent in whatever form is most helpful; a name, a thought, a picture, an idea, or perhaps just a feeling of reaching out to someone somewhere. The joining is in the hands of the Holy Spirit. It cannot fail to be accomplished. **P(20)**

P 4 A 4. A holy therapist, an advanced Teacher of God, never forgets one thing; he did not make the curriculum of salvation, nor did he establish his part in it. He understands that his part is necessary to the whole, and that through it he will recognize the whole when his part is complete. Meanwhile he must learn, and his patients are the means sent to him for his learning. What could he be but grateful for them and to them? They come bearing God. Would he refuse this Gift for a pebble, or would he close the door on the savior of the world to let in a ghost? Let him not betray the Son of God. Who calls on him is far beyond his understanding. Yet would he not rejoice that he can answer, when only thus will he be able to hear the call and understand that it is his? **P(21)**

B. Is Psychotherapy a Profession?

P 4 B 1. Strictly speaking the answer is no. How could a separate profession be one in which everyone is engaged? And how could any limits be laid on an[62] interaction in which everyone is both patient and therapist in every relationship into[63] which he enters? Yet practically speaking, it can still be said that there are those who devote themselves primarily to healing of one sort or another as their chief function. And it is to them that a large number of others[64] turn for help. That, in effect, is the practice of therapy. These[65] are therefore "officially" helpers. They are devoted to certain kinds of needs in their professional activities, although they may be far more able teachers outside of them. These people need no special rules, of course, but they may be called upon to use[66] special applications of the general principles of healing.

P 4 B 2. First, the professional therapist is in an excellent position to demonstrate that there is no order of difficulty in healing. For this, however, he needs special training, because the curriculum by which he became a therapist probably taught him little or nothing about the real principles of healing. In fact, it probably tried to teach[67] him how to make healing impossible. Most of the world's training follows[68] a curriculum in judgment, with the aim of making the therapist a judge.

P 4 B 3. Even this the Holy Spirit can use, and will use, given the slightest invitation. The unhealed healer may be arrogant, selfish, unconcerned, and actually dishonest. He may be disinterested and unconcerned with[69] healing as his major goal. Yet something happened to him, however slight it may have been, when he chose to be a healer, however misguided the direction he may have chosen. That "something" is enough. Sooner or later that something will rise in awareness[70] and grow; a patient will touch his heart, and the therapist[71] will silently ask him for help. He has himself found a therapist. He has asked the Holy Spirit to enter the relationship and heal it. He has accepted the Atonement for himself. **P(22)**

P 4 B 4. God is said to have looked on all He created and pronounced it good.[72] No, He declared it perfect, and so it was. And since His creations do not change and last forever, so it is now. Yet neither a perfect therapist nor a perfect patient can possibly exist. Both must have denied their perfection, for their very need for each other implies a sense of lack. A one-to-one relationship is not one Relationship. Yet it is the means of return; the way God chose for the return of His Son. In that strange dream a strange correction must enter, for only that is the call to awake. And what else should therapy be? Awake and be glad, for all your sins have been forgiven you. This is the only message that any two should ever give each other.

P 4 B 5. Something good must come from every meeting of patient and therapist. And that good is saved for both, against the day when they can recognize that only that was real in their relationship. At that moment it is[73] returned to them, blessed by the Holy Spirit as a gift from their Creator as a sign of His Love. For the therapeutic relationship must become like the relationship of the Father and the Son. There is no other, for there is nothing else. The therapists of this world do not expect this outcome, and many of their patients would not[74] be able to accept help from them if they did. Yet no therapist really sets the goal for the relationships of which he is a part. His understanding begins with recognizing this, and then goes on from there.

P 4 B 6. It is in the instant that the therapist forgets to judge the patient that healing occurs. In some relationships this point is never reached, although both patient and therapist may arrive at different[75] dreams in the process. Yet it will not be the same dream for both of them, and so it is not the dream of forgiveness in which both will someday wake. The good is saved; indeed is cherished. But only

---

[61] The *Urtext* manuscript has "but" typed. Handwritten mark-up and FIP change "but" to "for" which restores the *Notes* reading.

[62] *Urtext* manuscript has "a kind of" typed above the line, and crossed out by hand. It is not present in the *Notes*.

[63] The *Urtext* manuscript has "in" here but the *Notes* indicates "into" which is more appropriate.

[64] *Urtext* manuscript has "people" typed above the line, and crossed out by hand. The *Notes* also has two curious cross-outs in this line offering two alternate readings. See N 3:41:14-15.

[65] *Urtext* manuscript has "people" typed above the line, and crossed out by hand. The word "people" is in the *Notes*.

[66] Originally typed "give," *Urtext* manuscript mark-up suggests "offer" and finally "use" as seen here. The *Notes* has "use."

[67] Handwritten mark-up and FIP have "taught" instead of "tried to teach." The *Notes* has "tried to teach."

[68] Handwritten mark-up and FIP replace "training programs follow" with "training follows" which would more closely resemble the *Notes* which has "training follow" which has an obvious grammar problem. It would need to be "training follows" which is what the mark-up indicates.

[69] Handwritten mark-up and FIP have "may be uninterested in." The *Notes* has "may really be ~~act~~ unconcerned with healing as his major goal." The word really is written between the lines and appears to be an afterthought. The word "act" is crossed out.

[70] Handwritten mark-up crosses out "in awareness." FIP omits it. The *Notes* reads "sooner or later ~~that~~ it will rise and grow; a patient will …"

[71] *Urtext* manuscript has "he," handwritten mark-up and FIP substitute "therapist." In the *Notes* it is "he."

[72] **Genesis 1:31** Then God saw everything that He had made, and indeed it was very good. So the evening and the morning were the sixth day.

[73] *Urtext* manuscript has "it is" which is the same as the *Notes*. "The good" is handwritten in between the lines. FIP preserves that editing change.

[74] The word "not" is handwritten, it is not in the original *Urtext* manuscript. It is, however, present in the *Notes*.

[75] The *Urtext* manuscript has "may arrive at different dreams…" Handwritten mark-up and FIP replace that with "may change their dreams." The *Notes* has "may arrive at a different dream in the process." Also, the *Notes* appears to have initially said "the patient may arrive at a different dream in the process" with strikeout and interlinear writing changing that to "both patient and therapist may arrive at a different dream in the process."

little time is saved and[76] the new dreams will lose their temporary appeal and turn to dreams of fear, which is the content of all dreams. Yet no patient can accept more than he is ready to receive, and no therapist can offer more than he believes he has. And so there is a place for all relationships in this world, and they will bring as much good as each can accept and use. **P(23)**

P 4 B 7. Yet it is when judgment ceases that healing occurs, because only then it can be understood that there is no order of difficulty in healing. This is a necessary understanding for the healed healer. He has learned that it is no harder to wake a brother from one dream than from another. No professional therapist can hold this understanding consistently in his mind, offering it to all who come to him. There are some in this world who have come very close, but they have not accepted the gift entirely in order to stay and let their understanding remain on earth until the closing of time. They could hardly be called professional therapists. They are the Saints of God. They are the Saviors of the world. Their image remains, because they have chosen that it be so. They take the place of other images, and help with kindly dreams.

P 4 B 8. Once the professional therapist has realized that minds are joined, he can also recognize that order of difficulty in healing is meaningless. Yet well before he reaches this in time he can go toward it. Many holy instants can be his along the way. A goal marks the end of a journey, not the beginning, and as each goal is reached another can be dimly seen ahead. Most professional therapists are still at the very start of the beginning stage of the first journey. Even those who have begun to understand what they must do may still oppose the setting-out. Yet all the laws of healing can be theirs in just an instant. The journey is not long except in dreams.

P 4 B 9. The professional therapist has one advantage that can save enormous time if it is properly used. He has chosen a road on[77] which there is great temptation to misuse his role. This enables him to pass by many obstacles to peace quite quickly, if he escapes the temptation to assume a function that has not been given him. To understand there is no order of difficulty in healing, he must also recognize the equality of himself and the patient. There is no halfway point in this. Either they are equal or not. The attempts of therapists to compromise in this respect are strange indeed. Some utilize the relationship merely to collect bodies to worship at their shrine, and this they regard as healing. **P(24)** Many patients, too, consider this strange procedure as salvation. Yet at each meeting there is One Who says, "My brother, choose again."

P 4 B 10. Do not forget that any form of specialness must be defended, and will be. The defenseless therapist has the strength of God with him, but the defensive therapist has lost sight of the Source of his salvation. He does not see and he does not hear. How, then, can he teach? Because it is the Will of God that he take his place in the plan for salvation. Because it is the Will of God that his patients be helped to join with him there. Because his inability to see and hear does not limit the Holy Spirit in any way. Except in time. In time there can be a great lag between the offering and the acceptance of healing. This is the veil across the Face of Christ. Yet it can be but an illusion, because time does not exist and the Will of God has always been exactly as it is. **P(25)**

C. The Question of Payment

P 4 C 1. No-one can pay for therapy, for healing is of God and He asks for nothing. It is, however, part of His plan that everything in this world be used by the Holy Spirit to help in carrying out the plan. Even an advanced therapist has some earthly needs while he is here. Should he need money it will be given him, not in payment, but to help him better serve the plan. Money is not evil. It is nothing. But no-one here can live with no illusions, for he must yet strive to have the last illusion be accepted by everyone everywhere. He has a mighty part in this one purpose, for which he came. He stays here but for this. And while he stays he will be given what he needs to stay.

P 4 C 2. Only an unhealed healer could[78] try to heal for money, and he will not succeed to the extent to which he values it. Nor will he find his healing in the process. There will be those of whom the Holy Spirit asks some payment for His purpose. There will be those from whom He does not ask. It should not be the therapist who makes these decisions. There is a difference between payment and cost. To give money where God's plan allots it has no cost. To withhold it from where it rightfully belongs has enormous cost. The therapist who would do this loses the name of healer, for he could never understand what healing is. He cannot give it, and so he does not have it.

P 4 C 3. The therapists of this world are indeed useless to the world's salvation. They make demands, and so they cannot give. Patients can pay only for the exchange of illusions. This, indeed, must demand payment, and the cost is great. A "bought" relationship cannot offer the only gift whereby all healing is accomplished. Forgiveness, the Holy Spirit's only dream, must have no cost. For if it does, it merely crucifies God's Son again. Can this be how he is forgiven? Can this be how the dream of sin will end?

P 4 C 4. The "right to live"[79] is something no-one need fight for. It is promised him, and guaranteed by God. Therefore it is a right the therapist and patient share alike. **P(26)** If their relationship is to be holy, whatever one needs is given by the other; whatever one lacks the other supplies. Herein is the relationship made holy, for herein both are healed. The therapist repays the patient in gratitude, as does the patient repay him. There is no cost to either. But thanks are due to both, for the release from long imprisonment and doubt. Who would not be grateful for such a gift? Yet who could possibly imagine that it could be bought?

P 4 C 5. It has well been[80] said that to him who hath shall be given.[81] Because he has, he can give. And because he gives, he shall be given. This is the law of God, and not of the world. So it is with God's healers. They give because they have heard His Word and understood it. All that they need will thus be given them. But they will lose this understanding unless they remember that all they have comes only from God. If they believe they need anything from a brother, they will recognize him as a brother no longer. And if they do this, a light goes out even in Heaven. Where God's Son turns against himself, he can look only upon darkness. He has himself denied the light, and cannot see.

P 4 C 6. One rule should always be observed: No-one should be turned away because he cannot pay. No-one is sent by accident to anyone. Relationships are always purposeful. Whatever their purpose may have been before the Holy Spirit entered them, they are always His potential temple[82]; the resting place of Christ and home

---

[76] Handwritten mark-up and FIP delete "and" and begin a new sentence with "The". The *Notes* has it as the *Urtext* was originally typed.

[77] *Urtext* manuscript has "chosen a role on which." handwritten mark-up changes that to "chosen a road on which," and then changes it again, with FIP to "chosen a road in which." Temptations aren't "in" roads, but rather are "on" them, so we're going with the second option. The *Notes* has "road on which."

[78] Handwritten mark-up and FIP suggest "would." The *Notes* clearly has "could."

[79] Handwritten mark-up and FIP delete quotation marks. They are present in the *Notes*.

[80] *Urtext* manuscript has "be said." Handwritten mark-up corrects this to "been said." This corrects an apparent typo and restores the reading found in the *Notes*.

[81] **Matthew 13:12** "For whoever has, to him more will be given, and he will have abundance; but whoever does not have, even what he has will be taken away from him."

[82] **1 Corinthians 3:16** Do you not know that you are the temple of God and that the Spirit of God dwells in you?

of God Himself. Whoever comes has been sent. Perhaps he was sent to give his brother the money he needed. Both will be blessed thereby. Perhaps he was sent to teach the therapist how much he needs forgiveness, and how valueless is money in comparison. Again will both be blessed. Only in terms of cost could one have more. In sharing, everyone must gain a blessing without cost.

P 4 C 7. This view of payment may well seem impractical, and in the eyes of the world it would be so. Yet not one worldly thought is really practical. How much is gained by striving for illusions? How much is lost by throwing God away? And is it possible to do so? Surely it is impractical to strive for nothing, and to attempt to do what is impossible. Then stop a while, long enough to think of this: **P(27)** You have perhaps been seeking for salvation without recognizing where to look. Whoever asks your help can show you where. What greater gift than this could you be given? What greater gift is there that you would give?

P 4 C 8. Physician, healer, therapist, teacher, heal thyself.[83] Many will come to you carrying the gift of healing, if you so elect. The Holy Spirit never refuses an invitation to enter and abide with you. He will give you endless opportunities to open the door to your salvation, for such is His function. He will also tell you exactly what your function is in every circumstance and at all times. Whoever He sends you will reach you, holding out his hand to his Friend. Let the Christ in you bid him welcome, for that same Christ is in him as well. Deny him entrance, and you have denied the Christ in you. Remember the sorrowful story of the world, and the glad tidings[84] of salvation. Remember the plan of God for the restoration of joy and peace. And do not forget how very simple are the ways of God:

You were lost in the darkness of the world until you asked for light. And then God sent His Son to give it to you.[85]

---

1 Corinthians 6:19 Or do you not know that your body is the temple of the Holy Spirit who is in you, whom you have from God, and you are not your own?

[83] **Luke 4:23** He said to them, "You will surely say this proverb to Me, "Physician, heal yourself! Whatever we have heard done in Capernaum, do also here in Your country."
[84] **Luke 1:19** And the angel answered and said to him, "I am Gabriel, who stands in the presence of God, and was sent to speak to you and bring you these glad tidings."
[85] **Romans 8:3** For what the law could not do in that it was weak through the flesh, God did by sending His own Son in the likeness of sinful flesh, on account of sin: He condemned sin in the flesh,

Urtext Volume VI: *Song of Prayer*

Urtext Volume VI: *Song of Prayer*

Table of Contents

1. **PRAYER** 1
    A. Introduction: 1
    B. True Prayer 1
    C. The Ladder of Prayer 2
    D. Praying for Others 3
    E. Praying with Others 4
    F. The Ladder Ends 4
2. **FORGIVENESS** 4
    A. Introduction 4
    B. Forgiveness of Yourself 5
    C. Forgiveness-to-destroy 5
    D. Forgiveness-for-Salvation 6
3. **HEALING** 7
    A. Introduction 7
    B. The Cause of Sickness 7
    C. False versus True Healing 8
    D. Separation versus Union 8
    E. The Holiness of Healing 9

Urtext Volume VI: *Song of Prayer*

1. PRAYER

A. Introduction:

S 1 A 1 Prayer is the greatest gift with which God blessed His Son at his creation. It was then what it is to become; the single Voice Creator and creation share; the song the Son sings to the Father, Who returns the thanks it offers Him unto the Son. Endless the harmony, and endless too the joyous concord of the Love They[1] give forever to each other. And in this creation is extended. God gives thanks to His extension in His Son. His Son gives thanks for his creation, in the song of his creating in his Father's Name. The Love They share is what all prayer will be throughout eternity, when time is done. For such it was before time seemed to be.

S 1 A 2 To you who are in time a little while, prayer takes the form that best will suit your need. You have but one. What God created one must recognize its oneness, and rejoice that what illusions seemed to separate is one forever in the Mind of God. Prayer now must be the means by which God's Son leaves separate goals and separate interests by, and turns in holy gladness to the truth of union in his Father and himself.

S 1 A 3 Lay down your dreams, you holy Son of God, and rising up as God created you, dispense with idols and remember Him. Prayer will sustain you now, and bless you as you lift your hearts[2] to Him in rising song that reaches higher and then higher still until both high and low have disappeared. Faith in your goal will grow and hold you up as you ascend the shining stairway to the lawns of Heaven and the gate of peace. For this is prayer, and here salvation is. This is the way. It is God's gift to you.[3] **S(2)**

S 1 A 4 Asking is holy, and it is holy because it is a way of reaching God. He is the Answerer because you are in need of an Answer. No-one can[4] ask for another and receive the Answer for him. But you can, and indeed you must, help him by offering your love and support that his answer[5] be holy and his true need recognized. That is prayer; it is the same for yourself or for another. There is no difference. If you received the answers for another, there would be a difference.

S 1 A 5 This does not mean that you cannot get messages for another, if it is God Who chooses this way of reaching him. This will usually happen unexpectedly, generally in the form of a sudden feeling that you have something to tell him; a message to deliver. You have not been wrong in the past about how you have asked, but you are ready for a step ahead now. There are joint decisions in which unanimity of response is a good indication of authenticity. This should not be abandoned. But asking is a lesson in trust, and no-one can trust for another. He can only strengthen another's trust by offering it to him and having faith in his ability to hear for himself.

S 1 A 6 Asking is the way to God because it offers us[6] His Will as He would have us[7] hear it. We will have a series of lessons on asking because you have not understood it. But do not think because of that that you have been mistaken in your attempts. You have done well and will do better. **S(3)**

S 1 A 7 Any specific question involves a large number of assumptions which inevitably limit the answer. A specific question is actually a decision about the kind of answer that is[8] acceptable. The purpose of words is to limit, and by limiting to make a vast area of experience[9] more manageable. But that means manageable by YOU. For many aspects of living in this world that is necessary. But not for asking. God does not use words and does not answer in words. He can only "speak"[10] to the Christ in you, Who translates His Answer[11] into whatever language you can understand and accept. Sometimes words will limit fear; sometimes not. That is why some people hear words, some[12] receive feelings of inner conviction, and some do not become aware of anything. Yet God has answered, and His Answer will reach you when you are ready.

S 1 A 8 Answers are not up to you. Any limit you place on[13] them interferes with hearing. God's Voice is silent and speaks in silence.[14] That means that you do not phrase the question and you do not restrict the answer.

S 1 A 9 Asking is[15] prayer. It is not a demand. It is not questioning. It is not limitation. The only real request is for God's Answer. It[16] needs the humility of trust, not the arrogance of false certainty. Trust cannot lie in idols, for that is merely faith in magic.[17] Trust requires faith that God understands, knows, and will answer. It means a state of peace. For this you can[18] safely ask. In fact, if you do not feel that you[19] have it, asking for it is the only real request[20] you can make.

B. True Prayer

S 1 B 1 Prayer is a[21] way offered by the Holy Spirit to reach God. It is not merely a question or an entreaty. It cannot succeed until you realize that it asks for nothing. How else could it serve its purpose? It is impossible to pray for idols and hope to reach God. True prayer must avoid the pitfall of asking to entreat. Ask rather to receive what is already given;[22] to accept what is already there.

S 1 B 2 You have been told to ask the Holy Spirit for the answer to any specific **S(4)** problem, and that you will receive a specific answer if such is your need. You have also been told that there is only one problem and one answer. In prayer this is not contradictory. There are decisions to make here, and they must be made whether they be illusions or not. You cannot be asked to

---

[1] Schucman had a policy of capitalizing all pronouns and some attributes of any of the three persons of the Trinity. In this document the capitalization is very inconsistent. Generally we've adjusted it to fit her policy without footnoting each of the many instances.
[2] **Lamentations. 3:41** Manuscript has "hearts," handwritten mark-up crosses out the "s";
[3] FIP omits the next six paragraphs
[4] Handwritten mark-up suggests "You cannot"
[5] Handwritten mark-up suggests "asking"
[6] Typed in brackets (you)
[7] Typed in brackets (you)
[8] "G" replaces "the kind of answer that is" with "what kind of answer would be". In these footnotes for the *Song of Prayer* "G" refers to a version of this volume published by Gene Ward Smith which footnotes variant readings from an undetermined source. Unfortunately I have been unable to identify precisely what Smith's source was but I suspect it is another and different typed scribal manuscript, giving these footnotes some genuine authority. This is a matter which will have to be clarified with further research.
[9] "G" omits "of experience"
[10] FIP omits quotation marks
[11] "G" doesn't capitalize "His Answer"
[12] FIP adds "people"
[13] "G" has "upon" instead of "on"
[14] **1 Kings 19:12, Ps. 46:10**
[15] Handwritten mark-up suggests "a form of"
[16] Handwritten mark-up suggests "Thus it" or perhaps this is suggesting "This" in place of "it" … it is somewhat ambiguous.
[17] Handwritten mark-up suggests paragraph break here.
[18] FIP has "may"
[19] "G:" omits "feel that you"
[20] Handwritten mark-up suggests "that"
[21] Manuscript does not have the "a" here, it is a handwritten correction
[22] **Matthew 7:7** "Ask, and it will be given to you; seek, and you will find; knock, and it will be opened to you."

accept answers which are beyond the level of need that[23] you[24] recognize.[25] Therefore it is not the form of the question that matters, nor how it is asked. The form of the answer, if given by God through His Voice,[26] will suit your need as you see it. This is merely an echo of the reply of His Voice. The real sound is always a song of thanksgiving and love.[27]

S 1 B 3 We[28] cannot, then, ask for the echo. It is the song that is the gift. Along with it come the overtones, the harmonics, the echoes, but these are secondary. In true prayer you hear only the song. All the rest is merely added. You have sought first the Kingdom of Heaven,[29] and all else has indeed been given you.[30]

S 1 B 4 The secret of true prayer is to forget the things you think you need. To ask for the specific is much the same as to look on sin and then forgive it. Also in the same way, in prayer you overlook your specific needs as you see them, and let them go into His[31] hands. There they become your gifts to Him, for they tell Him that you would have no gods before Him;[32] no Love[33] but His.[34] What could His Answer be but your remembrance of Him? Can this be traded for a bit of trifling advice about a problem of an instant's duration? God answers only for eternity. But still all little answers are contained in this.

S 1 B 5 Prayer is a stepping aside; a letting go; a quiet time of listening and loving. It should not be confused with supplication of any kind, because it is a way of remembering your holiness. Why should holiness entreat, being fully entitled to everything love has to offer? And it is to Love one goes[35] in prayer. Prayer is an offering; a giving up of oneself[36] to be at one with Love. There is nothing to ask because there is nothing left to want. That nothingness becomes the altar of God. It disappears in Him. **S(5)**

S 1 B 6 This is not a level of prayer that everyone can attain as yet. Those who have not[37] need your help in prayer because their asking is not yet based upon acceptance. Help in prayer does not mean that another mediates between you and God. But it does mean that another can stand[38] beside you and help[39] to raise you up to Him. One who has realized the goodness of God prays without fear. And one who prays without fear cannot but reach Him. He can therefore also reach His Son, wherever he may be and whatever form he may seem to take.

S 1 B 7 Praying to Christ in anyone is true prayer because it is a gift of thanks to his Father. To ask that Christ be but Himself is not an entreaty but it IS[40] a song of thanksgiving for what you are. Herein lies the power of prayer. It asks nothing and receives everything. This prayer can be shared because it receives for everyone. To pray with one who knows that this is true is to be answered. Perhaps the specific form of solution[41] for a specific problem will occur to either of you; it does not matter which. Perhaps it will reach both, if you are genuinely attuned to one another. It will come because you have realized that it does not matter. Therein lies its only truth.[42]

C. The Ladder of Prayer

S 1 C 1 Prayer has no beginning and no end. It is a part of life. But it does change in form, and grows with learning until it reaches its formless state, and fuses into total communication with God. In its asking form it need not, and often does not, make appeal to God, or even involve belief in Him. At that level[43] prayer is merely wanting, out of a sense of scarcity and lack.

S 1 C 2 The prayer, or asking-out-of-need,[44] always involves feelings of weakness and inadequacy, and could never be made by a Son of God who knows Who he is. No-one, then, who is sure of his Identity could pray in this form.[45] Yet it is also true that no-one who is uncertain of his Identity could[46] avoid praying in this way. And prayer is as continual as life. Everyone prays without ceasing.[47] Ask and you have received,[48] for you have established what it is **S(6)** you want.

S 1 C 3 It is also possible to reach a higher form of asking-out-of-need, for in this world prayer must be used for reparation,[49] and so it must entail levels of learning. Here, the asking may be addressed to God in honest belief, though not yet with understanding. A vague and usually unstable sense of identification has generally been reached, but it[50] tends to be blurred by a deep-rooted sense of sin. It is possible at this level to continue to ask for things of this world in various forms, but[51] it is also possible to ask for qualities[52] such as honesty or goodness, and particularly for forgiveness for the many sources of guilt that inevitably underlie any prayer of need. Without guilt there is no scarcity. The sinless have no needs.

S 1 C 4 At this level also comes[53] that curious contradiction in terms known as "praying for one's enemies." The contradiction lies not in the actual words, but[54] in the way they are usually interpreted. While you believe you have enemies, you have limited prayer to the laws of this world, and[55] limited your ability to receive and[56] accept to the same narrow margins. And yet, if you have enemies you have need of prayer, and great need, too. What does the phrase really mean? Pray for yourself, that you may not seek to imprison Christ and thereby lose the recognition of your own Identity. Be traitor to no-one, or you will be treacherous to yourself.

---

[23] Handwritten mark-up crosses out "that"
[24] FIP inserts "can" here
[25] Handwritten mark-up indicates paragraph break at this point.
[26] Handwritten mark-up crosses out "through His Voice"
[27] FIP has "of Love"
[28] "We" is crossed out and "You" is penciled in.
[29] Handwritten mark-up appears to cross out the comma.
[30] **Matthew 6:33** "But seek first the kingdom of God and His righteousness, and all these things shall be added to you."
[31] Handwritten mark-up and FIP change this to "God's"
[32] **Exodus 20:3** "You shall have no other gods before Me."
[33] Manuscript is in lower case, handwritten mark-up corrects it to upper case.
[34] The word (Him) is typed in brackets and crossed out.
[35] Handwritten mark-up and FIP suggest "you go"
[36] Crossed out with "yourself" penciled in.
[37] FIP adds "reached it still", handwritten mark-up adds "still." the original typing is crossed out and reads "Until they (He) do they …"
[38] Handwritten mark-up crosses out "can" and pluralizes "stand" to "stands"
[39] Handwritten mark-up and FIP have this as "helps" instead of "help"
[40] Handwritten mark-up crosses out "but it is", FIP inserts sentence break after "entreaty" and leaves out "but" and the handwritten mark-up may do that also, legibility is not good.

[41] FIP changes "solution" to "resolution"
[42] Handwritten mark-up suggests "Christ is in both of you. That is its only truth."
[43] Handwritten mark-up suggests "these levels"
[44] Handwritten mark-up replaces "for" with "or". FIP rewrites this as "These forms of prayer, or asking… involve" Some think it was supposed to be "That prayer, or asking out of need, always involves" as this requires the fewest alterations of the text to achieve grammatical and logical sense. Manuscript has "The prayer for asking-out-of-need"
[45] FIP changes "this form" to "these forms"
[46] Handwritten mark-up suggests "can"
[47] **1 Thessalonians 5:17** "Pray without ceasing,"
[48] **Matthew. 7:7-8** "Ask, and it will be given to you; seek, and you will find; knock, and it will be opened to you. For everyone who asks receives, and he who seeks finds, and to him who knocks it will be opened." Also see **Luke. 11:19;John 17:7;16:23**
[49] FIP has "is reparative" instead of "must be used for reparation"
[50] Handwritten mark-up crosses out "it"
[51] FIP replaces "but" with "and"
[52] Handwritten mark-up replaces "qualities" with "gifts"
[53] Handwritten mark-up crosses out "comes" and adds "begins" at the end of this sentence. FIP retains original reading.
[54] Handwritten mark-up inserts "rather"
[55] Handwritten mark-up inserts "have also"
[56] FIP adds "to"

An enemy is the symbol for[57] an imprisoned Christ. And who could He be except yourself?

S 1 C 5 The prayer for enemies thus becomes a prayer for your own freedom. Now it is no longer a contradiction in terms. Rather it is[58] a statement of the unity of Christ and a recognition of His sinlessness. And now it has become holy, for it acknowledges the Son of God as he was created.

S 1 C 6 Let it never be forgotten that prayer at any level is always for yourself. If you unite with anyone in prayer, you make him part of you. The enemy[59] is you, as is the Christ. Before it can become holy, then, prayer becomes a choice. You do not choose for another. You can but choose for yourself. Pray truly for your enemies, **S(7)** then, for herein lies your own salvation. Forgive them for your sins, and you will be forgiven indeed.

S 1 C 7 Prayer is a ladder reaching up to Heaven.[60] At the top there is a transformation much like your own, for prayer is part of you. The things of earth are left behind, all unremembered. There is no asking, for there is no lack. Identity in Christ is fully recognized as set forever, beyond all change and incorruptible. The light no longer flickers, and will never go out.

S 1 C 8 Now, without needs of any kind, and clad forever in the pure sinlessness which[61] is the gift of God to you, His Son, prayer can again become what it was meant to be. For now it rises as a song of thanks to your Creator, sung without words, or thoughts, or vain desires, unneedful now of anything at all. So it extends, as it was meant to do. And for this giving God Himself gives thanks.

S 1 C 9 God is the goal of every prayer, giving it timelessness instead of end. Nor has it a[62] beginning, because the goal has never changed. Prayer in its earlier forms is an illusion, because there is no need for a ladder to reach what one has never left. Yet prayer is part of forgiveness as long as forgiveness, itself an illusion, remains unattained. Prayer is tied up with learning until the goal of learning has been reached. And then all things will be transformed together, and returned unblemished into the Mind of God.

S 1 C 10 Being beyond learning, this state cannot be described. The stages necessary to its attainment, however, need to be understood, if peace is to be restored to the Son of God,[63] who lives now with the illusion of death and the fear of God.

D. Praying for Others

S 1 D 1 We said that prayer is always for yourself, and this is true.[64] Why, then, should you pray for others at all? And if you should, how should you do it? Praying for others, if rightly understood, becomes a means for lifting your projections of guilt from your brother, and enabling you to recognize it is not he who is hurting you. The poisonous thought that he IS your enemy, your evil counterpart, your nemesis, must be relinquished before YOU can be saved from guilt. For this the means is prayer, of rising power and with ascending **S(8)** goals, until it reaches even up to God.

S 1 D 2 The earlier forms of prayer, at the bottom of the ladder, will not be free from envy and even[65] malice. They call for vengeance, not for love. Nor do they come from one who understands that they are calls for death, made out of fear by those who cherish guilt. They call upon a vengeful god, and it is he who seems to answer them. Hell cannot be asked for another, and then escaped by him who asks for this.[66] Only those who are in hell can ask for hell. Those who have been forgiven, and who have[67] accepted their forgiveness, could never make a prayer like this.[68]

S 1 D 3 At this level,[69] then, the learning goal must be to recognize that prayer will bring an answer only in the form in which the prayer was made. This is enough. From here it will be an easy step to the next level.[70] It[71] begins with this:

"What I have asked for for my brother is not what I would have. Thus have I made of him my enemy."[72]

S 1 D 4 It is apparent that this step cannot be reached by anyone who sees no value nor[73] advantage to himself in setting others free. This may be long delayed, because this step[74] may seem to be dangerous instead of merciful. To the guilty there seems indeed to be a real advantage in having enemies, and this imagined gain[75] must go, if enemies are to be set free. Guilt must be given up, and not concealed. Nor can it be[76] without some pain, and a glimpse of the merciful nature of this step may for some time be followed by a deep retreat into fear. For fear's defenses are fearful in themselves, and when they are recognized they bring their fear with them.

S 1 D 5 Yet what advantage has an illusion of escape ever brought a prisoner? His real escape from guilt can lie only in the recognition that the guilt has gone. And how can this be recognized as long as he hides it in another, and does not see it as his own? Fear of escape makes it difficult to welcome freedom, and to make a jailer of an enemy seems to be safety. How, then, can he be released without an insane fear for yourself? You have made of him your salvation and your **S(9)** escape from guilt. Your investment in this escape is heavy, and your fear of letting[77] go is strong.

S 1 D 6 Stand still an instant, now, and think what you have done. Do not forget that it is you who did it, and who can therefore let it go. Hold out your hand; this enemy has come to bless you. Take his blessing and feel how your heart is lifted and your fear released. Do not hold on to it, nor onto him. He is a Son of God, along with you. He is no jailer, but a messenger of Christ. Be this to him, that you may see him thus.

S 1 D 7 It is not easy to realize that prayers for things, for status,[78] for external "gifts" of any kind, are always made to set up jailers[79] and to hide from guilt. Yet these things, too,[80] are used for goals that substitute for God, and therefore distort the purpose of prayer. The desire for them IS the prayer. One need not ask explicitly. The goal of God is lost in the quest for lesser goals of any kind, and prayer becomes requests for enemies. The power of prayer can be quite clearly recognized even in this. No-one who wants an enemy will fail to find one. But just as surely will he lose the only true goal

---

[57] FIP changes "for" to "of"
[58] Handwritten mark-up crosses out "Rather" and changes "it is" to "It has become".
[59] Handwritten mark-up suggests quotation marks around "enemy"
[60] **Genesis 28:12** "And he dreamed, and behold a ladder set up on the earth, and the top of it reached to heaven: and behold the angels of God ascending and descending on it. "
[61] FIP replaces "which" with "that"
[62] Handwritten mark-up suggests "a beginning", Manuscript omits "a"
[63] Handwritten mark-up suggests "God's Son"
[64] FIP replaces "true" with "so"
[65] FIP omits "even"
[66] Handwritten mark-up, FIP suggests "it"
[67] FIP omits "have"
[68] FIP replaces "this" with "that"
[69] Handwritten mark-up and FIP have "these levels"
[70] Handwritten mark-up and FIP change "level" to "levels"
[71] Handwritten mark-up and FIP replace "it" with "The next ascent"
[72] FIP omits quotes
[73] FIP has "or" instead of "nor"
[74] Handwritten mark-up and FIP replace "this step" with "it"
[75] Manuscript has "game" corrected by handwritten mark-up and FIP to "gain"
[76] FIP and handwritten mark-up suggest "this be done"
[77] FIP has "letting it go"
[78] The word "attributes" is typed and struck out, the word "status" being put in its place. Handwritten mark-up and FIP suggest adding "for human love," here.
[79] initially typed "a jailer" this is crossed out and "jailers" typed above.
[80] Handwritten mark-up and FIP change "Yet these things, too, to "These things are"

that is given him. Think of the cost, and understand it well. All other goals are at the cost of God.

E. Praying with Others

S 1 E 1 Until the second step[81] at least begins, one cannot share in prayer,[82] for until that point, each one must ask for different things. But once the need to hold the other as an enemy has been questioned, and the reason[83] has been recognized if only for an instant, it becomes[84] possible to join in prayer. Enemies do not share a goal, and it is here[85] their enmity is kept. Their separate wishes are their arsenals; their fortresses in hate. The key to rising further still in prayer lies in this simple thought; this change of mind:

We go together, you and I.

S 1 E 2 Now it is possible to help in prayer, and so reach up yourself. This step begins the quicker ascent, but there are still many lessons[86] to learn. The way is open, and hope is justified. Yet it is likely at first that what is asked for even by those who join[87] in prayer is not the goal that prayer **S(10)** should truly seek. Even together they[88] may ask for things, and thus set up but an illusion of a goal they[89] share. They[90] may ask together for specifics, and not realize that they[91] are asking for effects without the cause. And this they[92] cannot have. For no-one can receive effects alone, and choose[93] a cause from which they do not come to offer them to him. Even the joining, then, is not enough, if those who pray together do not ask, before all else, what is the Will of God. From this Cause only can the Answer[94] come in which are all specifics satisfied; all separate wishes unified in one.

S 1 E 3 Prayers[95] for specifics always ask[96] to have the past repeated in some way. What was enjoyed before, or seemed to be, -- what was[97] another's and he seemed to like,[98] -- all these are but illusions from the past. The aim of prayer is to release the present from its chains of past illusions; to let it be a freely chosen remedy from every choice that stood for a mistake. What prayer can offer now so far exceeds all that you asked before that it is pitiful to be content with less.

S 1 E 4 You have[99] a newborn-chance each time you pray. And would you stifle and imprison it in ancient prisons, when the chance has come to free yourself from all of them at once? Do not restrict your asking. Prayer can bring the peace of God. What time-bound thing can give you more than this, in just the little space that lasts until it crumbles into dust?

---

[81] Handwritten mark-up and FIP replace "step" with "level" and omit "at least"
[82] FIP inserts sentence break here.
[83] FIP inserts "for doing so"
[84] Handwritten mark-up suggests "at least"
[85] Handwritten mark-up and FIP remove "and", beginning a new sentence with "It is in this their enmity"
[86] The word "yet" is overstruck out in the Manuscript here.
[87] Handwritten mark-up suggests "sometimes"
[88] FIP changes "they" to "you"
[89] FIP changes "they" to "you"
[90] FIP changes "they" to "you"
[91] FIP changes "they" to "you"
[92] FIP changes "they" to "you"
[93] Handwritten mark-up suggests "ask", FIP uses "asking"
[94] Handwritten mark-up and FIP change "Answer" to "answer"
[95] FIP has the singular "Prayer"
[96] FIP has "asks"
[97] Manuscript has "is", handwritten mark-up and FIP correct this to "was"
[98] FIP has "love"
[99] FIP inserts "chosen"

F. The Ladder Ends

S 1 F 1 Prayer is a way to true humility. But[100] here again it rises[101] up, slowly at first,[102] and grows in strength and love and holiness. Let it but leave the ground where it begins to rise to God, and true humility will come at last to grace the mind that thought it was alone and stood against the world. Humility brings peace because it does not claim that you must rule the universe, nor[103] judge all things as you would have them be. All little gods it gladly lays aside, not in resentment, but in honesty and recognition that they did[104] not serve.

S 1 F 2 Illusions and humility have goals so far apart they cannot coexist, **S(11)** nor share a dwelling place.[105] Where one has come the other disappears. The truly humble have no goal but God because they need no idols, and defense no longer has[106] a purpose. Enemies are useless now, because humility does not oppose. It does not hide in shame because it is content with what it is, knowing creation is the Will of God. Its selflessness is Self, and this it sees in every meeting, where it gladly joins with every Son of God, whose purity it recognizes that it shares with him. Now prayer is lifted from the world of things, of bodies, and of gods of every kind, and you can rest in holiness at last. Humility has taught[107] you how to understand your glory as God's Son, and recognize the arrogance of sin. A dream has veiled the face of Christ from you. Now can you look upon His sinlessness.

S 1 F 3 High has the ladder risen. You have come almost to Heaven. There is little more to learn before the journey is complete. Now[108] you say to everyone who[109] joins in prayer with you:

"I cannot go without you, for you are a part of me."

And so he is in truth. Now must[110] you pray only for what you truly share with him. For you have understood he never left, and you, who seemed alone, are one with him.

S 1 F 4 The ladder ends with this, for learning is no longer needed. Now you stand before the gate of Heaven, and your brother stands beside you there. The lawns are deep and still, for here the place appointed for the time when you should come has waited long for you. Here will time end forever. At this gate eternity itself will join with you. Prayer has become what it was meant to be, for you have recognized the Christ in you. **S(12)**

2. FORGIVENESS

A. Introduction

S 2 A 1 Forgiveness offers wings to prayer, to make its rising easy and its progress swift. Without its strong support it would be vain to try to rise above the[111] bottom step, or even to attempt to climb at all. Forgiveness is prayer's ally; sister in the plan for your salvation. Both must come to hold you up and keep your feet secure; your purpose steadfast and unchangeable. Behold the greatest help that God ordained to be with you until you reach to Him. Illusion's end will come with this. Unlike the timeless nature of its sister prayer, forgiveness has an end, for it becomes unneeded when the rising up is done. Yet now it has a purpose beyond which you cannot go, nor

---

[100] Handwritten mark-up and FIP change "But" to "And"
[101] Handwritten mark-up and FIP insert "slowly"
[102] Handwritten mark-up and FIP delete "slowly at first"
[103] Manuscript has "or" corrected to "nor" by handwritten mark-up
[104] FIP has "do"
[105] Handwritten mark-up and FIP insert "where they can meet" "G" notes that insertion creates IP
[106] FIP changes "has" to "serves"
[107] Handwritten mark-up, FIP suggest "has come to teach"
[108] Handwritten mark-up, FIP suggest "can"
[109] Handwritten mark-up, FIP suggest "comes to join"
[110] Handwritten mark-up, FIP suggest "can" instead of "must"
[111] FIP replaces "the" with "Prayer's"

have you need to go. Accomplish this and you have been redeemed. Accomplish this and you have been transformed. Accomplish this and you will save the world.

B. Forgiveness of Yourself

S 2 B 1 No gift of Heaven has been more misunderstood than has forgiveness. It has, in fact, become a scourge; a curse where it was meant to bless, a cruel mockery of grace, a parody upon the holy peace of God. Yet those who have not yet elected[112] to begin the steps of prayer cannot but use it thus. Forgiveness's[113] kindness is obscure at first, because salvation is not understood, NOR TRULY SOUGHT FOR. What was meant to heal is used to hurt because forgiveness is not wanted. Guilt becomes salvation, and the remedy appears to be a terrible alternative to life.

S 2 B 2 Forgiveness-to-destroy will therefore suit the purpose of the world far better than its true objective, and the honest means by which this goal is reached. Forgiveness-to-destroy will overlook no sin, no crime, no guilt that it can[114] find and "love." Dear to its heart is error, and mistakes loom large and grow and swell within its sight. It carefully picks out all evil things, and overlooks the loving as a plague; a hateful thing of danger and of death. Forgiveness-to-destroy IS death,[115] and this it sees in everything[116] **S(13)** it looks upon and hates. God's mercy has become a twisted knife that would destroy the holy Son He loves.

S 2 B 3 Would you forgive yourself for doing this? Then learn that God has given you a[117] means by which you can return to Him in peace. DO NOT SEE ERROR. Do not make it real. Select the loving and forgive the sin by choosing in its place the face of Christ. How otherwise can prayer return to God? He loves His Son. Can you remember Him and hate what He created? You will hate his Father if you hate the Son He loves. For as you see the Son you see yourself, and as you see yourself is God to you.[118]

S 2 B 4 As prayer is always for yourself, so is forgiveness[119] given you. It is impossible to forgive another, for it is only your sins you see in him. You want to see them there, and not in you. That is why forgiveness of another is an illusion. Yet it is the only happy dream in all the world; the only one that does not lead to death. Only in someone else can you forgive yourself, for you have called him guilty of your sins, and in him must your innocence[120] be found. Who but the sinful need to be forgiven? And do not ever think you can see sin in anyone except yourself.

S 2 B 5 This is the great deception of the world, and you the great deceiver of yourself. It always seems to be another who is evil, and in his sin you are the injured one. How could freedom be possible if this were true?[121] You would be slave to everyone, for what he does entails your fate, your feelings, your despair or hope, your misery or joy. You have no freedom unless he gives it to you. And being evil, he can only give of what he is. You cannot see his sins and not your own. But you can free him and yourself as well.

S 2 B 6 Forgiveness, truly given, is the only way in which your[122] hope of freedom lies. Others will make mistakes and so will you, as long as this illusion of a world appears to be your home. God[123] has given all His Sons a remedy for all illusions that they think they see. Christ's vision does not use your eyes, but you can look through His and learn to see like Him. Mistakes are tiny shadows, quickly gone, which[124] for an instant only seem **S(14)** to hide the face of Christ, which still remains unchanged behind them all. His constancy remains in tranquil silence and in perfect peace. He does not know of shadows. His the eyes that look past error to the Christ in you.

S 2 B 7 Ask then His help, and ask Him how to learn forgiveness as His vision lets it be. You are in need of what He gives, and your salvation rests on learning this of Him. Prayer cannot be released to Heaven while forgiveness-to-destroy remains with you. God's mercy would remove this withering and poisoned thinking from your holy mind. Christ has forgiven you, and in His sight the world is[125] holy as Himself. Who sees no evil in it sees like Him, for what He has forgiven has not sinned, and guilt can be no more. Salvation's plan is made complete, and sanity has come.

S 2 B 8 Forgiveness is the call to sanity, for who but the insane would look on sin when he could see the face of Christ instead? This is the choice you make; the simplest one, and yet the only one that you can make. God calls on you to save His Son from death by offering the love of Christ[126] to him. This is your need, and God Himself[127] holds out this gift to you. As He would give, so must you give as well. And thus is prayer restored to formlessness, beyond all limits into timelessness, with nothing of the past to hold it back from re-uniting with the ceaseless song that all creation sings unto its God. **S(15)**

S 2 B 9 But to achieve this end you first must learn, before you reach where learning cannot go. Forgiveness is the key, but who can use a key when he has lost the door for which the key was made, and where alone it fits? Therefore we make distinctions, so that prayer can be released from darkness into light. Forgiveness's[128] role must be reversed, and cleansed from evil usages and hateful goals. Forgiveness-to-destroy must be unveiled in all its treachery, and then let go forever and forever. There can be no trace of it remaining, if the plan that God established for returning be achieved at last, and learning be complete.

S 2 B 10 This is the world of opposites. And you must choose between them every instant while this world retains reality for you. Yet you must learn alternatives for choice, or you will not be able to attain your freedom. Let it then be clear to you exactly what forgiveness means to you, and learn what it should be to set you free. The level of your prayer[129] depends on this, for here it waits its freedom to ascend above the world of chaos into peace.

C. Forgiveness-to-destroy

S 2 C 1 Forgiveness-to-destroy has many forms, being a weapon of the world of form. Not all of them are obvious, and some are carefully concealed beneath what seems like charity. Yet all the forms that it may[130] take have but one[131] goal; their purpose is to

---

[112] FIP has "chosen"
[113] FIP and the Manuscript both have "Forgiveness'", or "s apostrophe" which would be correct if "forgiveness" were a plural possessive case, but it is a singular possessive case, so it should be "apostrophe s" -- From "A Manual of Style" (12th ed., University of Chicago Press, 1969):
[114] Handwritten mark-up, FIP add "seek and"
[115] **Romans 6:23** "For the wages of sin is death, but the gift of God is eternal life in Christ Jesus our Lord."
[116] Handwritten mark-up and FIP change "everything" to "all"
[117] FIP changes "a" to "the"
[118] **Matthew 25:40** "And the King will answer and say to them, 'Assuredly, I say to you, inasmuch as you did it to one of the least of these My brethren, you did it to Me.'"
[119] Handwritten mark-up and FIP suggest "always"
[120] FIP suggests "now"
[121] FIP suggests "so"

[122] Handwritten mark-up and FIP insert "only" here, removing the immediately previous instance of "only"
[123] Handwritten mark-up and FIP suggest "Yet God Himself"
[124] FIP changes "which" to "that"
[125] Handwritten mark-up and FIP suggest "becomes as"
[126] Handwritten mark-up and FIP suggest "Christ's Love"
[127] Handwritten mark-up and FIP delete "Himself"
[128] FIP and the Manuscript both have "Forgiveness'", or "s apostrophe" which would be correct if "forgiveness" were a plural possessive case, but it is a singular possessive case, so it should be "apostrophe s" -- From "A Manual of Style" (12th ed., University of Chicago Press, 1969):
[129] Originally plural, the typist overstruck the "s" making it singular. FIP keeps it singular.
[130] Handwritten mark-up and FIP suggest "seem to"

separate and make what God created equal, different. The difference is clear in several forms where the designed comparison cannot be missed, nor is it[132] meant to be.

S 2 C 2 In this group, first, there are the forms in which a "better" person deigns to stoop to save a baser[133] one from what he[134] is. Forgiveness here rests solely on the base[135] of gracious lordliness so far from love that arrogance could never be dislodged. Who can forgive and yet despise? And who can tell another he is steeped in sin, and yet perceive him as the Son of God? Who makes a slave to teach what freedom is? There is no union here, but only grief. This is not[136] mercy. This is death.

S 2 C 3 Another form, still very like the first if it is understood, does not appear in quite such blatant arrogance. The one who would forgive the S(16) other does not claim to be the better. Now he merely[137] says[138] that here is one whose sinfulness he shares, since both have been unworthy and deserve the retribution of the wrath of God. This can appear to be a humble act,[139] and can[140] indeed become[141] a rivalry in baseness[142] and in guilt. It is not love for God's creation and the holiness that is His gift forever. Can His Son condemn himself and still remember Him?

S 2 C 4 Here the goal is to separate from God the Son He loves, and keep him from his Source. This goal is also sought by those who seek the role of martyr at another's hand. Here must the aim be clearly seen, for this may pass as meekness and as charity instead of cruelty. Is it not kind to be accepting of another's spite, and not respond except with silence and a gentle smile? Behold, how good are you who bear with patience and with saintliness the anger and the hurt another gives, and do not show the bitter pain you feel.

S 2 C 5 Forgiveness-to-destroy will often hide behind a cloak like this. It shows the face of suffering and pain, in silent proof of guilt and of the ravages of sin. Such is the witness that it offers one who could be savior, not an enemy. But having made him[143] enemy, he must accept the guilt and heavy-laid reproach that thus is put upon him. Is this love? Or is it rather treachery to one who needs salvation from the pain of guilt? What is it for,[144] except to keep the witnesses of guilt away from love?

S 2 C 6 Forgiveness-to-destroy can also take the form of bargaining and compromise. "I will forgive you if you meet my needs, for in your slavery is my release." Say this to anyone and you are slave. And you will seek to rid yourself of guilt in further bargains which can give no hope, but only greater pain and misery. How fearful has forgiveness now become, and how distorted is the end it seeks. Have mercy on yourself who bargained[145] thus. God gives and does not ask for recompense. There is no giving but to give like Him. All else is mockery. For who would try to strike a bargain with the Son of God, and thank his Father for his holiness? S(17)

S 2 C 7 What would you show your brother? Would you try to reinforce his guilt and thus your own? Forgiveness is the means for your escape. How pitiful it is to make of it a[146] means for further slavery and pain. Within the world of opposites there is a way to use forgiveness for the goal of God, and find the peace He offers you. Take nothing else, or you have sought your death, and prayed for separation from your Self. Christ is for all because He is in all.[147] It is His face forgiveness lets you see. It is His face in which you see[148] your own.

S 2 C 8 All forms forgiveness takes that do not lead away from anger, condemnation, and comparisons of every kind are death. For that is what their purposes have set. Be not deceived by them, but lay them by as worthless in their tragic offerings. You do not want to stay in slavery. You do not want to be afraid of God. You want to see the sunlight and the glow of Heaven shining on the face of earth, redeemed from sin and in the Love of God. From here is prayer released, along with you. Your wings are free, and prayer will lift you up and bring you home where God would have you be.

D. Forgiveness-for-Salvation

S 2 D 1 Forgiveness-for-salvation has one form, and only one. It does not ask for proof of innocence, nor pay of any kind. It does not argue, nor evaluate the errors that it wants to overlook. It does not offer gifts in treachery, nor promise freedom while it asks for death. Would God deceive you? He but asks for trust and willingness to learn how to be free. He gives His Teacher to whoever asks, and seeks to understand the Will of God. His readiness to give lies far beyond your understanding and your simple grasp. Yet He has willed you learn the way to Him, and in His willing there is certainty.

S 2 D 2 You Child of God, the gifts of God are yours, not by your plans but by His holy Will. His Voice will teach you what forgiveness is, and how to give it as He wills it be. Do not, then, seek to understand what is beyond you yet, but let it be a way to draw you up to where the sight[149] of Christ becomes the eyes[150] you choose. Give up all else, for there IS nothing else. When someone S(18) calls for help in any form, He is the One to answer for you. All that you need do is to step back and not to interfere. Forgiveness-for-salvation is His task, and it is He Who will respond for you.

S 2 D 3 Do not establish what the form should be that His[151] forgiveness takes. He knows the way to make of every call a help to you, as you arise in haste to go at last unto your Father's house.[152]

---

[131] Handwritten mark-up and FIP suggest "this single"
[132] Handwritten mark-up and FIP insert "really"
[133] FIP adds quotes around "baser"
[134] Handwritten mark-up suggests really, crossed out and replaces with "truly" which FIP keeps.
[135] Handwritten mark-up and FIP replaces "solely on the base" with "on an attitude"
[136] Handwritten mark-up and FIP insert "really"
[137] Handwritten mark-up and FIP delete "merely"
[138] Handwritten mark-up and FIP insert "instead"
[139] FIP changes "act" to "thought"
[140] FIP changes "can" to "may"
[141] FIP changes "become" to "induce"
[142] Handwritten mark-up and FIP change "baseness and in" to "sinfulness and guilt"
[143] Handwritten mark-up and FIP change "made him" to "been made"
[144] Handwritten mark-up and FIP change "is it for" to "could the purpose be"
[145] FIP changes this to the present tense, "bargains"
[146] FIP changes "a" to "the"
[147] **1 Corinthians 15:28** "Now when all things are made subject to Him, then the Son Himself will also be subject to Him who put all things under Him, that God may be all in all."
[148] Manuscript does not contain "you see", but this correction is handwritten in.
[149] Handwritten mark-up and FIL change "sight" to "eyes" and the verb "becomes" is changed to "become"
[150] Handwritten mark-up and FIP change "eyes" to "sight"
[151] Handwritten mark-up and FIP change "His" to "Christ's"
[152] **Luke 15:11-32** Then He said: "A certain man had two sons. And the younger of them said to his father, "Father, give me the portion of goods that falls to me.' So he divided to them his livelihood. And not many days after, the younger son gathered all together, journeyed to a far country, and there wasted his possessions with prodigal living. But when he had spent all, there arose a severe famine in that land, and he began to be in want. Then he went and joined himself to a citizen of that country, and he sent him into his fields to feed swine. And he would gladly have filled his stomach with the pods that the swine ate, and no one gave him anything. "But when he came to himself, he said, "How many of my father's hired servants have bread enough and to spare, and I perish with hunger! I will arise and go to my father, and will say to him, "Father, I have sinned against heaven and before you, and I am no longer worthy to be called your son. Make me like one of your hired servants."'
"And he arose and came to his father. But when he was still a great way off, his father saw him and had compassion, and ran and fell on his neck and

He will direct[153] your footsteps surely,[154] and [155]your words sincere; not with your own sincerity, but with His Own. Let Him take charge of how you would forgive, and each occasion then will be to you another step to Heaven and to peace.

S 2 D 4 Are you not weary of imprisonment? God did not choose this sorry path for you. What you have chosen still can be undone, for prayer is merciful and God is just. His is a justice He can understand, but you cannot as yet. Yet[156] will He give the means to you to learn of Him, and know at last that condemnation is not real and makes illusions in its evil name. And yet it matters not the form that dreams may seem to take. Illusions are untrue. God's Will is truth, and you are one with Him in Will and purpose. Here all dreams are done.

S 2 D 5 "What should I do for this,[157] Your holy Son?" should be the only thing you ever ask when help is needed and forgiveness sought. The form the seeking takes you need not judge. But[158] let it not be you who sets the form in which forgiveness comes to save God's Son. The light of Christ in him is his release, and it is this that answers to his call. Forgive him as the Christ decides you should, and be His eyes through which you look on him, and speak for Him as well. He knows the need; the question and the answer. He will say exactly what to do in words that you can understand[159] and you can also use. Do not confuse His function with your own. He is the Answer; you the one who hears.

S 2 D 6 And what is it He speaks to you about? About salvation and the gift of peace. About the end of sin and guilt and death. About the role forgiveness has in Him. Do you but listen, for He will be heard by anyone who calls upon His Name, and **S(19)** places his forgiveness in His hands. Forgiveness has been given Him to teach, to save it from destruction and to make the means for separation, sin and death become again the holy gift of love.[160] Prayer is His Own right hand, made free to save as true forgiveness is allowed to come from His eternal vigilance and Love.

S 2 D 7 Listen and learn, and do[161] not judge. It is to God you turn to hear what you should do. His Answer will be clear as morning, nor is His forgiveness what you think it is. Still does He know, and that should be enough. Forgiveness has a Teacher Who will fail in nothing. Rest a while in this; do not attempt to judge forgiveness, nor to set it in an earthly frame. Let it arise to Christ, Who welcomes it as gift to Him. He will not leave you comfortless,[162] nor fail to send His angels down to answer you in His Own Name. He stands beside the door to which forgiveness is the only key. Give it to Him to use instead of you, and you will see the door swing silently open upon the shining face of Christ. Behold your brother there beyond the door; the Son of God as He created him. **S(20)**

3. HEALING

A. Introduction

S 3 A 1 Prayer has both aids and witnesses which make the steep ascent more gentle and more sure, easing the pain of fear and offering the comfort and the promises of hope. Forgiveness's[163] witness and an aid to prayer, a giver of assurance of success in ultimate attainment of the goal, is healing. Its importance should not be too strongly emphasized, for healing is a sign or symbol of forgiveness's[164] strength, and only an effect or shadow of a change of mind about the goal of prayer.

B. The Cause of Sickness

S 3 B 1 Do not mistake effect for cause, nor think that sickness is apart and separate from what its cause must be. It is a sign, a shadow of an evil thought that seems to have reality and to be just, according to the usage of the world. It is external proof of inner "sin," [165] and witnesses to unforgiving thoughts that injure and would hurt the Son of God. Healing the body is impossible, and this is shown by the brief nature of the "cure." The body yet must die, and healing it is but a brief delay in its return[166] to dust,[167] where it was born and will go back.[168]

S 3 B 2 The body's source[169] is unforgiveness of the Son of God. It has not left its source, and in its pain and aging and the mark of death upon it this is clearly shown. Fearful and frail it seems to be to those who think their life is tied to its command and linked to its unstable, tiny breath. Death stares at them as every moment goes irrevocably past their grasping hands, which cannot hold them back. And they feel fear as bodies change and sicken. For they sense the heavy scent of death upon their hearts.

S 3 B 3 The body can be healed as an effect of true forgiveness. Only that can give remembrance[170] of immortality, which is the gift of holiness and love. Forgiveness must be given by a mind which understands that it must overlook all shadows on the holy face of Christ, among which sickness should be seen as one. Nothing but that; the sign of judgment made by brother upon brother, and the Son of God upon himself. For he has damned his body as his prison, **S(21)** and forgot that it is he who gave this role to it.

S 3 B 4 What he has done now must God's Son undo. But not alone. For he has thrown away the prison's key; his holy sinlessness and the remembrance of his Father's Love. Yet Help is given to him in the Voice his Father placed in him. The power to heal is now his Father's gift, for through His Voice He still can reach His Son,

---

kissed him. And the son said to him, "Father, I have sinned against heaven and in your sight, and am no longer worthy to be called your son.'
"But the father said to his servants, "Bring out the best robe and put it on him, and put a ring on his hand and sandals on his feet. And bring the fatted calf here and kill it, and let us eat and be merry; for this my son was dead and is alive again; he was lost and is found.' And they began to be merry.
"Now his older son was in the field. And as he came and drew near to the house, he heard music and dancing. So he called one of the servants and asked what these things meant. And he said to him, "Your brother has come, and because he has received him safe and sound, your father has killed the fatted calf.'
"But he was angry and would not go in. Therefore his father came out and pleaded with him. So he answered and said to his father, "Lo, these many years I have been serving you; I never transgressed your commandment at any time; and yet you never gave me a young goat, that I might make merry with my friends. But as soon as this son of yours came, who has devoured your livelihood with harlots, you killed the fatted calf for him.'
"And he said to him, "Son, you are always with me, and all that I have is yours. It was right that we should make merry and be glad, for your brother was dead and is alive again, and was lost and is found."'

[153] Handwritten mark-up and FIP change "He will direct" to "Now can he make"
[154] Handwritten mark-up and FIP change "surely" to "sure"
[155] Handwritten mark-up and FIP omit "and"
[156] Handwritten mark-up and FIP replace "Yet" with "still"
[157] Handwritten mark-up and FIP change "this" to "him"
[158] Handwritten mark-up and FIP change "But" to "And"
[159] The original Manuscript inserts, apparently in error "that you can use as well and that you can also use."
[160] Handwritten mark-up and FIP replace "love" with "God"
[161] T I B 26b (4)

[162] **John 14:18** "I will not leave you orphans; I will come to you."
[163] FIP and the Manuscript both have "Forgiveness'", or "s apostrophe" which would be correct if "forgiveness" were a plural possessive case, but it is a singular possessive case, so it should be "apostrophe s" -- *From "A Manual of Style" (12th ed., University of Chicago Press, 1969):*
[164] Ibid.
[165] FIP chances "sin" to "sins"
[166] Handwritten mark-up and FIP change this line to "and so its healing but delays its turning back"
[167] **Genesis 2:7** "And the LORD God formed man of the dust of the ground, and breathed into his nostrils the breath of life; and man became a living being."
[168] Handwritten mark-up and FIP change "go back" to "return"
[169] Handwritten mark-up and FIP change "source" to "cause"
[170] Manuscript spells this "rememberance"

reminding him the body may become his chosen home, but it will never be his home in truth.

C. False versus True Healing[171]

S 3 C 1 Distinctions therefore must be made between true healing and its faulty counterpart. The world of opposites is healing's place, for what in Heaven could there be to heal? As prayer within the world can ask amiss and seeming charity forgive to kill, so healing can be false as well as true; a witness to the power of the world or to the everlasting Love of God.

S 3 C 2 False healing merely makes a poor exchange[172] of one illusion for a "nicer" one; a dream of sickness for a dream of health. This can occur at lower forms of prayer, combining with forgiveness kindly meant but not completely understood as yet. Only false healing can give way to fear, so sickness will be apt[173] to strike again. False healing can indeed remove a form of pain and sickness. But the cause remains, and will not lack effects. The cause is still the wish to die and overcome the Christ. And with this wish is death a certainty, for prayer IS answered. Yet there is a kind of seeming death that has a different source. It does not come because of hurtful thoughts and raging anger at the universe. It merely signifies the end has come for usefulness of body functioning. And so it is discarded as a choice, as one lays[174] by a garment now outworn.

S 3 C 3 This is what death should be; a quiet choice, made joyfully and with a sense of peace, because the body has been kindly used to help the Son of God along the way he goes to God. We thank the body, then, for all the service it has given us. But we are thankful, too, the need is done to walk the world of limits, and to reach the Christ in hidden forms and clearly seen at most in lovely flashes. Now we can behold Him without blinders,[175] in the light that we **S(22)** have learned[176] to look upon again.

S 3 C 4 We call it death, but it is liberty. It does not come in forms that seem to be thrust down in pain upon unwilling flesh, but as a gentle welcome to release. If there has been true healing, this can be the form in which death comes when it is time to rest a while from labor gladly done and gladly ended. Now we go in peace to freer air and gentler climate, where it is not hard to see the gifts we gave were saved for us. For Christ is clearer now; His vision more sustained in us; His Voice, the Word of God,[177] more certainly our own.

S 3 C 5 This gentle passage to a higher prayer, a kind forgiveness of the ways of earth, can only be received with thankfulness. Yet first true healing must have come to bless the mind with loving pardon for the sins it dreamed about and laid upon the world. Now are its dreams dispelled in quiet rest. Now its forgiveness comes to heal the world and it is ready to depart in peace,[178] the journey over and the lessons learned.

S 3 C 6 This is not death according to the world, for death is cruel in its frightened eyes and takes the form of punishment for sin. How could it be a blessing, then, and how could it be welcome when it must be feared? What healing has occurred in such a view of what is merely opening the gate to higher prayer and kindly justice done? Death is reward and not a punishment. But such a viewpoint must be fostered by the healing that the world cannot conceive. There is no partial healing. What but shifts illusions has done nothing. What is false cannot be partly true. If you are healed your healing is complete. Forgiveness is the only gift you give and would receive.

S 3 C 7 False healing rests upon the body's cure, leaving the cause of illness still unchanged, ready to strike again until it brings a cruel death in seeming victory. It can be held at bay a little while, and there can be brief respite as it waits to take its vengeance on the Son of God. Yet it cannot be overcome until all faith in it has been laid by, and placed upon God's **S(23)** substitute for evil dreams; a world in which there is no veil of sin to keep it dark and comfortless. At last the gate of Heaven opens and God's Son is free to enter in the home that stands ready to welcome him, and was prepared before time was and still but[179] waits for him.

D. Separation versus Union

S 3 D 1 False healing heals the body in a part, but never as a whole. Its separate goals become quite clear in this, for it has not removed the curse of sin that lies on it. Therefore it still deceives. Nor is it made by one who understands the other is exactly like himself, for it is this that makes true healing possible. When false, there is some power that another has, not equally bestowed on both as one. Here is the separation shown. And here the meaning of true healing has been lost, and idols have arisen to obscure the unity that is the Son of God. **S(24)**

S 3 D 2 Healing-to-separate may seem to be a strange idea. Yet[180] it can be said of any form of healing that is based on inequality of any kind. These forms may heal the body, and indeed are generally limited to this. Someone knows better, has been better trained, or is perhaps more talented and wise. Therefore, he can give healing to the one who stands beneath him in his patronage. The healing of the body can be done by this because, in dreams, equality cannot be permanent. The shifts and change are what the dream is made of. To be healed appears to be to find a wiser one who, by his arts and learning, will succeed.

S 3 D 3 Someone knows better; this the magic phrase by which the body seems to be the aim of healing as the world conceives of it. And to this wiser one another goes to profit by his learning and his skill; to find in him the remedy for pain. How can that be? True healing cannot come from inequality assumed and then accepted as the truth, and used to help restore the wounded and to calm the mind that suffers from the agony of doubt.

S 3 D 4 Is there a role for healing, then, that one can use to offer help for someone else? In arrogance the answer must be "no." Yet[181] in humility there is indeed a place for helpers. It is like the role that helps in prayer, and lets forgiveness be what it is meant to be. You do not make yourself the bearer of the special gift that brings the healing. You but recognize your oneness with the one who calls for help. For in this oneness is his separate sense dispelled, and it was this that made him sick. There is no point in giving remedy apart from where the source of sickness is, for never thus can it be truly healed.

S 3 D 5 Healers there are, for they are Sons of God who recognize their Source, and understand that all their Source creates is one with them. This is the remedy that brings relief which cannot fail. It will remain to bless for all eternity. It heals no part, but wholly and

---

[171] FIP moves this section heading one paragraph forward.
[172] Manuscript initially has "substitution" which is overstruck, "poor exchange" being typed above. The latter is better IP.
[173] Handwritten mark-up and FIP change "apt" to "free"
[174] Manuscript has "lies" and handwritten mark-up and FIP correct this to "lays"
[175] **1 Corinthians 13:12** For now we see in a glass darkly, but then face to face. Now I know in part, but then I shall know just as I also am known.
[176] Original is "earned"
[177] **John. 1:1-5** "In the beginning was the Word, and the Word was with God, and the Word was God.
The same was in the beginning with God. All things were made through him; and without him was not anything made that hath been made. In him was life; and the life was the light of men. And the light shineth in the darkness; and the darkness apprehended it not.
[178] **Luke. 2:29** "Lord, now You are letting Your servant depart in peace, According to Your word;"

[179] Typewritten alternative to "but" is "must"
[180] FIP adds "And" before "Yet"
[181] FIP changes "Yet" to "But"

forever. Now the cause of every malady has been revealed exactly as it is. And in that place is written now the holy Word of **S(25)** God. Sickness and separation must be healed by love and union. Nothing else can heal as God established healing. Without Him there is no healing, for there is no love.

S 3 D 6 God's Voice alone can tell you how to heal. Listen, and you will never fail to bring His kindly remedy to those He sends to you, to let Him heal them, and to bless all those who serve with Him in healing's name. The body's healing will occur because its cause has gone. And now without a cause, it cannot come again in different form. Nor will death any more be feared because it has been understood. There is no fear in one who has been truly healed, for love has entered now where idols used to stand, and fear has given way at last to God.[182]

E. The Holiness of Healing

S 3 E 1 How holy are the healed! For in their sight their brothers share their healing and their love. Bringers of peace - the Holy Spirit's voice,[183] through whom He speaks for God, Whose Voice He is - such are God's healers. They but speak for Him and never for themselves. They have no gifts but those they have from God. And these they share because they know that this is what He wills. They are not special. They are holy. They have chosen holiness, and given up all separate dreams of special attributes through which they can bestow unequal gifts on those less fortunate. Their healing has restored their wholeness so they can forgive, and join the song of prayer in which the healed sing of their union and their thanks to God.

S 3 E 2 As witness to forgiveness, aid to prayer, and the effect of mercy truly taught, healing is blessing. And the world responds in quickened chorus through the voice of prayer. Forgiveness shines its merciful reprieve upon each blade of grass and feathered wing and all the living things upon the earth. Fear has no haven here, for love has come in all its holy oneness. Time remains only to let the last embrace of prayer rest on the earth an instant, as the world is shined away. This instant is the goal of all true healers, whom the Christ has taught to see His likeness and to teach like Him.[184]

S 3 E 3 Think what it means to help the Christ to heal! Can anything be holier **S(26)** than this? God thanks His healers, for He knows the Cause of healing is Himself, His Love, His Son, restored as His completion and returned to share with Him creation's holy joy. Do not ask partial healing, nor accept an idol for remembrance[185] of Him Whose Love has never changed and never will. You are as dear to Him as is the whole of His creation, for it is[186] in you as His eternal gift. What need have you for shifting dreams within a sorry world? Do not forget the gratitude of God. Do not forget the holy grace of prayer. Do not forget forgiveness of God's Son.

S 3 E 4 You first forgive, then pray, and you are healed. Your prayer has risen up and called to God, Who hears and answers. You have understood that you forgive yourself and pray for you[187] and[188] in this understanding you are healed. In prayer you have united with your Source, and understood that you have never left. This level cannot be attained until there is no hatred in your heart, and no desire to attack the Son of God. Never forget this; it is you who are God's Son, and as you choose to be to him so are you to yourself, and God to you.[189]

S 3 E 5 Nor will your judgment fail to reach to God, for you will give the role to Him you see in His creation. Thus have you become "creator"[190] in His place, and He becomes[191] no longer Cause but only an effect. Now healing is impossible, for on Him lies the blame[192] for your deception and your guilt. He Who is Love is now[193] the source of fear, and[194] only fear can now be justified. Vengeance is His.[195] His great destroyer, death. And sickness, suffering and grievous loss become the lot of everyone on earth, which He abandoned to the devil's care, swearing He will deliver it no more.

S 3 E 6 Come unto Me, My children, once again, without such twisted thoughts upon your heart.[196] You still are holy with the Holiness which fathered you in perfect sinlessness, and still surrounds you in[197] the arms of peace. Dream now of healing. Then arise and lay all dreaming down forever. You are he your **S(27)** Father loves, who never left his home, nor wandered in a savage world with feet that bleed, and with a heavy heart made hard against the Love that is the truth in you. Give all your dreams to Christ and let Him be your Guide to healing, leading you in prayer beyond the sorry reaches of the world.

S 3 E 7 He comes for Me and speaks My Word to you. I would recall My weary Son to Me from dreams of malice to the sweet embrace of everlasting Love and perfect peace. My arms[198] are open to the Son I love, who does not understand that he is healed, and that his prayer has[199] never ceased to sing his joyful thanks in unison with all creation, in the holiness of God.[200] Be still an instant.[201] Underneath the sounds of harsh and bitter striving and defeat there is a Voice that speaks to you of Me. Hear this an instant and you will be healed. Hear this an instant and you have been saved.

S 3 E 8 Help Me to wake My children from the dream of retribution and a little life beset with fear, that ends so soon it might as well have never been. Let Me instead remind you of eternity, in which your joy grows greater as your love extends along with Mine beyond infinity, where time and distance have no meaning. While you wait in sorrow Heaven's melody is incomplete, because your song is part of the eternal harmony of love. Without you is creation incomplete.[202] Return to Me Who never left His[203] Son.

S 3 E 9 Listen, My child, Your Father calls to you. Do not refuse to hear the call of[204] Love. Do not deny to Christ what is His Own.

---

[182] **1 John 4:18** "There is no fear in love; but perfect love casts out fear, because fear involves torment. But he who fears has not been made perfect in love."
[183] Manuscript has this in lower case.
[184] **Genesis 1:26** "And God said, Let us make man in our image, after our likeness: and let them have dominion over the fish of the sea, and over the birds of the heavens, and over the cattle, and over all the earth, and over every creeping thing that creepeth upon the earth. And God created man in his own image, in the image of God created he him; male and female created he them."
[185] Manuscript has "rememberance"
[186] Handwritten mark-up and FIP replace "is" with "lies"
[187] Handwritten mark-up and FIP replace "pray for you" with "pray but for yourself."
[188] FIP starts a new sentence here.

[189] **Matthew 25:40** "And the King will answer and say to them, 'Assuredly, I say to you, inasmuch as you did it to one of the least of these My brethren, you did it to Me.'"
[190] Handwritten mark-up and FIP replace "Thus have you become" with "Do not choose amiss or you will think that it is you who are"
[191] Handwritten mark-up and FIP replace "becomes" with "is then"
[192] Handwritten mark-up and FIP replace "on Him lies the blame" with "He is blamed"
[193] Handwritten mark-up and FIP replace "is now" with "becomes"
[194] Handwritten mark-up and FIP replace "and" with "for"
[195] **Romans 12:19** "Beloved, do not avenge yourselves, but rather give place to wrath; for it is written, "Vengeance is Mine, I will repay," says the Lord."
[196] Manuscript has "heart" singular, FIP changes this to plural "hearts"
[197] FIP replaces "in" with "with"
[198] FIP capitalizes "Arms"
[199] FIP changes this to "prayers have"
[200] FIP changes "God" to "Love"
[201] **Psalm 46:10** "Be still, and know that I am God; I will be exalted among the nations, I will be exalted in the earth!"
[202] Handwritten mark-up and FIP replace "incomplete" with "unfulfilled"
[203] FIP changes "His" to "My"
[204] FIP has "for" instead of "of"

Heaven is here and Heaven is your home. Creation leans across the bars of time to lift the heavy burden from the world. Lift up your hearts to greet its advent. See the shadows fade away in gentleness; the thorns fall softly from the bleeding brow of him who is the holy Son of God.[205] How lovely are you, Child of Holiness! How like to Me! How lovingly I hold you in My heart and in My arms. How dear is every gift that you have given Me,[206] who healed My Son and took him from the cross.

S 3 E 10 Arise and let My thanks be given you. And with My gratitude will come the gift first of forgiveness, then eternal peace. So now return your holy **S(28)** voice to Me. The song of prayer is silent without you. The universe is waiting your release because it is its own. Be kind to it and to yourself, and then be kind to Me. I ask but this; that you be comforted and live no more in terror and in pain. Do not abandon Love. Remember this; whatever you may think about yourself, whatever you may think about the world, your Father needs you and will call[207] to you until you come to Him in peace at last.

---

[205] **Matthew 27:29** "When they had twisted a crown of thorns, they put it on His head, and a reed in His right hand. And they bowed the knee before Him and mocked Him, saying, 'Hail, King of the Jews!'"
[206] Handwritten mark-up and FIP change "that you have given Me" to "to Me that you have made,"

[207] **Matthew 22:14** "For many are called, but few chosen."

Urtext Volume VII: *Gifts of God*

Urtext Volume VII - *Gifts of God*

Table of Contents

1. THE DREAM OF FEAR 1
2. THE TWO GIFTS 3
3. THE ENDING OF THE DREAM 4
4. OUR GIFT TO GOD 6
5. THE FATHER'S LOVE 8

Urtext Volume VII - *Gifts of God*

1. THE DREAM OF FEAR

G 1 A 1. Fear[1] is the emotion of the world.[2] It has but one.[3] Its forms are many – call them what you will – but it is one in content. Never far, even in form, from what its purpose is, never with power to escape its cause, and never but a counterfeit of peace,[4] it rests uncertainly upon a bed of lies. Here it was born and sheltered by its seeming comfort. Here it remains where it was born, and where its end will come.[5] For here is nothingness, where neither birth nor death is real, nor any form in the misshapen mind that spawned it has any meaning in the Mind of God.[6]

G 1 A 2. If you were certain – wholly sure and with consistent grasp of what the world can give – fear would be laid aside as easily as joy and peace unite on love's behalf. But first there must be certainty that there can be no love where fear exists, and that the world will never give a gift that[7] is not made of fear, concealed perhaps, but which is[8] surely present somewhere in the gift. Accept it not, and you will understand a gift far greater has been given you.

G 1 A 3. Let not the world deceive you. It was made to be deception. Yet its snares can be so easily escaped a little child can walk through safely, and without a care that would arrest its progress. Dreams are dreams, and every one is equally untrue. This is the only lesson to be learned. Yet will fear linger until every one is recognized as nothingness, and seen exactly as it is and nothing more. There is no person, thing, or circumstance that you can value as your own without the "gift" of fear arising in your heart. For you have seen them all as they are not, and love for them has fled as if from you. And you will think that God has ceased to care for you who have betrayed the Son He loves, and chosen fear and guilt to be their friends.[9]

G 1 A 4. Does God deceive or does the world? For it is sure that one must lie. There is no point at which their thoughts agree, their gifts unite in kind or purpose.[10] What you take from one the other will obscure. There is no hope of compromise **G(2)** in this. Nor can there be a shifting of the mind between the two without the fear that every dream must bring. How fearful it must be to see yourself as maker of reality and truth, the lord of destiny and time's domain, and arbiter appointed for the world.[11]

G 1 A 5. Dreams never change. Remember only this, but do not let it slip away at times and let yourself give way to fear again. Deny the dream but do not fail the truth, for[12] what is true alone[13] will never fail. All else deceives,[14] all else will terrify, and even when it seems to please the most it brings with it a heavy cost of pain. Be free of suffering now. There is no cost for any gift that comes to you from God. His way is certain, for His gifts remain forever as He gave them. Do not think that fear can enter where His gifts abide. But do not think His gifts can be received where fear has entered[15] and has touched your sight with gross distortions that the world thinks real.

G 1 A 6. There are no scraps of dreams. Each one contains the whole of fear, the opposite of love, (in all its ways),[16] the hell that hides the memory of God, the crucifixion of His holy Son. Therefore, be vigilant against them all, for in their single purpose they are one, and hell is total. It can seem to be[17] forever for this lesson to be learned, and yet it need not be. I came to speak in time of timelessness. Have you not learned the pain of dreaming yet? There is no need to hug it to your heart, and to forget the dreadful cost of salvaging despair and building up deceptions once again.

G 1 A 7. The tiniest of dreams, the smallest wish for values of the world is large enough to stand between you and the sweet release that God would offer you. He cannot choose to change His Son, nor make your mind accept the perfect freedom He has given you. Yet it is certain you will turn to Him and suddenly remember. But be sure of this and do not let it slip away:[18]

> What God has joined is one. And one as well is everything that fear has made to be the great deceiver and the substitute for God's **G(3)** creation. You can choose but one, and which you choose is total. Everything the world can offer promises some joy that it will never give. And everything that God has promised you will never fail in anything. No need will be unmet, no hurt unhealed, no sorrow kept unchanged, no darkness undispelled. The smallest pain will vanish suddenly before His gifts.[19]

---

[1] February 8, 1978
[2] The *Urtext* manuscript has the word "one" handwritten in to make the sentence "Fear is the one emotion of the world."
[3] This sentence is crossed out.
[4] The *Urtext* manuscript has "peace" crossed out and "joy" handwritten in.
[5] Handwritten mark-up suggests "here it will remain" in place of "here it remains."
[6] Handwritten mark-up suggests "spawned its seeming life" in place of "spawned it"
[7] Handwritten mark-up suggests "which" in place of "that."
[8] The words "which is" are handwritten in between the lines.
[9] It would appear that "their" in "their friends" is first crossed out and replaces with "your." Then the whole phrase is crossed out and "to be your friends" becomes "in place of him."
[10] **Luke 16:13** No servant can serve two masters: for either he will hate the one, and love the other; or else he will hold to one, and despise the other. Ye cannot serve God and mammon.
[11] the word "ruler" is typed in brackets between "lord" and "of" and then crossed out.
[12] Handwritten mark-up suggests changing "for what is true" to "for only what is true" between the lines
[13] Handwritten mark-up crosses out "alone" apparently in conjunction with adding "only" as above.
[14] Handwritten mark-up puts a sentence break here.
[15] Handwritten mark-up inserts a comma here
[16] the bracketed words "in all its ways" are crossed out.
[17] the word "be" is crossed out and "take" is handwritten in between the lines.
[18] Handwritten mark-up indicates "no indent" here and adjusts paragraph breaks in this segment
[19] Handwritten mark-up indicates "no intent" and makes this all a continuous paragraph.
Isaiah 25:8 He hath swallowed up death for ever; and the Lord GOD will wipe away tears from off all faces; and the reproach of his people shall he take away from off all the earth: for the LORD hath spoken it.

Volume VII - Gifts of God

G 1 A 8. An unremembered world will leave no trace behind its going, when God's gifts have been accepted as the only thing[20] you want.[21] "Choose once again"[22] is still your only hope. Darkness cannot conceal the gifts of God unless you want it so. In peace I come, and urge you now to make an end to time and step into eternity with me. There will not be a change that eyes can see, nor will you disappear from things of time. But you will hold my hand as you return because we come together. Now the hosts of Heaven come with us, to sweep away all vestiges of dreams and every thought that rests on nothingness.

G 1 A 9. How dear are you to God, Who asks but that you walk with me and bring His light into a sickened world which fear has drained of love and life and hope.[23] Surely you will not fail to hear my call,[24] for I have never failed to hear your cries of pain and grief,[25] and I have come to save and to redeem the world at last from fear. It never was, nor is, nor yet will be what you imagine. Let me see for you, and judge for you what you would look upon. When you have seen with me but once, you would no longer value any fearful thing at cost of glory and the peace of God.

G 1 A 10. This is my offering: A quiet world, with gentle ordering and kindly thoughts, alive with hope and radiant in joy, without the smallest bitterness of fear upon its loveliness. Accept this now, for I have waited long to give this gift to you. I offer it in place of fear and all the "gifts" of fear.[26] Can you choose otherwise, when all the world is standing breathless, waiting on your choice? Come now to me and we will go to God. There is no way that we can go alone. But when we come together there can be no way in which the Word of God can fail. For His the Word that makes us one in Him, and mine the Voice that speaks this Word to you. **G(4)**[27]

---

[20] Handwritten mark-up makes "thing" into "things"
[21] Handwritten mark-up suggests paragraph break at this point.
[22] **T 31H 1** Temptation has ONE lesson it would teach, in ALL its forms, WHEREVER it occurs. It would persuade the holy Son of God he is a body, born in what must die, unable to escape its frailty, and bound by what it orders him to feel. It sets the limits on what he can do; its power is the only strength he has; his grasp cannot exceed its tiny reach. Would you BE this, if Christ appeared to you in all His glory, asking you but this, "**Choose once again** if you would take your place among the Saviors of the world, or would remain in hell, and hold your brothers there." For He HAS come, and He IS asking this.
T 31H 6 You ARE as God created you, and so is every living thing you look upon, REGARDLESS of the images you see. What you behold as sickness and as pain, as weakness and as suffering and loss, is but temptation to perceive YOURSELF defenseless and in hell. Yield NOT to this, and you will see ALL pain in EVERY form WHEREVER it occurs but disappear as mists before the sun. A miracle has come to heal God's Son, and close the door upon his dreams of weakness, opening the way to his salvation and release. **Choose once again** what you would have him be, remembering that every choice you make establishes your own identity as you will see it, and believe it IS.
[23] Handwritten mark-up suggests moving the paragraph break here.
[24] As originally typed there is a full sentence break here, which handwritten mark-up changes to a comma. This appears to be a correction since a full stop is not required here.
[25] typed in brackets and then crossed out is "(agony)."

[26] Handwritten mark-up crosses out "of fear" and inserts "that fear has given you."
[27] 2/9/78

2. THE TWO GIFTS

G 2 A 1. How[28] can you be delivered from all gifts the world has offered you? How can you change these little, cruel offerings for those that Heaven gives and God would have you keep? Open your hands, and give all things to me that you have held against your holiness and kept as slander on the Son of God. Practice with every one you recognize as what it is. Give me these worthless things the instant that you see them through my eyes[29] and understand their cost. Then give away these bitter dreams as you perceive them now to be but that, and nothing more than that.

G 2 A 2. I take them from you gladly, laying them beside the gifts of God that He has placed upon the altar to His Son. And these I give to you to take the place of those you gave away[30] in mercy on yourself. These are the gifts I ask, and only these. For as you lay them by you reach to me, and I can come as savior then to you. The gifts of God are in my hands, to give to anyone who would exchange the world for Heaven.[31] You need only call my Name,[32] and ask me to accept the gift of pain from willing hands that would be laid in mine,[33] with thorns laid down and nails long thrown away as one by one the sorry gifts of earth are joyously relinquished. In my hands is everything you want and need and hoped to find among the shabby toys of earth. I take them all from you and they are gone. And shining in the place where once they stood there is a gateway to another world through which we enter in the Name of God.

G 2 A 3. Father we thank You for these gifts that we have found together. Here we are redeemed. For it is here we joined, and from this place of holy joining we will come to You because we recognize the gifts You gave and would have nothing else. Each hand that finds its way to mine will take[34] Your gifts from me, and as we look together on the place whereon I laid your worthless gifts for you, we will see nothing but the gifts of God reflected in the shining round our heads.[35] Holy are we who know our holiness, for it is You Who shine Your light on us, and we are thankful, in our Father's **G(5)** Name,[36] that You have not forgotten. What we thought we made of You has merely disappeared, and with its going are the images we made of Your creation gone as well. And it is finished.[37] Now into Your Hands we give again the spirit[38] of Your Son who seemed to lose his way a little while but never left the safety of Your love. The gifts of fear, the dream of death, are done.[39] And we give thanks. And we give thanks, Amen. **G(6)**[40]

---

[28] 2/9/78 (February 9, 1978)
[29] Typed in brackets and then crossed out is "(sight)."
[30] The words "gave away" are crossed out and "give to me" is handwritten in.
[31] **T 11 D 9**. Long ago we said that God so loved the world that He gave it to His only-begotten Son. (that whosoever believeth on him should never see death). God DOES love the real world, and those who perceive its reality cannot see the world of death. For death is not of the real world, in which everything is eternal. God gave you the real world in exchange for the one you made, out of your split mind, and which IS the symbol of death. For if you could REALLY separate yourselves from the Mind of God, you WOULD die. And the world you perceive IS a world of separation.
T 11 I 9. The real world was given you by God, in loving exchange for the world YOU made, and which you see. But take it from the hand of Christ, and look upon it. Its reality will make everything else invisible, for beholding it is TOTAL perception. And as you look upon it, you will remember that it was always so. Nothingness will become invisible, for you will at last have seen truly. Redeemed perception is easily translated into knowledge, for ONLY perception is capable of error. And perception has never been. Being corrected, it gives place to knowledge, which is forever the ONLY reality. The Atonement is but the way back to what was never lost. Your Father could not cease to love His Son.
[32] typed with a capital "N" that is struck through indicating lower case
[33] The theme of holding hands is frequently used in the *Text* as a metaphor for loving relationship between humans, and between man and God. In particular Jesus and the Holy Spirit are characterized as leading us by the hand. Here are a few examples:
T 8 E 23 I DO go before you, because I AM beyond the ego. Reach therefore for my hand because you WANT to transcend the ego. My will, will NEVER be wanting, and if you want to share it YOU WILL. I give it willingly and gladly, because I need YOU as much as you need ME.
T 17 F 10. In your newness, remember that you have started again, TOGETHER. And take each other's hand, to walk together along a road far more familiar than you now believe. Is it not certain, that you will remember a goal unchanged throughout eternity? For you have chosen but the goal of God, from which your true intent was NEVER absent. Throughout the Sonship is the song of freedom heard, in joyous echo of your choice. You have joined with many, in the holy instant, and THEY have joined with you. Think not your choice will leave YOU comfortless. For God Himself has blessed your special relationship. JOIN in His blessing, and withhold not yours upon it. For all it needs now IS your blessing, that you may see that in it rests salvation.
T 18 D 4. You who hold each other's hand also hold mine, for when you joined each other you were not alone. Do you believe that I would leave you in the darkness you agreed to leave with ME? In your relationship is this world's light. And fear MUST disappear before you now. **T 18 D 5** Be tempted not to snatch away the gift of faith you offered to each other. You will succeed only in frightening yourselves. The gift is given forever, for God Himself received it. You CANNOT take it back. YOU HAVE ACCEPTED GOD. The holiness of your relationship is established in Heaven. You do not understand what you accepted, but remember that your understanding is not necessary. All that was necessary was merely the WISH to understand. That wish was the desire to be holy. The will of God is granted you. For you desire the only thing you ever had, or ever were.
T 24 C 7 [...] Here stands your brother with the key to Heaven in his hand, held out to you. Let not the dream of specialness remain between you. What is one IS joined in truth.
T 31 H 10 Salvation's song will echo through the world with every choice they make. For we are one in purpose, and the end of hell is near. In joyous welcome is my hand outstretched to every brother who would join with me in reaching past temptation, and who looks with fixed determination toward the light that shines beyond in perfect constancy.
[34] Several illegible words are typed and crossed out
[35] Handwritten mark-up suggests paragraph break here.
Acts 26:13 at midday, O king, I saw on the way a light from heaven, above the brightness of the sun, shining round about me and them that journeyed with me.
[36] Handwritten mark-up crosses out "our Father's Name" and then is typed "Your ancient Name."
[37] **John 19:30** "When Jesus therefore had received the vinegar, he said, It is finished: and he bowed his head, and gave up his spirit."
[38] Handwritten mark-up revises this phrase to "For we now commend into Your Hands the spirit" after, apparently first changing "give again" to "offer up" then crossing that out.
Psalm 31:5 Into thine hand I commend my spirit: thou hast redeemed me, O LORD, thou God of truth.
Luke 23:46 And Jesus, crying with a loud voice, said, "Father, into thy hands I commend my spirit:" and having said this, he gave up the ghost.
[39] This sentence is typed between the lines and handwritten mark-up points it to this location.
[40] February 11, 1978

3. THE ENDING OF THE DREAM

G 3 A 1. Illusions[41] are made as substitutes for truth, for which no substitutes are possible. Creator separate from creation was the first illusion, where all gifts of fear were born. For now creation could not be like its Creator, Who could never leave what He Himself created part of Him. Now must there be a substitute for love, which cannot have an opposite in truth and, being all, can have no substitute.[42] So fear was made, and with it came the need for gifts to lend the substance to the[43] dream in which there is no substance. Now the dream seems to have value, for its offerings appear as hope and strength and even love, if only for an instant. They content the frightened dreamer for a little while, and let him not remember the first dream which gifts of fear but offer him again.[44]

G 3 A 2. The seeming solace of illusions' gifts are now his armor, and the sword he holds to save himself from waking. For before he could awaken, he would first be forced to call to mind the first dream once again.[45] It is not God Who asks a price of him, but having drawn a veil across the truth, he now must let the veil be drawn away so that its lack of substance can be seen. No one would hesitate to leave[46] a dream of shock and terror, merciless decay and sickening contortions,[47] with despair always in sight and death not far behind, if he believed that it <u>was</u>[48] but a dream. Yet if he thinks that he must first go through a greater terror still, he must see hope in what will now appear the "better" dream.

G 3 A 3. And now he seeks within his dream to find what gifts it may contain. What can you get within its shadows? Who can save you now by giving you the love you threw away? What can you learn to do to make yourself a master over others? What is there that is your special gift within the dream? Find these and do not waken from the dream, for it can give you what you think you lack. And[49] if you waken all its gifts will go, your armor and your sword will disappear, and vultures, always circling overhead, will claim you as their lawful prey at last. **G(7)**

G 3 A 4. Oh children of the Father you forgot, you have not put your idols in His place, nor made Him give the gifts of fear you made. Let me be Savior from illusions. Truth may be concealed from you by evil dreams, but it is only from the dreams that you have need of[50] saving. Truth is still untouched by your deceptions. But[51] you cannot go past that first dream without a Savior's[52] hand in yours. Each gift of fear would hold you back unless you let me lift it from your mind by showing you that it is but a dream within a larger dream of hopelessness in which there <u>is</u> no hope. Take not its gifts, for they condemn you to a lasting hell which will endure when all the seeming joy the gifts appeared to give has[53] passed away.

G 3 A 5. Do not be tempted. Do not fall away into the shadows, and a deeper sleep in which the waking seems to be the dream. Help me give you salvation. Let us share the strength of Christ, and look upon the dream in which illusions started, and which serves[54] to keep their birthplace secret and apart from the illumination of the truth. Come unto me. There is no need to dream of an escape from dreaming. It will fail. For if the dream were real, escape would be impossible, and there would be no hope <u>except</u> illusions. Do not yield to this. It is not so. For I am not a dream that comes in mockery. Salvation needs your help as well as mine. Do not forget you do not answer for yourself alone.

G 3 A 6. My call to you is that you offer help from all the dreams the holy Son of God imagines, from the time that first of dreams was given false reality until all dreaming ends forever. Could a gift be holier than this? And could the need within a world of dreams be more acute or more compelling? Give me help in this, and not one gift the world may seek to give, or[55] one illusion held against the truth, can bind you longer. Time can have no sway upon you, nor can any laws of earth have power over you. Your hands[56] will heal, and give the gifts that you accept of me.

G 3 A 7. How joyful and how holy is our way when death has no dominion, and the **G(8)** dream of separation, agony and loss has been dispelled forever. Do not think that anything the gifts of fear hold out is worth an instant's hesitation, when the gate of Heaven stands before you and the Christ of God is waiting your return. Be still and hear Him, for His call to you could not be more insistent nor more dear, for it is but the call of Love Itself, Which[57] will not cease to speak of God to you. You have forgot,[58] but[59] He is faithful still, because He is so like His Father He remembers Him forever in His Love. And He cannot forget creation is inseparable from Creator, so He understands that you are part of God and of the Son created like Himself.

G 3 A 8. How dear are you to Him, a part in which is every gift of God forever laid, without whom is Christ incomplete, Who[60] is completion of His Father. Can a dream destroy a truth so holy and so pure that it encompasses all truth, and leaves nothing beyond Itself?[61] Can you betray a love so perfect that its gifts become Itself[62] in oneness, and this single gift is all there is to give and to

---

[41] February 11, 1978
[42] Handwritten mark-up appears to change full stop to an em dash.
[43] the word "the" is crossed out and "a" handwritten in.
[44] Handwritten mark-up indicates removal of paragraph break.
[45] Handwritten mark-up suggests paragraph break here.
[46] the word "let" is crossed out and "leave" handwritten in. Since "let" makes little sense here, we're calling this a correction.
[47] Typed and then crossed out is "(~~convulsions, corruptions~~)."
[48] Handwritten mark-up crosses out "was" and inserts "<u>were</u>".
[49] The word "And" is crossed out and "But" handwritten in.
[50] The manuscript has "from" but it appears to be a typo, since "of" is grammatically much better.
[51] Handwritten mark-up replaces the period with a comma, and "But" with "yet."
[52] Initially typed with lower case, the capital "S" is handwritten in.
[53] The manuscript has "have" but this leads to an agreement in number problem. It must be "has" or the word "joy" must be "joys."
[54] The manuscript has "serve" but this leads to an agreement in number problem. It must be "serves" or the preceding instance of "dream" must be "dreams."
[55] Handwritten mark-up crosses out "or" and writes in "nor."
[56] **T 1 A 1** "You will see miracles through your hands through Me."
[57] Handwritten mark-up strikes the capitals from two words making it "Love itself, which."
[58] Perhaps this should be "forgotten."
[59] Handwritten mark-up replaces the comma with a period and starts a new sentence "But he is …"
[60] This sentence is massively marked up with a footnote offering the following modified reading: "How dear are you, a part of Christ, in Whom is every gift of God forever laid, without which is He incomplete, Who…"
[61] Handwritten mark-up strikes the capital.
[62] Handwritten mark-up strikes the capital.

receive? Oh come and let creation be again all that it always was and still will be forever and forever.[63] Let the dream of time be given its appointed end,[64] and let God's Son have mercy on himself.

G 3 A 9. There is a silence covering the world that was an ancient dream so long ago no one remembers now. Its time is done, and in the little space it seemed to have[65] is nothingness. The dream has gone, and all its dreams of gifts have disappeared as well. The first dream has been seen and understood for merely an illusion of the fear on which the world was based. Behind[66] the dream, reaching to everything, embracing all, creation and Creator still remain in perfect harmony and perfect love.[67]

G 3 A 10. This is beyond the gate at which we stand. And shall we stay to wait upon a dream? Your holiness is mine, and mine is His.[68] Here is His gift, complete and undefiled. It is Himself He gives, and it is this that is the truth in you. **G(9)** How beautiful are you who stand beside me at the gate, and call with me that everyone may come and step aside from time. Put out your hand to touch eternity and disappear into its perfect rest. Here is the peace that God intended for the Child[69] He loves. Enter with me and let its quietness cover the earth forever. It is done. Father, your Voice has called us home at last: gone is the dream. Awake, My Child,[70] in love. **G(10)**

---

[63] **Psalm 148:6** He hath also established them for ever and ever: he hath made a decree which shall not pass away.
Isaiah 30:8 Now go, write it before them on a tablet, and inscribe it in a book, that it may be for the time to come for ever and ever.
[64] **T 1 B 13.** A miracle is a beginning and an ending. It thus abolishes time. It is always an affirmation of re-birth, which seems to go back, but really goes forward. It undoes the past in the present, and thus releases the future.
T 1 B 15. Each day should be devoted to miracles. God created time so that man could use it creatively, and convince himself of his own ability to create. Time is a teaching device, and a means to an end. It will cease when it is no longer useful for facilitating learning.
[65] Handwritten mark-up crosses out "have" and the brackets around the originally typed "(own)."
[66] Handwritten mark-up crosses out "Behind" and the brackets around the originally typed "(Beyond)."
[67] Handwritten mark-up shifts paragraph break two sentences later.
[68] Handwritten mark-up crosses out "His" and replaces it with "God's."
[69] Handwritten mark-up crosses out "Child" and the brackets around the originally typed "(Son)."
[70] Handwritten mark-up strikes the capital.

4. OUR GIFT TO GOD

G 4 A 1. There[71] is no gift of faith that God does not accept with gratitude. He loves His Son. And as He gives His gifts to him, so is He grateful for the gifts His Son gives Him. Gratitude is the song of Heaven,[72] the single harmony of[73] all creation at one with its Creator. For gratitude is love expressed in joining; the necessary condition[74] for extension and the prerequisite for peace. And who can be in conflict and love God?

G 4 A 2. We have discussed the gifts of God to you. Now we must also speak of those that you can give to Him. For it is[75] these that render[76] His giving, complete,[77] as it is His to you that make you whole. Giving is joy and holiness and healing. Here is your answer to the world, and God's as well. For here it is you join with Him, His likeness being yours in this alone.[78]

G 4 A 3. How can you give to Him Who has no lack, no need, no emptiness,[79] no unlit place which needs a light that you can offer Him? He saves your gifts for you. He does not know of giving and receiving. What is love, or comes from love, or offers love a gift, is one to Him because it is of Him. To Him and from Him are not different to One Who has no opposite. For love is all there is and everything there is. A gift to love is given everyone, not lessening the giver, nor in truth adding to the receiver. More than love there cannot be. But this a gift becomes if it is truly given and received by both to both who know that they are one:

> a key to silence and the peace of God,
> a glad acknowledgement of love of Christ,
> a greeting to the Holy Spirit's help,
> an invitation that He enter in
> and lift the Son of God unto Himself.[80]

G 4 A 4. What more would God hold dearer,[81] than this? These are His gifts as **G(11)** much as they are yours, for in them giver and receiver join. A gift is holy only when there is no sense of[82] all of who will gain thereby, and not a shadow of a thought of loss. It is not easy in the world to know what giving means, and how to give a gift that God and all creation will accept as shining outward from a thankful heart and inward to the altar of its God.

G 4 A 5. God gives the[83] grace to give as He must give, for He must give the only way He knows, and what He knows is everything He is. Christ gives as He does, being like Himself. And nothing stands outside the gifts They give, for every gift is all-encompassing and lifts the universe into Their arms.[84]

G 4 A 6. Yet what of you[85] who seem to be on earth, and do not understand what giving is because you have forgotten what love means? What gifts are there that you can give to God? My brother, there are many calls to you from those who lost their way and need your help in finding it again. It seems to you that you are helping them if you respond to what they ask and what you think they need. Yet it is always God Who calls to you, and he who[86] asks your help is but yourself. Who is the giver and the[87] receiver then? Who asks the gift and who is given it?

G 4 A 7. This is the only lesson that the world must teach in giving. It is not the one the world was made to teach. And yet it is the one the Holy Spirit sees in it, and so it is the only one it has. Forget the other devastating ways the gifts of earth are given and received. Forget the cost, the thoughts of loss and gain, the bargaining, the counting of the score, the world associates with every gift it gives in strict accordance with its laws. The money-changers of the marketplace have been your teachers.[88] Now they need a gift they could not give. Be savior now to them because you have another Teacher now.[89]

G 4 A 8. Count not the cost of giving. There is none. Your teachers have deceived. **G(12)** But do not think that their mistakes were not your own as well. To all who do not understand the gifts of God and Christ are one, be yours the voice that echoes what the Voice for God would say:

> *"Save Me, My brother, as you save yourself,*
> *And let <u>Me</u> give to God your gifts for you*
> *Because My[90] altar waits for them in love,*
> *And God[91] is asking that <u>We</u> place them there."*

There is no love but God's; no gifts but His. We but return his Own unto Himself. But as we do, He comes to call His Son from the far country where he threw away the memory[92] of all his Father's gifts, and ask him to return again to Him.

G 4 A 9. Child of Eternal Love, what gift is there your Father wants of you except yourself? And what is there that you would rather give, for what is there that you would rather have? You have forgotten Who you really are. What but that memory is dear to you? What trifling gifts made out of sickly fear[93] and evil dreams of suffering and death can be the substitute you really want for the remembrance of Christ in you? In the far country you were lost indeed, but you were not forgotten. Hear the call of love to love, by

---

[71] March ~~18~~ 5 (ca.) 1978
[72] Handwritten mark-up strikes "Heaven" and writes in "Heaven's gift."
[73] Handwritten mark-up strikes "of" and writes in "that is sung by."
[74] Handwritten mark-up changes "condition" to "precondition."
[75] Handwritten mark-up strikes out "it is."
[76] Handwritten mark-up strikes out "that render" and writes in "complete."
[77] Handwritten mark-up strikes out "complete."
[78] (March 18 1978)
[79] Handwritten mark-up suggests switching the phrases to make it "no emptiness, no need."
[80] Handwritten mark-up suggests (no indent) for this segment.
[81] Handwritten mark-up suggests "then,"
[82] Handwritten mark-up strikes "of" and writes in "at."
[83] The words "~~gift of~~" are struck out in the original manuscript.
[84] Handwritten mark-up capitalizes "Arms."
[85] Originally "us" is typed in brackets here and then crossed out.
[86] The words "he who" were capitalized originally and then corrected to lower case in handwritten mark-up.
[87] Handwritten mark-up strikes out "the."
[88] **Matthew 21:12** And Jesus entered into the temple of God, and cast out all them that sold and bought in the temple, and overthrew the tables of the money–changers, and the seats of them that sold the doves;
[89] **Matthew 23:8** "But be not ye called Rabbi: for one is your teacher, and all ye are brethren."
[90] Handwritten mark-up crosses out "My" and strikes the brackets from the originally typed "His."
[91] Handwritten mark-up strikes out "God" and writes in "He."
[92] The words "the memory" are typed between the lines, apparently the correction of an inadvertent omission.
[93] Handwritten mark-up crosses out originally typed "(~~sick despair~~)."

love, in love to you, and rise with love beside you to return[94] the gift of love that He[95] has given you, and you have given Him in gratitude.

G 4 A 10. Do not forget the Source of what you are, and do not think He has forgotten you. Love does not waver,[96] and does not forget the gifts[97] it gives that it would have you keep. Return them, then, for it is

dark indeed in the far country, where God's memory has seemed to disappear. Yet Christ has come wherever you have gone. For you are His, and being His you are His Father's too. He brings with Him the gifts His Father gave, and giving them to you He teaches you how to return them in the way He gives. Light knows no limit; love no lessening. Return, My Child,[98] to Me. For Christ is He Who is My Son and you are one with Him. You are My gift, for you are one with Me.[99] **G(13)**

---

[94] Handwritten mark-up crosses out originally typed "(to God)."
[95] Handwritten mark-up strikes "He" and writes in "God."
[96] **1 Corinthians 13:4-8** Love suffereth long, *and* is kind; love envieth not; love vaunteth not itself, is not puffed up, doth not behave itself unseemly, seeketh not its own, is not provoked, taketh not account of evil; rejoiceth not in unrighteousness, but rejoiceth with the truth; beareth all things, believeth all things, hopeth all things, endureth all things. Love never faileth: but whether *there be* prophecies, they shall be done away; whether *there be* tongues, they shall cease; whether *there be* knowledge, it shall be done away. For we know in part, and we prophesy in part: but when that which is perfect is come, that which is in part shall be done away.
[97] Handwritten mark-up strikes the "s" on "gifts" which leads to an agreement in number problem since the word "them" in the next sentence appears to refer back to these "gifts."

[98] Handwritten mark-up strikes the capital.
[99] **John 17:22** "And the glory which thou hast given me I have given unto them; that they may be one, even as we *are* one;"

5. THE FATHER'S LOVE

G 5 A 1. There[100] is a secret place in everyone in which God's gifts are laid, and his to Him. It is not secret to the eyes of Christ Who sees it plainly and unceasingly. Yet it is hidden to the body's eyes, and to those still invested in the world and caring for the petty gifts it gives, esteeming them and thinking they are real. Illusions' gifts will hide the secret place where God is clear as day, and Christ with Him. Oh let this not be secret to the world so full of sorrow and so racked with pain. You could relieve its grief and heal its pain, and let the peace of God envelop it as does a mother rock a tired child until it sighs and slips away to rest.

G 5 A 2. Rest could be yours because of what God is. He loves you as a mother loves her child; her only one, the only love she has, her all-in-all, extension of herself, as much a part of her as breath itself. He loves you as a brother loves his own, born of one father, still as one in him, and bonded with a seal that cannot break. He loves you as a lover loves his own; his chosen one, his joy, his very life, the one he seeks when she has gone away, and brings him peace again on her return. He loves you as a father loves his son, without whom would his self be incomplete, whose immortality completes his own, for in him is the chain of love complete – a golden circle that will never end, a song that will be sung throughout all time and afterwards, and always will remain the deathless sound of loving and of love.

G 5 A 3. Oh be at peace, beloved of the Lord! What is your life but gratitude to Him Who loves you with an everlasting Love? What is your purpose here but to recall into His loving arms[101] the son He loves, who has forgotten Who his Father is? What is your only goal, your only hope, your only need, the only thing you want, but to allow the secret place of peace to burst upon the world in all its joy, and let the Voice within it speak of Him whose love shines out and in and in between, through all the darkened places to embrace all living things within its golden peace? **G(14)**[102]

G 5 A 4. You are My Son, and I do not forget the secret place in which I still abide, knowing you will remember. Come, My Son, open your heart and let Me shine on you, and on the world through you. You are My light and dwelling-place. You speak for Me to those who have forgotten. Call them now to Me, My Son, remember now for all the world. I call in love, as you will answer Me, for this the only language that we know. Remember love, so near you cannot fail to touch its heart because it beats in you. Do not forget. Do not forget, My Child. Open the door before the hidden place, and let Me blaze upon a world made glad in sudden ecstasy. I come, I come. Behold Me. I am here for I am you;[103] in Christ, for Christ, My Own beloved Son, the glory of the infinite, the joy of Heaven and the holy peace of earth, returned to Christ and from His hand to Me. Say now Amen, My Son, for it is done. The secret place is open now at last. Forget all things except My changeless Love. Forget all things except that I am here.

---

[100] April 11, 1978
[101] Handwritten mark-up capitalizes "Arms."
[102] 4/11/79
[103] Handwritten mark-up capitalizes "You."

Appendix I: The *ACIM* Version/Edition Family Tree

Table of Contents

1. INTRODUCTION 2
2. VERSION HISTORY IN BRIEF 4
   THE MANY EDITIONS, A CONFUSING PROLIFERATION 4
   TERMINOLOGY AND NOMENCLATURE 5
3. THE SCRIBAL VERSIONS AND EDITIONS IN DETAIL 6
   THE SHORTHAND NOTES 6
   THE THETFORD TRANSCRIPT 7
   THE URTEXT VERSION 7
   THE HLC VERSION 7
   THE NUN'S VERSION (FOUNDATION FOR INNER PEACE VERSION) 8
4. THE SEVEN VOLUMES 8
5. POST-SCRIBAL VERSIONS 9
   THE ECLECTIC CRITICAL VERSION 9
   CIMS' INTERPRETIVE "ORIGINAL EDITION" 9
6. DIFFERENT KINDS OF EDITIONS 11
7. PUBLISHER CONTACT INFORMATION 14

Appendix I: The *ACIM* Version/Edition Family Tree

Family Tree: 5 Scribal Versions, 25 Editions

by Doug Thompson

1. Introduction

Most of the currently available editions of *A Course in Miracles* (listed on the next page) are at least honest attempts to produce a reasonably accurate copy of a particular scribal version, and, except for the ***facsimile*** and ***replica*** editions, all introduce some changes, correcting at least some of the most obvious unintentional typos, although several add a number of new ones and a few go beyond the "obvious typos" to address some more subtle problems such as apparently inadvertent omissions.

Editions which document editorial "interventions" are generally referred to as "**Scholarly Editions**" or "**Critical Editions**." There is no single generic term for editions which fail to meet the standard of "scholarly edition" although the terms "recreational edition" and "reader's edition" and "popular edition" are sometimes used. When dealing with a very inaccurate, sloppy and amateurish productions, and there have been some of them, a variety of unflattering terms are sometimes used.

Unfortunately for the reader, very few editions of the *Course* document the changes they introduce and several make statements indicating there are far fewer changes present than is actually the case.

One early English translation of the Bible in the 16th Century suffered from serious proofreading problems. In the Ten Commandments, for example, the unfortunate wording "Thou shalt commit adultery" appeared. It ended up being called the "*Wicked Edition.*"

The "editions" listed in the "*Family Tree Chart*" then are those which at least attempt to reproduce one of the original scribal versions with alterations limited to dealing with actual errors. They are of widely varying quality, accuracy and professionalism.

In the "*Family Tree Chart*" the five main headings list those primary scribal versions which are known either because copies are available or there are credible published and oral reports that, in the case of the *Thetford Transcript,* it did at least exist at one time and a copy may yet surface. Under each of the five scribal version headings, there is a list of all distinct editions of that version of which I am aware which are (or at one time were) publicly available either as a file distributed on the net or as a book or CD available for purchase. A number of the print editions are out of print and while copies may be found in libraries or used bookstores, there is otherwise no current commercial source for them. There is some indication that there may be yet other pre-publication manuscripts which have not yet surfaced.

There is at least one "*edition,*" a recent transcript of the *Notes,* which reliable sources indicate exists, but which is not available to the public, or even to me. Due to its unavailability, it is not listed.

In addition to the 25 editions of the historical scribal versions, there are two other editions, one in print and one planned, which do not attempt to reproduce any one scribal version but draw on two or more and in that sense are **Post-Scribal Eclectic Versions** (see Section 5, page 12 of this Appendix). Setting out to achieve very different things than any reproduction of a scribal version they cannot be evaluated, for instance, as to how "accurately" they represent any particular version since they don't attempt to represent any single version. These are discussed in section 5 (page 13 of this appendix). As serious textual scholarship on A Course in Miracles begins to be done, we can expect more "post-scribal versions."

The ACIM Family Tree
Editions of the Historical Scribal Versions

This list is current as of March 2009

1.	**_Shorthand Notes_**	1965-1978 *(some of this remains unavailable)*		
	a)	→ MPF 5 CD Facsimile Edition		(2007)
	b)	→ The Greene Facsimile Edition		(2007)
	c)	→ MPF cross-referenced "Toolbox" Edition	(e-text)	(2008)
	d)	→ MPF "Toolbox" partial transcript	(e-text)	(2008)
2.	**_Thetford Transcript_**	*(little if any of this has surfaced)*		(1965-197?)
	a)	→ No positively identified copies known		
3.	**_Urtext_**	1968? *(roughly the same length as the Notes, some "personal material" was removed and some "dictated without notes" material was added)*		
	a)	→ Legacy Facsimile Edition		(2000)
	b)	→ Legacy E-text	(e-text)	(2000)
	c)	→ MPF "Toolbox" Facsimile Edition		(2008)
	d)	→ MPF "Toolbox" 7 Volume Urtext	(e-text)	(2008)
	e)	→ MIAP Complete 7 Volume Urtext	(print)	(2008)
4.	**_Hugh Lynn Cayce Version_**	1972 *(~40,000 words removed from the Urtext)*		
	a)	→ Legacy Facsimile Edition		(1999)
	b)	→ Legacy E-text	(e-text)	(1999)
	c)	→ JCIM	(print)	(2000)
	d)	→ Blue Sparkly	(print)	(2003)
	e)	→ MPF "Corrected HLC"	(print)	(2006)
	f)	→ MPF "Corrected HLC"	(e-text)	(2006)
	g)	→ MPF Replica Edition	(e-text)	(2006)
	h)	→ MIAP "Annotated HLC" (2nd Ed.)	(e-text)	(2009)
	i)	→ MIAP "Annotated HLC" (2nd Ed.)	(print)	(2009)
5.	**_Nun's (FIP) Version_**	1975 *(~10,000 words removed from the HLC)*		
	a)	→ Criswell Facsimile (Xerox) Edition		(1975)
	b)	→ FIP First Edition	(print)	(1976)
	c)	→ FIP Second Edition	(print)	(1996)
	d)	→ FIP Electronic ACIM	(e-text)	(1997)
	e)	→ Legacy E-text (based on above)	(e-text)	(2000)
	f)	→ EA Edition	(print)	(2006)
	g)	→ Raincoast Edition	(print)	(2007)
	h)	→ FIP Third Edition	(print)	(2007)
	i)	→ MPF "Toolbox" FIP^2 cross-referenced	(e-text)	(2008)

See section 3 for descriptions of each edition.

Legend of Nomenclature:

Blue Sparkly:	Thetford Foundation's 4 volume hardcover edition (available in Australia and N.Z. only)
E-text:	A manuscript copied to a computer text-file copy which can be searched for text strings
EA:	Endeavor Academy
Facsimile:	A digitized photocopy of an original manuscript. Usually a PDF file, may also be printed
FIP:	Foundation for Inner Peace: FIP^1: First Edition FIP^2: Second Edition FIP^3: Third Edition
Greene:	Raphael Greene's publication of the *Shorthand Notes*
HLC:	Hugh Lynn Cayce (son of Edgar Cayce), the *HLC* Version was first shared with Cayce
Legacy:	E-text or facsimile first published anonymously on the net in the early days (2000)
MIAP:	Miracles in Action Press
MPF:	Miracles Pathway Fellowship publication
Nun's:	The 1975 abridged manuscript was first typed by a Nun, and thus named "*Nun's Version*"
Raincoast:	Raincoast Press
Replica:	An e-text which attempts keystroke for keystroke fidelity to source, including typos

For contact and ordering information for these editions please see the end of this document.

Appendix I: The *ACIM* Version/Edition Family Tree

2. Version History in brief
The Many Editions, a Confusing Proliferation

The proliferation of versions and editions of *A Course in Miracles* can be very confusing because while they differ substantially, they all **claim** a degree of "originality" few of them actually possess. To help the student navigate this very confusing scene, the "*Family Tree Chart*" chronologically traces the origins and lineage of each version. In section 3 there are brief descriptions offering an outline of the distinguishing features and major differences between them. Several of these versions are available in multiple editions, each of which is in its own way unique.

The Scribes, Helen Schucman and William Thetford, were involved in the production of five significantly different versions. Photocopies of only four of those five have come to light so far. While there is strong evidence of the fifth, little or none of it has yet surfaced. These four primary source versions reveal a great deal about how the Course evolved from the first *Shorthand Notebooks*.

Until 1999 there was only one version of *A Course in Miracles* generally available. That was the Foundation for Inner Peace (FIP) *First* and *Second Editions* of the *Nun's Version*. The *Nun's Version* earned its name because the final typing was done by a nun. While it was widely known that there were "earlier versions," there was little interest in these due to the fact that the spokespersons for FIP claimed there were "virtually no changes." In any event, the earlier versions were not made available. In 2000 two older manuscripts, the *Hugh Lynn Cayce (HLC)* version and the *Urtext* were published on the net and in 2007 the original *Shorthand Notebooks* emerged. We now have copies of these four distinct versions distinguished by substantial differences in length, organization, and wording.

Numerous published and oral accounts strongly suggest there is at least one other version – and possibly more than one – which has not yet surfaced. The uncertainty here arises due to published accounts indicating that two typed manuscripts were made for some volumes where only one has surfaced, and that three typed manuscripts were made for the *Text* where only two are known. This indicates that there is, or at least once was, at least one additional typed manuscript for each volume which has not yet come to light. There is some difference of opinion as to whether A) these accounts are inaccurate, that all manuscripts are present and accounted for or B) we're missing an intermediate re-typing or C) we're missing the original *Thetford Transcript*. After a careful examination of the evidence currently available, the weight of probability points to "C" that there is a missing manuscript, and the missing manuscript is in fact the original transcript Bill Thetford typed to Helen Schucman's oral dictation of her *Notebooks*. That same evidence suggests that the published accounts indicating that the *Urtext* **is** that *Thetford Transcript* are, in fact, mistaken.

Whether one agrees with this conclusion[1] or not, in interpreting this "*Family Tree Chart*," the *Urtext* is considered as the first known re-typing of the *Thetford Transcript* and not that original transcript itself. Should that ultimately prove to be incorrect, the labels will, of course, need adjusting.

To some extent, each of these five historical "scribal versions" is the progenitor of the next. From one version to the next the Scribes copied from the immediately previous version and while copying, they modified the material. Unfortunately, due to a lack of proofreading many of the inevitable copying mistakes from one to the next were never detected and thus never corrected. In addition, intentional changes were made, some of which were genuine corrections of earlier errors, but many of which were actually the introduction of new errors. While some have argued that the earlier versions were "rough drafts" and the last version was a "finished product," the textual evidence lends more support to the view that they are all "rough drafts." Each contains mistakes not found in the others. Each also contains corrections of previous mistakes, some of which are not found in other versions. In a very real way then for *A Course in Miracles* there is no "finished product" since rather obviously a "finished product" would involve thorough proofreading to identify and correct all the mistakes and would include the complete original dictation. No such version yet exists.

There are a few facts about the Course's history on which all credible accounts agree.

- the *Notes* represents the first written form.[2]

- the *Thetford Transcript* is always described as a verbatim, orally proofed copy of the *Notes* and if that is true, isn't *really* a different "*version,*" but just a typed copy. This can't really be verified until a copy of that *Thetford Transcript* becomes available for study.[3]

- the *Urtext* is the earliest typed manuscript currently available.

- the *HLC* is a later abridgement of the *Urtext,* with some 40,000 fewer words

- the 1975 *Nun's Version* was an even later abridgement of the *HLC,* with about 10,000 fewer words than the *HLC.*

- the Foundation for Inner Peace (FIP) *First, Second* and *Third Editions* involve only minor corrections to the 1975 edited *Nun's Version* and as such can be considered as editions of that version rather than as unique versions in their own right.

To add to an inherently confusing situation, while there are only five substantially different versions involved, there are dozens of different names being used for them leading to the impression that there are many more than five. Since many editions don't actually indicate which version they are presenting, and some actually make inaccurate claims in that regard, it's not always easy to tell which version any particular copy represents.

The "*Family Tree Chart*" includes all the editions of each of these five "scribal versions" of which I am aware at the time of writing (March 2008). There are other e-text editions circulating on the net which are generally of such erratic quality as to be undeserving of inclusion in the list. It's quite possible other editions exist which deserve mention. Should you know of another edition or be preparing to release one, please let us know! We'll certainly take a look at any new editions with an eye to their inclusion in this list.

---

[1] The evidence is briefly presented and reviewed in Appendix II.

[2] There is some indication that a few portions of the *Notes* may have been written twice, possibly with some editing, as we do see a few passages repeated. However these instances appear more likely to be exceptions than evidence indicating the existence of two, different versions of the handwritten *Notes*.

[3] Insofar as these reports of the *Thetford Transcript* being a very accurate copy of the *Notes* are true, it may seem rather unimportant since we have the original *Notes*. There are, however, some parts of the *Notes* where legibility of available copies is poor, and generally handwriting doesn't always provide a precise reading. One significant value of the *Thetford Transcript* lies in helping to correctly read those places in the *Notes* where legibility makes the reading questionable.

Appendix I: The *ACIM* Version/Edition Family Tree

Terminology and Nomenclature

While many different names have been applied to each version and edition, only the most original, historical names used in the earliest historical records, and where applicable, those used by the Scribes themselves, are used here.

Some terminology is used in this discussion which may be unfamiliar to some, particularly terms relating to different kinds of editions. For those interested in a brief description of these various kinds of editions, the last section of this discussion (see section 6) will provide additional background information.

The words *"version"* and *"edition"* can be, and often are used interchangeably. The reader should be aware that the word *"version"* is used in this discussion to indicate **substantive content differences** beyond the correction of errors, which leaves us with five historical *"scribal versions."* The word *"edition"* is used to indicate each distinct rendition of any particular *"version."* So any given version could have any number of *"editions."* While each edition will inevitably contain some differences from any other, the extent of those differences along with the intentions of the publisher determines whether it is classified as a new *version* or a new *edition* of an existing version.

One could almost as easily swap the words "edition" and "version" and speak of five primary historical "editions" of which there are any number of different "versions" of each available. This is not so much a matter of "correct English" as it is one of "defining our terms" for the purposes of clarity and precision in this discussion.

The model here is derived from Biblical scholarship where people speak of such things as the *"King James Version"* and the *"Revised Standard Version"* and the *"New English Version"* of the Bible. Each is a unique translation of the original Hebrew and Greek manuscript copies of the Bible. Each of those "versions" has been published in many different "editions." While the various editions may look very different, all contain pretty much exactly the same words although they may differ substantially in terms of appendices, commentary, footnotes, etc. As soon as there is any significant modification of the actual wording, beyond "correcting typos," however, the result is defined as a "new version."

We find that in the many editions of the numerous versions of the Bible, there is almost no difference at all in the actual wording, punctuation, reference structure, etc. You will also find that some "different versions" are in fact very similar to each other, having introduced only minor wording differences such as modernization of archaic terminology or introducing corrections based on new primary scholarship which was not available to the original translators. In short, *any changes* beyond correcting errors lead us to define the result as a new **version** rather than a new **edition** of an existing version. This does not include *documented changes*. For instance, since 1611 when the *King James Version* was first published, primary Biblical scholarship has corrected a number of errors in the manuscripts the 1611 translators used. Modern editions of the *KJV* generally include those corrections but they are footnoted or set in a different typestyle such that the reader can readily recognize them. This kind of change isn't considered a "new version" because we are still in the realm of "correcting errors" in an existing version rather than generating a "new version."

Inevitably the border between "version" and "edition" as those words are defined in this discussion is going to be a bit fuzzy and some works may indeed straddle that border. How many differences do there have to be before a document ceases to be a "new edition" of an existing version and becomes a "new version" entirely? It is probably impossible to achieve a precise answer. The basic indicator is the presence and frequency of intentional undocumented differences which go beyond "correction of errors."

There are some additional guidelines which are used here to answer the question. It should be remembered that all of the four available "historical versions" referred to here as "scribal versions" are roughly 85% identical. The intentional modifications can be classed as "corrections" or as "errors" or as "stylistic" changes which don't actually correct or introduce any error in terms of overt content, they just fiddle with the wording. Simply generating a copy with inadvertent mistakes does not a new "version" make. That's just an inaccurate edition. Where there are numerous intentional modifications of the material beyond simply correcting verified mistakes, well that *does* represent a new version. Of course determining whether a change is "minor" is subjective; what may seem "minor" to one might seem "substantive" to another. And how many do there have to be for us to say they are "numerous?"

The *Corrected HLC* introduces variant readings for example, but each substantive change is a "correction" based on evidence of a mistake and not a newly minted original variant, and each one is documented showing the original wording so the complete original *HLC* is intact within that edition. Being confined to "corrections" where there is genuine evidence of a likely error, the differences do not constitute a "new version." It is thus an **annotated** or **critical** edition of one scribal version. Other changes involve spelling and capitalization standardization which aren't classed as "substantive" changes. Many English words have variant spellings approved of by dictionaries. It's standard publishing practice to use a single variant in any particular volume. Since Schucman often used multiple different spellings, any editor of this work has to tackle this issue, one way or another. At the Miracles Pathway Fellowship we've generally chosen the spelling variant which US dictionaries say is the most commonly used in the USA since this work was produced in the USA by Americans and those spellings would be the most common in that place at that time. Further, it is easy for anyone anywhere in the world to find out what the most common US spellings are so as to predict how any given word might be spelled in our editions. There are a few exceptions where clarity argued for a spelling other than the most common in the USA.

In the historical scribal versions one can be distinguished from another because, *in addition to correcting or introducing typos* from one version to the next, the editors have done some or all of the following:

1) removed and/or added and/or re-arranged a significant amount of material

2) made numerous adjustments to wording

3) made extensive changes in punctuation and/or paragraphation

4) introduced or altered chapter and section divisions

5) changed the words which are emphasized, adding or deleting emphasis

The reader will note imprecise and subjective terms such as "significant" and "numerous" here. I wish to repeat and stress that I consider "correction of error where there is solid evidence of a real error" a very different kind of editorial intervention than alterations which do not involve any error in what is being altered. Given that every version has "errors" we'd rather hope every edition would correct these, except of course for **facsimile** and **replica** editions whose unique purpose is to reproduce a manuscript as exactly as possible with *no* modifications. While I think we'd all agree that two or three changes wouldn't constitute a new version although several thousand certainly would, just where do you draw the line? There remains a degree of subjectivity and even controversy in this.

For instance there is a "grey area" in the FIP *Second Edition* where we have the term "each other" in the original changed to "you and

Appendix I: The *ACIM* Version/Edition Family Tree

your brother" a number of times. Is that considered one change applied dozens of times or dozens of changes? While it can't be considered a "correction of error" it certainly can be considered "minor." In this case it is being judged as "below the threshold" for considering this a "new version." It should also be noted that the changes in the FIP Second Edition are documented in an *Errata* which purports to list each modification. I did mention that some editions might "straddle the border" and this one does. On the other extreme, as noted already, if the *Thetford Transcript* turns out to be what is claimed for it, a precise copy of the *Notes* then it really isn't a separate "version" it's just another "edition" or the same material in a different form. Until we have a copy to check however, we have to assume that like all the other known copies produced by the Scribes, it has some differences and must therefore be classified as a separate version.

There is also an enormous difference between "changes" which are not documented and those which are. An undocumented change is invisible to the reader. Documented changes are obvious. Invisible differences leave most readers with the impression what they're reading is the "original" even when it is not, and that is the source of a great deal of confusion.

The extent of each kind of change varies greatly from version to version and section to section within versions. Some material has never been changed at all and other material is changed almost beyond recognition, when it is preserved at all. We have as many as six variant readings of some passages, when the manuscript mark-up is taken into account. This is how one can distinguish the *HLC* from the *Urtext* for instance. Most of the time they are actually identical, but the paragraphation is different, the emphasis is different and sometimes the wording is different and many pages of material from the *Ur* are not included in the *HLC*. Similarly, there is material in the *HLC* which is not found in any earlier version. These differences are how we identify which scribal version we're looking at.

Should someone set out to reproduce *A Course in Miracles* and intentionally modify the material in any of the five ways noted above, this would be a "new version" unless of course the instances were "few" and "minor." For instance, if one were to reproduce the *Urtext* version but change most of the emphasis, the punctuation and some of the paragraph breaks it would be misleading to say this is still the *Urtext*, even if one left all the wording intact, because numerous of the defining characteristics of that version have been altered.

This is why Tom Whitmore's "*Original Edition*" is not considered to be an edition of the *HLC* even though the wording is mostly the same. In the *Text*, much of the punctuation and emphasis and some of the paragraph and section breaks are Whitmore's own original creative work and derive from no known scribal version. Some of the wording isn't the *HLC*, it's the *Urtext*. Some is simply "original." In the *Text* volume alone Whitmore has introduced over 7,000 original variant readings, none of which are documented. The *Workbook* and *Manual* in that edition draw from several versions and confine themselves to none. Regardless of how one views these original modifications, they are so numerous as to make it an "original" version and not an attempt to reproduce any particular scribal version with precision. I anticipate we will see many more eclectic "original editions" which are really new versions in the future as various people wrestle with the variant readings between the scribal versions and develop different ideas as to what it really should say.

Some have criticized this "*Original Edition*" as being a highly inaccurate representation of the *HLC*. I think that criticism is misplaced since it is very obvious that the intent here was not to produce an edition of the *HLC* but rather something "original."

Similarly if the *King James Version* of the Bible was altered in just that way, the result could be said to be *based on* the *KJV* but it would still be a "new" and "original version."

If one were to adopt the emphasis, paragraph breaks and punctuation from the *HLC* while preserving the wording of the *Urtext* it would be an "*Eclectic Version*" but it would not be **either** the *HLC* or the *Urtext*. It would be a new hybrid version containing characteristics of each of its parents. Were one to invent entirely new paragraphation, punctuation and emphasis, it would be an original "*Interpretive Version*" based on, but not even attempting to accurately reproduce the *Urtext*. If, in addition to selecting readings from more than one scribal version one introduced new and original variants of one's own, it would be an "*Original Edition.*"

However, when one takes a scribal version and inserts the *HLC* reference points, such as we have done with the *Urtext*, the fact that this overlay is documented means that the result is not a new "version" but rather a new "*Annotated Edition.*" The reader is never left in any doubt as to what derived from the manuscript and what is an editorial overlay.

There is another way of introducing extensive changes without the result being a "new version." That is to footnote each and every change such that the original reading is preserved along with the modification. Arguably the "altered" form is a "new version" but since the edition retains the precise original material, that form is an "existing version." This would be called an "annotated edition."

3. The Scribal Versions and Editions in detail

The Shorthand Notes

The *Notes* is the earliest written form of *A Course in Miracles*, but is the most recent of the versions to become available. Due to the fact that it is handwritten, partly in shorthand, it is much more difficult to read and render as an e-text than the later typed manuscripts. Further, it is only within the last year[4] that it has been generally available to scholarship. While I have been told that a complete transcript (e-text) of the *Notes* of good quality has been produced, it is not available so can't be considered to be a "published edition." The "partial transcript" **(1d)** listed is my own transcription which at the moment includes all of the *Notes* for the *Use of Terms*, *Song of Prayer*, and the first two and last chapters of the *Text*. It is my hope that anyone who is in possession of any transcriptions of any of the *Notes* will make that material public such that a complete searchable e-text can soon be available to scholarship. Such an e-text of the *Notes* is not a substitute for the original manuscript, it is more of an **index** to it since it provides a searchable text which is easy to read, a great convenience to anyone reading the *Notes*. Without a searchable text it is difficult and time-consuming to find anything in the facsimile editions.

Generally however the *Urtext* is mostly an accurate transcript of the *Notes*. It is far from perfect but using the MPF *e-text* and the MPF *facsimile* editions which use the same chapter, section and paragraph reference system, it is very easy to look up most passages in the *Urtext* e-text and then find the corresponding *Notes* page. Both of these are available in e-text form on the *Scholar's Toolbox* data disk.

The cross-referenced "*Toolbox*" edition **(1c)** organizes the *Notes* according to the volume, chapter, and section divisions used in all MPF primary source publications. The material is also cross-referenced according to the volume and page number in the "*22 Volumes of Helen Schucman's Unpublished Writings.*" This collection fits on a single CD and to squeeze it all in the resolution of the

---

[4] The first general publications of *Notes* material took place in August 2007. This Appendix was written in March 2008.

Appendix I: The *ACIM* Version/Edition Family Tree

image files had to be reduced. While the resolution is generally high enough for reading on screen or printing at 100%, if greater magnification is desired, one should turn to the *5 CD Facsimile Edition*.

This material is presented in PDF format. "Bookmarks" are used to indicate all the volume, chapter, and section divisions, making this a very convenient tool for quick reference except for the high resolution *5 CD Facsimile Edition* **(1a)** of the *Notes* which is referenced only by the original volume and page number designations. These designations also appear in the e-text and the *Scholar's Toolbox* editions for easy cross-referencing. The images are of higher quality than any of the other known publications and maximum readability of segments with poor legibility can be found here.

The *Greene Facsimile* **(1b)** uses an entirely unique reference system and is not readily amenable to cross-referencing to other editions or versions. It also omits the volume identifiers and title pages from the *22 Volumes*. Otherwise it is largely identical in content. Resolution is good but contrast is excessive turning "grey areas" either white or black. This makes for a "crisp" looking image but actually degrades faint images such that areas of poor legibility lose definition although it preserves areas of good legibility quite well.

The Thetford Transcript

The issues relating to the identification of both the *Thetford Transcript* and the *Urtext* are dealt with in detail elsewhere[5]. While positive identification is elusive, there is some evidence that the *Psychotherapy* and *Song of Prayer* volumes **might be** the *Thetford Transcript* as they do bear some signs of oral dictation. There is little to suggest that any of the other typed manuscripts represent an original manuscript typed to oral dictation while there is much to suggest that they are later edited re-typings. The MPF "*Toolbox*" **(2a)** collection contains those typed manuscripts which may be part of that original *Thetford Transcript*.

The Urtext Version

There are eight separate typed manuscripts labelled "*Urtext*", one each for the *Text, Workbook, Manual for Teachers, Use of Terms, Psychotherapy, Song of Prayer, Gifts of God* and *Special Messages*. The word "*Urtext*" in this discussion refers to that entire collection. Some use *Urtext* to refer only to the *Text* volume. Some refer to this collection as "the typescript" but, since all the manuscripts except for the handwritten *Notes* are "typescripts" this causes more confusion than clarity.

I suspect that the Scribes may indeed have only referred to the *Text* volume as an "urtext." However this material is categorized as "urtext" in the original and we've chosen to try to minimize confusion by **not** attempting to dream up yet another new name. The only publication to include all of this material in both facsimile and e-text editions is the "*Toolbox*" edition **(3c** and **3d)**. The MPF editions all include cross-referencing based on the original scribal chapter and section divisions of the *HLC*.

Seven of these *Urtext* volumes are widely, but not universally, considered "canonical" although the *Special Messages* are viewed as suspect by many.[6] The *Special Messages* are not included as canonical but are included in the *Scholar's Toolbox* on disk as an interesting supplement.

Beginning in the summer of 2000, portions of these *Urtext* facsimile **(3a)** copies were circulated on the net. Obtaining the complete collection has been a challenge and it's difficult to be sure it has all been located. To date I am not aware of anything missing in the *Urtext* collection. We can only be certain when the entire collection of original primary source material finally becomes available for scholarly scrutiny. The *"Legacy Facsimiles"* which have been circulating since 2000 **(3a)** are of varying quality and completeness. It is difficult to determine their number since no catalogue of such different unique collections exist, but there are at least several. The difference is in the total number of pages and the sequencing of those pages. The MPF "*Scholar's Toolbox*" **(3c)** and **(3d)** compilation includes, as far as can be ascertained, all of the material in its original sequence with two minor exceptions dealt with in the *Editor's Notes* in those volumes in which segments of the *Special Messages* are inserted into the text in the exact location the Scribes themselves inserted this material in the *HLC*. Although labelled "*Special Messages*," these segments are deemed to be later "dictated corrections and clarifications" in our view and also apparently in the view of the Scribes. In short, rather than being deemed "special" and of a personal or private nature, these segments are considered to be canonical material "dictated without notes."

In August of 2000 the *"Legacy E-text"* **(3b)** of the *Urtext* appeared on the net. Portions of this document are quite accurate reproductions of the *Urtext* manuscript but large portions are actually the *HLC*. The MPF "*Toolbox*" e-text edition **(3d)** is not 100% accurate but is vastly more accurate than its predecessor since it has all been proofed, although not proofed to the degree of thoroughness which is desirable. The proofing of that document is an on-going project.

The MPF *Complete Seven Volume Urtext* **(3e)** is available in print. Including some segments of the *Notes* which were omitted in the *Urtext* apparently inadvertently, it is the most complete print edition of *A Course in Miracles* writings known.

The HLC Version

The only facsimile copy of the *HLC* manuscript which has been published is that which was found in November 1999 at the Association for Research and Enlightenment Library in Virginia Beach, Virginia, USA. **(4a)** The *HLC* includes only the *Text* volume. An e-text of poor quality **(4b)** was hastily created within weeks of the discovery and began circulating on the net on January 6, 2000. Additional proofing of that document was undertaken in the following months and it appeared in print as *"Jesus' Course in Miracles"* (*JCIM*) **(4c)** in March of 2000. The proofing was not complete. There were several hundred typos which went uncorrected. It is otherwise a substantially accurate reproduction of the *HLC* manuscript.

In 2003 the *Thetford Foundation* in Australia produced a handsome print edition called "Blue Sparkly" **(4d)** after its cover design. This included the *HLC* text which is nearly identical to the *JCIM* **(4c)** text, typos and all. It also includes the *Workbook, Manual,* and *Use of Terms* derived from *Urtext* e-texts. No precise tabulation of the accuracy of this volume is available but it appears to be an honest effort to publish an accurate presentation with the inadequate proofing which is so typical of *A Course in Miracles* publishers since the beginning. Most of the *Legacy Edition* typos persist, for instance, although some have been corrected. Spelling is sometimes altered, but inconsistently.

In 2006 the *Corrected HLC*, **(4e)** a thoroughly proofed edition of the *HLC Text* volume was published. It is available in both print

---

[5] The evidence is thoroughly reviewed in Appendix II.
[6] There are differences of opinion as to what material is or isn't "canonical." Initially *ACIM* appeared in three volumes, *Text, Workbook,* and *Manual for Teachers*. At that time, in 1975, the other material had not yet been written. Shortly thereafter a fourth volume, *Use of Terms* was added, but wasn't called a fourth volume, it was called an appendix to Volume III. There is some dispute as to whether the *Use of Terms* should be considered canonical. Whitmore's three volume *Original Edition*, for instance, doesn't include it. The *Blue Sparkly* moves it to the front of the book as a kind of introduction. FIP included all four volumes in all of its editions, while still calling the fourth volume an appendix to Volume III, until the *Third Edition* in which the *Psychotherapy* and *Song of Prayer* volumes were added, but the *Gifts of God* was not added. Two of the *HLC* editions include only the *Text* volume because the *HLC* is only the *Text* volume. To date no edition has included the *Special Messages* as "canonical."

Appendix I: The *ACIM* Version/Edition Family Tree

and e-text formats. This includes a number of "corrections" of apparently inadvertent omissions and other errors which arose in the scribal copying from the *Urtext*. All deviations from the manuscript are footnoted and explained such that the reader can readily distinguish between the original scribal text and editorial "correction." This volume also includes two complete reference systems. One is based on the traditional "chapter/section/paragraph" numbering and one is based on the original manuscript page numbers. This makes it very easy to check the manuscript facsimile against either the e-text or paper editions and facilitates cross-referencing to other editions and versions. The MPF *"Toolbox"* contains a significantly enhanced PDF format facsimile edition **(4f)** which includes bookmarks for all the chapter and section breaks in order to assist quick cross-referencing with other editions.

Also in 2006 MPF released an *"HLC Replica"* **(4g)** edition which attempts to reproduce the original manuscript keystroke for keystroke with no corrections. All of the original spelling mistakes and other typos are preserved. This was initially created as a proofing tool and can be used to quickly check any e-text of the *HLC* to see where differences exist. It is currently available as an e-text only.

The Nun's Version (Foundation for Inner Peace version)

From 1975 until 2000 this was the only version of *A Course in Miracles* generally available and was advertised as, and widely but mistakenly believed to be, "virtually unchanged" from the original dictation. In fact it is about 60,000 words shorter than the *Urtext* in the *Text* volume and roughly 10,000 words shorter than the *HLC*. After chapter eight of the *Text* the magnitude of the differences declines dramatically such that later portions can fairly be described as at least "substantially unchanged."

Portions of the original *Nun's Version* manuscript in facsimile form have been circulated on the net. **(5d)**

In June of 1976 the Foundation for Inner Peace (FIP) undertook the first large-scale printing of this book in what has become known as the *"First Edition."* **(5b)** In fact the first printing of several hundred copies occurred in August of 1975 in what is known as the *"Criswell Edition"* sometimes nicknamed the *"Xerox Edition."* **(5a)** This was a facsimile edition in which the manuscript pages of the *Nun's Version* were photocopied at 50% of their original size. In each of the multiple re-printings of the FIP *First Edition* minor differences involving corrections of typos appeared, making each slightly different. In 1992 FIP released its *Second Edition* **(5c)**. This involved even more corrections of earlier typos and was the first to include a reference system printed in the margins. It was also the first known attempt to proofread any version against the original manuscripts. While hundreds of errors were detected and corrected, hundreds more, including some glaringly obvious ones, were missed. It was "proof-reading" but it wasn't "thorough proof-reading." This is meant less as a criticism than an observation intended to draw attention to the very large need for thorough and more professional proof-reading.

Recently FIP has produced a *Third Edition* **(5g)** which includes the *Psychotherapy* and *Song of Prayer* volumes.

Since 2003 at least two other publishers, *Endeavor* **(5e)** and *Raincoast* **(5f)** have introduced print editions of at least portions of the *Nun's Version*, although without the FIP reference system.

In editing the *HLC* into the *Nun's Version,* some chapter and section breaks and names were changed from the original *HLC* values. To facilitate cross-referencing all other versions an e-text of the FIP *Second Edition* was created which restores the original reference points where that was possible. In the early chapters it is not always possible due to the massive removal and re-arrangement of the material in that version. The only reason for restoring these reference points was to provide a research tool to make it easier to check material in the FIP edition against other versions. This edition is the complete text of the *Second Edition* with references from the *HLC*.**(5h)**

There is one additional edition which is worthy of mention but doesn't readily fit into any of our categories. That is the *Sonship Gift* three-column parallel edition of the first eight chapters of the *Urtext, HLC,* and *FIP*[2] produced by Raphael Greene in 2002. The first eight chapters are where most of the editing took place. This edition, distributed as a PDF file, allows for a text search of all three of those versions across the first eight chapters and makes it easy to tell at a glance whether a given passage was ever altered. The base texts Greene used were carefully proofed near-replicas of the respective manuscripts which attempt to reflect not only every original keystroke, but also the handwritten mark-up.

4. The Seven Volumes

Just to make it a bit more confusing, each of the seven volumes included in the *Urtext* collection has a somewhat unique history of its own. The previous discussion of "versions" applies primarily to the *Text* volume. The *HLC* version includes only the *Text* volume. There is no reliable evidence that the *HLC* ever included any other volumes.

The other volumes were all scribed later, in the case of the *Gifts of God*, several years later. Here's a brief summary of the other volumes.

In the first printing of *A Course in Miracles,* the 1975 *Criswell Edition* of the *Nun's Version,* we find the first three volumes, *Text, Workbook* and *Manual for Teachers*. In 1976, the FIP *First Edition* was published as three separate books, and a fourth volume, which Schucman scribed after the *Criswell* publication, called *Clarification of Terms,* was added to the smallest of the three, the *Manual for Teachers*. We call the *Clarification of Terms* by its original name, *Use of Terms* except when dealing explicitly with the FIP version.

In subsequent FIP editions this fourth volume is treated as an appendix to Volume 3, rather than as a separate volume. However, in the FIP Concordance, it is treated as a separate volume. Since it was written two years later than Volume 3, and is no more related to Volume 3 than any other volume, we've opted to deal with it as a distinct volume rather than as an appendix.

Subsequent to the *First Edition's* publication in 1976, Schucman scribed or completed the scribing of three additional volumes, *Psychotherapy, Song of Prayer* and *Gifts of God*.

In 2005 in the *Six Volume Concordance* published by MPF, volumes 5 and 6, *Psychotherapy* and *Song of Prayer,* were included in the *A Course in Miracles* canon as they are in the FIP Concordance.

In its 2008 *Third Edition,* FIP followed this practice and included its own edited versions of volumes 5 and 6. Previously these were published as separate "pamphlets" by FIP.

In 2008 the *Gifts of God* was added as a seventh volume. This has also previously been published by FIP in a collection of Schucman's own poetry under the same name. In the view of many this is also "scribed" material rather than Schucman's own composition and it is a thoroughly fitting "conclusion" to *A Course in Miracles.* No *Notes* material for this seventh volume has yet been located. Unlike the other volumes, we have only a single primary source for Volume 7. That is the collection of *Urtext* manuscripts in the *22 Volumes of Helen Schucman's Unpublished Writings*.

Appendix I: The *ACIM* Version/Edition Family Tree

Opinions do vary on the "authenticity" of some of the later volumes, most notably *Use of Terms*. Some do not consider it "canonical" at all while the Thetford Foundation includes it as a preface to their *Blue Sparkly* edition. We adopted an inclusive policy. Where there is a substantial body of opinion viewing material as authentic, despite the fact that opinions do vary, we chose to include it.

And this concludes the brief descriptions of the 25 editions of the five scribal versions which are currently known outlined in the "*Family Tree*" on page 3.

5. Post-Scribal Versions

As noted previously, a distinction is made between editions of *A Course in Miracles* which honestly attempt to reproduce an historical scribal version with no changes beyond correcting apparently inadvertent mistakes and those editions which differ frequently in any of five ways: wording, punctuation, paragraphation, reference divisions, or emphasis. The two versions discussed here do indeed differ in all five ways from any known historical scribal version. Thus neither can be called an "edition of this version" or an "edition of that version." Each is a unique, original, new version with a particular relationship to one or more of the historical scribal versions, or as is the case with one, no relationship to any historical scribal version at all at many points.

The Eclectic Critical Version

While not yet complete, the "*Eclectic Critical Version*" is a goal towards which some of us have been working for years. A group is being formed to coordinate this work.[7] It will not be an "edition" of any existing version although nearly every word, comma and paragraph break in it will likely derive from at least one of the historical scribal versions. The plan for this *Critical Edition* is to examine all variant readings between all historical scribal versions and using the methodology of textual scholarship, attempt to establish which of the variants is the most authentic. The objective is not to invent entirely new readings or "change" the content. Rather, where the content has already been changed, the intent is to sift through the changes and at least clean up the inadvertent errors. In short, where the respective scribal versions differ, the objective of a *Critical Edition* is to determine which variant is the best; which is the "correction" and which is the "error."

This project is modeled on the work of Biblical scholarship in dealing with the many variant readings which arise in ancient manuscript copies of the Bible. The variants are catalogued and carefully studied with the aim of establishing which variant is the most authentic. The result is a "consensus text" of the Hebrew and Greek Bible. It is not entirely an exact copy of any particular original historical source but if the scholars have done their work well, it is actually closer to the "original" than any of them.

When dealing with material of extraordinary spiritual and religious significance such as *A Course in Miracles* or the Bible, it can be *important*, even if not *crucial*, to establish as closely as possible what the authentic wording really is.

When this methodology is applied to the Course, the result will be a version with the most authentic reading which scholarship can achieve. Every instance of variant readings will be documented so that the reader can see what the variants are and why the scholars came to the conclusions they did. All available historical versions and relevant primary source materials will be consulted and compared. In that process at the very least, all the inadvertent copying errors should be detected and corrected. In all cases the reader will be able to see each variant and make up her own mind. Where it is unclear whether a given change was a correction of a previous mistake or the introduction of a new mistake, the editorial board will have to determine relatively probabilities and inform the reader of the residual uncertainty.

Rather clearly a work with such attributes cannot be considered an "edition" of any particular historical "version" but rather an entirely new, post-scribal version even though every word and comma might derive from one or another of the historical scribal versions. Relative to any particular scribal version it will differ in number of words, specific wording, emphasis, paragraphation and punctuation. It is "post-scribal" because while it will consist entirely of the Scribes' own words and introduce no variant not found in one of their versions, it won't have the benefit of their direct participation and consultation. Although **based** on their work it will not actually **be** their work since they aren't here to consult with. The overriding objective will be to ascertain the "author's intent."

In time any number of such "versions" may appear in which publishers draw on two or more of the historical versions and combine elements from each.

CIMS' Interpretive "Original Edition"

"CIMS" stands for the "Course in Miracles Society" which was founded in 2000 shortly after the *HLC* manuscript was discovered. One of its purposes was the publication of the *HLC*. In the year 2000 the "*JCIM*" edition of the *HLC* was published by CIMS. While suffering from a few hundred mostly very minor typos, *JCIM* is otherwise an accurate representation of the original *HLC* manuscript. In this second CIMS edition, accurate representation of the *HLC* has been replaced by an interpretive approach which introduces 7,971 undocumented variations from the *HLC* in the *Text* volume, and many more original variants in the other volumes.

The word "original" can trip us up here. It can refer to two entirely opposite things: 1) the earliest, *first* or "original" among a chronological series of variants or 2) the latest, most recent and "original" newly created variant, i.e. the *last* in a chronological series of variants.

Rather obviously, the *HLC* is in no way the "original" version of the Course. There are at least two earlier, larger and *more original* versions of which we have copies, and reports of at least one other earlier version of which no copies have yet surfaced. So the *Original Edition* is not in any way the "original course" and is in fact an "original" rendering of the second to last of the historical scribal versions.

By the working definitions of "*edition*" and "*version*" used in these discussions, this would be called an original *version* since it is not in fact an "edition" of any of the historical scribal versions but an eclectic combination of elements of three of them. This is not to say it's a mistake to call it an "*edition*" just to point out that these two words can be and are often used interchangeably and to be clear as to which meaning is intended. CIMS calls it an "*Original Edition*" but within the definitions of this discussion, it is an "*Original Version*."

To thoroughly discuss all the 7,971 deviations from the *HLC* in the *Text* volume alone would require an entire book. The discussion here is necessarily a very brief summary. Much more detail on this and other editions is provided on the website.

---

[7] Should you be interested in lending a hand, e-mail dthomp74@hotmail.com

Appendix I: The *ACIM* Version/Edition Family Tree

The "*Original Edition*" includes entirely original **eclectic interpretive** versions of the *Text, Workbook,* and *Manual for Teachers* which differ significantly from any known historical scribal version.

While CIMS claims the *Workbook* is the *Urtext,* and sometimes it is, it also sometimes reflects the FIP version instead and sometimes reflects none of the historical scribal versions. It truly is "original" in that the paragraphation, punctuation, and emphasis are frequently original creative work. It is this introduction of original new unexplained and undocumented variant readings, roughly seven thousand of them in the *Text* volume alone, that makes it an "***interpretive***" version and its selection of variants from more than one scribal version which makes it an "***eclectic***" version.

It draws both on several scribal versions and introduces unique original material, some examples of which are discussed below. If the variations from any particular version were merely accidental, and were few in number, one might call any of these volumes "editions" of an historical version with inadequate proofing. But while there appear to be a few hundred such inadvertent changes, there are many thousands of apparently intentional changes. Since none of them are documented, it is a matter of guesswork to determine which changes are copying mistakes and which are intentional editing changes. Either way, it's not an "edition" of a scribal version nor does it appear that the editors aspired to the goal of accurate reproduction, despite what they say in their *Preface*.

By and large the *Original Edition* contains the *HLC* wording in the *Text* volume, and includes, but doesn't document, some of the error corrections from the earlier *Corrected HLC* **(4e)** derived from the *Urtext*. Many of the words emphasized in the *HLC* are not emphasized in the *Original Edition* and many of the words emphasized in the *Original Edition* are not emphasized in the *HLC* or, for that matter, in any historical scribal version.

Punctuation is significantly transformed, apparently at random, which, in some cases, changes the meaning. Again this is done with no reference to any scribal version. In some cases "spelling" changes alter the tense or disrupt contractions which were needed for iambic pentameter. Spelling, capitalization, grammar and emphasis are largely "original" creative work and sometimes, so is the wording. Subjunctive verbs are changed to past tense or past conditional tense, for instance. None of the 7,971 deviations from the original *HLC* manuscript in the *Text* volume are documented or explained except in the cryptic phrase in the *Preface* which states that

> "The only changes that have been made to the edition [or version] of the Course as completed by Shucman [sic] and Thetford have been to correct obvious typographic errors and misspellings, to modernize and render consistent punctuation and capitalization, and to format the material for print publication."

While that could be a description of a *Critical Edition* of a scribal version, what CIMS produced is in fact a highly original *Interpretive Eclectic Version*. This is truly an "original" way of using the words "modernize" and "consistent" since the spelling, capitalization and punctuation modifications introduced in this work are neither "modern" nor even remotely "consistent."

For instance, in the case of commas being used with conjunctions, at one time "newspaper style guides" dictated getting rid of commas since they generally aren't strictly necessary. In newspapers every bit of space counts and reducing commas saves space. It can also encourage reporters and editors to write more succinctly and avoid complex compound sentences that require commas. It's possible that removal of commas beside conjunctions could be considered "modernizing" in that sense. Recent research has shown however that the average reader can read faster, and with higher comprehension if the commas are left in, since they provide visual cues to the clause structure within a compound sentence. It's almost always possible to parse the clauses *after* reading the sentence with no punctuation. The commas allow one to identify clause divisions *before* reading the sentence, which increases reading speed and comprehension. In the case of the sometimes highly complex sentence structure of ACIM, removing commas often introduces ambiguity in material that was originally quite clear.

"Modern" style guides advise the use of commas wherever they enhance clarity and readability. Whitmore has removed many of the commas that appeared alongside conjunctions, but did not do so consistently. While that is usually not a hugely significant alteration, it's not reasonably described as "modern." Kenneth Wapnick, who helped Schucman in the final editing, describes how comma usage was discussed and the decision was made to go heavy on the commas in order to enhance readability, which as noted, is exactly what it does. Interestingly, in the four scribal versions we have to compare, we can see that the Scribes made rather few changes to the original punctuation found in the *Notes*. When they do it is usually the replacement of one "pause" mark for another, such as the replacement of a comma with a period, colon, or semi-colon, which changes would not influence "how it sounds." Some commas were added later, but not many. And remember, this work began as an oral dictation, and if the Scribe taking it down inserted a "pause mark" where the Voice paused, then is a strong case for leaving it there because it is part of the "original oral content." In most cases it is clear from the character spacing in the *Notes* that Schucman usually inserted the commas as she wrote the words and did not often go back later to figure out where the punctuation should be. Given that, I see no reason to suppose the punctuation was Schucman's arbitrary decision rather than her recording actual pauses in what she "heard."

In the case of poetry, and much of the Course is blank verse poetry in iambic pentameter, rare indeed is the editor who would presume to alter or "modernize" any poet's punctuation according to the dictates of ***any*** prose style guide! There are no "style guides" for the punctuation of blank verse poetry and the attempt to edit any poet's composition to any prose standard can certainly be described as "original."

The *Original Edition* also includes an entirely original reference system of paragraph numbers within chapters rather than the conventional technique of counting paragraph numbers within sections. Sadly, the original manuscript page numbers are removed making it extremely cumbersome to cross-reference this version to ***any*** other. Due to the fact that Whitmore did not always maintain the same paragraph structure as that found in the *HLC* manuscript, these references are not amenable to use on any other edition or version of *A Course in Miracles*. For example, on the first page of the *Original Edition* we see the three paragraphs of the *Introduction* but the third paragraph actually contains three paragraph numbers such that the first line of the third paragraph is counted as one paragraph, the two lines of the inset epigraph are counted as paragraph four, and the last line is counted as paragraph five. This pattern is repeated frequently such that the paragraph count in the chapters of the *Original Edition* will not match the actual paragraph count of the *HLC*.

For those interested, several of the *HLC* editions are available in e-text form on the website and each is compared to the *HLC* replica which is an exact, keystroke for keystroke transcript of the *HLC* manuscript. The creation of the exact replica has proven very useful for proofreading *HLC* editions because with it one can find every difference and make sure it was intended and is properly documented. These comparisons show each instance where each edition introduced changes, and of course exactly what the change is. What's provided here is just a brief summary of what the comparison of the *Original Edition* to the *HLC* manuscript itself reveals.

http://www.miraclesinactionpress.com/dthomp74/2007/REVIEW/CIMS%202nd%20Edition%20A.htm

Appendix I: The *ACIM* Version/Edition Family Tree

6. Different kinds of editions

A Course in Miracles is a different sort of book than those most of us usually deal with. Most new books are written by a human, edited to some extent, submitted to a publisher, edited a bit more by the publisher with the collaboration of the author, and then they appear in print more or less exactly as the author wishes them to appear. It's fairly rare for a book to go to a second printing and rarer still to go to a second edition. For most books no question ever arises as to what the "authentic text" is, it is what is on the page! But then most books don't claim authorship by Jesus of Nazareth. That fact, if no other, demands that every effort be made to precisely and accurately reproduce the original with no undocumented deviations.

Then there are "classics" whose authors have passed away which, while they also always begin with a manuscript and then are printed in a "First Edition," end up becoming available in numerous editions and versions of various kinds, some of which are briefly mentioned below. In a few cases multiple early "versions" with variant readings of a classic emerge making it less than immediately obvious what the "authentic" or "original" text actually is. Where such questions arise, textual scholarship begins. Where the author is not available to consult and multiple "versions" of a text turn up, questions inevitably arise as to which of the variant readings should be considered most "authentic," which result from later copying mistakes, and which results from later corrections introduced by the author.

Different versions and editions are generally intended for different audiences and different applications as discussed below.

Facsimile Editions are essentially photocopies, often in colour and of very high quality, of original historical documents. Good ones are almost as useful for many purposes as the originals themselves and can save scholars a great deal of travel to inspect the originals. Especially with handwriting, there is "content" in the original manuscript page that no typed copy can fully capture. Facsimiles can capture most, but never all of that. For instance, it is sometimes only possible to tell whether a "dot" is an original pen stroke or a speck of dirt by microscopically inspecting the original manuscript, but not from any photographic copy. Similarly, if dating is an issue, the original medium is more helpful than any photocopy. Short of those physical issues with the original medium, facsimile editions are exceedingly useful for many purposes. Facsimile editions are of primary interest to serious scholars who want to check and double-check against the most primary of sources for previously undetected interpretive clues, or indeed simply to check a given copy's accuracy. Given that there are known inaccuracies in every extant edition, "checking accuracy" is a regrettable necessity.

Replica Editions are a character by character typed e-text representation with original typos preserved. Nothing is changed; it is a "slavish copy" as exact to the original in all regards as possible. Being "machine searchable" these can be useful as "indices" to a facsimile and for analysis with pattern recognition software. They are principally research tools of interest to primary textual scholarship. Few readers want the spelling mistakes preserved, but some do! The spelling inconsistencies may themselves contain information.

Critical (or scholarly) ***Editions*** include an "annotation apparatus" in which any "problem readings" are subject to scholarly commentary. These annotations are basically compendia of previous scholarship and are useful to subsequent scholarship. They provide the reader with some of the results of previous scholarship on these "problems" and may identify areas of uncertainty which require further research. These are generally produced by scholars for scholars, but "scholars" aren't confined to professionals who get paid for it. Anyone seriously interested in investigating possible nuances of meaning in any passage will find such a resource to be useful. Good

Critical Editions form the basis for all serious secondary scholarship and subsequent primary scholarship.

Interpretive Editions may or may not be scholarly, although those which achieve significant influence usually are. They are characterized by a degree of "editorial intervention" beyond merely correcting apparent errors. Rather than works of primary scholarship intended to reproduce an historical version accurately, these are "interpretive works" of secondary scholarship, are generally based on the best available primary scholarship, and are intended to mine subtle nuances of meaning. They reflect the ***opinion*** of their editors on the intended meaning rather than trying to capture the precise original text. Their objective is not reproduction; it is "interpretation."

It should be understood that the purpose of an ***Interpretive Edition*** is entirely different than that of a ***Critical Edition.*** Each reflects a very different approach. ***Interpretive Editions*** tend to be more accessible and easier to tackle for those new to the material while ***Critical Editions*** focus on precise accuracy, and sometimes this is at the expense of readability. With any book, if you just want to quickly skim through it to get a sense of it, you certainly will find footnotes distracting. When it comes time to delve into a particular passage in depth, however, those footnotes can prove helpful.

Popular Editions are generally based on a scholarly edition but omit the scholarly apparatus such as footnotes, marginalia and explanatory essays. This makes it possible to publish a less expensive, more compact product for a non-professional audience. The same attention to accuracy is expected, but they are "stripped down" for a general readership.

Urtext Editions ("urtext" is a German word meaning literally "pre-text") are common with classical musical scores and the word is applied to some editions of literary works. The term "***urtext edition***" is often used as an approximate synonym for a kind of "***scholarly edition***" which draws from multiple primary sources with the intent to reproduce the author's original intent. This can also be, and often is, referred to as an "***eclectic edition.***" Again, it is not intended to reproduce any single source, but is intended to capture "the intended meaning" as deduced from a rigorous comparison of multiple primary sources.

Eclectic Editions compare multiple primary sources and select from the variant readings according to some set of editorial principles, rather than attempting the direct reproduction of a single historical version. Those who select among variants rather obviously have as their intent the selection of the best or most authentic of the known variants. If the editorial principles are sound, and if their application is rigorous and methodical, and if the editors are skilled, the result can actually be a more authentic and accurate rendering than any of the individual primary sources. In the absence of sound scholarship, the result can be mere subjective whim which tells us more about the editor than the material being edited.

Of course any particular edition may reflect more than a single category.

Perhaps there is no better example than the Bible. The "original manuscripts" of Biblical books were all written well over 1800 years ago, in some cases much more. None of the original autographs has survived. Some Biblical material may have originated orally and have been passed down through many generations before ever being written down, during which time any number of variants might have arisen and been lost. What has survived from antiquity is a large collection of manuscripts and manuscript fragments, mostly ***at least*** several hundred years removed from their first being written down, all of which are copies of vanished copies through an unknown number of generations of vanished copies of a vanished original. In the process of repeated copying over centuries, variant readings arise

Appendix I: The *ACIM* Version/Edition Family Tree

both my mistake and by design. This results in a large number of variant readings or differences between various copies of the same material.

Primary Biblical scholarship is the discipline which, using techniques sometimes reminiscent of crime scene investigators, sifts through the archaeological evidence for the clues these fragments can provide as to what the "original text" might have been.

Virtually all contemporary Bible translations, for instance, work from "**eclectic critical editions**" of the *Hebrew Old Testament* and *Greek New Testament* known as a "**consensus text**."[8] A consensus text is created by a panel of scholars who evaluate variant readings and discuss and debate their merits until they establish a "consensus" as to which is the most authentic variant.

This represents the consensus among many scholars as to the best (most original and authentic) of the known variant readings for any passage in the Bible rather than any particular ancient manuscript. Such "consensus texts" are the fruits of primary textual scholarship and are the raw materials for secondary textual scholarship, two closely related but very different branches of textual scholarship. Primary scholarship has as its aim the establishment of the authentic text and comes into play wherever there are variant readings or questions about textual authenticity. In the case of the Bible it is a vast field because there are so many variants among available ancient source materials. Secondary scholarship seeks to interpret the text and, of course, starts with the best and most authentic text primary scholarship can produce. Of course there is some spill-over between the two. In the process of interpreting a passage a secondary scholar may delve into primary scholarship issues and question the authenticity of particular variants and in the process of sifting variants, primary scholars may well look at "interpretive clues" which derive from secondary scholarship.

The situation of the Bible is very similar to that of *A Course in Miracles* although it is often perceived very differently. Course students debate "which version is best" but rarely do Christians debate which ancient "version" of a Biblical passage is the best, when there are differences. Rather they look to primary scholarship and such things as scholarly "consensus texts" for the "most authentic reading." Course students don't do that for one simple reason: there is, to date, almost no respectable primary textual scholarship on *A Course in Miracles*. Instead there are multiple reproductions of historical versions with varying degrees of accuracy, all claiming, some quite misleadingly, to be "authentic."

In a nutshell, primary scholarship deals with 'what it says" and secondary scholarship deal with "what it means." Rather obviously the two are complementary and also rather obviously you can't begin to analyse "what it means" without first knowing "what it says!"

The four available historical scribal versions of *A Course in Miracles* present thousands of "variant readings." No one has yet identified all of them or made a *Catalogue of Variant Readings* although many variants have been identified and studied to some extent. Many of the variants are corrections of earlier scribal errors. Yet other variants involve re-working previous material for style. Some involve the deletion of "too personal" material whose removal was directed by the "Voice." A huge proportion, however, are simply inadvertent copying mistakes resulting from frequent recopying of the material without proofing. It is unlikely that the Scribes were even aware of most of these inadvertent errors although in some cases they were noticed and "fixed," but frequently not by restoring the material to the original, rather by "re-writing" the material to correct a grammar flaw resulting from the omission. While such editorial interventions cured the grammar problem, they did not restore the material to its original wording, and frequently they did not restore the original meaning either.

The first task of primary scholarship for *A Course in Miracles* is simply to gather and sort and index all of the available source material and develop that *Catalogue of Variant Readings*. The variant readings have to be identified before they can be analysed.

It seems clear that in the years of recopying and editing those involved were sincerely trying to "clean up" and "perfect" the material while preserving its "purity and integrity." However it is difficult to avoid the conclusion that due to inadequate proofing, although they did in fact "fix" some earlier problems, they introduced even more new ones, and they were almost certainly *unaware* that they had done so in many if not most cases.

In some cases their deletions are highly questionable and it is not always possible to be certain if they were intended or inadvertent. It is difficult to explain the removal of the huge section on sex and possession as "inadvertent." It's also impossible to explain the removal as "directed by the author" since the material is so clearly ***intended*** to be part of the Course and even says so explicitly.

Each of the several versions, then, contains "correct" material not present in any other and no single one of them is without mistakes. Yet in comparing all of them, the mistakes tend to show up readily enough and the "original intended reading" is often not at all difficult to discern from among the variants. There are only a few cases where it's not reasonably clear which of the available variants is the "best." However, what is obvious to one observer is not always obvious to all. This is where "scholarly consensus" comes in. Various opinions may exist but as many scholars examine, study and debate the issues, a "consensus" usually emerges, and if not a consensus, at least a clear majority opinion.

In order to produce a "consensus text" or an "eclectic version" of *A Course in Miracles* in which all of the mistakes are identified and corrected, and all the variants compared and analysed, it is exceedingly useful to begin with entirely accurate machine-readable copies of each of the versions to be compared.

Of course consensus texts were being made long before there were computers, but computers are much more efficient at identifying small differences between two texts than are humans. We don't yet have a single complete collection of thoroughly proofed texts. From a complete and accurate collection of source material, a *Catalogue of Variant Readings* can be compiled, and with the help of computers, it can be compiled quite quickly and easily. It essentially involves a list of all passages for which there are variations between versions, and what those variations are. This will make it simple to identify all variants in the extant sources for any passage which does, in fact, have variants. And there are thousands.

Any edition may appear as a printed book or an "e-text" edition or both. An "e-text" is generally a computer file in one of several formats which can be searched for text strings, displayed on a computer screen, or even printed. This mechanical searchability is enormously useful for reference purposes and for scholarship.

In the case of *A Course in Miracles* there are at least four "authorities" or "primary sources." These are the documents in which the Scribes themselves had a hand. These are the "scribal versions." These include the first print editions and several radically different manuscript versions, both hand and typewritten, some portions of which are well endowed with handwritten mark-up indicating editorial changes suggested some time after the document was first written. Where a typed manuscript has substantial mark-up there are really two versions on a single sheet of paper, the "pre-mark-up" version as originally typed or written by hand and the "post-mark-up" version as emended by the handwritten editing instructions. These instructions frequently suggest the movement of paragraph breaks

---

[8] Unfortunately for Course students, no such "consensus text" of *ACIM* yet exists, rather there are several different versions which vary enormously in length and wording. Hopefully this discussion will at least provide the student with some critical awareness of what the differences, strengths and weaknesses of each are.

Appendix I: The *ACIM* Version/Edition Family Tree

and sometimes involve wording changes. The evidence suggests there have been five principal versions, of which copies of four are presently available. Each of these four has at least two different variants, one with and one without mark-up. In the case of the *HLC* the mark-up is very minor and almost entirely involves corrections of typos. There is so little it can be largely disregarded. In the case of the *Urtext Workbook* by contrast, the mark-up is extensive but mostly relates to paragraphation. In the case of the *Nun's Version* there are multiple editions, each of which contains corrections of some typos in the earlier editions, and some which contain entirely, albeit mostly minor, original new variations. Indeed, each of the several printings of the *First Edition* included some corrections of earlier typos.

So, within several of the "four versions" there are in fact **two or more** "sub-versions."

In all the primary sources there are typos, obvious spelling and punctuation mistakes and other inconsistencies and every editor of a new edition has to decide how these will be handled. They can be ignored, as would be the case in a **replica edition** or some of them may be corrected according to strict or lax editorial principles which will vary depending on the kind of edition being prepared. Alternatively, as we can see in some editions, editors may simply "correct" material according to subjective whim.

One of the problems with some editions of the *Course* is that the "editorial principles" used to define errors and the methodology applied for correcting them appear fuzzy and are inconsistently applied. Part of the explanation for this is that many of the publications were produced by people with little if any publishing experience and with resources which were inadequate to the task. Brimming with "good intentions" and an eagerness to make the *Course* more available, they sometimes lacked the discipline and skill or simply the resources required to produce a result of consistently high quality.

The early publishing history of the Bible reveals some rather similar problems including a lack of proof-reading. Often the problem is simply lack of resources. Thorough proofreading is a labour-intensive process and small mistakes are very easy for humans to miss. When dealing with a huge book like *A Course in Miracles* we are talking about many thousands of hours of labour to achieve "thorough proofreading." One either has to mobilize, organize and train a substantial team of volunteers or one needs a budget adequate to hire professional proofreading services. Many of those involved in *A Course In Miracles* publishing since its beginnings in 1975 had neither!

Once you set out to correct even one error, however obvious, you need some guidelines to determine what is an "error" and what is an *intentional* idiosyncratic wording, or even spelling. "Correcting obvious typos" sounds simple until one encounters those situations where in one opinion it is a typo and in another it is perceived as intentional use of an unusual grammatical or literary form. Determining just what is really an error in the original and what is an intentional form is by no means always simple, nor is there always unanimous agreement. Various editions reflect various different ways of understanding "error." Some editions explain their guidelines and even document the changes they chose to make, while others make no visible distinction between precise replication of the original and their own editorial modifications.

I can sympathize with these problems because when I first set out to "edit" a Course manuscript I wanted to change a great deal. Having worked as an editor I think I know what "good English" is and what "proper grammar" is and my instinct was to make the text I was looking at conform to me ideas of "good style."

I can also empathize with Schucman's comment "I wanted to change everything." The style and structure and vocabulary in the Course is unique and conforms only to its own "style guide." Anyone with editorial experience or inclinations is itching to use that orange editor's pencil a great deal. In my first editing pass on the *HLC* for instance I had a huge list of proposed changes. As these were discussed back and forth among a number of people the list kept getting smaller and smaller as I became convinced that what was on the page, while very **unusual** was also usually very much **intended**. Based on comments made on the first edition of the *Corrected HLC*, the list has grown smaller still.

Any team producing a contemporary edition of *A Course in Miracles,* then, has a lot of decisions to make and as can be seen from the great variation in the several editions, these can be made in a variety of different ways. Each edition reflects a particular set of 'editorial principles' which range from 'subjective whim' to clearly articulated and well-recognized standards of textual scholarship which are applied with some degree of rigour.

7. Publisher Contact Information

EA
Endeavor Academy
501 E. Adams St
Wisconsin Dells
Wisconsin USA 53965
Telephone: (608) 253-6898
Fax: (608) 253-2892

FIP
Foundation for Inner Peace
PO Box 598
Mill Valley, California
USA 94942-0598
email info@acim.org

MIAP
Miracles in Action Press, LLC
52 Fitzgerald Drive,
Jaffrey, NH USA 03452
URL www.miraclesinactionpress.com
Email: doug@miraclesinactionpress.com

MPF (Doug Thompson)
Miracles Pathway Fellowship
160C Arthur St. N.,
Guelph, Ontario
Canada N1E 4V5
Telephone: 519-780-0922
E-mail dthomp74@hotmail.com

Raincoast
Raincoast Books
9050 Shaughnessy Street
Vancouver, British Columbia
Canada V6P 6E5
Telephone: 604-323-7100
Fax: 604-323-2600
Email: info@raincoast.com

Raphael Greene
Raphael Greene
email: task.hope@gmail.com

CIMS (Tom Whitmore)
7602 Pacific Street, Suite 304
Omaha, Nebraska
USA 68114
Telephone: 800-771-5056
fax: 402-391-0343
email: tom@whitmorelaw.com

Appendix II: Identifying the *Urtext* Manuscript

Table of Contents

1	WHAT IS THE *URTEXT*?	2
2	HOW IS THE WORD "URTEXT" USED IN *ACIM* WRITINGS	3
3	VERSION HISTORY FROM THE FIP/WAPNICK ACCOUNT	4
4	HOW IS THE WORD "URTEXT" USED ELSEWHERE?	4
5	IS THE "*ACIM URTEXT*" REALLY AN "URTEXT?" … FIRST IMPRESSIONS	6
6	WHAT DOES THE TEXTUAL EVIDENCE ITSELF TELL US?	6
	1. CHARACTERISTICS OF VISUAL COPYING ERRORS: DROPPING WORDS AND PHRASES	6
	2. CHARACTERISTICS OF ORAL TYPING: WRONG WORD TYPING MISTAKES	7
	3. IDIOSYNCRATIC ERRORS	8
	4. DUPLICATIONS	8
	5. EVIDENCE FROM THE PAGINATION	9
	6. CONTRA-INDICATIONS	11
7	CONCLUSION: THE *URTEXT* IS NOT ENTIRELY THE *THETFORD TRANSCRIPT*	12
8	HOW COULD SUCH A MISTAKE BE MADE AND PERSIST?	13
9	WHY IT IS IMPORTANT TO DETERMINE THE PROVENANCE OF THESE MANUSCRIPTS	13

1 What is the *Urtext*?

by Doug Thompson

Most students of *A Course in Miracles* have heard the story of the origins. Helen Schucman heard a "Voice" and took what she called "inner dictation" in her shorthand notebooks. Periodically she dictated those notes to her colleague William Thetford who typed them up, and then read them back to her to ensure accuracy. This first typed transcript has been referred to as the "*Urtext.*" Later this first transcript was edited and retyped several times before the book was first printed. While the story was widely circulated, the original *Notebooks* and the *Thetford Transcript* were kept secret. The word "urtext" then has been widely understood to be synonymous, in terms of the Course, with the term *Thetford Transcript.*

When a collection of digitized photocopies of early typed manuscript copies of the Course labelled "*Urtext of a Course in Miracles*" surfaced in 2000 it was of course assumed to be that first *Thetford Transcript* of the original *Shorthand Notebooks,* and it was assumed to be a highly accurate copy of that original dictation.

While I think some of the *Urtext* material may well be that original *Thetford Transcript,* after seven years of studying it, I have gradually come to doubt that much of it is. There is considerable evidence that at least some of it is a later retyping. In this essay I shall attempt to review and discuss the relevant evidence which has come to my attention.

It is the second oldest manuscript of *A Course in Miracles (ACIM)* currently available, that much is beyond dispute. The most widely recognized authorities such as Kenneth Wapnick and Judith Skutch's Foundation for Inner Peace (FIP) have repeatedly asserted that the original *Thetford Transcript* was called by the name "urtext."

Two serious scholarly analyses of the differences between the "versions" published to date, by Robert Perry[1] and Richard Smoley,[2] have both accepted, without question, the identification of the *Urtext* as the *Thetford Transcript.* Neither author had access to the *Notes* when these articles were written, however.

I am not aware of anyone – except me – who has seriously challenged the identification of the *Urtext* with the *Thetford Transcript.* On this and a number of other questions there has been a tendency, which I have often shared, to simply accept the declarations of Wapnick and FIP as authoritative and not requiring corroboration. One reason for this has been the lack of access to the primary source materials without which corroboration is difficult.

It was only after nearly a decade of investigation, and with enormous reluctance, that I finally accepted that much of the *Urtext* is very likely ***not*** the *Thetford Transcript,* but rather a later retyping.

Because I am now convinced this is not the *Thetford Transcript,* and I am very aware that there is a widespread belief that it is, I feel it essential to at least present the evidence which can help us correctly identify this significant manuscript collection.

Within weeks of its release in August of 2000, a few questions began to be raised as to whether or not it really was that original *Thetford Transcript* or a later, edited re-typing, or even a combination of parts of several re-typings. Further study cast progressively more doubt on the identification of this document as the *Thetford Transcript.* The ultimate test is to simply compare the various documents in detail. Yet much of the primary source material was not available to scholarship. Since comparisons with unavailable documents obviously couldn't be done there was a widespread feeling that there was no way to tell so that Wapnick's identification simply had to be accepted.

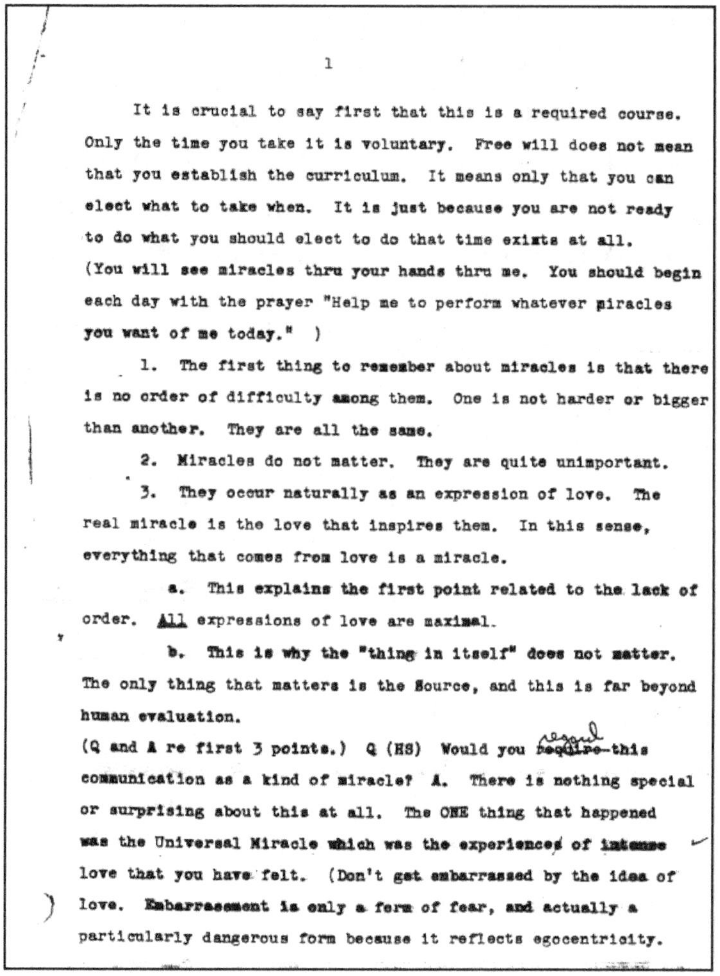

1

It is crucial to say first that this is a required course. Only the time you take it is voluntary. Free will does not mean that you establish the curriculum. It means only that you can elect what to take when. It is just because you are not ready to do what you should elect to do that time exixts at all.

(You will see miracles thru your hands thru me. You should begin each day with the prayer "Help me to perform whatever miracles you want of me today.")

1. The first thing to remember about miracles is that there is no order of difficulty among them. One is not harder or bigger than another. They are all the same.

2. Miracles do not matter. They are quite unimportant.

3. They occur naturally as an expression of love. The real miracle is the love that inspires them. In this sense, everything that comes from love is a miracle.

a. This explains the first point related to the lack of order. All expressions of love are maximal.

b. This is why the "thing in itself" does not matter. The only thing that matters is the Source, and this is far beyond human evaluation.

(Q and A re first 3 points.) Q (HS) Would you ~~require~~ regard this communication as a kind of miracle? A. There is nothing special or surprising about this at all. The ONE thing that happened was the Universal Miracle which was the experience~~s~~ of ~~intense~~ love that you have felt. (Don't get embarrassed by the idea of love. Embarrassment is only a form of fear, and actually a particularly dangerous form because it reflects egocentricity.

Figure 1: The first page of the *Urtext* manuscript of the *Text* volume

Now that we can compare much of it with the *Notes* we see that the *Urtext* is not an exact transcription of the *Notes.* Nor are many of the differences "inadvertent" discrepancies which could be explained as oral transcription errors. This *Urtext* is heavily edited in portions and a great deal of it shows clear, and in some cases utterly indisputable, evidence of being a "re-typing" with editing and sequencing changes and copying errors rather than an original transcript.

[1] Robert Perry: *The Earlier Versions and the Editing of A Course in Miracles,* Circle of Atonement.
http://www.circleofa.org/articles/EarlierVersions.php

[2] Richard Smoley: *A Comparison of Miracles*, Fearless Press

Appendix II: Identifying the *Urtext* Manuscript

2 How is the word "urtext" used in *ACIM* writings

The source for the notion that the *Urtext* is the original *Thetford Transcript* is not hard to find. In the "*Errata for the Second Edition*"[3] published by the Foundation for Inner Peace (FIP) in 1992 we read:

> "Helen took down her internal dictation in notebooks, and regularly dictated these to her colleague and collaborator, Dr. William Thetford, who typed out her words. This original typing of the three books came to be called the "urtext,"[4] a word denoting an original manuscript."

Wapnick, for his part, offers a slightly more detailed set of observations. The following quote comes from his introduction to the 32-part cassette tape series entitled: "*Classes on the Text of A Course in Miracles*":

> "Let me say a few words about the relationship of the early chapters of the text to what Helen had originally taken down. Briefly – since most of you know the story – Helen had written down the dictation from Jesus in notebooks. […] She then dictated what she had written down to Bill Thetford, who typed it out. What Bill typed out is what we usually refer to as the urtext. *The word "ur" comes from the biblical story of Abraham, who was born in Ur of the Chaldees. Basically it is used to symbolize the beginning of something.* (emphasis mine)

> "So when we speak of an urtext, we mean the first version of a manuscript. Thus there are famous urtexts of Shakespeare's works and many other literary masters. With regard to *A Course in Miracles*, we used that term to denote what Bill had typed, the original typed manuscript that was based on Helen's notebooks. Helen then re-typed the manuscript of the text twice. And then there was the penultimate version, which was the version I saw when I met Helen and Bill. That is the version[5] Helen and I edited into the finished copy -- the published copy."

The two primary documentary sources explicitly say the *Urtext* is the *Thetford Transcript*. Since it was Wapnick who filed the "*Urtext*" material at the copyright office,[6] it seemed to be a reasonable assumption that he understood what he was filing to be the *Thetford Transcript*. Wapnick, who probably had more and better access to a vastly wider range of primary source material than anyone else, and who knew the Scribes and their work as well as anyone alive, was presumed to be "The Authority" on this matter. Indeed, it was only after the evidence of the mistake became overwhelming that I reluctantly concluded that, incredible as it might seem, Wapnick was perhaps mistaken on this point.

The typed *Urtext* manuscript of the *Text* volume which appeared in 2000 was obviously earlier and much larger than any version of *ACIM* then public, and it was labelled "*Urtext.*" Naturally, given these "authoritative" descriptions of the *Urtext* from FIP and Wapnick, it was first assumed to be the *Thetford Transcript*.

Also from the "*Errata*" we read:

> "After each of these typing sessions, Bill read back to Helen what he typed to ensure that no mistakes were made. Thus, the urtext can be considered to have been carefully checked, and to be an accurate copy of Helen's original notes. Helen later re-typed the manuscript of the Text twice and the Workbook and Manual once, and none of these re-typings was [sic] ever proofread."

If the FIP "history" here is correct, and there is independent corroboration of some key points, this is a fairly high level of "proofreading" and would certainly catch most inadvertent errors such as omitted words or phrases. William Thetford is on tape stating much the same thing about the careful proofreading. Schucman read her *Notes* to him aloud, he typed them up and read them back to her to ensure accuracy.

We would therefore **assume** it to be accurate as Wapnick suggests. However, most notably in the early chapters, this *Urtext* is not nearly as accurate a copy of the *Notes* as we might expect from these accounts. To date no thorough comparison of the *Notes* and the *Urtext* has been done in order to completely catalogue the differences, but in the few chapters I've compared, the differences are numerous.

We'd expect any mortal typist to make some errors, and that would be a reason for this proofreading, to catch and correct typing mistakes. We'd expect that proofreading to identify some errors which we'd see as pencilled-in corrections but in the *Urtext* documents overall there is little which looks like the corrections we'd expect to see from such proofreading. In marked contrast, the short *Psychotherapy* volume, in just 29 pages, has several instances of precisely what we'd expect from an orally proofed transcript. In the 1072 pages of the *Urtext Text* volume, there is proportionately much less of this sort of editing.

While FIP and Wapnick disagree on the number of retypings, they both agree there were **at least two** typed manuscripts made, the original *Thetford Transcript* and one or more retypings of it, for every volume, with the *Text* having at least one more than the other volumes. The "other volumes" here may relate only to the *Workbook, Manual for Teachers*, and possibly the *Use of Terms*. So far, however, we only have a single typed manuscript earlier than the *HLC* for a total of two for the *Text* and only a single pre-1975 typed manuscript for the other volumes. These are the ones from *22 Volumes* material labelled "*Urtext*."

So our sources say two or more typed manuscript copies of the Course were made. What we have here labelled "urtext" is a typed copy of the *Notes* with some material added, some material omitted, and some material re-sequenced. It is almost certainly one of the several early typed copies, but which one?

---

[3] http://www.miraclestudies.net/Errata.html (errata to the FIP Second Edition)
[4] It is interesting to note that FIP reserves the name "*Urtext*" for volumes 1,2, and 3 only, and does not include the other volumes.
[5] http://www.miraclestudies.net/HLV.html
[6] 22 Volumes of "*Helen Schucman's Unpublished Writings*" were filed at the United States Copyright Office in 1990 by Kenneth Wapnick at the request of Helen Schucman's husband Louis Schucman. That material includes eight separate manuscripts labelled "*Urtext of A course in Miracles and Related Material,*" one each for the *Text, Workbook, Manual, Use of Terms, Psychotherapy, Song of Prayer, Gifts of God* and *Special Messages*.

Appendix II: Identifying the *Urtext* Manuscript

3 Version History from the FIP/Wapnick account

While FIP seems to indicate that the *HLC* may be the second re-typing, from Wapnick's descriptions the *Text* "version history" includes **six** versions:
1. *Notes*
2. *Thetford Transcript* (mistakenly called the *Urtext*?)
3. *First Re-typing* (which may actually be the *Urtext*?)
4. *Second Re-typing* (this may refer to the *HLC*?)
5. *HLC*
6. *Criswell/FIP* Editions

What we actually have copies of for the *Text* is only *four*:
1. *Notes*
2. *Urtext* (likely one of the re-typings)
3. *HLC*
4. *Criswell/FIP* Editions

From both the FIP and Wapnick descriptions, the other volumes "version history" involves *four* versions:
1. *Notes*
2. *Thetford Transcript* (which they called *Urtext?*)
3. *First Re-typing* (which more likely is the *Urtext?*)
4. *Criswell/FIP* First Edition

What we actually have copies of for the other volumes is only *three*:
1. *Notes*
2. *Urtext* (we can't be entirely certain which re-typing it is. Some portions may be the *Thetford Transcript*)
3. *Criswell/FIP*

Wapnick and FIP disagree on the number of additional retypings, but agree that there was more than one. The physical evidence appears to support their assertion that more exist than have so far come to light. There certainly is physical evidence of another retyping for the *Text* and in the extant *Urtext* we can see that some sections appear to have been re-worked multiple times while other sections appear exactly as they do in the *Notes*. It would appear that some portions were more heavily edited, and perhaps more frequently re-typed, than other segments. There thus may be (or at one time may have been) several partial retypings reflecting different stages of editing, or different versions, for some portions of the Course.

In any event, if the FIP and Wapnick reports of multiple complete or even partial retypings are correct, and I know of no evidence to suggest they are not, the question arises as to which of those multiple retypings the manuscripts labelled "urtext" represent. Are they the original typed transcripts or a later re-typed copy, or a combination of two or more originally distinct manuscripts, or even something else entirely?

Wapnick and the FIP *Errata to the Second Edition* were really the only published sources from which we could assess what this "*Urtext*" material in the *22 Volumes* was. While they disagree on a key point, that being how many retypings there were in total, they agree on what an "urtext" is. On this point however, it would seem that they may both be mistaken.

Wapnick said: "The word 'ur' comes from the Biblical story of Abraham, who was born in Ur of the Chaldees. Basically it is used to symbolize the beginning of something." He also says "urtext" is "a word denoting an original manuscript."

Every dictionary consulted, along with several encyclopaedias state that the term "urtext" derives from the German word "ur" (pronounced "oor") which means "original." It has nothing to do with Ur of the Chaldees or Abraham. As for "denoting an original manuscript" well … not *exactly* and certainly not *necessarily*.

4 How is the word "urtext" used elsewhere?

While dictionaries generally indicate that "ur" means "original" and "urtext" means "original text" this in no way means that "urtext" means the author's original autograph or any precise copy of it. It must be noted that it is easy to assume from such a brief dictionary definition that this is exactly what it means, and that may explain part of how the word "urtext" became connected with the *Thetford Transcript*.

If "urtext is taken to mean "original manuscript," the *Notes* would have to be considered "the urtext" since they are the original. A precisely accurate typed transcript could be considered the "same thing" or an "urtext transcript" but any subsequent edited version could not be considered "an urtext." Yet, when we find "urtext versions" of musical scores being published, they are **neither** "original manuscripts" **nor** precise copies of original autographs.

This is crucial to our understanding of the *ACIM Urtext*. In fact, as we shall see, the word "urtext" is far from precise and may refer to a variety of "earlier" things, but only rarely to "original autographs" or exact typed copies of them.

The most common usage of the word "urtext" seems largely, but not entirely, confined to classical musical scores. It comes from the German root for "original," "source," or "earlier." It is a prefix, much like "pre" in English. This meaning is not drawn from a dictionary, but from consultation with native German speakers who insist it **may** mean "original" or "earli**est**" but also **may** more generally mean "previous" or "earli**er**" – in short it is a relative, not a superlative term. Something may be both "earlier" than something else and also, but not necessarily, the "earliest."

There is more evidence that it is not necessarily a superlative term. In the *Britannica* definition (below) it is described as something "pieced together" from earlier sources with the intent to reflect the "original" meaning, but that is quite different from "the original autograph" or "earliest primary source."

In fact there seems little difference between the meaning of the term "Critical Edition" as applied to a literary work and "urtext" as applied to a musical score in that they share the overall intent to **reconstruct** or "piece together," as *Britannica* puts it, the "original intent" as closely as possible from extant primary sources.

In that sense of being a scholarly work piecing together primary sources, far from being the most primary source of all, which is the connotation of the word "original," it would in fact be a secondary source derived from primary sources, albeit with the intent to reflect an original document or at least the author's original intent which was presumed to have existed, at least hypothetically.

I say "hypothetically" because while the author of any work may be presumed to have had "an intent" which is at least theoretically knowable, no single one of that author's written drafts may actually represent it entirely. But, in sorting through the available evidence with the aim of representing that author's original intent, the result is called an "urtext." In short, it represents the **opinion** as to the author's original intent of those who pieced it together by examining all

Appendix II: Identifying the *Urtext* Manuscript

relevant documents rather than the "author's original statement" in any particular document.

This is a crucial, if subtle, distinction. By this definition the *Thetford Transcript* and the *Notes* would not be considered "urtexts." However, the document we refer to as the *Urtext* appears to genuinely be a "pieced together" urtext.

The document known as the *ACIM Urtext*, whatever it is, is not a precise copy of the *Notes*. It has many differences beyond what can be explained as copying errors. It shows clear signs of editing and many signs of visual copying errors and other evidence of retyping, but rather little sign of "oral errors" except in the *Psychotherapy* volume.

Yet it may well be the result of the Scribes "piecing together" earlier hand and typewritten drafts to reflect their idea of the author's original intent. In fact, that is ***exactly*** what it looks like! If it ***is*** that then it ***is*** precisely and exactly an "urtext" of the "pieced together" sort. But it's neither the *Thetford Transcript*, nor a precise typed transcript of the "original autograph" which is the *Notes*.

The *Britannica* definition (below) is also quick to point out that "urtext" does not necessarily mean "original autograph" but "may lead the uninitiated to suppose" that it does!

This came as quite a shock to me and I expect many others will be very surprised also. Before I read Wapnick I'd never encountered the term "urtext" and like many I simply *assumed* he knew what he was talking about and I didn't question either his definition or his statement that the *Urtext* was the *Thetford Transcript*. I've learned many times that one must be careful of assumptions in this field. Many well-meaning people have passed on their untested assumptions, perhaps in good faith, but sincere good faith does not always equal accuracy.

From Britannica:

"The word **Urtext** ("original text") may lead the uninitiated to suppose that they are being offered an exact reproduction of what Bach wrote. It must be understood that the autographs of many important works no longer exist. Therefore, Bach's intentions often have to be pieced together from anything up to 20 sources, all different. Even first editions and facsimiles of autograph manuscripts are not infallible guides to Bach's intentions. In fact, they are often dangerously misleading, and practical musicians should take expert advice before consulting them. ..."

While the primary use of the term appears to be for a kind of scholarly reconstruction of classical musical scores, some sources allow for its use on "a musical sore *or a literary work*."

From Encarta:

"Urtext (German for "original text"), edition of music that tries to capture the original intentions of the composer and minimizes editorial interpretation as much as possible. Urtext editions are usually based upon the composer's sketches and manuscripts, as well as original and early editions of the works."

From Wikipedia:

"An urtext edition of a work of classical music is a printed version intended to reproduce the original intention of the composer as exactly as possible, without any added or changed material. Other kinds of editions distinct from urtext are facsimile and interpretive editions [...].

"The word "urtext" is of German origin; "ur-" means "original". Occasionally the word "urtext" is capitalized, following German spelling practice."

From Oxford Literary Dictionary:

"Urtext, the German term for an original version of a text, usually applied to a version that is lost and so has to be reconstructed by textual criticism. Some scholars believe that Shakespeare's Hamlet is based on an earlier play that has not survived even in name; this hypothetical work is referred to as the Ur-Hamlet."

On that note, Henning Diedrich observes "there is the *Ur-Faust*, which is a proper, valid play on its own. There is *Faust I, Faust II*, and *Ur-Faust. Ur-Faust* was written decades earlier, probably never published, and was prose, as opposed to the verses of Faust I and II."

In this later sense of "ur" the German word's connotation of original, early document is clearly dominant. The "*Ur-Hamlet*" and "*Ur-Faust*" however do not really refer to "urtexts" (pieced together reconstructions) of either *Hamlet* or *Faust*! The meaning of "*Ur-Hamlet*" isn't "the first text (original copy) of *Hamlet*" so much as it is "the first *Hamlet*" or even "the literary origin or basis for *Hamlet*" which is something rather different. This is neither an "original autograph" nor a "pieced together" secondary work, so much as an earlier, previous, and even hypothetical precursor or prototype.

The difference is subtle but crucial. Assuming we had the first and original autographs of both *Hamlet* and *Ur-Hamlet*, we'd find them different, even if one was based on the other. And we could do an "urtext" (of the pieced together sort) of *Ur-Hamlet* as well as an "urtext" of *Hamlet*, if we had enough source material to work with.

Similarly with *Ur-Faust* ... it's not the same play as *Faust I* and we could presumably do an "urtext" for each play.

There are then these two somewhat divergent connotations to the German prefix "ur." Both relate to "originality" but in the first case the reference is to the scholarly reconstruction, through textual criticism, of something that is lost or never actually existed. The second refers to an earlier, more 'original' draft or version which may or may not still exist.

It's not a common word, it is not present in many dictionaries, so it is not surprising perhaps that Wapnick thought it might have to do with Abraham. Like me, he may have never heard the word before coming in contact with *ACIM* and like me he may have made assumptions about what it meant without checking.

Assuming for many years that Wapnick's definition was correct, the steadily increasing evidence that much of the "urtext" material in the *22 Volumes* was not the *Thetford Transcript* left me more and more puzzled. I was simply unprepared to accept there could be an error at this level for some years. I concede that it seems very unlikely and I fully expect there will be widespread scepticism of this hypothesis.

It seems possible the mistake was simply in the definition of the word "urtext." The word is sufficiently uncommon, imprecise and subject to variable usage that such a mistake is very understandable. I made it myself. That mistake was not recognized and corrected perhaps because they never checked. I can understand that also. It was only very recently that I began to suspect the word did ***not*** mean "autograph" and began to seriously check.

Getting the definition of a word wrong is one thing. Being unaware that the "urtext" was not in fact the *Thetford Transcript* while telling people for years that it was is a little more amazing. How could they have not known? Could it be that they never seriously checked that and several other assumptions they made and repeated, perhaps even in good faith, but without verifying them? Could it be that the actual *Thetford Transcript* no longer exists? Whatever misunderstandings of the definitions of unusual words might occur, it strikes me as highly improbable that one could fail to notice a difference between that original transcript and an urtext derived in part from it if one had both in one's hands.

In summary then, here's our problem: there is a "story" about the origins of the Course which comes from people who are in a position to know. So we believe it, having no reason not to, and besides it's not easy to check that story due to the fact that the documentary sources by which it could be checked are not available. As the documentary sources become available, we use the "story" to identify the documents but as we study the documents, various elements of the "story" are called into question. The origins of the word "urtext" with Abraham is simply not correct. The definition of the term "urtext" is not necessarily correct. The identification of the *Urtext* manuscript as the *Thetford Transcript* is almost certainly not

Appendix II: Identifying the *Urtext* Manuscript

entirely correct at least. And our two sources disagree with each other as to the number of retypings.

"The Authorities" on these matters appear less reliable than we'd like. This doesn't mean the rest of their information is incorrect, but it does remind us that anyone can err and verification is required.

5 Is the *"ACIM Urtext"* really an "urtext?" ... first impressions

Now Helen Schucman, who had some familiarity with classical music and might well have been familiar with **precisely** what an "urtext" is in that field, may well have adopted that word since it loosely described what she and Thetford had done with the "primary sources" which were her *Notes* and his *Transcript* as they edited those into a manuscript which I strongly suspect is in fact what we are referring to here by the name *Urtext*. They had corrected some typos in the earlier material, added to them segments "dictated without notes" and applied some of the corrections the Author had dictated. In short, the *ACIM Urtext* is, actually, an "urtext" in the "pieced together" meaning of the word, insofar as a term derived from music publishing can be applied to literature. Its use in literature is uncommon but not unprecedented. The *American Heritage Dictionary* does allow that while it normally applies to musical composition it can be used to refer to a "literary work."

When you look at the *ACIM Urtext* the expression "piecing together" immediately comes to mind. It is obviously assembled from bits and pieces of several different drafts, it has multiple internal pagination systems, was typed on at least two different typewriters, contains some duplication, and even has some pages marked "retyped," rather proving it wasn't a "single typing." It includes material not in the *Notes* while omitting some material that is in the *Notes*. While this is not wholly conclusive by itself, it does raise doubts about this being the *Thetford Transcript*.

Now if we had a document typed up by Thetford, incrementally day by day, simply copying down what Schucman dictated from her *Notes*, we'd not expect to see such "piecing together." Sure, some anomalies might arise from any number of causes, and Thetford may have re-typed the occasional page, but we aren't seeing anomalies within a document that looks like what we'd expect, the whole thing is anomalous, and little of it, aside from the *Psychotherapy* volume, looks like it is a document dictated orally, and then orally proofed.

It looks just like an "urtext" based on visually copying without proofreading, which we are told is how the first retyping came into being.

So let's probe the evidence further.

6 What does the textual evidence itself tell us?

Aside from the fact that it doesn't look like an orally dictated transcript, or what we'd expect to see in such a transcript, is there any other evidence? What it "looks like" and that "it looks all wrong" may raise questions but questions are not proof.

1. Characteristics of Visual Copying Errors: Dropping Words and Phrases

When one makes a copy by typing by eye one typically makes different errors than one makes when typing from oral dictation. I worked for years as a newspaper typesetter, where much of the work in the shop involved copy-typists manually copying typed and handwritten paper documents. It's the same kind of technology I presume Schucman had available for her "re-typing" work on *ACIM*. The typist sits at a keyboard (typewriter or typesetting machine, the latter is just a more sophisticated typewriter) with a "copy stand" on which sits the paper "original." At the newspaper the "original" is generally the reporter's typed story as marked up and "edited" by the editor. The copy-typist reads it and types what the reporter wrote as adjusted by the editor. Secretaries in office typing pools and typesetters in publishing firms were doing vast amounts of that labour-intensive copy-typing all over the world until computers and scanners and OCR technology almost entirely replaced that copy-typing activity in the past two decades. Now reporters type into computer files instead of onto paper and editors simply modify the reporter's file on screen and send it straight to production, with no re-typing required. There's a huge saving in labour and a huge reduction in "copying mistakes."

There are a number of exceedingly common mistakes when humans copy type by eye, and they show up frequently in the *ACIM* manuscripts. I saw these every day for years in the typesetting shop which is why I noticed them immediately. It is very easy to leave out words and phrases and even sentences and whole paragraphs. This is especially the case when there are two instances of the same word in close proximity. If, when the words between those two instances are left out, the result is still grammatically and factually correct, as is often the case, it's far from obvious that a mistake has been made at all. It's difficult from reading the result to notice the omission. There are many instances of this in *ACIM* from version to version, and this is utterly typical of the most common of visual copy-typing errors.

This does not mean that every omission is an "error." Some may well be intentional. Very few of the omissions appear to be intentional however.

I'll cite just one of many hundreds of examples where a line is left out, almost certainly unintentionally, while visually copy-typing. This is from the *Text* chapter 2. The *Urtext* reads:

> "T 2 C 8 The body, if properly understood, shares the invulnerability of the Atonement to two-edged application. This is not because the body is a miracle, but because it is not inherently open to misinterpretation. The body is merely a fact. Its ABILITIES can be, and frequently are, overevaluated. However, it is almost impossible to deny its existence. Those who do are engaging in a particularly unworthy form of denial. (The use of the word "unworthy" here implies simply that it is not necessary to protect the mind by denying the un-mindful. *There is little doubt that the mind can miscreate.* If one denies this unfortunate aspect of its power, one is also denying the power itself.)"

The emphasized line does not appear in the *HLC* or the later FIP editions. It is, however, in both the *Notes* and the *Urtext*. Without that sentence, the antecedent for "this unfortunate aspect" in the last sentence is gone, rendering it meaningless. What then does "this unfortunate aspect" refer to? The "unfortunate aspect" is, of course, the mind's ability to miscreate.

This is a classic example of an "inadvertent omission" copy-typing mistake. Usually, when the effect of an omission is to leave the following sentence incoherent, as in this case, it gets caught. I am quite surprised this one didn't get caught.

Appendix II: Identifying the *Urtext* Manuscript

In the case of the *Urtext* to the *HLC* we presume it was visually re-typed and we see hundreds of these small omissions. They are entirely predictable in human copy-typing which has not been proofed but very rare in proofed material. In the *Urtext* when compared to the *Notes* we see the same pattern of numerous, and usually small omissions which do not appear to be intentional.

One of the many omissions of *Notes* material in the *Urtext* typical of copying by eye is found in chapter 16 of the *Text*, in the first paragraph. Both the original *Notes* and the partly proofed FIP *Second Edition* include as the fourth sentence of that paragraph "His way is very different." It's underlined in the *Notes*. Neither the "*Urtext*" manuscript nor the *HLC* manuscripts include this sentence, nor does the FIP *First Edition*.

That's not the kind of error we get when typing to oral dictation and then proofing it by reading it back! First, such omissions which are a kind of optical illusion are much less likely when typing to oral dictation that is pacing itself to your typing speed. We used to do that sometimes in newspapers too. Reporters who could not physically transport a typed story on paper back to the office in time would "phone it in" and someone at the office, sometimes me, would type what the reporter read over the phone, and then of course read it back to him to ensure accuracy.

That "reading it back" will almost always catch missing words and phrases. The kind of errors we get with oral dictation involve words which sound similar and whose substitution sounds plausible. Obvious errors can still occur because they aren't obvious until the sentence or paragraph is complete, but they get caught, crossed out, and the correct word is typed or handwritten in.

There actually are a few of these in the *Text* which may stem from the original oral dictation and which never got caught. But there aren't many. It's also possible to mistype when copying by eye such that the resulting word is wrong, but still makes sense and sounds similar. The *Psychotherapy* volume is a complete contrast to the *Text* volume. We see several "oral" errors, sound alike words being substituted, crossed out, with the correct word handwritten in, which is precisely what we'd *expect* in pages typed from oral dictation. It is both the presence of these in that volume which leads to its tentative identification as, in fact, the *Thetford Transcript* and the absence of them elsewhere in the *Urtext* manuscripts which raises doubts about those other volumes being the *Thetford Transcript*. From what we've been told about the process of transcribing, such mistakes should be present and should be corrected. In fact they simply aren't there in the numbers expected, except in *Psychotherapy* and to a lesser extent in *Song of Prayer*.

In this example and most of the many other cases, deliberate omission appears unlikely as one can see no reason to suppose the words were not authentic or would otherwise be disagreeable to the Scribes.

While any particular mistake could have been made by anyone for any number of reasons and by itself proves nothing, a *pattern* of mistakes is powerful evidence, though it may well still fall short of being conclusive proof. The examples I've cited are typical, and there are hundreds of the same sort. Were there only one or two, I'd say it wouldn't mean much. Where one sees the same pattern time and again, it becomes strongly suggestive, just as where one fails to see a pattern that should be there.

2. Characteristics of Oral Typing: Wrong Word Typing Mistakes

Because I've done a lot of it, I have a sense of the kinds of errors which occur when typing to oral dictation. I'd say that almost any kind of mistake can occur. But when you read it back, most get noticed and corrected. Typing to oral dictation, even for a good typist, means numerous errors which of course are easy to fix and make vanish on a computer, but when typing onto paper, they leave visible traces on that original copy, no matter how you correct them. They might be corrected with handwriting or with overstriking, as might any errors, but you'd expect a much higher rate of error and you'd also expect any errors to be caught in the oral proofing, except possibly for ones that you can't hear.

Since we have reason to believe that Schucman typed the *HLC* we can see she was an excellent typist. Her error rate is very low. There are very few typos. Her typing is clean and largely error free. Yet in the *Urtext* we do see some pages which don't reflect such clean typing and which do include a lot of mistakes that were fixed, most notably in the *Psychotherapy* pamphlet.

For example, there is one on the first page of *Psychotherapy* where we find "Light" and we see "Life" written in, and it does not appear to me to be Schucman's handwriting. "Light" and "Life" sound enough alike that when either "makes sense" in the context, it is an easy "hearing error" to make but one which could well be caught in the proofing. This one, it seems, was caught.

Another example appears on page 9 of *Psychotherapy*. Figures 2 and 3 show the two lines in question, bottom of the second paragraph of section 3 E, *The Process of Illness*.

If you look closely (Fig. 3) you see that the last words were initially typed "*shadow be except the form.*" That's very typical of an "oral" error, "*the form*" and "*deformed*" sound very similar. The result makes grammatical and logical sense, so it could easily be missed. It is very unlikely that kind of mistake would be made by

Figure 2 *Psychotherapy* 3 E from the *Notes*.

Figure 3 the same words as in figure 2 from the *Urtext* manuscript

Appendix II: Identifying the *Urtext* Manuscript

visual copying, however, since the two forms do not *look* at all alike. The *Notes* reads "*shadow be except deformed?*" This is exactly the kind of mistake we'd **expect** to find in oral dictation that had been proofed. We'd expect it and in *Psychotherapy,* we see it, and we see it several times in a mere 29 pages! However, this kind of mistake and correction is very rare in the *Text* volume. This kind of error would of course be caught usually and would not often survive into a visually re-typed copy. Interestingly, however, the handwriting is obviously that of the same person, presumably Schucman. And that is not what we'd expect to see if Thetford is reading to her what he had just typed and marking corrections himself. Possibly this mistake was not detected in their oral proofing but was caught by Schucman later. We may never know for sure.

Another example of typical "oral mistakes" occurs on page 10 of the typed *Psychotherapy* manuscript. (see Figure 4) We see "illness lies instead" being corrected to "illness rise instead." That is what is in the *Notes*. But again "rise" and "lies" sound very much alike. These are typical of the sort of **hearing errors** which we'd expect of

```
is a meaningful concept.  Yet must their cures remain temporary, or another illness
              rise
lies instead, for death has not been overcome until the meaning of love is understood.
                                                           by
And who can understand this without the Word of God, given in Him to the Holy Spirit
as His gift to you?
```

Figure 4 In the second line "lies" is crossed out and becomes "rise" in the *Psychotherapy* manuscript which is characteristic of a hearing error rather than a visual copying error.

a manuscript typed to oral dictation.

Their presence here in the *Psychotherapy* manuscript is strongly suggestive that this may indeed be the *Thetford Transcript* and not a later re-typing. The fact that such mistakes, common in this document, are very rare in the *Urtext Text* volume would seem to indicate it is what it appears to be, a later re-typing and not the original *Thetford Transcript*. Those are just three examples. We even find corrections written into the *Notes*, such as exchanging "seek" for "find"

also written into the *Psychotherapy* manuscript which suggests the "correction" was made in both at the same time. Unless this typed manuscript was proofed against the *Notes* later, it is hard to explain how the same handwritten correction would occur in both documents. It could well have been done during the initial transcription as Schucman decided a change was needed after she dictated the word, and then made it in both her *Notes* and the transcript. It's very rare that we find editing changes in the typed manuscript reflected in the *Notes* that way. Of course it is difficult to be certain, but this is plausible and might well be expected in oral dictation and proofing, that Schucman would decide to introduce a change after first dictating it, while hearing it read back.

I've only noticed one other example of visible editing on a typed page being reflected in visible editing on a page of the *Notes*. That is actually in the *Text* volume. There may be others but they certainly are not common. The vast majority of editing we see on the typed manuscripts does not show up in the *Notes*. A possible explanation is that it was done some time later, during or after a re-typing. What we don't find here that we do find in the *Text* is numerous dropped words and phrases. The correspondence, word for word, comma for comma, between the typed manuscript of *Psychotherapy* and the *Notes* is higher than the average for the other typed manuscripts.

These, I submit, are powerful indicators which help us distinguish documents which have been copied "by ear" from the spoken word and documents which have been copied "by eye" from the written word.

3. Idiosyncratic Errors

Thetford described how he made certain typical typing errors, such as typing "bother" instead of "brother" and "slavation' instead of "salvation" and "crucifiction" instead of "crucifixion." Only in the *Psychotherapy* pamphlet have I found any of those "ideosyncratic errors." There are none in the rest of the *Urtext* material that I've spotted. Their absence in other volumes of the *Urtext* suggests a re-typed copy in which those sorts of errors were, of course, corrected. This is perhaps the most powerful evidence that in the *Urtext* we aren't looking at Thetford's original typing but at a re-typing with some editing, at least to the extent of fixing his spelling mistakes. There are two explanations for the lack of the patterns of idiosyncratic errors Thetford said were there: either this isn't the document he typed with those errors or he just made the story up. The latter seems extremely unlikely. The former is consistent with most of the other evidence.

4. Duplications

In the *Urtext* manuscript we find several instances where the same material is typed twice, not duplicate photocopies of the same page, but the same words typed on different typewriters, or with different line endings or on different parts of the page, but otherwise exactly the same words. Where the page beginning and ending are the same, this indicates that to some extent at least, this document is a combination of at least two distinct typed documents, and some of the material, at least, is re-typed and is not the "original" typed transcript. Where the duplication involves shifting page breaks, as in the example in figures 5 and 6, we see evidence which is more consistent with visual re-typing than with oral transcribing.

For instance, to pick just one of several examples, if we look at the bottom of page 454 and the top of page 455 (marked 281-282) we see the last two sentences of page 454 repeated on 455 and then crossed out by hand. (see figures 5 and 6)

It is perhaps impossible to be entirely sure of what has happened here, but it seems unlikely we'd see Thetford, while listening to Schucman read from the *Notes*, pause to change paper and then resume typing on a new page 18 words before where he'd stopped on the previous page, in the middle of a sentence! This sort of error appears much more consistent with visual re-typing than aural transcription.

It is quite possible that in re-typing, the typist got an extra two lines on the page such that the new page finished 18 words later than the page being copied. Then, perhaps having been distracted, when resuming typing on the next page the copyist began where the next

Appendix II: Identifying the *Urtext* Manuscript

page began, 18 words before where she'd left off previously. Later, this was noticed and the extra words were crossed out.

And in case you were wondering, the *Notes* (8:144-145) page break doesn't occur between "His call" and "for love" but actually a few words later, between "is" and "answered." Note that in the first copy on page 454, the word "is" is misspelled as "in." This is another sign of visual rather than aural copying. It also suggests a tired or distracted copy-typist.

It is also interesting to note that while the first two lines on p 282 (fig. 6) are the same as the last two on the previous page, there is one small difference. In the first, (fig. 5) there is a comma after "Father" which is not there in the second copy. This is illustrative of a general pattern seen where we have multiple typed copies: there are generally numerous small differences of this sort.

This isn't certain proof due to the fact that anyone can make almost any sort of error for almost any reason now and then. We weren't there at the time and cannot be entirely sure how any *particular* error arose. This is just one of many indications that we are dealing with a re-typed copy and not an original typed manuscript, however.

One or two such indications here and there are certainly not conclusive, but when we have a consistent pattern involving hundreds, the weight of "suggestive" evidence begins to add up to "conclusive proof."

The "error pattern" is consistent with visual copy-typing which was not proofed, and not aural transcription which was subsequently proofed.

---

5. Evidence from the Pagination

Further evidence lies in the pagination. It is important to note that my observations here are not based on any attempt at a thorough analysis of the pagination anomalies. It is the fact of the anomalies and the patterns I *have* noticed which are directly relevant. I strongly suspect that a very careful analysis of the pagination issues might yield significant new insights into the process by which the *Text* volume was created.

In the first 382 pages many pages bear at least two and often more page numbers, with all but one crossed out.

After page 84 the number marked on the page does not correspond exactly to the actual page number. The page numbering in the *Text* volume up to approximately the end of chapter 8 is utterly chaotic, starting, stopping, and restarting, with some pages having as many as four different numbers written, then crossed out. At the 174th page the numbering restarts at "1" and at the end of chapter 8, 382 pages from the start, the page is marked 209 and from that point to the end the numbering continues with substantial consistency and few multiple page numbers.

There are a few pagination anomalies in the latter three quarters of the manuscript. In chapter 18, section H, we have three pages of later material inserted out of chronological sequence to reflect the *HLC* ordering. It should be noted that this particular anomaly reflects the *HLC* editing and my attempt to match the *Urtext* manuscript page order to that of the *HLC* for the purpose of aligning chapter and section divisions identically between the two. Those three pages are part of the *Special Messages* material but bear page numbers and dates which would put them between 22 F and 22 G. This is not, then, an anomaly in the *Urtext* manuscript proper. This reflects subsequent scribal editing which relocated these three pages from their original sequence. The Scribes ended up including this material where we do in later editing, apparently accepting it as a "dictated correction" or "expansion" of earlier material.

In chapter 20 we have page 567a between 567 and 568 (absolute page number 744) and we have the page marked 583a between 583 and 584 (absolute page number 761). In chapter 21 we have 596a (absolute page 775). In chapter 22 we have 617a (797). Further study is required to begin to guess exactly why the Scribes needed to number some pages as "a" rather than assign a new page number but this may indicate pagination variation between an earlier copy and a new copy being made which required the insertion of extra pages. It may also indicate later insertion of material.

In chapter 26 Section F we have the page marked 732 followed by 740 with page numbers 733-739 (913-914) missing. However, there is no other indication of missing material here. The text across the "missing page numbers" is identical in the *Notes*. The anomaly here appears to be only in the page numbering. At page 731 (912) we also have an obvious change in typewriter from elite to pica. These clues suggest that possibly one segment is a later copy than the other.

In chapter 29 section E the marked pagination goes from 824 (998) back to 813 (999), reusing the page numbers 813-824. This sort of thing could happen if two or more "versions" whose pagination was slightly different due to editing or the use of different typewriters and margins were being combined later.

Careful study of these numbering anomalies and other physical clues such as changing typewriters may allow us to ultimately surmise more about the pattern of copying and recopying here. We can for instance easily discern at least two different typewriters being used and that may turn out to be an important clue as to the "generation" in copying. It may be that the shift from one typewriter to another happened at a certain point in time and that the relative age of the page may be indicated by which typewriter was used. It's also possible that Thetford used a different typewriter than Schucman did. Further study will be needed to determine if those hunches have any merit. If they do, we may be able to discern a great deal more about the actual creation of these physical pages in terms of when it was done and by whom.

The numbering anomalies in the last three quarters of the *Text* may appear numerous when listed here but are fewer than those in the first one quarter where there are too many to list.

In that latter section we also see very little handwritten mark-up. The page marked 209 is actually the 382nd page of the *Text* volume! From page 209 to the end, page 886, which is actually the 1072nd page of the *Urtext* manuscript, the numbers also very closely approximate those of the later *HLC* version. The material on page 209 of the *Urtext* occurs on page 219 of the *HLC*. Just 10 pages off. The material on page 886 of the *Urtext* occurs on page 866 of the *HLC*. Just 20 pages off. After factoring in the previously indicated pagination anomalies, the last three quarters of the *Urtext* is then just 47 pages longer than the *HLC*. Most of the page count difference is explained by differing average page length, however.

If we do a word count we find that the *Urtext* has 224,238 words from page 209 to the end and the *HLC* from the same point to the end has 223,222 words. That's a difference of 1,016 words or about 0.45% or the equivalent of roughly 3 average typed manuscript pages out of the 690 manuscript pages involved.

The reason why the actual page counts show a greater difference is that in contrast to the *HLC* manuscript, in the *Urtext* a great many pages have only a single paragraph and thus a lot of blank space. This is another of the oddities about the manuscript which may provide clues as to its origins. It is more likely in a retyping that one would not stop to replace the paper after only one paragraph whereas in the original transcript we might assume that the typist would stop at the end of that day's scribing and pick up again on a new sheet of paper for the next segment. It seems equally possible, however, that in a retyping process following editing, one might well try to keep the page breaks the same which could result both in our "a" page numbers and in pages with only a few lines, if different typewriters

Appendix II: Identifying the *Urtext* Manuscript

and different margin settings were used. This would most particularly be the case if one were retyping only a few pages within a larger segment, and there is some evidence that this in fact happened on at least one occasion. There would be a strong incentive in that case to keep the pagination as close as possible to the original.

As with other physical evidence, further research may well yield further answers.

However, the first quarter of the *Urtext* is 163 actual pages longer than the corresponding *HLC* material. *Urtext* 209 is really 382 pages from the beginning. Because the number of words per page is variable, the word count is more meaningful. The *Urtext*, from the beginning to chapter 8 section K is 108,659 words. The *HLC* is 79,552 or 29,107 words shorter. That means this first segment of 8 chapters of the *Urtext* is 26.78% longer than the *HLC* compared to 0.45% longer in the last 23 chapters. This is an enormous difference and reflects the relative extent of the editing between the two segments.

All in all these two segments are radically different from each other in several major characteristics strongly suggesting they reflect different generations of the editing and copying process.

The early manuscripts were stored by the Scribes in sets of four three-ring binders, we are told, roughly eight chapters to a binder. Thus this dividing point (end of chapter 8) is approximately the end of the first binder. Were the pages from 209 to the end found separately, in the three binders they represent, the obvious inference one could draw would be that we were missing the first binder, and that we had an edited copy which immediately preceded the *HLC* and from which most of the "personal" material had already been removed and otherwise showed relatively little difference. The differences between these last three binders of the *Urtext* and the *HLC* are really mostly minor re-writing and substantial paragraph break adjustment. In addition we find there are numerous dropped words, phrases, sentences, etc. This is typical of visual copy-typing. In fact, the bulk of the 1,016 word difference in length between the final 23 chapters of the two versions can be accounted for by these inadvertent omissions of words and phrases.

There is little or nothing about this latter three quarters of the material which, if it didn't bear the name "*Urtext*" would lead anyone to think it was the original *Thetford Transcript* as opposed to one of the later retypings, indeed the one immediately preceding the *HLC*. The latter three quarters of the material bears few hallmarks of "oral dictation" but does show numerous signs of visual copying errors.

Were one to find the first 382 pages by themselves one might well think, due to the chaotic numbering, that we had bits and pieces of several partial retypings presumably made during editing, pieced together in preparation for a further retyping or further editing, both of which we know did occur with this material. Yet the later *HLC* reduces these 382 pages to 219 pages. So quite a bit of editing took place between the *Urtext* and the *HLC*. A huge amount in fact. But when we compare these 382 pages with the *Notes* we see that there are large parts omitted, but also significant amounts of material, more than a dozen pages, **added!** This is rather what we'd expect from an "urtext" if that word is used in the Britannica sense of "piecing together" from earlier sources, but not at all what we'd expect from the original *Thetford Transcript*.

Of course it's not at all impossible that Schucman might have skipped some of the more "personal" material in her *Notes* while dictating to Thetford. That can't be ruled out entirely. It does seem doubtful however because she certainly did include a great deal of personal material which probably should have been omitted. So we have no certain *evidence* that she "omitted on the fly" rather than removing material later. She certainly removed material later, increasingly so as the years and copying went on.

The pagination chaos in the early material is somewhat baffling and difficult to explain at first glance. Some of it is explained by the "dictated without notes" segments which are inserted in the *Urtext*. Each such insertion generally commences with the page number 1.

It appears as if the material was reorganized and renumbered multiple times. Where pages have as many as four different numbers written and crossed out, we cannot readily tell which number was written first. Given that most of the editing, save for the insertion of obvious "dictated without notes" segments, resulted in the removal of material, we can guess that where we have multiple page numbers crossed out, the larger numbers might generally be the earlier and the smaller numbers the later.

In the process of editing which involved both removing and adding multiple pages, if the scribes paused to renumber things from time to time, this would pretty much explain a good deal of the renumbering that we see. In time, a more thorough examination of the many crossed out page numbers may enable us to reconstruct the stages of compilation with more confidence.

The real mystery is how it is that the 382nd page bears the number 209! And then that latter numbering system remains largely consistent to the end. How did they come up with the number 209? The mostly obvious explanation is that there is another document, 208 pages long, which is a condensed and edited retyping of the first eight chapters, one we don't have! In fact that appears exceedingly likely to me. There are certainly other possibilities. On the 174th page, the start of Chapter 3 Section H, the numbering restarts at 1. The previous page is numbered 172. That second numbering system is reasonably consistent through to the end with only minor anomalies. That page is dated Dec. 10, 1965. So, for whatever reason, at page 172 on Dec 10, 1965 it appears the Scribes started the numbering all over again from 1 and thereafter more or less stuck to it.

I think it should be obvious by now that further research is required to explain the numbers that we see but also that the numbers we see don't tend to support the idea that this is the first typed transcript. If it were, and Thetford added pages to the total each time he transcribed new material, why would some pages bear as many as four different page numbers? And why would he restart the numbering at 1 less than two months into the process?

If this *Urtext* is the "first retyping" that "missing document" would be the second retyping, and we do have some evidence here then which is consistent with Wapnick's claim that there were two retypings after the *Thetford Transcript* and before the *HLC*. It is possible that the early editing was largely confined to the first 8 chapters and that after page 209, what we see is at least a "first retyping" of the *Thetford Transcript*.

It's also possible that there are, or at least once were two entire retypings and what we're looking at is the first binder of one and the last three binders of the other.

It is possible that in the history of this *Urtext* document, that "first binder" of 208 pages of abridged chapters 1-8 was substituted, intentionally or inadvertently, for the 381 page collection we now see in the *Urtext*. It's also possible that there was never anything more than 381 pages to that document. It may be an early "partial retyping" of the first eight chapters.

It should be remembered that the scribing of the *Text* volume took place over a three year period and there is every indication that the earlier material was being edited and retyped as the later material was being dictated.

It seems that while we're told there were two retypings of the *Thetford Transcript* prior to the retyping we call the *HLC*, in fact the early chapters may have been reworked more often than the later chapters. Certainly that is where the bulk of the editing differences occur.

Due to the fact that we rather obviously don't have a "single retyping" here but a combination of at least two, and possibly many more partial retypings, it would seem clear that some of the material is certainly not the original *Thetford Transcript*. But that doesn't mean that all of it necessarily isn't.

Life would be much simpler if we simply had access to all the primary source material. It would be much easier to tell which was earlier and which was later when compared side by side than to try to

Appendix II: Identifying the *Urtext* Manuscript

discern from a single document whether it is the earlier copy, the later copy, or bits of both.

A careful analysis of the page numbering chaos might indeed provide evidence of several different uniquely identifiable drafts, at least one of which just might possibly be a part of the original *Thetford Transcript*.

I can offer one theory which does explain the evidence.

This material is **not** a direct transcript of the *Notes* entirely. Not only are portions of the *Notes* missing, but there is material present here which is not present in the *Notes*. However many of its pages might represent the first *Notes* transcript, this collection of pages has been edited, with material both added and removed.

We would expect an original transcript typed by Thetford and proofed orally to have considerable mark-up indicating corrections of original typing errors. We see very little of that sort of thing.

With the *Thetford Transcript* and with the "dictated without notes" fragments, Schucman, with an unknown degree of help from Thetford, may have pieced together the typed pages for small segments from time to time and then re-typed those segments with some editing changes so as to have a "clean copy" to share with others. We know that from quite early on, certainly as early as 1968, she was sharing at least portions of the material with a number of other people.

The frequent "short pages" may actually mark the boundary of such a re-typed segment.

Understandably, when sharing, she'd want a reasonably clean typed manuscript to xerox and share, rather than one full of editing marks, cut out portions, insertions, handwritten corrections, etc.

It is understandable to me how she could think of what she was doing in that process as 'preparing an urtext' from the earlier drafts since she would in fact be "piecing together" discreet source documents and producing what she felt to be something closer to what the Author intended than any one of those sources.

I say "Schucman edited" here but of course we don't know how much Thetford participated in that editing. It might have been a great deal, it might have been very little. We have very little information on that. Wapnick and FIP state that the retypings were done by Schucman, with only that first transcript being done by Thetford. Verifying this may not be easy. For the moment since I have no evidence to the contrary, I'm simply accepting it as a working hypothesis.

If we assume that she undertook this kind of process several times with different segments of the first eight chapters, each time producing a unique document for circulation which was numbered page 1 to whatever, and then later collected these separate edited and re-typed segments together in their chronological sequence, we can perhaps begin to explain the page numbering we do in fact see.

In this theory, they didn't wait until the dictation was finished to edit and re-type it. The editing proceeded on previously dictated material as new material was being received. This initial editing produced re-typed segments of varying sizes, from time to time. These segments were initially "stand alone documents" with their own specific pagination, prepared by Schuman for distribution to others. Later these several segments were collected together along with subsequent "dictated without notes" segments and become what we now know as the *Urtext*. It's important to remember that the Scribes had no idea how long the dictation would be until it was finished. Certainly in the first few months where the material is most chaotic and heavily edited, their way of handling the material likely would have been evolving.

After collecting two or more such re-typed and edited segments, a new numbering system for the collection would be needed. Earlier numbers would be crossed out and new ones manually written in, all this in preparation for yet another retyping. If we imagine this process was repeated several times, we end up with several page numbers on some pages. And that **is** just what we see.

What I'm suggesting here is that rather than sitting down and "re-typing the whole thing" with some editing, she may well have edited it segment by segment, at different times, retyping those small segments, quite possibly more than once for some of them, and then collected the most recent edited segments into a whole which was then further edited and again re-typed later.

This is, I suggest, what the *Urtext* appears to be, and this account of its creation explains what we see. There is nothing in what we see to suggest, however, that this is entirely, or even mostly, the original *Thetford Transcript*.

I don't *know* how it came to appear as it does, obviously, but at least I can visualize **some** plausible means of processing which would explain what we see. It is not impossible that in this process some of the original *Thetford Transcript* pages were used without retyping. The fact that some of the material is certainly a later edited re-typing doesn't prove that all of it is.

---

6. *Contra-indications*

Now so far all this evidence points to the *Text* volume being a later re-typing rather than an original oral transcript, but there are contra-indications on some pages. In these we see a variety of evidence which is quite consistent with the material being an oral dictation. Some handwritten corrections are of minor typing mistakes which could be oral errors and appear to be in handwriting other than Schucman's. I don't have enough of Thetford's handwriting to be sure it is his, but it could be from what I can tell so far. There is at least one crossed out line which is also crossed out in the *Notes*, suggesting the correction might have been made in both the *Notes* and the original transcript at the same time. It seems unlikely such a correction would be "copied" in a "retyping" so this suggests that the page in question, at least, might be the original *Thetford Transcript*. The contra-indications are sufficiently numerous in some segments to strongly suggest that at least portions of the *Text* volume may in fact be copies of that original *Thetford Transcript*.

The key element here is that the *Urtext* is a collection of different pieces, and the specific creation history of the various segments might well be rather different. While some pages are almost certainly later re-typed copies, other pages may well be Thetford's original transcript.

Appendix II: Identifying the *Urtext* Manuscript

7 Conclusion: The *Urtext* is not entirely the *Thetford Transcript*

Any conclusions based on a less than exhaustive examination of evidence that is sometimes fragmentary cannot be a "final" conclusion. There is definitely a need for further study and clarification of this question but based on the evidence examined so far, it seems indisputable that what emerged in 2000 as the *"Urtext" of a Course in Miracles* was assembled from at least two and almost certainly more discreet, earlier documents and that some of this, perhaps the majority of this, is almost certainly not the original *Thetford Transcript* although some portions may well be just that. While the evidence is strong, one way or the other on some pages, for other pages the evidence is less clear.

The conclusion that there is – or at least once was – additional typed material from the Scribes is corroborated by other evidence, notably Wapnick's enumeration of Schucman's retypings. Should copies of that material ever become available, it will be much easier to determine which is "original" and which is the "copy." Without actual copies to compare, most "evidence" is indirect and is more suggestive than conclusive. However there is such a preponderance of "suggestive" evidence indicating that some pages at least are later retypings that we can with some certainty say that the *Urtext* is not entirely the *Thetford Transcript* and indeed most of it does not appear to be.

The bulk of the analysis I've done has been on two volumes, the *Text* most (or all) of which I believe is likely a re-typed, edited copy of the *Thetford Transcript* and the *Psychotherapy* volume which I suspect may well be an original orally produced transcript of the *Notes*. A few brief comments on the *Workbook* are in order. While I have done only a cursory examination of that manuscript with the "generational question" in mind I've seen considerable evidence of "visual" retyping and editing in the single typed manuscript I have available. I've also noted an absence of "oral typing errors" where homonyms (words that "sound alike") are typed and then are corrected, although there are a few. Where changes are marked, either handwritten or typed between lines, they very rarely correct an inaccurate copying of the *Notes*. Most mark-up involves either a deviation from the *Notes* or simply changes to paragraph breaks which are exceedingly numerous. Changes of that sort are suggestive much more of later editing rather than early proofing. We would fully expect that in an oral transcript that had been proofed, the typist would make errors which deviate from the *Notes* and the corrections or marked-up changes would restore the material to the reading in the *Notes*. In the *Workbook* we see a few of these but the vast preponderance of handwritten changes alters typed material that is an accurate reflection of the *Notes*. In short, it's not a correction of an error in copying the *Notes*, it is subsequent copy-editing. And the handwriting is Schucman's. We also do see some examples of "dropped phrases" between two instances of the same word on adjacent lines, which is typical of visual copying mistakes.

The extensive mark-up for paragraph changes, most of which is preserved in the FIP editions, would more likely have been done late in the editing process with the most recent retyping rather than on the earliest, first typed transcript. This would also suggest that if there were two different typed manuscripts of the *Workbook* as Wapnick suggests, we're looking at the second and not the first.

In summary, then, most of the mark-up in the *Workbook* appears to be late copy-editing just before going to press rather than early proofing of an oral transcript.

Much closer and more thorough scrutiny on these other volumes is required before anything conclusive can be said of them, but the preliminary indications certainly suggest that except for *Psychotherapy* and possibly *Song of Prayer*, we are dealing with an edited copy of the first transcript, and not the first *Thetford Transcript* itself.

Little of what we've seen in the *Urtext*, outside of the *Psychotherapy* volume, is consistent with what we've been told about the *Thetford Transcript*. Rather, it is mostly consistent with a visually typed copy and Wapnick's information states that such a copy was made. In the *Text* volume we appear to have bits and pieces of several different retypings. None of that excludes the possibility that some pages may in fact be that original *Thetford Transcript*. Now that the *Notes* are available we can see that there are large gaps in the *Urtext* which we'd not expect to appear in the original *Thetford Transcript*. We also find that while the *Urtext* is **mostly** a very faithful transcript of the *Notes* (so is every version, for that matter), there are differences of a frequency and nature which suggest both inadvertent **visual** copying errors *and* intentional editing, neither of which should be present in the first transcript.

While there is generally much less editing of the "re-writing" sort between the *Notes* and the *Urtext* than between the *Urtext* and the *HLC* or between the *HLC* and the *FIP Abridgement*, there is still a good deal more editing than we'd expect from the *Thetford Transcript* original copy.

Basically everything we've been told about the *Thetford Transcript* by people who we suppose to have seen it, including Thetford himself, doesn't fit the *Urtext* in one or more critical ways. The reservations are so numerous and serious in nature that it must be considered extremely unlikely that this is the *Thetford Transcript*. Its identification as at least mostly the (or one of the, or a combination of two or more of the) later retyping(s) by Schucman is indicated.

My best guess is that the first 381 pages are Schucman's first retyping and the second 677 pages are her second retyping, assuming that Wapnick's statement that there were two retypings is correct. Whether the first one ever went past chapter eight is open to question. Wapnick did say the material was re-typed twice, but he didn't specify that **all** of the *Text* volume was re-typed twice. That is implied, but that is not stated. That the second retyping included chapters one to eight is strongly suggested by the page number 209 at the beginning of that second part, roughly the start of Chapter 9. From that point on the typing is cleaner, more consistent and the page number anomalies are much fewer indicating that most of it at least may be a "single retyping."

There is evidence then that we are missing the first eight chapters of the second retyping and possibly that we're missing the last three quarters of the first retyping and the whole of the *Thetford Transcript*.

The main evidence suggesting this is the *Thetford Transcript* is the label *"Urtext"* and the assertion by Wapnick and FIP that "urtext" means "original transcript." But, as we've seen, Wapnick and FIP may have been mistaken on that point, that's not at all what the word "urtext" necessarily means. It's not even certain that if the Scribes used that word, they were referring to the original *Thetford Transcript*. The word could be as correctly or even *more correctly* applied to an edited re-typing in which they understood themselves to be cleaning up mistakes in an earlier, first rough transcript. It is not impossible that Wapnick *assumed* it meant the original transcript but never confirmed that assumption.

Appendix II: Identifying the *Urtext* Manuscript

8 How could such a mistake be made and persist?

My argument is that the balance of evidence would likely convince any random jury that this is not, or at least largely not, the *Thetford Transcript*.

I can offer a theory which can account for this misidentification.

We can recall that Wapnick says the first version of the Course he saw was the *HLC*. He and Helen worked on this from May of 1973 until late in 1975, abridging it into what became the FIP *First Edition*. It's not known when he first saw any earlier material but that may not have happened until after Helen's death or at least well after he'd formed the belief that "urtext = original transcript."

I'm guessing that Helen and or Bill may have spoken to him of there being an "urtext" which was earlier than the *HLC* and of which the *HLC* was an edited abridgement. From the available evidence it would certainly appear that this is correct: Helen and Bill edited the *Urtext* and produced the abridged *HLC* version.

It is possible that Helen and or Bill may have spoken to him about the early scribing and transcribing and he may simply have made a mistake many others have made, and *assumed* that the first transcript and the "urtext" were one and the same thing rather than the latter being a derivative of the former. While he does speak of two retypings by Schucman prior to the *HLC*, he may be repeating what he was told, and that may be correct, but he may never have seen those other typed manuscripts.

If sorting out the early versions and identifying them was not important to him, and it would appear that it was never very important to him at the time, then it is not surprising that he never bothered to actually check. The question simply wasn't worth the effort for him. Further, he'd have no reason to even suspect that his identification was mistaken, so there'd be no particular reason to check.

Since the primary source material was withheld from scholarship, others who were interested did not have the opportunity to do the checking which would have cleared up the confusion.

Thus a very simple and mundane misunderstanding which is eminently understandable persisted because no one who had the means to check had a reason to check and no one who had a reason to check had the means to check.

That could quite plausibly explain how a misidentification arose and didn't get corrected.

It is not known to me if, among the papers of Helen and Bill which survive, any copy of that original transcript still exists. Nor do I know if Wapnick is in possession of a copy. If it does exist, it should be readily obvious with a side by side comparison which is the earlier and more original. If it doesn't still exist, and I am not aware of any evidence to suggest it does, then the confusion is even more understandable.

I know full well that many people have been told this document is the *Thetford Transcript* and have simply believed that and never thought to question it. Why not Wapnick? In fact, having been told that myself, I was inclined to believe it for years even as my study of the document kept revealing evidence that it wasn't. It was some years before I lined up all the evidence on both sides and concluded that most of this material simply couldn't be the *Thetford Transcript*. This rather shows that the human mind, having accepted a certain assertion as correct, sometimes requires rather a LOT of evidence of error before even considering there might be an error *especially when the presence of error appears to be highly unlikely* as it most certainly did in this case.

I would submit then that Wapnick, not having access to the original documents and not being particularly interested in them at first, may easily have misunderstood what the Scribes meant by the use of the unusual word "urtext" just as so many others have. That he was unfamiliar with the term is strongly indicated by his assertion that it comes from Abraham and "Ur of the Chaldees." It doesn't. Then, never having any reason to suspect a misunderstanding, he never felt the need to check and so continued to believe it was the *Thetford Transcript*.

How could Wapnick be wrong? Just as any of us could be and all of us have been wrong a times; a simple misunderstanding which was never checked and so never corrected.

The weight of evidence then is on the side of this being for the most part a later re-typed, edited manuscript rather than the original *Thetford Transcript*. I do not consider the question resolved however and it probably won't be until all relevant surviving documentation has been very thoroughly scrutinized.

I think it is beyond doubt that *some* of the *Urtext* is not the original transcript, but rather a later retyping. I'm reasonably convinced that some of it is likely the original transcript and I'm entirely uncertain about some portions of it.

9 Why it is important to determine the provenance of these manuscripts

There are some who are thinking "so what?" What makes it important to know whether this is a first or second or even third typed copy?

First off if we are going to claim, as many have done, and are still doing, that this is the "original" unedited dictation then we should know that the evidence does not really support that claim and in making that claim we are asserting what is almost certainly a falsehood. Eventually the truth generally comes out and it serves no one's real interests to propagate disinformation. It certainly feeds the reservations of sceptics when they find out that they haven't been told the truth. However "innocent" the reasons for a misunderstanding are, the suspicion will always haunt the minds of some that there has been some deliberate dishonesty and deception.

The credibility of the Course generally is hurt when falsehoods are propagated. The credibility of the Course is also hurt when the most "primary" of the primary sources are unavailable. How can we be certain that the later copies are "right" when we can't check the originals and we know that there are some inadvertent copying mistakes? And how can we expect people not to wonder what we're trying to hide when we won't allow inspection of the primary sources?

If we are going to make claims about provenance it behooves us to do more than believe the claims, we should also exercise due diligence to verify them.

That's one of the jobs of scholarship, check all the sources and evidence, look for mistakes, and correct the mistakes.

Another importance involves the work of transcribing the original *Shorthand Notebooks*. Bill Thetford's original transcript would be of enormous value in those areas where legibility is a problem in the *Notes*. Legibility is problematic sometimes because of bad photocopies, missing pages, and pages out of order but also because much of it is shorthand and abbreviations. In the later case some abbreviations can be expanded in more than one way and still be good grammar. The shorthand isn't always unambiguous. Looking

Appendix II: Identifying the *Urtext* Manuscript

to any later copy can certainly give us clues as to what Schucman intended but any later copy is more subject to possible copying mistakes than the original transcript would be. That original transcript then has more "authority" as a tool to interpret the *Notes* than any later copy or indeed than all later copies. We could have a higher degree of confidence that what's in the original transcript is what was originally intended than with any subsequent copy.

Even if it should prove that the later copies are ***always*** identical to the *Thetford Transcript* in areas of uncertainty, that original transcript is still useful in ways that the later copies aren't. With it we can ***know*** whether it is the same or different. Without it we can only wonder. And wonder about the motives of those who possess copies but refuse to let us see them.

In some ways that *Thetford Transcript* would enable us to "ask Helen what she meant" where the reading in the *Notes* is ambiguous and ask her within days of her first writing the material down. We do know that her idea of what she meant changed sometimes over time and became very different from it had been originally. Whatever you make of her later editing changes, knowing what she originally intended to commit to paper has some value and the original transcript can be expected to help us there in ways and with a degree of confidence no later retyping can.

Finally, if we think we have a copy of the *Thetford Transcript* then we won't go looking for it. If we think we don't have a copy and we recognize any importance to it, then we might go looking for it. According to several sources Thetford made multiple photocopies of his original transcript plus at least one carbon copy. At one time then there were several copies in existence. While I have no evidence indicating that any have survived it seems quite possible that at least one might have and that continued searching might eventually locate it.

In closing I would say, with Jesus in the *Urtext* that getting every word right is not crucial, but it is meaningful!

Appendix III – Referencing Explained

Table of Contents

1. **REFERENCING SUMMARY** 2
   - (1) Paragraph references 2
   - (2) Urtext Manuscript Page Number references 2
   - (3) Notes Manuscript Page Number references 2
   - (4) Page Number of the current volume 2
   - (5) Page Number of the whole book 2
2. **THE DESIGN OF THE REFERENCING SYSTEM** 2
   - INTRODUCTION 2
3. **VOLUME SPECIFICS** 3
   1. THE TEXT 3
   2. WORKBOOK 4
   3. MANUAL FOR TEACHERS 4
   4. THE USE OF TERMS 4
   5. PSYCHOTHERAPY 4
   6. SONG OF PRAYER 4
   7. GIFTS OF GOD 4
4. **USING UNREFERENCED EDITIONS** 4
   - CROSS-REFERENCING TO FIP 4
   - CROSS-REFERENCING TO BLUE SPARKLY 5
5. **OTHER SYSTEMS INCLUDED** 5
   - (1) The 22 Volumes 5
   - (2) Notes Archival Page Number 5
   - (3) Notes PDF page number 5
6. **BASIC HOW-TO** 6
7. **URTEXT TO NOTES CROSS-REFERENCE** 7
   - (1) Text 7
   - (2) Workbook 9
   - (3) Manual 10
   - (4) Use of Terms 11
   - (5) Psychotherapy 11
   - (6) Song of Prayer 11
8. **URTEXT TO FIP CROSS-REFERENCE** 12
   - (1) Text 13
   - (2) Workbook 19
   - (3) Manual 20
   - (4) Use of Terms 21
   - (5) Psychotherapy 21
   - (6) Song of Prayer 22
   - (7) Gifts of God 22

Appendix III – Referencing Explained

1. Referencing Summary

On the pages of the *Seven Volume Urtext* you will find several different reference systems printed.

(1) Paragraph references

in bold type at the start of each paragraph. For example, **T 14 B 12**. Each paragraph is referenced by Volume (**T**ext, **W**orkbook, **M**anual, **U**se of **T**erms, **P**sychotherapy, **S**ong of Prayer, **G**ifts of God) Chapter number, Section letter, and Paragraph number. The *Workbook* is done a little differently due to its anomalous structure. See below for specifics.

(2) Urtext Manuscript Page Number references

in bold type have been inserted in-line exactly where the manuscript page break occurs. For example **T(544) - 371** - means *Text*, 544th page which is marked 371. These are to facilitate cross-referencing this copy to the actual manuscript. In the *Text* volume the marked page numbers do not correspond to the actual page number after page 83. There are thus two numbers in the *Text*, the actual or Absolute Page Number and the marked page number.

(3) Notes Manuscript Page Number references

are inserted at the end of each section heading. These are of the form **(*N 1208 9:45)**. This means the 1208th *Notes* page of the current volume, *Text*, *Workbook*, etc., volume 9 of the 22 volumes, 45th page of volume 9 of 22.

(4) Page Number of the current volume

in the outside bottom corner of each page. These are of the form "I-22" where "I" is the volume number (I-VII) and 22 is the page number of the current volume.

(5) Page Number of the whole book

bottom of page in the centre.

---

2. The Design of the Referencing System

Introduction

Biblical scholars have it easy. In 1560 the *Geneva Bible* was the first print edition to use the familiar system of chapter and verse divisions. It has been used in nearly all editions of all versions of all Bibles in all languages ever since. While the reference divisions are often arbitrary, you can take a Biblical reference, such as "John 3:16" and find exactly the same passage in almost any edition of any version of the Bible in almost any language.

ACIM scholars have a tougher time. There are at least nine different reference systems I've seen used in published work and several more which I know to exist. And new ones keep popping up.

This speaks to a general problem associated with the lack of – and the need for – an effective standard universal reference system. When I set out to cross-reference the various ACIM versions, I carefully examined every reference system which had been used in ACIM in the attempt to find the best available. In the end I found them all wanting, but I did adopt some features from several.

Like every other ACIM reference standard in use, it is different from all the others. Unlike every other ACIM reference standard in use, it is consistent, intuitive and predictable. Anomalies are minimized and it can be readily used on any edition of any version of ACIM in any language *most of the time* except where:
- the original scribal chapter and section or paragraph breaks were moved
- the original sequence of material was altered
- the original material being referenced was omitted

Each individual historical primary source document (*Notes, Urtext, HLC,* etc.) has a unique "native reference system" based on such physical characteristics as page and line numbers or other physical textual landmarks. Since no two sources have the identical physical structure, such references are of little or no cross-referencing value. The goal here was to develop a system that would not only be effective on a particular version, it would be maximally adaptable as a cross-referencing system for *all* versions.

For the *Text* volume the chapter and section breaks William Thetford introduced into the *HLC* were taken as the standard and these were "retro-fitted" to all versions. Insofar as the content is

Appendix III - 2

Appendix III – Referencing Explained

similar between versions then, the same reference will take you to the same content in all versions.

There are several reasons for doing so:
- This system is familiar to many and has for years been a de-facto standard and it uses the same underlying logic as the widely known FIP system. It differs from the FIP system not in basic logic, but rather in the consistent application of that basic logic in a fixed-tier implementation.
- It has a high degree of "scribal authority" being the original insertion of textual division points in the *Text* by the Scribes
- It is suitably sized and structured for a "universal reference system."

While it would not have been impossible to use the FIP reference system for the earlier versions, it would have been much more difficult in the early chapters. There are several other reasons why that option was not chosen. Most notable among them is its inconsistent component numbering within tiers and the fact that it uses floating tiers such that one cannot always determine from the position of a given field in a reference, precisely which tier that field specifies. It should also be pointed out that the system is legitimately copyrighted and the copyright holder has gained some notoriety for a propensity to sue. While that is less of a concern today, at the time the system was being developed, that was a major consideration. It was not deemed to be legal to simple adopt the FIP system.

If there is one thing almost all Course students can agree upon, it is that the FIP *Second Edition* reference system is awkward, confusing and often very difficult to use. These difficulties experienced by students do not derive from the basic logic inherent in dividing the material up into three or four hierarchical tiers. The difficulties derive from doing so **inconsistently**. **Adapting** the FIP system while ironing outcome of its anomalies and inconsistencies seemed to be a better approach than simply **adopting** it.

A fixed three-tier referencing system within each volume has been used. The tiers are **chapter, section** and **paragraph**. The structure of some volumes makes this a little awkward at some points, but generally it works well. The fields are fixed, not floating, so that the field position in the reference always tells you whether the field is a chapter, paragraph or section designator. The designators alternate from numeric to alphabetical. Volume level designators are always letters, chapter level designators are always numbers, sections are always letters, paragraphs are always numbers. So if a field has been dropped at the beginning or the end to abbreviate the reference, it's still obvious what's left.

A fourth tier is the volume, of which there are seven: *Text, Workbook, Manual, Use of Terms, Psychotherapy, Song of Prayer* and *Gifts of God*. The first letter of the volume name is generally used to identify it. So a reference of **T 1 A 1** means *Text volume, Chapter 1, Section A, Paragraph 1*. One can always add a sentence number after the paragraph number if required.

In the *Text* volume there is one major anomaly in *Chapter 1, Section B, Principles of Miracles*. That anomaly required a unique approach, and is explained below under *Volume Specifics*.

In the *Workbook* the basic structure is of course the lesson numbers at the "chapter" tier. The *Workbook* isn't only lessons however. In addition to lessons, there are 24 "non-lesson" segments which occur between lessons which are a bit awkward to reference. To solve that problem the "inter-lesson" material is referenced to the preceding lesson number as a second section, for reference purposes, except for the *Introduction* which occurs before Lesson 1. These anomalies are discussed more thoroughly below under *Volume Specifics*. The other four volumes present much more minor referencing problems in large part due to their small size and straightforward organization.

In the e-texts of the source documents the original *Urtext* manuscript page numbers are indicated, either in margins or inline in bracketed numerals or the original pagination is simply maintained. In the *Notes* the *Urtext* page and paragraph references are marked in the margins except in the *Notes Workbook* facsimile where the paragraph level is not always marked. The *Notes* also have line numbers marked.

Due to the fact that paragraph breaks are not consistent across versions, the lower tier of referencing which is the paragraph number doesn't always match between the versions. Between the *Urtext* and the *Notes* however, it **usually** does. Also, between the *HLC* and *FIP* it **usually** does. The *Urtext* paragraph breaks have been marked in the margins of the *Notes*.

3. Volume Specifics

The Text

The *Text* volume is cross-referenced across the *Notes*, and both the *Urtext* manuscript facsimile and the e-text by *HLC* chapter, section and in the *Notes* and *Urtext*, by *Urtext* paragraph number.

The major anomaly is in the *Text* volume and applies only to section B of Chapter 1, the "*Miracle Principles*." Rather than counting the enormous number of paragraphs in that section and using a paragraph number, the ***miracle principle number*** is used for the third tier. Where a miracle principle has more than one paragraph, as several do, the second paragraph is marked as "b" and the third paragraph "c" etc. In a few cases there are more than 26 paragraphs so that the 26th paragraph is numbered, **37z** in the case of miracle principle 37 and the 27th is numbered **37aa**, the 28th **37ab**, etc.

Many of the first 55 pages of the *Notes* which include this difficult section have been "**Bookmarked**", so that you can, using the **Bookmarks**, get within a page or two in the *Notes* from the page reference in the *Urtext* e-text for this section. Thus you simply need identify the passage of interest in the *Urtext*, note the page number, and click on the "**Bookmark**" closest to it in the *Notes* to land within a page or so of the point you seek. Paragraph breaks and manuscript page numbers from the *Urtext* are marked in the margins of the *Notes* for convenient cross-referencing.

Of course there is material, particularly in early chapters, which is not present in the *Urtext* and vice versa, and for the moment, that material is not addressed by this cross-referencing system, and won't be until that material is transcribed into an e-text and added to the *Urtext*.

Appendix III – Referencing Explained

In the limited segments of the *Notes* omitted from the *Urtext* for which direct transcripts, or e-texts of the *Notes* are unavailable, the material original to the *Notes* which is not present in other versions is referenced only by the original *Notes* volume, folio and line numbers.

Workbook

The *Workbook* is both the easiest and the most difficult volume to reference. The *Workbook's* lesson numbers, which form the dominant structure of this volume, provide an obvious means of cross-referencing. *Lesson 10 is Lesson 10 in all versions!* Nothing more is needed to reference it. Not all 361 lessons in the facsimile copies are **Bookmarked**, but in all copies all the ***Review*** breaks and in Part II the 14 "***What Is***" breaks are marked. This sub-divides the *Workbook* into portions of a manageable size. Once you find the lesson number for a quote you've found in any of the e-texts, it is not difficult to locate it in the facsimiles.

The main trick in referencing for the *Workbook* is that in addition to the 361 lessons, which provide a basic top tier reference grid for the volume, there are 24 additional small segments of text between lessons. These include *Review* introductions, the "*What is?*" homilies in part 2, etc. These items occur between actual lessons. One easy way to refer to them is by the preceding lesson number, such as "after lesson X."

This is how it was done. After a great deal of discussion and the testing of many alternatives, the least awkward option was found to be referencing these "non-lesson" segments as a second section of the preceding lesson. To distinguish the lesson proper from the non-lesson material following it, the "section" designation "**L**" is used for the lessons proper, and for the 24 non-lesson segments, informative abbreviations indicating the nature of the content are used as section level designators as follows: "**IN1**" for the first *Introduction*, **R1** through **R6** for the six *Review* introductions, **IN2** for the *Introduction to Part 2*, **W1** through **W14** for the 14 "*What is*" segments in *Part 2*, **FL** for *Final Lessons* and **EP** for the *Epilogue*.

Each of those 24 "non-lesson" segments of text is referenced to the immediately preceding lesson number. So the first paragraph of *Review 1* which immediately follows *Lesson 50* is **W 50 R1 1**. The first paragraph of *Lesson 50* is referenced as **W 50 L 1**. In the *Workbook* then, there are 361 top level divisions of which 24 have "section" divisions other than just "**L**" which designates the lesson proper. Whenever something ***other*** than "**L**" appears in a *Workbook* reference, it refers to one of those 24 "non-lesson segments" and the "chapter level" value indicates the lesson number which it ***follows*** for ease of look-up.

Now generally individual lessons have no need of subdividing into sections, they are such small "chapters." The "section" tier is largely irrelevant for the lessons proper. This leaves it available to reference the non-lesson segments.

Since all versions are bookmarked identically, this should not present particular difficulty.

Manual for Teachers

Although slightly different than the FIP system, in that all segments are numbered sequentially rather than referencing first segments as "Introduction" to keep things simple and consistent, all chapter and section breaks are **Bookmarked** identically in the *Urtext*, both the e-text and the manual facsimile copies, and the *Notes*. *Urtext* page numbers are also indicated on the **Bookmarks**.

The Use of Terms

All the section and paragraph and page breaks in the *Use of Terms* are either **Bookmarked** or annotated in the margins in all three versions, the *Notes*, and the *Urtext* manuscript facsimile and the *Urtext* e-text.

This is the only volume for which there presently is a largely complete transcription or e-text of the *Notes*. In addition to its organization according to the original volume, folio and line numbers, these basic "chapter and section" references are also included for easy of cross-referencing.

Psychotherapy

All the chapter and section breaks are **Bookmarked** in all versions. This volume has delightfully small sections, making cross-referencing a snap.

Song of Prayer

Very little of the *Song of Prayer* volume is available to us in the original *Notes*. The five pages currently available are all annotated with the corresponding *Urtext* chapter, section and paragraph numbers.

Gifts of God

In this volume each of the five discreet, dated segments is counted as a "chapter," and within these short segments there is no need for divisions at the "section" level.

---

4. Using Unreferenced editions

Cross-Referencing to FIP

The FIP reference system has been around since 1992 and has been widely used. It would be great if that could have just have been used to reference the earlier versions.

In the first few chapters however, the FIP editions are massively abridged. There are then some 60,000 words in earlier material which are not present, and therefore are not referenced in the FIP editions. Further, FIP changed the sequence of some of the material it did preserve. This makes it impossible to maintain any direct, sequential relationship between FIP and the earlier, larger versions.

When first trying to apply the FIP referencing system to the *HLC* it was realized it simply can't be done in any way that is sensible for the *HLC*. Chapter and section divisions sometimes have to be moved or renamed. A great deal of material in the *HLC* isn't in

FIP or isn't there in the same sequence. The same *logic* can be applied to the *HLC*, but not the same actual chapter and section division points in many cases. The *HLC* has its own chapter and section divisions which are more original and have considerably greater "scribal authority" than those of the later abridgment.

A second problem with using the FIP system without modification is that it is inconsistent, contains many anomalies, and is anything but intuitive.

There are several criteria which a "good" referencing system should meet:

It should first be simple and intuitive so it is easy to use. Secondly it should be maximally usable on the many existing copies of ACIM which do not have any referencing system, or don't have the

Appendix III – Referencing Explained

same one. Thirdly, it would ideally be "universal" in that it could be readily used or at least adapted to any version.

The *logic* of the FIP system has the potential to meet these requirements reasonably well, but its inconsistent application fails to be simple and intuitive and fails to be "universal."

The FIP system is based on a simple three tier-logic but unfortunately, doesn't apply it consistently. It is this lack of consistency which makes it confusing. Sometimes the first section of a chapter is *Section I*, which is intuitive. Other times it is called "*Section In.*" In the original manuscript of the *HLC* (*Text* volume) every chapter has up to 12 sections and the first section is never given a title. FIP takes that model, keeps it most of the time, but sometimes gives the first sections new titles and other times just calls them "introduction."

Those first unnamed sections in each *HLC* chapter are simply labelled "*Introduction*" and they are referenced as "*Section A.*" The second section in each chapter is "*Section B.*"

This pattern of removing the "introductions" from the three tiers and not counting them as numbered elements is more pronounced in later volumes. Due to this anomaly in the FIP referencing system, while the references in our material generally look like FIP references and have the same underlying logic, the numerical values are often offset by one wherever FIP has declined to number a component and called it something else. While that is often "*In*" it can be other things as well.

However, if you actually examine the *Tables of Contents* you will generally recognize instantly where FIP has failed to number an element and thus where its numbers are offset by one.

In Appendix II of this document conversion charts for the first six volumes can be found.

Cross-Referencing to Blue Sparkly

The chapter and section divisions in the *Sparkly* correspond to the original *HLC* manuscript. Simply count the sections, and label them A B C etc. Make sure to number as "A" the first, untitled section in each chapter. This can be done with any copy of the *HLC* which has the chapter and section and paragraph breaks marked correctly. For the Whitmore *Original Edition* most of the chapter and section breaks can be used, but the paragraph breaks are sometimes rather scrambled and are numbered in an entirely novel and original way. Thus the relative position of a unique *Original Edition* paragraph designation within a chapter really cannot be correlated with any other copy of ACIM in any consistent way. So ignore those numbers and treat it as if there were no numbers other than chapter numbers. To a large extent, Whitmore's *Original Edition* preserves the actual original chapter and sections divisions making those "textual landmarks" a useable basis for referencing.

---

5. Other Systems included

(1) The 22 Volumes

In an effort to be inclusive of other means of referencing, and due to the fact that the *Notes* are organized into a volume and page number system unique to that collection, those volume and page numbers are included in the header for each *Notes* facsimile page. The original volume/folio information for the *Urtext* manuscript facsimile cannot be provided because it is not currently available.

In the *Urtext* e-texts the *Notes* volume/folio references are included section by section for ease of cross-referencing.

This system is based on the physical notes pages which are identified by their volume and page numbers, followed by an optional line number.

(2) Notes Archival Page Number

T the "**Archival Page Number**" for the *Notes* within each of the six canonical volumes, *Text, Workbook, Manual for Teachers, Use of Terms, Psychotherapy* and *Song of Prayer*.

The volume divisions of the "*22 Volumes*" do not correspond to the volume divisions of the "*7 volumes.*" The word "volume" here can get a bit confusing. There are these two ways of organizing the *Notes* material into volumes. One is the system found in the "*22 volumes*" and the other is the more common and familiar arrangement of the seven canonical volumes. The *Notes* material is referenced according to **both**.

So, each folio (individual sheet of paper of the single-sided photocopy) of the *Notes* has a number of different unique identifiers, each of which is best for particular applications. You will need the volume and page number (*22 volumes*) to instantly locate the high resolution scans in the 5-CD set of high resolution *Notes* scans, for instance, as that is the basic "native" referencing in the *Notes* collection.

Within any given canonical (the 7 volumes) volume, the **Archival Page Number** can be useful as it is an actual count of the actual individual folios. That page number may or may not correlate to any other numbering system in any other edition of any version. It is not known, for instance, if other copies of the *Notes* have the same number of pages, but it is known that some pages are missing from the original *Shorthand Notebooks*. This number is, then, relevant only to this particular collection. Since the numbering was created, for instance, several pages have turned up which were not present in our first copy. The whole scheme can't be redone each time a single page shows up.

This numbering follows a pattern a bit different from ordinary book numbering. It numbers every sheet of paper in this specific collection of documents as a discreet artefact whereas the more common approach with ordinary books is to not put numbers on cover pages, nor include – let alone number – duplicate pages. When dealing with "archaeological specimens" and in the *Notes* material that really is closer to what we've got than any conventional "book" then every element, regardless of our initial assessment of its importance, needs to be labelled and there is no simpler system than to start at one end and call that component 1 and then increment the number by 1 for each succeeding component until the end.

(3) Notes PDF page number

Having put two *Notes* facsimile pages on one page of the PDF file for more convenient display on a computer monitor, there is an additional page number for the PDF file itself, which is always exactly one half the actual *Notes* page number. The limitations of this reference are obvious.

Appendix III – Referencing Explained

The PDF page number is useful strictly for navigation within Acrobat Reader for the two pages per sheet copies in the *Scholar's Toolbox*. The **Go To Page** command, if given a number ½ of the **Archival Page Number** will land you at that page.

6. Basic How-To

The e-texts for the *Notes, Urtext, HLC, HLC Replica* and *FIP* editions of all volumes are **searchable**. If you wish to "look up" any quote in the *Notes*, first locate it in one of those e-texts. The *Urtext* is all we have for the portions of the *Notes* for which no transcripts are presently available since it is usually identical to the *Notes*. However, since it is sometimes worded differently than the later *HLC* and *FIP* versions, a quote you recall from reading one of the later versions may be easier to find in those versions due to different wording.

Once you find it, note the chapter, section and paragraph numbers. In fact you can copy the *Urtext* chapter, section and paragraph reference into your clipboard.

Then load the appropriate volume of the *Notes* facsimile and use the **Bookmarks** to get to the same chapter and section. Most of the *Notes* which corresponds to canonical material has the *Urtext* chapter, section and paragraph references marked. In *Acrobat Reader* you can press CTRL + F and "paste" the reference into the search box. Press RETURN (ENTER) and in a moment you should see the same paragraph in the *Notes*.

In *Notes* material that is not referenced to the *Urtext* by counting paragraphs, you'll quickly be able to identify the same paragraph in the *Notes* if it is, in fact, there.

This approach will work more often than not from any version to get you at least within a page. Even where paragraph breaks are moved, the average length of paragraphs doesn't often change a great deal. So paragraph 11 in one version might be paragraph 9 or 13 in another, but it won't likely be off by more than that.

Due to the fact that the *Urtext* is not word-for-word identical to the *Notes* in all cases, there are times when the passage you're looking for either isn't in the *Notes* or is worded differently. Remember too that there is material in each version not present in any other so it is always possible that the specific passage for which you seek simply isn't in the version you're searching.

When you run into that problem, locate an adjacent paragraph in the *Urtext* e-text, and then use that reference to find the corresponding spot in the *Notes*. Having found the corresponding spot, you can then determine if the material is simply not there, or is worded differently, or if there is some other discrepancy.

Usually however, the material is identical and it's very easy to locate the *Notes* segment desired.

Chapter and section breaks in the FIP version don't always correspond to those in the others, so sometimes those references won't be very useful. Usually, however, once you allow for the "FIP offset" (the fact that FIP fails to number "introductions" and certain other elements) the FIP reference will closely match the universal reference after chapter 14. In the first half of the *Text* volume there are many differences in the number and location of chapter and section breaks.

Mostly however, you can take a FIP reference, use the relevant cross-reference chart below, and find what the corresponding reference in the *Urtext* and *Notes* is.

Note: you can search for *Urtext* manuscript absolute page numbers in the *Notes* material also through the seven canonical volumes, just as you would search for paragraph references.

Appendix III - Urtext to Notes Cross-Referencing

7. Urtext to Notes Cross-Reference

(1) Text

Notes p#	Urtext:Ref	Urtext: Page	Notes Ref.
1*	T 1:1:1	(1)1	Volume 4 - 28
100	T 1 B 30g.3	(18)18	Volume 4 - 127
200	T 1 B 41ag.2	(51)51	Volume 5 - 49
223*	T 2:A:1	62	Volume 5 - 72
266	T 2:D:1	(97)96	Volume 5 - 115
296*	T 3 A 1	(120) 119	Volume 5 - 145
300	T 3 A 9.1	(121)120	Volume 5 - 149
389*	T 4 A 1	(185)C 12	Volume 5 - 238
391	Text 5b		Volume 5 - 240
394*	T 4 A 2	(185)C 12	Volume 5 - 243
400	T 4 A 8.1	(187)?23 ?C 14	Volume 5 - 249
497	T 4 G 21.1	(228)C 55	Volume 6 - 61
500	not in Urtext		Volume 6 - 64
507	T 4 G 22.7	(228)C 55	Volume 6 - 71
518*	T 5 A 1	(233)C 60	Volume 6 - 82
599*	T 6 A 1	(271)C 98	Volume 6 - 164
670	Text 8a		Volume 7 - 2
675*	T 7 A 1	(303)C 130	Volume 7 - 7
700	T 7 E 5.1	(314)C 141	Volume 7 - 32
758*	T 8 A 1	(346)C 173	Volume 7 - 90
800	T 8 G 3.8	(363)C 190	Volume 7 - 132
834	T 9 A 1	(386)213	Volume 7 - 166
900*	T 9 K 2.1	(415)- 242 –	Volume 8 - 4
909*	T 10 A 1	(419)- 246 -	Volume 8 - 13
997*	T 11 A 1	(449)- 276 -	Volume 8 - 101
1000	title page "Text 12b"		Volume 8 - 104
1001	T 11 B 3.1	(450)– 277 –	Volume 8 - 105
1075*	T 12 A 1	(485)312	Volume 8 - 179
1100	T 12 E 2.2	(496)- 323 –	Volume 8 - 204
1132*	T 13 A 1	(510)337	Volume 8 - 236
1196*	T 14 A 1	(538)365	Volume 9 - 33
1200	T 14 B 3.1	(540)- 367 –	Volume 9 - 37
1254*	T 15 A 1	(563)- 390 -	Volume 9 - 91
1300	T 15 G 7.6	(582)- 409 –	Volume 9 - 137
1350	Text 15b		Volume 9-187
1351	Nothing that relates to a specific relationship belongs in the notes		
1354*	T 16 A 1	(601)428	Volume 9 - 191
1397*	T 17 A 1	(630)457	Volume 9 - 234
1400	T 17 B 3.4	(631)458	Volume 9 - 237
1454*	T 18 A 1	(659)486	Volume 10 – 14
1500	T 18 I 10.3	(687)C 511	Volume 10 - 60
1502	Text 16b		Volume 10 - 62
1512	T 18 K 4	(693)517	Volume 10 - 72
1513*	T 19 A 1	(694)518	Volume 10 - 73

Appendix III - Urtext to Notes Cross-Referencing

		TEXT	
Notes p#	Urtext Ref	Urtext Page	*Notes* Ref.
1552	T 19 F 10	(713)537	Volume 10 -112 (missing)
1557	Not in *Urtext* (appears to be a letter with transcript following)		
1559	*Text 17a*		*Volume 10 - 119*
1560 – 1566 multivariate analysis Oct 14 1966. Volume 10 -120			
1567	*Text 17b*		*Volume 10 -127*
1568	T 21 D 9	(775)596a	Volume 10 - 128 (missing)
1600	T 21 I 5.1	(794)615	Volume 10 -160
1601*	T 22 A 1	(795)- 616 -	Volume 10 - 61
1627	*Text 18a*		*Volume 11 - 2*
1628	T 22 E 5	(809)628	Volume 11 - 3
1647*	T 23 A 1	(819)638	Volume 11 - 22
1683*	T 24 A 1	(838)657	Volume 11 - 59
1687	T 24 B 5	(839)658	Volume 11 - 62
1688	*Text 18 b*		*Volume 11- 63*
1694	T 18 H 10	(684)(631c)	Volume 11 - 69 (missing)
1695	T 24 C 1	(842)661	Volume 11 - 70 (missing)
1700	T 24 C 8.7	(844)663	Volume 11 - 75
1735*	T 25 A 1	(864)683	Volume 11 - 110
1800	T 25 J 6.3	(898)717	Volume 11 -175
1803*	T 26 A 1	(901)720	Volume 11 - 178
1868*	T 27 A 1	(934)760	Volume 13 - 3
1900	T 27 E 6.6	(948)774	Volume 12 - 35
1936*	T 28 A 1	(967)793	Volume 12 - 71
1983*	T 29 A 1	(990)816	Volume 12 - 118
2000	T 29 D 5.4	(998)824	Volume 12 - 135
2029*	T 30 A 1- B 1	(1016)830	Volume 12 - 164
2083-43	T 29 H 1 …		Volume 12 - 173-178
2045	T 30 B 10	(1019)(833)	Volume 12 - 179
2046	T 30 C 1	(1021)835	Volume 12 - 181
2088*	T 31 A 1	(1042)856	Volume 12 - 223
2100	T 31 B 5.1	(1047)861	Volume 12 - 235
2155	T 31 H 11	(1072)886	Volume 12 - 290 <Text ends>

31 shading indicates chapter break
24 shading indicates missing material
* indicates *HLC* chapter breaks

Appendix III - Urtext to Notes Cross-Referencing

(2) Workbook

	WORKBOOK		
Notes p#	Urtext Ref	Urtext Page	*Notes* Ref.
1	WIn1		Volume 13 - 1
135	W 51 R 1	88	Volume 13 - 26
241	W 77 L 1	152	Volume 14 - 1
258	W 81 R 2	162	Volume 14 - 17
370	W 111 R 3	228	Volume 14 - 130
480	W 135 L 18	288	Volume 15 - 1
524	W 141 R 4	311	Volume 15 - 45
650	W 171 R 5	381	Volume 15 -171
671	W 182 L 1	394	Volume 16 - 1
777	W 201 R 6	552	Volume 16 - 107
789	W 221 In2	459	Volume 16 - 119
797	W 220 W 1	462	Volume 16 - 127
809	W 230 W 2	473	Volume 16 - 140
823	W 240 W3	484	Volume 16 - 153
835	W 250 W4	494	Volume 16 - 165
849	W 260 W5	506	Volume 16 - 179
863	W 270 W6	517	Volume 16 - 193
875	W 280 W7	528	Volume 16 - 206
889	W 290 W8	539	Volume 16 - 219
902	W 300 W9	550	Volume 16 - 232
913	W 307 L 1	557	Volume 17 - 1
919	W 310 W10	561	Volume 17 - 7
932	W 320 W11	528	Volume 17 - 20
945	W 330 W12	539	Volume 17 - 33
958	W 340 W13	594	Volume 17 - 46
971	W 350 W14	605	Volume 17 - 59
990	W 361 Ep	619	Volume 17 - 78
994	end of WB	620	Volume 17 - 80

Appendix III - Urtext to Notes Cross-Referencing

(3) Manual

	MANUAL		
Notes p#	Urtext Ref	Urtext Page	*Notes* Ref.
1	M 1 A 1	1	Volume 17 - 83
5	M 2 A 1	3	Volume 17 - 87
7	M 3 A 1	4	Volume 17 - 89
10	M 4 A 1	6	Volume 17 - 92
13	M 5 A 1	8	Volume 17 - 95
31	M 6 A 1	18	Volume 17 - 113
37	M 7 A 1	22	Volume 17 - 119
39	M 8 A 1	23	Volume 17 - 121
43	M 9 A 1	25	Volume 17 - 125
47	M 10 A 1	27	Volume 17 - 129
48	M 11 A 1	28	Volume 17 - 130
52	M 12 A 1	30	Volume 17 - 134
56	M 13 A 1	32	Volume 17 - 137
59	M 14 A 1	34	Volume 17 - 141
64	M 15 A 1	37	Volume 17 - 146
67	M 16 A 1	39	Volume 17 - 149
69	M 17 A 1	40	Volume 17 - 151
77	M 18 A 1	43	Volume 17 - 159
83	M 19 A 1	47	Volume 17 - 165
85	M 20 A 1	48	Volume 17 - 167
89	M 21 A 1	51	Volume 17 - 171
92	M 22 A 1	52	Volume 17 - 174
95	M 23 A 1	53	Volume 17 - 177
100	M 24 A 1	56	Volume 17 - 182
106	M 25 A 1	58	Volume 17 - 188
110	M 26 A 1	60	Volume 17 - 192
114	M 27 A 1	62	Volume 17 - 196
117	M 28 A 1	63	Volume 17 - 199
121	M 29 A 1	66	Volume 17 - 203
129	M 30 A 7	70	Volume 17 - 213

Appendix III - Urtext to Notes Cross-Referencing

(4) Use of Terms

	USE OF TERMS		
Notes p#	Urtext Ref	Urtext Page	*Notes* Ref.
1	U 1 A 1	1	Volume 3 - 27
2	U 2 A 1	4	Volume 3 - 30
7	U 3 A 1	4	Volume 3 - 48
10	U 4 A 1	6	Volume 3 - 33
13	U 5 A 1	7	Volume 3 - 36
14	U 6 A 1	9	Volume 3 - 40
18	U 7 A 1	11	Volume 3 - 44
26	U 8 A 1	13	Volume 3 - 52
27	U 8 A 2	13	Volume 3 - 100
28	U 8 A 5	13	Volume 3 - 99
29	U 8 A 6	14	Volume 3 - 96

(5) Psychotherapy

	PSYCHOTHERAPY		
Notes p#	Urtext Ref	Urtext Page	*Notes* Ref.
2	P 1 A 1	1	Volume 3 - 102
2	P 2 A 1	1	Volume 3 - 102
6	P 3 A 1	3	Volume 3 - 106
8	P 3 B 1	4	Volume 3 - 108
10	P 3 C 1	5	Volume 3 - 110
16	P 3 D 1	8	Volume 3 - 116
18	P 3 E 1	9	Volume 3 - 118
24	P 3 F 1	12	Volume 3 - 124
28	P 3 G 1	14	Volume 3 - 128
33	P 3 H 3	16	Volume 3 - 133
37	P 4 A 1	19	Volume 3 - 138
41	P 4 B 1	21	Volume 3 - 141
48	P 4 C 1	25	Volume 3 - 148

(6) Song of Prayer

	SONG OF PRAYER		
Notes p#	Urtext Ref	Urtext Page	*Notes* Ref.
1	S 1 A 4	2	n/a
2	S 1 A 6	2	n/a
3	S 1 A 7	3	Volume 3 - 90
4	S 1 A 9	3	Volume 3 - 91
5	S 2 A 1	12	n/a

8. Urtext to FIP Cross-Reference

The following chart gives a basic section by section cross referencing of the *Urtext* to the FIP *Second Edition*. It's very rough in the first five chapters because so much has been re-written and removed in the FIP editions that it is quite difficult to align regions of correspondence. This is not guaranteed to be 100% accurate, but it will usually provide a helpful guide for translating between the two reference systems. This chart, of course, only translates to the resolution of section break at best. You're on your own when it comes to translating paragraph numbers within sections.

After chapter 14 the correspondence between the versions is generally high. Before that there are many differences.

- (1) Text 13
- (2) Workbook 19
- (3) Manual 20
- (4) Use of Terms 21
- (5) Psychotherapy 21
- (6) Song of Prayer 22
- (7) Gifts of God 22

Appendix III - Urtext to FIP Cross-Referencing

(1) Text

		Urtext Reference	FIP Reference	
1)	Introduction to Miracles	T 1	T-in.1	Introduction
	A. Introduction	T 1 A 1	T-in.1	Introduction
	B. Principles of Miracles	T 1 B 1	T-1.I.1	
	C. Distortions of Miracle Principles	T 1 C 1	T-1.VI.5.3	The Illusion of Needs
2)	The Illusion of Separation	T 2	T-1	
	A. Introduction	T 2 A 1	n/a	
	B. The Re-interpretation of Defenses	T 2 B 1	T-2.II.1.4	The Atonement as Defense
	C. Healing as Release from Fear	T 2 C 1	T-2.IV.1	
	D. Fear as Lack of Love	T 2 D 1	T-2.VI.1	Fear and Conflict
	E. The Correction for the Lack of Love	T 2 E 1		
	F. The Meaning of the Last Judgment	T 2 F 1	T-2.VIII.2	
3)	Retraining the Mind	T 3	T-3	The Innocent Perception
	A. Introduction	T 3 A 1		
	B. Special Principles for Miracle Workers	T 3 B 1	T-2.V.A.1	
	C. Atonement without Sacrifice	T 3 C 1	T-3.I.1	
	D. Miracles as Accurate Perception	T 3 D 1	T-3.II.1	Miracles as True Perception
	E. Perception vs. Knowledge	T 3 E 1	T-3.III.1	
	F. Conflict and the Ego	T 3 F 1	T-3.IV.1	Error and the Ego
	G. The Loss of Certainty	T 3 G 1	T-3.V.1	Beyond Perception
	H. Judgment and the Authority Problem	T 3 H 1	T-3.VI.1	
	I. Creating vs. the Self-Image	T 3 G 1	T-3.VII.1	
4)	The Root of all Evil	T 4	T-4	The Illusions of the Ego
	A. Introduction	T 4 A 1		
	B. Right Teaching and Right Learning	T 4 B 1	T-3.VI.7	
	C. The Ego and False Autonomy	T 4 C 1	T-4.II.1	
	D. Love without Conflict	T 4 D 1	T-4.III.1	
	E. The Escape from Fear	T 4 E 1	T-4.IV.1	This Need Not Be
	F. The Ego-Body Illusion	T 4 F 1	T-4.V.1	
	G. The Constant State	T 4 G 1		
	H. Creation and Communication	T 4 H 1	T-4.VII.1	
	I. True Rehabilitation	T 4 G 1		
5)	Healing and Wholeness	T 5	T-5	
	A. Introduction	T 5 A 1	T-5.in.1	
	B. Healing as Joining	T 5 B 1	T-5.I.1	The Invitation to the Holy Spirit
	C. The Mind of the Atonement	T 5 C 1		
	D. The Voice for God	T 5 D 1		
	E. The Guide to Salvation	T 5 E 1	T-5.III.1	
	F. Therapy and Teaching	T 5 F 1		
	G. The Two Decisions	T 5 G 1	T-5.V.1	The Ego's use of Guilt
	H. Time and Eternity	T 5 H 2	T-5.VI.1	
	I. The Eternal Fixation	T 5 I 1	T-5.VII??	The Decision for God
6)	Attack and Fear	T 6	T-6	
	A. Introduction	T 6 A 1	T-6.in.1	
	B. The Message of the Crucifixion	T 6 B 1	T-6.I.1	
	C. The Uses of Projection	T 6 C 1	T-6.II.1	
	D. The Relinquishment of Attack	T 6 D 1	T-6.III.1	
	E. The Only Answer	T 6 E 1	T-6.IV.1	
	F. "To Have, Give All to All"	T 6 F 1	T-6.V.1	The Lessons of the Holy Spirit
	G. "To Have Peace, Teach Peace to Learn it."	T 6 G 1		
	H. Be Vigilant only for God and His Kingdom	T 6 H 1		

Appendix III - Urtext to FIP Cross-Referencing

			Urtext Reference	FIP Reference	
7)		The Consistency of the Kingdom	T 7	T-7	
	A.	Introduction	T 7 A 1	T-7.I.1	
	B.	Bargaining versus Healing	T 7 B 1	T-7.I.4	
	C.	The Laws of Mind	T 7 C 1	T-7.II.2	The Law of the Kingdom
	D.	The Unified Curriculum	T 7 D 1	T-7.III.1	The Reality of the Kingdom
	E.	The Recognition of Truth	T 7 E 1	T-7.III.2	Healing as the Recognition of Truth
	F.	Healing and the Changelessness of Mind	T 7 F 1	T-7.V.1	
	G.	From Vigilance to Peace	T 7 G 1	T-7.VI.1	
	H.	The Total commitment	T 7 H 1	T-7.VII.1	The Totality of the Kingdom
	I.	The Defense of Conflict	T 7 I 1	T-7.VIII.1	The Unbelievable Belief
	J.	The Extension of the Kingdom	T 7 J 1	T-7.IX.1	
	K.	The Confusion of Strength and Weakness	T 7 K 1	T-7.X.3	The Confusion of Pain and Joy
	L.	The State of Grace	T 7 L 1	T-7.XI.1	
8)		The Journey Back	T 8	T-8	
	A.	Introduction	T 8 A 1	T-8.I.1	The Direction of the Curriculum
	B.	The Direction of the Curriculum	T 8 B 1	T-8.I.3.4	
	C.	The Rationale for Choice	T 8 C 1	T-8.II.1	The Difference between Imprisonment and
	D.	The Holy Encounter	T 8 D 1	T-8.III.1	
	E.	The Light of the World	T 8 E 1	T-8.IV.1	The Gift of Freedom
	F.	The Power of Joint Decision	T 8 F 1	T-8.VI.1	The Treasure of God
	G.	Communication and the Ego-Body Equation	T 8 G 1	T-8.VII.1	The Body as a Means of Communication
	H.	The Body as Means or End	T 8 H 1	T-8.VIII.1	
	I.	Healing as Corrected Perception	T 8 I 1	T-8.IX.1	
	J.	The Acceptance of Reality	T 8 J 1	T-9.I.1	Ch. 9 The Acceptance of the Atonement
	K.	The Answer to Prayer	T 8 K 1	T-9.II.1	
9)		The Correction of Error	T 9	T-9.III	Ch. 9 The Acceptance of the Atonement
	A.	Introduction	T 9 A 1	T-9.III.1	The Correction of Error
	B.	Sanity and Perception	T 9 B 1	T-9.III.4	
	C.	Atonement as a Lesson in Sharing	T 9 C 1	T-9.IV.1	The Holy Spirit's Plan of Forgiveness
	D.	The Unhealed Healer	T 9 D 1	T-9.V.1	
	E.	The Awareness of the Holy Spirit	T 9 E 1	T-9.VI.1	The Acceptance of your Brother
	F.	Salvation and God's Will	T 9 F 1	T-9.VII.1	The Two evaluations
	G.	Grandeur vs. Grandiosity	T 9 G 1	T-9.VIII.1	
	H.	The Inclusiveness of Creation	T 9 H 1	T-10.in.1	Ch. 10 The Idols of Sickness
	I.	The Decision to Forget	T 9 I 1	T-10.II.1	At Home in God
	J.	Magic vs. Miracles	T 9 J 1	T-10.IV.1	The End of Sickness
	K.	The Denial of God	T 9 K 1	T-10.V.1	
10)		God and the Ego	T 10	T-11	God or the Ego
	A.	Introduction	T 10 A 1	T-11.in.1	
	B.	Projection vs. Extension	T 10 B 1	T-11.in.3	
	C.	The Willingness for Healing	T 10 C 1	T-11.II.1	The Invitation to Healing
	D.	From Darkness to Light	T 10 D 1	T-11.III.1	
	E.	The Inheritance of God's Son	T 10 E 1	T-11.IV.1	
	F.	The "Dynamics" of the Ego	T 10 F 1	T-11.V.1	
	G.	Experience and Perception	T 10 G 1	T-11.VI.1	Waking to Redemption
	H.	The problem and the Answer	T 10 H 1	T-11.VII.1	The Condition of Reality
11)		God's Plan for Salvation	T 11	T-12	The Holy Spirit's Curriculum
	A.	Introduction	T 11 A 1	T-12.I.1	The Judgment of the Holy Spirit
	B.	The Judgment of the Holy Spirit	T 11 B 1	T-12.I.3	
	C.	The Mechanism of Miracles	T 11 C 1	T-12.I.9	The Way to Remember God
	D.	The Investment in Reality	T 11 D 1	T-12.III.1	
	E.	Seeking and Finding	T 11 E 1	T-12.IV.1	
	F.	The Sane Curriculum	T 11 F 1	T-12.V.1	
	G.	The Vision of Christ	T 11 G 1	T-12.VI.1	
	H.	The Guide for Miracles	T 11 H 1	T-12.VI.1	Looking Within
	I.	Reality and Redemption	T 11 I 1	T-12.VIII.1	The Attraction of Love for Love
	J.	Guiltlessness and Invulnerability	T 11 J 1	T-13.in.1	Ch. 13 The Guiltless World

Appendix III - Urtext to FIP Cross-Referencing

		Urtext Reference	FIP Reference	
12)	The Problem of Guilt	T 12	T-13.II	The Guiltless World
	A. Introduction	T 12 A 1	T-13.II.1	The Guiltless Son of God
	B. Crucifixion by Guilt	T 12 B 1	T-13.II.3	
	C. The Fear of Redemption	T 12 C 1	T-13.III.1	
	D. Healing and Time	T 12 D 1	T-13.IV.1	The Function of Time
	E. The Two Emotions	T 12 E 1	T-13.V.1	
	F. Finding the Present	T 12 F 1	T-13.VI.1	
	G. Attainment of the Real World	T 12 G 1	T-13.VII.1	
13)	From Perception to Knowledge	T 13	T-13.VII	The Guiltless World
	A. Introduction	T 13 A 1	T-13.VII.1	From Perception to Knowledge
	B. The Role of Healing	T 13 B 1	T-13.VII.3	
	C. The Shadow of Guilt	T 13 C 1	T-13.IX.1	The Cloud of Guilt
	D. Release and Restoration	T 13 D 1	T-13.X.1	Release from Guilt
	E. The Guarantee of Heaven	T 13 E 1	T-13.XI.3	The Peace of Heaven
	F. The Testimony of Miracles	T 13 F 1	T-14.in.1	Ch. 14 Teaching for Truth (Introduction)
	G. The Happy Learner	T 13 G 1	T-14.II.1	
	H. The Decision for Guiltlessness	T 13 H 1	T-14.III.1	
	I. The Way of Salvation	T 13 I 1	T-14.IV.1	Your Function in the Atonement
14)	Bringing Illusions to Truth	T 14	T-14.IV.7	
	A. Introduction	T 14 A 1	T-14.IV.7	Your Function in the Atonement
	B. Guilt and Guiltlessness	T 14 B 1	T-14.IV.10	The Circle of Atonement
	C. Out of the Darkness	T 14 C 1	T-14.VI.1	The Light of Communication
	D. Perception without Deceit	T 14 D 1	T-14.VII.1	Sharing Perception with the Holy Spirit
	E. The Recognition of Holiness	T 14 E 1	T-14.IX.1	The Reflection of Holiness
	F. The Shift to Miracles	T 14 F 1	T-14.X.1	The Equality of Miracles
	G. The Test of Truth	T 14 G 1	T-14.XI.1	
15)	The Purpose of Time	T 15	T-15	The Holy Instant
	A. Introduction	T 15 A 1	T-15.I.1	The Two Uses of Time
	B. The Uses of Time	T 15 B 1	T-15.I.3	
	C. Time and Eternity	T 15 C 1	T-15.II.1	The End of Doubt
	D. Littleness and Magnitude	T 15 D 1	T-15.III.1	
	E. Practicing the Holy Instant	T 15 E 1	T-15.IV.1	
	F. The Holy Instant and Special Relationships	T 15 F 1	T-15.V.1	
	G. The Holy Instant and the Laws of God	T 15 G 1	T-15.VI.1	
	H. The Holy Instant and Communication	T 15 H 1	T-15.VII.1	The Needless Sacrifice
	I. The Holy Instant and Real Relationships	T 15 I 1	T-15.VIII.1	The Only Real Relationship
	J. The Time of Christ	T 15 J 1	T-15.X.1	The Time of Rebirth
	K. The End of Sacrifice	T 15 K 1	T-15.XI.1	Christmas as the End of Sacrifice
16)	The Forgiveness of Illusions	T 16	T-16	
	A. Introduction	T 16 A 1	T-16.I.1	True Empathy
	B. True Empathy	T 16 B 1	T-16.I.4	
	C. The Magnitude of Holiness	T 16 C 1	T-16.II.1	The Power of Holiness
	D. The Reward of Teaching	T 16 D 1	T-16.III.1	
	E. Illusion and Reality of Love	T 16 E 1	T-16.IV.1	
	F. Specialness and Guilt	T 16 F 1	T-16.V.1	The Choice for Completion
	G. The Bridge to the Real World	T 16 G 1	T-16.VI.1	
	H. The End of Illusions	T 16 H 1	T-16.VII.1	
17)	Forgiveness and Healing	T 17	T-17	Forgiveness and the Holy Relationship
	A. Introduction	T 17 A 1	T-17.I.1	Bringing Fantasy to Truth
	B. Fantasy and Distorted Perception	T 17 B 1	T-17.I.3	
	C. The Forgiven World	T 17 C 1	T-17.II.1	
	D. Shadows of the Past	T 17 D 1	T-17.III.1	
	E. Perception and the Two Worlds	T 17 E 1	T-17.IV.1	The Two Pictures
	F. The Healed Relationship	T 17 F 1	T-17.V.1	
	G. Practical Forgiveness	T 17 G 1	T-17.VI.1	Setting the Goal
	H. The Need for Faith	T 17 H 1	T-17.VII.1	The Call for Faith
	I. The Conditions of Forgiveness	T 17 I 1	T-17.VIII.1	The Conditions of Peace

Appendix III - Urtext to FIP Cross-Referencing

			Urtext Reference	FIP Reference	
18)		The Dream and the Reality	T 18	T-18	The Passing of the Dream
	A.	Introduction	T 18 A 1	T-18.I.1	The Substitute Reality
	B.	Substitution as a Defense	T 18 B 1	T-18.I.4	
	C.	The Basis of the Dream	T 18 C 1	T-18.II.1	
	D.	Light in the Dream	T 18 D 1	T-18.III.1	
	E.	The Little Willingness	T 18 E 1	T-18.IV.1	
	F.	The Happy Dream	T 18 F 1	T-18.V.1	
	G.	Dreams and the Body	T 18 G 1	T-18.VI.1	Beyond the Body
	H.	"I Need do Nothing"	T 18 H 1	T-18.VII.1	
	I.	The Purpose of the Body	T 18 I 1	T-18.VIII.1	The Little Garden
	J.	The Delusional Thought System	T 18 J 1	T-18.IX.1	The Two Worlds
	K.	The Passing of the Dream	T 18 K 1	T-18.IX.11	
19)		Beyond the body	T 19	T-19	The Attainment of Peace
	A.	Introduction	T 19 A 1	T-19.I.1	The Attainment of Peace
	B.	Healing and the Mind	T 19 B 1	T-19.I.3	Healing and Faith
	C.	Sin vs. Error	T 19 C 1	T-19.II.1	
	D.	The Unreality of Sin	T 19 D 1	T-19.III.1	
	E.	Obstacles to Peace - I	T 19 E 1	T-19.IV.1	The Desire to Get Rid of It
	F.	The Attraction of Guilt	T 19 F 1	T-19.IV.A.10	
	G.	Obstacles to Peace II	T 19 G 1	T-19.IV.B.1	The Belief the Body is Valuable
	H.	Pleasure and Pain	T 19 H 1	T-19.IV.B.9	The Attraction of Pain
	I.	Obstacles to Peace III	T 19 I 1	T-19.IV.C.1	The Attraction of Death
	J.	The Incorruptible Body	T 19 J 1	T-19.IV.C.3	
	K.	Obstacles to Peace IV	T 19 J 1	T-19.IV.D.1	The Fear of God
	L.	The Lifting of the Veil	T 19 L 1	T-19.IV.D.8	
20)		The Promise of the Resurrection	T 20	T-20	The Vision of Holiness
	A.	Introduction	T 20 A 1	T-20.I.1	Holy Week
	B.	Holy Week	T 20 B 1	T-20.I.2	
	C.	Thorns and Lillies	T 20 C 1	T-20.II.1	The Gift of Lilies
	D.	Sin as an Adjustment	T 20 D 1	T-20.III.1	
	E.	Entering the Ark	T 20 E 1	T-20.IV.1	
	F.	Heralds of Eternity	T 20 F 1	T-20.V.1	
	G.	The Temple of the Holy Spirit	T 20 G 1	T-20.VI.1	
	H.	The Consistency of Means and end	T 20 H 1	T-20.VII.1	
	I.	The Vision of Sinlessness	T 20 I 1	T-20.VIII.1	
21)		The Inner Picture	T 21	T-21	Reason and Perception
	A.	Introduction	T 21 A 1	T-21.in.1	
	B.	The Imagined World	T 21 B 1	T-21.I.1	The Forgotten Song
	C.	The Responsibility for Sight	T 21 C 1	T-21.II.1	
	D.	Faith, Belief and Vision	T 21 D 1	T-21.III.1	
	E.	The Fear to Look Within	T 21 E 1	T-21.IV.1	
	F.	Reason and Perception	T 21 F 1	T-21.V.1	The Function of Reason
	G.	Reason and Correction	T 21 G 1	T-21.VI.1	Reason vs. Madness
	H.	Perception and Wishes	T 21 H 1	T-21.VIII.1	The Last Unanswered Question
	I.	The Inner Shift	T 21 I 1	T-21.VIII.1	
22)		Salvation and the Holy Relationship	T 22	T-22	
	A.	Introduction	T 22 A 1	T-22.in.1	
	B.	The Message of the Holy Relationship	T 22 B 1	T-22.I.1	
	C.	Your Brother's Sinlessness	T 22 C 1	T-22.II.1	
	D.	Reason and the Holy Relationship	T 22 D 1	T-22.III.1	Reason and the Forms of Error
	E.	The Branching of the Road	T 22 E 1	T-22.IV.1	
	F.	Weakness and Defensiveness	T 22 F 1	T-22.V.1	
	G.	Freedom and the Holy Spirit	T 22 G 1	T-22.VI.1	The Light of the Holy Relationship

Appendix III - Urtext to FIP Cross-Referencing

			Urtext Reference	FIP Reference	
23)		The War Against Yourself	T 23	T-23	
	A.	Introduction	T 23 A 1	T-23.in.1	
	B.	The Irreconcilable Beliefs	T 23 B 1	T-23.I.1	
	C.	The Laws of Chaos	T 23 C 1	T-23.II.1	
	D.	Salvation Without Compromise	T 23 D 1	T-23.III.1	
	E.	The Fear of Life	T 23 E 1	T-23.IV.1	Above the Battleground
24)		Specialness and Separation	T 24	T-24	The Goal of Specialness
	A.	Introduction	T 24 A 1	T-24.in.1	
	B.	Specialness as a Substitute for Love	T 24 B 1	T-24.I.1	
	C.	The Treachery of Specialness	T 24 C 1	T-24.II.1	
	D.	The Forgiveness of Specialness	T 24 D 1	T-24.III.1	
	E.	Specialness and Salvation	T 24 E 1	T-24.IV.1	Specialness Vs. Sinlessness
	F.	The Resolution of the Dream	T 24 F 1	T-24.V.1	The Christ in You
	G.	Salvation from Fear	T 24 G 1	T-24.VI.1	
	H.	The Meeting-Place	T 24 H 1	T-24.VII.1	The Meeting Place
25)		The Remedy	T 25	T-25	The Justice of God
	A.	Introduction	T 25 A 1	T-25.in.1	
	B.	The Appointed Task	T 25 B 1	T-25.I.1	The Link to Truth
	C.	The Savior from the Dark	T 25 C 1	T-25.II.1	
	D.	The Fundamental Law of Perception	T 25 D 1	T-25.III.1	Perception and Choice
	E.	The Joining of Minds	T 25 E 1	T-25.IV.1	The Light You Bring
	F.	The State of Sinlessness	T 25 F 1	T-25.V.1	
	G.	The Special Function	T 25 G 1	T-25.VI.1	
	H.	Commuting the Sentence	T 25 H 1	T-25.VII.1	The Rock of Salvation
	I.	The Principle of Salvation	T 25 I 1	T-25.VIII.1	Justice Returned to Love
	J.	The Justice of Heaven	T 25 J 1	T-25.IX.1	
26)		The Transition	T 26	T-26	
	A.	Introduction	T 26 A 1	T-26.I.1	
	B.	The "Sacrifice" of Oneness	T 26 B 1	T-26.I.2	The "Sacrifice" of Oneness
	C.	The Forms of Error	T 26 C 1	T-26.II.1	Many Forms; One Correction
	D.	The Borderland	T 26 D 1	T-26.III.1	
	E.	Where Sin has Left	T 26 E 1	T-26.IV.1	
	F.	The Little Hindrance	T 26 F 1	T-26.V.1	
	G.	The appointed Friend	T 26 G 1	T-26.VI.1	
	H.	Review of Principles	T 26 H 1	T-26.VII.1	The Laws of Healing
	I.	The Immediacy of Salvation	T 26 I 1	T-26.VIII.1	
	J.	For They Have Come	T 16 J 1	T-26.IX.1	
	K.	The Remaining Task	T 26 J 1	T-26.X.1	The End of Injustice
27)		The Body and the Dream	T 27	T-27	The Healing of the Dream
	A.	Introduction	T 27 A 1	T-27.I.1	The Picture of Crucifixion
	B.	The Picture of the Crucifixion	T 27 B 1	T-27.I.3	
	C.	The Fear of Healing	T 27 C 1	T-27.II.1	
	D.	The Symbol of the Impossible	T 27 D 1	T-27.III.1	Beyond All Symbols
	E.	The Quiet Answer	T 27 E 1	T-27.IV.1	
	F.	The Healing Example	T 27 E 1	T-27.V.1	
	G.	The Purpose of Pain	T 27 F 1	T-27.VI.1	The Witnesses to Sin
	H.	The Illusion of Suffering	T 27 G 1	T-27.VII.1	The Dreamer of the Dream
	I.	The "Hero" of the Dream	T 27 H 1	T-27.VIII.1	
28)		The undoing of Fear	T 28	T-28	
	A.	Introduction	T 28 A 1	T-28.I.1	The Present Memory
	B.	The Present Memory	T 28 B 1	T-28.I. 4	
	C.	Reversing Effect and Cause	T 28 C 1	T-28.II.1	
	D.	The Agreement to Join	T 28 D 1	T-28.III.1	
	E.	The Greater Joining	T 28 E 1	T-28.IV.1	
	F.	The Alternate to Dreams of Fear	T 28 F 1	T-28.V.1	
	G.	The Secret Vows	T 28 G 1	T-28.VI.1	
	H.	The Beautiful Relationship	T 28 H 1	T-28.VII.1	The Ark of Safety

Appendix III - Urtext to FIP Cross-Referencing

			Urtext Reference	FIP Reference	
29)		The Awakening	T 29	T-29	
	A.	Introduction	T 29 A 1	T-29.I.1	
	B.	The Closing of the Gap	T 29 B 1	T-29.I.4	
	C.	The Coming of the Guest	T 29 C 1	T-29.II.1	
	D.	God's Witnesses	T 29 D 1	T-29.III.1	
	E.	Dream Roles	T 29 E 1	T-29.IV.1	
	F.	The Changeless Dwelling-Place	T 29 F 1	T-29.V.1	
	G.	Forgiveness and Peace	T 29 G 1	T-29.VI.1	Forgiveness and the End of Time
	H.	The Lingering Dream	T 29 H 1	T-29.VII.1	Seek not Outside Yourself
	I.	Christ and Anti-Christ	T 29 I 1	T-29.VIII.1	The Anti-Christ
	J.	The Forgiving Dream	T 29 J 1	T-29.IX.1	
30)		The New Beginning	T 30	T-30	
	A.	Introduction	T 30 A 1	T-30.in.1	
	B.	Rules for Decision	T 30 B 1	T-30.I.1	
	C.	Freedom of Will	T 30 C 1	T-30.II.1	
	D.	Beyond All Idols	T 30 D 1	T-30.III.1	
	E.	The Truth Behind illusions	T 30 E 1	T-30.IV.1	
	F.	The Only Purpose	T 30 F 1	T-30.V.1	
	G.	The Justification for Forgiveness	T 30 G 1	T-30.VI.1	
	H.	The New Interpretation	T 30 H 1	T-30.VII.1	
	I.	Changeless Reality	T 30 I 1	T-30.VIII.1	
31)		The Simplicity of Salvation	T 31	T-31	The Final Vision
	A.	Introduction	T 31 A 1	T-31.I.1	The Picture of the Crucifixion
	B.	The Illusion of an Enemy	T 31 B 1	T-31.II.1	Walking with the Christ
	C.	The Self-Accused	T 31 C 1	T-31.III.1	
	D.	The Real Alternative	T 31 D 1	T-31.IV.1	
	E.	Self-Concept vs. Self	T 31 E 1	T-31.V.1	
	F.	Recognizing the Spirit	T 31 F 1	T-31.VI.1	
	G.	The Savior's Vision	T 31 G 1	T-31.VII.1	
	H.	Choose Once Again	T 31 H 1	T-31.VIII.1	

Appendix III - Urtext to FIP Cross-Referencing

(2) Workbook

		Urtext Reference	FIP Reference
1)	Introduction	W 1 IN1	W-in
2)	Review 1	W 50 R1	W-pI.rI
3)	Review 2	W 80 R2	W-pI.rII
4)	Review 3	W 110 R3	W-pI.rIII
5)	Review 4	W 140 R4	W-pI.rIV
6)	Review 5	W 170 R5	W-pI.rV
7)	Review 6	W 200 R6	W-pI.rVI
8)	Introduction to Part II	W 220 IN2	W-pII.in
9)	What is forgiveness?	W 220 W1	W-pII.1
10)	What is Salvation?	W 230 W2	W-pII.2
11)	What is the World?	W 240 W3	W-pII.3
12)	What is Sin?	W 250 W4	W-pII.4
13)	What is the Body?	W 260 W5	W-pII.5
14)	What is the Christ?	W 270 W6	W-pII.6
15)	What is the Holy Spirit?	W 280 W7	W-pII.7
16)	What is the Real World?	W 290 W8	W-pII.8
17)	What is the Second Coming?	W 300 W9	W-pII.9
18)	What is the Last Judgment?	W 310 W10	W-pII.10
19)	What is Creation?	W 320 W11	W-pII.11
20)	What is the Ego?	W 330 W12	W-pII.12
21)	What is the Miracle?	W 340 W13	W-pII.13
22)	What am I?	W 350 W14	W-pII.14
23)	Final Lessons	W 361 FL	W.fl.in.1
24)	Epilogue	W 361 EP	W.ep

In the *Workbook,* of course, the basic reference grid is the 361 individual lessons which are always of the form **W 200 L *n*** where *n* is the paragraph number. Although lessons always have a single section, the section designator "**L**" is used to distinguish the numbered lesson from the following non-lesson material in the 24 instances, listed above, where material other than lessons is included in the *Workbook*. After lesson 200, for instance, we have the sixth review. That segment is referenced as **W 200 R6 *n*** where *n* is the paragraph number. This provides the information most critical to actually finding it in a printed book; it *follows* lesson 200!

Appendix III - Urtext to FIP Cross-Referencing

(3) Manual

		Urtext Reference	FIP Reference
1)	Introduction	M 1 A 1	M-in.1
2)	Who are God's Teachers?	M 2 A 1	M-1.1
3)	Who are their students?	M 3 A 1	M-2.1
4)	What are the Levels of Teaching?	M 4 A 1	M-3.1
5)	What are the Characteristics of God's Teachers?	M 5 A 1	M-4.1
	A. Introduction	M 5 A 1	M-4.1
	B. Trust	M 5 B 1	M-4.I.1
	C. Honesty	M 5 C 1	M-4.II.1
	D. Tolerance	M 5 D 1	M-4.III.1
	E. Gentleness	M 5 E 1	M-4.IV.1
	F. Joy	M 5 F 1	M-4.V.1
	G. Defenselessness	M 5 G 1	M-4.VI.1
	H. Generosity	M 5 H 1	M-4.VII.1
	I. Patience	M 5 I 1	M-4.VIII.1
	J. Faithfulness	M 5 J 1	M-4.IX.1
	K. Open-Mindedness	M 5 K 1	M-4.X.1
6)	How is Healing Accomplished?	M 6 A 1	M-5.1
	A. Introduction	M 6 A 1	M-5.1 - M-5.2
	B. The Perceived Purpose of Sickness	M 6 B 1	M-5.I.1
	C. The Shift in Perception	M 6 C 1	M-5.II.1
	D. The Function of the Teacher	M 6 D 1	M-5.III.1
7)	Is Healing Certain?	M 7 A 1	M-6.1
8)	Should Healing be Repeated?	M 8 A 1	M-7.1
9)	How can the Perception of Order of Difficulties be …	M 9 A 1	M-8.1
10)	Are changes required in the life situations of God's Tea..	M 10 A 1	M-9.1
11)	How is Judgment Relinquished?	M 11 A 1	M-10.1
12)	How is Peace Possible?	M 12 A 1	M-11.1
13)	How many Teachers of God are needed to sae the world?	M 13 A 1	M-12.1
14)	What is the Real Meaning of Sacrifice?	M 14 A 1	M-13.1
15)	How will the World end?	M 15 A 1	M-14.1
16)	Is each one to be judged in the end?	M 16 A 1	M-15.1
17)	How should the Teacher of God spend his day?	M 17 A 1	M-16.1
18)	How do God's Teachers deal with their Pupils' thoughts	M 18 A 1	M-17.1
19)	How is Correction Made?	M 19 A 1	M-18.1
20)	What is Justice?	M 20 A 1	M-19.1
21)	What is the Peace of God?	M 21 A 1	M-20.1
22)	What is the Role of Words in Healing?	M 22 A 1	M-21.1
23)	How are Healing and Atonement Related?	M 23 A 1	M-22.1
24)	Does Jesus have a Special Place in Healing?	M 24 A 1	M-23.1
25)	Is Reincarnation True?	M 25 A 1	M-24.1
26)	Are Psychic Powers Desirable?	M 26 A 1	M-25.1
27)	Can God be Reached Directly?	M 27 A 1	M-26.1
28)	What is Death?	M 28 A 1	M-27.1
29)	What is the Resurrection?	M 29 A 1	M-28.1
30)	As for the rest…	M 30 A 1	M-29.1

Appendix III - Urtext to FIP Cross-Referencing

(4) Use of Terms

		Urtext Reference	FIP Reference
1)	Introduction	U 1 A 1	C-in.1
2)	Mind-Spirit	U 2 A 1	C-1.1
3)	The Ego-The Miracle	U 3 A 1	C-2.1
4)	Forgiveness- The Face of Christ	U 4 A 1	C-3.1
5)	Perception-Knowledge	U 5 A 1	C-4.1
6)	Jesus-Christ	U 6 A 1	C-5.1
7)	The Holy Spirit	U 7 A 1	C-6.1
8)	Epilogue	U 8 A 1	C-7.1

(5) Psychotherapy

			Urtext Reference	FIP Reference
1)	An Introduction to Psychotherapy		P 1 A 1	P-in.1
2)	The Purpose of Psychotherapy		P 2 A 1	P-1.in.
	A.	Introduction	P 2 A 1	P-1.in.1
3)	The Process of Psychotherapy		P 3 A 1	P-2.1
	A.	Introduction	P 3 A 1	P-2.in.1
	B.	The Limits on Psychotherapy	P 3 B 1	P-2.I.1
	C.	The Place of Religion in Psychotherapy	P 3 C 1	P-2.II.1
	D.	The Role of the Psychotherapist	P 3 D 1	P-2.III.1
	E.	The Process of Illness	P 3 E 1	P-2.IV.1
	F.	The Process of Healing	P 3 F 1	P-2.V.1
	G.	The Definition of Healing	P 3 G 1	P-2.VI.1
	H.	The Ideal Patient-Therapist Relationship	P 3 H 1	P-2.VII.1
4)	The Practice of Psychotherapy		P 4 A 1	P-3.I
	A.	The Selection of Patients	P 4 A 1	P-3.I.1
	B.	Is Psychotherapy a Profession?	P 4 B 1	P-3.II.1
	C.	The Question of Payment	P 4 C 1	P-3.III.1

Appendix III - Urtext to FIP Cross-Referencing

(6) Song of Prayer

			Urtext Reference	FIP Reference
1)	Prayer		S 1 A 1	S-in.1
	A.	Introduction	S 1 A 1	S-in.1
	B.	True Prayer	S 1 B 1	S-1.I.1
	C.	The Ladder of Prayer	S 1 C 1	S-1.II.1
	D.	Praying for Others	S 1 D 1	S-1.III.1
	E.	Praying with Others	S 1 E 1	S-1.IV.1
	F.	The Ladder Ends	S 1 F 1	S-1.V.1
2)	Forgiveness		S 2 A 1	S-2.
	A.	Introduction	S 2 A 1	S-2.in.1
	B.	Forgiveness of Yourself	S 2 B 1	S-2.I.1
	C.	Forgiveness-to-destroy	S 2 C 1	S-2.II.1
	D.	Forgiveness-for-Salvation	S 2 D 1	S-2.III.1
3)	Healing		S 3 A 1	S-3.1
	A.	Introduction	S 3 A 1	S-3.in.1
	B.	The Cause of Sickness	S 3 B 1	S-3.I.1
	C.	False versus True Healing	S 3 C 1	S-3.II.1
	D.	Separation versus Union	S 3 D 1	S-3.III.1
	E.	The Holiness of Healing	S 3 E 1	S-3.IV.1

(7) Gifts of God

The Foundation editions do not include the Gifts of God.

Appendix IV: The Nature and Significance of the Version Differences

The Nature and Significance of the Version Differences

by Doug Thompson

Those new to the Course will likely soon discover what long-time Course students generally know about: there are multiple versions of *A Course in Miracles* and some people have some rather strong opinions about which is "best." As one who uses – and publishes – all the versions I have access to, I wish to shed some light on a debate which often seems to generate more heat than light.

First I want to say that whatever version you have, read it and study it! If you come across a passage that leaves you wondering … see if it is the same in the other versions. Sometimes that experience is an eye-opener. Sometimes you're puzzling over a typo.

Second I want to say that there is no "perfect version" and none without errors and flaws. Nor is there one without unique merits. The *Scholar's Toolbox* contains four **Scribal Versions**, which is to say versions one or both of the Scribes had a hand in creating, and I'm pretty sure there exists at least one more we haven't yet seen. Each is an important "primary source" which helps us see more clearly what the elusive "original dictation" really was, and how it was that none captured it perfectly.

When looking at the various versions, these questions often come to mind:

What is the nature of the differences?

What is their significance?

Which version is the best?

First off we must remember that no one has even identified, let alone carefully examined all the differences. Every opinion on this topic is therefore based on fragmentary data if it is based on data at all. Of the thousands of differences between versions I've personally looked at I can say that among the frequent fairly minor differences, some are anything *but* minor. The differences fall into two broad categories:

1) Many appear to be simply inadvertent copying mistakes which are easy to correct and are mostly, but not entirely, rather minor.

2) Many others appear to be intentional changes of wording and punctuation three kinds:

   a. those which appear to be dictated corrections

   b. those which change the wording but do not appear intended to change the meaning significantly; in short editing for style

   c. those which appear to be editing mistakes, in that the meaning is changed but incorrectly changed

   d. those which are not obviously either corrections or corruptions

With the majority of the differences it is fairly obvious, at least to me, whether it is a "correction" or a "corruption." There will be differences of opinion about some of those but a great many really *are* obvious. With many, the editing appears to be unnecessary, making no significant change at all. Rather obviously there is a certain subjectivity in assessing a change as "error" or as a "correction" and these questions warrant careful study and extensive discussion.

Every version has mistakes and every version has material which is very clearly more authentic and accurate than any other. There is no version with a monopoly on authenticity or accuracy. Of the thousands of variant readings, the "best" can only be ascertained by checking all the variants. Each version then is a source and a "witness" to the original dictation. No version is free of error, no version is without unique value. Each version contains some material not present in any other. Each version omits some material which is present in one or more others.

This is not a hockey match in the "league of versions." It's not a competition between versions. This is a quest for the truth in which we have four witnesses who do not always agree on everything, but always sincerely attempt to point us to the truth, with varying degrees of reliability. It is possible to overestimate the significance of the differences but with fragmentary data it is even more likely to under-estimate the differences. Without examining a great many, it is impossible to come up with any sort of reliable estimate at all. And until they are all examined, any appraisal is an "estimate" and falls short of being conclusive.

From the fact that most differences are relatively minor some infer that "therefore the differences aren't very important." If one looks at a handful of minor differences that impression is understandable, but it would be misleading.

For instance, one difference is that some 60,000 words of the original dictation didn't make it into the 1975 abridgement, including the entire section on sex and possession. That's about the number of words in the average novel. That can hardly be considered a "minor" difference. It's an enormous difference. If all that material was "wrong" as some suppose, then its removal was a very significant correction, not an inconsequential "minor difference." If the removal of that material was a mistake, as others suppose, then its removal was a very major omission. Either way, it isn't a "minor difference."

A second aspect of the "quality" of the differences is simply the "quantity" of the differences. If you put a small splatter of mud on the Mona Lisa, it is "minor" but if you put several thousand splatters of mud on the Mona Lisa, even if all of them are "minor" by themselves, the overall effect of so many minor problems adds up to a rather major problem. The clarity of the message suffers from a large quantity of "minor" errors. In the category of "minor" differences there are at least several thousand.

Thirdly, while *most* of the editing changes are minor, a few have rather greater significance, in that they really do substantially change the content. If these really are "corrections" it is important to confirm them, but if these are editorial mistakes, it is important to correct them.

We have then three "major" differences: 1) a huge amount of very important material that was left out and 2) a huge number of "minor" alterations that add up to a very significant degree of difference between the original dictation and the final, substantially abridged and re-written publication in 1975, and 3)

Appendix IV: The Nature and Significance of the Version Differences

there are a few very significant changes in the content which need to be carefully studied.

All in all then, while *most* of the differences will not strike most people as hugely important individually, some are of very great importance indeed, and an accurate assessment of their merits is equally important to the goal of establishing the authentic text of A Course in Miracles as accurately as possible.

Unless you are going to simply accept the editor's decisions as always correct – which is problematic since they weren't always correct – then it becomes very important indeed to determine if any given change was made in error or not. This edition of the *Seven Volume Urtext* is offered in that Spirit: enhancing access to the material so that it is actually available for study.

In the year 2000 when earlier and less edited versions of *A Course in Miracles* first became public, intense controversy immediately arose about the extent, nature and importance of the differences between the versions. In a way that was funny because strong opinions emerged long before anyone had appraised more than a handful of the actual differences. It was as if the conclusions pre-dated the evidence!

On one side of the debate it is said that the shorter, heavily edited version published by the Foundation for Inner Peace in 1975 is the form in which the author wished the material to appear, and the differences in the earlier manuscripts represent errors which were subsequently corrected. In this view there is something "wrong" with even looking at the earlier material. Many who hold that view feel that the primary sources should have been kept secret. That thought is sometimes accompanied by projections of guilt, that those who are working on the primary sources are somehow "guilty" of violating Schucman's privacy or expressed wishes in daring to suggest that in her editing she might have erred. One will even hear it said that the earlier manuscripts were "stolen." If that is the case I'd like to know when the police were called and just who, as result of that oft-alleged "theft" has been denied access to the material thereby!

On the other side of the debate one hears the argument that the original wording is always the more authentic and that the later editing corrupted the message of the original dictation. This opinion is also sometimes accompanied by various kinds of guilt projections directed at those responsible for making the changes and then claiming that there were "virtually no changes." Given that those who did make the changes denied having done so for decades and appear to have deliberately kept the truth secret, it is perhaps not surprising that notions of "guilt" enter into the debate.

If "theft" is depriving the legitimate owner of access to his property the question may be asked "who owns the words of Jesus of Nazareth and just who has attempted to deprive whom of access to those words?"

There is an unpleasant fact about the Course's history which I'm not going to try to deny, hide, or paper over. For reasons which I don't claim to understand in detail, there are some who have gone to considerable lengths to obscure, deny, and intentionally falsify the truth about the Course's history and origins, and even the text of the Course itself, sometimes even lying under oath in court. There are others who have been misinformed and repeat incorrect information in good faith, believing it to be true. In such an environment, it is necessary to independently corroborate every claim of "fact" before accepting it as more than "potentially true" because some of what is being said isn't actually true, even though those who repeat it may sincerely *believe* it to be true.

Many books which refer to the Course, including such works as Gary Renard's best-seller *Disappearance of the Universe*, conspicuously draw attention to the claim that the 1975 edition was "virtually unchanged" from the original dictation.. Although Renard puts those words into the mouths of his fictional "Ascended Masters" which include no less than his own reincarnated self, I think it is safe to assume that when he penned those words he believed them to be true. He heard that line from a source he trusted. There is only one problem with it: it's not true.

Untruths, repeated again and again with sincere conviction by people who actually believe them to be true, can result in severe distortions being widely accepted as fact and thus being repeated all the more.

As the Course itself teaches us, guilt is always an illusion and never useful in determining the truth. The attempt to find fault and project guilt on individuals only obstructs any sincere attempt to discern the truth here. Avoiding guilt projection doesn't mean condoning and repeating error, however.

After eight years of studying many of the editing changes it is my opinion that the truth lies somewhere in between and just to the side of the two poles of opinion mentioned above. There is some truth to each of those polar opposite opinions, but each leaves out some crucial facts and is an incomplete account.

The first idea we need to deal with is that of "infallibly." If Jesus spoke to Helen as many suppose, and Helen was able to hear and record his words correctly at all, then one might – and some do – infer that surely Jesus would have made sure that any errors were corrected so we can be confident that the result in 1975 was flawless. There is no problem with the logic there.

On the basis of that belief one could then reasonably surmise that the editing must have been as flawless as the dictation, and just as completely directed by Jesus, and therefore the result of the editing is flawless. But wait, the editing *changed the dictation* massively, so the dictation wasn't flawless in the editors' view. Could the editing have suffered from the same flaws that the editors felt the original dictation suffered from?

The infallibility hypothesis is plausible enough but we can test it and when we do the evidence does not support it. Helen's hearing was sometimes erratic and she did not always follow the instructions of the Author. To that extent *she* introduced errors and failed to make corrections at times. There is at least one example of Schucman recording a dictated correction in her Notes which was never actually made in subsequent copies. A simple enough oversight but, infallibility admits of no such oversights! Helen Schucman was human and fallible especially when she, for whatever reasons, ignored the Author's instructions and proceeded on her own with what she was in later years to call "my book." She was both frightened by it and possessive of it. The hazards of the possession fallacy are well explained in the 60,000 words she chose to omit.

It is apparent to most readers that the grandeur of the poetry and prose in ACIM reflects a sublime intelligence which

Appendix IV: The Nature and Significance of the Version Differences

Schucman was clearly able to hear and record on paper with a high degree of accuracy – at least sometimes. This savant-like capacity to hear with extraordinary clarity and record with exceptional accuracy was not consistent, however. For a variety of reasons, including her own ego, her fears, and even medication the message she heard sometimes came through garbled.

This is clearly visible in her shorthand notebooks where we can see that she sometimes crossed out a line and re-wrote it with changes, occasionally several times. Either she "got it wrong" the first time and the author dictated a correction or she "got it right" the first time but then decided on her own to change it afterwards. Either way, we see that she was not a "flawless recording device" operating with consistent mechanical precision, recording the Author's words with 100% accuracy, but rather a human being applying a rare degree of skill with varying reliability. Her accuracy sometimes appears to have been 100%, her reliability was far short of that as she herself readily enough acknowledged.

She even recorded the Voice commenting on difficulty getting through because she was not as "right-minded" as needed and another commenting on her hearing difficulty being associated with her being "all doped up."

As we examine the differences between versions it is abundantly clear that Schucman's savant-like ability to hear and record iambic pentameter dictation did not extend to skill in copying or editing. As a copy-typist she was better than average but she certainly made her fair share of very human copying mistakes. As an editor she was compulsive and exercised a degree of "licence" with the material which went well beyond – and even directly disobeyed – the Author's very explicit instructions, according to Kenneth Wapnick's account in *Absence from Felicity*. A great many of the differences between the versions are not intentional editing of any kind, they are simply copying mistakes. The idea that a supernatural author "would have ensured all errors were corrected" collapses when we see that quite simply that is not what happened.

The idea of "infallibility" of the 1975 version is a wish projected onto facts which simply don't support it.

While the prose and poetry of the Course is sublime and even super-human at times, the editing often appears erratic, hurried, and even sloppy, sometimes to the point of recklessness. The "divine inspiration" or whatever unusual ability one might suppose Helen Schucman brought to bear for the composition of the Course did not extend to the copying and editing. One of the early instructions the Author gave to the Scribes was that Thetford should make the decisions about editing, not Schucman. It's not clear how much Thetford assumed that responsibility initially but it is clear that as the editing proceeded in later years he was not only not in charge, he wasn't even always informed and clearly did not carry out his assignment. I won't even try to explain why that was the case, but it is unquestionably the case.

Schuman herself said, in her still unpublished autobiography, that she wanted to change nearly everything while Thetford wanted to change little. We can see why Thetford was assigned the job of editing. Yet it was Schucman who did much of it, and this may explain a great deal of the problem we do in fact see with the "version differences." In instructing the Scribes to give the editing job to Thetford the Author *did* act to ensure accuracy, but in disobeying the instruction the Scribes opened the door to inaccuracy. In their "collaborative" undertaking Helen's role is explicitly that of "taking dictation" and Bill's specifically that of editing. In the end Helen "took possession" of the entire enterprise, collaboration ceased, and I think that explains a good deal of the problem we are trying to unscramble today.

In not even adequately proofing through multiple re-typings, the Scribes acted to *ensure* a high level of blatant and obvious errors which entirely explode the infallibility myth for anyone who looks on the evidence without blinders.

However much "divine guidance" might have been present in the editing, it is incontrovertible that it wasn't 100% reliable and that a great many very obvious mistakes were introduced. I don't dispute that there was a divine element. I can prove there was also a rather large – and far from infallible – "human" element also. Sorting out the wheat from the chaff here is the challenge.

It is simply a fact that a huge number of differences, many of them inadvertent mistakes, exist in the later versions. It is also a fact that the Author apparently was more concerned to get the book into print, errors and all, than to clean up all the mistakes. We have his own words to explain this: "errors are not crucial."

The first argument then, that the 1975 Abridgement is exactly the way both Schucman and the Author wanted it is obviously incorrect unless we are to suppose that both wanted a high level of inadvertent typos which Schucman almost certainly didn't even know were there. It has crossed my mind that the Author ay have been very much aware that the presence of such a large number of such obvious mistakes would ensure that eventually someone would come along who was receptive to the idea of fixing the mistakes *and* that the "infallibility" illusion would collapse upon itself rather quickly.

There certainly were mistakes made by the Scribes at every point in the long process of editing and retyping the original dictation. Their editing and copying is far from flawless *but* they certainly *did* find and correct some mistakes in the editing process. While it may have been excessive, inconsistent and even reckless at points, at other points it was quite adequate. In addition to obvious and probable editing mistakes, there are some obvious and probable genuine corrections and enhancements which resulted from the editing. It is a mixed bag.

In terms of "which version is best" what this means is that depending on the passage in question, the "best rendition" may be found in ***any one of them***! None has a monopoly on correctness, and none is free of obvious mistakes. The original wording is in my view ***usually*** better than the later, but by no means ***always***. The problem isn't a simple "either-or" choice between versions. To determine the "best version" of any passage with variant readings it is necessary to compare them all carefully in context. In most cases the "best" is fairly obvious to anyone. In some cases the choice is more subjective and there are different opinions. In a few cases the arguments supporting one are equally persuasive to me as the arguments supporting the other and I simply have no idea which is the more authentic. Further research may well solve such riddles however.

Don't overlook that line regarding the importance of "further research." God knows, as do I, that I don't have all the answers. But I have a list of questions that could keep an army of researchers busy for generations.

Appendix IV: The Nature and Significance of the Version Differences

The second argument then, that the earlier variant is *always* the better is also rather obviously disproven by the evidence.

In the debate about which version is "best" – the answer to the question is "it depends."

In a segment of the *Shorthand Notes* which didn't make it into any of the later typed manuscripts nor any print version of the Course to appear so far we can read the following words:

```
As long as you take accurate
notes, every word is meaningful. But
I can't always get through. Whenever
possible, I will correct retroac-
tively. Be sure to note all later
corrections.
```

(N 4:67) right after T 19 B 20

Fifty-five pages later in the *Notes*, and ten pages later in the *Urtext* we read a thought which did make it into the *Urtext* and which follows up on this idea:

```
Contradictions in My words
means1 lack of understanding, or
scribal failures, which I make every
effort to correct. But they are
still not crucial. The Bible has the
same problem, I assure you. And it's
still being edited. Consider the
power of my Word, in that it has
withstood all the attacks of error,
and is the Source of Truth.
```

(N 4:122-123) T 1 B 30d

The message seems very clear in three regards: 1) *"every word is meaningful"* but 2) scribal failures are *"not crucial"* and 3) *"I will correct retroactively"* along with *"I will make every effort to correct."* The third theme, that of correction, is repeated.

And there is the fourth theme about "retroactive correction" which I shall get to presently.

"Errors are not crucial." I've often thought that if you were to tear out every second page of the Course and give one group of students one half the pages and a second group the other half, and then gave each a multiple choice quiz, it's unlikely there'd be much, if any difference in their understanding of what the Course says. Careful textual scholars would likely extract the same basic ideas from either the odd or even numbered pages! It would just be a great deal more difficult and there'd be much more room for uncertainty if you're missing half the text.

"Every word is meaningful" in this regard: getting the words right clarifies the message and makes it easier to understand, not that every word is *crucial* to correct understanding. Not crucial, just meaningful. It's like the difference between a crisp, sharp movie image in full colour and a faded, scratched black and white still photo of your father. You'd recognize him in either but the clarity of the one would be better than the other.

"The power of my Word" is such that the truth can get through despite errors and omissions. The word the author chose here isn't "words" but "Word." And there is a difference. "Words" are what we read on pages and digest with our brains. "Word" is direct soul-level communication reflected, always with imperfections, in "words on the page." No matter how badly the "words" are scrambled the "Word" can still get through!

"I will correct retroactively" isn't given a time limit and from the second expression of the theme of correction, *"I will make every effort to correct"* we can perhaps surmise that the effort will continue until complete. I don't foresee it being complete in my lifetime.

If those are the words of the Author and they are true then he will make "every effort to correct" any scribal errors that remain. We can presume he is doing so right now. If there are remaining scribal errors then he *is* making every effort to correct them.

There are scribal errors. We know that.

Therefore he is making every effort to correct them. We know that too.

The "fact" is that however remarkable and even miraculous the accomplishments of the Scribes and their early helpers, and however valid their guidance was at points, their proofreading was inadequate to non-existent resulting in innumerable inadvertent copying mistakes. There are other differences which appear to be intentional editing or omission but given the lack of proofreading, it is necessary to "retroactively" review each and every change in order to find and correct the large number which clearly *are* mistakes and just as importantly, to identify those changes which are legitimate corrections of previous mistakes!

Inquiring minds do what to know what's a typo and what isn't!

That is not a particularly difficult challenge for a great many of the editing changes, in my opinion. With most it is quite obvious whether it is a mistake or a correction.

This fact of extensive and problematic editing, which is fairly well known, has generated an enormous amount of controversy in Course circles since it first emerged in 2000. Tempers have flared and arguments have raged in response to this fact but it is perhaps useful to remember the words of the Course: *"no one can be angry at a fact. It is always an interpretation that gives rise to negative emotions, regardless of their seeming justification by what appear as facts."* **M 18 A 4**

The idea that the Scribes and their work was infallible and entirely and always divinely guided and that they were incapable of human error is a "sacred cow" for some, and one which cannot survive in face of the facts. It is an idea which has been stated many times and accepted by many people and is repeated in best-sellers. But the fact is, the Scribes were human and there is plenty of very conspicuous human error in their work. In Course terms the problem here is straightforward: the *belief* in the infallibility of the Scribes is an illusion. The fact that there is so much anger associated with the "facts" which correct the illusion points to ego-attachment or what the Course calls *specialness*. One form that the specialness error can take is seeing some

---

[1] Some might regard this as a grammar error. However, the clause "contradictions in my words" can be construed as a singular noun clause, and if so, the grammar is correct.

Appendix IV: The Nature and Significance of the Version Differences

person at fault which results in guilt projection. An equally serious error is to see someone as infallible and incapable of error in the here and now.

Given the fact of editing errors, and the Author's previously quoted comments about errors and retroactive corrections, it should come as no surprise that today there are folks undertaking to identify and correct those errors, not because doing so is "crucial" to understanding the work at all, but because "every word is meaningful" and I don't think I need to argue that the "more clear" has advantages over the "less clear." Will anyone really argue that copying mistakes, when conclusively identified, should *not* be corrected?

Often when I quote the Bible I am met with the response "oh well we know the Bible isn't accurate, we can't be sure those words are authentic." That too is a "fact." For centuries Bible Scholars have been poring over ancient manuscript fragments in response to that fact trying to discern the "original" text which underlies centuries of copying mistakes. That effort to identify and correct such errors is ongoing and in many respects the Course is part of it, correcting as it does a number of mistaken interpretations of the Bible.

In those quotes above there is a fifth idea, in which Jesus himself directly compares the Course and its problems with accuracy to the Bible and its problems with accuracy.

Yet some people still preach – and believe – that "every word of the Bible is God-breathed and literally true." The belief collapses with even a cursory examination of the evidence *and* because the idea of specialness, of an infallible text, appeals to the ego the belief also persists because some simply find reasons not to examine the evidence. A commonly cited reason is that scholars are "too intellectual" and "insufficiently spiritual" to be trusted. Yet without centuries of Biblical scholarship, we wouldn't have the Bibles we do have today which really *are* considerably more accurate than those available 500 years ago.

Yet that critique of "scholarship" is not entirely without a valid basis. Scholars can only deal with "words." When it comes to the "Word" scholarship may well stumble over itself. There is not yet on earth any genuine "scholarship of the Soul." Textual exegesis on the nature of the "Holy Instant" is never going to replace the *experience* of the Holy Instant.

That's my academic background, Biblical Studies. Trained in scholarship in the Humanities, it's the "words" I study. Trained in Biblical Scholarship I know those words are at best the portal to the "Word" to which they try to point. I've spent a lifetime studying the "words" of men and women who had experienced the "Word" and try to tell me about it I mere "words."

The "words" of the Course are very much "not crucial" though they may be "meaningful." What's crucial is the "Word!" The mere "words" are important only if they do or fail to do their job, which is that of communicating the "Word!"

And it's partly from that background that I developed this mindset that errors in the "words" of Holy Writ should be identified and corrected where possible. How can you interpret a text if you don't know what it is? And what point is there in trying to interpret typos? When I discovered in 1999 that the Course suffered from some of the same copying mistakes as Biblical manuscripts, it was as natural as breathing to me to apply myself and my academic training to the problem of identifying and correcting the copying mistakes. And from my academic background I had a clear idea of at least one way of doing that, a way generally called *Primary Textual Scholarship.* An obvious starting point is to identify and track copying mistakes. Like any human undertaking, scholarship is far from perfect. But it's also far from useless. When we find one of the thousands of copying mistakes, we can sometimes fix it! We won't find them all and we might even mistake a correction for a copying mistake now and then, but textual scholarship certainly *can* clean up a lot of the problems and produce a *more accurate* if still imperfect result.

What we *do* have for the Course is what we *don't* have for the Bible, most of the original written documentation. Comparison allows us to readily identify exactly where copying errors arose and exactly what they are and usually allows us to correct those earlier errors with a very high degree of confidence.

And that's the task I feel called to undertake for *A Course in Miracles.* Clean up as many of the "words" as we can. Do what the Scribes were unable to do decades ago for reasons we may never fully understand.

When the Scribes asked for "guidance" as to how to proceed in publishing the material back in 1975 they reported having received several clear instructions. Among them was that the original dictation should be published without modification. I take that to mean not that they should include typos but rather that they should correct any mistakes *they had introduced* in order to publish *what had originally been dictated*, correctly with no scribal errors. I will also assume they came as close to that as they were able at the time with the resources available to them. I'm also quite certain they were unaware of many of the copying mistakes. In light of the above-quoted statement that copying errors are not *crucial* it is quite conceivable to me that it was more important to the Author to get the books into print promptly than it was to find and correct every last mistake.

Today, with more time and resources to apply, and the benefit of 20-20 hindsight, it is possible to come closer to that original instruction from the Author. I take it that what Helen and Bill published in 1975 was the closest they *could* come to following that guidance. Today, 33 years later, I can come a bit closer. It's still not perfect. But it's closer to that original dictation they were instructed to publish. It has been, to some extent, "retroactively corrected."

I emphasize "to some extent." The job is by no means complete. This is not perfect and there is a long road ahead of which I am aware and perhaps a longer one of which I am not yet aware. The road ahead involves the careful, diligent, prayerful and scholarly examination of every editing change. We don't even know yet what all the changes were! To discover that we must carefully examine all the primary source material.

So far I've dealt mostly with the simplest of the version problems, inadvertent copying mistakes or "scribal error." Some of the most important changes in content fairly obviously were quite intentional. In some cases it is just as obviously mistaken as the inadvertent omissions. In other cases it is less clear.

There is another vital concept in the previously cited quote, that "contradictions" may derive from *either* an incorrect understanding *or* scribal failure. A significant proportion of the later editing appears to have been intended to rectify apparent contra-

Appendix IV: The Nature and Significance of the Version Differences

dictions. These are among the most substantial alterations, where the content really is changed. In many of these instances it is my opinion that the "contradiction" being "corrected" derived from a lack of understanding of the material on the part of the editors rather than a failure of the Scribes to correctly record the Author's words. In short, while I can see how they perceived a contradiction and how they tried to fix it, I don't think the contradiction was in the text itself, I think it arose from their misunderstanding of the text.

I might be wrong on that and I might be right but I mean to find out.

I have looked at numerous examples of re-writing which change the meaning of a passage I don't think was originally an "error." I think the editor misunderstood the material and projected a perception of error onto the material and then conformed it to the editor's own misunderstanding. In some cases I think the evidence is so overwhelming there will be no debate. They simply blew it totally and it is obvious. In other cases it's much less clear.

In short, some of the editing changes derive from a "faulty understanding" and change the text of the Course to reflect that faulty understanding. If I am correct that such mistakes do exist, while they might not be *crucial*, surely their correction is desirable and *meaningful*.

Some of these may be as obvious to you as they are to me but I'm rather sure there will be differences of opinion with relation to others. These are questions which warrant much deeper scholarly research and textual analysis. We are not talking about simple and obvious copying errors here. We are talking about instances of replacing "Spiritual Eye" with "Holy Spirit" or "Soul" with "Spirit" where the original meaning of a passage is entirely transformed, often in error, in my view. I am not prepared to assume as a given either that the editors were always right or always wrong: rather I assume that we have to carefully appraise each editing change because sometimes they were right and sometimes they *very obviously* weren't!

Regardless of whether the "interpretive editing" which re-writes some passages and changes their meaning was "correct" or "mistaken" it is a fact that the general message of the Course is changed by it in the many passages affected. Most of these changes occurred rather late in the process. The early editing was mostly just omissions, many of which appear to me to be entirely justified omissions of "strictly personal" material. The most extensive re-writing which changes the actual content and message occurred in the last phase of the editing. It is thus the case that the "earlier the version" the less of this "re-writing" kind of editing exists.

If my hypothesis is correct, that most of it was unwarranted and "corrupts" the intended meaning, this would make the earlier versions more reliable than the later versions, *on average*. If my view is mistaken, and most of that re-writing corrects genuine scribal errors in the earlier material, then the later versions are in that respect closer to the Author's intended meaning, *on average*.

Which is it? Given time scholarship can provide an answer.

This is a question, however, which every student can answer for herself by looking at the differences and following her own Inner Guide. It is not a question which has been sufficiently researched by a sufficient number of scholars for anyone to provide a definitive answer based on scholarly research. It is however the case that there is considerable evidence to support the hypothesis that much of the re-writing that occurred in the last phase of editing is more reflective of editorial interpretation of the Author's dictation than the Author's dictation itself.

Let me restate that a bit more bluntly. Where the most significant changes in content occur, in the last phase of the editing, we see more of the interpretation of the editors being imposed on the text than we see correction of genuine mistakes in taking down the Author's own words. After studying "the differences" for the better part of a decade, that is what I think. Can I prove it? In many cases I think I could convince any jury. Am I right? Further research will establish that.

Whichever point of view is true, it is surely apparent that determining which is correct has some importance!

A scholarly consensus will no doubt emerge, but only when that research is done

The goal here then is not a "definitive edition" of A *Course in Miracles* but rather an accurate and accessible publication of an important part of the primary source material, the *Urtext* manuscripts. The goal here is not the "last word" on "The Word." The goal is simply to move toward the humbler goal of "getting the words right."

Since one can hardly make that determination without actually reading the material, in question, it is obviously crucial that the material be made available for study in the most accurate form possible.

In the case of Biblical scholarship, the original documents were either destroyed or are lost in desert sands or ruined cities. In the case of Course scholarship, much of the original documentation exists but those who have copies refuse to permit their inspection.

Of course in order to research these questions in the name of confirming genuine corrections and correcting genuine errors, scholars need access to all of the best primary source material which exists. Not only has this access been systematically withheld to date, the very idea of researching these questions has been viewed by some as an attack on the Scribes. It's not that. If it "attacks" anything, it "attacks" the illusion of their infallibility because they were infallible only in illusion, not in fact. As the Course tells us, the ego can become vicious when its pet illusions are confronted by truth.

The argument has not been so much that the numerous errors *shouldn't be corrected* as it has been a *denial that there are numerous errors at all* along with an enormous effort to suppress the evidence that they are there and attack those presenting the evidence when it cannot be suppressed.

Appendix V: Editorial Policies

The preparation of a rough historical manuscript for print production requires that editorial decisions be made regarding typos and handwritten mark-up. Working with a living author, an editor would simply consult the author directly regarding any uncertainties. When working with a channelled manuscript of one who has departed this plane, uncertainties cannot always be resolved so easily. We can guess, or compare the passage across other versions, compare discussions of the theme in other sections, or we can consult widely. More extensive textual research will no doubt clarify a number of areas where the manuscripts are ambiguous, and the work to date has added clarity to many uncertainties.

The handwritten mark-up in particular presents a challenge. Some clearly corrects typing mistakes. Much of the mark-up however, alters the wording, punctuation, sentence, or paragraph structure of material which contains no obvious errors and which is also an exact copy of the handwritten *Shorthand Notes*. This could represent channelled corrections to earlier scribal errors or it could be Schucman's infamous "compulsive editing," the sort of which she was later to say "always had to be undone." Although she *said* she wanted to change "everything" and that her changes had to be undone, there is very little evidence that her changes ever *were* undone and each instance could be either a correction or unwarranted editing. The goal of this work is not that of evaluating the variants as to their authenticity, the goal is to simply identify and present them *for* subsequent consideration. We can either *include* the mark-up modifying the material as marked, accepting this as the editorial decision of the Scribes, we can largely *ignore* the mark-up, or we can *pick and choose* which mark-up to accept and which to reject.

After months of head-scratching on this one, I decided to reproduce what was originally typed while footnoting any handwritten mark-up other than the most obvious typing and spelling corrections. So I've included, excluded, and picked and chosen all at the same time. Except for the most trivial, I've also footnoted exactly what was ignored in case that material is of some real value.

Editions of the Course available today fall into two categories:

1. Those which reproduce every keystroke as accurately as possible, including all the mistakes. This results in a "replica" of the original text, and
2. Those which fix "apparent" errors by making undocumented modifications to the original.

The former approach can be considered "accurate," and if well done it is certainly honest. The result however, is likely to be of interest only to a handful of scholars. The latter approach results in a neater, cleaner appearance and generally renders most of the material accurately but the reader can't determine what words are from the original manuscript and what is editorial "fixing," nor can the reader see where the original is ambiguous. In order to reproduce the manuscripts as accurately as possible and clean up the most obvious mistakes to have a reasonably consistent book, I have used a middle ground between the two approaches.

Generally I've tried to take a very "light" hand in determining what is an "error." Only the most obvious and clear "typos" are corrected. The author is fond of neologisms and novel word structures, including the largely archaic subjunctive mood. Many consider errors, as did I initially. It was only after consultation with grammarians that I discovered these errors to be perfectly correct English. Wherever there is any chance the form present on the page is what was intended, in particular when the *Notes* has the same form, it is not "corrected" to a more conventional usage. If I'm in doubt about something, I leave it as it is or possibly add a footnote. Only the most obvious typing and spelling mistakes are changed.

Where there is an obvious spelling mistake or inconsistency, it is corrected and/or standardized. For research and text search purposes, it does help if the same word is always spelled the same way. With a very few exceptions noted below, when Schucman used more than one spelling, that which US dictionaries indicate is the most common form in the USA is the one chosen, since that is where Schucman was working. Given that there are many hundreds of instances, instead of footnoting each, they are documented here.

Where handwritten mark-up corrects obvious typos, we simply employ the correction and do not footnote the fact. In many cases the typos were caught before the manuscript reached us and handwritten mark-up indicates the correct form. Most of these are trivial, represent "corrected typing mistakes" and footnoting each one would result in a vast number of entirely useless footnotes. Those who are interested in the study of the manuscripts at this level really need to work directly with the originals or facsimiles as no other kind of copy can really deal adequately with that kind of data.

Where there is handwritten mark-up indicating a change in the wording which is not obviously a correction of an error, that is to say where there is no apparent "typo" in what was originally typed, we use what was originally typed and footnote the variant suggested by the mark-up. That way the reader can see the variants contained in the manuscript, both the material as it was originally typed and the material as amended by the mark-up.

Where there are variant readings, I've tried to check each of these mark-up variants against the *Notes*. Where the mark-up alters material which is different than the *Notes* in such a way as to reconcile it with the *Notes* then we use the *Notes* reading, and footnote the variant, while noting the fact that the choice was based on the *Notes*. In some cases I'm sure some readers will form the opinion that another of the variants is the better, and I'm rather certain that in some cases further research will prove that to be the case. Because I can't possibly tell with certainty **which** variant is the best in all cases, the policy is to footnote them all. In this way the reader can tell in an instant that either the reading is clear and certain, or that there is some doubt and what the variants actually are. Of course I might be mistaken at times when selecting among variants. That is why it is crucial to let you know what the variants are so you can decide for yourself by whatever criteria you choose to apply. In time, as we consider these variants, a consensus is likely to emerge as to which is the more authentic.

Many paragraph break changes are indicated by handwritten mark-up. Generally the practice has been to use the original paragraph break structure and ignore the mark-up. However, in the most recent round of proofing we've begun to footnote the presence of paragraph break mark-up rather than ignore it. In future editions all such mark-up should be noted but in this edi-

Appendix V: Editorial Policies

tion most of it is not footnoted. In a few cases in the early work I adopted the mark-up paragraph breaks where they seemed preferable to the typed breaks. Later, I standardized to the original breaks. During future proofing this policy will be the standard and some paragraph break points may move by a few lines.

Biblical references where recognized are footnoted and readers are encouraged to advise us of any additional ones you find. Some themes, such as love and forgiveness are used so frequently in both the Course and the Bible that to footnote every one would result in thousands of identical footnotes. In such situations the policy is to reference the first instance and not repeat the footnote.

What I have *not* done is re-write the material based on what I think it should say. Only obvious spelling and grammar typing mistakes are corrected. Other ACIM editors, when convinced a passage is mistaken, have replaced it with their own original composition believing theirs is better. Where the Scribes provide variant readings in the various versions of their manuscripts, we can evaluate which is most likely to be authentic. Of course it is possible that the Scribes got it wrong in all variants, and something else entirely was intended. That moves beyond the arena of primary scholarship into the field of interpretation. In this work, we simply don't go there.

In the history of ACIM publishing, proofing has almost always been inadequate to non-existent. The reason is fairly obvious: it is time-consuming and either the resources to do a very thorough job were not available or if they were, other matters were considered (perhaps quite reasonably) of more importance. What we strive for is accuracy and we never adjust the material from what appears on the original manuscript pages without documenting that change, save for the rather few minor exceptions noted. Any undocumented changes are errors on our part and will be corrected for future editions as they are identified. Online editions will be corrected immediately. With publication and more eyes upon the pages, remaining errors are likely to be found much more quickly and you are invited to send reports of any suspected errors to Doug Thompson <dthomp74@hotmail.com>. We ask only that you check the online version first to be sure the correction has not already been made.

I wish to stress that this edition is not published as a substitute for or replica of the original historical manuscripts. It is rather published as a more accessible "index" and searchable companion to them. The original manuscripts involve thousands of typed pages with no referencing. Most don't even have page numbers and where they do, for the most part they are unusable because they are repeated and inconsistent. Yet those manuscripts remain the authority on what the *Urtext* says. For this reason we've *included* facsimiles of the manuscripts with rationalized "absolute page numbers" in addition to the sometimes chaotic page numbers marked on the original pages, and those page numbers are printed in the text in-line in bold type. This is to make it simple and easy for the reader to check the actual original manuscript facsimile any time any doubt as to the accuracy of this copy might arise.

While many variant readings from the *Notes* are mentioned in the footnotes, it should be noted that no complete comparison between the *Urtext* and the *Notes* has been undertaken. There are many more variants in the *Notes* than are indicated in this edition. The detailed comparison of all available versions and the compilation of a *Catalogue of Variant Readings* which will indicate all editing changes is the next major phase of the overall project which is to eventually produce a genuinely 'definitive' edition of *A Course in Miracles.*

In summary then, while not 100% accurate, this is far and away the most complete and accurate edition of *A Course in Miracles* of which we are aware. This is not to say that accuracy won't be improved with further scholarship, it will be. Where the manuscript contains variant or uncertain readings we have sought to document that fact, although it is certain that we have missed a few. Despite its known shortcomings, it is still far and away the most accurate rendition of the Course in print.

Spelling Standardization

These are the words whose spelling is routinely changed. You will note that few are really "errors," they are just alternate spellings.

1) `cancelling` becomes `canceling`
2) `marshaled` becomes `marshalled`
3) `no one` becomes `no-one`
4) `O` becomes `Oh`
5) `saviour` becomes `savior`
6) `till` becomes `'til`
7) `selfsame` becomes `self-same`
8) `re-awaken(s/ed/ing)` becomes `reawaken(s/ed/ing)`
9) `re-inforce` becomes `reinforce`
10) `re-inforcement` becomes `reinforcement`
11) `re-interpretor` becomes `reinterpreter`
12) `thru` becomes `through`
13) `towards` becomes `toward`
14) `whisp` becomes `wisp`
15) `yolk` becomes `yoke`

An Introduction to the *Scholar's Toolbox* on DVD

An essential collection of Reference Material in a "Toolbox" for Teachers, Students and Scholars

- **The most complete library of A Course In Miracles primary sources in facsimile (photocopy) and e-text (searchable) form**
- All 4 Historical *Scribal Versions* cross-referenced to each other.
- The Exhaustive Concordance allows look-up of any word or phrase in *A Course In Miracles*.
- An MP3 *Synthesized audio reading* of the entire Text of the Hugh Lynn Cayce Version.

For all four versions, THE **Scholar's Toolbox** *makes it easy to:*

Display,

    Search,

        Compare,

            Cross-reference,

                Cut,

                    Paste,

                        Quote,

                            Cite

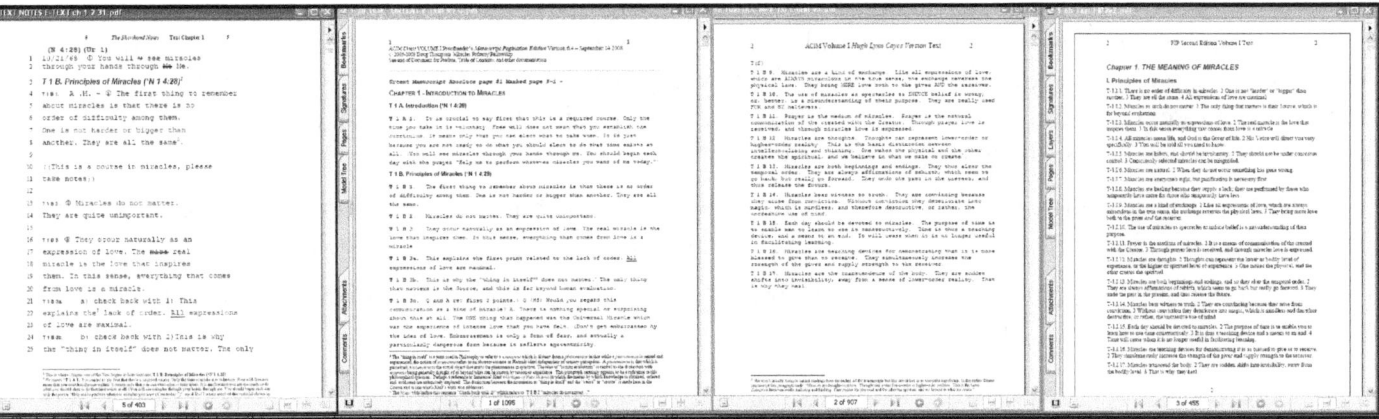

Shorthand Notes   **Urtext**   **Hugh Lynn Cayce**   **Foundation for Inner Peace**

Global Menu of primary source documents

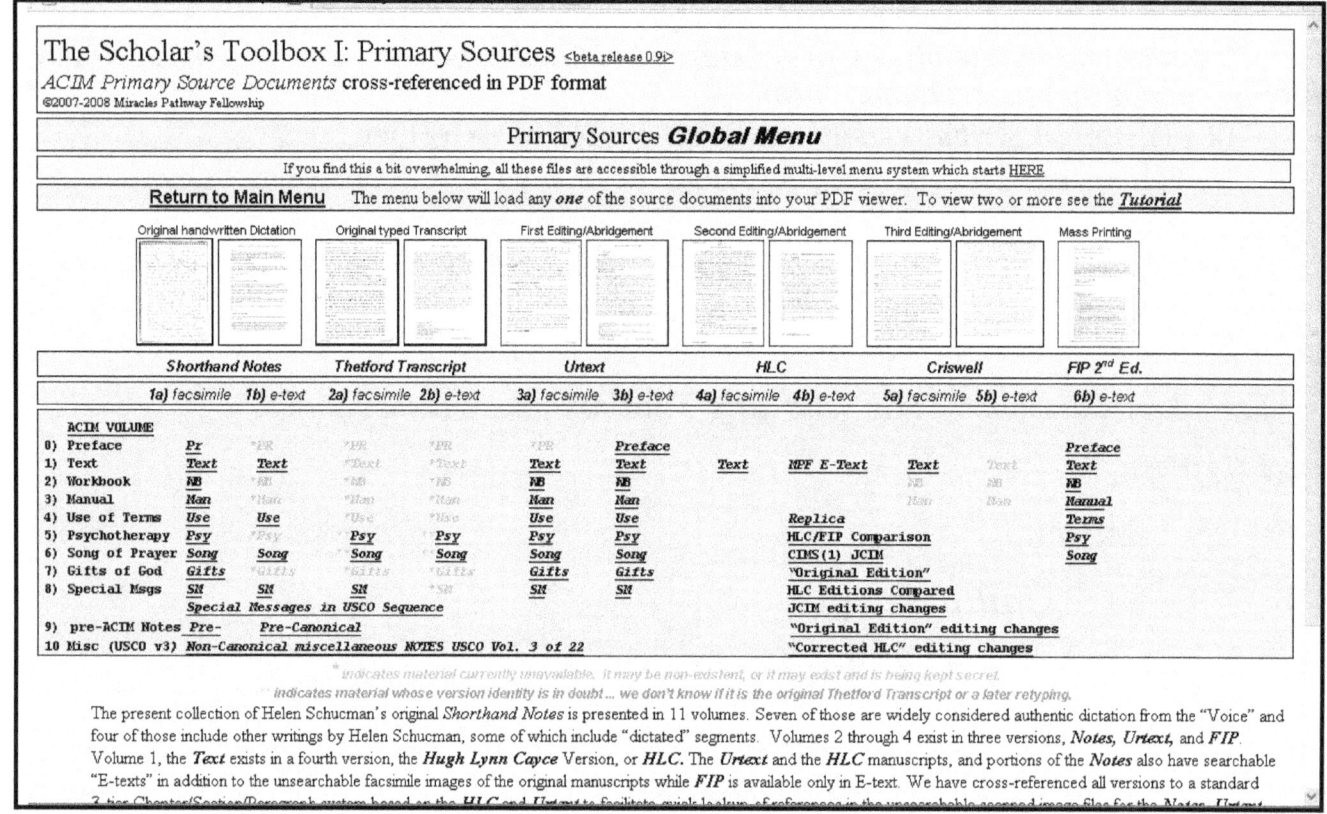

A principal feature of the *Scholar's Toolbox* is reproductions of many Course primary sources including most of the *Shorthand Notes, Urtext, and Hugh Lynn Cayce* manuscripts.

In this screenshot of the **Global Menu** each of the primary source files is listed by *version*. Each version is available both in *facsimile* copies which are photographic reproductions of original source manuscripts and *e-text* copies which are typed, machine-searchable copies. The *facsimile* is the "real McCoy" but the *e-text* is searchable and useful for locating particular words or passages. Having found a passage in the *e-text* one can then instantly locate the same spot in the *facsimile* by page number or paragraph reference due to the thorough cross-referencing.

Reduced to fit on the page, this menu looks a bit too busy, but it is much more readable on the computer screen. There are also sub-menus which show the source files sorted by volume and by version.

Clicking on any document name causes that document to be displayed. Let's start with the *Shorthand Notes*, page one of the *Text* volume.

What's on the DVD?

Searchable primary source documents displayed for inspection

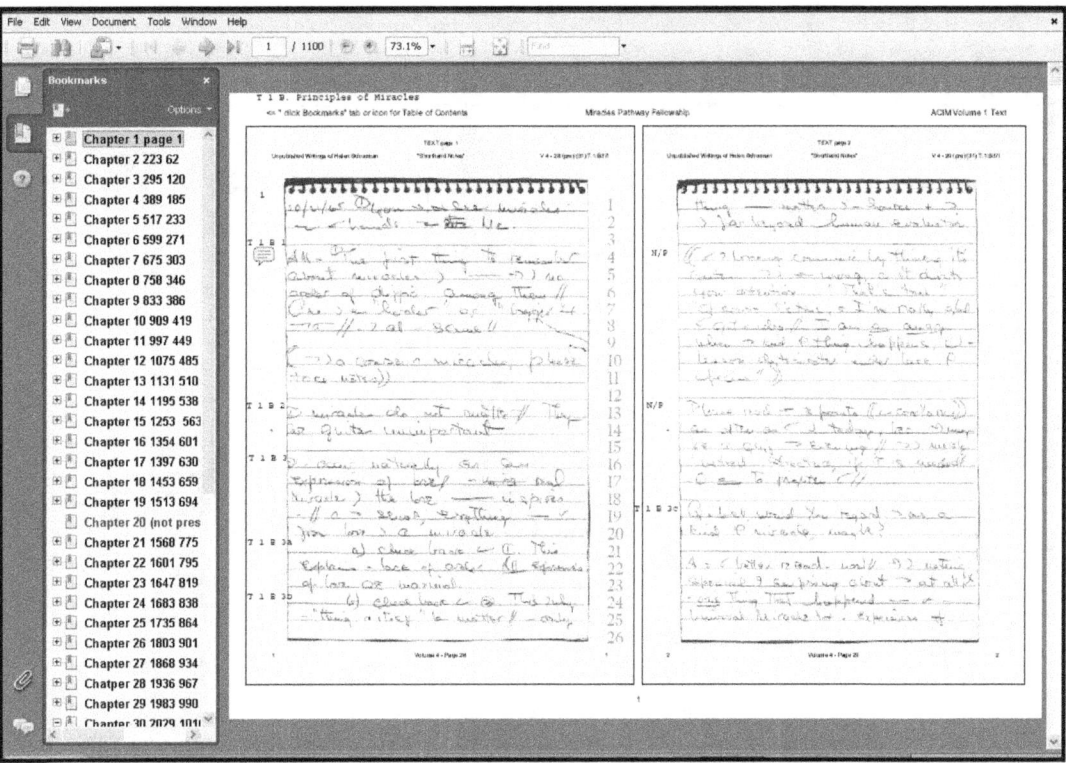

Above we see the *Notes* facsimile opened for viewing in *Acrobat Reader.* Below is the *Urtext* facsimile. Note that every chapter and section break is identically **"Bookmarked"** in each file.

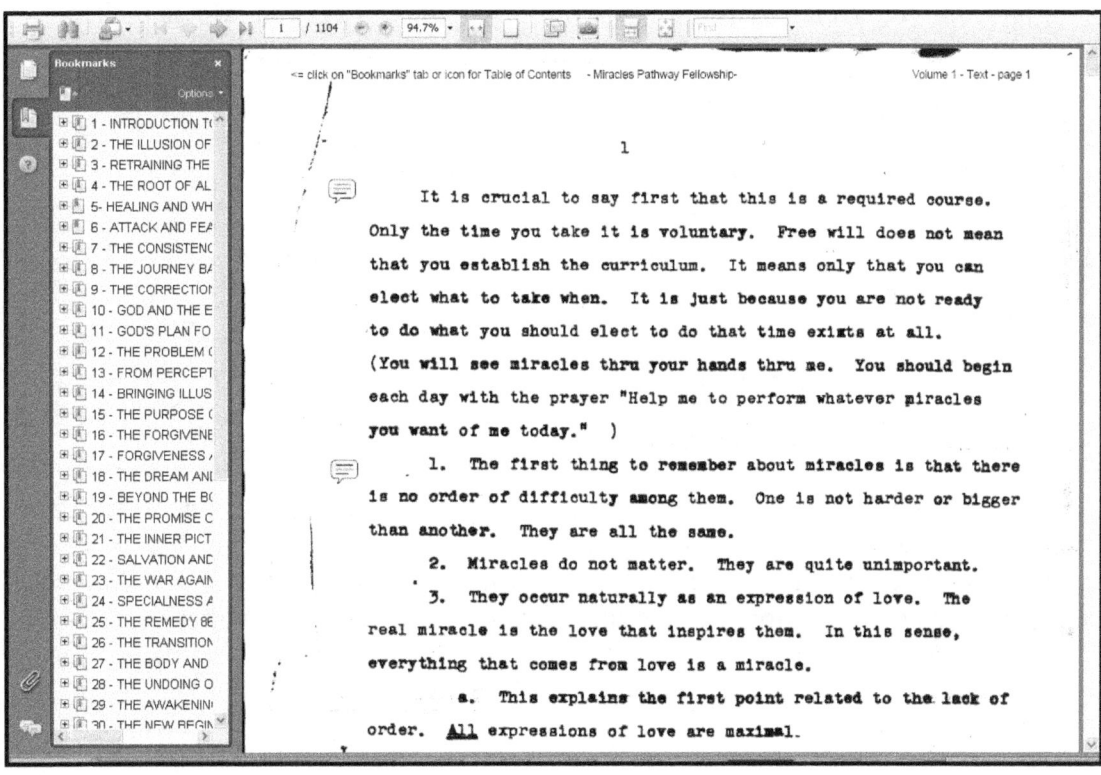

Appendix VI - iii

E-texts enable quick side by side version comparison

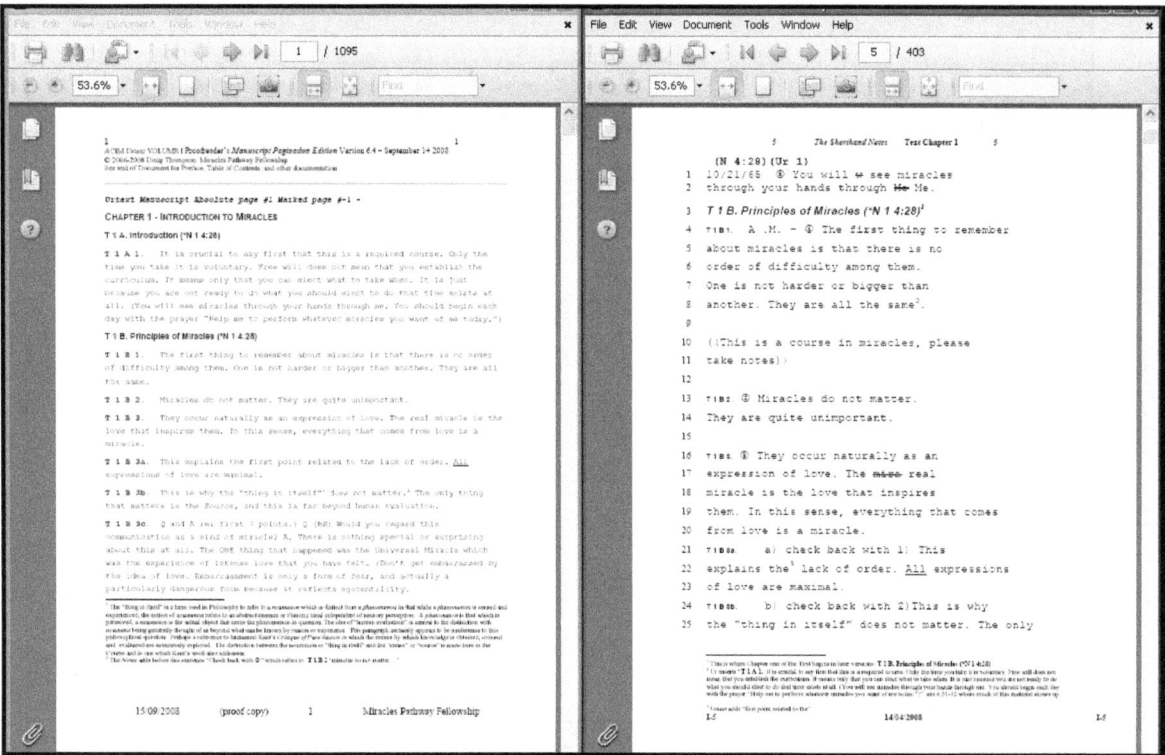

In this screenshot we see a side by side comparison with the *Urtext* (left) and *Notes* (right) *e-texts* of chapter 1. The DVD contains a **Tutorial** explaining how to use *Acrobat Reader* for multi-document display. If you wish to see two versions side by side for analysis, it's a snap for any volume of any version with the *Scholar's Toolbox*. If you want *four* versions side by side, see below!

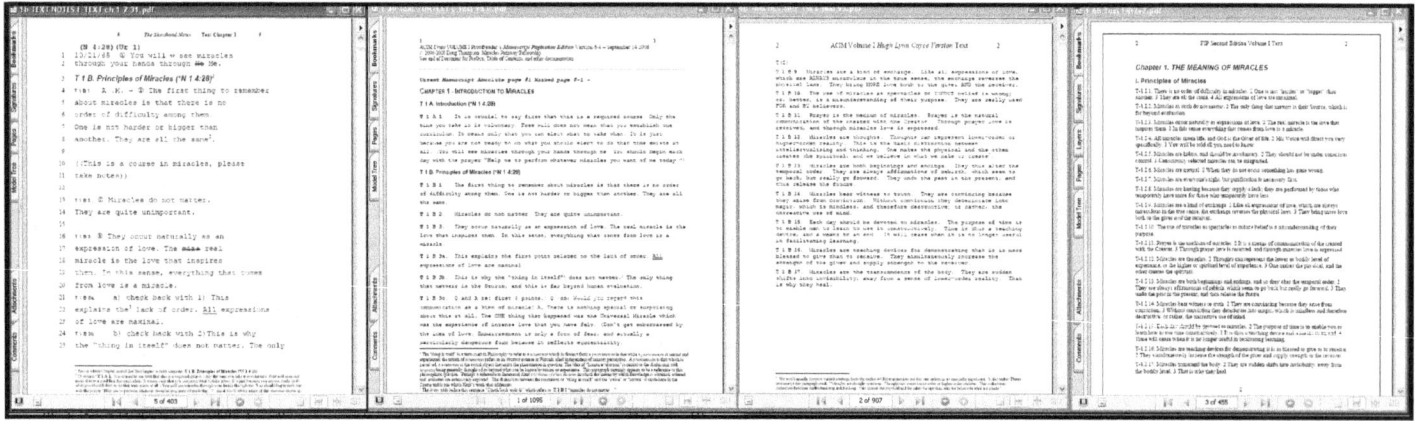

This screenshot of the e-texts of the *Notes, Urtext, HLC* and *FIP* versions is from the dual-head computer I use for document comparison. If you want to line up four versions side by side as seen here, that's a snap also *but* you need a dual-head computer with two monitors, otherwise things get too small to read. Ideally get *very large* monitors for this sort of work. The bigger the better.

What's on the DVD?

Facsimiles enable side by side primary source comparison

Locating a particular paragraph in the primary source *facsimile* files can be exceedingly tedious without the cross-referencing tools provided in the *Scholar's Toolbox* DVD.

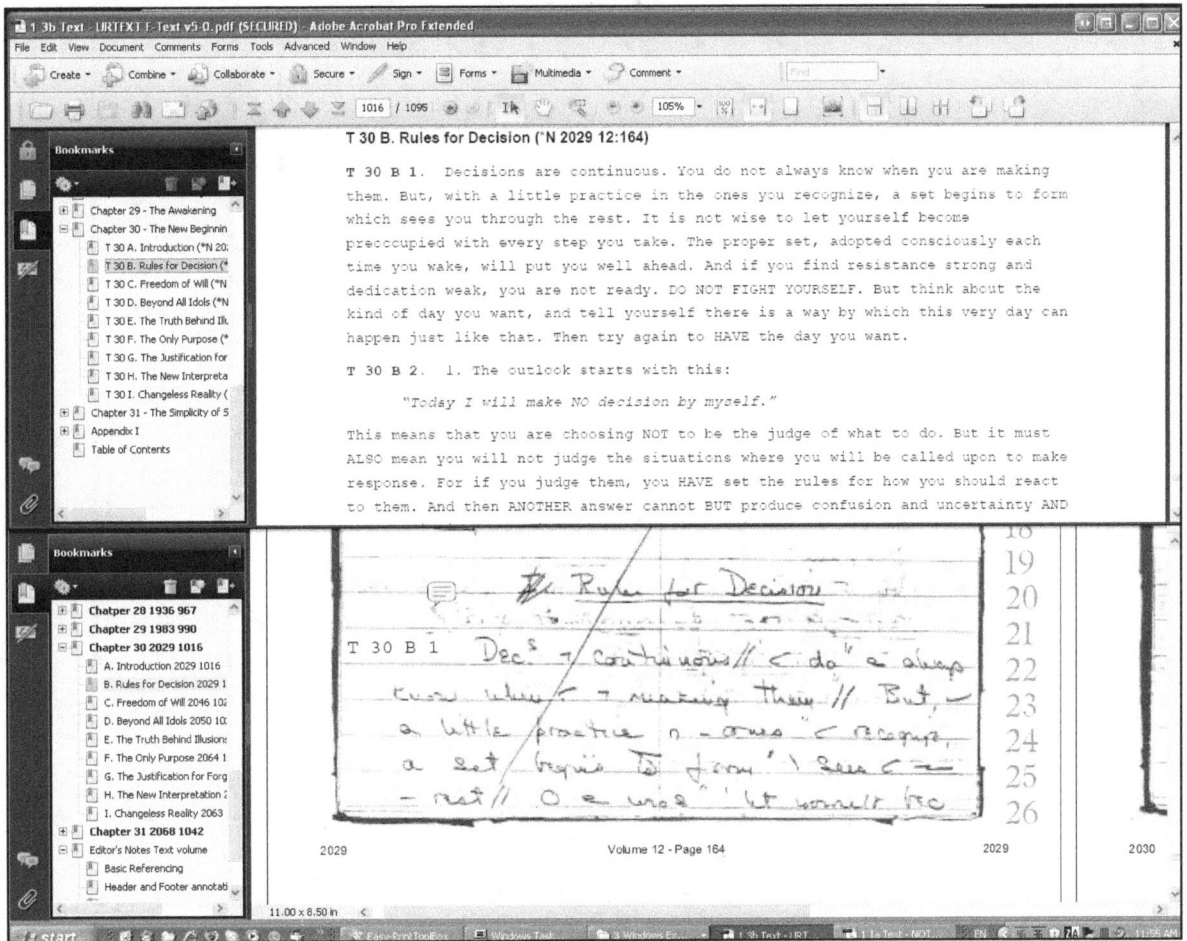

In this screenshot we see *Acrobat Reader 9* displaying two source documents, the *Shorthand Notes* and the *Urtext e-text* for the *Text* volume, both opened to paragraph **T 30 B 1**, in a tiled window on a single monitor. You will note on the left in the "**Bookmarks**" pane, both documents are identically bookmarked. These "**Bookmarks**" enable you to open any of the primary source documents to any particular chapter or section. The *e-text* shown in the upper frame is fully searchable, so you can search for any word or phrase or reference with the *Acrobat* "**Search**" and "**Find**" buttons. The lower frame is a *facsimile* or image file which is actually a photograph of the handwriting. Photos are not directly searchable. However the "typed" reference you see added in the left margin (**T 30 B 1**) of the *Notes facsimile* in the lower frame *is* searchable text. Having found a passage of interest by searching the *e-text* or Concordance, you can then "search" the *facsimile* file for that same reference and within seconds locate the same passage in the original manuscript facsimile.

A basic reference and look-up tool –

The *e-texts* are searchable in *Acrobat Reader*…

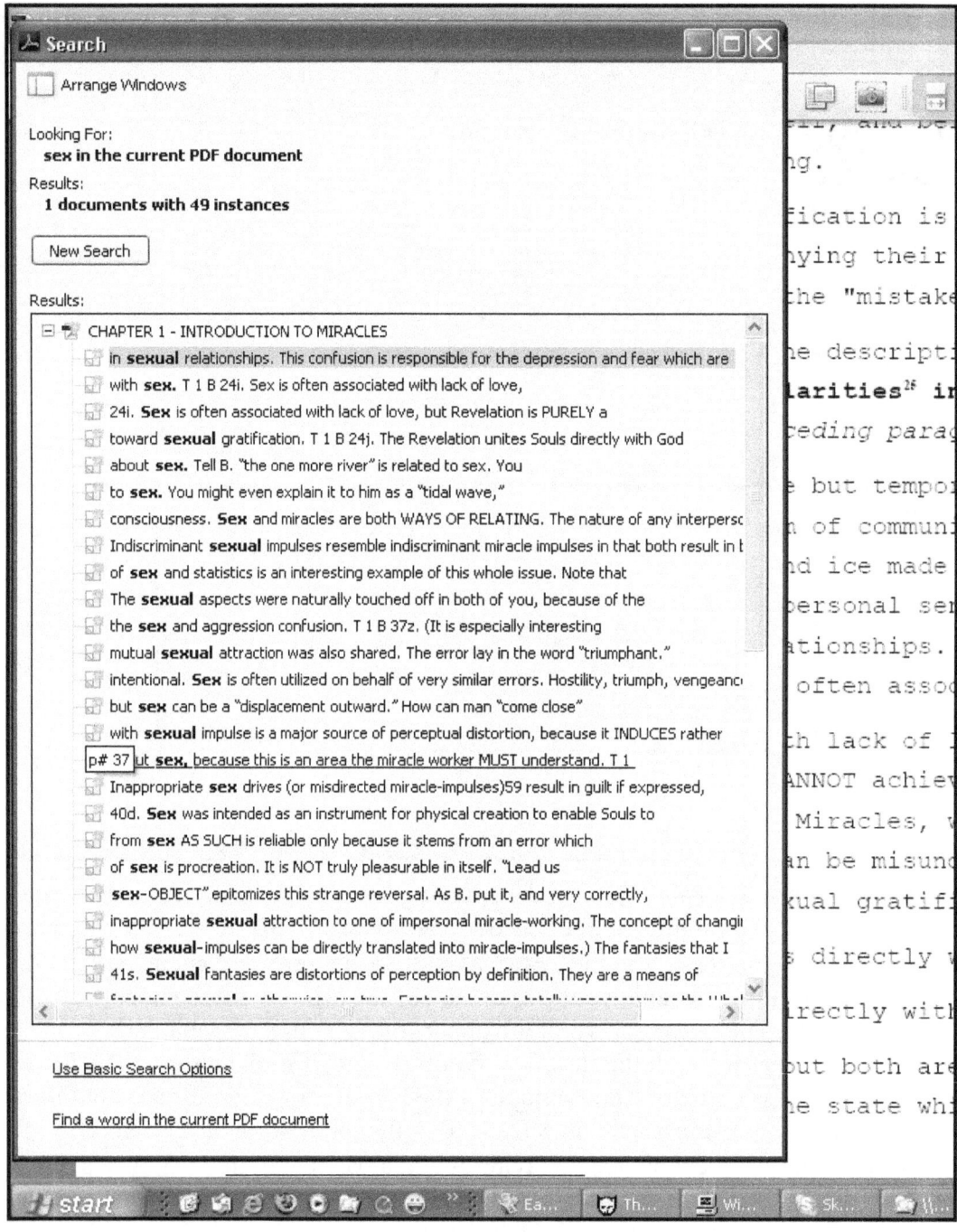

This screenshot shows the internal *Adobe Acrobat Reader* **Search** function in action. Type in the word or phrase to search for and *Acrobat Reader* will find every instance in a single file or across multiple files. Click on the one you want and the document opens to that line.

What's on the DVD?

A more powerful reference and look-up tool –
The Seven Volume *Urtext HTML* Concordance

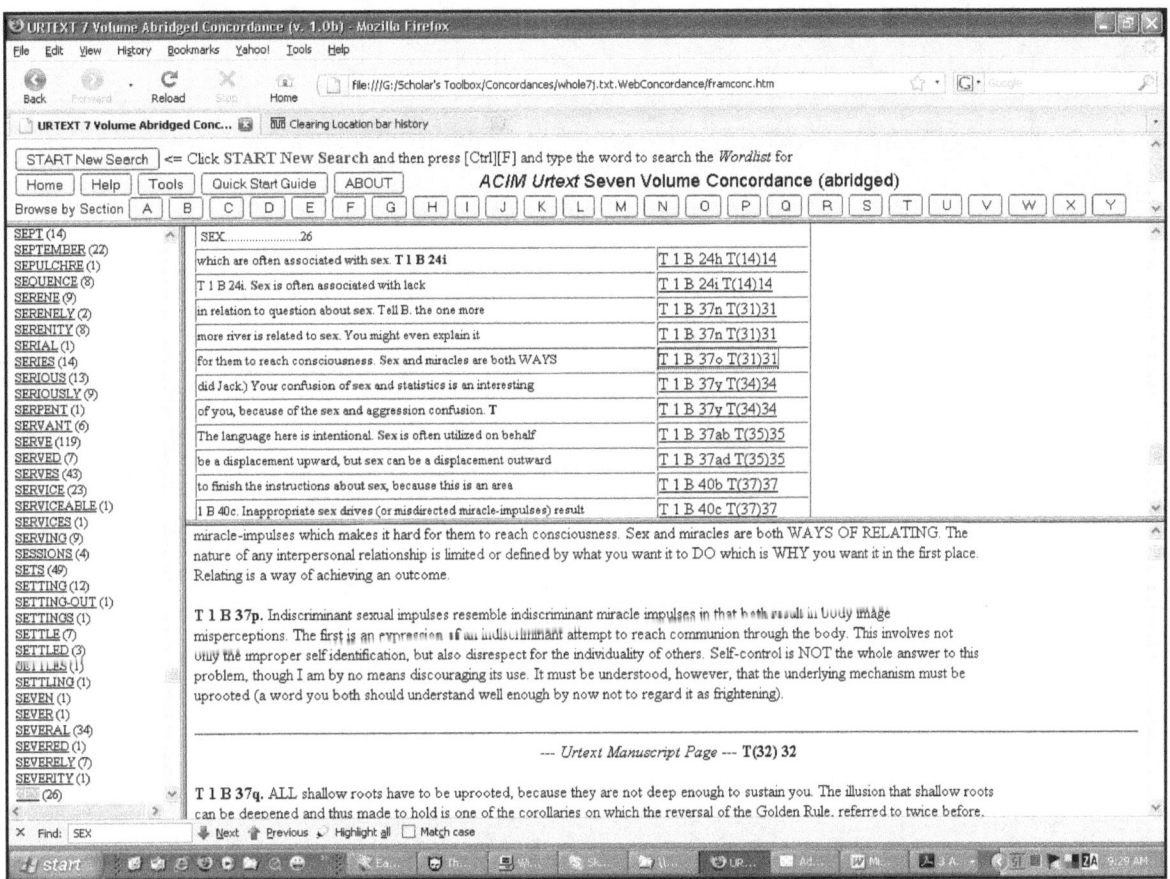

In this screenshot we see the ***Concordance*** conducting the same search we just did in *Acrobat Reader*. The ***Concordance*** is much faster, provides better context and provides the paragraph reference and manuscript page number for each result. Also, unlike the search results in *Acrobat Reader*, the results in the ***Concordance*** can be cut and pasted into other documents. This makes it ideal for citation, for quoting, and for cross-referencing. As with *Acrobat Reader*, just click on any "hit" and the *Text Frame* scrolls to that spot in the source file.

The ***Concordance*** to the *Seven Volume Urtext* comes in an abridged form on the DVD which is smaller and faster but leaves out the most common words, all the ifs, ands and buts. The ***Exhaustive Concordance*** is much larger, demands a faster computer, but includes everything. Except for this exclusion of common words, they are identical.

In the left ***Wordlist*** frame are all the words in the Course, along with their frequency. You can search this or any other frame for a particular word or phrase. Click on the word when you've found it, and all instances of that word *along with five words of context on either side* appear in the upper *concordance* frame.

The ultimate reference and look-up tool –
The FULL Concordance to the Seven Volume *Urtext*

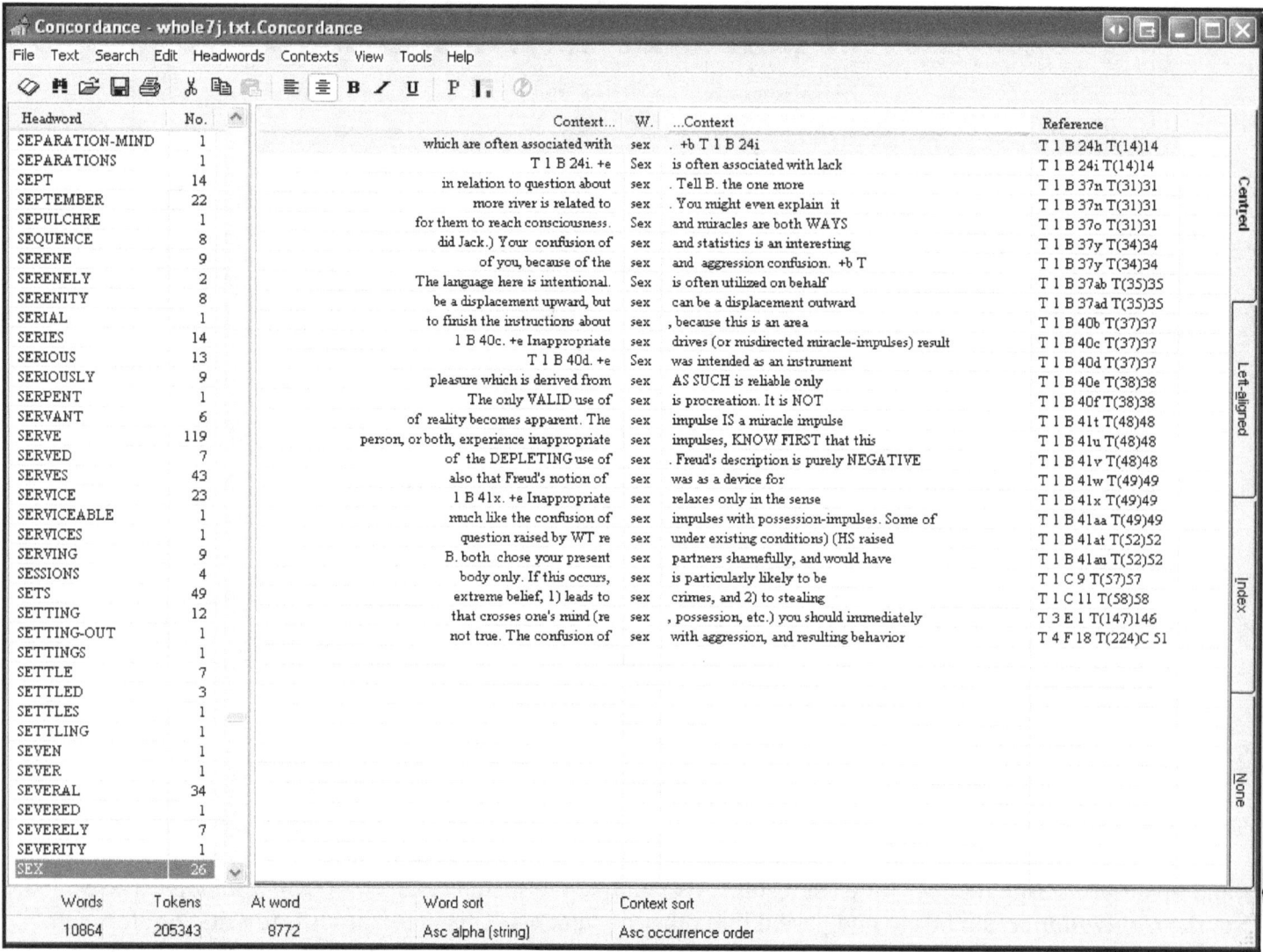

In this screenshot of the **Full Concordance** user interface we see the same look-up as before. It has all the features of the **HTML Concordance**, and a vast array of additional sophisticated text analysis capabilities. Unlike the **HTML Concordance**, the **Complete Concordance** allows complex proximity, context and hierarchical searching. We supply the data-base but not the application software for the **Complete Concordance**. This software and the data-base we supply is a must for every serious student however.

Scholar's Toolbox DVD (for PC or Mac) Order Form

If you have a copy without DVD or wish to order additional copies, you can do so on-line at miraclesinactionpress.com or use this order form.

√	Qty	Price to ship	Subtotal
☐	1	@ 24.00 ship 1 DVD to US Address	$
☐	1	@ 28.00 ship 1 DVD international	$

Some countries may assess import fees which must be paid by buyer $

Shipping: included

Total: $

Credit card Name:

Credit card Address:

CityState/Prov.Country

PhoneZip/Postal Code

e-mail address (not shared with 3rd parties)

Method of Payment: (Please allow 10 business days for checks to clear before shipping)

☐ Check*☐ MasterCard

☐ Money Order**☐ American Express

☐ Visa

Credit Card No.

SignatureExp. Date

* Checks must be in US funds drawn on a US bank
** International Postal Money Orders in US funds are acceptable

Please copy (or remove) and mail, fax or email this page with payment.
For payment by Check, Money Order or Credit Card mail this page with payment to:

Miracles in Action Press, LLC
52 Fitzgerald Drive
Jaffrey, NH 03452 USA

Or fax to: 866-683-6858 (toll free from USA only, credit card only)
Or scan & email to: mypurchase@miraclesinactionpress.com (credit card only)

Shipping Address: (this will become your shipping label, please ensure the address is precisely correct)

To: _____
(Name)

_____
(Address)

_____/_____/_____/_____
(City)(State, Province)(Country)(Postal Code or Zip)

www.ingramcontent.com/pod-product-compliance
Lightning Source LLC
Chambersburg PA
CBHW080402300426
44113CB00015B/2381